Twentieth-Century Literary Criticism

Topics Volume

Guide to Gale Literary Criticism Series

For criticism on	Consult these Gale series
Authors now living or who died after December 31, 1999	**CONTEMPORARY LITERARY CRITICISM (CLC)**
Authors who died between 1900 and 1999	**TWENTIETH-CENTURY LITERARY CRITICISM (TCLC)**
Authors who died between 1800 and 1899	**NINETEENTH-CENTURY LITERATURE CRITICISM (NCLC)**
Authors who died between 1400 and 1799	**LITERATURE CRITICISM FROM 1400 TO 1800 (LC)** **SHAKESPEAREAN CRITICISM (SC)**
Authors who died before 1400	**CLASSICAL AND MEDIEVAL LITERATURE CRITICISM (CMLC)**
Authors of books for children and young adults	**CHILDREN'S LITERATURE REVIEW (CLR)**
Dramatists	**DRAMA CRITICISM (DC)**
Poets	**POETRY CRITICISM (PC)**
Short story writers	**SHORT STORY CRITICISM (SSC)**
Literary topics and movements	**HARLEM RENAISSANCE: A GALE CRITICAL COMPANION (HR)** **THE BEAT GENERATION: A GALE CRITICAL COMPANION (BG)**
Asian American writers of the last two hundred years	**ASIAN AMERICAN LITERATURE (AAL)**
Black writers of the past two hundred years	**BLACK LITERATURE CRITICISM (BLC)** **BLACK LITERATURE CRITICISM SUPPLEMENT (BLCS)**
Hispanic writers of the late nineteenth and twentieth centuries	**HISPANIC LITERATURE CRITICISM (HLC)** **HISPANIC LITERATURE CRITICISM SUPPLEMENT (HLCS)**
Native North American writers and orators of the eighteenth, nineteenth, and twentieth centuries	**NATIVE NORTH AMERICAN LITERATURE (NNAL)**
Major authors from the Renaissance to the present	**WORLD LITERATURE CRITICISM, 1500 TO THE PRESENT (WLC)** **WORLD LITERATURE CRITICISM SUPPLEMENT (WLCS)**

ISSN 0276-8178

Volume 202

Twentieth-Century Literary Criticism

**Commentary on Various Topics
in Twentieth-Century Literature, including Literary
and Critical Movements, Prominent Themes and
Genres, Anniversary Celebrations, and Surveys
of National Literatures**

**Thomas J. Schoenberg
Lawrence J. Trudeau**
Project Editors

GALE
CENGAGE Learning

Detroit • New York • San Francisco • New Haven, Conn • Waterville, Maine • London

Twentieth-Century Literary Criticism, Vol. 202

Project Editors: Thomas J. Schoenberg and Lawrence J. Trudeau

Editorial: Dana Ramel Barnes, Tom Burns, Elizabeth A. Cranston, Kathy D. Darrow, Kristen A. Dorsch, Jaclyn R. Hermesmeyer, Jeffrey W. Hunter, Jelena O. Krstović, Michelle Lee, Russel Whitaker

Data Capture: Frances Monroe, Gwen Tucker

Indexing Services: Laurie Andriot

Rights and Acquisitions: Beth Beaufore, Jocelyne Green, Aja Perales

Composition and Electronic Capture: Amy Darga

Manufacturing: Cynde Bishop

Associate Product Manager: Marc Cormier

For product information and technology assistance, contact us at
Gale Customer Support, 1-800-877-4253.
For permission to use material from this text or product,
submit all requests online at **www.cengage.com/permissions.**
Further permissions questions can be emailed to
permissionrequest@cengage.com

While every effort has been made to ensure the reliability of the information presented in this publication, Gale, a part of Cengage Learning, does not guarantee the accuracy of the data contained herein. Gale accepts no payment for listing; and inclusion in the publication of any organization, agency, institution, publication, service, or individual does not imply endorsement of the editors or publisher. Errors brought to the attention of the publisher and verified to the satisfaction of the publisher will be corrected in future editions.

Gale
27500 Drake Rd.
Farmington Hills, MI, 48331-3535

LIBRARY OF CONGRESS CATALOG CARD NUMBER 76-46132

ISBN-13: 978-0-7876-9977-2
ISBN-10: 0-7876-9977-2

ISSN 0276-8178

Contents

Preface vii

Acknowledgments xi

Literary Criticism Series Advisory Board xiii

Preface

Since its inception *Twentieth-Century Literary Criticism* (*TCLC*) has been purchased and used by some 10,000 school, public, and college or university libraries. *TCLC* has covered more than 1000 authors, representing over 60 nationalities and nearly 50,000 titles. No other reference source has surveyed the critical response to twentieth-century authors and literature as thoroughly as *TCLC*. In the words of one reviewer, "there is nothing comparable available." *TCLC* "is a gold mine of information—dates, pseudonyms, biographical information, and criticism from books and periodicals—which many librarians would have difficulty assembling on their own."

Scope of the Series

TCLC is designed to serve as an introduction to authors who died between 1900 and 1999 and to the most significant interpretations of these author's works. Volumes published from 1978 through 1999 included authors who died between 1900 and 1960. The great poets, novelists, short story writers, playwrights, and philosophers of the period are frequently studied in high school and college literature courses. In organizing and reprinting the vast amount of critical material written on these authors, *TCLC* helps students develop valuable insight into literary history, promotes a better understanding of the texts, and sparks ideas for papers and assignments. Each entry in *TCLC* presents a comprehensive survey on an author's career or an individual work of literature and provides the user with a multiplicity of interpretations and assessments. Such variety allows students to pursue their own interests; furthermore, it fosters an awareness that literature is dynamic and responsive to many different opinions.

Every fourth volume of *TCLC* is devoted to literary topics. These topics widen the focus of the series from the individual authors to such broader subjects as literary movements, prominent themes in twentieth-century literature, literary reaction to political and historical events, significant eras in literary history, prominent literary anniversaries, and the literatures of cultures that are often overlooked by English-speaking readers.

TCLC is designed as a companion series to Gale's *Contemporary Literary Criticism,* (*CLC*) which reprints commentary on authors who died after 1999. Because of the different time periods under consideration, there is no duplication of material between *CLC* and *TCLC*.

Organization of the Book

A *TCLC* entry consists of the following elements:

- The **Author Heading** cites the name under which the author most commonly wrote, followed by birth and death dates. Also located here are any name variations under which an author wrote, including transliterated forms for authors whose native languages use nonroman alphabets. If the author wrote consistently under a pseudonym, the pseudonym is listed in the author heading and the author's actual name is given in parenthesis on the first line of the biographical and critical information. Uncertain birth or death dates are indicated by question marks. Single-work entries are preceded by a heading that consists of the most common form of the title in English translation (if applicable) and the name of its author.

- The **Introduction** contains background information that introduces the reader to the author, work, or topic that is the subject of the entry.

- The list of **Principal Works** is ordered chronologically by date of first publication and lists the most important works by the author. The genre and publication date of each work is given. In the case of foreign authors whose works have been translated into English, the English-language version of the title follows in brackets. Unless otherwise indicated, dramas are dated by first performance, not first publication. Lists of **Representative Works** by different authors appear with topic entries.

- Reprinted **Criticism** is arranged chronologically in each entry to provide a useful perspective on changes in critical evaluation over time. The critic's name and the date of composition or publication of the critical work are given at the beginning of each piece of criticism. Unsigned criticism is preceded by the title of the source in which it originally appeared. All titles by the author featured in the text are printed in boldface type. Footnotes are reprinted at the end of each essay or excerpt. In the case of excerpted criticism, only those footnotes that pertain to the excerpted texts are included. Criticism in topic entries is arranged chronologically under a variety of subheadings to facilitate the study of different aspects of the topic.

- A complete **Bibliographical Citation** of the original essay or book precedes each piece of criticism. Source citations in the Literary Criticism Series follow University of Chicago Press style, as outlined in *The Chicago Manual of Style,* 15th ed. (Chicago: The University of Chicago Press, 2003).

- Critical essays are prefaced by brief **Annotations** explicating each piece.

- An annotated bibliography of **Further Reading** appears at the end of each entry and suggests resources for additional study. In some cases, significant essays for which the editors could not obtain reprint rights are included here. Boxed material following the further reading list provides references to other biographical and critical sources on the author in series published by Gale.

Indexes

A **Cumulative Author Index** lists all of the authors that appear in a wide variety of reference sources published by Gale, including *TCLC*. A complete list of these sources is found facing the first page of the Author Index. The index also includes birth and death dates and cross references between pseudonyms and actual names.

A **Cumulative Topic Index** lists the literary themes and topics treated in *TCLC* as well as other Literature Criticism series.

A **Cumulative Nationality Index** lists all authors featured in *TCLC* by nationality, followed by the numbers of the *TCLC* volumes in which their entries appear.

An alphabetical **Title Index** accompanies each volume of *TCLC*. Listings of titles by authors covered in the given volume are followed by the author's name and the corresponding page numbers where the titles are discussed. English translations of foreign titles and variations of titles are cross-referenced to the title under which a work was originally published. Titles of novels, dramas, nonfiction books, and poetry, short story, or essay collections are printed in italics, while individual poems, short stories, and essays are printed in roman type within quotation marks.

In response to numerous suggestions from librarians, Gale also produces a paperbound edition of the *TCLC* cumulative title index. This annual cumulation, which alphabetically lists all titles reviewed in the series, is available to all customers. Additional copies of this index are available upon request. Librarians and patrons will welcome this separate index; it saves shelf space, is easy to use, and is recyclable upon receipt of the next edition.

Citing *Twentieth-Century Literary Criticism*

When citing criticism reprinted in the Literary Criticism Series, students should provide complete bibliographic information so that the cited essay can be located in the original print or electronic source. Students who quote directly from reprinted criticism may use any accepted bibliographic format, such as University of Chicago Press style or Modern Language Association (MLA) style. Both the MLA and the University of Chicago formats are acceptable and recognized as being the current standards for citations. It is important, however, to choose one format for all citations; do not mix the two formats within a list of citations.

The examples below follow recommendations for preparing a bibliography set forth in *The Chicago Manual of Style,* 15th ed. (Chicago: The University of Chicago Press, (2003); the first example pertains to material drawn from periodicals, the second to material reprinted from books:

Morrison, Jago. "Narration and Unease in Ian McEwan's Later Fiction." *Critique* 42, no. 3 (spring 2001): 253-68. Reprinted in *Twentieth-Century Literary Criticism.* Vol. 127, edited by Janet Witalec, 212-20. Detroit: Gale, 2003.

Brossard, Nicole. "Poetic Politics." In *The Politics of Poetic Form: Poetry and Public Policy,* edited by Charles Bernstein, 73-82. New York: Roof Books, 1990. Reprinted in *Twentieth-Century Literary Criticism.* Vol. 127, edited by Janet Witalec, 3-8. Detroit: Gale, 2003.

The examples below follow recommendations for preparing a works cited list set forth in the *MLA Handbook for Writers of Research Papers,* 5th ed. (New York: The Modern Language Association of America, 1999); the first example pertains to material drawn from periodicals, the second to material reprinted from books:

Morrison, Jago. "Narration and Unease in Ian McEwan's Later Fiction." *Critique* 42.3 (spring 2001): 253-68. Reprinted in *Twentieth-Century Literary Criticism.* Ed. Janet Witalec. Vol. 127. Detroit: Gale, 2003. 212-20.

Brossard, Nicole. "Poetic Politics." *The Politics of Poetic Form: Poetry and Public Policy.* Ed. Charles Bernstein. New York: Roof Books, 1990. 73-82. Reprinted in *Twentieth-Century Literary Criticism.* Ed. Janet Witalec. Vol. 127. Detroit: Gale, 2003. 3-8.

Suggestions are Welcome

Readers who wish to suggest new features, topics, or authors to appear in future volumes, or who have other suggestions or comments are cordially invited to call, write, or fax the Associate Product Manager:

Associate Product Manager, Literary Criticism Series
Gale
27500 Drake Road
Farmington Hills, MI 48331-3535
1-800-347-4253 (GALE)
Fax: 248-699-8054

Acknowledgments

The editors wish to thank the copyright holders of the criticism included in this volume and the permissions managers of many book and magazine publishing companies for assisting us in securing reproduction rights. Following is a list of the copyright holders who have granted us permission to reproduce material in this volume of *TCLC*. Every effort has been made to trace copyright, but if omissions have been made, please let us know.

COPYRIGHTED MATERIAL IN *TCLC*, VOLUME 202, WAS REPRODUCED FROM THE FOLLOWING PERIODICALS:

Extrapolation, v. 42, spring 2001. © 2001 by The Kent State University Press/ v. 43, winter 2002; v. 45, fall 2004. Copyright © 2002, 2004 by UTB/TSC. Both reproduced by permission.—*Foundation,* v. 28, summer 1999 for "The Thing: Of 'Monsters, Madmen, and Murderers'—A Morality Play on Ice" by John Trushell. Copyright © 1999 by the Science Fiction Foundation on behalf of John Trushell. Reproduced by permission of the author.—*Journal of Religion and Film,* v. 2, October 1998. Copyright by the *Journal of Religion and Film* 1998. Reproduced by permission.—*Literature/Film Quarterly,* v. 29, 2001. Copyright © 2001 Salisbury University. All rights reserved. Reproduced by permission.—*Science Fiction Studies,* v. 33, March 2006. Copyright © 2006 by SF-TH Inc. Reproduced by permission.—*Textual Practice,* v. 16, 2002 for "The Contemporary London Gothic and the Limits of the 'Spectral Turn'" by Roger Luckhurst. Copyright © 2002 Taylor & Francis Limited. All rights reserved. Reproduced by permission of Taylor & Francis, Ltd., www.informaworld.com and the author.

COPYRIGHTED MATERIAL IN *TCLC*, VOLUME 202, WAS REPRODUCED FROM THE FOLLOWING BOOKS:

Alessio, Dominic. From "Redemption, 'Race,' Religion, Reality, and the Far-Right: Science Fiction Film Adaptations of Philip K. Dick," in *The Blade Runner Experience: The Legacy of a Science Fiction Classic.* Edited by Will Brooker. Wallflower Press, 2005. Copyright © Will Broker 2005. Reproduced by permission.—Bignell, Jonathan. From "Another Time, Another Space: Modernity, Subjectivity and *The Time Machine*," in *Liquid Metal: The Science Fiction Film Reader.* Edited by Sean Redmond. Wallflower Press, 2004. Copyright © Sean Redmond 2004. All rights reserved. Reproduced by permission.—Booker, M. Keith. From *Alternate Americas: Science Fiction Film and American Culture.* Praeger, 2006. Copyright © 2006 by M. Keith Booker. All rights reserved. Reproduced by permission of Greenwood Publishing Group, Inc., Westport, CT.—Bruhm, Steven. From "The Contemporary Gothic: Why We Need It," in *The Cambridge Companion to Gothic Fiction.* Edited by Jerrold E. Hogle. Cambridge University Press, 2002. Copyright © Cambridge University Press 2002. Reprinted with the permission of Cambridge University Press.—Chapman, James. From "'A bit of the old ultra-violence': *A Clockwork Orange,*" in *British Science Fiction Cinema.* Edited by I. Q. Hunter. Routledge, 1999. © 1999 James Chapman. Reproduced by permission of Taylor & Francis Books UK.—Dawson, Graham. From *Soldier Heroes: British Adventure, Empire, and the Imagining of Masculinities.* Routledge, 1994. Copyright © 1994 Graham Dawson. All rights reserved. Reproduced by permission of Taylor & Francis Books UK and author.—Edwards, Justin D. From *Gothic Passages: Racial Ambiguity and the American Gothic.* University of Iowa Press, 2003. Copyright © 2003 by the University of Iowa Press. All rights reserved. Reprinted from *Gothic Passages* with the permission of the University of Iowa Press.—Fedorko, Kathy A. From *Gender and the Gothic in the Fiction of Edith Wharton.* University of Alabama Press, 1995. Copyright © 1995 The University of Alabama Press. All rights reserved. Reproduced by permission.—Grant, Barry Keith. From "'Sensuous Elaboration': Reason and the Visible in the Science-Fiction Film," in *Alien Zone II: The Spaces of Science-Fiction Cinema.* Edited by Annette Kuhn. Verso, 1999. © Barry Keith Grant. All rights reserved. Reproduced by permission.—Green, Martin. From *The Great American Adventure.* Beacon Press, 1984. Copyright © 1984 by Martin Green. All rights reserved. Reprinted by permission of Beacon Press, Boston.—Gross, Louis S. From *Redefining the American Gothic: From* Wieland *to* Day of the Dead. UMI Research Press, 1989. Copyright © 1989 Louis Samuel Gross. All rights reserved. Reproduced by permission.—Haggerty, George E. From *Gothic Fiction/Gothic Form.* Pennsylvania State University Press, 1989. Copyright © 1989 The Pennsylvania State University. All rights reserved. Reproduced by permission of The Pennsylvania State University Press.—Haggerty, George E. From *Queer Gothic.* University of Illinois Press, 2006. Copyright © 2006 by George E. Haggerty. All rights reserved. Reproduced by permission of the University of Illinois Press.—Hassan, Ihab. From "Quest: Forms of Adventure in Contemporary American Literature," in *Contem-*

Gale Literature Product Advisory Board

The members of the Gale Literature Product Advisory Board—reference librarians from public and academic library systems—represent a cross-section of our customer base and offer a variety of informed perspectives on both the presentation and content of our literature products. Advisory board members assess and define such quality issues as the relevance, currency, and usefulness of the author coverage, critical content, and literary topics included in our series; evaluate the layout, presentation, and general quality of our printed volumes; provide feedback on the criteria used for selecting authors and topics covered in our series; provide suggestions for potential enhancements to our series; identify any gaps in our coverage of authors or literary topics, recommending authors or topics for inclusion; analyze the appropriateness of our content and presentation for various user audiences, such as high school students, undergraduates, graduate students, librarians, and educators; and offer feedback on any proposed changes/enhancements to our series. We wish to thank the following advisors for their advice throughout the year.

Adventure Literature

The following entry presents critical discussion of adventure literature in the twentieth century.

INTRODUCTION

Adventure narratives have been a mainstay of literature from ancient times, and epics such as the *Odyssey* and *Gilgamesh* have inspired many generations of writers with their grand themes, which often include pitting humankind against supernatural forces, or against natural elements and human enemies. Scholars of the adventure genre have pointed out readers' enduring fascination with this kind of writing, but have also charted changes in attitudes toward adventure literature over time. Whereas the genre flourished in the late-nineteenth century, with such novels as Robert Louis Stevenson's *Treasure Island* (1883) and H. Rider Haggard's *King Solomon's Mines* (1885) enjoying enormous popularity and brisk sales, many writers adopted a more ironic stance toward adventure fiction in the years following World War I.

Adventure texts generally exhibit several common characteristics. They tend to be escapist, in the sense of offering the reader the opportunity to be transported to a "world elsewhere," distant either in terms of geography, like E. M. Forster's *A Passage to India* (1924), or in terms of its personages and events, like Edgar Rice Boroughs's *Tarzan of the Apes* (1917). Critics agree that adventure fiction must in some way encompass action—for example, exploration of unknown territory, as in T. H. Huxley's works; military action, as in Stephen Crane's *The Red Badge of Courage* (1895); or fantastic tales such as J. R. R. Tolkien's *The Hobbit* (1937) and Arthur Conan Doyle's *The Lost World* (1912). The adventurer hero is almost always male, whether a soldier, a scientific pioneer, or a memoirist, and tends to be an eccentric or social misfit who questions existing social values and norms. The main personage in adventure narratives often professes to be on a quest or mission. Critic Ihab Hassan has added that the hero is very often marked by a physical or psychic "wound" that motivates him to pursue his goal relentlessly. That drive to transcend personal, natural, and social limitations contributes to the reading public's fascination with adventure fiction, since, as Paul Zweig has written, "a man's essential moment comes in the midst of danger, when all of his life must be translated into action."

Following the enormous loss of human life, the failures of diplomacy, and the waning of British imperialism in the period after World War I, the adventure genre came to be regarded in a negative light because of its links with violence, nationalism, and expansionism. Successful novels such as Ernest Hemingway's *The Green Hills of Africa* (1935), André Malraux's *La Voie royale* (1930; *The Royal Way*), and George Orwell's *Burma Days* (1934) portrayed colonial adventure ironically, while straightforward adventure fiction began to be censured for its fostering of escapism as a means of avoiding dealing with political, social, and gender issues, for its outmoded sensationalistic style, and even for its vast popularity, the result of the mass marketing of cheap editions.

Modern scholars continue to find much of interest in adventure fiction. Recently critics have explored juvenile fiction as the typical and customary introduction to adventure literature, and have sought to analyze how the genre shapes Western culture's notions about masculinity and gender roles. The interplay between adventure fiction and colonialism has provided a focus for numerous contemporary studies as well, with special emphasis placed on its slightly different development in Britain and in the United States. Whereas reviewers were proclaiming the death of the adventure novel in England in the mid-twentieth century, it continued to flourish in the United States in, among other forms, the western story. The relationship between adventure fiction and the realist novel, too, has received much critical attention, with scholars examining adventure texts' seemingly contradictory claims to hyper-realism and anti-realism.

REPRESENTATIVE WORKS

Pierre Benoit
L'Atlantide [*Atlantida*] (novel) 1919

Edgar Rice Boroughs
Tarzan of the Apes (novel) 1917

Ralph Connor
The Doctor: A Tale of the Rockies (novel) 1906

Joseph Conrad
Heart of Darkness (novella) 1899

Stephen Crane
The Red Badge of Courage (novel) 1895

James Dickey
Deliverance (novel) 1970

Isak Dinesen
Den afrikanske Farm [Out of Africa] (novel) 1937
Skygger på Graesset [Shadows in the Grass] (novel) 1960

Arthur Conan Doyle
The Lost World (novel) 1912

Richard Ford
Rock Springs (novel) 1987

C. S. Forster
The Happy Return (novel) 1951

E. M. Forster
A Passage to India (novel) 1924

Wilfred Grenfell
Down to the Sea: Yarns from Labrador (short stories) 1910

H. Rider Haggard
King Solomon's Mines (novel) 1885

Ernest Hemingway
The Green Hills of Africa (novel) 1935
The Old Man and the Sea (novel) 1952

Michael Joseph
A Ship of the Line (novel) 1938

T. E. Lawrence
The Seven Pillars of Wisdom (nonfiction) 1922

Norman Mailer
The Naked and the Dead (novel) 1948
Why Are We in Vietnam? (nonfiction) 1967

André Malraux
Le Voie royale [The Royal Way] (novel) 1930

Peter Matthiessen
The Snow Leopard (nonfiction) 1978

Cormac McCarthy
Blood Meridian (novel) 1985

John McPhee
Coming into the Country (novel) 1978

V. S. Naipul
A House for Mr. Biswas (novel) 1961

George Orwell
Burma Days (novel) 1934

Paul Scott
A Division of the Spoils (novel) 1975

J. R. R. Tolkien
The Hobbit (novel) 1937

Percy F. Westerman
Winning His Wings: A Story of the R.A.F. (novel) 1919

OVERVIEWS AND GENERAL STUDIES

Paul Zweig (essay date 1974)

SOURCE: Zweig, Paul. "Conclusion." In *The Adventurer,* pp. 223-52. New York: Basic Books, 1974.

[*In the following excerpt, Zweig presents his conclusions about common traits of adventure writing from Homer to Norman Mailer, noting that in all of them "the adventurer's quest must be its own goal."*]

[Elsewhere] I have defined adventure simply as a physical challenge, a confrontation with bodily risk. The adventurer has chosen to meet death as an enemy. With his action, the adventurer says: "Death, thou shalt die." He will have won, finally, more often than he has lost. In the fullness of his act, he will have proved that death is fallible; that a man, crippled by mortality, can nonetheless win out against the limits of his nature. In the *Iliad,* an Achaean warrior asks his companion why they are risking their lives in battle. The companion answers: we risk our lives because we are mortal; we choose combat because it is the fate of man to die. Because death's ambush incites him to caution and fearfulness, the warrior chooses to stalk the stalker. That is why his acts do not need to be explained or justified. On the contrary, in mythologies, epic, and folklore, they are the source of meanings. The warrior's duel with death provides culture with its essential tools, its founding myths, its knowledge of the world.

It is in these terms that we have approached the great works of adventure literature, and the act of storytelling itself. But the questions we ask of past traditions are different from those we ask ourselves. Because our lives have not yet arranged themselves into history, we feel a deep connection to whatever is unfinished, groped toward. The clumsy novel, the bad movie, the flawed poem, if they are contemporary, struggle with the same bulky meanings that we struggle with. Listening to them, we hear our own voice speaking, full of stumbles and rough tones, and we are caught up in its struggle. Now, when the storyteller sets up in the marketplace, we are the ones who squat around him in a circle, dragging our past and dragged by our future. Historically speaking, literature has been the unique footprint of adventure, its definitive trace, like Friday's footprint on the sand. But here suddenly is Friday, his body oiled and naked, and here are we, clothed in caution, obsessively social. We cultivate simulacrums of danger in the interstices of our lives. We remark the self-serving energies of certain men who provoke actions we admire but also resent, wondering what it would be like to experience our own lives under the aspect of adventure. It is true that we have our small dramas of escape: our love affairs, our exotic vacations. But we also have a sense that alternatives have gradually been sealed shut as years pass; that every commitment we make has bricked us into a familiar, often comfortable identity, but one we can no longer choose to leave. Our uneasy fascination with adventure grows as the domestic walls become smoothed by use, until finally they resemble a mirror. Beyond the mirror, as beyond the hillcrest of primitive legend, exists a world of encounters, a magic world we imagine but never reach. Yet we glimpse it now and then. It erupts without warning and recedes in a blend of excitement and terror: a near accident in a car; a chance meeting with an old lover; a robbery. The world beyond the mirror breaks in upon us, wounding our methodical but fragile surfaces; and before the wound can heal, we glimpse an abyss of possibilities, a pit of otherness which is dizzying or frightening, but unforgettable.

Sometimes we feel that we have paid too high a price for our comfort; that the network of relationships and names which we have become does not leave us room to breathe. The limits which define us for others then seem like prisons. And we suspect, momentarily, that we live in exile from the best part of ourselves.

It is to this suspicion that adventures appeal. We daydream them, watch them in movies, follow them in newspapers, hear about them from friends, and tell our own modest stories under the guise of adventures. We allow ourselves this small measure of "irresponsibility," because we know that we have no choice. We need to find a defense against continuity. Adventure, we suspect, is our secret failing, as it was for Robinson Crusoe and Candide; it represents our inability simply to be ourselves; our "childish," illicit, but definite need also to be someone else, at least in our dreams. This is not simply a "literary" matter. Indeed, "serious" literature, as we have seen, does not encourage this vein of fantasy. Instead we must rely on our "bad taste" to let in pulp magazine stories, second-rate movies, sports events; or else, in another register, fast cars, gambling casinos, hikes in the wilderness: small vertical escapes from the chain gang of our days; parentheses of unreal intensity, which later seem dreamlike. Yet these side ventures have a reality of their own, an aura of released energy which is joyful even if it can be terrifying. These are our adventures: our "frivolous," necessary moments, like brief myths, which descend upon us, transposing us into their wholeness and vanishing.

Yet the scope of these daily adventures often seems fleeting and private; our bubbles of grandeur form and burst without applause, in a thin medium scarcely able to sustain our tall tales and our gossip. They are not adventures to sing about or live by, but to entertain in a minor key. Like Defoe, we have domesticated adventure. It has become a fillip for our identities; a wash of exotic color in our lives. Where in the modern world must we look, then, to witness the Nietzschean confrontation which Conan Doyle's romantic hero mused about in *The Lost World*:

> . . . it is only when a man goes out into the world with the thought that there are heroisms all round him, and with the desire all alive in his heart to follow any which may come within sight of him, that he breaks away as I did from the life he knows, and ventures forth into the wonderful mystic twilight land where lie great adventures and great rewards.[1]

What answer do we have for Conan Doyle's earthy newspaper editor, who objects: "I'm afraid the day for this sort of thing is rather past. . . . The big blank spaces in the map are all being filled in, and there's no room for romance anywhere."[2]

A few years before, Marlow, in *Heart of Darkness*, had told of his childhood fascination for those "white spaces" on the map. There were not many of them left by the end of the nineteenth century, but those that remained evoked a sense of mystery and confrontation with the unknown which Conrad conveyed with passionate skill. When another English writer, Charles M. Doughty, made his way into the Arabian desert, in the 1880s, it was, he said, to revive the splendor of the English language, by discovering a subject matter worthy of the high style. The result, *Travels in Arabia Deserta*, is a classic of adventure literature. Doughty devised a baroque style which transformed the desert into a world of heightened perceptions, like the magic countries of the *Odyssey*, or Gilgamesh's land of Faraway. For Doughty as for Conrad, the power of imagination and the resources of style were able to transform distance once more into an ontological fact.

Conan Doyle's hero in *The Lost World* sets out for the Amazon jungle, but, in fact, he travels further, into a fantastic valley inhabited by Stone Age tribes and prehistoric monsters. In Conan Doyle's popular idiom, the "blank spaces" were not merely undiscovered portions of the earth; they were gateways into another order of experience. The same was true for the French novelist, Pierre Benoit in his famous romance, *L'Atlantide.* For Benoit, the unexplored Hoggar mountains in the southern Sahara became a slate wiped clean of geographical perceptions, in which his vision of lost Atlantis could arise, as if by the natural motion of reality itself. The unknown still flourishes in the interstices of the known. Even in the twentieth century, distance can acquire a supernatural dimension and become a proper scope for adventure.

But as the mysteries of geographical distance have been solved by camera safaris, tourist cruises to the Antarctic, and the grim banalities of jungle warfare, the measure of distance has changed. Its horizon has come increasingly to exist in the emotional style of the adventurer, not in the "white spaces" which the map no longer contains. Already in *Heart of Darkness,* it is Marlow's narration which turns the Congolese jungle into a mythic wilderness. He sees it as a place of demonic confrontations, and he conveys his vision with dense language which describes not so much a place as a way of experiencing. The substance of adventure has been displaced inward, so that *Heart of Darkness* must also be read as a precursor of modernism, and Marlow's voyage up the Congo River as a voyage into the depths of the psyche. As Robinson Crusoe discovered that shipwreck and a desert island could not remove him from his mind, which held to the "middle station of low life," so our modern sense of adventure has discovered that an exploit's interior face contains its true potency.

This discovery prepared the way for several possibilities. The adventure story, which Mérimée, Robert Louis Stevenson, and Kipling had trimmed to a swift, bouyant genre, became slow and atmospheric; action swam in an elaboration of imagery and extreme emotions which became the architecture of a highly literary genre. The complex resources of style were devoted to myth-building of a new sort. Now, the magnifications of myth lay not in the framework of great exploits, but in the interior rhythm which the adventurer imposed upon the world of his experience. Instead of epic clarity, we had baroque developments of language. Instead of narrative swiftness, we had Gothic amplifications of atmosphere, a mythicization not of events but of sensibility. The classic adventure stories of this new genre present an unexpected anomaly: they tell tales of splendid courage and exotic actions in a style which secretes complexity and slowness, until the actions recede and become a background for the elaborate frescos of style. The greatest example of this new epic stylization is, of course, *Moby Dick,* in which the grandeur of the action is conveyed through an elaborate ground-swell of digressions

and stylistic asides. Doughty's *Travels in Arabia Deserta,* Conrad's early novels and stories, T. E. Lawrence's *Seven Pillars of Wisdom,* much of Malraux's work, especially *The Royal Way,* Genet's prose in *Thief's Journal,* are other examples of the genre.

The case of T. E. Lawrence is especially interesting to consider, from this point of view, because we have what amounts to two separate portraits of his career: one a product of the popular imagination, transmitted by newspapers, heightened by eyewitness accounts of famous people who knew him well; the other buried in the involute prose of his masterpiece, *Seven Pillars of Wisdom.*

The outward facts of his career are as simple as they are fascinating. Lawrence played a crucial role in a minor episode of World War I. While historic massacres were taking place in the trenches at Verdun and elsewhere, the British Arab Office in Cairo organized a campaign of harrassment against Germany's Middle Eastern ally, Turkey. The idea was to encourage a nationalist uprising in the Arab territories of the old Ottoman Empire. The enterprise might well have gone unnoticed, if an American journalist, Lowell Thomas, had not come across the Arab campaign and written a series of dispatches about a small, blue-eyed Englishman, who wore an Arab bridal costume, and out-bedouined the Bedouins on excruciating raids across the desert to blow up Turkish railway stations and destroy bridges. Suddenly this unimportant backwater of the Great War was news, and "Lawrence of Arabia" became a hero larger than any created by Kipling or Conrad.

It is hard now for us to imagine the enthralled atmosphere in which Lawrence's legend thrived. Crowds came regularly to hear Lowell Thomas lecture in London. For years after the war, newspapers were filled with rumors of new exploits and dark manipulations. Indeed, every colonial disturbance in the world during the 1920s seems to have been connected to Lawrence, who had conveniently disappeared from view. During the time of his legend, Lawrence enlisted as a recruit in the air force, under the assumed name Shaw, and he spent the rest of his life in a provocative sort of half-concealment, as an enlisted man in the armed forces. This private, almost invisible quality of Lawrence's post-Arabian years left the public free to create a troubling fantasy, which was never trimmed to size by real acts committed by the real man. The legend billowed in public, while Private Shaw kept half in and half out of his anonymous shelter in the armed service, like a secular monk, at least partly guilty of the Augustinian sin of pride at his excessive humility.

The popular craving for adventure reached an extraordinary peak during the 1920s and 1930s, in pulp magazines like the Doc Savage series, in Westerns, in the soaring cult of movie stars, in the creation of instant legends around figures like Rupert Brooke and Lawrence in England, and Lindbergh in the United States. Perhaps the catastrophic scope of World War I had something to do with it. The course of the war had been so vast and machinelike, and its results so paltry, that a certain conception of national life became suspect. One was eager to admire the heightened figure of heroes, but war, the traditional field for heroic endeavor, inspired horror. One wanted destiny scaled to the will of individuals, not cataclysms which made a joke of individuality, however brave or reckless. Also, one wanted to reaffirm an ancient sense of the unmediated struggle with fate, the primitive face-to-face between the Homeric hero and the god, between Beowulf and the monster: the demonic short circuit by which the heightened man swept aside religion, language, and morality, stepping beyond them into a sphere of solitary challenges. In this sense, adventure represents a sort of "Protestantism" of action, as opposed to the mediated, institutionalized bravery of heroes. But World War I had tarnished the mediating ideals; it had wounded the very notion of bravery. Death in such vast, faceless numbers could no longer be an adversary; it became a plague, a dissemination of poisons. Lawrence himself understood the problem, when he called the strategies of the European theater "murder war" and defined his own aims in terms which we have since come to identify as guerrilla warfare: an extended, minimally organized version of individual combat, on the model of medieval romance. By his own account, Lawrence stood in the shadow of Saladin, not Napoleon; his measure was legendary, not military. Even his military strategy, which the British military historian B. H. Liddell Hart particularly admired, presented a chivalric model: "Every enrolled man should serve in the line of battle and be self-contained there. The efficiency of our forces was the personal efficiency of the single man. . . . Our ideal should be to make our battle a series of single combats, our ranks a huge alliance of agile commanders-in-chief."[3] Against the backdrop of trench warfare, Lawrence's desert tactics, as he describes them in *Seven Pillars of Wisdom*, represent a sort of adventure war. We will never know how much of Lawrence's theorizing was done in the midst of the action, as he claims it was, and how much during the early 1920s, when he wrote three versions of his book, against the never-mentioned background of his immense fame. In any case, Lawrence identified unerringly the quality of solitary conflict, of "antinomian"[4] fluidity, which made his venture so appealing to the British public.

Lawrence's antinomian aura was not limited to his conception of military tactics. It was essential to the legend which magnified his obsessive personal qualities into a demonic portrait, owing as much to Gothic fantasy as to actual fact. Lawrence was perceived not only as a hero and a patriot, but as something of a monster: a homosexual, an uncontrolled killer, a masochist, a sadist, a cool manipulator. There is a certain comic-book exaggeration in the fascinated distrust, as well as the worship he inspired. Indeed, one genuine mystery is the extraordinary variety of opinions he fostered around him: Intellectuals like Robert Graves and George Bernard Shaw thought he was an excellent writer; Winston Churchill thought he was a great diplomat; Liddell Hart believed him to be one of the great military innovators of all time; the Arab warrior, Auda Abu Tayi, called him "the world's imp"; Allenby, the British commander-in-chief in the Middle East, suspected he was a "charlatan"; the French military attaché in Arabia, Colonel Bremond, thought he was a psychiatric case; many Arabs thought an "aurens" (their pronunciation of Lawrence) was a tool for blowing up trains. Perhaps the most troubling impression is one he relates in *Seven Pillars of Wisdom*. An old Bedouin woman, staring at him for a long time, marveled at his "white skin and the horrible blue eyes which looked, she said, like the sky shining through the eye-sockets of an empty skull."[5]

There is a question, itself part of the Lawrence legend, as to how much Lawrence was an accomplice in fostering these variously skewed impressions. He tells, in the *Seven Pillars*, of his genius for manipulation. Sitting one night around a tribal fire, he and his men preach the ideology of revolt:

> After dark we gathered around Auda's hearth, and for hours I was reaching out to this circle of fire-lit faces, playing on them with all the tortuous arts I knew.[6]

> Our conversation was cunningly directed to light trains of their buried thoughts; that the excitement might be their own and the conclusions native, not inserted by us. Soon we felt them kindle: we leaned back, watching them move and speak, and vivify each other with mutual heat. . . . They turned to hurry us, themselves the begetters, and we laggard strangers: strove to make us comprehend the full intensity of their belief; forgot us; flashed out the means and end of our desire. A new tribe was added to our comity.[7]

What he practiced with the Arabs, he seems to have practiced compulsively, perhaps even consciously, with everyone, always interposing a willed impression between himself and his interlocutors. As he writes: "I must have had some tendency, some aptitude, for deceit, or I would not have deceived men so well."[8] After Lawrence's initial notoriety was established, it is surely this element of refracted vision, as if the man had too many faces, too many shapes, for one to be sure he had any of them, that kept him in the public eye. He seems to be a man with too many biographies for us to believe he had any biography at all.

It is perhaps at this point that popular legend and Lawrence's involute self-portraiture intersect: The demonic voluptuary of pain, capable of extraordinary suffering and of inflicting extraordinary suffering, serving his country, and yet, perceptibly, making his country serve his own compulsive needs; providing an image of epic proportions to ignite the patriotism in the English soul, yet icily detached from the community of passions which the war drew upon, devoted only to his cruel privacy. All of this, like a page from a Gothic novel, made Lawrence the complicated, somewhat sinister figure of which England was both proud and afraid.

The impression we get from *Seven Pillars of Wisdom* is not entirely different. Indeed, the public and the private Lawrence are profoundly linked to one another, but there is a shift in emphasis which makes *Seven Pillars* an extremely curious book. It is, in some ways, an epic without any action; an elaborately crafted structure of impressions scaled to the stature of myth, within which the Arab revolt and Lawrence's reckless exploits proceed almost invisibly, as traces of feeling, modifications of the landscape. One sees why the Bloomsbury group was so interested in Lawrence. *Seven Pillars* is a book which Virginia Woolf might have written; its ability to mythicize the feelings of a very complicated man is oddly Proustian, too. Lawrence is by no means a master of his instrument as were these writers, but the resemblance of intention is striking. Precisely what made him so visible to the English public, his warrior qualities, blends in the book with the elaborate experience of the desert itself, with portraits of self-inflicted pain and troubled conscience, so as to be present only in the most elusive way.

Let me take a central example from the book. The march to Akaba is a turning point in the Arab revolt. Its daring conception and execution put the Turks on the defensive once and for all, and projected Lawrence into a central role in the war. By crossing hundreds of miles of impenetrable desert, by creating an army as he went from nomad tribes who distrusted each other almost as much as they hated the Turks, by drifting unnoticed behind the Turkish defenses, like a "gas" as he describes it, and then coalescing at the proper moment to carry the assault, Lawrence overturned the balance of power in Arabia. He demonstrated to the English that an irregular force using the desert the way pirates use the ocean, and held together by the fervor of an ideal, could do what no regular army could have done. Liddell Hart, a connoisseur in the matter, considers the Akaba expedition to be one of the important pages in the history of military strategy. In any case, it made Lawrence famous in Arabia and gave him almost unlimited credit with the Arab commander, Feisal, whose advisor he was. Yet it is precisely this bold relief which is missing from Lawrence's description of the Akaba expedition. The crucial actions of the march and its goal are present, in a sense, only as negatives, shadows cast against the densely colored atmosphere of the desert which Lawrence evokes on page after page in all its intricate variation:

> . . . we re-entered the volcanic ground. Little pimply craters stood about, often two or three together, and from the spines of high, broken basalt led down like disordered causeways across the barren ridges; but these craters looked old, not sharp and well-kept like those of Ras Gara, near Wadi Ais, but worn and degraded, sometimes nearly to surface level by a great bay broken into their central hollow. The basalt which ran out from them was a coarse bubbled rock, like Syrian dolerite. The sand-laden winds had ground its exposed surfaces to a pitted smoothness like orange rind, and the sunlight had faded out its blue to a hopeless grey.[9]

> We marched on, over monotonous, glittering sand; and over those worse stretches, "Giaan," of polished mud, nearly as white and smooth as laid paper, and often whole miles square. They blazed back the sun into our faces with glassy vigour, so we rode with its light raining direct arrows upon our heads, and its reflection glancing up from the ground through our inadequate eyelids.[10]

These desert passages, modeled after Doughty, but surpassing him by far, call upon all of Lawrence's artistry as a writer. In some sense they constitute the true subject matter of his book. The desert becomes a locus of values for Lawrence, but also a vision, a place of epic clarities within which the soft monotony of the town is brutally pared away.

Lawrence's desert is as far from England as Gilgamesh's cedar forest from Uruk and Grendel's cave from Hrothgar's brightly lit halls. The desert is "elsewhere," it is the essential elsewhere, and the desert traveler, like the archaic adventurer, is for Lawrence a traveler between the worlds. There is a visionary energy in *Seven Pillars*. Like Marlow steaming up the Congo River, like Ishmael sliding through the South Seas, Lawrence describes his entry into an order of mythic reality. Often, in the course of the book, the desert warrior is offered as an antitype which fascinated Lawrence, and which he tried, throughout his years in Arabia, to become, even to the point of madness. The Bedouin, writes Lawrence, exist in a world of moral and spiritual certainties, as stark and as vividly wrought as the desert landscape itself:

> They were a people of primary colors, or rather of black and white, who saw the world always in contour. They were a dogmatic people, despising doubt, our modern crown of thorns. They did not understand our metaphysical difficulties, our introspective questionings. They knew only truth and untruth, belief and unbelief, without our hesitating retinue of finer shades.[11]

Because values and their source in God stood about him like natural formations, a sort of divine geography, so to speak, the Bedouin nomad was not introspective or ceremonial; places were not sacred to him, domestic boundaries were merely conveniences to be erected and demolished; he was at home nowhere and everywhere, because each place he was and each place he wasn't was equally inscribed in the element of holiness:

The Bedouin could not look for God within him: he was too sure that he was within God. He could not conceive anything which was or was not God . . . yet there was a homeliness, an everydayness of this climatic Arab God, who was their eating and their fighting and their lusting. . . . Arabs felt no incongruity in bringing God into the weaknesses and appetites of their least creditable causes.[12]

The desert, for Lawrence, was an epic medium, generating perfect actions as naturally as the fertile land generated agriculture. Lawrence saw the Bedouin warrior as a man of pure acts that were ends in themselves: acts without pattern or long-range goal. Wherever the Bedouin was, became his goal; his life was essentially picaresque. He was an adventurer from birth. This was the ideal Lawrence longed for and learned to imitate by a ferocious act of will.

Yet he never could lose his trapped self-awareness. When he considers the great Arab warrior, Auda Abu Tayi, it is from a distance, and the distance, he felt, measured his failure to become another self: "The epic mode was alien to me, as to my generation. Memory gave me no clue to the heroic, so that I could not feel such men as Auda in myself. He seemed fantastic as the hills of Rumm, old as Mallory."[13] Lawrence drove himself to feats of endurance. He outdid the Bedouins in rough living, in ferocity, in the stealth and canniness of the desert. He planned and executed raids with all the skills of old Auda himself. He tried, too, to remake himself from within: to simplify the knot of "introspective questionings" which locked him into his European self ("The war held for me a struggle to side-track thought"[14]) and made him strangely exterior to the epic self for which the Arabs mistook him. But he could never succeed in this effort, and the failure became an obsession. A sense of his fraudulence plays through Lawrence's story like a leitmotif, paralyzing not so much his actions as his solidarity with them, his experience of being one with them. He felt that he was a put-up Bedouin. He apparently also guessed that the goal of Arab nationalism would be sold short in negotiations after the war, despite England's promises to the contrary. By serving Feisal he also betrayed him. Lawrence's adventures, therefore, were tarnished by a bad conscience. By an extraordinary irony, Lawrence created in *Seven Pillars of Wisdom* an epic world into which he had no entry. His longing for action exhausted itself in the delineation of a complex, stylistically dense "song" inhabited not by adventures, but by his failure to have had any, except, perhaps, at certain moments when a substitute for the Bedouins' naturally "thoughtless" nobility occured to him: pain, sheer mindless endurance which Lawrence came to value as a joust against nature, an essentially spiritual act. Suffering released him from doubts and betrayals; it was a divine drunkenness, a berserker rage turned inward. Suffering became a momentary access to the grandeur of the epic world. If Lawrence had a flaw as a military commander,

it was his inclination to undertake unimportant but excruciatingly painful missions; to throw himself into ordeals of endurance for the sheer pain of it. His description of a violent sandstorm conveys his sense of exaltation in suffering:

By noon it blew a half-gale, so dry that our shriveled lips cracked open, the skin of our faces chapped; while our eyelids, gone granular, seemed to creep back and bare our shrinking eyes. The Arabs drew their head-cloths tightly across their noses, and pulled the brow-folds forward like visors with only a narrow looseflapping slit of vision . . . for my own part, I always rather liked a khamsin, since its torment seemed to fight against mankind with ordered conscious malevolence, and it was pleasant to outface it so directly, challenging its strength, conquering its extremity.[15]

Lawrence has been called a masochist. He is frank about his erotic sensations when he was tortured at Deraa. But, in *Seven Pillars*, pain becomes a back door into Auda's world, a form of the adventurer's active passiveness, tinged by the longing for death:

Step by step I was yielding myself to a slow ache which conspired with my abating fever and the numb monotony of riding to close up the gate of my senses. I seemed at last approaching the insensibility which had always been beyond my reach: but a delectable land: for one born so slug-tissued that nothing this side fainting would let his spirit free.[16]

Seven Pillars of Wisdom is penetrated by a passion for adventure, but also by a sense of the fraudulence of adventure for the modern Englishman, condemned to a life of inner complexity. It also presents, in a brilliant stylistic fresco, the paradox of the modern adventurer: his actions ramify not into a story, but into a portrait of his sensibility, an aggrandized mythology of his self-awareness. The difference between the adventure story and the modernist epic of sensibility dwindles, as the authenticity of the adventurer's quest comes to lie not in the grandeur of acts themselves, but in the "form of experiencing" which encompasses the acts from within. *Seven Pillars of Wisdom*, like *Ulysses*, *Remembrance of Things Past*, and *The Man Without Qualities*, creates a constellation of inward space, a vast paralysis of style within which Lawrence's actual exploits move imperceptibly, almost irrelevantly.

Lawrence's eccentric prose embodies the paradox of our culture: its longing for great acts, combined with a sense of their irrelevance. Action creates values, yet it is a fraud; it represents the essential Nietzschean struggle, yet it is inauthentic, for authenticity exists only in the leisure of sensibility. What Lawrence himself experienced as a double bind verging on tragedy, became, a generation later, an intellectual passion, simplified eventually into an ideology.

André Malraux and Jean-Paul Sartre divide Lawrence's paradox between them. For both, the values of the domestic world seem false and confining. Claude Vannec, in Malraux's novel *The Royal Way,* has no love for the penitentiary society he fled when he came to the jungles of Cambodia:

> Although he was not naïve enough to be surprised by it, he had thought, in former days, about the conditions of a civilization which gives such a place to intellect that those who make a steady diet of it undoubtedly become overstuffed and are slowly brought to ever cheaper meals. Then what? He had no desire to sell cars, stocks, or speeches like those friends of his whose slicked-down hair signified distinction; or to build bridges, like those whose rough-cut hair signified science. What were they working for, if not to earn respect, but he hated the kind of respect they valued.[17]

In Sartre's *Nausea,* too, the world of social values and inherited gestures has become thin and scratchy, like the jazz record Roquentin listens to over and over again; each time it is played, the record becomes more deformed. For Roquentin, the community of shared words is no closer to the rich voice of the singer than this cunning imitation on the record player.

Yet, having judged the domestic world as severely as Nietzsche or Lawrence ever did, Sartre and Malraux draw opposite conclusions. Standing clearly in Lawrence's shadow, Malraux became not only a novelist, but a philosopher of adventure. In *The Royal Way,* we are told that Perken, an aging soldier of fortune, has carved out a fragile empire among the dissident tribes of Indochina. Behind Perken stands the legend of Meyrena, a nineteenth-century French adventurer, who made himself king over a confederation of jungle tribes. Both figures echo Lawrence's adventure in Arabia, and it is interesting that Malraux, only a few years ago, in *Antimemoirs,* should have retold the story of Meyrena in great detail, showing how much, even now, he is haunted by a vision of power and self-transformation of the kind Lawrence mythicized in *Seven Pillars of Wisdom.*

The central character in *The Royal Way,* Claude Vannec, is an intellectual and a student of history, like Lawrence himself. He has come to Cambodia to unearth valuable sculptures which he is sure adorn temples as yet undiscovered along the ancient royal way, deep in the Cambodian jungle. His plan is to steal and sell the sculptures, in order to buy his freedom from the domestic servitudes of a career. But Claude's quest in the jungle quickly becomes more real than any goal, more real than Europe or money. His adventure itself becomes the escape. When the carts loaded with sculpture are taken away by Moïs tribesmen, Claude has already forgotten them amidst the encroaching tragedy of Perken's death and Claude's own anguished insight into the cost, but also the necessity, of adventure:

> These worn-out ideas of men who believed that their lives served the end of some salvation; the words they say in conforming their lives to a pattern: they were

corpselike and dead, and what had he to do with corpses. The absence of a set goal in life had become a condition for action. Let others confuse this painful premeditation of the unknown, with a surrender to chance. All he wanted was to wrench his own images from a stagnant world. . . . "What they called adventure," he thought, "isn't a flight, it's a hunt: the established order does not yield to chance, but to the will to profit by it."[18]

> Being killed didn't frighten him: he didn't care much about his own skin; even in defeat he would have found his combat. But to accept the vanity of his existence, like a cancer; to go on living with the lukewarm feel of death in his hand: that he couldn't do. . . . What was this need for the unknown, this temporary destruction of the relationship of master to prisoner, which those who know nothing about it call adventure, if not a defense against those very things? . . . To possess more than himself, to escape the dusty life of the men he saw every day. . . .[19]

Adventure, for Claude, is a struggle against the diminished values of the modern world; but it is also, as he learns from Perken, a struggle against time, against age, against solitude, against the physical humiliation of death. Adventure alone can restore values which have been worn thin by domesticity. As he penetrates into the fetid atmosphere of the jungle, Claude enters into a primitive confrontation with the burgeoning power of life, thrusting itself upon him in all its viscous formlessness:

> As if into an illness, Claude sank into the fermenting forms that swelled, stretched, and rotted beyond the world where men count for something, and which divided him from himself with the force of darkness. . . . Now the oneness of the forest dominated; for six days, Claude had given up distinguishing beings and forms, life that moves from life that oozes; an unknown power bound fungus growths to the trees, made all those temporary things seethe over the ground like foam of the tide, in these steaming woods of the world's beginning. Could any human act have a meaning here? Could any will preserve its integrity? Everything ramified, softened, tried to adjust itself to a world that was both ignoble and fascinating, like the gaze of an idiot, assaulting the nerves with the same abject power as the spiders hanging between the branches, which it was so hard for Claude not to look at.[20]

The jungle has become the essential battleground, the element of life revealed to Claude in all its naked hostility. Against this "clenched fist,"[21] only a man of action can survive, returning blow for blow. As Claude strikes desperately at the stone wall of the temple, trying to detach the massive sculptures he has found, his act generates an ecstasy of pain; he flexes his very being against the forest, striking "almost unconsciously, the way a man walks when he is lost in the desert."[22] "He needed all the exaltation of his will to keep on going, to keep advancing against the forest, against men. . . ."[23]

To be sure, Malraux knows that a certain sort of adventure can be as fraudulent as the penitentiary morality from which Claude is escaping. Perken accuses Meyrena of having been a comic-opera figure, parading himself like a story, "a man intent on playing his own biography."[24] The captain of the ship which brings Claude and Perken to Cambodia formulates a judgment which Lawrence himself would have recognized: "Tout aventurier est né d'un mythomane," every adventurer starts out as a liar, a storyteller who wants to believe his own stories, and therefore needs to act them out. In this sense, the escape from culture becomes a coy act of culture, a dissimulated round trip; it is a going which is covertly a coming. The adventurer as *mythomane* has, in fact, never let go. He has simulated the radical separation of the traveler, but he persists in sending back messages which are stepping stones across the demonic seas, in view of his own safe return. We have seen that this traditionally has been an integral part of the adventurer's act, but Malraux challenges the tradition, and creates an adventurer who is committed to silence, or rather to a total act which does not need to be told in order to leave its imprint on the map of reality. Unlike Meyrena, Perken does not want to be a king, he wants to leave a "scar on the map."[25] Neither Claude nor Perken tells his story. As articulate as they are to each other—*The Royal Way* often resembles an essay on adventure—they tell nothing to anyone else, and nothing to us, who learn the story from a conventional novelistic narrator. Having abandoned the comic opera of storytelling, Malraux's adventurer is locked into a solitary combat with the viscous element of the jungle, with the fever of decay which saps his body, with the irreducible solitude which constitutes *la condition humaine*. Only in the mode of combat is it possible to know these enemies and to acknowledge them, without the interposed veil of customs and conventions, without the false comfort of society.

In *The Royal Way*, Malraux has simplified adventure into an act of revolt, which is also an act of truth. In the process, the epic desire to humanize the inhuman, extending the net of language ever further into the demonic darkness, has altered its focus. The act of Malraux's adventurer is not accomplished for man, but for self, because the adventurer has learned that "man" does not exist, but only selves. Name making and home going are not intertwined, as they were for Odysseus, for Gilgamesh, and for Beowulf. Malraux's adventurer refuses to have a home. He is not willing to die like Homer's Odysseus, at his fireside in the peace of old age, but rather like Dante's Odysseus, in mid-Atlantic. Malraux's morality of adventure sets aside T. E. Lawrence's concern about the fraudulence of action. Adventure circumscribed by silence becomes a crucial answer, perhaps the only fully human answer, to the problem of existence.

In these terms, we approach the most moving critique of the adventure morality in our century: that of Jean-Paul Sartre, for whom Malraux appears to be the perfect antitype, a dark and opposite twin in the manner of Gilgamesh and Enkidu. Like Malraux, Sartre expresses distrust of the intricate deceptions which bind men into a language, a set of principles, a routine of acts: in short, into society. Like Malraux, he pronounces a desperate judgment upon the "bad faith" of conventional attitudes, which conceal from each of us the terrible simplicity of "existence." Little by little, the shell of artifacts, names, and ambitions peels away from Sartre's hero, Roquentin. Against his will, Roquentin breaks through into a fetid vegetative life which had always been there, concealed by the enormous prestidigitation of culture: "A confusion of soft, monstrous bulks were left—naked, frighteningly, obscenely naked."[26] "Everywhere budding, blossoming, my ears droned with existence, my very flesh trembled and opened; it surrendered to the universal flowering. . . ."[27] The language might be Malraux's in *The Royal Way*, describing the jungle that closes in upon Claude Vannec. But where Claude saw a "closed fist," and struck back with hammer blows, Roquentin sees a limp flow of "marmalade," filling everything with its "jelly-like collapse."[28] This elemental larva-life does not call for acts; it is not a closed fist, but a jelly, dissolving acts, making them ludicrous. On the contrary, Roquentin's illumination requires that he "not . . . make the least movement,"[29] that he abandon himself to the overflow of a world without names, unmediated by acts and purposes. Instead of hammer blows, his response is "nausea" which is the bad taste of truth. As for the closed fist theory, Roquentin laughs bitterly:

> Imbeciles talk to you about the will to power, and the struggle for life. Hadn't they ever looked at an animal or a tree? This plane tree with its layers of peeling bark, this half-rotted oak, I was supposed to take them for harsh young energies spurting toward the sky. And what about this root? Should I imagine it as a hungry claw, tearing the earth, ripping out its food?
>
> I couldn't see things that way. Softnesses, weaknesses, yes. The trees floated; more like a collapse; from minute to minute, I expected to see the trunks become wrinkled, like weary rods, shrinking and falling to the ground in a soft, black, folded heap.[30]

This is not the only place in *Nausea* where Sartre seems to be answering Malraux. Indeed, if *The Royal Way* resembles an essay on adventure, *Nausea*, developing a similar insight into "existence," resembles an essay against adventure, and against Malraux. The character of Roquentin counterpoints that of Claude Vannec. Like Claude he is an intellectual, and a historian; like Claude too, he has been to Indochina. When Roquentin was younger, we learn, he had longed for a life of action, but something happened in Indochina to bring about a change in his thinking. As a result, he has chosen to live in a claustrophobic little town, Bouville (literally "Mudville") in Normandy, where he is writing the biography of an early nineteenth-century figure named Rollebon, a Casanova-like character whose life was devoted to intrigue.

Although he does not yet know it, Roquentin has begun his retreat from "action" into "existence." From acts, he has withdrawn to a history of acts; from adventure, he has withdrawn into leisure, made conveniently possible by a modest personal fortune. Having begun his retreat, however, Roquentin finds that it has taken him further than he meant. For his provincial routine gives way suddenly to "nausea," which is Roquentin's entry into the raw leisure of "existence."

The same insight which plunged Claude Vannec into action immobilizes Roquentin with a profound conviction that action of any kind is fraudulent. Willful violence was Claude's answer to the fetid encroachment of existence, but Roquentin, looking at a roomful of busy people, thinks: "They each had their small personal stubbornness that kept them from noticing that they existed."[31] The personal stubbornness, the obsession which focuses their lives, serves only to mask existence, not to confront it. The notion that "it is best to act first, to throw oneself into things,"[32] is precisely the lie out of which culture is made. As for adventure, it is simply a more flamboyant example of the same lie. Roquentin had been proud of the dangers he had sought out in Hanoi, Morocco, and elsewhere. They were luminous heights, moments of "melody" which he valued. But now it seems to him that the quest for such moments is not essentially different from the "personal stubbornness" of the toothpaste salesman. Roquentin may have sought out danger, he muses, but:

> I never had any adventures. Complications, events, incidents, anything you like. But not adventures. I'm beginning to see that it's not simply a question of words. Something was more important to me than all the rest, and I hadn't noticed. Not love, or God, or glory, or wealth, but . . . I had a feeling that at certain moments my life could take on a rare and precious quality. Extraordinary circumstances weren't necessary: all that I required was just a little discipline. There is nothing particularly brilliant about the life I'm leading: but from time to time, for example, when they played music in a café, I thought back, and said to myself: once in London, Meknes, Tokyo, I had fine moments, I had adventures. That's what they're taking away from me now. For no apparent reason, I've suddenly seen that I lied to myself for ten years. Adventures happen in books. And naturally, what they say in books can actually occur, but not in the same way. It was the way of occurring that was so important to me.[33]

At least one of Sartre's aims, in *Nausea,* is to discredit adventure as an alternative to the facile comforts of culture. If Malraux chose to express one side of T. E.

Lawrence's paradox—adventure as a program of existence—Sartre, with the sorrow of a disappointed lover chooses the other: the fraudulence of adventure, its quality of a willed artifact.

Yet it is clear that Roquentin's adventurous past has a bearing upon his fall into existence. His travels, the longing to organize his life into a "melody," even his fascination with the episodic career of the adventurer Rollebon, express embryonically his inability to accept the essential "dishonesty" of culture, its perspective of goals and purposes which stares with outrageous self-confidence from the portraits of local notables in the Bouville art museum. For Sartre, in *Nausea,* adventure is not an answer; it is a symptom, a first delirium of the nausea to come. Roquentin, returned from Indochina, is Claude Vannec who has entered into a more desolate wisdom. From the standpoint of nausea, the escape into adventure is a doomed attempt to use the tools of culture against culture itself. Leaving a "scar" on the map is ultimately not a form of silence, Perken and Claude to the contrary. It is a braver, yet stagier way to make a book. For "existence" to be an enemy, it must be seen with the eyes of fever, as Claude and Perken still see it. Roquentin has moved beyond fever, into the massive indifference of a larva-world which presses in upon him without will or intention, no longer as an enemy, but as a presence.

When the Autodidact wonders timidly if he might one day be ready to have an adventure, there is poignance in Roquentin's anger, for adventure had represented his last illusion that a victory might be won. Without an enemy there can be no victory. In Bouville, the will to adventure has become Bovaryesque, a gesture of escape reeking of the prison. The adventurer, for Sartre, is John the Baptist in the desert, announcing the negative dispensation of existence, but unable to let go of the last comfort which culture can offer: the book of his exploits.

The adventure of sensibility, developed in various ways by Melville, Conrad, and T. E. Lawrence, self-destructs in the immense passiveness of *Nausea.* As the adventurer explores the labyrinth of his sensations, he discovers that the labyrinth is no jungle, but merely a ramification of culture, another cell in the vast prison of continuity from which he thought to escape. Sartre, more radically than Lawrence, against the magniloquence of Malraux, announces the dead end of adventure. Unlike characters in the classical novel, Roquentin's leisure exists not this side of adventure, but beyond it, in a sort of negative beatitude.

The inward complication of the adventure story belongs to what may be called a vast imperialism of the mind, culminating absurdly, if splendidly, in the culture of the twentieth century. Since Descartes and Montaigne, a new space has been proclaimed for the accomplishment of aims, situations, and events; a space as complex as the material world, and as unfathomable as the cosmos of the Greeks: it is the space of personal experience. Whereas older, more humble conventions taught men to interrogate their experience in order to learn the nature of the world which impinged upon them in the form of events and situations, now men interrogate their experience in order to develop an interior geography, which has become the only locus for essential moments. If the Greeks suspected, uneasily, that they were guests among the higher mysteries of the world, the modern suspicion is different; today we suspect, uneasily, that it is the world which intrudes as a guest among the higher mysteries of the mind. The inward has accomplished an imperial victory over the outward. That is why storytelling has become a quaint and minor art, offering an antiquarian sort of pleasure: the pleasure of recalling a more ancient time when the world existed, and men could read it, according to the lexicon of signs which today serve only as metaphors for our experience of ourselves.

Pascal's image of man perched at the balance point between two infinities has taken on a strange literalness for us. We live with the firm conviction of the roominess of our interior space. We believe it to be largely unexplored, perhaps even inaccessible. We are fascinated by attempts to clarify it. We admire a sort of "travel literature" which has sprung up describing daring descents into the unknown element, for which the oceans, the heavens, and the depths of the earth provide metaphoric analogies. Coleridge's *Kubla Khan*; De Quincey's *Confessions of an English Opium-Eater*; Baudelaire's *Poeme du Hashish* and his *Paradis Artificiels*; the Romantic association of insanity with a form of adventure: All of these literary idioms borrow the traditional expectations of adventure to express our most daring enterprise: the exploration of interior space.

The very movement inward, which undermined the traditional framework of adventure, created in its place the medium for a new exploit, and a new simplicity. Alongside our Proustian, our Freudian, and our existential complication, we have circled back to a level of primitive certainties. By blurring the distinction between inner and outer space, by reversing our standards of value and authenticity, we have returned once again to the shamanistic origins of adventure.

If shamanism can be understood as a system of techniques for mastering the insecurity of personal experience by organizing its "absences" into a story, then the tradition of hallucinatory fantasies from Gerard de Nerval's *Aurelia,* to Hesse's drug narrative in *Steppenwolf,* and the "interior voyages" which form a vigorous element of contemporary literature, reassert once again a shamanistic vision of the psyche. The divorce between inward and outward adventure, consecrated by epic literature and reiterated by the Western tradition of storytelling, has ended in the nineteenth and twentieth centuries, so that we are faced today with an archaic insight: Once again we believe that the collapse of human limits—in the psyche as well as in the world—is a nightmare from which man perpetually awakens, by turning his terror into a story.

While T. E. Lawrence and Sartre grappled with the vanishing authenticity of "action," another, more naïve tradition asserted itself, founded on the shamanistic premise that the mind offers a shortcut into the invisible world which the psychic adventurer, using drugs, dreams, or trance, is not afraid to take, because he possesses the skill of safe returns, the skill of storytelling. Raymond Roussel and the surrealists; Herman Hesse; Henri Michaux; William Burroughs; more recently Carlos Castaneda's Indian sage, Don Juan: All of these, and others, have given rise to an idiom of adventure which has had a profound influence upon our cultural attitudes. Divorced from "action" by the enforced leisure of his self-awareness, the modern adventurer enters boldly into "interior space." Whereas Gilgamesh opened the great cedar gate, and Odysseus slipped compulsively into unknown seas, the shamanistic hero charms open the gate in his mind. The way out of the Gothic confinement of Sartre's no-exit world and Proust's cork-lined room has become not "action" in the old sense, but "absence" in the still older sense.

Indeed, the escape from continuity has become our most powerful cultural idiom, not only in Thomas Pynchon's and Norman Mailer's flirtation with adventure narrative, or in the immensely popular revival of medieval-style romance by Tolkien, but in the episodic sensibility of so much contemporary literature. The memorable works of fiction of the past decade have not been novels at all, but fragmentary forms, short stories, dream fantasies. I am thinking of Isaac Bashevis Singer's demonic tales; William Burroughs' *Naked Lunch* and *Nova Express*; Jerzy Kosinski's *The Painted Bird* and *Steps*; the pervasive influence of Borges; Norman Mailer's autobiographical journalism. It may be that William Faulkner was our last novelist. Since then, we have lost our interest in the extended metaphor of character which presides even over modernist novels like *Ulysses*.

One way to describe the change is this. The novel has traditionally set out to reassure the reader that a form exists in every life, giving it meaning and direction. The aesthetic wholeness of the novel, its beginning, middle, and end, make this meaning palpable. Every event in the novel, every emotion, no matter how seemingly arbitrary or spontaneous, has been kindled in advance by the impending satisfaction of an end, a palpable, inherently artistic conclusion.[34] What no man can grasp from within—the sense of an elaborate wholeness, a fully woven pattern—is offered comfortably, re-alistically, by the novel. Recently, however, we have begun to expect another pleasure from the stories we read. The spectacle of life's hidden form emerging from the vagaries of experience no longer warms our hearts. On the contrary, it chills us just a little, as if the form were a prison, and the novel's end-informed story the evidence for a failure of spirit. What Singer, Burroughs, and Borges express in their work are disruptive moments, flashes of illuminating intensity. It is not the end which is important, but the episode; not the form, of which the end is the final clarity, as when a sculptor unveils a statue, but the illumination itself, unruly and momentary, not casting a new light over what has been lived, but compressing life itself into its absoluteness, and bursting.

Robert Jay Lifton has written: "Such things as the drug revolution among the young, and their general stress upon intense experience, or upon what could be called experiential radicalism—whether in politics, art or life style—all these may well be quests for new forms of experiential transcendence."[35] Adventure, too, as we have defined it, is clearly a form of "experiential transcendence." In the midst of action, each move is dense with the weight of a lifetime, and is a lifetime, blazing with momentary intensity. Action fuses the moment into a separate whole, its parts powerfully compressed and interrelated, as in a dream. It is no surprise, therefore, that the popularity of episodic forms has been accompanied by a renewed fascination with adventure. The declining popularity of detective novels among the young is one evidence for the change. Whereas an older generation found its pleasure in the proposition that mysteries are puzzles which can be solved by "ratiocination," the young today show a marked preference for science fiction, or Tolkien-like fantasies; that is, for versions of romance, in which the mysteries exist not to be explained, but to be vanquished.

Perhaps the most interesting recent argument for the episodic has been made by Norman Mailer. In a sense, he is the historian of the change, and a main figure in it. Mailer became famous twenty-five years ago for exploiting the last subject matter in which a serious novelist and popular fantasy could meet: warfare. *The Naked and the Dead* is probably our last nineteenth-century novel, a kind of subspecies of *War and Peace,* and the final act of our nostalgia for novelistic wholeness. Ever since then, Mailer has floundered in and out of narrative, acknowledging his passion to tell a story, but recognizing, too, the campiness of "plot" with its mannered scenery, its characters busy doing nothing, its web of penitentiary relationships.

During those years, Mailer made an important discovery for himself. He discovered that he could no longer believe in the novelistic relationship between writing and life. The proposition that any man's existence, properly translated into language, could become a field of mysteries worthy of epic, was untrue, and worse, uninteresting. The net of syntax can be cast with intricate skill, but Leopold Bloom will still, ultimately, be a boring man, and Stephen Dedalus a sensitive but small-time aesthete.

The true "existential" exploit is not to make subject matter out of your life, but to make your life over and over again, into subject matter. In *Advertisements for Myself,* and *The Presidential Papers,* one sees a personality rising to the occasion of language, performing erratically, self-indulgently, because without the episodic heroism and the bizarre self-enlargements, he would not be subject matter; as if Mailer felt that to be the "hero" of a story, one had to be a hero in the archaic sense, the kind songs are sung about. Mailer's satisfaction as a writer resembles that of Odysseus at the feast in Phaiakia, when he tells the long story of his adventures. Mailer's public personality has been that of a man endlessly picking a fight: prizefighting has been his image of what it feels like to be a writer, but also of what it feels like to be a man. Who can forget the extraordinary description of Benny Paret's death in his fight with Emile Griffith? The climax of blows is hypnotic, like a sexual climax. It is Mailer's archetypal scene: a man facing death or humiliation, and therefore revealed in the fullness of his mystery.

A question is inevitably raised by this shift in the values of fiction. What adventures are there left to have? Where must one look to discover those gaps in the net of reality through which the adventurer slips? We know that forests are composed of ecological balances, not tree-gods and snake-spirits. We know that the horizon is not an ontological barrier. We know that all the places in the world are connected by lines of longitude and latitude, and most likely by politics, too. Yet the taste for adventure persists. Frivolous heroisms erupt when and where we least expect them. A man rows a dinghy across the Atlantic, or floats on a ship made of Egyptian papyrus from Africa to the Caribbean. Sir Francis Chichester sails alone around the world in a small sailboat. Mountain climbers scramble up a sheer cliff face, "because it's there." Young men and women hitchhike around the world, cross the Sahara, build primitive farms in remote areas of the Rocky Mountains, or hole up in isolated hamlets in Nepal.

The heroic explorations of Scott and Rasmussen, the muscular ambitions of Hemingway and Malraux, the intensities of Faulkner, appear even now to belong to a naïve age of belief, admirable but not wholly available to us. World War II seems to have been the watershed. Before then a residual confidence in adventure remained a firm part of the popular imagination, expressed in the old pulp magazines, in movies, in the sphere of political revolution, even in the fascination for great criminals like Dillinger and Al Capone. Since then, the world has gotten smaller and more businesslike. Even espionage and crime have become encased in the ordinary. James Bond amuses us precisely because we don't believe anything about him, because he is a kind of joke.

Mailer has said that he admires Hemingway and Malraux. He likes to imagine himself as a continuer of the tradition which they represent, the tradition of great adventurers. As a novelist, in works like *The Naked and the Dead, The American Dream,* and *Why Are We in Vietnam?,* he evokes the extravagant energies inhabiting moments of risk and extremity. But as his subject matter has intertwined itself with his own life, as Mailer has become the episodic hero of his "song," it has become clear that his personal exploits do not at all resemble those of Hemingway or Malraux. He does not go hunting in Africa, write battlefield reports from Indochina, or participate in revolutions. The heroism he builds in the interstices of his life and the extravagance of his style are elusive, often composed of a flirtation with ridicule. As if he earned rights to the heroic violence of his prose, by odds and ends of violence in his life, which are all that a "serious" man can manage these days.

Mailer's willful blundering describes the paradox of the episodic morality. Its exploits are not exotic journeys, crimes, even revolutionary violence. Its energy is aimless. Yet this is precisely what links it to the ancient energies of adventure, for the adventurer's quest must be its own goal. Like Odysseus, Gilgamesh, and the knights of medieval romance, the episodic heroes go nowhere in particular. The world may or may not harbor spacious possibilities, but the adventurer's magnificence lies in the going itself.

Notes

1. Conan Doyle, *The Lost World* (New York: Berkley, 1965), p. 11.

2. Ibid., p. 12.

3. T. E. Lawrence, *Seven Pillars of Wisdom* (New York: Dell, 1962), p. 341.

4. Ibid., p. 197.

5. Ibid., p. 220.

6. Ibid., p. 402.

7. Ibid., p. 546.

8. Ibid., p. 550.

9. Ibid., p. 245.

10. Ibid., p. 254.

11. Ibid., p. 37.

12. Ibid., p. 40.

13. Ibid., p. 547.

14. Ibid., p. 448.

15. Ibid., p. 251.

16. Ibid., p. 451.

17. André Malraux, *La Voie Royale* (Paris: Livre de Poche, 1959), pp. 36-37 (all translations mine).

18. Ibid., p. 37.

19. Ibid., pp. 37-38.

20. Ibid., pp. 65-67.

21. Ibid., p. 49.

22. Ibid., p. 82.

23. Ibid., p. 92.

24. Ibid., p. 12.

25. Ibid., p. 60.

26. Jean-Paul Sartre, *La Nausé* (Paris: Livre de Poche, 1959), p. 180 (all translations mine).

27. Ibid., p. 187.

28. Ibid., p. 189.

29. Ibid., p. 180.

30. Ibid., p. 188.

31. Ibid., p. 158.

32. Ibid., p. 159.

33. Ibid., p. 58.

34. Frank Kermode, *The Sense of an Ending* (London: Oxford University. Press, 1966).

35. Robert Jay Lifton, *Boundaries: Psychological Man in Revolution* (New York: Vintage, 1967), p. 28.

Ihab Hassan (essay date 1987)

SOURCE: Hassan, Ihab. "Quest: Forms of Adventure in Contemporary American Literature." In *Contemporary American Fiction,* edited by Malcolm Bradbury and Sigmund Ro, pp. 123-37. London: Edward Arnold, 1987.

[*In the essay below, Hassan explores the characteristics and aims of twentieth-century American adventure literature.*]

I

Quest? Adventure in the waning years of the twentieth century? In this era of satellites and supersonic jets, of the ubiquitous McDonald's and pervasive Panasonic? In our jacuzzi culture, in our cybernetic if not yet cyborg society, where *accidie* measures lives between hype and fix? Indeed, the very topic of quest seems now rather quaint, lacking, in academic circles at least, the glamour of feminism or poststructuralism, lacking even the glitz of Marxism.

Yet the subject endures, boasting a venerable pedigree. Think of Magellan and Drake, Marco Polo and Odysseus. Think, more recently, of Burton, Doughty, T. E. Lawrence and Freya Stark. Their tradition reaches, in postwar England alone, to Wilfred Thesiger, Francis Chichester, Chris Bonington. From rain forests, across oceans, steppes, savannahs, saharas, to the heights of the Andes or Himalayas, men and women still test the limits of human existence. They test spirit and flesh in a timeless quest for adventure, for meaning really, beyond civilization, at the razor edge of mortality. And they return, with sun-cracked skin and gazes honed on the horizon, to tell us all.

Adventurers can be eloquent, even loquacious. I shall, therefore, limit myself here to contemporary American prose writers whose work absorbs the traditional forms of quest, adventure, and autobiography into a somewhat esurient genre. And I shall address mainly one large query: what kind of symbolic option does this genre provide at the present time? So vague a query may be focused into three discrete questions:

(i) what are the literary features of the genre?

(ii) what is its historical motive in the American experience?

(iii) what does the genre finally reveal about contemporary individuals and their society?

Even then, our answers will remain probative, at very best, small, vicarious ventures into the lives we lead, dream to lead, in the closing moments of our century. The answers, in any case, will lead us from some general considerations of quest to selective literary examples.

II

The genre in which autobiography, adventure, and quest meet remains mapless. It draws on a wide region of experience, which we can try gradually to imagine, if not to define.

Consider autobiography first, now so abundant. Why this rage for self-witness? Perhaps because we live in a self-regarding age; perhaps because through autobiography we deny the obsolescence of the self in mass society, and hope to refute Nietzsche who proclaimed the self a fiction; perhaps because we lack consensus in our values, and so must ground our deepest articulations on the self, on death itself, the invisible ground of every

autobiography. But perhaps, too, we choose autobiography because it expresses all the ambiguities of our postmodern condition.

Autobiography is, of course, literature itself, the impulse of a living subject to testify in writing, as the Greek etymology of the word shows. But in the current climate of our ironic self-awareness, autobiography loses its innocence; it becomes the vehicle for our epistemic evasions, our social and psychic vexations. The innate contradictions of autobiography emerge to confirm the cunning of our histories. This is evident in the questions that theoreticians of autobiography now ask. For instance:

(i) Can a life ever be translated into words? Is there no irreconcilable tension between word and deed? Was St John or Goethe right about 'the beginning'?

(ii) Can a life still in progress—the dead don't write autobiographies, they only have biographies written about them—ever grasp or understand itself? Isn't autobiography doubly partial, twice biased, in the sense of being both personal and incomplete, partisan and fragmentary?

(iii) Can we clearly distinguish between fact and fiction in autobiography, any more than we can in news media? Isn't memory a sister to imagination, kin to nostalgia or self-deceit?

(iv) Isn't autobiography, therefore, itself a quest rather than the record of a quest, a labour of self-cognizance no less than of self-expression?

(v) And doesn't this quest, this labour of self-discovery, in turn affect the real, living, dying subject? Put another way, isn't autobiography shifty in that a first-person present (I, now) pretends to be a third-person past (he/she, then), and in the process alters both persons' character?

(vi) To that extent, isn't all autobiography both an act of dying (pretending to round off one's life in writing) and also a wager on immortality (aspiring to remembrance through print)? A false ending as well as a pseudo-eternity?

(vii) Lastly, how does autobiography transform the most private confession into public expression? Doesn't autobiography—however idiosyncratic, indeed, often *because* it is idiosyncratic—offer us the best mirror of a society, even of an age?

These conundrums of autobiography betray our graphomania, betray even denser complexities of our self-conscious age. Still, all the difficulties fail to inhibit the primal powers of adventure and quest, so frequently interactive. For if autobiography is the central impulse of literature, adventure and quest both revert to myth, which prefigures literature and still breathes life into all its shapes. Originally, adventure and quest related to such mythic narratives as the shamanistic flight, the hero's night journey, his trials in search of ultimate knowledge. Later, these narratives provided the structures and archetypes of epic, romance and novel. To this day, they inform the gothic novel, science fiction, the detective story, all manner of travel and action tales, which find rich analogues in the *Mahabharata* or the *Gilgamesh.*

Yet raw action is not really their point. In the most resonant adventures we find a spiritual element, a mystic or ontic affirmation, a sense of the sacred that confirms the order of Creation. As Paul Zweig remarks: 'The gleams of intensity which invest [these moments of being] have an other-worldly quality, as if a man's duel with risk were not a 'vocation' at all, but a plunge into essential experience. . . . Adventure stories transpose our dalliance with risk into a sustained vision.'[1]

We can suppose, then, that autobiography, adventure, and quest coalesce in a contemporary genre that conveys both the perplexities of the postmodern condition and the ancient, visionary powers of myth. This genre, defying any comfortable distinction between fiction and fact, employs the sophisticated resources of narrative to raise fundamental problems of human existence, problems personal, social and metaphysical. At its centre stands the 'hero with a thousand faces', as Joseph Campbell called him, an ontological voyager, a doer, prophet, and over-reacher, at once an alien and founder of cities, with whom we can still identify. Thus the 'I' that speaks to us through contemporary quests—henceforth I will use quest and adventure interchangeably—is both knowing and naive, historic and primordial, worldly and insubstantial. Its words constitute reality even as they confess its entrapments; its confessions draw us into a circle of experience which remains perilously distant from ours. In a sense, then, this is a genre of literature that hints its own abolition—in death, in silence, in extreme spiritual risk, in all those final conditions that make literature superfluous. Moments of pure being, like the 'great adventure', leave us mute.

III

But it is time now to engage the second question, regarding quest in its historic assumptions, its American milieu. Certain commonplaces of criticism offer us rough clues. American literature, critics have maintained, is largely autobiographical, a literature of the Self, from Poe's Arthur Gordon Pym through Melville's Ishmael, Twain's Huck Finn, and Whitman's Myself, to Salinger's Holden Caulfield or Bellow's Augie March. It is also a symbolic, visionary literature, less social than metaphysical, with a penchant for myth and romance. As such, it is an 'Adamic literature', with a bias for innocence and wonder, as the titles of even scholarly books intimate: *The American Adam, The Reign of Wonder, The Virgin Land, A World Elsewhere, Radical Innocence.* Finally, it is literature, though Adamic, of extremity, of intense and brooding modernity. Thus D. H. Lawrence notes in what remains the best book on

the subject: 'The furthest frenzies of French modernism or futurism have not yet reached the pitch of extreme consciousness that Poe, Melville, Hawthorne, Whitman reached. The great Americans I mention just were it. Which is why the world funks them, and funks them today [1923].'[2]

Such critical commonplaces indicate that quest is very much in the American grain. Its motive is in the wilderness, in the eternal search of misfits, outlaws, scalawags, crackpots, vagrants, visionaries, individualists of every stripe, for something they can hardly name: Eldorado, the New Jerusalem, the Earthly Paradise, the Last Frontier. 'Philobats' (walkers on their toes), as Gert Raiethel argues in his psychohistory of *voluntary* American immigrants, they form weak attachments to objects, persons, places; they relish movement, exposure, transgressive fantasies.[3] Yet Americans no more exempt themselves from history than anyone else. Their quests, therefore, reveal certain social attitudes, historical patterns, that we also need to ponder.

Here Martin Green's *The Great American Adventure,* which reviews a series of classic stories from Cooper through Dana, Melville and Parkman, to Hemingway and Mailer, proves relevant. Green contends that such stories manifest certain dispositions—I would not hesitate to say manners. These include a pagan, anti-intellectual, anti-pacifist outlook; a masculinist, often mysogynist, stance; a concept of manhood linked to nationalism, patriotism, America's Manifest Destiny; and a strong sense of caste, if not class, led by military aristocrats *and* democratic woodsmen (hunters, trappers, Indian fighters) who magnificently possess the frontier virtues of valour, self-reliance, knowledge of the wilderness, and, above all, a rude *ecological ethic.* This prompts Green to conclude that venturesome quests mark 'the highest achievement of American literature', indeed, offer 'the equivalent of the Great Tradition that British critics [like F. R. Leavis] found in the line of great novelists beginning with Jane Austen.'[4]

The thesis is suggestive, the social analysis moot. In any event, though adventure became secular and non sectarian in the last century, possibly even 'anti-Christian' as Green insists, it often took a spiritual, even mystic, turn. Green understands this; he says: 'Although hunting is an activity of the aristo-military caste, being a hunter in the American sense is in some ways not a caste activity, in that it takes place in a non-social space, outside the frontier of society. . . . Just for that reason, however, it represent more vividly the sacramental function of the man of violence. . . . Thus, if the hunter fails to represent the social aspect of caste, he nonetheless represents its religious aspect vividly.'[5] The religion in question is, I believe, 'natural,' the kind we sometimes see shimmer through the paintings of Thomas Cole, Frederick Edwin Church, Winslow Homer, or Albert Pinkham Ryder.

Spirit, then, is no stranger to violence, the violence of nature herself, the sacramental violence, too, of the hunter or primitive warrior who breaks the taboo against killing on behalf of his tribe. Indeed, some historians of the American frontier have come to consider the notion of 'sacramental violence' crux. Thus, for instance, Richard Slotkin claims that 'the myth of regeneration through violence became the structuring metaphor of the American experience.'[6] He continues: 'an American hero is the lover of the spirit of the wilderness, and his acts of love and sacred affirmation are acts of violence against that spirit and her avatars.'[7]

Slotkin's use of the feminine pronoun with reference to nature is instructive. The American hero loves nature but must also violate 'her', either profanely—exterminating the buffalo, wasting the land—or sacramentally. This ethos also affects the hero's attitude toward women, as Leslie Fiedler has famously argued in *Love and Death in the American Novel*. For quest always tempts the hero to abandon hearth, family, friends, leave society behind, a willed alienation aggravated by frontier conditions which released one kind of desire (freedom) only to constrain another (love).

Still, we can plausibly conclude that the historic experience of America proved singularly congenial to the spirit of quest. That experience conjoined energy and wonder, violence and sacrament, alienation and reverence, in unique measure. It is as if the 'complex fate' of which Henry James spoke at the turn of our century really entailed, more than a confrontation between Europe and America, a spiritual adventure into the uncharted wilderness of both the New World and of the Old Adam, Caliban, who Lawrence derisively invoked:

> Ca Ca Caliban
> Get a new master, be a new man.[8]

IV

Quests express our desires, betray our insufficiencies even more. For in quests, contemporary reality—personal or collective—finds a critique more stringent than in any Marxism.

We can commence with the solitary adventurer. What impels him to risk or seek? No single answer will do. Adventurers have adduced manhood, curiosity, rivalry, rage, the drive to excel, the need to experience extremity, the lure of things difficult and strange, the urge to confront death and master, if only for an instant, their own fate. Their motives may be ultimately, as we have seen, ontological: some profound affirmation of reality under the aspects of *both* harmony and strain, surrender and defiance. Chris Bonington reflects:

> The basic satisfaction of climbing is both physical and mental—a matter of coordination similar to any other athletic attachment. But in climbing there is the extra ingredient of risk. It is a hot, heady spice, a piquance that adds an addictive flavour to the game. It is accentuated by the fascination of pitting one's ability against a personal unknown and winning through. . . . It also gives a heightened awareness of everything around. The pattern of lichen on a rock, a few blades of grass, the dark still shape of a lake below, the form of the hills and cloud mountains above might be the same view seen by the passenger on a mountain railway, but transported to his viewpoint amongst a crowd, he cannot see what I, the climber, can. This is not an elitist ethic, but rather the deeper sensuous involvement that the climber has with the mountains around him, a feeling heightened by the stimulus of risk.[9]

There it all is: pride, risk, self-sufficiency, strenuous will, but also a 'coordination', some sensuous apprehension of being, beyond egoism. In its most intense awareness, the self opens, becoming everything that it is not.

Such solitary intuitions, however, scarcely exhaust the motives of quest. Men also venture in exclusionary groups, finding in male brotherhoods of power and peril alternatives to a society they contemn. Often, they avoid their own sahib-kind, drawn to 'natives', perhaps erotically, in associations that even racism may subtly excite. Often, they escape their own postindustrial societies, societies marked by bureaucratic chaos, collective alienation, immanent media, the deadly paradox of our time: 'unremitting [social] organization and the unleashing of vast destructive energies against civilization'.[10] In short, they flee the modern world itself, flee Western history, discovering another time in another place. Their quests, then, are as much judgements on the West as essays in utopia. Yet the best of them know that their intrusion on primitive 'utopias' alters them; their acts of exploration change the lands they explore. Applied to geopolitics, this Heisenbergian Principle—we affect what we observe—can be also called Colonialism.

This relates to what I term the adventurer's 'wound.' Frequently this is a literal, if obscure, infection, a mysterious disease almost like the Grail King's. Herman Melville suffers it in *Typee,* Francis Parkman in *The Oregon Trail,* Ernest Hemingway in *The Green Hills of Africa.* They all endure some debility, some 'pathetic' (the word is Melville's) flaw, a failure in their pampered immune systems. It is as if, in each seeker, two organic as well as social orders struggle more than meet. Call them Self and Other; call them the West and all *its* Others, those people it has discovered and deformed in the name of modernization. Thus 'the wound', secret agon of the blood, throbs also with the drama of colonial contamination. Is this the wound of postwar history, the revenge of the repressed, on an earth caught between enforced planetization and virulent retribalization? Khomeinis—and all their terrorists—believe they know the answer.

Yet 'the wound' is not only external, a gash in history, cicatrix of cultures. 'The wound' is also in the observer's mind, in his divided consciousness. It is in his enterprising gaze, a gaze without innocence, at once wounded and wounding. Encroaching on primal societies, the explorer finds, indeed *brings,* a serpent in every 'paradise'. Being human, he disturbs the pleroma of existence. Being, in addition, a Western seeker, adventurer, writer, he roils 'paradise'—it never was one—even more. Is this what the pathetic dis-ease of the adventurer conveys as it goads him on?

Note, though, who conveys, who speaks. It is not the wilderness nor its aborigines. Note who ventures and seeks. It is not the 'native'. In the Middle Ages, Arabs and Vikings raided the earth, roamed the seas. But since Renaissance voyagers, natives became 'natives' precisely because they remained where they had been born. They were dis-covered; like children, they were not meant to be heard, only seen. The winsome Bushmen and gentle Tasaday may have perfected an irenic mode of life. But they have not travelled far from the Kalahari Desert or rainforests of Mindanao—nor far from the Stone Age. It took another kind of curiosity, drive, aggression, ingenuity to speak them so that we all could hear. And as the Western explorers spoke them, everyone heard, everyone changed.

The adventurer/seeker, then, is a Westerner. Quest is the motive of his history and its deep wound. But it is the wound from which history flows, sometimes suppurates. His flight from modernity can not avail. His yearnings for desolations of sand or snow, in Arabia or Antarctica, lead him to an abandoned Coke can which rules that desolation more than Stevens's jar ever did the hills of Tennessee. Yet his will, malaise, disequilibrium, some radical asymmetry in his being, has made our world knowable, made the world we know.

V

We have reached the midway point; now abstractions must yield to selective examples. I have space for only five. Three would be labelled traditionally fiction, two non-fiction; all prove how fiction and fact, how quest, adventure, and autobiography, mingle in this avid genre.

Saul Bellow had never travelled in Africa when he wrote *Henderson the Rain King* (1959), possibly his best novel, no more than Defoe had visited the Americas when he wrote *Robinson Crusoe.* Bellow's book, we know, is a romance of ideas, a quest for reality, full of ordeals, initiations and rituals in the midst of mythic Africa. Its hero, Henderson, who speaks in the first person, is big, rich and strong, though past middle-age, with a face 'like an unfinished church', a truly exceptional 'amalgam of vehement forces'.

But Henderson's own heroes are not simply adventurers. They are men of universal service, like Albert Schweitzer and Wilfred Grenfel; they seek to give. For

Henderson has grown weary of the voice within him that always cries: 'I want, I want, I want.' He wants to conjugate it: 'I want, you want, she wants.' In the end, he goes back to study medicine at the age of 55. Before that, however, he must find his truth, which always comes to him in blows; he must overcome his chaos, his fear of death, his raging desires.

The search takes him to the Dark Continent. This is not only an exotic and distant place; not only the land we exploit or colonize; but also the space where we meet our darker self or double. There his bungling adventures lead him finally to a kind of terrible self-knowledge, terrible and tranquil at the same time. Like Daniel, he enters a lioness's den, and lives deeply in her mysterious presence; an avoider all his life, he tries to become like her 'unavoidable'. He enters Being, which alone enables Love, and learns to move with the rhythms of things—no more *grun-tu-molani,* as huge Queen Willatale enjoins him—not against them. And incidentally, he fulfils the quotation he once read in his father's library, which has haunted him throughout his life: 'The forgiveness of sins is perpetual and righteousness first is not required.'[11]

Quest, here, requires temporary exile from civilization, with all its clutter and distractions; it also compels Henderson to desert Lily, his second wife, the only person with whom he has a vital, struggling relation. Hence the recurrent prophecy from the Book of Daniel: 'They shall drive you from among men, and thy dwelling shall be with the beasts of the field.' But this archetypal movement into the wilderness must complete itself in a return. Having learned self-acceptance at last, having slain the monsters within him and without, and overcome his own death (frozen image of an octopus), the hero goes back to society. Thus Bellow encompasses both 'Africa' and 'America', nature and society, with his multiple moral as well as increasingly mystic vision. Thus, too, he shows that the garrulous, querulous, greedy 'I' can learn to become, through risk, something other than itself. Here is the passage:

> The odor was blinding, for here, near the door where the air was trapped, it stank radiantly. From this darkness came the face of the lioness, wrinkling, with her whiskers like the thinnest spindles scratched with a diamond on the surface of a glass. She allowed the king to fondle her, but passed by him to examine me, coming round with those clear circles of inhuman wrath, convex, brown, and pure, rings of black light within them. Between her mouth and nostrils a line divided her lip, like the waist of the hourglass, expanding into the muzzle. She sniffed my feet, working her way to the crotch once more and causing my parts to hide in my belly as best they could. She next put her head into my armpit and purred with such tremendous vibration it made my head buzz like a kettle.
>
> Dahfu whispered, 'She likes you. Oh, I am glad. I am enthusiastic. I am so proud of both of you. Are you afraid?'[12]

Here Henderson's wound—not literal though damaging enough—begins to heal. At least, so Henderson tells us in a fiction no less open than life.

Norman Mailer's *Why Are We in Vietnam?* (1967) is even more ambiguous as a fiction. Despite its title, the novel concerns Vietnam only obliquely. Ostensibly, the book relates a rousing hunt for grizzly in the Brooks Range of Alaska. Actually, it renders the initiation of a 16-year-old Texan, called D. J., into the violence within him and around him, a quest for manhood and identity, which will permit him to confront the war in Vietnam two years later.

D. J. is, of course, in the tradition of questing, adolescent heroes—Huck Finn (Twain), Henry Fleming (Crane), Nick Adams (Hemingway), Ike McCaslin (Faulkner), Holden Caulfield (Salinger)—whose initiation into reality also provides a critique of American society. Thus, in the remote wilderness of Alaska, under the Aurora Borealis, D. J. learns something about the betrayals of his father, the corruptions of America, the merciless laws of nature, the love and fear he harbours toward his friend, Tex—learns, above all, something about the intractable mystery of existence. Love, Power, Knowledge, Magic, Nature, and Death are all intimately bound; when their vital relations decay, we enter the universe of waste: cancer, excrement, money, Vietnam.

Once again, the hero learns from a beast. Here is the message in the grizzly's dying eyes:

> At twenty feet away, D. J.'s little cool began to evaporate. Yeah, that beast was huge and then huge again, and he was still alive—his eyes looked right at D. J.'s like wise old gorilla eyes, and then they turned gold brown and red like the sky seen through a ruby crystal ball, eyes were transparent, and D. J. looked . . . and something in that grizzer's eyes locked into his, a message, fellow, an intelligence of something very fine and very far away, just about as intelligent and wicked and merry as any sharp light D. J. had ever seen in any Texan's eyes any time (or overseas around the world) those eyes were telling him something, singeing him, branding some part of D. J.'s future, and then the reflection of a shattering message from the shattered internal organs of that bear came twisting through his eyes in a gale of pain, and the head went up, and the bear now too weak to stand up, the jaws worked the pain.[13]

As in Bellow's novel, so in Mailer's, social criticism blends easily into the metaphysics of quest. Mailer's satire of America—this 'sweet beauteous land' which has allowed plastic to enter its soul (materialism) and bureaucratic violence to shape its policy (Vietnam)—can be savage as well as obscene. No one, nothing, is spared in the 'United Greedies of America', as its messages collect nightly in the E.M.F. of the North Pole, and an 'hour before sunrise' begin 'to smog the pre-

dawning air with their psychic glug, glut and exudations, not to mention all the funeral parlors cooling out in the premature morn. . . .'[14] In the end, though, Mailer slyly introduces a radical uncertainty into his account. We never really know who tells the story: D. J., the white, athletic son of Dallas millionaires, or some 'mad genius spade' up in Harlem, a crippled disc jockey? Who speaks for America? Mailer will not say, though clearly his prose sings, no less a critique of America than a paean to it. Or is the whole book, this breezy, hip, sarcastic, poetic 'I', the voice of some demiurge, more beast than man, yet immaterial enough to speak its warning to the whole world, not just about Vietnam, through the Aurora Borealis?

In contrast to Bellow's and Mailer's fictions, James Dickey's *Deliverance* (1970) seems less a quest than a brutal tale of survival. The reader may wonder: deliverance from what? From moral complacencies, social pieties, perhaps from civilization itself? The clues are scattered, and in one place they become nearly explicit. Making love to his wife on the morning of his fateful adventure, the narrator, Ed Gentry, imagines—he is on the whole steady, unimaginative—the golden eye of a girl, a studio model: 'The gold eye shone, not with the practicality of sex, so necessary to its survival, but the promise of it that promised other things, another life, deliverance.'[15] Another life, deliverance: there lies the book's knot which links its two heroes, Ed Gentry and Lewis Madlock, doubles.

Ed—all are called by their first names—is practical and forthright, given to the task at hand, as Lewis is visionary. Lewis seeks immortality, and learns finally to settle for death. Meantime he trains himself implacably, trains his instincts, will and powerful body, to survive an atomic holocaust in the Georgia woods. He insists on turning the canoe trip of four urban businessmen into a moral, a life principle, a way, a provocation to everything Western civilization has achieved in 3000 years. He wants to recover something absolutely essential, and in doing so perform some superhuman feat that beggars eternity. But Lewis breaks his leg early on the trip—again that wound—and it is Ed who pulls the survivors through, after two murders and one death by drowning.

The scene is perfectly set for the encounter between nature and civilization, instinct and law, *within* the West itself. An entire region of the north Georgia wilderness is about to drown, turned into a serviceable lake. The Cahulawassee River, with its horrendously beautiful whitewater rapids, must vanish. Ageless cemeteries of hillbillies must be moved to higher ground. Marinas and real estate developments will appear on the dammed lake. On the eve of their departure, the four white, married, middle-class men pore over a coloured map of the region, intuiting the secret harmonies of the land, thinking that, henceforth, a fragment of the American wilderness will survive only in archives and the failing memories of old woodsmen.

Excepting Lewis, though, these businessmen are unfit to venture; they have learned to meet existence mainly on legal, domestic, or social terms. Still, they sense obscurely an alternative to their humdrum lives. 'Up yonder', as Lewis tells them, life *demands* to be taken on other terms. This they discover in scene after harrowing scene, in encounters with the stupendous force of nature (the rapids) and malevolence of man (hillbilly outlaws). Yet, too, they experience a strange happiness at the heart of violence. Three of them survive, irrevocably altered.

Dickey's novel is a masterpiece in the poetry of action and menace. Relentlessly, it renders, in a prose at once tight, elusive, and earthy, the atavism and terror of two autumn days in the Georgia woods. The book spares us no detail in the struggle of life for itself. But the book also reveals instants of subtle intimacy, moments of pure being. Having climbed, with bare hands, the sheer face of a gorge to kill a man at daybreak, Ed suddenly exclaims:

> What a view. *What* a view. But I had my eyes closed. The river was running in my mind, and I raised my lids and saw exactly what had been the image of my thought. For a second I did not know what I was seeing and what I was imagining; there was such an utter sameness that it didn't matter; both were the river. It spread there eternally, the moon so huge on it that it hurt the eyes, and the mind, too, flinched like an eye. What? I said. Where? There was nowhere but here. Who, though? Unknown. Where can I start? . . . What a view, I said again. The river was blank and mindless with beauty. It was the most glorious thing I have ever seen. But it was not seeing, really. For once it was not just seeing. It was beholding. I *beheld* the river in its icy pit of brightness, in its far-below sound and indifference, in its large coil and tiny points and flashes of the moon, in its long sinuous form, in its uncomprehending consequence. What was there?[16]

Perhaps this is the 'selflessness' of every mountaineer, every adventurer, at his moment of truth, healing all wounds.

Dickey prefixes an epitaph from Georges Bataille, which proposes a 'principle of insufficiency' at the base of human existence. The radical lack may underlie all life *as perceived by man*. Something is always buried, hidden, lost to us: murdered bodies lying under forest leaves, the forest itself flooded beneath a lake, hillbillies invisible, colonized within their own state, some part of our own nature, concealed and irreclaimable. Ed and Lewis—Ed *becomes* Lewis—manage to discover this perilous part of existence, and manage through great pain to reclaim it. But they must also face the or-

dinary world again, which Ed sees, at the end, in the image of a policeman: 'When we reached town he [the policeman] went into a cafe and made a couple of calls. It frightened me some to watch him talk through the tripled glass—windshield, plate glass and phone booth—for it made me feel caught in the whole vast, inexorable web of modern communication.'[17] The feeling passes, for Ed possesses the river permanently: 'Now it ran nowhere but in my head, but there it ran as though immortally.'[18] So ends his quest.

The transition from fiction to non-fiction seems almost imperceptible: the next two works share so many assumptions with the first three. Perhaps the authorial voice in the novels is less meddlesome; perhaps their interest in narrative, character, dialogue is more vivid or intense. Perhaps their imaginative freedom, a gaiety of reality, is more consciously felt. But these are matters of degree, conveyed in nuance more than in formal definition. In all, quest takes the language of the self to task and witness, and words walk in the shadow of death.

John McPhee's *Coming Into the Country* (1978) takes us to Alaska again, this time under the aspect of fact. As a reporter, an inspired essayist really, McPhee speaks in his own voice and gives us a luxuriance of precise detail, naming every flower, shrub, tree, bird, and beast in 'the last American frontier'. Yet the book often reads like a fable or romance because its characters are haunted by a dream of freedom, a stubborn intuition of possibility.

The Alaskan settlers—not the ones who go to make big bucks on the oil pipeline or a killing in real estate—all want space, independence, a chance to prove their worth. They seek a meaning in life, to which money, power, possession or celebrity is irrelevant. They want to live off the land, under the most exigent conditions, survive like Indian or Eskimo. They want to learn something about the final truths which civilization masks or distorts.

Their character, then, is solitary, anarchic, anti-authoritarian: no State or Federal interference, please! They are not socialists, not feminists, not joiners of any kind. But they obey the ecological ethic, without sentimentality or abstraction, like Cooper's Leatherstocking. Ecology? It is 'something eating something all the time out there', the wife of a settler says—eating out of need, without malice or waste. The voices of these uncommon men and women deserve to be heard in their own timbre:

> I want to change myself thoroughly 'from a professional into a bum'—to learn to trap, to handle dogs and sleds, to net fish. . . . It isn't easy to lower your income and raise your independence. . . . I've had to work twice as hard as most people.

I wanted to get away from paying taxes to support something I didn't believe in, to get away from big business, to get away from a place where you can't be sure of anything you hear or anything you read.

The czars exiled misfits to Siberia. The Soviets do that, too. . . . Alaskans are inheritors of determinative genes that took people out of Europe to the New World. [We're] doers. [We] don't destroy, we build.

The bush is so far beyond what anybody has been taught. The religious power here is beyond all training. There are forces here that a lot of people don't know exist.

Life and death are not a duality. They're just simply here—life, death—in the all-pervading mesh that holds things together.[19]

Does it all seem too literary? These pioneers, many of them college graduates, are articulate. McPhee himself joins them, drawn by their fierce vision. He knows that in their demesne, the grizzly stands as a symbol of freedom, the totem of all natural men who accept the rules of the wilderness, survival, death. (Like Faulkner's Ike McCaslin, McPhee doesn't carry a gun to see the grizzly.) But McPhee is also sufficiently clear-eyed to perceive their ineluctable contradictions. For the Alaskans end by reproducing the same conflicts they presume to leave behind. They bring with them alcoholism, envy, wife-stealing, even murder. And they dramatize the acute political dilemmas of our world in the four-way struggles between Federal Government, the State of Alaska, Corporate Enterprise, and the Individual, struggles that bush-planes and snow-mobiles carry to them at the edge of the Arctic.

In short, *Coming Into the Country* conveys tensions within both the Individual and American society—Freedom vs Equality, Progress vs Conservation, Libertarianism vs Liberalism, State vs Federal rights—tensions that even the immense Alaskan wilderness cannot resolve, dissolve. But the book also captures another persistent motive of the American Dream, the spirit of quest, an anarchic/religious impulse, still vibrant, still unappeased.

The motive in Peter Matthiessen's *The Snow Leopard* (1978) is explicitly religious, in fact Buddhist. Mathiessen tracks the rare, shy, nearly invisible snow leopard in the high fastness of the Inner Dolpo in Nepal. The animal becomes a symbol of spiritual knowledge or attainment, though Matthiessen never manages to see it. His Zen teacher had warned him before starting, in New York: 'Do not expect too much': that is, 'You may not be ready yet.' But in Zen, the admonition could also be taken to mean: to see or not see the leopard is the same, *satori* simply comes.

Matthiessen begins his journey in a troubled state. His young, beautiful wife, from whom he is about to be divorced, suddenly dies of cancer, leaving him a young son. The widower resolves to undergo the perilous journey nonetheless, as if to cleanse himself, come to terms with his guilt or pain. He gives us, in diary form, the record of his two-month mountain trek to the holy Crystal Monastery in the company of a professional biologist, George Schaller—who *does* see the leopard—as well as various Himalayan tribesmen and Sherpa guides.

The journey proceeds in several symbolic dimensions: horizontal (from Kathmandu to the Crystal Mountain), vertical (from valleys through mountain passes to unassailable peaks), temporal (present to past and back), cultural (West to East), generic (alternating between the forms of autobiography and didactic essay), and spiritual (a 'journey of the heart', toward enlightenment). The diary appears as a continuous dialogue of heterocosms, straining for peace between the One and the Many in all their manifestations.

This symbolic journey, however, is not without many complications and lapses. It confronts Matthiessen with the obdurate vanity of the self, its voracity, its tenacious fear of death. The journey also puts him in constant interactions with 'natives', including monks, lamas, and Sherpas, who form a loose caste system—lamas and Sherpas at the top. (Yet Tukten, the rogue Sherpa, a trickster figure and outsider, strikes Matthiessen as the most spiritually 'advanced'.) In them, he finds a tacit critique of his own society, its 'corrosive money rot', its 'retreat from wonder', its 'proliferations without joy'. Indirectly, he comments on race, sex, drugs, violence, illusion in America, with particular reference to the culture of the 60s, seen now from the austere, wholly essential—no dross there of any kind—perspective of the Himalayas.

How successful, finally, is this quest which subsumes the spirit of so many other quests? True to its moment, it seems ruled by ambiguities. Matthiessen relapses frequently into black moods; when he reaches the remote Crystal Monastery, he finds it empty; he never glimpses the snow leopard; he even begins to suspect that the willed act of searching may preclude the finding; he worries also that entrusting his experiences to the written word may falsify them irrevocably; and in Patan, after journey's end, he waits for Tukten at a Buddhist monastery in vain. Sometimes, even, he wonders if he has not been spared 'the desolation of success'. On the last day, he sees his face in the mirror: 'In the gaunt, brown face in the mirror—unseen since last September—the blue eyes in a monkish skull seem eerily clear, but this is the face of a man I do not know.'[20] Yet that stranger's face may also be the face of a being within us all, who neither error nor death can disfigure.

VI

Quests have no conclusion; they are extreme enactments of our fate in the universe. Everything is gathered in them, from existential meetings with death to the geopolitical conditions of our epoch, from the mythic experience of America to the facticity of post-industrial societies, from the literary problems of auto-biography to the nature of ultimate reality. As a symbolic option in the contemporary world, quests recover something essential to human life, often in encounters with animals (lion, grizzly, leopard), almost always in encounters with nature. However ravaging or equivocal, quests somehow pluck the nerve of human existence; they dispel the amnesia and anaesthesia, the complacent nihilism, of our cossetted lives. And they do so no-where more vividly than in contemporary American and British letters. It is not clear that they change the world: Thor Heyerdahl burned his reed boat, *Tigris,* as a pro-test against the conditions of our world, a flaming sig-nal of his disenchantment. But they may suggest a way for literature to renew itself, rise into bright forms from the ashes of postmodern ironies, parodies, pastiches, of all our vain verbal frolics. Perhaps Zweig will prove right, after all, when he says: 'The very movement in-ward, which undermined the traditional framework of adventure, created in its place the medium for a new exploit, and a new simplicity. Alongside our Proustian, our Freudian, and our existential complication, we have circled back to a level of primitive certainties.'[21]

But perhaps, too, all that will remain from quest is the indefectible perception of an individual alone, a percep-tion that, in our best selves, speaks of us, speaks to us, all. Thus Matthiessen:

> In other days, I understood mountains differently, see-ing in them something that abides. Even when ap-proached respectfully (to challenge peaks as mountain-eers do is another matter) they appalled me with their 'permanence', with that awful and irrefutable *rock*-ness that seemed to intensify my sense of my own tran-sience. Perhaps this dread of transience explains our greed for the few gobbets of raw experience in modern life, why violence is libidinous, why lust devours us, why soldiers choose not to forget their days of horror; we cling to such extreme moments in which we seem to die, yet are reborn. In sexual abandon as in danger, we are impelled, however briefly, into that vital present in which we do not stand apart from life, we *are* life, our being fills us; in ecstasy with another being, loneli-ness falls away into eternity. But in other days, such union was attainable through simple awe.[22]

Notes

1. Paul Zweig, *The Adventurer: the Fate of Adven-ture in the Western World* (Princeton, NJ, Prince-ton University Press, 1974), p. 4.

2. D. H. Lawrence, *Studies in Classic American Lit-erature* (Garden City, NY, Doubleday Anchor, 1955), p. 8.

3. Gert Raiethel, 'Philobatism and American Culture', *Journal of Psychiatry* VI (1979), pp. 462-96.

4. Martin Green, *The Great American Adventure* (Boston, Beacon Press, 1984), p. 18.

5. Green, *Adventure,* p. 110.

6. Richard Slotkin, *Regeneration Through Violence: The Mythology of the American Frontier* (Middletown, Conn., Wesleyan University Press, 1973), p. 5.

7. Slotkin, *Violence,* p. 22.

8. Lawrence, *American Literature,* p. 15.

9. Chris Bonington, *Quest for Adventure* (New York, Clarkson N. Potter, Inc., 1982), pp. 11f.

10. Ihab Hassan, *Radical Innocence: The Contempo-rary American Novel* (Princeton, NJ, Princeton University Press, 1961), p. 14. See also Erich Kahler, *The Tower and the Abyss* (New York, George Braziller, 1967), pp. xiii, 9, 22-3.

11. Saul Bellow, *Henderson the Rain King* (New York, Viking, 1959), p. 3.

12. Bellow, *Henderson,* p. 261.

13. Norman Mailer, *Why Are We in Vietnam?* (New York, Putnam, 1967), pp. 146f.

14. Mailer, *Vietnam,* p. 206.

15. James Dickey, *Deliverance* (Boston, Houghton Mifflin), p. 28.

16. Dickey, *Deliverance,* pp. 170f.

17. Dickey, *Deliverance,* p. 252.

18. Dickey, *Deliverance,* p. 275.

19. John McPhee, *Coming Into the Country* (New York, Bantam Books, 1979), pp. 177f., 178, 302, 255, 397.

20. Peter Matthiessen, *The Snow Leopard* (New York, Bantam Books, 1979), p. 328.

21. Zweig, *The Adventurer,* pp. 246f.

22. Matthiessen, *Leopard,* pp. 256f.

Andrea White (essay date 1993)

SOURCE: White, Andrea. "Adventure Fiction: A Spe-cial Case." In *Joseph Conrad and the Adventure Tradi-tion: Constructing and Deconstructing the Imperial Subject,* pp. 39-61. Cambridge: Cambridge University Press, 1993.

[*In the following excerpt, White provides an overview of popular travel and adventure fiction in England just prior to and during Joseph Conrad's time, stressing its connections with imperialism.*]

Once more the spirit of the age has found literary expression and the result is a whole revolving bookcase of literature charged with the spirit of imperialism.

(*Blackwood's Edinburgh Magazine,* February, 1899)

Closely related to travel writing was the adventure fiction of [Conrad's]. . . . In fact the line between the two discourses was often a thin one. Both constructed the imperial subject similarly, applauding the same heroic virtues of pluck and forthrightness in the conqueror, Othering the native in familiar ways, and making use of similar expressions, images, and plots. As Martin Green demonstrates, Victorian adventure fiction chronicled, as did . . . travel writing . . . , "dreams of adventure and deeds of empire." Both genres were tremendously popular, and both were well represented, side by side, in the flourishing periodical literature of the day. The reviewer quoted above, in *Blackwood's* celebratory millenial number, refers to works by such popular writers as W. W. Jacobs and Rudyard Kipling, and to Henry Newhall's *Drake's Drum* as examples of the current interest in books "charged with the spirit of imperialism." He also recommends a Mr. Vandervell's *Shuttle of an Empire's Loom* in which the British tar is depicted as having "unfailing pluck" and "indomitable good-humour" (p. 264), a familiar formula in travel writing and adventure fiction alike. The enthusiasm of the reviewer's contention that this "imperial" discourse was a literary expression of the spirit of the age promoted the readers' desire for the literary products while compelling their agreement with the beliefs that inhered in the age's spirit. More dangerously, . . . such authorizing of this discourse worked to silence any questions that might have suggested themselves about the European intrusion into non-European countries in the first place, for, in fact, both the travel writing and the adventure fiction of the day served to naturalize that intrusion and subsequent expansion "while inscribing difference into the very body of discourse and social relations in far from obvious ways" (Humphries, "Discourse," p. 114).

Blackwood's itself was a hearty participant in the imperial fervour, and the accompanying pieces in this 1,000th number evince this interest. For example, "From the New Gibbon" speaks triumphantly of the British Empire now at "the highest pitch of its prosperity," "its authority extended alike over the most dutiful of daughter peoples and the wildest and most sequestered barbarians," and boasts that even "two centuries of empire had seemed insufficient to oppress or enervate the virile and adventurous spirit of the British race" (p. 241). A piece on Jamaica constructs the imperial subject in a manner familiar to readers of travel writing in terms of the effaced European author and the homogenized, dehistoricized Other; this writer calls upon his readers to enjoy the sight of happy "negroes in their little log-huts . . . all seemed to be busy with something or another. At the doors women were sewing or men were cob-

bling" and "little picaninies in a state of nature" could be seen chasing chickens and pigs (p. 304). The facile and patronizing dismissal of "them," as contented and busy children—the "dutiful daughter peoples" presumably—in their "little" houses congratulates white writer and reader alike as representatives of a truly benevolent, productive empire. With "in a state of nature," we perceive the conspiratorial wink of writer to reader, both of whom understand the euphemism; not only are the children literally naked, and therefore uncivilized, but all these people are in their natural state—i.e. under the gaze of the European intruder and chronicler of imperial, civilized order. Other articles here include several pieces—stories and travel articles—on India, and on Malaysia, one by Hugh Clifford. All depict the white man as "Sahib" or "Tuan" against a generalized native population. Only the third item in *Blackwood's* 1,000th number failed to sound imperialism's triumphant note, the first installment of Joseph Conrad's "Heart of Darkness." Why its subversion was not felt by most readers is central to this study and will be the direct concern of later chapters.

In its construction of the imperial subject, then, adventure fiction derived its authority not only from its popular appeal but also from societal approval of its basic, and rather non-fictional, claims to be educational and inspirational, for the extent to which this discourse resembled the travel writing of the day, gave a special status to adventure fiction. So closely allied with travel writing, a genre that aspired to fact, after all, adventure fiction came to be viewed as a special case, demanding more credibility than other fictions. That both appeared not only in such an important publication as *Blackwoods*—as we have seen—but also side by side in such popular periodicals as *The Graphic,* the *Illustrated London News, Cassel's, Cosmopolis, Cornhill, Fraser's, Longman's,* and *T.P.'s Weekly,* earned for both a special status, marking them as part of the factual, workaday world of newsprint, not fanciful but part of the informational machinery of the day. In fact, both adventure fiction and travel writing were considered far preferable to novels about which general suspicion traditionally hovered, and book reviewers in the various newspapers and journals recommended the fiction as educational. By mid-century, the abundance of "penny-dreadfuls," cheaply printed, sensational novels aimed at the working classes (Hogarth, *Artist,* p. 16), such as *Black Bess, Tyburn Dick,* and *Mysteries of London,* to which almost narcotic-like qualities were ascribed, made most works of imaginative fiction generally suspect.[1] Religious Evangelicals and Dissenters, whose influence grew throughout the nineteenth century, went so far as to condemn the novel as "the Devil's bible" (Cruse, *Victorians,* p. 67f). The utilitarian argument against fiction which prevailed was particularly strong in reference to the working classes. The 1878 issue of *Publishers' Circular* expressed this view:

Free libraries, which should only be provided for the poor and helpless, not for those who can help themselves, should be resorted to for education and inspiration, and should begin at elementary works, long antecedent to works of imaginative fiction. If the ratepayers are to provide imaginative fiction, or the luxuries of the mind, for slightly poorer classes, why should they not also provide free games, free plays, *panem et circenses,* free cakes and nuts for the boys?

(Altick, *Common Reader,* p. 232)

"Luxuries of the mind," novels served no useful purpose. In his autobiography, *The Days of my Life,* H. Rider Haggard noted that in the year *King Solomon's Mines* appeared, 1886, the annual publication of novels was about 800. By 1894, Conrad could write his aunt in France that he had accepted his publisher's low terms for *Almayer's Folly*—£20—because publication itself was becoming so difficult; "every week some dozens of novels appear" (Karl, *Letters,* I, p. 178). By 1912, the annual publication of novels was up to about 3,000, reflecting a significant change in attitudes towards fiction, or simply a growing disparity between professions of belief and actual behavior. But in 1884, career novelists such as Henry James still felt they had to argue for the respectability of the novel and commented that while "the old superstition about fiction being 'wicked' has doubtless died out in England . . . the spirit of it lingers" (James, *Future of the Novel,* pp. 4, 5).

To avoid the stigma of being "merely a story," then, adventure fiction purported to be informational and often came equipped with the same appurtenances of fact as travel writing—appended maps, scholarly footnotes and explanatory prefaces. While having an interpretive stance that espoused imperial views, adventure fiction, like travel writing, was perceived as primarily factual, reliable reporting within a narrative enacted by fictional or semi-historical characters. Indicative of this perception was its considered suitability for a newly enfranchised populace, and interestingly, travel narratives and adventure fiction were considered together in this respect also. One of the innovations resulting from the Reform Bill of 1867, empowering school inspectors to examine the students in the higher grades on works other than the Bible, was that works such as "*Robinson Crusoe,* Voyages and Travels, or Biographies of eminent men," were approved of because these texts were all read as fact (Altick, *Common Reader,* p. 7). Fiction, as we have seen, was a frowned-upon frivolity, "free cakes and nuts"; the literacy needs of the working classes in particular, it was argued, should be confined to practical information that would make them more devout in their religious duties and more productive, obedient, subjects. Like *Robinson Crusoe,* Charles Kingsley's *Westward Ho!* was also read as a healthy corrective to the moral blight caused by novel-reading, and in at least one case of a youth "seduced" by fiction, that novel was offered as a solution to his destructive addiction. Upon reading it, according to a contemporary report, he abandoned his former life, reformed, and soon was respectably employed, filling "an important post in a large City printing office" (Greenwood, *Sunday School,* p. 6)—a convincing utilitarian argument, indeed.

Again the moral and economic arguments get collapsed here, for the century's literacy battles—in a manner familiar to us today—equated the democratization of knowledge with national prosperity. Since the 1840s, reformers in the wake of the first reform bill advocated only educational material that praised contentment with one's appointed station as a patriotic duty; any call for education as a means of social mobility would have been a voice in the wilderness. Rather, teaching the working classes their role in the scheme of things, and giving them useful knowledge laced with warnings against dissatisfaction were the goals of educational reform. Arithmetic—particularly for boys—was stressed as was geography, in order to "stimulate enterprise at home and swell the stream of colonialization" (Kay-Shuttleworth, *Popular Education,* p. 101).

That particular stream had been swollen with the poor, the idle, the criminal and had served as a convenient solution to England's rising population problem; Peggoty and Little Emily emigrated to Australia as a kind of punishment, to escape her disgrace in a new life. But by the second half of the century, settling in the empire's outposts was being spoken of as a kind of duty for the best representatives of all classes, but increasingly for the upper-middle classes, so important had the project become. Professor of Modern History, Charles Kingsley, warned his Cambridge undergraduates against the corrupting effeteness and frivolousness of contemporary life in England, and advocated instead manly activities abroad. As we have seen, he wrote admiringly of Brooke of Sarawak and also of his own son who "is now working with his own hands at farming, previous to emigrating to South America, where he will do the drudgery of his own cattle-pens and sheepfolds; and if I were twenty-four and unmarried I would go out there too, and work like an Englishman, and live by the sweat of my brow" (Lang, *Essays,* p. 158. See also Green, *Dreams of Adventure,* p. 218). Thus, the belief that the stream of colonization should be swelled because it was morally improving was inscribed in the discourse, urged in such patriotic terms by such authorities as Professor (and later Canon) Kingsley, so as to effectively naturalize the colonist's presence and conceal the fact of his intrusiveness. In even loftier terms John Ruskin would appeal to the Oxford undergraduates as fellow members of a "race mingled of the best northern blood," who must, as "youths of England, make [their] country again a royal throne of kings; a sceptred isle, for all the world a source of light, a centre of peace; mistress of Learning and of the Arts . . ." If England was not to perish, he told them, "she must found colonies as fast and as far as she is able, formed of her most energetic and worthiest men;—seizing every piece of fruitful waste ground she can set her foot on, and there teaching these her colonists that their chief virtue is to be fidelity to their country, and that their first aim is to be to advance the power of England by land and sea" (Ruskin, *Works,* p. 42). Consider the appeal: the moral obligation, the "destiny," of such a chosen people is to confer her light everywhere—and however—possible. This call to export British subjects, labor and ideas also repeated itself many times over in the magazine stories and adventure fiction of the day. Words are deeds and have consequences; whether Cecil Rhodes heard about Ruskin's lecture or read it—reportedly, Rhodes' library at Groot Schuur, Capetown included the works of Ruskin (Cloete, *African Portraits,* p. 151)—the discourse generally made a Rhodes inevitable, even though Ruskin later protested against the kind of empire-building he represented.[2] This appeal, then, was authorized in the educational discourse addressed to all classes, for a variety of reasons, under the guise of non-fictional Truth.

Travel narrative and adventure fiction, then, both enjoyed an elevated status and were read as similar discourses, subject to similar rules. Because of this association, the credibility and respectability of the one was also attributed to the other, thus gaining for adventure fiction an influential power that its predecessor, the Romance, lacked, one that shaped, with real consequences in attitude and policy, the outlook of generations of readers towards the imperial subject. Paradoxically though, adventure fiction and the travel writing that informed it were inscribed within the romance tradition. Both discourses were often framed as quest romance, thus necessitating the reader's view of the central protagonist as heroic and his endeavor as authorized, even divinely ordained. Interestingly, readers today respond with great strength to the travel adventure as romantic quest, particularly in regard to that paradigmatic saga of Livingstone and Stanley. Out of a possible multitude, a few examples: Marianna Torgovnick sees Livingstone as Stanley's "Grail" (*Gone Primitive,* p. 26), and similarly Jeal writes that Livingstone's search for the source of the Nile "had become a quest" and that it "would confirm the Sacred Oracles" (*Livingstone,* p. 329). Jacques Darras reads Stanley's quest for Livingstone as Marlow's for Kurtz, thus connecting the Belgian endeavor to the English one. Patrick Brantlinger locates common motives of quest romance in imperial adventure from *Treasure Island* to *Nostromo* (*Rule of Darkness,* p. 192f).

Victorian readers did not have to be familiar with medieval romance to understand the ideological appeal thus made, for Scott's historical romances had updated the genre for them, and by mid-century, the "Victorian mania for Scott had whetted the appetite for other adven-

ture" (Cruse, *Victorians,* p. 296). Adventure was the essential plot element of romance; the successful quest included the perilous journey and the crucial struggle and exaltation of the hero (Frye, *Anatomy,* pp. 186-187), certainly a familiar feature to readers of both travel writing and adventure fiction as was the impetus of romance towards "grave idealizing of heroism and purity" (Frye, *Anatomy,* p. 306). And as Michael Nerlich shows, from its beginning as twelfth-century knightly romance, the discourse argued that adventure was the exclusive property of a special class (Nerlich, *Ideology,* p. 6). In fact, as he goes on to show, the discursive power of the genre developed over the next few centuries as a justification of the existence of an embattled upper class (which might otherwise have been considered unnecessary, even parasitic), and as a glorification of its deeds (which might otherwise have been viewed as disruptive). In Haggard, this appeal is overt, for his protagonists Quatermain and Curtis write as members of an embattled squirearchy. Thus to invoke the romance, was to divinely authorize the questor's mission and place it beyond interrogation. But the Gradgrindian emphasis on facts authorized works of adventure fiction as "realistic" and "true-to-life," even though the writers' traces marked their stories "the way the handprints of the potter cling to the clay vessel" (Benjamin, *Illuminations,* p. 92).

Furthermore, adventure fiction generally announced itself as fact. Part of the particular pleasure afforded by the genre was that it concerned real places with geographically verifiable names, not airy habitations without names. In the prefaces and throughout the discourse too, this fiction promoted itself as chronicles of actual experience. From *Robinson Crusoe* on, adventure fiction had purported to work directly from original sources, and thus made claims on its readers' belief, presenting itself as having the force of actual experience behind it. As a contemporary writer, Andrew Lang observed, these writers had been there; as the "new conquerors," they had gone out of "the streets of the over-populated lands into the open air" and had "seen new worlds for themselves." This claim to provide eyewitness, and therefore reliable, information can be seen in the writing of Captain Frederick Marryat, Robert Ballantine, G. A. Henty, and H. Rider Haggard in their major works of adventure fiction that span the second half of the nineteenth century. In each case, the claim for reliability also serves to re-inscribe the imperial subject already constructed by the travel writing.

After serving in the Royal Navy for twenty-four years, from the age of fourteen, Marryat retired in 1830 and started writing novels that came directly out of those years at sea. In the preface to his first children's book, *Masterman Ready* (1841-42), Marryat describes his work as written in the "style" of *Swiss Family Robinson*, but he quickly moves to distance himself from that work, explaining his chief objection, its improbability:

> I pass over the seamanship, or rather the want of it, which occasions impossibilities to be performed on board of the wreck, as that is not a matter of any consequence: as in the comedy, where, when people did not understand Greek Irish did just as well, so it is with a large portion of the seamanship displayed in naval writers.

(p. v)

The preface makes further claims for the writer's authority. In it, Marryat goes on to object to the plants and animals inhabiting the supposed "temperate latitudes" of *Swiss Family Robinson,* plants and animals that he, from first-hand experience, knows are found only "in the interior of Africa or the torrid zone." These errors are inexcusable, he argues, for especially in works for children, "the author should be particular in what may appear to be trifles, but which really are not, when it is remembered how strong the impressions are upon the juvenile mind. Fiction, when written for young people, should, at all events, be based upon truth. . . ." However, that "realism" is relative and not absolute is borne out by Robert Louis Stevenson's comment several years later that he aimed to avoid what he felt were the great improbabilities that marred Marryat's *The Phantom Ship* when he was at work on *Ebb Tide,* a novel he intended to be grimly realistic (Hillier, *South Seas Fiction,* p. 134).

Ballantyne's claims are similar. Most of his books celebrated a cause of some kind, either supporting missionary efforts in Canada (*Hudson Bay,* 1848), the South Seas (*The Coral Island,* 1857), and Africa (*Black Ivory,* 1873), or a testimonial to the good work of the Ship wrecked Mariners' Society (*Shifting Winds,* 1866), or the suppression of the slave trade in Africa (*Black Ivory*). But all of them, didactic and polemical as they are, claim to be fact rather than fiction. Another "new conqueror," Ballantyne went out of "the streets of the over-populated lands into the open air" of North America with the Hudson's Bay Company at the age of sixteen; his first book *Hudson Bay* was actually a travel diary kept during his years with the Company. He continued to travel the rest of his life, as clerk, trader, fireman, or miner, in search of authentic settings for his fiction. So chagrined was he after *The Coral Island*'s publication to learn of a factual error he had written into that book—that coconuts grew on trees in the same form as Englishmen at home saw them in the shops—an error caused by his never having been to the South Seas himself, that he determined never again to write of places about which he lacked first hand knowledge (Quayle, *Ballantyne,* pp. 142, 143). In his first three books, *Hudson Bay,* an autobiographical account of

"everyday life in the wilds of North America," *The Young Fur-Traders* (1856) and *Ungava* (1857-58), Ballantyne assures his readers that his primary purpose is to inform, and he works to establish his credentials as an authority in prefaces, references to documented sources, footnotes, and purely informational asides. In his preface to *Ungava,* for example, he maintains that most of the major incidents are facts—"fiction being employed chiefly for the purpose of weaving these facts into a readable form," and that the intention of the story is "to illustrate one of the many phases of the fur-trader's life in those wild regions of North America which surround Hudson's Bay." He thanks the "Leader of the adventurous band" for his "kindness in placing at our disposal the ground work on which this story has been reared" (p. xi).

Interestingly, Ballantyne images books as factually informational within his fictions also. But he works to distance himself from those other, unreliable fictions; his heroes, he insists, are real, not heroes of "romance" (*Shifting Winds,* p. 17). Jack, the oldest of the trio of boys who shipwrecks on the Coral Island, frequently teases the youngest, Peterkin, that he would know more if he had read more. Because Jack has read a great deal, he has a store of handy information. "I have been a great reader of books of travel and adventure all my life, and that has put me up to a good many things that you are, perhaps, not acquainted with" (*CI* [*The Coral Island*], p. 25). Thus he knows how coral is formed, he can identify the breadfruit tree and knows its many useful products, and he knows the coconut can contain a delicious liquid, to the awed delight of his two younger, thirsty friends. Like Marryat's Masterman Ready and Ned in Henty's *Under Drake's Flag,* Jack has that valued commodity in adventure fiction, practical lore. But he credits books with his knowledge, particular ones at that. Later when Ralph, the middle boy who tells the story, finds himself in sole charge of a schooner, he happens to find an old volume of Captain Cook's voyages from which he learns "much interesting knowledge about the sea in which I was sailing, but I had many of my own opinions, derived from experience, corroborated, and not a few of them corrected" (*CI,* pp. 268-269). Travel narratives, then, are represented in this fiction as so reliable that they are to be read as information manuals and trusted more than experience itself. Rhetorically, this internal self-endorsing works well; it privileges the genre from within while arguing convincingly for its reliability. And it certainly functions to silence any notions that might disturb a contemporary reader as to the presence of these British boys on an island in the middle of the Pacific Ocean. The only "unnatural" aspect of this encounter, it is made clear, are the "barbarisms" practiced by the inhabitants themselves.

In his preface to *Shifting Winds,* Ballantyne thanks "the Secretaries of the 'Shipwrecked Mariners' Society' and of the 'Sailors' Home,' Well Street, London, for their kindness in supplying me with reports, magazines, and other sources of information." And in introducing *Black Ivory,* he qualifies the "fictional" quality of the work by assuring his readers he has examined the "Parliamentary Blue-books which treat of this subject" as well as "various authoritative works to which reference is made in the foot-notes sprinkled throughout this book" (*BI*, p. 10). These texts and their accompanying apparatus of quoted sources, maps, prefaces and footnotes urge their readers' belief and demand their effectual complicity in validating the fiction and its imperial justifications. Ballantyne often used his fiction to argue against the deplorable lack of contemporary emphasis on geography. Interestingly, his boy-hero, Martin Rattler, who excels in school in only one subject, his favorite one—geography—anticipates Conrad's experience as a student.

G. A. Henty's titles themselves claim a direct relationship with actual experience: *The Young Franc-Tireurs and Their Adventures in the Franco-Prussian War* (1872), *Under Drake's Flag* (1882), *With Clive in India* (1884), *With Roberts to Pretoria* (1902), and *With Kitchener in the Soudan* (1903), to name a few. They represent historical or still living figures of national import in real places. His prefaces sustain the claim. Addressed to "My dear lads," they are manly chats in which the author establishes his credentials as a teller of important truths. But what else is to be expected from a discourse that set such store by truth-telling generally? Henty's lads, as we shall see, are above all, honest. In fact, such truth-telling is an essential ingredient in the adventure hero's depiction generally. The preface to *The Young Franc-Tireurs* is typical in assuring the readers that in the following narrative, in the "guise of historical tales," he wants "to give . . . full and accurate accounts of all the leading events of great wars . . . While names, places and dates have been changed, circumstances and facts are true." Furthermore, he promises, he was there himself. He knew many of these irregulars or franc-tireurs personally, he promises his readers, and uses their own words often to tell his story, a story that would not otherwise have been recorded by main-stream historians. But we need to remember here, as Allen points out, that these were the days when the war correspondant was considered a gentleman adventurer, dependent usually on second hand information gleaned at day's end from the participants in cafés, beer gardens and barracks (Allen, "Henty," pp. 80-81). *By Sheer Pluck, A Tale of the Ashanti War* (1884) operates similarly, weaving together the fates of the fictional hero, Frank Hargate, with that of Sir Garnet Wolseley and his English troops. If Henty cannot give a first hand account himself, he cites eye-witnesses as sources, as in the preface to *On the Irrawaddy, A Story of the First Burmese War* (1897). Those witnesses include a Major Snodgrass,

"the military secretary to the commander of the expedition." That such a source can only strengthen his claim for authenticity is Henty's conviction apparently; that it might indicate a severe bias is a question whose investigation the author-reader contract established in these prefaces does not permit. And his appeal was persuasive. As a biographer notes, as late as 1955 in Britain, Henty was being reproduced in the Collins Schoolboys' Library, and in American schools as well his works were read as history for many decades (Arnold, *Held Fast,* p. 19).

H. Rider Haggard makes another kind of claim on his readers' credibility, an almost conventional one by the time he wrote in 1885, the travel writer's apology. In his preface to *King Solomon's Mines,* Allan Quatermain, Haggard's narrator, apologizes for his "blunt" way of writing. More accustomed to a rifle than a pen, he is incapable of

> the grand literary flights and flourishes which I see in novels—for I sometimes like to read a novel. I suppose they—the flights and flourishes—are desirable, and I regret not being able to supply them; but at the same time I cannot help thinking that simple things are always the most impressive, and books are easier to understand when they are written in plain language, though I have perhaps no right to set up an opinion on such a matter. 'A sharp spear,' runs the Kukuana saying, 'needs no polish'; and on the same principle I venture to hope that a true story, however, strange it may be, does not require to be decked out in fine words.
>
> (p. 20)

The disclaimer reminds us of Cook's who also felt that a plain style was appropriate for informational writing and hoped that "candour and fidelity [would] counterbalance the want of ornament" he was unable to provide. His authority, he maintains, derives from experience but also from factual travel accounts. If the travel writing of Cook and Livingstone informed Ballantyne, then Stanley was an important source for Haggard. *In Darkest Africa* certainly helped shape Haggard's belief in "the dark continent."

By thus disdaining any "literary" appeal, Haggard wisely broadens his audience and in fact disengages himself from the more literary *Treasure Island* on which he had originally modeled *King Solomon's Mines* (Cohen, *Rider Haggard,* p. 89). When Henry James referred to Haggard as Stevenson's "nascent rival" (Smith, *James and Stevenson,* p. 184), he acknowledged that those two writers were working in a similar vein, their chief difference being Haggard's lack of literary merit. While his remark intended to discredit Haggard for that failure, such was in fact Haggard's intention and one he often stated. The differences between those two works is revealing. Both were read as "adventure," but Haggard's followed the popular formula more closely and, consequently, enjoyed more success. In fact, Stevenson's quintessential adventure story, first published in *Young Folks* (October 1881), did not even sell well enough to boost the circulation of that periodical (Swearingen, *Stevenson*, p. 66). Certainly more literary than its companion pieces in *Young Folks*—"Sir Claude the Conqueror" or "Don Zalva the Brave"—it also refused to moralize, to include the "sayings of [Jim's] father or his mother" and passages of "a religious character" that Stevenson's father had advised him to add as a way "of harking back to something higher than mere incident" (Swearingen, *Stevenson,* p. 66). But it also refused to be "true-to-life" in certain ways. Its setting was distant but unnamed, and although inspired by Kingsley's *At Last* and well researched, it seemed improbable to many. Many readers found it too "fantastic" that a ten year old boy should be the hero of such bloody adventures and that the squire and doctor—English gentlemen, after all—should be so blind and gullible (Cohen, *Rider Haggard,* p. 89). Accused of not being factual, it was simply delivering the wrong fiction. That its sales were slow—a second edition was not required for two years—points up the essential ingredients of adventure fiction: at least a pretension to informational education and inspiration.

But eschewing the literary is also consistent with Quatermain's persona as a plainspoken, practical elephant hunter. In *Allan Quatermain* (1885), Haggard, in the guise of Editor, even corrects his narrator in a footnote, pointing out an instance of misquoted poetry (*AQ,* p. 90). To distance his telling from that of a novel—a work that needs added ornamentation to compensate for the barrenness of its content—also works to establish him as a reliable narrator of these events he took part in. Haggard acknowledges the tradition that holds that novels are frivolous fictions in order to characterize his narrator and the nature of his endeavor, but also to help counter objections to the believability of the events narrated. Such a disclaimer works for credibility, for it is an admission that the narrator has not the inventive powers necessary to bedeck and ornament, that his talents limit him to saying simply what happened. Like some simple primitive, his analogy suggests, all he can do is to trust that the unpolished spear he throws is so sharp and essentially sound that it will hit its target. He then goes on to construct his narration from his journal, from which he includes the occasional entry, to remind us of the journal's presence and therefore of the actuality of the events themselves.

In books Allan Quatermain does not narrate, Haggard avoids pretensions to the literary and sustains the fiction in other ways. In *She* (1886), for example, he establishes himself as "only the editor of this extraordinary history" (*She,* p. 17), working from papers left him by the original adventurer, including that writer's explanatory footnotes and only occasionally appending his own,

citing learned Egyptologists and other scholars to corroborate otherwise amazing pieces of information. In some of those footnotes and throughout the discourse, careful and accurate descriptions of indigenous flora and fauna and explanations of various physical phenomena common to Africa but unknown to readers at home, inform and earn the readers' belief that these narratives are based on facts. Haggard's narrator frequently deplores his inability to describe the essentially indescribable; beyond "the wild invention of the romancer" (*She,* p. 306), these events, although stranger than fiction, did indeed occur.

This claim to realism, then, gave the genre great persuasive power. Again, Lang speaks favorably of works such as Kipling's which "like all good work, is both real and romantic." While admitting of the possibility of adventure, it reveals "the seamy side of Anglo-Indian life" (Lang, *Essays,* p. 201). In fact the works themselves often addressed their readers' misinformation and sincerely tried to re educate. Ballantyne, Henty, and Haggard all expressed concern that the English reading public knew so little about geographical matters. Isabella Bird, an intrepid late Victorian adventurer/writer, and Conrad also, complained that Europeans generally knew nothing about geography and were extremely short-sighted to place so little value on it. For Conrad it was not even a set subject but the only one he remembers being very interested in (*Last Essays,* p. 2). So concerned was Stevenson with the widespread lack of accurate information that he wrote a series of letters to the *London Times* over a period of several years to try to correct illusions about Samoa that readers at home labored under.

Although read as Truth, then, and resembling travel writing in certain particulars, adventure writing was certainly constructing fictions, ones that worked to justify the European, particularly the British, presence in other lands. Those writers who "had seen with their own eyes," as Lang had noted approvingly, had done so in such a way that their view was often predetermined. And perhaps as André Gide observed in his *Travels in the Congo* (1927), dedicated to "the Memory of Joseph Conrad,"

> experience rarely teaches us anything. A man uses everything he comes across to strengthen him in his own opinion and sweeps everything into his net to prove his convictions. . . . No prejudice so absurd but finds its confirmation in experience.
>
> (p. 95)

These adventure writers, like other readers of travel narratives, were directly predisposed by those writers to view these other lands and the people who inhabited them in particular, predetermined ways. Like Kipling, Henty was a newspaper man, who, as a war correspondent for *The Standard* covered many colonial wars and on one such assignment joined up with H. M. Stanley, a fellow correspondent on the campaign and soon to become Commander of the Anglo-American Expedition for Exploration of Africa in charge of charting the Congo (Allen, "Henty," p. 90). Henty was covering the Ashanti campaign with Sir Garnet Wolseley (Gilbert's "model of a modern major general")—a campaign that left 4,000 Ashanti dead and 220 British and allied fatalities. "Covering" the war, as we have seen, is something of a euphemism, dependent as he was on second hand information. But even that term is too disinterested, for Henty certainly had attitudes already formed, and his accounts comprised less than objective reporting. Stanley returned to London and wrote *Through the Dark Continent* (1878), and whether Henty read Stanley's work or not is difficult to determine. The books Henty wrote out of the experience, *The March to Coomassie* (1874), *By Sheer Pluck* (1884) and much later *Through Three Campaigns* (1904) claimed to be factual accounts of historical, and fictional, characters in real places. But the attitudes towards the native and the Anglo-American presence in Africa were similar to those of Stanley and to many of the other writers of travel writing already discussed.

These writers, moreover, saw their fiction as continuations of real-life discussions in which they were personally participating. Kingsley, whose *Westward Ho!* celebrated Elizabethan England's imperialist ventures and successes, had read the journals of Rajah Brooke of Sarawak, as mentioned in the last chapter, and must have found himself in deep accord with that benevolent believer in progress, for he dedicated his work to Brooke, claiming he was "at once manful and godly, practical and enthusiastic, prudent and self-sacrificing . . ." (*WH*). As discussed earlier, Kingsley himself was a great promoter of colonization, issuing the call to England's youth in newspaper articles, fictions, and lectures. For Kingsley, Brooke was the colonizer *par excellence,* one Kingsley felt should be an inspiration to England's youth. Ballantyne also read much of the travel writing of his time; in *The Coral Island,* as we have seen, Jack extolls the virtues of Captain Cook's journals to Ralph, the central character, recommending it as containing much useful information. In Ballantyne's *Black Ivory,* the central characters frequently refer to Livingstone's work on the Zambesi, and editorial references are made in footnotes to other published works of "missionary enterprise." Haggard's first trips to Africa too were on official business; he accompanied Shepstone to South Africa to annex the Transvaal in 1877 and stayed on for a few years as a colonial officer (Cohen, *Rider Haggard,* p. 41). And since, as we have seen, the travel writers had their own reasons for defending the imperial project, from escaping the drabness of everyday life to establishing religious missions, their writing is other than objective. Whether these writ-

ers did "see new worlds for themselves," then, is doubtful. Even as they looked with their own eyes, they could not help, as we shall see, but view the landscape as beautiful and therefore worth annexing—or pestilential and thus in need of improving—the natives as inferior and therefore in need of enlightenment, and their own endeavors as benevolently heroic.

These writers were not spinning purely imaginary romances but were also informing the stay-at-homes in urban England of sunny foreign lands lately come into England's consciousness as acquisitions of empire. At the same time, however, adventure fiction argued powerfully for a particular interpretation of those realities, that the benefits of civilization merited British incursion into these lands. Influenced by the perspective from which travel narratives were often written, and by their own experiences in the outposts of empire, the writers of adventure fiction were intent both on revealing strange worlds to their readers, seen first-hand and additionally carefully researched, and also on shaping particular attitudes towards the imperial subject. That they did so with considerable effect derived in great part from the close association of adventure fiction with the highly esteemed and believed travel writing of the day. Indeed, this was "discourse" in Said's sense of writing that while manufacturing attitudes, rendered the machinery invisible.

But even though works such as *Masterman Ready, Westward Ho, The Coral Island, Under Drake's Flag,* and *King Solomon's Mines* worked in all these ways to be read not as novels, they were, in fact, clearly read as fictions, as exciting adventure stories about, in large part, fictionally constructed characters. Then why, in a culture that so distrusted novel-reading, did they become not only so popular and abundant but also officially validated? For they did indeed become recommended reading, especially for the young, and were, in fact, the prizes the culture conferred upon the young for good behavior. The answer must lie in their usefulness as inspirational literature, for they served the various utilitarian purposes of dispensing practical and historical information and of promoting an ideology of patriotic heroism and Christian dutifulness compatible with imperialistic aims.

The genre's ideology served imperial concerns so well, in fact, that it often became required reading. According to a biographer of Marryat, officers in H.M.S. Britannia were obliged to read and to memorize passages from *Peter Simple,* chapter 15 in particular, for in illustrating the value of a crew's unswerving obedience to a knowledgable, dutiful captain at sea, it both instructed and inspired (Warner, *Marryat,* p. 157). In this chapter, the frigate Peter is serving on has just captured two or three French vessels when "we had an instance showing how very important it is that a captain of a man-of-war should be a good sailor, and have his ship in such discipline as to be strictly obeyed by his ship's company" (p. 99). The device of a fifteen year old midshipman who is too young to participate in some of the action but has the perfect vantage point for narrating is effective. A kind of Joseph Andrews ingénu, his youthful inexperience is a good part of his appeal, and he takes as his models, as the readers also should, the captain and the admirable Mr. Chucks, "the best boatswain in the navy," the first lieutenant tells the Captain (p. 129). During this particularly life-threatening maneuver, absolute obedience is demanded and received, even by the mate who had not agreed with the captain's orders but had obeyed, for

> he was too good an officer, and knew that there was no time for discussion, to make any remark; and the event proved that the captain was right.
>
> 'My lads,' said the captain to the ship's company, 'you have behaved well, and I thank you; but I must tell you honestly that we have more difficulties to get through.'
>
> 'Mr. Falcon,' said he, at last, 'we must put the mainsail on her.'
>
> 'She never can bear it, sir.'
>
> 'She *must* bear it,' was the reply.

(p. 103)

The mainsail is set and the ship careens so in the storm that the first lieutenant, still a "good officer" presumably, cannot restrain himself: "'If anything starts, we are lost, sir,' observed the first lieutenant." He is practically certain of death yet maintains his observance of the code, never forgetting his place in the hierarchy— "Sir"—and "observing" rather than "screaming," or "complaining." Calmly, the captain replied, "'I am perfectly aware of it . . .'" (p. 105). A reader would not have to memorize this passage in order to learn the lesson here; if anyone in this situation had neglected his duty, all would suffer, and it is the indomitable Mr. Chucks who concludes "'Private feelings must always be sacrificed for the public service'" (p. 108), the message officers and readers alike should heed.

Kingsley's *Westward Ho!* was also put to good use, as we have seen, to reform wayward youths. Its writing was inspired, he admitted, by the enthusiastic support he felt for England's participation in the Crimean War. He thought of *Westward Ho!* as "containing doctrine profitable for these times" (Kingsley, (ed.), *Letters,* p. 214), for it espoused the same anti-Catholicism that was an important force behind the war and, for Kingsley, helped to justify that war. A year later, in 1856, he wrote "Brave Words for British Soldiers and Sailors," a tract that was distributed among the troops in Crimea, the only one of many such inspirational tracts the men actually read, a correspondant assured him. As a result of its success, he was made one of the Queen's chaplains and was presented to Victoria and the Prince Consort.

In shaping attitudes essential to the imperial subject, then, adventure fiction was extremely useful. Increasingly abundant and popular, it came to be "the energyzing myth of English imperialism . . . the story England told itself as it went to sleep at night" (Green, *Dreams of Adventure,* p. 3). Even though much of this discourse was aimed at a general audience—only three of Marryat's twenty-seven books were specifically for "young people"—much of it was addressed particularly to future empire builders and often appeared in periodicals such as *Young Folks, Union Jack* and *Boy's Own Magazine.* And what Orwell was to note of the Boy's Weeklies in the early twentieth century pertains to their Victorian counterparts as well, that even more than the national dailies with large circulation, they "reflect[ed] the minds of their readers" (Orwell and Angus (eds.), *Collected Essays,* p. 461). Imperial literature, in fact, bore the same relationship to its readers as parents to children; it espoused a similar ideology of duty, discipline, honesty, obedience and responsibility. In fact we see the same relationship reflected in the language of the adventure fiction that starts to deal with the subject peoples, especially the exotic subjects of the empire's outposts, Mother/country and Daughter/colonies. If, as Brantlinger suggests, Africa let men act like boys ("Victorians and Africans," p. 190), then similarly the fiction about Africa and other colonial outposts provided vicarious pleasures not only to young readers but also their fathers.[3]

G. A. Henty's more than eighty novels about the achievements of the British army in colonial settings were usually prefaced with "My dear lads." He actually aroused those dear lads to such a patriotic pitch that the generation reading him as Christmas gifts in 1900 were ready for the trenches fourteen years later (Allen, "Henty," p. 97). (See also Fussell, *Great War,* p. 155f). In his preface, Ballantyne presents *The Coral Island* "specially to boys" and signs it "Ralph Rover," the involved narrator of the tale. Others of his novels are entitled after their young heroes such as *Martin Rattler,* or *The Young Fur-Traders* (1856), making their intended audiences apparent. *Treasure Island* was addressed to "the wise youngsters of today" in the hope that youth had not become so studious as to forget its "ancient appetites" for Kingston or "Ballantyne the brave," and was signed "Captain George North." One of the great appeals of this fiction, then, was that it was delivered as truths passed on from one generation to the next. The persona of the speaker, a kindly and experienced older chap who appeared to know exactly what he was talking about and whose heart was obviously in the right place, did nothing to encourage disbelief or disobedience. The tone sustained in all of these works was of a manly chat or a kindly paternal lecture; as the dominant, officially approved discourse, it was appropriately men speaking to other men, or boys. Perhaps Benjamin's distinction between story and novel helps account for the nature of this fiction's appeal. Rather than the absent author of novels which described the modern world's perplexities, the story-teller—he who comes from afar—imparts practical counsel and the accumulated wisdom of the tribe (Benjamin, *Illuminations,* p. 84f).

Thus it came packaged as advice from a wise, good-natured father-figure. As espousing Truth and the requisite ideals, then, the culture used it as the prize for good behavior and in so doing conferred even more authority upon it. For taking academic firsts, for good conduct, for achievements in sports, this fiction was given as the prize. For example, a copy of Henty's *The Young Franc-Tireurs,* given as a Christmas present from "Momma and Papa" for "Xmas, 1901," must have been one of innumerable such parental gifts. A copy of Henty's *On the Irrawaddy* was also awarded as a prize on October of 1911 by the County Borough of Northampton's Education Committee to Arthur C. Tye, of the 2nd class "For excellent Work" and was signed by the Head Teacher. Pasted inside the cover of a copy of *Martin Rattler* is a bookplate from Glascow Academy, awarding this book as a Prize to H. M. Kay for "good work" in the First English Class and signed, E. Temple, Rector, 1916-17.[4]

These fictions arrived, then, with the blessings of the authorities; they and the ideals they espoused were not only endorsed by family, school and church, but were also promoted by the periodical publications that made this fiction so available. *The Illustrated London News* issue for November 30, 1901 in its article "Christmas Books for Boys," praised the "indefatigable Mr. Henty [who] has so skillfully blended fact with fiction in 'With Roberts to Pretoria'" and recommended it for being not only exciting but also educational. The other recommendations for Christmas fare for boys are other war books, *At the Point of the Bayonet,* about the Mahratta War and *To Herat and Cabul* about the first Afghan War, both by Henty. The genre arrived with great authority and all branches of the establishment endorsed it.

That it was a shaping fiction for several generations of Englishmen is easily attested to. Not only did the officers in H.M.S. Britannia read Marryat's *Peter Simple* and read it as a kind of rule book, but Conrad also admitted to an early admiration for that writer. In an early, laudatory article, "Tales of the Sea" (1898), he referred to Marryat as "the enslaver of youth" (*Notes,* p. 53). That frequent immersions in that writer, in abridged, translated versions, formed part of Conrad's obstinate resolve to go to sea, as suggested in *A Personal Record,* helps to support Martin Green's assertion that "Marryat was often said to be the best recruiting officer the British Navy had" (Green, *Dreams of Adventure,* p. 5). Marryat's influence on Conrad can also be measured in his writing itself. Conrad and Ford's collaborative effort,

Romance, for example, contained obvious echoes of *Peter Simple*; a contemporary reader would certainly have remembered Seraphina and O'Brien from Marryat's novel. Kipling's allusions to Marryat, too, reveal that earlier writer's pervasive influence. In his story "At the End of the Passage" (1890), Kipling likens one of his characters, a civil servant in India, overburdened with the tasks of civilizing the natives, to "Chucks," recognizing in Marryat's common seaman—"the best boatswain in His Majesty's service" [*PS* [*Peter Simple*], p. 129]—something akin to the figures he himself drew so well, the common soldier and the class-conscious civil servant, who, like Chucks, "had a great idea of bettering himself socially" (*Life's Handicap,* p. 161). Not only does Kipling assume his readers' ready understanding of "Chucks" and the world that comes with that allusion, but he also knows that the reference, made by one white man to three others within the fiction, is an illuminating one for them; these three Englishmen in India will hear the comparison and know exactly what the speaker means as will the readers of the fiction. Marryat was the common possession of a whole class of Englishmen involved in the Empire's business, and such invocations served indirectly to recall that "private feelings must always be sacrificed for the public service." Once that belief was in place, the idea of the White Man's burden as the selfless duty of responsible colonizers made perfect sense.

Writers and statesmen alike spoke as adults of the enormous influence these works exercised upon them throughout their lives. Speaking of his unhappiness at St. James School, Winston Churchill recalled many years later that reading provided him the greatest pleasure in his otherwise unhappy school days. When he was nine-and-a-half, his father gave him *Treasure Island* and that book particularly he remembered "devouring" "with delight" (Heath (ed.), *Churchill,* p. 22). So powerful were these books that they often preempted actual experience itself; not only were they shaping the metropolitan Englishman's ideas about these foreign places coming within England's sphere of influence, but they also predisposed the actual travellers themselves . . . to view these outposts in terms that derived more from travel writing, from the writers' own particular point of view as involved and therefore biased participants, and from adventure fiction, than from strictly factual information manuals. When Churchill, now a young British officer, first spotted Cuba from aboard ship, his vision of it was already colored:

> When first in the dim light of early morning I saw the shores of Cuba rise and define themselves from dark-blue horizons, I felt as if I sailed with Captain Silver and first gazed on Treasure Island. Here was a place where real things were going on. Here was a scene of vital action. Here was a place where anything might happen. Here was a place where something would certainly happen. Here I might leave my bones.
>
> (*A Roving Commission,* p. 77)

Churchill also remembered reading *Kidnapped* while a prisoner of war of the Boers, and being so immersed in it that he felt David Balfour's adventures and mishaps as though they were his own (p. 290). So real was this fiction for many of its readers, that it exerted a kind of immediacy that life did not.

Even earlier Churchill had been reading Haggard, although he owns up to his reading of Stevenson more readily than to that of Haggard. But Haggard himself included a letter from the young Winston, aged fourteen, to the writer in his 1926 autobiography *The Days of My Life* (p. 8).

> Thank you so much for sending me "Allan Quatermain," it was so good of you. I like AQ better than "King Solomon's Mines"; it is more amusing. I hope you will write a great many more books.
>
> I remain,
> Yours truly
> Winston S. Churchill

Many attitudes held and espoused by the later Churchill can certainly be found in this fiction that promoted imperial prestige, expansion, and heroism. The same claims could be made about Harold Macmillan, who asserted in his *Winds of Change*, that "Henty was the prize," although he ranked Henty equally with Scott, Dickens, Conan Doyle and Haggard as the authors he most enjoyed (p. 176). In his critical biography of Haggard, Morton Cohen speaks of other prominent people who have acknowledged an admiration for Haggard in particular, among them, King Edward VII, who claimed to prefer Haggard to Hardy and Meredith. Cohen refers to the many writers who spoke of their debt to Haggard—D. H. Lawrence, C. S. Lewis, and Henry Miller (Cohen, *Rider Haggard*, p. 231). In his Introduction to a 1957 reprint of *She*, Stuart Cloete, a South African writer, maintains that he "was brought up on Rider Haggard and G. A. Henty," and that their books "were the literary milk of my boyhood from which I have never been weaned." But Haggard's influence was not purely literary. In remembering the impact on him of his early reading, Graham Greene recalls that the book "above all other books at that time of my life" was *King Solomon's Mines*.

> This book did not perhaps provide the crisis, but it certainly influenced the future. If it had not been for that romantic tale of Allan Quatermain, Sir Henry Curtis, Captain Good, and above all, the ancient witch Gagool, would I at nineteen have studied the appointments list of the Colonial Office and very nearly picked on the Nigerian Navy for a career?
>
> (*The Lost Childhood*, p. 14)

But Greene was a reader, rather than a consumer, for whom, finally, the heroes seemed inordinately good.

> They were men of such unyielding integrity (they would only admit to a fault in order to show how it might be overcome) that the wavering personality of a child could not rest for long against those monumental shoulders. These men were like Platonic ideas: they were not life as one had already begun to know it.
>
> (*The Lost Childhood*, p. 9)

But for many readers, as we have seen, the books were as palpable and convincingly real as actual experience itself, and in some cases, more so. Many of those who were persuaded to devour the fiction whole went into the military or government. Green was rather exceptional in doing neither; instead, he became a writer, a writer as it turned out, of a very different colonial fiction, one that challenged adventure fiction's construction of the imperial subject.[5] But at the moment, particularly the 1880s and 90s, the spirit of the age was expressing itself in a literature that applauded Britain's imperial ventures. . . .

Notes

1. The enemies of public libraries, that is, free libraries supported by public rates, in the 1870s, 80s, and 90s often compared those public libraries to public houses; the one was declared to be as great a cause of wasted lives as the other (Altick, *Common Reader*, pp. 232-233). See Louis James, *Fiction for the Working Man* for the availability and variety of working-class fiction.

2. The story that Rhodes was in the audience that day at Oxford in 1870 and upon hearing Ruskin's call to duty set off for South Africa with fire in his eyes is such an irresistible one that it survives in spite of the fact that he had already returned to Kimberly when Ruskin delivered this lecture, the first in his Slade professorship at Oxford. Rhodes had been at Oxford earlier and returned in 1873. Although he was not present for the lecture, however much we would like him to have been, the lecture was written, published and much discussed.

3. The creator of that eternal youth, Peter Pan, attests in his Introduction to the 1913 edition of *The Coral Island* to his admiration for Ballantyne: "[He] was for long my man, and I used to study a column in *The Spectator* about 'forthcoming books,' waiting for his next as for the pit door to open." And the excitement generated by Ballantyne's adventures survived, for Barrie, into adulthood. He goes on to recall his anticipation of meeting, at his "solemn London club . . . a learned American who had vowed that he would show me how to make a fire as Jack made it in *The Coral Island*. We adjourned to the library (where we knew we were not likely to be disturbed), and there from concealed places about his person, he produced Jack's implements . . . in half a minute my friend had made fire, at which we lit our cigars and smoked to the memory of Ballantyne and *The Coral Island*" (*CI*, pp. vi-viii).

4. These cited examples are from copies in my possession; see bibliography.

5. Jeffrey Meyers' study, *Fiction and the Colonial Experience,* considers the colonial novels of Greene, along with those of Conrad, Kipling, Forster, and Cary as comprising one of two distinct "streams"; the other, he claims, is made up of the adventure fiction of Haggard, Henty, Buchan, and the early Kipling, among others. As I argue throughout, it is Conrad's fiction in large part that causes the initial divergence, but the streams are intimately related, nonetheless. Greene, in his *Journey Without Maps,* follows consciously in both Haggard's and Conrad's steps. Early in that work, he speaks of the attractions that motivated his trip to Africa, the willingness "to suffer some discomfort for the chance of finding—there are a thousand names for it, King Solomon's Mines, the 'heart of darkness' . . ." (p. 19). Towards the conclusion, he remarks again: "The need, of course, has always been felt, to go back and begin again. Mungo Park, Livingstone, Stanley, Rimbaud, Conrad represented only another method to Freud's, a more costly, less easy method, calling for physical as well as mental strength. The writers Rimbaud and Conrad were conscious of this purpose, but one is not certain how far the explorers knew the nature of the fascination which worked on them in the dirt, the disease, the barbarity and the familiarity of Africa" (p. 248). Behind Greene's trip to Africa is Conrad's, but behind Conrad—for Greene, as for so many other readers—is African travel writing and the adventure fiction of Haggard.

Bibliography

Altick, Richard D. *The English Common Reader: A Social History of the Mass Reading Public 1800-1900.* Chicago: The University of Chicago Press, 1957.

James, Louis. *Fiction for the Working Man, 1830-1850.* London: Oxford University Press, 1963.

Meyers, Jeffrey. *Fiction and the Colonial Experience.* New Jersey: Rowman and Littlefield, 1973.

JUVENILE ADVENTURE NARRATIVES

William H. Green (essay date spring 2001)

SOURCE: Green, William H. "King Thorin's Mines: *The Hobbit* as Victorian Adventure Novel." *Extrapolation* 42, no. 1 (spring 2001): 53-64.

[*In the essay below, Green compares J. R. R. Tolkien's* Hobbit *and H. Rider Haggard's* King Solomon's Mines *as adventure novels.*]

In 1881, when Robert Louis Stevenson, then a little-known writer of travel books, short stories, and essays, serialized *Treasure Island* in the periodical *Young Folks,* his story attracted little attention (McLynn 1980). Polished in style and almost static in its violence, much like a masterfully condensed Scott novel, *Treasure Island* was by design a children's book, a continuation of a tradition pioneered by Frederick Marryat and R. M. Ballantyne—the ripping tales of pirates and buried treasure that were already staples of juvenile fiction for boys. However, not until the story was printed in book form in 1883, penetrating the adult market, did it attract critical praise. *Treasure Island* was a product of literary alchemy, a series of stale juvenile devices, or ephemera, transmuted into a classic appreciated by adults, "an utterly original book" (Fraser 214).

H. Rider Haggard—also an author of failed fiction and travel books—is said to have written *King Solomon's Mines* in 1885 after a brother challenged him to write a story half as good as Stevenson's (L. R. Haggard 121-22). Haggard's own account makes an even stronger connection: "I read in one of the weekly papers a notice of Stevenson's *Treasure Island* so laudatory that I procured and studied that work and was impelled by its perusal to try to write a book for boys" (Karlin xii). *King Solomon's Mines,* Haggard's landlocked imitation of *Treasure Island,* also exploited the stock characters and plot devices of boys' fiction, and yet at its time also seemed startlingly original, marketed as "The most amazing story ever written," (Cohen 87). Haggard translated the voyage to a pirate island into a trek across the Dark Continent. *Treasure Island* and *King Solomon's Mines* revived adventure fiction and, as points of imitation, typify boy's action books in the decades to follow—the worlds of Mowgli, the Time Traveller, Tom Swift, Tarzan, Flash Gordon, and Conan.

But the most influential and innovative heir of Stevenson and Haggard may be J. R. R. Tolkien,[1] whose 1937 first novel was also a tale for boys and whose imitators constitute a major genre of post-modern fiction. His stories of Middle-Earth revitalized adventure fiction, which had again become stagnant. His first published novel, *The Hobbit,* shares with *Treasure Island* and *King Solomon's Mines* the distinction of being a children's book, yet presently appearing on adult bookshelves. Like *Treasure Island* and *King Solomon's Mines,* Tolkien's adventure story is impossible to confuse with any previous one and was the model for thousands of imitations, including his own great sequel, *The Lord of the Rings.* Yet *The Hobbit,* like *Treasure Island,* emerged from a popular tradition and exploits stock devices. Much as Haggard's book is *Treasure Island* reinvented in the African veldt, *The Hobbit* is *King Solomon's Mines* reinvented in Tolkien's great linguistic and geographical subcreation, Middle-Earth.

Like Stevenson and Haggard,[2] Tolkien invented stories by a largely unconscious method, letting them grow autonomously. He "had the sense of recording what was already 'there,' somewhere" and claimed to have been oblivious of obvious literary influences. He denied, for instance, consciously imitating *Beowulf* (about which he had just written an essay) when he described Bilbo's stealing a precious cup from the hoard of a sleeping dragon, a clear echo of line 2405 in the Old English poem (*Letters* 145, 31). Extremely well-read, Tolkien drew from a vast literary tradition—what he called the "Tree of Tales"—and his self-reporting of literary influence is obscure and contradictory, not because he plagiarized, but because his creative method involved impulsive inattention, deliberate ignoring of analogues as he cultivated an autonomous fantasy world using the method that Carl Jung called *visionary* (*Tree* 56).[3] Thus, even though Tolkien apparently did not describe himself as imitating Haggard, many parallels between *King Solomon's Mines* and *The Hobbit* argue that Haggard's work fed Tolkien's creative process.[4]

Reading either book after having read the other creates deja vu, a parade of familiar motifs in new dress and altered order. The reluctant heroes of both stories, Tolkien's Bilbo Baggins and Haggard's Allan Quartermain, are repeatedly said to be small and timid but are, nevertheless, hardy, strong-willed, and ethical—reluctant to kill but loyal to the death. Both heroes are distinguished by their alertness: Bilbo repeatedly wakes just in time or notices details that others miss, and Quartermain's Zulu name means "the man who gets up in the middle of the night, or, in vulgar English, he who keeps his eyes open" (*King* 47). Both are of good birth, with modest wealth and education. If these traits are typical of boy heroes, what sets both Allan and Bilbo apart is that both are, like Don Quixote, about fifty years old. Their suicidal quest for treasure is driven, not by youthful bravado or greed, but by a muted form of Quixotic madness: they are old boys seizing the trailing edge of youth to escape their dead-end pasts. Quartermain, a hunter, has lived hand-to-mouth for decades in this dangerous occupation and wishes to provide for his son's medical education (39). Bilbo, a bachelor in his dead father's house, has never been outside the neighborhood of his birth. He has, in effect, rejected life. The treasure hunts are last chances to enlarge their lives in the face of old age and death.

The two proposals for adventure are remarkably similar, presented unexpectedly by tall, bearded travelling strangers: Allan is approached by an English aristocrat met accidentally on shipboard, Bilbo by a wizard at his door. And Sir Henry Curtis, like the wizard Gandalf, already knows the hero's name and history. The Curtis-Gandalf figure in both stories is the architect of the adventure and recruits the hero for his supposed cleverness: Allan as a wilderness guide and Bilbo as an "expert treasure-hunter" (31). Moreover, Curtis and Gandalf travel with smaller men who provide comic relief—Gandalf with the dwarf Thorin and his followers, Sir Henry with the vain, monocled Captain Good. Sir Henry is searching for a lost brother, and Gandalf is helping Thorin to regain his ancestral home; so both expeditions are motivated by family honor, obligations that override the fact that neither has much hope of success. And (although we do not know this until late in Haggard's book) both expeditions return exiled kings—Ignosi in *King Solomon's Mines* and Thorin in *The Hobbit*.

Both heroes at first reject the proposed quests as suicidal. When Thorin tells Bilbo that his party "may never return," the hobbit collapses screaming on the floor (23). Allan, more self-controlled of himself, refuses Curtis' first offer with similar feelings: "I am, as I think I have said, a cautious man, indeed a timid one, and I shrunk from such an idea. It seemed to me that to start on such a journey would be to go to certain death" (32). Allan (who tells his own story) repeatedly claims to be timid and at one point bursts into tears, and Bilbo repeatedly regrets joining the expedition; but both act bravely and with cool attention when called on (288). Their early timidity emerges as sane caution, a measured courage that makes them better guides in the end. Timid courage is wiser than, for instance, the rush to adventure that betrays Dr. Livesey and Squire Trelawney in *Treasure Island*. Even as Bilbo naively frets over leaving behind money and handkerchiefs, his anxiety over details links him with Allan, who itemizes his party's munitions and concludes, "I make no apology for detailing it at length, for every experienced hunter will know how vital a proper supply of guns and ammunition is to the success of an expedition" (34, 45). Bilbo and Allan are practical, believable heroes, more likely to survive suicide missions because they admit their fear and avoid risks.

In the first chapter of *The Hobbit*, Gandalf produces a map of the treasure mountain, a map printed in the book. At the end of Tolkien's book is a second map showing the terrain of Bilbo's journey across a range of mountains and through a desolate forest. Maps, as guides to hidden treasure, have an literary genealogy through Poe's "The Gold-Bug" and Dumas's *The Count of Monte-Cristo*—both of which influenced Stevenson—and, of course, *Treasure Island*. But Tolkien's maps most closely resemble the map in *King Solomon's Mines*, with traits of Haggard's single map split between Tolkien's two (McLynn 5, 199). The first map, the one carried by the adventurers, gives local access to the treasure but does not chart a path of travel. The second, printed but never mentioned in the story, charts the dangerous trek from "The Edge of the Wild" to Thorin's treasure mountain, and thus directly parallels the map in *King Solomon's Mines*.

Tolkien's first map, like Haggard's, is said to have been drawn long before the time of the story (Tolkien's about 170 years before, Haggard's 300 years) by the last of his race to see the treasure chambers. In *The Hobbit,* this is Thorin's grandfather Thror, and in *King Solomon's Mines* it is the Portuguese adventurer José da Silvestra. Both documents were passed to descendants and then handed over to strangers when one of the descendants—having failed on a rash adventure—is delirious and dying (*Hobbit* 30; *King* 25-26). At the beginning of each book, it has been years since this transfer, but the present holder of the map—Gandalf in *The Hobbit,* Allan in *King Solomon's Mines*—has kept its existence secret while carrying the map (or a copy) on his person and only shares it with his co-adventurers after they have independently committed to a trek for which they need it (a pattern significantly different from *Treasure Island*). Both maps include wording that must be interpreted—Tolkien's runes and moon-letters, Haggard's Portuguese. Both indicate isolated mountains in the midst of plains and point to tunnel entrances with ruins nearby: labeled "hidden passage to the Lower Halls" in Tolkien and "mouth of the treasure cave" in Haggard (*Hobbit* 26; *King* 27).

Tolkien's second map, printed in the back of most editions, is a topographical road map of a region; however, if we trace the route of his adventurers on the map, we see strong analogues to José da Silvestra's. Both parties travel in more-or-less straight lines in compass directions (east in Tolkien, north in Haggard) over geographic barriers at right angles to the line of travel so that the travelers must cross them. Both routes cross a river, an alpine range, and a deadly wasteland. Also, both maps indicate hidden places of refreshment essential to the party's survival (Rivendell and Beorn's house in Tolkien, the "pan bad water" in Haggard), an ancient road, and a town near the destination. And, of course, at the far edge of each map (the top of Haggard's, the right of Tolkien's) is the mountain. Details from Haggard map are reoriented by Tolkien. However, the analogues make a strong case, at least, for cryptomnesia, or "concealed recollection" on Tolkien's part (See Jung et al. 23-26), his reproducing a half-forgotten pattern without (according to his letters) being conscious of its source.

Another remarkable similarity involves business contracts in the two stories. After Thorin explains that Bilbo is to be the expedition "burglar," the reluctant hero responds in "his business manner" that would like "to know about risks, out-of-pocket expenses, time required and remuneration, and so forth" (27). Faking professionalism to cover confusion, Bilbo exposes the dwarves' poor preparation in a comic analogue to *King Solomon's Mines.* When Allan Quartermain agrees to join Curtis' dangerous trek, he states his terms as three numbered items: (1) Curtis must pay all expenses, with

"ivory or other valuables" evenly divided between Allan and Captain Good; (2) upon receiving a £500 retainer, Allan will remain with Curtis to the end of the expedition; and (3) if Allan is killed or disabled, his son will be put through medical school (37-38). The last item requires a lawyer because Curtis will be at risk on the expedition (41).

Thorin leaves a virtual parody of this contract under Bilbo's parlor clock on the morning of departure, one that guarantees "traveling expenses," with profits to be divided between all participants and funeral costs paid by Thorin "or our representatives" (33). Since most of the perils of the journey involve being eaten or lost, this last provision is hardly practical; rather, it is the punch line of a darkly comic sequence. What "representatives" have been contacted since breakfast or are likely to turn up in the wilderness? The reference to "representatives" echoes the last item in Allan's contract by providing for the death of Bilbo's employer. There is no equivalent of Allan's second item, no retainer—another comic contrast, for the dwarves are exiles, poor except in pride.

Both expeditions are planned in clouds of smoke, and tobacco is a tool of male bonding throughout both books—as in adventure tales as diverse as *A Journey to the Center of the Earth, Treasure Island, A Connecticut Yankee in King Arthur's Court, The Lost World, Prester John, Green Mansions,* and *Lost Horizon.* In *King Solomon's Mines,* Allan hears about the expedition after Sir Henry Curtis invites him to "smoke a pipe," and Allan decides to join Curtis "before the burning tobacco had fallen into the sea" (15, 37). Interludes of pipe smoking punctuate the African tale—idyllic scenes such as when the old boys "by the light of the full moon" feast on elephant steaks around a campfire, "and then we began to smoke and yarn" (54). Bilbo is such an old boy. Smoking a long pipe on his doorstep when he first meets Gandalf, he shows off with a manly display of smoke rings, only to be shamed by the wizard's superior display the next day. The only non-cloth objects the hobbit takes with him from home are a pipe and tobacco, and his companions blow smoke rings for amusement when they rest at night. At the end of *The Hobbit,* Gandalf visits Bilbo years later and (in the very last line), the hobbit renews old bonds by handing the wizard a jar of tobacco.

Claudia Nelson discusses a trend in late Victorian boys' schools and fiction toward shunning the influence of women, and *The Hobbit* is, in this sense, a belated echo of *fin de siècle* values. G. A. Henty, who wrote nearly eighty late Victorian boys' books in a study "full of pipe-smoke," declared, "I never touch love interest" (M. Green 221). When his hero marries, the wife is hardly more than an empty sign of heterosexuality and social connection (Nelson 220). *Treasure Island, King Solomon's Mines,* and *The Hobbit* all represent defeminized worlds. Though Jim's mother is a blurry presence in early chapters of *Treasure Island,* a letter from Stevenson expresses a defeminizing plan—"No women in the story" (128)—and Haggard, in the words of Allan, makes the same claim: "there is no woman in it" (10). This, Allan admits, is an overstatement: *King Solomon's Mines* includes a crone, dancing girls, and a tragi-comic romance. But the overstatement does indicate how a Henty-like adventure differs from a conventional romantic story, an absence of the sort of love interest that, for instance, Stevenson includes in *The Black Arrow* and that Deborah Kerr gives Allan Quartermain in the 1950 film of *King Solomon's Mines. The Hobbit* goes a step further. It is really womanless, has no living female character, even a minor one. Bilbo's dead mother, discussed in the first chapter, is not mentioned later, and the few other references to women are anonymous or generic. Tolkien, as if reading "there is no woman in it" literally, created an all-male world.

In each story an early, almost gratuitous, episode occurs on the edge of the wilderness, a adventure that—except for providing an early cliffhanger (and, in Tolkien's more cumulative story, elvish swords)—might be omitted with little effect. The episodes are high points of weeks of slow travel from the comfortable homes through half-empty lands, travel otherwise dismissed in summary. Before Haggard's party reaches "the real starting-point of our expedition," the old boys pause to slaughter elephants. In the climax of this episode, Captain Good—comic companion of the expedition's organizer and thus equivalent to Tolkien's dwarves—falls before a charging elephant "as the sun was just going down in its reddest glory" (63, 61). Good seems as good as dead until a Zulu spears the elephant and is killed in place of Good. This gives Allan and Curtis (the Bilbo and Gandalf figures) time to dispatch the animal.

Bilbo's group encounters, not elephants, but giant trolls, a species he recognizes "from the great heavy faces of them, and their size, and the shape of their legs" (37). The dwarves foolishly approach these monsters and are captured, but Gandalf distracts the trolls (until the rising sun turns them to stone). These are, of course, very different episodes. What connects them is that both center on cliffhangers involving elephantine foes, parallel characters, and a solar epiphany in a summarized outward journey. Both episodes yield treasure—"a wonderfully fine lot of ivory" in *King Solomon's Mines* and "pots of gold" in *The Hobbit*—that both parties bury in anticipation of their return (*King* 63; *The Hobbit* 44). Here the echo becomes exact. The ivory is buried "carefully in the sand under a large tree . . . hoping that we might one day return," and the gold is buried "secretly not far from the track . . . in case they ever had the chance to come back" (*King* 63; *The Hobbit* 45).

The Hobbit soon echoes the next main episode in Haggard's story. Allan's people are staggering across a desert, their canteens empty. They hope to find a spring located nearby, according to José da Silvestra's old map. "If we do not find water we shall die" (83). Suddenly, the rising sun lights mountains they must climb to reach the treasure, tantalizingly clear but too far away to reach with empty canteens. Soon after, the expedition's tracker finds a pool at the top of a scrub-covered hillock in the desert. They drink, eat, smoke, and are refreshed. Allan's desert ordeal, from the cry *"trek"* with full canteens to "that blessed pool," is an exemplar of realistic but mythic adventure writing, and Tolkien seems to pay tribute to it in a briefer episode just after the escape from the trolls. Bilbo's company is trekking across a "silent waste" with food bags almost empty, led by Gandalf along a faint trail to Rivendell, their only hope: "We must not miss the road, or we shall be done for" (45-46). As they climb out of a stream bed (starvation, not thirst, is the peril), mountains loom suddenly near, seeming "only an easy day's journey" away though actually much farther. Soon after, Gandalf, the company's tracker, suddenly finds Rivendell (45-46).

Tolkien's description of the mountains is much leaner than Haggard's but suggests it. Haggard writes, "the morning lights played upon the snow and the brown and swelling masses beneath" (86), and Tolkien writes, "there were patches of sunlight on its brown sides and behind its shoulders the tips of snowpeaks gleamed" (46). Haggard's mountains are explicitly anatomical (snow-covered hillocks correspond "exactly . . . to the nipple on the female breast" (85)), while Tolkien only writes of gleaming "tips." The mountains ("Sheba's Breasts" in Haggard) combine with the foreground desert to suggest a supine woman, so that the pool of dark lifesaving water (in Tolkien's story, a hidden ravine with a stream) becomes a womb of rebirth. Haggard's nurturing womb is elevated on an altarlike hill, and its absence kills; Tolkien's is hemmed by bogs and sudden ravines, but he repeats in muted language Haggard's imagery of the earth as woman.

Tolkien wrote often of tunnels and subterranean travel. Three times Bilbo enters the west side of a mountain and passes through to the east, the "night sea journey" associated with mythological heroes, and *The Hobbit*'s exploits parallel underground action in *King Solomon's Mines.* In the desert Allan's party finds "grateful shelter" from the sun under "an overhanging slab of rock," and Bilbo's party evades a storm by "sheltering under a hanging rock" (*King* 76; *Hobbit* 55). Later Allan's party rests for the night in a mountain pass in a cave with a "hole in the snow" for a door. During the night their Hottentot tracker dies, and then they find the frozen corpse of the Portuguese cartographer who drew the treasure map. In a parallel sequence, Bilbo and his party take shelter for the night in a cave in a mountain pass, a cave entered through a low arch. Just as Haggard's cave does "not appear to be very big" and is "not more than twenty feet long," Tolkien's cave "isn't all that big and it does not go far back" (*King* 96-97; *Hobbit* 57). In Tolkien's cave the outcome is similarly grim—goblins attack at night, and Bilbo and his companions are almost killed, their ponies eaten.

In Tolkien's book, after Gandalf rescues Bilbo from the goblins, he is abandoned in a maze of lightless tunnels and must find his way out. This parallels the plight of Allan, Curtis, and Good after they escape Solomon's treasure chamber. Like Bilbo, they are in a "stone labyrinth" of narrow tunnels that bend and are intersected by other tunnels (*King* 294).[5] Allan has three matches, which he lights at crucial points, otherwise moving in pitch blackness; and as if alluding to this, Bilbo notices (anachronistically) that he has no matches. Both are utterly lost. Allan's companion observes, "We can only go on till we drop," and Bilbo plods on, "not daring to stop, on, on, until he was tireder than tired" (*King* 296; *Hobbit* 67). Suddenly both heroes run splash into an underground body of water, a dead end. Turning back up the tunnels and taking an alternate route, both finally see light—"a faint glimmering spot"; "a glimpse of . . . pale out-of-doors light"—and escape through a hole so narrow they must "squeeze" out (King 297; Hobbit 80). "A squeeze, a struggle, and Sir Henry was out," Haggard writes (297). Bilbo, on the other hand, "squeezed and squeezed, and he stuck!" (81) Only by bursting the buttons on his coat does he escape outdoors. Soon after, when Bilbo rejoins the dwarves and Allan's people rejoin their guides, there is surprise and joy. The dwarves have been wondering whether Bilbo is "alive or dead," and an African guide cries out, "Oh, my lords, my lords, it is indeed you come back from the dead!" (*Hobbit* 84; *King* 299) The parallels here are so many that, if Tolkien did not consciously imitate Haggard, we have a classic instance of cryptomnesia.

Both books also involve treasure chambers, cathedral-like rooms, and corpses in the mid-part of a passage through a hollow mountain. On one end of the passage is a large, well known public entrance, on the other a secret tunnel. In both stories parties of helpful natives conduct the outsiders to the vicinity of the treasure, but only the outsiders visit the fabulous chamber of diamonds. "The great chamber of Thror," with its rotting tables, skulls, and bones, recalls Haggard's cavern like "the hall of the vastest cathedral" with its side chapel where corpses sit around a table (*Hobbit* 205; *King* 262-67). Both parties enter the treasure chamber by a heavy stone door that blends into the wall when closed. Before the door opens, Allan says, he "looked for the doorway, but there was nothing before us but the solid rock," and when Bilbo's dwarves find their stone door, it looks like wall with no "post or lintel or threshold" (*King* 271; *Hobbit* 177). Each party is trapped behind such a door, under a snow-capped mountain in the silent earth (*King* 286; *Hobbit* 199). Allan's party is trapped by Gagool, a crone who is called "Mother, old mother" and who looks like a cobra and moves like a vampire bat or a snake (162). Bilbo's party is trapped by a batlike, snake-like dragon—a creature associated by Jungian analysts with the devouring mother.[6]

Similar bits of underground stage business and wording connect the two stories: Good, like Bilbo, is struck in the face by a flying bat, Allan and Bilbo both put large jewels in their pockets, and in both stories a giant gem from the mountain is associated with the local king. Both parties are taunted with threats of starvation in the treasure caves: Gagool says, "There are the bright stones that you love, white men, . . . *eat* of them, hee! hee! *drink* of them, ha! ha!" and a messenger tells the dwarves, "we leave you to your gold. You may eat that, if you will" (*King* 278, *Hobbit* 224). Perhaps Tolkien's most unmistakable echo of *King Solomon's Mines* is his Battle of Five Armies. Battles in the two books use the same strategy on like terrain: an outnumbered force executes a pincers movement to win against odds, attacking from two arms of high ground into a plain. Haggard's battleground is between two arms of a steep, flat-topped hill "shaped like a horse-shoe"—Tolkien's between narrow spurs of a solitary mountain (188).

The army of Haggard's good king, camped on the hilltop, initially holds off a force double its size thanks to the defensive advantage of high ground, but is weakened in the process; and, as the army of the evil king, Twala, is reinforced, the good are surrounded and without water. So the good king, Ignosi, plans to attack immediately, and he shrewdly deploys his force in four units: one to rush suicidally down toward the open end of the horseshoe, one to stand in reserve behind that one, and two to mass, hidden, on the flanking ridges. The plan is for the first unit, which Allan calls the Greys, to take grave losses and retreat, drawing the enemy army into exposed ground where it can be enveloped from three sides. Ignosi, who waits with the reserves, describes the plan thus: "when I see that the horns are ready to toss Twala, then will I, with the men who are left to me, charge home in Twala's face" (211-14).

The pincers movement, flanking an enemy with forces on both sides of a lagging middle, is an ancient tactic used successfully by the Athenian Miltiades against the Persians and the Roman Scipio Africanus against Hannibal, but the most direct model for Ignosi's tactic is the Zulu general Shaka, who consolidated an empire larger than Napoleon's and held back the British using flanking and rugged terrain (O'Sullivan 88, 93-94). Shaka deployed the same four units as Haggard's Zulu-raised king Ignosi: (1) a "chest" of older warriors with white shields (Haggard's "Greys"), (2) reinforcements behind them, and (3-4) two "horns" of younger warriors (Bryant 501; Krige 275). Haggard modeled his fictional African kingdom on the Zulus, whom he knew from his British colonial service, and his fictional battle is an exact implementation of Shaka's tactics—Tolkien's a very close approximation.

In *The Hobbit*, armies of men, elves, and dwarves are between two arms of the mountain when a hoard of evil goblins is seen approaching. The good armies quickly devise a plan similar to Ignosi's: to lure the goblin hoard "into the valley between the arms of the mountain" (237). Elves are positioned on one arm, Dwarves and men on the other, and "brave men" (like Haggard's Greys) meet the Goblins and draw them into the pincers. When the armies on the "arms" (Ignosi's horns) simultaneously attack the goblin's flanks, the evil army panics (239). This parallels events in *King Solomon's Mines*; Ignosi's plan is successful. After terrible loss of life among the Greys, the attack of the horns seals victory. Tolkien's battle, however, is more convoluted: the successful attack on the goblin's flanks is followed by another reversal as goblin reinforcements swarm over the mountain and outflank the flankers. For the several pages—narrated in the summary style of a chronicle—there is reversal after reversal in the tide of victory.

However, details in this convoluted battle echo Haggard's simpler one. As Twala's host is drawn between Ignosi's horns, the Greys are so reduced in numbers that they circle around a knoll to fight off attacks from all sides, a "doomed band" (223). Similarly, Thorin and his supporters form a ring, attacked from all sides by goblins. In both stories, however, the encircled fighters survive thanks to a single hero identified with the "berserks" of old Norse sagas. Tolkien's son Christopher summarizes the myth: "Berserks were said to fight without corselets, raging like wolves with the strength of bears, and might be regarded almost as shape-changers, who acquired the strength and ferocity of bears" (93). Haggard's Allan compares Curtis, whom he believes to be of Danish ancestry, to "his Berserkir forefathers." Fighting with the "doomed band," Curtis is a "wizard" who "killed and failed not" (226). The berserk in Tolkien's story is Beorn, a man who can change into a bear and thus epitomizes the berserk myth. Beorn mows down the goblins who have encircled the dwarves and, killing their king, Bolg, routs the evil armies. This moment in Tolkien's battle aligns with the moment in Haggard's when Sir Henry Curtis faces in single combat the evil king Twala just as Ignosi's pincers movement takes effect. In both stories the "berserk" hero confronts the evil king at the exact moment that resolves the battle—the onset of the last ebb in the rhythm of the battle. Curtis does not kill Twala at this moment—as Beorn kills Bolg—but does a few hours later in ritual combat.

Motifs of chain mail and unconsciousness further connect the battles. Allan and his companions receive "shining" coats of mail in the African kingdom, armor reserved for royalty and of such workmanship that it forms "a mass of links scarcely too big to be covered with both hands" (157). They wear the mail under their "ordinary clothing," and it repeatedly saves their lives, though there is reference to bruised flesh (158, 187, 241). Captain Good almost dies of contusions. Similarly, after Bilbo and the dwarves enter the dragon's treasure chamber, they don ancient armor, the hobbit receiving a silver shirt of marvelous workmanship, "a small coat of mail, wrought for some young elf-prince long ago" and a helmet (203). Bilbo and the dwarves, like Allan's party, wear the armor under their ordinary clothing, and the helmet saves Bilbo's life. The ancient armor protects but does not save Thorin. The dwarf king's "rent armour" lies beside the bed where, like Captain Good, he lies feverish after the battle (243). Finally, Allan and Bilbo are both knocked out by blows to the head in battle, lost for a time on the battlefield after victory, and feared dead. In both stories unconsciousness allows narrative compression through flashbacks as both heroes (and their readers) hear summaries after the fact of the respective victories.

There are more similarities between *King Solomon's Mines* and *The Hobbit*: "biltong" Allan's party grows sick of on the trail and the "cram" of Bilbo's party," the catalogs of descriptive names (*King* 91, 195; *Hobbit* 225, 190), and the narrative pacing of dangers and rescues—what Haggard calls "shaves" and Tolkien *eucatastrophes* (*King* 312; *Tree* 68-69). These situate stories within a broader tradition, for Stevenson's sailors chew "biscuit" and "junk," his pirates have descriptive aliases, and he is a master of the cliffhanger. The many parallels between Haggard's first successful fiction and Tolkien's are specific enough, however, to draw a line of descent from Stevenson through Haggard to Tolkien in the family tree of fiction. An entire clan of fantasy descends from *The Hobbit* and its sequels, and another clan, including the Tarzan books and Michael Crichton's *Congo*, descends independently from Haggard. The link between Haggard and Tolkien marks the kinship between these clans in the genealogy of influence.

Notes

1. Giddings and Holland argue persuasively for the influence of Haggard on *The Lord of the Rings* and place it accurately within a tradition of adventure fiction. However, they mention *The Hobbit* only briefly as biographical introduction. Though they make two questionable assumptions—that influences are conscious and that Tolkien's debt to adventure fiction can be narrowed to three novels—Giddings and Holland catalog impressive analogues between Tolkien's work and *King So-*

lomon's Mines, The Thirty-nine Steps, and Lorna Doone. An interesting application of their work is that The Hobbit echoes King Solomon's Mines more consistently than its sequel does (indeed, most of the Haggard analogues in The Lord of the Rings also occur in The Hobbit but not vice versa) and yet shows little influence of The Thirty-nine Steps or Lorna Doone.

2. Stevenson developed story ideas from dreams and attributed much of his best work to the "Brownies" who inspired him—for instance, when he wrote Dr Jekyll and Mr Hyde at a rate of perhaps eight thousand words per day (McLynn 254-59). Haggard is said to have written King Solomon's Mines and She each in about six weeks, and of the latter he said, "it was written at white heat, almost without rest. . . . I remember that when I sat down to the task my ideas as to its development were of the vaguest" (Cohen 97).

3. Jung praised writing "after the manner of Rider Haggard" because it "offers the richest opportunities for psychological elucidation." Such visionary novels were, in his view, deeper than psychological novels that consciously set out to explain character and thus obscured "the psychic background." A visionary tale "is constructed against a background of unspoken psychological assumptions, and the more unconscious the author is of them, the more the background reveals itself in unalloyed purity to the discerning eye" (Spirit 88-89).

4. Some of the analogues discussed in this article are mentioned at various points in my 1995 book, The Hobbit: A Journey into Maturity.

5. Jules Verne's A Journey to the Center of the Earth, is a primal novel of travel in an underground maze where the relationship between the leading characters suggests that between Bilbo and Gandalf, and the inexperienced hero is also "lost in a vast labyrinth" of tunnels (147).

6. The dragon as a central symbol of the devouring mother is developed at length in two of Erich Neumann's books, The Origin and History of Consciousness and The Great Mother: An Analysis of the Archetype.

Works Cited

Bryant, A. T. The Zulu People. Pietermaritzburg: Shuter and Shooter, 1967.

Cohen, Morton. Rider Haggard: His Life and Works. London: Hutchinson, 1960.

Fraser, G. S. "Afterword." Robert Louis Stevenson. Treasure Island. New York: Penguin, 1981.

Giddings, Robert, and Elizabeth Holland. J. R. R. Tolkien: The Shores of Middle-Earth. Frederick, MD: Aletheia, 1981.

Green, Martin. Dreams of Adventure, Deeds of Empire. New York: Basic, 1979.

Green, William H. The Hobbit: A Journey into Maturity. New York: Twayne, 1995.

Haggard, H. Rider. 1885. King Solomon's Mines. New York: Oxford UP, 1989.

Haggard, Lilias Rider. The Cloak That I Left. Ipswich: Boydell, 1976.

Jung, C. G. The Spirit in Man, Art, and Literature. Princeton: Princeton UP, 1966.

Jung, C. G. et al. Man and His Symbols. New York: Dell, 1964.

Karlin, Daniel. "Introduction." H. Rider Haggard. She. New York: Oxford UP, 1991.

Krige, Eileen Jensen. The Social System of the Zulus. Pietermaritzburg: Shuter and Shooter, 1965.

McLynn, Frank. Robert Louis Stevenson. New York: Random, 1993.

Nelson, Claudia. Boys Will Be Girls: The Feminine Ethic in British Children's Fiction, 1857-1917. New Brunswick, NJ: Rutgers UP, 1991.

Neumann, Erich. The Great Mother: An Analysis of the Archetype. Princeton: Princeton UP, 1963.

———. The Origin and History of Consciousness. Princeton: Princeton UP, 1970.

O'Sullivan, Patrick. Terrain and Tactics. New York: Greenwood, 1991.

Stevenson, Robert Louis. Treasure Island. New York: Penguin, 1981.

Tolkien, Christopher, trans. The Saga of King Heidrek the Wise. London: Nelson, 1960.

Tolkien, J. R. R. The Hobbit. Boston: Houghton Mifflin, 1966.

———. Letters. Ed. Humphrey Carpenter. Boston: Houghton Mifflin, 1981.

———. Tree and Leaf. Boston: Houghton Mifflin, 1965.

Verne, Jules. A Journey to the Center of the Earth. New York: Signet, 1986.

ADVENTURE LITERATURE AND IMPERIALISM

James W. Tuttleton (essay date 1996)

SOURCE: Tuttleton, James W. "American Manhood and the Literature of Adventure." In Vital Signs: Essays on American Literature and Criticism, pp. 26-41. Chicago: Ivan R. Dee, 1996.

[In the excerpt below, Tuttleton critiques Martin Green's conclusions in The Great American Adventure that

American adventure literature displays nationalistic and expansionistic tendencies.]

It isn't often that one is asked, in a volume of literary criticism, a question on the order of *What is the most important event in modern history?* But this is precisely what Martin Green asks toward the end of *The Great American Adventure* [see below, in War and Adventure], a book about American fiction. I shall return to his question in due course, but first let me say that Green's study, which is described as dealing with "action stories from Cooper to Mailer and what they reveal about American manhood," is not a work of historical analysis. It is instead a study of a dozen American adventure books seen as a reflection of America's "caste system" and her "imperialism," as these have shaped American "manliness." In fact, *The Great American Adventure* is merely the first of a trilogy of attacks on Western civilization and on its masculine underpinnings. The other two books in the trilogy are (à la William Empson) *Seven Types of Adventure Tale* and *The Adventurous Male: Chapters in the History of the White Male Mind.*

In subjecting these cultural phenomena to a political critique, Green offers a pretense of historical coverage by organizing his books into a triadic scheme. THREE FROM PHILADELPHIA: Cooper's *The Pioneers* (1823), Irving's *A Tour on the Prairies* (1832), and Robert Bird's *Nick of the Woods* (1837); THREE FROM BOSTON: Richard Henry Dana's *Two Years Before the Mast* (1840), Melville's *Typee* (1846), and Parkman's *The Oregon Trail* (1849); THREE ANOMALIES: Kit Carson's *Autobiography* (1856), Mark Twain's *Roughing It* (1872), and Theodore Roosevelt's *Autobiography* (1913); and what Green calls THREE AESTHETES: Hemingway's *The Green Hills of Africa* (1935), Faulkner's "The Bear" (1942), and Mailer's *Why Are We in Vietnam?* (1967).

Even a cursory glance will reveal that these triads are not subdivisions of a single whole and form no coherent logical entity. The first two suggest a regional connection; but the third denies any connection altogether; and the fourth—dealing with three of the greatest moralists in American fiction—misdefines them as, of all things, aesthetes. Since logic and intellectual coherence are not Professor Green's long suit, why even bother with Green's lucubrations about the adventure tale? That is a fair question; and it may seem churlish to single out Green when there are so many contemporary literature professors for whom intellectual coherence is a problem. But Green's criticism is worth attending to as an instance of the modern intellectual's loathing of Western civilization, even while he exploits the prestige and creature comforts it affords to the intellectual elite. To fathom this detestation of Western civilization and to trace the weird distortions it produces in our literary criticism is at once to understand what is happening to-day in the academy and to grasp a salient fact about the modern intelligentsia. What do these adventure tales reveal to Martin Green?

According to Green, these stories disclose a common type of protagonist engaged in a series of exciting or violent events—often far from home or civilization—that call for "such virtues as courage, fortitude, cunning, strength, leadership and persistence." Now, most of us would probably be disposed to admire these qualities as indeed worth cultivating. But to Green these are not virtues at all but rather qualities of an "aristo-military caste" derived from the European class system and therefore implicitly supportive of it. The values of this caste are said by Green to be celebrated by our culture and acclaimed by the specific writers he has adduced here. Reading these books, he says, is recommended by the "establishment" as a means of preparing boys to become leaders, rulers, and accomplished experts in the use of force. For Green, even the Boy Scouts of America is a doubtful organization, no doubt because of its aversion to gays but certainly because it advocates roughing it with tent and backpack. Green sees such groups and these authors as, in effect, servants and sponsors of American imperialist or nationalist objectives, which he describes as capitalist, anti-Christian, and antidemocratic. In consequence, he indicts them as complicit in an immoral and violent American expansionism.[1]

Two personal observations in the foreword of this book may help us to understand the astonishing premise of this study. First, Green, an Englishman by birth but a longtime professor at Tufts University, remarks that as boy and man he has always preferred domestic fiction to adventure tales. By domestic fiction he means the stories of O. Douglas, Charlotte Brönte, Mrs. Gaskell, George Eliot, Jane Austen, and others who have written what he calls the "serious novel": "stories about marriage and domesticity written in a form of moral realism and woman-centered whereas adventure was man-centered." This preference made Green feel out of step with other boys: "I was not a manly boy." Second, Green is a practitioner of "an English school of criticism, whose major present exponent is Raymond Williams; it looks at literature with strong political and social concerns of a left-wing kind." (He means of a Marxist kind, but no matter.) To Green's left-wing political orientation is added something else. He has been deeply affected by the radical moralism of Gandhi and the later Tolstoy, and he makes admiring references to "radical Christianity" (of a dissenting kind), to Quaker pacifism, and to Eastern nonviolence. What Tolstoy and Gandhi "would ask of a teacher of literature" also informs this critique of American adventure tales (*GAA,* 18, vii, ix). In view of the argument I shall develop, the extraordinary intellectual gyrations by which Martin Green got to this position deserve some brief description.

I

After writing comparatively optimistic, if idiosyncratic, literary analysis in *A Mirror for Anglo-Saxons* (1960), *Reappraisals* (1965), and *The Problem of Boston* (1966), Green was apparently unhinged by the general convulsions of the Vietnam era. *Cities of Light and Sons of the Morning* (1972) showed a man embracing, as the subtitle suggests, "A Cultural Psychology for an Age of Revolution," while abandoning his Catholicism, optimism, and ambivalent love for his adopted country. Following *The Von Richtofen Sisters* (1974), and *Children of the Sun* (1976), Green launched himself into a trilogy of books under the general title *The Lust for Power.* Each, he promised us, would deal with the immorality of adventure and the exploitations of imperialism in the West. In the first of these, *The Challenge of the Mahatmas* (1978), he weighed Western civilization against the pacifist teachings of Gandhi and the later Tolstoy, the two "mahatmas," and found it wanting. In the second, *Dreams of Adventure, Deeds of Empire* (1979), he found English literature before 1918 to be the aesthetic support of an empire-building that created the moral and spiritual crisis of our times. In the third, *Tolstoy and Gandhi, Men of Peace: A Biography* (1983), he returned to his spiritual heroes for a "joint biography" of two models offering a single solution to the destructive pursuit of power in the West. That trilogy, however, did not exhaust the moral fervor of Green's literary analysis. He followed with *The Origins of Non-Violence: Tolstoy and Gandhi in Their Historical Setting* (1986) and *Gandhi in India: In His Own Words* (1987). *The Great American Adventure*—the study of American fiction with which I am most concerned here—puts American writing on the axis where Marx and the mahatmas meet in Green's mind. Can the Marxist call to violent revolution and pacifist nonviolence be reconciled? On theoretical grounds alone, the task would seem to be formidable.

Given his contradictory premises, it is not surprising that Professor Green has no great admiration for the politics and morality of the adventure books in question, although—like Raymond Williams, Terry Eagleton, and the other left-wing Brits—he thinks them worth a "dialectical" unmasking. What we get, though, is principally the critical distortion produced by looking at them through pink spectacles. The distortions of our literature span a range from minor to major and would not be worth talking about if the literature he invokes did not have a permanent claim on our attention.

A minor distortion is Green's preposterous claim that Washington Irving and James Fenimore Cooper belong to "that Philadelphia school of writers that gave birth to American literature in the generation before Boston established its dominance as a writing and publishing center . . ." (*GAA*, 24). As scholarship, this is non-

sense. First, American literature originated in Boston and—from the days of the *Bay Psalm Book* to the 1880s—Boston was the intellectual center of American literature. Second, both Irving and Cooper were deep-dyed New Yorkers, not Philadelphians. That printers in Philadelphia produced some of their books does not make them members of some "Philadelphia school." There was no such school. To suggest this is on a par with describing Louis Auchincloss's Park Avenue and Wall Street fiction as Boston novels of manners because Houghton Mifflin is his publisher. Cooper and Irving selected publishers who promised satisfactory royalties and other benefits. Third, to press this point further, Melville is not a Boston author, though some of his in-laws came from Massachusetts. Melville's essential links were always with New York. Green knows this, I have reason to believe, for in his study of the literature of The Hub in Melville's time, *The Problem of Boston,* Green scarcely ever mentions Melville. These misrepresentations of the regional affiliations of his authors are stupefying in a cultural historian of Green's wide reading and suggest the perils of too procrustean and schematizing a mind-set. Forcing books and writers into doubtful categories, however, is only part of the problem of Green's ongoing literary project.

II

Green's treatment of Cooper's *The Pioneers* offers an instance of how not merely the facts but also the meaning of facts in a narrative can be distorted. According to Green, Cooper's "sense of values is based on adventure, manliness, and patriotism, and he gives Americans a picture of society that assigns a leading part to the aristo-military caste that embodies these values." These caste values are said to be embodied in Judge Temple, Oliver Edwards, and Natty Bumppo (Leatherstocking). To them is contrasted Elizabeth Temple, the Judge's winsome daughter, whom Green astonishingly calls "the social and moral tuning fork" of the novel (*GAA*, 29, 35). I shall return to her in a moment, for she is one of the most interesting characters in the novel. But first we must attend to the central event of the book, the event that provokes Green's accusation about the American penchant for violence.

The central issue in *The Pioneers* is the arrest of Natty Bumppo for shooting a deer in the teeming season. Cooper's point is the tension between the natural liberty that exists for the nomadic hunter in the wilderness, on the one hand, and civilization's constraint upon it when the rise of settlements requires the institution of the law, on the other. At what point can other people in the wilderness, who have now organized for themselves a set of laws, impose their legalities on a hitherto unconstrained hunter who is said by the critic to be a representative of the "aristo-military" caste? This is an important question for criticism, for sociology, and for the law. Let's take a look at this hunter. Natty Bumppo is far from a glamorous aristo-military type. A balding old man of seventy, sporting a single tusk of yellow bone, clad in ratty deerskin leggings, the sartorial wonder "Natty" is a near comic travesty of the vanishing woodsman. About the riskiest adventure in the novel is the hackneyed rescue of Elizabeth from a wild varmint in the woods. Elizabeth tells her father that Natty, her rescuer, saved her life and ought therefore to be pardoned of the charge that he killed a deer out of season. The Judge's reply, in view of Green's spurious claim for Elizabeth's centrality to the moral design of the novel, deserves the greatest attention.

Elizabeth Temple argues that "those laws that condemn a man like Leatherstocking to so severe a punishment [one hour in the stocks, a $100 fine, and a month in jail], for an offence that even I must think venial, cannot be perfect in themselves." For the Judge, however, "the sanctity of the laws must be respected." "Society," he tells her, "cannot exist without wholesome restraints," and "it would sound ill indeed, to report that a judge had extended favour to a convicted criminal because he had saved the life of his child." Speaking *in propria persona*, Cooper says that Miss Temple spoke with "a logic that contained more feeling than reason." And into the Judge's mouth Cooper puts the concluding, decisive argument. After giving Elizabeth money to pay Natty's fine, the Judge remarks: "Thou hast reason, Bess, and much of it too, but thy heart lies too near thy head. . . ." He asks her to "try to remember, Elizabeth, that the laws alone remove us from the conditions of the savages; that he has been criminal, and that his judge was thy father."[2] The general construction of plot and character confirm this viewpoint. At the end of the novel, Leatherstocking strikes deeper into the wilderness, leaving civilization and its laws behind, unable to conform to these newfangled legalities meant to socialize us.

Of course it could be argued, I suppose, that in structuring the plot in this way, Cooper is embodying in the Judge this "aristo-military" threat to humane values. But this approach would in my view need to assume the paranoid proposition that laws are per se unfair, that the socialization of individuals through legislation is inherently oppressive, and that the judicature must always be subverted in favor of an anarchical libertarianism. Is the Judge a front for The System? Is he simply a tool for the moneyed interests and the class-oriented power structure? Only in the sense that he is an educated, thoughtful, and articulate spokesman for civilized values. In making his claim for these values he of course defends the institution of the law and the rights of property. Such constitutional principles were for Cooper inseparable from a true American democracy. As *The American Democrat* (1838) makes plain, men of the Judge's type, members of the American gentry, are

democratic gentlemen, from whom, as a class, we have less to fear than from any other class in society.[3] Green doesn't like gentlemen, however, for they imply the English class structure, and they defend property rights with the support of the military. But if the Judge's reasoning is an instance of the "aristo-military" mind, I can only commend it. The idea of natural liberty is an interesting proposition in one's cozy study, but in the state of lawless nature, life is nasty, brutish, and short: it is the liberty of every man for himself. We see this in Cooper's *The Prairie,* where certain frontiersmen, having pushed too far ahead of civilization, regress to barbarism and savagery. Every witness to deep penetration into the Western wilderness—see particularly the Western works of Parkman and Irving—has testified to the kind of barbaric regression that often produced "white Indians."[4] But Green thinks the century's natural fear of atavistic regression a mere capitalist's trick.

III

Many of the tales dealt with by Green pose just this kind of tension between anarchy and order, between lawlessness in the wilderness (or on the remote prairie, the high seas, or on a Polynesian isle) and the necessary legal codes of conduct that must be introduced when a society begins to form in that lawless space. In the conflicts that result (whether with savage Indians, cannibals, mutinous sailors, or wild animals) most authors have preferred order to anarchy and have approved the imposition of humane law and even the judicious use of force, if necessary, to guarantee the conditions under which civilized existence can be nurtured. Green finds the resultant society not worth the immoral price. He sees in the expansion of Western civilization (through the Americas, Polynesia, and the Orient) a bloody record incompatible with Christian pacifism, Gandhian nonviolence, and universal brotherhood; and he has recoiled in disgust.

In any clime, coexisting with cannibals and Apaches, panthers and bears, has been harder in practice than the moral absolutist will allow. Green falls back on the old accusation that "white culture is built on guns and explosives." (Cooper thought it was built on liberty, law, and the rights of property.) For Green, "Officer or pioneer, the hero is a man of blood" (*GAA,* 37). This tiresome canard reminds us of another Englishman, D. H. Lawrence, who also reduced the typical American of our classic literature to the blue-eyed killer: "The essential American soul is hard, isolate, stoic, and a killer."[5] Green finds the image of his disgust everywhere—in kindly Irving, in Dana, Faulkner, Mailer, and the rest. They are all complicit in glorifying bloodlust, the social caste system, and the capitalist extermination of aborigines.[6]

So sweeping an indictment of our action stories of course prevents Green from making any moral discriminations whatsoever. But for us the task of the ethical sensibility is precisely to make moral discriminations, and, in respect to most of these writers, Green's indictment can have little value. Virtually every one of these writers abhorred anarchic violence and affirmed the sanctity of the law. With Mailer, however, Green is absolutely right. He has got his target right in the center of the cross hairs. *Why Are We in Vietnam?* does legitimate, without remorse, the acting out of murderous impulse, in Mailer's case as a means of discovering one's so-called "existential being." Even so, Green's reading of Mailer is off to the left in its emphasis on his supposed aestheticism. Mailer's thinking is eccentric and morally incoherent. But his concerns in the novels of the 1960s were moral concerns and involved a theology of Manichean struggle in the cosmos between God and the Devil. He cannot be written off as intending merely to "aestheticize violence." Nor is it appropriate to claim such an intention for Hemingway and Faulkner.

It is a hard saying but a true one that we live in a complex world of predation and death-dealing. Nature red in tooth and claw can horrify; and it will not change matters much if we euphemize this nature-system as an ecological food chain, rather than calling it the bloody arena of Darwin's "struggle for survival." (All the more reason to affirm the law: to restrain human predation.) But if Hemingway and Faulkner ritualize the ubiquity of death-dealing, in their hunting stories, they do so for a religious rather than for an aesthetic purpose. Sam Fathers in "The Bear," and Ike McCaslin, his young protégé initiated into the hunter's code, both articulate a reverence for life—for all being—that is communicated in their sympathetic identification with the magnificent buck, the towering bear, and other such creatures, and in the guilt they feel upon killing animals.

Something of the same religious identification with the order of being itself is expressed in Hemingway's elaborate rituals of hunting and fishing, not to speak of bullfighting. I cannot defend bullfighting here, but anyone opposed to this "sport" must engage with the evident fact that the rites and rules of the *corrida,* which have compelled the Mediterranean imagination for at least four thousand years, formalize the inevitability of death-dealing in an obscurely moral and primordially religious way. Like Faulkner, Hemingway expresses the immense pity of the human plight in knowing, consciously, its place in this scheme of predation. This pity is movingly expressed in *The Old Man and the Sea,* a work that Green avoids because it obviously cannot serve as ammunition for his left-wing attack. Old Santiago loves and respects the fish he kills, calls it his brother, and begs its pardon as he reels it in. "Perhaps it was a sin to kill the fish," he thinks to himself, "even though I did it to keep me alive and feed many people." Later he thinks, "You did not kill the fish only to keep alive and to sell for food. . . . You killed him for pride and because you are a fisherman. You loved him when

he was alive and you loved him after." He wonders, "If you love him, it is not a sin to kill him. Or is it more?"[7] The meaning of such moral reflection—which points to the ineluctable fatality of the human condition in a world where life feeds on life—is beyond Green's understanding. He is impatient and dismissive of all such anguished moral struggle as so much macho rationalization.[8]

Of course "The Bear" and *The Old Man and the Sea* may be accused of a false primitivism, of presenting an extinct animism, a regression to some pantheistic morality now obsolete for urban critics like Green, who have left errant humanity behind for the higher planes of sainthood, where Mahatma Gandhi, Tolstoy, and Albert Schweitzer abide. But in terms of practical morality, what do we do when the tsetse fly is about to bite, when the bear is about to kill the livestock, when game presents itself to one whose family must be fed? For most of us there is no escaping this human dilemma, however much it may be disguised in city life. It will not serve to reduce this universal problem to the excesses of individualism, capitalism, and imperialism. Most American pioneers tried to be good Christians, but the doctrine of turning the other cheek presented too many problems to (let us say) the peaceful immigrant farmer from Yorkshire whom the Iroquois warrior had got by the throat.

Green's anti-imperialism is that of an Englishman who feels guilt at the moral cost of his country's worldwide imperial adventures. But Americans never had a world empire and, in my view, never wanted one. Even the forays into Mexico in the 1840s and the Cuban and Philippine hullabaloos at the *fin de siècle* were short-lived anomalies. Green treats the slow and spreading settlement of the American West as if it were identical with a planned, armed British military takeover in India or Africa, when in fact the American militias were called out essentially to protect from Indian savagery peaceable settlers on the frontier.[9]

IV

If American adventure stories condone or aestheticize violence, what kind of fiction does Green admire? Green most values the social novel which deals with money, property, class, marriage, and the domestic scene. One may sympathize with this preference. James, Wharton, Austen, and George Eliot—practitioners of this kind of fiction—*are* artists of a major order. But even here rigid generic distinctions are perhaps unwise. Cooper wrote some of our best early novels of manners—for example, *Satanstoe* and *Home As Found*; and James's "The Beast in the Jungle" is an adventure tale transcendently superior to most of Green's examples. Indeed, as James asks in "The Art of Fiction," "What is adventure, when it comes to that, and by what sign is the listening pupil to recognize it?"[10] Green can recognize adventure only by tracking down the aristo-military type. But for James, the drama of a rejected marriage proposal was adventure incarnate. And as he remarked of Isabel Archer's midnight vigil, when she reflects on the failure of her marriage in *The Portrait of a Lady,* the "representation simply of her motionlessly *seeing,*" "the mere still lucidity of her act," was "as 'interesting' as the surprise of a caravan or the identification of a pirate."[11]

It is true that the attempts by Howells, James, Wharton, and other novelists of manners to register the adventure of the mind, to catch the finer vibrations of the moral sense, may seem rarefied to readers demanding the kind of violent adventure reflected in the books of Mailer, Faulkner, Hemingway, and others. Our appetite for them leads Green to characterize books of this kind—in the language of his mentor, F. R. Leavis—as "the great tradition, the central tradition, in American literature."[12] But this formulation makes too much of the romance as *the* tradition, a mistake that Richard Chase inaugurated in *The American Novel and Its Tradition.* I for one think that the great tradition in America, as in England, is in the social novel and have so argued at some length.[13] But there is no denying that our frontier experience has produced compelling fictive representations and that the romance genre is marked by some splendid instances of the form.

I find interesting Green's direct appeal to English teachers, especially academic feminists, to turn away from these adventure stories "toward others—those about 'strong women'—who can do more to build up the communal pride and energy of readers who want to resist imperialism and to change the meaning of 'America'" (*GAA,* 219). Except for "The Bear," I suspect that the works of Green's "great tradition" of violent adventure are not widely taught, except perhaps in the odd doctoral seminar at Tufts.

In any case, if English teachers do transform the canon as Green proposes, they will finally feminize American literary culture.[14] This would appear to be Green's objective, for he has elsewhere quoted Gandhi's call for more feminized men:

> I have repeated times without number that nonviolence is the inherent quality of women. For ages men have had training in violence. In order to become nonviolent they have to cultivate the qualities of women. Ever since I have taken to nonviolence, I have become more and more of a woman.[15]

No one can object to the growth of women's wise influence on American culture. Certainly we need all the wisdom we can get, especially if the effect is a decline in violence. But I am not convinced that those in our society who wish to emasculate males—especially white males, of which I am one—or who wish to effect an an-

drogynous merger of genders so that men and women become less distinguishable, are really speaking in the best interests of either sex or of their relationship to each other or of the future of the race. All too often what is at work is a sexism directed at men, not only by feminist ideologues but even by "liberated" men. A typical instance is this remark of W. P. Day, whom Green cites with approval: "Violence is, of course, the natural expression of the masculine in its purest form, the application of force to the world to assert its power and identity."[16] But is violence *the* natural expression of masculinity? Is it identical with "force," and, if so, what is force? Does it mean energy? If so, I see no moral flaw inherent in the application of *energy* to the world, so as to assert power, effect change, and actualize identity. That is what produced the Chartres cathedral, Mozart's sonatas, the vaccine of Jonas Salk, the four-minute mile, the moon landing, and *The Old Man and the Sea.* Of course, many intellectuals have a problem with the exertion of physical energy, which they must be at pains to discredit as they are not good at it. And of course, in some strains of oriental thought, all exertion of energy is vain. But most boys and men are not Eastern passivists or armchair intellectuals. And the attempt to neuter them through discrediting the active life is, as Camille Paglia has shown, a form of sexual decadence.[17] But sexual decadence offers a critical thrill for English teachers nowadays. The freakish is now "in." Thus academic intellectuals are usually the least trustworthy guides as to what forms of conduct and being constitute man- and womanhood. Yet the manly women, the feminized men, and the whole carnival of lesbians and homosexuals now proclaiming what is pretentiously and risibly called "Queer Theory" do not scruple to tell us what, genderwise, we ought to be.

What will be the case if, as I suspect it to be, women readers and teachers admire adventure stories too, even as men admire good novels of manners? As James remarked in "The Art of Fiction": "There are some subjects which speak to us and others which do not, but he would be a clever man who should undertake to give us a rule—an index expurgatorius—by which the story and the no-story should be known apart."[18] Yet Green and like-minded ideologues want to declare as forbidden and undesirable our classic tales of adventure.

It is perhaps a sign of the times that Green must be so apologetic about his preference for the novel of manners. The prisoner-of-sex syndrome seems to have affected a good many male critics as well. In an essay called "The Ways of a Wimp," the novelist Thomas Flanagan has expressed uneasiness over his liking for Austen, Proust, and James because he thinks that Americans automatically identify such a preference with something less than full masculine intelligence and aesthetic understanding. Of course Flanagan does not consent to this charge of wimpiness, but the uneasiness is still there. Something of the same discomfort arises in Alfred Habegger's *Gender, Fantasy, and Realism in American Literature* (1982), which contains a chapter called "Henry James and W. D. Howells as Sissies." Doubtless some adventure-writing he-men, like Frank Norris and Jack London, disliked the domestic realism of Howells and James, with its "drama of a broken tea-cup, the tragedy of a walk down the block, the excitement of an afternoon call, the adventure of an invitation to dinner," as Norris described it.[19] But Norris, London, and the others were merely trying to make a critical space for their own brand of fiction, a sensational naturalism intended to shock genteel Victorian America, or what was left of it. No wonder Alexander Harvey in *William Dean Howells* (1917) put Howells "at the head of the sissy school of American literature." But need anybody be troubled in his manhood by the macho posturing of the naturalists?

As it turns out, both Harvey and Habegger, as well as Martin Green, really like the domestic realism of Howells and James. So do I. There is a great deal of sheer aesthetic pleasure to be derived from Howells's modest comedies of manners like *A Chance Acquaintance* or *The Lady of the Aroostook*. There is also stunning depth of human understanding disclosed in novels like *The Wings of the Dove* and *The Golden Bowl*. And I would not give up Cooper's *Satanstoe* as a portrait of colonial domestic manners. But one is frankly appalled at the morbid self-consciousness, the sexual anxiety, and the embrace of hysterical thinking about manliness and womanliness evident in these critics and projected by them onto the whole of American culture. I can see no necessary contradiction between the pleasures of a good narrative about a wilderness hunt and the pleasures of a domestic narrative about pride and prejudice. James had it right in saying that there is simply good fiction and bad fiction.

V

A central issue here is the pleasure of the text. Green can get no pleasure from a novel in which an Osage Indian or a blue-coated cavalryman bites the dust, or in which the hunt for game in the wilderness turns sanguinary. He cannot have us read these narratives "with total assent or complicit enjoyment" (*GAA*, ix). Pleasure is capitalist corruption, and literary pleasure corrupts absolutely. But this fear of pleasure neither allows the author his *donnée* nor permits the reader any willing suspension of disbelief, even for the moment. The *reductio* of Green's dour moralism is Tolstoy's "What Is Art?"—which insists that the only justification of art is its promotion of brotherhood and human happiness.[20] But in fact Tolstoy wasn't even content with *that* formulation and eventually renounced the vanity of all literature, including his own; and Gandhi had no use whatsoever for the fruits of aesthetic invention. Green is

sincere enough to know that his continued preoccupation with art constitutes a rejection of the lesson of the mahatmas, but he rationalizes his lecturing and writing about art as a mode of "contemplation" in which his unmasking of the literature of empire somehow saves his honor and redeems his refusal of their oriental asceticism. But this activity is not contemplation, in the Eastern meaning. The renunciation commanded by Gandhi is quite plain: "All attachment to the senses is death."[21] If Green cannot yet submit himself to it, which of us could, even if we wanted to? Meanwhile, both the Tolstoyan and Marxist instrumental views of literature are hopelessly reductive of art's rich complexity of being. And the danger of adopting this functionalist view of art is that it impels us headlong toward the *index expurgatorius* with the clever left-wing authoritarian telling us what we can and cannot read.

Green's moralism runs counter to the whole affective psychology of "violence in art." I have in mind here Aristotle's observation, in the *Poetics,* that such is the pleasure of poetic *mimesis,* or imitation, that, although "there are some things that distress us when we see them in reality," "the most accurate representations of these same things we view with pleasure—as, for example, for forms of the most despised animals and of corpses."[22] Likewise, Sir Philip Sidney in "An Apology for Poetry" speaks of "the sweet violence of a tragedy."[23] And Dr. Johnson remarks that "the delight of tragedy proceeds from our consciousness of fiction; if we thought murders and treasons real they would please no more."[24] Wallace Stevens has even suggested, in *The Necessary Angel,* that the literature of violence, when it achieves true aesthetic nobility, may have a genuine existential value: "It is a violence from within that protects us from a violence without. It is the imagination pressing back against the pressure of reality. It seems, in the last analysis, to have something to do with our self-preservation; and that, no doubt, is why the expression of it, the sound of its words, helps us to live our lives."[25]

But Green won't draw a line between fiction and reality. He would make us feel guilty for the pleasure we take in literature's capacity to represent life, including life's violence. That capacity, for him, amounts to aesthetic hedonism, literature as "a pleasure garden for the socially privileged" (*GAA,* viii). Like Plato, or like the commissars whose politics Green espouses, he would deny such pleasurable adventure stories and admit to his utopia only tales that emphasize the pastimes of the domestic circle, the joys of economic production, the drama of social justice triumphant, the elimination of class conflict. These, for Green, express *the most important event in modern history,* which he identifies, following "Sartre and most Marxists (and most modern intellectuals)," as "Europe's industrialization of its economy" (*GAA,* 228).

I confess here to a sense of deflation at the answer to this great question about the most important event in European history. Sartre is hardly an economic historian, and no rational argument for this astonishing proposition is offered. The industrialization of Europe's economy was a fine thing—achieved without Marx's help, thanks to aggressive entrepreneurs building a better mousetrap. But the application of industrial techniques to production, distribution, and consumption, as an answer to a question about the most important event in human experience, grotesquely materializes history and robs it of the transcendental meaning it had for Gandhi and Tolstoy. In reality, *The Great Adventure* has unwittingly led us to believe that *the westward expansion of civilization* was the major event in modern history. But Green will have none of this because to assent to the literature of expansion is to recognize the rise of civilization in wilderness and prairie, the extension of law, the creation of wholesome socialized existence where once there was anarchy and savagery. This grand movement, afoot since 1492, is advancing Western civilization, and Green detests it for its ideology of personal liberty, its individualistic energy and success, its foundation on private property and the protection of the law, and its resignation to the inescapable fact, on the individual level, of human inequality. Behind Green's detestation of Western civilization is a racist self-loathing, reflected in his approval, in *The Challenge of the Mahatmas,* of Susan Sontag's calumny that "the white race is the cancer of human history."[26] Behind Green's work lies an undeclared romance with the utopian antithesis of the West, never quite defined, that inheres in the "countercultures" that he praises—the world of Tolstoy's peasants, the Quakers' Holy Experiment in Pennsylvania (1682-1775), Ascona, or in the ashrams of Gandhians in India.[27]

Can Green's Gandhism be reconciled with his left-wing politics, with what he calls "Marx and his revenge, his call to action, to praxis, to political rising"? This book certainly fails to harmonize them. Indeed, it cannot be done. Even Green has to confess in *The Challenge of the Mahatmas*: "Marxism-modernism is no option for a man opposed to violence; and Gandhism is antiintellectual and antiaesthetic."[28] My complaint here is not with the dedicated Marxist. He knows what he wants—a violent revolutionary overthrow of the capitalist system. Nor do I fault the Christian pacifist and nonviolent Gandhian. Both are sincere in believing that the martyr to faith will shame into conversion his violent oppressor. Such men of faith and private conviction can at times effect useful moral change. But what one faults here is the intellectual muddlement of a critic who tries to have it both ways: a nonviolent overthrow of the capitalist system in which those who have accumulated property through hard work or inheritance will somehow peacefully allow themselves to be stripped of it by intellectual leftists like Green. He has painted himself into a

corner from which he cannot escape, and his work reflects this paralysis. The sensible option would be to abandon Marxism, but Green has not to my knowledge renounced it despite its call to violence.

When Marx *has* had his revenge, when left-wing revolutions have erupted, men of moral conscience, of pacifist belief, and of Christian conviction have been among the first to be liquidated as reactionary vestiges of obsolete bourgeois morality. One of the greatest moral abominations of modern history was the wholesale slaughter of millions of Tolstoy's peasants, civil servants, doctors, merchants, artists, liberal humanists, and even dedicated Marxist functionaries (and their wives and children) in the name of that leftist ideology that now permeates the American university; our intellectual life is rotten with its false pieties and bogus sentimentality. In *The Challenge of the Mahatmas,* Green confesses: "I could not describe even theoretically the kind of political radicalism that I could subscribe to authentically."[29] When we think about the totalitarianism of Cuba and China and about how democracies perish, such confusion in our university intellectuals is instructive. Given the social wreckage produced by Marxist revolutions in this century, no one pretending to call himself a humanist can ignore the ways in which political radicalism has created an intolerant and repressive Marxist praxis. By every rational, religious, and humanly civilized criterion, that ideology has proven itself totally and horridly bankrupt. We need a better dream of the future; the Marxist polity, in all its bloody actuality, has been and is still a nightmare.

Notes

1. Martin Green, *The Great American Adventure* (Boston: Beacon Press, 1984), pp. 1, 11. Citations from this work will hereafter be given as *GAA,* in parentheses, in the text.

2. Cooper, *The Pioneers,* ed. Leon Howard (New York: Rinehart, 1959), pp. 394-95

3. Cooper, *The American Democrat,* ed. Robert Spiller (New York: Vintage, 1956), p. 89.

4. For an impressive treatment of Irving and the topic of adventure, see Peter Antelyes, *Tales of Adventurous Enterprise: Washington Irving and the Poetics of Western Expansion* (New York: Columbia University Press, 1990). On Parkman, see the previous essay and *La Salle and the Discovery of the Great West.*

5. D. H. Lawrence, *Studies in Classic American Literature* (Harmondsworth, England: Penguin, 1977), p. 68.

6. A cogent answer to the disgust with civilization found in certain contemporary leftist literary critics, of whom Green is merely typical, will be

found in Peter Shaw's splendid critical study *War Against the Intellect: Episodes in the Decline of Discourse* (Iowa City: University of Iowa Press, 1989), especially "Literary Scholarship and Disparaging American Culture" and "Civilization's Malcontents: Responses to *Typee*" (pp. 91-120).

7. Ernest Hemingway, *The Old Man and the Sea* (New York: Scribner's, 1952), pp. 50, 54, 105.

8. On the matter of the food, Green opines that meat-eating *produced* the warrior class. But vegetarianism also involves the killing of life forms for our alimentary sustenance. So vegetarians cannot claim, in my view, any moral superiority to meat-eaters, nor does vegetarianism deliver us from the offense of killing.

9. European colonial masters in the Third World could be a brutal lot; but anyone reflecting on the history of postcolonial life in India and Africa must be horrified at what has happened since the European oppressors left: the pervasive increase in poverty; the decline of the standard of living; the breakdown of law and order; the lack (indeed loss) of political liberties that originated with the colonial administrations; the rise of savage strong-men; and the constant tribal, ethnic, and religious warfare that has produced horrific widespread starvation and, in fact, wholesale regressions to barbarism. But of course there will always be those who see in American foreign policy, like the rescue of starving Somalis, some kind of covert imperialism.

10. Henry James, *Literary Criticism: Essays on Literature, American Writers, English Writers* (New York: Library of America, 1984), p. 61.

11. Henry James, *The Art of the Novel: Critical Prefaces,* ed. R. P. Blackmur (New York: Scribner's, 1934), p. 57.

12. F. R. Leavis, *The Great Tradition* (New York: George W. Stewart, [1948]).

13. James W. Tuttleton, *The Novel of Manners in America* (New York: W. W. Norton, 1974.)

14. See Ann Douglas's treatment of the nineteenth-century forces working to effeminize our society in *The Feminization of American Culture* (New York: Alfred A. Knopf, 1977).

15. Quoted in Martin Green, *The Challenge of the Mahatmas* (New York: Basic Books, 1978), p. 42. In calling women inherently nonviolent, the mahatma had clearly never visited a public junior high school in New York City.

16. Quoted in Martin Green, *The Adventurous Male: Chapters in the History of the White Male Mind* (University Park: Pennsylvania State University Press, 1993), pp. 18-19.

17. Camille Paglia, *Sexual Personae: Art and Decadence from Nefertiti to Emily Dickinson* (New Haven: Yale University Press, 1990), *passim*.

18. Henry James, "The Art of Fiction," p. 60.

19. Frank Norris, "A Plea for Romantic Fiction," *The Responsibilities of a Novelist* (New York: Doubleday, Page, & Co., 1903), p. 215.

20. Leo Tolstoy, "What Is Art?" in *Critical Theory Since Plato,* ed. Hazard Adams (New York: Harcourt, Brace, Jovanovich, 1971), p. 716.

21. Quoted in Green, *The Challenge of the Mahatmas,* p. 230.

22. Aristotle, *Poetics,* trans. Leon Golden (Englewood Cliffs, N.J.: Prentice-Hall, 1968), p. 7.

23. Sidney, "An Apology for Poetry," in *Critical Theory Since Plato,* p. 106.

24. Samuel Johnson, "Preface to Shakespeare" (1756), in *Criticism: Major Statements,* eds. Charles Kaplan and William Anderson (3rd ed., New York: St. Martin's Press, 1991), p. 233.

25. Wallace Stevens, "The Noble Rider and the Sound of Words," in *The Necessary Angel: Essays on Reality and the Imagination* (New York: Vintage, 1951), p. 36.

26. Green, *The Challenge of the Mahatmas,* p. 179.

27. See Green's *Mountain of Truth: The Counterculture Begins, Ascona, 1900-1920* (Hanover, N.H.: University Press of New England, 1986.)

28. Green, *The Challenge of the Mahatmas,* pp. 229, 87.

29. Green, *The Challenge of the Mahatmas,* p. 150.

Jamie S. Scott (essay date 2001)

SOURCE: Scott, Jamie S. "Doctors Divine: Medicine and Muscular Christianity in the Canadian Frontier Adventure Tale." In *Colonies-Missions-Cultures in the English-Speaking World: General and Comparative Studies,* edited by Gerhard Stilz, pp. 24-40. Tübingen, Germany: Stauffenburg Verlag, 2001.

[*In the following essay, Scott discusses how narratives written by missionaries and doctors in nineteenth- and early twentieth-century Canada propagated Christianity and Western culture in frontier territories.*]

1. INTRODUCTION

Following a pattern repeated around the empire, Christian missionaries played key roles in British and British-sponsored settlement in Canada (Grant: 1989). By the middle of the nineteenth century, Oblate and other Roman Catholic organisations had joined Anglican, nonconformist and lay Christians in the mission fields of Newfoundland and the Labrador, Upper and Lower Canada, and the Canadian prairies, sub-arctic and west coast.[1] Published in 1824, just after his return to England, John West's *The Substance of a Journal During a Residence at the Red River Colony, British North America, in the Years 1820-1823,* gives us an early first-hand account of the efforts of "British Christians" to export "the advantages of civilised and social life, with the blessings of Christianity" (West: 1824, xv).[2] His missionary civilising goals are clear: to eradicate the corrupting influence of those "Europeans" who "have borne scarcely any other mark of the Christian character than the name"; to overcome the "idolatry and ecclesiastical tyranny" of "the Church of Rome"; and to lead the Native peoples "to the culture of the field as a means of subsistence" by establishing "the principle, that the North-American Indian of these regions would part with his children, to be educated in the white man's knowledge" (50, 114, 139, 13).[3]

Although West's keen eye does not miss the degree of devastation brought to these communities by European diseases, we should hardly be surprised if his account of the Red River settlement shows little scientific concern with the health and sanitary conditions of either Europeans or Natives.[4] His judgments are of a moral order, and western medicine and sanitation generally bore little resemblance in the early nineteenth century to the scientifically informed and professionally managed institutions of the later nineteenth and twentieth centuries. During West's time in Canada, for example, various versions of Galen's miasmatic doctrine of atmospheric corruption still dominated theoretical debates about the causes of disease; indeed, "in the hands of some writers [this doctrine] was reduced to the simple proposition that bad smells breed diseases" (Youngson: 1979, 23). Microbial theories of contagion had received little attention. As John and Jean Comaroff have noted of the period, sickness seemed "a matter of excess or deficiency," and treatment for the most part assumed the "formulaic" character of "bloodletting, drastic purgatives, and emetics," accompanied by "the compensatory management of diet, dress, and exposure to volatile winds" (Comaroff and Comaroff: 1997, 327). Whether members of the Royal Colleges of Physicians and Surgeons or of the Society of Apothecaries, "[m]ost doctors before 1850, and many as late as 1870, it would seem, simply did not observe or think scientifically" (Youngson, 17). Within a few years of West's return to England, however, the Anatomy Act (1832) clarified the legal status of cadavers made available for dissection, in an effort to end the "resurrectionist" trade in "subjects" stolen from graves (Reader: 1966, 39). A circulation of influences saw swift advances in pathology, which led to demands for improvements in the quality of microscopes and other instruments, which in turn produced further progress in pathology. Advances in medical and sanitary theory and practice followed, and quickly began to take hold in Canada.

2. MEDICINE AND MISSIONARIES

The mid nineteenth to the early twentieth century saw radical changes in four major areas of western medical and sanitary theory and practice. First, James Y. Simpson's use of chloroform at the Edinburgh Royal Infirmary heralded the general practice of anaesthesia in Britain, especially after 8 April, 1853, when John Snow administered chloroform to Queen Victoria to ease the birth of her eighth child, a son, Prince Leopold.[5] Canadian doctors learned about anaesthesia from both their British and American colleagues, and by the third quarter of the nineteenth century, chloroform and ether were widely employed (Roland: 1967, 250). Secondly, in 1867, Joseph Lister published his theory and practice of antisepsis.[6] In 1877, T. G. Roddick, who visited Edinburgh several times to observe Lister, imported the complete antiseptic system, using it with great success in the Montreal General Hospital (MacDermot: 1967, 28-29). Thirdly, standardised procedures for the professional qualification of doctors, more stringent academic requirements, and fee structures all became British law with the Medical Act (1858), its Amending Bill (1878), and a second Medical Act (1886). Likewise, the founding of the Canadian Medical Association in 1867 signalled greater professionalism, although separate provincial jurisdictions over medical education and registration were not harmonised until the Canada Medical Act of 1912, and the Royal College of Physicians and Surgeons of Canada was formed only in 1929 (MacDermot: 1935, 53-58; 1967, 128-30).[7] Fourthly, a series of health and safety laws culminating in a comprehensive Public Health Act (1875) combined to regulate everything in Britain from slaughter houses, burial grounds, clean water supplies and sewage disposal to infant vaccination, quarantine for infectious diseases and inspection of prostitutes for contagious diseases (Porter: 1997, 409-15). In a similar fashion, Canada, too, saw the creation of organised departments of health. In 1872, for example, the city of Toronto established a Local Board of Health, and in 1882, Ontario's Public Health Act set up a Provincial Board of Health. Emended in 1884, this provincial act empowered William Canniff, Toronto's crusading Medical Health Officer from 1883 to 1890, to "Canadianize [. . .] the sanitary idea," although federal standards "for the improvement of environmental sanitation, and for the provision of safe food and water" only appeared with the creation of the Canadian Department of Public Health in 1919 (MacDougall: 1988, 83, 87; MacDermot: 1967, 81).

British ecclesiastical organisations had long recognised the connection between healing and preaching. "The

Order for the Visitation of the Sick, and the Communion of the Same" in Thomas Cranmer's first Anglican *Book of Common Prayer* makes an explicit connection between sin and sickness.[8] Early nineteenth-century doctors, divine and medical alike, will have been familiar with the Methodist John Wesley's evangelical association of their vocations in his *Primitive Physic; or, An Easy and Natural Method of Curing Most Diseases,* published in 1791. So also, in colonial New England, seventeenth-century Puritan divines had taken the notion of God—the great physician of Israel—very much in the plain sense; to be properly Christian was to be a physician (Watson: 1991, 7). And Cotton Mather's *Magnalia Christi Americana; or the Ecclesiastical History of New England* cites the gospel example of the disciple Luke, speaking of an "angelical conjunction" whereby preacher-physicians through the ages have "administered unto the *souls* of the people the more effectually, for being able to administer to their *bodies*" (Mather: 1702, I, 439). For early Victorian England, David Livingstone's celebrated autobiographical *Missionary Travels and Researches in South Africa,* published in 1847, embodies this vocational association in the colonial and imperial mission fields. In a letter, Livingstone advises fellow clinician, John Kirk, never to overlook "the opportunity which the bed of sickness presents by saying a few kind words in a natural respectful manner and imitate as far as you can the conduct of the Great Physician, whose followers we profess to be" (Foskett: 1964, 43).

In 1841, however, such occasional encounters between the medical and clerical callings received institutional form, when Sir John Abercrombie founded the nondenominational Edinburgh Medical Missionary Society. A professional literature followed. In 1878, for example, the Medical Missionary Association, set up in London on the model of the Edinburgh society, began publishing a quarterly journal, *Medical Missions: At Home and Abroad.*[9] In the "Introduction" to its first issue, the journal reveals its *raison d'être*:

> But in the sense in which the term [medical missionary] is generally used, a medical mission means an agency in which the doctor and those who work with him use the influence they have acquired over their patients by their medical skill to recommend the religion of Christ. In this they are following closely in the footsteps of their Lord and Master, who gave us the example of combining preaching with healing.
>
> (*Medical Missions* 1 (1878): 1)[10]

In 1879, the first contribution from Canada appears in the journal. The Right Rev. Dr. John Horden, Bishop of Moosonee, tells of two doctors employed by the Hudson's Bay Company. The doctors treat the company's employees, as well as those natives who come to the fort to trade. Horden holds the medical missionaries in high esteem:

> [O]ur young medical men [. . .] who are firm believers in Christ [. . .] must ever be numbered among the most valuable of our missionaries, for the healing of the body softens the prejudices of unbelief, and leads the devotee of superstition to believe that a system which can induce men freely to exercise their professional skill to relieve his physical ailments, must have some good secrets connected with it, a something which ennobles human nature, stimulating charity and self-sacrifice. Does he not see these qualities personified in the person of him now ministering to his needs?
>
> (1879, 88)

Incarnations at once of "the great Physician" himself and of the evangelising strategies developed in earlier ecclesiastical literature like West's *Journal,* these doctors also embody white colonial convictions about the universal relevance of their own knowledge (88). "The natives themselves possess no medical knowledge whatsoever," writes Horden (87). Accordingly, by the end of the nineteenth century, Canadian churches were sending their own medical missionaries into western and northern Canada, as evidenced in such autobiographical works as the Methodist A. E. Bolton's *Medical Work among the Indians* (1896) and the Presbyterian Arthur Barner's pseudonymous *Surgeon of the Skeena: A Brief Resumé of the Life and Work of Rev. Horace C. Wrinch* (1910) (Barner: 1910; Bolton: 1896; see also Large: 1968).

3. WRITING THE MEDICAL MISSIONARY

3.1. HIRAM A. CODY'S THE FRONTIERSMAN: A TALE OF THE YUKON

The heroic figure of the Christian missionary was quite familiar to late nineteenth- and early twentieth-century Canadian readers from the work of Ralph Connor, whose novels, *Black Rock: A Tale of the Selkirks* (1898) and *The Sky Pilot: A Tale of the Foothills* (1899), pioneered the melodramatic celebration of Christian missionary heroism on the northern and western frontiers.[11] These novels turn to expressly Christian proselytising ends a literary fashion established in the frontier romances of writers like R. M. Ballantyne and Horatio Gilbert Parker, who between them published numerous titles set in northern and western Canada. But what of those Canadian colonial writers who chose to celebrate the *medical* missionary in their work? To begin with, I would like to look quickly at Hiram A. Cody's *The Frontiersman: A Tale of the Yukon* (1910), the main protagonist of which—Keith Steadman—is a medical missionary to the Yukon.[12]

Cody casts Steadman as "the traditional noble, lone traveller, the fearless fighter, and the chaste lover," one of the "simple, strong-hearted, evangelical heroes" typical of the adventure story genre (Klinck: 1965, 1: 347). *The Frontiersman* proceeds from action scene to action scene, exciting the sensibilities of a cloistered urban audience with descriptions of wolf attacks, gold robberies, bar brawls, natural calamities, and other frontier trials. A couple of short paragraphs from a chapter entitled "Where Is My Flock?" convey a clear impression of a generation of white Christian attitudes towards Native peoples in Canada:

> Here the Indians were living their wild life, sunk in degradation and superstition, when found by Keith Steadman, medical missionary from eastern Canada. At the command of his veteran Bishop of the Mackenzie River, he had forced his way over the Rocky Mountains, sought out these wandering sheep of the wilderness, and for ten long years lived in their midst.
>
> [. . .]
>
> It was uphill work to root out old ideas, to plant new seeds, and to overcome the jealousy of the Medicine Men. Often his life was in great danger, but in the end he conquered and won the confidence of the natives.
>
> (Cody: 1910, 34-35)

Notice the dominant military trope informing these paragraphs—the "veteran" bishop giving a "command," the missionary forcing his way through the Rockies, eventually conquering the old ways of the Indians, like Moses bequeathing to Joshua the Israelite conquest of Canaan (*Joshua*, 1: 2-9). Notice also the image of husbandry, likening the destruction of Native culture to clearing and cultivating the land. This trope, too, derives from early biblical narratives—Adam is commanded "to dress [Eden], and to keep it," then when expelled, "to till the ground from whence he was taken" (*Genesis* 3: 15, 23).

In this same aggressive, paternalistic tenor, Steadman has to defend his flock from the evil influences of the saloon-keeper, Jim Perdue, when the Indians succumb to the influences of the Frenchman's grog. Here is the encounter between the missionary and Perdue:

> 'What is the meaning of this?' he [Steadman] demanded. 'What are you doing with my Indians? Where is my flock which I left in peace and quietness?'
>
> 'Who in h-l are you, and what business is it of yours what we do with the Indians?' replied Perdue in a surly manner, at the same time shrinking back from those searching blue eyes, which seemed to pierce his very soul.
>
> 'Man,' came the response, as a yearning arm reached out toward the natives, 'they are mine. Through long years of travail I have borne with them, and I love them. I am Keith Steadman, the missionary.'
>
> (Cody: 1910, 450)

Notice how the Indians are doubly disempowered. Seduced by Perdue's alcoholic blandishments, their souls are in danger of joining his in eternal damnation, as the French-Canadian's name none too subtly implies. The Indians thus become commodities in the ongoing colonial struggle between the Roman Catholic French and the Protestant English. In the logic of this colonial economy, at once religious and political, the missionary claims outright ownership of the Indians—"my flock," "they are mine." Steadman's bald assertion of his own identity is so sure, so absolute, that it erases all other identities. "I am Keith Steadman, the missionary," reverberates with the revelation at Sinai. Yet Cody makes next to nothing of his hero's medical credentials.

3.2. RALPH CONNOR'S THE DOCTOR: A TALE OF THE ROCKIES

The second text I would like to consider is Ralph Connor's *The Doctor: A Tale of the Rockies* (1906).[13] Like Cody's fiction, "Connor's novels adhered to a single and highly successful formula—the playing out of a morality in a magnificent natural setting, with colourful characterizations and vivid descriptive passages to put flesh on the archetypal confrontation of men with their unruly souls" (Thompson and Thompson: 1972, 159). Though published four years before *The Frontiersman*, *The Doctor* offers a more complex picture of relations between the missionary and medical vocations on the Canadian frontier. To begin with, Connor's novel introduces some scientific realism to the adventure story genre. We hear, for example, that the "dread of [microbes] was just beginning to obtain in popular imagination" (Connor: 1906, 73). Capitalising on this sense of realism, *The Doctor* goes on to tell the story of rural Ontario brothers, Bernard ("Barney") and Richard ("Dick") Boyle. Connor portrays both young men in appropriately heroic terms: "Barney's jaw ran along the side of his face, ending abruptly in a square-cut chin, the jaw and the chin doing for his face what a ridge and a bluff do for a landscape," while Dick "was a good man to look upon, with his springy step, his tan skin, his clear eye, but chiefly because out of his clear eye a soul looked forth clean and unafraid upon God's good world of wholesome growing things" (66, 112). But the brothers fall out over the love of Margaret, the beautiful "daughter of the manse" (13).

Wishing to become a doctor, Barney enters the tutelage of old Dr. Ferguson, who encourages him to become a surgeon, since he has "got the fingers and the nerves" (68). Following mid-Victorian professional distinctions, Ferguson differentiates a physician, who "guesses and experiments, treats symptoms, trys [sic] one drug then another, guessing and experimenting all along the line," from the surgeon for whom "[t]here's no guess at the knife point! The knife lays bare the evil, fights, eradicates it!" (68). Battling "evil," that is to say, the surgeon in some sense does God's work. But Ferguson's old books do not prepare Barney well for his exams, which he fails twice. Coached by Dr. Trent, "the most brilliant surgeon on the staff," Barney finally qualifies, quickly proves his surgical genius, and takes up a teaching position at the Johns Hopkins Medical School in

Baltimore (115). Meanwhile, Dick has been preparing to enter the Presbyterian ministry, though he, too, must overcome obstacles. At the Presbytery examination for his minister's license, the Rev. Alexander Naismith, "went after Boyle on every doctrine in the catalogue," finally insinuating that he was a man of low morals because he smoked a little and did not subscribe to "total abstinence" (189, 193, 194). Eventually, however, Dick becomes a missionary to crews building the Crow's Nest railroad on the western frontier in the Calgary Presbytery. The railroad's General Manager, however, has been requesting a medical missionary, so Dick, lacking Barney's medical training, does the next best thing and uses his clerical influence to raise funds to build Kushinook Hospital. At the same time, the railroad workers are all talking about a courageous new physician called "Dr. Bailey" (228). Dr. Bailey, of course, is really Barney, and the point of Connor's plotting here is to dramatise the relationship between the medical and the missionary—the body and the soul—in the civilising colonial agenda.

On the medical side, Barney has to deal with an outbreak of diphtheria at the railroad workers' camp. A series of scenes dramatises the medical procedures for coping with the disease: building an isolation camp, disinfecting the bunkhouse, keeping the infected men away from the cookhouse, and administering injections of "antitoxin" (249, 262). The diphtheria retreats, and Barney suggests sanitation measures to prevent typhoid:

> 'Look at the location of the camp. Down in a swamp, with a magnificent site five hundred yards away,' [Barney says,] pointing to a little plateau further up the hill, clear of underbrush and timbered with great pines. 'Then look at the stables where they are. There are no means by which the men can keep themselves or their clothes clean. Their bunks, some of them, are alive with vermin, and the bunk-house is reeking with all sorts of smells. At a very little more cost you could have had a camp here pleasant, safe, clean, and an hospital ready for emergencies.'
>
> (271)

But the real appeal of such reforms to the railroad company, Barney argues, ought to lie first in their economic return, and secondly, in their publicity value:

> 'Why it would pay,' continued the doctor. 'You would keep your men in good condition, in good heart and spirits. They would do twice the work. They would stay with you. Besides, it would prevent scandal.'
>
> (272)

Unable to resist Barney's logic, the camp manager agrees to relocate the camp. But the same reforms which result in healthy conditions for the men also benefit the company, of course. A healthier workforce translates into greater profits. Further, when Barney's reforms do in fact result in improved economic performance, the railroad company makes him medical superintendent of the line, thus silencing the lone voice of protest if not with wealth, then at least with the rewards of power. Medicine thus serves colonial capital.

The story does not end here, however. Barney finds Dick washed up on the shore after a bad tumble in the rapids of the Big Horn River. He coaxes life back into Dick: "With his swift fingers he filled his syringe with the whiskey and injected it into the arm" (309). Barney gets Dick to Kushinook Hospital, and he survives. Barney confesses he has misjudged his brother, and they are reconciled. When the injured Dick is unable to lead the next Sunday service, Barney volunteers. The church is packed to hear Barney testify to the miraculous change God has wrought in his life. Now more missionary than medical, Barney sets out to make right the wrongs of the past by reforming the "red-light" culture of the west (379). "To his former care for the physical well-being of men," writes Connor, "he added now a concern for their mental and spiritual good, and hence the system of libraries and clubrooms he had initiated throughout the camps and towns along the line" (379). A reformed barman even identifies Barney with Christ himself: "You're like—Him, I think . . . You make me think o'Him" (388). Exhausted, the self-sacrificing Barney dies of a ruptured appendix in Dick's hospital, his last words binding Dick and Margaret one to another. The minister's daughter, Margaret, and the heroic frontier missionary, Dick, continue to run Kushinook Hospital, and after a respectable interval, they marry, "for love's sake" (1906: 399). Medical care thus remains safely within the control of religious authority—the body regulated by a manly Christian ethic.

3.3. *Wilfred Grenfell's* Labrador Tales

Wilfred Thomason Grenfell's *Labrador Tales* provide my third area of enquiry.[14] A fully trained and qualified medical doctor himself—unlike Cody or Connor—for Grenfell the life of the manly Christian missionary means first and foremost the life of medical service. As a result, many of Grenfell's stories dramatise physical human suffering with the detached intensity of the clinical eye. For instance, "How We Did without a Doctor," in the collection *The Harvest of the Sea,* tells us that although Labrador is naturally a healthy place, where "bracing air, the freedom from infectious germs and the sea-life make new men of worn-out material," a fisherman may easily lose his livelihood because "cuts, sea-boils and ulcers from the poisoned water round their [fishing] stages [. . .] often lead[s] to abscess, gangrene and the loss of a hand" (Grenfell: 1905, 132). The next story, "Preach the Word—Heal the Sick," suggests an answer for much of this suffering—the mission's hospital-ship, *Strathcona.* With "Preach the Word" painted on the starboard rail, "Heal the Sick" on the port, and the biblical apothegm, "Jesus saith, follow Me, and I will make you fishers of men," engraved round her "great oak wheel," the ship seems to symbolise a comfortable isomorphism between the medical and the missionary vocations (140). We cannot ignore the commodity value of Grenfell's writing here. With one eye each on fundraising in Britain and the United States, he describes *Strathcona* as "English from her truck to her cut-water, though she was smart enough to be an American pleasure yacht" (163). Yet the genuine humanitarian concern for the poor and helpless is inescapable, too.

Grenfell's attitudes towards the native Inuit are equally ambiguous. "The Labrador Eskimo and the Moravian Mission," in *The Harvest of the Sea,* for instance, describes the Inuit as "a queer, merry little brown people [. . .] almost always fat and jolly" (126). At the same time, however, Grenfell quite openly expresses his admiration for their integrity and communitarian values: "The eskimo are very honest and seldom if ever steal: indeed, they hold most things in common" (128). "The Missions," in *Labrador: The Country and Its People,* presents these ambiguities still more starkly. Grenfell describes the reactions of a group of Inuit upon first encountering a hospital:

> At first the "Innuits" would not subject themselves to the necessary hospital regulations. We carried thither the first patients in our little hospital steamer. A severe epidemic of grippe (with heart troubles and other complications) was killing many. We had picked up a full load, and dumped them on the new doctor. It was a new experience to see an Eskimo trying to accommodate himself to a bed. The warmth of the ward was objectionable. The additional heat of bedclothes was intolerable. Washed to fine nut-brown, with their jet-black hair and large, dark eyes, they formed a most pleasant contrast to the white sheets on which they lay when we paid our first morning visit. Covering of any kind they had long ago disposed of, and even then they were perspiring and panting. Nature seems to have taught them what civilization has made us forget,—the value of fresh air
>
> (Grenfell: 1909a, 230-31)

Made impersonal as "a full load," the "[w]ashed" Inuit bodies of "fine nut-brown, with their jet-black hair and large, dark eyes" contrast sensually, even sexually, with "the white sheets on which they lay." The clinician's expressed admiration for traditional Inuit healthiness— "Nature seems to have taught them what civilization has made us forget,—the value of fresh air"—only increases our sense of this repressed attraction. But then this admiration turns, ironically enough, upon an accord between the traditional ways of the Inuit and vying western medical theories about "the value of fresh air." Perhaps removal to Grenfell's sanitary hospital improved the health of the Inuit; but they "eventually recovered," he tells us, "in spite of me" (231).

In these respects, the demands placed upon the medical missionary in such remote and inhospitable regions leads inexorably to an authoritarian assumption of responsibility for all aspects of people's lives, whether white or native, even though, ironically, the manly Christian gospel enjoins an ethic of disciplined self-sufficiency. "Where Poverty Means Starvation," in *The Harvest of the Sea,* editorialises on this situation. "Could anything be done to preach the gospel on economic lines?" Grenfell writes (1905, 156). "Should he go on preaching the salvation of the soul in the next world, while he witnessed the damnation of the body in this, without making an effort to mitigate the situation, however feeble it might prove?" (156). Elsewhere, Grenfell describes his efforts to "mitigate the situation." The Labrador mission sets up cooperative enterprises for the fishing communities, to free them from economic dependency on rapacious suppliers and fickle government; for the sick, he builds hospitals and provides transport to them; for the naked, clothes; for the wronged, justice; for the illiterate, schools; for orphans, foster care; against temptation, "[o]pen hostility to the liquor traffic"; and finally, for the lonely and isolated, a network of Christian correspondents in Britain and the United States (Grenfell: 1909a, 246-49). He looks forward to "the time when no mission need work among those men of Labrador, for they will be self-sustained and powerful in their simple, wholesome life by the sea" (Rompkey: 1991, 278; Grenfell: 1909a, 250). Till then, he writes: "Christ would interpret the love of the Father in Heaven to His children on this coast by the erection of churches, the duplication of religious services, then insisting on an orthodox intellectual attitude by doctrinal methods, has not been the premise on which the [mission] work has been developed" (Grenfell: 1909a, 249). Instead, Grenfell interprets "the love of the Father in Heaven" as a mandate to establish what he sees as a kind of benevolent Christian dictatorship over the fishing communities of northern Newfoundland and the Labrador, his *credo* a muscular Christian version of the Juvenalian apothegm, *mens sana in corpore sano,* which so captured the humanist imagination of the Renaissance. In fact, an American admirer sees Grenfell as a modern incarnation of the Renaissance man:

> Sailor, surgeon, engineer, industrial leader, manufacturer, explorer, and policeman, as well as teacher and preacher, he combines in one person, all, or nearly all, the activities that make the best modern missions a centre of civilization and a bringer of life wherever they are established.
>
> (Abbott: 1903, 692)

4. CONCLUSION

What are we to make of these various portrayals of the medical missionary in Canadian colonial writings? Well, to begin with, we need be under no misapprehension of the extent to which the vision of Christian missionary heroism pervades late nineteenth-and early twentieth-century Canadian society and culture. Though only Hiram Cody's first attempt at a novel, *The Frontiersman,* received almost unqualified plaudits.[15] In this regard, only Ralph Connor's success exceeded Cody's.[16] On the other hand, *The Frontiersman* and *The Doctor* represent different perspectives upon the medical missionary operating on the Canadian frontier. In its use of the popular adventure story as a vehicle for propagating the ethical and theological principles of those aggressive forms of Christian proselytising variously called muscular or manly Christianity, Cody's novel projects an uncompromising image of the missionary as an instrument of colonial and imperial hegemony. As for such familiar Victorian proponents of this species of Christianity as the Thomas Hughes of *Tom Brown's Schooldays* or the Charles Kingsley of *Westward Ho!,* so for Cody physical prowess serves as "an index of psychological, moral and spiritual health" (Vance: 1989, 110). At the same time, however, *The Frontiersman* fails fully to develop our sense of the missionary Steadman's status as a medical man. Not exactly invisible, his clinical skills seem nonetheless little more than a nominal addition to his manly Christian prowess. In its projection of the heroic colonial image of the Christian medical missionary, Cody's *The Frontiersman* thus leaves unexplored the theological and ethical tensions implicated in the phrase "medical missionary," tensions between medical knowledge in the service of colonial and imperial capital and the missionary's supposed focus upon ethical reform and spiritual metamorphosis.

By contrast, the narrative of *The Doctor* enacts Ralph Connor's theological and ethical judgement on the nature of the relationship between the medical and the missionary. Note the economy of the plot: Barney is sacrificed, though not before he is redeemed; and the pure of heart—Margaret and Dick—live on, blessed with success and happiness in this life as well as the next, though not before their self-sacrificial moral fibre has been severely tested. As for Cody's Keith Steadman, so for Connor's Dick and Barney Boyle, both medical and missionary vocations are manly Christian pursuits, enactments of what Daniel Coleman has called "the allegory of manly maturation that precedes, pervades, and succeeds turn-of-the century-Canadian expansionism" (1997, 85). At the same time, these vocations constitute vying, even mutually contradictory spheres of European professional knowledge. In Connor's story, we thus find little or no mention of the need to missionise an almost invisible indigenous population; rather, settling whites are the objects of a civilising drive preoccupied with settling its own missionary priorities. In fact, in a telling reversal of tropes, a native name is given to Kushinook Hospital, which has displaced the mission station as the centre of medical missionary power and authority. At the same time, however, *The Doctor* makes it clear that no matter how

noble, even essential, physical care is, spiritual care will always transcend it. Margaret finally chooses the missionary, Dick, not the doctor, Barney; and Dick, not Barney, controls the hospital. *The Doctor* subjects both vocations to that project's agenda, but rules firmly and unequivocally in favour of missionary over medical priorities—"of the 'spirit' versus the 'body,' of 'preaching' versus 'practice'" (Comaroff and Comaroff: 1997, 329). On the other hand, precisely for this reason, Connor's missiology differs little from Cody's; in the last analysis, both writers stress the priority of saving souls over healing bodies.

The picture becomes more complicated when we come to Grenfell. His contemporaries detected in Grenfell himself a high imperial embodiment of the heroic missionary ideal. Here, for example, is the portrait of early biographer—better, hagiographer—James Johnston:

> The age of romance in Missions is by no means passing away. Heroes on the field are as numerous today, if not more so, than at any period since the dawn of the missionary enterprise over a century ago. To this company Dr. Grenfell of Labrador belongs [. . .] He is unquestionably the embodiment of a type of heroic manhood at once courageous, resourceful, vigilant, pitying, for the sake of the human wreckage on Labrador's rugged shores. What wonder that he is altogether regarded as the greatest man who has hitherto appeared in Labrador.
>
> (Johnston: 1904, 11)

But Grenfell's Christianity has no clear denominational attachments, and his missiology is much less orthodox than Cody's or Connor's. In *Labrador: The Country and Its People,* for instance, he describes his mission's mandate:

> The *raison d'être* of the Mission is to commend to men who daily face the perils and privations of the sea, the Gospel of Christ as the practical rule of life. It labours to form no church. It seeks to inculcate no submission to any theories or shibboleths. It aims at adherence to no intellectual dogma.
>
> (Grenfell: 1909a, 238)

There is ideological naiveté here, of course; whatever the apparent disinterestedness of Grenfell's ecumenical magnanimity, ideological presuppositions of some kind must permeate his medical and missionary practices. In fact, we find that this freelance theological status translates into an easy isomorphism between Grenfell's medical missionary goals and the Anglo-Saxon civilising agenda, not only of British, but also of American late nineteenth and early twentieth century colonial and imperial Christianity.

More specifically, an Anglo-American ideology of racial supremacy becomes quite explicit in Grenfell's life and work. Nowhere does this ideology appear more starkly than in Grenfell's whole-hearted subscription to the writings of Lyman Abbott, the turn-of-the-century Christian social philosopher to whom he once wrote: "I do not think, as far as theology goes, there can be a pin of difference between your views and my own" (Grenfell: 1909b; qtd. in Rompkey, 110). As an American Congregationalist minister and "theistic evolutionist," Abbott wrote extensively on social and political issues (Rompkey, 109). In a chapter on "The Growth of Democracy," in *The Rights of Man: A Study in Twentieth Century Problems,* he spells out his thoughts on Anglo-Saxon Christian civilising:

> It is said that we have no right to go to a land occupied by a barbarian people and interfere with their life. It is said that if they prefer barbarism they have a right to remain barbarians. I deny the right of a barbaric people to retain possession of any quarter of the globe. What I already said I reaffirm: barbarism has no right, which civilization is bound to respect. Barbarians have rights which civilized people are bound to respect, but they have no right to their barbarism. A people do not own a continent because they roam through its forests, travel across its prairies, and hunt on its hillsides; no people own a continent unless they are using the continent. The world belongs to humanity, not to the men who happen to be in one quarter of the globe. And the people who are living in a place and not utilizing the place have no right to warn all other people off as trespassers. The dog has not a right to the manger, even if he is a barbarian dog and the ox is an Anglo-Saxon ox.
>
> (Abbott: 1901, 274)[17]

From these remarks it is not a long step to Grenfell's unabashed avowal of Christian authoritarianism. In opposition to self-determination for Newfoundland and the Labrador, for example, he wrote: "Even in the New World, doubts are rising as to whether autocratic power may not have some advantages if tempered by a Christian spirit, if exercised under wise advisers, and if administered with courage" (1934, 68). In Grenfell's case, at least, the combined authority of the medical and the missionary over individual and collective bodies and souls leads to such conclusions. Late in life, Grenfell maintained that he did not "personally regard the hospital work as the first work of the mission, and never did," that he was "far more interested in making a new man than a new body" (1940; qtd. in Rompkey, 295). But perhaps his writings muddy this self-evaluation, even if an exact assessment of Grenfell's sense of relations between the spirit and its corporeal temple is difficult to fathom.

Of the cultural construction of modern medicine, Michel Foucault has written: "To the army of priests watching over the salvation of souls would correspond that of the doctors who concern themselves with the health of bodies" (Foucault: 1973, 32-33). But perhaps Foucault might have considered the priest who *is* a doctor—the medical missionary, for whom the discursive exchange

sometimes seems to flow both ways between the clinical and the clerical. When, for instance, Grenfell chooses to describe a list of sanitary guidelines for children as a "Catechism of Simple Rules of Health for Use in Newfoundland and Labrador Schools," he is investing the medical with the sort of uncompromising certainty we might elsewhere associate with religious authority.[18] Grenfell seems well aware of the likely effects of such transpositions. As he notes in a story titled "A Physician in the Arctic," collected in *Down to the Sea: Yarns from the Labrador,* successful surgery on a "double cataract" might be "quite as miraculous to the [patient's] neighbours as the restoring of sight to the blind in Our Saviour's time" (1910a, 190). Incarnating—if you will—the Protestant ethic and the spirit of medicalism, this dialectical blurring of the boundaries between the medical and the missionary works produces, at least in Grenfell and his vocationally doubled disciples and patient-converts, "just the kind of disciplined worker of whom [colonial and imperial] policymakers dreamed" (Comaroff and Comaroff: 1992, 232).

Notes

I wish to thank the Social Science and Humanities Research Council of Canada for funding this research.

1. For an early account of Anglican missionising in Canada, for example, see Gould (1905).

2. The Christian Missionary Society sent West out with the Hudson's Bay Company in 1820. As the first Anglican missionary in the Red River settlement, the *Journal* tells us, he was to attempt "to seek the instruction, and endeavour to meliorate the condition of the native Indians" (West, 3). His writings reveal West to have been a careful, if incredulous observer of the religious life of Native Americans, and he respects their close attachment to the "native soil" (West, 109).

3. In recent years, a large literature has developed on the residential school system consequent to this religious ideology (Haig-Brown: 1988; Lascelles: 1990; Knockwood: 1992; Miller: 1996; Blake: 1999).

4. On one occasion, West notes of the Indians how "the measles [. . .] carried off great numbers of them, in different tribes," while generally, although Europeans find "the climate of Red River [. . .] to be remarkably healthy," "the natives of the country" commonly die of "pulmonary consumptions [. . .] the unavoidable consequence of privations and immoderate fatigue, which they endure in hunting and war; and of being continually exposed to the inclemency of the seasons" (West, 37, 106).

5. Collegial resistance to anaesthesia affected especially the clinical status and treatment of women. On the question of the gendering of Victorian

medicine, see Jordanova (1989), and with reference to Canada, see Mitchinson (1991). For various interpretations of gender and imperialism, see Midgley (1998).

6. In a series of short articles, Lister moves from the occasional use of carbolic acid as an antiseptic, through the articulation of the "antiseptic principle," to a full-fledged surgical "system" (Lister 1867a, 1867b, 1867c, 1867d, 1869, 1875).

7. For details about local and regional medical societies in Canada before and after the founding of the Canadian Medical Association, see MacDermot (1967: 152-55, 217). The earliest society—the Medical Association of Nova Scotia—was formed in 1854.

8. "The Order for the Visitation of the Sick, and the Communion of the Same" instructs the minister to exhort "the sicke person after this fourme, or other lyke" (Cranmer: 1549): "DERELY beloved, know this that almighty God is the Lorde over lyfe, and death, and over all thynges to them perteyning, as youth, strength, helth, age, weakenesse, and sickenesse. Wherfore, whatsoever your sickenes is, knowe you certaynly, that it is Gods visitacion. And for what cause soever this sickenesse is sent unto you; whether it bee to trye your pacience for the example of other, and that your fayth may be founde, in the day of the Lorde, laudable, glorious, and honourable, to the encrease of glory, and endelesse felicitie: Orels it be sent unto you to correcte and amende in you, whatsoever doeth offende the iyes of our heavenly father: knowe you certainly, that if you truely repent you of your synnes, and beare your sickenes paciently, trusting in Gods mercy, for his dere sonne Jesus Christes sake, and rendre unto him humble thankes for his fatherly visitacion, submytting yourselfe wholy to his wil; it shal turne to your profite, and helpe you forewarde in the ryght waye that leadeth unto everlastyng lyfe" (Cranmer: 1549).

9. Other medical missionary organs soon appeared. In 1897, for example, the Church Missionary Society began monthly publishing of *Mercy and Truth: A Record of the Church Missionary Society Medical Missionary Work.* Tellingly, in 1924, *Medical Missions: At Home and Abroad* was renamed *Conquest by Healing.*

10. For a revealing instance of the militaristic tactics of medical missionising, see Dr. W. Thomson Crabbe's article in the tenth issue of *Medical Missions* (1880, 145-52).

11. Other instances of this genre include William H. Withrow's *Neville Trueman, the Pioneer Preacher* (1880), Egerton Ryerson Young Snr.'s *Oowikapun; or, How the Gospel Reached the Nelson River Indians* (1895), Basil King's *Duncan Polite* (1905),

and Ernest Thompson Seton's *The Preacher of Cedar Mountain: A Tale of the Open Country* (1917).

12. Originally titled *God's Frontiersman, The Frontiersman* fictionalises aspects of Cody's own Anglican missionary service in the Diocese of Selkirk, later the Yukon, from 19 June, 1904, to 31 December, 1910, under the celebrated Bishop William Carpenter Bompas, a biography of whom became Cody's first published book (1908). Cody's clerical career epitomises the blending of the religious and the colonial, of frontier Christian missionising with British imperial expansionism; the Colonial and Continental Church Society of England paid $500 of Cody's $1,200 stipend (Jones: 1981, 177).

13. "Ralph Connor" is the pseudonym of the Reverend Charles Gordon. Born in Glengarry County, Ontario, Gordon studied at Knox College, in Toronto, and then at the University of Edinburgh. Ordained in 1890, he spent four years as a Presbyterian missionary in the frontier communities of Alberta, followed by a year back in Scotland chasing funds for Canada's western mission fields. In 1894, until he retired in 1924, Gordon served as minister of the mission church of St. Stephen's, in Winnipeg, Manitoba, where he preached a form of Social Gospel Christianity (Allen: 1971). Under the name "Ralph Connor," Gordon began writing short stories for the Presbyterian magazine, *The Westminster,* as another way of raising money for domestic frontier missions.

14. Brought up in an Anglican household in Cheshire, England, Grenfell undertook medical studies at the London Hospital, then, in 1893, joined the National Mission to Deep Sea Fishermen, which was founded in 1881, and was later granted a royal charter. His spiritual testimony, "What Christ Means to Me," tells us of a youthful admiration for the muscular Christianity of Charles Kingsley. "Kingsley was not interested so much in doctrines," Grenfell writes. "To him a Christian was a man who cleaned out the filth in his own backyard himself, and not the man who asked God to keep away typhoid from his house while he himself did nothing" (1926, 452). Like Cody and Connor, Grenfell wrote in large part to raise funds for the mission field, and like the stories of his contemporaries, Grenfell's writings draw directly upon his own missionary experiences.

15. For example, writing in the October 1910 issue of Canada's *Busy Man's Magazine,* which became *MacLean's* just five months later, in March 1911, Arthur Conrad hailed Cody as "A New Literary Luminary" (Jones: 1981, 180).

16. F. W. Watt has reminded us that "one publisher, George Doran, built his house on a foundation of

Connor novels, and by 1937, when Connor died, his fame well on the decline, the total of copies sold was over five millions" (1959, 26).

17. Abbott's writings are full of the sort of views we find in Grenfell's work. A chapter in *Christianity and Social Problems,* titled "Christianity and Labour," for example, addresses of the Judaic roots of labour as honourable and of the first followers of Jesus as "a church of hard-working men [fishermen, Paul the tent-maker, Jesus the carpenter] [. . .] a working-men's organization" (1896, 165-66).

18. Here is the first sequence of Grenfell's "Catechism"—"The Air": "Is fresh air good for me? I cannot live without it. / Is air ever bad? Yes, it gets very poisonous. / What makes it poisonous? Every time any one breathes he throws poison into the air. / What are these poisons like? Some are poisonous gases, some like tiny seeds. / Will they hurt me? Yes, they will kill me in time. / How can I avoid these poisons? By always keeping in fresh air." Other sequences are concerned with "Sunshine," "The Window," "Washing," "Spitting," and "Wounds" (qtd. in Johnston: 1904, 129-30).

Works Cited

Abbott, Lyman (1896). *Christianity and Social Problems.* Boston: Houghton, Mifflin and Co.

Abbott, Lyman (1901). *The Rights of Man: A Study in Twentieth Century Problems.* Boston: Houghton, Mifflin and Co.

Abbott, Lyman (1903). "Wilfred Grenfell." *Outlook* 74: 692-94.

Allen, Richard (1971). *The Social Passion: Religion and Social Reform in Canada, 1914-1928.* Toronto: U of Toronto P.

Barner, Arthur (1910). *Surgeon of the Skeena: A Brief Resumé of the Life and Work of Rev. Horace C. Wrinch/ [Arthur Barner].* Toronto: Committee on Missionary Education [and] Literature Department, Woman's Missionary Society, United Church of Canada.

Blake, Lynn A. (1999). "Pastoral Power, Governmentality and Cultures of Order in Nineteenth-Century British Columbia." *Transactions, Institute of British Geographers New Series* 24: 79-93.

Bolton, Albert E. (1896). *Medical Work among the Indians.* Toronto: Woman's Missionary Society of the Methodist Church, Canada.

Cody, Hiram (1908). *An Apostle of the North, Memoirs of the Right Reverend William Carpentier Bompas: With an Introduction by the Most Reverend S.P. Matheson.* London: Seeley.

Cody, Hiram (1910). *The Frontiersman: A Tale of the Yukon.* Toronto: W. Briggs.

Coleman, Daniel (1997). "Immigration, Nation, and the Canadian Allegory of Manly Maturation." *Essays on Canadian Writing* 61. Toronto: ECW. 84-103.

Comaroff, John L., and Jean Comaroff (1992). *Ethnography and the Historical Imagination.* Boulder Westview P.

Comaroff, John L., and Jean Comaroff (1997). *Of Revelation and Revolution: Christianity, Colonialism, and Consciousness in South Africa.* Vol. 2. *The Dialectics of Modernity on a South African Frontier.* Chicago: U of Chicago P.

Connor, Ralph (1898). *Black Rock: A Tale of the Selkirks.* Toronto: Westminster.

Connor, Ralph (1899). *The Sky Pilot: A Tale of the Foothills.* Toronto: Westminster.

Connor, Ralph (1906). *The Doctor: A Tale of the Rockies.* Toronto: Westminster.

Crabbe, W. Thomson (1880). "Medical Missions: The Importance of Individual Dealing." *Medical Missions: At Home and Abroad* 10: 145-52.

Cranmer, Thomas (1549). *Book of Common Prayer.* <http://justus.anglican.org/resources/bcp/BCP_1549.htm>.

Foskett, R., ed. and intro. (1964). *The Zambesi Doctors: David Livingstone's Letters to John Kirk, 1858-1872.* Edinburgh: Edinburgh UP.

Foucault, Michel (1973). *The Birth of the Clinic: An Archaeology of Medical Perception.* Rpt. 1975. Trans. A. M. Sheridan Smith. New York: Vintage.

Gould, Sydney (1905). *Inasmuch: Sketches of the Beginnings of the Church of England in Canada in Relation to the Indian and Eskimo Races.* Toronto: Missionary Society of the Church of England in Canada.

Grant, John Webster (1982). *Moon of Wintertime: Missionaries and the Indians of Canada in Encounter since 1534.* Toronto: U of Toronto P.

Grenfell, Wilfred T. (1905). *The Harvest of the Sea: A Tale of Both Sides of the Atlantic.* New York: Fleming H. Revell.

Grenfell, Wilfred T. (1909a). *Labrador, the Country and Its People.* New York: Macmillan.

Grenfell, Wilfred T. (1909b). "Letter to Lyman Abbott. 17 November." Lyman Abbott Memorial Collection. Bowdoin College Lib. Brunswick, ME.

Grenfell, Wilfred T. (1910). *Down to the Sea: Yarns from the Labrador.* New York: Fleming H. Revell.

Grenfell, Wilfred T. (1926). "What Christ Means to Me." *British Weekly* 80: 447, 452, 473, 479, 487, 516, 523, 542; 82: 8, 16, 40.

Grenfell, Wilfred T. (1934). "Dictatorship by Consent: The New Government of Newfoundland and Labrador." *Among the Deep Sea Fishers* 32: 68.

Grenfell, Wilfred T. (1940). "Letter to Cecil S. Ashdown. 16 April." *Wilfred Thomason Grenfell Papers,* Sterling Lib., Yale U, New Haven, CT.

Haig-Brown, Celia (1988). *Resistance and Renewal: The Residential School.* Vancouver: Tillicum Library.

Horden, Rt. Rev. Dr. John (1879). "Letter, 23 June, 1879." *Medical Missions: At Home and Abroad* 6 (Oct.): 87-88.

Hughes, Thomas (1857). *Tom Brown's School Days at Rugby, by an Old Boy.* Rpt. 1859. Boston: Ticknor and Fields.

"Introduction" (1878). *Medical Missions: At Home and Abroad* 1: 1.

Johnston, James (1904). *Grenfell of Labrador.* London: S.W. Partridge.

Jones, Ted (1981). *All the Days of His Life: A Biography of Archdeacon H. A. Cody.* Saint John, New Brunswick: The New Brunswick Museum.

Jordanova, Ludmilla (1989). *Sexual Visions: Images of Gender in Science and Medicine between the Eighteenth and the Twentieth Centuries.* London: Harvester Wheatsheaf.

King, Basil (1905). *Duncan Polite.* Chicago: H.S. Stone.

Kingsley, Charles (1855). *Westward Ho! or, The Voyages and Adventures of Sir Amyas Leigh, Knight, of Burrough, in the County of Devon in the Reign of Her Most Glorious Majesty Queen Elizabeth, Rendered into Modern English by Charles Kingsley.* Rpt. 1969. New York: Airmont.

Klinck, Carl F. (1965). *Literary History of Canada: Canadian Literature in English.* Rpt. 1976. 4 vols. Toronto: U of Toronto P.

Knockwood, Isabelle (1992). *Out of the Depths: The Experiences of Mi'kmaw Children at the Indian Residential School at Schubenacadie, Nova Scotia.* Lockeport, Nova Scotia: Roseway.

Large, R. Geddes (1968). *Drums and Scalpel: From Native Healers to Physicians on the North Pacific Coast.* Vancouver: Mitchell.

Lascelles, Thomas A. (1990). *Roman Catholic Indian Residential Schools in British Columbia.* Vancouver: Order of OMI in BC.

Lister, Joseph (1867a). "On a New Method of Treating Compound Fracture, Abscess, etc., with Observations on the Conditions of Suppuration." *The Lancet* 1: 326-29, 357-59, 387-89, 507-509.

Lister, Joseph (1867b). "On a New Method of Treating Compound Fracture, Abscess, etc." *The Lancet* 2: 95-96.

Lister, Joseph (1867c). "On the Antiseptic Principle in the Practice of Surgery." *The Lancet* 2: 353-56.

Lister, Joseph (1867d). "Illustrations of the Antiseptic System of Treatment in Surgery." *The Lancet* 2: 668-69.

Lister, Joseph (1869). "Observations on Ligature of Arteries on the Antiseptic System." *The Lancet* 1: 451-55.

Lister, Joseph (1875). "On Recent Improvements in the Details of Antiseptic Surgery." *The Lancet* 1: 434-36.

Livingstone, David (1857). *Missionary Travels and Researches in South Africa.* London: Murray.

MacDermot, H. E. (1935). *The History of the Canadian Medical Association.* Vol. 1. Toronto: Murray.

MacDermot, H. E. (1967). *One Hundred Years of Medicine in Canada, 1867-1967.* Toronto: McClelland and Stewart.

MacDougall, Heather (1988). "Public Health and the 'Sanitary Idea' in Toronto, 1866-1890." *Essays in the History of Canadian Medicine.* Eds. Wendy Mitchinson and Janice Dickin McGinnis. Toronto: McClelland and Stewart. 62-87.

Mather, Cotton (1702). *Magnalia Christi Americana; or the Ecclesiastical History of New England.* London: Thomas Parkhurst.

Midgley, Clare, ed. (1998). *Gender and Imperialism.* Manchester: Manchester UP.

Miller, J. R. (1996). *Shingwauk's Vision: A History of Native Residential Schools.* Toronto: U of Toronto P.

Mitchinson, Wendy (1991). *The Nature of Their Bodies: Women and Their Doctors in Victorian Canada.* Toronto: U of Toronto P.

Porter, Roy (1997). *The Greatest Benefit to Mankind: A Medical History of Humanity from Antiquity to the Present.* London: HarperCollins.

Reader, W. J. (1966). *Professional Men: The Rise of the Professional Classes in Nineteenth-Century England.* London: Weidenfeld and Nicolson.

Roland, Charles G. (1967). "The Early Years of Antiseptic Surgery in Canada." Rpt. 1981. *Medicine in Canadian Society: Historical Perspectives.* Ed. S. E. D. Shortt. Montreal: McGill-Queen's UP. 237-53.

Rompkey, Ronald (1991). *Grenfell of Labrador: A Biography.* Toronto: U of Toronto P.

Seton, Ernest Thompson (1917). *The Preacher of Cedar Mountain: A Tale of the Open Country.* London: Hodder and Stoughton.

Thompson, J. Lee, and John H. Thompson (1972). "Ralph Connor and the Canadian Identity." *Queen's Quarterly* 79: 159-70.

Vance, Norman (1985). *The Sinews of Spirit: The Ideal of Christian Manliness in Victorian Literature and Religion.* Cambridge: CUP.

Watson, Patricia A. (1991). *The Angelical Conjunction: The Preacher-Physicians of Colonial New England.* Knoxville: U of Tennessee P.

Watt, F. W. (1959). "Western Myth: The World of Ralph Connor." *Canadian Literature* 1: 26-36.

Wesley, John (1791). *Primitive Physic; or, An Easy and Natural Method of Curing Most Diseases.* Rpt. 1960. Intro. A. Wesley Hill. London: Epworth.

West, John (1824). *The Substance of a Journal During a Residence at the Red River Colony, British North America, in the Years 1820-1823.* Rpt. 1967. Vancouver: Alcuin Society.

Withrow, William H. (1880). *Neville Trueman, the Pioneer Preacher.* Toronto: W. Briggs.

Young, Egerton Ryerson (1894). *Oowikapun; or, How the Gospel Reached the Nelson River Indians.* New York: Hunt and Eaton.

Youngson, A. J. (1979). *The Scientific Revolution in Victorian Medicine.* London: Croom Helm.

WAR AND ADVENTURE

Martin Green (essay date 1984)

SOURCE: Green, Martin. "Introduction: Adventure, Manliness, Nationalism." In *The Great American Adventure,* pp. 1-19. Boston: Beacon Press, 1984.

[*In the following excerpt, Green examines how adventure writing supported general attitudes toward expansionism, nationalism, and the power of the ruling class.*]

Adventure can, of course, mean both a certain kind of experience and the literary form built around that kind of experience. It is an adventure, of a passive kind, if your ship gets wrecked in a storm, and you alone of all aboard are thrown up by the waves upon the shores of a desert island. It is also an (active) adventure if you thereupon set to work, and build a hut, tame some animals, grow some vegetables, bake bread, build boats, make your own clothes of skins, set up little outposts all over the island, design your own daily, seasonal, annual routines, and make the island blossom like a rose, your property. But something else we call an adventure is the story of such experience, told even by a man who is making the whole thing up.

Conceptually I would define the adventure experience as a series of events, partly but not wholly accidental, in places far from home—most often also far from civilization—which constitute a challenge to the person they happen to. In the adventure tale, that person responds to that challenge with a series of exploits which make him/her a hero/heroine, that is, eminent in such virtues as courage, fortitude, cunning, strength, leadership, and persistence.

I said him/her, but in fact it nearly is nearly always him (and for that reason I propose to use "him" as the pronoun for the adventure reader). That is, the adventure tale was written almost exclusively for a masculine audience. It has been the main literary means by which males have been taught to take initiatives, to run risks, to give orders, to fight, defeat, and dominate; while females have been taught, both by being ignored by the genre and by being reduced to passive roles within it, *not* to do those things.

Less obviously, but just as importantly, adventure writing has been linked to the expansion of certain political societies. To enjoy adventures was (and is) to prepare oneself in imagination to go out to a frontier, whether it was overseas or in the western part of this continent, and to advance that frontier—against native populations or natural barriers—to extend the domain of civilization. (And "civilization" was usually a pseudonym for one's own country.) Some thrillers, of course, have no connections with this political theme, but, as I hope the rest of this book will show, many *have* such connections, though they are sometimes of a hidden kind.

Thus "adventure" is linked to both "manliness" and "patriotism"; linked as critical concepts, in our minds, now studying the adventure tale, but also linked, as articles of faith, in the minds of those who read these tales with avidity. And I do not mean, by putting these words in quotation marks, to make fun of them. They are ideas that have motivated great historical actions and great moral virtues. I only mean to put them into question.

We think first of all, no doubt, of popular adventure stories; of the paperbacks at the drugstore and the shelves at the public library marked "Mysteries," "Westerns," "Thrillers," and "Spy Stories." "Adventures" are for men what "Romances" are for women; and taking the two together, they amount to a very large part of "American literature," if we understand that phrase sociologically, to include all the books of narrative printed in this country. Books of this sort continue to flow out of the publishing houses and to be bought and read in enormous numbers, as they have for many generations.

But I am interested in literature in that other sense—the books we take seriously because they embody an intelligence equal to our own. There *are* adventures that embody such intelligence and seriousness, although we tend to forget that when we are being literary. But in fact nearly every man reads *some* adventures, and even the best of them have a lot in common with the worst; just as even the most serious novels of, say, Doris Lessing, have a lot in common with the most fomularized Harlequin or Gothic romances. The best and the worst are both parts of the same enterprise, whether they be adventures or romance novels; and the serious adventure writers are in time imitated by the formula writers—although the reverse also happens sometimes. So I have chosen twelve American adventures which I do take seriously and will try to show how some of the political secrets of America are revealed in the way they are written and in what they borrow from the history of their own times.

We can, of course, distinguish between different kinds of adventure in literature. The most important distinction is between two main kinds; to explain them I must for a moment refer to British authors, because the Americans took their bearings from traditions established by the British. The Robinson Crusoe adventures (of which many have been written since the first one of 1719) are quite unlike the Waverley adventures. (Walter Scott's *Waverley* (1814) tells the story of the 1745 Jacobite Rebellion in Scotland.) One can distinguish the two kinds by the number of participants (Defoe's Crusoe story has one man alone, while Scott's Waverley novels have crowd scenes and, usually, a romantic pair); the kind of setting (the Crusoe story is set on an island, the Waverley story has scenes at court and a generally "historical" flavor); and the kind of narrative (Crusoe's is a plain-man's autobiography, Waverley is elaborately literary and cites historical sources and folklore).

These different adventures address different parts of society as their primary audiences: Defoe's story is written by, about, and for the English merchant; Scott's is by, about, and for the British aristocrat—the bearer of arms, in both senses of arms. But both serve a national purpose, and are aimed at a national audience (the one sees the nation as primarily a trading community, the other sees it as primarily a political organism) and both are versions of the energizing myth of British society, the dream that made young Britons want to go out and spread the empire.

One more distinction must be made to avoid confusion later. The energizing myth of America, like that of the other nations of the modern world-system, has been ambiguous. On the one hand, it has been passionately anti-imperialist; born in rebellion against the British empire, America has detested tyranny, aristocracy, militarism, courts, and castes, and has suspected every elegance that seemed to speak of social privilege, even the purely intellectual. On the other hand, it has been triumphantly imperialist; it has not only spread westwards like a prairie fire to take a whole continent away from its original inhabitants but has spread American styles of technology and discourse all over the world, to displace other indigenous cultures. It has become an empire, relying on its own military caste, while thinking of itself as an egalitarian democracy. Adventure has been the energizing myth of both aspects of America, and thus has recommended both plain, peaceable manliness and triumphant imperial militarism. Usually the first meaning is overt, the second covert (visible only to readers who cannot or will not identify with the audience for whom the story was written); but both meanings are there, and in the long run they are interdependent. In nearly all the narratives I discuss, I shall have to turn from the one meaning to the other.

In all of them, adventure is the energizing myth of empire, taking empire to mean any expanding society dominant over others. This myth most obviously energizes a society when that society is expanding territorially, as the United States was doing throughout the nineteenth century. The American adventure stories represented, in attractive and individualized form, the policies and compromises, the punishments and rewards, and the stresses and problems involved in advancing a frontier at the expense of native populations and against natural obstacles. To read the adventures was to prepare oneself to go west and take part in the national work. Yet such stories are also relevant to the culture of any society which is still expanding economically and politically, even if it has stopped its territorial growth, as the United States has in the twentieth century. On the other hand, adventure stories become less relevant and attractive to a society which has ceased to expand and has begun to repent its former imperialism. Thus Britain after 1918 stopped enjoying adventure stories and told them only ironically and bitterly. (The abrupt decline in Kipling's reputation exemplifies this change.)

Unlike Britain, America in the twentieth century was still—is still—a world power, a world ruler, and a world leader. And America has never *not* been an expanding society; it has been, from its inception and conception, a land of adventure. It was Europe's land of adventure before it was its own. It was the place Englishmen, Germans, Spaniards, and Frenchmen came to, seeking the adventures they could not find in their overcivilized home countries. That is why the adventure story is a peculiarly American form; although, if we look at the world as a whole, and at literature as a whole, we see that adventure is also a European form, because of the great story of Europe's establishment of hegemony over the rest of the globe. American stories were often written by and for Europeans. Even today, one of most widely read writers of Westerns is the German Karl May, who never saw America. Thus *American* adventure is just the most striking version of this European (or white) form of literature.

Adventure tales are in fact where the two cultures come together. I mean the most important pair of opposed cultures, that of reflection (enshrined in our universities) and that of action or violence (institutionalized in our army, our police, our prisons). I do not mean the cult of violence, but the imaginative preparation to manage, employ, and engage in conflict and force. Because of the split between these two cultures, adventure has been neglected, intellectually. Even though it has been the major imaginative form and educative force for men of action, they have had little help in thinking about it from men or women of reflection. For example, the adventure tale, the literary version of adventure, has been studied, if at all, only in terms of popular culture, and "Popular Culture" is a kind of study that refuses to respond to the writer's intentions in anything like his own language. This book attempts to work out a critical method that takes the significant adventure tales seriously, to create an imaginative context for them equivalent to that we have for "serious literature"—a method that combines form, content, and historical criteria.

Significant literary adventures consist of three elements, the first two of which are frontier anecdote (or seafaring anecdote or shipwreck anecdote) and the long tradition of literary romance. We have adventure when those two elements fuse, and the romance motifs of treachery and revenge, disguise and mystery, a great wrong righted, and true love frustrated and then consummated are interwoven with the specifying details of wigwam and warpaint, the log cabin and the covered wagon, or the ocean and the storm and the footprint in the sand. This fusion becomes significant, can be taken seriously, when a third element is added: when the adventure makes the reader/writer contemplate his/her own status anthropologically. (I use the term *anthropological* to suggest the way adventures compare "civilized people"—that is, people of the writer's own culture—with other groups.) What distinguishes us from the Other? How do we measure up against Him, in warmth of heart, keenness of mind, firmness of courage? How would we measure up to the challenges he meets, as well as those he himself offers? How exactly has our nature changed as a result of this immense modern civilization we have built up around ourselves? And how do we feel about that change? These are the questions that, for instance, *Robinson Crusoe* makes us ask and helps us answer; and obviously they are as serious as any questions raised by what we call serious fiction.

Significant adventure also raises the question of violence, which serious literature (notably the domestic novel) by and large evades. Of course, there are episodes of suffering in novels of all sorts; but there is nothing problematic about violence, however appalling its scope, so long as it is merely suffered. The difficult questions about it are only raised when the reader is asked to engage in it himself, via a character or an institution with whom he has identified. In many adventures, of course, the violence merely occurs, and is enjoyed—often as a corrupt excitement. But the significant adventure always raises the moral question, even though it usually resolves that question in the affirmative.

That is why adventure (the experience) has been the great rite of passage from boyhood to manhood, as in the Boy Scout movement; and why adventure (in books) has been the ritual of the religion of manliness, which was the unofficial religion of the nineteenth century, if not of the twentieth. In mainstream books it quite displaced the Christian values. Adventure experience was the sacramental ceremony of the cult of manhood. (That is why adventure writers put such stress on the coarse food and the rough conditions of sleeping, and so forth—all the experiential and initiatory rituals by which a boy becomes a man.) From Cooper's *The Pioneers* and Bird's *Nick of the Woods* to Mailer's *Why Are We in Vietnam?* a crucial set of images and concepts relates to manhood. The man of the woods—from Natty Bumppo and Nathan Slaughter to Big Luke Fellinka—is more of a man than those he meets, and the genteel heroes of those novels, from Oliver Effingham to Roland Forrester to Randall Jethroe, have to measure up to him, to show themselves worthy to be his heirs.

"Manhood" was also paired with some contrasting term—as the affirmed or superior value—in dozens of polarities of thought. Any male had to strive always to be a man and not a boy, in Hemingway adventures; a man and not an animal, in religious exhortation; a man and not a slave, in slavery narratives; and similarly, a man and not a coward, a man and not a mouse, a man and not a woman. At the same time, manhood also—*being* such a sacred value—spread out to mean all humanity, spread out beyond these antitheses to include the inferior or rejected term in each case; manhood/humanity thus included boys and slaves and women and cowards.

This anthropocentric and androcentric religion penetrated literature gradually during the eighteenth century; there is no sign of it in *Robinson Crusoe,* and in *Waverley* it is mild and modest; but in the American adventure from Cooper on it is evangelical in its fervor. And the political expression of that religion, which was very intimately related to manhood, was nationalism. The political system as a whole was emotionally and spiritually animated by the religion. Congress was an assemblage of national elders, who exerted actual power over the nation's young adventurers, but who—in terms of the national myth—lived in imaginative dependence upon them. The young adventurers were more "American" than any professional politician.

I have defined adventure as the energizing myth of empire (in another book, I develop this idea at length), but it will be to our advantage, here, to use the idea of nationalism as much as, or more than, imperialism; partly because Americans thought of their politics and literature as nationalist and partly for other reasons that will become clear as we look at the specific adventures. In any case, the idea of a nation was closely related to the idea of empire—of the modern world-system. Nationalism was what was talked about, because imperialism was morally shady. "Nations," as the nineteenth century used the term, were the members of that family of states which ruled the modern world-system. It was the British, the Dutch, the French, and so on, who were thought of as nations; and the Germans, the Poles, the Greeks, the Italians, the proto-nations, were summoned to join them, to become nations, to throw off the yoke of the old empires—Turkey, Austria, and Russia—and join us in exploiting the unclaimed world out there—Asia, Africa, Australia, and so on. (The latter areas were not inhabited by *nations*.) This summons was carried by the adventure tales of Scott and his European successors, and nationalism was not felt to be at odds with empire of the modern kind. The Austrian empire was the enemy of the nations it ruled over, but the British empire was the friend of all true nationalism—it ruled only over tribes or mutually hostile groups like Hindus and Muslims. Thus, when Scott showed Scotland how to accept her destiny as a nation, it was as a partner *within* the British empire.

It will perhaps be agreed without much protest that the Anglo-Saxons always felt there to be close natural connections between the love of adventure, the writing of adventures, the progress of democracy, and the expansion of trade, between adventure and, for example, the expansion of the American empire in this modern sense. It will be easily agreed, I suggest, that such activities supported and strengthened each other in the great new republic as much as in the constitutional monarchy of England. That idea was always more or less acknowledged.

To give an example, two sentences from the chapter entitled "The Advocate" in *Moby Dick* will show the close connections which Melville took for granted, between world democracy and commercial enterprises like whale fishing, between free trade and the modern empire that was driving out colonies of the old kind.

> Until the whale fishery rounded Cape Horn, no commerce but colonial, scarcely any intercourse but colonial, was carried on between Europe and the long line

of the opulent Spanish colonies on the Pacific coast. It was the whalemen who first broke through the jealous policy of the Spanish crown, touching these colonies; and, if space permitted, it might distinctly be shown how from those whalemen at last eventuated the liberation of Peru, Chili, Bolivia from the yoke of Old Spain, and the establishment of eternal democracy in those parts.[1]

It will be the argument [elsewhere] that Melville was himself an adventure lover and adventure writer, although an ambivalent one; and to suggest that even *Moby Dick* was, at one level of intention, a work of literary propaganda for the modern world-system, a literary version of the energizing myth of the nineteenth century.

It may be more difficult to accept the idea that there is an equally close connection between adventure and caste; adventure was the means by which men of the ruling class justified their claims to represent America. Yet this is true of adventure in both senses: as action and experience, and as literary form.

Adventure (the experience) is always an escape from, an alternative to, settled civilized city life. But settled life has two aspects, which from some points of view are very different; for this reason, adventure, as the alternative to it, also takes on different meanings. On the one hand, settled life is a matter of limitations, rules, and privileges—of hierarchy—and so an escape from it can be a pursuit of egalitarian democracy. On the other, settled life is organized under the aegis of bourgeois commercial work, industriousness and productivity; so that an escape from it can serve the purposes of aristocracy, of the warrior virtues, and of romanticism. Egalitarian democracy and what I shall call the "aristomilitary" virtues were usually held to exclude each other; but in this context they did not.

Adventure as a written form has served both these purposes—sometimes *either* one *or* the other, sometimes both in the same story—and Americans have often confused the two, in consequence. But the most interesting adventures from a literary point of view have predominantly served the second purpose, perhaps because literature itself as a social entity is committed to manifesting and conferring high-culture status. Readers and writers are always, willy nilly, members of the ruling class.

Literature is, after all, an activity of one particular class, who can be defined economically as the book buyers. And in America in the early nineteenth century when the book buyers included neither an intelligentsia nor an academia, they could perhaps be named, in terms of their ideology, the responsible class—meaning those who felt themselves responsible for their culture, felt it their duty to look after their country's sense of values, its cultural standards, its ideology. The main geographical locus of this class in nineteenth-century America was, in the first 40 years, Philadelphia, in the later years, Boston. It was no mere accident that these were the publishing centers of America, and the first three of the authors I shall discuss published at Philadelphia; the second three, at Boston. The ideology of this class was nationalist, adventurous, and humanist—meaning that it made a cult of manhood.

Hidden in this ideology—which I shall sometimes call just nationalism—was an antidemocratic tendency that will be important for our argument. A nation was conceived of as, or felt to be, an organic entity; the different groups in society were felt to be natural growths and to be mutually complementary, rather than mutually competitive; it was thus implicitly a caste and not a class theory of society. I use the world "class," by contrast, to signify that sense of society we associate with democracy, in which all social distinctions are felt to be unjust or at least unfortunate, and in which the ideal is universal equality and social mobility—lack of differentiation. Nationalism, however, insisted on differentiation. For instance, "the American nation," as Cooper understood it, assigned an important function to the soldier and the aristocrat, even though society disapproved of them. (I am reporting Cooper's view of America's attitude toward its soldiers and aristocrats. But can we say he was wrong?) According to the strictly economic theory of society, which modern bourgeois experience tends to generate, soldiers and aristocrats are idle consumers and/or destroyers of wealth. Cooper's heroes, however, were soldiers and aristocrats, and he wanted his readers to prefer them to those mean and envious "democrats" among his characters who resented his heroes. Since nationalism connotes relation with other states (as democracy and society do not) and so implies a nation's need for military defense and/or aggression, it reconciles the middle-class reader to the aristo-military caste. (This is why Scott's novels were felt to be so nationalist and were so often imitated, by Cooper in America and by other writers in other countries, because their primary drive was just to bring together the merchant and the soldier.)

Nationalism also carried with it an anti-Christian tendency; that is, a tendency opposed to any form of religious radicalism, any sect (in America the classic example was Quakerism) that renounced war and empire and "the world." The most striking expression of this theme in American adventures is the implicitly hostile treatment of Quakers and Moravians in Cooper, Irving, and Bird. There was a British precedent, in Defoe's *Captain Singleton,* but the theme is much more developed in the American works. No doubt this is because the issue of peace versus patriotism had been sharpened by the War of Independence, when the Quakers of Pennsylvania had refused to fight; Franklin tells some anti-

Quaker stories in his autobiography, mocking their pacifism. The relation of this issue to nationalism is thus very clear. Cooper discusses it quite explicitly in the first Natty Bumppo romance, gently criticizing the Quakers and deploring the Moravians' "Christianizing" of the Delawares—which meant their emasculation as a tribe. The message of this novel, and of many others, was that in order to be manly and to become a nation, Americans had to give up the Christian devotion to peace. They could not go on being, as they had been in the seventeenth and eighteenth centuries, a congeries of idealistic sects (seekers of political "alternatives," to use a modern term), refugees from the various European evils of tyranny, hierarchy, luxury, latitudinarianism, and so on. They had to recognize that they too had become a military people and to accept the leadership of an aristo-military caste.

Nineteenth-century fiction as a whole taught this lesson, including the domestic or serious novel, though in a discreet and disguised way. The hero, the man fit to marry the heroine (who, in these novels, is the true center) must be a man of adventures, with a fiery and in some sense aristocratic temperament. He cannot be a Quaker or religious zealot. Scott's treatment of low-church enthusiasts is markedly unsympathetic—they are the enemy for his sensibility. Dickens and Trollope, but also Charlotte Brontë and even George Eliot, consistently drew unfavorable portraits of evangelicals, and preferred ardent young gentlemen, full of natural fire, as their heroes. But the serious novel's values are—in oblique and attenuated form—erotic, not political; only in the adventure is the connection made clear between these fiery heroes and militarism and nationalism.

In nineteenth-century America, above all, it is striking how many adventures (in both senses) served the purposes of its ruling class; most notably, served the purpose of legitimizing its aristo-military function. America had of course an unusual preponderance of "democrat-adventurers" in its population—people in revolt against all social hierarchy. Most frontiersmen thought themselves the opposite of aristocrats. Moreover, the culturally dominant class were ex-Puritans, at least in New England, and hostile to "the men of blood," as their seventeenth-century ancestors had called the aristo-military caste. More than other countries, America needed propaganda on behalf of that caste.

There had been a development away from Puritanism even in New England in the course of the eighteenth century; one that especially affected attitudes towards soldiers. We may date the decline of clerical influence from 1691, when the governors of Massachusetts began to be appointed by the King and voting rights were determined by property ownership, not church membership.[2] Merchants made huge profits in the wars that were so frequent from 1690 to 1715, and the attitude to war changed; it was now said to stimulate inventiveness and manly qualities. Military discipline was seen as moral, and Christianity itself was praised for transforming "effeminate Cowards" into "valiant Heroes." Army officers became culture heroes, a pattern begun in Colonel Church's *Entertaining Passages.*

One striking example of this shift is found in the comment of John Adams, in the middle of the century, that he "longed more ardently to be a Soldier" than a lawyer; at the First Continental Congress, he grew impatient with those who "shuddered at the prospect of blood." He said he would have been a soldier himself had he come from any colony south of New England, "where the martial Spirit is but just awakened and People are unaccustomed to Arms." He described the military regimen as "a mixture of the Sublime and the Beautiful" and declared that an independent America "must adopt the great, manly, and warlike virtues." My source for this account concludes that "now the soldier was idealized, for he had come to embody the masculine and sacrificial virtues which Americans believed essential for maintenance of the new nation and its new republican freedoms."[3] An important change had taken place, but the antimilitary and antiaristocratic feeling stayed strong in New England, and the conflict of loyalties was often renewed.

It was therefore the task of American "culture" to reconcile that conflict, to combine in authoritative images the Brahmin with the aristo-military virtues; and literature, as we shall see, was a major means to that end. So the American adventure, in its written form, was often a gesture of ideological rebellion against Christian tradition (though a gesture also of caste piety) whereby ruling-class men subverted their Brahmin heritage while asserting new claims for it. This was especially true in New England, which took culture most seriously, and we shall see it in the autobiographical narratives of Dana and Parkman, but Cooper and Bird had contributed to the same cause through their fiction. The political-historical climax to this century-long process could be said to be Theodore Roosevelt's career. Roosevelt made himself fit to represent America though born to the upper class, fit to become President—by virtue of his adventures, both enacted and written.

In all these narratives we see the implicit conflict between the claims of different classes to represent adventure (and thus to represent America) as well as the implicit assertion of the claims of the rulers, the responsible or gentlemanly class, over those of the irresponsible or frontier class. In *Dreams of Adventure* I tried to show how Cooper's characterization of Natty Bumppo amounts to such a claim. Natty, Cooper's hero, may be called a definition of the "true American"; Cooper is making a claim on his behalf that it is *this* type that represents America, not the uncultured frontiers-

man represented by Davy Crockett and other "wild men of the West" (their own phrase). Cooper's hero is a figure of responsibility, a reincarnation of ruling-class, classical, Republican virtues in democratic guise. Crockett's picture of himself, in his autobiography, and in campaign speeches, is culturally anarchic. Dana and Parkman (and most of the other writers I shall discuss [elsewhere]) endorse both of Cooper's claims: that the best Americans are gentlemen—that there is no intrinsic conflict between being an American and being a gentleman—and that the gentleman is not essentially Brahmin (that is, a man of peace and learning) but rather a leader, a captain, a hero, a man of fire and fierceness.

Thus Cooper (and his successor, Bird) uses aristocratic terms to explain the workings of command, discipline, courage, and so on. Leaders, even in the wilderness, should be aristocrats. Born gentlemen (or Virginians, or English officers), because they are of the warrior caste, know how to give courage to others, how to impose discipline on a group, and how to maintain its spirit.

Dana and Parkman often use aristocratic terms, too; and they also use an idealized caste-consciousness to the same effect. Men of courage may be low born, but they are *nature*'s gentlemen. This does not mean that snobbery blinded these writers to reality. They present decadent aristocrats and lion-hearted plebians quite insistently, but they see them as anomalies within nature's caste system. They see the phenomena of command as analogous to those of caste, and they understand the former in terms of the latter. Nobility of nature may be found at any social level, but nobility will always be the dominant value. Such "democratic" sentiments (very typical of nineteenth-century liberalism) employ caste terms as a matter of course and imply that, given a chance, nature's aristocrats will end up on top. They will know how to give orders and keep order—as if they were born to it.

Melville, in *Redburn*, describes a sailor (Jackson) who derives his power to command from depths of malignity, not nobility. This upsets the hierarchy I just described. But that is because Melville was in some ways deeply hostile to the adventure ethos. His was quintessentially a divided mind. In other passages, moreover, he says just the reverse. In *White Jacket* he more comfortingly confirms that Virginians make better captains than other Americans, and that English ships are happier than American ones because an English captain belongs—as a captain ought to belong—to the aristo-military caste. (The phrase is mine, but his idea is the same.) The terms of this old-fashioned and chivalric sociology were indeed better adapted than those of progressive democracy to explaining the phenomena of authority and leadership.

Of course, there are differences between what "gentleman" means to different writers. Although all claim to be gentlemen, they do not all define the concept the same way. Melville, like Irving, usually demonstrates a sophistication of taste and a range of reference, especially in literary matters, that establishes him, the writer, as a belletrist, a man of taste, something of a scholar. In his satirical and self-distinguishing way, Twain aims in the same direction. Bird and Cooper, however, are more inclined to assert a noble and spirited temperament, a character implicitly martial and neither bookish nor commercial. Their gentility is not so essentially literary. Their joking references, in letters and so on, to their books as objects of commerce, as commodities with prices and sales sheets may be read as protests against the ignominy of their position. (You find the same sharp-edged jokes in Pushkin and Byron, two arrant aristocrats.) Dana and Parkman too, although they do it more discreetly, stress their own qualities of command, courage, and endurance.

The class idea of the gentleman can thus be assimilated to two different social entities, two different castes, the Brahmins and the warriors; Melville, Irving and Twain incline to the first, the other four to the latter. But in all of their books, the fateful question, gentleman or not-gentleman? is always asked. Both the Brahmins and the warriors are, after all, twice-born castes; the crucial distinction is between them and the once-born laborers, the masses. That alternative is the dynamic of the modern system's disguised caste structure, as much as it is the dynamic of Hinduism; in Europe it can be found forcefully expressed in, for example, Defoe's work. That system has made a basic dynamic out of the drive to become a gentleman and to avoid being the opposite, and literature has been one of the principal mechanisms by which the drive has been transmitted. . . .

[Cooper], Irving, and Bird, wrestle in literary ways with the myths of the frontier, subduing them to the purposes and advantages of the ruling class. (They invented very important lower-class characters, like Natty Bumppo and Nick of the Woods, but their own representative in their books is a romantic-genteel hero.) . . . Dana, Melville, and Parkman, wrestled with those myths more existentially, risking their lives to conquer them, to acquire them for gentlemen. Dana showed what the life of the common man, as sailor and beachcomber, was really like, and how gentlemen could succeed in that life. Melville showed what cannibals were really like, and how a gentleman could deal with them; Parkman what Indians and emigrants were really like, and how a gentleman could deal with them.

The dates and occasions of the books discussed coincide with the growth of American empire. Dana's voyage of 1839 placed California on the American map; Melville dates his narrative, or his voyage, from the French annexation of the Marquesas Islands in 1841 (and the subtler American-missionary imperialism

there); and Parkman's narrative is dated by the Mexican War of 1846, as well as by the land migration to Oregon and California. Each relates obliquely to a further step of empire, and each develops the adventure genre in significant ways.

[Carson], Twain, and Roosevelt . . . extend and exemplify this pattern but who are in one way or another exceptions to it. They employ various forms of narrative and none of them are represented by a single literary text. Carson was a man of action, not of letters, and his narrative is less interesting, *as narrative.* Twain, the opposite, is so *much* the man of letters that his relations with adventure are hostile and mocking, as well as enthusiastic. They must be examined thematically throughout his work. Finally, Roosevelt is interesting primarily as a political phenomenon. A self-made man, self-formed in the image of the adventure hero, he coined that lore and legend into political gold; he was the manly leader America had been looking for, at least since *Two Years Before the Mast.*

What they have in common is that all three make the nation-state, as much as the individual, the adventurer or the locus of adventure. The United States as a whole is seen on the move in their narratives. They represent the period in which the historians of Parkman's group were writing the adventure legend of the Anglo-Saxon nations, the white race's epic of world domination. We associate this legend with concern over the closing of the frontier—elucidated in the famous 1893 essay by historian Frederick Jackson Turner, the heir of Parkman—and with the replacement of the frontier as the locus of adventure on foreign soil—the sites of imperialist adventure like Roosevelt's "splendid little war."

The period of Carson, Twain, and Roosevelt was, therefore, militaristic, or at least military, and may be said to have begun with the Civil War and ended with World War I. Even during years of peace between, books made Americans aware that their army was employed in either fighting Indian tribes or enforcing white American policy toward them. These were the decades of Custer and his last stand and of Buffalo Bill Cody—Custer's guide—and his Wild West Show. This was the period, everywhere in the modern world-system, of *militarism* and *imperialism.* The two words were first employed together by critics of Napoleon III's empire and adopted in England in 1864, and in Germany in 1870.

Thus nationalism was transformed into, or unmasked as, imperialism. (When Germany finally achieved national unity in 1870, Bismarck named it the Second Reich, the Second German Empire.) *Imperialism,* however, was a sinister word, which set a moral obstacle between writers and the adventure theme; at the same time it gave the theme a fatal allure for them. At least in politics, and to some degree in literature also, the obstacle was overcome by Theodore Roosevelt.

If we associate Roosevelt with Dana, rather than with Natty Bumppo, it is because he was a Harvard man; it was the gentleman-as-adventurer who finally entered the White House in the twentieth century. This was also the period of the adventure's greatest popularity as reading matter, the period of the dime novel. After his death, partly because of the pendulum movement of taste, and partly because of the Great War's character as nightmare rather than adventure, there was a reaction against the form. In England this led to a complete divorce between adventure and literature, but in America, it led to a new alliance under the aegis of art—an aestheticization of adventure. The evolution began with Crane's *The Red Badge of Courage,* and was carried to triumph by Hemingway, Faulkner, and Mailer ("Three Aesthetes").

It was natural that, as America entered upon her career as a world power, and then world ruler, the character of her written adventures should also change. Her writers became more concerned about the artistic status of their forms; they could write adventure only if it was also myth or metaphor. *Because* they were now the artist-representatives of a world-empire, they had to make their art proud, mysterious, and autonomous. Their rhetoric became more esoteric and aesthetic, and the figure of the adventurer approached that of an artist—and vice versa as they made themselves adventurers-as-artists. Not superficially, but profoundly, this change resembled one that had occurred in English writing at the end of the nineteenth century, when Kipling briefly imposed himself upon the reading public as the bard of empire. The subtler imperialization of American literature occurred fifty years later and corresponded with the transfer of world leadership (or, more exactly, the leadership of the modern world-system) from Great Britain to the United States.

Kipling had no heirs among his fellow-countrymen, but in America he found a follower in Hemingway, as Conrad did in Faulkner. Between 1920 and 1960, after all, America still had a calling to rule the world, which England had lost; and it had no strong tradition of the serious novel to resist adventure. The literary coup d'état, which had failed in Kipling's hands but which had intended to make adventure the dominant genre of fiction, and so of all literature, triumphed in America in the middle of the century.

Despite all these historical changes, a remarkable continuity runs through these narratives, fictional and nonfictional. Similar, even identical, themes and motifs recur, like guns, nature, and Crusoe, in the early narratives. California is described in Dana, the Marquesas Islands in Melville, and both recur in Twain. The hunter's passions and his great animal antagonists appear in Parkman, and again in Faulkner and Hemingway. The ocean and the prairie, the cannibal and the Indian, the whale and the buffalo, the bear and the lion, all clearly manifest the same values in the different narratives.

This sequence of books, moreover, has some claims to be considered the highest achievement of American literature in this 150-year period—that is, in the history of the United States. They are the equivalent of the Great Tradition that British critics found in the line of great novelists beginning with Jane Austen and the concurrent line of culture theorists beginning with Burke.

In England in the nineteenth century adventure was an entertainment genre, as far as literature went. The serious literary work was done in the genre of the novel—stories about marriage and domesticity written in a form of moral realism, and woman-centered whereas adventure was man-centered. The works of Charlotte Brontë, Mrs. Gaskell, George Eliot, and Thomas Hardy will show what I mean. But the nineteenth-century novel was also a function of "culture"—that is, a principled criticism of and resistance to "civilization" (understood as society's aggressive and repressive forces). And culture, at least in the nineteenth century, drew much of its strength from continuities, cyclical rhythms in nature and social life (in, for instance, marriage), which continued from the preindustrial era. Culture seemed to transcend class conflicts and to harmonize all the nation's values. Tolstoy and Lawrence, probably the two greatest writers of the cultural novel, exemplify these characteristics for nineteenth-century Russia and twentieth-century England.

In America, however, because it remained a frontier society (receiving new citizens all the time, changing its physical limits, and acquiring new resources), the serious novel did not establish itself. Continuities were not characteristic of American life. Moreover, at least in nineteenth-century America, the very concept of culture was debased to a slogan or battle cry in the struggle between the two classes that claimed to represent the country: the gentleman and the frontiersman. The frontiersman knew he was not cultured and did not want to be. Culture never escaped the reproach of being sectarian, never seemed to transcend class as it did in England. It was adventure that seemed to transcend class in America and to bring all the conflicting interests of Americans into harmony. In consequence, adventure could command some of the best energies of men of letters. Thus the sequence of books [I have mentioned] here constitutes the central achievement of American literature.

Notes

1. Herman Melville, *Moby Dick* (Boston, 1956), p. 101.

2. John Ferling, "The American Soldier," *American Quarterly* 33(1):26-45.

3. As quoted in ibid., p. 44.

Graham Dawson (essay date 1994)

SOURCE: Dawson, Graham. "Self-Imagining: Boyhood Masculinity, Social Recognition, and the Adventure Hero." In *Soldier Heroes: British Adventure, Empire, and the Imagining of Masculinities*, pp. 259-81. London: Routledge, 1994.

[*In the excerpt below, Dawson offers a personal reminiscence, pointing out how adventure writing—and especially the soldier hero—influenced and nurtured notions about masculinity and nationalism in England.*]

IMAGINING MYSELF IN THE SOCIAL WORLD

As a very small boy, I became notorious in the family as an inveterate wearer of hats. I had a number of different kinds, but my favourites were black felt cowboy hats that could be tied under the chin with cord, of which I had several over the years, worn until they were quite battered and unserviceable. I am wearing cowboy hats in a number of photographs from the family album, all taken between 1958 and 1961 in the house and garden in Doncaster, or on seaside holidays on the north-east coast near Scarborough. . . . The earliest were taken when I was about 2 years old. I am wearing dungarees, clutching a glove-puppet and wearing that first cowboy hat. How did I get it? Was I given it? Did I find it lying around somewhere? Did I see it in a shop? None of the family remembers, but it is clear that the wearing of hats in general, and cowboy hats in particular, rapidly became a sign of my individuality—a way of identifying myself, of saying: 'This is me, Graham; I am someone who wears hats'. I can recall with precision the feeling of satisfaction and composure that accompanied the purchase of a new hat. With this feeling, another is mingled: that of being affirmed and basking as the centre of attention within the family. My family enjoyed my wearing of hats, appreciated me as a hat-wearer. I remember my father at the seaside, chuckling and marvelling at it.

This attitude of approval is also evident in the photographs. I am wearing a cowboy hat and looking very pleased with myself in an affectionate family portrait with my parents taken in 1959. Further photographs catch me wearing them (undoubtedly with parental approval) in public places like the beach or a fairground, as well as in the privacy of our back garden. In some, the hat is supplemented by other basic features of 'the cowboy'. In one, dated 1959 (when I was 3), I am standing on a quay holding a shiny toy six-gun. In another, I am sitting on a white-painted wooden horse called Snowy, made by my father, wearing a black 'Lone Ranger' face mask. Dependent as my public appearance was upon parental approval, it is inconceivable that, without it, my hat-wearing would have been recorded for posterity at all. The achievement of such approval was an important part of the cowboy hat's meaning for me as a little boy.

The other part of its meaning, invisible to the camera, derived from the use made of hats and other dressing-up materials in play fantasies in which I acted out adventures featuring myself as hero. Whether I was riding Snowy or being shot by my friend, Janet, the hats and guns were accessories to this central imaginative process. They were not indispensable: I remember galloping round the new garden, after our move to Hemel Hempstead, on a broomstick horse with a tablecloth thrown over my shoulders as a cloak, a feather stuck in my hat for a plume and a stick for a sword, as a cavalier serving under Prince Rupert in the English Civil War. The representational form of play-clothes and toys, though, made these identificatinos more 'realistic', and so over the years I acquired a sizeable collection of hats, dressing-up clothes and toy weapons.[1]

My basic cowboy gear was fleshed out by further items: a 'Lee Enfield' rifle, a sheriff's badge, holster and bullets, a bow and arrows and, one Christmas, a whole US cavalry uniform of matching blue-cotton blouse and trousers with yellow stripes and a yellow neckerchief, which I wore with a toy sword and scabbard. After we moved to Hemel Hempstead, Wild West outfits were gradually superseded by Second World War ones. My favourite hat now became a plastic, American-style 'steel helmet' complete with camouflage netting. Accessories included a plastic tommy-gun, a hand grenade and a combat knife on a belt. These various items, of course, were all commodities produced for a mass market and designed for their compatibility with the currently popular genres of adventure.

Like my play-fantasies with toy soldiers, the imaginative identifications that I made in dressing up drew upon the available cultural repertoire of stories and heroes like the Lone Ranger. In dressing-up narratives, however, projective identification and third-person narration were replaced by introjective identification and first-person narration.[2] Wearing a cowboy hat, a cavalry outfit or a soldier's helmet, I was imagining myself to be the cowboys, cavalrymen and soldiers of the comics and television, and I acted out adventures of which I was the protagonist as well as the creator. Through introjective identification, whereby words, images and stories already charged with my own projective investments were now incorporated into my own sense of self, I was quite literally composing 'myself'. Whereas in solitary and introverted play with soldiers my imagined narratives were significant only in reference to my own internal world, in dressing up and acting a part I was representing this imagined self to others and assuming the shape in which I wanted to appear in the world. My imaginings were taking on a more fully social form.

This social imagining of the self was not something neatly contained within a special activity called 'play', but continually affected all aspects of everyday life. Being an adventure hero empowered me to go out into the public world beyond the garden gate. I remember, as a 5-year-old on the front of my father's bike, turning to wave encouragement to my troops marching behind, and becoming a great and magnanimous military commander at the head of his column. As a compliant world of troops and horses took shape around me, I embodied in my own person the fulfilment of a wish: to be bigger, stronger, more powerful and effective in the world. The narrative expressed a phantasized domination over imagos which I projected onto the landscape and figures around me, controlling them, ordering them around and subordinating them to my own desire and will. My father, who sat out of sight behind me, pedalling the bike that actually carried us forward, also featured in this narrative as the commander's driver. His presence, of course, rendered safe my being 'in public', thus underpinning the possibility of such a fantasy. However, on this occasion my father refused to play the part allotted to him, and instead asserted his real authority: seeing my wave, he scolded me for making traffic signals, and the great and magnanimous military commander deflated in tears.

This bruising deflation of my imagined self occurred through an encounter with the rules of a sociocultural order that governed public behaviour, but that I knew little about (in this case, the Highway Code as mediated by my father's authority). It would be wrong, though, to read in this the simple predominance of 'reality' over 'fantasy', or the re-imposition of my 'real' identity as a small boy onto my imagined identity as a soldier hero. All identities must be imagined, and the great and magnanimous soldier was merely one among several other current identities, formed under the impact of a splitting that also produced the foolish, irresponsible and powerless little boy whom I felt myself to be after scolding. Bossed around and made to feel small by my big, powerful father, I now imagined *him* to be controlling *me,* ordering me around and subordinating me to his desire and will. Both narratives were imaginative responses to my real social relations. While the latter might appear to correspond more accurately to the actual power relations pertaining between my father and myself, it was nonetheless a phantasy governed by defensive splitting, that retained in reversal those same two roles and produced an experience of my father as a punitive figure in the black-and-white terms of my own preoccupations with authority. Where imagining myself was governed by splitting, then, I moved in and out of various incompatible and even dichotomous identities, each of which required the projection of 'other' qualities in order to sustain itself.

Whereas in solitary play with toys, identities are imagined through projection directed at omnipotently controlled, purely symbolic objects, these social imaginings position real others, inviting approval and affirmation and running the risk of refusal and negation. At stake here is the winning and withholding of social recognition: 'who I can imagine myself to be' becomes inseparable from 'who they will recognize me as'. My father's scolding was, in effect if not intention (he was not a party to this particular fantasy), to withdraw recognition of me as a great and magnanimous soldier, such that I could no longer sustain this identity in public. The deflation of fantasies through encounters with other people constitutes the means to discover which imaginings can be recognized and so sustained in particular public worlds and which will elicit the experience of misrecognition. The difference between these two outcomes is itself dependent on the social imaginings of the other: on, that is, the reciprocity or discrepancy between the form in which I identified myself and the form in which I was imagined by my father.

Neither self-imagining nor recognition is an arbitrary product of individual whim or tolerance. Both are governed by norms and taboos, definitions of what is possible or 'appropriate' for people occupying different positions within social relations, as these are furnished by cultural imaginaries. Just as I drew from available cultural imaginaries in imagining myself, so other people did in investing imaginative significance in me as a son, a brother, a boy. The composition of sustainable public identities involved a negotiation between my own wishes and other people's recognitions of me: who they wanted me to be, and who they would allow me to be. This process is deeply bound up with power—to elicit recognition or to refuse it, to impose or to contest it. It is therefore shaped by the relations of power that constitute the social divisions and conflicts of the wider hegemonic order. Children, while peculiarly dependent upon affirmative recognition, are relatively powerless to determine its conditions or forms.[3]

Some of the most powerful adult investments that impinge on the identities children can imagine for themselves are to do with gender. Since gender identity is so important in our culture, a child's need for affirmative recognition from others gives rise to a pressure to make him or herself clearly recognizable as 'a boy' or 'a girl'. This makes attractive those cultural forms that identify the self most clearly according to current definitions of appropriateness. The effects of this process have been described in a story told by Michelle Cohen about her son:

> When D was about 3 he decided one morning to wear a woman's smock . . . [that] he loved to 'dress up' in. He put it on, but when his father realized D wanted to wear it to walk (with me) to the CCC [Children's Community Centre], he became furious and yelled that D was not to go out with a dress on. He refused to explain why he was so violently opposed to this. I was very upset but told D that he could wear the dress if he wanted, comforted him, and we left. When we arrived

at the CCC a male visitor greeted us and said to me 'Is she your child? What's her name?' (D also had, at this time, long blonde curly hair which both I and his father loved). I retorted that my child was a boy called D but D turned to me, gripped me intensely and whispered 'take off the dress, take off the dress'. No amount of comforting could persuade him to change his mind. He has never worn a dress since.[4]

This story testifies to the anxieties that surround the imaginative acquisition and maintainance of an 'appropriate' gender identity. Whatever identity D imagined for himself whilst wearing that dress—whatever self it enabled him to be—he cannot sustain it against the public threat to his gender identity that it brings about. His transgression of the codes that mark him as a boy prompt anger and then misrecognition, both crucially coming from men, including his father. His mother's affirmative recognition, tolerance and encouragement cannot offset D's desire to identify himself as a boy and to be recognized as such by men in particular. Crucially, this leads to a withdrawal of D's investment from a form in which he had previously secured recognition from his mother. It establishes conflict between competing recognitions.

My parents may have refused my imaginings on 'inappropriate' occasions like the bike-ride to school but, in contrast to D, I met no essential rejection of my imagined self as a cowboy-soldier. Not only did it meet with the approval of both my parents, it also furnished the clothes I felt comfortable in, and so affected the ways I liked to appear in the wider public world. As a 6-year-old, my blue cavalry blouse did service as a 'real' shirt, while a new check shirt, to which I had taken an instant dislike such that I refused to wear it, became a favourite after my mother had suggested its likeness to the check shirts worn by cowboys. Her recognition enabled me to 'see' myself in that shirt; and so powerful was this identification that some of the clothes I wear today, in my thirties, continue to echo this childhood style. This experience is the polar opposite of D's experience with the dress. The cowboy-soldier repertoire furnished a range of significant styles that were then considered 'appropriate' for a boy. It provided the forms that enabled me to imagine myself *as* 'a boy' because these invited, through long convention and use, recognition as a boy from others; both from my parents and from the wider culture. To use or 'inhabit' those forms made it possible to elicit such recognition and to avoid the distress of scenes like D's encounter at the Children's Centre.

Anxieties about gender identity, and the desire to locate myself clearly and firmly in a world of sexual difference, would seem to have driven me towards precisely the most conventional forms and styles. The cowboy, the soldier, the adventurer, were not only 'masculine' forms but had come to be signs of masculinity as such.

As popular, recognizable boyhood forms, they were already widely available in 1950s culture and were there lying in wait for me. In imagining myself in their terms, I entered into them, tried them on for size and cut myself to fit them. But at what price? When, in a panic, D takes off his dress for the last time, he takes off a part of himself with it, securing a 'masculine' identity by separating himself, through psychic splitting, from a 'femininity' that is associated with the rejected forms. The process of splitting is made manifest through this cutting of the self to fit these recognizable cultural forms.

But this is not the end of the story. In the first place, while every boy has to learn to cut himself to fit, some 'manage' this more thoroughly than others; and all inhabit those styles and use those forms in different ways, making (within limits) their own versions of masculinity. Second, imagining an identity is not a fixed, once-and-for-all achievement, but is subject to continual reworking and transformation. The fixities of a clear and unambiguous gender identity are something desired as much as achieved; a wished-for end to the confusion and distress produced by a world divided by gender. In the ordinary course of growing up, children encounter new social situations and new publics, which bring about new anxieties and pressures on identity, as well as new sources of affirmative recognition and pleasure. Among these, school looms largest.

BOY CULTURE

Recognition, of course, is not the monopoly of adults. Children play with other children: siblings, relatives, the children of neighbours and parents' friends all provide possible playmates, and opportunities for more equal and reciprocal recognitions than are possible between children and adults. My earliest playmate was a girl, Janet, a year older than me, whose garden backed onto ours. Photographs confirm that we used to dress up and play cowboys and Indians together. . . . While this confounds any simple identification of these as exclusively or necessarily boys' forms, our play did nevertheless have to negotiate sexual difference. I registered Janet's difference from me in terms of the frilly white braid around her cowboy hat. This made it, to my mind, not a 'real' cowboy hat, just as she was not a 'real' cowboy but a 'cowgirl', an Annie Oakley skilled with the six-gun.[5] Partly due to the distance I had to travel to my first school, I had no other regular playmate during my Doncaster years. But after our move to Hemel Hempstead in 1962, I became one of some thirty children attending a brand-new school that opened at the bottom of our road. As the school rapidly expanded, along with the housing estate that it served, a steady stream of new children joined my class. After a couple of years, this settled down into a cohesive and stable group that remained together for my four years in junior school, between the ages of 7 and 11. In this rich, new public world, all my most significant friendships were with other boys.[6]

Despite the school's egalitarian ethos and the friendships that flourished between boys and girls within the classroom, playtimes saw the formation of sharply gendered groups with distinctive forms of shared play. Chief amongst our boys' games were 'British Bulldog' (the tag game), playground football—and playing at war. All these games involved a large group which divided itself into two sides. When playing at war, each side would attack and defend agreed 'bases' using a variety of tactics—charging, creeping up, outmanœuvring, holding strong defensive positions, counter-attacking and retreating—the aim being to capture the base and 'kill' all the enemy. Physically, the play was not unlike games of tag, the major difference residing in our narrative imaginings, amongst which Second World War themes were especially popular.

Since we were not allowed to bring toys to school or to use sticks, our weapons in all these narratives were completely imaginary, being represented for others by particular hand and arm positions; mostly those appropriate to each weapon, 'as if' we were holding a tommy gun at the hip or a sword in the hand. How these imaginary weapons were to be used, and the distances at which they would be effective, was governed by elaborate conventions, called 'taking your shots'. When 'using guns', for example, the convention was to catch the eye of your enemy whilst simultaneously 'firing' by making the appropriate sign at whomever you were shooting. 'Taking your shots' meant acknowledging when you were the target of a successful hit and falling down dead (with a cry reminiscent of the 'a-a-a-rghs' and 'u-u-u-rghs' much loved by the war comic-strip writer). You were then out of the game for the duration of that particular attack. If there was any ambiguity, you could claim to be 'only wounded' and continue the game partly immobilized. Anyone 'not taking their shots' would be pursued by a clamour to that effect. Disputes were resolved verbally between the two boys involved, and in serious cases the game would halt and others be brought in to pass a group judgement. 'Taking your shots' not only regulated the public interaction, but also set limits to private fantasy. Within these bounds, however, a great deal of give-and-take sharing occurred, whereby friends would reciprocally allot and be allotted places in each others' fantasies, regularly stepping out of self-absorption in the role in order to provide a commentary on 'what is happening now', so as to enable the other to respond appropriately.

At school, play became a social relation. To be successful, playing together necessarily involved the sharing of narratives and self-imaginings. These assumed a social form, governed by conventions and rules, through active negotiation with others who were also investing their own imagined selves in a narrative that was at one and the same time determined by numerous internal worlds and had a public existence. Since my own imaginings had to respond to the doings of others, the fantasies of shared play involved a significant giving-up of omnipotent control. In recompense, to allow an other to enter into and share in some of my most significant fantasies, and to be allowed to enter into and share in his, promoted a very powerful kind of social recognition: one that depended on trust, mutual enjoyment and the reciprocity and equality of the exchange. Through shared play and the negotiations that sustained it, we could give each other a kind of recognition that was available nowhere else. Our play identities as soldier heroes, recognized and affirmed by others, became 'real' in the sense that our play relationships and play itself were central components of our real, developing friendships. Just as we could move fluidly between absorption of the self in play and the explanation and negotiation needed to secure its shared character, so the medium of our friendship could shift fluidly between being a soldier hero and being the boy who explained, negotiated and helped resolve disputes.

As this kind of reciprocity developed, and my group of boy friends began to provide an alternative basis of affirmative recognition, playground war games became increasingly important in my life. The pleasures of war play were a significant factor in attracting me away from the security of the domestic sphere into a more fully committed participation in the public world of the school: as a 7-year-old, it was their lure that prompted me to ask my mother if I could begin to stay for school dinners. My independence from the family household, and perhaps especially from my mother, was strengthened to the extent that I could belong, with mutual recognition, among other boys with similar needs, in a group that bonded together around common interests and practices. The shared forms of this distinctive 'boy culture' were those of a collectivity defined by age and gender, in and through which we affirmed our 'masculinity'.[7] As its influence spread beyond the school gates, the connotations of distance and independence from domesticity became increasingly attached to its forms. From the age of 7 or 8 years old, as we were trusted farther afield without parental supervision, we began calling for each other not only to stay in and play in our various houses and gardens, but also to 'go out to play'. Boy culture gradually came to occupy the wider public spaces of the neighbourhood: the streets, alleys and garage-areas of the estate, the apple-orchard behind the shops, the green and, given our semi-rural location, the nearby country lanes, farmers' fields and woods.

These became an adventure world, invested with excitement by frontier narratives of exploration, survival and combat like the Crusoe story. Indeed, in a sense these narratives functioned here as an energizing myth, no longer inspiring men to go out to the imperial frontiers, but now inspiring boys to invest their own neighbourhood with all the characteristics of a wilderness. We made secret camps in trees and in thickets of ferns that rose above our heads, followed paths and tracks to see where they would lead, and played war games with extended scope for hiding, ambushing and tracking. The imagining of adventure offered the means for us to move away from the safety of home and garden into an engagement with a real public world that was as new and unknown to me as Crusoe's island was to him. Learning to inhabit that world as a significant and exciting place was not entirely an imaginary act, but involved the acquisition of actual skills and knowledges: orienteering, exploring, building.[8] Entering into it also enabled an actual freedom, from parental control and the tasks of the domestic home, to do what I wanted, with my friends. This is a distinguishing mark of boyhood that contrasts with the more restricted mobility of little girls, a result of the greater responsibility that they are often given for the care of younger children and other domestic labour.[9]

My remembering of boy culture during the four-year period of my time at junior school is vivid with excitement and pleasure. I see it as the period when my overall self-confidence blossomed and when, especially as a 9- and 10-year-old, I enjoyed being popular with other children in the class.[10] Two 'best friends', Michael and Patrick, stand out from a number of other close friendships as being especially long-lasting and significant. Alongside our sharing of adventure fantasies, what I remember most clearly is an easy physical warmth and closeness, often expressed in wrestling; indeed, my feelings for Patrick had all the passionate intensity of a love not fully recognized as such. I retain a nostalgic yearning for this lost boyhood intimacy, and this period of my life has assumed in memory the ideal quality of a golden age when all was happiness and contentment. At one point during it, however, my father was treated in hospital for a serious illness and was off work for some months. I was badly affected by this, and among the unspoken anxieties of family life at the time, I became an insomniac in need of sleeping pills and a night-light. The discrepancy between these anxieties and my idealized memories of boy culture in this period, from which they are utterly dissociated, suggests that my self-imagining as an adventure hero, and my recognition as such by other boys, was the cultural form of a psychic splitting in manic defence against them.

In Kleinian terms, defensive idealizations of this kind are not necessarily a bad thing and, in the protection they provide against the unravelling effects of anxiety, may have important psychic benefits. These benefits may be augmented in imaginings that are shared with others. In contrast to the omnipotent control exercised in wish-fulfilling play with toys, the reciprocal recognitions that occur in shared play fantasies offer possibilities for the introjection of qualities derived from real other people rather than from one's own projected wishes. According to Klein, these are the kinds of introjection upon which any effective integration of the internal world depends: they make possible the 'modification of imagos' into more complex and less dichotomous figures, and thus enable a greater capacity for subjective coherence.[11] While the adventure fantasies of boy culture can be understood in terms of psychic splitting and the operation of manic defence against anxiety, the social recognition involved in their sharing may help to promote an increased cohesion and security of the inner world that in turn facilitates the facing and working-through of difficulties encountered in social life.

Yet my identification with this particular cultural form of idealization was not without its costs. Whilst I was an adventure hero, other aspects of my social world literally disappeared. Participation in boy culture took me out into the 'adventure worlds' of school and neighbourhood which were predicated increasingly upon their separation, both physical and psychic, from the world of domestic life. The composure of self-imagining as a hero, the pleasures of war play and the recognitions of boyhood friendship all came to depend upon this distance. But of course I did not thereby cease to live in that domestic world: at home I continued to be involved in intense and tangled relationships with my mother, father and brother, and to participate in the extended family circle. Locating myself in these social relations required an altogether more complicated kind of self-imagining, one capable of negotiating the full range of adult recognitions and misrecognitions. Similarly, the exclusion of girls from boy culture did not mean that we boys ceased to relate to them within the public space of the classroom. Friendship with girls made other kinds of demands upon our self-imagining, and the presence of teachers insisted on other kinds of recognition, in forms that were 'policed' by the educational and egalitarian ethos of the school. Even within boy culture, the adventure hero coexisted with those other selves who played football or marvelled at the natural world. Seen within the context of my experience as a whole, the adventure hero appears as one split form among many other selves, between which 'I' would fluctuate. These were at once the inhabitants of a complex and divided social world and of the fractured inner world correlated to it.

To understand my boyhood self-imagining as a soldier hero, then, it is necessary to enquire into its relation to these other selves. In the Kleinian model, the various split parts of the self coexist within a more extensive subjectivity for which further integration is a psychic option both feared and desired: feared, because splitting offers distinct benefits, that render forms like the idealized adventurer so attractive to inhabit and so difficult to relinquish; desired, because greater psychic coherence holds out the promise of a fuller and more effective participation in social life. The social and psychic costs of preserving defensive splits become visible at moments of schism between different selves, when temporarily their connectedness cannot be denied, so that their incompatibility is experienced as a contradiction: one self is exposed to consequences brought about by the actions (or imaginings) of another. To explore these moments of schism as they break open the apparently seamless coherence of my boyhood adventure heroes is to step outside the pleasurable memories of past investments into more difficult and troubling memories of discord and distress. These are precisely the experiences against which the adventure hero offered a defence, but which inevitably occurred, despite him.

One painful memory of my boyhood concerns the collision between two worlds, and two selves, when I was 10 years old. It features my best friend Patrick, who lived nearly a mile away from our house and the school at the bottom of our road. One Friday I had made an arrangement with him to play down the lanes after school. He wanted to go home and change into his soldier's gear, and would then walk all the way back to my house to call for me *en route* to the lanes. When I arrived home, however, my parents insisted that I went shopping with them in town, forbade me to go out and overrode all my protests about Patrick. I felt dismayed and humiliated at my inability to honour our arrangement. Through no fault of my own, I was going to let Patrick down and betray our friendship. He would come all this way for nothing, and (in the days before we acquired a telephone) I could do nothing to prevent it. When Patrick arrived, eagerly expectant and togged out in his soldier's kit, helmet and gun, and I had to give him the news, I burst into tears.

The intensity of my memory repeats the intensity of the original experience: a moment of irresolvable contradiction when the splitting between alternative selves was exposed as such, and my powerlessness in relation to my parents was seen to override the self I wished to be. I felt my parents to be unfair, but more importantly, to be denying my autonomy by refusing to recognize the importance—and the forms—of my friendship with Patrick. This sense of my powerlessness in the face of parental authority was heightened by its explicit negation of the powerful, even omnipotent, soldier hero whom I would become on leaving behind the controlled space of the home in Patrick's company. Feeling the distress arising from this contradiction only made it worse, since my would-be bravado in the face of danger and adversity was replaced by the actual tears of a small boy resigned to defeat. Worst of all, these tears were shed, not in front of my parents alone, nor in front of Patrick in his ordinary clothes, but at the sight of a Patrick who had already become a soldier hero. Dressed up, he was the very image of what I wished to be but had now been denied; and instead of exchanging the empowering recognitions of shared adventure, I stood before him as the very image of what we both hoped to escape.

Both the desirability of splitting and its costs as a defensive strategy are captured in this image of two boys facing each other through an open doorway. One remains inside experiencing distress and wishing to escape over the threshold, but is powerless to 'go out'; while the other, already over that threshold, is powerless to help. For adventure, as we knew it, could only handle such conflicts by offering escape from them. The imaginary coherence of the kind of adventure hero whose forms we inherited depends upon its clearly occupying the 'public' side of the public-private division. The price of this coherence is the splitting-off of the adventure hero from the imaginary selves who inhabit the 'private' side of the division. When I was called away from the exciting world of adventure down the lanes to go shopping at Tesco, the mundane and boring tasks of the domestic household were reaffirmed *as* mundane and boring by comparison; and the reciprocity of boy friendship appeared so much more preferable to the complicated relationships of the family, saturated as they were with controlling power and resistance to it.

In another memory of boyhood discomposure, my discomfort also derived from the temporary impossibility of shared adventure, this time with a girl. Within the structured context of school activities, friendships between girls and boys flourished: one of my own favourites was a girl named Anne, with whom I shared a double-desk during my second year in the juniors. Outside that context, so many of our pleasures, pursuits and imaginings were gender-exclusive that it was hard to find common ground. Gender separatism in playground and neighbourhood was such that Anne and I never called for each other at home, and my efforts to remember anything about girls' culture or any shared forms of play have drawn the blankness born of difference. Certainly I and the boys in my group did not extend the recognitions of shared adventure to girls. On the unusual occasions when girls and boys did meet outside school—at birthday parties and suchlike—the atmosphere was charged with a peculiar kind of excitement and permeated by a very different kind of imagining: romance. Contrary to the assumptions of some cultural critics, masculinities are also imagined in 'feminine romance'.[12] The chief vehicle of my own introduction to these narratives of heterosexual love and desire—in a form that was easily split-off at a safe distance from the adventure world—was pop music: the radio charts, but especially my older brother's Beatles' albums that I listened to over and over again on his tape-recorder. Here, at least, was a possible common ground.

Romance hung uneasily in the air on one extraordinary occasion when, as an 8-year-old, I was chosen together with Anne to accompany the headmaster on behalf of the class on a shopping trip to buy a leaving-present for our class teacher. This unusual contact with her augmented the excitement of the occasion, but when we eventually found ourselves left alone together in the Headmaster's van, we were suddenly shy of each other and sat tongue-tied and vacuous. How much easier it would have been, with a boy, to share the excitement of the trip as an imagined adventure! By comparison, the self I could imagine through romance was so much more tentative and uncertain of itself. I felt the adventure hero to be the most powerful of my self-imaginings because it enabled the avoidance of such difficulties in a world where these other relationships did not (or should not) exist. The dangers inherent in the collision between boyhood adventure and romance were to be demonstrated a year or so later when, one day in the school playground, Anne became the first girl I ever kissed romantically, and the other boys ridiculed me mercilessly as a 'softie' (one who was 'soft' on girls). Construed in terms of romance, this could be seen as an expression of friendship with positive connotations. In terms of the 'harder' codes of an exclusive boy culture, however, it was an act of weakness that invited projective disavowal of the adventure hero's denigrated other. Here, the masculinity of the idealized adventure hero appears to have been, not one choice among many possible selves, but a form that was installed as the norm, to be policed by group recognitions and by the withdrawal of affirmation.

The common factor in my distressing memories about Anne and Patrick is the collision between two very different imagined selves, and the exposure of limitations and inadequacies in the adventure hero as a mode of defensive self-imagining. These contradictions can be closely related to splitting in cultural imaginaries and the different positions occupied by boys and girls in relation to the public sphere. Far from enabling me to locate myself effectively within these social divisions, and to handle the many kinds of recognition generated by them, adventure tended to render these complexities invisible. These difficulties became magnified once I left the juniors for secondary school, and entered adolescence.

HORNBLOWER MEETS THE SKINHEADS: THE ABANDONING OF ADVENTURE

In contrast to my memories of primary school as a nostalgic golden age of happiness and contentment, I remember my first three years at secondary school (1967-9) as a time when I was lonely and unhappy and lost a good deal of confidence. Allocated to different schools in various parts of town, my group of primary-school friends was split up. None accompanied me to the grammar school some twenty minutes' walk away, where I followed my older brother, and under the demands of a new way of life, losing touch with them seemed inevitable. In my new school-public I encountered new kinds of recognition, not all of it affirmative, and experienced new anxieties. I sought to make friends among boys who mostly lived on an estate neighbouring the school—an estate that I found distinctly 'rough' in comparison with our 'respectable' area—or who were bussed in from the 'posh' parts of nearby Abbot's Langley. In this new school I had to confront and live out the ambiguities and contradictions of my family's class position, experienced in terms of my encounter with different forms of adolescent masculinity.

My father was a primary-school teacher whose promotion to a Deputy Headship had enabled our 'escape' from Doncaster and the claustrophobia of a traditional working-class family network. My mother, after working for several years in low-skilled jobs on the local industrial estate, became a school dinner-lady and eventually trained as a teacher herself. Our own tentative social mobility, as we gradually settled into the lifestyle of an aspiring, lower-middle-class professional family, was paralleled and to some extent obscured by the more general expansion of horizons and opportunities characteristic of many working people's lives in the 1960s.[13] Our New Town housing estate and primary school, with its uprooted mixture of skilled and unskilled, working-class and middle-class families, was typical of these transformations in class and culture. My experience there left me utterly unprepared for the degree of physical intimidation and fighting, as well as the overt and, to my sheltered sensibility, rather brutal, masculine sexuality, that were part and parcel of my new school's culture. From basking in the centre of positive recognition and approval at primary school, I now found myself increasingly marginalized within a new public of tough, sporty skinhead lads who defined successful masculinity in terms that I felt myself unable to meet. Afraid of some, while admiring and wishing to emulate others, I gained little affirmation from any of them.

In response, I sought solace in the comfort of adventure, but found even this to have changed. While continuing to play with my soldiers into my twelfth year, I became increasingly conscious of their 'childishness'. Having lost the friends with whom I once shared adventure play fantasies, I was now confronted by adolescent, subcultural expectations of real masculine prowess and by the impossibility of recognition as an adventure hero without the performance of actual rather than imagined deeds. In these circumstances, my adventure fantasies became solitary once again. The forms that gave me pleasure, however, were ones that related to these new dilemmas.

I have a vivid memory of a particularly satisfying game that I played by myself as a 12-year-old, during the summer holiday following my first year at secondary school, while camping in the Lake District with my family. With a carefully chosen stick I would absorb myself for long periods in swathing down dense banks of nettles, some as tall as myself. The stick was a sword, the nettles were the massed enemy hordes, whose unpleasant sting justified their destruction. They would outnumber in quantity, but not outmatch in quality, the gallant and deft swordsman who would cut a path through them back to the family tent and evening meal, defying sting-wounds which, if received, were never more than a scratch. This swordsman was Captain Hornblower RN, the naval hero of C. S. Forester's famous sequence of novels set in the Napoleonic Wars, in which I immersed myself for the first time on that very holiday (and would reread several times over the next few years).[14]

In Hornblower, I found a hero relevant to the new conflicts and anxieties that I faced at secondary school. Anxieties about not fitting in and my lack of affirmative recognition were augmented by a feeling that I was somehow responsible for this, that I must be at fault. I came to experience conflicts stemming from my relationships with other boys as a conflict in myself, between the rather pathetic and inadequate boy I now felt myself to be and the powerful, well-liked boy I wanted to be and saw in others. The form of my misrecognition by the skinhead lads coincided with and reinforced denigrated imagos with which I now began to identify myself, establishing a vicious circle of lowering self-esteem. I could counter these anxieties, however, in wish-fulfilling fantasies in which I became omnipotently powerful and triumphed over all enemies and obstacles. Playing the part of Hornblower in solitary play, and swathing down compliant nettles in a most satisfying manner, I became the hero I wished to be.

The Hornblower novels appealed to me as a 12-year-old because of the greater realism of their characterization in comparison to many other adventure stories. The simple splitting that produces hero and enemy in narratives like 'Attack on Marzuk' or *Bugles in the Afternoon* is tempered into a more complicated and troubled hero who spoke more directly to my own anxieties. The novels that I read first—coincidentally the earliest in the sequence to be written—tell of Hornblower as an up-and-coming junior captain in the Royal Navy. Like my own long-established play fantasies and many other public adventure narratives, they deal explicitly with the desire-for-recognition theme and invest martial rank with intense significance. Hornblower's worth is not yet recognized and he sets out to prove himself through military adventure. As a captain commanding his own ship, he is sent on individual missions to distant waters, where his initiative is given full scope but where the opportunity for success always carries a high risk of failure. In order to succeed, besides defeating the French and Spanish enemy, he must also negotiate the navy's hierarchy of authority and prestige. He becomes engaged in a constant struggle to win the respect, obedience and loyalty of his officers and crew, and—in a familiar evocation of persecutory anxiety—he finds his risks magnified by orders from above that are seemingly arbitrary, often ill-judged and always punishingly demanding.[15] Performing the impossible against all the odds of course enables Hornblower to become a hero. But even when successful, his achievements are not given the recognition they deserve by the Admiralty. In *A Ship of the Line,* for example, the story begins with Hornblower lamenting his ill-fortune at being granted no prize money for his victory over a much larger Spanish warship, narrated in the previous novel, *A Happy Return.*[16] Social recognition of the hero is withheld—to fuel further adventures.

Another factor that helps to explain my attraction to Hornblower is the way his struggle for respect and recognition is given explicit class connotations throughout the novel-sequence. In subsequent volumes, Forester fleshes out his hero's past as a boy-midshipman and service-orphan—echoes of the orphan phantasy so prevalent in girls' comics, here—from a poor family with no influential connections. Upwardly mobile and of middling rank, Hornblower's original class location always renders him vulnerable in a highly stratified society even as he rises through it by promotion. As a captain he lives in constant fear of being ruined, and at the start of *A Ship of the Line* his 'poverty-stricken condition' gives rise to anxieties regarding status and prestige. What other captains take for granted—the trappings of status, the outward signs of power—Hornblower cannot afford and has to fight for. Since he moves in circles above his station, almost every social encounter with his colleagues and superiors involves some degree of shame, unease and social doubt, which fuel his self-criticism and his need to prove himself. Material security, his naval reputation and an established position in society are all dependent on his success as a fighting captain. At the same time, in dealings with his own subordinates he has to win the respect of tough ordinary-seamen whose expectations and standards of behaviour are equally alien to him.[17]

The question of masculine identity lies at the centre of Hornblower's struggle for recognition. Here again his attraction, for me, lay in the unconventional characteristics that disadvantage him for the achievement of ideal heroism. Just as I failed to achieve the required masculine standard in terms of physical prowess, Hornblower is apparently a non-starter as a soldier hero. As a midshipman he is gauche and gangling, while as a captain he remains physically weedy, with spindly legs and poor arm-strength—and invariably he gets sea-sick at the start of every voyage. Like my own adolescent self-identification in terms of brain rather than brawn, Hornblower's natural bent is as an intellectual: he has a calculating, analytical mind and an extensive knowledge of seamanship and naval strategy, which he applies in careful planning of any sortie or attack. All his adventures involve moments of carefully realized calculation and risk-taking, as he devises daring solutions to the tasks and dangers before him. Nevertheless, Hornblower does make himself into a fighting man. Not content to be the distant tactician, and refusing to order his men to do anything he has not proved himself capable of doing, he insists on himself leading the missions and expeditions he has designed; and this in the teeth of his own palpable fears and sense of physical inadequacy. A fighting hero by effort of will, who demonstrates courage and integrity as qualities to be struggled for, Hornblower made it possible for me to imagine their achievement. Combining in himself qualities that I struggled to hold together—intellectual and physical achievement; fear and courage—he offered me the possibility of integrating what might otherwise be split between different imagos (one an impossibly idealized hero and the other a contemptible rival or enemy), and so of modifying the more extreme features of my own self-denigration.

Hornblower, too, is a figure torn by warring parts of the self and constantly strives for that elusive masculine integrity himself. His own self-esteem remains low, and he is engaged in a constant struggle to live up to his own impossibly high ideals and to cope with his own savage self-criticism. This inner conflict only ceases when he is involved in the problem-solving associated with running a ship, following an order or fighting a battle. The start of novels often finds him itching to get into his ship and set sail. Once at sea, he achieves a mode of 'being himself' that is constantly thwarted on land. Action and adventure, then, provide the means by which inner conflict and self-doubt can be imagined as overcome, enabling Hornblower to attain his ideal self and win public recognition. The heroic fantasies that accompanied my sword-fights with nettles did the same for me. When I imagined myself as Hornblower, not fitting-in had its own recompense.

Like Sergeant Miller from the *Victor* story, Hornblower succeeds in winning the admiration and affection of the men he commands; and as the novel-sequence progresses, even the naval hierarchy is gradually brought to bestow recognition and honour upon him. At the culmination of this public recognition, Hornblower becomes a Lord and an Admiral.[18] To this extent, he remains a conventional, wish-fulfilling adventure hero. Even as a Lord, however, he never inhabits positions of

status and prestige comfortably, and never quite belongs either in aristocratic circles or among the seamen he commands. Like myself at that time, he is an essentially lonely figure. In Hornblower the self-made man, self-contained and self-reliant, able to negotiate successfully the cultures he never really belongs in, but never escaping a background that marks him out as different, I found an ideal hero relevant to my own experiences.

With hindsight, however, the ideal appears more problematic. The earlier novels reproduce the damaging split between the worlds of adventure and domesticity by closely associating Hornblower's escape to sea with escape from the demands of his wife, Maria.[19] She is described as a plain and dumpy woman who simultaneously nags and adores him. Her presence in the narrative makes Hornblower into a stereotypical henpecked husband. He observes the forms of marriage with dutiful resignation, but guiltily wishes to leave Maria far behind. This conventional 'escape from domesticity' motif gave me little help in coming to terms with my own contradictory relation to domestic life. However, it is complemented by the introduction into the Hornblower adventures of a love interest. To his great surprise, Hornblower exercises a great charm and attraction for women, who fall in love with him easily, despite his own uncertainties and lack of initiative. In the very first book, Hornblower finds himself in a hopeless mutual passion with the glamorous, highborn Lady Barbara. In a later novel, the contradictions in Hornblower's class position are resolved on this rather effortless romantic terrain when Forester conveniently kills off Maria and their children with the smallpox. The narrative displaces Hornblower's grief and guilt into excitement at the possibility, and eventual achievement, of marriage with Lady Barbara. The female characters in the Hornblower novels are split in this way into an idealized romantic aspect and a denigrated, ultimately dispensable domestic aspect.[20] This corresponds closely to the dominant forms of recognition for girls and women within the culture of adolescent boyhood at my school: forms that were becoming increasingly problematic for me as I began to turn to friendship with girls as an alternative source of pleasure and affirmation.

It also seems significant in retrospect that, unlike my earlier identification as the Lone Ranger, Hornblower is a British hero. For it is by virtue of intensely personal fantasies and meanings of the kind that I have explored in these last two chapters that British military masculinity becomes a figure of excitement and pleasure for boys and men. Hornblower is sustained throughout his career by an ideology of service to King and Country, which gives meaning to his life, and to which he submits his personal destiny. In many respects, he is a deeply conservative figure, and it would not be difficult to produce a reading of the novels that demonstrated their affinity with a number of themes central to the discourse of conservative British nationalism. Duty, freedom, the individual and self-help all feature prominently. They are linked to an uncritically 'patriotic' popular memory of the Napoleonic Wars as a struggle for national survival against continental tyranny. This found a powerful contemporary echo in the British response to the Soviet invasion of Czechoslovakia in summer 1968, when I was first reading the novels. Horatio Hornblower himself bears some striking resemblances to Nelson, that pillar of the conservative nationalist military pantheon.[21] In projective identification of myself with Hornblower, I was opening myself to the introjection of these conservative values and this version of Britishness.

That the national military masculinity represented by Hornblower failed to attain a lasting purchase into my teens was not due to any inherently radical political leanings on my part, but because my identification with the soldier hero failed to provide the composure and affirmative recognition that I now needed in the public worlds of school and beyond. Abandoning my deeply attractive but solitary adventurer, I looked elsewhere in search of new heroes. I discovered alternative possibilities in the counter-culture that began to develop a foothold in my school in the late 1960s and early 1970s. I was drawn to this by the attraction of possible new friendships with boys who were esteemed within the school, but who subscribed to a very different set of values and inhabited a different style of masculinity from the skinhead lads. There was scope in this for new ways of relating to people, new kinds of self-expression and new narratives that explored rather than sought to escape from the complexities of the self. I began to write poetry and play the guitar, to practise yoga and enjoy the world of psychedelia, to read Tolkien and Herman Hesse, to grow my hair long and wear flared trousers and brightly coloured T-shirts.[22]

Although the Women's Liberation Movement would subsequently criticize the supposed 'sexual revolution' stimulated by the counter-culture for reproducing established gender relations, in my experience it offered forms of masculinity that were less polarized in opposition to femininity than those I had known. The more emotional and vulnerable masculinity of the post-Beatles John Lennon, and the overtly 'feminine' style of musical heroes like Marc Bolan and David Bowie, offered new ideals to aspire towards in the early 1970s. Consequently, friendship with girls that went beyond romance became imaginable and increasingly important to me. Indeed, in psychic terms, my involvement with the counter-culture facilitated an identification with 'feminine' aspects of myself. In its espousal of liberation, self-fulfilment and 'playpower', and in its critique of the structures and values of 'straight society', the counter-culture and its successors in the 1970s made

possible a rebellious assertion of independence which called in question masculinity along with everything else.[23] This rebellion was directed against my parents and the school authorities, but also against their internalized imagos from whom I had sought recognition in adventure fantasies.

The counter-culture was furthermore inimical to the adventures of soldier heroes in its critique of militarism and wholehearted support of pacifism.[24] Two fixed memories from this period mark my transition from *The Guns of Navarone* in 1969 to *The Politics of Ecstasy* in 1971.[25] The first is a feeling of intense revulsion at a scene in a war film (the last I watched for many years). An American soldier, fighting the Japanese in the Burmese jungle during the Second World War, rests in the sun by a roadside, takes off his boots, enjoys a beautiful butterfly—and has his throat cut from behind by the enemy. The second is of my mother, furious, shouting at me to remove the white poppy I wore on my school blazer during Remembrance Week, and refusing to listen, in her rage at my disrespect for the nation's dead, to my explanation that I wished there to be no more war. The depth of my new-found revulsion in the first memory, and my sense of unfair misrecognition in the second, suggests a shift in the significance that war held for me, that was deeply bound up with attempts to compose a new sense of self. By belonging to the counter-culture, I could become someone different, both independent from my parents and better able to cope with the pressures of adolescent masculinity at school. Social recognition within the counter-culture depended upon inhabiting various shared beliefs and practices, and if these proved incompatible with my enjoyment of the masculine pleasure-culture of war, then the latter would have to be relinquished. Drawn into the forms of this new cultural imaginary, I abandoned my investments in adventure.

THE RETURN OF THE SOLDIER

But is it ever possible to 'abandon' an identity that has become so deeply rooted in the psyche? The wish to rid oneself of an identification now felt to be an encumbrance is the concomitant of the process described earlier as 'cutting oneself to fit'. In order to inhabit one form, other parts of the self are trimmed away and consigned to the waste-bin. Rubbishing, denigration, disavowal: these are the psychic accompaniments of splitting and defensive projection, turned now against the once-idealized form as the idealizing investment is transferred on to its replacement. The hippy and the pacifist, just as well as the soldier hero, may become the forms assumed by the self as it 'searches for the secrets' of a painless and coherent identity.[26] However, those aspects of contradictory subjectivity that are denigrated and disavowed in this process do not thereby cease to exist. Their psychic reality remains, even if unacknowledged, to perpetuate psychic conflict along new alignments, with implications for the possibility of social relationship.

In effect, while attempting to renounce the adventure hero, I maintained its existence as a split imago but simply reversed its value from positive to negative. There was more than a hint of a retreat from unresolved Oedipal dilemmas in this: my identification with the feminine also involved a new intimacy between myself and my mother, while the abandoning of my identification with adventure heroes would seem to have involved a projection of this now-denigrated imago into my father, whom I began to experience as the antithesis of my new self. Just as there had always been aspects of my life about which the adventure hero had nothing to say, relationships with which it could cope only by shutting them out, so the sustenance of my new oppositional identity now involved a rejection, not only of a part of myself, but also of a popular form of imagined masculinity and those boys and men identified with it. Among the problems this would generate for my future relationships with other men, the first and greatest difficulty that it delivered me into was an overt and damaging conflict with my father. It was he who bore the brunt of my rebellion, and in reacting to this, only exacerbated a conflict that came close to blows on one occasion in my later teens, when he contested my right to wear long, shoulder-length hair.

These conflicts, both psychic and social, ensured that the counter-cultural identity of my teenage years could only be—like any other identity—a provisional and semi-resolved response to the contradictions of subjectivity. I sustained it, nevertheless, through to my second year at university in 1975-6, after which the need to find some means of integration became pressing. When I was introduced at university to Marxist cultural studies, alternative ways of understanding my history and that of my family, within the broader context of socialist and feminist politics, became available. These helped me to begin building bridges between my father and myself: to begin to effect reparation of the damage done through defensive splitting to us both. Our arguments about whether or not *The Dirty Dozen* was just harmless escapism played an early part in this process. My encounter with psychoanalysis and psychotherapy has been one of the directions it has taken subsequently; writing this book, and rethinking my own relation to adventure and its significance in my past, has been another.

In the course of this investigation I have been surprised by the potential of my long-renounced identification with the soldier-hero imago to revert to its original positive value. [Elsewhere] I touched on the pleasures of remembering boyhood adventure, and the obstacles that this transference placed in the way of my endeav-

ours to attain a critical distance on masculinity.[27] One manifestation of this ambivalence has been my difficulty in achieving a flexible writing voice when exploring these memories, a voice that could enter into the unconscious investments that have transferred on to my descriptions of boyhood forms, without getting caught up in them. My first drafts invariably tended to reproduce boyhood excitements in overelaborate and uncritical detail, while many of the gaps and silences that marked the parameters of those original investments were repeated in the writing. My first discussion of women characters in adventure stories, for example, took the form of a paragraph tacked on at the end, as an afterthought to the serious business of analysing the hero. The crucial domestic context of play and its connection to family dynamics and my relationship to parents has proved especially difficult to recover.

I have come to see these transferential investments at work in my writing as the site of an active contradiction. My analysis of the adventure hero and masculinity has developed in fruitful dialogue with feminism. Feminist ideas and politics have profoundly influenced my understanding of gender relations and my own sense of myself as a man. They have contributed to my growing awareness of how my 'socialization' as a boy and a man has involved benefits, privileges and opportunities less readily available (at the very least) to girls and women, but also how it has subjected me to a variety of negative pressures, that have stultified and limited me, caused me unhappiness and contributed to failures of understanding and communication. To tease open this process and explore its contradictory results can be a positive and challenging experience that opens out masculinities to constructive change; this being one of the motivating desires behind my investigation of adventure. In remembering my own boyhood, however, I found myself defining my approach to the soldier hero and adventure *against* feminist approaches, many of which have tended to be overtly critical, even hostile, to these forms of narrative and subjectivity. This was particularly the case in my writing about boy culture, which I sought to rescue from charges of misogynistic 'male bonding' and of fostering masculine aggression.[28] There was more to this than rational academic or political disagreement. In effect, my writing functioned here as a defensive reaction against criticism of war play that seemed to threaten the value I had invested in those memories. It became charged with a sense of my misrecognition as a man by women, and with a corresponding wish to overcome this by composing a positive account of boyhood masculinity that would elicit more favourable recognition instead.

Soldier heroes are not only kept alive by the reproduction of public narratives that tell their stories, as in the unbroken reprinting of *Seven Pillars of Wisdom*, or the twentieth-century history books featuring Indian Mutiny generals. Introjections of the idealized heroes and heroines of children's culture persist as imagos in the internal worlds of adults, where they retain the potential to become active once again. While each new generation of boys will encounter only the very latest heroes or those handed down to them from the past, others live on in the psyches of their fathers and grandfathers. These latter are altogether more ambivalent phenomena, which give rise to some unexpected conflicts.

One notable instance is that of the Kenyan novelist and playwright, Ngũgĩ wa Thiong'o, who has written about the 'drama of contradictions' that he had unwittingly played out as a 16-year-old reader of the Biggles books in mid-1950s Kenya.[29] While Ngũgĩ at his colonial high school was thrilling to the adventures of Captain W. E. Johns' fictional RAF hero, his brother was fighting for Kenyan independence with the Mau Mau guerrillas in a war that was eventually won for the Empire by RAF bombers.

> Biggles . . . would have been pitted against my own brother who amidst all the fighting in the forest found time to send messages to me to cling to education no matter what happened to him. In the forests they, who were so imbued with Kenya nationalist patriotism, had celebrated my being accepted into the same Alliance High School where I was to meet Biggles, an imaginary character so imbued with a sense of British patriotism. . . . The flag which we saluted every day accompanied by God Save the Queen, may she long reign over us, was central to the Biggles enterprise.

Thirty-six years later, the contradiction can be named and understood as such: 'The Royal Air Force? That should have alerted me, should have made Biggles my enemy.' Yet Ngũgĩ also testifies to the power of these stories to cut across the more obvious political identifications by evoking a more direct and exciting fantasy:

> The Biggles series were full of actions, intrigues, thrills, twists, surprises and a very simple morality of right against wrong, angels against devils, with the good always triumphant. It was adventure all the way, on land and in the sky. . . . The books did not invite meditation; just the involvement in the actions of the hero and his band of faithfuls. They were boy's books really. I could never think of Biggles as an adult. He remained an adolescent, a Boy Scout . . . a boy daring to try, never giving up, stretching the boundaries of what was credible, but still inviting his boy readers to join in the adventure.

Ngũgĩ's memories evoke the pleasures of Biggles in terms of a utopian, adolescent longing for an uncomplicated, unthreatening world of boundless possibility where the harsh realities and ferocious conflicts of colonialism need not intrude and where everyone is still a boy.

Although Ngũgĩ does not say whether the memory of these past investments in the cultural forms of the colonizer poses any problems for him today, his essay implies that the reality of this contradiction became evident to him as he left boyhood to fully enter the adult world, where he learned to recognize who his enemies really were. But what of cases where the contradictions cannot be named as such—where the conflicting identifications are not worked through to some fuller understanding? What of those of us formed on the other side of the colonial divide, and whose national imaginary has become so profoundly nostalgic for the days when 'Britain was . . . the nation that had built an Empire and ruled a quarter of the world'?[30]

Something of the utopian excitement, the manic triumphalism of a boyhood adventure magically transferred to the real world, characterized the national-popular mobilization that sustained the Falklands-Malvinas War. Without seeking to reduce the complex determinations of that conflict to a simple matter of identity-politics, I want to suggest that this mobilization depended upon narratives whose psychic charge tapped the childhood bases of subjectivity in generations brought up on either the national heroics of the Second World War or the imperial epic before it. It is no accident that the Falklands War, like so many others, was fought in the name of the past, in defence of an idealized value—'our way of life'—that was imagined to be under threat. The extraordinary conditions of wartime encouraged the transference, on a collective scale, of anxieties and fears of destruction and loss that might otherwise have had no occasion to manifest. The idealizations recalled in defence against them were familiar, recognizable forms from the national imaginary: brave and righteous soldier heroes who fought the good fight against their moral inferiors, under a leader who, although disturbingly a woman, was closely identified with Churchill, the great masculine protector. At this psychic level, the Falklands-Malvinas War was conditional upon the condensation of national and colonial imaginaries that occurred during and after the Second World War, and would have been unimaginable without it. However much we might wish that the national past would cease to haunt us, soldier heroes like these will keep on returning, until such time as we can face the conflicts and contradictions of our position in the contemporary world more realistically.

Notes

1. See P. Wollen, 'Do Children Really Need Toys?', M. Hoyles (ed.), *Changing Childhood,* Writers and Readers, 1979.

2. See M. Klein, 'Personification in the Play of Children', *Contributions to Psycho-Analysis 1921-45,* Hogarth Press/Institute of Psycho-Analysis, 1948.

3. For a study of the impact of power relations upon the recognition of children by parents, see V. Walkerdine, 'Video Replay: Families, Films and Fantasies', in *Schoolgirl Fictions,* Verso, 1990.

4. M. Cohen, 'Gender Rules OK?', in Hoyles, *Changing Childhood,* p. 182.

5. In workshop discussions of earlier drafts of this chapter, a surprising number of women remembered girlhood desires in the 1950s and 1960s to 'be a cowboy', and their thwarting, for no other reason than that they were girls, as a traumatic moment of misrecognition. Exclusions of this kind may become part of the taken-for-granted order of things for boys.

6. The following analysis is derived from a more detailed account of boy culture in and out of school, in G. Dawson, 'Soldier Heroes and Adventure Narratives: Case Studies in English Masculine Identities From the Victorian Empire to Post-Imperial Britain', doctoral thesis, University of Birmingham, 1991, pp. 473-91.

7. I have been influenced here by Paul Willis's work on the cultures of masculinity among older boys and young adults. See P. Willis, *Learning to Labour: How Working Class Kids Get Working Class Jobs,* Saxon House, Farnborough, 1977; 'Male School Counterculture', in Open University (U203), *The State and Popular Culture One,* Open University, Milton Keynes, 1982.

8. These classic themes of boy culture—involving a transplanting of the Crusoe story from Empire to English rural neighbourhood—are explored in B. B.'s children's story, *Brendon Chase,* Ernest Benn, 1968. I am grateful to Bob West for sharing and analysing his memories of 'Harding's Wood' with the Popular Memory Group during our autobiographical work together.

9. The history of childhood suggests that its vaunted freedoms have always been closely circumscribed by class and gender inequalities. See Hoyles, *Changing Childhood;* S. Firestone, *The Dialectic of Sex: The Case For Feminist Revolution,* Paladin, St Albans, 1972, pp. 73-102; L. Davidoff and C. Hall, *Family Fortunes: Men and Women of the English Middle Class 1780-1850,* Hutchinson, 1987, pp. 343-8, 385-8, 403-5. With the increasing perception of dangers posed to unsupervised children in public spaces in the 1980s and 1990s, it seems likely that the freedom of independent mobility enjoyed by children is currently undergoing a further historical shift.

10. There is some documentary evidence of this in school reports, which had once worried about me as a classroom 'daydreamer', but now registered my energetic participation in most activities at school.

11. See Chapter 2, pp. 41-2 and note 40 above.

12. See the analyses of 'masculine' and 'feminine' romance in J. Batsleer, T. Davies, R. O'Rourke, C. Weedon, *Rewriting English: The Cultural Politics of Gender and Class,* Methuen, 1985, pp. 70-105; and my summary in Chapter 3, pp. 63-4 above.

13. See A. Marwick, *British Society since 1945,* Penguin, Harmondsworth, 1982, pp. 114-85.

14. C. S. Forester, *The Happy Return,* Penguin, Harmondsworth, 1951; *A Ship of the Line,* Michael Joseph, 1938; and *Flying Colours,* Penguin, Harmondsworth, 1951. For Forester's debt to G. A. Henty, see J. M. MacKenzie, *Propaganda and Empire: the Manipulation of British Public Opinion, 1880-1960,* Manchester University Press, Manchester, 1984, p. 220.

15. Cf. the use of martial rank to symbolize the internal world and its conflicts in the naval officer's dream quoted at the head of Part IV above; and the significance of rank in both adventure stories and my play-fantasies, Chapter 9, pp. 246, 251, 254 above.

16. Forester, *Ship of the Line,* pp. 38-9.

17. ibid., p. 39. All these themes can be found ibid., pp. 7-20.

18. C. S. Forester, *Lord Hornblower,* Penguin, Harmondsworth, 1964.

19. See *Ship of the Line,* pp. 8, 42-3; C. S. Forester, *Hornblower and the Atropos,* Companion Bookclub edition, no date, pp. 34-50; C. S. Forester, *Hornblower and the Hotspur,* Penguin, Harmondsworth, 1968, pp. 5-26.

20. See the contrast established in, for example, *Ship of the Line,* pp. 26-39.

21. Forester also wrote *Nelson: A Biography,* Bodley Head, 1929—a further instance of the intertwining of biographical and fictional narratives that has interested me throughout this book.

22. For the counter-culture in Britain, see E. Nelson, *The British Counter-Culture 1966-73: A Study of the Underground Press,* Macmillan, 1989; D. Glover, 'Utopia and Fantasy in the Late 1960s', in C. Pawling (ed.), *Popular Fiction and Social Change,* Macmillan, 1984, pp. 185-211. Among its key texts were H. Hesse, *Steppenwolf,* Penguin, Harmondsworth, 1965; H. Hesse, *The Glass Bead Game,* Penguin Books, 1972; J. R. R. Tolkien, *The Lord of the Rings,* George Allen & Unwin, 1968.

23. For feminism and the counter-culture, see J. Mitchell, *Women's Estate,* Penguin, Harmondsworth, 1971; R. Morgan, 'Goodbye to All That', in J. C. Albert and S. E. Albert (eds), *The Sixties Papers: Documents of a Rebellious Decade,* Prae-

ger, New York, 1984; M. Wandor (ed.), *The Body Politics: Writings from the Women's Liberation Movement in Britain 1969-72,* Stage 1, 1972. For Lennon, see H. Kureishi, 'Boys Like Us', *The Guardian* (Weekend supplement), 2-3 Nov. 1991, pp. 4-7. For Bowie, Bolan and the 'gender-bending' styles of 1970s glamrock, see D. Hebdige, *Subculture: The Meaning of Style,* Methuen, 1979. The phrase 'playpower' was used by Richard Neville, an editor of the underground magazine, *Oz,* to describe an alternative to the work ethic governing 'straight society'. Neville became one of my new heroes during the famous 'Oz Trial' in summer 1971, when he and the other editors were charged with conspiracy to corrupt the public morals. I followed developments on television, and was scandalized when Neville's hair was forcibly cut while he was on remand. See R. Neville, *Playpower,* Paladin, St Albans, 1971; and T. Palmer, *Trials of Oz,* Blond & Briggs, 1971.

24. For the peace movement, including opposition to the Vietnam War, see C. Harman, *The Fire Last Time: 1968 and After,* Bookmarks, 1988.

25. A. Maclean, *The Guns of Navarone,* Fontana, 1959; T. Leary, *The Politics of Ecstasy,* Paladin, St Albans, 1969.

26. See Chapter 2, pp. 43-4 above.

27. See Chapter 9, pp. 243-4 above.

28. See Dawson, 'Soldier Heroes', pp. 481-4, for examples.

29. Ngũgĩ wa Thiong'o, 'Ambivalent Feelings about Biggles', *The Guardian,* 13 Aug. 1992. For an ideological analysis of Biggles, see B. Dixon, *Catching Them Young 2: Political Ideas in Children's Fiction,* Pluto, 1977, pp. 105-10.

30. See Margaret Thatcher, Speech to a Rally at Cheltenham Racecourse, 3 July 1982, discussed in Chapter 1. . . .

Marilyn C. Wesley (essay date 2003)

SOURCE: Wesley, Marilyn C. "Lacanian Westerns: Richard Ford's *Rock Springs* and Cormac McCarthy's *Blood Meridian.*" In *Violent Adventure: Contemporary Fiction by American Men,* pp. 62-80. Charlottesville: University of Virginia Press, 2003.

[*In the following excerpt, Wesley explores two novels—Ford's* Rock Springs *and McCarthy's* Blood Meridian—*as works that challenge the formulaic Western tradition by focusing on its psychological underpinnings in family drama.*]

The Western adventure occurs at a special point in the emergence of "American civilization." Previous "savagery and lawlessness" are threatened by an "advancing wave of law and order" but retain enough power "to pose a momentarily significant challenge" according to Cawelti (*Six-Gun Mystique* 65). As a result, the hero of Western adventure is poised between the competing alternatives of East and West, cast as justice and outlawry. In the traditional Western narrative, he manages to negotiate a changing ideological landscape by dramatizing appealing aspects of both binary terms. He is frequently called upon to defend nascent justice by using the violence practiced by the outlaw, and much of his popular appeal is a result of his ability to support the morality associated with the bonds of community while practicing the transgressive individuality attributed to the bandit. Enjoying this intermediate status between the responsibility of the socialized adult and the freedom of the unruly child, the Western hero is, regardless of age, a successful version of the archetypal boy.

Contemporary texts by Richard Ford and Cormac McCarthy, however, expose the psychological and social irresolution of the Western genre. In stories set in the Western middle ground between boyhood and manhood, *Rock Springs* (1987) and *Blood Meridian* (1985) use male violence as theme and form to portray the failure of masculine development. Whereas Tobias Wolff and Pinckney Benedict expose the predicament of the young man unable to complete his development because of the absence of appropriate Freudian fathers, the boys in *Rock Springs* and *Blood Meridian* are stalled in an emotional position that does not anticipate patriarchal empowerment. Overwhelmed by the inefficacy or the sheer destructiveness of the violence they encounter, the protagonists of these narratives may be understood through their attachments to the integrative projection of childhood that Jacques Lacan has theorized as the Imaginary mother. In Ford's text this preoccupation suggests the developmental impossibility facing individual young men, while McCarthy employs this theme to challenge the assumptions of national myth.[1]

"A Border Between Two Nothings"

The title of Richard Ford's collection of short stories, *Rock Springs,* the name of a working-class town in Montana, places them within the narrative space of the Western, the genre "defined by its setting" (Cawelti, *Six-Gun Mystique* 62). In a modern age bereft of either genuine wilderness or promising institutions, Ford's stories recast the Western drama as a point in male development, the perceptual predicament of a young man transversing the border-state between idealizations of a mother's affectionate integrity and a father's constitutive violence. Whatever the protagonist's actual age and circumstance, the focus is the boy's negotiation of the issues this position generates. Like the traditional Western hero, Ford's composite boy wants to put his violent heritage in the service of an emergent civilization, but he never manages to balance the gendered divergences experienced in his relations with mothers and fathers, and the memories that comprise the stories replay moments when his dilemma is most evident.

The title of the story "Great Falls," the name of another Montana town, invokes the symbolic Western location to establish the dramatis personae of *Rock Springs*: the father, the mother, and the boy. In this story, the father, Jack Russell, is an airplane mechanic, a fisherman, a duck hunter, and a part-time professional poacher. As his son, Jackie, recalls, he could "catch a hundred fish" during a "weekend" (30) and a "hundred ducks" in twenty seconds (31)—illegal game that he sold to a local caterer. Jack's proficiency in slaughter connects him to the Western ideology of male violence as a means to masculine empowerment, but the flaw in this position is intuited by his son: The "true thing" he knows about his father is that he didn't "know limits" (30). Ford's major thematic preoccupation is the boy's alignment to the problem of "limits" defined through the gendered roles of his parents. In the action of the story, the father has brought Jackie back early from hunting to confront the man with whom the mother leaves the marriage. The father comes near to killing Woody, the other man, but finally does not do it. As he explains to his rival, he would like to find a way to "hurt" him but cannot think of any and feels "helpless" as a result (42).

The key to the deficiency of Ford's men is precisely this kind of choice. They understand that violence is expected, so choosing the pacifistic option, accepting moral "limits," typically unmans them. The father in "Great Falls" wants to know if Woody considers him a "fool" (42). Abdicating the masculine resolution of a Western "showdown" is also a motif in one other story. In "Sweethearts," Arlene's first husband, a man who does transgress lawful limits, stops by to have Arlene and her second husband drive him to jail to begin a three year sentence for issuing bad checks. Russell, the second husband, cares for his young daughter and makes breakfast for Bobby, the first husband. For the first three pages of the story, gender role reversal and ambiguous pronouns make it unclear as to whether the narrator, who is eventually revealed as the second husband, is a man or a woman. His maternal care does, however, place Russell's consideration as the antithesis of Bobby's lawlessness. At the end of the story, outside the jail, Bobby reveals that he has a gun and wants to kill Arlene, but a shoot-out with the watching deputy is avoided by Russell's deflection of the Western script Bobby is trying to set into motion. Similarly, in "Fireworks," the protagonist thwarts possible conflict with a competitor by simply refusing to meet with his wife's former husband. The men in *Rock Springs* try, usually

without much success, to maintain effective limits, because when the expected male confrontation does occur, the outcome is disastrous. In "Optimists" the boy sees his father slay a provocateur with one deadly punch, an act that also destroys the family relationship. Male violence in these stories is presented as unresolvable masculine dilemma: To avoid violent action is to be "helpless" and unmanly, but to act violently, as in the modern anthology *Stories for Men,* is destructive rather than constructive.

Unlike the father, whom the son understands, in the *Rock Springs* stories the mother remains an attractive mystery throughout. In "Great Falls," for example, the mother is effectively lost to the boy. On the day after she has left with Woody, she arranges a meeting to say good-bye to her son. He perceives her abandonment as a turning point that precipitates the uncertainty that characterizes him. Although everything may be "fixed by staying," to leave and not return "hazards life" because things can get out of control (48).

"*Great* Falls," certainly an ironic superlative title in view of the father's helplessness and the boy's loss, concludes with a series of questions about the pivotal event that the narrator has never been able to answer. He wonders why his father would not allow his mother to come home, why the other man would risk his life for a woman he apparently doubted, and why his mother had left. Although Jackie had never been able to answer the questions, their enigma might be approached, he suggests, through the philosophic observation that concludes the story. There is some "low-life . . . coldness" in everyone, a "helplessness" that prevents an understanding of life and that makes people behave like wary "animals—watchful, unforgiving, without patience or desire." And it is this destructive condition that turns "existence" into a "border between two nothings" (49).

One of these "nothings" between which the psyche of the boy is suspended is evidently a missing mother. In eight of the ten stories of the collection, an absent mother is a fact of life, and that primary absence is a condition the protagonists can never fully come to terms with. Besides the loss of the mother reported directly in "Great Falls" and "Optimists," in "Rock Springs" and "Sweethearts" the father abdicates traditional aspects of masculinity to care for a mother-abandoned child; in "Children" both the boy narrator and his foil have been left behind by mothers; in "Going to the Dogs" the focal character, whose wife has left him, seeks comforting from two women willing to mother him; in "Winterkill," in which feminine solicitude is a more important value than sexuality, the story begins with reference to the narrator's impossible project of going home to his mother; and in "Communist" the forty-one-year-old narrator recalls a troubling event when he was sixteen years old, which he continues to ponder, noting that he and his mother didn't ever really talk again (235). In the gendered terms of the Western genre, the woman associated with the civilizing community that establishes limits in the wild West is simply unavailable.

In six of the ten stories a man is out of work, and in "Optimists" the pressure of the imminent loss of the father's railroad job is the underlying motivation for the murderous response the story recounts. Thus, the other defining negation affecting the boy is the father's characteristic economic marginalization, which makes his legendary capacity to assert power through violence actually ineffectual. This failure is treated most extensively in "Communist," the final story in the collection. In the story, the deceased father is replaced by Glen Baxter, a Vietnam vet, who takes the boy and his mother, Aileen, to hunt Canada geese. In retrospect, the boy, Les, recognizes his first hunt as a kind of initiation, a realization that "something important" would "happen" to him on a "day" he would never forget (219). What happens is that at the very point when Les is being inducted into the male ideology of violent power, the polarized meaning of the masculine and feminine ethical positions are enacted for him by Glen and his mother. Aileen, who is disturbed by the hunt because of her objection to killing the "special birds" who "mate for life" (219), is eventually captivated by the beauty Glen's expedition has made it possible for her to witness, the migrating geese turning silver in the setting sun (228).

Using his dead father's shotgun, Les proves a proficient hunter, a capability that reminds him of other lessons his father had provided through teaching him to box: to "tighten" his fists, to "strike" from his shoulder, never to hit while "backing up," to snap his fist inward, to hold his "chin low" and, to move toward a fighter as he falls in order to be in position to punch him "again." Most significant is the instruction not to shut his eyes when he is hitting an opponent in the face and "causing damage," because he will need this sight to "encourage" himself (226).

This education in pugilistic violence is supposed to instill masculine competence and clear-sighted evaluation, but that ideal is annulled by the problem of violence as unnecessary destruction and the absence of "limits" introduced by the boy's description of the father in "Great Falls." This problem finds expression in "Communist" when the mother discovers that Glen has shot a last goose by "mistake" and that it is still swimming wounded. She demands that Glen finish it off because that's the "rule" (230). Glen insists that it "doesn't matter" (231). In "The Short Happy Life of Francis Macomber," Ernest Hemingway memorably coded the uncompleted kill as a failure of masculine potency. To this allusion Ford adds the onus of the failure of human sympathy. The already troubled relationship of the

couple ends with the mother's accusation that because her lover does not possess a "heart," there is really "nothing to love" in him (231).

"Communist" opposes two Western ideals: male violence, which signifies an absence of rules, and female love, which portends the possibility of moral integrity. The absence of masculine limits produces the killer's irresponsibility. But the incident also implies the failure of violence to produce genuine empowerment. When Glen comments on the beauty of the geese and observes to Les that he doesn't know why he shoots them, Les admits a definitive confusion: "Maybe there's nothing else to do with them" (228). That is, for the adult male, violence, the only option, is evidently ineffective. Already implicated in the violence of such "helpless" fathers, Ford's boys also recognize the necessary morality assigned to absent mothers and long for an apparently impossible combination that includes the failed possibilities of each.

This contradictory attempt to retain the imagined integrity of the unavailable mother while practicing the destructive violence of the ineffectual father is staged as oedipal drama in the story "Children," a title that suggests the truncation of masculine development as a consequence of this dilemma. The young male narrator and his boxing pal, Claude, participate in a scheme to keep secret from his mother the fact that Claude's father has a lover. Sherman, a railroad man of Indian blood who has twice been to prison for brawling and theft, has been sleeping with the young girl at a local motel (71). When the boys take her fishing, the story intimates that she may come to harm. After a confrontation with his father, Claude says that he thinks they ought to "kill her . . . just to piss him off" (75). The father-son rivalry culminates in Claude's sexual connection with the girl who belongs to his father, but the possible violence is deflected. At the crucial instant when Claude thrusts his knife at the girl, ostensibly for her to use to remove the hook from a fish, he is excited by two possibilities: that they could kill her and "Who'd know about it?" or that she could kill him when he gives her the knife (92). She averts the crisis by calmly tossing Claude's knife into the creek, taking off her clothing, and having intercourse with him.

Claude exemplifies the boy who is beginning to follow the trajectory of Freud's Oedipus complex, in which fear of castration by the powerful father causes the boy to renounce his attachment to his mother and bury his resentment toward his father in order to gain masculine authority on his father's terms. If his son gives him any "trouble," Sherman warns, "I'll break you up" (77). The father's implicit transference of access to the girl (Claude asks if his father is "giving" her to them as a "reward" [74]) signals the benefits available at the conclusion of this negotiation. But the story also introduces an alternative pattern. The narrator's relationship with the girl, Lucy, takes on the features of what E. Ann Kaplan calls "romantic" love rather than genital conquest. While Claude fishes to demonstrate his masculine prowess, the narrator and the girl sit together on a blanket to share confidences and a gentle kiss.

Lucy's significance may be understood through Jacques Lacan's interpretation of Freud's account of masculine development. During the Lacanian oedipal process, the boy loses not the mother but the illusions of coherent selfhood that the mother has fostered by her nurturance of the child through the stage of identity Lacan calls "Imaginary," although the desire for this fundamental integrity always remains an important component of the Lacanian unconscious. According to both Freud and Lacan, the provocation for the oedipal passage is the realization of the mother's "castration," which for Lacan is the understanding of her lack of power within the social system. However, the exclusive relationship of mother and child temporarily excludes the power arrangements the father's presence introduces. Therefore a competent female can lend meaning to the boy's projections of wholeness, and thus it is the "phallic" mother of his infancy rather than the castrated mother figure of his later experience who is the object of the preoedipal boy's yearnings.[2] Lucy, who simply takes the symbolic phallus Claude is trying to claim and invalidates its authority, enacts the role of empowering mother to the narrator, who is fixated on the elusive fantasy of maternal integration.

In her analysis of the narrative patterns of rock videos, Kaplan defines the type that corresponds to the preoccupations of Ford's boy narrators as "romantic" because of the "yearning quality" depicted toward a love relationship: "The address is to the absent or loved one, or the video plays out the pain of separation" (59). For Kaplan the appeal of such productions derives from their representation of the Lacanian "transition between the pre-Oedipal and the phallic phases" (94), the intermediate position of the narrator of "Children," who does not share his friend's phallic pretensions.

After the boys have helped the girl get a bus out of town, Claude brags that he is "strong" and "invincible" and that he doesn't have anything on his "conscience." Although Claude's egotistic claims suggest he has not fully experienced the dissolution of self concomitant to the Lacanian Symbolic order, and his denial of "conscience" indicates he has not realized the superego that concludes oedipalization as Freud has defined it, he evidently aspires to the only masculinity structured by the generic Western—that of the violent male. The narrator, in contrast, is understandably leery of a paternal disorganization founded on ineffectual violence. Not preoccupied with Claude's illusions of genital conquest, he describes himself regretfully as lacking the consolida-

tion of even a specious phallic identification: "What was *I* good for? What was terrible about me?" (98).

The boy's longing for the absent phallic mother who is capable of supplying the limits the father's violence lacks is the characteristic concern of Richard Ford's *Rock Springs* stories. The title, with its connotations of both masculine obdurateness and feminine nurturance, may symbolize this desire. Perhaps the appeal of the oedipal allegory found in the formula Western is that the hero—the cowboy as the American boy—can participate in the abrogation of limits, the unlimited power promised through male identification, at the same time he supports the communal creation of civilization by the feminized order of the settlement. But unlike Freud's oedipal young man, the cowboy hero never has to choose. Like The Lone Ranger, after saving the town, never fully identified, he can get back on his beautiful phallic horse and ride away. Themes of preoedipal longing signal the need for order in the face of adult male violence in *Rock Springs*, but unlike traditional Westerns, Richard Ford's stories recount the costs of such holding actions in his protagonists' lives. "I think of the characters . . . as being rather unfixed, I think of them as changeable, provisional, unpredictable, decidedly unwhole," the author confided in an interview (Lyons 43). The narrator of "Children" further articulates this sense of displacement and incompletion: "Outside," he explains, is an "empty" "place" that didn't even seem to "exist," somewhere you could occupy for a "long time and never find a thing you admired or loved or hoped to keep. And we were unnoticeable in it" (98).

This quotation conveys a preoccupation with "lack" within the project of masculine development that Ford dramatizes and Lacan theorizes. Lacan's formulations relate to the complex negations of Ford's family drama, because unlike the social scientists and psychologists . . . ., Lacan, like Ford, problematizes the concept of developmental progression. Nevertheless, there are important differences. The Lacanian subject is shaped by two contiguous occurrences. The first, the Imaginary, is the intuition of an integrated personality, an illusory selfhood that is shattered by the second, the Symbolic, the realization of subjectivity within the social order imposed by linguistic practice. Although Lacan narrates these conditions as the chronological events of infantile experience he borrows from Freudian theory, they are conceived as inseparable and permanent conditions of the human psyche. That is, for Lacan, culture and community are not, as in the Western, projected in terms of feminized spaces to be loved and left. Inevitably conveyed through the structure of language, they are the foundations of paternal power, which in Western adventure is supposed to be generated by male violence.

Unlike both the Freudian father and the Lacanian paternal signifier, which derive their authority from culture and language, the Western male archetype is defined outside the feminized community through aggressive intervention. Although communal order with its accompanying loss of phenomenal identity is the inevitable fate of the Lacanian subject, the generic Western structures the failure of socialization. The revelation of that failure is the project of both *Rock Springs* and *Blood Meridian.* And if the development of the young male is apparently doubtful within the negations of Ford's family relationships, it is patently impossible within the phantasmal parental void of Cormac McCarthy's novel. *Blood Meridian,* by situating its unnamed protagonist in a field of phenomenal saturation, exposes asocial violence as a ruinous basis for both personal manhood and communal integrity.

THE MASCULINE IMAGINARY

What happens when a boy is reared by wolves? In the myth of the founding of Rome, a society of war and law emerges, but McCarthy's *Blood Meridian; or The Evening Redness in the West,* a tale of war without law, tells the story of a boy who joins an itinerant band of wolfish scalp hunters,[3] whose predatory violence does not presage any kind of civil order. McCarthy's Western novel, based on historical accounts of the Texas-Mexico border in the decades before the Civil War, does not present the Western hero in the generic role of mediator between the "civilization" of the town and the "wilderness" of the outlaw (Cawelti, *Adventure* 193).[4] The central issue of the traditional Western, according to Cawelti, is the victory of the "good violence" exercised by the hero in defense of emergent culture over the "bad violence" perpetrated by "villains" with "evil aims" (*Six-Gun Mystique* 15). *Blood Meridian,* however, is a different kind of Western that repudiates constructive violence.[5] In it there are only villains, and theme and form establish the awful preponderance of "bad violence" as the dominant feature of a historical period of American conquest through a narrative of boyhood staged as the Lacanian Imaginary without the concurrent Symbolic order.[6]

McCarthy's revised Western excises any source of moral authority through the enigmatic figure of "the judge" derived both from the stock Western character and from actual history. Judge Roy Bean is the figurative grandfather of this motif. Having appointed himself justice of the peace in 1882, he held court in his Texas saloon. A convicted rustler as well as the only "law west of the Pecos," he represents not only the difficult struggle to establish law in a new territory but the contradictions of the concept of "law" in a lawless region.

In "'What kind of indians was them?': Some Historical Sources in Cormac McCarthy's *Blood Meridian,*" John Emil Sepich reports that McCarthy's character was based on the real Judge Holden described in Samuel Chamberlain's account of Captain John Joel Glanton's gang of bounty hunters: "[A] cooler blooded villain never went unhung; he stood six feet six in his moccasins" and had a face "destitute of all hair." A speaker of many languages and an expert in botany, geology, and mineralogy, "the best educated man in Northern Mexico," the actual judge was, paradoxically, also the "ravisher" of children (Sepich 125-26).

In addition to exaggerating the judge's bizarre appearance, McCarthy mystifies his combined violence and erudition. What Chamberlain calls an "appetite" for "blood" (Sepich 125) McCarthy styles as seeming capricious viciousness, which is really fundamental philosophy. In one instance the fictional judge purchases a pair of pups from a ragged child only to immediately toss them into the river. Perhaps the most appalling example occurs after white raiders harvested the "long locks" of the Indians to leave the dead "rawskulled" in "bloody cauls" (157). When the judge discovers one living Apache child among the mutilated tribe, he carries the half-burned boy before him on his saddle. Two days later the judge is observed dandling the child on his knee one minute and apparently murdering and scalping it in the next. The destruction of such obvious victims as the dogs and the Apache boy indicate that the judge's brutality is motivated by more than the economic reward offered for Indian scalps.[7] To McCarthy's judge, murder is the instrument of effective "ritual," which always involves the "letting of blood," and death is merely "agency" (329).[8]

The judge's blood rituals are attempts to define himself through the assertion of power over everyone and everything else, which also find expression in his scientific observations of the Western landscape. The judge's constant measuring, sketching, recording, and collecting supports the ambition of total control. Because "nature" can subdue mankind, he seeks its subjugation. Only when every "entity is routed out" and exposed to him, he explains, will he become "suzerain of the earth" (198). Toward that end he must control all "pockets of autonomous life" (199). What abides beyond his "knowledge," he declares, "exists without" his "consent" (198). To attain the ultimate power to which he aspires, "nothing" must be allowed to exist on earth except through his "dispensation" (199).

Imperial Eyes, Mary Louise Pratt's landmark analysis of the travel discourses of European colonialism, equates eighteenth-century studies of natural history with the imperialist exploitation of the very territories the naturalists were exploring, often in the same expeditions as soldiers and merchants. Despite so-called scientific objectivity, natural history functioned, she charges, as an adjunct to imperialism by itemizing the exploitable wealth of a "new" region and by introducing the pattern of acquisitive knowledge that made projects of global economic power imaginable. The portrayal of the judge crossing the "virgin" West with his journals and specimens harks back to a type that precedes the cowboy. He is the fictive American heir of the European naturalists whose totalizing descriptions helped convert world into empire,[9] but whereas their domination served the economic expansion of the home society, his serves the egoistic aggrandizement of the homeless self.[10]

The judge's narcissistic naturalism has parallels with Linnaen science and Lacanian psychology. Linnaeus, Pratt argues, arranged all plant life through its conformity to or difference from twenty-six "basic configurations" (25). "One by one the planet's life forms were to be drawn out of the tangled threads of their life surroundings and rewoven into European-based patterns of global unity and order. The (lettered, male, European) eye that held the system could familiarize ('naturalize') new sights/sites immediately upon contact, by incorporating them into the language of the system" (Pratt 31).

Linnaeus's system, as Pratt interprets it, is similar to Lacan's theory of the Symbolic order, into which the young man is incorporated through the oedipal process. Both Linnaen taxonomy and the Lacanian Symbolic are hierarchical regimes patterned after the similarities and differences structuring language, and both operate to reproduce the authority of the dominant male class. But the judge, separate from any order except that of his own devising, a burlesque of Linnaen science, is also a parody of Lacan's Law of the Father. According to James M. Mellard, "The Symbolic order, like language, permits human relations to occur on a plane of mediation that is exemplified in the figure of the judge, the ruler, the arbitrator, the authority" (17). Yet McCarthy's judge is the antithesis of the social mediator. Because the judge has no source save his own will, his titular name is in fact a mockery of the masculine system of Symbolic authority. His self-serving violence, which assigns all externals to the illusion of his own absolute power, and his strange reciprocal relation with the boy demonstrate a more complex position in the male maturational drama.

Just as the judge's private desires differ from the public effect of natural science, the protagonist's experience with the judge differs significantly from the achievement of Symbolic order. Lacan dramatizes a boy's entry into culture as the emergence from the private world of the mother into the public realm of the father. But in McCarthy's novel the maternal solicitude that lends support to Imaginary integration does not exist, and a paternal order independent of egotistical will is inconceivable.[11] *Blood Meridian* begins with the significant fact that the boy's mother died at his birth in 1833, and his father, a besotted former schoolmaster, does not even teach him to read or write. In these details McCarthy thwarts the two rudimentary necessities for Lacanian maturation—a supportive mother figure and a father figure who embodies the communal system inscribed in language.

In McCarthy's novel, the figuration of the asocial judge denies the possibility of his Symbolic representation of the Father, the Lacanian personification of the patriarchal system of culture. The absence of a mother for whom the boy can imagine a romantic attachment precludes the interpretation of the judge as the "imaginary father,"[12] whose competition for maternal relation institutes oedipalization. Because he displays the control that the unformed protagonist requires, the judge is cast instead as a grotesque projection of the phallic mother. Indeed, the judge in *Blood Meridian* plays a phallic mother run amuck. The novel depicts what happens when, rather than an integrating mother, a castrating father operates as the dyadic authorizing figure of the boy's mirror stage, for such is the role of the judge in the psychic life of the immature protagonist known only as "the kid." As a result, the judge and the kid are locked into a circular relationship of dangerous dualism, from which the boy gains neither the sense of personal integration of the normative Imaginary phase nor the induction into social regulation of the Symbolic order.

The most important episode of the Lacanian Imaginary is the mirror stage, in which the protection of the mother inspires the child's vision of himself as complete, an identification symbolized by his image in the mirror—a representation of self that appears whole, but is only an ideal created through the agency of reflection.[13] Based on dualistic and unstable mirroring, the scopic events of this period are experienced as repetitious similarities rather than definitive differences. In *Blood Meridian* this destabilizing reflection is characteristic of the strange relationship between the judge and the boy.[14] Although there is no communication acknowledged between them until the end, they observe each other throughout: "The kid was watching the judge" (79), and "Watching him" across the dim and smoky room "was the judge" (325).

At the conclusion of the book, the boy and the judge finally speak to each other about the effects of their participation in reciprocal and destructive mirroring. Watching the boy, the judge asks if it was always the kid's belief that if he didn't "speak" he wouldn't "be recognized." Ignoring the kid's claim that the judge *had* "seen" him, the judge explains that although he had "recognized" the boy the time first he "saw" him, the kid was a "disappointment" to him and remained so. "Even so at the last I find you here with me," he concludes. But the boy demurs: "I ain't with you" (328).

For Mellard "the Imaginary order is evidenced in the subject's awareness of 'two-ness,' of others caught in either a narcissistic or an aggressive relation with the ego of the subject" (28). The dyadic relation of the judge and the boy is both narcissistic from the point of view of the boy ("You seen me") and aggressive from the perspective of the judge ("You were a disappointment to me"). "Aggression is produced in response to the mirror stage" through the "rivalry over which is the self and which is the other, which the ego and which the replica," as Jane Gallop explains (62). For Lacan, "Aggressivity is the correlative tendency of a mode of identification that we call narcissistic," and this inevitable aggression "determines the formal structure of the ego and the register of entities characteristic of his world" (*Écrits* 16). Thus the threatening mirroring of the boy and the judge represents relationship in a world dominated by the need of the ego to secure its power. Nevertheless, according to Gallop, "Lacan's writings contain an implicit ethical imperative to break the mirror, an imperative to disrupt the imaginary in order to reach 'the symbolic'" (59). McCarthy's "psychodramatization" (Lacan, *Écrits* 9), however, denies the possibility of a culturally constructed revision of the extreme egotism represented by the judge.

As Lacan defines it, the appeal of the scopic drive that dominates the Imaginary situation is that it "most completely . . . eludes castration" (*Fundamental Concepts* 78). That is, the boy seeks the supportive reflection of identification sustained through the gaze of the mother in order to counter the "castration" from illusory integration threatened by the father. In Lacan's revision of Freud's oedipal story, the threatened castration by the "father" representing culture forces the boy into the Symbolic order of definitions and laws that contradict his false sense of personal value. But McCarthy's vicious judge, the opposite of the integrating mother, is also an inversion of the potentially castrating father. In Freud's description, it is the threat, not the act, of castration that moves the boy out of narcissistic dualism into the system of social authority internalized as the superego. Yet the judge is himself stuck in the mirror stage of aggressive narcissism and has no law to transmit, so when the boy begins to differentiate himself from their mirroring relation, the judge makes good on the threat of paternal castration by apparently killing him. The judge destroys what he cannot control after the kid makes two significant moves away from scopic reciprocity near the end of the novel.

First, despite the dominant violence of his surroundings, the boy futilely attempts to fashion his own moral order, as evidenced by his promise to aid the mother figure he discovers among a company of murdered penitents. Coming upon their mangled corpses, he spies what appears to be an old woman at prayer. Without recognizing that she has been dead a long time, the kid pledges to save her. The second deadly move occurs during the interview with the judge when the boy asserts his separation: "I ain't with you." In the Imaginary register of the violent judge, those "not with him" are against him, and what he cannot incorporate as reflection of his own ego he systematically destroys.

As the boy's death implies, the emotional extremes of the Western Imaginary are not in *Blood Meridian* a preliminary to any kind of social order. The anonymous kid evidently dies without ever being named; that is, without ever assuming his place within the Name-of-the-Father of the Symbolic organization of language and community.[15] McCarthy's work suggests that pervasive violence begets only violence. Without a paternal order to move into, the kid's attempt "to break the mirror" cannot result in his entrance into the communal salvation he naively promises to the effigy of the absent mother.

THE VIOLENT SUBLIME

The boy's developmental failure makes *Blood Meridian* an antioedipal parable. Although it does not endorse the anarchic supervention of social regimens that Gilles Deleuze and Felix Guattari theorize in *Anti-Oedipus*,[16] the novel's form inscribes an eternal Imaginary through repeatedly enacting the undifferentiated pulsations of experience they endorse. Repudiating the rising action and climax of the conventional novel, McCarthy's tour de force endlessly replicates free movement across vast prairies, hostile deserts, and dangerous mountains. And his rhetorical intensity simulates for the reader the protagonist's peculiar psychological predicament.

"They rode . . ." is the formulaic commencement of countless paragraphs and chapter divisions in *Blood Meridian*,[17] and, as in the following example, it establishes the rhythmic metonomy that organizes the novel: "They rode" through windy mountain passes and forests of pine, the "shoeless mules slaloming" through dry grass and pine needles, through the shaded "coulees" of northern "slopes" with their light dustings of snow. "They rode" through the fallen leaves of dark trails and "they rode" through the narrow passes "shingled" with ice. Crossing a high ridge at sundown where wild doves rocketed "down the wind" to veer between the horses and drop "into the gulf below," "they rode" into a forest of dark firs, the "little Spanish ponies sucking" at the weak "air" (136).

Even this condensation of a lengthy passage demonstrates the poetic effects Longinus is assumed to have described as "the sublime"—the audacious and passionate use of poetic language that "flashing forth at the right moment scatters everything before it like a thunderbolt." The description of nature, the rhythm, the imagery, the synaesthetic appeal to the senses, the striking diction of "slaloming" mules and ice-shingled leaves contribute to a poetic texture denoting, according to Longinus, a "plenitude" that demonstrates rhetorical "power" (77).

The effect of this sublime passage, that literally moves its characters upward, also connotes transcendence in the Romantic tradition of natural description.[18] But Mc-Carthy rescinds the transcendental promise through both structural repetition and the contravening violence that always follows description in his novel. At the very crest of the passage, Glanton, the leader of the band of outlaws, encounters a bear "with dim pig's eyes," and violent mayhem ensues. When his horse rears up, Glanton draws his gun. The horse behind him falls as the Delaware riding it struggles to regain its footing by hitting the horse's head with his fist. At this point, the bear swings toward Glanton "stunned . . . beyond reckoning, some foul gobbet dangling from its jaws and its chops dyed red with blood." When Glanton shoots the animal in the chest, it snatches the Indian off his reeling horse, meeting the next shot, the body still hanging from its bloody maw. Throughout this melee, the forest resounds with the shouts of men and the loud "whack" of their efforts to beat the "screaming" ponies into "submission." As Glanton gets ready to fire a third round into the bear's arcing shoulder, the enraged animal rolls over him, a "sea of honey colored hair" reeking of "carrion" (137).

This second passage is also sublime in its heightened effects—the precise description, the graphic imagery, the exploitation of senses—but its fullness of expression of all aspects of violence promises repetitious horror rather than climactic transcendence. The unresolvable intensity illustrated by this passage, typical of the Imaginary order, structures the entire novel. *Blood Meridian* endlessly varies the same poetic sequence of extreme sensation leading to violent actions. In the same way the judge contracts knowledge to murder, the structural pattern of the novel reduces human experience to sensational violence. This paradoxical reduction, a repeated figure that fills the whole field,[19] obliterates any other possible organization through the exhibition of obsession. And just as the sublimity of style does not lead to transcendence, the repeating pattern denies the possibility of progress.[20] For order, which depends on the differentiation of the Symbolic system, cannot be born of the endless similarity imposed by the reiterative structure of this novel. Although the sublime depiction of violence may appeal to a hunger for sensation, the replication of intensity is, in effect, cloying. In the Imaginary condition, to which identity is confined, violence leads not to meaning but to chains of endless sensation drained of significance.

McCarthy, who uses standard Western conventions in his novels of *The Border Trilogy,* at first seems to be evoking in *Blood Meridian* the cinematic sweep of the typical Western setting, with open plains and vast "snow-covered peaks" (Cawelti, *Six-Gun* 67). This definitive setting, according to Cawelti, signals the hero's "epic courage and regenerative power" (68) to destroy the old ways and secure a "settled society," action that "almost invariably requires a transcendent and heroic violence" (Cawelti, *Adventure* 193-94). But it is precisely the ideology of transcendence through a violence conceived as heroic—the illusion that the aggressiveness of the hero can install an advancing civilization—that *Blood Meridian* disputes. By representing the brutal events of a particular era, McCarthy substitutes a degrading history for a progressive myth. His allusion to a figurative Western landscape connoting promise is rescinded by the violent abridgement of signification in repetitive scenes of exploitation. The depravity of the judge, the death of the boy, and the sterility of the setting all inscribe the absence of a moral order.

Critics charge that the Edenic setting of the mythologized Old West and the idealization of the Western hero obscure the violent elimination of its native inhabitants (Jewett and Lewis 44 ff.). McCarthy's settings, however, filled with appalling historical violence, obviously reverse this omission. But they do something more. Tzvetan Todorov describes the process *Blood Meridian* turns into story: "in some remote place where the law is only vaguely acknowledged. . . . Far from central government . . . all prohibitions give way, the social link, already loosened, gives way, snaps, revealing not a primitive nature, the beast sleeping in each of us, but a modern being, one with a great future in fact, restrained by no morality and inflicting death because and when he pleases" (*Conquest* 145).

THE PSYCHOTIC WESTERN

In form and theme McCarthy's phantasmal novel dramatizes Lacanian psychosis. The kid's story enacts this condition because he experiences the inability of a father figure to embody social order ("the foreclosure of the Name-of-the-Father in the place of the Other") that "gives psychosis its essential condition" and "structure" (*Écrits* 215). As Lacan explains it, in the static situation of the psychotic, "the lack of the Name-of-the-Father in that place which, by the hole that it opens up in the signified, sets off the cascade of reshapings of the signifier from which the increasing disaster of the imaginary proceeds" (*Écrits* 217), a description that accounts well for the repeating nontranscendent structure of *Blood Meridian.* According to Lacan, psychosis exhibits "the subject's topographical regression to the mirror stage" as an instance of "a relation to the specular other . . . reduced to its fatal aspect" (*Écrits* 209), a psychological location duplicated in the retrogressive Western setting of *Blood Meridian* and its protagonist's deadly encounter with the destructive judge.

If the psychotic condition, as Lacan contends, provides the novelist with "situations [that] are his true resource" (*Écrits* 216),[21] McCarthy's novel is a stunning realization of novelistic potential. Enjoying cult status since its publication in 1985, *Blood Meridian* has already provoked much excellent commentary. To read this enigmatic and nihilistic text once more, this time in light of Lacanian theory, is useful because Lacan stresses the necessary connection between private experience and public meaning that the extraordinary exaggeration of the novel also brings into focus.

For Lacan it is the almost unimaginable failure of the institution of community as an organizing system that is the cause and content of psychosis—and, I am arguing, it is that failure that provides the central theme of McCarthy's narrative. The generic kid's inability to mature into the Western hero is rooted in a context of extreme violence, a landscape of ethical sterility presented as a place and time that contradicts a Western mythology of incipient civilization. Nothing less than the disclosure of the political unconscious of the Western genre and the romance of Western history, *Blood Meridian,* a psychotic parable of the violent past, serves as a warning to the violent present: Social value cannot develop out of personal or public aggression. McCarthy's plot and structure speak to the absence of a culture and community that model and promote genuine power in the lives of American men. Masculine maturity cannot proceed from violence, and social system does not develop out of the abrogation of communal order.[22]

Richard Ford's *Rock Springs* and Cormac McCarthy's *Blood Meridian* challenge the formula Western.[23] The Imaginary encounters of their protagonists in private relationships and public exploits uncover the defects of male violence in the developmental transaction of American boys and refuse to vindicate them through the solace of Western adventure. Ford's realism depicts in ordinary, contemporary Western life a parental failure of power and order that cannot nurture the adult development of his sonlike characters, while McCarthy's sublime re-presentation of Western history emblematizes a politics of destruction that cannot be rewritten as progress. . . .

Notes

1. See comparable studies of adaptations of the Western genre in Jane Tompkins's *West of Everything*; Paul Smith's "Eastwood Bound"; and chapter 5, "Westerns," in Roger Horrocks's *Male Myths and Icons.*

2. See Lacan, "The Meaning of the Phallus," (*Feminine* 76, 83) as to the child's initial expectation that the mother will possess the phallus. What is at issue in this scene is the boy's desire to retain this illusion. The "discovery of the castration of the mother" and the consequent loss of the illusion of integrity she authorizes in the mirror stage inaugurates the Symbolic definition of self in the binary divisions of language. See Lacan, *Écrits,* 282.

3. Wolves, a primary motif throughout *Blood Meridian,* also appear as an important symbol in *The Crossing* (1994). The central male character, also a Western boy, is introduced through his almost otherworldly experience of a wolf pack and the plot develops as an attempt to rescue a wolf.

4. See Slotkin and Drinnon for historical analysis of the violence in Western texts.

5. McCarthy told Richard B. Woodward in a 1992 interview that "there's no such thing as a life without bloodshed" and that the expectation of some kind of improvement "is a really dangerous idea" (36).

6. Horrocks reads the violence in the conventional Western as the ethical justification of imperialism (58, 77), an ideological premise that *Blood Meridian* exposes and exploits.

7. John Emil Sepich cites Ralph A. Smith's "The 'King of New Mexico' and the Doniphan Expedition" for these horrifying statistics on the outlay of one frightened Mexican town that paid a large bounty on Comanche scalps:

   > Pay as a private in the United States army at [the time of the novel] averaged about fifteen dollars a month, when bonuses were included. A group of Indian hunters averaging about fifty men and paid two hundred dollars a scalp would have to bring only four scalps into Chihuahua City in order to exceed the army's rate of pay. . . . [James] Kirker's group was known to have killed as many as two hundred Indians on a single trip, bringing in one hundred and eighty-two scalps. Taking the averages, this is sixty times more than the men would have earned in other employment. At one point Chihuahua owed James Kirker about $30,000.

   (124)

8. See Steven Shaviro on the importance of ritual in the novel.

9. See also Thomas Pughe's "Revision and Vision: Cormac McCarthy's *Blood Meridian,*" in which he interprets the figure of the judge in McCarthy's anti-Western as the "link between the barbarization of the gang and the European civilization that Lukacs associates with 'progress'" (378).

10. See also Brian Evenson's "McCarthy's Wanderers: Nomadology, Violence, and Open Country," in which he links the judge's homelessness to the practice of extreme exploitation (47).

11. See also Nell Sullivan's "Cormac McCarthy and the Text of Jouissance," which in closing suggests the centrality of a Lacanian representation of "unassuageable lack" in McCarthy's novels (122).

12. Julia Kristeva explains this Lacanian figure as the "father in individual prehistory," a "Third Party" whom the boy's Imaginary mother desires (23, 251).

13. Lacan provides this description of the normative mirror stage:

> This jubilant assumption of his specular image by the child at the *infans* stage, still sunk in his motor incapacity and nurturing dependence, would seem to exhibit in an exemplary situation the symbolic matrix in which the *I* is precipitated in a primordial form, before it is objectified in the dialectic of identification with the other, and before language restores to it, in the universal, its function as subject.
>
> This form would have to be called the Ideal-I, if we wished to incorporate it into our usual register . . . But the important point is that this form situates the agency of the ego, before its social determination, in a fictional direction.
>
> *(Écrits* 2)

14. Rick Wallach's observation of both the emphatic immaturity, "the pediatric symbolism" (127) of feature in the representation of the judge and the "troubling complementarity" of the kid and the judge (128) supports a reading of the suspension of progress and the nondifferentiation of self and other of the Imaginary stage.

15. This destructive denouement may be understood as one outcome of the condition Julia Kristeva calls "abjection." As Stephen Frosh glosses it: "The fragility of [the] early subject/object boundary is extreme, making the first motion of the subject-to-be one that can be overwhelmed, producing a state of genuine abjection, of being devoured . . . Without mediation, this is precisely what happens in the relationship between the desiring mother and the despairing child" (135).

16. See also Shaviro 145-46 on the relation of *Blood Meridian* to Deleuze and Guattari.

17. Dana Phillips also notes the repetition of this phrase: "The most often repeated sentence in *Blood Meridian*," she observes, "is 'They rode on'" (443).

18. Tompkins interprets the typical Western setting as a dramatization of psychological impulse: "The monolithic, awe-inspiring character of the landscape seems to reflect a desire for self-transcendence, an urge to join the self to something greater" (76).

19. Dee Brown's *Bury My Heart at Wounded Knee* and Michael Lesy's *Wisconsin Death Trip* employ comparable repetition of horrific pattern to the study of Western history.

20. See also Joseph Tabbi's *Postmodern Sublime: Technology and American Writing from Mailer to Cyberpunk* (1995), which theorizes the sublime in contemporary fiction as an expression of "nonverbal technological" realism (xi), and Barbara Claire Freeman's *The Feminine Sublime: Gender and Excess in Women's Fiction* (1995), which reads sublimity of theme and style as liberating "encounters with excess" (3). In "Sublimity and Skepticism in Montaigne" (1998), David L. Sedley helpfully summarizes the current debate about the concept of sublimity as an effect, suggesting transcendence of epistemological limits or as the figuration of skepticism about that capacity. McCarthy's use of the figure suggests the latter position. Of the collection of articles on this issue in *Of the Sublime: Presence in Question* (1993), edited by Jean François Courtine and others, Jacob Rogozinski's discussion of violence and Kantian indeterminacy in "The Gift of the World" is most relevant to my position.

21. Ironically, it is the psychotic effusions of another defective judge, Judge Schreber, whom Freud studied, that led Lacan to his theory of psychosis. See *Écrits: A Selection*, "On a question preliminary to any possible treatment of psychosis" 179-225.

22. See Phillips's "History and the Ugly Facts of Cormac McCarthy's *Blood Meridian*" for an analysis that articulates, as does this essay, the novel's refusal of conventional narrative pattern but insists that the predominant violence portrayed cannot be read as any kind of "sign or symbol" (435) and that *Blood Meridian* cannot be understood politically (449), a conclusion disputed here.

23. The revisionary forms of the Western that Cawelti examined in his 1976 *Adventure, Mystery, and Romance* depart from the formula of benign aggression enough to present "a sense of human depravity and corruption that almost seems to take a delight in the destructiveness of violence by accepting it as an inevitable expression of man's nature." However, even this type of Western continued to present violence as "the product of morally purposeful individual action in defense of the good group" (259). Ford and McCarthy rescind this principle.

Works Cited

Brown, Dee Alexander. *Bury My Heart at Wounded Knee: An Indian History of the American West.* New York: Holt, Rinehart & Winston, 1970.

Cawelti, John G. *Adventure, Mystery, and Romance: Formula Stories as Art and Popular Culture.* Chicago: U of Chicago P, 1976.

————. *Adventure, Mystery, and Romance: Formula Stories as Art and Popular Culture.* Chicago: U of Chicago P, 1976.

Courtine, Jean François, et al. *Of the Sublime: Presence in Question.* Tr. Jeffrey S. Librett. Albany: State U of New York P, 1993.

Drinnon, Richard. *Facing West: The Metaphysics of Indian-Hating and Empire-Building.* Norman: U of Oklahoma P, 1997.

Evenson, Brian. "McCarthy's Wanderers: Nomadology, Violence, and Open Country." *Sacred Violence: A Reader's Companion to Cormac McCarthy.* Ed. Wade Hall and Rick Wallach. El Paso: U of Texas at El Paso, 1995.

Freeman, Barbara Claire. *The Feminine Sublime: Gender and Excess in Women's Fiction.* Berkeley: U of California P, 1995.

Frosh, Stephen. *Sexual Difference: Masculinity and Psychoanalysis.* New York: Routledge, 1994.

Horrocks, Roger. *Male Myths and Icons: Masculinity in Popular Culture.* New York: St. Martin's, 1995.

Kristeva, Julia. *Powers of Horror: An Essay on Abjection.* Tr. Leon S. Roudiez. New York: Columbia UP, 1982.

Lacan, Jacques. *Écrits: A Selection.* Tr. Alan Sheridan. New York: Norton, 1977.

————. "The Meaning of the Phallus." *Feminine Sexuality: Jacques Lacan and the* école freudienne." Ed. Juliet Mitchell and Jacqueline Rose. Tr. Jacqueline Rose. New York: Norton, 1982.

Lesy, Michael. *Wisconsin Death Trip.* London: Allen Lane, 1973.

Phillips, Dana. "History and the Ugly Facts of Cormac McCarthy's *Blood Meridian*." *American Literature* 68.2 (June 1996): 433-60.

Pughe, Thomas. "Revision and Vision: Cormac McCarthy's *Blood Meridian.*" *Revue Francaise d'Etudes Americaine* 17.62 (Nov. 1994): 371-82.

Sedley, David L. "Sublimity and Skepticism in Montaigne." *PMLA* 113.5 (Oct. 1998): 1079-92.

Sepich, John Emil. "'What kind of indians was them?': Some Historical Sources in Cormac McCarthy's *Blood Meridian.*" *Perspectives on Cormac McCarthy.* Ed. Edwin T. Arnold and Dianne C. Luce. Jackson: UP of Mississippi, 1993.

Shaviro, Steven. "'The Very Life of the Darkness': A Reading of *Blood Meridian.*" *Perspectives on Cormac McCarthy.* Ed. Edwin T. Arnold and Dianne C. Luce. Jackson: UP of Mississippi, 1993.

Slotkin, Richard. *Gunfighter Nation: The Myth of the Frontier in Twentieth-Century America.* New York: Harper, 1992.

————. *Regeneration through Violence: The Mythology of the American Frontier, 1600-1860.* Middletown, CT: Wesleyan UP, 1973.

Sullivan, Nell. "Cormac McCarthy and the Text of Jouissance." *Sacred Violence: A Reader's Companion to Cormac McCarthy.* Ed. Wade Hall and Rick Wallach. El Paso: U of Texas at El Paso, 1995.

Tabbi, Joseph. *Postmodern Sublime: Technology and American Writing from Mailer to Cyberpunk.* Ithaca: Cornell UP, 1995.

Tompkins, Jane. *West of Everything: The Inner Life of Westerns.* New York: Oxford UP, 1992.

Wallach, Rick. "Judge Holden, *Blood Meridian*'s Evil Archon." *Sacred Violence: A Reader's Companion to Cormac McCarthy.* Ed. Wade Hall and Rick Wallach. El Paso: U of Texas at El Paso, 1995.

Woodward, Richard B. "Cormac McCarthy's Venomous Fiction." *New York Times Book Review* 19 Apr. 1992, 28-31, 36, 40.

FURTHER READING

Criticism

Bruzelius, Margaret. Introduction to *Romancing the Novel: Adventure from Scott to Sebald,* pp. 13-39. Lewisburg, Penn.: Bucknell University Press, 2007.

> Presents an overview of adventure narrative criticism and focuses on "the tension between realist aspirations and romantic plotting" in various literary works.

Butts, Dennis. "Imperialists of the Air-Flying Stories 1900-1950." In *Imperialism and Juvenile Literature,* edited by Jeffrey Richards, pp. 126-43. Manchester, England: Manchester University Press, 1989.

> Discusses the ways in which British juvenile fiction about flying written between 1910 and 1950 mirrored and supported the values of imperialism.

Dawson, Graham. "The Blond Beduin: Lawrence of Arabia and Imperial Adventure in the Modern World." In *Soldier Heroes: British Adventure, Empire, and the Imagining of Masculinities,* pp. 167-90. London: Routledge, 1994.

> Discusses the details of the literary depictions of Lawrence of Arabia and argues the he "has continued to fascinate over such a long period because he embodies contradictions and enigmas that have remained potent and unresolved into late- and post-imperial Britain."

Dixon, Robert. "Imperial Romance: *King Solomon's Mines* and Australian Romance." In *Writing the Colonial Adventure: Race, Gender, and Nation in Anglo-Australian Popular Fiction, 1875-1914.* Cambridge: Cambridge University Press, 1995.

 Presents an overview of the works of Australian authors who imitated H. Rider Haggard's famous novel and asserts that these works display "the fractures and divisions around discourses of race, gender, nation and empire characteristic of colonial nationalism."

Green, Martin. "In the Trough of the Wave of Imperialism: Adventure Images after 1918." In *Dreams of Adventure, Deeds of Empire,* pp. 320-37. London: Routledge & Kegan Paul, 1980.

 Discusses how adventure narratives changed in England after 1918, with many writers adopting anti-imperialist stances that resulted in more satirical and ironic literature.

———. "Hemingway's *The Green Hills of Africa* (1935)." In *The Great American Adventure,* pp. 167-83. Boston: Beacon Press, 1984.

 Analyzes Hemingway's treatment of the adventure tale in *The Green Hills of Africa* and notes that because he "associated his work with that of Gertrude Stein rather than with [Theodore] Roosevelt . . . he redeemed adventure for American literature."

Harrison, James. "Kipling's Jungle Eden." In *Critical Essays on Rudyard Kipling,* edited by Harold Orel, pp. 77-92. Boston: G. K. Hall & Co., 1989.

 Analyzes Kipling's treatment of the theme of Eden, noting that even though he associated it with the jungle, his view of it is "essentially post-lapsarian."

Holtsmark, Erling B. "Tarzan: Literary Background and Themes" and "Tarzan: Characters." In *Edgar Rice Burroughs,* pp. 33-52; 53-75. Boston: Twayne Publishers, 1986.

 Examines the context, influences, themes, and characterizations in Burroughs's Tarzan novels.

Inness, Sherrie A. "Girl Scouts, Camp Fire Scouts, and Woodcraft Girls: The Ideology of Girls' Scouting Novels, 1910-1935." In *Nancy Drew (r) and Company: Culture, Gender, and Girls' Series,* edited by Sherrie A. Inness, pp. 89-100. Bowling Green, Ohio: Bowling Green State University Press, 1997.

 Examines fiction and nonfiction written in connection with scouting for girls in the period from 1910 to 1935, suggesting that the scouting movement "function[ed] as a disciplinary agent of the state."

Moss, Robert F. "Clash of Loyalties: Kipling's Men in Conflict." In *Rudyard Kipling and the Fiction of Adolescence,* pp. 91-106. New York: St. Martin's Press, 1982.

 Discusses Kipling's novels *Soldiers Three* and *Light* in terms of his "schizophrenic" conflict between a desire for the comforts of home and a desire for adventure.

Sampson, Robert D. "In Appreciation of 10-Cent Pleasures." In *Deadly Excitements, Shadows and Phantoms,* pp. 1-4. Bowling Green, Ohio: Bowling Green State University Poplar Press, 1989.

 Presents some introductory remarks on pulp magazines of the 1930s as adventure narratives.

Spilka, Mark. "Victorian Keys to the Early Hemingway: Captain Marryat" *Novel* 17, no. 2 (winter 1984): 116-40.

 Traces parallels in the works and lives of Hemingway and British adventure writer Frederick Marryat.

White, Andrea. "Conrad and the Adventure Tradition." In *Approaches to Teaching Conrad's "Heart of Darkness" and "The Secret Sharer,"* pp. 31-9. New York: The Modern Language Association of America, 2002.

 Traces Joseph Conrad's strong, self-conscious connection to the canon of adventure literature.

Gothic Literature

The following entry presents critical discussion of Gothic literature in the twentieth century.

INTRODUCTION

Gothic literature originated as a genre in the eighteenth century, with Horace Walpole's *The Castle of Otranto* (1764) its first bestseller. Popular with readers from its inception to the present day (Bram Stoker's *Dracula* has never been out of print since its initial publication in 1897) and varied in terms of its style and content, Gothic has evolved in theme and technique, and has become interconnected with the detective fiction and the science fiction genres in the twentieth century.

The term Gothic typically refers to the occurrence of supernatural or horror elements in fiction, as in ghost stories like Arthur Conan Doyle's *The Hound of the Baskervilles* (1902), Shirley Jackson's *The Haunting of Hill House* (1959), and Henry James's *The Turn of the Screw* (1898), or in works of terror like Robert Louis Stevenson's *The Strange Case of Dr. Jekyll and Mr. Hyde* (1886). As is traditional for Gothic texts, strange events are presented in a stylized, formal, sometimes ritualistic manner. Yet the term Gothic is also used for works imbued with a weird or troubling atmosphere such as William Faulkner's *Light in August* (1932) or the short stories of Flannery O'Connor.

In the modern era, Gothic has come to denote pieces that feature mankind's "dark side"—whether violent, erotic, nonconformist, or bizarre. Scholars have pointed out that contemporary Gothic is always driven by desire and complex human psychological states, even in science fiction works involving the use of science for perverse purposes, or detective works that explore notions of sin, retribution, and redemption. Unlike earlier Gothic works that relied on physical phenomena for effect (haunted houses, ghosts, vampires, crazed and murderous individuals), contemporary Gothic turns inward to explore the buried emotions that motivate individuals to pursue their secret obsessions and guilty pleasures. In effect, the imminent danger has shifted to internal rather than external origins. Writers like Djuna Barnes, Angela Carter, H. P. Lovecraft, and Edith Wharton recognized and successfully made literary use of this change in the Gothic paradigm.

Theorists of Gothic literature are divided into two camps: one group considers Gothic texts generally conservative, since the events they portray ultimately end with the restoration of social order; the other group regards the ultimate goal of the genre to be the subversion of social order in order to bring about change. Contemporary scholars of Gothic have also explored its connections with feminism, particularly in regard to definition of gender roles and women's search for identity. Analyzing Gothic works through the filter of Freudian psychology, some have written about the role of both adult and children's sexuality in Gothic works. In the novels of Anne Rice and Stephen King commentators also glimpse an examination of the role of the author and of the act of writing itself as the fulfillment of some half-acknowledged, potentially dark desire. Applying the elements of the Gothic to other kinds of texts, for example social and political works, scholars have, in addition, identified and discussed what they have termed "City Gothic," "Schoolhouse Gothic," and "Political Gothic."

REPRESENTATIVE WORKS

Djuna Barnes
Nightwood (novel) 1936

Angela Carter
Honeybuzzard (novel) 1966

Louis-Ferdinand Céline
Voyage au Bout de la Nuit [*Journey to the End of the Night*] (novel) 1932

Philip K. Dick
Ubik (novel) 1969

Arthur Conan Doyle
The Hound of the Baskervilles (novel) 1902

William Faulkner
Light in August (novel) 1932

Christopher Fowler
Darkest Day (novel) 1993

M. John Harrison
The Course of the Heart (novel) 1992

Shirley Jackson
"The Lottery" (short story) 1949
The Haunting of Hill House (novel) 1959

Henry James
"Owen Wingrave" (short story) 1892
The Turn of the Screw (novella) 1898
"The Jolly Corner" (short story) 1908

M. R. James
Ghost Stories of an Antiquary (short stories) 1904

Stephen King
Rage (novel) 1971
The Shining (novel) 1978
Pet Sematary (novel) 1983

H. P. Lovecraft
*Dragon and Other Macabre Tales (short stories) 1987

Flannery O'Connor
The Complete Short Stories of Flannery O'Connor
    (short stories) 1974

John Rechy
City of Night (novel) 1963

Anne Rice
Interview with the Vampire (novel) 1976
"The Master of Rampling Gate" [published in *Redbook*
    magazine] (short story) 1984
The Vampire Lestat (novel) 1985

Muriel Spark
Driver's Seat (novel) 1970

Bram Stoker
Dracula (novel) 1897

Oliver Stone and Zachary Sklar
JFK: The Book of the Film (nonfiction) 1992

Edith Wharton
Hudson River Bracketed (novel) 1929
The Gods Arrive (novel) 1932

*Most of Lovecraft's tales were written between 1905 and 1935.

OVERVIEWS AND GENERAL STUDIES

Roger Luckhurst (essay date 2002)

SOURCE: Luckhurst, Roger. "The Contemporary London Gothic and the Limits of the 'Spectral Turn.'" *Textual Practice* 16, no. 3 (2002): 527-46.

[*In the essay below, Luckhurst examines the characteristics of a group of novels he terms London Gothic.*]

Rupert Davenport-Hines, in his suitably uncontrolled history *Gothic: 400 Years of Excess, Horror, Evil and Ruin,* enthusiastically asserts that 'in the 1990s, gothic has sustained a strong revival'. His eclectic texts range from Poppy Z. Brite, The Cure and David Lynch to Damien Hirst and that hellish duo Jake and Dinos Chapman. In the main, he suggests that it is contemporary America that 'has been profoundly reinfiltrated by goth ideas'.[1] Patrick McGrath and Bradford Morrow, in their Poe-worshipping introduction to *The New Gothic* in 1991, include more representatives of a British tradition; like Davenport-Hines they emphasize psychological extremity as the keynote of this contemporary Gothic revival.[2] In both books, such 'counter-reactions to the prevailing emotional environment' are protean enough to ensure that the Gothic persists in transgressing 'dominant cultural values' across different national contexts and aesthetic forms—a sort of principled derangement that refuses to be ensnared by history or locale.[3] In the same diffuse spirit, a certain strand of cultural theory in France, Britain and America embraced a language of ghosts and the uncanny—or rather of anachronic spectrality and hauntology—following the publication of Jacques Derrida's *Specters of Marx* in 1993 (translated into English in 1994). This text has proved extremely influential, prompting something of a 'spectral turn' in contemporary criticism. When Martin Jay wished to sum up recent directions in cultural theory he chose the title 'The Uncanny Nineties' in deference to *Specters*. 'Are you a scholar who deals with ghosts?' Martin McQuillan asked Derrida's translator, Peggy Kamuf. 'Yes . . . although I'm not sure I would have said so with as much conviction before *Specters of Marx*', she replied. She was answering, as we shall see, for a sizeable band of cultural critics.[4]

This essay is partly a response to Martin Jay's questions 'Why . . . has the uncanny become a master trope available for appropriation in a wide variety of contexts? What are the possible drawbacks of granting it so much explanatory force?'[5] These questions have been crystallized, for me, by trying to reflect on the notable revival over the past twenty years of a newly Gothicized apprehension of London. I want to argue that the critical language of spectral or haunted modernity that has become a cultural-critical shorthand in the wake of *Specters of Marx* can go only so far in elaborating the contexts for that specific topography of this London Gothic—that, indeed, the generalized structure of haunting is symptomatically blind to its generative loci.

What follows is in two parts. In the first, I want to suggest an *oeuvre* of texts that might be included in this new London Gothic, and to explore it in relation to the discourse of spectralized modernity. The second part launches itself from the limits of this account, offering a reading of the work of Iain Sinclair and Christopher Fowler.

I

W. G. Sebald's extraordinary novel *Austerlitz* hinges on a moment that has become typical—even stereotypical. Austerlitz tells the anonymous narrator of his attempts to fend off the collapse of his identity by trudging through the city of London at night. As he crosses Liverpool Street station, then undergoing modernization, Austerlitz becomes attuned to the successive erasures enacted on the site. The station is built on the site of the asylum, St Mary of Bethlehem: 'I kept almost obsessively trying to imagine—through the ever-changing maze of walls—the location in that huge space of the rooms where the asylum inmates were confined, and I often wondered whether the pain and suffering accumulated on this site over the centuries had ever really ebbed away.'[6] The Broad Street excavations have similarly uncovered the compacted bodies of old burial grounds, and such locations prompt Austerlitz to speculate: 'It does not seem to me . . . that we understand the laws governing the return of the past, but I feel more and more as if time did not exist at all, only various spaces interlocking according to the rules of a higher form of stereometry, between which the living and the dead can move back and forth as they like.'[7] Given these Gothic reflections on inheritance, indebtedness and the returning dead, it is fitting that Austerlitz uncovers the encrypted memories of his own orphaned Jewish origins in an abandoned waiting room scheduled for demolition in the station. This is London's psychic topography: traumatic memory is recovered on the ground of the city's buried history.

The site of Austerlitz's revelation comes at the end of twenty years of the elaboration of a newly Gothicized London. Consider: in Will Self's version of the city, the dead have spilled over from Crouch End in his early tale 'The North London Book of the Dead' to occupy a variety of 'cystricts' from Dulston in the northeast to Dulburb in the south in *How the Dead Live*. In *Mother London,* Michael Moorcock suggests that redemption for the traumatized city lies in a gaggle of telepaths, psychotically open to the lost voices of metropolitan history. Ghosts are inhumed in a Victorian terraced house in Michèle Roberts' *In the Red Kitchen.* In M. John Harrison's novel *The Course of the Heart,* an occultist living above the Atlantis Bookshop in Museum Street engages in elaborate rituals in anonymous north London houses, hoping for access to the plenitude of the Gnostic 'pleroma'. His reluctant, psychically damaged circle of initiates suffers punitive decades of haunting for their uncomprehending participation in these rites—obscene protrusions of the psychotic Real into dreary urban spaces. The horror writers Christopher Fowler and Kim Newman have unleashed vampires, personal daemons, reanimated corpses, undead media executives and murderous secret societies on to the London streets. In Neil Gaiman's *Neverwhere* one can

fall through the cracks of cruel London indifference to find oneself in the parallel space of the Underside, or London Below. China Miéville's *King Rat* also invokes a wholly other system of networks and rat-runs inches away from the human dominion of the city. In *Perdido Street Station,* Miéville reimagines London as New Crobuzon, a metropolis of alchemy and magic. Marcello Truzzi notes that an important strand in occult belief is 'the inference of strange causalities among otherwise ordinary events'.[8] The poet, novelist and essayist Iain Sinclair has generated a tangle of these occulted causalities, often marking out trajectories through the East End of London. With undecidable intent (he is a dead-pan mythographer), Sinclair claims to unearth hidden lines of force and meaning—most notoriously in his poem sequence on the secret significances of Hawksmoor's churches, *Lud Heat,* undoubtedly one of the *ur*-texts for this resurgence of London Gothic since its publication in 1975. This opaque text, published by Sinclair's own Albion Press, gained kudos from its programmatic re-functioning by Peter Ackroyd in *Hawksmoor* in 1985 (*Lud Heat* gained even more kudos from being impossible to get hold of until its mass market reissue in 1995—it worked its effect as a rumour as much as an actually read text). Sinclair has continued to conduct investigations into the marginal and the vanished through the language of lost inheritance and ghostly debt. The novel *Downriver* repeatedly stages forms of séance communication with London's disappeared. Forgotten and despised areas, abandoned buildings or empty rooms work as conductors to revivify buried histories. Sinclair entwines his own project with a host of other psychogeographers of London's occlusions, from the poets Aidan Dun and Allen Fisher to the film-makers Chris Petit and Patrick Keiller and the avant-garde provocateur Stewart Home.[9]

Many of these contemporary texts engage in historical excavations that self-reflexively incorporate knowledge of the Gothic genre itself. Robinson, Keiller's eccentric urban detective in the film *London,* navigates the city by turning again and again to its eighteenth-century traces, bad-temperedly fantasizing the erasure of Victorian London other than for the precious residues of Poe, Stoker or Rimbaud. Ackroyd omnivorously roams the centuries, but readers of this genre soon note that it is the Gothic revival of the late Victorian era that turns up repeatedly, clearly because this was the moment when a distinctively urban Gothic was crystallized. The parallel explosion of Gothic scholarship in the 1990s (the International Gothic Association was founded in 1991) tracked the movement of the genre from the wild margins of Protestant Europe to the imperial metropolis of the Victorian *fin de siècle*—precisely the trajectory that brings Count Dracula from the Carpathian mountains to the populous streets of London, or Arthur Machen's corruptive Helen Vaughan from the Celtic fringes of England to the wealthiest streets of Piccadilly in *The*

Great God Pan. Christopher Fowler's most impressive novel to date, *Darkest Day,* traces a sequence of modern-day killings back to events in the newly built Savoy Theatre in 1888. Alan Moore and Eddie Campbell's influential graphic novel about the 1889 Whitechapel 'Ripper' murders, *From Hell,* condensed every available conspiracy theory into a supernaturalized account that included lengthy disquisitions from the killer on the occult power of place (this meta-commentary was largely excised from the 2001 film version).[10] Sinclair wrote his own contribution to the Ripper mythology, *White Chapell, Scarlet Tracings,* but *Downriver* also picks up traces of the dead of the 1878 *Princess Alice* disaster (in which over 600 people drowned in the sinking of a Thames pleasure-cruiser). Another séance conjures the seventeen dead from the fire at the Whitechapel Hebrew Dramatic Club in 1887. 'Fire is the essence of voices,' we are told. 'It is what you cannot reduce to ash.'[11]

Is this Gothic revival and its fascination with its own generic past anything other than self-referential involution—a kind of return of the repressed 'return of the repressed' as empty postmodern pastiche? This is the thrust of Michael Moorcock's short satirical tale, 'London Bone', in which the rapacious demand for authentic London history begins to disinter the bones of the dead from London graveyards for escalating market prices. The collapsed economy and exhausted imaginary of contemporary London can only feed on its own dead.[12] Yet the pervasiveness of Gothic tropes on the imagining of London across a diversity of discursive modes seems to be undertaking far more cultural work than empty repetition might suggest. Patrick Wright's *A Journey Through the Ruins: The Last Days of London* stitches together a jeremiad against the London of the 1980s in true Gothic fashion, by haunting places of inner-city ruin left to the vagaries of the market or hurriedly redesignated as 'heritage' sites. 'An interest in debris and human fallout is part of the New Baroque sensibility', he claims.[13] Peter Ackroyd's best-selling *London: A Biography* transposed his novelistic explorations of the strange rhythms of London time and space into a method for apprehending a city apparently resistant to the cognitive regimen of history. The temporal slippages at certain specific locales in London in *Hawksmoor* and *The House of Doctor Dee* (which are figured through the Gothic very precisely as visiting derangement on their inheritors) become the principal device for the historian of the city. London origins are lost in semi-mythical or visionary accounts, and historiography is further mocked by the patterns of disappearance and return that crumple linear time into repeating cycles or unpredictable arabesques. 'The nature of time in London is mysterious', Ackroyd claims, pointing to the 'territorial imperative or *genius loci*' that ensures certain zones retain their function across the centuries—not just the clusters of trades, but the homeless of St

Giles, or the occultists of Seven Dials.[14] There is, Ackroyd affirms, 'a Gothic *genius loci* of London fighting against the spirit of the classic' (p. 580)—understanding the Classical mode as that which always wants to order and regiment the life of the city. This spirit exists 'beyond the reach of any plan or survey': we have to understand that 'the city itself remains magical; it is a mysterious, chaotic and irrational place which can be organised and controlled only by means of private ritual or public superstition' (p. 216). The 'spirit' of London survives the apocalyptic fires that periodically revisit it, and it will certainly outlast any of the passing political interventions dreamt up by the Westminster village. 'It does not respond to policy committees or to centralised planning. It would be easier to control the elements themselves', Ackroyd states in his conclusion, thus essentially naturalizing (or rather supernaturalizing) London 'muddle' (p. 764).

We might begin to sense something more purposive in the contemporary London Gothic here. One of Ackroyd's most attentive readers, Julian Wolfreys, suggests that London has encouraged these tropes since the huge expansion of the metropolis in the nineteenth century. As the first megalopolis of the modern era, London becomes a sublime object that evokes awe and evades rational capture. The 'London-effect', for Wolfreys, is the sense that there is 'always a mysterious supplement that escapes signification'. Writers since Blake and Dickens have understood that London is not a city that can be encompassed by the panoptical ambitions of novelistic realism but requires a writing that evokes 'the ineffability and lack which is always at the heart of London'.[15] This 'crisis of representation' argument is regularly rehearsed in postmodern urban theory—although it is usually the sprawl of Los Angeles or the ribbon developments of Phoenix that are the focus.[16] London is different, the argument proceeds, and is more amenable to the disorderly mode of the Gothic, because the creative destruction of its specific embodiment of modernity is peculiarly hidebound by the ancient commands and ancestral inheritances that live on amidst the mirrored glass and cantilevered concrete. These traces, Wolfreys argues in *Writing London,* are 'spectral through and through: they are the marks of already retreating ghosts who disturb any certain perception we may think we have concerning the city's identity'.[17]

This theory of a spectralized modernity is shared by a number of urban theorists. James Donald presents a more gestural notion of a 'haunted city', with the ghost acting as a supplement that evades totalized planning.[18] 'We need,' Christine Boyer concurs, 'to establish counter-memories, resisting the dominant coding of images and representations. . . . We are compelled to create new memory walks through the city, new maps that help us to resist and subvert the all-too-programmed and enveloping messages of our consumer culture.'[19]

The more indifferent to history the ruthless transformation of city-space, the more likely it is, Anthony Vidler suggests, that 'the uncanny erupts in empty parking lots around abandoned or run-down shopping malls . . . in the wasted margins and surface appearances of postindustrial culture'.[20] Never far away from contemporary urban theory is Michel de Certeau's *The Practice of Everyday Life,* and sure enough de Certeau neatly condenses all of these strands in the passing comment:

> Haunted places are the only ones people can live in—and this inverts the schema of the *Panopticon.* But like the gothic sculptures of kings and queens that once adorned Notre-Dame and have been buried for two centuries . . . these 'spirits', themselves broken into pieces in like manner, do not *speak* any more than they *see.* This is a sort of knowledge that remains silent. Only hints of what is known but unrevealed are passed on 'just between you and me.'[21]

The buried Gothic fragment thus operates as the emblem of resistance to the tyranny of planned space, but this resistance is necessarily occluded and interstitial, passed on only between initiates. (Indeed, given the embrace of obscurity and scarcity by a number of recent London 'visionaries', this transaction 'just between you and me' seems uncannily apt.)

We have the beginnings of an explanation situating the use of Gothic tropes within a larger critique of amnesiac modernity. Jean-François Lyotard wrote of the ghosts that structurally haunted any total or totalizing system, and of the commitment of thought to open to 'the anguish . . . of a mind haunted by a familiar and unknown guest which is agitating it'.[22] Jean-Michel Rabaté concurs: 'we might say that "modern" philosophy has always attempted to bury [its] irrational Other in some neat crypt, forgetting that it would thereby lead to further ghostly reapparitions.' For him, 'a whole history of our spectral delusions remains possible, even urgent and necessary.'[23] Any proclamation of self-possessed modernity induces a haunting. This becomes, for David Glover, a 'spectrality effect' by which the Gothic haunts modernity in general.[24] From a somewhat different context, the science theorist Bruno Latour also joins this conjuncture by arguing that 'modern temporality is the result of a retraining imposed on entities which would pertain to all sorts of times and possess all sorts of ontological statuses without this harsh disciplining'. Because this project was an imperious imposition on heterogeneity, 'symptoms of discord are multiplied': 'The past remains, therefore, and even returns. Now this resurgence is incomprehensible to the moderns. Thus they treat it as the return of the repressed.'[25] Perhaps the global time zone system, zeroed on Greenwich in 1884, makes London particularly subject to magical and superstitious beliefs, as Maureen Perkins has recently argued.[26] Within these contexts, Gothic tropes can be exemplary symptoms of the horrors that beset an uncomprehending modernity, or can act as devices that acknowledge London as (in Latour's term) a polytemporal assemblage. In this set-up the past 'is not surpassed but revisited, repeated, surrounded, protected, recombined, reinterpreted, and reshuffled'.[27] 'There are little bubbles of old time in London', one character in Gaiman's *Neverwhere* explains, 'where things and places stay the same, like bubbles in amber. . . . There's a lot of time in London, and it has to go somewhere—it doesn't all get used up at once.'[28] Critical discourse makes similar claims: as Lynda Nead puts it in her discussion of London modernity, 'the present remains permanently engaged in a phantasmatic dialogue with the past'.[29] The comments in *Austerlitz* on the spatial ordering of time, the localized temporalities of London in Ackroyd, or Patrick Wright's observation that 'On Dalston Lane time itself seems to lie around in broken fragments: you can drop in on previous decades with no more effort than it takes to open a shop-door', are thus given a common root.[30] They can all be countersigned by Derrida's assertions in *Specters of Marx* regarding the 'non-contemporaneity of the present time with itself (this radical untimeliness or this anachrony on the basis of which we are trying here to *think the ghost*)'.[31]

De Certeau's assertion that unearthing gothic fragments might contribute to an *aesthetic of resistance* also helps explain more avant-garde interest in Gothic topology. There has been a long association of the metropolitan avant-garde with occult investigation. The Surrealists adopted the methods of the spiritualist trance-medium to unleash the revolutionary delirium of the unconscious. The city was explored in the same way: in André Breton's *Nadja,* for instance, chance encounters and certain zones of Paris become charged with occult significance. Breton's subjectivity was doubled or ghosted as a consequence of this exercise in the urban uncanny.[32] The Situationist International, formed from the European postwar rump of Surrealism, also reinvented the city through the *dérive,* a delirious or drunken drifting that tore up the tyranny of abstract city-space.[33] Claiming direct descent, the London Psychogeographical Association was formed in the early 1990s. Stewart Home, associated with the Neoist avant-garde, eventually edited a collection of LPA texts, which evidenced a fascination with occult modes of explanation. In one communication, 'Nazi Occultists seize Omphalos', the election of a British National Party representative in the Isle of Dogs is attributed to the exercise of Enochian magic. The BNP have tapped into the ley-line that runs between the Greenwich Observatory and Queen Mary College in Mile End. This line of occult force, the conspiratorial text informs us, has powered the formation of the British Empire, at least since John Dee's alchemical service to Elizabeth I.[34] Jenny Turner has suggested that Home "is fascinated by the way that official, admired, respectable forms of knowledge are structurally identical to their occult, reviled shades, and in his best work shakes hard at the barriers between them'.[35] In *The House of Nine Squares,* a set of letters and texts on Neoism, Home records his delight that the dead-pan missives of the London Psychogeographical Association have been mistaken as products of 'an occult group': 'This type of misunderstanding makes it much easier for us to realise our real aim of turning the bourgeoisie's weapons back against them.'[36] Elsewhere, in response to critical comment from other radical avant-garde groupings, the LPA declared: 'We offer no attempt to "justify" or "rationalize" the role of magic in the development of our theories. It is sufficient that it renders our theories *completely unacceptable.*'[37]

Mystification and unlikely counter-factual histories, it would seem, are dialectically motivated by the creeping uniformity of commodified London. The LPA, Iain Sinclair comments, is 'the revenge of the disenfranchised. Improvisations on history that are capable of making adjustments in present time. Prophecy as news. News as the purest form of fiction.'[38] Sinclair, now in a curiously anomalous position as a hegemonic counter-culturalist, works the same line of ambivalence as Home. The fractured lyric persona in Sinclair's *Lud Heat* defends the discovery of 'the secret routines' in the East End through a method of 'high occulting' against the languages of '*the objective*', '*the scientific approach*' and 'scholarly baby talk'.[39] Sinclair dowses along ley-lines and conducts séances in *Downriver,* yet the same text rants against 'stinking heritage ghosts', myths sustained 'only to bleed the fund raisers' (p. 122). The character given narratorial authority for the conclusion of *Downriver* expresses contempt for 'necrovestism: impersonating the dead, spook-speaking' (p. 399). The mysterious Spitalfields figure David Rodinsky—whose room was allegedly left untouched on his disappearance in 1969 and 'rediscovered' in 1987—is mockingly debunked as a conjuration of heritage hype in one text, then becomes the basis for full-scale mythologizing in another.[40] The ambiguity is deliberately nurtured, for if 'the occult logic of "market forces" dictated a new geography' of London, Sinclair implies that his project is a necessary counter-conjuration, a protective hex against the advancing armies of orthodoxy.[41]

The framework of spectralized modernity can thus integrate widely divergent instances of the London Gothic—it makes unlikely bedfellows of Peter Ackroyd and Stewart Home. Yet it is the very generalized economy of haunting that makes me suspicious of this spectral turn. Jodey Castricano's reading of 'familiar Gothic tropes and topoi . . . in Derridean deconstruction' toys with calling the philosopher a 'Gothic novelist'—one that speaks with a decided affinity to a popular and distinctively *American* tradition of obsessive returns from the dead that stretches from Poe to Stephen King.[42] Transposed in space by Castricano,

Jean-Michel Rabaté's *Ghosts of Modernity* uncovers the same spectral reiteration by tracking across temporal moments, from Spinoza in 1674 via Marx and Engels to Beckett in 1952.[43] In Julian Wolfreys' work spectrality exceeds the Gothic as merely 'one proper name for a process of spectral transformation', and becomes a generalized deconstructive lever discernible everywhere.[44] No concept, no self-identity, no text, no writing that is not haunted: 'the spectral is at the heart of *any* narrative of the modern', the latest addition to his *oeuvre* states.[45] This extension is clearly legitimated by Derrida's own view that 'it is necessary to introduce haunting into the very construction of a concept. Of every concept, beginning with the concepts of being and time. This is what we would be calling here a hauntology.'[46] What is proclaimed by this structure is, as Martin Jay observes, 'the power of haunting *per se*': 'in celebrating spectral returns as such,' he continues, 'the precise content of *what* is repeated may get lost.'[47] Unable to discriminate between instances and largely uninterested in historicity (beyond its ghostly disruption), the discourse of spectralized modernity risks investing in the compulsive repetitions of a structure of melancholic entrapment. In this mode, to suggest an inevitably historicized mourning-work that might actually seek to lay a ghost to rest would be the height of bad manners. And because the spectral infiltrates the hermeneutic act itself, critical work can only replicate tropes from textual sources, punning spiritedly around the central terms of the Gothic to produce a curious form of meta-Gothic that elides object and instrument. This has happened from the very beginning of this spectral turn: 'Impossible, at least for me,' Nicholas Royle comments, 'to review this book about apparitions, phantoms, spectres, without feeling a need to respond in kind. . . . A phantom book calls for a phantom review.'[48]

The way in which *Specters of Marx* has been received and mobilized by literary critics shows some marked differences from the Marxist and broader political-philosophical response. Respondents from the Marxist tradition tend to concentrate on Derrida's deferred readings of Marx and the proposals for a largely spectral 'New International' in the latter half of the book. Kate Soper is typical in excoriating the emptying out of any possibility of a political ontology by Derridean hauntology once *Specters* gets around to filling out the generalized structure of the spectro-political.[49] Literary critics, as we have seen, tend to elaborate on the figurations of ghosts and hauntings, principally developed in the opening section of *Specters.* The play with Hamlet's father's spirit here makes things suitably homely for literary types, even if, as John Fletcher has carefully noted, Derrida rather misreads the import of the ghost in *Hamlet.*[50] What Derrida himself makes of this literary-critical mobilization may be hinted at in his lengthy response to the Marxist critiques collected in *Ghostly Demarca-*

tions. In an essay that barely mentions spectres at all, the most sustained discussion of the term is in response to Fredric Jameson's judgement of it as 'aesthetic': 'to all those—they are legion—who think they can "re-aestheticize" matters in this book, reducing its concepts (the concept of the "spectre", for instance) to figures of rhetoric, or my demonstrations to literary experiments and effects of style: none of what matters to me, and, above all, may matter to the discussion under way . . . can be reduced to, or elucidated by, this "aesthetic" approach.'[51] Nevertheless, what Derrida's hauntology has spawned, at least in Gothicized literary criticism, is the punning search for a textual reading machine for variously termed cryptomimetics (Castricano), spectrography (Rabaté), Gothic spectro-poetics (Wolfreys) or phantomistics (Royle) that largely recirculates Gothic-aesthetic tropes. This certainly 'respects' texts, but it rarely goes beyond what Derrida has elsewhere termed 'doubling commentary'.[52]

In order to read something of the *specificity* of the contemporary London Gothic I want to aim at breaking through this meta-Gothic discourse. When Chris Baldick proposes that Gothic tales evoke 'a fear of historical reversion; that is, of the nagging possibility that the despotisms, buried by the modern age, may yet prove to be undead', this could be taken as another generalized conjuring of haunted modernity.[53] In fact, it is part of a counter-move to the spectralization of the Gothic that situates it rather more precisely as a grounded manifestation of communities in highly delimited locales subjected to cruel and unusual forms of political disempowerment. A geography of the genre thus observes clusters at the colonial edges of England—Anglo-Irish Gothic, or a Scottish Gothic that speaks to 'issues of suppression in a stateless national culture'.[54] And surely what the contemporary London Gothic most evidently articulates is not simply empty structural repetitions of polytemporal spookiness: these are themselves symptoms of that curious mix of tyranny and farce that constitutes London governance.

II

In Christopher Fowler's novel *Darkest Day* (1993), the ancient Whitstable family, the aristocratic 'backbone of England' and stalwarts of the Goldsmith's Guild in the City of London, begin to be killed off in elaborate, anachronistic ways.[55] It transpires that the founding father of their modern wealth, James Makepeace Whitstable, had in 1888 constructed a murderous device to kill off any threats to their financial empire. Whitstable's arcane knowledge combined the technical skill of the watchmaker and electrician with occult sciences learned in India: his machine tracks the markets and then dispatches reanimated corpses to assassinate business rivals. Age and water damage from the buried River Fleet have miscalibrated the machine, so turning it on its unknowing beneficiaries. When Fowler's detectives Bryant and May uncover the machine beneath the medieval guild-hall, concealed in a sub-basement, they knew 'they were looking at the cold damaged heart of the Whitstable empire, a manufactured embodiment of everything that had grown flawed and failed in imperialist England' (p. 491). Fowler's later *Disturbia* (1997) is similarly concerned with a murderous group operating from a privileged position in London. The apparatus of this text is not supernatural; instead, the Gothic is evoked to reflect on the labyrinthine secrecy of the Establishment and the growing occultation of the public sphere in London: 'Its keys are hidden because the key-holders are invisible to the public.'[56] Fowler's plot involves a young wannabe journalist investigating the secretive right-wing League of Prometheus. Unmasked as an agitator, the League sets him a challenge to solve ten riddles about the city that pits Vince's 'secret' knowledge of London against the League's networks of power and privilege. Vince's journey allows Fowler to entertain the reader with obscure aspects of London history—a love of the local, preserved detail (and their eccentric custodians) that ensures Vince survives the abstracted, panoptical control of London by the League.

Fowler's populist Gothic pits a young, mobile generation against the dead weight of inherited traditions. Hip, trashy and saturated with references to 1990s culture, Fowler's work nevertheless resonates richly with the original impetuses of the Gothic: the fears of reversion to arbitrary and oppressive rule. In 1986, representative metropolitan government in London was extinguished, explicitly (as the White Paper said) to 'remove a source of conflict' with central government.[57] As one historian of Thatcherism has remarked, 'the absolute sovereignty of parliament had never in the twentieth-century been so markedly revealed during peacetime as during the debates over the abolition of the metropolitan authorities'.[58] Some 272 non-elected quangos replaced the GLC; the 'London Residuary Body', staffed by four employees, sold off 9,000 GLC properties before dissolving itself. In 1990, the Inner London Education Authority was abolished as one of the few remaining pan-London bodies that 'abolitionists saw . . . as implicitly subversive'.[59] In the same year as abolition, 1986, the progressive deregulation of financial controls on the City of London culminated in the 'Big Bang'—the full opening of London markets to the borderless flows of international capital and their final severance from the social fabric of London itself. 'Freedom for finance was but the restoration of ancient privileges', Will Hutton has observed.[60] The City Corporation has preserved its essentially medieval system of governance and its twelfth-century Royal Charters, having been economically powerful enough to resist all forms of municipalization over the centuries. The guild system, abolished across Europe in the late eighteenth century as an element of the formation of the modern state, was left untouched within the City of London: family inheritance still operates to fill guild posts, and the calendar of feast-days orchestrates a structure of fraternal contacts that oils the machinery of influence.[61] The Labour opposition promised to return both metropolitan governance and regulation of the City in its 1996 *A Voice for London* document. By 1997, the City had persuaded New Labour to abandon such 'inefficient' controls. The griffins marking the boundaries of the 'Square Mile' of the City (joined after the 1992 Bishopsgate bomb by the 'Ring of Steel' and the CCTV system that makes these the most extensively surveilled streets in the world) are, after all, the mythological beasts that defend treasure.

'It is impossible to accept at face value' the economic historian (and free-market advocate) Ranald Michie benignly comforts, 'a hypothesis that blames difficulties on a mysterious group—the City—who managed to dominate economic, social and political life for at least a century'.[62] Yet this is precisely the imaginary specific to a London-based Gothic. As Alexandra Warwick has observed, it is difficult to transpose narratives of the 'planned space' of urban modernity from Hausmann's Paris to a London that had no centralized governance, and a City Corporation that actively resisted any grand urban redesign. Instead, in the London Gothic, 'the relation of the individual to London's urban space is one of paranoia; the fragmentary and tentative internal pattern created is projected outward onto the map of the city but the inscription of the pattern is unstable; it further fragments and then returns to menace'.[63] Thus, the League of Prometheus in *Disturbia* or the Masonic machinations behind the Ripper killings in *From Hell* (or even the killing of the poet Chatterton by Masons in Aidan Dun's *Vale Royal*) are fantasized condensations of persecutory agency.

That the Gothic provides ideal tropes for this becomes explicit in the ninth tale of Iain Sinclair's *Downriver*, 'Isle of Dogs (*Vat City Plc*)'. Here, Sinclair and friends attempt to penetrate the security cordon around the heart of Docklands at Magnum Tower (Canary Wharf), a site now purchased by the Vatican, guarded by armed monks and Swiss guards. It is a place of black magic ceremonies. The Isle 'lets slip its ghosts' (p. 276), who are demons and demagogues: Martin Bormann, Idi Amin, Baby Doc Duvalier. A ritual in the pyramid that tops Magnum Tower aims 'to halt time, wound its membrane, and give them access to unimagined powers' (p. 283). The intruders glimpse a ceremony that mixes Stephen Hawking's quantum physics with a 'mock-Cawdor millennial rap' delivered from a dais of human skulls (p. 294). Sinclair literalizes the voodoo economics at work in the City, and transposes the tyranny of one era on to another: the London Docklands Development Corporation—Michael Heseltine's 'enterprise zone' established in 1981 and given freedom from all planning restrictions and any need to include social or infrastructural provision—is refracted through the eighteenth-century Gothic.

Pre-modern, Gothicized languages seem peculiarly apposite to Docklands. Janet Foster's ethnographic study of the Isle of Dogs speaks of the 'benevolent feudalism' of the developers Olympia and York towards the marginalized residents of the Island.[64] Bill Schwarz examines the slippages between sites of futuristic developments and failed social housing as the starkest instance of 'regressive modernization' in London. Writing in 1991, in the wake of O&Y's collapse, Schwarz wonders if Docklands might become 'a ghost city'.[65] The context for this spectral Docklands is far from the abstracted modernity evoked in recent critical theory, or the benign, Ackroydian experience of crumpled temporalities in the 'magical' city. It points, instead, to the deliberate evisceration of London's democratic public sphere marked out on the physical landscape of the city.

Sinclair's vision of a city ruled over by the undead Widow—eventually staked by her own party—is more jaggedly trenchant than the populist Gothic of Christopher Fowler. Yet *Darkest Day* directs us to another important locus for the ways in which contemporary Gothic allegorizes stalled representative government in London. The Whitstable family secret is traced back to events in 1888, hooking up all the appurtenances of the late Victorian Gothic (murderous defence of aristocratic inheritance, the vengeful undead of the imperial periphery and so on) with the present day. The year 1888 was also the one in which Parliament finally passed the bill establishing the London County Council, despite, as David Owen records, fears of mob rule after the extension of the franchise to include more working-class votes in the 1884 Reform Act, and the City Corporation's attempts throughout the 1880s to bribe Members of Parliament and the hire of thugs to break up meetings of the Municipal Reform League.[66] A Tory government pre-empted the inevitable and established the LCC, ensuring, as ever, no jurisdiction over the City. When the Progressives famously used London as the test-bed for collectivism and socialist municipalization throughout the 1890s, an 1899 Act established the metropolitan boroughs in ways that designedly undercut the centralizing plans of the LCC.[67]

The kinds of statistics that shocked social reformers into philanthropic and democratic measures were also those that generated Gothic fictions within the topography of London. The positivist mapping of London, street by street, undertaken by Charles Booth in the seventeen volumes of *Life and Labour of the People of London* between 1889 and 1903, was inextricably linked with the Gothic landscapes of Stevenson, Wilde, Machen or Wells. These discourses converged in the metaphorics of the primitive urban jungle, the penumbra of unknown Darkest London.[68] 'Is this monster city again to double and treble itself?' asked the social commentator Frederic Harrison in 1887. 'Are its dead still more to endanger the living?'[69] While the cemeteries overflowed, James Cantlie identified 'urbomorus' as the city disease that sent Londoners into degenerate decline.[70] Sidney Low similarly saw 'a vast dark city . . . spreading hideously over the face of England', sapping the 'strength and stamina' of naturally rural Teutons.[71] W. T. Stead's London was a 'Modern Babylon' of sexual slavery and the sacrifice of young girls, the decadent West feeding off the souls of the East. Amidst these Gothicized apprehensions, Sidney Webb composed *The London Programme* for the newly elected Progressives of the LCC, a project to respond to 'political helplessness' by animating 'a greater sense of common life'.[72] Even Webb, though, resorted to Gothic terminology as the pressure on London collectivism grew, speaking of the LCC as 'the Frankenstein creation which [the Tories] are now so anxious to destroy'.[73] The reanimated corpse of London governance again turned on its master a hundred years later. After fourteen years with no direct municipal governance, a disenchanted populace rebelled against the New Labour gerrymandering of the selection and election of the Mayor and Assembly in May 2000. The powers of the Greater London Authority, however, had already been sufficiently shorn of effect to ensure fiscal control from Westminster. Tony Blair vetoed the return of the GLA to County Hall, despite the offer of space from Shirayama Shokusan, its corporate owners. Rejecting the historic symbol of municipal socialism, a spokesman for the Prime Minister, who plainly had not read any Gothic novels, informed the press that 'There is no room for ghosts from the past'.[74]

The echoes between the late Victorian and contemporary Gothic convey more than the empty repetitions or returns of a spectralized modernity, but it is also important to recognize the fundamental incoherence of these Gothic reflections on London governance. The genre may always be expected to exceed the hope of uncovering any fixed allegorical substratum, and my intention here has not been to recruit the contemporary Gothic to some kind of coherent political analysis of London ills. The unstable valences of the London Gothic just as often flip fantasies of persecutory tyranny into a nostalgia for those very spaces of unregulated violence or disorderly conduct. This is certainly the case in the 1890s, as the LCC unleashed an increasingly paternalistic and somewhat puritanical set of moral interventions into the life of the city, often framed within social Darwinian and eugenic terms. Arthur Machen, the minor Decadent now revived as the quintessence of the degenerate *fin-de-siècle* Gothic by critics, in fact came to use accesses to the supernatural as a means of escaping the banal levelling imposed by the stern gaze of the schools or health inspector. 'Our age, which has vulgarised everything, has not spared the unseen world, and superstition, which was once both terrible and picturesque, is now thoroughly "democratised".'[75] In *The London Adventure,* Machen trudges the grey streets of London to conjure epiphanic moments of escape: 'We, it appears, are to learn of high things, if at all, through little things,

and things of low estate. If we are to see the vision of the Grail, however dimly, it must no longer be in some vaulted chamber in a high tower . . . [but] through the Venetian blinds in some grey, forgotten square of Islington.'[76] Thomas Burke similarly titillated Edwardians with the transgressive delights of a rapidly vanishing Chinese Limehouse, where nubile young white girls fell in thrall to the Chinaman, a carnivalesque space put to an end by the interventions of the state.[77] The advent of a knowable and governable London in the late nineteenth century thus encourages a discourse of lost pleasures, of nostalgic evocations addressed to those who live in the wake of 'vanished' London.

Nostalgia for the secret or hidden burns through contemporary London fictions too. 'I mourn the loss of another secret locale,' the narrator of *Downriver* complains, 'another disregarded inscape has been noticed and dragged from cyclical time to pragmatic time' (p. 33). Patrick Wright is undoubtedly correct to see Iain Sinclair as 'less an abracadabra man than a poet of the Welfare State, the laureate of its morbidity and failure'.[78] Yet an occultism that conjures counter-spells is itself intrinsically anti-democratic in its love of the arcane. As Georg Simmel commented long ago on the secret society, Sinclair's advocacy of London's hidden cabal of lunatic scribblers and dowsers might well hold off 'the violent pressure of central powers', but it does so only by reifying and repeating the hierarchies it ostensibly opposes.[79] This, too, is the culmination of Fowler's *Disturbia*: Vince triumphs over the aristocratic sociopath who heads the League of Prometheus, yet rather than demolishing its networks of privilege, Vince becomes the new leader of the League, aiming to make it 'truly invisible again', 'doing pretty much what government ministers did, only more so' (p. 338). The final homily of Fowler's text—that Vince's knowledge of the city converts into power, an exemplary trajectory for Londoners to become 'finally free to plot a course through the maze of glass and steel and flesh' (p. 341)—is pure fantasy fulfilment, cancelled by the novel's heavy investment in secrecy and privilege. It reveals precisely why the Gothic provides such resonant ways of apprehending contemporary London. So etiolated is any idea of a metropolitan public sphere that we have turned instead to the private experiences of hidden routes, secret knowledges, flittering spectres, the ghosts of London past. London is already 'vanished and vanishing' in 1905; the 1980s see another cluster of texts on *London's Secret History* or *The Ghosts of London*.[80] The allure of these languages has, I have aimed to show, a precise if ambivalent genealogy in questions of London governance.

The spectropoetics or hauntological frameworks encouraged by *Specters of Marx* routinize specificity beneath a general discourse regarding the spooky 'secret sharer' of Enlightenment modernity. This is a curious product of a thinker so often insistent on singularity and a resistant residue of untranslatability in every event. Perhaps, then, it is worth recalling that ghosts are held to haunt specific locales, are tied to what late Victorian psychical researchers rather splendidly termed 'phantas-mogenetic centres'. This might suggest that the ghosts of London are different from those of Paris, or those of California (where *Specters of Marx* was first delivered in lecture form). To uphold their liminal status between life and death, presence and absence is, in this case, to forget the other cultural convention about ghosts: that they appear precisely as *symptoms,* points of rupture that insist their singular tale be retold and their wrongs acknowledged. To respect the 'asymmetrical' demand of the spectre ('This spectral someone other looks at us, we feel ourselves being looked at by it, outside of any synchrony'), or to keep to a generalized account of temporal disadjustment ('here anachrony makes the law') is in my reading of the London Gothic to miss the point of its contemporary insistence.[81] The spectral turn reaches a limit if all it can describe is a repeated structure or generalized 'spectral process'—perhaps most particularly when critics suggest the breaching of limits is itself somehow inherently political.[82] The politics of such moves is, very exactly, *vacuous*: empty and without discernible content. If, as Derrida constantly proclaims in 'Marx & Sons', the whole thrust of *Specters of Marx* is to aim for a 'repoliticization' then surely we have to risk the violence of *reading* the ghost, of cracking open its absent presence to answer the demand of its specific symptomatology and its specific locale.

Notes

1. Rupert Davenport-Hines, *Gothic: 400 Years of Excess, Horror, Evil and Ruin* (London: Fourth Estate, 1998), pp. 9 and 375.

2. Patrick McGrath and Bradford Morrow (eds), *The New Gothic: A Collection of Contemporary Gothic Fiction* (London: Picador, 1991), p. xii.

3. Davenport-Hines, *Gothic,* p. 346.

4. Peggy Kamuf, 'Translating specters: an interview with Peggy Kamuf', *Parallax* 7:3 (2001), p. 45. I would include myself as a minor member of this band, having contributed to collections on ghosts, the Gothic and Derrida in the 1990s. I note this not as a narcissist, but as someone who can cast no stones: any critique undertaken by this essay is an auto-critique too.

5. Martin Jay, 'The uncanny nineties', in *Cultural Semantics: Key words of our Time* (London: Athlone Press, 1998), p. 157.

6. W. G. Sebald, *Austerlitz,* trans. Anthea Bell (London: Hamish Hamilton, 2001), p. 183.

7. Ibid., p. 261.

8. Marcello Truzzi, 'Definition and dimensions of the occult: towards a sociological persepective', *Journal of Popular Culture* 5:2 (1971-2), p. 638.

9. For some commentary on these groupings, see Peter Barry, 'Revisionings of London in three contemporary poets: Iain Sinclair, Allen Fisher, and Aidan Dun', in Holger Klein (ed.), *Poetry Now: Contemporary British and Irish Poetry in the Making* (Tubingen: Stauffenberg Verlag, 1999), and Robert Sheppard's review of Sinclair's anthology *Conductors of Chaos* in 'Elsewhere and everywhere: other new (British) poetries', *Critical Survey* 10:1 (1998), pp. 17-32.

10. Alan Moore and Eddie Campbell, *From Hell, Being a Melodrama in Sixteen Parts* (London: Knockabout, 1999).

11. Iain Sinclair, *Downriver (Or, The Vessels of Wrath): A Narrative in Twelve Tales* (London: Paladin, 1991), p. 143. All further page references in parentheses in the text.

12. Michael Moorcock, *London Bone* (London: Scribner, 2001).

13. Patrick Wright, *A Journey through the Ruins: The Last Days of London* (London: Radius, 1991), p. 12.

14. Peter Ackroyd, *London: A Biography* (London: Chatto & Windus, 2000), pp. 661 and 141. All further page references in parentheses in the text.

15. Julian Wolfreys, *Writing London: The Trace of the Urban Text from Blake to Dickens* (Basingstoke: Palgrave, 1998), pp. 8 and 25.

16. See e.g. William Sharpe and Leonard Wallock on the 'crisis of terminology' for the contemporary city in 'From "Great Town" to "Nonplace Urban Realm": reading the modern city', in Sharpe and Wallock (eds), *Visions of the Modern City* (Baltimore, MD: Johns Hopkins University Press, 1987), p. 1.

17. Wolfreys, *Writing London,* pp. 204-5.

18. James Donald, *Imagining the Modern City* (London: Athlone, 1999), pp. 17-18.

19. M. Christine Boyer, *The City of Collective Memory: Its Historical Imagery and Architectural Entertainments* (Cambridge, MA: MIT Press, 1996), pp. 28-9.

20. Anthony Vidler, *The Architectural Uncanny* (Cambridge, MA: MIT Press, 1992), p. 3.

21. Michel de Certeau, *The Practice of Everyday Life,* trans. Steven Rendall (Berkeley, LA: University of California Press, 1984), p. 108.

22. Jean-François Lyotard, 'About the human', in *The Inhuman: Reflections on Time,* trans. Geoffrey Bennington and Rachel Bowlby (Cambridge: Polity Press, 1991), p. 2.

23. Jean-Michel Rabaté, *The Ghosts of Modernity* (Gainesville: University Press of Florida, 1996), pp. xviii and xxi.

24. David Glover, 'The "spectrality effect" in early modernism', in Andrew Smith and Jeff Wallace (eds), *Gothic Modernisms* (Basingstoke: Palgrave, 2001), pp. 29-43.

25. Bruno Latour, *We Have Never Been Modern,* trans. Catherine Porter (Hemel Hempstead: Harvester, 1993), pp. 72 and 69.

26. Maureen Perkins, *The Reform of Time: Magic and Modernity* (London: Pluto, 2001).

27. Latour, *We Have Never Been Modern,* pp. 74-5.

28. Neil Gaiman, *Neverwhere* (London: Headline Publishing, 2000), pp. 235-6.

29. Lynda Nead, *Victorian Babylon* (New Haven, CT: Yale University Press, 2000), p. 8.

30. Wright, *A Journey through the Ruins,* p. 12.

31. Jacques Derrida, *Specters of Marx: The State of the Debt, the Work of Mourning, and the New International,* trans. Peggy Kamuf (New York: Routledge, 1994), p. 24.

32. André Breton, *Nadja,* trans. Richard Howard (New York: Grove Press, 1960). For commentary on the 'ghosted' subject in *Nadja,* see Margaret Cohen, *Profane Illumination* (Berkeley, LA: University of California Press, 1993) and Jean-Michel Rabaté, *The Ghosts of Modernity,* 'André Breton's ghostly stance', pp. 42-66.

33. For original documents, see *The Situationist International: An Anthology,* ed. and trans. Ken Knabb (New York: The Bureau of Public Secrets, 1989).

34. Stewart Home, *Mind Invaders: A Reader in Psychic Warfare, Cultural Sabotage and Semiotic Terrorism* (London: Serpent's Tail, 1997), pp. 29-32.

35. Jenny Turner, 'Aberdeen Rocks' [Review of Stewart Home, *69 Things to do with a Dead Princess*], *London Review of Books* (9 May 2002), p. 38.

36. Stewart Home, *The House of Nine Squares: Letters on Neoism, Psychogeography and Epistemological Trepidation* (London: Nine Squares, 1997).

37. LPA document, cited in Simon Sadler, *The Situationist City* (Cambridge, MA: MIT Press, 1999), p. 165. Home has extended these investigations into an overheated pulp fiction about sex magic and London topography in *Come Before Christ and Murder Love* (London: Serpent's Tail, 1997).

38. Iain Sinclair, *Lights Out for the Territory: 9 Excursions in the Secret History of London* (London: Granta, 1997), p. 26.

39. Iain Sinclair, *Lud Heat and Suicide Bridge* (London: Vintage, 1995), p. 113.

40. See Iain Sinclair, 'The mystery of the disappearing room', in *Downriver,* and Rachel Lichtenstein and Iain Sinclair, *Rodinsky's Room* (London: Granta, 1999), perhaps particularly '"Mobile invisibility": Golems, Dybbuks and unanchored presences', pp. 171-200.

41. Sinclair, *Downriver,* p. 265.

42. Jodey Castricano, *Cryptomimesis: The Gothic and Jacques Derrida's Ghost Writing* (Montreal: McGill-Queen's University Press, 2001), pp. 6 and 26.

43. Rabaté, *The Ghosts of Modernity,* 'The "moderns" and their ghosts', pp. 216-33.

44. Julian Wolfreys, *Victorian Hauntings: Spectrality, Gothic, the Uncanny and Literature* (Basingstoke: Palgrave, 2002), p. 7.

45. Ibid., p. 3 (emphasis added).

46. Derrida, *Specters of Marx,* p. 161.

47. Jay, 'The uncanny nineties', p. 162.

48. Nicholas Royle, 'Phantom Review' [Review of *Specters of Marx*], *Textual Practice* 11:2 (1997), p. 387.

49. Kate Soper, 'The limits of hauntology', in 'Spectres of Derrida: Symposium', *Radical Philosophy* 75 (January/February 1996). For other Marxist responses see Michael Sprinker (ed.), *Ghostly Demarcations: A Symposium on Jacques Derrida's Specters of Marx* (London: Verso, 1999), and the special issue of *Parallax* entitled 'A New International?' 7:3 (2001).

50. John Fletcher, 'Marx the uncanny: ghosts and their relation to the mode of production', *Radical Philosophy* 75 (1996). Fletcher concludes by arguing that 'the ghost in *Hamlet* is different from the tropes of spectrality in Marx, [and] this difference dramatizes issues of the epochal and the historical that are foreclosed and misrecognized by Derrida's transcendental "hauntology"' (p. 36). (One might disagree with the characterization of hauntology as 'transcendental' here, but Fletcher's point remains a powerful one.)

51. Jacques Derrida, 'Marx & Sons', in *Ghostly Demarcations,* p. 248.

52. Jacques Derrida, *Of Grammatology,* trans. Gayatri Spivak (Baltimore, MD: Johns Hopkins University Press, 1976), p. 158.

53. Chris Baldick, 'Introduction', in *Oxford Book of Gothic Tales* (Oxford: Oxford University Press, 1992), p. xxi.

54. See Robert Mighall, *A Geography of Victorian Gothic Fiction: Mapping History's Nightmares* (Oxford: Oxford University Press, 1999) and some of the contributions to Glennis Byron and David Punter (eds), *Spectral Readings: Towards a Geography of the Gothic* (Basingstoke: Macmillan, 1999). See also Margot Backas, *The Gothic Family Romance: Heterosexuality, Child Sacrifice and the Anglo-Irish Colonial Order* (Durham, NC: Duke University Press, 1999). Citation from David Punter, 'Heart lands: contemporary Scottish Gothic', *Gothic Studies* 1:1 (1997), p. 101.

55. Christopher Fowler, *Darkest Day* (London: Warner Books, 1993), p. 223. All further references in parentheses in the text.

56. Christopher Fowler, *Disturbia* (London: Warner Books, 1997), p. 3.

57. Citation from 1983 White Paper, *Streamlining the Cities* (October 1983), quoted in 'London after the GLC: an editorial foreword', *London Journal* 10-11 (1984-5), p. 6.

58. Eric J. Evans, *Thatcher and Thatcherism* (London: Routledge, 1997), p. 61.

59. Ben Pimlott and Nirmala Rao, *Governing London* (Oxford: Oxford University Press, 2002), p. 50.

60. Will Hutton, *The State We're In* (rev. edn London: Vintage, 1996), p. 28.

61. See William F. Kahl, *The Development of London Livery Companies* (Boston, MA: Baker Library, 1960).

62. Ranald C. Michie, *The City of London: Continuity and Change, 1850-1990* (London: Macmillan, 1990), p. 10.

63. Alexandra Warwick, 'Lost cities: London's apocalypse', in *Spectral Readings*, p. 84.

64. Janet Foster, *Docklands: Cultures in Conflict, Worlds in Collision* (London: UCL Press, 1999), p. 229.

65. Bill Schwarz, 'Where horses shit a hundred sparrows feed: Docklands and East London during the Thatcher years', in John Corner and Sylvia Harvey (eds), *Enterprise and Heritage: Crosscurrents of National Culture* (London: Routledge, 1991), p. 90.

66. David Owen, *The Government of London 1855-89: The Metropolitan Board of Works, the Vestries, and the City Corporation* (Cambridge, MA: Harvard University Press, 1982).

67. See Susan D. Pennybacker, *A Vision for London 1889-1914: Labour, Everyday Life and the LCC Experiment* (London: Routledge, 1995). There are also useful contributions on the LCC era in David Feldman and Gareth Stedman-Jones (eds), *Metropolis—London: Histories and Representations since 1800* (London: Routledge, 1989).

68. See Gareth Stedman-Jones, *Outcast London* (Harmondsworth: Penguin, 1971) and Joseph McLaughlin, *Writing the Urban Jungle: Reading Empire in London from Doyle to Eliot* (Charlottesville: University Press of Virginia, 2000). For selections of contemporary documents, see 'Outcast London', in Sally Ledger and Roger Luckhurst (eds), *The Fin de Siècle: A Reader in Cultural History 1880-1900* (Oxford: Oxford University Press, 2000), pp. 25-51.

69. Frederic Harrison, 'London in 1887', in *The Meaning of History and Other Historical Pieces* (London: Macmillan, 1894), p. 435.

70. James Cantlie, *Degeneration Amongst Londoners* (London: Field & Tuer, 1885).

71. Sidney Low, 'The Rise of the suburbs', *Contemporary Review* 60 (1891), p. 550.

72. Sidney Webb, *The London Programme* (London: Swan Sonnenschein, 1891), pp. 4 and v.

73. Sidney Webb, 'The work of the London County Council', *Contemporary Review* 67 (1895), p. 130.

74. Pimlott and Rao, *Governing London*, p. 87. For a rapid response to these farcical events see M. D'Arcy and R. MacLean, *Nightmare: The Race to Become London's Mayor* (London: Politico's, 2000).

75. Arthur Machen, 'Science and the ghost story', *Literature* (17 September 1898), p. 251.

76. Arthur Machen, *The London Adventure* (London: Martin Secker, 1924), pp. 77-8.

77. See esp. Thomas Burke, *Limehouse Nights: Tales of Chinatown* (London: Grant Richards, 1917), and for London lost to the regulative interference of the Defence of the Realm Act his *Out and About: A Notebook of London in Wartime* (1919). I am indebted here to Anne Witchard's as yet unpublished work on Burke's fantasy Limehouse for these points.

78. Wright, *A Journey through the Ruins,* p. 164.

79. Georg Simmel, 'The sociology of secrecy and secret societies', *American Journal of Sociology* 11: 4 (1906), p. 472.

80. Philip Norman, *London Vanished and Vanishing* (London: Adam & Charles Black, 1905); Peter Bushell, *London's Secret History* (London: Constable, 1983); J. A. Brooks, *Ghosts of London,* 2 vols (Norwich: Jarrold, 1982).

81. Parenthetical citations from Derrida, *Specters of Marx,* pp. 6 and 7.

82. I am thinking here in particular of Julian Wolfreys' comments in the introduction to his *Victorian Hauntings,* where the 'spectral mechanism' of the Gothic is held to be 'a subversive force . . . through which social and political critique may become available' (p. 11).

Steven Bruhm (essay date 2002)

SOURCE: Bruhm, Steven. "The Contemporary Gothic: Why We Need It." In *The Cambridge Companion to Gothic Fiction,* edited by Jerrold E. Hogle, pp. 259-76. Cambridge: Cambridge University Press, 2002.

[*In the following essay, Bruhm surveys numerous works in order to reach some conclusions about the characteristics of modern Gothic, especially noting the influence of Freudian psychology.*]

My title suggests a rather straightforward enterprise: I want to account for the enormous popularity of the Gothic—both novels and films—since the Second World War. However, the title proposes more questions than it answers. First, what exactly counts as "the contemporary Gothic"? Since its inception in 1764, with Horace Walpole's *The Castle of Otranto,* the Gothic has always played with chronology, looking back to moments in an imaginary history, pining for a social stability that never existed, mourning a chivalry that belonged more to the fairy tale than to reality. And contemporary Gothic does not break with this tradition: Stephen King's *IT* (1987) and Anne Rice's vampire narratives (begun in the 1970s) weave in and out of the distant past in order to comment on the state of contemporary American culture, while other narratives foreground their reliance on prior, historically distant narratives. Peter Straub's *Julia* (1975), Doris Lessing's *The Fifth Child* (1988), and John Wyndham's *The Midwich Cuckoos* (film version: *The Village of the Damned* [1960]) all feed off *The Turn of the Screw* (1898) by Henry James, itself arguably a revision of Jean-Jacques Rousseau's *Emile* (1762), a treatise on the education of two children at a country house. And as many contributors to this volume demonstrate, the central concerns of the classical Gothic are not that different from those of the contemporary Gothic: the dynamics of family, the limits of rationality and passion, the definition of statehood and citizenship, the cultural effects of technology. How, then, might we define a contemporary Gothic? For to think about the contemporary Gothic is to look into a triptych of mirrors in which images of the origin continually recede in a disappearing arc. We search for a genesis but find only ghostly manifestations.

Nor is the idea of origin the only problem here, for there is also the problem embedded in my title: why we need the contemporary Gothic. Certainly its popularity cannot be disputed—films like *Rosemary's Baby* (1968), *The Exorcist* (1973), and *The Silence of the Lambs* (1991) take home Oscars, and Stephen King habitually tops the best-seller lists—but why are we driven to consume these fictions? Is this craving something structural or social? Does it stem from our desire to see the political tyrant bested or the weak, deformed, or unfortunate (as in Shirley Jackson's *The Lottery* [1949]) scapegoated in a ritual purgation of blood? The Gothic has always been a barometer of the anxieties plaguing a certain culture at a particular moment in history, but what is the relationship between these general social trends and particular individual psyche? When the children of *Nightmare on Elm Street* (1984) conjure Freddy Kruger in their dreams, are they expressing a personal nightmare about what lies beneath their consciousnesses, a social nightmare about how America treats its dispossessed, or some amorphous combination of the two? For that matter, do we need to see each child's Freddy Kruger as the same Freddy Kruger? The "we" who needs the Gothic is by no means a unified, homogeneous group. I do not necessarily need the same things you do. I do not necessarily take the same things from a Gothic narrative as do the others who have bought the book or the theatre ticket. Like the question of origin I addressed above, the basis of need and desire is not only a theme in Gothic narratives but a theoretical quandary for the spectators and readers who consume those narratives.

We can best address the question of audience need by placing the contemporary Gothic within a number of current anxieties—the ones we need it both to arouse and assuage. One of these anxieties, taken up by Stephen King in his nonfictional *Danse Macabre* (1982), is political and historical. He discusses at length the degree to which the Second World War, the Cold War, and the space race gave rise to particular kinds of horror in the 1940s and 1950s. Central to this horror is the fear of foreign otherness and monstrous invasion. We need only consider Ira Levin's *The Boys from Brazil* (1976), William Peter Blatty's *The Exorcist* (1971), or Stephen King's *The Tommyknockers* (1988) to see the connection between national purity and the fear of foreign invasion, be it from Germany, the Middle East, or outer space. Another anxiety, not unrelated to the first, is the technological explosion in the second half of the twentieth century. Advances in weaponry—both military and medical—have rendered our culture vulnerable to almost total destruction (as in Boris Sagal's *The Omega Man* [1971] or King's *Firestarter* [1980] and *The Stand* [1978]) or have helped us conceive of superhuman beings unable to be destroyed (the cyborgs and animate machines of *2001: a Space Odyssey* [1968], the *Terminator* series [1984, 1991], or *Dark City* [1998]). Third, the rise of feminism, gay liberation, and African-American civil rights in the 1960s has assaulted the ideological supremacy of traditional values where straight white males ostensibly control the public sphere. In the midst of this onslaught comes a further blow to Euro-American culture: the heightened attack against Christian ideology and hierarchy as that which should "naturally" define values and ethics in culture. The Satanism of *Rosemary's Baby,* the continued cult worship of the Dracula figure in all his manifestations, and the popularity of anti-Christ figures from Damien Thorne of *The Omen* (novel, 1976; film, 1976) to Marilyn Manson all attest to the powerful threat (and attraction) posed by our culture's increasing secularity. And regardless of whether one loathes the anti-Christian figure in these narratives or cheers him on, one cannot help but be impressed by the degree to which this "attack of the Gothic" has infiltrated our culture and fractured any ideologically "natural" state of personal or social well-being.

The Gothic texts and films I have already mentioned circle around a particular nexus: the problem of assimilating these social anxieties (which I will momentarily discuss in terms of "trauma") into a personal narrative that in some way connects the Gothic protagonist to the reader or spectator. What becomes most marked in the contemporary Gothic—and what distinguishes it from its ancestors—is the protagonists' and the viewers' compulsive return to certain fixations, obsessions, and blockages.[1] Consequently, the Gothic can be readily analyzed through the rhetoric of psychoanalysis, for many the twentieth century's supreme interpreter of human compulsions and repressions. In both theory and clinical practice, psychoanalysis is primarily attributed to the work of Sigmund Freud, for whom the Gothic was a rich source of imagery and through whom the Gothic continues to be analyzed today.[2] Psychoanalysis provides us with a language for understanding the conflicted psyche of the patient whose life story (or "history") is characterized by neurotic disturbances and epistemological blank spots. More often than not, such psychoanalytic accounts are intensely Gothic: "The Uncanny" (1919) and "A Seventeenth-Century Demonological Neurosis" (1922),[3] along with a number of Freud's case studies, make the figure of the tyrannical father central to the protagonists' Gothic experiences, as does Matthew Lewis's *The Monk* (1796) or Stoker's *Dracula* (1897); "On Narcissism: an Introduction" (1914) and *Group Psychology and the Analysis of the Ego* (1921) offer us purchase on the person in society looking for acceptance while at the same time remaining abject and individualized, a central problem in Gothic novels; and the phantasms generated by the Wolf Man or Dr. Schreber, like those experienced by the grieving subject in *Mourning and Melancholia,* cannot be dissociated from the Gothic ghost, the revenant who embodies and projects the subject's psychic state.

But perhaps what is most central to the Gothic—be it classical or contemporary—is the very process of psychic life that for Freud defines the human condition. While the id finds its narrative expression in the insatiable drives of the desiring organism (Dean Koontz's Bruno in *Whispers* [1981], the mutant child in the film *It's Alive* [1974]), the superego takes monstrous form in the ultrarational, cultured figures of Hannibal Lecter, Damien Thorne, or Anne Rice's blood-drinking literati. The battle for supremacy between the ravenous id and the controlling superego translates in myriad ways into the conflicts of the Gothic. Indeed, what makes the contemporary Gothic contemporary, I hope to show, is not merely the way Freudian dynamics underlie Gothic narratives (for this, uncannily, is also the condition of classical eighteenth-century Gothic), but how contemporary Gothic texts and films are intensely *aware* of this Freudian rhetoric and self-consciously *about* the longings and fears it describes. In other words, what makes the contemporary Gothic contemporary is that the Freudian machinery is more than a tool for discussing narrative; it is in large part the subject matter of the narrative itself. A major theme of the Gothic has always been interior life, as in the paranoid Gothic of William Godwin's *Caleb Williams* (1794) or James Hogg's *The Private Memoirs and Confessions of a Justified Sinner* (1824), but the rise of psychoanalysis in the twentieth century has afforded Gothic writers a very particular configuration of this internal life. To the degree that the contemporary Gothic subject is the psychoanalytic subject (and vice versa), she/he becomes a/the field on which national, racial, and gender anxieties *configured like Freudian drives* get played out and symbolized over and over again.

The unconscious, Freud postulates, is born from the moment the child first encounters a prohibition or law against satisfying desires. In Freud's work, the most important desire is that of the (male) child to have uninterrupted access to his mother. The Oedipus complex arises, Freud suggests, when the boy wants to continue to use his mother as an uninterrupted source of pleasure and nourishment as well as the provider of the physical tactility that will ensure this safety. The father interrupts this infantile desire—what Freud calls "primary narcissism"—by prohibiting the child's continued desire for the mother. In the interests of fashioning the child's masculinity and his individuality, the father forces him to submit to the patriarchal law of finding his own other-sexed partner, thereby leaving the mother to return her affections to the father rather than lavishing them on the son. But, true to the Freudian schema, the child's desires for the mother, and his attendant aggression, hatred, and fear of the father, do not disappear. They are put away in a space where they are no longer socially visible (lest the child appear "queer"[4]) but where they structure the developing personality and help control what that child will come to desire, both socially and sexually. This is the key point to a Freudian understanding of the Gothic in general: as human beings, we are not free agents operating out of conscious will and self-knowledge. Rather, when our fantasies, dreams, and fears take on a nightmarish quality, it is because the unconscious is telling us what we *really* want. And what we really want are those desires and objects that have been forbidden.

What makes the contemporary Gothic particularly contemporary in both its themes and reception, however, is that these unconscious desires center on the problem of a lost object, the most overriding basis of *our* need for the Gothic and almost everything else. That loss is usually material (parents, money, property, freedom to move around, a lover, or family member), but the materiality of that loss always has a psychological and symbolic dimension to it. When the Freudian father pries the son away from the mother and her breast, he is seen by the child to introduce a sense of *loss,* an absence that will then drive the child to try to fill the empty space that prohibition creates. In the psychoanalytic Gothic, we intensely desire the object that has been lost, or another object, person, or practice that might take its place, but we are aware at some level that this object carries with it the threat of punishment: the anger of the father, the breaking of the law, castration. When the desire for an object butts up against the prohibition against the fulfilling of that desire, the result is the contemporary human subject. Simply put, we *are* what we have become in response to the threat of violence from anything like the figure of the father. Furthermore, the mode in which the late modern subject most enacts this scene of prohibition—and the mode in which we as audience take it up—is the Gothic, itself a narrative of prohibitions, transgressions, and the processes of identity construction that occur within such tensions. Let us, then, consider first the themes of the contemporary Gothic before speculating on why we as an audience take it up with such relish.

Oedipal battles between parent and child are not new in the Gothic, to be sure; *Frankenstein* (1818) is just one progenitor of novels such as *The Exorcist, Pet Sematary* (1983) or *Interview with the Vampire* (1976). Even so, a novel such as Stephen King's *The Shining* (1977) offers an especially textbook case of the oedipal conflict. The oedipal family—a trinity of daddy, mommy, child—is trapped in a remote hotel where the caretaker goes mad and tries to kill the son he thinks is a traitor to him. While the horror story of cabin fever is clear, Stephen King is too consciously Freudian to allow the plot to stay there: "Freud says that the subconscious never speaks to us in a literal language," his protagonist Jack Torrance tells wife Wendy, "Only in symbols" (p. 264). Chief among these symbols is their son Danny's ability to read minds and to glimpse the future (a talent the novel calls "shining"). This ability is, among other

things, a way of looking into his parents' minds to see what they are thinking. In fact, this very act of looking corresponds to a famous Freudian moment called "the primal scene." In Freud's case study of the Wolf Man (1918), he postulated that his patient had seen his parents having sex *a tergo,* so that both parents' genitals were visible. The father was deemed to have a penetrating and violently aggressive penis while the mother had lost her penis (the male child being unable to imagine that not all people have a penis as he does) to the violating father.

In both Freud and *The Shining,* this hypothesis gives the primal scene a special Gothic undertone. For the boy-child, it is a primary threat: the father has the penis and can remove someone else's. For Danny Torrance, in particular, it shrouds shining—that is, sexual knowing—in a pall of disgust, transgression, and prohibition. Likening his talent for shining to "peeking into [his parents'] bedroom and watching while they're doing the thing that makes babies" (p. 83),[5] Danny also reads his father's mind to determine the level of paternal hatred toward him and his mother. In this primal shining, there is more than one lost object: mother and son lose phallic power *vis-à-vis* the father, and the family loses the bond that was supposed to keep them safe and close. It is small wonder, then, that when Danny begins to explore the Overlook Hotel and discovers/hallucinates its horrible ghosts—such as the dead woman in the bathtub—he does so out of a desire to heal the family: "Danny stepped into the bathroom and walked toward the tub dreamily, as if propelled from outside himself, as if . . . he would perhaps see something nice when he pulled the curtain back, something Daddy had forgotten or Mommy had lost, something that would make them both happy" (p. 217). Danny's desire to look—perhaps like ours, as desirous voyeurs of the Gothic—is ultimately the desire to find that which has been lost, that which will unify an otherwise fragmented subjectivity. And in Freud, as in King, it is the lost object (the penis) that constitutes the identity of the male: "normal" boys rigorously imitate masculine identity precisely because they fear the father will rob them of the marker of masculine entitlement, the penis, if they do not. Danny's, then, is a remarkably *contemporary* problem: whereas the original *Frankenstein* at least believed in the possibility of real fatherhood, real domesticity, and a real self, Danny is forced to operate in a psychological sphere where some crucial aspect of the self is always lost and must always be sought, but can never provide the happiness for which it is desired.

The contemporary Gothic, in other words, reveals the domestic scene in a world after Freud and the degree to which that domestic scene is predicated on loss. The ideology of family continues to circulate with as much atmospheric pressure as it did in the novels of Ann Radcliffe or Mary Shelley, but with a difference:

whereas financial greed, religious tyranny, and incestuous privation interrupt the smooth workings of the eighteenth-century family (only to exhort the importance of the family as a concept), the contemporary Gothic registers the (Freudian) impossibility of familial harmony, an impossibility built into the domestic psyche as much as it is into domestic materiality. For in such a novel as *The Shining,* everybody hates a parent and presumably the *wrong* parent. Wendy hates her mother and loves her father (as is the case with Susan Norton in *Salem's Lot* [1975]); Jack hated his mother but respected his abusive father; and even Danny, whose suffering at the hands of his father we have just noted, "loved his mother but was his father's boy" (King, *Shining,* p. 54). So why this bond with the tyrannical father? Why is the mother, Wendy, reduced to a walking talking breast to whom Danny can periodically run for solace (rocking, cooing, the singing of lullabies) but who holds little other value in Danny's emotion economy? Why this change from the classical Gothic, where the male child also hated the tyrannical father but without the same psychological complications?

The reason is Freud. In the contemporary psychological schema, we desire not only the lost object but the approval of the tyrant who took that object from us. Freud's *Totem and Taboo* (1913) maps the path by which the rebel sons become their hated father by consuming his body after they have killed him. In order to kill the father and thus establish their own autonomy, they first have to assume the father's strength beforehand, a psychological incorporation of the father/tyrant that will later be ritualized in the consuming of his body and later cannibalistic rituals like it, ranging from the Holy Eucharist to Gothic vampirism. *The Shining,* similarly, documents Danny's vacillation between child and man, or between parental appendage and autonomous adult. Here he vacillates between being the child who tears the father figure and being a father figure himself: both Jack and Danny are male figures responsible for taking care of Wendy; both Jack and Danny shine; and both Jack and Danny are caretakers of a hotel, although in the end it is Danny who will excel over Jack by remembering what his father forgot (how to take care of the boiler). This becoming-father, then, is an act both of homage and of transgression: the son adores the father to the degree that he must kill him in order to *become* him. King and the contemporary Gothic thus write into the family romance Oscar Wilde's quite modern realization that we kill the thing we love. Horror, mutilation, and loss thus become more than shock effect; they constitute the very aesthetic that structures the human psyche in the twentieth century, connecting the Freudian vision of the human mind generally to the dynamics of Gothic villainy and victimization.

Indeed, such ambivalence between the abusive parent and the desiring child is not limited to father-son dy-

namics. Although father and son constitute the usual scenario in Freud's phallically centered thinking, the Gothic provides equal opportunity for the monstrous mother as well. Famous girl stories in this vein include that of Carrie White and her mother in King's *Carrie* (1974) or Eleanor in Shirley Jackson's *The Haunting of Hill House* (1959); boy-centered versions appear in Norman Bates's relation to his mummified mummy in Hitchcock's *Psycho* (1960, based on the 1959 novel by Robert Bloch) and the castrating mother of Daniel Mann's *Willard* (1972).[6] A number of forces conspire to frame this contemporary mother. A narrative such as *The Exorcist,* for example, at least momentarily blames a child's demonic possession on her mother's feminism: Chris McNeil has left her husband, she supports herself and her daughter Regan through her successful acting career, and she has abandoned the usual religious and social codes of feminine propriety. For this she is punished, as a demon enters the body of her (maternally neglected) child. Moreover, Blatty's antifeminism resonates with another theory of the monstrous maternal, that of psychoanalyst Julia Kristeva. According to Kristeva, paternal prohibition is not the only reason the child must achieve distance from the mother. The child must "abject" the mother—discard or jettison the primal connection to her, deem her dangerous and suffocating—if she/he is to gain any autonomous subjectivity whatsoever. That thrown-off mother, at least in the child's fantasy, continually lures and seduces the child back to the primary bond where she/he is completely taken care of; in response, the child must demonize and reject her in order "to constitute [it]self and [its] culture" (Kristeva, *Powers of Horror,* p. 2).[7] And because that act of abjecting "is a violent, clumsy breaking away, with the constant risk of falling back into under the sway of a power as securing as it is stifling" (ibid., p. 13), the mother is continually reinvented as monstrous but in a way the child incorporates as much as she/he abjects. Regan McNeil comes to embody Chris's sexual knowledge, her foul language, and her refusal to adhere to conventional social codes governing women; Carrie White *becomes* the murderous, vindictive mother/God she hates. We come then not to be mere victims of the lost object—the mother—but active agents in the expulsion of that mother. We are creatures of conflicted desires, locked in an uncanny push-me-pull-you that propels us toward the very objects we fear and to fear the very objects toward which we are propelled. We must bond with our parents, but not too much; we must distance ourselves from our parents, but not too much.

That the persecuted subject should escape persecution either by returning to the maternal breast or by becoming the parent she/he fears marks a problem in that subject's personal history, a problem central to the contemporary Gothic. According to Freud, the obsessive return to the nurturing, safe mother is a *regression,* one that arrests the individual's psychological development. But taking the path forward toward adulthood by no means guarantees a happy growth or linear progress. Adults such as Jack Torrance of *The Shining,* Thad Beaumont of *The Dark Half* (1989), Clarice Starling from Thomas Harris's *The Silence of the Lambs* (1988), or Hannibal Lecter in Harris's sequel *Hannibal* (1999) are all to a great extent determined by the familial relations they experienced in childhood. At the level of the parental, Jack Torrance remains subject to his father's abusive control (he *becomes* his father), while Carrie White adopts the brutal, punishing, destructive power of her mother—although it might be more accurate to say that Carrie becomes Margaret's punitive angry God, new England's cosmic Father. And as Gothic children threaten the role of the parent by consuming or incorporating that parent's power, we find in them intellects that soar beyond what children are supposed to have. See, for example, the children of *Village of the Damned,* whose intellects far surpass those of adults, a condition we also find in Regan McNeil of *The Exorcist* or Gage Creed and Timmy Baterman of King's *Pet Sematary* (1983). Our domestic lives are supposed to be governed by a logic of chronology—older and wiser parents care for and instruct their innocent and vulnerable offspring—but not in the Gothic. Psychological subject positions shift and float, rearranging and destabilizing the roles assumed to belong to each person in the domestic arrangement.

This disruption of domestic history is ultimately based on a fluidity in the Gothic protagonist's personal history; contemporary Gothic characters often utterly confuse their childhood experiences with their adult lives. This confusion results from the unconscious as Freud described it, a repository of prohibited desires, aggressions, and painful or terrifying experiences. As these psychological experiences mesh with the sense of loss that accompanies them (loss of parent, loss of security, loss of ego or stable sense of self), they set up echoes of childhood in the subject's later life. What was repressed thus returns to haunt our heroes with the vivid immediacy of the original moment. And it is this moment of return, seminally theorized by Freud in *Totem and Taboo,* that highlights the key difference between the contemporary Gothic and its classical predecessors' understanding of personal and social history. In the late eighteenth-century Gothic of Ann Radcliffe or Matthew Lewis, moments from the historical past (often appearing as spectral figures) haunt the heroes in order to proclaim some misdeed regarding property or domestic relations. It is often the project of those novels to expose ancient tyrannies, to foil the characters perpetuating them, and to return property and persons to their divinely ordained spheres. In so doing, the classical Gothic returns its society to a logic of historical progression. The contemporary Gothic, conversely, cannot sustain such a program, precisely because of its characters' psychological complications. With the ravages of

the unconscious continually interrupting one's perception of the world, the protagonist of the contemporary Gothic often experiences history as mixed up, reversed, and caught in a simultaneity of past-present-future.[8] History has made a promise—that one will grow from a fragile, vulnerable child to an autonomous, rational adult—but it is unable to keep that promise in the twentieth century. It can only offer a future that is already suspended between present and past. While the Gothic may ostensibly plot the movement of chronological time, it really devastates any sense of linear progression that we might use to put together our "personal history."

Especially when viewed through the lens of psychoanalysis, then, the contemporary Gothic markedly registers a crisis in personal history: in the world depicted in such works, one is forced simultaneously to mourn the lost object (a parent, God, social order, lasting fulfillment through knowledge or sexual pleasure) and to *become* the object lost through identification or imitation. This history of repetition, I would argue, constitutes a sense of *trauma,* and it is finally through trauma that we can best understand the contemporary Gothic and why we crave it. Speaking of the Gothic as analogous to trauma, or even as the product and enactment of trauma, makes sense for a number of reasons. First, the Gothic itself is a narrative of trauma. Its protagonists usually experience some horrifying event that profoundly affects them, destroying (at least temporarily) the norms that structure their lives and identities. Images of haunting, destruction and death, obsessive return to the shattering moment, forgetfulness or unwanted epiphany ("you will remember what your father forgot," Tony tells Danny Torrance [King, *Shining,* p. 420]) all define a Gothic aesthetic that is quite close to Cathy Caruth's definition of trauma and its corollary, post-traumatic stress disorder (PTSD):

> there is a response, sometimes delayed, to an overwhelming event or events, which takes the form of repeated, intrusive hallucinations, dreams, thoughts or behaviors stemming from the event, along with numbing that may have begun during or after the experience, and possibly also increased arousal to (and avoidance of) stimuli recalling the event . . . [T]he event is not assimilated or experienced fully at the time, but only belatedly, in its repeated *possession* of the one who experiences it.[9]

Caruth has in mind survivors of Auschwitz and Vietnam, but her descriptions also remind us of a number of protagonists of the contemporary Gothic. Peter Straub's fictions habitually portray men (although *Julia* is an exception) who have endured some invasion, violation, or uncanny experience in younger life and have never comprehended the full effects of that experience. Sears James in *Ghost Story* (1979), the narrator of "The Juniper Tree" in *Houses Without Doors* (1991), and Tim

Underhill in *Koko* (1988) and *The Throat* (1994) all return to earlier experiences and only gradually "assimilate" them, if at all.

Gothic horrors in these texts are the distortions, hallucinations, and nightmares that proceed from these experiences. Memories of that moment flash before the Gothic hero's eyes only to be inaccessible minutes later: when Dr. Louis Creed of *Pet Sematary* loses his first patient at his new job, his mind immediately "seemed to be wrapping those few moments in a protective film—sculpting, changing, disconnecting" (p. 77). Similarly, as he prepares to disinter his dead child Gage, Louis "realized he could not remember what his son had looked like . . . He could see [Gage's features] but he could not integrate them into a coherent whole" (p. 334). The child-woman Claudia of *Interview with the Vampire* lives fully as a vampire but cannot recall the moment that made her one (unlike Lestat and Louis, who remember everything). *The Exorcist*'s Regan has experienced the "numbing" that characterizes the subject during trauma—Regan "herself" is inaccessible to herself, her mother, the doctors, and priests—and she remembers nothing of her experience after the exorcism. Time and again the contemporary Gothic presents us with traumatized heroes who have lost the very psychic structures that allow them access to their own experiences. As I have been suggesting, such narratives emphasize a lost object, that object being the self. Individual autonomy, unity of soul and ego, and personal investment in will and self reliance have all been shattered by the forces of the social and the ravages of the unconscious upon the ego in contemporary existence. The self is shattered into pieces, the "many" rather than the "one" that defines a character like Regan McNeil, who now is "no *one*" (p. 325, emphasis added), but rather "quite a little group," a "stunning little multitude" (p. 245).

That loss of wholeness, that destruction of the thing in favor of many things, so obsesses Gothic fiction in the later twentieth century that many such narratives are about the impossibility of narrative. Jack Torrance's writer's block (which Stanley Kubrick changes in his 1980 film to an obsessive repetition of the cliché "all work and no play makes Jack a dull boy") is not unlike Catharine Holly's inability to tell the story of Sebastian in Tennessee William's southern Gothic play, *Suddenly Last Summer* (1958, adapted as a film in 1959). Eleanor in *The Haunting of Hill House* is unable to narrate the death of her mother, and so the story is told only fleetingly in the words appearing on the walls of the mansion. King's *Pet Sematary* opens with a list of books written by people who have done important things in the world and follows with a list of people who attended the corpses of those famous authors but who have not written books or told their stories themselves. King concludes: "*Death is a mystery, and burial is a secret.*" Trauma collapses the ability to render experience in a narrative, as recent studies of concentration camp prisoners and child sexual abuse survivors are making very clear. Trauma destroys what Pierre Janet calls "narrative memory," the ability to apply principles of coherence and analytical understanding to one's life events.[10] Indeed, *Pet Sematary* implicitly compares the temporality of trauma (a forgetting that is interrupted by unwilled remembering) with the experience of a child learning a language: "babies make *all* the sounds the human voice box is capable of . . . They lose the capability as they learn English, and Louis wondered now (and not for the first time) if childhood was not more a period of forgetting than of learning" (p. 221). What Louis as adult will then come to "re-member" (his dead son Gage returned from the grave) is pretty horrific, but lest my analogy seem far-fetched, *The Exorcist* makes the same move and much more clearly. "Cryptomnesia: buried recollections of words and data" that Regan may have learned in early childhood come "to the surface with almost photographic fidelity" (p. 268), and by now no one needs to be reminded of what kind of verbal spectacle Regan makes of herself.

All of this together fashions a contemporary Gothic phenomenon. Words, the building blocks of stories, rise and fall in consciousness, constituting horrifying returns and traumatic suggestions. The very act of storytelling itself has the resonance of multiple traumas that we, like Louis Creed at the graveside, cannot integrate into a coherent whole. What gets left in this blank space where our narratives cannot be is, paradoxically, a massive production of other Gothic narratives. In the process of trauma shattering us from one into a "stunning little multitude," we are forced to confront our demons, our worst fears about the agents and influences that might control and create us.

It is here, too, that we can see the link between the domestic anxieties we have been discussing and more far-flung social anxieties. The Gothic mother who must be abjected and the authoritative tyrannical father who must be overthrown are, according to psychoanalysis, parts of one's self that must be feared because they define the self at the same time as they take one's self-definition outside, to an other and perhaps to many outside versions of that other. The volatile status of otherness, it is true, has come to haunt the Gothic mode since the eighteenth century. But in the contemporary moment, that otherness is often framed by a psychoanalytic model of the psyche that includes a larger social vision full of phobias and prejudices about many types of "others." Gothic plots such as *Ghost Story* or *The Hand That Rocks the Cradle* (1992) connect their *femmes fatales* to motherhood in general, meshing the need for abjection with a larger cultural misogyny and fear of too-powerful women. Same-sex bonding between men, which, as Eve Kosofsky Sedgwick argues, is the glue that cements capitalist relations in the west,[11] finds its Gothic counterpart in the homosexual panic of King's Jack Torrance, Robert Bloch's Norman Bates, or Peter Straub's Peter Barnes.[12] And in our contemporary imagination, where homosexuality is also pedophilia in the eyes of many, narratives from King's *Salem's Lot,* King and Peter Straub's *The Talisman* (1984) to Straub's "The Juniper Tree" and "Bunny Is Good Bread" (in *Magic Terror* [2000]) do more than tell a horror story about children's victimization at the hands of a monster; they project the Gothic terror of our culture's contemporary cult of child-worship.[13] Why else would Louis Creed, looking at his sexually arousing wife, think that "she looked amazingly like [their daughter] Ellie . . . and Gage" (King, *Pet Sematary,* p. 187)? Then, too, can we read the racist representation of vampires as Mexican immigrants in John Carpenter's 1998 film *Vampires* without seeing it as an up-to-date version of the fear of eastern Europeans in Stoker's *Dracula,* which additionally indicates the fear of the unknown, "foreign" parts of ourselves, be they sexual or "spiritual"? Or might we see in the gypsy who curses Billy Halleck in Richard Bachman's *Thinner* (1984), or in Dr. Rabbitfoot in Straub's *Ghost Story,* the fear of the "magical" animism, where internal thought can suddenly become external object or action, a process which to Freud constitutes the infantile thinking we never completely forget?[14] In the spaces left by many kinds of trauma, we rush in to supply all kinds of stories. We generate an industry of narrative fantasies that merge all too nicely with other social prejudices, and we do all of this to convince ourselves that the horror of consciousness is not ours, that it really comes from the outside.

Yet we have done so, in the end, without much psychological success. The Gothic continually confronts us with real, historical traumas that we in the west have created but that also continue to control how we think about ourselves as a nation (be it "America," "Canada," "Great Britain," or some other country). Ira Levin's *The Boys From Brazil* directly invokes the Jewish Holocaust, while *Carrie* at least briefly nods to the war in Vietnam, as if her personal trauma were somehow linked to America's great social trauma of that time. Whatever metonymic affiliations Carrie might have with Vietnam, in fact, it makes her telekinetic power analogous to the nuclear bomb, thus providing us with some of the same Cold War anxieties we see in *Village of the Damned* and Margaret Atwood's *The Handmaid's Tale* (1985). *Pet Sematary* may be about the personal trauma of losing a child, but it is also about American colonization. The Micmac burial ground that lies beyond the pet cemetery exerts a malignant and ancient spiritual influence over the environs of Ludlow, Maine; the Wendigo who presides over this burial ground is the amoral nature god who returns to reclaim what Christianity has taken from the natives. Hence the parody of resurrection: what returns from the grave is not the Christ-child but a murderous demon, an aboriginal trickster figure who, in the Gothic imagination, has been transmogrified into a knife-wielding killer. Each of these social and national traumas was caused by human agency, yet they have rendered humans unable to tell any kind of complete story about them. Thus the Gothic renders them in fits and starts, ghostly appearances and far-fetched fantasies, all attempting to reveal traumatic contradictions of the collective past that cannot be spoken.

In short, it seems that we are caught in what Freud would call a repetition-compulsion, where we are compelled to consume the same stories (with minor variations), experience the same traumatic jolts, behold the same devastating sights. So, to return to the questions I asked at the beginning of this chapter, why are we so drawn to the Gothic? Who is this "we" that are craving it? We find ourselves compelled to accept more than one answer. Clearly, there is some kind of comfort associated with repetition, but what kind of theory explains that comfort? Walter Benjamin might suggest that such horror narratives confirm for us that we are spectators, safely distanced onlookers whose integrity is guaranteed by the dissolution of another. As Benjamin puts it, "What draws the reader to the novel is the hope of warming his shivering life with a death he reads about,"[15] and the compulsive repetition of this hand-warming gives us the necessary assurance that the victim is not us. But the very seductiveness of Gothic fiction makes such a claim to being outside it impossible to sustain. We seem to want these fictions from the inside out; we crave them not for their distance but for their immediacy, for they make our hearts race, our blood pressure rise, our breathing become shallow and quick, and our stomachs roll. Like the traumatized subject, we physically roil when faced with a parade of uncontrollable and horrifying images that are strangely familiar, as uncanny as they are abject. We crave these "stimuli," to use Caruth's word, and we feel possessed by them. Indeed, as an individual reader or viewer, I may not *be* traumatized at the moment of reading, but I certainly join with the Gothic mode in *feeling like one who is traumatized.* Father Merrin of *The Exorcist* says of horror's agent, "I think the demon's target is not the possessed; it is us . . . the observers . . . every person in this house" (p. 369). So if the priests of *The Exorcist* can perform an exorcism on Regan, we need to consider that Gothic fiction in general can perform some kind of exorcism on us, the observers in this highly oedipal and traumatized house.

Perhaps the repetition compulsions underlying trauma can provide us with some insight. While both the Gothic and trauma are characterized by the inability to comprehend fully one's experience and to filter that experience through what Pierre Janet has called "narrative memory," they suggest more than the horrors of ineffability. Caruth argues that "trauma can make possible survival" by actually capitalizing on the distance one takes from the traumatic experience. We have already seen King's Louis Creed respond to disaster by partially removing himself from the anxiety-inducing scene: a "protective film" disconnects him from the moment. Caruth provides an interesting take on this phenomenon. "[T]hrough the different modes therapeutic, literary, and pedagogical encounter," she says,

> trauma is not experienced as a mere repression or defense, but as a temporal delay that carries the individual beyond the shock of the first moment. The trauma is a repeated suffering of the event, but it is also a continual leaving of its site . . . To listen to the crisis of a trauma . . . is not only to listen for the event, but to hear in the testimony the survivor's departure from it; the challenge of the therapeutic listener, in other words, is *how to listen to departure.*[16]

One thinks here of Louis in Rice's *Interview with the Vampire,* as he is compelled to tell the whole story of his life with Lestat as a means of displacing it into history and into a story that the listening boy eagerly wants to hear. According to Robert Jay Lifton, the subject shattered by trauma "struggles to put together the pieces, so to speak, of the psyche, and to balance the need to reconstitute oneself with the capacity to take in the experience."[17] But as we know, to repeat is to visit the same place but with a difference: in repetition, we relive an event but the intervening distance of time and space means that the repetition cannot be perfect or authentic, that it can only produce the original experience differently. Moreover, repetition with a difference must usually be performed through literature and fiction. When Lifton was researching his 1986 book *The Nazi Doctors,* he found himself having nightmares that *he* was an Auschwitz prisoner. At some level, he endured the horror of the traumatized survivor, in that both he and the survivor had a distanced presence to the "real" experience. Narrative, not corporeal presence, engaged him in a shattering moment through which, as Elie Wiesel told him, he could only begin to write about the Holocaust. Lifton was lured into his research in much the same way Rice's interviewer is seduced—and in fact wants to live out—Louis's narrative account of vampirism. Says Lifton, "it's being a survivor by proxy, and the proxy's important" (p. 145).

Surviving by proxy: Lifton's phrase begins to explain why we crave the Gothic. We crave it because we *need* it. We need it because the twentieth century has so forcefully taken away from us that which we once thought constituted us—a coherent psyche, a social order to which we can pledge allegiance in good faith, a sense of justice in the universe—and that wrenching withdrawal, that traumatic experience, is vividly dramatized in the Gothic. We do not seek out one Gothic experience, read one novel, or see one movie, we hunt down many. We do not tell one story, we tell many, even as all of them are knitted together by those famil-

iar, comforting, yet harrowing Gothic conventions. For our traumas, like Regan McNeil's demons, are legion: the tyranny of the lawgiving father, the necessity of abjecting the mother, the loss of history and a sense of pre-formed identity, and the shattering of faith in a world that can permit the Holocaust and genocide or reconstruct us as cyborgs or clone each of us into another self (the deepest anxiety in Cronenberg's *Dead Ringers* [1988]). What better venue can there be for working through our always vague sense of these traumas than a malleable form of fiction-making that cannot really grasp all its own foundations—indeed, that beholds fragments of them always receding into a distant past—just as we feel about ourselves in the west as we watch older ways of grounding our "natures" dissipate and disappear?

As we confront this underlying terror of our times, after all, the Gothic provides us a guarantee of life even in the face of so much death. Who is more alive than Regan when she is hurling a priest across the room? Who is more alive than Carrie when she is incinerating her graduating class? Who is more alive than I when I am thoroughly gripped by a horror story that actually changes my physiological condition as I read or watch? But the pleasantly terrifying thing may be that this life, this consciousness of being alive, is constantly shadowed by previous and imminent breakage and dissolution. Contemporary life constantly reminds us that we are moving toward death, or at least obsolescence, and that life we must continually strive to hold together. Paradoxically, we need the consistent consciousness of death provided by the Gothic in order to understand and want that life. This realization brings us back to the quandaries with which this chapter began: the problem of delimiting and thus anchoring both the "Gothic" and the "contemporary Gothic." But now we see why those problems still bedevil us. The Gothic's basic investment in ravaging history and fragmenting the past meshes with our own investments now as we attempt to reinvent history as a way of healing the perpetual loss in modern existence. "We" do this, moreover, as a western civilization shattered by personal and social traumas, yet "we" do not exist except as a collection of individual psyches whose personal histories are inflected by social history but not completely determined by it. We want *our* life and *our* death, and in that vacillation between wanting life and capitulating to destruction, we keep needing the Gothic to give shape to our contradiction. By now we have become like an Anne Rice vampire or a Stephen King family man: we crave presence, we crave departure, we *crave.*[18]

Notes

1. This pattern becomes especially apparent in the course of King's *Danse Macabre* and Skal's *The Monster Show.*

2. For a more complete discussion of Freud's relation to the construction of the Gothic, and vice

versa, see Fred Botting, "The Gothic Production of the Unconscious" in Glennis Byron and David Punter, eds., *Spectral Readings: Towards a Gothic Geography* (London: Macmillan, 1999), pp. 11-36.

3. In addition to the works by Freud in the guide to further reading below, see the following: "From the History of an Infantile Neurosis (The 'Wolf Man')" (1914) in *The Standard Edition of the Complete Psychological Works of Sigmund Freud*, ed. and trans. James Strachey (London: Hogarth, 1955-61), XVII, 1-122; "Group Psychology and an Analysis of the Ego" (1921) in *Standard Edition*, XVIII, 67-143; "Mourning and Melancholia" (1915), trans. Joan Rivière, in *Standard Edition*, XIV, 237-58; "On Narcissim: an Introduction" (1915) trans. C. M. Baines, in *Standard Edition*, XIV, 67-102; "Psychoanalytic Notes on an Autobiographical Account of a Case of Paranoia (Dementia Paranoides) (Schreber)" (1910) in *Standard Edition*, XII, 1-82; and "A Seventeenth-Century Demonological Neurosis" (1922), trans. E. Glover, in *Standard Edition*, XIX, 67-105.

4. In my use of the term *queer* here, I am thinking specifically of the Freudian explanation for male homosexuality. In his essay "On Narcissism: an Introduction" Freud theorizes that the proto-homosexual male child refuses to break the connection with the mother in time to develop "normal" relations. The result, Freud suggests, is that the child takes up the identity or subject-position of the mother and seeks a love object whom he can love the way his mother loved him. In this sense, Freud sees male homosexual desire as "narcissistic," in that the homosexual supposedly seeks himself in a love object.

5. For other textual connections between shining and various forms of the primal scene, see Stephen King, *The Shining* (Harmondsworth: Penguin, 1977), pp. 201, 297, and 303.

6. The mother, however, need not be a castrating bitch in order to produce a Gothic effect. Sometimes the horror is "caused" by her strong sense of love that becomes overindulgence. See for example Robert Aldrich's film *Whatever Happened to Baby Jane?* (1962) or Mervyn LeRoy's *The Bad Seed* (1956).

7. For a more complete analysis of maternal rejection and its relation to the Gothic, see Steven Bruhm, "The Gothic in a Culture of Narcissism" in *Reflecting Narcissus: a Queer Aesthetic* (Minneapolis: University of Minnesota Press, 2001), pp. 144-73.

8. This "history" is perhaps best allegorized in Danny Torrance's imaginary friend Tony. With hair like Danny's mother and a facial structure like his fa-ther, Tony is "the Daniel Anthony Torrance that would someday be—. . . a halfling caught between father and son, a ghost of both, a fusion" (King, *Shining*, p. 420). He seems to suggest a history that is not one, a future tense that is completely infected by the past.

9. Cathy Caruth, "Trauma and Experience: Introduction" in *Trauma: Explorations in Memory*, ed. Cathy Caruth (Baltimore: Johns Hopkins University Press, 1995).

10. For a discussion of Janet's thought, see Bessel A. van der Kolk and Onno van der Hart, "The Intrusive Past: the Flexibility of Memory and the Engraving of Trauma" in *Trauma*, ed. Caruth, pp. 158-82. For more on the problem of story-telling and trauma, see Elaine Scarry, *The Body in Pain: the Making and Unmaking of the World* (Oxford: Oxford University Press, 1985).

11. See Eve Sedgwick, *Between Men: English Literature and Male Homosocial Desire* (New York: Columbia University Press, 1985), especially chapters 5 and 6, for a powerful treatment of the homosocial bond in the Gothic.

12. For a more complete discussion of Gothic misogyny and contemporary homosexual panic, see Bruhm, "Gothic in a Culture of Narcissim."

13. The most intelligent books to date on child-worship and its manifestations in contemporary culture are both by James Kincaid—*Child-Loving: the Erotic Child and Victorian Culture* (New York: Routledge, 1992) and *Erotic Innocence: the Culture Of Child Molesting* (Durham, NC: Duke University Press, 1998).

14. See chapters 2 and 3 of Freud, *Totem and Taboo*, for his explanation of animism and totemism, as well as their relation to the demonic.

15. Walter Benjamin, *Illuminations*, trans. Harry Zohn (New York: Schocken Books, 1969), p. 101. In Steven Bruhm, *Gothic Bodies: the Politics of Pain in Romantic Fiction* (Philadelphia: University of Pennsylvania Press, 1994) I make a similar argument about the late eighteenth-century Gothic and its functions within the discourse of sentimentality and moral sense philosophy.

16. Caruth, "Trauma and Experience," p. 10.

17. Caruth, "An Interview with Robert Jay Lifton" in *Trauma*, p. 137.

18. I want to thank the Social Sciences and Humanities Research Council of Canada for financial assistance in the preparation of this [essay].

THE EVOLUTION OF GOTHIC STYLE

Louis S. Gross (essay date 1989)

SOURCE: Gross, Louis S. "Surpassing Loves." In *Redefining the American Gothic: From* Wieland *to* Day of the Dead, pp. 53-64. Ann Arbor, Mich.: UMI Research Press, 1989.

[*In the following essay, Gross analyzes John Rechy's* City of Night *as a modern Gothic work driven by the themes of sexuality and change.*]

In *Love and Death in the American Novel* Leslie Fiedler writes, "The subject par excellence of the novel is love or, more precisely—in its beginnings at least—seduction and marriage. . . ."[1] What then is to be said of the Gothic novel where terror is the subject and loneliness the emotional stance? Perhaps that by their absence love and marriage are everywhere in the Gothic novel, serving as a distant possibility of salvation. Because Gothic narrative depends on the reader's sense of dislocation and anxiety it moves things dimly perceived into the spotlight: the marginal becomes central. Likewise, twisted reflections are the only ways of perceiving reality. While sentimental romance has its place in this genre, it is never the locus of intense emotion; such emotion resides in those exchanges most imbued with mystery and terror for Western culture, the incestuous and the homoerotic. In addition, the Gothic has always retained an uneasy alliance with pornography. Their view of sexuality is essentially similar: a concentration on the economy of sexuality, the uses of power and torture inherent in certain structures. From Horace Walpole to Anne Rice, the power of sexual desire is a constant in Gothic narrative and a vehicle for the inescapable transformation that overcomes the quester. The agents of this fear reside in shadows and margins, and the Gothic quest forces confrontation with them. As in pornography, the Gothic at once wallows in these "perverted" desires yet retains society's righteous horror at their practice. The attraction and repulsion at the heart of Gothic fears are best served by "abnormal" sexuality, however much decorous writers like Ann Radcliffe might wish otherwise.[2]

The significance of incest in Gothic narrative illustrates the power of taboo sexuality in these texts. Aside from the universal social strictures against incest which imbue it with awful mystery, there is a particular use of this theme in terror fiction.[3] In *Dreadful Pleasures* James Twitchell writes, "The early gothic usually tells the story of a single and specific family romance run amok: 'father' has become monstrous to 'daughter.' It seems to make little difference if the father role is shunted to uncle, priest, duke, landlord, or devil, as long as his relationship with the young female is one of paternal dominance. Nor does it seem to make much difference how he is introduced or dispatched as long as he can confront her and, in so doing, dislocate her already vulnerable sense of sexual identity. This often barely disguised incestuous interaction forms the core of horror art which continues unabated to this day."[4] Incestuous relationships in American Gothic fiction are primarily adult brother-sister pairings; they rarely involve children (though *The Turn of the Screw's* ambiguity may involve hints of childhood incest) or parents and children (Alfred Hitchcock's *Psycho* (1960) is an important exception here). Perhaps as an influence from the early Romantic movement, incestuous longing in our Gothic is often spiritual in nature. Characters who have a sense of fragmentation or incompleteness seek an image to complete themselves. What more logical one than a blood relative who may look like him and share his history. The passion is never consummated, indeed sexual caresses are replaced by murderous attacks as in *Wieland* or *Night of the Living Dead*. Undoubtedly the most famous incident of incest in American Gothic fiction is Poe's "The Fall of the House of Usher," yet the theme is treated so ambiguously as to contradict Twitchell's definition. Here is no sadistic patriarchal attack nor confrontation with budding sexuality but an inevitable because longed-for annihilation. In many ways, Poe's story is a tale of an incestuous double, a portrait of family as prison and grave. Roderick Usher's inability to exist in a world other than that conscribed by family history is reflected in the living response of building to mind and spirit a terrifying vision of spiritual imprisonment. The forced confrontation with this fearful double, embodied in sister Madeline, involves the possibility of transgressive sexuality.

While Poe never overtly states the nature of Roderick and Madeline's relationship, we may deduce it from certain hints in the text: the insistence on the "evil" of the Ushers as a hereditary blood disease; the fact that the family has put forth no "enduring branch." These may be read as symptoms of vampirism as well,[5] but in Poe passion is a vampiristic emotion: it seeks total absorption and annihilation in the lover.[6] It is Usher who introduces the information critics seize on to read incest into the tale. The narrator and Roderick are gazing on the corpse of Madeline: "A striking similitude between the brother and sister now first arrested my attention: and Usher, divining, perhaps, my thoughts, murmured out some few words from which I learned that the deceased and himself had been twins and that sympathies of a scarcely intelligible nature had always existed between them."[7] What a perfectly Gothic phrase to describe sexual exchange: "sympathies of a scarcely intelligible nature." Poe's use of this unsettling mystery is brilliantly illuminated by the tale's climax when the pair sway in the throes of an embrace at once erotic and deathly while their world, the House of Usher, collapses around them. Poe's handling of a traditional Gothic theme may be the most famous use of it in American Gothic fiction but his deeply ambiguous style precludes using this tale as our only illustration of incest in American Gothic fiction.[8]

Nathaniel Hawthorne's story "Alice Doane's Appeal" (1835) is a more remarkable illustration of the contrary uses to which American Gothic puts this elementary trope. This story, long regarded as one of Hawthorne's most complex (or muddled, depending on one's critical stance), is a direct meditation on the uses of European Gothic cliché in American fiction. The central narrative involves a triangle composed of Leonard and Alice Doane and Alice's mysterious "suitor" Walter Brome who is revealed as their long-lost brother. These three draw ever closer to the violent confrontation engineered by an evil Wizard. The story's frame device involves a young writer who despairs of ever making people truly feel through such traditional Gothic means, and who seeks to enliven his audience's sense of darkness about America's past by making national experience a part of the Gothic mode. Hawthorne's story announces a particularly American response to the Gothic: acknowledging it as a view of national experience rather than a collection of manipulative literary effects.

Much of the controversy over "Alice Doane's Appeal" centers on the extent to which the frame and inner narrative reflect or contradict each other.[9] The particularly deliberate way in which the narrator undercuts the tale of incestuous longing and violence forces the reader to consider the teller's relation to his tale as important as the tale itself. He selects a properly atmospheric spot to recite his tale of the Doanes—Gallows Hill—but the "gayety of girlish spirits" insures a rather skeptical audience. Throughout the recounting of this traditional Gothic folktale, the frame narrator measures and broods on the emotional effect of his dark narration. His lack of faith in this tale's power to affect the audience results in a transformation not only of literary tradition but of his own perception.

Let us first look at the interior narrative. It opens with the discovery of a corpse beside the road to Boston. The narrator then retraces the path that has led to the murder. It is a tale of two orphans, brother and sister, who, having lost their parents in an Indian raid, have become all to each other. The brother is "characterized by a diseased imagination and morbid feelings";[10] the sister is "beautiful and virtuous" but unable to impress her virtue on her brother. Thus far the tale seems a most ordinary one, the characters properly emblematic and ripe for transformation. The tale's "turn of the screw" involves the mystery of a traveler who sets himself up as Alice's erstwhile suitor.

Leonard Doane makes his passionate affection for Alice quite clear in his first appearance, speaking of "the closeness of the tie which united him and Alice, the concentrated fervor of their affection from childhood upwards, their sense of lonely sufficiency to each other, . . . his discovery, or suspicion of a secret sympathy between his sister and Walter Brome, and how a distempered jealousy had maddened him" ("ADA," 209).[11] Leonard reasons that Alice is attracted to Brome because of his resemblance to Leonard. In fact, Brome and Doane are clearly doubles. Not only do they look alike, they share the same "diseased" moral faculty even though Brome has been raised in the Old World of manners and culture: "Nay! the very same thoughts would often express themselves in the same words from our lips, proving a hateful sympathy in our secret souls" ("ADA," 209). The tale appears to splinter into two tales—one about incest, the other about a doppelgänger—but the revelation of Brome's true identity collapses these separate tensions into one. Brome is revealed as the Doanes' brother, miraculously saved from the Indian raid that had claimed the rest of the family. Thus, his "secret sympathy" with Alice and Leonard's "hateful sympathy" with him reflect the incest narrative's polar movement of attraction and repulsion for that which will restore a fragmented personality. The inappropriate family that Leonard and Alice form is threatened by the danger of the character who attempts to actualize the sexual bond between brother and sister.

Leonard, still unaware of Brome's true identity, murders him and consults the local Wizard for help against the "dark impulses" that seem to command him to kill Alice as well ("ADA," 212). The Wizard, promising to unravel the mystery, takes both the Doanes to a graveyard, where the tale's conclusion is set. Here, "where all the dead had been laid, from the first corpse in that ancient town, to the murdered man who was buried three days before" ("ADA," 213), they receive their Gothic epiphany: the whole plot was engineered by the Wizard for no apparent reason but for demonic mirth. The graves give up their dead, and the faces of friends and neighbors long departed turn to shrill mockery as they reveal their sympathy with the evil Wizard, and with the Doanes, for they show a "ghastly smile of recognition" ("ADA," 214). An infernal orgy of shrieks and blasphemy forms the climax of this final scene, at which point the narrator loses interest in the outcome and hastily summarizes the conclusion: "The story concluded with the Appeal of Alice to the specter of Walter Brome; his reply, absolving her from every stain; and the trembling awe with which ghost and devil fled as from the sinless presence of an angel" ("ADA," 214). Why does the narrator, eager as he is to affect his listeners, skimp on horrific detail in what should be his tale's climax? One can imagine what Matthew Lewis would have done with the infernal riot of the graveyard. An answer may be found in the frame narrative, which initially is subservient to the incest tale but which finally transforms its terrors to something altogether more disturbing.[12]

The frame narrative concerns a young writer who ventures to Gallows Hill with two young women, there to read them "Alice Doane's Appeal," a tale he had written many years ago but not published.[13] Throughout his recitation the narrator gauges the extent to which his friends are involved in the tale: "Their bright eyes were fixed on me; their lips apart" ("ADA," 212). As a Gothicist he is quite properly concerned with the uneasy equation of reader with suffering victim. We sense in his narration, however, a lack of faith in Alice Doane's plight that is borne out in the conclusion. Having told of the demonic orgy and Alice's answered prayer, the narrator points to a mound of earth near the ladies' seats as the grave of that evil Wizard: "The ladies started; perhaps their cheeks might have grown pale, had not the crimson west been blushing on them; but after a moment they began to laugh, while the breeze took a livelier motion, as if responsive to their mirth" ("ADA," 214). Momentary fear and embarrassed laughter, are these not the rewards of most Gothic narrative? Only the gifted Gothicist whose vision is black enough can hold off final mirth. For the narrator of "Alice Doane's Appeal," as for Nathaniel Hawthorne, the momentary fear is not enough; the Gothic vision must be deeper, broader, inescapable.

To achieve this goal, the frame narrator transforms the locus of terror from the "literary" fear of Alice Doane to the historical one of American history. The agent of transmission is memory; the victim, "girlish spirits" to be attacked as earlier Gothic heroines suffered physical abuse. The narrator's choice of Gallow's Hill as the place of his recital seems intended as preparation and reinforcement for the dark mood of his Doane tale, and it does prepare the reader in anxiety. What Hawthorne actually does, however, is to have the inset tale prepare us for the true fear of the frame narration—evil done in historical time and sealed in the inherited American historical imagination. The juxtaposition of the narratives is the structural link between Gothic tradition and Hawthorne's transformation of it. The graveyard climax of the Doane tale is the thematic link to the victims of the Salem witch trials, whose existence in American memory fulfills a haunting function in the frame narrative.

This is perhaps the explanation for the "unsatisfying" quality of the Doane story, for Hawthorne is concerned not with the resolution of Alice's plight but with the scene in the village graveyard where "all the dead had been laid" and historical evil reveals itself. Chief among the risen dead are "old defenders of the infant colony . . . starting up [as if] at an Indian war cry" and "pastors of the church, famous among the New England clergy, . . . ready to call the congregation to prayer" ("ADA," 213). These pillars of the community, rather than condemn the incestuous longings of the Doanes, revel in them. The fear of "abnormal" sexuality as a transforming agent is given full play as the dead are contorted in "pain and hellish passion" and "unearthly and derisive merriment." As in the terrifying paranoiac conclusion to "Young Goodman Brown," the face of piety and honor hides a demonic leer. The sinful brother and sister are faced with the manifestation of the web of evil in which they are enmeshed. Their transgression of sexual boundaries lets loose chaotic transformation of character, as revealed in Leonard's murder of Brome and the resurrection of the revered dead as "sinful souls and false spectres." Whether the reader understands these souls as evil in themselves or the result of Leonard's sinful perception, the point is clear: perverse sexuality is demonically transforming of character. This theme is a traditional component of Gothic fiction; what Hawthorne does with it is decidedly untraditional.

While allowing a common sexual anxiety to do its work of unsettling the reader, Hawthorne pulls back from the "soothing" dispersal of fear by a traditional conclusion. Instead, he abruptly cuts off the conclusion of the Doane tale and forces us into the narrator's imaginative recreation of a monument in American history, another group of people leering and cursing those to be hanged as witches. Here we have no invented victims such as Alice Doane but women who lived in a time and place, women with names like Ann Hibbins and villains like Cotton Mather whose evil dwarfs that of the Wizard. Here, perhaps, the narrator speaks for all American Gothicists:

> And thus I marshalled them onward, the innocent who were to die, and the guilty who were to grow old in long remorse—tracing their every step, by rock, and shrub, and broken track, till their shadowy visages had circled round the hilltop, where we stood. I plunged into my imagination for a blacker horror, and a deeper woe, and pictured the scaffold—

> But here my companions seized an arm on each side; their nerves were trembling; and sweeter victory still, I had reached the seldom trodden places of their hearts, and found the wellspring of their tears. And now the past had done all it could.

("ADA," 216)

The sought-after emotional response of Gothic narrative, fear and terror, is achieved in this story by imbuing historical memory with the Gothic fear of transforming character, the sense not of Gothic art and American history as separate reflections of a people but of inscribing fear through historical imagination.[14] In its dialectic between Gothic convention and a transformation of that convention, "Alice Doane's Appeal" is a central text in American Gothicism.

While we cannot say if any Gothic writers lived the drama of incest in their personal lives, the case of homoeroticism and Gothic narrative is different. From its inception, gay writers have found the Gothic a congenial home. The list of gay Gothicists includes Horace Walpole, Matthew G. Lewis, William Beckford, Oscar

Wilde, James Whale, John Rechy, and others of more ambiguous sexual identity such as Henry James and Herman Melville. What is the connection between marginal social status and the development of this genre? In *Between Men: English Literature and Male Homosocial Desire*, Eve Kosofsky Sedgewick writes: "If we look at the history of distinctively homosexual roles in England, we find that something recognizably related to one modern stereotype of male homosexuality has existed since at least the seventeenth century—at least for aristocrats. The cluster of associations about this role . . . include effeminacy, connoisseurship, high religion, and an interest in Catholic Europe—all links to the Gothic. . . . The genre as a whole . . . came in the nineteenth century to seem a crystallization of the aristocratic homosexual role. . . ."[15] In American tradition the cluster of associations differs somewhat—childhood, cosmopolitan longings, artistic sensibility, among others—but most association is with "decadent" art. In fact, the entire Southern Gothic movement of Tennessee Williams, Truman Capote, Carson McCullers and William Inge is shaped by those qualities culturally associated with gays, and therefore defined as unhealthy. No other genre so welcomes culturally defined "sickness" and horror as the Gothic.

Gay writers, constricted by censorship laws and the marketplace, still had to wait till the middle of the twentieth century for a frank reflection of the "unspeakable" in gay life and it came in the work of John Rechy, whose career has taken him through the sexual underground. From *City of Night* (1963) to *Numbers* (1968), *The Sexual Outlaw* (1970), *The Vampires* (1973) and *Bodies and Soul* (1983) Rechy has inscribed his vision of gay life in America, and the genre in which he first found critical and popular success is the Gothic. *City of Night* is Rechy's most famous and influential novel. In its depiction of a man's journey through the gay underworld of prostitution, drugs, and violence, the novel inscribes a vision of dark despair that fuels the Gothic flame even as it records a moment in a history of social oppression.

Rechy's unnamed narrator—"I" to himself, "Youngman" to others—is a contemporary Texas Everyman. He is born to wandering, dissatisfied with the world he is given, and unable to forge a new one. Though his travels take him to the rings of Hell, he searches for a meaning there. The Gothic quest in this novel does not involve a search for familial identity as in *The Castle of Otranto* or national identity as in *Lionel Lincoln* but the knowledge of spiritual identity and the possibility of transfiguration through the body. Rechy's characters hunger for human and divine love but the hunger drives them to the outer limits of sexuality, that place where the Gothic is most at home.[16]

For a novel published in 1963, *City of Night* is startlingly frank in its depiction of homoerotic activity;

little concession is made to the heterosexual audience and the book is relentless in its depiction of sexual compulsion. The book's structure is little more than a series of sexual encounters in various urban American locales: El Paso, New York, Los Angeles.[17] Each city is vividly described but they finally all become one, the City of Night, the Gothic world's prisonhouse where the forbidden is the only mode of communion. Rechy's America is not one of endless renewal but endless consumption, a chrome and neon jungle through which the traveller "would go to freedom: New York!—embarking on that journey through nightcities and nightlives—looking for what—perhaps some substitute for salvation."[18]

In "John Rechy's Tormented World," Ben Satterfield makes an insightful diagnosis of Rechy's world: "What makes Rechy's characters different from the 'outsider' figure popular in American fiction is that Rechy's people are alienated from themselves and nature as well as society; and what makes Rechy's world crueler than, for instance, Dreiser's is its unrelenting hostility. Rechy evokes not just the indifference of society to pain and suffering, but the outright malignancy of the world at large, a world in which death is final, religion is false, and love is seldom found."[19] What Satterfield fails to mention is that this is a definition of the world we find in the Gothic. What Rechy does in this novel is to use the emotionally resonant if politically repressive iconography of gay life, shared imaginatively by straights and gays alike, to reveal a rich strain in Gothic narrative, the attraction/repulsion of transforming traditional sexual roles and thereby gaining demonic power. Just as the transforming woman of Gothic fiction is heiress to the knowledge of the demonic, so is the man or woman who passes over sexual boundaries open to transforming power.[20]

The men of Rechy's novel do not journey to the place of transformation (Udolpho, Transylvania, the Bates motel), they exist in it. The narrator of *City of Night* is the journeyer but he does not admit his homosexuality to us or to himself. He is simply a hustler, using the gay world (for it is the reader's assumption that the Gothic world is the only gay world that gives the novel its emotional power). The men of Rechy's City have no family, no social position, at least none when they are transformed by homoerotic desire. They exist solely in the frantic (a resonant Rechy image) search for salvation through the transfiguring power of physical attraction. In this world there are a number of modes of confronting the disappointing reality of the body but two stand out: the violent abuse of it leading to masochism and the imaginary willing it into otherness of transvestism. These two modes of perception are of course very much a part of Gothic narrative here turned to a specific lived perception.

The abuse of the body in Gothic narrative is pervasive and shocking. The body is cut, whipped, beaten, burned, trampled upon, stabbed, hanged—a litany of pain and mutilation unmatched in more respectable genres. Torture is not practiced merely for sensation value, however. The Gothic is concerned with human experience at the brink, and the body in pain is a body heightened in perception, both mortal and physical. The twisted bodies of these characters are offered by their creators for the reader's entertainment, a sign of the fascination and revulsion for the flesh that binds reader and writer alike.[21] In *City of Night* the desire for physical abuse is offered as a mode of transforming the pleasurable to the painful (and vice versa) and somehow finding love. Of course, there is no love for these characters to find, only the frantic struggling to be transformed. For the narrator, this cycle of violence is something to avoid being caught up in. Early in the book he is picked up by a middle-aged man who offers him money to beat him. The narrator makes a show of revulsion and walks out. As he leaves, the man offers a curselike judgment: "You will eventually . . . if not with me, with some one else." This phrase haunts the narrator, indicating as it does the inevitability of his transformation and the futility of it. Throughout his travels the narrator is attracted to the weak and pitiful men who seek abuse but he withholds it, refusing to cross the boundary separating him from the "queers" who pay for his services. But as the man prophesied, the narrator does cross over in a terrifying scene late in the book.

Neil, one of the narrator's San Francisco acquaintances, seduces him into compliance by telling him, "'I know you're intrigued by violence. I could sense your excitement when I presented you to the mirror. You saw yourself. Then, as you should be—as you would like to be—as you could be! Out of my clothes, you know, you're very ordinary—like hundreds and hundreds of others. (You're really not my cup of tea),' he added cuttingly, 'But I can transform you—if you Let Yourself Go!'" (*CN*, 264-65). Neil dresses the narrator in the vestments of sado-masochistic iconography: boots, leather, heavy studded belt! "Suddenly he has flung himself on the floor, his head rubbing over the surface of the boots, the tongue licking them, he falls on his back, his face looks up pleadingly at me . . . his eyes as if about to burst into flame, his tongue like an animal desperate to escape its bondage—I stand over him as he reaches up grasping, urgently opening the fly of my pants—'Please—on me—please do it!' he pleaded" (*CN*, 266). The signs of transformation are clear—flaming eyes and animal tongue—but what is it Neil transforms into? The narrator is frightened and pauses but the ritual once begun must continue.

Neil begs and tears at the narrator's clothing, forcing his boot into his groin and howling with pain. The narrator then has his moment of transforming vision:

> . . . it was I who was being seduced by him—seduced into violence: that using the sensed narcissism in me . . . he had played with all my hungry needs . . . to leave behind that lulling, esoteric, life-shuttered childhood, that once-cherished place by the window—to which, despite all those things, I had, I know, still clung: to compassion, to pity—and knowing only that this was the moment which could crush . . . whatever of innocence still remained in me . . . that . . . I could prove to the hatefully initiating world that I could join its rot, its cruelty—I saw my foot rise over him, then grind violently down. . . .
>
> (*CN*, 267)

But the moment of transfiguration is revealed as pathetic failure by Neil's response:

> He let out a howl. . . . Tears came to his eyes in a sudden deluge which joined the perspiration and turned his face into a gleaming mask of pain. And he sobbed:
>
> "Why . . . hurt? . . . Why . . . Wanted lo—. . . ."
>
> I was seized by the greatest revulsion of my life . . .—for myself, for him. . . . I bent down over him, extending my hand to him, to help him up—to help him—as if he were the whole . . . sad, sad crying world, and I could now, at last, in that moment, by merely extending my hand to him in pity, help him—and It. . . .
>
> And as the man sobbing on the floor in the disheveled wet costume saw my hand extended to him in pity, the howling stopped instantly as if a switch had been turned off within him, and his look changed to one of ferocious anger.
>
> And he shouted fiercely:
>
> "No, no: You're not supposed to care!"
>
> (*CN*, 267-68)

At the moment of transformation the unremitting despair of Rechy's vision reveals the futility of transcending the City of Night, the disintegration of hope that is the Gothic quester's epiphany.

The second major mode of metamorphosis in this work is transvestism. The figure of the man or woman who blurs traditional sexual distinctions is, of course, not restricted to Gothic or any narrative but it is central to them in a unique way. The transvestite is the marginal figure par excellence: living in the lines between distinctions and offering in his very existence a critique of such concepts as the "natural," he illustrates a transformation made of equal parts imagination and will. For the gay narrative, he serves as the radical embodiment of any self-parody and oppression; for the Gothic, he serves as the carrier of demonic transforming power. The character of Matilda/Rosario in Lewis's *The Monk* is a most striking example of the demonic transforming power. The demon who seduces monk Ambrosio is a shape shifter who uses his/her alternating sexual identities to initiate him into malefic power.[22]

While the demonic power of nontraditional sexuality is evident in Gothic narrative it is also evidently politically repressive, fostering notions of transformations as physical manifestations of evil. Even Rechy is unable to extricate himself from open-mouthed horror in contemplating the pitiful shape shifters who totter through his City on spiked heels, searching for the love they will never find. The novel's most memorable transvestite is Miss Destiny, whose search for a "husband" leads her to the narrator. Her Fabulous Wedding is the subject of monologue after monologue, all meant to attract a partner who will give her an identity. Stanton Hoffman writes of the way in which Rechy's world "functions as a metaphor for a destructive and despair-ridden American reality."[23] While this seems a facile equation, the truth is that Rechy's world is the dark underside of that reality, the place where love is unattainable and acts of the will initiate the discovery of disintegration that underlies the Gothic.

At the center of the novel stands the narrator, the "hero" on his Gothic quest. In traditional fashion he is an orphan and his journey through the novel is an attempt to connect with something that will give him a boon, a gift he can take back from his journey. He is, therefore, an observer and an inscriber of the pain he encounters. His contact with those marked by failed transformations results in his gradual education to the City of Night. Through this character's narration, Rechy shapes the imaginative vision of urban gay life to Gothic form. An example of this style is the narrator's description of a prototypically decadent gay/Gothic party:

> Tim and I ended up together at another party—much later: toward early morning—in a house somehow like Death—or like that house in the Gloria Swanson movie where she went Mad . . . From somewhere, weird organ music is being played. On the floor, male couples danced holding tight to each other . . . gliding over the waxgleaming floor like shadowy sailboats on a frozen black lake . . . and figures that I took to be statues would move occasionally? come together, separate like dark clouds . . . The host came to us. Appropriately he looked like Dracula with piercing unclothing eyes and red red lips.

> (*CN,* 200)

In such scenes Rechy manages to turn the well-worn cliché of Gothic art to new purpose: an illumination of modern life and a reappraisal of the ways in which gay life and perception have influenced this genre. No longer is the Witches' Sabbath a quaint Old World myth, here it is New World entertainment, Count Dracula is the evening's host and the dead, soulless guests the leftovers from the bar and bath set. While critics argue whether there is still life in the Gothic novel, life has become a Gothic novel.

The narrator's final act is to return home to El Paso carrying the City of Night within him. The life he has witnessed is inscribed in a specific literary style: the education of a young man. Because it is an education into despair, the form is properly Gothic. Likewise, as the story of modern gay America the form is fitting. *City of Night* is one of those rare works where the conventions of a genre connect with a group perception, revealing both the imaginative power and the political complexities of alternate sexualities. The demonic transformation of the hustler and the transvestite is finally empowering only if one accepts the Gothic vision as social reality, which the policy makers of the world do not. While gay artists and readers have found in the Gothic a mirror for the sense of mystery and loss forced on them by society, that same society has accepted the dark vision as justification for a political agenda. In this way gay writers and readers have been imprisoned in the Gothic world they helped create. While alternate, "abnormal" sexuality such as incest or homoeroticism gives the genre a shorthand for demonic transformation, it cannot affirm anything; it can, however, illuminate a history of sexual oppression and terror. That is in the real world. For the narrator of Rechy's novel, as for all sojourners in the Gothic City of Night, the prison is still locked:

> And I returned to El Paso.

> Here, by another window, I'll look back on the world and I'll try to understand. . . . But, perhaps, mysteriously, it's all beyond reasons. Perhaps it's as futile as trying to capture the wind.

> And its windy here now.

> No matter how you close the windows or pull the curtains or try to hide from it, it's there. It's impossible to escape the Wind. You can still hear it shrieking. You always know its there. Waiting.

> And I know it will wait patiently for me, ineluctably, when inevitably I'll leave this city again.

> And what has been found?

> Nothing.

> A circle which winds around, without beginning, without end.

> (*CN,* 379)

Notes

1. Leslie Fiedler, *Love and Death in the American Novel* (New York: Stein and Day, 1966), p. 27.

2. For more on sexual figures in Gothic narrative see Nicholas K. Kiessling, "Demonic Dread: The Incubus Figure in British Literature," in *The Gothic Imagination,* ed. by G. R. Thompson (Pullman: Washington State University Press, 1974), pp. 22-41; Coral Howells, *Love, Mystery and Misery: Feeling in Gothic Fiction* (London: Athlone Press, 1978); Walter Evans, "Monster Movies: A Sexual Theory," *Journal of Popular Culture* 11 (1973): 124-42; and Gail Griffin, "'Your girls that you all

love are mine': *Dracula* and the Victorian Male Sexual Imagination," *International Journal of Women's Studies* 3, no. 5 (1980): 454-64.

3. For analyses of the meaning of incest in Western culture see Elizabeth Janeway, "Incest: A Rational Look at the Oldest Taboo," *Ms.,* November 1981, p. 61, Jeffrey Masson, *The Assault on Truth; Freud's Suppression of the Seduction Theory* (New York: Farrar, Straus, and Giroux, 1984); Judith Lewis Herman, *Father-Daughter Incest* (Cambridge: Harvard University Press, 1981), and Robin Fox, *The Red Lamp of Incest* (New York: Dutton, 1980).

4. James B. Twitchell, *Dreadful Pleasures: An Anatomy of Modern Horror* (New York: Oxford University Press, 1985), p. 42.

5. See J. O. Bailey, "What Happens in 'The Fall of the House of Usher'?" *American Literature* 35 (1964): 445-66.

6. Poe's poem "Annabel Lee" is a good illustration of the convergence of love and vampirism in his work.

7. Edgar Allan Poe, *The Fall of the House of Usher and Other Tales* (New York: Signet Classic, 1960), p. 125.

8. The same obtains in Herman Melville's *Pierre,* which contains substantial incestuous elements, but Melville's sardonic irony removes the incest from the mode of the fearful to that of burlesque.

9. Nina Baym argues that the two parts of the story "form a contrast, and cannot be considered as parts of a cumulative effect . . ."; "Hawthorne's Gothic Discards: Fanshawe and 'Alice Doane,'" *The Nathaniel Hawthorne Journal* 1974 (Indian Head, Inc., 1975), pp. 105-15. For a contrary reading of the story, see Roy Harvey Pearce, "Hawthorne and the Sense of the Past," *Historicism Once More* (Princeton: Princeton University Press, 1969), pp. 150-52; Robert H. Fossum, "The Summons of the Past: Hawthorne's 'Alice Doane's Appeal,'" *Nineteenth Century Fiction* 23 (1965): 294-303; Stanley Brodwin, "Hawthorne and the Function of History: A Reading of 'Alice Doane's Appeal,'" *The Nathaniel Hawthorne Journal* 1974 (Indian Head, Inc., 1975), pp. 116-28.

10. "Alice Doane's Appeal," in *Nathaniel Hawthorne: Tales and Sketches* (New York: The Library of America, 1982), p. 208. All subsequent text references, designated by "ADA," are to this edition.

11. Note also the similarity between Doane's suspicion of "secret sympathy" and the "sympathy of a scarcely intelligible nature" that has passed between Roderick and Madeline Usher.

12. Note the similarities to Brockden Brown's *Wieland,* which also tells of a particularly American inappropriate family.

13. The similarities to Hawthorne's own history with this story lead us to recognize the "I" narrator as a fictional double of Hawthorne in his struggles as an American Gothicist. For background on the various incarnations of this story see Nina Baym (note 1), p. 105. For discussions of incest in Hawthorne's own life see Philip Young, *Hawthorne's Secret* (Boston: David R. Godine, Pub., Inc., 1984) and Gloria Erlich, *The Tenacious Web: Family Themes and Hawthorne's Fiction* (New Brunswick: Rutgers University Press, 1985).

14. For a detailed analysis of this theme in American Gothic narrative see chapter 2 of this work.

15. Eve Kosofsky Sedgewick, *Between Men: English Literature and Male Homosocial Desire* (New York: Columbia University Press, 1985), pp. 934.

16. Part of the reason that Gothic fiction has a clouded reputation is its liaison with sensationalist elements of varying disrepute; works like *The Monk* and *The Quaker City* are surely the most pornographic and uneasily approved "literary" works.

17. Rechy continues this relentless, ritualistic sexual odyssey in works such as *The Sexual Outlaw* and *Numbers.* These books are remarkable for their use of episodic structure to support theme.

18. John Rechy, *City of Night* (New York: Ballantine Books, 1963), p. 19. All subsequent text references, designated by *CN,* are to this edition.

19. Ben Satterfield, "John Rechy's Tormented World," *Southwestern Review* 67 (Winter 1982): 78.

20. This demonic bond is clearly portrayed in William Burroughs's *City of the Red Night* (1981), in which the Magician engages in anal intercourse with his acolyte while reciting his incantations. Note also the similarity with Rechy's title.

21. A modern master of such inclination is the Canadian filmmaker David Cronenberg whose films maim and mutilate the body in a frenzy of love and hate. His most successful film, *They Came from Within* (1975), concerns aphrodisiac parasites that lodge in people's stomachs turning them into sex-crazed beasts infecting each other and spreading disease. See *The Shape of Rage: The Films of David Cronenberg* (New York: Zoetrope Books Ltd., 1981).

22. The figure of the transsexual is an even more awe-inspiring and terrible one, combining the mutilation and imaginative will of the two major modes. The way in which books and films on the lives of

transsexuals present them is close enough to any horror narrative to qualify as Gothic. The link between them is the subject of numerous comedic sketches in which the Frankenstein Monster is fitted with a female brain and suffers the torments of Christine Jorgensen, Renee Richards, and company. The hermaphrodite is, however, not a part of Gothic narrative. In his "natural" transsexualism he bears the mark of God's truly transcendent power, as Flannery O'Connor illustrates in her haunting story, "A Temple of the Holy Ghost."

23. Quoted in Satterfield. See note 19.

George E. Haggerty (essay date 1989)

SOURCE: Haggerty, George E. "James's Ghostly Impressions." In *Gothic Fiction/Gothic Form*, pp. 139-68. University Park: Pennsylvania State University Press, 1989.

[*In the excerpt below, Haggerty explores Henry James's handling of Gothic subjects and themes in his short fiction, focusing on his shift from physical devices to emotional states produced by uncanny phenomena.*]

The greatest of Hawthorne's early critics and the one most sensitive to the nature of his achievement was, of course, Henry James. James learned a great deal from Hawthorne, and various aspects of James's work have been interestingly related to that of his predecessor.[1] From very early in his career James experimented with the tale form; therefore he was alive to the technique whereby Hawthorne had heightened the affective power of his own tales. In his study of Hawthorne for the English Men of Letters series, James describes those tales in terms that give us a crucial, if not surprising, insight into his interpretation of Hawthorne's technique:

> The charm—the great charm—is that they [Hawthorne's tales] are glimpses of a great field, of the whole deep mystery of man's soul and conscience. They are moral, and their interest is moral; they deal with something more than the mere accidents and conventionalities, the surface occurrences of life. The fine thing in Hawthorne is that he cared for the deeper psychology, and that, in his way, he tried to become familiar with it. . . . This air, on the author's part, of being a confirmed *habitué* of a region of mysteries and subtleties, constitutes the originality of his tales.

> (*Hawthorne* 64)

James echoes Hawthorne's own terminology here: *moral* interest, *something more* than conventionality, a *deeper* psychology; all these remind us of Hawthorne's affective technique and his manner of engaging the reader in Gothic experience. The "mysteries and subtleties" James found in Hawthorne's tales are vastly intensified in his

own, especially in the ghostly tales, which include his most important examples of the form.[2] James's concern for "the whole deep mystery of man's soul and conscience" surfaces everywhere in his tales, rendering them intellectually and emotionally sophisticated. James's own rewriting of morality, his own handling of the conflict between Gothic experience and narrative convention, carry him beyond the formal difficulties that confounded his eighteenth-century predecessors and enable him to refine, if not revolutionize, the achievement of his American forebears. James was committed to integrating Gothic concerns into the novelistic tradition without diluting them in intensity or fierceness. It was possible for him to accomplish this goal because James understood the problems inherent in Gothic expression and knew how to create a narrative form precisely suited to the eerie formlessness of his material. If there is something cold—at times almost diabolical—about his Gothic enterprise, we must still admire the brilliance with which he makes his own version of horror so thoroughly harrowing.

James was from the first committed to the tale as a serious literary form. Throughout his career he made remarks such as that to be found in his *Notebooks* for Sunday, 19 May, 1899:

> But [Taine's] talk about [Turgenev] has done me a world of good—reviving, refreshing, confirming, consecrating, as it were, the wish and dream that have lately grown stronger than ever in me—the desire that the literary heritage, such as it is, poor thing, that I may leave, shall consist of a large number of perfect *short* things, *nouvelles* and tales, illustrative of ever so many things in life—in the life I see and know and feel.

> (*NHJ* 101)

A glance at his *Notebooks* reveals, however, that it was no easy task for James to create the "perfect short thing." He repeatedly finds himself faced with short tales expanding, through his developmental impulse, into *nouvelles* or short novels.[3] Control becomes the admonitory imperative throughout the *Notebooks*; moreover, we can watch him trying to "control" himself in his attempts to delineate the method of compression necessary to keep a particular work within certain bounds. This process of self-regulation for effect suggests a wariness on James's part. It also suggests a certain distance from those effects themselves. Perhaps it is this distance that allows James to gauge his effects so precisely. In the Preface to "The Coxen Fund," for instance, he says of the tale that as a "marked example of the possible scope, at once, and the possible neatness of the *nouvelle,* it takes its place for me in a series of which the main merit and sign is to do the complicated thing with a strong brevity and lucidity—to arrive, on behalf of the multiplicity, at a certain science of control" (*AN* 231). Here is the Jamesian revision of the doctrine of "single effect": "To do the complicated thing with a strong brevity and lucidity"—instead of narrowing his scope and presenting only one side of experience, James intends to acknowledge the multiplicity of his material, but still to represent it so that a single purpose is maintained. He associates brevity with strength and distinguishes *nouvelle* from novel as a way of marking out an area of (literary) experience for which the novel is unsuited.

"The Coxen Fund" itself, as well as James's reports on its progress in his *Notebooks,* illustrates this process. The strong first person narrator of this tale works in a way that would not be unknown to Poe:

> The formula for the presentation of it in 20,000 words is to make it an *Impression*—as one of Sargent's pictures is an impression. That is, I must do it from my own point of view—that of an imagined observer, participator, chronicler. I must picture it, summarize it, impressionize it, in a word—compress and confine it by making it the picture of what I see.
>
> (*NHJ* 160)

James's careful use of the term *impression,* suggesting as it does the subjective focus of earlier Gothic tales, begins to elucidate James's own technique. For James, an observer is a participator, and in an impression the creator and the observer meet. "When James writes [in the Preface to *The Ambassadors*] about 'the terrible *fluidity* of self-revelation,'" William R. Goetz tells us, "he is referring less to the problem of dramatic construction . . . than to the extratextual question of the relations between author, reader, and work."[4] But this question is not "extratextual" for James. Indeed, his elaborate system of Notes and Prefaces assures our engagement in the process of creation as well as the dramatic intricacies of "self-revelation." James is certainly as sensitive to the affective implications of his narrative structure as any of the writers we have considered. An impression, if finely wrought, is perfectly recreated in the reader. That is the basis of James's Gothic technique.

He speaks further in this entry about "condensed action," "*intensification,*" and "summarized exhibition," all techniques crucial to the Gothic tale as I have described it. For James a tale could only be perfectly short by being perfectly realized as an impression. His description makes it sound as though he is doing what he does in novels in miniature, but condensation and intensification are telling expressions that begin to hint at the essence of James's conception of the tale. Condensation and intensification result in a world as uncanny as it is seductive and magical.[5]

In his study of Hawthorne, James speaks of "the magnificent little romance of *Young Goodman Brown*" as "not a parable, but a picture, which is a very different thing" (93). James emphasizes the visual in Hawthorne because as a picture the tale has greatest effect. This helps us further to distinguish Jamesian Gothic: A picture, vivid enough and carefully drawn, can create an impression as no amount of "meaning" can. James saw a picture not only as an objective artifact, but as an expression of the most intimate subjective vision. If Hawthorne suggests an inner reality that recedes as we pursue it, James's realities are so profoundly internalized that it is the exterior that threatens to recede.

Leon Edel quotes James (at twenty-two) as saying that "a good ghost story must be connected at a hundred points with the common objects of life," and that he preferred the "terrors of the cheerful country house and the busy London lodgings" to the clanking trapdoor ghosts of the Gothic romance (quoted in "Introduction," *Ghostly Tales* xxv). By defying Gothic convention in this way, James seems to suggest a deeper and more fully articulated sense of Gothic material, which could be brought into the realm of realist fiction, or in effect brought out in it, without losing any of its intensity. James's ghosts appear without disrupting the surface reality of his tales because "the common objects of life" have no meaning for him beyond the impression that they so compliantly help him to create. James does not devalue the real, as Hawthorne seems sometimes to do; rather, he insists that it is always more than realistic fiction has allowed it to be. Subjective and objective distinctions begin to fade in James's work because he already understands that such distinctions need to be deconstructed before a truly powerful Gothic fiction can emerge. He harnesses the horror that Kristeva describes as resulting from such a dissolution (141) and uses it for his own affective ends.

While earlier examples of the Gothic, according to Todorov, have as their "principle and explicit theme the hesitation of the protagonist, in James's work the representation of such hesitation is virtually eliminated, and only survives in the reader" (Todorov, "The Structural Analysis of Literature" 86). For Edel, this is James's "little expedient of inviting the reader to participate in the terror or hauntedness that he seeks to evoke" ("Introduction" xxix). These observations are by no means unjust, but they fail to explain the full extent of James's mastery of the Gothic. For it is not only that he engages the reader directly in the Gothic situation, but rather that he makes the Gothic situation a part of the reader, makes it "exist" in his or her consciousness as it has never before existed. He does this by refusing to give special value to specific readings or levels of meaning in his tales, while at the same time encouraging us to look for the key to meaning. But as he himself says of Hawthorne, these tales are not parables, they are pictures. He makes certain that they become pictures of ourselves.

Jauss says that "even the extreme case of an open-structured fictional text, with its quantity of indeterminacy calculated to stimulate the imagination of the active reader, reveals how every fresh response links up with an expected or supposed meaning, the fulfillment or nonfulfillment of which calls forth the implicit question and so sets in motion the new process of understanding" (69). For James, however, a "new process of understanding" begins with the author's attempt to defy the very concept of "supposed meaning" by means of a narrative that has no meaning but that which is constituted in the response of the reader. We can, of course, talk about the "meaning" of any of James's Gothic tales, but no articulation of meaning can take the place of the Gothic experience itself. James challenges such literary assumptions as a way of carrying us beyond ourselves into a public/private world both uncanny and, finally, liberating.

James describes this aspect of his Gothic technique as follows:

> With the preference I have noted for the "neat" evocation—the image, of any sort, with fewest attendant vaguenesses and cheapnesses, fewest loose ends dangling and fewest features missing, the image kept in fine the most susceptible of intensity—with this predeliction, I say, the safest arena for the play of moving accidents and mighty mutations and strange encounters, or whatever odd matters, is the field, as I may call it, rather of their second than of their first exhibition. By which, to avoid obscurity, I mean nothing more cryptic than I feel myself show them best by showing almost exclusively the way they are felt, by recognising as their main interest some impression strongly made by them and intensely received.
>
> (*AN* 256)

Here an effect we have observed in the most powerful Gothic tales is fully articulated. The greatest impression is conveyed by depicting the impression only, and allowing the reader to imagine the cause. The "intensely received" impression that James here describes as occurring *within* his tales gives rise to a response in the reader that direct presentation of the supernatural would make impossible.

James goes on to explain that there would be an inevitable thinness in the direct technique: "We want it clear, goodness knows, but we also want it thick, and we get the thickness in the human consciousness that entertains and records, that amplifies and interprets it" (*AN* 256). James then cites Poe as an example of a writer whose effects "coming straight, as I say, are immediate and flat." Hawthorne, one would imagine, approaches the richness James describes in a tale such as "Rappaccini's Daughter," but even Hawthorne does not quite recognize the affective possibilities that James attests to:

> The moving accident, the rare conjunction, whatever it be, doesn't make the story; . . . the human emotion and the human attestation, the clustering human condi-

tions we expect presented, only make it. The extraordinary is most extraordinary in that it happens to you and me, and it's of value (of value for others) but so far as visibly brought home to us.

> (*AN* 257)

James hereby shifts the focus of Gothic fiction from the inhuman to the human and from the supernatural to the natural; or perhaps it would be more precise to say that he breaks down the division between such artificial distinctions. It is "how" to articulate the human element in Gothic that so baffles James's early predecessors. By rejecting the dichotomies that they so carefully establish, James liberates Gothic fiction from its position as a qualified form and places it within the great tradition itself. The "moral" force of James's Gothic tales is more than an intensification of that concern for "the deeper psychology" he recognized in Hawthorne. It is, instead, a transformation of the Gothic from a passive to an active form: "Only make the reader's general vision of evil intense enough," James says in the Preface to "The Turn of the Screw," ". . . and his own experience, his own imagination, his own sympathy . . . and horror . . . will supply him quite sufficiently with all the particulars. Make him *think* the evil, make him think it for himself, and you are released from weak specifications" (*AN* 176).

By evoking the reader's own horror, James avoids the pitfalls of conventional Gothic expression. The existence or nonexistence of ghosts is a moot issue in one of his tales, for ghosts and such conventional devices are understood as a means to an expressive end that lies in the reader's own response.[6] Unlike those writers, however, who, for instance, used the sublime as a technique for evoking a psychological reaction, James is not seeking a response to something that he articulates within the tale; rather, the reader must experience the tale so as to provide its detail him- or herself. Affective technique, therefore, has come as far as possible from Lewis's gruesome corpses and Radcliffe's waxen images. James is of course still trafficking in fear, but it is the fear of real as opposed to fear of imagined experience. It has no parameters beyond the individual experience of each reader; it is neither subjective nor objective, internal nor external, but merely an intense expression of who we are and how we know ourselves.

James's Gothic tales, in other words, provide a peculiarly Jamesian answer to the Gothic dilemma that Walpole articulated. Fact and fancy, reality and imagination, are blended in these tales with a subtlety that renders them as inevitable as they are unnerving. Although their subtlety seems effortless, James can at times in the *Notebooks* be seen to be working out his conception of the Gothic tale and expanding our sense of the significance of the form.

"Owen Wingrave," for instance, concerns a tall, athletic-looking, but sensitive young man who reads Goethe's poetry on a bench in Kensington Gardens. He belongs to a family that has made the military its "religion," but he is himself unwilling to serve. We might at first ask where we are to find Gothic material in a tale about a young man who resists the army. James answers this question for us himself. In his *Notebooks,* we see James conceiving of an Owen who "fights, after all, exposes himself to possibilities of danger and death for his own view—acts the soldier, *is* the soldier, and of indefeasible soldierly race—proves to have been so—even in his very effort of abjuration" (*NHJ* 119).

James sensed, however, that such a tale needed "to be distanced, relegated into some picturesque little past when the army occupied more place in life—poeticized by some slightly romantic setting" (*NHJ* 120). James's impulse, then, was to "romanticize" his material to heighten its effect. But the terms of this distancing become even more suggestive as James develops his idea:

> Even if one could introduce a supernatural element in it—make it, I mean, a little ghost-story; place it, the scene, in some old country-house, in England at the beginning of the present century—the time of the Napoleonic wars.—It seems to me one might make some *haunting* business that would give it a colour without being ridiculous, and get in that way the sort of pressure to which the young man is subjected. I see it—it comes to me a little. He must die, of course, be slain, as it were, on his own battle-field, the night spent in the haunted room in which the ghost of some grim grandfather—some bloody warrior of the race—or some father slain in the Peninsular or at Waterloo—is supposed to make himself visible.

(*NHJ* 120)

James's idea to make the tale "a little ghost-story" seems at first to suggest that the supernatural element was here extraneous to the original idea. But as James works out the story for himself, the supernatural emerges naturally as a means to express "the sort of pressure to which the young man is subjected." But this pressure can by no means be expressed in any other way. Here we see James working out the form of the tale in terms that assure us that Owen's death is a metaphorical vehicle, which will lead us in our search for meaning into the shadowy precincts of self-confrontation.

This simple suggestion in the *Notebooks* is rendered most powerfully in the tale. Because Owen is of the heroic ilk, James avoids telling us too much of the tale from that perspective. Instead, Spencer Coyle and his wife provide the "human attestation" to the emerging Gothic interest of the tale, especially as the scene shifts to Paramore, the family mansion, where familial pressure is being (officially) applied. They note the "sinister gloom" of the place, and Mrs. Coyle even goes so far as to call it "wicked and weird" (*HJSS* 332).

James is doing more than laying the groundwork for a haunting here. He is demonstrating that Gothic fears and hysterical imaginings are indeed part of an everyday world and need little more than an "admirable" old house to excite them. The human element in the tale insists that a house is more than a house, that its meaning is complicated by the terms of human perception. The uncanny is oddly available here as a way of apprehending experience. James is moreover suggesting the kind of challenge Owen will be prepared to face: This is what will happen, he seems to be saying, when a young man is trapped between events and a demand for meaning.

Owen is peculiarly aware of "the house—the very air and feeling of it." "There are strange voices in it that seem to mutter at me—to say dreadful things as I pass," he tells his friends. "I mean the general consciousness and responsibility of what I'm doing. . . . I've started up all the old ghosts. The very portraits glower at me on the walls" (*HJSS* 336). Owen's expression of his predicament has no meaning without its suggestion of the ghostly: His "general consciousness" becomes itself the metaphorical vehicle beyond which stand "all the old ghosts." What has happened, then, is that James has so identified metaphorical and metonymical structures in this tale that neither can exist without the other. Everything about Owen's predicament implies a confluence of the realistic and the uncanny. It remains for him to attempt to distinguish them.

James accomplishes more than a literalization of the ghostly metaphor. He also suffuses the literal itself with metaphorical implications. Owen must struggle with these ghosts as he struggles with his family. Each represents the other in an intimate and indestructible bond. The intensity of this situation is only increased when James introduces us to what otherwise would be an unthreatening, contextualizing, dinner party, which at first seems intended to introduce a few diverting characters to the family group. Owen's friend Kate Julian belies this impression, however, by taking the military issue so seriously as to retort "Ah let him prove it!" to Coyle's claim that Owen is at heart a fighting man (*HJSS* 345). Her remark is cryptic and suggestive enough to remind us that she is merely reasserting the challenge of the house itself, and that social relations will only intensify Gothic concerns.

When other guests such as Owen's friend Lechmere attempt to counteract this impression by talking about the haunted room, trying not to take it seriously, we are reminded of a Gothic technique that goes back at least to Lewis's tale of the Bleeding Nun, where defiance of the supernatural leads only to blatant victimization. But what was a mere means to an end in Lewis's hands is for James an end in itself as well. Lechmere and the others are clearly afraid of the "risk" that the haunted room implies—the risk not just of a ghostly presence, but of meaning itself. For if there are no ghosts, their fears and their challenges are merely self-reflexive and without objective meaning. Miss Julian herself leads the campaign to determine the nature of truth.

Through Lechmere we indirectly hear a report of her challenging Owen to pass a night in the haunted room. It is furthermore Lechmere's impression that Owen has already spent the previous night there and that "he *did* see something or hear something" (*HJSS* 350). Lechmere and Coyle confront this possibility helplessly. "Why then shouldn't he name it?" Coyle asks in defiance. "Perhaps it's too bad to mention," the young man suggests (*HJSS* 351). Lechmere's response is reasonable as well as alarming, but it is Coyle's that is more fully in touch with James's Gothic concern. By not naming what he has seen—that is, by not giving public expression to his private experience—Owen attempts to separate the metaphorical and the metonymical functions of language in the tale. He attempts to internalize the ghostly presence as a way of silencing it. The outcome is inevitable.

The long, culminating paragraph of the tale realizes this inevitability in terms that are by now familiar. Instead of witnessing Owen's supernatural confrontation, we are, with Spencer Coyle, trapped by the baffling architectural complexity of the house itself and unable to do more than let the fear possess us as it does our interlocutors. By insisting on the nature of the house itself, James is reminding us of his Gothic heritage. At the same time, however, the Coyles' homely inability to do more than chat about the situation and then succumb to sleep reminds us how very much this world is like our own. If we are tempted to suggest that James is therefore creating the same dichotomy of subjective and objective as his predecessors, though, events in the tale quickly remind us that for James such a dichotomy is not only unnecessary but untrue. Coyle wakes to an agonized cry for help, which at once gives meaning to the maze of corridors and brings life to the decrepit edifice:

> He rushed straight before him, the sound of opening doors and alarmed voices in his ears and the faintness of the early dawn in his eyes. At a turn of one of the passages he came upon the white figure of a girl in a swoon on a bench, and in the vividness of the revelation he read as he went that Kate Julian, stricken in her pride too late with a chill of compunction for what she had mockingly done, had, after coming to release the victim of her derision, reeled away, overwhelmed, from the catastrophe that was her work—the catastrophe that the next moment he found himself aghast on at the threshold of an open door. Owen Wingrave, dressed as he had last seen him, lay dead on the spot on which his ancestor had been found. He was all the young soldier on the gained field.
>
> (*HJSS* 352)

The full measure of the horror of the tale does not rest solely in the stricken pose of Kate Julian or even in the corpse of young Owen. Spencer is "aghast," as we should be, not just at the fact of Owen's death, but at the horror of the circumstances surrounding it. In fulfillment of our greatest fears, the metaphorical level of the tale has assumed an uncanny air of reality. Owen's death insists on the power of the forces working against him, forces we have come to understand as house, family, and tradition. These forces are "objectified" in the ghost we never see. Owen's corpse both brings strains of significance into focus and renders them inseparable. Tenor and vehicle, metaphor and metonymy, subjective and objective, inside and outside—all such dualisms are broken down, and we are left confronting the horror of a world in which boundaries are meaningless and subjective horror assumes public form. Donna Przybylowicz suggests that "when one brackets the natural world in order to examine the intricacies of the mind, what is revealed is the dialectic of self and other, of the differential relations between manifest and latent contents of the psyche" and that James's late texts emphasize "the relativity of all experience and . . . the functioning of the mind" (9). In his Gothic texts, it is especially true that mind and world are pathologically inseparable, and that self becomes threateningly exposed to the misconstructions of other. Still, the functioning of mind matters less in these tales than the horror that privacy finally implies. Mind ceases to function, in fact, when confronted with the implications of its own nature.

Owen dies a hero—both his sense of himself and the family claim are vindicated. Those who remain behind, however, are left confronting a world in which "catastrophe" can be fully articulated. Jamesian ghosts, then, reside in neither a purely objective nor a purely subjective realm. Todorov says that in James's tales "perception and knowledge take the place of the object which is, or is to be, perceived" ("The Structural Analysis of Literature" 86). Perception and knowledge are crucial in these tales; but as "Owen Wingrave" suggests, rather than replace objective experience, they become the field within which the complex nature of experience is realized.

If the ghost is a matter of fact in "Owen Wingrave" (for even if we wish to force the ghostly confrontation into Owen's private psyche, we must still acknowledge its objective power), and the issue of perception a secondary one, a tale like "Sir Edmund Orme" suggests a more complex but nonetheless single-minded presentation of Gothic concerns. The ghost in this tale is that of Sir Edmund Orme, a lover whom Mrs. Marden had jilted several years before. Now as she and the young man who narrates the tale are trying to win her daughter Charlotte's acceptance of his proposal of marriage, this ghost keeps appearing to them as some kind of warning. They both seem comfortable enough with the ghost, but their big fear is that Charlotte should see it. For Mrs. Marden this would imply that Charlotte has inherited her romantic guilt, and for the narrator that she has inherited her faithlessness. "I believe it will all pass," Mrs. Marden says to the narrator, "if she only loves you" (*HJSS* 164).

Our perspective on the ghostly situation, then, is the reverse of what it was in "Owen Wingrave." That is, we now see things on the side of those who bring their own haunted personalities, their own questioning faithlessness, to bear on an innocent girl. Like Giovanni in "Rappaccini's Daughter," these characters push toward a resolution of the question of whether or not Charlotte sees the ghost, just as they push toward a marital commitment from her. The ghostly obsession, however, displaces any direct interest in Charlotte, and, as in Hawthorne's tale, Charlotte is more a victim of experiment and speculation than she is an object of love. "I want to understand what I see" (*HJSS* 158), says the narrator, and out of that desire comes the Gothic force of the tale.[7]

Again, the ghostly material in the tale assumes a role beyond that of compartmentalized subjectivity. For a moment, the ghost becomes objective fact and, in so doing, challenges the world of privacy and subterfuge. It appears at those moments when Mrs. Marden has attempted to separate her subjective experience from the public world that she has created for her daughter. Such a dichotomy is false, and experience itself returns to "haunt" Mrs. Marden in the form of Sir Edmund Orme. Mrs. Marden and the ghost depart simultaneously: She dies suddenly once her secret has been revealed, and the ghost ends his visitations. Nevertheless, the ghost has liberated Charlotte from her enforced parochialism and offered her an authentic vision of reality. The idea that Charlotte has finally seen what is going on around her gives the tale a real Jamesian interest. The moral and psychological concerns are complex: James generates greater horror from the human relationships here because he has created a convincing ghost. What we perceive in this tale is how appropriate hauntedness can be as a means of talking about characters' relations to the past and explaining their actions in the present. James makes us recognize that such ghostliness is woven into human experience. Mrs. Marden was about to make her daughter the second victim of her lovelessness. The intrusion of a ghost into the world of this tale is for James a way of making us feel what things are really like in our own world. James's ghosts do not stretch our imaginations, they enrich our conception of who we are.

Such an appreciation of James's Gothic technique is useful in approaching his most widely known Gothic tale, "The Turn of the Screw." The clearest fact about this tale is that it has given rise to an overwhelming amount of critical exegesis. While the same is perhaps true of all great works of literature, rarely is it the case that critical discussion of a work hinges on a single issue so prominently. The issue, of course, amounts to whether or not the ghosts "really" exist in this tale—whether the children, Miles and Flora, are in fact threatened by supernatural presences or whether these presences are merely the hallucinatory projections of the governess who narrates the tale. The history of criticism of the work shows that for several years after the publication of the tale the governess was taken seriously and that an anti-governess faction sprang up in the thirties, largely thanks to Edmund Wilson, creating a critical controversy that has been raging ever since.[8] Shosana Felman has said, "If the strength of literature could be defined by the intensity of its impact on the reader, by the vital energy and power of its *effect, The Turn of the Screw* would doubtless qualify as one of the strongest—i.e., most *effective*—texts of all time" (143). In the realm of Gothic fiction, where effect is all, "The Turn of the Screw" remains unparalleled.

This critical heritage itself helps to illuminate the nature of "The Turn of the Screw." The disagreement over the tale arises from an ambiguity that is inherent to its affective technique. The tale is the record of an unnamed woman whose tenure as governess to two small children at Bly, an isolated country house, is fraught with fear and horror. At first her problems seem fairly simple. Miles has been sent home from school for reasons that neither the governess nor her companion, Mrs. Grose, the housekeeper, are able to comprehend. The governess is powerless to turn to the children's guardian, a man for whom she has developed a certain affectionate devotion, because he has very clearly stipulated that she is to handle all problems on her own. The problems become more serious, however, when the governess sees first one and then another "ghost" of previous servants at Bly. With Mrs. Grose's seeming encouragement she supposes them to be Peter Quint, former valet to the master, and Miss Jessel, her predecessor as governess. Mrs. Grose suggests that they were an evil pair, both in their own liaison and in their influence on the children. The governess becomes obsessed with the fear that these ghosts will appear to the children, and it gradually becomes apparent to her, in answer to these fears, not only that the ghosts have appeared to the children but also that the ghosts and the children are somehow in league.

At every stage of the tale the governess protests the veracity of her visions: "It was not, I am as sure to-day as I was sure then, my mere infernal imagination . . ." ("Turn" 50). But we are never allowed to see things as clearly as she does, nor are we left without doubt that perhaps the experience is in her imagination. We do see, however, her various methods of exposing the children's ghostly attachment, which only result in upsetting the children, or so it seems, and alienating Mrs. Grose. Her frenzy culminates in a final confrontation with Miles, which results in the boy's demise, dispossessed of the ghost, as she would have us believe, or simply frightened to death.

Freudian critics have made much of the sexual implications of the tale and the possibility that the governess's reactions are basically hysterical. "The one characteristic by which a 'Freudian reading' is generally recognized," Felman tells us, "is its insistence on the crucial place and role of sexuality in the text" (150). "The Freudian critic's job," she says, "is but to pull the answer out of its hiding place—not so much to give an answer *to* the text as to answer *for* the text: to be *answerable for* it, to answer *in its place,* to replace the question with an answer" (152). Felman, in other words, argues that "sexuality is the *division and divisiveness of meaning*; it is meaning *as* division, meaning *as* conflict" (158). But meaning in this sense, Felman says, can only fail to mean and must give rise to a conflict of interpretation like that surrounding "The Turn of the Screw" (159). We have already seen the degree to which an insistence on precise and rigid "meaning" has been a source of conflict in Gothic fiction and how a clash of interpretation has been one response to the unsettling narrative effect of the kind of horror that Gothic fiction produces. What Felman so wittily exposes as the collective hysteria of the critics of the tale is surely a measure of its uncanny power. The haunting power of "The Turn of the Screw" has no more specific a meaning than any of the *other*worldly hauntings I have considered. James uses the threatening possibilities of meaning, however, to render our own relation to the text so harrowing. As a result, the tale achieves what so many other Gothic works aspire to: It challenges our concept of reality itself.[9] In "The Turn of the Screw" the very nature of subjectivity is thrown into doubt, as is the basis on which we can establish our relation to the unknown.[10]

The plight of the governess is so familiar to us as readers of Gothic fiction that we can but wonder that such a controversy has been granted so marked a level of critical credence. The crisis that the tale explores is similar to the crises of other Gothic tales. James is so deft, however, in rendering the ghostly in realistic terms that it is impossible not to take the governess seriously, at least at first, and not to question her when she comes to be questioned. That there is no way of deciding her case is a critical commonplace. That this is precisely the measure of James's success in the tale has even yet not been fully explored.

Within the tale, subject and object are identified so intensely that they become almost interchangeable. "The moving accident . . . doesn't make the story," I have quoted James as saying, "the human emotion and the human attestation . . . only make it" (*AN* 257). In this case, human attestation represents an artistic fusion of the subjective and objective in the tale, at the same time that the governess narrates the story of what was for her the brutal struggle between them. The tale, that is, objectifies subjectivity and gives the object a subjective presence, while the governess attempts to determine her relation to both inside and outside, and therefore to "truth." Were she to address "The Turn of the Screw," Kristeva's terms of analysis would be more to the point than most others. Her analysis of "abjection" explores the psychological implications of the governess's obsession with such relations: "Owing to the ambiguous opposition I/Other, Inside/Outside—an opposition that is vigorous but pervious, violent but uncertain—there are contents, 'normally' unconscious in neurotics, that become explicit if not conscious in 'borderline' patients' speeches and behavior" (7). The governess inhabits this border region and makes her own abjection palpable for the reader in the terms that Kristeva describes.

"How can I retrace to-day the strange steps of my own obsession?" the governess asks ("Turn" 52), and we very quickly realize that nearly a century of critical controversy was anticipated in her own reaction to the situation at Bly. The ambiguity of events is not only a critical concern, it is present in the text itself:

> There were times of our being together when I would have been ready to swear that, literally, in my presence, but with my direct sense of it closed, they [the children] had visitors who were known and were welcome. Then it was that, had I not been deterred by the very chance that such an injury might prove greater than the injury to be averted, my exaltation would have broken out. "They're here, they're here, you little wretches," I would have cried, "and you can't deny it now!" The little wretches denied it with all the added volume of their sociability and their tenderness, just in the crystal depths of which—like the flash of a fish in a stream— the mockery of their advantage peeped up.

("Turn" 52)

The governess here articulates the problem for which critics have indicted her: She very clearly sees that her own effect on the children, were she to spring the ghosts on them, might in fact be worse than the influence of the ghosts themselves. She is frightened for the children as much as she is frightened by them. The ambiguity as to whether or not the children are in league with the ghosts is not an accident; it is exactly what James wants to heighten.[11] This odd situation gives rise to the real horror of the tale. For Felman,

> The governess naturally . . . postulates that the signified she is barred from, the sense of what she does not know, exists and is in fact possessed by—or possessing—someone else. Knowledge haunts. The question of meaning as such, which seems indeed to haunt the pages of *The Turn of the Screw,* can thus be formulated as the question: *"What is it that knows?"*

(201)

Like Giovanni Guasconti, the governess is beset with an ontological crisis that results in the fusion of objective and subjective states in the tale, and in turn of the metonymical and metaphorical functions of language. This situation establishes the anxiety that pervades the tale. Earlier Gothicists, in experimenting with ghostly convention, used metaphorical and metonymical language alternately. James has here created a world in which the two are indistinguishable. Hence the mystique of "ambiguity" surrounding the tale: The ultimate Gothic effect is of course an inability to know what is true beyond the confines of private experience. Here private is public and vice versa. And while it would be nice, both for the governess and for us, to know the answer to the grand question she poses, the beauty of the tale is its defiance of such desires. For after all, what is truly horrifying about human experience in James's terms is that the subjective is the only objectivity we can know.

For the governess, the tale must seem to assume the form of an elaborate self-defense because her anxiety and confusion, again and again articulated in her narration, insist on the shape of proof. But of course she can prove nothing to herself nor to the reader. For in Miles's death her struggle ceases: Subjective and objective divide again into unfathomable duality, creating a void of meaning that is as impossible to cross as her experience is to interpret.[12]

In order to recreate her anxiety, the governess rightly focuses on the danger to the children and her fears on their behalf. As the passage quoted above makes clear, however, the fears are self-directed. That is, it is her responsibility to decide what to do about the children, and in deciding she must try to determine the limitations of her own perceptions or risk acting in a world in which such determinations are impossible. It is easy for the reader to share in this anxiety because James creates for us a position exactly analogous to that which the governess narrates. We are forced to determine the indeterminate relation of objective fact and subjective fantasy in the tale and to decide her culpability or innocence and the culpability or innocence of the children. Such decisions are potentially as horrifying as the decisions she herself makes. We must face the crisis she faces and judge for ourselves; that is, if the governess does not do what is best for the children, what would we do in her place? The tale involves us to the degree that whether or not the ghosts exist we believe that the children are in danger. Psychologically we are implicated in that danger ourselves, for we are incapable of seeing any more than the governess sees.

In thus participating in the experience of Bly, we recreate the tale's great achievement: its harrowing resolution of subjective and objective states. We internalize the governess's plight and understand the terms of her obsession intimately. That is why so many readers resent critical attacks on the governess and indeed why so many critics exult in them. For by condemning the governess, critics condemn our own pleasure in a tale that has so perfectly avoided the linguistic and structural pitfalls of its predecessors. Moreover, such condemnation seems to deprive us of our own experience of this struggle between the public and the private, which James has been so careful not to resolve. We almost dread that he will.

We can discover the nature of this dread in "The Turn of the Screw" by examining the closing pages of the tale, where James's affective technique is most vivid. Felman says that "in this final chapter the entire effort of the governess aims at *reading* the knowledge of the child, and thus at naming truth and meaning" (209). When the governess finds herself alone with Miles after Flora and Mrs. Grose have fled Bly, she confronts him over the disappearance of the letter she had written to the uncle:

> My grasp of how he received this suffered for a minute from something that I can describe only as a fierce split of my attention—a stroke that at first, as I sprang straight up, reduced me to the mere blind movement of getting hold of him, drawing him close and, while I just fell for support against the nearest piece of furniture, instinctively keeping him with his back to the window. The appearance was full upon us that I had already had to deal with here: Peter Quint had come into view like a sentinel before a prison. The next thing I saw was that, from outside, he had reached the window, and then I knew that, close to the glass and glaring in through it, he offered once more to the room his white face of damnation. It represents but grossly what took place with me at the sight to say that on the second my decision was made; yet I believe that no woman so overwhelmed ever in so short a time recovered her command of the *act*. It came to me in the very horror of the immediate presence that the act would be, seeing and facing what I saw and faced, to keep the boy himself unaware. . . . It was like fighting with a demon for a human soul, and when I had fairly so appraised it I saw how the human soul—held out, in the tremor of my hands, at arms' length—had a perfect dew of sweat on a lovely childish forehead.

> ("Turn" 84-85)

The fierce split of her attention, with which the governess begins the final chapter of "The Turn of the Screw," signals the Gothic crisis as I have described it. In her hands she holds one tangible, seemingly objective version of reality; without the window there stands a profoundly threatening different, seemingly subjective presence attempting to assert itself. But for the governess these two worlds are dangerously confused and hideously inseparable. Quint's "white face of damnation" expresses this confusion perfectly: Damnation works as both a metaphor for the influence of the unseen on the seen, and as a metonymic suggestion of how this experience connects to our own sense of things. By so transforming his sentinel-like presence, the governess renders action both necessary and impossible. We too feel the necessity of action and the horror of having to act. For action will define one's relation to these conflicting forces in a permanent and possibly devastating way. This is the kind of paralysis Kristeva describes as objection: "There looms, within abjection, one of those violent, dark revolts of being, directed against a threat that seems to emanate from an exorbitant outside or inside, ejected beyond the scope of the possible, the tolerable, the thinkable" (1).

When the governess says that "it was like fighting with a demon for a human soul," she is using metaphorical language that is absolutely identical to her real situation. She is trapped, that is, in a situation that defies the distancing of metaphor, or rather substitutes equivalence for analogy, ultimately baffling her search for truth. Inside and outside are confused both literally and figuratively here.[13] The governess's "very horror of the immediate presence" draws her into a battle as vivid and desperate as any I have considered. What does it mean to say that these are her hysterical imaginings? Does not the power of the scene emerge from the governess's need to discover the truth of her experience and her terror at confronting it? Felman speaks of "the madness of interpretation" surrounding the tale. She says that "while it points to the possibility of two alternative types of reading, it sets out, in capturing *both* types of readers, to eliminate the very demarcation it proposes" (227). But that is precisely what it does first within the tale to the governess herself; it eliminates the kinds of demarcation that would make it possible for her to escape the horror that this collapse of boundaries make inevitable: "It was for the instant confounding and bottomless, for if he *were* innocent what then on earth was I?" ("Turn" 87). This "bottomless" fear—this abyss of meaning that opens before the governess at her moment of crisis—is what the tale is all about.

The events at the close of the tale confound our own increasing desire for meaning and resolution. The nearly physical interaction between Miles and the governess remains impossible to untangle. Miles bursts out in a "white rage," either of fury or of fear. His frantic searching is either in a spirit of disbelief or exposure. His invective jeer ("You devil!") could be directed at the governess or at Quint; and it could be uttered in sheer terror, or in recognition that she has found him out. The governess reads his inability to see Quint as a sign that she has triumphed. "I have you," the governess says to signal her possessive triumph, and yet she speaks of the moment as one of loss: "With the stroke of the loss I was so proud of he uttered the cry of a creature hurled over an abyss" ("Turn" 88). She seems to know that in liberating Miles from Quint she has lost him as well. She catches him and holds him for a minute before she

realizes that Miles has succumbed to his own liberation. And his death leaves us ever to wander in the darkness of our own confusion.

The affective technique of "The Turn of the Screw" could thus be said to involve us in the subjective horror of an experience and to insist that we take that subjectivity as fact. We are therefore confronted with our own inability to explain, or explain away, the Gothic experience. The degree to which we push for a resolution to this confusion, the very degree to which we desire that resolution still, is the degree to which we are part of the horror of the tale.[14]

This tale could be said to expand the subjective nature of discourse and through its use of language to involve the reader in its Gothic nature. The governess articulates a horror of her own, but that becomes encompassed in our experience of the tale with her as a function in it. James has taken the doctrine of "single effect" and extended it beyond the devices within the work to the work itself.[15] That is, the whole experience of the tale is meant to be its own climactic event. Affect becomes everything: What the tale has accomplished in affective terms is all that it means, and our own horrifying confusion becomes what the tale is "about." Nothing exists in the tale except to complicate our feelings about what transpires there. It is "an *amusette* to catch those not easily caught" (*AN* 172), and all the details of our experience of the tale are but the bait for the epistemological crisis that we experience as the ultimate horror of this tale and of Gothic fiction in general.

James did not, however, leave the form of the tale in such a subjective wilderness for posterity. In his final Gothic tale he went on to show that experiences of Gothic proportions need not lead to destruction and dilemma. In other words, in what is in some ways his most deeply personal Gothic tale—the one that comes closest to his own experience—James suggests the manner in which horror can be confronted and accommodated within a world of what I have been calling novelistic dimension. He presents the Gothic confrontation in a way that we can finally understand, and in doing so, to speak in less theoretical terms, he shows us how we can live with the unknown.

In "The Jolly Corner," as Leon Edel tells us, James "created one of his finest phantoms—the ghost of a man in search of himself, and of that side of himself which he has repudiated" (*HJSS* 721). But the phantom itself is not only what is fine; the fineness exists rather in the tension-fraught anticipation of the "presences" that Spencer Brydon feels in the abandoned New York home of his childhood, to which he has returned after a life abroad.[16] The confrontation with these presences— with the life that might have been—forms the basis of the action in this tale, but the excruciating anticipation is in some ways an end in itself: and there the full force of Jamesian interest resides.

> It had begun to be present to him after the first fort-night, it had broken out with the oddest abruptness, this particular wanton wonderment: it met him there—and this was the image under which he himself judged the matter, or at least, not a little, thrilled and flushed with it—very much as he might have been met by some strange figure, some unexpected occupant, at a turn of one of the dim passages of an empty house.
>
> (*HJSS* 730)

Note the subtlety of James's technique. An unspecified "it" haunts a description of wonder until that wonder itself becomes analogous to the confrontation with a ghost. For James even the method of relating the tale—a method far less obvious than the mood-setting of Poe or even Hawthorne—embodies his Gothic concerns. Form and subject, style and content, become one, just as the states he describes become an indeterminate realm consisting of both subjectivity and objectivity. We are not surprised, then, when James transforms analogical language into a version of the real:

> The quaint analogy quite hauntingly remained with him, when he didn't indeed rather improve it by a still intenser form: that of his opening a door behind which he would have made sure of finding nothing, a door into a room shuttered and void, and yet so coming, with a great suppressed start, on some quite erect con-fronting presence, sometimes planted in the middle of the place and facing him through the dusk.
>
> (*HJSS* 730)

Spencer Brydon first introduces the ghostly presence in language, as a metaphorical expansion of experience, and then finds himself substituting tenor for vehicle, lit-eralizing the metaphor and confronting the ghostly with-out its distancing effect.[17] Within the house, as subjec-tive and objective experience become suffused, the languages of metaphor and metonymy become virtually interchangeable. Experience is handled so deftly in the tale that, when a ghost does finally appear, whether or not it has an objective presence is an insignificant con-cern.

Przybylowicz says that in his late works James "begins . . . to experiment with the idea of the deconstructed, fragmented self and to concern himself with the interro-gation and disintegration of accepted values and institu-tions. The whole notion of 'reality' no longer exists" (21). She says of Spencer Brydon as well that his "fren-zied pursuit of ontological disequilibrium" (23) leads him from the "natural-fact-world" to an "imaginary realm of phantasy" (117). It is true that the experience of this tale challenges our sense of the everyday world; but unlike earlier Gothic works, it insists on retaining the "natural-fact-world" both in Brydon's private expe-rience and in the narrative structure of the tale. James

does not therefore abandon the uncanny power of the "I-Thou" mode here. Rather, he challenges the very dis-tinctions between tale and novel that I have been mak-ing. What is most haunting about this tale, in other words, is the degree to which the everyday world is not sacrificed to effect but rather transformed by it.

The one character who exists as a finely drawn *ficelle* to bring out Brydon's inner experience could serve to dismiss the ghostly presence with her cool rationality. But instead Alice Staverton, observing and testing Bry-don's ideas as she does, works primarily to intensify and support the formal achievement. She becomes as intimately involved in the haunting as he—she sees and accepts the ghost of what he "would have been"—and as a result she has the singular distinction of being able to contextualize the Gothic nightmare, just as James's language has been doing all along. The harrowing self/other dichotomy, elsewhere so destructive, here seems only helpful and supportive. Alice saves Brydon be-cause she can see the truth about him; in fact, she sees this ghost before he does:

> "Well, *I've* seen him."
>
> "You—?"
>
> "I've seen him in a dream."
>
> "Oh a 'dream'—!" It let him down.
>
> "But twice over," she continued. "I saw him as I see you now."
>
> "You've dreamed the same dream—?",
>
> "Twice over," she repeated. "The very same."
>
> This did somehow a little speak to him, as it also grati-fied him. "You dream about me at that rate?"
>
> "Ah about *him!*" she smiled.
>
> His eyes again sounded her. "Then you know all about him." And as she said nothing more: "What's the wretch like?"
>
> She hesitated, and it was as if he were pressing her so hard that, resisting for reasons of her own, she had to turn away. "I'll tell you some other time!"
>
> (*HJSS* 738)

Of course this is meant to heighten suspense, but at the same time it shows us how unsensational James can be. There never seem to have been two less likely subjects for a haunting. Yet the very concerns that oppress each of them separately, and in their relationship to one an-other, are the material out of which Jamesian ghosts are made. For Kaston, such conversations are the sign of mutuality in late James: By building on these fragments of understanding, characters begin to understand.[18] Alice emphasizes the *alter* of Brydon's alter ego, partly to underline the crucial difference, as he will discover, but also as a means of suggesting just what kind of a personal threat such a presence can be. She seems to understand the nature of Brydon's abjection and to offer him solace as an escape from its terms. The horror of his situation could come between them, as any reader familiar with James expects, but in this case, somehow, it draws them together. No characters in Gothic fiction learn to approach one another so directly.

The nature of this communion depends chiefly on the setting in which the story is laid. The house on the "jolly corner" is a cause of mutual concern to hero and heroine. It represents the vestiges of a past age—the time, at least, before life had changed them. ("They had communities of knowledge, 'their' knowledge [this discriminating possessive was always on her lips] of presences of the other age . . ." [*HJSS* 729].) The house offers them a sentimental reflection on the life that might have been ("'Oh,' he said, 'I *might* have lived here; . . . I might have put in here all these years. Then everything would have been different enough—and, I dare say, "funny" enough'" [*HJSS* 733]). "The great gaunt shell" takes on a personality of its own, "as . . . some lifelong retainer's appeal for a character" (*HJSS* 731), and that is the basis of the haunting that ensues. We understand that it comes to represent the "past" for both of them, and as such it haunts them with the possibilities of a different present.

The physical house almost seems to aspire to the state of metaphor. The "great grey rooms," as physically oppressive as they can be, indeed very quickly become the mental landscape that all Gothic settings aspire to. That James effects this transformation is not surprising, and has been often remarked.[19] What is more interesting, though, is the method whereby James breaks down the distinction between interior and exterior states here:

> He always caught the first effect of the steel point of his stick on the old marble of the hall pavement, large black-and-white squares that he remembered as the admiration of his childhood. . . . This effect was the dim reverberating tinkle as of some far-off bell hung who should say where?—in the depths of the house, of the past, of that mystical other world that might have flourished for him had he not, for weal or woe, abandoned it. On this impression he did ever the same thing; he put his stick noiselessly away in a corner—feeling the place once more in the likeness of some great glass bowl, all precious concave crystal, set delicately humming by the play of a moist finger round its edge. The concave crystal held, as it were, this mystical other world, and the indescribably fine murmur of its rim was the sigh there, the scarce audible pathetic wail to his strained ear, of all the old baffled foresworn possibilities. What he did therefore by this appeal of his hushed presence was to wake them into such measure of ghostly life as they might still enjoy.

> (*HJSS* 740)

James focuses on a precise physical detail, just as the memory would recreate a former home, and uses that physical detail to ring in the past.[20] Depths of house, past, and mystical other world clearly reside in the same imaginative place. The delicacy of the image that James suggests is appropriate because of the narrative delicacy with which he sets these wheels in motion. A tap of steel on marble becomes a "dim reverberating tinkle" and then a "scarce audible pathetic wail." Brydon's imagination transforms the house into his memory—it is as clearly an interior landscape for him as it is for the reader. The "moist finger" is Brydon's own, playing on his inner consciousness, as it is James's playing on the tension of the situation. The emphasis here is on "impression": both the one Brydon creates and the one created in him. The wail that springs out of the place in his imagination is the measure of his suffering. The place, in Kristeva's terms, cries out for him. The "stylistic intensity" here represents Brydon's horror, what Kristeva calls "the incandescent [state] of a boundary-subjectivity" (141), which in other contexts has been the uncanny experience of a mystical presence. Here it is the void of memory.

Setting, then, in its very physicality, becomes the springboard of the imagination. James had praised Hawthorne's subjects for their "picturesqueness, their rich duskiness of colour, their chiaroscuro" (*Hawthorne* 60), and in this tale we can see him putting such effects to use himself. Light and dark assume metaphorical significance, and the house becomes the medium for self-discovery:

> With habit and repetition he gained to an extraordinary degree the power to penetrate the dusk of distances and the darkness of corners, to resolve back into their innocence the treacheries of uncertain light, the evil-looking forms taken in the gloom by mere shadows, by accidents of the air, by shifting effects of perspective; putting down his dim luminary he could still wander on without it . . . and . . . visually project for his purpose a comparative clearness.

> (*HJSS* 742)

Physical and mental processes are identified here to such an extent that each has metaphorical potential for the other. This linguistic balance intensifies descriptions in both directions. Brydon presses on with a determination to know what other Gothic heroes have fled in fear of. By so equating the public and the private, James not only heightens the Gothic nature of this quest but interprets it exclusively in its own terms. When Brydon loses confidence, therefore, and experiences fear, it is not fear that takes the form of the house, but rather the house that takes the form of fear:

> The house, withal, seemed immense, the scale of space again inordinate; the open rooms, to no one of which his eyes deflected, gloomed in their shuttered state like mouths of caverns; only the high skylight that formed the crown of the deep well created for him a medium in which he could advance, but which might have been, for queerness of colour, some watery under-world.

> (*HJSS* 753)

"Seemed," "created *for him*," "might have been": Although James insists on the subjective nature of the Gothic experience here, there is none of the ambiguity of "The Turn of the Screw." We understand the Gothic nature of Spencer Brydon's world strictly in terms of his own relation to it.

In the Gothic novel, the Radcliffean heroine, for instance, seems dwarfed by the dimensions of her surroundings, and she is terrified. Here Brydon expands the dimensions of the house by means of the importance he places on the impending confrontation. The narrative analogies that emerge in this description, such as "it might have been, for queerness of colour, some watery under-world," suggest more clearly Brydon's own sense of his Gothic quest. In Radcliffe, then, the sources of the Gothic are objective and isolated, while James makes them inseparable from the inner experience of his character. We are not free to step back and analyze the Jamesian Gothic experience, because its objective reality is indistinguishable from Brydon's subjective interpretation of it. As a result, we have no escape from its Gothic intensity. Indeed, James has created an affective situation that so undermines our distance from the Gothic experience that our only alternative is to experience it exactly as Brydon himself experiences it in this scene.

The Jamesian Gothic character is more luridly exposed than any I have considered. We experience Brydon's response to his situation directly and with more unmediated intensity than we experience anything in Gothic fiction. "Some impressions strongly made . . . and intensely received" remain the key to James's Gothic technique. Here we see such a technique developed to its fullest. Instead of standing back in amazement at Frankenstein or Heathcliff, puzzling over the stupor of Roderick Usher, or even finding ourselves alienated from the judgment of Giovanni Guasconti, we feel with Brydon each turn in the passageways of his search for himself. Even the intensely engaging nature of James's other tales seems pallid beside the intensity of this inner confrontation. Far from defusing the force of the tale, this technique heightens the degree to which the reader becomes involved in it. We come to know Brydon intimately, so that we can experience the force of his fear more fully.

James makes us familiar with the workings of Brydon's mind so that we can appreciate the dimensions of his terror and experience his Gothic nightmare as our own:

> . . . an appearance produced, he the next instant saw, by the fact that the vestibule gaped wide, that the hinged halves of the inner door had been thrown far back. Out of that again the *question* sprang at him, making his eyes, as he felt, half-start from his head, as they had done, at the top of the house, before the sign of the other door. If he had left that one open, hadn't

he left this one closed, and wasn't he now in *most* immediate presence of some inconceivable occult activity? It was as sharp, the question, as a knife in his side, but the answer hung fire still and seemed to lose itself in the vague darkness to which the thin admitted dawn, glimmering archwise over the whole outer door, made a semicircular margin, a cold silvery nimbus that seemed to play a little as he looked—to shift and expand and contract.

(*HJSS* 754)

The technique of the opened door in itself is so simple that it is almost laughable. We do not laugh, however, and this is a signal that James has so intensely involved us in Brydon's plight that such simple effects have become profound. The panic of Brydon's response is something we can feel intensely. The movement from exterior detail to interior reaction has been intensified to the point of hysteria, while at the same time we watch, for Brydon and for ourselves, the hard surfaces of the house become suffused with the silvery nimbus of dawn. Mental and physical states are reaching the climax of such a process of suffusion as well: The play of Brydon's mind colors the scene as much as does the play of dawn light.

Because we have been able to see Brydon from the outside, with the help of Alice Staverton, as well as to know him from within, there is a dual process at work here. Emotionally we fear the ghost as Brydon has come to fear it. We also know instinctively, much as Alice Staverton knows, that this confrontation must take place, and, again like Alice, we know its significance. No interpretation is required here, because the tale interprets itself. James has so linked the metaphorical and metonymical functions of language that although meaning remains absent and indeterminate in this overdetermined text, its significance is implicit within the tale and articulated in the terms in which the tale is told. This is not "meaning" in the sense of a "detachable message" (Iser, *Act of Reading* 7), but rather "the referential totality which is implied by the aspects contained in the text and which must be assembled in the course of reading"; and which according to Iser must be combined with "the reader's absorption of the meaning into his own existence" (151). In "The Jolly Corner," there is no abyss of interpretation and little possibility of interpretive distortion: The tale offers us no alternative but to understand it in its own terms. The ghostly confrontation is the reality that the tale proposes, and we accept it.

If this confrontation casts a negative shadow over similar moments in the Gothic novel—one need only think of the lockstep progress of the Bleeding Nun and Lewis's bald assertion of her ghostly presence ("God Almighty! It was the bleeding nun!") to generate such a feeling—it is only because James's narrative technique offers a convincing solution to the problem of direct supernatural portrayal. Spencer Brydon "sees" a ghost, and we see it with him. "Rigid and conscious, spectral yet human, a man of his own substance and stature waited there to measure himself with his power to dismay" (HJSS 755). Everything in the tale has led us to anticipate this confrontation, an objective presentation of subjective experience as well as a subjective understanding of the objective, and we are not disappointed.

We do not stop to question whether or not the ghost is "real," because it stands so clearly before us and we accept it as an expression of Brydon's struggle with himself. He is responsible for the ghost, literally and figuratively; and that is exactly how we understand it. That it is not what Brydon expected ("It was unknown, inconceivable, awful, disconnected from any possibility . . ." [HJSS 756]) suggests the degree to which it is "one of those violent, dark revolts of being, directed against a threat that seems to emanate from an exorbitant outside or inside" (Kristeva 5). Brydon is as deeply horrified as is possible, and we understand, for ourselves, what that horror implies. The alter ego has made its devastating point. When Spencer Brydon finally "sees," it is a moment of vision for us as well.[21]

And, one might add, for Alice Staverton, who, at the moment of the ghost's appearance (he appears to her in another dream), knows that Brydon knows, at last, what he would have been. "It had brought him to knowledge, to knowledge—yes, this was the beauty of his state" (HJSS 758). The closing pages tell us the full extent of this knowledge. That the ghost was more horrifying than Brydon ever imagined is the final measure of the power of self-deception. We share the extremity of Brydon's horror because James has caused this sudden subversion, for him and for us, of our control. This experience is not totally devastating because of Alice Staverton's reassuring refusal to abandon the hero and her faithful presence at his side.

"You brought me literally to life" (HJSS 758-59), Brydon tells her. She becomes his tutor ("Isn't the whole point that you'd have been different?" [HJSS 761]), his mother (as she holds him to her breast), his lover (as she fully accepts him). For Brydon she offers a rebirth unusual in James's world:

> "I could have liked him. And to me," she said, "he was no horror. I had accepted him."
>
> "'Accepted'—?" Brydon oddly sounded.
>
> "Before, for the interest of his difference—yes. And as I didn't disown him, as I knew him—which you at last, confronted with him in his difference, so cruelly didn't, my dear—well, he must have been, you see, less dreadful to me. And it may have pleased him that I pitied him."
>
> (HJSS 762)

Her understanding is both literal and figurative response. And because Alice herself equates them, we find our-

selves confronting a heightened sense of reality here. Brydon, like so many Gothic heroes, panics at the fact of difference. But Alice redeems that difference with her love.

This denouement is in some ways a reversal of the ultimate Gothic concern of works like "Rappaccini's Daughter" or "Sir Edmund Orme." Alice sees the horror and yet is not horrified by what she sees. She does not push to understand, she merely lovingly accepts; and this is the key to the salvation her love offers. At the same time James has surpassed the inherent awkwardness of these earlier Gothic effects. Epistemological confusion enhances the affective technique there. Hawthorne's allegorical perspective keeps us a certain distance from final explanations. Beatrice's "poison" affects Giovanni in a way we can never fully understand; indeed our efforts at understanding are the very source of Gothic power. The power of "The Jolly Corner," however, arises out of an acceptance of Brydon's plight. He has at no time alienated us. As the story closes, we understand him as a man who has had to face the dreadful truth about his inner self but who is at the same time liberated from the horrifying confines of the private. Gothic fiction as well ceases to inhabit the realm of private fantasy and emerges as a form with profound public significance, liberated again from the limits of formal conventionality.

"Such compositions as 'The Jolly Corner,'" James says, "would obviously never have existed but for that love of 'a story as a story' which had from far back beset and beguiled their author" (AN 252). The "story" of "The Jolly Corner" is more than a sensationalistic rendering of a man's inner search. James uses his ghostly effects to expand the expressive possibilities of fiction without subverting the fictive concerns that are most important to him. With James we have witnessed the full legitimization of the Gothic. He has seamlessly incorporated ghostly effects into serious fiction, without either diminishing the power of the Gothic or diluting the seriousness of his work. The keystone to this technique is of course the form of the tale. There the "story" remains unencumbered of everything but its bare essentials. Impressionize, says James, and it is because the impressions he creates are so powerful that his tales achieve such greatness.

> The charm of all these things for the distracted modern mind is in the clear field of experience . . . over which we are thus led to roam; an annexed but independent world in which nothing is right save as we rightly imagine it. We have to do that, and we do it happily for the short spurt and in the smaller piece, achieving so perhaps beauty and lucidity; we flounder, we lose breath, on the other hand—that is we fail, not of continuity, but of an agreeable unity, of the "roundness" in which beauty and lucidity largely reside—when we go in, as they say, for great lengths and breadths. And this, oddly enough, not because "keeping it up" isn't abundantly within the compass of the imagination appealed to in

certain conditions, but because the finer interest depends just on *how* it is kept up.

(*AN* 171)

How it is kept up in "The Jolly Corner" and the other tales I have considered is not only through our excitement at the hands of a deft manipulator of the Gothic, but also through our understanding of what concerns are most intensely his own:

> Essentially . . . excited wonder must have a subject, must face in a direction, must be, increasingly, *about* something. Here comes in then the artist's bias and his range—determined, these things, by his own fond inclination. About what, good man, does he himself most wonder?—for upon that, whatever it may be, he will naturally most abound. Under that star will he gather in what he shall most seek to represent; so that if you follow thus his range of representation you will know how, you will see where, again, good man, he for himself most aptly vibrates.

(*AN* 253-54)

Nowhere is this more apparent than in James's own Gothic tales. He uses the form to clarify areas of concern which pervade his work. As a result the tales themselves assume a seriousness that their powerful effects do not belie. James's tales most clearly show us that the Gothic can offer serious fiction an expanded literary vocabulary for the expression of the most deeply human concerns.

While James's tales achieve a level of sophistication outside the ken of early Gothic visionaries, they do at the same time offer a practical solution to the challenge of Walpole's Gothic dream. Walpole sought to create a form that would blend two modes of literary discourse. With James such a blending is finally accomplished, not just in terms of literary convention, but also in accordance with the truth of human experience. For James develops a form that combines the haunting forces of an unreal and subjective world with an objective fictional world both palpable and real. In James's tales the unreal is granted legitimacy because it is more than merely metaphorical. It becomes a part of the human context. James thereby teaches us the degree to which the Gothic is part of human experience and indeed instructs us in the Gothic dimensions of our own natures. We understand his tales not as sensationalistic pieces acting on us from without, but as deeply moving works that affect us most powerfully from within. They are so powerful because they convey directly in emotional as well as intellectual terms the very concerns James seeks to evoke. The didacticism of these tales is at heart emotional: Whatever we come to know as a result of the Jamesian Gothic experience, we have first been made to feel.

The ultimate achievement of Gothic fiction, therefore, is to raise such purely emotional affective concerns to a level of sophistication that liberates them from the realm of the sensational and earns them a place in the literary canon. James's tales demonstrate the kind of affective sophistication a Gothic writer can aspire to: In his works there is nothing that is not perfectly commensurate with the truth of the situation he is depicting. He haunts us with the Gothic force of the world we know. James sees no need to distance his ghosts beyond the human consciousness that apprehends them. Nevertheless, his tales strike the chord that his Gothic predecessors were straining toward. For what do ancient castles, monks, prisons, or murderers express beyond the truth they convey about human emotions? James evokes all the ghostliness of the Gothic by suggesting that we consider the motivation for these metaphors in the first place. Here the uncanny potential of the tale form is fully realized. When Buber talks about the uncanny moments that disrupt our settled assumptions about the nature of experience (*I and Thou* 34), he could be talking about the kind of intensity we witness in these tales.

The measure of Gothic success lies not in any objective inventory of props and devices, James would say, but in the power of emotion generated in tales such as "The Turn of the Screw" or "The Jolly Corner." These tales truly have the harrowing power of the epigraph to this study, because they make their appeal exactly where our emotions are most vulnerable. When we begin to lose faith in our own ability to distinguish what is real, we are in a Gothic world ourselves. Walpole's Gothic dream becomes a reality in James's fiction because James makes it a reality for every one of us. The Jamesian Gothic metaphor has as its tenor not only the consciousnesses of the characters within his tales, but also the consciousnesses of those reading them. There is a reality that realism can only capture—paradoxically—by means of an impression of ghostliness; as a result of this ghostliness we are led into a more direct and a more horrifying knowledge of ourselves.

Notes

1. See Bewley; R. W. B. Lewis; Poirier. The work of these critics provides a rich context for this study, but none of them addresses the particular concerns at issue here.

2. The conventional selection of eighteen tales is that made by Leon Edel in *Henry James: Stories of the Supernatural*. The tales included are: "The Romance of Certain Old Clothes," 1868; "De-Grey: A Romance," 1868; "The Last of the Valerii," 1874; "The Ghostly Rental," 1876; "Sir Edmund Orme," 1891; "Nona Vincent," 1892; "The Private Life," 1892; "Sir Dominic Ferrand," 1892; "Owen Wingrave," 1892; "The Altar of the Dead," 1895; "The Friend of the Friends," 1896; "The Turn of the Screw," 1898; "The Real Right Thing," 1899; "The Great Good Place," 1900;

"Maud-Evelyn," 1900; "The Third Person," 1900; "The Beast in the Jungle," 1903; "The Jolly Corner," 1908. Edel uses the latest published edition of each tale.

3. For a discussion of the tale, the anecdote, and the *nouvelle* as generic distinctions, see Vaid 1-10. The tale, for James, could be very short or relatively long. In this study, I will consider examples that range from 10,000 words ("Sir Edmund Orme") to 44,500 words ("The Turn of the Screw"). Also see Good, and Cowdery, especially 19-34.

4. *AN* 321; Goetz 114.

5. Buber's *I and Thou* (33-34) informs my description here.

6. Todorov emphasizes this affective technique in his discussion of James's tales, and suggests that the hesitation he has seen as crucial to the "fantastic" is in that James made both the method of the tale and its subject. The hesitation is transferred from character to reader, and the quest for the supernatural becomes replaced by a desire to understand ("The Structural Analysis of Literature" 82-87).

7. Todorov's reading of the tale would take this statement on its own terms. In the narrator's quest for understanding, he would say, resides the "fantastic" interest of this tale. Indeed, the ambiguity about Charlotte's relationship to the ghost makes this concern somewhat engaging. But to make that the crucial interest of the tale is particularly inhumane. In my reading of the tale, this ambiguity can be seen as a way of heightening the effective force of far more central and powerful a concern. For whether or not Charlotte has seen the ghost, in terms of the action of the tale, we understand the ghost not as a measure of narrative confusion but as a measure of Charlotte's victimization.

8. For a discussion of this controversy, see Willen. See also Sheppard; McElroy; and, most importantly, Felman 141-247.

9. "The verb *to be* has lost one of its functions," Todorov tells us, "that of affirming the existence or non-existence of an object" ("The Structural Analysis of Literature" 87).

10. "Madness is in a sense the final issue raised by the first-person narrator in James," Goetz says, ". . . this narrative method also raises fundamental questions of the artistic imagination and narrative authority" (115).

11. Felman tells us that "'Knowing' . . . is to 'seeing' as the signified is to the signifier: the signifier is the *seen,* whereas the signified is the *known.* The signifier, by its very nature, is ambiguous and obscure, while the signified is certain, clear, and unequivocal. Ambiguity is thus inherent in the very essence of the act of seeing" (200).

12. See Schleifer: "The void stands behind the world—behind nature and behind language—ready to expose itself in the intensity of silence, in the forceful arguments of absence" (309-10).

13. What Kristeva says of Céline could apply as well here as it has at other moments of Gothic intensity: "Céline's narrative is a narrative of suffering and horror, not only because the 'themes' are there, as such, but because his whole narrative stance seems controlled by the necessity of going through abjection, whose intimate side is suffering and horror its public feature" (140).

14. "Following [Edmund] Wilson's suggestions," Felman says ironically, "there seems to be only one exception to this circle of universal dupery and deception: the so-called Freudian literary critic himself. By avoiding the double trap set at once by the unconscious and by rhetoric, by remaining himself *exterior* to the reading-errors that delude and blind both characters and author, the critic thus becomes the sole agent and the exclusive mouthpiece of the *truth* of literature" (229). But of course such critics are as implicated in the significance of "The Turn of the Screw" as those who read it as a simple ghost story.

15. In discussing "The Turn of the Screw," James says: "The grotesque business I had to make her [the governess] picture and the childish psychology I had to make her trace and present, were, for me at least, a very difficult job, in which absolute lucidity and logic, a singleness of effect, were imperative" (*Henry James: Letters* 4:86).

16. In discussing this tale and "The Beast in the Jungle," Goetz says that "What is striking is not that they internalize second consciousness but that they project the hero's own self, or part of it, onto an alter ego" (164). We have seen that such projection has been implicit in Gothic fiction all along.

17. On the imagery and implication of vacancy in the tale, see Auchard 50-51: "Here the voids are charged" (51).

18. Kaston 14; see also Yeazell 64-99.

19. See, for instance, Sheldon; and Buitenhuis 214-20.

20. Przybylowicz says that Brydon has "a mnemonic relationship to his past self" (125).

21. For an interpretation of this encounter as an "ordeal . . . of reading and writing," see Esch.

Works Cited

Bewley, Marius. *The Complex Fate: Hawthorne, Henry James and Some Other American Writers.* London: Chatto & Windus, 1952.

Buber, Martin. *I and Thou.* 2d ed. New York: Scribner's, 1958.

Buitenhuis, Peter. *The Grasping Imagination: The American Writings of Henry James.* Toronto: University of Toronto Press, 1970.

Cowdery, Lauren T. *The Nouvelle of Henry James in Theory and Practice.* Studies in Modern Literature, no. 47. Ann Arbor: UMI, 1986.

Esch, Deborah. "A Jamesian About-Face: Notes on 'The Jolly Corner.'" *ELH* 50 (1983): 587-605.

Felman, Shoshana. *Writing and Madness [Literature/ Philosophy/Psychoanalysis].* Trans. Martha Noel Evans and Shoshana Felman. Ithaca: Cornell University Press, 1985.

Goetz, William R. *Henry James and the Darkest Abyss of Romance.* Baton Rouge: Louisiana State University Press, 1986.

Good, Graham. "Notes on the Novella." *Novel* 10 (1977): 197-211.

James, Henry. *Henry James: Letters.* Ed. Leon Edel. 4 vols. Cambridge, MA: Belknap-Harvard, 1974-84.

Kaston, Carren. *Imagination and Desire in the Novels of Henry James.* New Brunswick, NJ: Rutgers University Press, 1984.

Kristeva, Julia. *Powers of Horror: An Essay on Abjection.* Trans. Leon S. Roudiez. New York: Columbia University Press, 1982.

Lewis, R. W. B. "Hawthorne and James: The Matter of the Heart." In *Trials of the World: Essays in American Literature and Humanistic Tradition,* 77-96. New Haven: Yale University Press, 1965.

McElroy, John Harmon. "The Mysteries at Bly." *Arizona Quarterly* 37 (1981): 214-36.

Poirier, Richard. "Visionary to Voyeur: Hawthorne to James." In *A World Elsewhere, the Place of Style in American Literature,* 93-143. New York: Oxford University Press, 1966.

Przybylowicz, Donna. *Desire and Repression: The Dialectic of Self and Other in the Late Works of Henry James.* University, AL: University of Alabama Press, 1986.

Schleifer, Ronald. "The Trap of the Imagination: The Gothic Tradition, Fiction, and 'The Turn of the Screw.'" *Criticism* 22 (1980): 297-319.

Sheldon, Pamela Jacobs. "Jamesian Gothicism: The Haunted Castle of the Mind." *Studies in the Literary Imagination* 7 (1974): 121-34.

Sheppard, E. A. *Henry James and* The Turn of the Screw. Oxford: Oxford University Press, 1974.

Todorov, Tzvetan. *The Fantastic: A Structural Approach to a Literary Genre.* Trans. Richard Howard. Cleveland: Case Western Reserve University Press, 1973.

Willen, Gerald. *A Casebook on Henry James's "The Turn of the Screw."* 2d ed. New York: Crowell, 1969.

Yeazell, Ruth Bernard. *Language and Knowledge in the Late Novels of Henry James.* Chicago: University of Chicago Press, 1976.

Abbreviations

Works frequently cited in the text and notes have been identified by the following abbreviations:

AN: James, Henry. *The Art of the Novel: Critical Prefaces.* Ed. Richard P. Blackmur. New York: Scribner's, 1934.

CEWNH: Hawthorne, Nathaniel. *The Centenary Edition of the Works of Nathaniel Hawthorne.* Ed. William Chavaret et al. 19 vols. to date. Columbus, OH: Ohio State University Press, 1962-

CWEAP: Poe, Edgar Allan. *The Complete Works of Edgar Allan Poe.* Ed. James A. Harrison. 17 vols. 1902. New York: AMS, 1965.

HJSS: James, Henry. *Henry James: Stories of the Supernatural.* Ed. Leon Edel. New York: Taplinger, 1970.

LMWS: Shelley, Mary. *The Letters of Mary Wollstonecraft Shelley.* Ed. Betty T. Bennett. 3 vols. Baltimore: Johns Hopkins University Press, 1980-88.

MSJ: Shelley, Mary. *Mary Shelley's Journal.* Ed. Frederick L. Jones. Norman: University of Oklahoma Press, 1947.

NHJ: James, Henry. *The Notebooks of Henry James.* Ed. F. O. Matthiessen and Kenneth B. Murdock. 1947. New York: Galaxy, Oxford, 1961.

TSEAP: Poe, Edgar Allan. *Collected Works of Edgar Allan Poe.* Ed. Thomas Ollive Mabbott. 3 vols. to date. Cambridge, MA: Harvard University Press, 1969-. Vol. 2: *Tales and Sketches, 1831-42.* Vol. 3: *Tales and Sketches, 1843-49.*

"Turn": James, Henry. *The Turn of the Screw.* 1898. Ed. Robert Kimbrough. New York: Norton, 1966.

GENDER AND THE GOTHIC IMAGINATION

Kathy A. Fedorko (essay date 1995)

SOURCE: Fedorko, Kathy A. "The Gothic Text: Life and Art." In *Gender and the Gothic in the Fiction of Edith Wharton,* pp. 1-21. Tuscaloosa: University of Alabama Press, 1995.

[*In the excerpt below, Fedorko examines Wharton's treatment of family, marriage, incest, and houses in her*

Gothic stories written in the 1920s and 1930s, as well as in some of her biographical writings. The critic suggests that Wharton used the Gothic mode to write about women's self-definition.]

Wharton's conflicting and conflicted views of women and men and feminine and masculine reflect a complicated interweaving of family and social environment, historical time, and individual psychology. These conditions and the gender tension they foster in turn provide the impetus for Wharton to use and recast Gothic conventions and narratives in her fiction as a way to dramatize psychic conflict. Indeed, as a dreamlike interaction among parts of the self, the Gothic in her fiction allows Wharton both to mirror and to revise issues that inform her life as well as the genre: an ambivalent terror of/attraction to the supernatural and the threatening; a fascination with incest; a fearful ambivalence about marriage, about breaking out of social restraints, about being "different"; and an attraction to houses as signs of self and to the "abyss" as a state of being beyond the rational. Wharton's handling of these issues distinctly evolves throughout her career. In the process, Wharton progressively imagines a fe/male self, moving from gender-bound women and men in the Gothic-marked fiction written early in her career to characters in the later fiction who struggle toward or even attain a degree of gender mutuality.

FAMILY AND SOCIETY

Wharton's autobiographies—the published version, *A Backward Glance* (1934) and the unpublished version, "Life and I"[1]—and her autobiographically colored nonfiction *French Ways and Their Meaning* and *The Writing of Fiction* document the personal and professional struggles that drew Wharton to a Gothic perspective. "Life and I" also vividly dramatizes that perspective, for in it Wharton remembers her child self as a Gothic heroine—trapped in suffocating interiors, suppressed by patriarchal restraints embodied by her mother, isolated by her writing and tortured by her acute sensibilities, but at the same time pleasurably, even erotically, charged by those sensibilities. As a passionate, secret lover of words and literature, Wharton felt herself to be the isolated, emotionally orphaned heroine, alone in her "other side," a supernatural world where the flow and energy of words brought ecstatic release while producing inordinate guilt because she was so "different" ("Life" 23, 36). This intermingling of eroticism and fear, pleasure and pain, is the quintessential Gothic psychology.

"Life and I" demonstrates Wharton's uneasiness with the patriarchal value system that tells women they are worthwhile only if they are attractive, especially to men, and that they risk being excluded if they are intelligent or strong willed or in any other way "unfemi-

nine."[2] "To look pretty" is one of the "deepest-seated instincts of my nature," Wharton writes there. Her clarification of this instinct identifies her as both gazed-at (female) art piece and (male) artist: "I say 'to look pretty' instead of 'to be admired,' because I really believe it has always been an aesthetic desire, rather than a form of vanity. I always saw the visible world as a series of pictures, more or less harmoniously composed, & the wish *to make the picture prettier* was, as nearly as I can define it, the form my feminine instinct of pleasing took" ("Life" 1-2).

Wharton's earliest memory, with which she begins *A Backward Glance,* is of being dressed beautifully while walking with her father and realizing for the first time the value of being a "subject for adornment" (2). Yet at the same time, in "Life and I," she confesses humiliation about being laughed at by her brothers for her red hair and the "supposed abnormal size" of her hands and feet; she was, she felt, "the least good-looking of the family" and therefore intensely conscious of her "physical short comings" (37).

Though pronouncing at a young age that when she grew up she wanted to be "the best dressed woman in New York" like her mother, Wharton felt herself no match and no daughter for the elegant Lucretia Jones (*BG* 20). While she recalls her "tall splendid father" as "always so kind," with strong arms that "held one so safely," and her childhood nurse Doyley as "the warm cocoon" in which she "lived safe and sheltered," she remembers that her mother's abounding interest in flounced dresses and ermine scarves was accompanied by her indolence and capriciousness, that her mother stressed politeness and reserve rather than nurturing (20, 26). This model of old New York womanhood upheld the patriarchy with her "shoulds" and "musts," her withering judgmental demeanor, and her physical reserve, an outcome, perhaps, of her own "internalized oppression" that she encouraged in her daughter (Wehr 18). Sandra Gilbert describes Wharton's situation in her comment that "the more fully the mother represents culture, the more inexorably she tells the daughter that she cannot have a mother because she has been signed with and assigned to the Law of the Father," the law that means "culture is by definition both patriarchal and phallocentric" ("Life" 358).

Even speaking was a hazardous business for the precocious, acutely sensitive young Edith, because, in Wharton's view, her mother scorned verbal imperfection and risk taking. Over sixty years later the daughter writes, "I still wince under my mother's ironic smile when I said that some visitor had stayed 'quite a while,' and her dry: 'Where did you pick *that* up?'" (*BG* 49). The anger is palpable in the memory that "my parents—or at least my mother—laughed at me for using 'long words,' & for caring for dress (in which heaven knows she set me the example!); & under this perpetual cross-fire of criticism I became a painfully shy self-conscious child" ("Life" 37). And a shy adult. For throughout *A Backward Glance* runs the theme of her "incorrigible shyness" that she blames time and again for missed opportunities of intimacy. The mute girl is mirrored in the passive female Gothic character, holding her tongue, afraid to question, unable to defend herself.[3]

It is worth remembering that "the image of the repressive mother is the daughter's *creation*" and that Wharton's autobiographies should not be assumed to be factual documents (Fryer 359-60 n.4).[4] Although there are hints in *A Backward Glance* about Lucretia's difficult childhood, we have no "backward glance" from Lucretia to counter her daughter's perspective and to help us understand her own childhood pain and losses. Still, however skewed Wharton's memories of her mother, her perception was that she was rejected by a cold mother who criticized and restrained more than she accepted and nurtured. From her Wharton learns the intense self-criticism, the self-hating voice, that women internalize from patriarchal judgment of them as inadequate. Wharton's reiteration in "Life and I" that she "frankly despised" little girls clearly seems to include herself (12). This "self-hater" turns up in her Gothic short stories as the female victim who colludes in her own destruction and as the villainous male who oppresses the passive woman (Wehr 20).[5]

As a child Wharton is beset by "the most excruciating moral tortures" instilled by her internalized mother ("Life" 2). She illustrates this point with an anecdote about telling a little boy in her dance class that their dance teacher's mother looks like an old goat. When she admits to the teacher that she made the remark, she gains a scolding and the tormented sense that her own mother would have thought her "naughty" not to have known how to do the "right" thing ("Life" 7). Noting that she had two "inscrutable beings" to please, God and her mother, and that her mother was the most inscrutable of the two, Wharton confesses that "this vexed problem of truth-telling, & the impossibility of reconciling 'Gods' standard of truthfulness with the conventional obligation to be 'polite' & not hurt anyone's feelings" plunged her into a "darkness of horror" (6-7).

Wharton's intense moral anxiety resembles the impetus for traditional Gothic fantasy of the eighteenth century, springing as it did from uneasiness about "problems of personal moral responsibility and judgement, questions of restrictive convention, and a troubled awareness of irrational impulses which threatened to subvert orthodox notions of social and moral propriety" (Howells 7). Wharton's girlhood, as she perceives it, thus is haunted by a late nineteenth-century version of the "grim realities" of eighteenth-century womanhood that inspired Ann Radcliffe's and Fanny Burney's Gothic, "the re-

straints on her freedom, all the way to actual imprisonment; the mysterious, unexplained social rituals; the terrible need always to appear, as well as always to be, virtuous; and, over all, the terrible danger of slippage from the respectable to the unrespectable class of womanhood" (Moers 206-207).

Bourgeois men were actors in the eighteenth-century world, and women were passive possessions whose good behavior was often the deciding factor in their material well-being. Female respectability involved passive obedience to male authority, since women were seen as "inescapably Other" (Day 95). Societal emphasis on reason and repression of feeling, the "male" sphere, made that which was repressed, the "female" sphere, all the more threatening and thereby in need of destruction or imprisonment. The rebellious Gothic probed fears, spoke the unspeakable, meddled in the taboo, like rape, sex among the clergy, and, especially, incest. Social institutions like the church and the family, symbolized by the ruined church or castle, were considered claustrophobic and hypocritical because they suppressed and denied part of human experience.

Initially Wharton's "devastating passion" for "making up" stories as a child was a way of finding release from a threatening, confining, judgmental world into a supernatural one ("Life" 11). The sound and sight of words produced "sensuous rapture," regardless of her inability to understand them (10). She writes in "Life and I" that words "sang to me so bewitchingly that they almost lured me from the wholesome noonday air of childhood into some strange supernatural region, where the normal pleasures of my age seemed as insipid as the fruits of the earth to Persephone after she had eaten of the pomegranate seed" (10). Wharton might well be describing immersion in *le sémiotique*, Julia Kristeva's term for a pre-Oedipal, preverbal, sensual state associated with the maternal voice and bodily rhythms. The sensuousness of language thus provides the young Wharton with a haunted maternal bower, a "secret garden."[6]

Even when Wharton learns the meanings of words, it isn't intellectual discourse but rather the language of erotic secrecy and mystery, of supernatural otherworldliness that pervades her descriptions of immersion in books. She feels a "secret ecstasy of communion" with the books in her father's library: Coleridge; Goethe's *Faust* and *Wilhelm Meister*; *The Duchess of Malfi*; *The White Devil*; the "Song of Solomon"; Irving's *Tales of the Alhambra,* no small dose of the romantic, the erotic, the Gothic (*BG* 69). These "enraptured sessions" with poetry, philosophy, religion, and drama become part of her "secret retreat" within her where she "wished no one to intrude" (70). "Words and cadences haunted it like song-birds in a magic wood," nurturing the way her mother did not (70). Her father's library becomes analogous to "my strange inner world," conflating the symbolic and spiritual, the paternal and maternal (72). In Wharton's Gothic, startling, disorienting, and often erotic discoveries take place in libraries, as intellectual knowledge is expanded by intuitive, uncanny awareness.[7]

Wharton's dilemma as female child and woman is that intellectual knowledge and activities endow male-identified power at the same time that they estrange her from her female self as it has been defined by her society and her mother. Discovering Sir William Hamilton's *History of Philosophy* in her brother's room gives the young Wharton the hope that "now I should never be that helpless blundering thing, a mere 'little girl,' again!" ("Life" 32-33). But her intense intelligence and engagement with language also increase her sense of abnormality. As she confesses, "it humiliated me to be so 'different'" (36). The social ramifications of difference were clear. According to an 1882 story in the *Newport Daily News* the engagement between Edith Jones and Harry Stevens, when she was nineteen, was broken because of "an alleged preponderance of intellectuality on the part of the intended bride" (Lewis, *Biography* 45).

Her own writing intensified Wharton's gender conflict. This public, and thereby unfeminine, act was met with silent disapproval: "My literary success puzzled and embarrassed my old friends far more than it impressed them, and in my own family it created a kind of constraint which increased with the years. None of my relations ever spoke to me of my books, either to praise or blame—they simply ignored them; and among the immense tribe of my New York cousins, though it included many with whom I was on terms of affectionate intimacy, the subject was avoided as though it were a kind of family disgrace, which might be condoned but could not be forgotten" (*BG* 143-44). In having her own writing avoided as though it were a "family disgrace," Wharton faced the quintessential woman writer's dilemma. Writing is a fearful, "naughty" thing to do, for it involves honesty of feeling, assertiveness, and noticing and talking of things not polite to acknowledge. Like sex, it is fraught with guilt, this uncontrolled, unladylike, other-worldly act. Hélène Cixous, in urging women to "write her self," shows that Wharton's dilemma is still a current one for women: "Where is the ebullient, infinite woman who, immersed as she was in her naiveté, kept in the dark about herself, led into self-disdain by the great arm of parental-conjugal phallocentrism, hasn't been ashamed of her strength? Who, surprised and horrified by the fantastic tumult of her drives (for she was made to believe that a well-adjusted normal woman has a . . . divine composure), hasn't accused herself of being a monster? Who, feeling a funny desire stirring inside her (to sing, to write, to dare to speak, in short, to bring out something new), hasn't thought she was sick?" ("The Laugh" 876).[8]

The denial by silence of Wharton's writing by her extended family and their dread of creativity is not unlike the denial of intense and sometimes supernatural experiences by characters in her Gothic stories. Their attempted suppression of disorienting awareness is undermined when the reader joins Wharton in an act of voyeurism and recognition as the story plays itself out.[9]

Her family relationships and experiences were not Wharton's only impetus for using Gothic conventions and narratives in her fiction as a way to tell the disallowed story of female sexuality and power. Her Victorian/Post-Victorian Anglo-Saxon society, with its penchant for ignoring what it considered inappropriate human experience, was an impetus as well. In *French Ways and Their Meaning,* Wharton describes maturity in a society as the ability to face primal terrors. "Intellectual honesty, the courage to look at things as they are," she writes, "is the first test of mental maturity. Till a society ceases to be afraid of the truth in the domain of ideas it is in leading-strings, morally and mentally" (58-59).

One of the main aspects of life to which Wharton refers in the phrase "things as they are" is sexuality. The French, she observes, are criticized by Anglo-Saxons for talking and writing freely about sexuality, as if to do so were "inconsistent with . . . purity and morality." Wharton notes approvingly that the French just take sex for granted "as part of the great parti-coloured business of life" (60, ellipsis mine).

Wharton felt that Anglo-Saxon literature had been no better than the society at acknowledging female sexuality in particular. In *The Writing of Fiction* she argues that English novelists create women whose passion is banked by prudery. Scott, for instance, "became conventional and hypocritical when he touched on love and women," substituting "sentimentality for passion" and reducing his heroines to "'Keepsake' insipidities" (5). Thackeray, Dickens, Brontë, and Eliot were also affected by the "benumbing" restraints of their time (63).

Wharton's own portrayal of passionate women in her novels was hindered not only because, as Elizabeth Ammons argues, she felt the American woman she wrote about "was far from being . . . a whole human being" but also because her society, her background, and the very form of realism resisted such portrayal (3, ellipsis mine). In *A Backward Glance,* Wharton recounts that early in her career she had a reader protest, "have you never known a respectable woman? If you have, in the name of decency write about her!" (126) Those were the days, she remembers, when an editor stipulated that no "unlawful attachment" should appear in her projected novel and when her friend Charles Eliot Norton warned that "no great work of the imagination has ever been based on illicit passion" (126-27). But decades later the situation remained unchanged. The

Saturday Evening Post, Liberty, and *Collier's* wouldn't publish *Hudson River Bracketed* and *The Gods Arrive* because of the "illicit liaison" in them, and the editor of *Delineator,* which finally did publish them, commented that "the situation, that of a man and woman unmarried and living together, is a little startling for magazine publication" (Lewis, *Biography* 502).

Wharton's anger about the problem of portraying sexuality in literature surfaced most heatedly when she chided younger novelists for not realizing that portraying whole people, complete with passions, had been difficult for their predecessors. In a 1931 letter to Sinclair Lewis she rebukes him for the depreciatory comments he had made about Howells in his Nobel acceptance address; Wharton points out that Howells had to contend with a country "reeking with sentimentality and shuddering with prudery" (Dupree 265). She returns to the matter in *A Backward Glance,* commenting bitterly that "the poor novelists who were my contemporaries . . . had to fight hard for the right to turn the wooden dolls about which they were expected to make believe into struggling suffering human beings. . . . The amusing thing about this turn of the wheel is that we who fought the good fight are now jeered at as the prigs and prudes who barred the way to complete expression" (127, ellipsis mine).

Contemporary critical discussion of realism has shown that the difficulty of portraying passions in realistic fiction that Wharton pinpointed (and a reason why she relied on a Gothic subtext to show passion constrained) is a problem inherent in the form. The dilemma is the very strength of realistic fiction, Leo Bersani has argued; its recreation of social structures militates against a full portrayal of the forces that would deny their validity. "The technical premises of realistic fiction—the commitment to intelligible, 'full' characters, to historical verisimilitude, to the revealing gesture or episode, to a closed temporal frame—already dooms any adventure in the stimulating improbabilities, of behavior which resists being 'placed' and interpreted in a general psychological or formal structure" (67). Because it keeps characters coherent, "the containment of desire is a triumph for social stability" (73).

Feminist criticism has enlarged the conversation about how this "containment of desire" in deference to "social stability" is a culturally created gender issue, a containment of the "natural" feminine/maternal by the "symbolic" masculine/paternal. Often "submerged meanings" appear in women's writing as surreal or uncanny eruptions in and interruptions of the text (Gilbert and Gubar, *Madwoman* 72). Grace Poole's intrusion into Jane's story in *Jane Eyre* is one of the most discussed examples. A novel such as *Villette,* as well, which seemingly doesn't recognize the Romantic or Gothic, nonetheless can be said to possess a "buried letter of Romanticism" and "the phantom of feminism" convey-

ing "the discourse of the Other, as the novel's unconscious . . . struggles for articulation within the confines of midnineteenth-century realism" (Jacobus, "Buried Letter" 42, 59; ellipsis mine).

Brontë's texts have been called examples of "new" Gothic in that intense feeling and extrarational experience are not only contained in "marvelous circumstance" but interpenetrate the "ordinary world" and thereby enlarge the sense of reality in the novels, especially the reality of women (Heilman 123, 121). Traditional Gothic male villains are deconstructed when "dark magnetic energy" characterizes female protagonists (127). Such a view privileges the realist form with which Wharton was comfortable in her novels but into which, like Brontë, she interwove a Gothic text to accommodate the gender tension central to her life as a writer.

THE ABYSS

Wharton's sense of being an outsider, the "separated one," as a precocious child and a woman writer, uncomfortable with the male-identified power of writing and the intellect while at the same time lured by the nourishing female-identified "rich world of dreams" and the sound and sight of words, helps explain her use of mystical/supernatural rather than "realistic" language to describe her creative process, the goddess's descent into the soul, as she puts it (Wilt 19; "Life" 12; *BG* 198). The moment of creation is akin to the mysterious moment just before sleep when "one falls over the edge of consciousness" (*BG* 198). Similarly, the storytelling process "takes place in some secret region on the sheer edge of consciousness" where characters haunt the brain and names spectrally appear without characters (205). The creative act is "like the mystic's union with the Unknowable" (121) or "that mysterious fourth-dimensional world which is the artist's inmost sanctuary (*WF* 119)."[10]

Wharton's language of creativity—the "unknown depths," the "sheer edge of consciousness," the mysterious and the spectral—is the language of her Gothic as well. Characters anxiously facing the dark abyss of preternatural knowledge or entering a mysterious life removed from society in the Gothic stories and the Gothic-marked novels replicate Wharton's creative process of entering the "unknown depths." Wharton's Gothic thus enacts the writing process as a plunge into awareness beyond the realistic, where the unexpurgated "real" story is told, the "unlabeled, disallowed, disavowed" of which her patriarchal mother and society would not approve (Stein 126).

The omnipresent Gothic abyss traditionally threatens damnation, a fall into "the demonic underworld" that leads to "the rejection of human identity and the embracing of the monstrous" (MacAndrew 49; Day 7).

Rather than this chaotic loss of humanity, the abyss as Wharton uses it is a plunge into a realm that threatens loss of the controlled self at the same time that it promises new understanding. And what realm could be more frightening and yet more alluring for this unmothered daughter of the patriarchy than the feminine/maternal darkness, with its overwhelming intimacy and primal power?

Wharton acknowledges the occult power of the maternal when she places the faculty for apprehending ghosts in "the warm darkness of the pre-natal fluid far below our conscious reason" (*G* vii). Her Gothic portrayals of inner journeys into threatening knowledge take characters into maternal places: houses, cabins, caves. Within the place within the mind of the character, an abyss opens, threatening annihilation at the same time that it promises self-awareness if s/he can acknowledge the experience.[11]

Facing the abyss is crucial to Wharton's Gothic, for the willingness of characters to face the maternal darkness indicates their willingness to understand the inner life, the loss of the known self that has opened before them. Arrogant intellectual men in her Gothic fiction are usually those least willing to acknowledge what they have seen in the abyss and most apt to ignore or deny their experience with the darkness. Wharton seems to be mirroring her sense of the limitations of her own rationality, of the patriarchal symbolic, her sense that, emphasized at the expense of respect for the maternal erotic darkness, such logocentrism becomes tyrannical and repressive.[12] Since the characters, especially in the stories, are themselves too timid to fully assimilate what they have experienced, Wharton depends on the reader to decipher their lost knowledge. Thus the woman's story is heard despite the attempts of the male narrator or other (usually male) character to deny or suppress it.

Contemporary feminist criticism of the Gothic argues that what draws a woman in particular to the "forbidden center" of the Gothic mystery is not threatened incest within the Oedipal plot, a reading that privileges the male reader, but rather "the spectral presence of a dead-undead mother, archaic and all-encompassing, a ghost signifying the problematics of femininity which the heroine must confront" (Kahane, "Gothic Mirror" 336).[13] The "ubiquitous Gothic precipice on the edge of the maternal blackness" thus draws female characters to a confrontation with the mysteries of identity (340).

Sexual maturity, the secret knowledge and power of the mother, is both feared and desired. "Bad" women the heroine confronts in the Gothic text are the "monstrous" other parts of herself, and the parts of the mother, that she cannot accept—her passions, her ambitions, her energy (Stein 123ff.). The Gothic gives "*visual* form to the fear of self," the dark, knowing mother/self who might appear in the fiction as a mad woman or a freak or a sexual monster and therefore beyond the pale of respectable society (Moers 163). Wharton gives such "visual form to the fear of self" when Lily Bart has her disturbing vision of herself in the mirror early in *The House of Mirth* and in the mirror of her thoughts after Trenor's attempted rape. Wharton's own fear of her sexual self is reflected in the exaggerated mirroring of Lily's vaguely erotic activities by the omnivorously sexual Bertha Dorset.

Wharton's use of the abyss in her Gothic fiction as a character's disorienting confrontation with primal human emotion or experience recalls Jung's theory of individuation, "the process by which a person becomes a psychological 'in-dividual,' that is, a separate, indivisible unity or 'whole,'" by assimilating knowledge from the unconscious as part of consciousness (9[1]:275). This process has been called an adaptation to inner reality as well as outer, to what one is "meant to be"; one recognizes the next step in what one is meant to be by looking for what attracts and frightens at the same time (Whitmont 48-49, 62). The "rebirth journey," as individuation has been called, brings to consciousness "the lost values of the psyche, which lie so largely in the realm of Eros, and by this means the human being becomes more complete" (Harding 245). The goal of the journey is an assimilation of gender selves, inner and outer worlds, consciousness with unconsciousness.[14]

Jung conforms with most androcentric Western theory in his association of consciousness with the masculine and unconsciousness with the feminine. "Psychologically the self is a union of conscious (masculine) and unconscious (feminine). It stands for the psychic totality" (9[2]:268). These realms accrue, however, the sexist associations of reasonable, reasoning masculine consciousness as opposed to feared, fearful feminine unconsciousness. In Jung's theory the male hero's plunge into the abyss of the unconscious involves confronting his "shadow," the hated, repressed side of the personality and thereafter the "anima," the archetypal image of the female in a man's unconsciousness, an awesome, organic power associated with the Terrible Mother or with a dual mother, part destructive, part creative (Wehr 59-67, 112-13). The ultimate encounter is thus with an Other that must be overcome to be assimilated.

Feminist archetypal critics have revised Jungian theory to make it more compatible with women's experiences as women themselves have written about them. The shadow a woman confronts often carries with it the gynophobia of the social world that fuses with the animus (the archetypal image of the male in a woman's unconscious) into "a masculine character who loathes the woman as much as she loathes herself" (Pratt, "Spinning" 104). Annis Pratt cautions that for women the rebirth journey entails psychological risk that is as likely to lead to madness as to renewal (*Archetypal* 142). But women may also overcome this self-destructiveness and assimilate a mother/self that engenders a sense of female power and erotic independence by accepting rather than fearing the life forces of sexuality, birth, and death. Thus "the woman's encounter with a feminine figure at the depths of her psyche . . . is more a fusion than an agon; the woman encounters a being similar to herself which empowers even as it exiles her from the social community," since she then becomes a woman unreconciled to a patriarchal world (Pratt, "Spinning" 106, ellipsis mine). In imagining this feminine archetype encountered in the inner world, women writers often draw on female-identified mythology: Demeter/Persephone, Celtic Grail legends, Ishtar/Tammuz rebirth legends, and witches and other wise women (Pratt, *Archetypal* 170). This is Wharton's practice in her Gothic-marked fiction.

While male reading of the Gothic places the "maternal blackness" beneath the ruined castle, "the crumbling shell of paternal authority," as imprisoning womb/tomb, feminist reading is more apt to identify the castle or other enclosure as the mother, "mother as nurturer, as sexual being, as body, as harboring a secret, as an indifferent hardness" (Fiedler 112; Holland and Sherman 289). The mother, especially for the woman reader, threatens nothingness, overwhelmingness, nonseparation (Holland and Sherman 283). The female Gothic character's entrapment in or exploration of a Gothic house is thus an extension of her relationship to the maternal body she shares (Kahane, "Gothic Mirror" 338).[15]

Kristeva's theory of the abject provides another way to read the abyss in Wharton's Gothic. Though Kristeva emphasizes the abject as a reiteration of *separation* from the maternal, her discussion of the self-awareness gained in the process of struggling against and being pulled into the abject sheds light on the response of Wharton's Gothic characters. Lying just on the edge of meaninglessness and nonexistence, the abject represents "our earliest attempts to release the hold of *maternal* entity even before ex-isting outside of her, thanks to the autonomy of language" (13). "The phantasmatic mother," constitutes, in the history of each person, "the abyss that must be established as an autonomous (and not encroaching) *place,* and *distinct* object, meaning a *signifiable* one," so that the person might "learn to speak" (100). In spite of this "placing," one does not "cease separating" from the abject; it retains the power to recreate the act of attempting to break away from the maternal entity punctuated by the pull back from it (13).

Reexperiencing the act of separation from the mother forces the limits of one's psychic world and the limits of self-knowledge. "The abject shatters the wall of re-

pression and its judgments. It takes the ego back to its source on the abominable limits from which, in order to be, the ego has broken away. . . . Abjection is a resurrection that has gone through death (of the ego). It is an alchemy that transforms death drive into a start of life, of new significance" (15, ellipsis mine).

Such a definition of the abject as a rebirth into new understanding through the pull of the maternal abyss helps explain why Wharton's characters are both terrified of and attracted to extrarational experiences. Wharton's Gothic emphasizes the maternal abyss as "repellent and repelled" to those most frightened by it, yet Wharton also emphasizes that it is also a state of being that one must assimilate within oneself rather than reject or pull away from (6). In dramatizing primal experiences in her Gothic fiction—of ghosts, madness, and sexual threat—Wharton is courting disorder. She is pressing the limits of rationality and having her characters risk temporary egolessness for the sake of greater awareness, particularly of the feminine. She is speaking about those things considered unspeakable by her family and society—the erotic, the antisocial, the grotesque, the energetic, the fearful—those emotions and conditions that, like the regression to the maternal, threaten to overwhelm one.[16]

Wharton dramatizes the power of the uncontrollable and overwhelming in her autobiographical account of recuperating, when she was nine years old, from a near-fatal bout of typhoid and of being given a book to read: "To an unimaginative child the tale would no doubt have been harmless; but it was a 'robber-story,' & with my intense Celtic sense of the super-natural, tales of robbers & ghosts were perilous reading. This one brought on a serious relapse, & again my life was in danger" ("Life" 17).

Thereafter, until she was a "young lady," she lived in "chronic fear" of an unexplained terror, "like some dark undefinable menace, forever dogging my steps" (17). Most terrifying was returning from daily walks outside with nurse, governess, or father and, while waiting for the door to her home to be opened, feeling the menace behind her, on top of her, and being "seized by a choking agony of terror" until she could escape inside (18). The memory suggests an overwhelming need to reconnect with the sheltering maternal body/house across the threshold. But the intensity of the "undefinable menace" that sends her to the mother also suggests an anxious fear of separation intensified by never having felt solidly connected in the first place. In Wharton's Gothic fiction, terror of the outside unknown is transmuted into terror of the internal unknown, within the house/mother rather than outside of it. Facing that terror is a courageous means of claiming and transforming it.

Wharton states, in "Life and I," that until the age of twenty-seven or twenty-eight, she "could not sleep in the room with a book containing a ghost-story" (19). Using the progressive tense of recent occurrence, she admits, "I have frequently had to burn books of this kind, because it frightened me to know that they were down-stairs in the library!" (19). Such a sensational reaction to the threat posed by the supernatural—such books almost killed me and I subsequently burned them—reveals how much Wharton feared the uncontrollable and how much power she granted fiction as a means of recreating the terror of uncontrollable forces. Julia Briggs's idea that "by recounting nightmares, giving them speakable shapes and patterns" in "stories of the terrific unknown," we hope to "control them and come to terms with them" might well account for both Wharton's autobiographical "confession" and her Gothic fiction that draws one into the "terrific unknown" (11).

In recasting the "abyss" as a restorative, regenerative place for those courageous enough to face it, Wharton reconceives its destructive power. Her several nervous breakdowns and her bouts of "occult and unget-at-able nausea" and overwhelming fatigue during the period when she was most conflicted about her identity as writer/wife/socialite/intellectual/homemaker made her familiar with the risks of the journey into the self (Wolff 52). Wharton's experience with the Weir Mitchell Rest Cure for her nervous collapse was more salutary than the experiences of Charlotte Perkins Gilman or Virginia Woolf, since she was encouraged to write during her time of separation from the outside world (Lewis, *Biography* 84). Nonetheless her imposed infantalization, during which she was barred from visitors yet felt "ghostly presences . . . peering in on her morning and night," reappears as a dominant theme in many of her Gothic stories (84). Walter Berry's comment in his letter of November 9, 1898, that he is "delighted to hear" that Wharton had "loosened the first stone in your cell toward an escape" suggests that Wharton saw herself as a prisoner during her "cure" (Beinecke).

Her visit with her dear friend Henry James during his period of despair in 1910 is another encounter with the abyss. She observes that his eyes are those of a man who "has looked on the Medusa," and as she sits beside him, she looks "into the black depths over which he is hanging—the superimposed 'abysses' of all his fiction" (Lewis and Lewis, *Letters* 202). Most notable for Wharton is that James is no longer in control of his emotions: "I, who have always seen him so serene, so completely the master of his wonderful emotional instrument . . . , I could hardly believe it was the same James who cried out to me his fear, his despair, his craving for the 'cessation of consciousness,' & all his unspeakable loneliness & need of comfort, & inability to be comforted!" (202, ellipsis mine).

Wharton later comments how "haunted" she has been by James's condition (203). The tension between complete mastery over one's emotions and being incapacitated by them is part of the gender-identified duality that Wharton dramatizes in her Gothic fiction. Ellen Olenska in *The Age of Innocence* is perhaps her most successful example of a character who exemplifies balance between the extremes, though it comes at the cost of "leaving home" for good. Because she has faced the Medusa and the darkness of the abyss, Ellen possesses a maturity of mind and spirit that Newland Archer admires, even marvels at. He himself skirts the edge and the Medusa's gaze, thereby sacrificing the "flower of life" (*AI* 350).

Confronting the Medusa, without the deflecting mirror in which Perseus sought refuge, is one of Wharton's favorite ways of describing the act of facing powerful femaleness directly, unflinchingly. Yet the drama and tension of traditional female Gothic is in good part dependent on the *concealment* of female knowledge, the mysteries of birth, death, and sexuality, within the threatening maternal space of dungeon, castle, or haunted room. One female reader of the form, Leona Sherman, describes recreating in the Gothic a figurative confrontational dance with her mother about the essence of femaleness: "I know she knows but she won't tell me. I know I know, but I doubt because she won't tell me. She says one thing, but I see another on her face. I feel we can't really talk about what we know, because she would be calling her whole past life into question and endangering her present. She thinks the concealment necessary for my survival, and finally, she loves me and wants to protect me above all. The mysteries are the issues of sex and birth and death and, too, the necessity of concealing them" (Holland and Sherman 287).

Wharton describes in "Life and I" just such an evasive encounter with her mother about sexuality. I quote this much quoted passage in its entirety because Wharton's dramatic, even melodramatic, rendering of her request for information about the secret of sexuality so uncannily mirrors Sherman's description of a woman reading/recreating a Gothic story:

> . . . a few days before my marriage, I was seized with such a dread of the whole dark mystery, that I summoned up courage to appeal to my mother, & begged her, with a heart beating to suffocation, to tell me "what being married was like." Her handsome face at once took on the look of icy disapproval which I most dreaded. "I never heard such a ridiculous question!" she said impatiently; & I felt at once how vulgar she thought me.

> But in the extremity of my need I persisted. "I'm afraid, Mamma—I want to know what will happen to me!"

> The coldness of her expression deepened to disgust. She was silent for a dreadful moment; then she said with an effort: "You've seen enough pictures & statues in your life. Haven't you noticed that men are—made differently from women?"

"Yes," I faltered blankly.

"Well, then—?"

I was silent, from sheer inability to follow, & she brought out sharply: "Then for heaven's sake don't ask me any more silly questions. You can't be as stupid as you pretend!"

The dreadful moment was over, & the only result was that I had been convicted of stupidity for not knowing what I had been expressly forbidden to ask about, or even think of!

["Life" 34-35]

Wharton recreates herself here as the traditional Gothic heroine probing the dread-producing mother/castle for answers about "the whole dark mystery" of sexuality, but she leaves both uninformed and humiliated because she is so uninformed.

Perhaps because Wharton didn't believe, as Sherman posits, that the mother/Gothic denies the knowledge to the questing daughter because she "loves me and wants to protect me above all," in her own Gothic fiction Wharton turns the "Gothic denial" of "the whole dark mystery" of sexuality, birth, and death figured by the woman/mother on its head (Holland and Sherman 292, 287). By denying access to the mother and thereby to femaleness, both women and men wield patriarchal power, power defied by characters such as Charity Royall in *Summer* and Lady Jane Lynke in "Mr. Jones." More often, a character shrinks from rather than claims this powerful knowledge, and the reader is left with an awareness of the sacrifice that the character has made because of her or his timidity.

WOMEN AND MEN

Wharton seems, at first glance, to be arguing for sexual equality on the social as well as the fictional front in her indictment, in *French Ways and Their Meaning*, that America's hypocritical Puritan heritage concerning "the danger of frank and free social relations between men and women" has been the main retardant to "real civilization" there (112-13). "The two sexes complete each other," Wharton insists (103). Yet *French Ways* reveals the same kind of gender tension that her autobiographies do as well as a denigration of women. Her stress on equal relations between women and men as keys to a mature culture is contradicted by her relegation of women, in the same book, to subservient roles of muse, patient listener, faithful attendant, and helpmate (113; see esp. pp. 112, 26, 121). Although herself a devotee of "good talk," one whose delight in it her friend Gaillard Lapsley once described as that of "an emancipated feminist conscientiously practicing free love" (Lubbock, "Memoirs"), Wharton writes in *French Ways* that a woman has "no place" in a conversation, "unless her ideas, and her way of expressing them, put her on an equality with the men; and this seldom happens. Women (if they only knew it!) are generally far more intelligent listeners than talkers" (25). After all, she adds, "intelligent women will never talk together when they can talk to men, or even listen to them" (26).

Wharton's accolades in *French Ways* go to the "man's woman," one "whose mind is attuned to men's minds" and so doesn't possess the fussiness and spitefulness of the woman who spends time with other women (119). This denigration of women is echoed in a 1923 letter to Minnie Jones in which Wharton writes that she is "not much interested in traveling scholarships for women" and that "they'd much better stay at home and mind the baby" (Beinecke). "Emancipated" young women are a "'monstrous regiment' . . . taught by their elders to despise the kitchen and the linen room," to their own demise (*BG* 60). It isn't difficult to see why an acquaintance of Wharton's would assume that "being a very normal person she preferred men to women, and often terrified the latter with a cold stare" (Lubbock, *Portrait* 28).

The impression was reinforced by Wharton's cultivation of a coterie of admiring male friends with whom she surrounded herself and for whom she often played the part of Great Mother. Adrienne Rich's discussion of the "motherless" woman seems particularly applicable to Wharton in this regard. Such a woman may deny her own vulnerability, deny she has felt any loss or absence of mothering by "mothering" others. In this way she gives to others what she has lacked. "But this will always mean that she needs the neediness of others in order to go on feeling her own strength. She may feel uneasy with equals—particularly women" (246).

At the same time, Wharton's misogynist talk and that of her acquaintances about her is belied by her strong and enduring friendships with many women, among them Sara Norton, "so beloved and frequent a visitor" to the Mount; sister-in-law Minnie Jones, of whom Wharton writes, "To me she became closer than a sister of my own blood"; Minnie Bourget, with whom, from their first meeting Wharton felt "a deep-down understanding established itself between us"; her niece and frequent correspondent the landscape architect Beatrice Farrand; Elisina Tyler, a companion in her war projects who was with her when she died; Rosa de Fitz-James, with whom she traveled; and of course her personal maid Elise and Gross, her housekeeper for forty-five years, "two faithful women (who) kept the heartfire burning" (*BG* 155, 104; Lewis, *Biography* 514). Fifteen years after *French Ways*, in *A Backward Glance*, Wharton admits her intense admiration and affection for the "intellectually ardent" Vernon Lee, "the first highly cultivated and brilliant woman I had ever known" (Lewis, *Biography* 321; *BG* 132). She also acknowledges that Lee, along with Matilde Serao, a Neapolitan journalist and novelist, and Madame de Noailles, a French poet, has the gift for great talk that she has heretofore only found in men.[17] Mary Berenson provides an illuminating glimpse into Wharton as a woman friend in her observation that Wharton "said she wasted her youth trying to be beautiful, but now that she has given up all hope she feels freer. She *is* heavy-handed, but when you like her it becomes rather endearing. I think she is a very good friend to her friends" (Strachey and Samuels 184).

Nonetheless, in her professional persona, Wharton usually disparages the intellect and strength of women. One reading of this disparagement is that she sensed the danger inherent in a woman's immersing herself in male-identified qualities, especially to the exclusion of the kind of nurturing relationships she could share with female friends. The dominance, severity, and self-engrossment that Wharton felt had distorted her own life and denied her needed nurturance were, after all, her mother's qualities. Another reading is that Wharton saw her professional self as male and special compared to that of all other women, a self Kathryn Allen Rabuzzi denotes a "pseudo-man" unable to risk acknowledging the vulnerability and weakness inherent in "typical" women (136).[18] Still another reading, and the one on which I build my discussion of Wharton's Gothic, is that this disparagement reflects her profound discomfort with these male-identified qualities in herself. So out of keeping with the expected norm of femininity are her ambition, drive, passion, and intellect that they must be continually disowned, distanced, and kept in their place by patriarchal severity and scorn directed at other women. Mary Daly calls such a response "feminine antifeminism," possessed by women whose internalized "patriarchal presence" leads them to express "disapproval and hostility" toward women who threaten the gender status quo (52). All of these readings speak of a dissonant relationship with both genders as Wharton defined them and a persistent fear of the aware self that would acknowledge and accept the multivalent nature of femininity that she herself possessed.

Marriage

In traditional Gothic, the heroine escapes self-knowledge and personal authenticity through marriage; "profound uncertainty gives way to confidence and reason: married love conquers fear" (Nichols 188). This "happy ending" allows the heroine and the reader to have it both ways; romantic love acts as a defense against male sexuality, which the woman both fears and desires, and so it provides a solution certified by society (Holland and Sherman 286). Although in *French Ways* Wharton extols marriage as a woman's badge of maturity, in her Gothic stories marriage is what causes fear and distress. The Gothic version is closer to Wharton's own marital experience. Edith Jones's passionless marriage to Teddy

Wharton, the handsome, compliant, and even supportive gentleman who so epitomized the restrained, unintellectual society that bred him, was physically draining for her and eventually mentally and emotionally imprisoning as well. Even as Wharton actively traveled, entertained, and bought and renovated houses, she perceived herself during her marriage as "a dim woman cloistered in ill-health" (Donnée Book). Attacks of asthma struck whenever she was forced to share a bedroom with Teddy (Wolff 51). Wharton uses the Gothic to speak, not about "melancholy, anxiety-ridden sentimental love" that ends in marriage, but rather about patriarchal restraints on the female person and spirit within the domestic setting (Howells 5). At the end of her Gothic stories the heroine is often dead or imprisoned rather than able and willing to resume the "quiescent, socially acceptable role" of the expectable Gothic ending (Kahane, "Gothic Mirror" 342). In Wharton's Gothic, marriage is therefore not a defense against the male, sexual forces that menace and attract a woman in traditional Gothic but rather is apt to be the very source of the threat against a woman because it controls her sexuality and sometimes even kills her (Holland and Sherman 286).

Wharton's Gothic consistently magnifies the constraining, even destructive effects of marriage on women, even though elsewhere in her writing she is as contradictory about marriage as she is about what a woman should be. Several references to marriage suggest Wharton's belief in the institution: her much cited remark about "the poverty, the miserable poverty, of any love that lies outside of marriage" during her affair with Morton Fullerton; her argument in *French Ways* that marriage completes a woman; and her comments in *The Gods Arrive,* via the intellectual, unmarried George Frenside, about the need for the framework of marriage—"Marriage may be too tight a fit—may dislocate and deform. But it shapes life too; prevents growing lopsided, or drifting" (Lewis, *Biography* 317-18; *GA* 311). Wharton's unpublished notebooks reveal a darker, more sardonic view of marriage, such as the 1913 dialogue insert:

> "Did you know that John and Susan committed suicide together on Tuesday?"
>
> "What? No—How?"
>
> "They got married."
>
> [Donnée Book]

The questionable ideal of marriage as the union of two "equal" souls in the early story "The Fullness of Life" is consistently refuted in the Gothic stories and the novels with a Gothic subtext, where marriage is more apt to be suffocating captivity. Eventually, in her last two completed novels, Wharton resolves the still-prominent question of whether such a union of equal souls is possible by showing that the true union must be *within* the woman and man, between the feminine and masculine parts of the self. A marriage of selves can occur when a person confronts and accepts the feminine/maternal within, an act that Wharton perceives as a *human* (rather than an exclusively female) act of courage.

INCEST

Wharton's allusions to incest and, in the "Beatrice Palmato" fragment, dramatization of it is in keeping with her use of the Gothic to probe the "unacknowledged, disavowed, disallowed" story about female sexuality (Stein 126). Her career-long attraction to incest has been discussed as an outgrowth of her own incest experiences.[19] But reading Wharton's Gothic as an exploration of gender, as I do, opens up other possible readings of the incest motif. Jung posits that whenever the drive for wholeness appears, that is, the union of feminine and masculine, "it begins by disguising itself under the symbolism of incest" (16:263). To a degree this tendency helps explain Wharton's interest in sexual union as a fusion of conflicting yet related forces. Since, however, incest is destructive to women in Wharton's Gothic fiction, her use of it seems instead to be a dramatization of the longing of a woman to lose her sense of powerlessness by merging with the masculine power that controls her. The warning that too often a woman "cannot distinguish between her unmothered need for the mother and her need for a male partnership," which she assumes will fill her with "patriarchal authority," helps explain the dilemma of unmothered characters such as Sybilla Lombard in "The House of the Dead Hand" and Beatrice Palmato in the fragment bearing her name (Perera 162). The desire of both women for self-definition results instead in absorption by those patriarchal figures who possess self-defined power and control.

HOUSES

Wharton's Gothic reveals that female self-definition is most successfully achieved, not through a man, but through the reclaiming of a house, which serves as her most powerful sign of body/self. This is in keeping with Gothic tradition. As Elizabeth MacAndrew notes, "The omnipresent old house or castle is one of the most stable characteristics of the Gothic," and as those who have written about female Gothic have subsequently argued, the house/castle embodies the feminine/maternal (48). In *A Backward Glance* Wharton recalls being frightened, as a small child, by the "intolerable ugliness" of her aunt's Hudson River Gothic estate called Rhinecliff (28). "From the first," she writes, "I was obscurely conscious of a queer resemblance between the granitic exterior of Aunt Elizabeth and her grimly comfortable home, between her battlemented caps and the turrets of Rhinecliff" (28). Within this female house/body, Wharton has a terrifying nightmare of a Wolf un-

der her bed, one of the first of her "other similar terrifying experiences" of being haunted by "tribal animals" (28). The adult Wharton hints at but skirts the observation that destructively uncontrollable power haunts the female body.[20]

In one of her earliest stories, "The Fullness of Life," which Wharton in a 1898 letter to Edward Burlingame, her Scribner editor, self-consciously called "one long shriek," the narrator, a dead woman and so the ultimate passive character, compares a woman's nature to a "great house full of rooms" (Scribner Collection; Lewis, *CSS* 1:14). In most of the rooms, friends and family come and go, "but beyond . . . are other rooms, the handles of whose doors perhaps are never turned; no one knows the way to them, no one knows whither they lead; and in the innermost room, the holy of holies, the soul sits alone and waits for a footstep that never comes" (Lewis, *CSS* 1:14, ellipsis mine).

The narrator's unresponsive husband never ventures into her inner self, "full of treasures and wonders" (14). The woman confers with the "Spirit of Life," about being granted a "soul-mate" for eternity, but she rejects the boring ideal for the unhappy but comfortable tension with her husband. When the Spirit points out that the choice is forever, she counters, "Choosing! . . . Do you still keep up here that old fiction about choosing? I should have thought that *you* knew better than that. How can I help myself?" (20, ellipsis mine) "How can I help myself?" is the central question, suggesting as it does that helping herself is both a possibility and an impossibility.

By 1917 this passive early character's creator has realized that a woman can nurture her own fulfillment rather than having to depend on a man for it. In a letter written to her close friend Mary Berenson urging her to help heal herself after a nervous collapse, Wharton again calls on the house/self image: "I believe I know the only cure, which is to make one's centre of life inside of one's self, not selfishly or excludingly, but with a kind of unassailable serenity—to decorate one's inner house so richly that one is content there, glad to welcome any one who wants to come and stay, but happy all the same in the hours when one is inevitably alone" (Lewis, *Biography* 413). Wharton's notebook entries about the blessedness of being alone at her home in Hyères illustrate how happily she had learned to live in her own inner house.

In "A Little Girl's New York," an essay written near the end of her life, Wharton reads women's sexually suppressed bodies in their overly decorated houses. In the 1890s the uniform brownstones marched up Fifth Avenue like "disciplined schoolgirls." Her description "penetrate[s] from the vestibule . . . into the carefully guarded interior" of one of the brownstones, which could easily have been her mother's on West Twenty-third Street:

> Beyond the vestibule (in the average house) was a narrow drawing-room. Its tall windows were hung with three layers of curtains: sash-curtains through which no eye from the street could possibly penetrate, and next to these draperies of lace or embroidered tulle, richly beruffled, and looped back under the velvet or damask hangings which were drawn in the evening. This window garniture always seemed to me to symbolize the superimposed layers of under-garments worn by the ladies of the period—and even, alas, by the little girls. They were in fact almost purely a symbol, for in many windows even the inner "sash-curtains" were looped back far enough to give the secluded dwellers a narrow glimpse of the street; but no self-respecting mistress of a house (a brownstone house) could dispense with this triple display of window-lingerie, and among the many things I did which pained and scandalized my Bostonian mother-in-law, she was not least shocked by the banishment from our house in the country of all the thicknesses of muslin which should have intervened between ourselves and the robins on the lawn.
>
> [358]

Wharton becomes the male-identified "penetrator" of this house and custom by becoming writer and house designer. Her first published book, *The Decoration of Houses,* written with Ogdon Codman and the source of her first royalty check, is a declaration of independence in several respects. In it Wharton stresses that the house is an "organism" and that decoration is not a "superficial application of ornament" but a branch of architecture that is itself an expression of the "tastes and habits" of the people living in the house (xxx, 17). Art and life are organically conjoined in successful house creating, she argues, and both are guided by symmetry, proportion, and simplicity.

These classical principles guided her creation of her "first real home," the Mount, a palatial house on a hill overlooking Lake Laurel outside Lenox, Massachusetts, whose building she designed and supervised herself and for which she paid in part from the earnings of *The House of Mirth* (*BG* 125). These principles also guided her renovation of her two French homes, Pavillon Colombe in St. Brice-sous-Forêt, outside Paris, France, and Ste. Claire du Vieux Chateau, in Hyères on the Mediterranean, self-created havens established after her divorce from Teddy. Part of the appeal of both places was their woman-centered histories, one sensual, one spiritual. Wharton was delighted that Pavillon Colombe had been named after two actress sisters of erotic fame "installed there" by their lovers around the mid-1700s. Ste. Claire, by contrast, was a former convent, built within the crenelated walls of an old château and overlooking Hyères and the sea, a place Wharton once called

"the garden of my soul" (Notebook 1924-34). Another part of the appeal of both houses was their need for extensive renovation; out of the ruins Wharton created classically ordered, impeccably orchestrated households.[21]

In her Gothic, Wharton seems to be deliberately testing and countering the classical control she imposed on her own houses. In the short stories and Gothic-marked novels, dilapidated, disordered, or eerie houses embody, for those who become aware of it, an alternative reality, a way of knowing that is visceral rather than rational, frightening more than soothing, disruptive of the status quo rather than supportive of it. Like castles in traditional Gothic, Wharton's Gothic houses hold secrets about ungovernable passions: greed, lust, rage, fear, jealousy. Locked up or otherwise kept inaccessible by patriarchal heavies, these houses embody the suppression of women's (and sometimes men's) stories and lives, to the detriment of women and men alike.

Thus the question of who controls the house and its environment is a crucial source of gender conflict in the Gothic fiction. Female protagonists in the early Gothic stories—"The House of the Dead Hand," "The Lady's Maid's Bell," "The Duchess at Prayer"—are held captive in houses as much by their own passivity as by patriarchal power, which in turn is partly a projection of their own feared assertive self. In *The House of Mirth, Summer,* and *The Age of Innocence,* a woman's search for a home is a search for a way of being in society that is defined by oneself rather than by society or by a man.[22] Judith Wilt's comment about place and the Gothic is appropriate to Wharton's view: "Power, the Gothic says, resides in place, and . . . overwhelmingly, the kind of power that resides in place, in placement, seems to be male, and the power that challenges it, evades it, or that seeks place from a position of place-lessness, is female" (276-77, ellipsis mine).

Wharton revises this dynamic in her Gothic stories and novels written in the 1920s and 1930s—"Miss Mary Pask," "Dieu d'Amour," "Bewitched," *Hudson River Bracketed,* and *The Gods Arrive*—by making houses more female-identified, or by having caves and cabins serve as female spaces. The timid, usually male, characters who enter these mysterious, dark, sensuous places, "the maternal body with its related secrets of birth and sexuality" as well as death, feel threatened by annihilation, and they flee in terror (Holland and Sherman 286). Male characters like Orrin Bosworth in "Bewitched" and Vance Weston in *Hudson River Bracketed* and *The Gods Arrive,* who are unafraid of female-identified places, are also able to hear and assimilate women's stories and respect female experience. Female characters who reclaim houses, such as Jane Lynke in "Mr. Jones" and Halo Spear in *The Gods Arrive,* reclaim their female history and control over their lives. Sara

Clayburn's anxious nighttime search for her servants through her cold, silent house in "All Souls'," written shortly before Wharton's death, vividly dramatizes a woman's terrified realization that her feminine self is alien and empty.[23] That Wharton never indicates the gender of the scholarly narrator who tells Sara's story, comforts her after her ordeal, and frames her surreal experience with references to women's supernatural powers is fitting as a coda to Wharton's career-long conversation about women and men and feminine and masculine in her Gothic fiction.

Notes

1. Cynthia Griffin Wolff posits that "Life and I" was written in 1920 or 1922 (417, n.3).

2. Wolff discusses the tension in Wharton between doing and being, between creating art and becoming a beautiful art object. See especially 40-43.

3. According to Wolff, Wharton's experiences taught her that "strong emotions of any kind were innately dangerous" (38). For the young Wharton nothing was worse than to be mute. "To be 'mute' . . . is to be vulnerable to pain," and words offered "the promise of an escape from loneliness and helplessness" (25-26, ellipsis mine). I argue that in the Gothic stories dangerous emotion is projected onto the dangerous man, preying upon the mute woman, whose imprisonment is partly a result of self-censorship. Although she doesn't mention the Gothic, Wolff discounts most of Wharton's ghost stories as inferior fiction.

4. Wolff also notes that the inclination "to fall into the formula of nasty mother and clever daughter" ignores the complexity of the relationship between Lucretia and Edith Jones (32). Erlich posits that Wharton's image of her mother may well have been "a projection of the child's need for punishment rather than an accurate description," but she acknowledges that whatever the "historical truth," Wharton's "internalized mother" was a "persecutory figure" (25, 26).

5. As Pablo Freire writes, "The oppressed suffer from the duality which has established itself in their innermost being. They discover that without freedom they cannot exist authentically. Yet, although they desire authentic existence, they fear it. They are at one and the same time themselves and the oppressor whose consciousness they have internalized" (32).

6. Several critics have noted that Wharton's use of "secret garden" in connection with her writing probably refers to Frances Hodgson Burnett's 1911 children's classic of the same name. What is important for my purposes are the similarities *The Secret Garden* bears both to Wharton's childhood

and to her Gothic. At the beginning of the novel, two emotionally abandoned children, Mary and Colin, are angry, pale, and lonely, living together in what Mary calls a "queer house," where "everything is a kind of secret. Rooms are locked up and gardens are locked up" (159). Both think the other is a ghost when they first meet, both live in their own world of stories and dreams. Together they enter the secret, neglected garden, care for it, and are rejuvenated by the activity. This plot resembles Wharton's Gothic heroes/heroines entering the spirit of the mother in a mysterious enclosure and being shaken and changed by the encounter.

7. Erlich calls Frederick Jones's library Wharton's "emotional center" (32). She notes that Wharton even makes the connection in "Life and I" between the library and her self or body and that books and libraries are thereafter "libidinized" (34, 154). Carol J. Singley and Susan Elizabeth Sweeney discuss Wharton's anxiety about reading, in her father's library, books forbidden by her mother. They quote Paula Berggeren as even suggesting that in disobeying her mother Wharton is figuratively gazing on her "father's nakedness" in the library (185).

8. Gilbert and Gubar also identify the "anxiety of authorship" that a woman writer experiences because of "her culturally conditioned timidity about self-dramatization, her dread of the patriarchal authority of art, her anxiety about the impropriety of female invention" (*Madwoman* 50). Singley and Sweeney discuss how Wharton expresses her anxiety about reading and writing in the narrative of "Pomegranate Seed." My sense of Wharton's gender discomfort in relation to writing differs slightly but significantly from both of these useful studies. I believe Wharton felt anxious about writing not only because she was a woman but because speech and writing *do* have the potential to be aggressive, harmful acts regardless of which gender engages in them. Lucretia Jones's power to wound with words was an early model for her daughter of this potential. Thus although the culturally constructed anxiety Wharton felt about writing influenced her projective creation of menacing intellectual men in her Gothic fiction, she is also responding to her discomfort with destructive verbal power.

9. Howells refers to readers of the Gothic as "literary voyeurs" (15-16), and Wolstenholme extensively discusses this quality of the Gothic experience.

10. Fryer discusses the haunted quality of Wharton's creative process (158-59).

11. Wolff talks about Wharton's realization that good art develops from the artist's courage to plunge

into the primal depths and confront "his most secret self" (9). Wolff stresses Wharton's need to outgrow and reject her relationship with her mother, however, while I see Wharton attempting to assimilate and recreate her maternal relationship and using the Gothic abyss as a locus of this interaction.

12. A key characteristic of ghost stories by American women, according to Lynette Carpenter and Wendy K. Kolmar, is that they not only expand "reason" to include the supernatural but more often replace reason with sympathy as the key interpretive faculty (13).

13. Fleenor notes that "this confrontation can be seen in a literary context as the confrontation of the female author with the problem of being an author, not the father of her work but the mother of it" (16).

14. Jung's tendency to ignore socially derived, sexist assumptions in the construction of his archetypes, which I discuss earlier, also colors his theory of individuation; this emphasizes the importance of feminist archetypal criticism of women's rebirth journeys as portrayed in their writing.

15. Kahane points out that the maternal body carries such "archaic fantasies of power and vulnerability" because society encourages it with its cultural divisions ("Gothic Mirror" 350).

16. Tzvetan Todorov discusses the fantastic as a means of combating social and internal censorship. The function of the supernatural in particular "is to exempt the text from the action of the law, and thereby to transgress that law" (159).

17. Susan Goodman looks closely at Wharton's relationship with Sara Norton in developing her thesis that Wharton's heroines struggle to define themselves "through connections with other women" (3). Katherine Joslin also points out that although Wharton's intellectual friendships with men are emphasized, her "awakening" to intellectual and literary life came in her contacts with women as well as men (17-18); see also 54-57. Joslin notes that few scholars have concentrated on Wharton's "kinship with women" (19).

18. Olin-Ammentorp also makes this point in "Wharton's View."

19. See White, *A Study,* and Erlich in particular.

20. Wolff discusses the Wolf as Wharton's symbol for her own strong emotions (see especially 38-39).

21. Joslin discusses the importance of Pavillon Colombe and Ste. Claire to Wharton's sense of self-possession. The latter, she notes, has "all the char-

acteristics of a satisfying lover" for Wharton (27). Gilbert and Gubar discuss Wharton's houses as symbolic alternatives to the House of Mirth (*No Man's Land,* 157-58).

22. Wendy Gimbel writes convincingly about houses as symbolic possibilities for female selfhood in *The House of Mirth, Ethan Frome, Summer,* and *The Age of Innocence.* She overlooks the importance of the dilapidated houses in this fiction, however.

23. In her essay on "All Souls'," Annette Zilversmit calls for Wharton criticism to explore "the world of the female that both sexes fear," the "wildness within." It is time, she argues, to reclaim "these forbidden selves, their buried texts, these alienated, tabooed, even most disagreeable desires and feelings," in our critical responses to Wharton. I see my study of the Gothic in Wharton's fiction as a possible response to this call ("All Souls'" 326).

Bibliography

CORRESPONDENCE AND MANUSCRIPTS

"Life and I." Edith Wharton Archives, Beinecke Library, Yale University, New Haven, Connecticut.

WORKS BY EDITH WHARTON

The Age of Innocence. New York: D. Appleton, 1920.

A Backward Glance. New York: D. Appleton-Century, 1934.

"Beatrice Palmato." In *Edith Wharton: A Biography,* by R. W. B. Lewis. New York: Harper & Row, 1975.

French Ways and Their Meaning. New York: D. Appleton, 1919.

The Gods Arrive. New York: D. Appleton, 1932.

The House of Mirth. New York: Charles Scribner's Sons, 1905.

Hudson River Bracketed. New York: D. Appleton, 1929.

"A Little Girl's New York." *Harper's Magazine,* December 1937-May 1938, pp. 356-64.

Summer. New York: D. Appleton, 1917.

The Writing of Fiction. New York: Charles Scribner's Sons, 1925.

SECONDARY SOURCES

Bersani, Leo. *A Future for Astyanax: Character and Desire in Literature.* Boston: Little, Brown, 1976.

Carpenter, Lynette, and Wendy K. Kolmar. *Haunting the House of Fiction: Feminist Perspectives on Ghost Stories by American Women.* Knoxville: University of Tennessee Press, 1991.

Cixous, Hélène. "The Laugh of the Medusa." *Signs* 1 (Summer 1976): 875-93.

Day, William Patrick. *In The Circles of Fear and Desire: A Study of Gothic Fantasy.* Chicago: University of Chicago Press, 1985.

Dupree, Ellen. "Wharton, Lewis, and the Nobel Prize Address." *American Literature* 6 (May 1984): 262-270.

Erlich, Gloria C. *The Sexual Education of Edith Wharton.* Berkeley: University of California Press, 1992.

Fiedler, Leslie A. *Love and Death in the American Novel.* New York: Criterion Books, 1960.

Fleenor, Juliann E., ed. *The Female Gothic.* Montreal: Eden Press, 1983.

Freire, Pablo. *Pedagogy of the Oppressed.* Trans. Myra Bergman Ramos. New York: Herder & Herder, 1971.

Fryer, Judith. *Felicitous Space: The Imaginative Structures of Edith Wharton and Willa Cather.* Chapel Hill: University of North Carolina Press, 1986.

Gilbert, Sandra M., and Susan Gubar. *The Madwoman in the Attic: The Woman Writer and the Nineteenth Century Literary Imagination.* New Haven: Yale University Press, 1979.

———. *No Man's Land: The Place of the Woman Writer in the Twentieth Century.* Vol. 2. *Sexchanges.* New Haven: Yale University Press, 1989.

Gimbel, Wendy. *Edith Wharton: Orphancy and Survival.* New York: Praeger, 1984.

Goodman, Susan. *Edith Wharton's Women: Friends and Rivals.* Hanover: University Press of New England, 1990.

Harding, M. Esther. *Women's Mysteries Ancient and Modern.* New York: Bantam Books, 1971.

Heilman, Robert B. "Charlotte Brontë's 'New Gothic.'" In *From Jane Austen to Joseph Conrad,* ed. Robert Rathburn and Martin Steinmann, Jr. Minneapolis: University of Minnesota Press, 1958.

Holland, Norman, and Leona Sherman. "Gothic Possibilities." *New Literary History* 8 (1976-77): 279-94.

Howells, Coral Ann. *Love, Mystery, and Misery.* London: Athlone Press, 1978.

Jacobus, Mary. "The Buried Letter: Feminism and Romanticism in *Villette.*" In *Women Writing and Writing About Women,* ed. Mary Jacobus. New York: Barnes & Noble, 1979.

Joslin, Katherine. *Women Writers: Edith Wharton.* London: Macmillan Education, 1991.

Jung, C. G. *Collected Works.* 20 vols. Ed. Gerhard Adler et al. Trans. R. F. C. Hull. Bollingen Series 20. Princeton: Princeton University Press, 1960-85.

Kahane, Claire. "The Gothic Mirror." In *The (M)other Tongue, Essays in Feminist Psychoanalytic Interpretation,* ed. Shirley Nelson Garner, Claire Kahane, and Madelon Sprengnether. Ithaca: Cornell University Press, 1985.

Kristeva, Julia. *Powers of Horror: An Essay on Abjection.* Trans. Leon S. Roudiez. New York: Columbia University Press, 1982.

Lewis, R. W. B. *Edith Wharton: A Biography.* New York: Harper & Row, 1975.

Lewis, R. W. B., and Nancy Lewis, eds. *The Letters of Edith Wharton.* New York: Charles Scribner's Sons, 1988.

Lubbock, Percy. "Memoirs." Edith Wharton Archives, Beinecke Library, Yale University, New Haven, Connecticut.

———. *Portrait of Edith Wharton.* New York: D. Appleton-Century Co., 1947.

MacAndrew, Elizabeth. *The Gothic Tradition in Fiction.* New York: Columbia University Press, 1979.

Moers, Ellen. *Literary Women: The Great Writers.* New York: Anchor Books, 1977.

Nichols, Nina daVinci. "Place and Eros in Radcliffe, Lewis, and Brontë." In *The Female Gothic,* ed. Juliann E. Fleenor. Montreal: Eden Press, 1983.

Olin-Ammentorp, Julie. "Wharton's View of Women in *French Ways and Their Meaning.*" *Edith Wharton Review* 9 (Fall 1992): 15-18.

Perera, Sylvia Brinton. "The Descent of Inanna: Myth and Therapy." In *Feminist Archetypal Theory: Interdisciplinary Re-Visions of Jungian Thought,* ed. Estella Lauter and Carol Schreier Rupprecht. Knoxville: University of Tennessee Press, 1985.

Pratt, Annis. "Spinning Among Fields: Jung, Frye, Lévi-Strauss, and Feminist Archetypal Theory." In *Feminist Archetypal Theory: Interdisciplinary Re-Visions of Jungian Thought,* ed. Estella Lauter and Carol Schreier Rupprecht. Knoxville: University of Tennessee Press, 1985.

Singley, Carol J., and Susan Elizabeth Sweeney. "Forbidden Reading and Ghostly Writing: Anxious Power in Wharton's 'Pomegranate Seed.'" *Women's Studies* 20 (1991): 177-203.

Stein, Karen F. "Monsters and Madwomen: Changing Female Gothic." In *The Female Gothic,* ed. Juliann E. Fleenor. Montreal: Eden Press, 1983.

Strachey, Barbara, and Jayne Samuels, eds. *Mary Berenson: A Self-Portrait from Her Diaries and Letters.* New York: W. W. Norton, 1983.

Todorov, Tzvetan. *The Fantastic: A Structural Approach to a Literary Genre.* Trans. Richard Howard. Ithaca: Cornell University Press, 1980.

Wehr, Demaris S. *Jung and Feminism: Liberating Archetypes.* Boston: Beacon Press, 1987.

White, Barbara A. *Edith Wharton: A Study of Her Short Stories.* New York: Twayne, 1991.

Whitmont, Edward C. *The Symbolic Quest: Basic Concepts of Analytical Psychology.* New York: G. P. Putnam's Sons, 1969.

Wilt, Judith. *Ghosts of the Gothic: Austen, Eliot, and Lawrence.* Princeton: Princeton University Press, 1980.

Wolff, Cynthia Griffin. *A Feast of Words: The Triumph of Edith Wharton.* New York: Oxford University Press, 1977.

Wolstenholme, Susan. *Gothic (Re)visions: Writing Women as Readers.* Albany: State University of New York Press, 1993.

Zilversmit, Annette. "'All Souls': Wharton's Last Haunted House and Future Directions for Criticism." In *Edith Wharton: New Critical Essays,* ed. Alfred Bendixen and Annette Zilversmit. New York: Garland, 1992.

Abbreviations

AI: *The Age of Innocence*

BG: *A Backward Glance*

CI: *Crucial Instances*

CP: *Certain People*

CSS: *Collected Short Stories*

DM: *The Descent of Man and Other Stories*

EF: *Ethan Frome*

G: *Ghosts*

GA: *The Gods Arrive*

HB: *Here and Beyond*

HM: *The House of Mirth*

HRB: *Hudson River Bracketed*

HW: *The Hermit and the Wild Woman and Other Stories*

"Life": "Life and I"

S: *Summer*

WF: *The Writing of Fiction*

X: *Xingu and Other Stories*

Helene Meyers (essay date 2001)

SOURCE: Meyers, Helene. "The Construction of the Sadomasochistic Couple." In *Femicidal Fears: Narratives of the Female Gothic Experience,* pp. 59-85. Albany: State University of New York Press, 2001.

[*In the excerpt below, Meyers discusses how Angela Carter and Muriel Spark "explore both the pervasiveness and the perversity of the gendering of masochism and sadism" in their Gothic novels* Honeybuzzard *and* Driver's Seat, *respectively*]

My overarching argument concerns the ways in which the strand of the contemporary female Gothic . . . stages and intervenes in debates between cultural feminism and gender skepticism. In this [essay], I take the risk of being charged with critical masochism and return to the scene where cultural feminists purportedly committed one of their most heinous "crimes": pornography. A great deal of feminist ink and bad blood has been spilled on the "sex wars"[1]; however, my primary concern here is that cultural feminists find in pornographic scripts the crystallization and reproduction of culture's desire for female victims. When Susan Griffin argues that "pornographic culture annihilates the female sex" and that "a woman inherits from culture a continual experience of fear" (217), she is reading culture as a femicidal plot. In *Pornography: Men Possessing Women,* Andrea Dworkin describes a pornographic photograph entitled "Beaver Hunters" that depicts a woman tied to the hood of a black jeep: the bound woman, whose genitals are exposed and foregrounded, is the "beaver," and two men who sit inside the jeep are clearly the hunters. According to Dworkin,

> Terror is finally the content of the photograph, and it is also its effect on the female observer. That men have the power and desire to make, publish and profit from the photograph engenders fear. That millions more men enjoy the photograph makes the fear palpable. That men who in general champion civil rights defend the photograph without experiencing it as an assault on women intensifies the fear, because if the horror of the photograph does not resonate with these men, that horror is not validated as horror in male culture, and women are left without apparent recourse.
>
> (27)

Dworkin's prose, her emphasis on female fear and female horror, suggests that the production, consumption, and cultural acceptance of pornography is a paradigmatic narrative of the female Gothic.[2]

Indeed, Ellen Moers's offhand comment that "the Marquis de Sade . . . is known to have admired Mrs. Radcliffe's works" (137) embeds a connection between the Gothic and the pornographic from the start.[3] However, whether or not one makes an argument about direct influence, it seems clear that these two genres overlap. Pornography, predicated as it is upon violations of the female body, acts out the worst fears of the Gothic heroine. Male villains and the young, attractive females whom they often cause to suffer are muted versions of sadists and masochists. As Edmundson quips, "S & M is where Gothic, in a certain sense, wants to go" (131).[4] From the point of view of feminist critics, such sadomasochistic tendencies of the Gothic point to the "cultural, psychoanalytic, and fictional expectation that [women] *should* be masochistic if they are 'normal' women" (Massé 2). Thus, hints of female masochism in the Gothic appear inextricably related to social conformity. For example, in *The Mysteries of Udolpho,* where protectors still exist, Emily could have saved herself a lot of trouble by eloping with Valancourt rather than traveling to Italy with Montoni and her aunt. However, since elopements aren't ladylike, she eschews Valancourt's protective and loving offer, hence becoming Montoni's dependent and prey.

Angela Carter's *Honeybuzzard* (1966) and Muriel Spark's *Driver's Seat* (1970) explore these inchoate connections among pornography, female Gothicism, and gender norms. In these two novels, the female Gothic experience is situated in the primary pornographic relationship, the sadomasochistic couple, and both authors use this couple to suggest that perversion and femicide are the logical outcome of hegemonic definitions of masculinity and femininity. Thus, like cultural feminist discourse, they use sadomasochism to make generalizations about gender.[5] However, by portraying masochistic female victims and men who struggle against their own sadistic tendencies, Carter and Spark considerably complicate the gendered roles of victim and victimizer that seem clearly defined and inevitable in O'Brien's *Casualties of Peace* and Bainbridge's *Bottle Factory Outing.* Ultimately, both Spark and Carter represent sadism and masochism as gendered strategies that assuage contemporary anxieties about identity and vulnerability. By reading sadism and masochism as perverse, culturally encouraged, and gendered forms of agency, Spark and Carter counter determinist, normalizing trends in psychoanalytic and cultural feminist thought. Significantly, however, Carter and Spark do not represent the cultural playing field for sadists and masochists as an equal one. Rather, the ready-made scripts for male sadists and female masochists make it doubly difficult, though not impossible, for women to simply refuse to be victims.

* * *

Of course, the spectre of female masochism has long haunted psychoanalysis and feminist thought. Freud recognized that masochism could exist in men; in fact, in his 1924 paper "The Economic Problem in Masochism," he concerned himself with feminine masochism only as it is found in men. Clearly, he linked masochism with femininity and passivity; even Juliet Mitchell, who defends Freud against feminist "misreadings," acknowledges this (115). However, for Freud, sex and gender often became problematically entangled. Thus even when Freud discussed male masochists, his remarks tended to associate this perversion with his perception of normal, biologically female bodies:

> But if one has an opportunity of studying cases [of male masochists] in which the masochistic phantasies

have undergone specially rich elaboration, one easily discovers that in them the subject is placed in a situation characteristic of *womanhood,* i.e. they mean he is being castrated, is playing the passive part in coitus, or is *giving birth.*

> (258—my emphasis).

The suggestion here and elsewhere is that masochism is part of both the female and the feminine personality. As Luce Irigaray puts it in her essay "Psychoanalytic Theory: Another Look," "As for *masochism,* is it to be considered a factor in 'normal' femininity? Some of Freud's assertions tend in this direction" (44).

Two of Freud's disciples, Helene Deutsch and Marie Bonaparte, intuited such tendencies and essentialized them.[6] Deutsch, who embraced Freud's idea of the castration complex, infamously believed that female masochism and biology are intertwined. According to Deutsch, "the absence of an active organ [penis] brought the turn toward passivity and masochism in its train" (251). Although Deutsch recognized that masochistic tendencies pose dangers to the ego, she asserted that female masochism is a necessary and natural means to prepare women for the pain of defloration and childbirth. As Deutsch put it in her reactionary 1944 study *The Psychology of Women,* "In one of her functions woman must have a certain amount of masochism if she is to be adjusted to reality. This is the reproductive function" (276).

Marie Bonaparte, in whose "enormously interesting" company Muriel Spark spent many hours during World War II, also believed that masochism is inherently female.[7] In *Female Sexuality* (1953), Bonaparte, too, pointed to the pain involved in menstruation, defloration, and childbirth as evidence of the need for female masochism. Yet her argument went even further; since the ova awaits the penetrating spermatozoa, she deemed that

> fecundation of the female cell is initiated by a kind of wound; in its way, the female cell is primordially masochistic. Now it would appear that these prototypal cellular reactions pass unchanged into the psychical apparatus of those who bear the same cells and, indeed, our psycho-sexual responses, whether male or female, seem thoroughly permeated with them.

> (78)

Bonaparte, like Deutsch, wholeheartedly accepted the castration complex in women and asserted the primacy of the penis and thus the inferiority of the clitoris. As the following quotation illustrates, the activation of female masochism was inextricably related to this theoretical castration complex:

> The girl . . . discovers the difference between the sexes and then must submit to the castration complex with all its disappointments as regards the too-small clitoris.

This, the executive organ, properly speaking of the infantile phallic sadism, soon therefore becomes depreciated and the envied penis, that big paternal penis with which the clitoris could never compare, must, in the little girl's eyes, take its place as the true representative of sadism. A sort of surrender of the clitoris to the greater and mightier power of the penis would occur, as it were. This is when the primary, passive masochistic drives dormant in the female are no doubt mobilized. The active clitoridal sadistic attitude, which now must be abandoned, is reversed, and the little girl desires the father's assaults and the blows of his big penis.

(82)

Psychoanalytically, Bonaparte imagined the penis as a great, mighty weapon capable of delivering blows; as women become masochistic, so does the penis become "the true representative of sadism." Thus reproduction, compulsory heterosexuality, female masochism, and male sadism become mutually constituting and reinforcing discourses, and psychoanalysis plays its part in normalizing the female Gothic by reading sadomasochism as *the* script of sexual difference.[8]

Significantly, while most cultural feminist thought has refuted such determinist and normalizing explanations for female masochism, the tendency to associate penises and penetration with violence has retained traces of an essentialized male sadism. Alice Echols highlights the contradictory problematic of such arguments: "Although some [cultural feminists] seem to attribute women's masochistic fantasies to their masochism, most argue that they are a patriarchal invention or that they reveal women's powerlessness and socialization rather than their masochism. Of course, men's sadistic fantasies are still seen as confirmation of their fundamentally murderous nature" ("New Feminism" 448). Clearly this cultural feminist double standard is contaminated by the same reactionary essentialism of the hyperFreudian Deutsch and Bonaparte. I purposefully modify the term *essentialism* here. My assumption is that not all forms of essentialism are equal, nor equally bad. However, a belief in the essence of male sadism invites a belief in the inevitability of female victimization, a self-defeating stance for a feminist vision of social change. Given that the charge of essentialism during the past decade has both served the forces of backlash *and* fueled productive and progressive feminist self-consciousness, it seems necessary to use the word with care.

In the work of Karen Horney lies a social constructionist response to such essentialist trends in Freudian psychoanalysis and, by extension, cultural feminism. In her paper "The Problem of Feminine Masochism" (1935), Horney suggested a cultural culpability in the formation of female masochists. Horney astutely pointed out that the female castration complex or "penis envy" is "an hypothesis, not a fact" (216). Hence she undermined arguments based on the assumption that the castration complex forces women to turn their aggressive drives inward and thus become masochistic. Even more importantly, Horney argued that large numbers of masochistic women do not automatically support theories of biologically essential female masochism; cultural as well as biological factors have to be considered, and Horney chided psychoanalysis for its denial tendencies:

> Whenever the question of frequency enters into the picture, sociological implications are involved, and the refusal to be concerned with them from the psychoanalytic angle does not shut out their existence. Omission of these considerations may lead to a false valuation of anatomical differences and their personal elaboration as causative factors for phenomena actually partially or wholly the result of social conditioning. Only a synthesis of both series of conditions can lead to a complete understanding.

(224)

Although Horney did not discount biology, her interest lay in determining the cultural conditions that may cause the development of female masochism. The conditions she cited include the "blocking of outlets for expansiveness and sexuality," the "estimation of women as beings who are, on the whole, inferior to men," the "economic dependence of women on men or on family," and the "restriction of women to spheres of life that are built chiefly upon emotional bonds, such as family life, religion, or charity work" (230). Obviously, such conditions are coterminous with traditional ideals of femininity, a fact that caused Horney to assert that "in our culture it is hard to see how any woman can escape becoming masochistic to some degree, from the effects of the culture alone, without any appeal to contributory factors in the anatomical-physiological characteristics of woman, and their psychic effects" (231). Thus Horney recognized female masochism as a phenomenon but viewed it as culturally constructed. Horney also shrewdly exposed the ideological power of psychoanalysis by noting that biologically deterministic theories of female masochism bolster androcentric cultures. Moreover, Horney strove to disrupt the seamlessness between sadomasochism and heterosexuality, even as she recognized their cultural entanglements. Horney included "biological differences in intercourse" as a factor that may "serve" but not cause the formation of female masochism. As if prescient of the cultural feminist critique of intercourse, Horney clearly stated, "Sadism and masochism have fundamentally nothing whatsoever to do with intercourse, but the female role in intercourse (being penetrated) *lends* itself more readily to a personal misinterpretation (when needed) of masochistic performance; and the male role, to one of sadistic activity" (232).

In their fictions, Angela Carter and Muriel Spark expose both the pervasiveness and the perversity of the gendering of masochism and sadism. Like Horney, they privilege the social implications of such sadomasochistic plots and reveal their characters' misinterpretations to be cultural ideology. Taken together, *Honeybuzzard* and *The Driver's Seat* suggest that hegemonic definitions of femininity and masculinity tend to construct female masochists and male sadists. Carter and Spark share cultural feminism's reading of the pornographic sadomasochistic couple as a cultural norm constituting Gothic horror.

* * *

Angela Carter's first novel *Shadow Dance* (1966; released in the United States as *Honeybuzzard*)[9] explores the connections among pornography, the female Gothic, and gender norms through the figure of the male sadist. However, by highlighting the process and the struggle of endorsing sadistic feeling and action, Carter reads sadomasochism as a Gothic gendered script but does not naturalize it as such. Indeed, in that early novel, Carter plays the role of the moral pornographer, an idea that she develops in *The Sadeian Woman and the Ideology of Pornography* (1978). In that work, Carter proposes that pornography might not only constitute the female Gothic but also have the potential to produce feminist effects. She imagines a "moral pornographer" who "might use pornography as a critique of current relations between the sexes" (19).

In *Shadow Dance*, Carter explores "a dimension of pure horror" as she depicts the violence of Honeybuzzard, a stereotypical sadist and part owner of a junk shop. Honeybuzzard chooses Ghislaine, his masochistic ex-girlfriend, as the main object of his violence. Early in the novel, we learn that Honeybuzzard has slashed Ghislaine's face and has permanently disfigured her. Despite such abuse—or perhaps because of it—Ghislaine craves Honeybuzzard's mastery over her and begs him to become her lover once more. Ghislaine is what Herod from *Casualties of Peace* erroneously assumed Willa and all women to be. Meanwhile, Honeybuzzard has begun a romantic relationship with another woman, Emily; the latter, who is initially unaware of Honeybuzzard's sadistic tendencies, is young, sexy, and emotionally self-sufficient. Honeybuzzard ultimately responds to Ghislaine's pleas by strangling her. Upon discovering her lover's capacity for violence, Emily betrays Honeybuzzard to the police and excises him from her heart, despite the fact that she is pregnant with his child.

Although the plot of this novel depends heavily on Honeybuzzard and Ghislaine's perversions, we are denied access to their consciousness. Occasionally, we derive information from Emily's point of view; however, the bulk of the narrative is limited to the consciousness of Morris Gray, Honeybuzzard's business partner and best friend. Morris is simultaneously attracted and repelled by Honeybuzzard's perversity, and the climax of the novel revolves around Morris's response to Honeybuzzard's murder of Ghislaine. Indeed, the meaning of this work lies in understanding and interpreting Morris's psyche. Carter uses Honeybuzzard's murderous perversity to expose the Gothic elements in Morris's more mainstream male imagination.

Angela Carter explicitly identified herself as a feminist in her life and work. In "Notes from the Front Line," Carter writes, "The Women's Movement has been of immense importance to me personally and I would regard myself as a feminist writer, because I'm a feminist in everything else and one can't compartmentalise these things in one's life" (69). For Carter, the study of philosophy and the social unrest of 1968 merged to form her feminist consciousness: "I can date . . . to that sense of heightened awareness of the society around me in 1968, my own questioning of the nature of my reality as a woman. How that social fiction of my 'femininity' was created, by means outside my control, and palmed off on me as the real thing" ("Notes" 70). Despite such self-identification and feminist self-consciousness, feminist controversy has sometimes surrounded her work. While Dworkin dubbed *The Sadeian Woman* "a pseudofeminist literary essay,"[10] Keenan reads that work—rightly, I think—as evidence of "Carter's extraordinary capacity to tap into crucial critical debates relevant to feminism and cultural politics, long before those debates had been fully staged" (132).[11] Significantly, the brutal violation of female bodies in Carter's fiction has made some critics question the efficacy of her feminist politics. As Gamble summarizes one strand of critical opinion, Carter's views on pornography along with "her graphic depictions of violence against women in her writing . . . have led some critics to conclude that . . . she actually only furthers reactionary portrayals of women as nothing more than the objects of male desire" (4).

Unlike a lot of other women's fiction written in the 1960s and the 1970s, *Honeybuzzard* is technically male-centered—as noted above, much of the narrative is from Morris's point of view—and this fact lends credence to another critical view that Carter's *early* work is male-identified. Indeed, responding to Carter's own comments about "patriarchal bias" in her work, Gamble writes, "It is in *Shadow Dance* that this bias is most disturbingly obvious, for this is a text in which women are resolutely denied the privilege of a narrative voice. By excluding them from the formation of discourse, they are rendered figments of a fevered male imagination, and become the targets of a disturbing blend of violence and eroticism" (54).

Certainly, Carter distinguishes between her pre- and post-'68 performances. As she puts it, "I was, as a girl, suffering a degree of colonialisation of the mind. Especially in the journalism I was writing then, I'd—quite unconsciously—posit a male point of view as a general one. So there was an element of the male impersonator about this young person as she was finding herself" ("Notes" 71). Thus Elaine Jordan, a critic who astutely notes the feminist pleasures and dangers that Carter provides, accepts such remarks as immutable fact: "[I]t's true that she started writing as a kind of male-impersonator, with a strong streak of misogyny" (119).[12] However, Carter's own accounting of her feminist consciousness suggests that male identification[13] and male mimicry need not be equated: "I realise, now, I must always have sensed that something was badly wrong with the versions of reality I was offered that took certain aspects of my being as a woman for granted. I smelled the rat in D. H. Lawrence pretty damn quick" ("Notes" 70). Lee comments that "it is useful to speculate whether Carter saw her own novels as fulfilling the demands of a moral pornography" (10); as I advance a reading of *Honeybuzzard* in the related terms of a female Gothic that does feminist work and a work of moral pornography, we might remember that Carter herself argued that sexual relations are symptomatic of social relations, and thus if the latter are "described explicitly [they] will form a critique of those relations, *even if that is not and never has been the intention of the pornographer*" (22—my emphasis).

Honeybuzzard is the prototype of the lupine masculine principle that pervades "The Company of Wolves," Carter's version of "Little Red Ridinghood." However, unlike the male beast whose murderous desires are harnessed by an aggressive female sexuality, Honeybuzzard seems untamable.[14] Even his physical appearance underscores his violent nature: "It was impossible to look at the full, rich lines of his dark red mouth without thinking: 'This man eats meat.' It was an inexpressibly carnivorous mouth; a mouth that suggested snapping, tearing, biting. . . . How beautiful he was and how indefinably sinister" (57). Thus Honeybuzzard is the repository of evil, and much of the plot revolves around his malevolent acts. Seemingly devoid of feeling, Honeybuzzard coolly slashes Ghislaine's face, unthinkingly humiliates Morris by creating a cardboard jumping jack in his image, and responds to the suicide of a pregnant woman (who mistakenly believed that her husband had slashed Ghislaine) with a practical joke.

Together, Honeybuzzard and Ghislaine represent the classic sadomasochistic couple, and their depiction exposes the co-implication of pornographic, psychoanalytic, and Gothic scripts. Feminist commentators on sadomasochism such as Susan Griffin and Jessica Benjamin have noted that the sadist and the masochist are complements, that the couple becomes the projection of a divided self.[15] In this case, that self is Morris, for the tension between Honey and Ghislaine represents the tension within Morris himself. Ultimately, Honey and Ghislaine are little more than cardboard figures; the

real power of this novel lies in Morris's relationship with the two members of this couple and his eventual decision to side with and protect the sadistic Honey.

Morris is the contemporary antihero *par excellence*. A failed artist, he occupies himself by scavenging through abandoned buildings with Honey and selling found objects in a jointly owned junk shop. Predictably, this business venture is less than profitable, and Morris relies on his wife, Edna, for economic stability. Morris self-consciously meditates on his own uselessness and impotence; he often alludes to his childless marriage, his disastrous sexual exploits with Ghislaine, and his dependence upon Honeybuzzard. Ultimately, Morris recognizes that the junk he gathers and sells is a metonym for his life.

Significantly, Morris's personal history prepares him for a life among the rubble. During World War II, a building in which he and his mother were staying was bombed. His mother, who was copulating outside the door of this building, was presumably killed; he was buried under debris for a time. Thus Morris's primal scene is set for profound ambivalence toward Mom, whom Morris loves but also hates for abandoning him in the act of loving another.

The specifics of Morris's childhood trauma inevitably connect sexuality with death, desire with abandonment and lack. Such connections inhere in the pornographic imagination, and thus Honeybuzzard's battle against Ghislaine's sexualized flesh becomes aligned with Morris's battle against his own vulnerability. Significantly, however, Morris's fear is also linked to Western cultural traditions of misogyny not readily identified as pornographic. In the opening scene of the novel, Ghislaine has just gotten out of the hospital—she was recovering from the wound Honeybuzzard inflicted on her—and Morris meets her in a bar. When Morris first sees her, he utters, "'Oh, God in Heaven,' as if invoking protection against her" (1). Repeatedly, Morris compares her to infamous female monsters. Thus Ghislaine reminds him of the Bride of Frankenstein, a Fury, a witch-woman, and Medusa. Threatened by her voracious desire, Morris thinks of her as a "candle flame for moths, a fire that burned those around her but was not itself consumed" (3). Morris also associates the phrase "memento mori" with Ghislaine; his consciousness is emblematic of a culture that links women with death, the womb with the tomb. Following such great traditions, Morris translates such fear of morality and vulnerability into aggression.

Clearly, Morris receives vicarious pleasure from Honeybuzzard's violence against Ghislaine. We find out that only hours before Ghislaine was mutilated, Morris, frustrated by his own impotence with Ghislaine, had told Honey to "take her and teach her a lesson" (34). After the opening scene in the bar, Morris returns home and surveys several pornographic photographs of Ghislaine; he, Honey, and Ghislaine had spent an afternoon together taking these pictures. Although Honey posed with Ghislaine for some of these photos, Morris's attention is fixated on the latter; indeed, he soon finds himself engaged in an act of imagistic mutilation:

> Yet, once he had the pen in his hand, he found he was finely, carefully, striping each image of her with a long scar from eyebrow to navel. All the time, he wondered why he was doing it; it seemed a vindictive thing to do and he had never thought of himself as a vindictive man. But he did not stop until he had finished marking them all in.
>
> (17-8)

Thus Morris has essentially done to Ghislaine's image what Honeybuzzard has done to her body.

Yet, unlike Honeybuzzard, Morris has flashes of guilt about and identification with Ghislaine, and thus his response to Honeybuzzard's brutality and his own sadistic feelings is complex and ambivalent. When Morris runs away from Ghislaine at the bar, someone throws a bottle at him but misses. Yet he imagines that he has been struck, and this vision reveals much about his relation to Ghislaine:

> He felt the bottle shattering against his face and, raising his hand, was bemusedly surprised to find no traces of blood from a gashed forehead on his fingertips. Why not? In a metaphysical hinterland between intention and execution, someone had thrown a bottle in his face, a casual piece of violence; there was a dimension, surely, in the outer nebulae, maybe, where intentions were always executed, where even now he stumbled, bleeding, blinded. . . . He walked on in a trance, *scarred like her.*
>
> (11—my emphasis)

Since Morris's own violent intentions toward Ghislaine have been executed by the sadistic Honeybuzzard, Morris imagines that he must be punished. Significantly, however, the envisioned punishment merely confirms that Morris shares Ghislaine's wounded status—he is "scarred like her." Morris's figurative wound surfaces again in a dream during which he cut Ghislaine's face with "a jagged shard of broken glass and blood was running on her breast not only from her but also from himself, from his cut head" (18). Here Morris figures himself as both victim and victimizer; in his psychic melodrama, Ghislaine, the female masochist, plays his wounded, needy self, and Honeybuzzard, the male sadist, is presented as an impenetrable and therefore invulnerable alter ego.[16]

Although Ghislaine and Honey are presented as parts of Morris, the latter attempts to strengthen his ties with the seemingly unassailable Honey and to sever his association with Ghislaine's vulnerable flesh. At one point, Morris thinks, "I am a second hand man; and [Ghislaine], now, is a second hand woman." Morris momentarily recognizes that Ghislaine's physical mutilation parallels his own psychic wounding. However, rather than sustaining this identification, Morris seeks to realign himself with Honey and to deny his own feelings of worthlessness and vulnerability. Hence Morris's next thought is that he and his sadistic business partner could display Ghislaine in their storefront window: "They would put her in the window arranged on a rug or a sofa, with a label Sellotaped to her navel: 'Hardly used'" (19). However, it is precisely Ghislaine's use that is underscored here. By dehumanizing Ghislaine and establishing her as an object of exchange, Morris strives to reassert his connection to Honey and thus his own value.

However, Morris's identification with Honey is not yet secure. On one of their junk-finding excursions in an abandoned building, Morris and Honey happen upon the living space of a waitress whom Morris has dubbed a "Struldbrug," a Swiftian allusion to those who are decrepit but immortal. Given that structures in the Gothic often represent the maternal body[17] and that Morris regards this waitress as a mother figure, it seems clear that the scene in this abandoned building is inextricably related to the rubble of Morris's youth, the abandonment and ambivalence he felt upon his mother's demise. As an equal opportunity sadist who does not distinguish between nurturing women and sexual women, Honey decides to have his fun. Thus when the waitress arrives home, Honey purposefully frightens her; as a result of this fright and her inebriation, she falls into a stupor. Fearing for her life, Morris wants to seek medical aid, but Honeybuzzard forbids such action. In a rare act of rebellion, Morris thwarts Honey's will and tries to run away to get help. Honey responds to such opposition with violence: he catches Morris, they wrestle, and Honey finally threatens to kill his partner with the same knife that he used to mutilate Ghislaine. Beaten into submission, Morris is forced to abandon the Struldbrug and is taken by Honey back to the junkshop.

Like Ghislaine, Morris has become the victim of Honey's sadism; thus Morris has not been freed from association with the female embodiment of his victim self. Moreover, Morris's inability to aid the Struldbrug provokes guilt about violent impulses that precede the events of this overdetermined evening. Indeed, during the delirium that results from his injuries, Morris moans that he has killed his mother. By refusing to make distinctions between sexualized flesh and maternal bodies, distinctions that Morris and the cultural psyche he represents have deployed to manage embodied vulnerability and matricidal impulses, Honey alienates Morris.[18]

Significantly, Emily, Honey's current girlfriend, represents the possibility of Morris sustaining this alienation and finding an alternative resolution to the ambivalence that causes him to identify with Honey. On the night that Honey and Morris fight about the Struldbrug, Emily comforts Morris by making love to him. Such use of sexuality clearly muddies the division between nurturance and carnality that Morris has internalized and that Honey has violated that very night. The fact that sexualized Emily, "a new-style matriarch" (Sage, *Angela Carter* 14) is also an expectant mother—Morris later finds out that she is carrying Honey's child—could further disrupt Morris's dichotomizing of women.[19] Thus in the figure of Emily, Morris is offered an alternative to Honey, a revision of the terms that originated Morris's interest in Honey's sadistic acts.

However, Morris's investment in Honeybuzzard is stronger than his identification with bodies capable of being scarred, buried, or terrified into oblivion. At the end of the narrative, as the threat of Honeybuzzard's violence against Ghislaine escalates, Morris bonds anew with his sadistic alter ego. When Emily, Honey's girlfriend, informs Morris that Ghislaine has returned and that Honey has gone with her, Morris experiences "a premonition of horror" (167). Although he suspects that Ghislaine is in grave danger, his chiding of Emily shows that his real concern is for Honeybuzzard:

> "You shouldn't have let him go alone!"
>
> "What?"
>
> "There's something wrong with him, *he* needs help. He oughtn't to go with Ghislaine, I know it. He—"
>
> "He's not a kid. What he does is his own business and if he wants to go off with that mad bitch, then it's up to him, isn't it."
>
> "But I don't know what he might do with her. Oh, God, if only I knew. . . . He's always seemed so essential to me, like a limb. You can't call your hand a friend, it's just there. And you don't bother to ask why it does things—picks things up, puts them down. And he was like *my* hand that belonged to me but I never understood how it functioned."
>
> (172—my emphasis)

Thus Morris acknowledges that Honeybuzzard is figuratively a part of himself, whom he seeks to protect rather than interrogate.

The climax of the novel underscores Morris's empathy with Honeybuzzard. Fearing the worst, Morris takes Emily to the abandoned building he and Honey visited on the previous night. Once inside, Morris and Emily discover the body of Ghislaine and understand that Honey has strangled her. Now that Ghislaine is dead, Morris's ambivalence toward her is nonexistent; since he no longer needs to fear her, he can feel "pity and tenderness, for the first time unmixed with any other feeling" (180). However, he still reserves most of his

concern for Honey, who has acted out Morris's desire by "doing what Morris had always wanted but never defined . . . filling up her voracity once and for all by cramming with death the hungry mouth between her thighs" (180-81). Gamble aptly notes that "[a]s a statement of murderous misogyny, this could hardly be bettered" (55).[20] Clearly, Morris has projected his own neediness onto Ghislaine and labeled it her "voracity"; to his mind, male vulnerability and the lack associated with female genitalia are inextricably connected.[21] Since Honeybuzzard has destroyed the emblematic cause of Morris's own hungry, childish mouth, Morris feels indebted to, and protective of, his murderous double: "But I wanted it. I am to blame, too, I should have guessed, I should have protected *him*" (181—my emphasis).

The details that surround Ghislaine's death clearly suggest that such hatred of sexualized flesh originates not in Morris, nor even in Honey, but rather in a dominant mythology of Western culture. Susan Griffin has argued that the underlying ideology of Christianity and pornography is the same—the hatred and flagellation of the flesh.[22] Carter fictionally makes the same point by repeatedly associating pornographic and Christian iconography. Ghislaine is the daughter of a minister; her obsession with the mortification of her flesh (at one point, she reopens her facial scar; even after Honeybuzzard has slashed her, she returns to him and proclaims him her master) seems ordained by family history. Significantly, Honeybuzzard murders Ghislaine in the room where he had previously shared with Morris his fantasy of raping Ghislaine on a plaster Christ. Indeed, Morris and Emily find Ghislaine's body on a table surrounded by candles; thus Ghislaine's death scene resembles a black mass. In addition, in the last glimpse we have of Honeybuzzard, he is cradling that plaster Christ. As Lee astutely notes, "Honeybuzzard finds religious images powerful; they incite his increasing perversity because they seem to sanction his treatment of women" (27).[23] Clearly images of sadistic violence and sacred sacrifice merge in this final scene, and thus Carter once again links mainstream culture with the pornographic imagination.

Unlike the narrator in *Rebecca* and Brenda in *The Bottle Factory Outing,* Emily refuses to be complicit in the death of another woman. Despite her involvement with Honey, she has managed to reject not only the dualities of the sadomasochistic script but also its violence; thus she flees the building to call the police. Morris, following her, is thrown into another psychic crisis. Appalled by Emily's betrayal of the father of her child, Morris wants to aid a clearly maddened Honey; yet Morris fears the consequences of such an action. To his mind, protecting Honey is a heroic act; hence he sees his dilemma as one of courage versus cowardice. Significantly, Morris looks to the mythological realm for guidance and nerve. At one point, he questions his responsibility to Honey and utters the legendary question: "Am I my brother's keeper?" Thus he sees his loyalty to Honey as an avoidance of Cain-like behavior. He also casts himself as Orpheus and his journey back into the abandoned building as a journey into the underworld. Interestingly enough, earlier in the novel when Morris is presented with the Orpheus/Eurydice myth, his response is to think "Orpheus was a fool, in the first place, to want to go and retrieve the silly bitch" (24). However, when Eurydice takes on a male form, this journey "to rescue or destroy a dear companion" makes sense to him.

Via such androcentric mythological visions, Morris finds the strength to align himself with Honey, and he returns to the literal and figurative shadows of the abandoned building. At this point, Morris knows that Emily has already contacted the police and that Honey will be caught. Nevertheless, Morris turns his back on Emily, who is overcome by the nausea of pregnancy, and embraces the Gothic underworld where he will excuse femicide and do battle against male vulnerability. Symbolically, Morris eschews sexualized maternity and instead chooses the ruins of a paternalistic culture where body and soul cannot meet. Carter's 1974 commentary—"We live in Gothic times. Now to understand is the main thing"[24]—reads like a metacommentary on her first novel. However, even as she represents the Gothic, she avoids naturalizing it. Indeed, by envisioning Morris's ultimate identification with, and defense of, the male sadist as a struggle and a choice (albeit a culturally overdetermined one), Carter refutes the essentialist tendencies of both psychoanalytic and cultural feminist discourses. About Carter's works, Peach generalizes: she "complicated the familiar villain/victim . . . binarisms while not eschewing the way in which pain and suffering are employed to dominate women" (167). That generalization is particularly apt for *Honeybuzzard*. Thus I would argue the feminist potential of her early Gothic work, too often dismissed as the misogynist product of male impersonation.

Significantly, Carter does not imagine that Emily has any trouble rejecting Ghislaine's masochism; indeed, although *Honeybuzzard* makes use of the sadomasochistic couple, it ultimately privileges the first member of that pornographic dyad. Hence Carter's text is complemented well by Muriel Spark's *Driver's Seat* (1970), a novel that focuses upon the other half of that couple, the female masochist, as it cautions against using victimization to establish one's identity.

* * *

The Driver's Seat, Spark's tenth novel, is the story of Lise, a thirty four-year-old woman who has worked most of her adult life in an accountant's office. At the beginning of the novel, Lise is preparing for a vacation in southern Italy; the novel follows her movements the day before and the day of her flight from Copenhagen to Rome. Early on in the novel, we find out that Lise will be murdered. Thus the reader is led to believe that only two questions remain: who has committed this femicide and why? By the end of the novel, these two questions are answered: we know that Richard, a fellow traveler on Lise's flight and a supposedly reformed victimizer of women, has committed the crime and that, ostensibly, he has only obeyed orders, since the climax of the novel reveals that Lise has suicidally planned her own femicide. This revelation indicates that the needs served by her masochistic performance constitute the real mystery of this novel.

Such concerns may seem unduly macabre and worldly for an author often characterized by her Catholicism and her vision of a transcendent realm. In an interview with Sara Frankel, Spark clearly identifies her unswerving religious faith as her life's compass:

> It's very important for me to have a point of departure, because in the modern world nobody has any fixed belief or fixed idea of anything, and in a world like that a fixed point is very important. And it's not that I took it on for convenience—it's that I can't *not* believe that there is this norm. What other norm could there be, for someone brought up in the Western world, really wanting something. Whether we like it or not, the Christian-Judaic tradition that grew up around the Mediterranean dictates what we think is good or evil, and defines all of the absolutes that we hold to be important. The idea of Christ as an example, for instance, was terribly important to the whole development of the West—sociologically, morally, even politically.
>
> (445)

Possibly Spark cannot imagine herself living without this "fixed point" because she can and does imagine the despair of characters who lack it. Indeed, Lise seems like a casualty of the modern world, a traveler without a literal or figurative compass. It is perhaps not incidental that Spark, suffering from "nervous exhaustion," finished *The Driver's Seat* in a hospital (Whittaker 36) and that Lise has appropriated the Christian strategy of martyrdom while neglecting the redemptive purpose of that act.

Significantly, Lise's search for her destroyer reflects her creator's belief that violence is both a fact of life and a novelistic necessity:

> I'm quite fascinated by violence. I read policiers, detective stories, all that sort of thing, and I think a lot of life is violent. A lot of my novels don't have violence, but sometimes it's necessary: you can't have novels without violence. For instance, in a lot of romantic novels—take Daphne du Maurier's—there's violence all over the place. But she weeps a lot over it, it's very romantically presented. And generally speaking you

find more violence in love story novelists, taking extreme cases. I don't know if you've ever read Barbara Cartland, but her books are full of violence, men whipping brides and oh my God, this is the romantic thing carried to its absurdity.

(Frankel interview 452)[25]

Clearly, Spark is familiar with the conventions of the Gothic romance and the ways in which this genre overlaps with pornography. *The Driver's Seat* seems indebted to, and a refinement of, such conventions, since in that novel Spark removes any trace of "weeping" and carries the connection between romance and violence to an even more absurd extreme than Barbara Cartland: Lise spends the last day of her life looking for Mr. Right, the man who will murder her. Thus the heterosexual horror that O'Brien's Willa and Bainbridge's Freda find when they least expect it is exactly what Lise actively seeks.[26]

In *The Driver's Seat,* Spark, unlike Angela Carter, has eschewed the conventions of the modernist psychological novel and has instead appropriated some of the strategies of the *nouveau roman.* Lise's story is told almost wholly in the present tense; as Bold and Whittaker note, this device promotes narrative tension and the illusion of immediacy. Yet the occasional flash-forward,[27] with its requisite use of the future tense, disrupts that illusion and irrevocably alters the hermeneutic code. The most dramatic use of this flash-forward technique occurs early in the novel when the narrator informs us that Lise will shortly become a murder victim: "She will be found tomorrow morning dead from multiple stabwounds, her wrists bound with a silk scarf and her ankles bound with a man's necktie, in the grounds of an empty villa, in a park of the foreign city to which she is travelling on the flight now boarding at Gate 14" (25). At this point, we do not yet know that Lise actively seeks this fate, that she is purposefully traveling to achieve this end, that a cause-effect relationship exists between the willful boarding of this plane and the pornographic pose of her dead body. Nevertheless, we do know what will happen to the protagonist as well as how it will happen ("multiple stabwounds"). By structuring the novel in this achronological manner, Spark assures her readers of the inevitability of Lise's victimization, but she does not use that victimization as the climax of the novel. While psychoanalysts, journalists, and Lise herself might fetishize a wounded female body, Spark's narrative does not.

Although the third-person narrator of *The Driver's Seat* knows and tells about Lise's imminent death, his/her knowledge of causality and psychological motivation is nonexistent. Early on, the narrator objectively describes Lise: "Lise is thin. Her height is about five-foot-six. Her hair is pale brown, probably tinted" (16). Note the last qualifying phrase. Although the narrator can report

the objective data of color, the source of this color (from genes or a bottle) remains unknown. Similarly, the narrator finds it impossible to ascertain the state of Lise's psyche. At one point, s/he reports Lise's actions but adds, "Who knows her thoughts? Who can tell?" (53).

Since *The Driver's Seat* is not a psychological novel and we do not have access to Lise's mental processes, it remains unclear why Lise plots her own murder. Unlike Carter, Spark does not provide us with a detailed personal history, with family background, with past pain that results in present pathology. However, the narrative does suggest that Lise has experienced mental illness in the past. During the first pages of the novel, she breaks down at work, and the reactions of her coworkers "conveyed to her that she had done again what she had not done for five years" (6). In addition, a conversation with Richard, her soon-to-be murderer who has only recently been released from a psychiatric hospital, reveals that she is familiar with the decor of such places as well as the habits of its inmates:

> "Were the walls of the clinics pale green in all the rooms? Was there a great big tough man in the dormitory at night, patrolling up and down every so often, just in case?"
>
> "Yes," he says.
>
> "Stop trembling," she says. "It's the madhouse tremble."

Thus Lise and her murderer have a shared experience, and Spark, like Carter, links the pathology of the sadist to the self-destructiveness of the masochist. Yet Spark's narrator cannot explicitly identify the forces that have driven these two characters to assume such perverse roles.

However, we are provided with information that may be construed as both symptoms and causes of Lise's desperation. We know that Lise has worked in an accountant's office for over sixteen years, a period that constitutes much of her adult life. "She has five girls under her and two men. Over her are two women and five men" (6). Lise has her place in a fairly strict hierarchy where gender plays a role, though not an absolute one. Such facts perhaps sketch Lise as an alienated, stultified middle manager. Even more telling is the description of her apartment:

> She has added very little to the room; very little is needed, for the furniture is all fixed, adaptable to various uses, and stackable. . . . The writing desk extends to a dining table, and when the desk is not in use it, too, disappears into the pinewood wall, its bracket-lamp hingeing outward and upward to form a wall-lamp. The bed is by day a narrow seat with overhanging bookcases; by night it swivels out to accommodate the sleeper. . . . A small pantry-kitchen adjoins this

room. Here, too, everything is contrived to fold away into the dignity of unvarnished pinewood. . . . Lise keeps her flat as cleanlined and clean to return to after her work as if it were uninhabited. The swaying tall pines among the litter of cones on the forest floor have been subdued into silence and into obedient bulks.

(12)

Clearly, Lise's living quarters are functional but sterile. Pinewood, a wood often used for coffins, dominates; thus the text suggests that in this cold, clean, impersonal space, Lise experiences death in life. If one's physical space reflects one's identity, then Lise doesn't seem to have one. She has a room of her own but precious little to add to it. The final image of this description intimates that the movement of nature has been processed into stasis. Like the pinewood of her apartment, Lise seems to have been "subdued into silence" and obedience. Apparently, she can only imagine breaking out of such an empty and superficially ordered life by actively seeking her death.

The encounters Lise has during the last day of her life demonstrate that bleakness and superficiality are the marks of contemporary existence as well as Lise's life. In an airport concession stand, Lise briefly talks with a woman who is dutifully searching for paperback novels with pastel-colored covers: she wants this reading matter to conform to the decor of her South African beach house.[28] Apparently, in the world in which Lise lives, books are literally judged by their covers, and one's facade renders one's interior moot.

Lise's experience with Mrs. Fiedke, Richard's aunt who fatefully ends up staying in the same *pensione* as the protagonist, also underscores the transitory and disconnected nature of human relationships.[29] Lise and Mrs. Fiedke meet, share a taxi, lunch together, shop together. And yet, when Mrs. Fiedke fails to emerge from a bathroom stall in a department store, Lise deserts her. A few pages later, Mrs. Fiedke reappears and finds Lise attentively watching a woman dancing in the music department:

> Mrs. Fiedke comes up behind Lise and touches her arm. Lise says, turning to smile at her, "Look at this idiot girl. She can't stop dancing."
>
> "I think I fell asleep for a moment," Mrs. Fiedke says.
>
> (65-66)

Lise is not surprised to see Mrs. Fiedke and does not ask what happened to her; Mrs. Fiedke is not angered by Lise's desertion and offers an unasked-for explanation. As Ian Rankin has noted, there is a Beckett-like quality to the conversations between Lise and Mrs. Fiedke (151). In this world, conversations are collections of utterances rather than dialogues dependent upon understanding and response. Shortly after this scene,

Mrs. Fiedke and Lise are separated during a student demonstration, and they do not meet again. Although Mrs. Fiedke contributes to the success of Lise's plan—she purchases the murder weapon (a letter opener) and gives Lise valuable information about Richard's past—she remains unaware of Lise's search for death in the form of a man. Ultimately, Lise's relationship with Mrs. Fiedke demonstrates that human contact does not ensure communication, continuity, or connection.

Significantly, sexual intercourse is presented as an especially alienating, mechanistic, and impersonal form of communication. Spark satirically dramatizes this point through her depiction of Bill, a macrobiotic enthusiast who meets Lise on the plane to Italy and decides that she is his "type." Subscribing faithfully to an Eastern doctrine that divides the world into yin and yang, negative and positive, passive and active, feminine and masculine, Bill decides that Lise will be the one to provide him with his orgasm (a yang experience) that night. Bill is a comic character; he obviously represents an alternative lifestyle—one that ascribes significance to everything. In order to counter the chaos and nothingness of modernity, Bill follows a regime that neatly divides the world into complementary opposites.

About Bill and his macrobiotic system, Rankin writes, "It is as if Spark were offering Lise a way out, another, radically different, life to which she might attach herself. It is a lifestyle which Lise cannot accept" (150). Thus Lise is presented as perversely refusing heterosexual romance as a life preserver.[30] However, it seems important to note why this purportedly "radically different life" is not a viable alternative for Lise. Although the Eastern doctrine of yin and yang is predicated upon complementarity, Bill's division of experience looks suspiciously like the traditional Western gender hierarchy. According to Bill's view of the world, pleasurable experiences such as orgasm are yang, and toxic foods such as salami and coffee are yin. In addition, Bill humorously manifests his belief in strict sexual difference by insisting that men are supposed to urinate three times a day and women twice. When Bill tries to force Lise to help him achieve his daily orgasm, it becomes obvious that this revolutionary lifestyle caters to male desire and exploits women:

> the tussle that ensues between Bill and Lise, she proclaiming that she doesn't like sex and he explaining that if he misses his daily orgasm he has to fit in two the next day. "And it gives me indigestion," he says, getting her down on the gravel behind the hedge and out of sight, "two in one day. And it's got to be a girl."
>
> (106)

Although Bill's macrobiotic way of life privileges bodily experience, it also propagates a false sense of intimacy and thus only adds to the disconnection that seems rampant in modern life. Lise underscores the disillusionment caused by sex when she tells Richard, "Most of the time, afterwards is pretty sad" (113). Thus Lise experiences postcoitus as a time of pain and loneliness; for her, the body is the site of vulnerability. Margaret Moan Rowe asserts that in *The Driver's Seat,* "one sees Spark's most extreme dismissal of sexuality. . . . [T]here in the most extreme form sex is without any meaning whatsoever" (174). However, the episode with Bill suggests that the problem might lie with what sex is revealed to mean here: the satisfaction of men's needs and the psychological and physical vulnerability of women. Ultimately, Spark implies that the sexual revolution may not be quite so revolutionary for women.

Paradoxically, although the objective, external style of this narrative precludes our knowing Lise's full story, it may well symbolize the source of her despair and pathology. Spark asserts that narrational choices are inevitably tied to the theme of each individual work.[31] In *The Driver's Seat,* the narrator seems capable only of observing and reporting, not of making or finding significant relationships. That narrative stance seems to mirror the plight of the characters in this novel. Indirectly, we are given to understand that Lise is invisible and vulnerable in this world; she lacks a "fixed point" and thus cannot find meaning in life. Hence she chooses death. Michelle Massé has argued that "masochism can work to create and preserve a coherent self" (45). By contriving her own murder, Lise will use the mutilated remains of her body to gain posthumous attention. In short, Lise will create an identity by becoming a victim.

Significantly, Lise's masochistic plan makes abundant use of the rites of traditional womanhood. First and foremost, Lise uses the romantic paradigm as the model for the search for her murderer. Whenever she meets a man, she tries to determine if he is her "type"; indeed, Mrs. Fiedke believes that Lise is looking for a boyfriend and tries to help her find her match. Although Lise wants to be in "the driver's seat," to be in control of her fate,[32] she can only imagine gaining that control through Mr. Right. The script that Lise writes for herself is ultimately an extreme and perverse form of the conventional romantic script. In that script, when you find your man, you find a respite from the dangers of the world; in Lise's script, when you find your man, you die and thus are rendered invulnerable and publicly visible. In both cases, compulsory heterosexuality mediates female fate and female identity. The very extremity of Spark's narrative exposes as it echoes the perverse underpinnings of Deutsch and Bonaparte's plot.

Lise's preparation for her death mainly revolves around shopping. In the first scene of the novel, Lise searches for the dress in which she will meet her man; this outfit will be her analogue of a wedding dress, and she de-

sires something that will draw attention. Initially, she is offered a stain-resistant dress, which she immediately and somewhat hysterically rejects—she can only be a spectacle in her death if the stains of her stigmata show.[33] She finally finds the brash outfit for which she has been looking: the dress consists of a "lemon-yellow top with a skirt patterned in bright V's of orange, mauve, and blue"; over this, she wears a "coat with narrow stripes, red and white, with a white collar" (6-7). Dressed in this way, Lise can ensure that people will notice her and thus that witnesses will be able to reconstruct the story of her death. Similarly, she assiduously shops for the accessories necessary for her murder. These include a scarf and neckties with which she expects to be bound at the moment of her death. Ultimately, Lise constructs her identity as a victim from the world of women's fashion[34] and gives new meaning to "shop 'til you drop"; like Freda in *The Bottle Factory Outing,* her desire involves using the status quo rather than changing it. Clearly, Spark is more interested in charting the effects rather than the origins of female masochism. However, by yoking the details of Lise's plan to heterosexual romance and conspicuous consumption, Spark, like Horney, intimates that female masochists are made, not born.

Indeed, Lise is a case study of a woman who has wholly internalized stereotypical assumptions of female masochism. The only way she can imagine taking control of her life is through self-destruction, and she extends her strategy into a general and familiar theory of female victimization. When Richard laconically tells Lise as she drives through a park that "a lot of women get killed" in such locations, Lise readily agrees: "Yes, of course. It's because they want to be. . . . Yes, I know, they look for it" (113-14). For Lise, blaming the victim equals the assumption of agency.[35] However, Richard's response to Lise's self-serving pronouncements on female masochism testify to the inadequacy and inaccuracy of such views: "No, they don't want to be killed. They struggle. I know that" (114). As a man who has formerly stabbed but not killed a woman, Richard knows all about imposing violence on others and the resistance that results from such imposition. Here the male sadist provides the best evidence against the omnipresence of female masochism.

Just as Spark refuses to blame the victim, so does she challenge a simplistic victim-victimizer dichotomy. Indeed, Lise's plan to be mistress of her own murder blurs that dichotomy considerably, and the linguistic level of the novel underscores that point. Early in the novel, the narrator states that "the combination of colours [in her outfit] . . . *drags* attention" to Lise (53—my emphasis). The verb "drags" seems like an odd choice here and certainly calls attention to itself. However, later, this word reappears in a context that illuminates its initial use. Lise gets a lesson on hunting from a man whom she temporarily mistakes for her "type." According to this man, the predatory habits of big game enable their own slaughter: "You've got to wait for the drag. They call it the drag, you see. It kills its prey and drags it into the bush then you follow the drag and when you know where it's left its prey you're all right. The poor bloody beast comes out the next day to eat its prey, they like it high" (95-96). A synchronic cycle of victimization is described here—at one moment, the same being is both predator and prey. Thus Lise's implication in such a cycle is subtly suggested by the first use of "drags."

Indeed, Lise's predatory instincts constitute her use of masochism to "regulate others as well as the self" (Massé 45). Richard, Mrs. Fiedke's nephew and Lise's murderer, had been Lise's right-hand seat companion on the plane to Italy. She had initially identified him as her "type." Discomforted by Lise and the flirtatiousness of Bill (who sits on Lise's left), Richard changes his seat.[36] When he arrives at the *pensione* where his aunt is staying and sees Lise, he immediately leaves in an attempt to elude her. Richard has just emerged from a six-year stint in a psychiatric hospital; treatment there served in lieu of a jail sentence for his assault on a young woman. This reformed slasher apparently senses that Lise can incite the sadism that is still within him but that he is determined to control. Nevertheless, when Lise encounters Richard later that night as he returns to the *pensione,* she is determined that he will put her plan into action. Despite his "fear" and "resistance," Lise pursues him. She commands him to follow her, "leads" him to the door, drives him to the spot she has selected for her murder, and instructs him in great detail how to murder her. Lise counts on her active masochism to provoke an act of passive sadism. She wants to control not only her murder but also her murderer.

Yet Richard's sadism becomes anything but passive. Lise gives Richard explicit directions: she tells him to first tie her hands together, next to tie her ankles together, and then to strike her with the letter opener. However, Richard does not follow instructions exactly, and thus comes the final, subtle twist to this macabre plot:

> He ties her hands, and she tells him in a sharp, quick voice to take off his necktie and bind her ankles.
>
> "No," he says, kneeling over her, "not your ankles."
>
> "I don't want any sex," she shouts. "You can have it afterwards. Tie my feet and kill, that's all. They will come and sweep it up in the morning."
>
> All the same, he plunges into her, with the knife poised high.
>
> (116-17)

The use of the phrase "all the same" indicates that Richard has violated Lise's instructions and her body. What initially plunges into her is "he," not the knife, although

the subtle rendering of this scene momentarily confuses the weapon with the male sex organ.[37] Although this confusion is not sustained, male sexual sadism is presented as a powerful weapon of control. By raping Lise, Richard asserts his authority in this script and thus figuratively replaces Lise in the driver's seat. In her final moments, Lise learns the hard way that not all women ask for what they get. Her desire to control her life by controlling her own victimization ultimately fails since Richard (a.k.a. "Dick") thrusts sexual violence into Lise's final act.

Not all critics agree that Lise has been victimized and thus has forfeited her place in the driver's seat; indeed, some ignore or render insignificant the sexual violence that occurs against Lise's will. Sproxton comments, "He performs the murder precisely to her instructions" (142). Rankin comments that Lise "is, in the end, not to be pitied too much, for her plan has worked. Her victim is more in need of sympathy" (154). And Rowe asserts that "at the end, Lise's plot has unfolded completely, and she remains in the driver's seat." However, in Muriel Spark's universe, no one takes the driver's seat for long. Richard, like Lise, is quickly ousted from that position: the ending of the novel indicates that the police will arrest him for murder, and although substantial evidence will corroborate his statement that "she told me to kill her and I killed her" (117), it is unlikely that he will lead a normal life hereafter. The novel ends with "pity and fear, fear and pity," and it seems clear that both parties involved in this sensational crime merit both reactions. The chiastic structure of the phrase "pity and fear, fear and pity" rhetorically represents an object and its reflected image and is perhaps meant to suggest the doubled and tragic nature of the sadomasochistic couple.

Spark's interviews underscore Ruth Whittaker's observation that "[t]he novels of Muriel Spark are written from a Roman Catholic standpoint, whether or not her religion is specifically mentioned" (37). Hence the theological implications of Lise's and Richard's story deserve note. For the feminist concerned about gendered patterns of violence against women, the female masochist commits a crime against herself, and the male sadist commits a crime against women; however, for Spark, the sadomasochistic couple also sins against God by not recognizing that divinity rather than humanity is in the driver's seat. By taking control of life and death, Lise and Richard attempt to usurp the power of God. Thus Spark thrusts them both from their illusion of mastery: Lise's death scene does not go as planned, and the power Richard derives from rape is transitory. Ultimately, from both a theological and feminist perspective, Lise and Richard are cautionary figures who seek agency and identity in all the wrong places.

Muriel Spark's *Driver's Seat* extends our understanding of the cultural work that scripts of female masochism do. For Deutsch and Bonaparte, masochism "naturally" produces a heterosexual, reproducing female subject. Horney, more schooled in a hermeneutics of suspicion, astutely notes that the naturalizing of female masochism reproduces patriarchy. Spark particularizes Horney's insights by depicting the forms of social control and social recognition that masochism offers. In a world where death is certain and violent crimes against women an increasing possibility, masochism becomes a perverse form of agency: if one can't avoid sadists, then one might be able to control how and when they strike. Similarly, in a world where the role of victim is an all-too-viable one for women, life in death produces a more glamorous identity than death in life. As Massé astutely notes, "Masochism . . . can be a psychic strategy that makes the best of a bad business, that insists on wresting identity and self-affirmation from the biased social contract that traumatizes women" (42). Although Spark explores the productive use of masochism, she certainly doesn't endorse it. Indeed, the story of Lise suggests that women who choose this strategy are fucked by both God and men.

* * *

Lise looks for death in the form of a man and finds it; Morris fears death, projects it onto Ghislaine's sexualized flesh, and thus supports her destruction. Such plots suggest that, within contemporary sexual politics, both men and women view death as inextricably connected with the other gender. However, as Chancer rightly emphasizes, *the organization of patriarchy itself necessitates that a group positioned masochistically, or women, cannot be truly equal to the one positioned sadistically, or men* (139). Indeed, as Carter's and Spark's texts show, cultural forces which align female identity with masochistic performance and male identity with sadistic activity ensure an abundance of dead female bodies. Ultimately, both Carter and Spark recognize that women's bodies constitute the objects of male sadistic violence, and thus they refuse to disassociate masochism and sadism from biological sex. They refuse to be gender skeptics. Yet they also stop short of seeing these perversions as inherent or desirable expressions of sexual difference, and hence they avoid falling into the traps associated with cultural feminism and hyper-Freudian psychoanalysis that might make such gender relations seem inevitable. Like Horney, Spark and Carter link cultural norms and gendered perversions.

By situating the sadomasochistic couple within a larger cultural context, Spark and Carter suggest that the primary pornographic relationship is embedded in our cultural consciousness; thus their texts implicate men and women in femicidal scripts. Such a move is risky feminist business: a serious consideration of female masochism perilously borders on blaming the victim, and empathy with male sadists raises the fear that those figures

will be exonerated. Since our culture already tends toward such blame and exoneration, many feminists rightly approach with caution any strategies that might reinforce such positions. Yet Carter and Spark adroitly negotiate such potentially antifeminist minefields. In *Honeybuzzard,* Carter focuses on the man who protects and identifies with the sadist, not the man who actually commits the heinous crime. Hence she distances her readers from sadistic action and focuses instead on sadistic feeling. Further, she offers Emily as a counter to Ghislaine.[38] In *The Driver's Seat,* Spark presents Lise's sickness as a societal symptom, and she emphasizes that Richard's sadism is incited by, but does not originate with, Lise's masochism. Spark and Carter carefully avoid indicting the dead; however, they also refrain from presenting femicide as a simple story of unrelenting and essential male aggression. These texts distance us from the resignation to the female Gothic represented in Willa's and Brenda's story. Taken together, *The Driver's Seat* and *Honeybuzzard* short-circuit scripts of male vice and female virtue. Indeed, these texts use stock characters from cultural feminism and the Gothic to offer a promising scenario: if culture and not nature constructs female masochists and male sadists, then the mutability of these Gothic beings perhaps becomes easier to imagine. Thus the understanding that there *are* ready-made Gothic plots but they need not be followed becomes a crucial part of refusing victimization.

Notes

1. Although the relationships between the Gothic and pornography that I will discuss shortly will only put me on the margins of the feminist "sex wars," I want to acknowledge that these wars have been and will continue to be waged, and I want to set forth some of my basic assumptions. I oppose censorship, and I sincerely doubt that antipornography ordinances could be drafted that would protect all the cultural documents that *need* protection in a culture that has strong puritanical roots. This point is relevant to the study at hand; I shudder to think how a conservative court might rule on the literary and theoretical voices at issue in this book. I also think antipornography ordinances put representations of gay and lesbian sexuality especially at risk. I certainly do not trust legislators who oppose including gays and lesbians in an employment nondiscrimination act and who rally for a homophobic defense of marriage act to write more laws that will affect how, whether, and which representations of queer sexuality are disseminated. Moreover, I do not believe that all pornography or representations of sadomasochism are equal or mean the same thing.

2. Hoeveler reads Dworkin as being at the end of a long line of Gothic feminists who "suggest in their

writings that they hate their flesh" (246); this is an example of the conflation of those who are designated as "Gothic feminists" with that which they expose/analyze (in this case, the hatred of female flesh). Even if one buys this reading of Dworkin (which I do not), it seems imperative to put it into dialogue with Dworkin's emphasis on masculine culture's power over, and abuse of, female bodies.

3. Moers is responsible for coining the term "female Gothic." Later feminist critics of the Gothic have built upon Moers' throwaway line. Michelle Massé's, *In the Name of Love: Women, Masochism and the Gothic* devotes a chapter to *Story of O*. As Massé puts it, "The depiction of explicitly genital sexual practice which is pornography's metier can be simply a difference in degree, not in kind, from the Gothic's more genteel abuse" (108). In *Art of Darkness: A Poetics of Gothic*, Anne Williams argues that the "line between Male Gothic and pornography is not easy to draw" (106). In *Gothic Feminism*, Hoeveler comments, "At many points *Udolpho* reads like sanitized pornography, as if Radcliffe had traced over all the monotonous sex in the Marquis de Sade and substituted extended descriptions of the landscape or the chase around the castle as more exciting" (100).

4. William Patrick Day, too, notes that "the pattern of all relationships in the Gothic fantasy . . . operates on the dynamic of sadomasochism" (19).

5. There is now, of course, a compelling body of scholarship that reads sadomasochism as a sexual play with power rather than a crystallization of gender hierarchy. Tania Modleski has sagely noted that the meaning of sadomasochism cannot be divorced from its context and participants. See her discussion in *Feminism without Women*, esp. 148-57.

6. My discussion of Helene Deutsch and Marie Bonaparte is indebted in great part to Kate Millett's work in *Sexual Politics*. For a related discussion of Freud and Deutsch, see Lynn Chancer, *Sadomasochism in Everyday Life*, 127-28.

7. See Spark's *Curriculum Vitae*, 138-39, for discussion of her relationship with Bonaparte. Most pertinent here is Spark's remembrance that "[w]e discussed literature, which she, having been a prominent pupil of Sigmund Freud, approached from a psychological point of view—something quite new to me. I was intrigued, but I felt it left too much unsaid" (138).

8. For other views on the relationship between psychoanalysis and the Gothic, see Williams, esp. 239-248; Judith Halberstam, *Skin Shows: Gothic Horror and the Technology of Monsters*, 8; William Patrick Day, *In the Circles of Fear and Desire*, esp. 177-190; Mark Edmundson, *Nightmare on Main Street*, esp. 32-36, 125-29; and Jerrold E. Hogle, "The Gothic and the 'Otherings' of Ascendant Culture: The Original *Phantom of the Opera*," esp. 822-26. Massé uses the structure of Freud's beating fantasy to organize her study of the Gothic, *In the Name of Love*.

9. As Marc O'Day points out, "The title switch between the British and American editions, from *Shadow Dance* to *Honeybuzzard*, reflects a shift of attention from the supporting cast to the monster himself" (27). My reading of this novel refocuses attention on one member of the "supporting cast," Morris.

10. Dworkin, *Pornography: Men Possessing Women*, 84. Dworkin situates Carter in a long line of Sadeian apologists.

11. Keenan reads *The Sadeian Woman* as a "reaction to the mythicization of female virtue" (139). Obviously, I think that argument—as well as the one about intervening in nascent critical debates—holds for *Honeybuzzard* as well. Perhaps significantly, although Keenan notes Carter's use of sexual violence in several texts, she does not mention *Honeybuzzard*. That omission may be due to the assumption, discussed in the next paragraph, that Carter's pre-'68 work is not of feminist interest.

12. In "The Dangers of Angela Carter," Jordan reviews and counters the critical history that reads Carter as a reproducer of patriarchal consciousness.

13. For a provocative theoretical challenge to the concept of male identification, see Judith Butler, *Gender Trouble*, esp. 30.

14. For a fascinating story of the vanquishing rather than the taming of a male sadist, see Carter's "Bloody Chamber."

15. See Susan Griffin, *Pornography and Silence: Culture's Revenge against Nature*, and Jessica Benjamin, "Master and Slave: The Fantasy of Erotic Domination."

16. In *Pornography and Silence*, Griffin argues that "the sadomasochistic ritual demands the invulnerability of the sadist and the vulnerability of the masochist" (48).

17. See Claire Kahane, "The Gothic Mirror." Lorna Sage, in her introduction to *Flesh and the Mirror*, writes that Carter reported in interviews that "houses stood in for mothers" (6).

18. For a discussion of the matricidal tendencies of Western culture, see Luce Irigaray, "Body against Body: In Relation to the Mother."

19. See Robin Ann Sheets, "Pornography, Fairy Tales, and Feminism," esp. 653-54, for a discussion of "the mother as sexual subject" in Carter's "The Bloody Chamber." Like Sage, Aidan Day reads Emily as "the new order that displaces the old reality" (20). In contrast, Linden Peach finds nothing redemptive about Emily, "who manifests her failure to develop the imaginary" (39). Peach reads Carter's work, especially her early work, as in dialogue with the "Euro-American Gothic" tradition (which he unself-consciously charts as a wholly male tradition) and with Fiedler's *Love and Death in the American Novel*. Such literary and critical frames may help to explain his assessment of Emily.

20. Gamble continues, "but the elaborate mythology which is built up around Ghislaine tends to obscure the fact that she has done very little, if anything at all, to deserve it. . . ." (55). This statement is consistent with Gamble's view of this novel as exemplifying Carter's pre-'68 "patriarchal bias." I tend to agree with Lee's assessment that, from the start of her career, Carter positions her reader to be an active and responsible interpreter: "Reading Carter's works is always an active process, and this equal exchange between reader and text finally allows new formulations to arise from the old" (11).

21. In *The Sadeian Woman*, Carter foregrounds the cultural equation of the female body with the wounded body: "The whippings, the beatings, the gougings, the stabbings of erotic violence reawaken the memory of the social fiction of the female wound, the bleeding scar left by her castration, which is a psychic fiction as deeply at the heart of Western culture as the myth of Oedipus, to which it is related in the complex dialectic of imagination and reality that produces culture. Female castration is an imaginary fact that pervades the whole of men's attitudes toward women and our attitude to ourselves, that transforms women from human beings into wounded creatures who were born to bleed" (23).

22. As Griffin provocatively puts it, "All the elements of sadomasochistic ritual are present in the crucifixion of Christ." See Griffin, *Pornography and Silence*, 68-69.

23. Aidan Day makes a similar point: Honeybuzzard's "cast of mind has been formed by a culture oppressive to women which is shot through with the attitudes of religious patriarchy" (16).

24. See the afterword to Carter's *Fireworks: Nine Profane Pieces*, 122.

25. *The Ballad of Peckham Rye* (1960) and *Not to Disturb* (1971) are among the violent plots au-

thored by Spark. Many of her early short stories also end in violence; a particularly interesting example is "The Portobello Road."

26. Lise's masochistic contriving of her murder should be distinguished from Rebecca's purported desire for death at Maxim's hands. If Maxim was correct in surmising that "Rebecca wanted me to kill her" (374), we need to remember that she would have been trying to preserve and reinforce her carefully constructed subversive identity in anticipation of the ravages of terminal cancer. Unlike Lise, Rebecca's primary mode of seeking recognition as a subject is not through victimization.

27. Ruth Whittaker uses this term in her discussion of the novel.

28. Spark lived in Rhodesia from 1937 through 1944. This reference may well be a commentary on Southern African white women.

29. Spark has a flair for creating wonderful old women. *Memento Mori* is full of such characters; Lady Edwina in *Loitering with Intent* is another marvelous example.

30. Judy Sproxton comments that Lise "repudiates Bill's advances, implying that she has no interest in sex. Since Bill professes to be merely concerned that he should keep up with his regime of a daily orgasm, his warmth towards her is hardly likely to change her attitude" (141). Thus Sproxton implies that Mr. Right might. Although Sproxton includes her discussion of *The Driver's Seat* in a chapter titled "Women as Victims," she reads Lise's story as an individual case history and concludes that "Lise's morbidity demonstrates the horror of the negative use of free will" (144). Such critical framing seems to reflect her view that "Spark is not a feminist in the sense that she asserts specific rights for women, nor is she interested in decrying a society which might seek to repress women" (18).

31. In the Frankel interview, Spark asserts, "That's the most difficult part of a novel: finding the tone, deciding who the unseen, invisible narrator is, and what role he's going to play for this particular book. You've got to consider then the theme, and what type of narration will best fit that theme and technique. I've got to think about this quite a lot before I begin" (454).

32. Relevant here is Massé's point that "by producing the script of the beating fantasy or a Gothic plot, the script writer works to assure her own agency" (47).

33. I use the word "stigmata" purposefully here. Although I would not want to overemphasize this idea, Lise does strike me as a false Christ figure.

34. Joanna Russ notes that popular Gothics feature detailed descriptions of women's clothing. She sees this convention as inextricably connected to the readership of these Gothics—housewives, who, among many other things, "shop for clothing for themselves and their children" (39). Here women's fashion represents masochistic norms of femininity and emphasizes the importance of (female) appearance. The issue of confused identity that results in Willa's death in *Casualties of Peace* is also effected through clothing, in that case a fur coat, a fetishized object of female consumption obtained through hunting for prey.

35. Lise's view constitutes an interesting though extremely problematic defensive strategy—by asserting that women who get killed actively pursue that fate, Lise refuses to recognize the ways in which female victimization compromises female autonomy. Thus Spark posits an extremely sophisticated rationale for *women* believing in female masochism.

36. I suspect that Spark has some fun with these seating arrangements. Richard on the right and Bill on the left suggests the thieves that flank Christ at Calvary. Of course, the man on the right would be Lise's "type."

37. Alan Bold points out Spark's subtle depiction of rape: "Readers aware of Spark's meticulous attention to language will realize that her pun on 'plunges' makes it plain that the murderer ignores Lise's request to desist from sexual penetration" (94). Margaret Moan Rowe, in her *Dictionary of Literary Biography* article on Spark, also mentions "the rape-murder" of Lise.

38. Thus I disagree with Lee when she writes that "the tragedy is offset only slightly by Emily's saving herself" (11).

Works Cited

Benjamin, Jessica. "Master and Slave: The Fantasy of Erotic Domination." Snitow 280-99.

Bold, Alan. *Muriel Spark*. London: Methuen, 1986.

Bonaparte, Marie. *Female Sexuality*. New York: International UP, 1953.

Butler, Judith. *Gender Trouble: Feminism and the Subversion of Identity*. New York: Routledge, 1990.

Carter, Angela. *The Bloody Chamber and Other Stories*. New York: Penguin, 1979.

Chancer, Lynn S. *Sadomasochism in Everyday Life: The Dynamics of Power and Powerlessness*. New Brunswick: Rutgers UP, 1992.

Day, Aidan. *Angela Carter: The Rational Glass*. New York: Manchester UP, 1998.

Day, William Patrick. *In the Circles of Fear and Desire: A Study of Gothic Fantasy*. Chicago: U of Chicago P, 1985.

Deutsch, Helene. *The Psychology of Women: A Psychoanalytic Interpretation*. New York: Grune, 1944. Vol. 1.

Dworkin, Andrea. *Pornography: Men Possessing Women*. New York: Perigee, 1981.

Edmundson, Mark. *Nightmare on Elm Street: Angels, Sadomasochism, and the Culture of the Gothic*. Cambridge: Harvard UP, 1997.

Gamble, Sarah. *Angela Carter: Writing from the Front Line*. Edinburgh: Edinburgh UP, 1997.

Griffin, Susan. *Pornography and Silence: Culture's Revenge against Nature*. New York: Harper, 1981.

Halberstam, Judith. *Skin Shows: Gothic Horror and the Technology of Monsters*. Durham: Duke UP, 1995.

Hoeveler, Diane Long. *Gothic Feminism: The Professionalization of Gender from Charlotte Smith to the Brontës*. University Park: Pennsylvania UP, 1998.

Hogle, Jerrold E. "The Gothic and the 'Otherings' of Ascendant Culture: The Original *Phantom of the Opera*." *South Atlantic Quarterly* 95 (1996): 821-46.

Irigaray, Luce. "Body against Body: In Relation to the Mother." *Sexes and Genealogies*. Trans. Gillian C. Gill. New York: Columbia UP, 1993. 7-21.

Kahane, Claire. "The Gothic Mirror." *The (M)other Tongue: Essays in Feminist Psychoanalytic Interpretation*. Ed. Shirley Nelson Garner, Claire Kahane, and Madelon Sprengnether. Ithaca: Cornell UP, 1985. 334-51.

Keenan, Sally. "Angela Carter's *The Sadeian Woman*: Feminism as Treason." *The Infernal Desires of Angela Carter: Fiction, Femininity, Feminism*. Ed. Joseph Bristow and Trev Lynn Broughton. New York: Longman, 1997.

Lee, Alison. *Angela Carter*. New York: Twayne, 1997.

Massé, Michelle A. *In the Name of Love: Women, Masochism and the Gothic*. Ithaca: Cornell UP, 1992.

Millett, Kate. *Sexual Politics*. 1970. New York: Ballantine, 1978.

Modleski, Tania. *Feminism Without Women: Culture and Criticism in a "Postfeminist" Age*. London: Routledge, 1991.

Moers, Ellen. *Literary Women*. 1976. New York: Oxford UP, 1985.

Peach, Linden. *Angela Carter*. London: MacMillan, 1998.

Rowe, Margaret Moan. "Muriel Spark." *Dictionary of Literary Biography*. Ed. Jay Lottalio. Detroit: Gale, 1983. Vol. 15, pt. 2.

Russ, Joanna. "Somebody's Trying to Kill Me and I Think It's My Husband: The Modern Gothic." *The Female Gothic*. Ed. Juliann Fleenor. Montreal: Eden, 1983.

Sheets, Robin Ann. "Pornography, Fairy Tales and Feminism." *Journal of the History of Sexuality* 1.4 (1991): 633-57.

Snitow, Ann. "A Gender Diary." Hirsch and Keller 9-43.

Snitow, Ann, Christine Stansell, and Sharon Thompson, eds. *Powers of Desire: The Politics of Sexuality*. New York: Monthly Review, 1983.

Spark, Muriel. *Curriculum Vitae: Autobiography*. Boston: Houghton Mifflin, 1993.

Sproxton, Judy. *The Women of Muriel Spark*. London: Constable, 1992.

Whittaker, Ruth. *The Faith and Fiction of Muriel Spark*. New York: St. Martin's, 1982.

Williams, Anne. *Art of Darkness: A Poetics of Gothic*. Chicago: U of Chicago P, 1995.

George E. Haggerty (essay date 2006)

SOURCE: Haggerty, George E. "'Queer Company': *The Turn of the Screw* and *The Haunting of Hill House*." In *Queer Gothic*, pp. 131-50. Urbana: University of Illinois Press, 2006.

[*In the following excerpt, Haggerty explores Henry James's* The Turn of the Screw *and Shirley Jackson's* The Haunting of Hill House *in terms of the authors' extending the Gothic tradition to include neurosis, female sexuality, and children's sexuality.*]

Henry James's *The Turn of the Screw* (1898) is the perfect gothic tale. Generations of critics have testified, either directly or indirectly, to its signal uncanniness.[1] Its position within the history of gothic fiction, however, is sometimes ignored. In the context of this study, where hystericized heroines are commonplace, the governess's uneasiness with her eerie surroundings is hardly surprising. What is more, the crisis James's heroine confronts, which concerns the haunting of children, Miles and Flora, under her charge, is not entirely unprecedented, but it brings into clear focus some of the central obsessions of the gothic literary tradition. Victimization of the young is, after all, a gothic staple, and concern for the safety of children has been there from the first.

Shirley Jackson's *The Haunting of Hill House* (1959) builds on some of James's insights and fashions a more fully "neurotic" gothic heroine. But there, too, house,

haunting, and even ghostliness are familiar to readers of gothic fiction. Eleanor Vance, Jackson's heroine, does not know why she must obey the dictates of the house any more than James's governess knows why she must torment the children in her charge. In both cases a kind of debilitated female sexuality wreaks havoc in the intimate world of family and responsibility. Both heroines are neurotic in their different ways, but in both cases the novelists make the reader aware of more than simple female hysteria. In each we learn how the context feeds these neuroses and how even the most well-meaning friends hasten the (self-) destruction that this particular form of madness entails.

Together, these works show the ways in which twentieth-century gothic could begin to revise familiar tropes and give them new energy in the spirit of late-nineteenth- and early-twentieth-century developments in psychology and psychoanalysis. Seen within the context of the gothic tradition, moreover, they fulfill rather than reimagine gothic potential.

James was writing in a gothic tradition that made it perfectly reasonable to place a young woman in a "haunted" house and confront her with demons beyond her conscious control. As if to signal this connection, James has the governess ruminate after her first confrontation with what she takes to be the ghost of Peter Quint, once a valet at Bly: "Was there a 'secret' at Bly—a mystery of Udolpho or an insane, an unmentionable relative kept in unsuspected confinement? I can't say how long I turned it over, or how long, in a confusion of curiosity and dread, I remained where I had had my collision" (148).[2]

Like Ann Radcliffe's Emily in *The Mysteries of Udolpho*, James's governess must on her own confront the unknown, and the mysteries she faces are the mysteries of her deepest fears. Also like Emily, she is victim of the delusions into which her intelligence and sensibility lead her.[3] Confronted with partial knowledge, that is, she draws conclusions that are unwarranted and perhaps dangerous. In the first chapter of this study I quoted Claire Kahane, for whom the woman hidden in the recesses of Udolpho is "a victimizer victimized by her own desire." "Laurentini is presented as Emily's potential precursor," Kahane says, "a mad mother-sister-double who mirrors Emily's own potential for transgression and madness."[4] James's governess is both a victimizing victimizer and a "mother-sister-double" to the children under her care. But she is also the innocent Emily, who remains sane but seems at the same time potentially mad and dangerous.

No critic can challenge the structural integrity of the tale. The reader is limited to the perspective of the governess, and the uncertainty she faces concerns ambiguity and uncertainty about who can see the ghosts and who is being haunted by them. She challenges herself repeatedly with the fear of madness, as is clear when late in the tale, in the company of Flora and a servant, Mrs. Grose, she sees the ghost of Miss Jessel, her predecessor, across the lake: "She was there, and I was justified; she was there, and I was neither cruel nor mad" (213). The governess is uneasy about her sanity to the degree that she cannot prove the objective existence of the ghosts without threatening the children or challenging them directly. When she does come close to exposing them to her reality, they in each case deny seeing what she sees, and they curse her in the process, as Flora does immediately after the scene above ("'I don't know what you mean. I see nobody. I see nothing. I never *have*. I think you're cruel. I don't like you!'" [215]).

Of course it is possible to question the honesty of the children in scenes like this, and various passages can be cited to suggest that they must be involved with the infernal, just as various passages can be cited to suggest that they are victims of the governess's hysteria. But my argument is analogous to that made about "explained gothic": If what we imagined to be a ghostly presence—in Clara Reeve, say, or Radcliffe—turns out to be a corpse, even a waxen image of one, or if it reveals incest or sadistic incarceration, then the interest is even more pointed in a specifically human direction. In this case it hardly matters whether the ghosts have an objective existence in order to understand that the governess suffers. It takes no inversion of the tale to see her plight as harrowing and debilitating. Her confusion and desperate attempt to challenge the unknown is even more painful because they involve victimization of children under her charge. The tale does not allow us to determine whether she is correct or incorrect in her suspicions. It simply dramatizes—vividly, in fact—how much the suspicions matter.

James's governess has been the brunt of critical discomfort since Edmund Wilson first posited her victimization of the children and her compromised interest in them and their guardian. Ellis Hansen has observed that this reading, like other seeming alternative ones, all depend on an unassailable notion of childhood innocence:

> In all three approaches to the novella and film—as a ghost story, as a Freudian case study, as a self-conscious meditation on literary ambiguity—the allure of gothic children remains intact. If it is a ghost story, then the ghosts *are fiends who corrupt the children's innocence*. If it is a psychological case study of a paranoid woman, then the governess is *a fiend who corrupts the children's innocence*. If it is an irresolvable exercise in ambiguity, then the naïve reader entertains lecherous fantasies and suspicions resembling those of the *fiends who corrupt the children's innocence*. The predicate is always the same. Innocence was never so vulnerable, yet never so unassailable. It was never so sexy.[5]

The erotics of childhood are wittily suggested in this critical *jeu d'esprit*, but surely the trope of childhood complicity with adult desire is a familiar one to students of gothic fiction. Hansen's analysis, like so many readings of *The Turn of the Screw*, implies that James's greatest innovation is his insistence on involving children in the haunting. But gothic fiction has dealt in haunted children from the first. Poor Conrad has barely reached puberty when he is crushed by a gigantic helmet in *The Castle of Otranto*; William Beckford's *Vathek* focuses on the erotics of childhood, understandably enough for this notorious pederast, and childhood innocence and its (not inevitable) demise are a central theme of the novel; Sophia Lee examines childhood and childhood memories at length in *The Recess*; the children Mary Shelly depicts in *Frankenstein* are haunted by the monstrous; Charlotte Dacre's characters in *Zofloya* begin their rapid decline because of the horrors of childhood; Ann Radcliffe considers her heroines as children and exposes violence upon children; Maria Regina Roche discusses the impossibilities of childhood; and Sheridan LeFanu articulates one of the most memorable hauntings of the nineteenth century when he introduces the eponymous Carmilla into the bedroom of Laura when she is still a little girl. Indeed, the examples are so numerous that one has to consider what sleight of hand led James to claim a distinction of this kind.

Hansen partly answers that question. Late-nineteenth and early-twentieth-century culture needed childhood innocence to fill out a certain kind of self-projection. Hansen adds that critics "scrutinize the children with a mixture of lasciviousness and impunity that is paradigmatic of the modern relation between adults and children: reading as child-loving without end, parental protection as paranoid pedophilia." James's children fall into this description in a way that Beckford's or Mary Shelley's do not, in part because he entered into a negotiation that renders their emerging sexuality as something always already taboo. Surely their "innocence" is the question that obsesses the governess. The ghosts she confronts, that is, are the specters of the possibility that these children are not as innocent as they seem. Their uncanny charm takes on a different, not to say nefarious, quality if the children have been consorting, in the past or in the haunted present, with the transgressive figures of Quint and Miss Jessel.[6]

From the very first the governess is trapped by the awkwardness of her situation at Bly. Unable to turn to her employer for help, she must rely on Mrs. Grose, an illiterate housekeeper; when the house starts to seem haunted, the governess is more and more harrowingly on her own. Having written herself into a romance that centers on her relation to her employer—"She was in love" (103) the narrator admits at the opening of the tale—she has no choice but to eroticize the details of her life at Bly and invest the children with this uncanny and unsettling power. The governess understands the situation as increasingly "queer." After the first encounter with Quint she muses, "Here it was another affair; for many days after, it was a queer affair enough" (149). What she means by "queer" is odd, strange, and uncanny, but as several critics have argued the term could also resonate with a hint of transgressive sexuality.[7] There is a queer mood in *The Turn of the Screw* to the degree that the governess is unable to confront the implications of what is going on around her.

When she talks to Mrs. Grose about their need to work together to protect the children from the ghosts, she makes the specific limits of her ability clear: "What was settled between us, accordingly, that night, was that we thought we might bear things together; and I was not even sure that, in spite of her exemption, it was she who had the best of the burden. I knew at this hour, I think, as well as I knew later what I was capable of meeting to shelter my pupils; but it took me some time to be wholly sure of what my honest ally was prepared for to keep terms with so compromising a contract. I was queer company enough—quite as queer as the company I received" (157).

The governess sees herself as queer because she has lost her footing in this bizarre world. She is not sure of the values that are implicit there, nor is she ready to interpret the goings-on in any way that criticizes her charges. In a sense, her desire to protect them queers her position more than any attack on their sensibilities. She becomes almost obsessed with the terms of their relations, and even their innocence she reads as uncannily complicated: "For if it occurred to me that I might occasionally excite suspicion by the little outbreaks of my sharper passion for them, so too I remember wondering if I mightn't see a queerness in the traceable increase of their own demonstrations" (173). There is something queer about the children, she is saying. There is something queer about their demonstrations of passion for her, and by implication there is something queer about their demonstration of affection for Quint and Jessel. These possibilities are described as queer because they are uncanny in a way the governess cannot fathom. Her tentative desire and frustrating isolation make it less likely that she will understand the erotics of childhood with anything but horror. When the governess confronts Miles about his behavior at school and his ultimate expulsion this motif becomes even more intense. She asks him to explain what happened:

> "Do you mean now—here?"
>
> "There couldn't be a better place or time." He looked round him uneasily, and I had the rare—oh, the queer!—impression of the very first symptom I had seen in him of the approach of immediate fear. It was as if he was suddenly afraid of me—which struck me indeed as perhaps the best thing to make him.
>
> (229)

Even here the governess discovers queerness in her impression of Miles's fear. She invokes queer as a modifier because Mile's fear is not something that she understands. She shifts from announcing a "rare" impression to announcing a queer one. What does that change imply? It seems to me that it articulates her deepest unspoken fear about Miles. She worries about his relation with Quint but does not know how to put it into words. An impression of queerness is the best she can do.

This queerness suffuses the text with a specific uncanniness the governess never fully understands. Her uneasiness fosters queer company; queer impressions; queer looks ("You looked queer," the governess tells Mrs. Grose when she is discussing the letter they received dismissing Miles from school; "I doubt if I looked as queer as you," the housekeeper retorts [171]); and queer elements ("I scanned all the visible shore while Mrs. Grose took again, into the queer element I offered her, one of her plunges of submission" [211]). This disquietude also forces her to act but makes it impossible for her to know how to do so.

Patricia White mentions Freud in her discussion of the film *The Haunting,* inspired by Shirley Jackson's *The Haunting of Hill House*: "Freud's essay on the uncanny draws on the literary gothic, particularly the work of E. T. A. Hoffman. In it he associates the sensation with the etymological overlap between definitions of the uncanny, *das Unheimliche,* and its apparent opposite *das Heimliche* (literally, the homey, the familiar), ultimately identifying this convergence with 'the home of all humans,' the womb. The woman provides the uncanny, her experience remains a shadowy area."[8]

The governess, like White's female spectator, "must undergo a constant process of transformation."[9] In her queer and uncanny world the familiar world of home and childhood is rendered unfamiliar because she cannot be sure that she is seeing what she thinks she sees. The potential "evil" of the children creates this uncanny context. As the governess tries to transform herself in order to come to terms with what is going on around her she is unequal to the demands the house has placed upon her. Like Eleanor Vance in *The Haunting of Hill House,* she finds herself drawn to its eeriness but is afraid of what that says about her.

One of the keys to her uneasiness is concern over what Miles did to be dismissed from school. She worries that his relations with Quint, either those of the past or those of a ghostly present, might have produced a quality in the boy that makes him dangerous to the others at the school, but she never discovers the nature of that behavior. When she confronts Miles, a confrontation that seems to be the cause of Miles's death, she refuses to understand him when he tries to answer her. She is in a realm that challenges all her assumptions, and that makes her react violently. Consider the encounter when she gets Miles to admit some sort of misbehavior at school:

> "What then did you do?"
>
> He looked in vague pain all round the top of the room and drew his breath, two or three times over, as with difficulty. He might have been standing at the bottom of the sea and raising his eyes to some faint green twilight. "Well, I said things."
>
> "Only that?"
>
> "They thought it was enough!"
>
> "To turn you out for?"
>
> Never, truly, had a person 'turned out' shown so little to explain it as this little person! He appeared to weigh my question, but in a manner quite detached and almost helpless. "Well, I suppose I oughtn't."
>
> "But to whom did you say them?"
>
> He evidently tried to remember, but it dropped—he had lost it. "I don't know!"
>
> He almost smiled at me in the desolation of his surrender, which was indeed practically, by this time, so complete that I ought to have left it there. But I was infatuated—I was blind with victory, though even then the very effect that was to have brought him so much nearer was already that of added separation. "Was it to everyone?" I asked.
>
> "No; it was only to—." But he gave a sick little headshake. "I don't remember their names."
>
> (232-33)

Coming as it does right before the tragic conclusion of the tale, the conversation gives crucial insight into what has happened. This key passage manages to amplify the governess's confusion in direct relation to Miles's revelations. Miles is "sick," trapped in the implications of his crime and afraid of what this confrontation will mean, and that causes him to panic. "He might have been standing at the bottom of the sea and raising his eyes to some faint green twilight," an image that suggests compulsion, suffocation, and despair. "Some faint green twilight" is the hope the governess holds out, the hope she will be able to deliver him from his torment whatever it happens to be. But that is precisely what she cannot do. Instead, she turns the casual encounter into a gothic confrontation and forces Miles to confront some truth about himself.

"Saying things" does not seem a terrible transgression to the governess, and she struggles to come to terms with the few details of his confession. She has trouble making sense of it at all. Pushing Miles to give details of the things he said and the people to whom he said them, the governess finds herself immediately out of her depth in this sea of truth. She seems to have him

where she wants him and thinks she might stop there. But even as she congratulates herself, she tries to push things further: "But I was infatuated—I was blind with victory, though even then the very effect that was to have brought him so much nearer was already that of added separation" (233). That leads to the final detail that leaves her confused and nearly helpless:

> "Were they then so many?"
>
> "No—only a few. Those I liked."
>
> Those he liked? I seemed to float not into clearness, but into a darker obscure, and within a minute there had come to me out of my very pity the appalling alarm of his being perhaps innocent. It was for the instant confounding and bottomless, for if he *were* innocent, what then on earth was *I*?
>
> (233)

As the governess floats into "a darker obscure," the source of the queer uncanniness of the text starts to come clear. Miles is all along suspected of some kind of unnatural relation with Quint. The governess has considered the degree to which Miles occupies an unnatural place in her imagination. She imagines that he could say to her, "'Either you clear up with my guardian the mystery of this interruption of my studies, or you cease to expect me to lead with you a life that's so unnatural for a boy.' What was so unnatural for the particular boy I was concerned with was this sudden revelation of a consciousness and a plan" (197).

It does not take too much imagination to see the relation between Miles and Quint as an erotic relation. Several critics have suggested this and often take it for granted.[10] But it may simply be the erotics of language that Quint has taught the boy. Miles does not say he did things with his schoolmates, which would hardly have been a surprise. Public schools were a sexual workshop for many young boys and still are. But the difference between mechanical sexual experimentation and "saying things" is profound. If Quint has taught Miles erotic language—the language of love—such language can threaten situations that are unemotionally sexual. Is that far-fetched? Well, imagine if Miles confessed to saying things to little girls whom he "liked." The erotically transgressive possibilities are immediately obvious. Because Miles says things to boys he liked, the governess is at a loss. But how could she not be? She is not prepared to understand Miles's position, nor is she able to see where his confession will take her. By closing the possibility of hearing what Miles is trying to say, by feeling lost in the darkness at his clear attempt to satisfy her request, the governess chooses the haunting rather than the simple reality of Miles articulating love for his friends. The famous ending of the tale vividly emphasizes this disjunction:

> "Is she *here*?" Miles panted as he caught with his sealed eyed the direction of my words. Then as his strange

"she" staggered me and, with a gasp, I echoed it, "Miss Jessel, Miss Jessel!" he with a sudden fury gave me back.

I seized, stupefied, his supposition—some sequel to what we had done to Flora, but this made me only want to show him that it was better still than that. "It's not Miss Jessel! But it's at the window—straight before us. It's *there*—the coward horror, there for the last time!"

At this, after a second in which his head made the movement of a baffled dog's on a scent and then gave a frantic little shake for air and light, he was at me in a white rage, bewildered, glaring vainly over the place and missing wholly, though it now, to my sense, filled the room like the taste of poison, the wide, overwhelming presence. "It's *he*?"

"Peter Quint—you devil!" His face gave again, round the room, its convulsed supplication. "*Where*?"

They are in my ears still, his supreme surrender of the name and his tribute to my devotion. "What does it matter now, my own?—what will he *ever* matter? I have you," I launched at the beast, "but he has lost you for ever!" Then, for the demonstration of my work, "There, *there*!" I said to Miles.

But he had already jerked straight round, stared, glared again, and seen but the quiet day. With the stroke of the loss I was so proud of he uttered the cry of a creature hurled over an abyss, and the grasp with which I recovered him might have been that of catching him in his fall. I caught him, yes, I held him—it may be imagined with what a passion; but at the end of a minute I began to feel what it was truly that I held. We were alone with the quiet day, and his little heart, dispossessed, had stopped."

(234-35)

This passage is quoted at length because it unfolds in such fascinating a way and in doing so reveals the misunderstanding that costs Miles his life. The governess insists that Miles sees what she sees, feels what she feels, but it is obvious that he does not. Trapped and compelled as he has been all along, for him the air is empty and the window is blank. Why should Quint as a spectral presence appear to the governess and not to Miles? It may be precisely because the governess fears what Quint represents—adult sexuality, emotional maturity, and queer victimization of a kind she does not understand—but Miles understands the past not as a threat but as an opportunity. He has "said things" because Quint introduced him to a world beyond his years, perhaps, but that does not mean Miles sees any of this as evil. The governess can only imagine evil in such a relationship because her experience of emotional relations is so limited. She clearly prefers the tale of an otherworldly gothic haunting to the brutal reality of boyhood erotics that Miles comes so close to representing. Miles is confused to the point of torment because the governess wants to challenge him with a past that he sees as innocent. He did not say things to torment his friends; he said things because he liked them. Quint has not tormented him; he liked him. And the boy learned from Quint what it means for two males to be attached to each other emotionally. This may be more threatening than any sexual liaison they might have had. In the end, emotional bonds between men, love between men, is what is truly threatening. That kind of love looms up in this final scene, but the governess can see it only as evil. And as evil it has the power to destroy Miles, and that is exactly what it does.

Earlier in the tale the governess confronts Flora over her secret relation with Miss Jessel. In doing so she earns the child's undying hatred. Why would that be? In part the governess is guilty of literalizing a relation that is primarily emotional. Young girls who spend too much time together are hunted down, branded, and exposed.[11] Again the fear seems to be one of the girl's complicity. In the lakeside scene, where Flora plays at the side of the water while "Miss Jessel" glowers from the other side of the lake, the governess sees Jessel as "a figure of quite as unmistakeable horror and evil: a woman in black, pale and dreadful—with such an air also, and such a face!" (164). She feels this horror because her authority is threatened to be sure, but she also feels horror at the possibility that Flora sees and accepts this dark and threatening presence. That defies the governess's primary dictum: "I was there to protect and defend the little creatures in the world the most bereaved and the most loveable, the appeal of whose helplessness had become only too explicit, a deep, a constant ache of one's own committed heart" (161).

The governess's relation to the children is queer because she never fully admits the implicit erotics of her intense voyeuristic pleasure in their lives. Nor can she directly confront the erotic context of her original employment. She chooses to see ghosts—she is haunted, that is—because she is unwilling to confront the complex erotics of her position. She imagines these alternative competing sexual liaisons because they exonerate her in some way. At the same time, the possibility of what she has imagined haunts her. Rather than confront it directly, though, for her it is simply "queer." What torments her is being confronted by a world that exposes her limitations. As her anxiety grows so does the tension in the tale. "If he *were* innocent, what then on earth was *I*?" (233) is the story's central anxiety. What would constitute innocence in the world that James has described? It is impossible to tell. What could be more harrowing than that? And what could more clearly represent the basic tropes of twentieth-century psychoanalysis?

Shirley Jackson's *The Haunting of Hill House* tells a similar tale of a young single woman and the children who haunt her. In this case the children are ghosts in Hill House, the "deranged house" (70) in which Dr.

Montague and his three assistants have gathered to pursue the unknown.[12] Eleanor Vance is central among those assistants. The reader gets to know her inner life directly and to experience Hill House primarily from her perspective. Like James's governess at Bly, Eleanor is out of her depth in Hill House, and the dwelling seems determined to undermine her sense of self and challenge her deepest fears. As the novel develops, these fears are articulated in three ways: the first is Eleanor's attraction to Theodora, the fashionable and self-possessed lesbian who has been invited to Hill House on account of her powers or ESP; the second is Eleanor's guilt over her mother's death; and the third is her identification with the house and the horrors that it reveals.

Theodora is as different from Eleanor as she could be: "Duty and conscience were, for Theodora, attributes which belonged properly to the Girl Scouts. Theodora's world was one of delight and soft colors" (8). Theo attracts Eleanor from the moment they meet. Just after unpacking, as they are dressing to spend some time outdoors, "Theodora came through the bathroom door into Eleanor's room; she is lovely, Eleanor thought, turning to look; I wish I were lovely. Theodora was wearing a vivid yellow shirt, and Eleanor laughed and said, 'You bring more light into this room than the window'" (47). Eleanor's attraction to Theodora's brightness often includes this hint of self-denigration and self-effacement. Part of the attraction she feels is to the difference between them. Theodora is beautiful, well-dressed, and self-assured, all things that suggest an ability Eleanor feels she lacks. Eleanor does not feel beautiful or self-assured, to say the least, and her clothes are an embarrassment to her. Her deficiencies are glaring, at least to herself, and at moments like these a kind of erotic relation emerges from the space between herself and Theodora. Eleanor turns the seemingly playful difference violently against herself as the novel proceeds.

Dr. Montague, the vague scholar of the paranormal, has rented the house and assembled the company. Luke Sanderson, a representative of the family that owns the house, with Eleanor and Theodora makes up the little group. Dr. Montague is an avuncular presence throughout. Making notes and trying to look at the larger picture, he keeps his distance from the other three. Young Luke, however, is a ladies' man, and he creates an odd dynamic by playing on the affections of both Eleanor and Theodora. The erotic dynamic among Luke, Theodora, and Eleanor is a central feature of the narrative, but Luke's key function is to create tension between the women, which he manages to do without really trying.

The reader never gets any more than Eleanor's impressions of Theodora's feelings toward her. Eleanor's attraction is immediate and vivid: "she was always shy with strangers, awkward and timid, and yet had come in no more than half an hour to think of Theodora as close and vital, someone whose anger would be frightening" (49). At times, Theodora is sensitive and caring, and at others she is ruthless. In a scene just after Eleanor imagines Theodora's anger she is treated sweetly and Theodora seems to care about her: "Eleanor turned and stared, and then saw amusement on her face and thought, She's much braver than I am. Unexpectedly—although it was later to become a familiar note, a recognizable attribute of what was to mean 'Theodora' in Eleanor's mind—Theodora caught at Eleanor's thought, and answered her. 'Don't be so afraid all the time,' she said as she reached out to touch Eleanor's cheek with one finger. 'We never know where our courage is coming from'" (50). This intriguing scene measures the women's mutual desire in terms of Eleanor's fear and endless self-questioning. Theodora seems to understand in a way that allows her to care for her friend and offer her support. Eleanor's vulnerability is almost attractive to Theodora, at least it becomes the basis of their intimacy in this way. By reaching out to touch Eleanor's cheek, moreover, Theodora tries to instill some of her personal strength on the weak and soon-to-be suffering Eleanor.

This intimacy is repeated in the company of their two companions and in private moments. Sometimes Eleanor gets it wrong: "Theodora had abandoned any attempt at a chair and had put herself down on the hearthrug, cross-legged and drowsy. Eleanor, wanting to sit on the hearthrug beside her, had not thought of it in time and had condemned herself to one of the slippery chairs, unwilling now to attract attention by moving and getting herself awkwardly down onto the floor" (68). But at other times she and Theodora seem perfectly in tune.

> "I went to private school where they made me learn to curtsy."
>
> "I always had colds all winter long. My mother made me wear woolen stockings."
>
> "*My* mother made my brother take me to dances, and I used to curtsy like mad. My brother still hates me."
>
> "I fell down during the graduation procession."
>
> "I forgot my lines in the operetta."
>
> "I used to write poetry."
>
> "Yes," Theodora said, "I'm positive we're cousins."
>
> (53-54)

The ease with which Eleanor and Theodora converse and share details of the past, the intimacy of the revelations, and the painful memories they reveal all suggest that the women want to find some common ground on which they may be able to construct an intimacy in which they can believe. The scene takes place before the women have met the others, and as a result it places them in a special relation to each other that continues throughout the novel. They are always aware of each other and can commune without speaking in the social setting as well as the paranormal one. The two are often the same. Even at this moment, for instance, they are threatened by the unknown. No sooner do they reach out to each other but they notice something odd move across the grass. They are momentarily "frozen, shoulders pressed together." Their fear of something they cannot see punctuates this moment of intimacy with the threat of the unknown. Indeed, the closer the two women move to one another, the more threatening the house becomes.

The growing intimacy between the women is hinted even at moments when they seem violently at odds. After the words "HELP ELEANOR COME HOME" (146) are found scrawled on the hallway walls, for instance, Eleanor nearly (and quite understandably) breaks down. Theodora taunts and teases her ("Maybe you wrote it yourself," [147]) until Eleanor retorts violently, "Maybe it was only addressed to me because no possible appeal for help could get through that iron selfishness of yours; maybe I might have more sympathy and understanding in one minute than—" (147). It is a tense moment until it becomes clear that Theodora's intention was to create an angry response in Eleanor in order to expel her fear. Everyone seems able to laugh off the tension—all, that is, except Eleanor, who is hurt and confused. The brutal truths used here are painful, to be sure, but they are couched in the care that Theodora has taken all along. Eleanor's fear of her friend seems justified at first, and it is difficult for Eleanor to get beyond that.

Much later, after they have endured a great deal, Theodora and Eleanor meet and almost break through the difficulties that surround them:

> "Theo," Eleanor said awkwardly, "I'm no good at talking to people and saying things."
>
> Theodora laughed. "What *are* you good at?" she demanded. "Running away?"
>
> Nothing irrevocable had yet been spoken, but there was only the basest margin of safety left them; each of them moving delicately along the outskirts of an open question, and once spoken, such a question—as "Do you love me?"—could never be answered or forgotten. They walked slowly, meditating, wondering, and the path sloped down from their feet and they followed, walking side by side in the most extreme intimacy of expectation; their feinting and hesitation done with, they could only await passively for resolution. Each knew, almost within a breath, what the other was thinking and wanting to say; each of them almost wept for the other. They perceived at the same moment the change in the path and each knew then the other's knowledge of it; Theodora took Eleanor's arm and, ahead of them the path widened and blackened and curved.
>
> (174-75)

In the midst of the horrors of Hill House these women find each other. This scene makes it seem as if they are on the verge of expressing mutual love. The emphasis on expectation and knowledge, on meditation and meaning, and on walking in tandem on a path in the woods are all elements that suggest desire thwarted by circumstance, an intimacy that would be realized were it not for other developments that seem determined to destroy it. "Do you love me?" are the words never spoken. Hill House ensures that they are not.[13]

Hill House does so, it seems, by revealing the deeply buried guilt Eleanor feels about her mother's death. At the opening of the novel the reader is told that Eleanor had lived with her mother and cared for her until the older woman's death. The connection between that event and the horrors of Hill House becomes apparent the first time the group goes exploring. Dr. Montague stops them at the front door to show them the library that opens off the front hall: "Then the Doctor said, 'Now *here* is something none of you anticipated,' and he opened a small door tucked in beside the tall front door and stood back, smiling. 'The library,' he said, 'in the tower.' 'I can't go in there,' Eleanor said, surprising herself, but she could not. She backed away, overwhelmed with the cold air of mold and earth which rushed at her. 'My mother—' she said, not knowing what she wanted to tell them, and pressed herself against the wall" (163). Whether her sense of loss, her anger, her unresolved feelings about the death, or her fear of her mother or her mother's corpse, something causes Eleanor to connect the graveyard smell with the mother. Readers familiar with gothic fiction are forced to ask whether the mother is walled up in the house in some literal or figural way.

When supernatural events start to enliven things even further, which happens most dramatically when something starts pounding on all the bedroom doors in the middle of the night, these fears become more vividly realized. When Eleanor first hears the knocking and someone calling her name she assumes that it is her mother calling:

> "Coming, mother, coming," Eleanor said, fumbling for the light. "It's all right, I'm coming." *Eleanor,* she heard, *Eleanor.* "Coming, coming," she shouted irritably, "just a *minute,* I'm *coming.*"
>
> "Eleanor?"
>
> Then she thought, with a crashing shock which brought her awake, cold and shivering, out of bed and awake: *I am in Hill House.*
>
> "What?" she cried out, "What? Theodora?"
>
> "Eleanor? In here." . . .
>
> "Something is knocking on the doors," Theodora said in a tone of pure rationality.

"That's all. And it's down near the other end of the hall. Luke and the doctor are probably there already, to see what is going on." Not at all like my mother knocking on the wall. I was dreaming again.

(127-28)

Eleanor connects the banging to her mother's knock and then feels that the fear she experiences is something alive. What she feels so intensely, however, is guilt that her mother's death has bequeathed her. The connection between Theodora and her mother is subtle but unmistakable. At first she thinks it is her mother when it is actually Theodora calling; even when she enters Theodora's room she is not sure what she is doing there. At the same time the women are thrown together violently to experience the banging, and as at other horrifying moments in the book they remain calm and in close touch.

Later, Eleanor expresses guilt about her mother more or less openly: "'It was my fault my mother died,' Eleanor said. 'She knocked on the wall and called me and called me and I never woke up. I ought to have brought her the medicine; I always did before. But this time she called me and I never woke up.' 'You should have forgotten all that by now,' Theodora said. 'I've wondered ever since if I did wake up. If I did wake up and hear her, and if I just went back to sleep. It would have been easy, and I've wondered about it'" (212). One source of the haunting of Hill House, then, is this tormenting guilt about her mother's death. Eleanor imagines this moment of transgression almost as if she needs guilt to give meaning to her existence.

When Mrs. Montague arrives to prepare everyone for communing with spirits, the planchette she uses spells out "Eleanor come home." Mrs. Montague is certain that she is hearing from a nun who must have been connected with Hill House, someone trapped in the house: "'I daresay she was walled up alive,' Mrs. Montague said. 'The nun I mean. They always did that, you know. You've no idea the messages I've gotten from nuns walled up alive'" (189). Invoking that same gothic tradition that James does in *The Turn of the Screw,* in other words, Mrs. Montague understands what kinds of mysteries haunt the female imagination. The connection between a nun walled up alive and the messages to Eleanor suggest that the house calls her out of a private guilt and into itself.

Eleanor feels she is becoming part of the house—or the house is becoming part of her—from the beginning of her sojourn there. "I don't think we could leave now if we wanted to" she tells the group after their first conversation about the history of the house (75). Later, when she hears that two young girls grew up in the house, she has a hard time imagining children there. But her name is written on the wall and appears in

other ways as well, so she feels the house is calling out to her. The most dramatic instance occurs when Eleanor finds her name splashed in blood on Theodora's bedroom walls and clothes:

Moving quickly, Eleanor ran into the hall and to Theodora's doorway, to stop aghast, looking over Theodora's shoulder. "What *is* it," she whispered.

"What does it *look* like, you fool?"

And I won't forgive her *that,* either, Eleanor thought concretely through her bewilderment. "It looks like paint," she said hesitantly. "Except the smell is awful."

"It's blood," said Theodora with finality. She clung to the door, swaying as the door moved, staring. "Blood," she said, "All over. Do you see it?"

(153)

Soon after this first encounter, when Dr. Montague and Luke have joined them, they notice writing on the wall: "All of them stood in silence for a moment and looked at HELP ELEANOR COME HOME ELEANOR written in shaky red letters on the wallpaper over Theodora's bed. . . . The smell was atrocious, and the writing on the wall had dripped and splattered. There was a line of drops from the wall to the wardrobe—perhaps that was what had first turned Theodora's attention that way—and a great irregular stain on the green rug" (155). As gruesome as any image in this novel, this blood-spattered room suggests the violence of homicidal rage that smolders beneath the surface of relations here. Eleanor does not perhaps want to spatter Theodora's blood on the walls, but she does let jealousy and desire torment her to excess. Moreover, her relation to her mother and her sister was one of hatred: "Eleanor Vance was thirty-two years old when she came to Hill House. The only person in the world she genuinely hated, now that her mother was dead, was her sister. She disliked her brother-in-law and her five-year-old niece, and she had no friends" (6). Perhaps the familial intimacy of the plea for her return is written in blood because that is what the family represents to her. She thought that Hill House was an escape from that world, but it seems more and more to be a return to it.

In *Powers of Horror* Julia Kristeva describes this state as abjection, a term that describes Eleanor's demeanor. For Kristeva, "There looms, within abjection, one of those violent, dark revolts of being, directed against a threat that seems to emanate from an exorbitant outside or inside, ejected beyond the scope of the possible, the tolerable, the thinkable. It lies there, quite close, but it cannot be assimilated. It beseeches, it worries, it fascinates desire."[14] Here the house beseeches and worries and fascinates. It creates an abjection into which Eleanor fits like hand in glove. As the house calls to Eleanor she feels that she must answer:

"Those letters spelled out *my* name, and none of you know what that feels like—it's so *familiar.*" And she gestured to them almost in appeal. "Try to *see,*" she said. "It's my own dear name, and it belongs to me, and something is using it and writing it and calling me with it and my own *name*. . . ." She stopped and said, looking from one of them to another, even down onto Theodora's face looking up at her, "Look. There's only one of me, and it's all I've got. I *hate* seeing myself dissolve and slip and separate so that I am living in one half, my mind, and I see the other half of me help-less and frantic and driven and I can't stop it, but I know I'm not really going to be hurt and yet time is so long and even a second goes on and on and I could stand any of it if only I could surrender—."

"*Surrender?*" said the doctor sharply, and Eleanor stared.

"Surrender?" Luke repeated.

"I don't know," Eleanor said, perplexed. I was just talking along, she told herself, I was saying some-thing—what was I just saying?

(160)

Eleanor wants to surrender to the house because she thinks she has no choice. She gives in to the voices calling her because she feels in her heart that she does not deserve the freedom she has started to feel. In this sense she is like James's governess and Miles or Flora. She is the one who is afraid of the implications of her desire. She both feels the desire and knows that she must stop doing so. A key moment in this transition is when Eleanor thinks it is Theodora's hand she grips as they hear voices in the night:

Eleanor took a breath, wondering if she could speak now, and then she heard a little soft cry which broke her heart, a little infinitely sad cry, a little sweet moan of wild sadness. It is a *child,* she thought with disbe-lief, a child is crying somewhere, and then, upon that thought, came the wild shrieking voice she had never heard before and yet knew she had heard it in her night-mares. . . .

Now, Eleanor thought, perceiving that she was lying sideways on the bed in black darkness, holding with both hands to Theodora's hand, holding so tight that she could feel the fine bones of Theodora's fingers, now, I will not endure this. They think to scare me. Well, they have. I am scared, but more than that, I am a person, I am human. I am a walking reasoning hu-morous human being and I will take a lot from this lu-natic filthy house but I will not go along with hurting a child, no, I will not; I will by God get my mouth to open right now and I will yell I will I will yell "STOP IT," she shouted, and the lights were on the way they had left them and Theodora was sitting up in bed, startled and disheveled.

"What?" Theodora was saying. "What, Nell? What?"

"Good God," Eleanor said, flinging herself out of bed and across the room to stand shuddering in a corner, "God God—whose hand was I holding?"

(162-63)

The child's voice seems to emerge from Eleanor's imagination in some way. The familiar nightmare shrieking she hears seems to be something from her own past as well. Is the suffering child herself in some way? Does she hear the cry of a solitary child in pain because that is what she feels? These questions pale be-side the central question that Eleanor asks, Whose hand was she holding? The point seems to be that although she imagines she is gripping Theodora tightly, she is actually gripping something out of the nightmare of confused identity that the house has become for her. In other words, the house emerges from her consciousness (subconscious?) to substitute itself as an object of de-sire and lure her to her demise. Eleanor finds herself at home because her repressed past returns in vivid clarity.

This end takes place in two parts. In the first, Eleanor sneaks out of her room at night and makes her way down to the library and up the rickety stairs to the top of the tower. Just before she makes her playful dash through the house she hears the sound of children sing-ing at their games: "Go walking through the val-ley. . . . Go in and out the windows. . . . Go forth and face your lover, / As we have done before" (225-26). It is almost in the spirit of this children's game that she runs around the dark house, seeking her mother and avoiding her friends as they desperately search for her. "I have broken the spell of Hill House," she tells her-self, "and somehow come inside" (232). When they fi-nally find her at the top of the tower they panic, and as Luke climbs up to help her down there is general disap-proval of her behavior.

When the next morning she is told to go home, she panics. Not wanting to leave, she pleads with the doctor to allow her stay: "The doctor took her by the arm and, with Luke beside her, led her to the car and opened the door for her. The carton was still on the back seat, her suitcase was on the floor, her coat and pocketbook on the seat; Luke had left the motor running. 'Doctor,' Eleanor said, clutching at him, 'Doctor.' 'I'm sorry,' he said. 'Good-bye.' 'You can't just *make* me go,' she said wildly. 'You *brought* me here'" (243). Her need to stay at Hill House is expressed by her desperate and suc-cessful attempt to crash her car into a tree along the drive and so kill herself. Even at the end, however, she is confused between the house and her need to become part of it and her new friends and her emotional and erotic attachment to them: "In the unending, crashing second before the car hurled into the tree, she thought clearly, *Why* am I doing this? Why am I doing this? Why don't they stop me?" (245-46).

The friends do not rush out to stop Eleanor because they know she does not belong in their world. Her so-lipsistic experience is brought into the fulfillment that the house has promised from the first. Eleanor accepts the hysteria that friends and family have assumed. At Hill House she is able to give it form. In hurtling her-self at the tree she accepts what it means. Desire, for Eleanor, is nothing more than death.

The first two of Foucault's "four great strategic unities"—"1. *A hysterization of women's bodies*" and "2. *A pedagogization of children's sex*"—come into vivid focus here.[15] *The Turn of the Screw* and *The Haunting of Hill House* both reveal the relation between the first and second "unities" Foucault describes and the degree to which hysteria and gender emerge naturally from gothic works like these. Gothic fiction, in other words, participates in the formation of "specific mechanisms of knowledge and power." Or perhaps it is more correct to say that gothic fiction sees through these mechanisms and invokes them for affective force at the same time that it exposes their limitations.

The Turn of the Screw and *The Haunting of Hill House* suggest that gothic novelists were at least as adept as Freud at exposing the workings of hysterical response. Indeed, in some ways the novelists make the cultural terms of female victimization clearer than Freud did. James's governess and Jackson's Eleanor Vance are victims because they are put in situations that are outside of their control. The world of desire confounds them. Abject and isolated, they confront the darkness that haunts them, but in the end it consumes them. They cannot accept intimacy because intimacy is exactly what haunts them in the first place. In that sense they each understand intimacy as something that threatens to destroy them. Had Freud understood that, the history of twentieth-century psychiatric treatment might have been different. The almost overly familiar gothic trope of the persecuted female imbues these outwardly neurotic women with a depth and a complexity they would otherwise lack.

These are not "case studies" because both fictions invoke the richness of the gothic tradition, and in doing so they tell a more complex story than any that emerges from strict psychosexology. Both James and Jackson use the energy of the gothic tradition to confront their heroines with a world beyond themselves. The results are rich because so many gothic heroines have paved the way for these intrepid heroines. The novelists invoke contemporary psychological interpretations of the neurotic mind, and they also invoke a tradition that goes deeper than twentieth-century psychology could ever allow itself to go.

Notes

I would like to thank my colleague Joseph Childers for his comments and suggestions for this chapter.

1. Studies of "The Turn of the Screw" that have informed this discussion include Ronnie Baillie, *The Fantastic Anatomist: A Psychoanalytic Study of Henry James* (Amsterdam-Atlanta: Rodopi Press, 2000), ch. 4, "Autopsy: *The Turn of the Screw*"; Ellis Hansen, "Screwing with Children in Henry James," *GLQ: A Journal of Lesbian and Gay Studies* 9, no. 3 (2003): 367-91; Stanley Renner, "Sexual Hysteria, Physiognomical Bogeymen, and the 'Ghosts' in *The Turn of the Screw*," *Nineteenth-Century Literature* 43, no. 2 (1988): 175-94; Allan Lloyd Smith, "A Word Kept Back in *The Turn of the Screw*," *Victorian Literature and Culture*, edited by John Maynard and Adrienne Auslander Munich (New York: AMS Press, 1996): 24: 139-57; and Elton E. Smith, "Pedophiles amidst Looming Portentousness: Henry James's *The Turn of the Screw*," in *The Haunted Mind: The Supernatural in Victorian Fiction*, edited by Robert Haas and Elton E. Smith (Lanham: Rowman and Littlefield, 1999), 123-30.

2. Henry James, *The Turn of the Screw*, in *The Portable Henry James*, edited by John Auchard (New York: Penguin, 2004), 137-235; further references in the text are to this edition.

3. Of course the reference might also apply to Charlotte Brontë's *Jane Eyre*, but James refers all the way back to Radcliffe herself. Brontë would have provided a more immediate and more accessible reference for James's readers.

4. Claire Kahane, "The Gothic Mirror," in *The Mother Tongue: Essays in Feminist Psychoanalytic Interpretation*, edited by Shirley Nelson Garner, Claire Kahane, and Madelon Sprengnether (Ithaca: Cornell University Press, 1985), 339.

5. Hansen, "Screwing with Children in Henry James," 372-73.

6. Ibid. In this context see James R. Kincaid, *Child-Loving: The Erotic Child and Victorian Literature* (New York: Routledge, 1994).

7. See especially Hugh Stevens, "Homoeroticism, Identity, and Agency in James's Late Tales," in *Enacting History in Henry James: Narrative, Power, and Ethics*, edited by Gert Buelens (New York: Cambridge University Press, 1997), 126-47. Stevens pays special attention to the force of the term *queer*. "There is, of course," Stevens says, "dispute as to whether 'queer' might have had a homosexual connotation for James at the turn of the century. The *OED* lists 1922 as the first date of this usage, which would, however, almost certainly have enjoyed considerable oral circulation before occurring in writing. It may be that James used 'queer' precisely because its connotation with 'homosexual' is tentative and uncertain. . . . Recent commentators who have argued that 'queer' already had homosexual connotations in the late nineteenth century include Elaine Showalter, in *Sexual Anarchy: Gender and Culture at the Fin de Siècle* (New York: Viking Press, 1990), 111-12;

Wayne Koestenbaum, in *Double Talk: The Erotics of Male Literary Collaboration* (New York: Routledge, 1989); and Joseph Bristow, in *Effeminate England: Homoerotic Writing after 1885* (Buckingham: Open University Press, 1995), 145n10. See also Eric Haralson, *Henry James and Queer Modernity* (New York: Cambridge University Press, 2003), 5-8. For Haralson, "One can no more pin down the first instance in which *queer* meant '(a) homosexual' in Anglo-American discourse than one can say 'modernity' commenced on or about December 1910, as in Virginia Woolf's famous formula" (9).

8. Patricia White, "Female Spectator, Lesbian Specter: *The Haunting*," in *Inside/Out: Lesbian Theories, Gay Theories,* edited by Diana Fuss (New York: Routledge, 1991), 142-72, quotation on 149. The internal reference is to Sigmund Freud, "The Uncanny" (1919), in *Art and Literature,* edited by Albert Dickson (Harmondsworth: Penguin, 1985), 335-76.

9. Mary Ann Doane, *The Desire to Desire: The Woman's Film of the 1940s* (Bloomington: Indiana University Press, 1987), 157.

10. For a succinct summary of this approach see Philip Brett, "Britten's Bad Boys: Male Relations in *The Turn of the Screw*," *repercussions* 1 (1992): 5-25, reprinted in *Music and Sexuality in Britten: Selected Essays of Philip Brett,* edited by George E. Haggerty (Berkeley: University of California Press, forthcoming).

11. The locus classicus of the danger of such relations is the account to be found in Sheridan Le Fanu's vampire story "Carmilla."

12. Shirley Jackson, *The Haunting of Hill House* (1959, repr. Harmondsworth: Penguin, 1984); further references in the text are to this edition.

13. Although Patricia White's article remains the richest discussion of lesbianism in the film version of the novel, her insights are too genre-specific to be quotable in this context, but I recommend the essay nonetheless. For a discussion of Jackson's attitude toward the novel ("I am always afraid of being alone") see S. T. Joshi, "Shirley Jackson: Domestic Horror," *Studies in Weird Fiction* 14 (1994): 9-28.

14. Julia Kristeva, *Powers of Horror: An Essay on Abjection,* translated by Leon S. Roudiez (New York: Columbia University Press, 1982), 1, see also 90-112 on the figure of death.

15. Michel Foucault, *The History of Sexuality,* vol. 1: *An Introduction,* translated by Robert Hurley (New York: Vintage-Random House, 1980), 103, 104-5.

LITERARY AND THEMATIC CONNECTIONS

Thomas H. Keeling (essay date 1980)

SOURCE: Keeling, Thomas H. "Science Fiction and the Gothic." In *Bridges to Science Fiction,* edited by George E. Slusser, George R. Guffey, and Mark Rose, pp. 107-19. Carbondale: Southern Illinois University Press, 1980.

[*In the following essay, Keeling draws parallels between Gothic and science fiction as he compares M. G. Lewis's* The Monk *and Philip K. Dick's* Ubik.]

Critical histories of science fiction usually link the development of this genre with that of the gothic novel. Tracing the genealogies of modern robots and androids through the labyrinths of gothic nightmare, scholars invariably lead us into Victor Frankenstein's "workshop of filthy creation"; in Hawthorne's "Birthmark" and "Rappaccini's Daughter," they find prototypes of the modern "man of science," the hero-villain of so much science fiction. Similarly, works such as Poe's *Narrative of Arthur Gordon Pym,* Stevenson's *Dr. Jekyll and Mr. Hyde,* and Wells' *Island of Dr. Moreau* frequently find their way into studies of both gothic and science fiction. Contemporary science fiction writers, moreover, appear to be fascinated by the gothic, as illustrated by the success with which Walter Miller, in *A Canticle for Leibowitz,* Ursula Le Guin, in *The Left Hand of Darkness,* and Stanislaw Lem, in *Solaris,* integrate traditional gothic motifs into science fiction narratives.

Recognition of the historical ties and apparent structural similarities that link these two genres has led a number of critics to speak of science fiction as if it were simply an "updated" gothic form that appeals to the same fantasies and expectations as the earlier gothic. Brian Aldiss asserts that science fiction, born of the gothic mode, "is hardly free of it now."[1] Both forms deal in enchantment and nightmare, he suggests, and both employ methods of narrative distancing, the only real difference being that gothicists set their fantasies in the past—usually in the Catholic south—while science fiction writers project their fantasies into future worlds, alien worlds, or alternate worlds. Leslie Fiedler offers the same argument and actually refers to science fiction as a "neogothic" form.[2] For such critics, the themes and motifs of science fiction are merely a futuristic displacement of the gothic: the old sorcerers become the modern physicists; demonic possession becomes telepathic control; corpses, once animated supernaturally, are now rejuvenated with the help of cryogenics; and time travel renders superfluous the elaborate rites once used to conjure up the spirits of the dead.

These suggestive surface-level parallels may be more clearly illustrated in a brief examination of two specific novels, M. G. Lewis's classic eighteenth-century romance *The Monk* and Philip Dick's *Ubik*. Rather than provide lengthy plot summaries of these two works, I shall move quickly to some of the more important structural, conceptual, and aesthetic parallels. Here it is sufficient to observe that *The Monk* is a weave of two tales, the first being that of a Capuchin monk, Ambrosio, whose sexual obsession weakens his resistence to demonic influence, leads him to commit "inhuman" crimes, and eventually precipitates his destruction. The subplot centers on two tormented lovers, Raymond and Agnes; while Raymond fights to free himself from the physical and psychological hold of an ancient specter called the "Bleeding Nun," Agnes endures excruciating torture in the subterranean tombs of a convent. Philip Dick's *Ubik* focuses on the hero's struggle to survive the chaos created by individuals possessing extraordinary psychic abilities and by the curious mental state known as "half-life," which results when people are frozen immediately after death.

The plots of both novels hinge upon the intervention of beings endowed with apparently supernatural powers. As a grisly phantom from Raymond's ancestral past, the Bleeding Nun is clearly a true supernatural, demonic agent, as are the Wandering Jew, whose exorcism frees Raymond, and Matilda, the demonic *femme fatale* who unleashes Ambrosio's suppressed sexual appetite. In *Ubik* the characters' frightening psychic abilities (including telepathy and precognition) result from an advance in human evolution. Jory, the half-lifer who is the ultimate "demon" in this story, seems to be a transformed gothic monster, not only in his strange cannibalism (reminiscent of the vampire's), but also in such physical traits as his pointed teeth and incongruous facial features.

The second and more significant parallel lies in the way these characters use their powers to violate those basic experiential premises we normally take for granted. By penetrating into the minds of others in order to influence their perception and behavior, the Bleeding Nun, Matilda, and Ambrosio all represent a threat to the long-cherished concept of the self as a discrete and inviolable category, just as Jory and the telepaths do in *Ubik*. Moreover, in both novels the violation of self produces temporal and spatial disorientation and an overall sense of what Wolfgang Kayser, speaking of the aesthetics of the grotesque, calls "alienation and estrangement."[3]

This transgression of boundaries normally considered discrete is usually accompanied by physical grotesquerie, which is the third major respect in which *The Monk* and *Ubik* resemble each other. In one of the most graphically grotesque scenes of Lewis' tale, Agnes awakens in darkness, grasps something soft, and advances it toward her: "In spite of its putridity, and the worms which preyed upon it, I perceived a corrupted human head."[4] Starving in a subterranean vault, she later clings tenaciously to the decaying, worm-infested corpse of her own infant. Scarcely less "gothic" are Philip Dick's descriptions of the remains of Jory's victims, dehydrated, almost mummified heaps of bones with leering, paper-like skulls and recessed eyes.[5]

These glances at *The Monk* and *Ubik* underscore the fact that gothic and science fiction may also share a common reader appeal. It does not follow from these observations, however, that science fiction is simply a neogothic form—that aside from the substitution of a fear of the future for a fear of the past, the narrative "formula" is essentially the same in both genres. Science fiction is not, in fact, an updated and disguised form of gothicism. In order to isolate the actual generic differences that separate gothic and science fiction, we must penetrate beyond the observable surface-level types and paraphernalia—the relentless and mysterious villains, the deranged scientists, the haunted castles, the starships, the ray guns, and the trap doors. They, after all, are but the "signs" by which we recognize these genres; they recur only because they are among the necessary correlates of other, deeper structures or because they most readily and convincingly image forth those underlying laws and conditions that truly define the fictional worlds of gothic and science fiction. If we are indeed looking at two distinct genres, then on the level of structural and aesthetic premises we expect to find some essential differences beneath the many suggestive but finally accidental similarities.

I. The first constant in the generic paradigm that defines the older genre, the gothic novel, is the presence of one or more "demonic agents," characters whose obsession (or "possession") radically restricts their vision and behavior, giving them the appearance of being driven by forces alien and external to them.[6] Demonic agents may be possessed by a certain "ruling passion" (lust, in the case of Ambrosio) or by a particular belief or image that becomes an *idée fixe* (as in the cases of Victor Frankenstein and Hawthorne's Aylmer). Of course, they may also be possessed by actual supernatural forces; for example, Ambrosio's psychological obsessions facilitate actual "possession" by the demon, Matilda, and eventually by Lucifer himself. Natural and supernatural types of possession function simultaneously in *The Monk* and in most other major gothic novels to produce a pattern of behavior that may be human in kind, but that is demonic in intensity and force.

Like St. Anthony and other ascetics, the demonic agent tends to generate his world around him. Action and setting are therefore largely the exteriorization of internal nightmare and obsession. Schedoni's shadowy machinations in Mrs. Radcliffe's *Italian* reveal more about the obsessed mind of Ellena, the heroine through whose fears we experience the events of the novel, than about Schedoni himself. Indeed, to the extent that the persecuted maiden creates the gothic villain out of her subconscious fears and desires, she is her own persecutor. So too, the nightmarish *Doppelgänger* of gothic fiction usually originates in the hidden recesses of the demonic agent's psyche. The images of decay, the haunted—seemingly animistic—landscapes, and the labyrinthine systems of vaults and passageways that recur frequently in gothic fiction are, on another level, metaphors revealing the interior landscape of the demonic agent.

Demonic agency *may* occur in any prose genre, including science fiction. (Indeed, Angus Fletcher has even suggested that the perfect agent is not a man possessed by a "daemon," but a robot such as Talus or those in Capek's RUR.)[7] Manipulated by forces completely beyond his comprehension or control, this kind of agent becomes little more than a puppet. In *Ubik* we happen to have a kind of demonic agent in the character of Jory, who is actually described as a monster in his attack on Joe Chips, the hero, and who is quite capable of engulfing others in a strange, projected world of his own.

However, demonic agency is not an essential element in science fiction, as it is in the gothic paradigm. The fictional world projected in science fiction, unlike that of the gothic, is not necessarily the revelation of hidden fear, nightmare, or supernatural force; more often it is the visual analogue for a configuration of abstract, philosophical ideas or an extrapolation based upon a given system or condition. In Le Guin's *Dispossessed,* for example, the model established with the contrasting worlds of Urras and Anarres reflects contrasting political, social, and philosophical points of view. Shevek, whose purpose is to reunite these two cultures, never approaches the inflexible, monomaniacal archetype of the demonic agent. Nor do we find demonic agency as a controlling vision or narrative device in works such as Larry Niven's *Ringworld* or Philip Dick's *Man in the High Castle,* where the focus is again on a particular matrix of ideas rather than on the expression of a single obsessed or possessed psyche.

When possession does occur in science fiction, moreover, it is frequently only a narrative device or embellishment. Consider Stapledon's *Last and First Men,* in which the speaker is a disembodied intelligence of the distant future who has "possessed," or "inspired," the twentieth-century man who is writing the narrative. Significantly, the novel does not focus on this possession at all; Stapledon refers to it as a "device": "only by some such trick could I do justice to the conviction that our whole present mentality is but a confused and halting first experiment."[8] "Mentality" here refers to that of the race or culture, for Stapledon's aim is "myth" in the cultural sense—not the exploration of an individual psyche. When such possession occurs in the gothic, as it does in Hogg's *Confessions* and in the Bleeding Nun episode of *The Monk,* it becomes the actual subject or focus rather than a "device" in Stapledon's sense. Demonic agency, an essential element of the gothic, is merely an accidental feature in science fiction, not one of the genre's structural prerequisites.

II. The gothic universe in which agents function is pandeterministic, and pandeterminism is the second constant in gothic fiction. In its most abstract sense, pandeterminism signifies that "the limit between the physical and the mental, between matter and spirit, between word and thing, ceases to be impervious."[9] Pandeterminism implies an unseen causal system in which relations exist on all levels, thus subverting our normal expectations of cause and effect; it is this aspect of the gothic that we call the "supernatural." A pandeterministic world is one in which the categories of experience that we regard as discrete (self and not-self, dream and reality, animate and inanimate, human and animal, and so on) become penetrable, their boundaries vulnerable to transgression. In such a world all causes and, therefore, all events, are related to one another by strict laws that are never fully revealed. The corollary to pandeterminism is thus pansignification; since relations exist on all levels, among all elements of the world, this world becomes highly significant—everything is charged with meaning: a blood-stained dagger, a lost manuscript, an offhand allusion to an heir presumed dead, a physiognomical resemblance—all details are significant and somehow related to one another.

In the gothic novel pandeterminism means that the relations between events defy both human logic and empirical cause and effect. We may "feel" as if events were linked by some divine or infernal logic, but this causation is beyond the laws of nature and altogether unknowable. No advance in physics or parapsychology will "explain" Lorenzo's prophetic dream, in which he sees Antonia ravished and destroyed by an enormous fire-breathing form. We cannot cite a new discovery in geriatrics to explain the mystery of the Wandering Jew, nor can we explain in empirical or psychological terms how his bizarre exorcism succeeds in ridding Raymond of the curse of the Bleeding Nun. The sciences of statistics and probability theory, even if they were perfected, could not account for the incredible series of coincidences that toss Raymond into the skeletal arms of the Bleeding Nun, who, as it turns out, is really the ghost of his grandfather's great-aunt. Nor could they explain why, of all the girls in the world, Antonia should be the one Ambrosio torments, rapes, and murders; Antonia, we discover, is really Ambrosio's sister, a fact that Lucifer reveals to Ambrosio in the final pages of the novel. We may, of course, discover the psychological or ethical "meaning" of such relations and patterns of causation, but the "how" remains mysterious and unknowable by definition. The violations and transgressions occur or appear to occur in outright defiance of our empirically determined experiential categories, without any pretension that they can be rationally understood.

Causation of this sort has no real place in science fiction, though it often seems to. In science fiction, as in the gothic, the categories of time and space are violated constantly. Wells' hero does so by means of a time machine, rocket commandos of space opera freely teleport themselves throughout the universe, and in *The Sirens of Titan* a strange "Chronosynclastic Infundibula" results in amazing leaps through time and space. Clearly, many of these "miracles" are no less implausible than Ambrosio's magic myrtle or his demon-assisted escape from the dungeons of the Inquisition. In order to distinguish action and causation in the gothic from action and causation in science fiction, we must look not to the events themselves—for they are equally fabulous—but to the rhetoric employed to account for these events.

Even in Anne Radcliffe's so-called Explained Supernatural, the aesthetics of terror (always related to the sublime and the grotesque) depend upon the impression that the natural laws and categories have been suspended—that dark, demonic forces have intruded into the natural world. Science fiction, on the other hand, relies upon the premise that all events—no matter how fantastic—have natural, that is, empirical or "scientific" causes. Consider the apparent pandeterminism of *Ubik*, where Philip Dick rivals any gothicist in his violations of the categories of time and self. Pat Conley's "talent" enables her not only to see alternate futures, "laid out side by side like cells in a beehive," but actually to change the past and, therefore, the present according to her needs or her whims. That her victim may be shifted from one existence to another without ever knowing it is a kind of violation far more radical than Matilda's manipulation of Ambrosio. Yet Dick demands that his readers accept the acquisition of such amazing talents and antitalents as a natural step in the evolution of the species.

Futhermore, the temporal disorientation experienced by Joe Chips is even more frightening than the demonic penetration of the past into the present that we find in the Bleeding Nun episode of *The Monk*; it is actually a deterioration of the present into archaic forms—a massive assault on the entire fabric of our physical and psychological existence. Yet neither Joe nor the reader is ever tempted to assume supernatural causation; the causes may be unknown, but they are not altogether beyond science. We soon discover that much of what Joe experiences is the result of his being in half-life and of being subjected to Jory's unusual powers. Even when there is no satisfying answer whatsoever—as in Lem's

Solaris and *The Investigation*, both novels concerned with the process of seeking answers to the unanswerable—we are not invited to conclude that causation is supernatural, only that our mental sets are inadequate, finally insufficient in dealing with the cosmos. In spite of many provocative but accidental similarities between the events in gothic and science fiction, the two genres differ in their essential causal premises.

III. The third constant in gothic fiction concerns the moral axis, the ethical perspective that the genre accepts, either implicitly or explicitly. Whatever is perceived as "alien" here—whatever seems to intrude into the otherwise stable and usually bourgeois world—is always perceived as "evil" as well. Behind demonic agency, behind gothic pandeterminism, and behind the grotesqueries of the gothic landscape, we inevitably encounter a vertical, dualistic, Manichaean world view, which, regardless of how complex the psychology or aesthetics may be, ultimately resolves the conflict in terms of good and evil. Obviously true of *The Castle of Otranto*, Radcliffe's romances, and *The Monk*, it is also true of such complex works as *The Turn of the Screw* and *Absalom, Absalom!*, where the old demons have been transformed and internalized or have retreated into the landscape.

This moral perspective has no necessary place in science fiction, however, where schisms are more likely to develop between the sterile and the generative, human logic and alien logic, "nature" and "science," man and science, or between contrasting socioeconomic and cultural systems rather than between absolute good and evil. Where would we locate absolute good and absolute evil in *The Dispossessed*? Though Le Guin cannot conceal implicit judgments regarding the relative merits of the cultures of Urras and Anarres, those judgments cannot be expressed in absolute moral terms. The interest in alternate worlds in Philip Dick's *Man in the High Castle* is speculative rather than normative, and man's urge to explain and evaluate reality in moral terms is effectively parodied in such works as *The War of the Worlds*, *The Sirens of Titan*, and *The Investigation*, where chance, evolution, Brownian motion, and whimsy replace the Christian moral order so essential to the gothic. Even in *Ubik*, where Pat Conley and Jory appear almost demonic at times, the conflicts between the Psis and the Norms and between Jory and the other half-lifers are formulated in terms of survival and adaptation rather than in terms of absolute good and evil.

The "evil" alien in gothic fiction is a form of chaos that disrupts the "good" and stable norm. Indeed, the plots of almost all early gothic romances, including *The Monk*, progress toward the restoration of order. The element of chaos (evil), although it is usually manifested in supernatural agency and causation and grotesque imagery, is almost invariably historical or psychological in origin. It threatens always to destroy or transform the positive norm, which is generally bourgeois in values and expectations. Chastity and "virtuous" love and marriage, cleanliness, financial security, the family, Christian ethics, and a kind of psychological sanctity and commonsense hold on reality—these are the values the gothicist must defend, however insincerely or ineffectively. Essentially conservative in its fear of the past, its fear of subconscious desires (a fear ironically at odds with the genre's effects and techniques), and its fear of innovations that might breed chaos, gothic fiction is an ideal form for the exploration of different psychological states and aesthetic points of view. However, its underlying values and perspectives generally render it useless as a vehicle for treating larger systems or problems of a sociological, economic, political, scientific, or philosophical nature.

If the gothic is a fundamentally conservative genre in this respect, science fiction can be viewed as potentially "subversive" insofar as it is not restricted to a moral vision of the world, and certainly not to a conventional Christian interpretation of reality. Furthermore, the science fiction writer, unlike the gothicist, has no necessary commitment to bourgeois reality as it is. In fact, the disrupting alien elements may actually be seen as part of an inevitable and desirable change. In Sturgeon's *More Than Human* and in Clarke's *Childhood's End,* for example, the emergence of "Homo Gestalt," supplanting "normal" humanity, represents a greater perfection of the species. The gothicist would regard Homo Gestalt as a physical and moral threat to the accepted norm, a manifestation of something indisputably evil. Lester del Rey asks that his Homo Mechanensis, "Helen O'Loy," be accepted as an "ideal" woman; for the gothicist, on the other hand, automata, puppets, and doubles figure among the most grotesque and threatening of all demonic creations.

Of course, the science fiction writer may adhere strictly to a good-versus-evil, hero-versus-villain moral perspective. This frequently results in futuristic "Cowboys and Indians" à la *Battlestar Galactica.* Where the absolute moral vision survives untransformed and unassailed in science fiction, we are not surprised to find ourselves trudging through naïve alien-invasion stories of the comic-book variety or space opera of the sort Harry Harrison parodies in "Space Rats of the CCC." In most serious works of science fiction, labeling the alien element "good" or "evil" would run counter to the authors' intentions. It is essential to Le Guin's purposes in *The Left Hand of Darkness* that Genly Ai, our "normal" persona, eventually understand and accept the strangely androgynous Gethenian, Estraven, for this study of an alien sexuality is really a study in the psychology and sociology of human sexuality. The gothicist, of course, would see Estraven as a grotesque bisexual, a living affront to the all-important categories of male and female.

Indeed, the confusion of masculinity and femininity in Lewis' Matilda—who is at one point the vaguely homosexual boy, Rosario—is one of the demon's most grotesque characteristics, a point that disturbs even Ambrosio.

Le Guin's fiction is subversive, not because of any reversal of moral polarities, but because the conventional moral axis becomes either an idea to be studied or an altogether irrelevant archaism. The elaborate future history of our species in Stapledon's *Last and First Men* treats as petty or genuinely foolish some of our most sacred cultural assumptions; it too is a subversive novel when compared to the gothicists' defenses of those assumptions. Philip Dick's *Man in the High Castle* challenges our rarely questioned assumptions regarding our desirable victory over the "evil" Japanese in World War II; *Ubik* obliterates, without apology, the distinctions between life and death and between self and not-self around which so much of our world view is oriented. These novels are analytical, speculative, and subversive at precisely those critical points at which a gothicist would have to be judgmental, didactic, and conservative.

In summary, then, the three *essential* elements of the gothic's generic paradigm—demonic agency, pandeterministic causation, and a clear Manichaean moral perspective—are, at best, accidental characteristics of science fiction. Pandeterminism, in fact, is actually incompatible with science fiction's conceptual and rhetorical premises. The gothic novel is an ideal form for the exploration of individual psychology, especially aberrant psychology, as well as of aesthetic concepts such as the sublime and the grotesque. However, the same structural elements that define the genre and that make gothic fiction such an effective means of examining the interior landscape also limit the genre, making it generally inadequate as a means of social criticism or of cultural, political, philosophical, or scientific speculation. These, of course, are the areas in which science fiction excels. Unhampered by the gothic's necessary moral perspective and unrestricted by its fairly narrow range of narrative assumptions and aesthetic premises, science fiction can move freely through a greater range of subjects and points of view and employ a greater variety of narrative structures than the gothic can.

It is not the purpose of this study to contribute to the proliferation of definitions of science fiction. The generic paradigm I have used in distinguishing between these two genres reveals much more about the gothic than about science fiction. However, any extended discussion of what science fiction is not raises the question of what it is, and several useful lines of definition do seem to have emerged from these comparative observations.

Science fiction's vision extends outward, away from the interior man, exploring instead man's relationship with his natural and artificial environments. In doing so, science fiction shares common ground with political novels, adventure novels, travel narratives, and satirical fantasies such as *Utopia, Gulliver's Travels,* and *A Connecticut Yankee in King Arthur's Court.* While such concerns in no way preclude close attention to psychological detail, they become secondary to the interplay of ideas on a larger scale. Even when science fiction appears to deal with the interior of a single psyche, its actual focus shifts from the mind *per se* to the mind as it responds to or is modified by some technical or scientific innovation.

If science fiction may be distinguished from the gothic and other confessional forms by its emphasis on "ideas" rather than on the labyrinthine depths of the individual mind, these "ideas" may, in turn, be defined by a specific rhetoric or perspective. Although the miracles of science fiction are frequently as implausible as those of the gothic necromancer, they are premised on a faith that the universe is an essentially "natural" phenomenon, ultimately accessible to the rational or scientific mind. This premise remains true even in works such as *Solaris,* which concludes that the universe is essentially unknowable to man because he is limited by his own perceptual and conceptual sets or lenses. In this respect, Lem's novels resemble Gödel's Theorem and the Heisenberg Principle: both challenge man's ability to arrive at absolute certainty with modern tools, yet they are, in themselves, impressive achievements of the scientific frame of mind and in no way invite prescientific or supernatural alternatives. Lem can arrive at his conclusions only through the literary equivalent of an "experiment": the controlled application of logic and scientific knowledge. This assumption of the validity of scientific reasoning holds also in works such as *A Canticle for Leibowitz* and *Brave New World,* which reflect our deepest fears of science and technology.

Science fiction, then, is a form of fiction that, unlike confessional or psychological fiction, focuses on man's relationship with his natural and man-made environments and that, unlike such works as *The Faerie Queene,* assumes that the scientific perspective—even though it is imperfect and is the frequent cause of our crises—is still our best tool in dealing with those environments. What this formulation lacks is something that would clearly differentiate science fiction from "realistic" novels dealing with man's sociopolitical environment (for example, *La Comédie humaine*) or fiction influenced by Zola's attempted application of scientific methods. Political and social novels examine directly the truth of man's condition as it is or has been in the historical past. Science fiction begins with a "What if?" proposition, locating its speculations in the future, in alien worlds, or in a past modified or reinvented by sci-

ence. The strategy is one of projection and extrapolation. Its strength lies in the fact that, although it rewards our deepest desires temporarily to escape reality as it is, it finally brings us back to a reexamination of the present.[10] Darko Suvin and others have argued that this "attitude of estrangement" has become essential to the structure of the genre. The projected setting becomes a displaced image of the present, a mirror that, as Suvin observes, both reflects and transforms the world as we know it.[11] The "sense of wonder" so often associated with science fiction originates in this strategy of displacement and extrapolation—not in the genre's concern with man and his environment or in its "scientific" premises.

Entertaining for a moment the idea that a genre has an absolute and immutable form, we might attribute to science fiction three primary characteristics: (1) Science fiction is that class of fiction that focuses upon man's relationship with his environment rather than upon individual psychology. (2) It accepts and uses the premises of modern science in its examination of phenomena and in its extrapolations. (3) The genre employs the narrative strategy of displacement or estrangement ("fabulation") in distancing the fiction. This three-part definition of science fiction acknowledges the genre's similarities to other genres at the same time it isolates or distinguishes it. Science fiction and gothic fiction share the third criterion but not the first two. The second criterion is the only one that separates science fiction from allegorical and satirical works such as *The Faerie Queene* and *Gulliver's Travels.* And only the third criterion distinguishes science fiction from much of what we call "realistic" or "naturalistic" fiction.

Of course, generic models should be formulated and applied with caution and humility, for it is easy to forget that taxonomy is not a goal in itself but, rather, a means with which we may better understand a particular type of literature. Moreover, literary genres are not fixed; they blend, disappear, and reemerge as something strange and new. It is possible for science fiction to use the gothic as a "mode," employing the gothic's peculiar atmosphere and psychological orientation for its own purposes. *A Canticle for Leibowitz* and *The Investigation* succeed admirably at this. On the other hand, the strategies of science fiction itself may be subordinated to other forms. C. S. Lewis's trilogy is an elaborate Christian parable that exploits science fiction techniques but that ultimately rejects the premise that the universe is a natural phenomenon approachable through scientific reasoning. Because the conditions under which fiction is written change and because the strongest authors usually modify inherited forms, fictional genres tend to diffuse and become less distinct. While authors today frequently exploit the gothic as a mode or stratagem, we must look back almost a century to find a serious novel that is unambiguously "pure" gothic. I suspect that in the next few decades science fiction will undergo similar transformations, becoming more versatile as a mode and less distinct as a genre.

Notes

1. Brian Aldiss, *Billion Year Spree: The True History of Science Fiction* (Garden City, N.Y.: Doubleday, 1973), p. 18.

2. Leslie Fiedler, *Love and Death in the American Novel,* 2d ed. (New York: Stein and Day, 1966), p. 500.

3. See Wolfgang Kayser, *The Grotesque in Art and Literature,* trans. Ulrich Weisstein (1963; reprint ed., New York: McGraw-Hill, 1966), pp. 179-89.

4. Matthew G. Lewis, *The Monk* (New York: Grove Press, 1952), p. 385.

5. Philip R. Dick, *Ubik* (New York: Bantam, 1977), p. 152.

6. My use of this term is based on Angus Fletcher's analysis and application of the concept of daemonic agency in the first chapter of *Allegory: The Theory of a Symbolic Mode* (Ithaca, N.Y.: Cornell University Press, 1964).

7. Ibid.

8. Olaf Stapledon, *Last and First Men* (1931; reprint ed., New York: Dover, 1968), p. 10.

9. Tzvetan Todorov, *The Fantastic: A Structural Approach to a Literary Genre,* trans. Richard Howard (Cleveland: Case Western Reserve University Press, 1973), p. 113.

10. Cf. Ursula K. Le Guin on *The Left Hand of Darkness*: "Yes, indeed the people in it are androgynous, but that doesn't mean that I'm predicting that in a millennium or so we will all be androgynous, or announcing that I think we damned well ought to be androgynous. I'm merely observing, in the peculiar, devious, and thought-experimental manner proper to science fiction, that if you look at us at certain odd times of day in certain weathers, we already are. I am not predicting or prescribing. I am describing. I am describing certain aspects of psychological reality in the novelist's way, inventing elaborately circumstantial lies" (Introduction to *The Left Hand of Darkness* [New York: Ace Books, 1976], p. v).

11. Darko Suvin, "On the Poetics of the Science Fiction Genre," *College English* 34 (1972), reprinted in *Science Fiction: A Collection of Critical Essays,* ed. Mark Rose (Englewood Cliffs, N.J.: Prentice-Hall, 1976), p. 59.

Robert Scholes speaks of this facet of science fiction as "fabulation": "Fabulation, then, is fiction that offers us a world clearly and radically discontinuous from the one we know, yet returns to confront that known world in some cognitive way" (*Structural Fabulation: An Essay on Fiction of the Future* [Notre Dame, Ind.: University of Notre Dame Press, 1976], p. 29).

Ronald Schleifer (essay date 1993)

SOURCE: Schleifer, Ronald. "Rural Gothic: The Sublime Rhetoric of Flannery O'Connor." In *Frontier Gothic: Terror and Wonder at the Frontier in American Literature,* edited by David Mogen, Scott P. Sanders, and Joanne B. Karpinski, pp. 175-86. Cranbury, N.J.: Fairleigh Dickinson University Press, 1993.

[*In the essay below, Schleifer discusses several of Flannery O'Connor's short stories, noting that she treats the rural countryside as a middle ground between the natural and the supernatural, where characters can learn lessons about themselves.*]

> There are two qualities that make fiction. One is the sense of mystery and the other is the sense of manners. You get manners from the texture of existence that surrounds you. The great advantage of being a Southern writer is that we don't have to go anywhere to look for manners . . . We in the South live in a society that is rich in contradiction, rich in irony, rich in contrast, and particularly rich in speech.
>
> —Flannery O'Connor

In *A Portrait of the Artist,* that most ungothic of literary works, Stephen Dedalus explains to his friend Lynch that although Aristotle had not defined pity and terror in the *Poetics,* he, Stephen, had:

> Pity is the feeling which arrests the mind in the presence of whatsoever is grave and constant in human sufferings and unites it with the human sufferer. Terror is the feeling which arrests the mind in the presence of whatsoever is grave and constant in human sufferings and unites it with the secret cause.[1]

Stephen is attempting to define tragic art, yet his definitions are useful in developing a sense of the larger movements of gothic fiction—of the serious contemplation of the supernatural in literature. The novel, I would argue, seeks to achieve some sense of Stephen's "pity," to create the texture of a social world in which we can join in sympathy with its human sufferers. What has characterized the great novelists in English—from Defoe through Fielding and George Eliot to the human comedy of *Ulysses* itself—is an abiding sense of sympathy for the human sufferer, or its opposite, a sense of irony toward him. Another way to say this is to argue that the novel seeks to hide and to erase its own origins, to present itself and its characters on their own terms within the context of "the texture of existence that surrounds" them,[2] whereas the gothic romance seeks to reveal its hidden origins. The novel deals with the middle between apocalyptic ends; it deals with ongoing life, with what William Spanos, following Kierkegaard, calls the "interesting . . . the intentionality of *inter esse* meaning '(i) "to be between," (ii) "to be a matter of concern."'"[3]

The gothic romance, on the other hand, seeks extremes; it seeks to articulate a sense—an "experience"—of the sublime, and to this end proceeds, as Peter Brooks has noted, by means of the logic of the excluded middle.[4] "It is not made from the mean average or the typical," Flannery O'Connor has written, "but from the hidden and often the most extreme" (MM, 58); "it is the extreme situation that best reveals what we are essentially" (MM, 113). The gothic romance, when it is serious, seeks essences; it seeks origins—both its own and its characters'. That is, it seeks Joyce's "secret cause" and achieves, in the course of that quest, the terror Stephen talks of. Origins are always supernatural; they are always beyond what can be known in a rational, logical way. That is why Stephen talks of the "mystical estate" of fatherhood as the basis of the Catholic Church in *Ulysses,* because "it is founded, like the world, macro- and microcosm, upon the void."[5] Origins always articulate what O'Connor calls "mystery" and what the literary tradition calls the "sublime": the manifestation and apprehension of the Sacred within quotidian reality. The gothic tradition arose, Brooks argues, "at the dead end of the Age of Reason, [when] the Sacred reasserted its claim to attention, but in the most primitive possible manifestations, as taboo and interdiction . . . [The gothic tradition] reasserts the presence in the world of forces which cannot be accounted for by the daylight self and the self-sufficient mind."[6] The daylight self and the self-sufficient mind are inhabitants of novels, where union with the human sufferer is enough and supernatural origins are beside the point: we need not know Moll Flanders' real parentage and name to feel the sympathetic understanding she occasions; and although Tom Jones's parentage is of some importance, it is precisely his indifference to such questions that makes him so appealing.

The gothic novel, however, presents precisely the need to discover origins: its characters, from *The Castle of Otranto* on, seek to find (or find thrust upon themselves) their parentage and their origins. The gothic is a haunted literature (it is no accident that both Joyce and O'Connor come from a Catholic tradition that takes the presence of the supernatural seriously), and what haunts it—whether it be Count Dracula, the Frankenstein monster, or the governess's ghosts in "The Turn of the Screw"—is some supernatural origin, some inhuman silence, forces beyond the self-sufficiency of the daylight self. These forces raise the question of identity and origin for the characters of gothic romance: "who and

what am I?" ask Frankenstein's monster and Lewis's Monk and Kafka's K.; "how can I discover those forces beyond myself that originate myself, my own 'secret cause'?" To put these questions in literary terms especially appropriate to Flannery O'Connor, how can we discover the origins of the power of literature, the originary force of metaphorical language? Such discoveries, as Stephen suggests, are made in terror, made in the loss of self within its secret cause. "To know oneself," O'Connor has written, "is, above all, to know what one lacks" (MM, 35): it is a way of exploring the self and the world in a manner different from sympathetic understanding, through terror, violence, and encounter with the supernatural. O'Connor goes on to say,

> St. Cyril of Jerusalem, in instructing catechumens, wrote: "The dragon sits by the side of the road, watching those who pass. Beware lest he devour you. We go to the Father of Souls, but it is necessary to pass the dragon." No matter what form the dragon may take, it is of this mysterious passage past him, or into his jaws, that stories of any depth will always be concerned to tell, and this being the case, it requires considerable courage at any time, in any country, not to turn away from the storyteller.
>
> (MM, 35)

Seeking the Father of Souls—the secret cause and origin of identity and the "rich speech" that manifests identity—the writer and the reader must pass the dragon outside; they must, as O'Connor continually insists, recognize the literal reality of the Devil, the poverty of our self-sufficiency, and the necessity of grace. Such self-knowledge is a form of agony; as O'Connor says in what I believe is her best story, "The Artificial Nigger"—a story whose plot literally repeats the plot of St. Cyril's parable, with the artificial nigger a silent figure on the side of the road—such knowledge grows "out of agony, which is not denied to any man and which is given in strange ways to children."[7] It is this "mysterious passage" that the gothic tradition offers us when it is most serious, a passage to and through origin and identity to their secret cause.

Nowhere are origins and identity more pressing problems, as Roy Male has shown,[8] than on the frontier, where one continually encounters "mysterious strangers" who raise questions about one's own as well as others' identity. One such modern frontier is O'Connor's South: it is especially a "frontier" for a Catholic writer in the predominantly fundamentalist Protestant South. Like the gothic romance Brooks describes, O'Connor seeks in her work to "reassert" the Sacred in the quotidian world, to situate her characters on the mysterious passage between the "manners" of novels and the "mystery" of union with secret causes. Tzvetan Todorov's study, *The Fantastic,* situates gothic fiction in the "frontier" between natural and supernatural understandings of experience. In fact, although he does not use it, "frontier" itself is an apt metaphor for the situation of the gothic as Todorov defines it: "the fantastic is that hesitation experienced by a person who knows only the laws of nature, confronting an apparently supernatural event."[9] This is O'Connor's "frontier," that of a fiction which is always

> pushing its own limits outward towards the limits of mystery, because . . . the meaning of a story does not begin except at a depth where adequate motivation and adequate psychology and the various determinations have been exhausted. Such a writer . . . will be interested in possibility rather than probability. He will be interested in characters who are forced out to meet evil and grace and who act on a trust beyond themselves.
>
> (MM, 41-42)

The gothic, that is, presents a world beyond the understandings of metaphor, a world of mysterious inhuman forces that cannot adequately be explained by the metaphors of psychology or sociology or well-meaning humanism. It is a literature of *presence* unmediated by the substitutions of language, presences which are inhuman, terrifying, secret, sublime.

Yet O'Connor's frontier is more literal than this: her constant gesture is to place her characters between the natural and the supernatural by locating them, often on a literal journey, between the cities and the rural country of the South. "What the Southern Catholic writer is apt to find, when he descends within his imagination," she notes, "is not Catholic life but the life of this region in which he is both native and alien" (MM, 197). Rufus Johnson in "The Lame Shall Enter First"—a character who embodies, as many of O'Connor's characters do, the *reality* of the Devil—has a history of "senseless destruction, windows smashed, city trash boxes set afire, tires slashed—the kind of thing . . . found where boys had been transplanted abruptly from the country to the city as this one had" (CS, 449). This is where the supernatural is most clearly and terrifyingly encountered—on those frontiers between the country and the city, faith and faithlessness, Protestant fundamentalism and cosmopolitan skepticism. Yet Rufus Johnson, as the well-meaning humanist-protagonist of the story learns, cannot be explained: he is simply a literal force, the force of the Devil, to be encountered on this "frontier." "I have found," O'Connor writes, "that anything that comes out of the South is going to be called grotesque by the Northern reader" (MM, 40), and she found this because the strangeness of that frontier in our culture—that location of the clashes between terror and pity—forces upon her characters confrontations with themselves and origins beyond themselves. "While the South is hardly Christ-centered," O'Connor says, "it is most certainly Christ-haunted" (MM, 40).

To speak of the "literal" force of characters is to speak of one particular aspect of rhetoric, of the *power* rhetoric has to make its effects as literal as events in the world. In such an examination of rhetoric the opposition between the literal and the figurative is beside the point: discourse creates *literal* effects that move us as effectively as nondiscursive events. In this understanding, discourse creates (or "occasions" or "provokes") experience,[10] and such experience is not subject to description in terms of the opposition between "literal" and "figurative" correspondence between discourse and its object. In this understanding, "rhetoric" is not the means of expressing pre-existing experiences; rather, it occasions experience.

O'Connor has precisely this concern with rhetoric. "The problem of the novelist who wishes to write about a man's encounter with this God," O'Connor has written, "is how he shall make the experience—which is both natural and supernatural—understandable, and credible, to his reader" (MM, 161). This is O'Connor's rhetorical problem, to make the Sacred literal in a world in which it seems at best metaphorical, originating in a mode of perception rather than in the created world. The problem of her rhetoric, then, is the problem of the gothic, the problem of the sublime.

The act of "facing oneself" is the recurrent action of O'Connor's stories, the action of gothic romance. Perhaps the most striking example of this is that of O. E. Parker in "Parker's Back," who literally "faces" his own back with a giant tattoo of Jesus, the eyes of which "continued to look at him—still, straight, all-demanding, enclosed in silence" (CS, 526). This is a representative gothic gesture: to make the metaphorical literal. Gothic romance does this, as Todorov and others have shown,[11] by narrating dream and nightmare as reality and projecting our deepest impulses and fears onto the landscape. The face on Parker's back—its "all-demanding" eyes—made Parker feel "that his dissatisfaction was gone, but he felt not quite like himself. It was as if he were himself but a stranger to himself, driving into a new country though everything he saw was familiar to him, even the night" (CS, 527). Such a feeling—a feeling that the reader is never sure Asbury achieves or not, hence the relative failure of "An Enduring Chill"—is what Freud calls the "uncanny," "That class of terrifying which leads back to something long known to us, once very familiar"; "the uncanny," Freud says, "would always be that in which one does not know where one is, as it were."[12] The uncanny is familiar and strange, just as Parker is both familiar and strange to himself with God's constant eyes literally upon him, and he is in a country in which he is both native and alien.

That country is the country of the frontier, between the familiar and strange, the natural and supernatural. One gets there in O'Connor by "facing" oneself, by seeking origins and seeing oneself, as Mr. Head does, with God's own eyes, with God's eyes *upon* one. The gothic, I have suggested, "literalizes" the metaphorical: like the more general category of the sublime, it deals in effects rather than meanings and thus is not subject to the distinction between literal and figurative description; in it, this distinction collapses in the "literalness" of experience. O'Connor effects this collapse in the highly figurative rural speech of her characters that they understand as fully literal. It is for this reason that her backwoods characters so often use country clichés in their speech: her act is to make us see the familiar as strange, to make us see literally and thus strangely what we usually don't see at all because it is so familiar. "Christ!" someone says in the pool hall when Parker reveals his tattoo (CS, 526), and suddenly—almost supernaturally—O'Connor creates Christ's presence, as literal as it is for Parker, by means of the cliché of astonishment. In "The River," Bevel learns of Jesus:

> He had found out this morning that he had been made by a carpenter named Jesus Christ. Before he had thought it had been a doctor named Sladewell, a fat man with a yellow mustache who gave him shots and thought his name was Herbert. . . . If he had thought about it before, he would have thought Jesus Christ was a word like "oh" or "damn" or "God," or maybe somebody who had cheated him out of something sometime. . . .
>
> (CS, 163)

Such a discovery is the terrifying revelation of what we already knew: "carpenter" in this context takes on the full presence of its literal meaning of a maker, and Bevel (something a carpenter makes) is faced with a terrifying prospect of seeing himself anew.

Such an "experience" of the literal—the confrontation with the literal self, its literal origin, a powerfully literal meaning—are the repeated actions in Flannery O'Connor, and they take place in what John Hawkes has called "her almost luridly bright pastoral world,"[13] on borderlines between the city and the country or between day and night. This is why so often O'Connor's stories end at sunset, as in "Revelation," when Mrs. Turpin watches her hogs as the sun goes down:

> Then like a monumental statue coming to life, she bent her head slowly and gazed, as if through the very heart of mystery, down into the pig parlour at the hogs. They had settled all in one corner around the old sow who was grunting softly. A red glow suffused them. They appeared to pant with a secret life.
>
> (CS, 508)

From this sight she looks up as the sun goes down and sees her vision of a vast hoard of souls going to heaven, "whole companies of white trash, clean for the first time in their lives, and bands of black niggers in white robes, and battalions of freaks and lunatics shouting and clapping and leaping like frogs" (CS, 508). The metaphor O'Connor uses is almost an allusion to

Otranto with its giant statue coming to life, but the language is that of Mrs. Turpin, another in O'Connor's procession of good country people. That language informs a rural vision, Hawkes's lurid pastoral world, with a sense of supernatural force so that the whole is seen in a new light. Here again O'Connor creates the *presence* of the supernatural, of mysterious forces beyond the daylight self, in pig and sunset. "Revelation" begins with Mrs. Turpin's confrontation with a Wellesley student in a doctor's office, yet it ends with her own uncouthness—her own rural sensibility—miraculously transformed on the frontier of a secret life.

That life is Mrs. Turpin's life, but dark, unknown, strange: it is the life revealed in the college girl's fierce remark: "Go back to hell where you came from, you old wart hog" (CS, 500). It is the inhuman life of wart hogs from hell that, literalized, leads strangely to Mrs. Turpin's vision of heaven. Mrs. Turpin "faces" herself with the hog; she sees her own secret life in the elemental life of her farm and discovers, as Parker had, the presence of God in and beyond His creation, in and beyond the hogs, the people, the peculiar light of the setting sun.

This is the light of grace, and it appears again at another sunset situated on the urban frontier at the end of "The Artificial Nigger." There Mr. Head and his grandson, Nelson, after the small inferno of their day in Atlanta, discover in the accidental image of suffering presented by a dilapidated statue of a Negro the "action of mercy." What is powerful in O'Connor is her ability to create the *presence* of Christ and grace felt through and beyond the world of nature. How she does this is the problem and the secret of her art. It is an art that is gothic and that depends, fully, on its situation on one of the frontiers of our culture. Herman Melville wrote in *The Confidence-Man*, "it is with fiction as with religion: it should present another world, and yet one to which we feel the tie."[14] O'Connor, like Melville, presents another world of white trash, black niggers, freaks, lunatics—in a word, a world of "good country people"—which is tied to ours yet strangely literal in its very landscape and language.

That tie with our world is the tie with what she calls the "action of mercy," and in her best work it is "tied" through her metaphoric language becoming literal.[15] Love is the burden of "The Artificial Nigger": face to face with a broken-down statue of a Negro, Mr. Head and his grandson are "faced with some great mystery, some monument to another's victory that brought them together in their common defeat" so that they "both feel it dissolving their differences *like an action of mercy*" (CS, 269, emphasis added). This encounter creates a sense of humility for Mr. Head until, three paragraphs later, "he stood appalled . . . while *the action of mercy* covered his pride like a flame and consumed it." In the course of these paragraphs (and in the course of Mr. Head's experience), simile is rendered as assertion until, before our eyes, grace manifests itself, the action of mercy, the secret cause, appears:

> [Mr. Head] stood appalled, judging himself with the thoroughness of God, while the action of mercy covered his pride like a flame and consumed it. He had never thought himself a great sinner before but he saw now that his true depravity had been hidden from him lest it cause him despair. He realized that he was forgiven for sins from the beginning of time, when he had conceived in his own heart the sin of Adam, until the present when he had denied poor Nelson. He saw that no sin was too monstrous for him to claim as his own, and since God loved in proportion as He forgave, he felt ready at that instant to enter Paradise.
>
> (CS, 269-270)

This is the "secret cause" that Joyce speaks of, a sense of God's presence and love in the heart of Mr. Head. But what is remarkable about this passage, I believe, is that we never question the fact that the realization described—its language and its theology—is simply beyond the frontier language and evangelical Christianity of Mr. Head. Head, hick that he is, believes that an inferno underlies Atlanta and fears to be sucked down the sewer: he literalizes his own metaphor (see CS, 259, 267). In other words, O'Connor is able, here and elsewhere, to create a sublimely literal irony. Throughout "The Artificial Nigger" the language of the narrator constantly paraphrases Mr. Head's thoughts and language in a rhetoric completely beyond his backwoods rhetoric. This paraphrase makes that language itself—its ignorance, its racism, its violence—entirely invisible.

What reveals itself here is that Catholic grace, like the Mormon's magical glasses, includes the ability to see "through" and to understand another language. Thus the narrator notes, "They stood gazing at the artificial Negro as if they were faced with some great mystery, some monument to another's victory that brought them together in their common defeat" (CS, 269), but Head simply breathes, "An artificial nigger!" and says "They ain't got enough real ones here. They got to have an artificial one" (CS, 268, 269). "Nigger" is Head's word, "Negro" the narrator's, yet O'Connor wants us to see *through* the rhetoric to the "literal" fact, wordlessly experienced by Head and narrated in a technical theological discourse far beyond Head's experience and understanding. In other words, O'Connor creates the rhetorical *effect* of godly presence by narrating in a language that implies its own transparence, implies that the literal *inhabits* the metaphorical so that, as another theological writer, Søren Kierkegaard says, "through a negation of the immediate phenomenon the essence remains identical with the phenomenon."[16]

Such an effect is created by being situated on a "frontier" between rural discourse and cosmopolitan theology. But more than this, O'Connor is *enacting* the "mystery" of grace as well. Throughout this story—as in most of her stories—O'Connor faces her cosmopolitan readers with the language and experience of rural ignorance. When Head tells Nelson that the sewers of Atlanta are literally hell, we *know* that we know more than these ignorant characters. But when the story finally presents the sure knowledge that Mr. Head, despite his racism and ignorance, can count himself among the saved—that "he was forgiven for sins from the beginning of time" and that "since God loved in proportion as He forgave, he felt ready at that instant to enter Paradise" (CS, 269-70)—at that moment its readers, like St. Cyril, are faced with a mystery which cannot be understood by the self-sufficient mind of humanistic intelligence. At such moments the cosmopolitan understanding of her readers is faced with a discourse whose power is beyond the comprehensions of the irony that had seemed to govern the story's narrative throughout.

This power is that of sympathy: the passage suggests that Head, like his cosmopolitan reader, can only understand the "secret cause"—here the sin of Adam—by experiencing the agony of his own egocentric denial of "poor Nelson" (or in the case of the reader, "poor" Mr. Head himself). Mr. Head is not truly a part of the world he lives in—neither is Mrs. Turpin, O. E. Parker, and most of O'Connor's protagonists—and his struggle, like that of the others and like our own, is to find some connection in a world that simply seems alien, other, without human response. It is a world, as the Misfit says in "A Good Man is Hard to Find," in which, without an answering Jesus, there's no pleasure but meanness, "no real pleasure in life" (CS, 133)—a world in which, as O'Connor says, we are native and alien.

How to discover a human response in such a world is the great problem: Mr. Head can, as he has done all his life, depend on himself and his ability to give "lessons" and be a "suitable guide for the young" (CS, 249), or he can discover, in terror or in love, but above all in humility, supernatural forces outside himself that lead him to other human sufferers who can respond to himself.

Most of O'Connor's heroes fall into terror: they find, as Parker does, the terrifying cost of God's enduring eye; or they find, as the Misfit does, the senselessness of not knowing God is there. As O'Connor herself says, "Often the nature of grace can be made plain only by describing its absence" (MM, 204), and such absence *is* inhuman; it leaves our world literally senseless and results in the senseless violence—the inhuman violence—of all those who do not fit: the Misfit, Rufus, Shiftlet, and all the rest. But others—Mrs. Turpin, Mr. Head, Bailey's mother—discover love amid their terror: they discover the literal language of God already in their own Southern slang. They achieve humility when they realize that they are not fully self-possessed, that their "calm understanding," in the narrator's paraphrase of Head's evaluation of himself, leaves out their own mysterious origins and leaves out forces—articulated by Head's exclamation, "An artificial nigger!"—beyond themselves.

The action of mercy, then, is the action of rhetoric that finds meaning in a senseless world, that suggests the literal in its figured values; it offers a sense of grace, a sense of the supernatural, in the world in which O'Connor characters, both native and alien, do not quite fit.

What the rural Southern frontier finally offers O'Connor is that position in the world—that situation—where the strangers you meet can be anyone, can, in fact, be supernatural: Jesus, the Devil, the Holy Ghost.

> "I can tell you my name is Tom Shiftlet and I come from Tarwater, Tennessee, but you never have seen me before; how you know I ain't lying? How you know my name ain't Aaron Sparks, lady, and I come from Singleberry, Georgia, or how you know it's not George Speeds and I come from Lucy, Alabama, or how you know I ain't Thompson Bright from Toolafalls, Mississippi?"
>
> (CS, 147-48)

All these names, as Roy Male has suggested, are filled with light,[17] and they set forth the action—sometimes the failed action—of O'Connor's gothic fiction: to discover or create light out of the dark frontier of rural Georgia. "I think," O'Connor wrote, "[the Catholic writer] will feel a good deal more kinship with backwoods prophets and shouting fundamentalists than he will with those politer elements for whom the supernatural is an embarrassment of sociology or culture or personality development" (MM, 207). That sense of supernatural force that the backwoods prophets feel in the world repeats itself in the uncanny force and presence O'Connor achieves within the cliché-ridden language of her fiction. Both acknowledge the supernatural and discover that it can be found on the edges of our culture, dark and empty as they may be, on the rural frontier.

Notes

This essay is a revised version of "Rural Gothic: The Stories of Flannery O'Connor," that originally appeared in *Modern Fiction Studies*, 28 (1982), 475-85. That essay was reprinted in *Critical Essays on Flannery O'Connor*, ed. Melvin Friedman and Beverly Clark (New York: G. K. Hall, 1985) and *Flannery O'Connor: Modern Critical Views*, ed. Harold Bloom (New York: Chelsea House, 1986). The present essay was especially revised for this collection.

1. James Joyce, *A Portrait of the Artist as a Young Man* (New York: Viking, 1969), 204.

2. Flannery O'Connor, *Mystery and Manners: Occasional Prose,* ed. Sally and Robert Fitzgerald (New York: Farrar, Straus, and Giroux, 1969), 103; future references, abbreviated MM, will be included parenthetically within the text.

3. William V. Spanos, "Hermeneutics and Memory: Destroying T. S. Eliot's *Four Quartets,*" *Genre,* 11 (1978): 532.

4. Peter Brooks, "Virtue and Terror: *The Monk,*" *ELH,* 40 (1973): 252. For a complementary treatment of the gothic tradition, see my "The Trap of the Imagination: The Gothic Tradition, Fiction, and 'The Turn of the Screw,'" *Criticism,* 22 (1980): 297-319.

5. James Joyce, *Ulysses* (New York: Random House, 1961), 207.

6. Brooks, 249.

7. *The Complete Stories of Flannery O'Connor* (New York: Modern Library, 1974), 269. Future references to O'Connor's stories will be to this edition, abbreviated CS and included parenthetically in the text.

8. Roy Male, *Enter, Mysterious Stranger* (Norman: University of Oklahoma Press, 1979).

9. Tzvetan Todorov, *The Fantastic,* trans. Richard Howard (Ithaca, NY: Cornell University Press, 1975), 25.

10. For a discussion of the collapsing of the distinction between literal and figurative use of language, see Ronald Schleifer, *A. J. Greimas and the Nature of Meaning* (Lincoln: University of Nebraska Press, 1987), ch. 5, esp. 201-08.

11. *The Fantastic,* treats this throughout; see also Leslie Fiedler, *Love and Death in the American Novel* (New York: Stein and Day, 1966).

12. Sigmund Freud, "The Uncanny," in *Studies in Parapsychology* (New York: Collier Books, 1963), 21.

13. John Hawkes, "Flannery O'Connor's Devil," *Sewanee Review,* 70 (1962): 399.

14. Herman Melville, *The Confidence-Man* (Indianapolis: Bobbs-Merrill, 1967), 260.

15. For Blake's similar transformation of simile to metaphor, see my "Simile, Metaphor, and Vision: Blake's Narration of Prophecy in America," *Studies in English Literature,* 19 (1979): 569-588.

16. *The Concept of Irony,* trans. Lee Capel (Bloomington: Indiana University Press, 1965), 265.

17. Male, 30.

Avril Horner (essay date 2002)

SOURCE: Horner, Avril. "'A Detour of Filthiness': French Fiction and Djuna Barnes's *Nightwood*." In *European Gothic: A Spirited Exchange, 1760-1960,* edited by Avril Horner, pp. 230-51. Manchester, England: Manchester University Press, 2002.

[*In the following essay, Horner examines how Djuna Barnes drew on the French Gothic tradition in* Nightwood, *which, in turn, influenced William Faulkner and Carson McCullers.*]

> The French have made a detour of filthiness—Oh, the good dirt! Whereas you are of a clean race, of a too eagerly washing people, and this leaves no road for you.
>
> (Barnes 1985: 123[1])

The inclusion of [an essay] about an American novel in a book on European Gothic writing might seem somewhat anomalous. However, in this [essay] I shall argue that Djuna Barnes's most famous work, *Nightwood,* which was written in Europe and published in 1936, engages with French literature in a number of ways in order to develop its own transatlantic Gothic agenda. I shall therefore try to retrieve Djuna Barnes's *Nightwood* as a Gothic text and, in so doing, trace its derivation from a French tradition of Gothic or quasi-Gothic writing. This tradition begins with the *roman noir* and the *roman frénétique,* which flourished respectively between 1790 and 1820 and between the 1820s and 1830s.[2] It continues with the work of authors such as Eugène Sue, whose novels were widely translated across Europe, and Lautréamont, whose emphasis on sadism and cruelty recuperates the radical agenda developed by de Sade some 80 years earlier. This disquisition on darkness influences, in turn, the work of 'decadent' *fin-de-siècle* authors such as Huysmans, whose cynicism and interest in excess are reflected in the novels of later writers such as Louis-Ferdinand Céline and Georges Bataille.

What we therefore see in *Nightwood* is an expression of anomie coloured by its author's exposure to a particular French literary tradition, described by Kristeva as 'a black lineage'. Exemplified for Kristeva by the works of Lautréamont and Artaud, this lineage is one in which 'inhumanity discovers its appropriate themes, contrary to all lyrical traditions, in horror, death, madness, orgy, outlaws, war, the feminine threat, the horrendous delights of love, disgust, and fright' (Kristeva 1982: 137). Barnes's embrace of such a lineage is inflected by her situation as a modernist. Like many of her contemporaries, she took to heart the radical experimentation with language which was central to the French symbolist movement and which constituted its most important legacy to modernism. It is curious that T. S. Eliot, who was himself profoundly influenced by French symbolism, ignored the impact of French writing on Barnes's work in his famous introduction to *Nightwood*. In so doing, he set in place a critical tradition which presents the novel as a bizarre and eccentric text owing more to English Renaissance drama than to French literature. Resisting this reading, recent feminist interpretations of *Nightwood* have retrieved it as an important American modernist and/or lesbian text. Mary E. Galvin, for example, in her book *Queer Poetics: Five Modernist Women Writers,* describes Barnes as a writer who:

> consistently presents lesbian sexuality as central to her urban settings and her depiction of her times; the 'otherness' her characters experience is integral to the modernist scene.
>
> (Galvin 1999: 102)

This championing of Barnes as an American lesbian modernist has had its uses. The current resurgence of interest in her work has coincided with the emergence of queer theory, which has been used to interpret her writings in a manner more sophisticated than that of earlier critics such as Field, who tended to conflate the works with a gossipy version of the life (Field: 1983). Nevertheless, there is still much work to be done on Barnes's debts to French literature.

However, before exploring the impact of certain aspects of French culture on Barnes's writing of *Nightwood,* we perhaps need first of all to establish briefly the novel's Gothic credentials. Lewis Gannett commented in 1937 in the *New York Herald Tribune* that 'It is a book of Gothic horror, not of Elizabethan tragedy' (Field 1983: 215)—thus taking issue with T. S. Eliot's claim in his 1937 introduction to Barnes's novel that its 'quality of horror and doom' related it to Elizabethan drama (Eliot 1937: 7). Leslie Fiedler also included *Nightwood* in his 'neo-gothic' category in *Love and Death in the American Novel* in 1966 (Fiedler 1992: 490) and Ellen Moers defined it as 'modern female Gothic' in *Literary Women* (Moers 1976: 108). In seeing *Nightwood* as a Gothic text, however, these critics have remained exceptions. In part, this neglect of the novel's Gothic elements may be due to the inclusion of *Nightwood* within the modernist canon: the early masculinist critical construction of modernism as a movement of 'high', experimental culture, which eschewed the melodramatic, the popular and the Gothic, has meant that texts canonized within modernism tend to be read in a certain way. Thus while Barnes has been coupled with Joyce and *Nightwood* with André Breton's *Nadja,* the novel's Gothic elements have been largely ignored. These include: the representation of Paris as a dark and labyrinthine space; the presentation of the Volkbeins' Viennese home (complete with ancestral fake portraits and a 'thick dragon's blood pile of rugs from Madrid' (p. 17)), as a Gothic house; a continual questioning of normality as benign; and, above all, a blurring of the boundaries between night/day, masculine/feminine, sacred/profane, real/surreal and human/animal. Furthermore, whilst Felix Volkbein is linked explicitly with the figure of the Wandering Jew (p. 20), Robin—through her restless night-time predatory wanderings during which she 'feeds off' her café victims—is implicitly associated with the figure of the Vampire. In particular, the novel's strange closure, which shows us Robin's union with a dog in a ruined chapel, both recalls the Gothic novel's fondness for the sacrilegious act and expresses the insight that modernism's anxieties concerning the fragmentation of the self are essentially Gothic.[3] Nevertheless, the critical resistance to seeing *Nightwood* as a Gothic work has persisted. Bonnie Kime Scott notes that the novel 'has been called, alternatively, surrealistic, Eliotic, Dantesque, fugal, Elizabethan, *even gothic*' (my italics) (Scott 1990: 23) and Diane Chisholm also argues for the novel's debts to surrealism rather than the Gothic tradition (Chisholm 1997: 185). This ambivalence concerning the strong Gothic legacy evident within *Nightwood* perhaps also derives from a rather limited conception of the nature of Gothic. Given the complex development of the Gothic mode over 250 years, it is clearly too reductive simply to equate it with suggestions of the supernatural or with the use of tropes such as the haunted house, the young female victim and the Bluebeard figure. Rather, it is now best defined in the spirit of Angela Carter who argues that the Gothic:

> grandly ignores the value systems of our institutions . . . (and) deals entirely with the profane   Character and events are exaggerated beyond reality, to become symbols, ideas, passions. Its style will tend to be ornate, unnatural—and thus operate against the perennial human desire to believe the word as fact . . . It retains a singular moral function—that of provoking unease.
>
> (Carter: 1974: 133)

This broad definition, together with David Punter's claim that Gothic authors are writers who 'bring us up against the boundaries of the civilized, who demonstrate to us the relative nature of ethical and behavioural codes' (Punter 1996: 183-184), allows us to locate *Nightwood* firmly within the genre of the Gothic—for the novel does nothing if not provoke 'unease' and 'bring us up against the boundaries of the civilised'.

Written mainly in England during the early 1930s, *Nightwood* nevertheless draws heavily on French literary and cultural legacies. This is not surprising, given the fact that Barnes lived in Paris—often seen as *the* modernist city—between 1921 and 1931, a period frequently presented as the defining moment of high modernism. Barnes felt what one biographer has described as 'an intense alienation from both family and nation' (Herring 1995: 85) and she looked to English and European culture for intellectual inspiration. Like other American expatriates, such as Ezra Pound, Ernest Hemingway and Gertrude Stein, Barnes was a writer whose residence in Paris had a catalytic effect on this desire to embrace Europe and European consciousness. It is, of course, impossible to know exactly what Barnes read during those eleven years in Paris but it seems likely that she would have absorbed much French, as well as English and American, literature. Certainly she was an eclectic reader. We know from her diaries and letters that during the 1930s she read the work of Proust, Fielding, Dostoevsky, certain Renaissance authors (including Sir Thomas Browne, Robert Burton and Donne), William James, Céline, Luther, Pascal, Montaigne, Bergson and Emily Brontë (Herring 1995: 139, 194-195, 219). Such reading patterns probably owed much to the fact that as a child she was exposed to a very wide range of literature, including much in translation. James Scott's interviews with Barnes revealed that her childhood evenings were often spent, along with other family members, listening to her grandmother, Zadel, read aloud from a broad selection of European and American authors; favourite writers included Dostoevsky, Dickens and Proust (Herring 1995: 38). Barnes even claimed that her own name, Djuna, 'came from Eugène Sue's *The Wandering Jew,* where there is an Indian prince called Djalma, which became spliced with Thurn's word for moon, "nuna"' (Herring 1995: 32). Given that Barnes had very little formal education, the literary diet made available at home through both her grandmother's and her parents' reading would have been the main influence on her as a creative child and adolescent. There is no doubt that this intellectual legacy helped shape the content and form of her work, although the emotional legacy of an unorthodox childhood—one scarred by a strangely intense and probably incestuous relationship with her grandmother—has aroused more interest and has been better documented (Dalton 1993; Herring 1993).

An early acquaintance with the works of Eugène Sue thus formed part of Barnes's intellectual legacy. Sue's *The Mysteries of Paris* (1842-43) was translated into several languages, including English, and remained immensely popular throughout the nineteenth and early twentieth centuries. It almost undoubtedly informs her portrayal of Paris in *Nightwood* as a dark and labyrinthine city, more reminiscent of the capital before Haussmann's transformation of it between 1852 and 1870 than during the period in which *Nightwood* is set (the novel opens in 1880 but its main focus is on Paris in the mid-1920s). Indeed, several elements of *Nightwood* can be tracked back not only to Barnes's time and friends in Paris (Matthew O'Connor being based on Dan Mahoney, an infamous resident of Paris during the 1920s, for example), but to the city as represented by nineteenth-century authors such as Dickens, Zola and Eugène Sue. In Sue's *The Mysteries of Paris,* the rural idyll of Bouqueval Farm offers a place where goodness, health and love flourish, in contrast to the capital, which is the scene of numerous cruelties, sadistic acts and criminal deeds. As in the work of Victor Hugo, the surface morality of Sue's novel hides a fascination with the criminal, a downwardly mobile figure who both lives outside the confines of bourgeois life and threatens it. Despite the hero's claim that 'the good and wicked, great and small, submit almost always to the influence of higher, nobler spirits' (Sue n.d.: 390), the moral ambiguity of Sue's novel resides in the fact that the relish and energy with which urban scenes of depravity and cruelty are described result in far more convincing scenarios than those offered by the rural idyll of Bouqueval Farm, meant to indicate a better life. In this sense, *The Mysteries of Paris,* whilst continuing to express a Romantic anxiety about the city as a place of exploitation and depravity, nevertheless positions itself as an early decadent city novel through its prurient and consistent interest in urban evil. *The Mysteries of Paris* and *Nightwood* both portray Paris as an urban Gothic space in the sense defined by Alexandra Warwick: 'The city is seen as uncanny, constructed by people yet unknowable by the individual' (Mulvey-Roberts 1998, 288-289).

Paris, Vienna, Berlin and New York as we see them in *Nightwood* are 'unknowable' in this sense; they are labyrinthine spaces where freedom exists more as an intellectual concept than an actuality. Guido Volkbein, a Jew of Italian descent and Robin's father-in-law, finds no peace of mind in his pseudo-Gothic mansion in Vienna, where anti-Semitic feeling runs rampant (as, in fact, it did during the 1920s[4]). Barnes's portrayal of the circus as an exotic event in Paris and New York enables the reader to experience the modern city through the eyes of the unconventional and the marginalized, categorized as unclean and abject by the bourgoisie who wish their cities to be clean, tidy and ordered. The perspective offered by such a spectacle—like that provided by carnival—is allowable, however, only within carefully defined city limits and definitions. Neither do the anonymity and sexual freedom offered by the city result in emotional fulfilment and liberation. The liberty to conduct a lesbian relationship in Paris means little to Nora since her lover, Robin, uses that freedom precisely to challenge Nora's desire for a monogamous love by finding other lovers in Parisian bars and cafés and by eloping with Jenny Petherbridge. In Barnes's novel, cities are informed by Sue's Paris and Dickens's London, worlds in which suffering and exploitation are commonplace and where freakishness and the grotesque indicate both the limits of, and a challenge to, urban order and bourgeois values. The idea of the city as the acme of urbane sophistication and cultural integrity is thus profoundly challenged by Barnes, as it was by Dickens and by nineteenth-century French novelists such as Sue, Balzac and Zola.

Interestingly, early readers of *Nightwood* were quick to point to the European legacy evident in the novel and, in particular, to parallels with certain French authors. For example, Rose C. Feld, reviewing the novel for the *New York Herald Tribune* in 1937, compared Barnes to Baudelaire whilst Theodore Purdy, in the *Saturday Review* during the same year, noted T. S. Eliot's 'failure to perceive that the atmosphere of decay in "Nightwood" stems from the fin-de-siècle Frenchmen rather than from the Elizabethans'; in the same year, the anonymous reviewer for the *Times Literary Supplement* likened Barnes to Céline (Marcus 1990a: 195-204). Later, in 1945, Joseph Frank claimed that *Nightwood* was constructed on the same principles as Proust's *A la recherché du temps perdu* (Field 1983: 145). Given this reception, it is strange that critics have engaged very little with the French dynamic of *Nightwood*. There are three notable exceptions to this statement. Jane Marcus, in her influential essay 'Laughing at Leviticus: *Nightwood* as Woman's Circus Epic', interprets the novel as exploring the political unconscious of the rise of fascism. Constructing Barnes as a subversive writer, she briefly draws attention to Barnes's debts to Rabelais, Victor Hugo and Eugène Sue (Marcus 1990b: 221-250). Diane Chisholm, in her article 'Obscene Modernism: *Eros Noir* and the Profane Illumination of Djuna Barnes', presents Barnes as an avant-garde author, carefully situating the novel in the context of modernism, obscenity and surrealism and paying particular attention to the parallels between *Nightwood* and Breton's *Nadja* (Chisholm 1997: 167-206). Erin G. Carlston, in her book *Thinking Fascism: Sapphic Modernism and Fascist Modernity,* charts *Nightwood*'s links with French *fin-de-siècle* decadence and a particular strain of what she calls 'romantic Catholicism' which she sees as ushering in the rise of fascism (Carlston 1998: 42-85). It is evident from these quite different readings that Barnes's 'detour' into a French 'filthiness' has divided these critics: whereas Marcus and Chisholm represent her as radical and subversive, Carlston sees her as an author who moved from a flirtation with fascism in the thirties to a final rejection of it in the 1950s. This recuperation of Barnes as either excitingly left- or dangerously right-wing suggests something about both the elusive nature of *Nightwood*'s 'meaning' and the continuing ambivalence of the American imagination in the face of a Gallic 'black lineage'. The French, of course, have a better track record than the Americans for accommodating dark desires—as Barnes's words, used as the epigraph to this chapter, indicate. Through its representation of 'Frenchness', the American novel has often embraced decadence and iniquity—aspects of human behaviour supposedly excluded from the agenda of the New World—by projecting them on to a European other (the writings of Henry James offer an obvious example). These elements, as Ahmed Nimeiri has pointed out, are signalled in *Nightwood* 'by such metaphors as the night, the forest, the beast and "filthiness'". Hence, as Nimeiri notes, Matthew O'Connor's admiration of the French as a people who can accept both night and day as 'two travels' and who are able to make 'a detour of filthiness' (Nimeiri 1993: 106-107).

In this respect, a key text for any evaluation of the impact of French literature on Barnes's creative imagination must surely be Lautréamont's *Les Chants de Maldoror* (1868-69) (translated as *Maldoror*). This strange Gothic text, described in the *New Oxford Companion to Literature in French* as celebrating 'the unbridled predatory misdeeds of a prowler monster whose shape is as indefinite as his age' (France 1995: 447), reaffirms the values of Eugène Sue's world, in which evil usually triumphs over good. It also continues the Sadeian tradition of portraying cruelty in order to explore the dynamics of power and control (Blanchot 1949; de Jonge 1973). Certainly both de Sade and Lautréamont relish the creation of nightmare scenarios as a way of probing the seductions of power in order to ask questions about the relationship between the governance of personal desires and the governance of peoples and nations. It is not surprising, then, that de Sade and Lautréamont were embraced by Surrealists such as André Breton and critics such as Maurice Blanchot, since their anti-Christian and anti-humanist agendas seemed to offer a very modern reaction to realism, rationalism and the optimistic faith in progress characteristic of modernity. Again, it is not surprising that such a reaction provoked fresh allegiance in the wake of World War I (Chisholm points out that de Sade enjoyed a revival in literary circles in Paris in the early 1920s; 1997: 201). However, whereas there is an explicit Sadeian element in *Nightwood*, signalled by the fact that at one point in the novel we find Robin Vote reading 'the memoirs of the Marquis de Sade' (p. 73), the connection with *Les Chants de Maldoror* is more tenuous—although given Barnes's own interest in surrealist thought, it is likely that she would have come across Lautréamont's work. Indeed, the parallels between Lautréamont's novel and *Nightwood* are, to say the least, highly suggestive. Certainly, like both de Sade and Lautréamont, Barnes uses Gothic paraphernalia in order imaginatively to challenge the definition of desire as it is socially constructed.

Maldoror is a disturbing work that eschews linear logic in favour of a nightmare scenario in which—as in the writings of de Sade—one episode of sadistic cruelty follows pell-mell upon another. Its anti-hero, Maldoror, is the perpetrator of these acts, which include rape, incest, bestiality and murder. In diabolic fashion, he sets himself against God, who is portrayed in the spirit of Goya's Saturn as a divinity who eats those he has made and who is careless of, and impervious to, man's suffering. Indeed, like the novel's anti-hero, Lautréamont's God seems to derive pleasure from both causing and watching human agony. Its excesses, like those of the

Gothic genre which it both mimics and parodies in places, give *Les Chants* a blackly humorous air. However, as Alex de Jonge, one of Lautréamont's most perceptive critics has suggested, the French author's use of sensationalism is harnessed to an intellectual end; as in the work of de Sade, the indulgence of excess is used to shock and to challenge cultural conventions:

> In forcing man's attention on his instinctive love of cruelty, no less real for being inadmissible, Maldoror appeals to man's repressed and secret self. Desires that normally have to be sublimated by culture into notions such as crime and punishment, law-enforcement, the obscene rituals of social justice and authoritarianism, are exposed by Maldoror for what they are: institutions created by society to permit its leaders to exercise their natural, instinctive desire to treat their fellows as their slaves, without abdicating from their role as do-gooders and pillars of the community: to behave, in short, like miniature versions of the eating God.
>
> (de Jonge 1973: 51)

Hence, of course, Maldoror's similarity to Milton's most famous character: 'most think that he is tortured by incommensurable pride, as Satan was, and that he would like to be God's equal' (Lautréamont 1973: 31). Milton's Satan and Lautréamont's Maldoror share the same intellectual impulse: a desire to expose the tenets of Christianity and Western civilization to a searing critique. In Lautréamont's text, however, there is no salvation for the deity. Indeed, de Jonge suggests that Lautréamont's work anticipates the Foucauldian insight that we are all trapped within an episteme which limits our self-understanding and knowledge: the only way out, intellectually, is to smash the metaphorical bars of the cultural prison thereby erected (de Jonge 1973: 15). To this end, Lautréamont eschews the world of daylight for the world of night, daytime logic for night-time imaginings, *civitas* for wildness, civilization for barbarism; in terms of style he draws attention to the text by baring the device and by poeticizing his language through linking words by shape and sound rather than by meaning. The resulting experimental nature of his writing gives it a very modern air, although clearly he draws on the works of Maturin, Poe, Scott and Eugène Sue in creating his strange fictional world. Indeed, in choosing his *nom de plume*, Isidore Ducasse presumably turned to Sue's historical novel, *Lautréamont*, published in 1837, the hero of which is described by de Jonge as 'a brutal, insolent officer, with a black and cynical sense of humour and distinctly mephistophelian characteristics' (de Jonge 1973: 29). Lautréamont's writing identity is thus textually haunted by that of an earlier rebel against law and order, just as is that of Barnes. For I want to suggest here that what have been perceived as the more bizarre elements of *Nightwood* derive from a French literary tradition in which *Maldoror* is an important element. In portraying same-sex love, bestiality and incestuous desire, Barnes is not simply writing a 'confessional' novel, which is how *Nightwood* has often been interpreted. Rather, she is also engaging with a European tradition, intellectually iconoclastic and quasi-Gothic in temperament, which seeks to deconstruct the morality of Western civilization in order to expose its hypocrisy and institutionalized cruelty.

This is certainly the aim of Lautréamont's text, which unsympathetic readers dismissed as full of freakishness, salacious acts of cruelty and gratuitous violence. The novel follows the wanderings of the malicious Maldoror, whose restlessness relates him to Melmoth and the Wandering Jew, and whose predatory instincts and thirst for blood relate him to Dracula:

> Heaven grant that his birth be not a calamity for his country, which has thrust him from its bosom. He wanders from land to land, hated by all. Some say that he has been a victim of some special kind of madness since childhood. Others believe that he is of an extreme and instinctive cruelty, of which he himself is ashamed, and that his parents died of grief because of it. There are those who maintain that in his youth he was branded with an epithet and that he has been inconsolable for the rest of his existence because his wounded dignity perceives there a flagrant proof of the wickedness of mankind, which manifests itself during their earliest years and grows continually. This epithet was *The Vampire!*

> (Lautréamont 1965: 30-31)

As I have already intimated, Robin Vote is also a vampiric figure, albeit a less obvious one, in so far as by night she preys sexually on the café inhabitants of Paris, draining her partners of love and energy. A wandering, emotionally estranged being, dislocated from her environment, Robin embodies a misanthropic cynicism. Eschewing the values of her unconventional companions as well as those of the bourgeoisie, she is an anarchic force even within the liberal and tolerant environment of *Nightwood*'s Paris. She is linked with the marginality of the circus people and with the social liminality of the Jew and the sexually 'deviant' (just as Dracula is linked with the Jew, the Gypsy and homosexual desire). Like Maldoror and Dracula (who is associated with wolves and bats), she sometimes seems closer to animals than to people—a feature emphasized by her silence (she speaks fewer than ten times in the novel). Arguably, she has an avatar in Maldoror, whose most fulfilling sexual encounter is coupling with a female shark (and, since Maldoror fantasizes himself as 'the son of a female shark' (Lautréamont 1965: 15), the deed also has a quasi-incestuous dimension). Indeed, Maldoror places dogs above humans in the hierarchy of living things:

> When you are in bed and you hear the howling of the dogs in the fields, hide yourself beneath your blankets, don't make a jest of what they are doing: they have the insatiable thirst for the infinite, like you, like me, like the rest of human beings with our long, pale faces . . . I, even as the dogs, feel a yearning for the infinite.

> (Lautréamont 1965: 15)

Maldoror even sees himself as half beast, half human, with the 'protruding bones of [his] emaciated face, resembling the bones of some great fish' (Lautréamont 1965: 15). Similarly, Robin's connection with animals in *Nightwood* reaffirms the breakdown of the boundary between beast and human represented throughout Barnes's novel. We first meet Robin in a room which looks like 'a jungle' (p. 56); she is described by the narrator as 'a woman who is beast turning human' (p. 59) and later, by the doctor, as 'a wild thing caught in a woman's skin' (p. 206).

This dissolution of the boundary between human and animal takes a particularly nasty turn in *Maldoror,* however, when Maldoror's dog, imitating his master, rapes a beautiful young girl, the daughter of Providence:

> Carrying out that order appeared to be difficult for the bulldog. He thought his master had commanded him to do what had already been done, and this wolf with the monstrous muzzle contended himself with violating the virginity of that delicate child in his turn. From her lacerated stomach the blood ran again down her legs and upon the meadow. Her cries mingled with the animal's yelps. The child held up the golden cross that she wore about her neck that he spare her; she had not dared to present it before the savage eyes of him who first conceived the idea of profiting by the weakness of her age.

> (Lautréamont 1965: 137)

The peculiar closure of *Nightwood,* which culminates in a strange union between Robin and Nora's dog, seems to rework this passage in a more benign manner:

> Sliding down she went; down, her hair swinging, her arms held out, and the dog stood there, rearing back, his forelegs slanting; his paws trembling under the trembling of his rump, his hackle standing; his mouth open, his tongue slung sideways over his sharp bright teeth; whining and waiting. And down she went, until her head swung against his; on all fours now, dragging her knees. The veins stood out in her neck, under her ears, swelled in her arms, and wide and throbbing rose up on her fingers as she moved forward.

> The dog, quivering in every muscle, sprang back, his lips drawn, his tongue a stiff curving terror in his mouth; moved backward, back, as she came on, whimpering too now, coming forward, her head turned completely sideways, grinning and whimpering. Backed now into the farthest corner, the dog reared as if to avoid something that troubled him to such agony that he seemed to be rising from the floor; then he stopped, clawing sideways at the wall, his forepaws lifted and sliding. Then, head down, dragging her forelocks in the dust, she struck against his side. He let loose one howl of misery and bit at her, dashing about her, barking, and as he sprang on either side of her he kept his head toward her, dashing his rump now this side, now that, of the wall.

> Then she began to bark also, crawling after him—barking in a fit of laughter, obscene and touching. The dog began to cry, running with her, head-on with her head,

as if to circumvent her; soft and slow his feet went. He ran this way and that, low down in his throat crying, and she grinning and crying with him; crying in shorter and shorter spaces, moving head to head, until she gave up, lying out, her hands beside her, her face turned and weeping; and the dog too gave up then, and lay down, his eyes bloodshot, his head flat along her knees.

(pp. 237-239)

Interestingly, the raped child in *Maldoror* holds up her cross before the dog 'that he might spare her', knowing that it would be useless to present it to the 'savage eyes' of Maldoror (who will later treat Mervyn, his young male victim, worse than a dog). Similarly, Robin's encounter with Nora's dog, whilst strangely disturbing, seems less threatening than most of the human encounters described in the novel which reveal the 'naturally' exploitative and manipulative manner of human behaviour. The behaviour of dogs, by contrast, ranges from an honest animality to the intellectual/ spiritual 'longing for the infinite' assumed traditionally to be the prerogative of human beings. Thus the Gothic agenda is the same for both episodes: to submit to scrutiny the power of the Church and the intellectual legacy of the Enlightenment which enables the categorization of every thing and every living thing into hierarchies, a supposedly 'objective' process which in fact conceals an agenda whereby particular aspects of life can be denigrated or abjected. An apparently 'innocent' activity, such categorizing underpins particular ideologies and social hegemonies, justifying certain barbarous acts, such as genocide or ethnic cleansing.

On one level, then, Robin, like Maldoror and Dracula, is the wild stranger who brings chaos into the city space and who threatens 'normal' hierarchies. And in the spirit of the Gothic text, Robin's final flight is into the wilderness. Dracula's last resting place is within the rocky wildness of the Carpathian mountains; Frankenstein's monster flees to the Northern Arctic wastes to die. *Nightwood*'s closure gives us Robin finally taking refuge on Nora's wild estate, where the ruined chapel indicates a lost faith and a crumbling civilization. The use of Gothic tropes in Barnes's work, however, is not simply derivative; like Lautréamont, she parodically adapts the Gothic mode in order to challenge convention, conservatism and institutionalized cruelty. Lautréamont's defence of the supernatural and of horror—'do not despair, for in the vampire you have a friend despite your opinion to the contrary' (Lautréamont 1965: 48)—is, finally, a defence of the right to attack the vile body of modernity. It is a sentiment with which Barnes would have been in sympathy.

The same fierce antagonism to contemporary society marks the novels of Huysmans and Céline. Although their works are less obviously Gothic than those of Lautréamont, their penchant for excess and their con-

viction that suffering is the natural condition of humanity place them in the same French tradition of intellectual disaffection. Moreover, even a cursory reading of Huysmans's *A Rebours,* published in 1884 (translated as *Against Nature*), and Céline's *Voyage au bout de la nuit,* published in 1932 (translated as *Journey to the End of the Night*), suggests their influence on *Nightwood.* For example, the *fin-de-siècle* extravagances of des Esseintes's house at Fontenay in Huysmans' *Against Nature,* including a jewel-encrusted tortoise and an organ from which one can draw off various alcoholic drinks in relation to the notes on its keyboard (Huysmans 1998: 35-40), find an echo in the eccentricities of Robin and Nora's apartment in the Rue du Cherche-Midi, which contains:

> circus chairs, wooden horses bought from a ring of an old merry-go-round, venetian chandeliers from the Flea Fair, stage-drops from Munich, cherubim from Vienna, ecclesiastical hangings from Rome, a spinet from England and a miscellaneous collection of music boxes from many countries

(p. 85)

Similarly, des Esseintes's predilection for unusual sexual partners (which include Miss Urania—an androgynous American circus acrobat—as well as a female ventriloquist and a strangely dressed young man) is reflected not only in Robin's sexual eclecticism but also in Barnes's portrayal of the circus in Paris and New York as curiously fascinating and erotic. Whilst Jane Marcus is no doubt right to suggest in 'Laughing at Leviticus' that the depiction of the circus as well as the opera in *Nightwood* indicates Barnes's Rabelaisian spirit and her desire to embrace low as well as high culture, it is worth remembering that there is in French art, as Nicholas White points out, a tradition of representing circus performers as objects of desire (as in the work of Degas, Rops and Seurat) which both Huysmans and Barnes exploited (Huysmans 1998: 208-209).[5] But perhaps the most striking similarity between Huysmans's novel and *Nightwood* is the strange conjunction of Catholic and Sadeian thought evident in both works. Whilst the works of Baudelaire and Edgar Allan Poe are evoked in *Against Nature* 'on account of their similar poetics, their mutual interest in the study of mental illness' (Huysmans 1998: 156), it is de Sade's ambivalent attitude towards religion which fascinates des Esseintes, in particular his desecration of 'a Divinity which he hoped would be willing to damn him, while yet declaring, as a further act of defiance, that this Divinity did not exist' (Huysmans 1998: 132). Not surprisingly, then, des Esseintes's drift towards Catholicism is clearly informed by a relish for suffering as well as beauty (as, indeed, was that of Huysmans himself). The religion that appeals to him is, by his own confession:

> a Catholicism gingered up with a little magic, as occurred under Henri III, and a touch of sadism, as happened at the end of the last century. This special brand

of clericalism, this depraved, artfully perverse mysticism towards which, at certain times of day, he was drawn, could not even be discussed with a priest, who would not have understood it, or who would have promptly, and with horror, rejected it.

(Huysmans 1998: 176-177)

This same ambivalence towards Catholicism is represented in *Nightwood,* where it is linked with Robin's furtive recourse to beautiful churches in Paris and with Matthew O'Connor's masturbating during mass (although this does not stop him describing himself as 'as good a Catholic as they make' (pp. 217-218)). For Erin G. Carlston, Barnes's debts to Huysmans link her with the rise of fascism, for she sees in the alliance between *fin-de-siècle* decadence, Catholicism and dandyism an alternative to Marxist or liberal positivism which ended in the rise of Hitler (Carlston 1998: 59). In order to sustain such a reading, however, Carlston has to ignore the self-reflexive irony of *Nightwood,* conveyed mainly through the musings of Matthew O'Connor who, Felix thinks, although he lies, is 'a valuable liar' (p. 49). O'Connor, who gave his 'kidney on the left side to France in the war' (p. 31), has come face to face with 'the Beast' in the wood of the night and expresses his cynical understanding of human nature in a series of elliptical philosophic musings. He knows that cruelty derives from unresolved fear and that at a social level this expresses itself in war: 'he berserks a fearful dimension' (p. 119). He also understands that the French embrace of 'filthiness' leaves 'a path for the Beast' (p. 123): that the fascinated interest shown by the French in horror and the abject is also symptomatic of a susceptibility to the agenda of fascism which embraces irrationality and cruelty. There is an understanding, however, that risking excess can engender insight: 'You beat the liver out of a goose to get a *pâté*; you pound the muscles of a man's *cardia* to get a philosopher' (p. 127). Or, in Kristeva's words, 'the danger of filth represents for the subject the risk to which the very symbolic order is permanently exposed, to the extent that it is a device of discriminations, of differences' (Kristeva 1982: 69). The American, in avoiding the risk, also eschews greater knowledge and understanding: 'The French are dishevelled, and wise, the American tries to approximate it with drink. It is his only clue to himself. He takes it when his soap has washed him too clean for identification' (p. 131). The American obsession with cleanliness, then, suggests a puritan nation which, whilst resistant to the dangerous seductions of fascist philosophy, demonstrates a cultural narrowness, naivety and intolerance that belie its political agenda of individual freedom (and which can result in McCarthyism). In this respect, whilst Carlston's critique of Barnes as a decadent writer (whom she links with Huysmans, Oscar Wilde and Céline), is extremely useful in properly contextualizing *Nightwood,* her claim that O'Connor's narrative position 'can rather easily be aligned with certain predomi-

nant impulses in fascist writing' (Carlston 1998: 67) is tenable only if one ignores the irony in O'Connor's monologues. If one reads them as ironic, however, they lead us to conclude that any description of *Nightwood* as a quasi-fascist text has already been preempted by O'Connor's own critique of American and French consciousness in relation to 'filthiness' and 'the Beast'. In order to accept Carlston's argument, readers have to close their ears to the element of Gothic parody in *Nightwood.*

I am not, however, trying here to recuperate Barnes as a radical, left-wing thinker. Rather, I would link Barnes's *Nightwood* with Céline's *Journey to the End of the Night,* an equally problematic text. Kristeva has described Céline's novels as expressing 'A yearning after Meaning together with its absorption, ingestion, digestion and rejection' (Kristeva 1982: 136). She has also defined his work as 'apocalyptic' in so far as it embraces 'suffering, horror and their convergence on abjection' (Kristeva 1982: 154): indeed, for her, 'his whole narrative stance seems controlled by the necessity of going through abjection, whose intimate side is suffering and horror its public feature' (Kristeva 1982: 140). Even sexual desire is presented as a form of 'debilitated suffering' (Kristeva 1982: 148). Such a nihilistic vision appealed to intellectuals of both the extreme Left and the extreme Right during the 1930s since, whilst not always agreeing on the causes of alienation (although capitalism became a shared scapegoat in the aftermath of 1929), the same feelings of disaffection from modernity's myth of progress informed opposite ends of the political spectrum.[6] Whilst *Nightwood* has continued to attract divided readings (as those offered by Marcus and Carlston illustrate most recently), *Journey to the End of the Night* has, in retrospect, frequently been seen as sounding a protofascist note which was later to develop into a virulent anti-semitism, tainting Céline's literary reputation and besmirching his life. It is therefore worth recalling that in 1932, Paul Nizan, then a Communist militant, reviewed *Journey* as offering a sinister, but recognizable, portrayal of the world: 'il arrache tous les masques, tous les camouflages, il abat les décors des illusions, il accroît la conscience de la déchéance actuelle de l'homme' ('he tears off all masks, all disguises, he destroys all illusory façades, he seduces us into believing in the total decline of humanity') (my translation) (Suleiman 1971: 45). Indeed, the novel even evoked a Christian defence by René Schwob (Noble 1987: 22). Both works resisted, and continue to resist, definitive readings. In this respect, Carlston's claim that *Nightwood*'s 'resistance to any totalizing "cultural vision" or interpretation' (including her own) is 'both wily and forceful' and her suggestion that its 'complexity' is 'dangerous' (Carlston 1998: 84-85)—as if the novel had a malignant life of its own independent of the reader—betray a strange nervousness. Such a reaction reveals more, perhaps, about a continuing American anxiety in the face of the 'black lineage' of French intellectual pessimism than it does about Barnes's most famous work.

Barnes's letters reveal that she read Céline's *Voyage au bout de la nuit* soon after it was published (Herring 1995: 219) and, indeed, the anonymous reviewer for the *Times Literary Supplement* likened *Nightwood*'s 'sickness of the soul' to 'M. Céline's otherwise quite different book "Voyage au Bout de la Nuit"' (Marcus 1990a: 200). There are certainly some striking parallels between Céline's novel and *Nightwood*. Both novels are structured through the restless picaresque activity of characters who feel emotionally dislocated from their home cultures, with Bardamu journeying between France, French Colonial Africa and the United States and Robin moving between Paris and New York. The self-reflexiveness of both works derives from their self-conscious and experimental use of language which destabilizes the realist dimension of the two novels; in this respect, they are clearly written within the modernist framework. Although Céline's *Journey* is not obviously Gothic, its fascinated delineation of horror and excess, together with what Nicholas Hewitt has described as 'the considerable presence of ghosts' in the text (Hewitt 1987: 75-84), give it a quasi-Gothic air.[7] Moreover, Céline's Bardamu and Barnes's O'Connor are alienated, cynical narrators who see the world as a place of hypocrisy which reeks of lies, suffering and mortality:

> When the grave lies open before us, let's not try to be witty, but on the other hand, let's not forget, but make it our business to record the worst of the human viciousness we've seen without changing one word. When that's done, we can curl up our toes and sink into the pit.
>
> (Céline 1997: 28)

In addition, the trauma of World War I hangs like a pall over both texts and whilst Catholicism is present as nostalgic whiff of incense, God is not. The pessimism of both novels is relieved, however, by a Beckettian humour which allows for despair to be expressed aphoristically: 'love is only infinity put at the disposal of poodles' (Céline 1997: 14); 'We are but skin about a wind, with muscles clenched against mortality' (p. 122). (O'Connor's definition of life as 'the permission to know death' (p. 122) even seems to anticipate the title of Céline's novel, *Mort à crédit*, published in 1936.) Characters survive rather than live in such worlds, which are as black as hell yet portrayed by their authors with what Céline described as a 'comic lyricism': the result is what Kristeva has defined as '(a) laughing apocalypse' or 'an apocalypse without god' (Kristeva 1982: 206). Both texts use the darkness of the night as a metaphor for anomie and despair and both use 'the Beast' to suggest the savagery at the heart of human darkness. Indeed, Céline's Baryton sees the twentieth century as a monster slouching towards annihilation:

> 'I saw the human mind, Ferdinand, losing its balance little by little and dissolving in the vast maelstrom of apocalyptic ambitions! It began about 1900 . . . mark that date! From then on, the world in general and psychiatry in particular have been one frantic race to see who could become more perverse, more salacious, more outlandish, more revolting, more creative as they call it, than his neighbour . . . A pretty mess! Who would be first to throw himself into the arms of the monster, the beast without heart and without restraint! . . . The beast will devour us all, Ferdinand, it's a certainty and a good thing too! What is this beast? . . . A big head that goes where it pleases! . . . Even now its wars and its flaming slobber are pouring in on us from all sides! . . .'
>
> (Céline 1997: 371)

O'Connor equates knowledge of the Beast with the knowledge of the worst that humans can perform and therefore with a true understanding of the human condition:

> The French have made a detour of filthiness—Oh, the good dirt! Whereas you are of a clean race, of a too eagerly washing people, and this leaves no road for you. The brawl of the Beast leaves a path for the Beast. You wash your brawl with every thought, with every gesture, with every conceivable emollient and savon, and expect to find your way again . . . There is not one of us who, given an eternal incognito, a thumbprint nowhere set against our souls, would not commit rape, murder and all abominations.
>
> (pp. 123-24; 128)

The 'detour' into 'filthiness', then, that we see so clearly in the work of de Sade, Lautréamont, Céline and Barnes represents a willingness to confront the abject as Kristeva defines it in *The Powers of Horror*: 'what disturbs identity, system, order. What does not respect borders, positions, rules. The in-between, the ambiguous, the composite. The traitor, the liar, the criminal with a good conscience, the shameless rapist, the killer who claims he is a savior . . .' (Kristeva 1982: 4). Drawing on the work of anthropologists and Freud's *Totem and Taboo*, Kristeva explores the key role of filth in the construction of social identities:

> It is as if dividing lines were built up between society and a certain nature, as well as within the social aggregate, on the basis of the simple logic of *excluding filth*, which, promoted to the ritual of *defilement*, founded the 'self and clean' of each social group if not of each subject . . . Defilement is what is jettisoned from the '*symbolic system*'. It is what escapes that social rationality, that logical order on which a social aggregate is based, which then becomes differentiated from a temporary agglomeration of individuals and, in short constitutes a *classification system or a structure*.
>
> (Kristeva 1982: 65)

To explore the relative nature of 'filth', and to question its categorization, is thus to question the construction of social orders and the basis on which individual subjectivity is founded. It is to probe at the very boundaries of what it means to be human: 'filth is not a quality in itself, but it applies only to what relates to a *boundary*' (Kristeva 1982: 69). The frailty of both collective and individual identities is thereby instantly exposed. That way madness—or at least the risk of it—lies; hence the interest in dislocated states of mind evident in the work of both Barnes and Céline. Such writing also exposes the fact that social morality derives from cultural constructions of the abject rather than philosophic objectivity. The inevitable conclusion that social-value systems are arbitrary and primitive results in both aggressive challenges to convention and profound cynicism. Thus, within the fictional worlds of Céline and Barnes, the usual taboo system is reversed so that darkness equals enlightenment, transgression equals liberty and the embrace of 'filth' signals intellectual integrity (for Bardamu war is to be rejected as 'filth' rather than to be welcomed as a noble venture and for Robin Vote promiscuity is true freedom). Or, as de Jonge notes of Maldoror's unsociable antics, 'Truth and freedom will be only achieved through basic transgression' (de Jonge 1973: 49). However, whereas exploration of the abject through transgression cannot be culturally tolerated as social deed, it can be tolerated as literary text: 'Because it occupies its place, literature may also involve not an ultimate resistance to but an unveiling of the abject: an elaboration, a discharge, and a hollowing out of abjection through the Crisis of the Word' (Kristeva 1982: 208).

This 'unveiling' is what links the work of the French authors briefly discussed here and whose writings seem to have influenced Barnes' creation of *Nightwood*. It should be clear, therefore, that I disagree with Chisholm, who locates Barnes's 'grotesquely pessimistic' eroticism solely within the modernist moment of surrealism, which she sees as outdoing 'its Romantic and Sadean precursors by using eros to invoke and release the revolutionary energies concealed in the detritus of industrialist-capitalist society' (Chisholm 1993: 187, 172). Rather, I see Barnes as aligning herself with a particular French intellectual tradition whose authors all share an obsession with '(a)bjection, or the journey to the end of the night' (Kristeva 1982: 58). (The exception here, perhaps, is Huysmans who turned, like des Esseintes, to Catholicism for consolation in the face of nihilism.) Moreover, in so far as their writings thereby face the void of meaninglessness, they also engage with Gothic notions of sublimity. 'No Beast is there without glimmer of infinity' in Victor Hugo's words (Kristeva 1982: 1). It is not surprising, then, to find that, in its turn, *Nightwood* influenced other writers of the Gothic, including Carson McCullers and William Faulkner, both of whom admired her writing style and her portrayal of the grotesque (Herring 1995: 299). It also seems to have left its mark on Jeanette Winterson's *Sexing the Cherry* and Carter's *Nights at the Circus*. The French

'detour' into 'filthiness', then, found its way across the Channel and the Atlantic via the '*Colonie américaine*' in Paris. European Gothic has a way of spiriting itself into even the cleanest of Anglo-Saxon beds.

Notes

1. All quotations are from this 1985 edition of the novel; page references will appear hereafter in the text. I would like to thank Paul Callick for first drawing my attention to Lautréamont's *Madorer* and Ursula Tidd for suggesting the link with Huysmans's *A Rebours*. I would also like to express my warm appreciation of help received from Ursula Tidd and Geoff Harris, who both provided detailed feedback on the final draft of the chapter. Any errors or misjudgements that remain are, of course, my own.

2. For more on the *roman noir*, see Hale 1998.

3. See Horner and Zlosnik 2001 for a fuller justification of Barnes's novel as a gothic text.

4. See Pulzer 1964 for the reasons for this.

5. It is perhaps also worth noting that the Hoffmannesque element in *Nightwood* noted by Marcus might well derive from Barnes's reading of *Against Nature*, in which the Coppelia of Hoffmann's *The Sand Man* is invoked.

6. See Sternhell 1983.

7. Hewitt argues that the portrayal of so many '*fantômes*' in the novel are Céline's way of representing Barmadu's alienation from contemporary society: 'Bardamu as the "fantôme burlesque de la médecine bourgeoise", demonstrates a profound and sensitive awareness on Céline's part of the historical significance of the First World War, which ushered in a new and increasingly rebarbative society and contrived to invalidate so many of the positive myths by which men live' (Hewitt 1987: 84).

References

Barnes, D. (1985) *Nightwood,* London, Faber & Faber [1936].

Blanchot, M. (1949) *Lautréamont et Sade,* Paris, Gallimard.

Carlston, E. G. (1998) *Thinking Fascism: Sapphic Modernism and Fascist Modernity,* Stanford, Stanford University Press.

Carter, A. (1974) *Fireworks,* London, Faber & Faber.

Céline, L.-F. (1997) *Journey to the End of the Night (Voyage au bout de la nuit)*, trans. Ralph Manheim, London, John Calder [1932].

Chisholm, D. (1997) 'Obscene Modernism: *Eros Noir* and the Profane Illumination of Djuna Barnes', *American Literature,* 69:1, 167-206.

Dalton, A. B. (1993) '"This is Obscene": Female Voyeurism, Sexual Abuse, and Maternal Power in *The Dove*', *Review of Contemporary Fiction,* 13:3, 117-139.

Eliot, T. S. (1937) 'Introduction', in D. Barnes, *Nightwood,* London, Faber & Faber, 1-7.

Fiedler, L. (1992) *Love and Death in the American Novel,* New York, Anchor Books.

Field, A. (1983) *The Formidable Miss Barnes: The Life of Djuna Barnes,* London, Secker & Warburg.

France, P. (ed.) (1995) *The New Oxford Companion to Literature in French,* Oxford, Clarendon Press.

Galvin, M. E. (1999) *Queer Poetics: Five Modernist Women Writers,* Westport, Greenwood Press.

Hale, T. (1998) 'Roman Noir', in M. Mulvey-Roberts (ed.), *The Handbook to Gothic Literature,* London, Macmillan, pp. 189-195.

Herring, P. (1993) 'Zadel Barnes: Journalist', *Review of Contemporary Fiction,* 13:3, 107-116.

————. (1995) *Djuna: The Life and Work of Djuna Barnes,* London and New York, Viking.

Hewitt, N. (1987) *The Golden Age of Louis-Ferdinand Céline,* Leamington Spa, Hamburg, New York, Berg Publishers.

Horner, A. and Zlosnik, S. (2001) 'Strolling in the Dark: Gothic Flânerie in Djuna Barnes's *Nightwood*', in A. Smith and J. Wallace (eds), *Gothic Modernisms,* London, Macmillan, pp. 78-95.

Huysmans, J.-K. (1998) *Against Nature* (*A Rebours*), trans. M. Mauldon, Oxford, Oxford University Press [1884].

de Jonge, A. (1973) *Nightmare Culture: Lautréamont and Les Chants de Maldoror,* London, Secker & Warburg.

Kristeva, J. (1982) *Powers of Horror: An Essay on Abjection* (*Pouvoirs de l'horreur*), trans. Leon S. Roudiez, New York, Columbia University Press.

Lautréamont (1965) *Maldoror* (*Les Chants de Maldoror*) trans. G. Wenham, New York, New Directions Publishing Corporation [1868-69].

Marcus, J. (1990a) 'Mousemeat: Contemporary Reviews of *Nightwood*', in M. L. Broe (ed.), *Silence and Power,* Carbondale and Edwardsville, Southern Illinois University Press, pp. 195-206.

————. (1990b), 'Laughing at Leviticus: *Nightwood* as Woman's Circus Epic', in M. L. Broe (ed.), *Silence and Power,* Carbondale and Edwardsville, Southern Illinois University Press, pp. 221-250.

Moers, E. (1986) *Literary Women,* London, The Women's Press [1976].

Mulvey-Roberts, M. (ed.) (1998) *The Handbook to Gothic Literature,* Basingstoke, Macmillan.

Nimeiri, A. (1993) 'Djuna Barnes's *Nightwood* and "the Experience of America"', *Critique: Studies in Contemporary Fiction,* 34:1, 100-112.

Noble, I. (1987) *Language and Narration in Céline's Writings,* Basingstoke, Macmillan.

Pulzer, P. G. (1964) *The Rise of Political Anti-Semitism in German and Austria,* New York and London, John Wiley & Sons.

Punter, D. *The Literature of Terror (Vol. 2) The Modern Gothic,* London, Addison Wesley Longman.

Scott, B. K. (1990) *The Gender of Modernism: A Critical Anthology,* Bloomington and Indianapolis, Indiana University Press.

Sternhell, Z. (1983) *Ni droite ni gauche: l'idéologie fasciste en France,* Paris, Le Seuil.

Sue, E. (n.d.) *The Mysteries of Paris* (*Les Mystères de Paris*), Sawtry, Cambridgeshire and New York, Dedalus/ Hippocrene (Dedalus European Classics).

Suleiman, S. (1971) *Paul Nizan: pour une nouvelle culture,* Paris, Editions Bernard Grasset.

RACE, SOCIETY, AND POLITICS

Justin D. Edwards (essay date 2003)

SOURCE: Edwards, Justin D. "Epilogue: Twentieth-Century Gothicism and Racial Ambiguity." In *Gothic Passages: Racial Ambiguity and the American Gothic,* pp. 110-14. Iowa City: University of Iowa Press, 2003.

[In the following excerpt, Edwards touches on William Faulkner's use of Gothic in Light in August *to depict the search for identity by the biracial character Joe Christmas.]*

While depictions of racial ambiguity existed in gothic discourse prior to Poe and have continued after Chesnutt, Poe's ideas about hybridity and racial amalgamation during the late 1850s mark a paradigm shift in the articulations of racial categories that flourished during the rest of the century. Indeed, Poe's use of the term "hybrid" in *Pym* to describe race mixture and identificatory ambiguity became an influential model for representations of racial mixture. These, in turn, were challenged and supplanted by the rise of popular forms of Darwinism in the late nineteenth and early twentieth centuries. Stephen Crane's *The Monster* (1899), for instance, resists the conflation of gothicism with racial ambiguity and moves toward a representation of blackness, whiteness, and the gothic which, a few decades later, would be picked up by African American writers such as Richard Wright and Ralph Ellison. In Crane's novella, Henry Johnson, a black man whose face is disfigured in a laboratory fire and who is then ostracized by his community, adopts a Darwinistic model of race and identity in a hybrid text that draws on both naturalist forms and gothic images. The effacing of Henry marks him as both an outcast and a weak man who cannot survive within a community where whiteness is equated with health and strength. The survival of the fittest, a repressive ideology that displaces Henry because of his black skin and disfigured face, is presented alongside the macabre setting of the doctor's giant, dark house and the monstrous community that banishes the victim, calling for his blood. More terrifying, however, is the image of Henry's "monstrousness," which is not a great remove from the formidable racist constructions of the black man as an "uncivilized animal" or an "ignoble savage," racist constructions which are, as Toni Morrison notes, dominant in American literature (59).

Crane connects racial difference, gothicism, and scientific ideologies when Henry's deformity arises out of an accident in Dr. Trescott's scientific laboratory, transforming Henry from man to monster. This metamorphosis, which echoes the scientific creation of the monster in Mary Shelley's *Frankenstein,* furthers the text's merger of gothicism and race when the doctor creates a grotesque life form, a figure whose descendants also include Dr. Jekyll and Dr. Moreau. Central to Shelley's and Crane's texts is the gothic depiction of the laboratory, which, in *Frankenstein,* is a gloom-drenched laboratory full of ominous equipment, and which, in Dr. Trescott's lab, inspires Henry's "fear" and "terror" (405). This lab is clearly a place where nature is manipulated and altered: Henry is given a monstrous new life here, for an acid compound shatters its glass container and "sizzles" upon Henry's "molten head" like a "red snake [that] flowed directly down into Johnson's upturned face" (406). The burning chemical, moreover, transforms into a snake—the original "monster" of Eden—that symbolically bites Henry, infecting him with a poison from which he will never recover. And just as the biblical snake robs innocence, the "liquid snake" is the final stage in the infliction of pain and oppression that disfigures Henry into the monster.

Crane's text is significant because it uses gothic conventions fraught with political symbolism—the fire also destroys an engraving of *The Signing of the Declaration*—by highlighting the contradictory American assertion, in the face of Henry's blackness, that all men are created equal (403). Crane's framing of Henry's burning with this engraving (which eventually drops to the floor, bursting with "the sound of a bomb") calls attention to Henry's disenfranchised position within the nation: the blaze is called Henry's "submission" and he is said to be "a creature to the flames" (405). The flames thus symbolize his weak position within American culture; he must submit to the fire just as he must submit to wealthy white men such as Dr. Trescott. The uncanny house, then, is haunted by national injustices of the past; its burning structure reflects the heated racial tensions that threaten to destroy the nation and consume the principles upon which the Declaration of Independence was signed. Just as Henry finds the fire-ravaged house inescapable, he is unable to escape the history of his fathers—not only the founding forefathers represented in the engraving—but those African American fathers whose lives were ravaged by slavery.

It is significant that Crane's text turns away from the gothicism of racial ambiguity found in earlier nineteenth-century texts. Henry's skin is unmistakably black, and the scenes of abuse are clearly inscribed on his body, which, like Sethe's chokecherry tree in Toni Morrison's *Beloved,* displays the tortures of a racial injustice written on the flesh as well as in the text. Henry's disfigured face fits this gothic pattern, but this physical abuse is compounded by the psychological abuses of segregation; that is, Henry is removed from the streets of Whilomville: first, he is confined to a house on the outskirts of town; and, second, after escaping from Williams's home, he is incarcerated in the local prison. The abuse that can be read on Henry's body engenders the desire to section him off from society, just as the 1896 *Plessy v. Ferguson* decision attempted to restrict the actions of a portion of the population. Crane's gothicism, then, attacks the segregation laws that deny the very existence of racial ambiguity; in fact, the theme of segregation merges with gothic conventions in the conclusion of the text where we find Henry (who now inhabits the room over Dr. Trescott's carriage house) wearing "a heavy crêpe veil" over his face (435). In this penultimate scene, Henry has taken on the physical characteristics of a phantom, while his face continues to be segregated from the town's field of vision.

The creation of this phantom presence is thus presented as a crime for which an outraged Mother Nature seeks revenge. Appearing at a time when lynchings and urban race riots were on the rise and in which theories of racial difference proliferated, *The Monster* responded to the pseudo-Darwinist theories that were motivated by a desire to restrict immigration on racial grounds. Such overtly racist works such as Lothrop Stoddard's *The Rising Tide of Color Against White World-Supremacy* (1922) and Madison Grant's *The Passing of the Great*

Race; or, the Racial Basis of European History (1916) attempted to define race in strictly biological terms. With this in mind, the creation of Henry as the ghastly Other may encompass the creation of an artificial racial binary that pits whiteness against blackness. The genesis of the monster, I suggest, comes to stand in for the genesis of pseudoscientific racial theories that justify the effacing of African Americans. Given that Crane's narrative questions essentialist racial divisions, the text implies that, just as the scientific laboratory transforms Henry into the beast, American "scientific" theories about racial difference work to create an inferior race through doctrines of white supremacy.

When one reads *The Monster* in this light, it is important to remember that anxiety over the early 1900s shift in American racial geography resulted in a revival of scientific attempts to prove that African American was a degraded race. And the dissemination of Darwinist theories throughout the United States provided a scientific frame of reference from which social critics could revive the debate over the place of black men and women in the human community. As a result, arguments that echoed antebellum proslavery diatribes of natural "Negro inferiority" were presented to the public by "objective social scientists." William P. Calhoun and Charles Carroll, for example, espoused "Aryan supremacy," claiming that "the negro was genetically inferior," a race that would never overcome "immorality, dishonesty, laziness or ignorance" (Carroll 54). It is also interesting to note that Calhoun and Carroll couched their racist ideas in gothic terms; blacks, they claimed, were "a fungus growth that the white man should totally destroy," for, they claimed, blacks were "the greatest menace" to the "Anglo-Saxon civilization" because of the potential for "pollution with the blood of the depraved Ethiopian" (Calhoun 139, 141). These racist ideologues asserted that African Americans of the early 1900s were "unreliable" and even "inhuman" (Carroll 56). Such discourses stemmed from northern migration and the subsequent restructuring of the Northern and Southern economies. The assumed instability generated by this "unreliable" race resulted in an anxiety about race relations. That is, by espousing the "unreliable" nature of African Americans, racist social scientists could circulate discourses of fear and anxiety based on social instability; if blacks were not loyal or reliable, these people claimed, white control in the United States would be vulnerable to attacks arising out of racial oppression.

While Calhoun and his contemporaries discouraged racial mixture and feared racial ambiguity, the early twentieth century also witnessed an increase in the number of African American authors who turned to biracial figures and narratives of passing. As M. Giulia Fabi has argued, racial ambiguity and passing became an important theme that laid the groundwork for the rise of the African American novel, but this theme was to be fully explored only by black writers of the twentieth century (12). Indeed, the trope of passing by, among others, James Weldon Johnson, Nella Larsen, Jessie Fauset, Walter White, and George Schuyler transformed representations of blackness and often celebrated racial ambiguity as a reaction to the restrictive myths of racial purity and the color line. Passing, for these writers, was not a source of fear and anxiety; it was an important subject in the dramatization of race as a cultural construct; it was a part of the quest for, and expression of, racial identity; and it was a challenge to the irrationalities of the American attempt to classify races biologically. To a large extent these novels, particularly those published during the Harlem Renaissance, explored the coding that interacts with America's basic attitudes toward racial intermixture.

One exception to this is William Faulkner's *Light in August* (1932), in which Joe Christmas's passing is depicted as a haunting presence that not only merges the binaries of blackness and whiteness but also joins together the past with the present and the South with the North. As a kind of tableau, a ghostlike figure, Joe generates anxiety in the town of Jefferson; his body is a testament to the ontological breakdown of American racial categories, and he symbolizes the return of a repressed history of slavery, rape, and miscegenation. As such, he is always potentially violent, and his relationship with Miss Burden, a white woman, culminates in his violent murdering of her and the burning of her plantation, an act that recalls the white antebellum anxieties over slave insurrections. Indeed, as a figure who is simultaneously "real" and "not real," he embodies an "in-betweenness" associated with a state of abjection that complicates the distinctions between self and other, subject and object. It is here that meanings begin to collapse; we are forced to see Joe Christmas as existing "beside himself," inside and outside of himself, as well as confounding the hermeneutics of language and racial difference.

The epistomological certainties of *Light in August* are always illusory, for there are multiple breakdowns in the transference of knowledge, exposing gaps in language and understanding. No light can be shed on Joe's heritage, for example, and we are thus left in the dark when it comes to ascribing him a fixed identity. Any "truthful" determination of selfhood is impossible and certainties are concealed by the text, just as lightness or darkness cannot be read on his body. The secrets and mysteries of the text's gothicism are never unveiled; we are never enlightened. Faulkner's gothic novel thus points back to nineteenth-century depictions of racial ambiguity that highlight an anxiety about the collapse of meaning and the erasure of racial binaries. Joe's lack of a stable or singular race identity and his failure to embody fully either race successfully, suggest the ontological impossibility that uneasily inhabits the structure of racial identity. Presenting himself at times as white and at other times as black locates him in relation to others, but the "being" that relates Joe to each of these terms of identity is actually a "not-being." That is, his failure to be either black or white is a failure to "be himself," a failure to realize himself authentically and a failure to identify himself with blackness or whiteness. This failure is not . . . a personal, subjective failure; rather, it is the failure of any form of rigid classification at the heart of the limited language of racial identity. Joe's identity, like so many of the passing figures [I have mentioned], exposes the fact that identity is not what one is but what one passes for—a vision of identity that has often been articulated in gothic terms.

Works Cited

Calhoun, William P. *The Caucasian and the Negro in the United States. They Must Separate. If Not, Then Extermination; A Proposed Solution: Colonization.* Columbia, SC. 1902. N.p.

Carroll, Charles. *The Negro a Beast, or, In the Image of God.* St. Louis. 1900. N.p.

Crane, Stephen. *The Monster.* In *Stephen Crane: Prose and Poetry.* New York: Library of America, 1996. 391-448.

Fabi, M. Giulia. *Passing and the Rise of the African American Novel.* Champaign: U of Illinois P, 2001.

Faulkner, William. *Light in August.* 1932. New York: Random House, 1959.

Grant, Madison. *The Passing of the Great Race; or, the Racial Basis of European History.* New York: Scribner's, 1916.

Morrison, Toni. *Beloved.* New York: Knopf, 1987.

Stoddard, Lothrop. *The Rising Tide of Color Against White World-Supremacy.* New York: Scribner's, 1922.

Gregory G. Pepetone (essay date 2003)

SOURCE: Pepetone, Gregory G. "Chronicles of Redemption." In *Gothic Perspectives on the American Experience,* pp. 135-68. New York: Peter Lang, 2003.

[*In the excerpt below, Pepetone identifies what he terms the "Political Gothic" genre and focuses on Oliver Stone's* JFK.]

The political Gothic imagination explores perverse power relationships, dialectical inequalities within our system of constitutional checks and balances, hidden histories, and the conspiratorial mechanisms whereby officially sanctioned versions of history, i.e., consensus histories, are shaped and rendered plausible. As a narrative genre, the political Gothic may function almost independently of other Gothic genres. Conversely, it may seek to achieve a blend of political, philosophical, psychological, and supernatural perspectives, as does the complex cinematic mythos of Oliver Stone's complementary pairing, *JFK* and *Nixon.* Whereas *JFK* seems a comparatively straightforward exercise in *cinéma vérité,* a docudrama that presents an alleged hidden history of the Cold War era, it is also a self-conscious exploration of what academic philosophy refers to as the epistemological question, i.e., an examination of the meaning and nature of truth itself. Moreover, Stone's film furnishes a compelling study of the psychological price exacted from authentic Gothic heroes who confront disturbing truths that most of us prefer to either ignore or deny. *Nixon,* meanwhile, is an almost classic instance of the interior drama on which psychological Gothic narrative thrives. Nevertheless, for much of its imagery and characterization it draws upon prototypes derived from literary and cinematic horror. These prototypes suggest the supernatural Gothic in ways that provide an archetypal dimension to Stone's portrayal of Richard M. Nixon as a half-crazed tyrant caught in the snares of his obsessive need to destroy his political "enemies," exorcise personal demons from his troubled past, and gain political mastery over the sinister forces of covert fascism that have lifted him to national prominence. The literary, journalistic, and cinematic antecedents of Stone's sophisticated and richly textured blend of Gothic genres are many.

In 1962, Fletcher Knebel and Charles W. Bailey II wrote a political thriller entitled *Seven Days in May* that was subsequently turned into a critically acclaimed film starring Burt Lancaster as the treasonous General Scott, Kirk Douglas as Colonel Jiggs, the thankless informer responsible for exposing Scott's planned coup, and Frederick March as the Kennedy-style President Jordan Lyman. John Frankenheimer, who also worked on *The Manchurian Candidate,* and screenwriter Rod Serling of *Twilight Zone* fame, collaborated on *Seven Days in May. The Manchurian Candidate,* adapted from another literary Cold War thriller, is premised on the ability of governments to create, á la Frankenstein, a programmed assassin. As attested by John Marks (see *In Search of the Manchurian Candidate: The CIA and Mind Control*), this capability is one that was being developed by the CIA's MK-ULTRA program at the very time Hollywood's cautionary Cold War parable was in production. Frankenheimer's film was informed by canons of political correctness that prevailed during the McCarthy era. Consequently, the sinister conspirators it features are communists from the Far East. The fictional plot of *Conspiracy Theory,* a more recent cinematic foray into the realm of the political Gothic, explores a similar premise, though the post-Warren Commission climate of opinion in America rendered it unnecessary for

Hollywood to identify the origin of those who are seeking to program Jerry Fletcher—a likable patsy portrayed by Mel Gibson—as emanating from any point further east than Langley, Virginia.

Conversely, *Seven Days in May* envisions a planned military *coup d'état* provoked by the decision of a liberal president to ratify a controversial peace treaty with the Soviets at the height of the Cold War. The dénouement of the novel includes the following short speech from a general loyal to his constitutional oath: "I did a lot of putting two and two together on the way over here, Senator, People always say it can't happen here, and I'm one of those people. But all of a sudden I figured out I was wrong. Given the right circumstances, it can happen anywhere, and don't quote me in the Senate, but the military has been riding awful high-wide-and-handsome in this country ever since World War II" (Knebel and Bailey II 311). This sentiment was forcefully, if somewhat belatedly, expressed by another prominent military man, President Dwight D. Eisenhower in his Farewell Address to the Nation on January 1, 1961: "The conjunction of an immense military establishment and a large arms industry is new in the American experience. . . . We must never let the weight of this combination endanger our liberties or democratic processes. We should take nothing for granted" (Stone and Sklar 1).

Documentary footage of Eisenhower's televised address comprises the opening segment of *JFK*, Oliver Stone's recreation of the Cold War at its most perilous hour. In it, Stone complies with Eisenhower's advice to take nothing at face value with regard to the events of that period. Interestingly, John F. Kennedy himself had offered to vacate the White House during the filming of *Seven Days in May*, predicting that the scenario it developed was one that could happen to him if another fiasco similar to the Bay of Pigs incident were to occur during his administration (Frankenheimer, director's commentary, DVD). Kennedy was, of course, referring to the unsuccessful, CIA-engineered invasion of Castro's Cuba in 1961. From the standpoint of America's shadow government, a similar disaster did, in fact, occur the following year when the Cuban missile crisis resulted in a pledge from Kennedy to Soviet Premier Khrushchev. In essence, Kennedy assured the Soviets that America would never again invade Cuba provided the Russian-supplied nuclear warheads were dismantled and permanently removed from that island. In Dallas on November 22, 1963, according to Oliver Stone, America's shadow government implemented the coup that President Kennedy anticipated in response to such a pledge.

What distinguishes Stone's efforts from those of the other entirely fictional films mentioned above is that he uses actual people and events as a springboard for his-

torical speculation, or revision, as some would prefer to call it, thereby polluting time-honored distinctions between fact and fiction, history and romance, art and propaganda. These distinctions, however, are neither so pure nor so time-honored as Stone's detractors would have us believe. Walpole's *The Castle of Otranto,* English fiction's first neo-Gothic novel, was originally presented as a true story. A short time later, MacPherson's *The Poems of Ossian,* another Gothic literary hoax passed off as the product of an antique Celtic bard, incited the intelligentsia on both sides of the Atlantic to heated controversy over its authenticity. To cite a more recent example, Whitley Streiber's 1987 best-selling novel *Communion,* which allegedly chronicles its author's encounters with an alien intelligence, is either an artful literary hoax or an astounding confirmation of Hamlet's Gothic assertion that there are indeed more things in heaven and earth than are dreamt of by scientists wedded to consensus understandings of the cosmos.

Stone's own defense against the charge of historical distortion vacillates, somewhat disingenuously, between the claim that he is a mythmaker not an historian, and the countercharge that his critics are inconsistent in signaling out *JFK* and *Nixon* while ignoring other dramas that are at least as flagrant in their distortion of history, such as Peter Shaffer's *Amadeus*—an historically questionable account of the alleged murder of Mozart. Nevertheless, Stone's arguments are essentially valid. In the manner of Shakespeare, Walter Scott, Charles Brockden Brown, and Nathaniel Hawthorne, he uses history as artistic raw material from which to fashion a modern political mythology, though his literary predecessors typically softened their criticisms of contemporary events by distancing them in time and/or geographical setting. Similarly, the harsh invective directed at Stone's work by lawyers, journalists, and historians such as Robert G. Blakey, George Wills, Anthony Lewis, George Lardner Jr., Gerald Posner, Stephen Ambrose, and many others, suggests levels of denial and disingenousness that run far deeper than any to be found in Stone's forthright, if not entirely convincing, rebuttals. Not unlike the assassins in the film's mythic reenactment of the Dallas conspiracy, Stone's character assassins often shoot from protective cover at their moving target—attacking his continually evolving perspective from so many angles as to render an effective response impossible.

Apart from Frankenheimer's successful Cold War fantasies and the more generic historical influence of silent filmmakers such as Sergei Eisenstein and D. W. Griffith, at least two modern Hollywood practitioners of the political Gothic influenced and anticipated Stone's work. In his commentary, included in the *Special Edition Director's Cut* of *JFK*, he refers specifically to Frank Capra and Orson Welles in this regard. Alluding to the essential "harshness of vision" that informed Capra's films during the 1930s, he takes pointed exception to the standard criticism of Capra as a purveyor of patriotic sentiment grounded in an idealized perception of America. Many critics were quick to compare Stone/Costner's portrayal of Jim Garrison, the New Orleans District Attorney who brought the only prosecution in the murder of President Kennedy, to Jefferson Smith, played by James Stewart in Capra's 1939 classic *Mr. Smith Goes to Washington*: "According to one such critic, Stone also made this comparison. 'The D.A.,' Stone said, was . . . someone who undertakes to investigate something that had been covered up. He makes mistakes. He has many frustrations. He has few successes. He is reviled, ridiculed, and the case he brings to trial crashes. . . . Capra's movie is a declaration of principles in the face of murderous odds. 'Lost causes,' as Mr. Capra says, 'are the only causes worth fighting for.'" Thus, according to Frank Beaver, "*JFK* resulted in a different kind of Stone film—one with more bathos than edge, a cause movie rather than a caustic one'" (Mackey-Kallis 37). The ahistorical nature of such criticism fails to take into account Capra's impact on his journalistic contemporaries. Similarly to *JFK, Mr. Smith* touched a popular nerve while managing to reduce pundits, diplomats, and politicians to a condition bordering on hysteria. Writing of this phenomenon in his autobiography, Capra comments wryly, "I took the worst shellacking of my professional life. Shifts of hopping-mad Washington press correspondents belittled, berated, scorned, vilified, and ripped me open from stem to stern as a villainous Hollywood traducer" (Capra 283).

One Democratic senator proclaimed that *Mr. Smith* was "exactly the kind of picture that dictators of totalitarian governments would like to have their subjects believe exists in a democracy" (Capra 287). Ironically, one of the film's most illustrious critics was none other than the American Ambassador in London, Joseph P. Kennedy, who upon viewing the film phoned a top executive at Columbia Pictures to complain that, in criticizing democracy, it furnished America's enemies with a propaganda weapon (Capra 289). Kennedy went on to urge that the film be withdrawn from Columbia's European market. Columbia's Harry Cohn responded that *Mr. Smith* was a "shot in the arm for all the Joes in the world that resent being bought and sold and pushed around by all the Hitlers in the world" (Capra 289). Obviously, Capra's vision of America seemed far less warm, fuzzy, and inoffensive to the guardians of truth in his own day than it does to their modern counterparts. Today's champions of consensus history have been similarly assertive in their denunciation of Stone's *JFK* as a dangerous attack on democracy itself. Often they have employed the very arguments used by critics of Capra's film in 1939.

In a scene reminiscent of the democratic letter campaign in Capra's film, Garrison/Costner, during his closing argument to the jury, holds up a handful of letters containing small cash donations. According to Garrison, these letters from ordinary men and women throughout America who wish to support his legal crusade attest to the people's hunger for truth and justice with regard to the murder of their president. In an impassioned appeal to the jury—and by extension, the viewing audience—Garrison/Costner refers to the Kennedy assassination as America's darkest moment and exhorts his audience in the following terms to uphold the authentic American dream: "Do not forget the young President who forfeited his life. Show the world this is still a government *of* the people, *for* the people, and *by* the people. (Stone and Sklar 178-79). Garrison's stirring tribute to the authentic American dream, which might have come directly out of Capra's earlier film, invokes the language of Thomas Jefferson as well as Jefferson Smith. In an earlier scene deleted from the final cut, Garrison's assistant, Numa Bertell, reads aloud from one of the thousands of letters Garrison later refers to in his closing argument: "Dear Mr. Garrison, God bless you for having the courage to go after the murderers of President Kennedy. . . . We have four kids and not an extra lot of money but we enclose a contribution to help with your work." Bertell comments, "That's what it's about, boss. For every lousy article in the press there's a hundred of these" (Stone and Sklar 95). Dramatizing the difference, not only between Garrison and his detractors but between the age of Capra and that of Stone, Bill Broussard, another, far more cynical assistant who would later betray Garrison, sarcastically reminds Bertell that Garrison's opponents are not corresponding (Stone and Sklar 95).

The most obvious and telling difference between Mr. Smith in Washington and Mr. Garrison in New Orleans is that, in the end, the former prevailed over the forces of greed, anomie, and corruption arrayed against him, whereas the latter did not. According to an arithmetic of the human spirit difficult to calculate, suggests Stone, that difference measures the defeat sustained by democratic idealism during a Cold War supposedly fought in its defense. Advocates of covert fascism have always accused their opponents of gross sentimentality. This charge was raised by critics of Dickens's appeal to human decency in *A Christmas Carol* and by critics of Capra's imaginative gloss on that appeal in *It's a Wonderful Life*. Similarly, it is raised by critics of Stone's insistence that anti-Communism and pro-capitalism together do not necessarily equal American patriotism. Indeed, according to Stone, the highly combustible chemistry of that Cold War formula may have destroyed the authentic American dream.

In the same DVD commentary on *JFK* in which Stone expresses his affinity for Capra, he asserts, "Orson

Welles should have made this film. He had the right kind of jigsaw mind." Although Garrison's impassioned plea on behalf of the truth as our most prized possession would seem to imply an infallible judgment, Garrison's Platonic idealism (and by extension that of Oliver Stone) implies no such thing. On the contrary, one of the obvious points of similarity between Stone and Welles is the way in which both filmmakers encode the allusiveness and complexity of truth into the very structure of their Gothic narratives. That structure consists of a kaleidoscope of episodes that are discontinuous in time, style, setting, and technique. These disjunctive episodes include actual documentary footage, pseudo-documentary footage, the use of surrealistic montage, rapid-fire time shifts, and confrontations between human perspectives that are mutually exclusive. By these disorienting means, Welles and Stone recreate the confusing welter of impressions that anyone who would gain so much as a fleeting glimpse of the truth must confront and master. In doing so, they pay homage to the impenetrable mystery of life that lies at the core of the philosophical Gothic paradigm.

Indeed, both *Citizen Kane* and *JFK* project a postmodernist conception of truth as something that is unknowable, or at least unverifiable. Both plots present their audiences with mysteries that are not only unsolved but unsolvable. The meaning of Kane's final utterance, "Rosebud," is rejected as a key to a definitive understanding of his character and motivations. Similarly, Garrison fails in his quest to define the exact parameters of the conspiracy that claimed Kennedy's life or to bring those responsible for it to justice. In the words of Susan Mackey-Kallis, "In many ways it [*JFK*] is . . . the most sophisticated and complicated of Stone's films, taking as its theoretical polemic the search for 'truth' with the realization that there is no single, ultimately knowable truth about the Kennedy assassination" (Mackey-Kallis 38). The truth about the Kennedy assassination, as David Ferrie—a complex and grotesque character unconvincingly portrayed by Joe Pesci—emphatically asserts is "a mystery wrapped in a riddle inside an enigma" (Stone and Sklar 93). Indeed, the painful paradox of the Gothic hero is that he or she is driven by a moral imperative to seek truth in a world in which such a quest is destined to fail.

Gothic heroes from legend and classical literature, e.g., Robin Hood and Hamlet, to more recent examples such as Stone's Jim Garrison and John F. Kennedy himself, are restless characters whose idealistic quest for enlightenment and justice is conditioned by a realization that the price they must pay, even for partial success, will be inordinately high. That is why, in Gothic terms, success is measured not so much by achievement as by authenticity of purpose. Norman Mailer once spoke of John Kennedy as "an outlaw sheriff." With that inspired characterization, he captured an aspect of the Kennedy myth that speaks to the charge of uncritical hero-worship so often leveled against Oliver Stone and other alleged Camelot loyalists. Many of those who dismiss Stone's countercultural perspective on the Cold War era would maintain that Kennedy's ambiguous political record and his well-publicized sexual exploits suggest that he was neither different from nor better than his immediate successors, Lyndon Johnson and Richard Nixon. Stone, of course, rejects this view, insisting that Kennedy's principled advocacy of democratic idealism, his intellectual distinction, and his growing disenchantment with the Pentagon, the CIA, organized crime, and big business not only set him on a collision course with Eisenhower's covertly fascist military-industrial complex, but set him far above those who would follow.

In assessing the question of Kennedy's character from Stone's perspective it is important to realize that Stone is a melodramatist, as are all exponents of the Gothic imagination. Melodrama is an unfairly maligned artistic genre that speaks the operatic language of dream and myth, as opposed to that of psychological realism (see *One Half of Robertson Davies* 143-60). Hyperbole is Stone's element and in some instances the modern-day classicists who object to his work are, one suspects, offended as much by the melodramatic manner in which his message is delivered as by the message itself. Accordingly, Stone paints the world as he experiences it, not in terms of subtle, finely drawn distinctions, but in boldly romantic, sharply defined contrasts and vivid emotions. Based on his other films, however, one suspects that, like Kennedy himself, Stone is an idealist without illusions, well aware of human complexity and ambiguity, i.e., the shadow side of the human condition. As Mackey-Kallis astutely observes, several of Stone's characters recognize that "growth requires a balancing of opposites, an acknowledgement of the human capacity not only to love but also to hate and destroy" (Mackey-Kallis 123) Indeed, in commenting on some of the minor characters in *JFK* from the seedier side of life in Dallas, Stone invokes the complex moral and psychological vision of Dostoevsky, claiming "There is redemption in everything, even in crime" (DVD commentary). The crime of high treason and its damning or redemptive effect on all of us is the subject matter of *JFK*.

Paradoxically, *JFK* is not about Kennedy in the sense that *Nixon* is about Nixon. Neither is it fundamentally about Jim Garrison. Its focus is the political climate within which Kennedy functioned and the matrix of opinion and emotion that coalesced to bring about his death. Garrison is merely the dramatic vehicle used to explore that matrix. Consequently, a psychologically nuanced portrait of either Kennedy or Garrison would have blurred Stone's essential insight, which is that the "dark side of Camelot" pales by comparison with the darkness that engulfed it. Stone's frequently noted idée fixe with the decade of the 1960s suggests that his thera-peutic quest for redemption from past traumas is being figuratively and literally projected upon a culture that shares his Gothic obsession as well as his need to tran-scend it.

The extent to which the Kennedy of history and myth will eventually merge or diverge is an issue that can only be resolved in the long councils of time. For Stone, and those who share his Gothic outlook, however, the issue is moot. Kennedy was, to them, a modern Robin of Locksley, an Earl's son who renounced the comforts of wealth and privilege to champion the cause of social justice. His stirring summons to excellence seemed to embrace and encourage America's disenfranchised, i.e., its youth, its artists, its intellectuals, its immigrants—the very classes and types who had participated in the original American experiment and who, according to Hoftstadter, were subsequently excluded from a sense of participation by the rise of America's plutocracy (see Hofstadter on the Mugwumps and the "status revolu-tion," 135). All Americans were once again invited to the banquet, summoned to participate in an American renaissance of art and learning as they had been two centuries earlier by the Founding Fathers. Henry Fair-lie, one of Kennedy's most severe, if fair-minded crit-ics, called this summons the "politics of expectation" (see Fairlie, *The Kennedy Promise*).

Whether warranted or not, the devastating sense of loss occasioned by Kennedy's death, the sense of having been suddenly and violently deprived of an historic op-portunity, evicted almost from the stream of time itself, has haunted an entire generation. Stone is a courageous and eloquent spokesperson for that lost generation, but he is not its only spokesperson. Chris Carter's *X-Files* television series offers an alternative conspiratorial my-thology to that of Stone in which the infamous Cigarette-Smoking Man, a sinister, all-powerful repre-sentative of America's shadow government, is identified as the assassin of both JFK and MLK (see *Musings of a Cigarette-Smoking Man*). The persistent yearning, in the wake of Kennedy's murder, to recapture a better, more hopeful time is poignantly expressed in a brief dream sequence from the prologue to one of the "Lone Gun-man" episodes of the *X-Files*. The protagonists are an oddly assorted trio of computer nerds, Byers, Frohike, and Langly, who write and publish their own conspiracy newsletter entitled *The Lone Gunman*—an ironic refer-ence to the Warren Commission's baseline conclusion that one lone assassin, Lee Harvey Oswald, murdered President Kennedy. The dream sequence, narrated by Byers, depicts a well-dressed young man about to enter a lovely suburban home, where he is enthusiastically greeted by his adoring family. The narration reads:

> My name is John Fitzgerald Byers. I was named after the thirty-fifth president, and I keep having this beauti-ful dream. In that dream the events of November 22,

1963 never happened. In it, my president was never as-sassinated. Other things are different too, in my dream. My country is hopeful and young again, young in spirit. My fellow citizens trust their government, never once having been betrayed by it. My government is truly of the people, by the people, and for the people. All my hopes for my country and for myself, all are fulfilled. I have everything a person could want. I have a family and love. Everything that counts for anything in life, I have it.

> *(Three of a Kind)*

At this point, the setting abruptly shifts to a barren desert in which the disoriented Byers stands alone and disconsolate, as the voice-over continues, "But the dream ends the same way every time . . . I lose it all."

Cited out of context, the outstanding feature of this vi-gnette is, perhaps, its overt sentimentality. This feature is mitigated, however, by the authenticity of Byers's quest for truth and by the many sacrifices he and his cohorts have made on its behalf, as depicted in earlier episodes. Moreover, the unabashed emotionalism of Byers's melodramatic dream language, in this instance, becomes a metaphor of the very openness and freedom of expression that are impossible in a post-Kennedy world presided over by covert government. Temporal displacement and the obsessive need to relive past trau-mas are recurrent Gothic themes. Both figure conspicu-ously in Byers's dream sequence. They signal either an insurmountable cycle of grief leading to despair or a transcendent impulse to attain redemption through achieving continuity and closure with the past. In *X-Files* episodes such as "Three of a Kind," "Musings of a Cigarette-Smoking Man," and "Operation Paper Clip," Carter fictionalizes documented government pro-grams, e.g., CIA's MK-ULTRA and the FBI's COIN-TELPRO to assassinate heads of state, experiment "sci-entifically" on unwitting civilian populations, and provide safe haven for Nazi war criminals.

Libra is a political Gothic novel, first published in 1988, that explores the allure of secrets and the predicament in which a patriotic young Marine by the name of Lee Harvey Oswald is landed by succumbing to their seduc-tive power. It provides yet another variation on the theme of conspiracy explored by Oliver Stone. As in *JFK,* Oswald is seen by Don DeLillo, *Libra*'s author, as an innocent patsy manipulated by CIA conspirators. The tragic twist in DeLillo's alternative to the consen-sus history of these events is that the original, compara-tively benign, conspiracy itself becomes a tool in the hands of a more sinister faction of covert operators gar-nered from organized crime, the CIA, and the Cuban exile community. The initial plan called for a bogus as-sassination attempt on Kennedy that would galvanize public support for another Bay-of-Pigs style invasion of Cuba, thereby sabotaging Kennedy's conciliatory policy toward Castro following the Cuban missile crisis. This possibility, along with several others, is a topic of discussion among Garrison's team of investigators in Stone's screenplay as well (see Stone and Sklar 134). DeLillo, Stone, and others who have agonized over these events seem preoccupied by the inconclusiveness of the Kennedy saga and the lack of closure that it imposes. In the absence of a more substantive explanation, they are forced to conclude that the veiled nature of hidden history, i.e. the seductiveness of esoteric knowledge, is itself a motivating factor to those who illicitly conspire to alter the course of human events. That there is a world inside the world, a conclusion gleaned from his infatuation with communist ideology, is one that the youthful Lee Harvey Oswald finds intoxicating.

The Gothic imagination seeks to uncover the secret wellsprings of human action, which is why so many Gothic narratives, including *Citizen Kane, JFK,* and *Nixon* puzzle over the obscure motivations of their protagonists and villains. Often, owing primarily to Sigmund Freud, these motivations are sought in the repressed experiences of early childhood. (For a particularly interesting discussion of Freud's influence on the Gothic imagination see Mark Edmundson's *Nightmare on Main Street*). Kane's craving for love and acceptance is therefore traced to "Rosebud" and all the childhood memories associated with it. Similarly, in Oliver Stone's *Nixon,* which is in many respects a modern retelling of *Citizen Kane*—the man gains the world only to lose his soul—Richard Nixon's pathetic attempt to substitute power for love is tracked to the losses and humiliations of his childhood. Indeed, Stone makes extensive use of many Wellesian devices throughout *Nixon,* such as audio and visual montage, documentary news footage, and an episodic structure replete with disorienting time shifts. DeLillo's *Libra* furnishes another instance of the "Freudian fallacy," i.e., an attempt to reduce complex psychological events to simple causes, often having to do with alleged sexual traumas in early childhood. In an extended trope of power and secrecy, the opening chapter explains Oswald's later attraction to the hidden, subterranean world of espionage with reference to his childhood predilection for riding the subways of New York City: "He was riding just to ride. The noise had a power and a human force. The dark had a power. . . . Never again in his short life, never in the world, would he feel the inner power, rising to a shriek, this secret force of the soul in the tunnels under New York" (DeLillo 13).

The 1973 film *Executive Action* starring Burt Lancaster, Robert Ryan, and Will Greer was the first major motion picture based on the Kennedy assassination. It was adapted from a book co-authored by Mark Lane, whose groundbreaking *Rush to Judgment* (1966) was the first best-selling nonfiction critique of the Warren Commission, and Donald Freed, who would later contribute a fictionalized exploration of the RFK assassination. The film's director, David Miller, also relied on well-known assassination researchers Penn Jones Jr. and David Lifton for detail and historical background. *Executive Action* is premised on a plot hatched by the CIA and funded by extreme right-wing Texas oil baron H. L. Hunt, once characterized as the richest man in America. Five political incentives to murder Kennedy are cited in this conspiratorial scenario: Fear of a liberal Kennedy dynasty; fear that Kennedy would disengage from Vietnam; fear that he would encourage rather than resist the civil rights movement ("the Black revolution"); fear that his Nuclear Test Ban Treaty signaled a policy of appeasement toward the Soviet Union; and fear that Kennedy's anti-business stance (as evidenced by his confrontation with U.S. Steel) would result in the elimination of the lucrative oil-depletion allowance. A sixth Malthusian motivation, darkly hinted at by one of the architects of the conspiracy, is a covertly fascist plan to use perpetual global war as a means of population control. Once again, the substance of Lane's scenario, though downplayed, is also considered in *JFK*. In retrospect, the most interesting feature of this comparatively plodding docudrama is its use of news footage of Kennedy speeches in which he articulates his commitment to democratic idealism. Music, costumes, characterization, and scene selection, though realistic up to a point, seem, on the whole, better suited to a Hollywood Western than a political Gothic thriller.

Two cinematic retellings of the Robin Hood legend, Kevin Reynolds's *Robin Hood: Prince of Thieves* and Robert Young's *Herne's Son,* neither of which garnered critical acclaim, deal, as does *JFK,* with the fate of a heroic leader who defies a corrupt government in order to serve the cause of justice for all. Both contain words that those who share Stone's sense of deprivation might subconsciously apply to Mailer's outlaw sheriff, John F. Kennedy: In the more recent of the two, Azeem—Robin Hood's Muslim sidekick played by Morgan Freeman—consoles his self-accusatory friend following a murderous attack on their forest retreat: "I once heard a wise man say, 'There are no perfect men in this world, only perfect intentions'" (*Robin Hood: Prince of Thieves*). In *Herne's Son,* which takes place several years subsequent to the capture and execution of England's prince of thieves, an embittered and still grieving John Little is asked to explain his belief in the fallen hero. He replies, "The fire burned bright in him, and for a while it warmed us all. Now he's gone and the fire went with him. It's all over." "No," says Robert of Locksley, "nothing's forgotten. Nothing is ever forgotten" (*Herne's Son*). The flame that fired Oliver Stone's youthful idealism was extinguished, though not forgotten, by the brutal murder of John F. Kennedy. For Stone, as for many others, the world has seemed a much darker and colder place ever since.

At the peroration of his final address to the jury in *JFK,* Garrison proclaims "We have all become Hamlets in our country—children of a slain father-leader whose killers still possess the throne. The ghost of John Kennedy confronts us with the secret murder at the heart of the American dream" (Stone and Sklar 176). This interesting comparison, which became the focus of a journalistic broadside, reminds us that *JFK* is a ghost story as well as a political thriller. Stone's troubling narrative speaks of an America haunted by a guilty awareness of subversion and betrayal. "Foul deeds will rise," says Hamlet, "Though all the earth o'erwhelm them, to men's eyes" (Act I Scene II). The secret murder that both Hamlet and Garrison investigate carries the weight that burdened Brockden Brown and Hawthorne, i.e., the Oedipal murder of a father/king, but also the curse of Cain/Kane, ("the primal eldest curse . . . A brother's murder," *Hamlet,* Act III Scene III). Small wonder that those who surround Hamlet prefer to bury the past, dissociate themselves from Hamlet's "unprevailing woe" and rationalize his behavior. It also comes as no surprise to Stone's defenders that "the media's strange rage for silence in this matter presents us with a textbook case of denial, disassociation, and double-think" (Oglesby 267). Essentially, the question that divides Stone from his critics is the same as that which divides Hamlet from his critics at Elsinore: Whose version of reality is delusional?

Is the ghost of Hamlet's father real; and if not, is Hamlet's obsession with avenging his father's death symptomatic of clinical paranoia? Brockden Brown's Wieland was prompted to commit murder by just such a disembodied voice. The tormenting apparition was similarly vivid and the injunction it delivered proved just as ruinous. Throughout the drama, Shakespeare toys with the ambiguity between Hamlet's feigned madness and behavior that suggests genuine lunacy. The guards on the watchtower see the ghost in the first act, as does Hamlet, but only Hamlet speaks to it. Later, in his mother's bedroom, Gertrude sees and hears nothing, while Hamlet, who will shortly commit his first murder, is driven to distraction by the visionary specter. In Gothic narratives, madness is often presented as being in the eye of the beholder. For example, is Fox Mulder, in the *X-Files* television series, truly paranoid, as many of his more conventional colleagues suspect, or is his apparent paranoia a mark of superior insight and intellect?

Gothic heroes often seem eccentric, restless, and obsessed, if not clinically unbalanced, to those around them. The "madness" of the heroine in Gilman's "The Yellow Wallpaper," however, is precisely what enables her to recognize the psychological double bind in which she has been placed by her husband. From his vantage point, of course, the tyrannical motives to which she attributes his actions are delusional. Stone's conspiratorial version of reality raises similarly disturbing doubts and questions. If his outlook is sound, then it is the officially sanctioned version of recent American history, i.e., consensus history, that is unsound. Similarly to Stone, both Hamlet and Garrison feel that the times are out of joint. They are burdened by "the cursed spite that ever they were born to set it right." In other words, both characters share a daunting sense of responsibility to set the public record straight and confront sinister forces that have conspired to change history. Ultimately, they share a disturbing intuition that the legitimacy of the state has been fatally compromised, despite comforting reassurances of continuity and normalcy tendered by their leaders, i.e., King Claudius and President Johnson. According to Stone, the death of Kennedy changed America and the world forever (Stone and Sklar 183). Stone perceives Kennedy's assassination as a point of impact that prompted an ever-expanding ripple effect. In *Hamlet,* Shakespeare gives pointed expression to Stone's contention that such deeds ultimately transform society:

> The cease of majesty dies not alone, but, like a gulf doth draw what's near it with it; it is a massy wheel, fix'd on the summit of the highest mount, to whose huge spokes ten thousand lesser things are mortis' and adjoin'd; which when it falls, each small annexment, petty consequence, attends the boisterous ruin. Never alone did the king sigh, but with a general groan.

> (*Hamlet* Act II Scene III)

In testimony given before Chief Justice Earl Warren, Oswald's murderer Jack Ruby, in fear for his life, pleaded to be removed from Dallas to Washington where he could tell the whole truth, asserting that a new form of government was taking over the country (Oglesby, *The JFK Assassination* 272). Stone/Garrison's primary insight concerning the effects of Kennedy's murder is that Ruby was accurate in his prediction. This new form of government, according to Garrison, proved to be an old and infamous form of government, the very form of government, indeed, that he and thousands of others fought to overcome in World War II. In a passage from his summation speech to the jury that was partially cut from the final version of the film, Garrison warns that fascism in America will assume the guise of national security. There will be no goose-stepping soldiers in the streets and no concentration camps, other than the "clever concentration camps of the mind" fashioned by journalists. He claims that America has arrived at a juncture in history, comparable to Germany in the 1930s, that is unrecognized as such because fascism in our country has assumed the benign form of liberal democracy (Stone and Sklar 177).

Clearly, if Garrison was right, the "hippies" of the sixties who took to the streets carrying protest signs denouncing "Amerika,"—a Teutonic misspelling intended to suggest that current policies were more in keeping with the precepts of Hitler than Jefferson—were not far wrong. The critical barrage leveled against Garrison's assertion that the Kennedy assassination has turned Americans into Hamlet figures grieving the loss of a slain father-leader came from the pen of Alexander Cockburn (see Stone and Sklar 379-83). As it happens, the Stone/Garrison analogy to *Hamlet* was lifted from an afterword written by historian Carl Oglesby to one of Garrison's two books on the assassination. Ironically, Cockburn finds a "fascist yearning" in Oglesby's analogy. Oglesby hotly denies this charge, pointing out that what he and most Americans yearn for is a democratic openness in government that has absolutely nothing to do with fascism. As for the charge that those who share his Gothic perspective are guilty of idolizing Kennedy, Oglesby reminds us that Hamlet's father was no more a moral paragon than was Kennedy himself. Indeed, he was cut off in the blossom of his sin. Quoting from *Hamlet,* Oglesby confirms that far from seeking to escape the harsher realities of politics, as Cockburn suggests, those who subscribe to a conspiratorial reading of Kennedy's death carry a special burden: "The bumper sticker of the Dealey Plaza revisionist movement reads 'The time is out of joint. O cursed spite, that ever I was born to set it right'" (Oglesby, *The JFK Assassination* 300).

Stone's cinematic narratives offer a cathartic mythology that respects evidence rejected out of prejudice and entertains speculation concerning the present and future status of our democracy that adherents of consensus histories dare not confront. Ultimately, as film critic Roger Ebert affirms, "*JFK* accurately reflects our national state of mind since November 22, 1963. We feel that the whole truth has not been told." Stone's film, insists Ebert, is not about the factual accuracy of Jim Garrison's case. "It is about Garrison's obsession. . . . The assassination of John F. Kennedy will obsess history as it has obsessed those whose lives were directly touched" writes Ebert. He concludes that, like other subversive narratives of the political Gothic imagination, "*JFK* is a brilliant reflection of our unease and paranoia, our restless dissatisfaction. On that level it is completely factual" (Ebert 234-38).

LEWIS IN NIXONLAND

Adlai Stevenson, twice Democratic contender for the presidency during the Cold War era and Ambassador to the United Nations under Kennedy, once referred to Richard M. Nixon's interior landscape as "Nixonland." He characterized it as "a land of slander and scare, of sly innuendo, of poison pen and anonymous phone call and bustling, pushing, shoving—the land of smash and grab and anything to win" (Summers 136). Nixonland was in many respects Sinclair Lewis's imagined land of American fascism made real. In examining Stone's

screenplay for *Nixon,* we will simultaneously consider the salient aspects of Nixon's personal and political legacy that parallel the coming of American fascism as depicted by Sinclair Lewis in *It Can't Happen Here.* Nixon's distrust of reason, for example, was attested by his own irrational behavior, which was noted and commented upon by advocates and adversaries alike. Author Anthony Summers has compiled an extensive list of primary sources close to Nixon who doubted his sanity. For instance, Henry Kissinger, Nixon's Machiavellian secretary of state, claimed that "Nixon seemed driven by his demons." Media news anchor Walter Cronkite, once voted the most trusted man in America, said that Nixon "actually seemed unbalanced." According to Kenneth O'Donnell, John Kennedy's special advisor, "JFK never trusted his [Nixon's] mental stability." *Newsweek*'s John Lindsay regarded Nixon as a "walking box of short circuits," and Robert Green, senior editor of *Newsday,* once referred to Nixon's "Hamlet-like moments" (Summers 95). In one such tragic/comic moment from Stone's screenplay, the unhinged president invites his alarmed secretary of state to kneel with him in prayer. Alluding to this scene, Gothic cultural historian Mark Edmundson writes: "Nixon—to me anyway—simply *was* a Gothic hero-villain, very light on the hero. . . . When the mad bomber of Cambodia gets on his knees late at night in a haunted White House and begins talking to the portraits of former presidents, we are with Monk Lewis and Horace Walpole" (Edmundson 22).

Edmundson's allusion to Nixon's Gothic penchant for conversing with works of art refers to a climactic moment in Stone's screenplay when the distraught president, realizing that congressional exposure of his crimes in connection with the Watergate burglary has left him with no viable alternative to resignation, apostrophizes the portrait of his former nemesis, John F. Kennedy. Padding over to the portrait in slippers very late at night and looking up he muses aloud, "When they look at you, they see what they want to be. When they look at me, they see what they are" (Rivele, Wilkinson, and Stone 303). Stone's fictional dialogue envisions a transcendent, if farfetched, moment of self-realization on Nixon's part that simultaneously gives expression to Stone's perception of Kennedy and Nixon as personifications of America's essential Gothic dilemma, i.e., its ongoing struggle to balance its utopian and dystopian tendencies. Fundamentally, Stone conceives of Nixon as Kennedy's *doppelganger,* his Jungian shadow. At one point, Watergate burglar, and former CIA operative E. Howard Hunt characterizes Nixon as "the darkness reaching out for the darkness" (263). In Stone's incarnational mythology, therefore, the excess of Nixon's demonic and unreasoning paranoia is presented as a dark mirror image of Kennedy's democratic restraint and reasonableness. In other words, Stone perceives these two men as projections, on a wide historical screen, of the deep divisions within American political consciousness. The psychodrama in which they are engaged is continually reenacted on a smaller scale within each of us. Their struggle for synergy defines the American experience from a Gothic point of view.

Edmundson's "the mad bomber of Cambodia" epithet suggests yet another strand in Stone's polyphonically textured parable. Among his closest circle of advisers, Nixon was known as "the mad monk" (one more coincidental link to Matthew Lewis—known as "Monk" Lewis—an eighteenth-century English novelist whose best-known work, entitled *The Monk,* is a literary landmark in the Gothic revival of that era). Nixon's Gothic nickname originated in a Hamlet-like strategy decision on Nixon's part to affect madness, to put on an antic disposition in order to confound and intimidate his enemies. Referring to the so-called Eastern Establishment, Kissinger tells Nixon that the communists respect only strength, and they will only negotiate if they fear the madman Richard Nixon. At which point, Nixon smiles darkly (191). A short while later, Nixon echoes Kissinger's grasp of realpolitik, affirming a view founded on years of red baiting, that the best way to gain the enemy's cooperation is to convey a predisposition for unpredictable violence (195). Based on several statements made by Stone subsequent to the release of his film, it seems probable that his understanding of Nixon in relation to both Kennedy and the Cold War establishment evolved over time. Expecting "demonization," critics who scoffed at Stone's earlier "idealization" of Jim Garrison and John F. Kennedy were pleasantly surprised to discover a sympathetic portrayal of Kennedy's chief political rival. Far from being the caricature anticipated by Stone's critics, the Richard Nixon of Stone's imagining is insecure, needy, bemused, and at times even anguished by his own personal and political dilemmas.

At the heart of his anguish, suggests Stone, lay a dark suspicion that he, no less than his immediate predecessors, was at the mercy of sinister and uncontrollable forces. Clearly, Stone's Nixon is haunted by the ghost of Kennedy, as evidenced by, among other things, his obsessive contention that he has nothing in common with his deceased predecessor. When his wife, Pat claims that her love for him is inadequate to compensate for the disapproval of his political adversaries, Nixon objects, asserting that, unlike Kennedy, he does not crave public approval. Later that same night he asks his young Cuban valet Manolo if he had cried when Kennedy was killed and, if so, why. Manolo admits that he did cry, but can offer no explanation other than that Kennedy somehow made him "see the stars." In an uncharacteristic moment of candor and self doubt, Nixon silently ponders the inspirational qualities of his former adversary (217). Later, when he confronts a small cluster of incredulous, bleary-eyed adolescents protesting

the Vietnam War during an impromptu late-night visit to the Lincoln Memorial, he tells them that neither he nor the Vietnamese want the conflict to continue. An earnest young woman replies that someone certainly does. realizing the chilling implications of this tacit admission that even the commander and chief is powerless to oppose a military-industrial system bent on war, she asks Nixon why, in that case, he should wish to be president. He nervously replies that there is more at stake than his own personal desire for peace or hers. The commentary of the screenplay at this point reads, *"The nausea of the Beast makes him reel"* (221). In humanizing moments such as these, we catch a glimpse of Nixon that differs from the mechanical, untrustworthy public figure with whom most of us are familiar. At such moments, Stone's Gothic villain seems to be reaching tentatively for the light. The question, of course, is whether the humanity with which Nixon is endowed by Stone and Hopkins belongs to Nixon or to them.

The "Beast," alluded to above, is another supernatural Gothic motif, comparable to the ghost of Oswald in *JFK,* a visual code that Stone contemplated but ultimately discarded. In the working script, however, he periodically calls for a brief image that will recur throughout the film, an image of evil identified as "the Beast" (40). What he evidently had in mind was a sequence of bestial or reptilian images that would be flashed on the screen in the manner of a subliminal message whenever Nixon was confronted by or reminded of the covert fascism that conspired to promote Vietnam and destroy Kennedy. It was to have occurred, for example, when he discussed his political prospects with a group of Texas oilmen and Cubans just prior to Kennedy's assassination (157). It is mentioned again when Nixon refers to the Bay of Pigs in a meeting with his political aide H. R. Haldeman (181)—who came to regard all such references as veiled allusions to the Kennedy assassination (50)—and again on the occasion of his visit to the office of CIA Director Richard Helms (208). Indeed, the entire sequence, i.e., scenes sixty-six through sixty-eight, involving Nixon and Director of Central Intelligence (DCI) Helms vividly illustrates Stone's method of using the conventions of supernatural Gothic to underscore his political Gothic message. When Nixon first arrives at Langley, he passes the Orwellian seal of the CIA—"You shall know the truth and the truth shall make you free"—a Biblical citation that eerily echoes the Nazi motto posted on the entrance to the concentration camps: "Work shall make you free." Indeed, the almost savage irony of this false tribute to honesty and openness is apparent when considered with reference to the authentic American dream. Jefferson made an informed public the cornerstone of democracy. For the CIA, an organization premised on deception and secrecy, to embrace such a motto carries a corollary implication that its true purpose is to enslave—to create, in the name of national security, a gulag of the mind that requires no barbed wire and within which dismay and confusion are the only guard dogs necessary.

When Nixon enters Helms' office by a "secret door," the viewer is subconsciously made aware that the forces of covert fascism are, in effect, an occult, i.e., hidden, priesthood whose power derives from its status as the keeper of state secrets. When Helms spots Nixon, he extends a welcoming hand and offers what the screenplay refers to as a "reptilian" smile. Throughout their conversation Helms occupies himself with his award-winning collection of orchids—a symbol of tropical decadence—that exude the sweet decay of death. As he bends to examine them, placing himself at eye level with the camera, his eye sockets turn completely black. In that instant, the dark abyss of America's cryptocracy is fleetingly revealed for what it truly is, a zombie-like monster from the annals of Gothic horror. In this chilling scene, Helms asks Nixon if he appreciates flowers. Nixon states emphatically that he does not, claiming that they remind him of death. He then informs Helms that there are, however, things in life more dreadful even than death, such as evil (212)—an observation that, once again, seems uncharacteristic of Nixon, though not of Stone.

Later in the screenplay, during a discussion of who would be most effective at obstructing the FBI investigation of the Watergate burglary, Nixon nominates Helms, who can scare anyone (114). The identification of the CIA with the Beast is made even more explicit in the final line of dialogue between Nixon and Helms in which Helms quotes a famous passage from William Butler Yeats' Gothic poem, *The Second Coming*: "What rough beast in its hour come round at last / Slouches toward Bethlehem to be born," concluding with the observation that, "Yes, this country stands at such a juncture" (Rivele, Wilkinson, and Stone 212). This allusion to Yeats was perhaps inspired as much by *Slouching Towards Bethlehem*, a well-known collection of essays on America in the 1960s by New York journalist and author Joan Didion as by the original poem that furnished the title of her book.

When the topic turns to covert operations and President Kennedy, Nixon tenses, suddenly sensing the presence of the Beast. Helms comments that Kennedy threatened to smash the CIA. In response, Helms receives the President's personal assurance that the Agency under Nixon's watch is secure, suggesting in the same breath that a communistic Cuba would be a small price to pay for stabilizing the balance of world power. When Helms menacingly reminds Nixon that President Kennedy shared this conviction, Nixon suddenly envisions Kennedy with his head blown off in Dallas and himself laid out in a coffin (211). According to Garrison, in Stone's screenplay, the murder of Kennedy reduced the president to the status of a mere public relations officer for the military-industrial-intelligence complex. Confronted by Helms and the sinister forces he represents, Nixon clearly realizes that the power of the presidency is slight compared with that of the Beast. Reflecting on the young woman with whom he spoke at the Lincoln Memorial, Nixon muses to Haldeman, "She understood something it's taken me twenty-five **** [expletive deleted] years in politics to understand. The CIA, the Mafia, the Wall Street bastards. . . . 'The Beast.' A nineteen-year-old kid. She understands the nature of 'the Beast'" (222). Just as the dark side of Camelot diminishes to almost zero, in Stone's estimation, against the backdrop of America's covert fascism, Nixon's darkness is mitigated by the abyss that opens before us in the presence of Helms. The reason for this is obvious: While, for Stone, the dualism of Nixon and Kennedy symbolize a potential synergy between America's dystopian and utopian dialectic, the covert fascism of men like FBI Director Hoover, DCI Richard Helms, and crime lord Johnny Roselli threaten to destroy the very dialectic on which that synergy depends.

In Nixonland, as Stone clearly demonstrates, respect for human rights is replaced by brute strength, just as integrity and openness are replaced by an accepted code of behavior premised on lies and covert operations. In response to the release of the *Pentagon Papers* by Daniel Ellsberg, Nixon expresses his admiration for the terrorist tactics of the Nazis, suggesting that those responsible for news leaks within his administration should be intimidated as members of indigenous resistance movements in German-occupied countries were intimidated by Nazi threats of arbitrary execution. In 1970, something very like this Nazi policy was implemented at Kent State University in Ohio, when, as shown in the film, a phalanx of National Guardsman opened fire on students and professors assembled on the campus lawn, killing four of them. In the film, as these events unfold on television, Nixon fumes at the spectacle of rioting guardsmen advancing on unarmed civilians, contemptuously referring to student dissidents as "bums" and asserting that these so-called flower children should be taken to the woodshed (193). Responding to Nixon's panegyric on Nazi war crimes, presidential aide, Chuck Colson replies, "Just whisper the word to me sir, and I'll shoot Ellsberg myself" (106).

From the "dirty tricks" campaign of Dwight Chapin to the oval office audience granted a delegation of hard hats who physically assaulted law-abiding antiwar protesters on Wall Street, the Nixon administration embraced and encouraged brown shirt tactics, deception, forgery, slander, stonewalling, burglary, arson, bribery, and illegal surveillance as legitimate political tactics. Did Nixon's political opponents do likewise? Yes, though to a significantly lesser degree. However, from the standpoint of democratic idealism, acceptable ends do not justify unacceptable means. Discussing this very point in the film, Nixon aide John Ehrlichman tells his cohort Bob Haldeman that Nixon is wrong in his assertion that Presidents Truman, Kennedy, and Johnson were guilty of using the same vicious methods that erupted into the Watergate scandal. He points out that none of Nixon's immediate predecessors would have dared forge a cable, as E. Howard Hunt did, implicating President Kennedy in the CIA-sponsored assassination of South Vietnamese President Diem. He goes on to question Haldeman concerning Nixon's evident dread whenever mention is made of the 1961 invasion of Cuba at the Bay of Pigs (259-60). Clearly, there is no room in Nixonland for constructive dissent. Democratic belief in the value of dialogue, according to Nixon's covertly fascist mind-set, is a left-wing fallacy. For Nixon, as one journalist points out, politics is war and one's political adversaries are viewed not as the loyal opposition but as the enemy (138).

Stone's Nixon sincerely believes that law and justice are unrelated, not just in practice but in principle. In *JFK*, Garrison, as he recounts the suspicious circumstances of Oswald's arrest, reminds the jury that Dr. Best, Himmler's right-hand man in the Gestapo, believed that as long as the police carry out the will of the government they serve, they are acting legally (Stone and Sklar 174). Similarly, when Haldeman tries to warn the president that by attempting to head off an FBI investigation he may be guilty of obstructing justice, Nixon replies that his decision is dictated by considerations of "national security." When Haldeman inquires as to the relevance of this doctrine to the situation at hand, he is told peremptorily that national security is involved whenever the president says it is (Rivele, Wilkinson, and Stone 115). Nixon's concise expression of the fascist leadership principle and its corollary belief in legally infallible government by an elite group was a cornerstone of Nazism (Ebenstein, Ebenstein, and Fogelman 73). Inevitably, one is reminded of Garrison's warning that national security is a concept as easily invoked in defense of fascism as democracy (Stone and Sklar 117). It is revealing in this regard that the president appeared on national television to announce his determination to learn the truth about Watergate no matter who was involved during the very period in which he and his people were desperately conspiring to obstruct justice (Rivele, Wilkinson, and Stone 268).

Racism, another cardinal tenet of both German fascism and its American counterpart as envisioned by Sinclair Lewis, is an obvious component of Nixon's outlook. This is attested by his many derogatory allusions to Jews and "niggers" in the Watergate tapes. At one point in Stone's screenplay, Nixon's Attorney General John Mitchell says of Henry Kissinger, "The Jewboy's a Harvard whore with the morals of an eel—sells himself to the highest bidder." Seemingly indifferent to Mitch-

ell's racial slur, Nixon commends Mitchell for his political savvy (149). Later, as he is constrained to listen to a sampling of his own racial slurs recorded on the White House tapes, a Nixon in denial vehemently protests that he never made those comments about Jews (292). In the opinion of some, Nixon's most flagrant expression of racism was his decision to widen an inherently racist war in Southeast Asia with his secret bombing campaigns in Laos and his infamous Cambodian "incursion" (more Orwellian language)—an event that provoked the Kent State massacre and led directly to the killing fields of Cambodia.

Nixon's disregard of constitutional and international law, as manifested in this flagrant violation of Cambodian neutrality and congressional intent, was originally listed as an impeachable offense on an indictment drafted by Congress, but later dropped because, as Nixon boasted to General Haig, the president can bomb whoever he wants (283). Similarly, the surprise Christmas bombing of Hanoi aroused the ire of the international political and journalistic community. Reporting these events, Stone makes use of documentary footage with a B.B.C. voiceover to the effect that the Nixon administration, in launching the most brutal bombing campaign in American history, has resorted to a Stone Age tactic worthy of a crazed tyrant (236). Credited in later years with having ended a war he did not begin, it has become politically correct in certain quarters to view the "rehabilitated" Nixon as more sinned against than sinning. Such flagrant revisionism fails to take into account the fact that the Eisenhower/Nixon administration pursued a policy with regard to the Geneva Accords of 1954 that made war in Vietnam inevitable. Moreover, Nixon's efforts to sabotage Johnson's peace initiative in 1968 for reasons of partisan political expediency may have prolonged that war unnecessarily. Countless American combatants as well as Asians, to say nothing of the young patriots murdered at Kent State and Jackson State for protesting an unjust war, paid with their lives for Nixon's pointless pursuit of a policy that promised "peace with honor" and ended in a chaotic flight from Saigon that delivered neither peace nor honor.

Though he ran for office as a staunch exponent of law and order, Nixon's covertly fascist domestic policy was consistent with that of his renegade foreign policy. Indeed, it was in the domestic arena that Nixon's contempt for democracy and his use of totalitarian tactics were most damaging to his administration. His efforts to obstruct justice in the Watergate affair extended from simple lack of cooperation and the payment of hush money to a contemplated Frankenheimer-style coup in which the military would be used to thwart Congress (see footnote, 297). Fortunately, the military was uncooperative. Stone's screenplay abounds in allusions to Lincoln and the Civil War. Clearly, Nixon saw the liberal counterculture, comprised largely of John F.

Kennedy's alienated constituency and the antiwar movement it spawned, as a latter-day Confederacy—with himself cast in the role of stalwart Abe Lincoln fighting to preserve the Union. In another Hamlet-like moment of Gothic introspection, Nixon soliloquizes on death as he stares up at a portrait of Lincoln. Who helped them both to power—God or death—asks Nixon rhetorically (184).

In his memoirs, Nixon evinces a seemingly inexhaustible capacity for denial: "If I could be hounded from office because of a political scandal like Watergate," he writes, "the whole American system of government would be undermined and changed. I never for a moment," Nixon reflects with a self-complacence reminiscent of the Nazi war criminals prosecuted at Nuremberg, "believed that any of the charges against me were legally impeachable" (Summers 466). Stone vividly dramatizes the psychotic split implicit in Nixon's perception of himself as an innocent defender of the American way at the very time he is actively engaged in subverting constitutional authority. As Nixon and his discomfited secretary of state, Henry Kissinger, kneel together in prayer, Nixon suddenly sobs out his sense of unmerited persecution. With a theatrical hypocrisy equal to that of Mr. Pecksniff, Nixon calls upon God to save America from its enemies, i.e., all those who disapprove of his conduct in office. Anticipating the revisionists who would later come to his defense, he recites a highly selective version of his resume according to which he brought peace in our time to a slavering horde of pinko liberals whose hatred of him epitomizes the ingratitude of a politically depraved Eastern establishment (Rivele, Wilkinson, and Stone 301-02). The climax of Nixon's Alice-in-Wonderland inversion of the issues raised by the overt Civil War of the 1860s and the covert civil war of the 1960s is dramatized in Stone's portrayal of the 1968 Republican National Convention. Nixon's Lincolnesque pledge to heal the wounds of war by bringing a divided nation together is interspersed with scenes of Gestapo-like police riots in Chicago, FBI attacks on Native American militants at Wounded Knee, and shots of George Wallace whipping a right-wing crowd of white supremacists into a frenzy. Against this totalitarian backdrop, Nixon's populist appeal to a "silent majority" in favor of war and the suppression of political dissent assumes the distinct aura of a party rally at Nuremberg.

Distrust of reason, denial of basic human equality, adherence to a code of behavior based on lies and violence, espousal of government by an elite group, racism, opposition to international law, and the use of totalitarian tactics: these were the political precepts of Nixonland. They are also the political precepts of the fascism that Sinclair Lewis foresaw as a plausible outcome of the political turmoil by which twentieth-century America was engulfed (see chapter 3 in *Today's ISIMS*

by Ebenstein, Ebenstein, and Fogelman). Despite the obvious differences between Nixonland and Nazi Germany, the following passage relating to fascism from Ebenstein's standard political science textbook should give Americans pause: "As long as the people did not make any trouble politically and did not interfere with the rule of the dictator and his henchmen, they could often lead their own lives relatively freely" (73). Cold War America did not have a dictator, of course; even Nixon was eventually compelled to abide by the rule of law. It did, however have a covert intelligence establishment based on Nazi protocols, a right-wing creed that justified immoral means in pursuit of allegedly moral ends, and a fervent belief that "only a small minority of the population . . . is capable of understanding what is best for the entire community" (72).

In effect, Nixon attempted to resist "the Beast" by duplicating the very sins that summoned it into existence—the original sins of America's Cold War fall from grace. He chose to fight communist evil with fascist evil, to defend a public code based on law, dialogue, and an open political process by adopting a private code premised on crime, intolerance, and secrecy. "Funny therapeutics," as Doremus Jessup might have said. The Gothic split between democratic idealism and covert fascism embraced by Nixon and the Cold War establishment he represented is explicitly denounced by Jefferson: "To say, in excuse, that gratitude is never to enter into the motives of national conduct, is to revive a principle which has been buried for centuries with its kindred principles of the lawfulness of assassination, poison, perjury &c. . . . *I know but one code of morality for men, whether acting singly or collectively*" (as quoted in Padover 37, italics mine).

The disparity between Jefferson's democratic idealism and America's subsequent Faustian bargain is clearly expounded in Robert Bolt's 1960 drama *A Man for All Seasons* concerning Sir Thomas More's principled protest against Henry VIII's politically expedient marriage to Ann Boleyn. Though set in Tudor England, it clearly addresses ethical and political dilemmas posed by the times in which it was written. When More's son-in-law, Roper, a Protestant fanatic cut from the same mold as later fundamentalist fanatics, angrily asks More whether he would give the Devil benefit of the law, More replies heatedly, "Yes, what would you do? Cut a great road through the law to get after the Devil?" Roper responds, "I'd cut down every law in Europe to do that." "Oh," says the aroused and indignant More, "And when the last law was down, and the Devil turned round on you— where would you hide, Roper, the laws all being flat? This country's planted thick with laws from coast to coast with man's laws, not God's—and if you cut them down—and you're just the man to do it—d'you really think you could stand upright in the winds that would blow then? Yes, I'd give the Devil benefit of the law, for my own safety's sake" (Bolt 38).

To the extent that both Kennedy and Nixon struggled against the Beast and lost, Stone's portrayal of the latter as the dark alter ego of the former is justified. However, to the extent that Nixon's code differed from that of the Beast in degree only, Stone's moral vision is perhaps blurred by his use of this *doppelgänger* motif. The tragedy of President Nixon is that he was a man who defined himself in terms of his enemies rather than his ideals. Like Roper, he had few scruples when it came to upholding the law, and when the Devil turned on him—as it inevitably will, according to the Gothic imagination—he had nowhere to hide. Nixon was a typical American in many ways. Similarly to a great many other Americans, he endorsed an inauthentic version of the American dream that confuses *excess* with *suc*cess and power with privilege. As he once proclaimed to Kissinger, his conception of geopolitics envisioned a world linked by enlightened self-interest and motivated by fear (Rivele, Wilkinson, and Stone 196). Ultimately, Nixon's American dream was about seizing and maintaining an advantage by whatever means, fair or foul. As Jim Garrison says to his wife Elizabeth in *JFK,* however, American democracy is fundamentally not about gaining the upper hand. It is, as John F. Kennedy suggested, about acknowledging a mutuality of interest that is mindful of our shared needs and our shared mortality (Stone and Sklar 140).

Indeed, the authentic American dream is about letting go—of property, security, wealth, privilege, power, celebrity, influence, and life itself if need be—in order to advance the cause of justice. It is not, as the warped ethic of Nixonland maintained, about holding on to those advantages at any cost, including the triumph of injustice. During the Kennedy years, Americans were called upon to uphold a faith in the ultimate vindication of right over might. Kennedy's tragedy, and ours, is that at the time of his death he seemed to be moving the nation toward a post-Cold War conception of the American experience that transcended the blinkered perspective of Nixonland. Indeed, this nascent conception may well have enabled him to transcend his own all too frequent surrender to the ethics of Nixonland, sometimes referred to as *The Dark Side of Camelot* (the title of a book on the subject of Kennedy's frailties by Seymour M. Hersh). What many of Kennedy's admirers and detractors alike seem not to realize is that his dark, shadow side—which undoubtedly existed—was an essential component of the Kennedy promise. The point is not that both he and Nixon possessed a dark side. According to the political Gothic imagination we all do, as Jung affirmed. The point is that unlike Nixon, Kennedy demonstrated a capacity to rise above the limitations that so often hamper the hero-villains of Gothic fiction

to become an authentic hero, i.e., one whose unique advantages are justified and redeemed in the service of others. That is why, as Stone's Nixon correctly observes, in Kennedy we saw ourselves not as we are, but as we might be.

As the end of the Camelot era approached—which to many seemed only a beginning—the pampered patrician and zealous cold warrior ready to pay any price and bear any burden to defend the cause of liberty was finally subordinate to the Kennedy who made us see the stars. Having at last tamed his own Cold War demons and emerged from beneath his father's shadow to become a mature statesman of imposing stature, he seemed to have attained within himself a synergy between a romantic need for self-assertion and a classical restraint imposed by his highly cultivated sense of historical perspective. Kennedy's pragmatism, which he defined as idealism without illusions, had finally reconciled republican and frontier conceptions of America, capitalism's dream and democracy's dream, in a way that, had he lived, might truly have benefited his country and the world. In 1963, the presidency was still a fulcrum of immense power. In an America unbalanced by the alliance of capitalism and covert fascism, Kennedy was the first and, in many ways, the last Cold War president to use that fulcrum on behalf of democratic idealism. By doing so, however, he became, as Oliver Stone's Mr. X maintains, a threat to the national security structure (Stone and Sklar 113). Moreover, his inherited wealth enabled him to largely skirt the polluted swamp of the American political process in which Nixon had been totally submerged from the outset of his career. By late 1963, Kennedy seemed intent on replenishing the forests of national and international law that had been leveled by the cold winds of a Cold War, winds that in all probability claimed his life. "President Kennedy was a work in progress when he was killed," writes historian Carl Oglesby. "It is a great loss that we never got to see the finished product, but it was also a kind of national disaster that he chose to treat the White House as a finishing school" (Oglesby, *The JFK Assassination* 302).

IMAGES OF THE BEAST

Though it was not included in the finished version of the film, in the uncut version the ghost of Lee Harvey Oswald, played by method actor Gary Oldman (the Count Dracula of Francis Ford Coppola's film remake of the vampire legend) takes the stand to address Garrison's jury on his own behalf. In an impromptu speech of heartfelt intensity, Oswald/Oldman passionately proclaims his innocence along with his undying love for his country, his young wife, and his family. Though personally moved by Oldman's Gothic improvisation, Stone realized that it was discordant with the note of documentary realism established throughout *JFK*. He

abandoned it, accordingly. That Stone's Gothic imagination is predisposed to such flights of supernatural fancy, however, is clearly evidenced in the working script of his second conspiratorial film, *Nixon*. Apart from the hidden histories, perverse power relationships, and conspiratorial agendas developed in *Nixon,* Stone makes ample use of supernatural Gothic conventions: We first encounter Stone's hero-villain alone in the White House Lincoln Sitting Room, which is compared to a tomb, besieged by Gothic weather (Rivele, Wilkinson, and Stone 88). Nixon, himself sits in shadow silhouetted by an open fire. As the stage directions explain, he hates the light (91). Incongruously, the air-conditioning is running full-blast. It is upon precisely such extreme contrasts and incongruities of imagery that the supernatural Gothic thrives. Darkness, within the context of the Gothic imagination, is a symbolic state of mind as well as a physical reality, as are the light and warmth Nixon seeks from his solitary hearth. Hearth-fire itself is an ambiguous emblem of enlightenment, human warmth, companionship, and the hard-won containment of a potentially destructive force.

Apropos of Stone's use of Gothic imagery, *Nixon*'s animal imagery comprises a cinematic bestiary of natural and supernatural creatures used to convey a political Gothic message. In a burlesque scene at the Oval Office between Nixon, Kissinger, Haldeman, and Erlichman, Nixon, who has been unsuccessfully coaxing a pet dog to accept a biscuit, turns the air blue with undeleted expletives, complaining that after two years the animal is still unresponsive and utterly useless as a public relations asset. Finally, Nixon turns on Kissinger, who has tried repeatedly to channel the conversation toward foreign policy matters, blaming him for the dog's uncooperative demeanor. The astonished Kissinger is completely nonplussed while the amused viewer is left to draw the obvious conclusion: Even man's best friend is understandably ill at ease in the presence of these snarling human beasts (103).

Another, more menacing, use of animal imagery occurs at the Del Mar Racetrack in scenes 47-49. FBI Director Hoover, who is earlier referred to as a lizard, is seated with his homosexual partner, Clyde Tolson, and Johnny Roselli, a mobster suspected of complicity in the JFK assassination. As the horses rush to the finish line, the bandaged front leg of one of the animals snaps, producing a sound like a rifle shot. The jockey is thrown from his mount as Nixon approaches Hoover, hoping for his support in his forthcoming political race against Robert Kennedy. Nixon, Tolson, and Hoover leave the bleachers in order to spare Nixon a politically embarrassing encounter with his former friend from Cuba, Roselli. As they walk in the vicinity of the stables, Nixon complains to Hoover that the 1968 race could be 1960 all over again with Bobby "riding his brother's corpse right into the White House" (177). Tolson helpfully suggests

that the former Attorney General should be shot. When Nixon obsequiously lobbies for Hoover's backing, the amused director of an institution that came close to being a state-sponsored secret police force explains that the system can only stand so much abuse. Implying that the Kennedys and Dr. King, who he characterizes as a moral hypocrite, constitute such an abuse, Hoover goes on to assert that the White House has already been inhabited by one radical, presumably JFK, and that in his opinion the country could not survive another.

At this point the stage directions suggest that the increasingly uncomfortable Nixon is once again plagued by vague but disturbing images. His discomfort is underscored aurally by the snorting and heavy breathing of the nearby horses (178). In this episode, the actual or potential violence done to and by animals reinforces the conspiratorial violence that has already been perpetrated against John Kennedy and Martin Luther King and that would shortly be visited upon Robert Kennedy. It is alleged that Hoover harbored a pathological fear of anyone stepping on his shadow, a particularly intriguing neurosis from a Jungian point of view. In the words of Anthony Summers, "That a man with a crippled psyche, capable of great evil, became the trusted symbol of all that was safe and good is a paradox of our time. So too is the fact that, in a tribute after Hoover's death, Chief Justice Warren E. Burger said he had 'epitomized the American dream' while renowned psychiatrists consider that he would have been well suited for high office in Nazi Germany" (Summers 6, 7). Obviously, Warren Burger's version of the American dream was not that of Thomas Jefferson and John Kennedy.

In addition to Stone's Gothic bestiary, *Nixon* features an array of standard Gothic archetypes including ghosts, monsters, zombies, robots, and vampires. In the wake of the so-called "Saturday night massacre" in which Nixon fired top officials rather than comply with a legal ruling to turn over the secret White House tapes to a special prosecutor, a television reporter asks if a government of laws has become a government of one man (Rivele, Wilkinson, and Stone 287). While an anxious America awaits an answer to the reporter's question, Nixon, again alone in the Lincoln Sitting Room, is accosted by the ghost of his long-departed mother. Speaking in the Quaker idiom familiar to his childhood, she asks what has happened to change her once devout son into the beleaguered "crook" he has since become. A distraught Nixon, desperate to avoid a confrontation with his repressed Quaker conscience, pleads with her to remain silent (289). In Nixon's case, this apparition is clearly a projection of his repressed guilt and denial—a denial so severe as to raise legitimate doubts as to the besieged president's mental stability. Ultimately, of course, the Gothic monster that stalks the pages of Stone's screenplay is the Beast of America's government-within-the-government, but at one point

this beast is explicitly identified with another classic monster: As presidential aides, Erlichman and Haldeman huddle together in a White House corridor discussing Nixon's obsessive, if veiled, allusions to the Kennedy assassination, i.e., the Bay of Pigs invasion, Haldeman confides to his counterpart that when the CIA went after Castro, the plot was somehow turned against Kennedy. Erlichman responds, "Christ, we created Frankenstein with those **** [expletive deleted] Cubans" (261).

Frequently, Nixon's movements and manner of speaking are described as robotic (117), or else he is likened to a living corpse, i.e., a zombie (118). The political Gothic message that informs such comparisons has to do with Nixon as a "hollow man" consumed by an insatiable lust for power. "Whenever a man has cast a longing eye on offices, a rottenness begins in his conduct," says Jefferson (as quoted in Summers 81). After Nixon lost the presidential race to Kennedy in 1960, his campaign manager Murray Chotiner confidently predicted that he will run again, not from a moral imperative to seek office but, "Because if he's not President Nixon, he's nobody" (Summers 123).

The most elaborate Gothic trope developed in the original screenplay has to do with vampirism. Often, the imagery associated with this motif is blood drenched. "The blood is the life," intones Bram Stoker's literary monster (though his readers know perfectly well that blood is just as often, in fact far more commonly, perceived as an accompaniment of death). In the screenplay of *Nixon,* the ambiguous fluid of life/death flows as freely as in those of *Dracula*. Indeed, the imagery used is often explicitly derived from vampire lore. When Nixon considers opening China, he does so in order to drive a stake through the heart of the alliance between communist China and the Soviet Union (196). Early in the screenplay, as Nixon discusses Cuba with political aide Herb Klein, the stage directions describe a Nixon who is besieged by inner demons in the form of persistent images of violent death. Later, in response to the release of the *Pentagon Papers,* Nixon the Impaler characterizes his anticipated vendetta against antiwar intellectuals as sudden death and vows to get them on the ground, stake them, and twist the stake mercilessly (228). Owing to the discovery of the White House tapes, his deepest secrets are about to be revealed. Realizing this, a sleepless Nixon awakens in the middle of the night to find himself covered in blood. He is rushed to a hospital where he experiences a hallucinatory episode rife with sanguine images of pain and death from his own family history and the history of the violent nation over which he has presided. Taken together, this dark overlay of surrealistic images and motifs suggestive of vampirism transform Stone's nominally realistic docudrama into a compelling horror story. In fact, from Stone's Gothic perspective, the "lyrical" 1960s, so often portrayed as a utopian idyll—a colorful era of rebellion, hedonism, and carefree social experimentation—was, in reality, just such a horrific episode. Oliver Stone's vision of the 1960s suggests a Gothic transformation scene straight out of Hollywood Gothic—a transformation scene in which the United States of America ultimately emerges as the United States of Amerika—a rapacious monster that feeds off the flesh and blood of its own sons and daughters.

It is important to understand that, contrary to what today's conservatives would have us believe, nuclear terrorism and anti-communist belligerency during the Cold War era had far more to do with the breakdown of respect for authority in American society than "liberal permissiveness." In terms of its emotional impact and divisiveness, the paradigm shift that took place during the 1960s, from a Newtonian to a Gothic perspective on the American experience, might almost be characterized as a Second Civil War. Overtly, this generational conflict was fought in homes and on the streets between a youth counterculture traumatized by the ever-present threat of nuclear holocaust and an older generation wedded to a politically obsolete conception of the world formed before the advent of nuclear weapons. Covertly, it was fought behind the scenes, so to speak, between Kennedy and the Cold War establishment itself.

At stake was the world as we know it versus a world in which—if Kennedy's diplomatic and social agenda had prevailed—the Cold War would have been phased out in favor of cooperation and peaceful coexistence with the Soviets—thereby preempting the recent proliferation of nationalistic factions—the Vietnam War would have ended before it truly began, the vigilante regime of an invisible government would have been brought within the purview of the Constitution, Dr. King's vision of the beloved community would have replaced the defacto racial segregation that reigns today, the economic anarchy of what came to be known as corporate globalization (and the breeding ground for terrorism it has spawned) would have been nullified by a commitment to democracy in the workplace and a policy of economic self determination for third world countries, the social pollution of organized crime would have been stopped before it could be effectively assimilated into the mainstream of the economy, and an authentic intellectual and aesthetic culture, rather than the ersatz consumer culture of McWorld and MTV, would have been nurtured at home and exported abroad. As the enigmatic Mr. X from *JFK* comments, however, that enlightened prospect ended on November 22, 1963. One could plausibly argue that Kennedy's utopian prospect, even had he lived, would have been imperfectly realized. However, one could just as plausibly argue that even an imperfectly realized version of that prospect would be preferable to the political and cultural dystopia we currently inhabit.

In the final analysis, critics who attribute the latter position to wishful thinking are unanswerable. Kennedy's murder saw to that. However, it is significant to note that in at least one instance, the postmortem attacks on his character can be laid to rest. With regard to the Cuban Missile Crisis, it is the duplicity and susceptibility to panic alleged against Kennedy that is myth and his patient and measured rationality under pressure that is confirmed by the historical record (see *The Kennedy Tapes* ed. by May and Zelikow and Roger Donaldson's film based on it, *Thirteen Days*). The attempt to arouse public support for a timely and conclusive reinvestigation of his assassination was partly defused by well-publicized and often tendentious exposés of the so-called Camelot myth. To an extent, these exposés were justified. However, in this instance, and perhaps others as well, it would appear that the autopsy on Kennedy's much-maligned character was as badly bungled as his fraudulent and misleading medical autopsy.

Works Cited

Bolt, Robert. *A Man For All Seasons*. New York: Vintage, 1960.

Cockburn, Alexander. "J.F.K. and *JFK*." *JFK: The Book of the Film*. Oliver Stone and Zachary Sklar. New York: Applause Books, 1992. 379-83.

DeLillo, Don. *Libra*. New York: Viking, 1988.

Didion, Joan. *Slouching Towards Bethlehem*. New York: Farrar, Straus and Giroux, 1968.

Ebenstein, Alan, William Ebenstein, and Edwin Fogelman. *Today's ISMS: Socialism, Capitalism, Fascism, Communism, and Libertarianism*. New Jersey: Prentice-Hall, Inc., 1985.

Ebert, Roger. *The Great Movies*. New York: Broadway Books, 2002.

Hersh, Seymour M. *The Dark Side of Camelot*. Boston: Little, Brown and Company, 1997.

Hofstadter, Richard. *The Age of Reform*. New York: Vintage Books, 1955.

Knebel, Fletcher, and Charles W. Bailey II. *Seven Days in May*. New York: Bantam Books, 1962.

Lewis, Matthew. *The Monk*. New York: Oxford University Press, 1998.

Lewis, Sinclair. *It Can't Happen Here*. New York: Signet, 1935.

Mackey-Kallis, Susan. *Oliver Stone's America: "Dreaming the Myth Outward."* Boulder, CO: Westview Press, 1996.

MacPherson, James. *The Poems of Ossian*. Boston: Crosby, Nichols, Lee & Company, 1860.

Marks, John. *In Search of the Manchurian Candidate: The CIA and Mind Control*. New York: Dell, 1977

May, Ernest R., and Philip D. Zelikow. *The Kennedy Tapes: Inside the White House During the Cuban Missile Crisis*. Cambridge, MA: Belknap, 1997.

Oglesby, Carl. *The JFK Assassination: The Facts and the Theories*. New York: Signet, 1992.

Rivele, Stephen J., Christopher Wilkinson, and Oliver Stone. *Nixon: An Oliver Stone Film*. New York: Cinergi Productions Inc., 1995.

Shakespeare, William. *Hamlet*. 1601. In *William Shakespeare: The Complete Works*. Ed. Stanley Wells and Gary Taylor. Oxford: Clarendon Press, 1986.

Stone, Oliver, and Zachary Sklar. *JFK: The Book of the Film*. New York: Applause Books, 1992.

Summers, Anthony. *The Arrogance of Power: The Secret World of Richard Nixon*. New York: Viking Penguin, 2000.

Walpole, Horace. *The Castle of Otranto and Hieroglyphic Tales*. Ed. Robert L. Mack. Vermont: Everyman, 1993.

Sherry R. Truffin (essay date 2004)

SOURCE: Truffin, Sherry R. "'Screaming while School Was in Session': The Construction of Monstrosity in Stephen King's Schoolhouse Gothic." In *The Gothic Other: Racial and Social Constructions in the Literary Imagination*, edited by Ruth Bienstock Anolik and Douglas L. Howard, pp. 236-48. Jefferson, N.C.: McFarland & Company, 2004.

[*In the following essay, Truffin examines several of Stephen King's works about teachers and students as examples of "Schoolhouse Gothic."*]

THE TEACHER AS MONSTROUS OTHER

Malevolent teachers who "would hurt the children in any way they could" are immortalized in Pink Floyd's *The Wall* and in numerous texts that exemplify the trend that I call the "Schoolhouse Gothic." Extraterrestrials attempt to colonize earth by inhabiting the bodies of high school teachers and terrorizing students in *The Faculty*. A demon disguised as a substitute teacher is sent to punish a lapsed satanic cult, that is also a parent-teacher association, by sacrificing cult members and their children/students in *The X-Files*. The "objective" nineteenth-century scientist and the white supremacist are fused in the sinister, slaveholding schoolteacher in Toni Morrison's *Beloved*. These texts suggest that in the popular imagination, schools serve the same social function as prisons and mental institutions—to define, classify, control, and regulate people—as Michel Foucault articulates in *Discipline and Punish*. In response, no area of contemporary culture—music, film, television, fiction, or scholarship—can escape the compulsion to return again and again to schools and teachers to dramatize a central fixation that locates these texts in the Gothic tradtion: a fixation on mystified power. The work of that most prolific contemporary Gothic writer, Stephen King, is no exception.

David Punter, who notes that the Gothic survives to this day because it continues to offer an "image-language in which to examine social . . . fears,"[1] observes that contemporary academic discourse shares with the Gothic a clear set of obsessions: power, alienation, dislocation, otherness (181-214). The Gothic, like the contemporary academy, has its origins in the Age of Reason yet offers what Fred Botting calls "counternarratives displaying the underside of enlightenment and humanist values."[2] Such counternarratives resonate with those of Foucault, whose work is preoccupied with, if not actually haunted by, the legacy of the Enlightenment. According to Anne Williams, Foucault's work reveals the way in which "Enlightenment thought [is] characteristically ordered and organized by creating institutions to enforce distinctions between society and its other, whether it resides in madness, illness, criminality, or sexuality."[3] In specifically Gothic terms, the relationship between the thinking, rational subject and its Other(s) works the same way: "the haunted Gothic castle . . . *creates* the haunted, dark, mysterious space even as it attempts to organize and control it" (Williams 248). Thus both the Gothic tradition and poststructuralist discourse interrogate the strategies of classifying and standardizing that is associated with the Enlightenment and question the institutions that reproduce these strategies, including the state, the family, the church, the laboratory, and, yes, the school.

The modern academy is one of the institutions entrusted with the construction of the contemporary subject. It functions as home, prison, and laboratory all at once and is, according to Foucault, a key site where Power and Knowledge intersect and reinforce one another. We do not, however, need Foucault's guidance to see that the modern school has assumed many of the socializing and penalizing functions traditionally associated with the court, the family, and the church. As a result, the teacher becomes a figure of immense power, dictating what children learn, when they work, when they play, and even when they take trips to the lavatory. More importantly, teachers determine which children are prodigies and which ones are problems. And so they wield an inexhaustible and inscrutable authority.

Schools and schoolteachers make frequent appearances in the fiction of Stephen King, whose Schoolhouse Gothic presents teachers as monstrous Others whose teaching breeds monstrous students who, in turn, strike out at the educational system that created them. This fiction equates teaching with crimes that have long prevailed in Gothic texts, even as it reflects shifting configurations and conceptions of power. King's *The Shining* and *Rage* displace the fears and rivalries that Freud ascribed to parent-child relationships (a pattern evident in earlier Gothic texts) onto educational institutions, portraying the teacher as an abusive surrogate parent and highlighting the power of the teacher to identify and isolate "bad" children and to administer punishment. *Rage* also likens modern education to another Gothic anxiety—rape—locating the male in the position of power over the docile, usually female figure. Images of teachers as abusers and rapists emphasize the way in which the teacher labels and victimizes the student. Other images, however, implicate the teacher and the school in larger systemic processes that *construct* the student as the monstrous Other. Both "Suffer the Little Children" and *Rage* develop the Gothic tradition by exploring the role of the school and schoolteacher in enforcing what Foucault calls the "Power of the Norm"[4]— established and legitimated through strategies of surveillance and consolidated in discourse.

The Shining sets the stage for the constant slippage between the roles of cruel teacher and abusive parent that recurs in King's fiction. Jack Torrence, an alcoholic writer and former English teacher, agrees to be the winter caretaker of what turns out to be a malevolently haunted resort hotel in Colorado, ultimately succumbing to the sinister influences of the hotel and attempting to bludgeon his wife, Wendy, and his son, Danny, to death. Jack takes the job to work on a play about a school headmaster who accuses a "saintly"[5] student of cheating on a final exam, eventually beating him to death; Jack has recently lost his teaching position after assaulting a rich, good-looking student named George Hatfield who slashed Jack's tires after being cut from the debate team because he stuttered. During his time at the Overlook, Jack is increasingly unable to write his play as he comes to see the student-hero of *The Little School* as "a monster masquerading as a boy" (273) and to identify with the schoolmaster who beats him to death.

As Jack becomes increasingly paranoid and violent, he repeatedly confuses his son, Danny—whose imaginative, clairvoyant power to "Shine" draws the envy of his artistically frustrated father—with George Hatfield, whose money, popularity, and good looks Jack had resented. In a trance, Danny imagines his father shaking him and screaming *"Don't Stutter!"* and is bewildered, since he has never stuttered (139). Later, Jack has a vision in which he bludgeons George Hatfield to death with a cane (much like the one his own abusive father had wielded), at which point Hatfield—to Jack's horror—transforms into a crying, pleading Danny (287).

Jack then encounters the ghost of Grady, a former care-taker who has murdered his wife and two daughters be-fore killing himself; Grady tells Jack that Danny plans to escape and therefore "needs to be corrected" (366). Ultimately, Jack roams the labyrinthine hotel,[6] brandish-ing a mallet, which he uses to break several of his wife's ribs and to threaten his son/student while screaming, *"You cheated! You copied that final exam!"* (444). In Jack, King fuses the cruel father with the sadistic teacher, who is instructed that "education always pays" (368); King thus shows us two monstrous educators who define instruction as violence.

LEARNING FROM MONSTROUS TEACHERS

King's "Suffer the Little Children" begins to suggest the ways in which monstrous teaching might create monstrous students. Echoing Foucault's argument in *Discipline and Punish: The Birth of the Prison,* a gene-alogy of Western penal practices, King, in "Suffer the Little Children," indicates parallels between the school and the prison or mental institution, explores the ways in which these institutions define deviance, and inscribes surveillance and forced confession at the heart of the teaching profession.

In *Discipline and Punish,* Foucault argues that the "dis-appearance of torture as a public spectacle" (7) during the late eighteenth and early nineteenth centuries is an index of the transformation of social power in Western culture. In pre-modern society, power, located in visible authorities, worked to punish physical bodies for spe-cific crimes; in a modern disciplinary society the hidden machinations of power define and regulate deviance through normalizing practices and strategies of surveil-lance. The aim of this power, in Foucault's formulation, is its own reproduction, which requires the construction of particular forms of subjectivity—the making, in short, of persons. The chief characteristic of these per-sons is, for Foucault, their homogeneity. Foucault de-scribes the human soul as no more and no less than "the present correlative of a certain technology of power over the body," a thing "not born in sin and subject to punishment, but . . . born rather out of methods of punishment, supervision, and constraint" (29). Fou-cault's rather astonishing claim here is that neither God nor nature nor parents nor mad scientists create people: rather, people are produced by Power, an impersonal force (or, rather, a complex network of related forces) that—despite all ideologies to the contrary—constitutes, legitimates, animates, and reproduces the institutions that, in turn, constitute and help to replicate modern culture. Thus, Foucault argues, power makes people.

Schools—like prisons, asylums, hospitals, factories, and other social institutions—play an important role in con-structing these modern subjects and in ensuring that most will be docile and "normal" while others will be unruly and "deviant." For Foucault, the modern disci-plinary society is a "punishable, punishing universality" (178) whose institutions individuate, distribute, and rank the human multiplicities whose lives they are charged with improving, rehabilitating, curing, and or-dering through "procedures that constitute the indi-vidual as effect and object of power, as effect and ob-ject of knowledge" (192). What unites these different "procedures" is "a relation of surveillance," which Fou-cault insists is "inscribed at the heart of the practice of teaching, not as an additional or adjacent part, but as a mechanism that is inherent to it and which increases its efficiency" (176). Surveillance is the most important mechanism, according to Foucault, by which Power is obtained, deployed, and transferred in modern Western culture. Surveillance "automatizes and disindividual-izes" (202) Power, dispersing and mystifying it. It re-produces the specific form of Power that Foucault calls the Norm, which, he argues, "since the eighteenth cen-tury, . . . has joined other powers—the Law, the Word (*Parole*) and the Text" (184). These powers are, in fact, intertwined: the power of the Norm is both translated into and enforced by discourse, by texts. In *The History of Sexuality,* Foucault argues that academic and medical discourses of the Victorian age "transform[ed] sex into discourse'" and implies that modern subjectivity can be understood in the same terms: our culture believes that the "truth" about a person is found not in intimate inter-action but rather in a confession or, better still, a file. Foucault's Power of the Norm—established and legiti-mated through strategies of surveillance and consoli-dated in discourse—turns out to be a major concern of King's Schoolhouse Gothic.

The protagonist of "Suffer the Little Children" is Miss Sidley, a rather severe elementary school teacher who, "like God, . . . seemed to know everything at once."[8] One way that she inspires this fear is by watching her students in her eyeglasses while writing on the chalk-board: "the whole class was reflected in [her] thick lenses and she has always been amused by their guilty, frightened faces when she caught them at their nasty little games" (82). In fact, she regards control over the students as her crowning professional triumph: "the success of her long teaching career could be summed and checked and proven by this one everyday action: she could turn her back on her pupils with confidence" (81). Miss Sidley becomes convinced that a student named Robert is a monster after she sees his distorted face in her glasses, and then sees him momentarily "chang[e]" (83) when they are face to face. Assuring herself that "she was not going to be one of those old-maid schoolmarms dragged kicking and screaming from their classes at the age of retirement," women who "re-minded her of gamblers unable to leave the tables while they are losing," she insists that *"she* was not losing. She had always been a winner" (83). Teaching, for Miss Sidley, is not occasionally punctuated by power struggles: it *is* a power struggle in which nothing less than the prerogative of definition is at stake.

However, Miss Sidley begins to suspect that the power structure has somehow been inverted; she can "feel the weight of their eyes on her like blind crawling ants" (84) when she writes on the board and despairs as her cold, alert, watchful eyes turn into "frightened, watching" (85) eyes. One day, she finds herself watching Robert transform into an ugly monster, and she is terrified. She pulls herself together and concludes that if her students are fiends "hiding behind masks" (85), and if Robert is "a monster, not a little boy," then "she must make him admit it" (87). She longs to grab the children and "shake them until their teeth rattled and their giggles turned to wails . . . thump their heads against the tile walls and . . . make them *admit* what they knew" (85). Significantly, it never occurs to her to contrive ways of placing the children in the care of colleagues in the hope that they will see what she sees: instead, she plots to make the children confess.

For Foucault, confession is a key component of the exercise of Power. It signals that a subject has internalized the definitions imposed upon him or her. In *The History of Sexuality,* he describes the confession as:

> a ritual . . . that unfolds within a power relationship, for one does not confess without the presence [or virtual presence] of a partner who is not simply the interlocutor but the authority who requires the confession, prescribes and appreciates it, and intervenes in order to judge, punish, forgive, console, and reconcile. . . .
>
> [61]

Thus, if Miss Sidley can get the children to confess, then her status as an authority will be unassailable, as will her judgment of the deviance of her students. Miss Sidley marches the class into the mimeograph room one by one for a "Test" ("Suffer" 90)—itself a ritual of definition and classification—and shoots them. Here, as in *The Shining,* King defines education as violence. Miss Sidley executes the children one by one until she is discovered by another teacher, and then she is sent to a mental institution, where the psychiatrist and the orderlies "watc[h] her for the first sign of an aggressive move" (92) just as she once watched her pupils. Eventually, she is allowed to interact with children under carefully controlled circumstances but "see[s] something which disturb[s] her" (92) and eventually commits suicide. Her psychiatrist, in turn, becomes absorbed in contemplation of the children—"hardly able to take his eyes off them" (92)—at which point the story ends. It is not clear from the text whether or not the children *actually* transform into the creatures seen by Miss Sidley (and, presumably, the psychiatrist) or whether these metamorphoses are delusions, brought on, perhaps, by the very power disparities in and through which the

teacher has learned to function. That is, to justify and to maintain her power, Miss Sidley needs to regard the children as monsters (at least potential ones), and her visions are depicted as a self-fulfilling prophecy of a most horrific order.

In this story, however, power does not go uncontested: Foucault claims that "where there is power, there is resistance, and yet, or rather consequently, this resistance is never in a position of exteriority in relation to power" (*HS* [*The History of Sexuality*] 95). In "Suffer the Little Children," students who have been subject to the power of "a dominating, overseeing gaze"[9] find a way (at least in Miss Sidley's mind) to resist, to turn that gaze around and thus to reverse the mechanism of surveillance and gain a measure of control—however fleeting and costly—over their tormentor. In this story, the classroom is depicted not as a value-free place in which benevolent teachers facilitate learning but rather as a site of institutional surveillance and control—not unlike the prisons, mental institutions, and hospitals described in *Discipline and Punish, Madness and Civilization,* and *The Birth of the Clinic*—institutions designed, according to Foucault, to objectify, classify, and discipline bodies and to construct persons (and, perhaps, monsters).

MONSTROUS PRODUCTS OF MONSTROUS EDUCATION

Rage, one of King's early novellas, goes much farther than "Suffer the Little Children" in exploring the ways in which the monstrosity of the teacher is reproduced in the student and revisited on the school. In *Rage,* the maladjusted Charlie Decker uses a pipe wrench to mangle a chemistry teacher who has forced him to solve a problem on the board and then mocked him for getting it wrong. When he is expelled, Charlie sets his locker on fire to create a diversion, shoots two teachers, and holds his algebra class hostage. After the initial shock subsides, his classmates join him in a strange form of group therapy that concludes with the ritual humiliation and abuse of the single straight-laced nonparticipant. As Charlie puts it, school was cancelled for the day, but "in Room 16, education went on."[10]

Rage employs many images to explore the monstrosity of teachers. Like *The Shining, Rage* reveals a Freudian subtext that parallels parents with teachers and presents both as monstrous. Charlie's relationship with his father is horrific—rife with unresolved, and irresolvable, Oedipal conflict. He reports that "my dad has hated me for as long as I can remember" (53). After Charlie encounters the primal scene, he begins to regard his father as a monster: he remembers hearing noises and imagining that "something terrible was coming. Coming for me through the darkness . . . creaking and creaking and creaking" (50). He realizes that "the Creaking Thing was in Mom and Dad's room," and, shortly thereafter, that "the Creaking Thing was my Father" (51). He "dare[s] to hate him back" (58) at age four, after his father hurls him to the ground in anger and then denies the act. The boy shrieks; his mother temporarily exiles his father, and Charlie admires the "practiced and dreadful ease" with which his mother sends his dad "stomping away like a surly boy" (58). In *Rage,* the Freudian subtext is far from subtle.

Charlie is unable to separate his family trauma from his troubles at school, and so he thinks of his schooling in familial terms, as being "caught for another day in the splendid sticky web of Mother Education" (11). More often, however, he conceives of school as decidedly masculine, as a sophisticated version of his father. As he leads his peers in a group intervention, Charlie is repeatedly distracted and disturbed by Mrs. Underwood's body, admitting to himself that "I wish it was [my father] I'd killed, if I had to kill anyone. This thing on the floor between my feet is a classic case of misplaced aggression" (155). Principal Denver's lecture comes to Charlie as "shark words at deep fathoms, jaws words come to gobble [him]. Words with teeth and eyes" (20). For Charlie, father and teacher are always one, and both are sinister, castrating forces against which he must fight for self-preservation.

Rage also likens modern education to rape, positioning the teacher as the powerful (usually male) subject in contrast to the docile (usually female) other. Anne Williams argues that much male Gothic fiction is about "horror of the female," a horror that is "figure[d]" and "control[led]" in Gothic texts by displays of masculine power, displays ranging from the penetrating male gaze to actual rape and murder.[11] Charlie Decker refuses to be feminized and victimized in this way, to play the docile victim that Williams describes as "an object . . . [that] may never be anything else but an object, and a focus of unconscious resentments against the feminine" (109). Charlie taunts the principal about his true role, which Charlie believes to be both sexual and sadistic. Charlie accuses Mr. Denver of "get[ting] a kick out of peddling my flesh" (*Rage* 21) but sarcastically excuses him by conceding that "everybody has to get it on, everybody has to have someone to jack off on" (21). Before leaving the office, Charlie untucks his shirt, unzips his pants, and tells the secretary that Mr. Denver "jumped over his desk and tried to rape me" (22). When the school guidance counselor, Mr. Grace, is asked to take over for the principal, Charlie refuses to answer his questions, believing that the counselor is "a man with a headful of sharp, prying instruments. A mindfucker" (67), always trying to "sli[p] it to you" (66). Charlie manipulates and reverses the power dynamic by insisting on being the one who gets answers: he tells Mr. Grace that he will shoot a student if Grace asks him any questions, then tricks him into asking a ques-

tion, at which point, Charlie shoots into the floor, shocking his peers out of their mesmerized states and terrifying the school officials. Charlie hears Mr. Grace crying over the intercom and congratulates himself on having "made [Grace] fuck himself with his own big tool" (75). Later, as his peers bond, Sandra—one of Charlie's smartest classmates—compares her education to an anonymous, somewhat violent sexual encounter that she has had, musing that teachers "want to stuff things into your head until it's all filled up. It's a different hole, that's all. That's all" (116). Thus *Rage* offers a conception of the school—of its disciplinarians, its counselors, and its teachers—as a power struggle of the sadomasochistic variety, and suggests that students, aware of themselves as sexual as well as pedagogical victims, are able to appropriate power and invert the power structure.

The paranoid vision of high school offered in *Rage* suggests, however, that the power by which the academy operates is more subtle, diffuse, and mysterious than that of either the abusive parent or the serial rapist. Charlie Decker, like Miss Sidley, fears the kind of surveillance that Foucault associates with modern Western culture and its chief normalizing institutions. Charlie suspects that he is even being watched in the restroom: "someone's always got to peek. People like Mr. Denver and Mr. Grace even get paid for it" (11). He remembers bringing his weapon to school "ever since [he] decided that people might . . . be following [him] around and checking up" (23). He recalls the day that he assaulted his chemistry teacher and how "everybody was *looking* at [him]. All of them *staring*" (150). He thinks of the aftermath of the attack, "the way people looked at [him] in the halls. The way [he] knew they were talking about [him] in the teachers' rooms" (155). Although Charlie has, in fact, done something to attract the attention of the school officials, the novella suggests that the school, like a prison, is designed not for isolated observation but rather for general, corporate surveillance and control. It is a place that assumes and, in a sense, *creates* deviance.

The physical plant, the daily routine, and the power structure of the school all help to reproduce the Foucauldian Power of the Norm by maximizing conformity. The lockers stand "in silent sentinel rows" (25) like prison guards. The ticking of the clock carves the day into intervals (85, 96, 143, 157), and "the clock buzze[s] away with a vague kind of determination" (52). According to Foucault, segmented time is central to the modern disciplines: "there is not a single moment of life from which one cannot extract forces" (*DP* [*Discipline and Punish*] 165). The school is especially sensitive about time: Foucault reports that "from the seventeenth century to the . . . beginning of the nineteenth, . . . the complex clockwork was built up cog by cog" so that "in the end, all the time of all the pupils was occupied . . . [and] [t]he school became a machine for learning" (165). This machine, Foucault goes on to explain, "requires a precise system of command" and a "technique of training" (166). This training involves "few words, no explanation, a total silence interrupted by signals—bells, clapping of hands, gestures, a mere glance from the teacher. . . . The pupil will have to have learnt the code of the signals and respond automatically to them" (166). It is not surprising to note, then, that when Charlie shoots the teacher and shuts the classroom door, only one student screams, and even she "stop[s], as if ashamed at screaming while school was in session, no matter how great the provocation" (*Rage* 33). Charlie and his peers tense up each time the schoolbell rings as they resist the automatic response of gathering their things and heading to the next class (85). In *Rage,* the diffuse power relations produced and reproduced in the school expand beyond the single figure of a teacher or a principal; they are, as anticipated by Foucault, ultimately internalized within the psyches of the students.

Constant surveillance—along with its discursive product, the permanent record—ensures that the student will become what Foucault calls "an effect and object of power, . . . effect and object of knowledge" (*DP* 192). Foucault claims that modern culture not only makes individuals out of bodies, but also "case[s]" (191) out of individuals. The *case* is "the individual as he may be described, judged, measured, compared with others, in his very individuality . . . and the individual who has to be trained or corrected, classified, normalized, excluded, etc" (191). Foucault argues that:

> for a long time ordinary humanity—the everyday individuality of everybody—remained below the threshold of description. To be looked at, observed, described in detail, followed from day to day by an uninterrupted writing was a privilege. The chronicle of man . . . formed part of the rituals of his power. The disciplinary methods reversed this relation, lowered the threshold of describable individuality and made of this description a means of control and a method of domination.
>
> [191]

The *caseness* of the student—or the prisoner or mental patient—is contained in and maintained by his file. During Charlie's visit to the principal's office, Mr. Denver looks at a paper "so he wouldn't have to look at" the boy, and the boy surmises that it is "something from my file, no doubt. The almighty file. The Great American file" (*Rage* 20). Later, when Mr. Denver is on the intercom, Charlie snarls at him, "I'm out of your filing cabinet now, Tom. Have you got it? I'm not just a record you can lock up at three in the afternoon" . . . "before the day's over, we are going to understand the difference between people and pieces of paper in a file" (43). Charlie, in short, recognizes that he has been constructed as a Foucauldian "case" by his teachers and

counselors over the years and that in "case" form, he resides in his permanent record. He resists this construction, perhaps because he believes that it is false and perhaps because he fears that it will become true, that its official bureaucratic sanction will *make* it so. Foucault insists that:

> [w]e must cease once and for all to describe the effects of power in negative terms: it "excludes," it "represses," it "censors," it "abstracts," it "masks," it "conceals." In fact, power produces; it produces reality; it produces domains and objects and rituals of truth. The individual and the knowledge that may be gained of him belong to this production.
>
> [*DP* 194]

Charlie's deepest anxieties come from an awareness that he is, in some sense, the object of such procedures, that he has been carefully observed, monitored, assessed, and classified—and from his suspicion not only that he cannot escape these judgments and classifications but also that they have had some mysterious role in making him the monster that he is.

Significantly, Charlie's drama ends as he leads his classmates in an attempt to force a confession of deviance from all-American boy Ted Jones. Now that he is in a position of power, Charles takes upon himself the prerogatives of Foucauldian power. When Ted refuses, he is accused of a variety of perversions and hypocrisies, then spat upon, punched, kicked, and tortured with the implements of the classroom: ink and notebook paper. He is left in a catatonic state, looking rather monstrous, with "blue black teardrops" all over his face, a bloody nose, and "one eye glar[ing] disjointedly toward no place" (*Rage* 162). King shows that the deviant becomes the Norm, that Power shifts, reproduces itself, endures.

Today, the headline "Horror in the Halls" is likely to announce neither the publication of a Gothic novel nor the release of a teen slasher flick, but rather a real-life school shooting. In light of the Columbine tragedy of 1999, as well as the seemingly ubiquitous school shootings around the U.S., Stephen King's 1971 *Rage*—if not his full inventory of Schoolhouse Gothic tales—appears decidedly prophetic. Ultimately, Charlie Decker may share with the student-gunmen of our time a common nightmare—that they're "another brick in the wall."[12] The same fear appears to plague scholars and teachers, judging from the way in which the contemporary academy has embraced the claustrophobic vision of modern Western culture and its institutions that Foucault offers in *Discipline and Punish,* deploying this vision as a basis for probing its own crimes and complicities. It remains to be seen whether academics will attempt to remake their institutions in such a way as to meaningfully address the sense of dis-ease that gives rise to such disturbing images of schools and teachers—to the horrifying alienation that constructs both teachers and students as the Other—or whether they will simply become bored with those images and develop new, less unsettling self-portraits. Either way, manifestations of the Schoolhouse Gothic will continue to circulate and to enthrall as long the paradigms resonate with the anxieties of the larger culture, as long as they give those anxieties structure and significance.

Notes

1. David Punter, *The Literature of Terror, vol. 2: The Modern Gothic.* 2nd ed. (London: Longman, 1996), 117.

2. Fred Botting, *Gothic* (London: Routledge, 1996), 2.

3. Anne Williams, *Art of Darkness: A Poetics of the Gothic* (Chicago: University of Chicago Press, 1995), 248.

4. Michel Foucault, *Discipline and Punish: The Birth of the Prison,* trans. Alan Sheridan (New York: Vintage, 1977), 184.

5. Stephen King, *The Shining* (New York: Signet, 1978), 271.

6. Evoking the typically labyrinthine Gothic structure.

7. Michel Foucault, *The History of Sexuality: An Introduction, Vol. 1,* trans. Robert Hurley (New York: Random House, 1978), 20.

8. Stephen King, "Suffer the Little Children," in *Nightmares & Dreamscapes* (New York: Signet, 1993), 81.

9. Michel Foucault, *Power/Knowledge: Selected Interviews and Writings: 1972-1977,* ed. Colin Gordon (New York: Pantheon Books, 1990), 152.

10. Stephen King, *Rage,* in *The Bachman Books* (New York: Signet, 1986), 44.

11. Williams, 114.

12. Roger Waters, "Another Brick in the Wall, Part II." *On The Wall* (New York: Columbia Records, 1979).

Works Cited

Botting, Fred. *Gothic.* London: Routledge, 1996.

Foucault, Michel. *Discipline and Punish: The Birth of the Prison.* Translated by Alan Sheridan. New York: Vintage, 1977.

———. *The History of Sexuality: An Introduction, Volume 1.* Translated by Robert Hurley. New York: Random House, 1978.

———. *Power/Knowledge: Selected Interviews and Writings, 1972-1977.* Edited by Colin Gordon. New York: Pantheon Books, 1990.

King, Stephen. *Rage.* In *The Bachman Books.* New York: Signet, 1977.

———. *The Shining.* New York: Signet, 1978.

———. "Suffer the Little Children." In *Nightmares & Dreamscapes.* New York: Signet, 1993.

Punter, David. *The Literature of Terror. Vol. 2: The Modern Gothic.* 2nd ed. London: Longman, 1996.

Waters, Roger. "Another Brick in the Wall, Part II." *The Wall.* 1979. Performed by Pink Floyd. Compact Disk C2K 68519. New York: Columbia Records, 1997.

Williams, Anne. *Art of Darkness: A Poetics of the Gothic.* Chicago: University of Chicago Press, 1995.

FURTHER READING

Criticism

Beer, Janet, and Avril Horner. "'This Isn't Exactly a Ghost Story': Edith Wharton and Parodic Gothic." *Journal of American Studies* 37, no. 2 (August 2003): 269-85.

Discusses several works by Edith Wharton that parody Gothic themes and circumstances.

Benefiel, Candace R. "Blood Relations: The Gothic Perversion of the Nuclear Family in Anne Rice's *Interview with the Vampire.*" *Journal of Popular Culture* 38, no. 2 (November 2004): 261-73.

Characterizes Anne Rice's *Interview with the Vampire* as a parody of family relations that allows the reader to imagine "alternative family structures and incestuous attraction."

Bloom, Clive, ed. *Gothic Horror: A Reader's Guide from Poe to King and Beyond.* New York: St. Martin's Press, 1998, 301 p.

Collection of essays on traditional as well as contemporary Gothic works.

Brabon, Benjamin, and Stéphanie Genz, eds. *Postfeminist Gothic: Critical Interventions in Contemporary Culture.* Basingstoke, England: Palgrave, 2007, 189 p.

Examines examples of women's Gothic in film and popular culture from a postfeminist perspective.

Hoeveler, Diane Long, and Tamar Heller, eds. *Approaches to Teaching Gothic Fiction: The British and American Traditions.* New York: Modern Language Association of America, 2003, 310 p.

Collection of background and thematic essays on various topics related to British and American Gothic.

Horner, Avril, and Sue Zlosnik. *Daphne du Maurier: Writing, Identity, and the Gothic Imagination.* Basingstoke, England: Macmillan Press Ltd, 1998, 235 p.
    Examines the breadth of du Maurier's work in terms of her handling of the interconnections between Gothic, writing, and identity.

Massé, Michelle A. *In the Name of Love: Women, Masochism, and the Gothic.* Ithaca, N.Y.: Cornell University Press, 1992, 301 p.
    Discusses the theme of women's masochism in relation to Gothic in such works as Charlotte Perkins Gilman's "The Yellow Wallpaper," Daphne du Maurier's *Rebecca,* and Charlotte Brontë's *Jane Eyre.*

Nash, Jesse W. "Postmodern Gothic: Stephen King's *Pet Sematary.*" *Journal of Popular Culture* 30, no. 4 (spring 1997): 151-60.
    Examines the style and themes of King's *Pet Sematary* in the context of the postmodern Gothic.

Ringel, Faye. "'Diabolists and Decadents': Lovecraft's Gothic Puritans." *LIT: Literature, Interpretation, Theory* 5, no. 1 (1994): 45-51.
    Discusses the American Puritan-influenced Gothic stories of H. P. Lovecraft, noting that he "simultaneously enshrines and demonizes" the traditions and superstitions he mines.

Roberts, Garyn G. "Gothicism, Vampirism, and Seduction: Anne Rice's 'The Master of Rampling Gate.'" In *The Gothic World of Anne Rice,* edited by Gary Hoppenstand and Ray B. Browne, pp. 55-70. Bowling Green, Ohio: Bowling Green State University Popular Press, 1996.
    Discusses Anne Rice's 1984 short story "The Master of Rampling Gate" as a reinterpretation of Gothic traditions and techniques.

Russ, Joanna. "Somebody's Trying to Kill Me and I Think It's My Husband: The Modern Gothic." *Journal of Popular Culture* 6, no. 4 (spring 1973): 666-91.
    Study of contemporary mass-market Gothic novels written by female authors expressly for women.

Sonser, Anna. "Consuming Passions in *The Vampire Lestat.*" In *A Passion for Consumption: The Gothic Novel in America,* pp. 136-44. Bowling Green, Ohio: Bowling Green State University Popular Press, 2001.
    Discusses Anne Rice's *Lestat the Vampire* as a postmodern Gothic work that blurs and questions the boundaries between the real and the imaginary.

Science Fiction Film Adaptations

The following entry presents critical discussion of feature films based on works of science fiction, which often utilize advanced special effects technology to explore characteristic science fiction themes.

INTRODUCTION

Science fiction films utilize cutting-edge technology to create spectacular images of human life in futuristic or alien worlds and explore distinctive science fiction themes, such as the existence of extraterrestrial life forms, the possibility and implications of time travel, the dehumanizing effects of technology, and the dangers of bioweapons and nuclear arms. Oftentimes science fiction films borrow elements from other genres, including fantasy, horror, or even detective fiction, thus blurring distinctions between various film genres. Film historians cite the first science fiction film as Georges Méliès's 1902 *Voyage dans la Lune* (*A Trip to the Moon*). Based on a novel by Jules Verne, the fourteen-minute film utilized visual trickery and illusion—the equivalent of today's special effects—to depict the journey of a spacecraft to the moon. The film captured the imagination of filmgoers and became a tremendous success, and science fiction film quickly became a staple of the burgeoning film industry.

In the early years special effects technology was crude, so filmmakers strived to provide exciting and creative images of other planets, futuristic societies, or alien life in order to appeal to Depression-era audiences wearied by their immediate economic and political circumstances. European filmmakers recognized early that science fiction films could be used as effective vehicles for social and political commentary. In one well-known example, Fritz Lang's *Metropolis* (1927) depicts a futuristic city where the stratification of the ruling and working classes has led to a dystopian society on the precipice of a class-based revolution. Science fiction films during these years also provided heroes as well as escapist entertainment, resulting in a host of films during the 1930s depicting the adventures of such comic-strip heroes as Flash Gordon and Buck Rogers. In general, these movies resulted in charges that science fiction movies were juvenile and insubstantial.

It wasn't until the tensions of the Cold War and the "Red Scare" that the science fiction film genre, which began to feature plots and situations that reflected those tensions, once again captured the imagination of filmgoers on a grand scale. Reviewers began to note that science fiction films reflected the social and political concerns of the era. In the 1950s alien invasion films exploited American fears of communism as a threat to the American way of life. They also echoed the widespread concern that there were enemies among us, paralleling the real-life anti-Communist hearings of the House Un-American Activities Committee in the late 1940s and Senator Joseph McCarthy's hearings about Communist influence on the U.S. government and army in the 1950s. Worries about the intensifying nuclear arms race were reflected in science fiction films that portrayed technology as out of control and world-threatening. Postapocalyptic films depicted life after a nuclear holocaust and often explored man's growing and discomforting dependence on technology. In the 1970s and 1980s a series of dystopian science fiction films were released, such as *A Clockwork Orange* (1971), *Soylent Green* (1973), and *1984* (1984). These films reflected the despondency of the post-Vietnam and Watergate eras.

The spectacular commercial success of the *Star Wars* series, however, belied that trend by combining elements of fantasy and science fiction to tell an inspiring story with breathtaking special effects. With the advent of computer technology during this period, special effects began to advance at a staggering pace and profoundly affect the look and feel of science fiction films. The growing importance of computers and the Internet also figured as prominent themes in science fiction movies in the 1990s, with the emergence of virtual-reality films such as Andy and Larry Wachowski's trilogy of *Matrix* movies. In recent years, CGI (computer-generated imagery) technology has played an integral role in science fiction film, providing invaluable services to such blockbuster movies as the *X-Men* movies. Despite concerns that technology overshadows the themes and performances in these movies, critics agree that the sophistication of science fiction films has grown over the years. Science fiction film has become a respectable topic for scholarly study; moreover, it is recognized for its potential to explore relevant and complex themes and provide stunning visual entertainment for its wide, enthusiastic audiences all over the world.

REPRESENTATIVE WORKS

Jack Arnold

It Came from Outer Space! [based on "Black Destroyer" and "Discord in Scarlet," by A. E. Vogt] 1953

John Carpenter
The Thing [based on "Who Goes There," by John W. Campbell, Jr.] 1982

Christian Duguay
Screamers [adapted from "Second Variety," by Philip K. Dick] 1995

Terence Fisher
Spaceways 1952

Richard Fleischer
Soylent Green [based on *Make Room! Make Room!*, by Harry Harrison] 1973

Philip Kaufman
Invasion of the Body Snatchers [adapted from *The Body Snatchers*, by Jack Finney] 1978

Stanley Kubrick
2001: A Space Odyssey [adapted from *2001: A Space Odyssey*, by Arthur C. Clarke] 1968
A Clockwork Orange [adapted from *A Clockwork Orange*, by Anthony Burgess] 1971

Fritz Lang
Metropolis 1927

Richard Linklater
A Scanner Darkly [adapted from *A Scanner Darkly*, by Philip K. Dick] 2006

George Lucas
Star Wars [Episode IV] 1977; also released as *[Star Wars: Episode IV] A New Hope*
[Star Wars: Episode V] The Empire Strikes Back 1980
[Star Wars: Episode VI] Return of the Jedi 1983
[Star Wars: Episode I] The Phantom Menace 1999
[Star Wars: Episode II] Attack of the Clones 2002
[Star Wars: Episode III] Revenge of the Sith 2005

Rudolf Maté
When Worlds Collide [adapted from *When Worlds Collide*, by Edwin Balmer] 1951

Georges Méliès
Voyage dans la Lune [based on *A Trip to the Moon* by Jules Verne] 1902
Le voyage à travers l'impossible [*The Impossible Voyage*] 1904

Christian Nyby and Howard Hawks
The Thing (from Another Planet) [adaptation of "Who Goes There," by John W. Campbell, Jr.] 1951

George Pal
The Time Machine [adapted from *The Time Machine*, by H. G. Wells] 1960

Irving Pichel
Destination Moon [adapted from *Rocket Ship Galileo*, by Robert Heinlein] 1950

Michael Radford
1984 [adapted from *1984*, by George Orwell] 1984

Franklin J. Schaffner
Planet of the Apes [adapted from *La Planète des singes*, by Pierre Boulle] 1968

Ridley Scott
Alien 1979
Blade Runner [based on *Do Androids Dream of Electric Sheep?* by Philip K. Dick] 1982

Don Siegel
Invasion of the Body Snatchers [adapted from *The Body Snatchers*, by Jack Finney] 1956

Brian Singer
X-Men [based on the *X-Men* comic series by Marvel Comics] 2000
X2: X-Men United [based on the *X2* comic series by Marvel Comics] 2003
X-Men: The Last Stand [based on the *X2* comic series by Marvel Comics] 2006

Steven Spielberg
Close Encounters of the Third Kind 1977
E.T.: The Extra-Terrestrial 1982
A.I.: Artificial Intelligence [based on "Supertoys Last All Night Long," by Brian Aldiss] 2001
War of the Worlds [based on *War of the Worlds*, by H. G. Wells] 2005

Rachel Talalay
Tank Girl [based on the British comic strip by Jamie Hewlett and Alan Martin] 1995

François Truffaut
Fahrenheit 451 [adapted from *Fahrenheit 451*, by Ray Bradbury] 1961

Paul Verhoeven
Total Recall [based on "We Can Remember It for You Wholesale," by Philip K. Dick] 1990
Starship Troopers [based on *Starship Troopers*, by Robert Heinlein] 1997

Andy Wachowski and Larry Wachowski
The Matrix 1999
The Matrix Reloaded 2003
The Matrix Revolutions 2003

John Woo
Paycheck [based on "Paycheck," by Philip K. Dick] 2004

Robert Zemeckis
Contact [based on *Contact,* by Carl Sagan] 1997

OVERVIEWS AND GENERAL STUDIES

Bryan P. Stone (essay date October 1998)

SOURCE: Stone, Bryan P. "Religious Faith and Science in *Contact.*" *Journal of Religion and Film* 2, no. 2 (October 1998): n.p.

[*In the following essay, Stone explores the relationship between religious faith and science as depicted in* Contact, *focusing on the role of technology in human life.*]

Religion and religious faith have not traditionally been a preoccupation of contemporary film, though they are becoming increasingly prominent these days. Directed by Robert Zemeckis (of Forrest Gump fame), *Contact* ranked eleventh in top grossing films in 1997, securing for itself a respectable position in contemporary American culture so far as popular film goes. *Contact* is based on the late Carl Sagan's novel by the same name that imagines the personal, religious, and political impact of an extraterrestrial encounter—a question that is certainly worth entertaining, especially with regard to its theological implications. Anyone who has paid attention to the work of Carl Sagan will recognize his perennial interests throughout the film. Sagan, who wrote more than two dozen books, hundreds of articles, and hosted the 1980 PBS series, *COSMOS,* was enormously successful in his lifetime at popularizing science and giving the search for extraterrestrial intelligence a measure of scientific respectability. Though Sagan had no place in his worldview for traditional religion and popular notions of God, he had a deep appreciation for the unresolvable mysteries of the universe. Sagan was actively involved in the transition of *Contact* from book to screenplay until his death at age 62 in December, 1996. Toward the beginning of the film, the central character of *Contact,* Eleanor "Ellie" Arroway, asks her dad whether he thinks there are people on other planets. In a line that is something of a Sagan mantra, her father replies, "I don't know . . . but I guess I'd say if it is just us . . . seems like an awful waste of space."

It is difficult to watch the film without being impressed by its special effects, especially the very beginning of the film where we are graphically transported backwards away from the planet earth for an incredible ride through the universe. However, *Contact* is much more subtle and intelligent on the "alien" side of things than other recent films and it does have a way of drawing the viewer in where the dimension of science is concerned. Roger Ebert refers to *Contact* as "the smartest and most absorbing story about extraterrestrial intelligence since *Close Encounters of the Third Kind.*" [*Chicago Sun Times,* 11 July 1997.] Of course, that may not be saying much since few science fiction films over the last two decades have taken it upon themselves to rise above the standard plot that include lots of people getting slimed by aliens and cosmic cowboys chasing interplanetary bad guys throughout the galaxy.

Still, as a uniquely modern genre, science fiction—whether in literature, film, or television—is uniquely suited for dealing with questions of faith. At first glance, we might take science fiction to be a distraction—a flight of fancy and escape from the real world. When science fiction first began to appear almost a hundred years ago it was considered little more than the product of end-of-the-century anxiety. Since that time, however, it has served as an important avenue for dealing with heavy questions such as the shape of ultimate reality, the meaning of life, and the place of human beings in the cosmos. *Contact* boldly places such questions at its front and center even though this can sometimes cause the film to become preachy, often straining under the weight of its own sense of self-importance. In brief, the film is about Ellie Arroway (Jodie Foster), a zealous radio astronomer who discovers a pulsing signal originating from the star system Vega, some twenty-six light years away (later in the film we see an Elvis look-alike holding up a sign that says "Viva Las Vega") The signal contains instructions for building a star-transport and most of the film traces the political, scientific, and religious complications that develop in response to the alien signal and Ellie's strong desire to be the one to go on the transport. Introduced into the story to provide roadblocks for Ellie are cardboard characters such as a glory-hogging science advisor to the president (Tom Skerritt) and a paranoid national security advisor (James Woods). Ellie is an atheist because she doesn't find any empirical evidence for the existence of God, but because the film develops her character so well, even the most devout theists will find themselves liking her and taking her side. Ellie finally gets to take the transport and after traveling through galactic wormholes at cosmic speeds she encounters an alien who, strangely enough, appears in the form of her father (I can just see Freud with a broad smile across his face). The alien has few answers for Ellie's questions and can only give her hints of the evolutionary process that has for millions of years brought them to this point. The alien doesn't even know how the transport system got there in the first place. Nonetheless, he comforts Ellie with the following words of wisdom:

> You're an interesting species. An interesting mix. You're capable of such beautiful dreams and such horrible nightmares. You feel so lost. So cut off. So alone.

See, in all our searching, the only thing we've found that makes the emptiness bearable . . . is each other.

Many viewers will likely be disappointed by the encounter. Twenty-six light years and all we get is a cure for interplanetary angst! And yet, perhaps an understated alien encounter is somewhat refreshing given some of the outlandish portrayals in other science fiction films. The film quickly turns to what is perhaps its most important segment—not the alien encounter, but Ellie's return to earth. To her fellow earthlings it appears that her star-transport never left—such is the nature of interstellar travel, I guess. Ellie is now left having to explain her experience not merely in the face of a lack of evidence, but in the face of controverting evidence. Ellie the atheist is reduced to the status of those poor religious folk who have no proof for their claims, but must simply live by faith and bear witness to their life-changing experiences in an unbelieving world. The other central character, Palmer Joss (played by Matthew McConaughey) shows up early in the film during Ellie's research at the Arecibo radio telescope site in Puerto Rico. McConaughey is completely unconvincing as a kind of new age ex-catholic theologian who got his Masters of Divinity, dropped out of seminary, and is now working on a book about how technology affects third-world cultures. Later in the film, we discover he has written another book entitled, *Losing Faith,* an indictment of modern culture that has lost its sense of direction and meaning despite its advances in science, technology, and creature comforts. According to Palmer, "We shop at home, we surf the Web, at the same time we're emptier."

Palmer is supposed to represent faith in the film and Ellie, of course, represents science. Their flirtations are the flirtations between science and faith. When they hold hands or kiss, we are watching the potential union of science and faith. And in a scene that is loaded with theological potential, faith gives science his number, but science never calls! The problem, however, is that we don't get to know Palmer well enough to understand, let alone identify with, his version of faith so that throughout the movie the "faith" that collides with and sometimes colludes with science remains abstract, meaningless, and void. We do know that Palmer couldn't, as he says, "live with the whole celibacy thing." He tells Ellie, "You could call me a man of the cloth . . . without the cloth." Following the standard Hollywood convention for communicating to viewers that the two have established a close caring relationship, they fall into bed for a one-night stand never to see each other again until four years later after Ellie has tuned in to the alien signal. By this time, Palmer has become, as Larry King describes him, "author and theologian . . . spiritual counselor of sorts and a recent fixture at the White House" or, according to the *New York Times,* "God's diplomat."

As a film that deals with the question of the existence of God, both of its central characters, Ellie and Palmer, supply the typical arguments for their respective positions on the topic. While their arguments are by no means profound, it is extraordinary to see a film today even allow itself to deal with such questions explicitly. Where the film gets muddled, however, is, first, in its attempt to portray authentic religious faith and, second, in its attempt to interface science with religious faith (which, of course, is a muddle that is the byproduct of the first muddle). Either the film does not really understand religious faith or, while pretending to remain neutral on the question, it so implicitly disagrees with religious faith that it finds it difficult to write well for it.

It is tempting to suggest that it is Carl Sagan's well known atheism that is the culprit here, but the truth of the matter is that authentic religious faith is notoriously difficult to depict accurately on screen. It is much easier to resort to caricature and distortion. Through the vehicle of the Palmer Joss character, *Contact* tries not to yield to the standard Hollywood convention of trivializing religion by presenting persons of faith as misinformed, confused, ineffective, fundamentalist, or fanatic. But it is not at all clear that it succeeds in doing this with Palmer. In the case of three other less prominent instances of religious figures in the film it finally does succumb to traditional Hollywood conventions altogether (and that doesn't even count the man holding the "Jesus is an alien" sign halfway during the movie!) The first figure is a priest who, in the beginning of the film, attempts to console Ellie, age 9, after her father has died. The priest tells her, "Ellie, I know it's hard to understand this now, but we aren't always meant to know the reasons why things happen the way they do. Sometimes we just have to accept it as God's will." Ellie responds matter of factly, "I should have kept some medicine in the downstairs bathroom . . . then I could have gotten to it sooner" and the priest is left with a helpless, confused stare on his face. It has now gotten to the point in popular film that if you see a man with a clerical collar you can go ahead and count on his being morally reprobate, inflexibly ruthless, or, in this case, sincere but intellectually helpless.

The second religious figure is the brief appearance of Richard Rank, leader of the Conservative Coalition who is thrown into the mix now and again to blabber this and that about not knowing whether the aliens have any moral values or to criticize science for "intruding into matters of faith." This, of course, is meant to be a parody of Ralph Reed and the Christian Coalition—a parody made all the more amusing by the casting of Rob Lowe (not exactly the epitome of righteousness). Finally, there is the fanatic cult member with a crucifix draped around his neck who blames science for all the world's woes and subsequently tries to nuke the entire project. But for what reason? "What we do we do for the goodness of all mankind. This won't be understood—not now—but the apocalypse to come will vindicate our faith." In other words, no answer is to be given. Instead the film merely falls back on one of the standard film conventions for portraying religious faith—a mixture of fanaticism and irrationality. Not that some future contact with extraterrestrial intelligence wouldn't occasion some very real conflict and tension between science and religion. One need not think long about doctrines central to all religions (such as soteriology, anthropology, or eschatology—not to mention christology, in the case of Christianity) to realize that each of them would be thrown into a tizzy with the advent of aliens. But, of course, these are not explored in the film. Rather, the focus of the faith versus science tension is an entirely anti-technology predilection.

So, then, are these the only candidates to be found for the relationship between religious faith and science: the befuddled priest, the political moralizer, the irrational fanatic, or the whatever-Palmer-Joss-is? Apparently so. *Contact is* a good example of how Hollywood creates and maintains popular attitudes toward religion and religious "faith" whether it intends to or not. What we find in the film, *Contact, is* an explicit message about science and religion that attempts a neutrality and maybe even a positive cooperation between the two. On the implicit level, however, where filmic conventions operate (See Margaret R. Miles, *Seeing and Believing.* Boston: Beacon Press, 1997), we find what is true of many popular films a consensus that traditional religious faith is deeply untrustworthy and to be placed at the margins of culture if not rejected altogether.

Furthermore, because of the implicit messages the film conveys to its viewers about the nature of religious faith, it never really is able to make the jump it wants to with regard to the relationship between that very faith and science. In the end, faith is not allowed to stand on its own two feet but is instead reduced to a caricature. As a byproduct, even the question of God's existence is throughout the film treated as if it were logically identical to the question of alien existence. As a byproduct, even the question of God's existence is throughout the film treated as if it were logically parallel to the question of alien existence. But just this confusion is what an authentically religious faith can never allow. The existence of God is not at all parallel to the question of whether there are aliens. The latter will always be an empirical question that is answerable, at least in principal, by empirical methods of discovery while the question of God's existence, as a properly metaphysical question, is in a different category altogether. It is almost as laughable as hearing once again of the Soviet cosmonaut who, having attained space orbit, proudly boasted that he saw no God. What we have here is a mixing of categories and a misunderstanding of the nature of faith.

But perhaps this film can teach us something about the uneasy relationship of faith and science in our world. As a general uneasiness about where our technocentric world is headed becomes increasingly widespread along with alteration after alteration in our understanding of the cosmos, we can expect more films to reflect our cosmic anxieties and the implications of those anxieties for religious faith. A faith that tries to achieve for its claims the certainty of science is perhaps as doomed as a science that pretends it begins with no faith claims of its own. There is a yearning in our world today for a philosophy—nay, a spirituality—that can resolve the tensions between faith and science with integrity and practicality. If *Contact is* unsuccessful in pointing the way to such an integral spirituality, it at least has the courage to try to imagine its possibility. Whether and how we decide to rise to that challenge is up to us. In a secular and scientific world that less and less requires metaphysical stop-gaps, the challenge of people of faith is to communicate that faith as pervasive, relevant, and meaningful rather than obscure, trivial, and silly. And perhaps the one point where that task will be most difficult but most important is, as the film itself suggests, at the intersection of the human spirit and technology.

Barry Keith Grant (essay date 1999)

SOURCE: Grant, Barry Keith. "'Sensuous Elaboration': Reason and the Visible in the Science-Fiction Film." In *Alien Zone II: The Spaces of Science-Fiction Cinema,* edited by Annette Kuhn, pp. 16-29. London: Verso, 1999.

[*In the following essay, Grant explores the relationship between the genre of science fiction and the medium of film.*]

In this [essay] I want to explore the relation of science fiction to the cinema—that is to say, the relation between the genre of science fiction and the medium of film.[1] As I shall argue, the inherent nature of cinema as a visual medium has tended to work against the distinctive dynamics of science fiction as a genre. My intention is not to claim, as indeed some critics have, that 'Science fiction film . . . is an intellectual impossibility.'[2] Clearly such a sweeping claim would be absurd, yet fans of science-fiction literature have lodged this complaint against science-fiction film frequently.

For my purpose here, we might begin to hack our way through what Darko Suvin calls the 'genealogical jungle' of science fiction by distinguishing it from horror.[3] Although the two genres share some of the same generic elements (iconography, character types, conventions), their treatment is notably different. So while the genres of science fiction and horror often overlap, even more so in film than in literature, the contrasts between them are rooted in the particular nature of science-fiction *film*.

Both science fiction and horror, along with fantasy, are types of narrative that have been called speculative fiction or structural fabulation.[4] Horror and science fiction are both rooted in the real world: the former works by positing something as horrifying in contrast to the normal, quotidian world; the latter by acknowledging to some extent contemporary scientific knowledge and the scientific method. Hence the close relationship between the two genres. Such works as Mary Shelley's novel *Frankenstein* (1817), Ridley Scott's *Alien* (1979), and the two versions of *The Thing* (1951, 1982) have been categorized as both science fiction and horror, for all employ iconography and conventions found in both genres. By contrast, fantasy narratives are based neither in the natural world nor in the supernatural, but the *supra*natural. As Robert Heinlein notes,

> Science fiction and fantasy are as different as Karl Marx and Groucho Marx. Fantasy is constructed either by denying the real world *in toto* or at least by making a prime basis of the story one or more admittedly false premise—fairies, talking mules, trips through a looking glass, vampires, seacoast Bohemia, Mickey Mouse.[5]

The distinctive aim of fantasy, then, according to Lester del Rey, is to present 'alternative *impossibilities*'.[6]

Despite the narrative relation between horror and science fiction, the two genres offer experiences and pleasures strikingly different, in fact almost opposite, in nature. As such critics as Robert Scholes and Bruce Kawin have argued, the appeal of science fiction is primarily cognitive, while horror, as the genre's very name suggests, is essentially emotional.[7] Linda Williams has discussed the horror film as a 'body genre'—that is, one of those genres (like pornography and melodrama) that works by eliciting pronounced emotional and physiological excitation. Science-fiction, by contrast, is often defined more cerebrally as a philosophical openness described as a 'sense of wonder'. Science-fiction critic Sam Moskowitz, quoting Rollo May, for example, invokes the phrase as the essential quality of science fiction and defines this sense of wonder as a heightened awareness and open attitude to new ideas.[8] Science fiction, quite unlike fantasy and horror, works to entertain alternative *possibilities*.

Perhaps, then, the fundamental distinction between the two genres is one of attitude: a closed response in horror, an open one in science fiction. Horror seeks to elicit terror and fear of something unknown or unacknowledged. According to Robin Wood's highly influential Freudian/Marxist analysis of the horror film, the genre's monsters represent a 'return of the repressed', forbidden desire disowned and projected outward by the protagonist.[9] Accordingly, in horror stories narrative consciousness is often trapped or contained, set in claustrophobic, enclosed places, as in the countless castles, vaults, tombs and chambers that typify the genre's dramatic spaces. And vision is often obscured, from Poe's 'The Pit and the Pendulum' (1843) to John Carpenter's *The Fog* (1979). Because the sleep of reason breeds monsters, horror tales emphasize darkness and night (Stephen King's *The Dark Half* [1990], the numerous movies entitled *Night of . . .*) and superstition (*Halloween* [1978], *Friday the 13th* [1980] and the various *Curse(s) of . . .*).

Tellingly, the narrator's struggle in Poe's story 'Descent into the Maelstrom' (1841) to employ empirical reasoning so as to prevent being sucked below the surface is paradigmatic of the horror tale. By contrast, the rapt upward gaze of faces bathed in beatific light in Steven Spielberg's *Close Encounters of the Third Kind* (1977) is emblematic of the expansive thrust of science fiction. Vision in horror tales tends to focus down and inward, as in Poe's 'The Premature Burial' (1844) or David Cronenberg's *Parasite Murders* (a.k.a. *Shivers/They Came From Within*, 1975), while science fiction gazes up and out—from man's one small step in Jules Verne's *From the Earth to the Moon* (1865) to the giant step for mankind through the stargate in Stanley Kubrick's *2001: A Space Odyssey* (1968). Kawin sums up the difference by comparing the last lines of *The Thing*—the dire warning 'Keep watching the skies!'—and *Brainstorm* (1983)—the hopeful and expansive invitation to 'Look at the stars!'[10] It is no coincidence that one of the first science-fiction movies of the sound era was entitled *Just Imagine* (1930).

For Damon Knight, 'Some widening of the mind's horizons, no matter in what direction' is what science fiction is all about.[11] In this sense science-fiction narratives are, to use Méliès's own phrase, *voyages extraordinaires* which, befitting their frequent setting in the future and/or on parallel worlds, emphasize the vastness of space and the fluidity of time. Thus in science fiction, narrative point of view expands to entertain rather than contain new possibilities. As in, say, Olaf Stapledon's novel *Last and First Men* (1930) or H. G. Wells's *The Shape of Things to Come* (1933) and the film version *Things to Come* (1936), which Wells scripted, the dramatic conflict in science fiction is quite often exactly this: the difficulty of accepting rather than combating forces larger than the individual will. According to Suvin, the genre works by providing us with an experience of 'cognitive estrangement': as in Russian Formalism, our attention is returned to reality by the premises of science-fiction tales, which make us question the givens of our world.[12]

In both Richard Matheson's *The Shrinking Man* (1956) and the film adaptation *The Incredible Shrinking Man* (1957), the mental perspective of the protagonist expands even as his body dwindles. At first Scott Carey is terrified by the new, challenging world in which he finds himself, but ultimately he achieves spiritual transcendence. His epiphanic perception, on the novel's final page, is that he has moved from the 'universe without' to the 'universe within': 'Why had he never thought of it; of the microscopic and the submicroscopic worlds? . . . He'd always thought in terms of man's concept, not nature's. . . . But to nature there was no zero. Existence went on in endless cycles' (or, as the film concludes: 'To God there is no zero').[13]

The horrible dangers of an enlarged world are embodied in both novel and film in the spectacular form of a spider that comes to seem monstrously large. Both horror and science fiction make generic claims to monster movies—'the Creature film sits (awkwardly, for some) between horror and SF', observes Vivian Sobchack[14]—but they are represented quite differently in the two genres. This difference follows from their respective orientations of vision. In horror, creatures are monstrous violations of ideological norms, while in science fiction monsters are often simply a different life form. Because of this difference in the treatment of the Other, as Sobchack observes, horror monsters threaten the disruption of moral and natural order, while those of science fiction address the disruption of the social order.[15]

So the monsters of horror are typically abject, occasionally even unnameable, as in Stephen King's *It* (1986); but in science fiction they may be subjects of rational scrutiny, as in John W. Campbell, Jr's novella 'Who Goes There?' (1938), the source of both versions of *The Thing*. Because the monsters of horror commonly represent 'the return of the repressed', they tend to be anthropomorphic (the vampire, the zombie, the mummy) and animalistic (the wolf man, cat people), to spring from our physical nature, albeit in unnatural or 'interstitial' form.[16] The Other of science fiction, however, frequently takes nonhumanoid forms, whether animal (*War of the Worlds*, 1953), vegetable (*The Andromeda Strain*, 1970), or mineral (*The Monolith Monsters*, 1957).

The fundamental difference between science fiction and horror is conventionally represented within the two genres themselves as a differing emphasis on the mind (science fiction) and the body (horror). Science fiction focuses on heady issues, as in such movies as *The Brain from Planet Arous* (1958) and *The Mind of Mr Soames* (1969). The premise in Poul Anderson's novel *Brain Wave* (1954) is that the human race is suddenly confronted with a quantum leap in intelligence. By contrast, horror commonly evokes our anxiety about the body, so vividly invoked in such horror films as *I Dismember Mama* (1972) and *The Texas Chain Saw Massacre* (1974). Indeed, contemporary horror movies focus on the graphic spectacle of the violated body to

such an extent that they have been referred to as 'meat movies'. For Philip Brophy, they tend 'to play not so much on the broad fear of Death, but more precisely on the fear of one's own body, of how one controls and relates to it'.[17] In many of these movies, such as the *Hellraiser* series, evisceration and flaying—that is, exposing the body as a visible site—are treated as the privileged moments of horror, the generic 'money shots'. (Indeed, it might even be argued that the history of the horror film traces a trajectory of gradual, inexorable surrender to the allure of the visible, and that this genre's current aesthetic impasse and moribund status is precisely the result of its wholesale capitulation to the representation of horror as that which is corporeal, physical—that is, *seen*.)

For Christian Metz, the chronological development from Lumière to Méliès marks an evolution of 'cinematography to cinema'—that is, from a conception of film as a recording tool to an artistic medium.[18] But it is perhaps more accurate to say that cinema is simultaneously Lumière and Méliès, science *and* fiction, for the film image is at once a concrete, scientific record of things in the real world ('*actualités*') and a selected account of that world ('*artificially arranged scenes*'). Dziga Vertov's Kino Eye, that unblinking machine capable of perceiving the world with a greater objective fidelity than the human eye, always open to that which is placed before it, would suggest that the cinema would be an ideal medium for conveying science fiction's sense of wonder. Indeed, cinema as a medium displays three central aspects central to the genre of science fiction: space, time, and the machine—or the apparatus, in the terms of materialist film theory. (We might note in passing that these themes appear much less often in the horror genre.)

In cinema, narration proceeds by manipulating time and space, elongating and condensing both for dramatic and affective purposes. The techniques for achieving such spatial and temporal distortions constitute the foundation of classic narrative film, but such manipulations are central to documentary and experimental cinema as well. Across the range of different film practices the camera, the recording apparatus itself, seems capable of moving through both dimensions at once. Terry Ramsaye has noted how much the cinema resembles a time machine in his discussion of H. G. Wells's description of travelling through time in *The Time Machine* (1895).[19] (Later in the year Wells's book was published, inventor William Paul, whom Wells knew, applied for a patent for a machine that would provide simulated voyages through time.)

The cinematic machine, like the Constructors in Stanislaw Lem's novel *The Cyberiad* (1967), is a device capable of imagining and 'building' (through special effects) other machines infinitely more sophisticated than itself. Science-fiction film has relied heavily on special effects, and these effects in turn constitute one of the particular pleasures of the genre. The genre's reliance on special effects is itself an enactment of science fiction's thematic concern with technology. It is therefore understandable that for many viewers the value of (that is to say, the pleasure derived from) science-fiction movies is determined by the quality (synonymous with believability) of the special effects. For these viewers, nothing destroys the pleasure of a science-fiction movie more than seeing the 'seams' in a matte shot or glimpsing the zipper on an alien's bodysuit. Even Richard Hodgens, an apparent purist who bemoans the lack of scientific knowledge in science-fiction movies, at several points seems to confuse the failure of some films' special effects to be 'convincing' with the plausibility and consistency of their narrative premises.[20]

Special effects are 'filmic moments of a *radically* filmic character',[21] for they seek to achieve unreality as realistically as possible—to engage 'our belief, not our suspension of disbelief', as Sobchack puts it. We marvel at special effects images at once for their fantastic content and for the power of their realization. They announce the powers of cinema while, paradoxically, taming the imagination through the very fact of visual representation. This visualization for the camera pulls the images from speculation to spectacle—in Sobchack's terms, it transforms the poetry of the possible into the prosaic realm of the visible.[22]

Because of the science-fiction film's emphasis on special effects, the genre's primary appeal has been the kinetic excitement of action—that 'sensuous elaboration' which Susan Sontag describes as 'the aesthetics of destruction . . . the peculiar beauties to be found in wreaking havoc, making a mess'.[23] (This pleasure is itself visualized in the 'bird's-eye view' shot in Alfred Hitchcock's 1963 (science-fiction?) thriller *The Birds,* as the viewer is placed with the hovering birds looking down in seeming satisfied contemplation of the picturesque destruction they have wrought in the town below.) At least one subgenre of the science-fiction film, the apocalyptic film, is founded on the promise of scenes of mass destruction. In these films, from *When Worlds Collide* (1951) to the recent *Armageddon* and *Deep Impact* (both 1998), we eagerly await the climactic tidal wave that will sweep over New York and its landmarks of western civilization.

The paradigmatic example of this difference between science fiction in the two media is, perhaps, *Frankenstein.* Shelley's novel is a central early text in the history of science-fiction literature—the 'first great myth of the Industrial age', in the words of Brian Aldiss[24]—while James Whale's 1931 movie is a classic horror film. In the film, philosophy is replaced by *frisson,* and the white magic of science becomes black.[25] Dr Fran-

kenstein's laboratory, with its battery of crackling generators and steaming German Expressionist beakers—clearly influenced by Rotwang's laboratory in *Metropolis* (1926)—evokes not enlightened scientific inquiry but the dark supernatural world of the Gothic. The creature is transformed from a nimble and articulate being, an effective metaphor for Romantic *hubris* and encroaching industrialization, into a lumbering, grunting monster. The movie is less interested in the moral implications of human artifice than in the frightening spectacle of Boris Karloff's stiff-legged strut, and so shifts the focus from, as it were, the doctor's dilemma to the revenge of the creature. The doctor's famous cackle, 'It's alive, it's alive', as uttered by actor Colin Clive, unmistakably marks him as an unhinged man—the familiar mad scientist of horror who has committed the hubristic sin of investigating phenomena 'Man was not meant to know'.

Monsters, phaser-gun gadgetry and large-scale destruction are staple motifs of science-fiction literature, but they have been more prominent in science-fiction cinema. If the cinema's BBBs (big bosomed babes, in the jargon of the genre), as represented by *Fire Maidens From Outer Space* (1956) and Jane Fonda as *Barbarella* (1967), cannot hope to match the depictions in the science-fiction pulps in the 'Golden Age' (approximately 1938 to 1950), it is only that actresses of flesh and blood could never equal the damsels in the fantastically stylized illustrations of the pulp covers—although Russ Meyer's amply endowed women in *Dr Breedlove* (1964) come close.

Because film is primarily a visual medium, it tends to concentrate on the depiction of visual surfaces at the expense of contemplative depth. Science fiction's characteristic sense of wonder thus works differently in film than in literature. According to Cyril Kornbluth, 'The science fiction writer churns out symbols every time he writes of the future or an alternate present; he rolls out symbols of people, places, things, relationships, as fast as he can work his typewriter or his pen.'[26] Indeed, writing in the interrogative mode of science fiction rather than the declarative mode of realism is necessarily to write symbolically, for it is the extrapolative kind of writing that contemplates the potential of things, how things *might* be regarded (Suvin's 'cognitive estrangement'). Unlike words, which are rendered either as sounds or marks on paper, representational images are first and always objects in the material world, the things themselves before being symbolic of something else.[27]

In other genres, inherent symbolism is provided by visual icons which carry 'intrinsic charges of meaning independently of whatever is brought to them by particular directors'.[28] But, as Sobchack notes, the common objects in science-fiction films, like spaceships, lack the iconographic consistency of other genres and are relatively 'unfixed'.[29] But science-fiction films are are shaped by the ideological constraints of the genre system, which typically features comfortable narrative closure. So even though science-fiction movies allow us the anarchic pleasure of witnessing civilization's destruction, the genre also offers us, at least in its classic form (similar to the gangster film, to which monster movies are closely related), the satisfaction of the restoration of social order. So in the monster movies that typified science-fiction film during the 1950s (the period John Baxter refers to as 'Springtime for Caliban'[30]), the creatures, which almost always appear as the result of nuclear testing, are often finally destroyed with an 'ultimate weapon' that uses similar technology. In other words, the unfortunate results of sophisticated and potentially lethal technology are defeated by the creation of even more sophisticated and lethal technology.

In *The Beast from 20,000 Fathoms* (1953), one of the movies that initiated the 1950s monster cycle, the elegiac atmosphere that informs Ray Bradbury's 1951 source story 'The Fog Horn' is emphatically sacrificed for visual spectacle. The story is a mood piece about a lonely prehistoric creature drawn from the sea to a lighthouse by the melancholy sound of its horn. Bradbury's prose is more suggestive than concrete in its description, but the movie features a radioactive, mutated Rhedosaurus that wreaks havoc in New York City, with the requisite shots of physical destruction and stampeding pedestrians. In the film's climax, the army pursues the creature to Coney Island, for no particular reason other than the visual interest in showing the creature in proportion to the famous Cyclone roller coaster, where it is killed with a new nuclear warhead. Thus our fears about the possibility of nuclear holocaust are at once aroused and assuaged in a narrative trajectory that in short order became a soothing ritual in the myriad movies featuring genetically altered insects, reptiles, and other asserted BEMs ('bug-eyed monsters') that soon followed. Of course, the ideological assurance of such narrative closure works across numerous genres, but in the specific case of science fiction it compromises the radical potential of the genre's extrapolative, speculative dynamic.

In recent years, the science-fiction film has placed great emphasis upon the child, and this is no accident. Robin Wood has argued convincingly that recent American cinema generally has tended to construct the viewer as childlike,[31] in thrall to the illusion. In science fiction specifically, the generic sense of wonder, and by extension the position of the spectator, has been located in the image of a wide-eyed child. This development, of course, is largely the result of the huge commercial success of George Lucas's *Star Wars* trilogy and Steven Spielberg's *Close Encounters* and *ET: The Extraterrestrial* (1982), all of which rank among the top box-office winners in film history. (The *Star Wars* cosmol-

ogy became even more firmly entrenched in American cultural consciousness when former President Ronald Reagan named his national defence programme after Lucas's film and referred to the Soviet Union as the 'Evil Empire'.) Subsequent science-fiction movies such as *Starman* (1984), *The Explorers* (1985), *Short Circuit* (1986), *Tron* (1982) and *The Last Starfighter* (1984) exhibited a new adolescent orientation, clearly showing the influence of the Lucas and Spielberg films. *Cocoon* (1985), with its premiss of alien lifeforms that change a swimming pool into a fountain of youth, even manages to make children of senior citizens.

Before Spielberg and Lucas, children were as sparse in science-fiction films as in the stylized towns of the classic Western. Aside from such rare exceptions as *Invaders From Mars* (1953) and *Village of the Damned* (1960, based on John Wyndham's *The Midwich Cuckoos,* 1957), until recently children tended to be neither heard nor seen in science fiction. In horror, however, children have been presented frequently as figures of evil rather than innocence. From *The Bad Seed* (1956) to Stephen King's *Pet Sematary* (1983), horror tales have depicted children as figures of demonic possession. Many of these movies, following upon the popularity of *Rosemary's Baby* (1968) and *The Exorcist* (1973), may be read as embodying adult fears of being 'possessed' by children—that is, of being obligated to them, an expression of cultural backlash against the centrality of the nuclear family in a period of dissolving marriages and more open sexual mores.

Discussing the infantilization that informed much of Hollywood cinema in the 1980s, Wood refers to special effects as the exhibition of technological 'magic'. Tellingly, Lucas's special effects company is called Industrial Light and Magic—the name itself suggesting the kind of totemic power the popular audience ascribes to the sophisticated technology required to produce such visual illusions. As Carl Freedman notes, special effects tend to 'overwhelm the viewer, to bathe the perceptual apparatus of the filmgoer in the very "filmicness" of film'.[32] This position is literalized by the placement of the camera (and hence the position of the spectator) in the genre's now-conventional special effects image described by Martin Rubin as 'a shot . . . of an enormous spacecraft rumbling over the camera position, so that the entire underside passes overhead, massive, ominous, bristling with special effects paraphernalia'.[33] (The convention is nicely parodied in the opening shot of Mel Brooks's 1987 science-fiction parody *Spaceballs,* with its enormous ship that rumbles past—and past, and past.)

The scopophilic pleasure of cinema is mobilized most intensely in special effects images, as viewers are swathed in their power. This wondrous dependence on special effects imagery is itself the subject of Paul Verhoeven's *Total Recall* (1990), based on Philip K. Dick's short story 'We Can Remember It For You Wholesale' (1966). Like Dick's story, the movie is a reflexive science-fiction film about the extent to which we look to the image to provide our reality. The protagonist, Douglas Quaid, because of his memory implant, becomes incapable of distinguishing reality from fantasy: he does not know whether his adventure is the program he requested at Rekall, Inc, or if his actual identity has been accidentally uncovered. Viewers share Quaid's lack of epistemological certainty since they are incapable of detecting—indeed, are virtually challenged to detect—a flaw in the state-of-the-art special effects, that is, of distinguishing between what is 'real' and what is 'imagination'. Inevitably, the viewer regresses to that earliest phase of childhood Jacques Lacan calls the pre-Oedipal Imaginary, unable to distinguish the nature of the visual field. The world of the film, with its domestic wall projections of make-believe environments, mechanical taxi drivers and holographic projections, is a postmodern simulacrum, just as the visual media are for us in the real world. The landscape of recent popular cinema offers ample evidence that, like Quaid, we enjoy imagining ourselves as Arnold Schwarzenegger in non-stop action movies—just like *Total Recall.*

Verhoeven follows the same approach in his more recent *Starship Troopers* (1997), based on Heinlein's 1959 novel. The book is a rather straightforward account of the military mindset and values in the future when the human race is threatened by an extraterrestrial army of giant intelligent insects. Without a trace of irony, Heinlein uses the story to offer extended passages about the benefits of a social order organized by militaristic principles. The film, however, completely subverts the book's conservative ideology by deconstructing military guts and glory even as it provides it so completely. Again with state-of-the-art effects, Verhoeven shows us graphic battles between bugs and humans as soldiers are impaled, eviscerated and dismembered. The protagonists are all played by beautiful young actors, with whom the audience can easily identify. But these scenes alternate with images of official government propaganda films (obviously inspired by the nationalistic fervour of Frank Capra's *Why We Fight* documentaries from World War II) that clearly contradict the bloody truths of the war. In the film, the young people still march off to war full of optimistic faith, just as audiences flocked to the film to see the much-touted violence of its battle scenes.

Apart from Verhoeven's postmodern critiques, much of contemporary science-fiction cinema has replaced the sense of wonder with the awe of mystification. Popular science-fiction movies like *The Terminator* (1984) and *Predator* (1987), offering almost continuous spectacular action, seem to have succumbed almost entirely to the siren call of the sensuous spectacle. Other science-fiction films like *Alien, Blade Runner* (1982, based on

Dick's 1968 *Do Androids Dream of Electric Sheep?*) and John Carpenter's 1982 version of *The Thing,* which propound ostensible humanist messages, are devoid of rounded characters and overwhelmed by production design and special effects, thus contradicting their own themes.

The starchild of *2001* looking down at Earth, returning our gaze to us for self-scrutiny, has become the regressive child/man of *Close Encounters* who, wanting to escape his adult responsibilities and enter the womb of the 'Mother' ship, gazes upwards, as if in religious devotion. If the reverential awe we accord science-fiction images is a debasement of science fiction's distinctive philosophical attitude, it is because the film medium, and the generic system which organizes so much of popular cinema, work to discourage the kind of speculative narrative that has challenged us to embrace what Arthur C. Clarke calls *Childhood's End.* Embodied in science-fiction films most fully in special effects, the genre's characteristic sense of wonder is perhaps the ontological fulfilment of the nature of science-fiction *cinema.*

Notes

1. This is a substantially revised version of an essay originally published in *Literature/Film Quarterly,* vol. 14, no. 3, 1986.

2. John Baxter, *Science Fiction in the Cinema,* New York: Paperback Library, 1970, p. 8.

3. Darko Suvin, *Metamorphoses of Science Fiction,* New Haven, CT: Yale University Press, 1979, pp. 16-36.

4. Science-fiction author Robert A. Heinlein uses the term 'speculative fiction' in his essay 'Science Fiction: Its Nature, Faults, and Virtues', in Basil Davenport, ed., *The Science Fiction Novel: Imagination and Social Criticism,* Chicago: Advent, 1969, pp. 14-48. 'Structural fabulation' is Robert Scholes's term in *Structural Fabulation: An Essay on Fiction of the Future,* Notre Dame, IN: University of Notre Dame Press, 1975.

5. Robert Heinlein, 'Preface' to *Tomorrow, the Stars,* New York: Doubleday, 1967, p. 8. See also Heinlein, 'Science Fiction'.

6. Lester del Rey, *The World of Science Fiction, 1926-1976: The History of a Subculture,* New York: Ballantine, 1979, pp. 6-9.

7. Scholes, *Structural Fabulation*; Bruce Kawin, 'Children of the Light', in Barry Keith Grant, ed., *Film Genre Reader II,* Austin: University of Texas Press, 1995, pp. 308-29.

8. Linda Williams, 'Film Bodies: Gender, Genre, and Excess', in Grant, ed., *Film Genre Reader II,* pp. 140-58; Sam Moskowitz, *Seekers of Tomorrow,* Westport, CT: Hyperion Press, 1974, p. 211.

9. Robin Wood, 'An Introduction to the American Horror Film', in Barry Keith Grant, ed., *Planks of Reason: Essays on the Horror Film,* Metuchen, NJ: Scarecrow Press, 1984, pp. 164-200.

10. Kawin, 'Children of the Light', p. 256.

11. Damon Knight, *In Search of Wonder,* 2nd edn, Chicago: Advent, 1967, p. 13.

12. Suvin, *Metamorphoses of Science Fiction.*

13. Richard Matheson, *The Shrinking Man,* New York: Bantam, 1969, p. 188.

14. Vivian C. Sobchack, *The Limits of Infinity: The American Science Fiction Film,* New York: A.S. Barnes, 1980, p. 47.

15. Ibid., p. 30.

16. For a discussion of Julia Kristeva's concept of abjection as applied to the horror film, see Barbara Creed, *The Monstrous-Feminine: Film, Feminism, Psychoanalysis,* London and New York: Routledge, 1993. On monsters as interstitial beings, see Noel Carroll, *The Philosophy of Horror, or Paradoxes of the Heart,* New York and London: Routledge, 1990, pp. 31-5.

17. Philip Brophy, 'Horrality—The Textuality of Contemporary Horror Films', *Screen,* vol. 27, no. 1, 1986, p. 8.

18. Christian Metz, *Film Language: A Semiotics of the Cinema,* trans. Michael Taylor, New York: Oxford University Press, 1974, p. 44.

19. Terry Ramsaye, *A Million and One Nights: A History of the Motion Picture through 1925,* New York: Touchstone, 1986, pp. 153-4.

20. Richard Hodgens, 'A Brief and Tragical History of the Science Fiction Film', *Film Quarterly,* vol. 13, no. 2, 1959, p. 31.

21. Carl Freedman, 'Kubrick's *2001* and the Possibility of a Science Fiction Cinema', *Science Fiction Studies,* no. 75, 1998, p. 305.

22. Sobchack, *The Limits of Infinity,* p. 88.

23. Susan Sontag, 'The Aesthetics of Destruction', in *Against Interpretation,* New York: Delta, 1966, p. 212.

24. Brian Aldiss, *Billion Year Spree: The True History of Science Fiction,* New York: Schocken Books, 1974, p. 23.

25. Hodgens, 'A Brief and Tragical History.'

26. C. M. Kornbluth, 'The Failure of the Science Fiction Novel as Social Criticism', in Davenport, ed., *The Science Fiction Novel,* p. 54.

27. Of course, the recent use of Computer Generated Imagery in science-fiction special effects complicates such claims about cinema's indexical fidelity to the real world.

28. Colin McArthur, *Underworld USA,* New York: Viking Press, 1972, p. 19.

29. Sobchack, *The Limits of Infinity,* pp. 64-87.

30. Baxter, *Science Fiction in the Cinema,* p. 100.

31. Robin Wood, *Hollywood from Vietnam to Reagan,* New York: Columbia University Press, 1986, p. 163.

32. Freedman, 'Kubrick's *2001*', p. 306.

33. Martin Rubin, 'Genre and Technology: Variant Attitudes in Science Fiction Literature and Film', *Persistance of Vision,* nos 3/4, 1986, p. 107.

Annette Kuhn (essay date 1999)

SOURCE: Kuhn, Annette. Introduction to *Alien Zone II: The Spaces of Science-Fiction Cinema,* edited by Annette Kuhn, pp. 1-8. London: Verso, 1999.

[*In the following essay, Kuhn delineates the various approaches to science fiction film criticism.*]

In 1997, a survey of science-fiction studies courses in North American universities and colleges revealed that *Blade Runner* was far and away the most widely assigned film. Its closest rival, *2001: A Space Odyssey,* received considerably fewer votes, while *Metropolis* came in at a close third place. The films in the *Alien* series were rated at fifth place, after *The Day the Earth Stood Still.* The absences from the list are interesting, too: the box-office successes *Star Wars* and *Close Encounters of the Third Kind,* for example, appear nowhere on it. While this survey makes no claim to representativeness, it is certainly indicative, at least as a snapshot of a science-fiction film canon in the process of formation.[1]

If this does constitute a canon, though, it is of a singular kind. A science-fiction buff's top ten films, for example, would quite probably be different from this pedagogic pantheon—which is not, of course, to say that a degree of 'fannish' investment must necessarily be absent from a university teacher's choice of films to screen on a science-fiction course. Nonetheless, given the genre's nature, history and characteristic modes of reception, a particular set of pedagogical imperatives, intertexts and cultural references comes into play whenever science-fiction cinema enters an educational context. Since most higher education courses in science-fiction studies concern themselves primarily with literary rather than with cinematic science fiction, their central theoretical and methodological agendas are rarely those of screen studies. At the same time, while the constituencies and agendas of, say, film studies, literary science-fiction studies, and science-fiction fandom may differ from one another, there are undoubtedly areas of overlap and common interest.

Within screen studies scholarship, for example, there has often been less interest in science-fiction cinema as a genre than in certain science-fiction films as self-contained objects of analysis. A rough count of publications in the field suggests that the screen studies science-fiction canon is headed more or less equally by the *Alien* films and *Blade Runner*,[2] but if these have become cultural icons, objects of fascination and fodder for commentary and analysis by film scholars, this is not necessarily, nor indeed only, because they are science-fiction films. Any scholarly or pedagogical canon of science-fiction cinema is ultimately bound up with other canons: in particular those of science-fiction studies more generally, and those of film scholarship. What then are, or ought to be, the objects and substantive concerns of a screen studies approach to science-fiction cinema? How—with what methodologies—are these objects most appropriately approached? Above all, perhaps, whom ought such studies to address?

Science-fiction cinema challenges several screen studies agendas, and the encounter between science-fiction studies and screen studies raises a number of as yet unanswered questions. A look at the literature suggests, for example, that within the broader study of film genres there is relatively little sustained reflection on science-fiction cinema, and that extensive studies of science-fiction cinema as a *genre* are few and far between. At the same time, and perhaps in consequence, discussions of individual science-fiction films are frequently uninformed by genre criticism or by awareness of science-fiction cinema's considerable history. This state of affairs clearly has implications for the manner in which criticism and analysis of science-fiction films is conducted. Such work is frequently confined to discussions of plot and character, for instance, paying relatively little attention to questions of film form and cinematic address. Where these latter are considered, it is usually in the context of readings of single films rather than treatments of the genre. In consequence, the key question as to whether there are modes of cinematic enunciation peculiar to, or particularly associated with, science-fiction cinema as against other film genres remains largely unaddressed by screen studies scholarship.

In generic terms, science-fiction cinema may be approached in four ways: in terms of its *themes,* its *iconographies,* its *modes of address,* and its *uses.* Vivian Sobchack, one of the few film scholars to have under-taken a systematic analysis of science-fiction cinema as a genre, has proposed that, thematically, science fiction offers a 'poetic mapping of social relations as they are created and changed by new technological modes of "being-in-the-world"'.[3] This suggests that science fiction's characteristic themes are basically twofold, having to do with technologies on the one hand and with modes of societal organization on the other. The preoccupation with technology gives the genre its peculiar fluidity, says Sobchack: for technologies—and, it might be added, the cultural attitudes and competences that go with them—are in constant flux. It is the emphasis on the social which gives science-fiction narratives their characteristic coolness, in that they display a tendency to eschew the motivations and psychological development of characters in favour of a detached, even Olympian, stance towards the social arrangements governing the fictional worlds they construct and the fictional characters who inhabit these worlds.

It is surely no coincidence, then, that among popular fictional genres science fiction above all appears to solicit critical commentary of a sociological kind. This is apparent in readings which in one way or another address the relationship between the social worlds of science fictions and the 'real' worlds outside them. Overviews of the genre, for example, very often adopt a historical approach in which science fiction's thematic preoccupations are tracked alongside social events and attitudes prominent at the time the work first appeared. With science-fiction cinema, the trajectory typically runs from the Cold War obsessions of American 1950s science fiction (*The Thing, Invasion of the Body-snatchers*), through the ecological disasters predicted in 1970s films like *THX-1138* and *Soylent Green,* to the post-industrial and postmodern cityscapes of more recent productions like *Blade Runner* and the *Terminator* films. In close analytic encounters with science-fiction films, critics mine thematic and iconographic subtexts for insights into their ideological workings.[4] It is in this spirit that Sobchack advances the view that contemporary science-fiction films offer 'new symbolic maps of our social relationship to others in what has become the familiarity (rather than the novelty) of a totally technologised world';[5] and that, with their rubbish-strewn ruined cityscapes, these films take for granted, even eroticize, the effects of disaster.

The social and technological thematics of science fiction often go hand in hand with certain iconographies—with dominant visual facts, motifs or symbols in a film's, or in the genre's, overall organization. Prominent in popular imaginings of science fiction are such familiar icons as spaceships, robots and aliens. These, however, are probably more prominent in science fiction in non-cinematic media, figuring particularly memorably in the science-fiction comics and pulp literature of the 1940s and 1950s. Indeed issues of narrative theme, as well as of iconography, cut across all the media forms in which science fiction finds expression: the themes and iconographies associated with science fiction, that is, are not confined to science-fiction cinema.

Is there, then, anything peculiarly distinctive about science-fiction in *cinema* as against science fiction in other media? Sobchack has suggested that the science-fiction film provides 'concrete narrative shape and visible form to our changing historical imagination of social progress and disaster':[6] in other words, the genre's fictions of progress—as well, *pace* Susan Sontag, of disaster[7]—are precisely rendered *visible* in science-fiction films. Visibility, of course, is not an attribute confined to cinematic science fiction: science fictions are told through visual media and matters of expression other than cinema, from comic books to television to computer games and the Internet. If it has this much at least in common with other media, then, how is cinematic science fiction different?

Perhaps the main site of potential distinctiveness is cinema's specific apparatus and modes of address—the manner and context in which films are consumed, and the ways in which they interpellate, or speak to, the spectator. When viewed in cinemas, science-fiction films foreground spectacle at the levels of both image and (if the term may be thus extended) sound. Big-budget science-fiction extravaganzas offer the total visual, auditory and kinetic experience of the *Gesamtkunstwerk*: the spectator is invited to succumb to complete sensory and bodily engulfment. Wherever cinema exhibits its own distinctive matters of expression—as it does with science fiction in displays of state-of-the-art special effects technologies—there is a considerable degree of self-reflexivity at work. Indeed, when such displays become a prominent attraction in their own right, they tend to eclipse narrative, plot and character. The story becomes the display; and the display becomes the story. Does it really matter, for example, that a film like *2001: A Space Odyssey* effectively lacks a plot? The enticement is not narrative involvement, nor even identification with characters, but rather the matters of expression of cinema itself, and this film's awe-inspiringly unfamiliar imagery. Spectators are invited to gape in wonder and abandon themselves to the totality of the audiovisual experience.

If this is the case, the singular address of science-fiction cinema rests on a particular gaze, a form of looking which draws in senses other than vision: hence Vivian Sobchack's suggestion that, more than any other film genre, science fiction repays analysis in terms of a phenomenonology of vision—analysis, that is, which attends to the sensuous immediacy of the viewing experience. Such vision-implicated sensuousness might well, of course, derive its power in part from its evocation of primal fantasies and pre-Oedipal pleasures.[8] These defining features of science-fiction cinema's metapsychology ground the uses and instrumentalities of science-fiction films as a body of cultural texts.

The 1990s have seen significant shifts in the central *topoi* of screen studies, shifts which have accompanied a general move away from grand theory towards more grounded and inductive approaches to the study of culture. This is evident, for example, in an increased attention to microhistories of cinema, of its institutions and intertexts, and in refinements in the ways in which interconnections between film texts and their contexts of production and reception are conceptualized. At the same time, the rise of cultural studies within the academy has energized debates around the cultural instrumentalities of a wide range of media forms; and a number of studies of science-fiction fandom and of the reception and uses of science fiction in cinema and other media have been conducted within this framework.[9] These studies raise urgent questions about the continuing cultural significance of distinctions between the various media in which science fiction finds expression.

One of the consequences of a shift of focus from the specifically cinematic to the more broadly cultural is a deflection of attention away from the cinematic apparatus, from cinema's own institutional and spectatorial mechanisms and their intersection in the conscious and unconscious psychical and affective processes evoked in the act of film spectatorship. This point is of some significance in light of the rise during the 1990s of new technologies of communication and vision, and of the revolution currently under way in systems for the delivery and reception of moving-image media. Science fiction figures prominently in this context, and not only at the level of media content: questions concerning metapsychology, textual specificity, and cultural instrumentality are in fact more centrally at issue here. Meanwhile, the very concept of science-fiction *cinema* is undergoing transformation at every level, from the metapsychological to the institutional to the economic.

Among screen theory's new *topoi* is space; and this is a development whose import for the study of science-fiction cinema goes far beyond mere wordplay. In classical film theory, cinematic space is codified primarily in terms of diegetic space and spectatorial space, each qualifier implying a particular locus. Diegetic space is the organization of space on screen, within a film's fictive world; in particular the mapping and rendering intelligible of a fictive geography. Assuming the act of viewing—as against the film text—as its locus, spectatorial space is the space between spectator and screen, the space which organizes the ensemble of screen, spectator and cinematic apparatus. If diegetic space is primarily about the film text, then, spectatorial space is primarily about the metapsychology of cinema.[10] For film theory which takes classical Hollywood cinema as its cornerstone, the spectator is not a passive recipient of messages but actively, if not necessarily consciously, involved in the relay of meanings and subjectivities produced within and by the cinematic apparatus.[11] In their construction of a fictive, or virtual, geography for the spectator, however, spectatorial space and diegetic space are conjoined and mutually dependent.

Classical film theory holds that a necessary condition of this imbrication of spectatorial and diegetic spaces is a distinctive type of viewing situation, involving a large cinema screen viewed in a darkened cinema auditorium. However, given that the cinema auditorium is now only one of a number of possible venues for viewing films, the classical configuration of diegetic and spectatorial space must be regarded as historically and culturally specific. Nonetheless, given the peculiar importance of sound and spectacle in science-fiction cinema, the classical spatial model arguably remains serviceable, in this context at least. As a set of institutions and a mode of textual organization, classical Hollywood cinema may indeed be history; and yet science-fiction films continue to demand certain engagements with diegetic, spectatorial—and perhaps also with other—spaces. Ironically perhaps, these engagements are rather different from those proposed by classical cinema and classical film theory. What, then, is distinctive about the spaces of science-fiction cinema? And how might these spaces be conceptualized in relation to science-fiction films when these are consumed outside the cinema auditorium? What, in other words, is the difference between the spaces inhabited by the spectator of science-fiction films in the cinema and those inhabited by the consumer of science fiction delivered in other moving-image media? To what extent do these spaces remain separate, and to what extent—and with what possible consequences—do they leak into one another?

Notes

1. *Science-Fiction Studies,* vol. 24, no. 1, 1977.

2. The count is based on publications listed in the Bibliography: see Appendix. *Metropolis* takes third place, well behind the leaders, and is followed by *Star Wars,* the *Terminator* films, *2001, Close Encounters of the Third Kind,* and *Robocop.*

3. Vivian Sobchack, 'Science Fiction', in Wes D. Gehring, ed., *Handbook of American Film Genres,* Westport, CN: Greenwood Press, 1988, p. 229.

4. See, for example, Peter Biskind, *Seeing is Believing: How Hollywood Taught Us to Stop Worrying and Love the Fifties,* New York: Pantheon Books, 1983; H. Bruce Franklin, 'Visions of the Future in Science Fiction Films from 1970 to 1982', in Annette Kuhn, ed., *Alien Zone: Cultural Theory and Contemporary Science Fiction Cinema,* London: Verso, 1990.

5. Sobchack, 'Science Fiction', p. 237.

6. Ibid., p. 231.

7. Susan Sontag, 'The Imagination of Disaster', in *Against Interpretation,* London: Eyre & Spottiswoode, 1966.

8. Vivian Sobchack, *Screening Space: The American Science Fiction Film,* New York: Ungar, 1987, ch. 4; Sobchack, 'Cities on the Edge of Time', in this volume; Daniel Dervin, 'Primal Conditions and Conventions: The Genre of Science Fiction', in Kuhn, ed., *Alien Zone.*

9. Kuhn, ed., *Alien Zone,* p. 9; Henry Jenkins and John Tulloch, *Science Fiction Audiences: Watching Star Trek and Doctor Who,* New York: Routledge, 1995; Constance Penley, 'Brownian Motion: Women, Tactics, and Technology', in Constance Penley and Andrew Ross, eds, *Technoculture,* Minneapolis: University of Minnesota Press, 1991.

10. Stephen Heath, 'Narrative Space', *Screen,* vol. 17, no. 3, 1976; David Bordwell, *Narration in the Fiction Film,* London: Methuen, 1985, ch. 7.

11. For a discussion of spectatorial space and the mobility of spectatorial subjectivity in relation to unconscious fantasy, see Elizabeth Cowie, 'Fantasia', *m/f,* no. 9, 1984.

J. P. Telotte (essay date 1999)

SOURCE: Telotte, J. P. Introduction to *A Distant Technology: Science Fiction Film and the Machine Age,* pp. 1-27. Hanover, N.H.: Wesleyan University Press, 1999.

[*In the following essay, Telotte surveys the key science fiction films produced in the major industrialized countries during the period between World War I and World War II, analyzing them as cultural texts that speak about the nature of film, the science fiction genre, and man's developing relationship to technology.*]

I

For this was the triumph of the machine—that in its capacity to produce imitations it could supply everything from entertainment to necessities in virtually unlimited quantities. But to the more thoughtful observers of change, it was precisely the machine's capacity to imitate that raised the knottiest issues. And the question first posed by industrial technology in the nineteenth century would become the question we are still trying to answer: how has the machine, with its power to produce replicas and reproductions, altered our culture?

—Miles Orvell, *The Real Thing* (36)

The Machine Age, that period which stretches roughly from the time of World War I to the start of World War II, is a watershed era for both American and world culture. It marks, as Richard Guy Wilson has offered, the coming "dominance of the machine in all areas of life and culture" and the emergence of a "special sensibility" that informs the twentieth century. It is also, many would argue, the moment at which the modern world first discovers its specifically modern character. Furthermore, and probably far more significantly for us today, it is the point at which the modern establishes the terms for the emergence of a contemporary, postmodern culture—one that draws much of its character from the technology that seems to be constantly reshaping our world, reworking our culture, even modifying our very humanity.

As the epigraph from Miles Orvell hints, the Machine Age is also a most crucial period for the movies. For film is itself one of those machines—indeed, for most of this century, the preeminent one—whose "power to produce replicas and reproductions" has "altered our culture" in ways we are only beginning to assess. During this era the way in which film functioned changed tremendously. From its earlier status as a curiosity or simple entertainment for the lower classes, from a "cinema of attractions," it became a worldwide medium of general communication and artistic expression. In this period too technology abruptly changed film's form, as the various apparatuses for sound recording, synchronization, and amplification converged, forcing a medium that had developed a highly conventional and effective practice of silent communication to shift gears, to acquire a voice, and in the process to explore new approaches to narration. In addition, the era saw the development of various technologies for color reproduction with the introduction of first the two-strip and later the three-strip Technicolor process.[1] The Machine Age thus becomes a special historical marker for film, a point at which it pushes definitively in the direction of André Bazin's "myth of total cinema,"[2] while also foregrounding, in an incipiently postmodern way, the very technologies involved in its efforts at reproduction, at actuating that "myth."

The resulting tensions, as film strives for a new level of realistic representation, for what has been described as a "transparent realism," while struggling with its own technological development, become particularly obvious in those films that clearly respond to and reflect the Machine Age. Specifically, the science fiction films of the era—which, in focusing on the technological, invariably foreground the machine, even the machinery of

the cinema—can help us sketch the tensions involved in that "special sensibility" of which Wilson speaks as it resonated in modern culture and in the cinema. In this period most of the major industrialized countries that were struggling with the new dominance of the machine and its accompanying sensibility also produced significant science fiction texts. Of course, I do not mean to suggest that there is a massive body of film work to rival the explosion of pulp literature in the era, much less to approach the great flood of science fiction movies that would appear in the early Cold War years. Still, the major industrialized countries, particularly the Soviet Union, Germany, France, the United States, and England, produced films that are often cited as key works in cinematic history, as well as classics of the genre. Yet while films like *Paris qui dort* (*The Crazy Ray,* 1924), *Metropolis* (1926), and *Things to Come* (1936) have figured substantially in discussions of the cinematic avant-garde (*Paris qui dort*), the expressionist movement (*Metropolis*), and the influence of literature (*Things to Come*), few of the period's other science fiction films, when they are mentioned at all, have received more than cursory critical attention.

Because they seem so central to that question Orvell poses, reflect so fundamentally the machine's subtle alterations of our culture, and look so obviously toward our current technological world—having helped to construct it—these films beg more careful consideration, and in some cases *a first* contemporary examination. In them we can find a catalogue of the various technologies that were already shaping the modern world and a forecast of those that would influence or become commonplace in our own time: the setback skyscraper, the automobile, the long-range airplane, the helicopter, high-speed trains, the radiotelescope, television, rocketships, robotics, and atomic power, among others. With these elements the films echoed the visionary work of established writers like Jules Verne and H. G. Wells, brought to life the highly popular pulp fiction of the period, found in the pages of publications like *Amazing Stories* and *Astounding Stories,* and drew into the cultural mainstream the imaginings of such figures as the avant-garde planner Le Corbusier, the architect Hugh Ferriss, and the industrial designer Norman Bel Geddes. They provide us with a telling record of our machine imaginings in the first half of this century, and thus rich material for beginning to study the ongoing cultural construction of the technological in America and other industrialized countries. From such a beginning, we might also better understand how that construction of the technological has shaped our contemporary world, which seems to live and breathe through its technology.

The period's science fiction films offer us more, however, than just a catalogue of appealing images and traces of various other cultural movements. For in them we can also begin to detect a curious ambivalence about the technological that seems to run counter to the supposed cultural embrace of a Machine Age ethos and to strike a rather different chord than we find in most of the technology-romanticizing pulps. As we shall see, the films tend in various ways to appear detached from and at times even skeptical of the very machines on which their narratives focus, and in some cases far more aware than mainstream movies of their own status as cinema, as products of a technology of reproduction. The tensions involved in the development of film technology and narrative in this period thus seem to intersect with those implicit in a Western world that was struggling with its own transition into the modern, into a Machine Age culture.

I want to look at the science fiction films of this period, then, as key cultural texts—texts that speak simultaneously about the nature of film, about the science fiction genre, and about our sense of the technological, particularly about the ways in which we were engaged in the cultural construction of the technological. That "special sensibility" of which Wilson speaks, and which he ties to the very meaning of the word "modern," is the key link here. For in this period, as he explains, "modern" implied "a complete break with the past," the abandonment of "outmoded" traditions and traditional styles in favor of a thoroughly contemporary aesthetic based largely on the properties of the machine—speed, regularity, efficiency—and its powers of reproduction, the implicit notion that "a whole new culture . . . could be built as readily as the machine" (23). Certainly, films, as the key aesthetic product of what Walter Benjamin has termed "the Age of Mechanical Reproduction," were engaged in all of these tasks. And along with the literature of science fiction, which found its name if not quite its origin in this period,[3] they often looked to the future, visualized various utopian possibilities, offered us schemes for building "a whole new culture." In effect, these films seem to have been involved in another kind of distancing project that was also a key part of Machine Age culture: detaching audiences from the familiar or traditional world, as well as from its associated values.

Yet as we shall see, that project was problematic, since the machine technology that was proving so pervasive came with its own problems. Mechanisms such as the airplane and the tractor, which promised so many benefits to modern life, also, as bombers and tanks, contributed massively to the slaughter of World War I. The introduction of Henry Ford's assembly-line techniques met with violent resistance in England and elsewhere. Literature of the early Machine Age, as Cecelia Tichi has shown, repeatedly evoked the image of technology "to represent uncontrolled, destabilizing power" (52). While such an attitude partly followed from a simple distrust of change, another factor was the sense that, as Tichi explains, "a dominant technology" effectively "re-

defines the human role," even threatens to redefine human nature (16)—a problem with which we continue to struggle today. Science fiction films from the Machine Age consequently faced the difficult task of fashioning an acceptable view of the technological, of presenting technology not as a distancing or alienating force, but as a means of bridging the distances that gaped all the more obviously in the modern world—distances between different nations and peoples, between the different classes in every nation, between men and women, between the individual and that natural world from which all of us were increasingly estranged. And they had to do so, as I have suggested above, while confronting their own distant perspective, their own skepticism about this technological work. As we shall see, the task was a rather paradoxical and difficult one, and in its ambivalences perhaps a revealing mark of modernism itself.

II

Of course, in order to begin exploring these tensions and that sense of distance from which they emanate, we do not have to look solely at the science fiction film. The Machine Age provides us with ample film texts that attest to the power, allure, and pervasiveness of the technological in this era, and that reflect the dynamic of its construction. The very appearance of certain other film genres, after all, testifies to one dimension of this technological development. The musical, most obviously, could find its voice only with the coming of sound technology. And the excitement of the gangster film relied on its characteristic combination of technological images and violent sounds—speeding cars, squealing tires, and chattering machine guns. On a thematic level, the biopic (biographical picture) explored the new appeal of the scientist and his struggles with science and technology, as films like *The Story of Louis Pasteur* (1936), *The Story of Alexander Graham Bell* (1939), *Young Tom Edison* (1940), and *Dr. Erlich's Magic Bullet* (1940) suggest. But even prior to these developments the silent comedy had demonstrated the appeal of certain technological imagery. Particularly, it showed that the automobile—or flivver—made a most apt prop for all sorts of humorous situations. If, as Henri Bergson claims, laughter commonly proceeds from the "encrustration" of the mechanical on the human,[4] then comedy, particularly under the guiding hand of Mack Sennett, could make great capital by depicting humans trying to conform to the logic of the auto and, in some cases, by attributing human characteristics to that same mechanism, as well as by repeatedly rendering characters as the offspring of machines.

A more complex response to the Machine Age shows up in the work of the three key comic filmmakers of this period, Harold Lloyd, Charlie Chaplin, and Buster Keaton. In both his shorts and early features, most notably films like *Get Out and Get Under* (1920) and *Hot Water* (1924), Lloyd works his own variations on the Sennett pattern, with his glasses character struggling to cope with Model-Ts that seem to have minds of their own. But Lloyd's greatest successes were never so much when his character is at odds with technology as when he embodies the very spirit of the Machine Age, as the title of one of his best features, *Speedy* (1928), implies. In fact, most often Lloyd's films chronicle his reckless exploits in the big city: driving various vehicles at breakneck speed through crowded streets, chasing runaway cars, buses, or trollies, climbing the sides of setback skyscrapers. Certainly, he is most remembered for the iconic image of his glasses character dangling from a clock face many stories up in *Safety Last* (1923), as he tried to emulate a key popular culture figure of the era, the human fly. It is an image that Lloyd knew would appeal to period audiences, since he had put his character into that same precarious situation in several of his most popular shorts—*High and Dizzy* (1920) and *Never Weaken* (1921)—and when trying to adapt to the new technology of sound, he naturally returned to this formula for success in *Feet First* (1930). In every instance Lloyd sought to offer his audience a reassuring image, that of a thoroughly modern man, able quite literally to "rise" to the challenge of the modern technological world, to master one of its foremost emblems, the setback skyscraper. And at least for his silent films, his audience responded with enthusiasm to that image.

If the Machine Age posed a challenge to the individual, then, it seems to have been a challenge that, Lloyd's films reiterate, the "speedy," optimistic individual could meet. Still, nothing came easily to the Lloyd persona. The modern world, as his movies depict it, is clearly marked by a sense of distance—the great heights his character must climb or cope with, the distances he must cover in various mad dashes to the rescue, the seemingly insurmountable obstacles that separate him from the success he both desires and deserves. But no distance or obstacle ever defeats this figure, in great part because Lloyd is so much a part of that Machine Age world, so driven by its spirit, as if he were himself a machine—or at least a construct of the times.

For Charlie Chaplin, whose little tramp character was by nature always shut off from the cultural mainstream and always seemed to be at odds with that spirit of the times, there was far less possibility of such accommodation. In his first film, *Kid Auto Races at Venice* (1914), the lines are not drawn so starkly. For here he happens upon a sure emblem of the era, a motion picture camera filming a local soap box derby. The comic confrontation that follows, as he repeatedly draws up close, studies the mechanism, and constantly positions himself between the camera and its erstwhile subject, suggests less the sort of conflict to be found throughout his fea-

ture films and more of the Sennett-like encounter between man and machine designed to make comic capital from human curiosity or vanity.

In his later films, with his tramp persona more elaborately drawn and thoroughly established with movie audiences worldwide, Chaplin turns that Machine Age world into a far more active antagonist. As its title implies, *Modern Times* (1936) offers probably the best gloss on this relationship. Here Chaplin's tramp is, from the start, out of step with the machine world, as he works on an assembly line, performing a mindless, repetitive task, tightening bolts. He becomes so much an extension of the line, so machine-like in his motions, that when given a break, a moment to become human again, he at first cannot control his body's near-automatic twisting motions. The assembly line has produced a physiological fallout, a twitch that makes it practically impossible for him even to eat during his lunch break. And when offered the solution of being fed by a product of the period's much-trumpeted efficiency movement, an automatic feeding machine, the tramp fares no better. Battered and beaten by the machine as it runs amuck, the tramp at one point even has bolts pushed into his mouth—perhaps the most appropriate food for someone who has become little more than an extension of the machine. By the end of the day, as the line has gotten faster and faster, it also produces a psychological fallout, as the tramp, just like the feeding machine, goes haywire, tightening everything on which his wrenches can be fitted: the noses of his coworkers, the bolts on a fire hydrant, the buttons on prominant parts of a woman's dress. And in both this scene and a later one, first the tramp and then a mechanic he is assisting are swallowed up by the factory machinery. In the first of these swallowings, we see the tramp stretched over cog wheels, impelled by the great gears of a machine, looking very much like a piece of film caught in the sprockets of a camera or projector, as he evokes the movie apparatus not as an object of curiosity, as in *Kid Auto Races,* but rather as yet another threatening machine.[5] The larger implication is clear; for Chaplin the world of the Machine Age is ultimately at odds with human nature, even destructive of that nature, and we should keep our distance. Thus he would end his last film of this era, *The Great Dictator* (1940), with his little tramp, here in the character of a Jewish barber mistaken for the Hitler-like dictator Hynkel, surrounded by storm troopers as he makes a passionate speech warning the people against "these unnatural men—machine men with machine minds and machine hearts."

Neither wholeheartedly embracing the spirit of the age, as did Lloyd, nor quite as alienated from it as Chaplin, Buster Keaton offers a more complex response to this modern, technological world, a kind of middle ground. For his persona is, apparently like Keaton himself[6]—

and, we might assume, like much of his audience—almost invariably curious and even enthusiastic about the machines that provide the backdrop or become the central props in many of his films: steamboats, trains, cars, cameras, projectors, ocean liners, and so on. Often, the Keaton persona even acts like a machine—fast, efficient, thoroughly predictable—as if he were one of those very "machine men" against whom Chaplin inveighs. The opening scene of what is probably his most famous film, the Civil War epic *The General* (1926), amply illustrates this character. As Johnnie Gray, the engineer of the locomotive "The General," he leaves his train to visit his girl, Annabelle Lee. On the way, he picks up two young admirers who fall in behind him as he walks; unnoticed, Annabelle Lee too joins the procession, picking up the rear of this human train. After reaching her house, Johnnie finds that to be alone with his girl, he must first get rid of the two boys, so he pretends to leave, they rise to follow, he marches them through the door, and then he falls back, shutting the door on them—effectively uncoupling several cars from the human train. His train-like behavior seems all the more fitting when we see a present Johnnie has brought Annabelle Lee—a photograph showing his face low in the foreground and "The General" in the background, dominating the composition and looking as if it were driving *through his head.* More than just an indication of how important the locomotive is to him, this picture tells us precisely what is on, or in, his mind, in fact, how much his mind is guided by a kind of machine model. He thinks in a very simple cause-and-effect, linear, train-like way, and he acts accordingly.

And yet a troubling undercurrent always threatens that characterization. In her discussion of the Machine Age in America, Cecelia Tichi describes a key shift that occurs in the era. While in the nineteenth century, she suggests, "machine technology, like the forces of nature," often came to represent instability, to suggest "horrific, destabilizing energies loosed in the universe," "chaotic natural energies" against which the individual seemed practically helpless (52, 53), with the coming of the Machine Age those same images were often transformed into ones of stability and efficiency, typically linked to the machine itself. In the Keaton world, there is no possibility for such easy demarcation. Machines are as tricky as they are efficient; instability and chaos are constant potentials in both the natural and the mechanical worlds. Hence Keaton's films offer the war setting of *The General,* the deadly feud of *Our Hospitality* (1923), the cannibal attack in *The Navigator* (1924), the cyclone of *Steamboat Bill, Jr.* (1928), and the great rock slide in *Seven Chances* (1925). As this last film illustrates, though, that instability and the energy involved are elements that the Keaton character can often turn to profit. In *Seven Chances* he is being pursued by a mob of women—all dressed in wedding gowns and veils—who have heard he will inherit a million dollars if he is married before day's end. In trying to escape this capitalist love connection, Keaton tumbles down a mountainside, dislodging several boulders, which, in turn, start a massive rock slide from which he must run for his life. As he runs from the rocks, he plunges headlong into the army of pursuing brides and momentarily freezes, trying to decide on the better of the two terrible fates—being crushed or married. As an alternative, he heads back toward the rocks, dodging them and letting the boulders chase off his female pursuers. He has simply turned that natural instability to his own end, using one chaotic element to negate another.

That same imaginative and transformative spirit underlies Keaton's relationship to the machine, which, for all of its often daunting power or puzzling character, remains a source of attraction, and at times even a vehicle of salvation. In *The Navigator,* for example, Rollo Treadway and his girl, attacked by cannibals, abandon their steamship and sink beneath the waves, only to be saved at the last moment by a passing submarine, which just happens to surface under them. In *The General* Johnnie Gray uses his train to rescue Annabelle Lee from her Union kidnappers, to warn the Confederate forces about a surprise attack, and to win this battle if not the Civil War. *Steamboat Bill, Jr.* (1928) concludes with Willie Canfield maneuvering his father's steamboat through a cyclone- and storm-swollen river to rescue his father, his girl, her father, and a drifting preacher who, we assume, will perform the expected marriage. And in *Sherlock, Jr.* (1924) we see another sort of rescue, as Keaton, a film projectionist, turns to the movie he is then showing for help when his girl suddenly shows up and suggests marriage. By sneaking quick glimpses at the film, he figures out how to hold her hand, embrace her, offer her a ring, and then kiss her, while he is also warned of what will surely, if rather inexplicably, follow—a hoard of children. Serving in such a supporting role, the machine never seems a true menace in Keaton's films. While it often signals his detachment from others—in *The General,* for instance, the train is one of his "two loves" and all too easily substitutes for his girl—and points up the folly of acting *too* machine-like, the machine more generally helps to measure his characters' gradual maturing and involvement in the modern world.

Keaton seems to have gauged better than any of his fellow comedians the very nature of the machine. While it may be fast and efficient, it is never totally reliable or free from its own instabilities, in part because of the larger instability of this world and the unpredictability of everything in it. What is probably his most representative Machine Age work, the two-reeler *The Electric House* (1922), well illustrates this view. In this film Keaton plays a recent college graduate—his degree is in Botany—who is mistaken for an electrical engineer and asked to convert the Dean's old house to a modern, totally electric residence. This narrative premise obviously echoes Wilson's description of the period's belief that everything "could be built as readily as the machine" itself. And the character's acceptance of the project, with a manual titled *Electricity Made Easy* as his only aid, seems to affirm that notion. However, when the Dean returns from vacation to inspect his "electric house," he finds it not only wired and equipped with multiple mechanical conveniences, but also a place of constant surprise. The escalator, for example, never seems to run at the same speed twice, and when he first tries it out, the mechanism vaults the Dean through a second-story window into the pool below.[7] The lights flicker off and on, and the train Keaton has rigged to serve meals jumps its track, dumping the main course in the lap of the Dean's wife. Further compounding this unpredictability is the appearance of a real electrical engineer, jealous of Buster's work, who tinkers with the wiring to make the entire house appear as if it had a mind of its own. The chaos that results, as all the household mechanisms run amuck and make the inhabitants think the place is haunted, drives home the film's key point: that modernizing the world—or a house—does not make it any less capable of surprise, any less challenging, any less human.

Outside of the comic world, that rather mixed view of the age's technological thrust seems all the more common. In that bellwether of an emerging Russian cinema, *Battleship Potemkin* (1925), the modern steel warship is a site of oppression and dehumanization in the hands of the Czar's officers, as well as a sign of the people's power and revolutionary spirit once it is commandeered by mutinying sailors. René Clair's social commentary *A Nous la liberté* (1930) on the one hand presents the modern manufacturing system, complete with its Fordian assembly line, as the surest sign of its escaped-convict protagonist's successful movement into the modern world and attainment of wealth and social standing. On the other, it suggests that such a status—and the conditions that make it possible—is something else from which he needs to escape, something from which we shall all eventually need "la liberté." In numerous films on World War I, that testing ground for "mechanized" warfare, the machine—whether airplane, dirigible, machine gun, or tank—becomes the key image of both human power and human destruction. Thus such works as *Hell's Angels* (1930), *All Quiet on the Western Front* (1930), *The Dawn Patrol* (1930, 1938), and *La Grande Illusion* (1937), among many others, use exciting aerial and combat sequences in large part to set the stage for antiwar and at times anti-machine messages. And in a host of period cartoons, perhaps most notably those of Max and Dave Fleischer (such as *Ko-Ko's Earth Control* [1928], *Come Take a Trip in My Airship* [1925, 1930], *Sky Scraping* [1930], *The Robot* [1932], *Crazy Inventions* [1933], *More Pep* [1936], and

especially the various Betty Boop and Grampy pairings) we repeatedly see a fascination not only with the latest technology, but also with the ways in which that technology plays tricks on people, renders them comic figures, component parts in an unpredictable Rube Goldberg machine.

Probably the most telling text in this regard is the air epic *Wings* (1927), a film historically renowned for winning the first Academy Award for Best Picture. Blessed with a large budget and an unparalleled level of assistance in both men and machines from the army,[8] director William Wellman fashioned a tribute to the pioneer aviators of World War I and the fragile machines in which they flew, drawing largely on his own experiences as a pilot with the Lafayette Flying Corps. More than just a film about the war, though, *Wings* explores the technological spirit that moved those early aviators, that spurred them to flight. Thus the film begins with a title card offering a tribute to Lindbergh, who had only recently accomplished his great transatlantic crossing, and quoting his praise for the fliers of World War I when "feats were performed and deeds accomplished which were far greater than any peace accomplishments of aviation." With that epigraph, the film links its recollections of the decade before to current events, indeed, to one of the signal events of the era, and in the process affirms its own Machine Age sensibility.

The narrative that follows further places its tale of mechanized warfare by framing it with two extensive home-town sequences. These not only introduce the key figures—Jack Powell, his neighbor Mary Preston, and David Armstrong, who is both Jack's rival for the love of Sylvia Lewis and also his best friend—but also establish what another title card terms "the dreams of youth," which inspire these people and have helped quicken the pace of modern life. Those dreams are all about speed and flight. After staring up at the sky, Jack turns to working on his car, stripping it, souping up the engine for more speed, all with the help of Mary, who also graces the car with an emblem, a shooting star. It is a vehicle with which, we learn, he has already "left the ground several times"—in accidents. More to the point, it is a kind of dream machine, a device that makes him dream of being up in the clouds, far away from his small-town home and its suggestion of a rural, agrarian America of earlier times. This dream leaves him so detached from this world that he hardly notices Mary, who has a crush on him, as he races off to show Sylvia his car. And this mad rushing about—"Life marched at the double quick," a title offers—prepares us for the speed with which, as war is announced, both he and David jump at the chance to sign up for the Army Air Corps and go to France.

That dream of distance and detachment from this world, though, is repeatedly punctured as Jack and David enter service in the Air Corps. The more experienced Cadet

White, with whom they are first billeted, dies in a crash on a routine training flight right after introducing himself and promising that they "will be seeing a lot of each other." On their first combat sortie, nearly the entire flight is shot down; Jack crashes in no-man's land and David is narrowly spared after his machine guns jam. During the big offensive thrust at St. Mihiel, Jack accidentally shoots down and kills David, who had been flying in a captured German plane—who had *become,* in Jack's eyes, that enemy machine. On this note, with the machine as emblem of alienation and destruction, the war narrative ends and we return to Jack's hometown, where he is lauded as a hero but must also face David's parents and return his effects. To complete the framing effect, the narrative shows Jack uncovering his old hot rod and encountering Mary. But instead of speeding away in the car, as he did in the opening sequence, now Jack treats it like a park bench, sitting on it with Mary, watching a shooting star in the night sky, and finally pledging his love to her. After his great dreams of speed and flight, of being much like that distant shooting star, he has definitely returned to earth and to life. These framing scenes thus acknowledge what we might term the special sensibility of the Machine Age, even define it as a dream of distance, speed, and power, but also trace its possible consequences and draw its dreamers back to reality.

III

That dream of distance chronicled in *Wings,* of a kind of transcendence available through the machine, and the eventual devastation of that dream compose a story hardly limited to the period's narratives of air warfare. It is, in fact, the driving pattern at work in the science fiction films of this era; yet that pattern and this whole body of work have largely gone unexplored. As we have already noted, most of the major industrialized nations, and thus most of the major film-producing countries, turned out in this era not only a number of texts *about* technology and its shaping power, but also a variety of science fiction films that parallel, in focus though not in the volume, the science fiction stories then appearing in the pulp literature. And with but a few notable exceptions, this segment of our cinematic and cultural history, as well as a potentially resonant element of the science fiction genre's history, has largely escaped critical notice.

Certainly, the science fiction literature of this era suffers from no similar lack of attention. As Edward James notes in his history of the genre, the period between the wars saw the science fiction genre become "fully recognized," having developed a readily identifiable set of concerns, "its own specialist magazines and its own specialist readership" (53), along with an enthusiastic and organized fandom.[9] As a result, no examination of the development or impact of the literary genre has

been able to overlook the remarkable convergence in this time of a traditional speculative literature, such as that of H. G. Wells; of the pulps, particularly Hugo Gernsback's *Amazing Stories, Astounding Stories* (especially under the editorship of John W. Campbell, Jr.), and *Wonder Stories*; and of what James terms "a boom in 'futurology'" (43), which produced a body of essays, pamphlets, and books attempting to assess the direction and future development of our culture and its institutions. Indeed, as Howard Segal reminds us, the "extraordinary final outpouring of faith in technological progress" (132) in the late Machine Age occurs across a broad range of texts, often blurring distinctions between fiction, informational text, and polemic, and all converging in their speculations on how technological development and planning might begin to reconstruct modern culture. These developments have all been seen as crucial to defining the literary genre and to placing it in our cultural history.

However, the films of this period have seldom been brought within that larger generic vantage and, with a few exceptions, have often become little more than footnotes to both film history and our speculations about technology in the era. Among many others, this relatively neglected body of Machine Age science fiction films includes works like France's (*Paris qui dort The Crazy Ray*) and *La Fin du monde* (1930); Germany's *Metropolis, Die Frau im Mond* (1929), *F.P. 1 Antwortet Nicht* (1932), *Gold* (1934), and various, largely forgotten films by Harry Piel, such as *Der Herr der Welt* (1934); Russia's *Aelita* (1924); the United States' *The Mysterious Island* (1929), *Just Imagine* (1930), and *The Invisible Ray* (1936); and England's *The Tunnel* (1935) and *Things to Come.* Of this group, only *Metropolis,* partly because of director Fritz Lang's auteur status and partly because of the film's standing as the earliest utopian/dystopian film, has previously received much detailed attention. Others draw only cursory consideration at best. *Paris qui dort,* for example, is at times mentioned in the context of early avant-garde filmmaking; *Just Imagine* has become little more than an object warning about merging genres, in this case the musical and science fiction; and *Things to Come* is cited for H. G. Wells's singular participation in the project. The rest of those mentioned above, since they are generally difficult to locate today and appeared at a time when film was in transition between the full flowering of the silent aesthetic and the awkward emergence of sound narrative, tend to be ignored and are practically absent from all standard histories of film.[10]

Of course, one reason for this relative neglect is that these are all essentially border films, and as such create difficulties for historians, who, because of the very requirements of their task, tend to focus on more definitive works. Yet precisely because of that border status, these films stand to reveal much about technologies, cultures, and indeed a cinema all in transition. Certainly as a group these films speak revealingly and perhaps surprisingly about Western culture in this period, as well as about its embrace of technology and even of the movies themselves. In these works, for example, we find a remarkable cultural convergence on technological issues, which were already perceived as remaking our world. Yet in that convergence, as we noted above, we can also sense a curious ambivalence about the technological, which, for the most part, runs counter to the supposed cultural embrace of a Machine Age ethos, and which certainly strikes a rather different chord than does the popular pulp fiction. In them too we find constant intersections with other popular genres of the period—for example, the disaster film, the horror film, even the musical and the western—that suggest a rather fluid and developing sense of these formulas. These border works thus promise to shed a revealing light on the cultural work of this genre.

To collect on that promise, we might first consider our conventional views of both the science fiction film and of the very mechanism of genre. As Susan Sontag has emphasized, the science fiction genre, especially in its American incarnations, has typically focused on a triad of elements: technology, science, and reason.[11] Perhaps its key semantic element—and thus one of the most basic signposts indicating we have entered science fiction territory—is the technology we typically encounter, the spaceships, robots, ray guns, futuristic architecture, and so on, which mark the form. That technology derives from a scientific world, typically from a culture that is intent on exploring, understanding, and codifying our world, as well as any others we might encounter. Behind that effort is a rational perspective, a thoroughly modernist view of the world, and indeed the universe, as essentially knowable, reducible to cause-and-effect terms, and thus accessible to human manipulation. Yet Sontag also reminds us how often that effort fails, how typically calamity or "disaster" follows from the application of this triad, as we see in the numerous alien invasion films of the 1950s, the atomic mutation movies of the same period, the post-apocalyptic works of more recent times, and the rather questionable portrayal of the scientist throughout the genre's history. Following her lead, yet arriving at a different end, Bruce Kawin has described the genre, in its best incarnations, as intent on vanquishing the unknown, overcoming limits— "it opens the field of inquiry, the range of possible subjects, and leaves us open" to wonder as well (321), he says. In contrast to Sontag, he views those films that cast our technology or the science behind it in a threatening light, films like *The Thing* (1951), *Invasion of the Body Snatchers* (1956), or *Alien* (1982), as horror, not science fiction films, concerned mainly with the dangers that attend such openness. Of course, both of these vantages have at their heart a fundamental tension between the professed aims of science/technology/reason and

their cultural products—a tension which each critic tries to resolve by pushing what may seem an absolutist view of the genre. In fact, this effort at resolution may be at the root of Sontag's ultimate dissatisfaction with the form; she finds that it usually offers "an inadequate response" to our more pressing cultural problems (211).

And yet the genre has, as have our other popular formulas, often served us well in doing the work of culture, that is, in providing the imaginative constructs we need—in this case, those revolving around technology, science, and reason—to cope with the problems of our culture. They offer, as Barry Grant simply puts it, "contemporary versions of social myth" (115). Those myths help us by imaginatively resolving the seemingly unresolvable problems with which we wrestle. Thus, even as our culture has struggled recently with issues of cloning, genetic manipulation, and artificial intelligence, our science fiction films have repeatedly offered up a central and multiply resonant image, that of the android/robot/cyborg, the image of human artifice, as a means of narratizing those concerns and rendering them less uncanny, less menacing, and, in the case of the *Star Wars* trilogy's almost cuddly robots, even comforting.[12]

I emphasize this cultural work because it may offer another clue as to why these films have generally received so little attention. Certainly in the Machine Age, with its pervasive machine culture, we might expect a genre whose very focus is the technological to be prominent in this "mythic" work of constructing a friendly image of technology and a comforting narrative of its place in our world. Western culture at every turn confronted signs of this new industrial civilization: new processes of production (Fordism, Taylorism), the prominence of the automobile, high-speed air travel, widespread electrification, the introduction of various labor-saving household appliances, an architectural emphasis on the setback skyscraper, literature in which, as Cecelia Tichi observes, machine metaphors were becoming pervasive, even a music that, Richard Guy Wilson reminds us, increasingly incorporated "nontraditional sounds that reflected the machine" (34). And yet the genre that seems best equipped for addressing these dizzying developments never fully rises to the occasion, never manages to become the sort of prominent formula we might expect, certainly not to the extent that the musical, gangster film, or comedy did in the same era. The absence of a large body of work to match that literary outpouring of the genre is itself an interesting symptom to consider.

Of course, as William Johnson has argued, we should not expect to understand the science fiction film simply by seeing it as an extension of the literary genre (2). The film form develops together with the cinema itself, and consequently is more fundamentally invested in the technological, more implicated in its cultural construction than the literature; it has more at stake. With this history in mind, Garrett Stewart suggests that "science fiction in the cinema often turns out to be, turns round to be, the fictional or fictive science of the cinema itself" (159), a form haunted by "the spirit of fabrication" (162)—technological, cinematic. As a result, the form's examinations of machine technology or its impact always evoke an element of reflexivity or self-consciousness from which a cinema, driven by an emphasis on seamless narrative and transparent realism, might inevitably recoil.

What I am suggesting is that on some level the science fiction *film* genre always seems to find its very subject matter—science, technology, or more generally, fabrication—challenging, even a bit troubling. Of course, in the Machine Age there were added anxieties with which our films and their audiences had to cope. A testing ground for much modern technology, World War I had also left a terrible fallout from the mechanized destruction that technology brought, as a film like *Wings* demonstrates. And later, with the Great Depression, as we see in Chaplin's *Modern Times,* technology was often associated with those cultural forces that seemed antithetical to labor, that seemed intent on eliminating the individual from the workplace or reducing him to a part in a machine. But while other films managed to dissolve those anxieties in their generic formulas (*A Connecticut Yankee* [1931], *Modern Times*) or blunt them with romantic or other compensations (*Wings, Dirigible* [1930]), the science fiction film seems, throughout much of the Machine Age, to have been almost too close to its subject, too marked by the same sort of tensions that typified modern culture, tensions that came with technology itself. What we find, consequently, is a form simply unable to fully or satisfactorily accommodate the very values associated with its subject, to solve the problem of distance.

IV

Yet what is this problem of distance? For much of my thinking about the position of technology in modern Western culture, I have drawn on the philosopher Robert Romanyshyn's analysis of the technological, which he describes in very nonmaterial terms—as a kind of "cultural-psychological dream of distance from matter" (194). That dream, he suggests, has at its core our desire for detachment from this world, for freedom from our human limitations. Jean Baudrillard, with his almost ahistorical perspective, describes that sort of distance not only as possible but as the inescapable condition of our postmodern, electronic culture, wherein the individual has come to resemble an "orbital satellite in the universe of the everyday" (*Ecstasy* 16), always removed from the world and thus never able to determine what is "real" in it. As Mark Dery has more recently assessed, ours is a culture longing to achieve "escape

velocity," the technological expertise necessary to escape from our very humanity, weighed down as it is by an environment and a mortality that clearly have their limits.[13] In line with these views, Romanyshyn argues that technology is "a matter [not just] of measure but of attitude" (21)—an attitude that represents a most telling "symptom" of all technological culture, both in its formative stages during the modern era and in its state of seeming exhaustion in our postmodern time. Ultimately, these two metaphors, of "dream" and "symptom," encompass his explanation of our modern-day technological condition.

Romanyshyn suggests, in a way that recalls the work of Martin Heidegger[14] and seems particularly fitting to a consideration of film, that we might think of technology not so much as a thing, but as "the enactment of the human imagination in the world." In its various manifestations, technology demonstrates how we have tried to "create ourselves" and the world we inhabit (10). In effect, he says, we "dream" through the technologies we produce; we dream of ways to alter material reality, including our own bodies, to make it correspond to our desires, and to banish our sense of limitation. Thus he describes the technological in a rather conventional way as "a work of reason," but reminds us that it is "reason lined with desire" (10). That description not only invites us to do a bit of dream analysis—examining the dream of technology according to its own logic, searching for any "repressed" significances it may have, while trying to access a kind of cultural unconscious—but also implicates the movies themselves as products of a "dream factory," as we still commonly describe the film industry.

At the same time, Romanyshyn views the technological as a key *symptom* of the modern—and indeed the postmodern—world. A symptom, he says, is "a way of saying not only that something is wrong, but also how that something can be made right" (13). Technology as symptom, then, speaks about that desire we share for what Stewart terms "fabrication"—for remaking the self, reshaping our world, overcoming our human limitations, or as Dery offers, simply escaping from those limitations—but in doing so it reveals the objectification, detachment, and distance built into that desire, attitudes that have become all the more obvious and troubling in the contemporary world, where, says Baudrillard, they have come to seem practically unavoidable. At the same time, the technological suggests a route back from or an alternative to those attitudes, what Romanyshyn would call a "recovery" from those symptoms. For through a mindfulness of our technological culture and its implications, through facing the doubleness of our technology and ourselves, he suggests, we might reenter a world from which we have become distant, alien, astronaut-like.

Of course, the science fiction film in general offers a natural field for exploring this pattern, for examining the traces of distance that mark the form and assessing the symptomatic status of these cultural texts. But by generally limiting our focus to the science fiction films of the Machine Age, I hope to stake out an especially revealing bit of territory. Their generic foregrounding of the technological brings into sharp focus this pattern of distance at a particularly formative time, when the modern world was preparing for the emergence of our contemporary, postmodern, and thoroughly technologized culture. In her study of the era, Cecelia Tichi notes how, by the turn of the century, popular culture and serious literature alike had already begun to reflect a whole new, Machine Age sensibility, particularly through the pervasive use of machine metaphors, even in the least likely places, such as descriptions of natural phenomena. The implication, she says, is that "knowledge of the workings of nature is . . . knowledge of machines"; that at least in Machine Age America our art had begun to suggest there was no easy "distinction" (40) to be drawn. While that same argument is a difficult one to make for many films of this period—indeed, a film like *Wings,* in both its title cards and images, repeatedly resorts to *nature* metaphors to describe the machines and mechanical endeavors it depicts—at least the science fiction films allow for no easy retreat, no way to draw back from a technological world, from an environment shaped by machines and machine attitudes. Instead, they confront us with the fact of fabrication, bring the technology itself up close for our inspection, and in the process hold our own, at times hesitant embrace of the technological up for examination as well.

What we repeatedly see in those Machine Age confrontations is a complex story of distance and detachment. For as we range across the science fiction films of several countries, trying to sketch the different contexts in which they confront the technological, we shall consistently encounter narratives about great physical, cultural, or epistemological distances and the struggle to overcome them—to move from the Earth to the moon, to span this world's barrier oceans, to unite different cultures or classes, to gain some great knowledge or distinction. And those narratives typically turn on technological devices—rockets, submarines, radio-telescopes, tunnels, aircraft, and various sorts of rays—for bridging these gaps, or, in some cases, for coping with a threatening distance. While those efforts sometimes fail (as in *La Fin du monde* or *The Mysterious Island*) and sometimes succeed (as in *The Tunnel* or *Die Frau im Mond*), the tension that hangs over the narratives, another sort of distance that haunts the point of success or failure, seems most telling in terms of what these films together reveal about attitudes toward the technological.

Even beyond this tension, the narratives themselves are obviously symptomatic, suggesting a modern culture that is intensely aware of a problem of distance. That problem is in part indicative of the more general modern sensibility, what Orvell terms "the central problem of the machine age," that "of man's alienation from the concrete world of experience" (*Real Thing* 172). It is also fallout from what Walter Benjamin in his landmark essay "The Work of Art in the Age of Mechanical Reproduction" describes as our modern detachment "from the domain of tradition" (221), from all that formerly carried authority or meaning—what he terms "aura." But it is also the problem of the technological sensibility itself, of the fact that technology, along with the great power it offers, intervenes between the self and the world, placing us, as Romanyshyn puts it, behind a "window on the world" (31). There we may feel in control of the world, but we also come to feel like something less than participants in it; we become observers and manipulators essentially *displaced* from the world. Orvell puts this attitude in more concrete terms when he describes a shift in the very function of machines in this period. In the nineteenth century, he argues, "the machine was used predominantly to create consumer objects that enthusiastically mimicked handcrafted things"—objects like clothing and furniture that retained a link to the natural world and a traditional way of life. However, in the twentieth century, the machine increasingly was employed "to manufacture objects that were themselves machines—telephones, phonographs, coffee makers, toasters, vacuum cleaners" (*Real Thing* 142); those machines, in turn, marked an ever greater distance from the natural world inhabited by previous generations. More subtly, they began to fashion a world that was fundamentally *defined by distance,* from the beliefs and values of those earlier generations, from the "aura" of things, even from each other.

As machine-made products themselves, the films we will study bear the marks of this problem, which we can begin here to trace. While they find their central attraction in technology and its power, in the constructs of reason that they visualize, that imagery always represents, in Romanyshyn's phrase, "reason lined with desire," in effect, a kind of wish fulfillment—just what we would expect from a dream factory. Yet it is a wish fulfillment that inevitably falls short. Thus while these films offer us images that emphasize the power and potential of technology—power and potential that modernism would claim as our birthright—they also typically reveal the shadow of technology, the problems that desire would overlook. When seen in the context of genre, the era's science fiction films do seem intent on carrying out the usual work of genre: helping audiences troubled by the rapid pace of technological development and the embrace of the machine in all areas of life find some accommodation with this modern situation, by offering them strategies for distancing themselves from their anxieties, by constructing the technological in accord with their desires. So while a film like the Will Rogers *Connecticut Yankee* offers us images of airborn destruction, of tanks, machine guns, and mechanized soldiers—all nightmarish leftovers of World War I and hints of wars yet to come—it marshals those images in defense of Western culture, as signs of how Yankee mechanical ingenuity can triumph over a barbaric spirit, here embodied in the treacherous figure of Morgan Le Fay.[15] Yet even as such films offer comforting strategies, they seem almost inevitably haunted by that sense of distance, as if it were built into the technology itself—hard-wired, to use a contemporary image. Thus, for all of the affirmations of the technological they offer, for all their reminders that, as cultural historian David Gelernter offers, "technology had accomplished breathtaking things" (262) and promised to do far more, the era's films also leave us strangely unsatisfied, never fully convinced, still apprehensive.

V

Before turning to the films themselves and measuring out their dream of distance, we might pause for a brief comment on methodology. This study aims to explore that ambivalence noted above, those abiding tensions in modern industrial culture and its films, by drawing both on Machine Age and postmodern assessments of the impact of technology. Thus, while it attempts to ground its speculations in the history and attitudes of the Machine Age, to draw as much as possible on the era's own ideas, it also hopes to suggest an element of continuity, one in which the Machine Age appears as an early development of patterns we would now identify as postmodern. To better identify this continuity, the study also adopts certain postmodern critical assumptions. Most important, it assumes Baudrillard's notion of seduction to suggest the subtle way in which the technological has always wielded its power. As he argues, "technology . . . doesn't push things forward or transform the world"; it very simply "becomes the world" (*Baudrillard Live* 44). And that "becoming," I would suggest, is essentially recorded on these science fiction films. At the same time, this study takes its central conceit from a complementary and more historically grounded view, Romanyshyn's study of how the technological has functioned in Western culture as a powerful distancing device, something that places us at "a distance from matter," including *human* matter. This view especially helps us describe a central pattern at work in the texts we encounter—a pattern of distance and detachment that affords these films a kind of double vision, as they both embrace and critique the technological and its growing hold on our lives. It also offers a new perspective on ways in which the technological has been implicated in oppositions between classes, races, and genders throughout much of this century.

More broadly conceived, then, this examination is situated in both contemporary cultural criticism and film history. On the one hand, it is concerned with the ways in which our technological consciousness has evolved, both empowering us and distancing us from the very world over which we would exercise that power, even distancing us from each other. That development in the modern era, in what we have come to call the Machine Age, has dramatically set the stage for our postmodern encounter with the technological, and particularly for our own conflicted attitudes toward an electronic, computer-driven technology that promises one day to "download" us into a machine. On the other hand, this examination tries to fill in a large gap of film history, a gap primarily in our study of the science fiction genre but also in film's encounter with its own technological base. As we have noted, the science fiction films of this era, with very few exceptions, go unmentioned in our histories, despite their implications for film in a crucial, formative period. Yet as Garrett Stewart puts it, in their technological thrust, our science fiction films can help us "peer into the mechanics of apparition that permit these films in the outermost and first place" (161). By at least partially filling in these gaps and grappling with that reflexive potential, we might better understand how a kind of cinematic imagination became so powerful in and symptomatic of modern life.

This simultaneously cultural and cinematic vantage could easily focus solely on the American cinema, providing a filmic complement to Tichi's examination of the Machine Age's literary impact, *Shifting Gears,* or a prologue to Vivian Sobchack's study of more recent science fiction films, *Screening Space.* To limit the focus in this way, though, would miss an opportunity for cross-cultural study to which this material readily lends itself. For despite the cultural differences we expect to find in films from countries such as the Soviet Union, Germany, France, the United States, and England, their science fiction films converge enough in their key images, concerns, and attitudes to suggest what Stuart Hall terms a cultural "conventionalization" (30) of technology's presentation, which helps show us how a broad technological perspective was being constructed. These films allow us to gauge both similar and different responses to the technological in different countries, as well as to glimpse the international circulation of meaning in this era. While the discussion that follows is organized on the basis of national origins, then, it also proceeds in a roughly chronological, if at times overlapping, way in its discussion of the films. With this vantage we might better observe the process of change—even radical transformation—that the industrialized cultures that produced key science fiction texts underwent as they tried to address the seemingly irresistible power of the machine and machine principles.

Finally, we shall carry out this investigation by assuming a fundamental dynamic that should be endemic to most cultural criticism. In genre study we often begin from the notion that every film represents a combination of *convention* and *invention*. The work draws on a vast pool of readily recognizable components—character types, objects, settings, attitudes, narrative turns, and so on; to this relatively stable base it adds its own particular developments, its own coloring, its own narrative trajectory, with which it addresses its specific temporal and cultural circumstances. For the purposes of this study we might consider another, similar dynamic at work, one of *reflection* and *construction*. Certainly, the films we shall consider are themselves historical artifacts and reflect their times and their societies, yet seeing them only as historical records can produce misperceptions and misconstructions. For even in their own times and places these films represented particular constructions of a cultural reality, constructions that at times drained technology of value, linked it to colonialism, or even ascribed its more negative elements to the feminine.[16] To better gauge the function of our science fiction films in this era, particularly as they helped accommodate the technological, we need to keep this reflection/construction dynamic in focus.

In the process, we shall be triangulating film, science fiction, and modern technological culture to reveal the significant reshaping that was underway, as the modern world, through its embrace of technology and its powers, was just beginning to point the way to a postmodern world. This is the point when, as Walter Benjamin has so neatly codified it, we were beginning to notice a fundamental shift in the way in which we viewed our world. As he formulated this change, the "cult value" we once saw in our world and especially its artistic products was being replaced by "exhibition value"; a world that assumed a certain essence or "aura" (221) in each work of art, in each act of reproduction—and indeed, in all that was the model for reproduction—was giving way to one that detached production from tradition and traditional meanings, and in the process asserted a whole new function, a materialist and political one, for the process of reproduction. Thus our art, and preeminently the cinema, according to Benjamin, would find its fundamental concern—and source of value—in our world's "reproducibility," as it set about chronicling or reproducing real events in order to make visible the relations governing that world (223).

What the Machine Age brought, in all aspects of modern technological culture, was a new dominance of the machine that effectively *re-placed* the human, that is, it put us in a *new* place. It shifted us from among the many creatures of nature, particularly of a divinely ordained natural order, to the movers and manipulators of that order, operating from a position outside of it—at a great psychological if not physical distance from it.

Thus Orvell, following Benjamin's lead, has argued that one of the era's key manifestations was the "discovery of new ways of looking" at things (*Real Thing* 222), ways that, it was thought, at least in America, might restore our "contact with reality" (241) and replace a cultural fascination with imitation with a new access to authenticity itself. Our technology—the technology of the movie camera most certainly, but also the work of industrial construction, architecture, processes of manufacture, and so on—provided us with "a new 'screen' or 'filter' through which the world was experienced" (*After* 10), and that new experience could conceivably enable us to rework our world in ever more productive and efficient ways. Through our technology, in other words, we might begin determining the function and teleology of all things, even the human, and manipulating them in accord with the values inherent in this new, technological way of seeing.

The key factor in this new positioning, as Romanyshyn observes, is that the individual is placed not at the center of the world, but rather *outside* it, there to become a kind of "spectator self" (117) or moviegoer, viewing the world as if through a window or screen—that of the technological—and thus seeing the self as separate from and unconnected to the fate of the rest of that world. Of course, instead of simply providing us with power over the world, the conditions of existence, and our own bodies, as our "technological dream" has long and seductively promised, that attitude of distance has opened the way for ecological abuses, estranged people from one another, and even promoted what Romanyshyn terms the "abandonment of the body" (20), an ongoing effort, which Dery describes, to distance ourselves from the frailties of the "human machine," from the conditions of our very humanity.

Yet another, perhaps more personal sort of problem also attends this Machine Age sensibility and repeatedly surfaces in the era's films. A felt separation or difference from the world, such as both Romanyshyn and Baudrillard describe, could well leave us unmoored in a traditionally conceived reality and prone to see the self as simply another sort of "invented . . . created . . . manufactured" thing (Romanyshyn 17). We might come to seem like the product of a far less efficient system than that which Frederick Winslow Taylor championed in his popular *Principles of Scientific Management* in 1911 or that Henry Ford demonstrated in his production techniques, or perhaps just one more of those "component parts" which, Tichi explains, were central to a developing aesthetic of the period (173). When exaggerated, the basic principles of what came to be known as Taylorism and Fordism, championed—and reviled—by many in this period can easily suggest what Carroll Pursell terms "a hegemonic culture of modernism run amok" (117). Certainly, those principles often enthroned by the Machine Age—motion and time studies, emphasis on efficient management, assembly-line techniques—contain attitudes that not only linked workers to the technology of the assembly line, but also subtly conflated them with the very products of that line—as Chaplin so well illustrated in the factory scenes of *Modern Times*. Such linking and conflating threatened to make workers not just the manipulators but the manipulated, not just contrivors but contrivances, not just the masters of the machine but the mastered as well. In that threat, we can begin to see the foundation of a typically postmodern anxiety, as our efforts to deploy the latest technological advances seemed to render us more and more "technologized," and our creation of all varieties of artifacts seemed to draw us further toward the artificial and further from the human.

And yet, our science and technology, particularly in the Machine Age, also have at their core our own desire to locate a place for the human—to put us in a position to better deal with our world, our situations, our selves, in effect, to construct a *better* place for us and our machines. In the Machine Age, we were already congratulating ourselves on "A Century of Progress" and planning out "The World of Tomorrow," as the themes for the two most significant World's Fairs of the era underscore. These fairs should remind us, Gelernter argues, of the extent to which in this era, despite all forebodings, when "people turned their minds to the future, what they saw was *good*. Technology in particular was good" (25). Our films of this period were employed precisely in doing the generic work necessary to accommodate these attitudes toward the technology of "progress" and "tomorrow." Yet that was hardly an unproblematic task, for before we could enter this "world of tomorrow," we had to distance ourselves from our anxieties about the machine—quite reasonable reactions for a period sandwiched between two great mechanized wars—while we also embraced a technological attitude that subtly fostered its own disconcerting sense of distance and detachment. As we shall see, the inevitable tensions and rather forced accommodations that resulted are a hallmark of this era's films, as well as of the troubled emergence of modern technological culture.

Notes

1. For a brief background on the development of color technology and its impact on film narrative, I recommend Richard Neupert's excellent article, "Exercising Color Restraint."

2. Bazin argued that the cinema represented an effort at satisfying "our obsession with realism" (12). That obsession begins, he says, with a myth, "the myth of total cinema" (22), a dream that we might perfectly reproduce "the world in its own image" (21). This dream or "myth" is one that Walter Benjamin, Miles Orvell, and other commentators have linked specifically to modernism and especially to the Machine Age, with its emphasis on mechanical reproduction.

3. While the appellation "science fiction" first appears in 1851 in a work by William Wilson, this genre was long known under a variety of terms. As Edward James explains, in the late nineteenth century the American publisher of dime novels, Frank Tousey, used the phrase "invention stories," a widely adopted term which was replaced in the next century by such titles as "pseudo-scientific stories," "scientific fiction," and, as popularized in the subtitle of the famous pulp *Amazing*, "scientifiction" (9). Hugo Gernsback, publisher of *Amazing*, is credited with finally establishing the current appellation "science fiction" in 1929, although a phrase like "scientification" lingers well into the 1930s in some of the pulps.

4. Throughout his discussion of the causes of laughter and ultimately his generalizations about comedy, Bergson refers to "mechanical inelasticity" as the fundamental factor. His oft-cited formula, the "mechanical encrusted on the living" (84), offers a useful way of seeing and thinking about the most basic appeal of silent comedy in which the human often becomes machine-like, while the machines—cars, planes, boats—repeatedly exhibit human characteristics.

5. Of course, at this point in his career, Chaplin did feel that he was being menaced by cinematic technology, that he was being forced to radically alter his films and especially his tramp portrayal due to the popular demand for "talkies." In *Modern Times*, as he literally does in the opening sequence of the earlier *City Lights* (1931), he essentially thumbs his nose at the vogue of talking pictures by having several of his characters speak not normally but through mechanisms: a television speaker, a phonograph record, a radio. And in the final scene, when the little tramp is forced to sing, he forgets the words of his song and sings gibberish instead, while miming actions that convey the song's implications and thereby wringing laughter from his audience. It is a final, fleeting moment of triumph for the strategies of silent comedy before Chaplin fully succumbs to the sound imperative—and in the process says goodbye to his little tramp persona—with *The Great Dictator* in 1940.

6. Many stories about Keaton attest to his personal fascination with the technological. As Rudi Blesh describes Keaton's first meeting with Fatty Arbuckle, Keaton's primary interest was not so much in the work of his fellow comedian as in the film apparatus, the camera, which he proceeded to disassemble and inspect in great detail (88). And as a

reflection of that fascination, Blesh sees the abiding story in the Keaton films as always "man at the mercy of both chance and The Machine" (xi).

7. The several serious injuries and close calls Keaton suffered while making his films—including a broken neck in *Sherlock, Jr.* (1924)—attest to a certain level of unpredictability that attended the technology of filmmaking itself. In the case of *The Electric House,* though, that element reflects on the larger thrust of the film, for the unpredictable escalator was in fact just as depicted. In early shooting, Keaton caught his foot in the mechanism and suffered a broken ankle that shut down work on the film for several months. See Blesh's account of this dangerous machine encounter in his biography of Keaton (154).

8. *Wings* used more than thirty-five hundred active-duty troops and sixty Army Air Corps airplanes, as well as various other government resources. As Wellman biographer Frank Thompson notes, the director "was given orders by the War Department that granted him authority to request whatever assistance he needed . . . No other military film ever made was to have such complete cooperation by the Armed Forces" (61). That cooperation was apparently due in large part to the public's turning away from the military in this time of peace and prosperity, which the military hoped to counter by its own sort of cultural construction, that is, by encouraging a view of the military that melded the heroic efforts of the Great War to the Machine Age's fascination with the technologies of flight and speed.

9. Since the late 1920s, an active science fiction fandom has influenced the shape and reception of the literary form. As Edward James notes, this "body of enthusiastic and committed readers . . . has had an appreciable and unique, if unmeasurable, impact upon the evolution of sf, influencing writers, producing the genre's historians, bibliographers, and many of its best critics, and, above all, producing many of the writers themselves" (130). We might also note that the first World Science Fiction Convention was held in New York in 1939, coincident with that watershed of the Machine Age, the New York World's Fair.

10. As an example of that relative neglect, we might note that in her broad-ranging overview of the American science fiction film, *Screening Space,* Vivian Sobchack makes no mention of the films on which we shall focus here: *The Mysterious Island, Just Imagine,* and *The Invisible Ray.* And of these three, only the last receives even a cursory treatment in John Baxter's dated but useful historical account, *Science Fiction in the Cinema,* although he does include brief discussions of several of the foreign works in this period and suggests some intriguing connections between them. For its comparative and cross-cultural focus, his book remains a valuable resource.

11. Sontag's essay, "The Imagination of Disaster," remains one of the most thoughtful and influential pieces on the genre. In it she explores the importance of those images of catastrophe and disaster that so dominated our science fiction films in the 1950s and 1960s, and attempts to link those images to a larger thrust of the genre.

12. For an extended account of this figure's function within the history of both literary and cinematic science fiction, see my *Replications.*

13. In his examination of various strains of "cyberculture," Dery sounds a note very similar to that of Baudrillard's work, as he describes how the latest technology "seduces us with its promise of delivery from human history and mortality" (10).

14. Heidegger's work, especially his key essays "The Question Concerning Technology" and "The Age of the World Picture," provides an important grounding for this notion of the technological as a way of thinking, as a fundamental human attitude. See *The Question Concerning Technology and Other Essays.*

15. This application of the technological clearly runs counter to the thrust of Mark Twain's original novel of 1889. In that work he emphasized the potential for mass destruction that our technology made possible and offered up horrifying images of slaughter, all achieved with the best of intentions by his Yankee protagonist.

16. In her essay "Technophilia," Mary Ann Doane argues that science fiction has always been "obsessed with the issues of the maternal, reproduction, representation, and history" (174). That "obsession," she claims, is rooted in a fundamental opposition between the feminine and the technological, with the latter always promising "to control, supervise, regulate" the former (163). It is an opposition that Romanyshyn sees as implicit in that distancing effect he imputes to the technological, which he reminds us is "not only a dream of escape from matter but also a flight from the feminine" (172).

Bibliography

Baudrillard, Jean. *The Ecstasy of Communication.* Trans. Bernard and Caroline Schutze. New York: Semiotext(e), 1988.

Benjamin, Walter. "The Work of Art in the Age of Mechanical Reproduction." In *Illuminations.* Trans. Harry Zohn, ed. Hannah Arendt, 217-51. New York: Schocken, 1969.

Dery, Mark. *Escape Velocity: Cyberculture at the End of the Century.* New York: Grove, 1996.

Gelernter, David. *1939: The Lost World of the Fair.* New York: Avon, 1995.

Grant, Barry Keith. "Experience and Meaning in Genre Films." In *Film Genre Reader II,* ed. Barry Keith Grant, 114-28. Austin: U of Texas P, 1995.

James, Edward. *Science Fiction in the Twentieth Century.* New York: Oxford UP, 1994.

Kawin, Bruce F. "Children of the Light." In *Film Genre Reader II,* ed. Barry Keith Grant, 308-29. Austin: U of Texas P, 1995.

Orvell, Miles. *The Real Thing: Imitation and Authenticity in American Culture, 1880-1940.* Chapel Hill: U of North Carolina P, 1989.

Pursell, Carroll. *White Heat: People and Technology.* Berkeley: U of California P, 1994.

Romanyshyn, Robert D. *Technology as Symptom and Dream.* London: Routledge, 1989.

Segal, Howard P. "The Technological Utopians." In *Imagining Tomorrow: History, Technology, and the American Future,* ed. Joseph Corn, 119-36. Cambridge: MIT Press, 1986.

Sobchack, Vivian. "Cities on the Edge of Time: The Urban Science Fiction Film." *East-West Film Journal* 3 (1988): 4-19.

———. *Screening Space: The American Science Fiction Film.* 2d ed. New York: Ungar, 1987.

Sontag, Susan. "The Imagination of Disaster." *Against Interpretation,* 212-28. New York: Dell, 1966.

Stewart, Garrett. "The 'Videology' of Science Fiction." In *Shadows of the Magic Lamp: Fantasy and Science Fiction in Film,* eds. George E. Slusser and Eric S. Rabkin, 159-207. Carbondale: Southern Illinois UP, 1985.

Tichi, Cecelia. *Shifting Gears: Technology, Literature, Culture in Modernist America.* Chapel Hill: U of North Carolina P, 1987.

Wilson, Richard Guy, Dianne H. Pilgrim, and Dickran Tashjian. *The Machine Age in America: 1918-1941.* New York: Abrams, 1986.

Elyce Rae Helford (essay date 2000)

SOURCE: Helford, Elyce Rae. "Postfeminism and the Female Action-Adventure Hero: Positioning *Tank Girl.*" In *Future Females, the Next Generation: New Voices and Velocities in Feminist Science Fiction Criticism,* edited by Marleen S. Barr, pp. 291-308. Lanham, Md.: Rowman & Littlefield, 2000.

[*In the following essay, Helford interprets Rachel Talalay's* Tank Girl *"as an instructive representation of the compromises and contradictions of the 1990s brand of postfeminism."*]

> I was READY to watch Lori Petty kick some men's asses—hell, I was ready to watch the movie as a damn instruction manual.
>
> —Suzanne Sullivan (Review of *Tank Girl*)

INTRODUCTION

"What Do Young Women Want?" is the subtitle of a 1995 article by Wendy Kaminer about the "third wave" and the changing face of feminism in the 1990s. Kaminer sees young women rejecting many of the basics of feminist politics and desiring personal empowerment. As a professor of English and women's studies, I find myself often asking this same question and feeling troubled at the similar conclusions I reach. The mass media's history of misrepresenting feminism's second wave, compounded by 1980s backlash and repudiation of feminism in favor of a more individualistic and essentialist postfeminism, have strongly molded what feminism is and can be for young women today, particularly the middle-class, predominantly white eighteen-year-olds I teach (in classes from first-year composition to introduction to women's studies) and find on the internet (in spaces from a soap opera chat forum to a feminist theory discussion group). In all of these spaces I frequently encounter the words (or the idea) "I am not a feminist, but . . . ," a sentence fragment Susan Douglas views as the refrain of young women who are definable as feminists but unwilling to take on the label for fear of being ostracized (294). Concerns involve lesbian baiting and accusations of "man hating" that are closely related to fears of losing dating options and male approval.

These young women I encounter and read about in articles by and concerning them fight against real and imagined boundaries of past and present patriarchies and feminisms as they attempt to articulate selves full of "choice," promise, and various kinds of success in the home and workplace. They are women who have been encouraged by the media and dominant threads of American history to value individualism and downplay communal efforts and activism, to see the American Dream as entirely attainable to those who just work hard enough. They envision their worlds as centered in what Elspeth Probyn calls "choiceoisie," an alternative to feminism that envisions all major life decisions as individual options rather than culturally determined or directed choices (quoted in Dow 99, 103). Women "choose" the life they want (to be stay-at-home mothers or career women, for example), making "choiceoisie" a clearly middle-class perspective (see Dow 99). These optimistic postfeminist opportunists have seen many glass ceilings broken by token individuals and, with reference to the media, are quick to tout the names of Madonna, Roseanne, or Oprah, seeing in these women (or rather their rhetorically constructed media personas) and in their individualistic, heroic ("bootstrap") efforts the promise of success equal to that of men.

The world such women can construct from these images is a patriarchy that does not obstruct their progress (changed enough by the 1970s women's movement) and access to choices. In favoring the individual exception rather than group struggle, they may find it easy to forget that tokenism not only reveals the strong individual's will but also oppressive structural forces (Cloud 117). You cannot have a token such as Oprah Winfrey if there is no structural subordination in the first place. Yet, through the token, systemic sexism, racism, and/or classism are repressed; in the token who "triumphs over adversity," focusing on the individual *triumph* can displace the importance of the group nature of the *adversity*. As Dana Cloud compellingly argues in her study of the rhetorical construction of "Oprah," the bootstraps philosophy that yields the token "obscures the collective nature of oppression and the need for collective social action . . . to remedy social injustice" (117). Instead, the token is held up not as exception but as proof that egalitarianism (the fully functioning American Dream) was present all along: "In popular culture . . . a token can be defined as a persona who is constructed from the character and life of a member of a subordinated group, and then celebrated, authorized to speak as proof that the society at large does not discriminate against members of that group" (123-124). Thus, if the token can be represented as an adequate example of gender, race, and/or class equality, feminism emerges as an overreaction to a nonexistent problem or as quaint reminder of the days when some folks didn't have it so good.

So what does our young woman want, especially she who does not think, for example, that one Oprah extinguishes the pay gap between women and men, one Ellen DeGeneres negates lesbian baiting, or one Madonna stops date rape? For many, the answer will still lie in individual action, in believing in what has come to be called postfeminism (a "new conservative feminism" [Stacey 559]), characterized in the 1980s in response to New Right backlash against feminism and liberalism. As Susan Douglas puts it, in the 1980s women were told they "had to make their peace with patriarchy and learn how to fit in" (238); postfeminism was one possible response. As I understand and interpret it, postfeminism has three key elements: (1) rejection of the (radical feminist) emphasis on "sexual politics"; (2) a consequential emphasis on individual efforts over group activism; and (3) a "pro-family" stance (because feminism is accused of being "anti-family"). Postfeminism leaves patriarchy in place, denouncing the idea that women are oppressed as a group and that the "personal is political" in "an attempt to avoid all forms of direct struggle against male domination" (Stacey 562). It affirms gender difference and celebrates traditionally feminine qualities, such as (maternal) nurturance (563). And, while acknowledging that feminism was necessary to create openings for women's success, this is no longer so because women's success "is dependent on individual initiative and does not require collective action" (Dow 93).

From the 1980s to the late 1990s, postfeminism has arguably been the dominant form of feminism for young, middle-class American women. We can hear it clearly in the beliefs of young "individualist feminist" Karen Lehrman, for example, who holds that "considering the ubiquity of equal opportunity laws, sex discrimination in the workplace should be considered a private matter between women and their employers" (quoted in Kaminer 23). Systemic critique is excluded from this brand of feminism in favor of the competitively driven woman who works within the system for personal improvement. The dangerous result is that "an excessively individualist feminism obliterates the political" (23). Thus, "it's easy to understand the appeal of a pure individualism to young women professionals imbued with confidence, an ethic of self-reliance and the headstart of a good education" (23); however, this brand of politics does nothing to ensure that *all* women receive ample education and opportunities. In fact, postfeminism, based as it is upon competition, guarantees that a power and privilege imbalance will exist among women. As Kaminer concludes, "it's hard to imagine a women's movement without at least a little 'gender consciousness' and some commitment to collective action" (23). Nonetheless, the individualist strain of feminism (whether named postfeminism or not) is what the media is feeding young feminists. In terms of entertainment programming, this ideology has been particularly well projected through the image of the female action-adventure hero. I wish now to turn my focus to her.

POSTFEMINISM AND THE FEMALE ACTION-ADVENTURE HERO

We would not have female action-adventure heroes without a feminist (not postfeminist) consciousness. The female action-adventure hero is composed equally of herstory, affirmative action, equal opportunity, and repudiation of gender essentialism and traditional feminine roles. To move from the objectification of women as helpless victims (saved by the male action-adventure hero) or as seductive villains (women's power as inherently sexual and evil) to, for example, Xena: Warrior Princess, women's emotional and physical strength, desire for empowerment, and relationships to strong women of the past, among other factors, must be asserted, at least indirectly. Women have to desire and then demand such figures from within a patriarchal media that is unlikely to create them without prompting and the assurance of an audience to watch them. So, the very presence of the female action-adventure hero (even when she is Barbarella) is noteworthy.

Nevertheless, the limitations of the female action-adventure hero are equally (or more) important to attend. The heroic figure is individualistic, most often a loner. But, even when working with others, s/he acts to right wrongs without insisting on greater cultural change. Xena, for example, travels with her respected partner, Gabrielle, but is the undisputed leader. And, when evil must be thwarted, it always appears in the form of an individual ruler to be dethroned or a warlord or monster to be stopped through physical combat. One king is replaced by another (however much kinder and gentler); there are always more warlords or monsters; and Gabrielle still follows Xena. Each village's problem is solved in isolation from the larger culture by an individual hero who proposes individualist solutions that never threaten the patriarchal and classist structure that is plainly evident in every episode. Xena never recommends, for example, that the people who call for her services try nonviolent noncooperation, abolish servitude (though she, like most heroes developed in and for a postcolonial audience, does overtly denounce slavery), or demand equal pay for equal work.

Heroes such as Xena (like the comic book or TV *Wonder Woman* before her) are part of the myth of the American Dream, of transcendence, of individual greatness done for the good of others. Thus, female heroes function well within the individualist discourse of postfeminism. This circumstance is made even more plain within the context of the development of the female action-adventure hero during the 1980s and 1990s. This is the era of Sigourney Weaver's Ellen Ripley in the *Alien* films—particularly heroic in the second film, *Aliens* (1986)—and Linda Hamilton's Sarah Connor in *Terminator 2* (1991). These survivors-turned-heroes (in the progression from the original film to its sequel/s) were both given life by Gayle Anne Hurd and James Cameron, the production team/couple that became famous in the 1980s and early 1990s for its action-adventure films featuring strong female characters. Ripley and Connor demonstrate such traditional heroic qualities as determination, self-sacrifice, stamina, and physical strength. And they shed traditional feminine traits, such as passivity, gentleness, and emotionality (other than anger). We see these women pump up their biceps, shoot off enormous phallic weapons, sweat bullets, and save the universe. Compassion is still present (a traditionally feminine trait, yet generally seen in male heroes as well), but only for members of the home team, for the children who will carry on the great traditions of individualism and "choice." Compassion rarely involves any emotional display once the hero goes into battle mode.

Interestingly, despite their nontraditional strength and use of violence, both Ripley and Connor have been deemed sexy by many male viewers. All actors in film wear makeup, but Weaver and Hamilton do not look made up in traditional ways (lipstick, eyeliner, mascara, etc.). *Aliens* and *Terminator 2,* instead, produce the "buns of steel" version of female appeal; these heroes who display their thin, fit bodies and prowess with a weapon are saved from being alienatingly strong by the camera's emphasis on their bodies. These are not traditional pinup, stripper, or model types. But they are sexualized in similar ways when the camera highlights their bodies during "unexpected" moments (when the characters seem not to know they are being watched). Audience members are invited to enjoy the voyeuristic pleasure of watching Connor do chin-ups on an overturned bed located in her prison cell, for example. In this scene, she does not see viewers as we stare at her body through the barred window, turned away from but on display for us, locked in her jail and filmic cell. Similarly, we catch Ripley in a moment otherwise reserved for privacy: when she emerges from her sleeping capsule in sweaty tank top and underwear. Here, however, our pleasure is less peep show than striptease, as our fellow (gender implications intended) voyeurs, the other marines, get to check out the merchandise as well.[1] Despite nonconventional feminine sexualization, the portrayals of Ripley and Connor still enlist the male gaze ("woman as image, man as bearer of the look"), still occasionally "freeze the flow of action in moments of erotic contemplation" (Mulvey 27). These texts describe their female hero stars as powerful, yet still objects controlled by the camera and the viewer, at times clearly "coding [the] women for strong visual and erotic impact so that they can be said to connote *to-be-looked-at-ness*" (27).[2]

In addition to the sexualization of these women within *Aliens* and *Terminator 2,* intertextual readings show how nontraditional presentations of the female might have been "softened" for audiences ahead of time. Fans of Sigourney Weaver, for example, could remember her more traditionally feminized/sexualized role in *Ghostbusters,* in which she portrays the love interest for the main male character (played by Bill Murray) and in which demonic possession turns her into a lustful creature impatiently awaiting completion of her evil function through sexual coupling with a possessed man. Though the possession is played largely for humor (Weaver writhes on a bed while Rick Moranis's desexualized "nerd" character tries to find and mate with her), Weaver's sexual allure is not displayed as ridiculous. She ends the film in a coupled relationship with her savior, Murray's womanizing antihero character. Similarly, Linda Hamilton would be well known to television audiences for her role in the television fantasy/romance serial *Beauty and the Beast.* Her hair, makeup, and clothing in this series suggest a soft, conventionally feminine beauty. The show's driving tension is her impossible love for the Beast, and Hamilton's character is often a victim needing to be rescued by him. In neither of these roles is the female character incompetent; Weaver and Hamilton both play professional women. However, their beauty and sexuality are far more traditionally feminine in representation than in *Aliens* and *Terminator 2*. Their primary male costars both dominate and are stereotypically masculine in behavior (Murray's character is clearly sexist whereas the Beast is strong and violent; both men are "tamed" through their attraction to the traditionally feminine aspects of the characters Weaver and Hamilton play).

Clearly, Ripley and Connor were not traditionally sexualized. But sexualization, as a central element of Western culture's definition of womanhood, is, as I have briefly illustrated, still a component of female heroic representation. And this trend in representing the female action-adventure hero has ensued well into the 1990s, with a return to emphasizing traditional feminine beauty. Ripley, for example, continues in the apparently never-ending *Alien* film phenomenon, most recently as a psychotic clone in *Aliens: Ressurection* (1997). Her sexuality is now more perverse, her clothing more leather fetish than military drab, her nails polished Goth green and lipstick dark and prominent; however, she is also no longer the heroic standard for women in the action-adventure genre. Hypermasculine women are not as hip as they once were. If we take other popular cultural images as examples, we see that aggressive Roseanne of the sitcom *Roseanne* has given way to a kinder, gentler talk show host Roseanne and even nicer Rosie O'Donnell. The tough women of *L.A. Law* have become the miniskirt-wearing, manchasing Ally McBeal. And Oprah glorifies her slimmer, trimmer body and increasingly trivially focused talk show. Increased emphasis on traditional femininity in looks and behavior (in various combinations and to various degrees) have again become a significant part of the media's normative image of the empowered woman. Ripley has been replaced by butch but sexily clad Xena; Connor is outdone by increasingly blonde teen heartthrob Buffy the Vampire Slayer.

Postfeminism's "Rock-Me" Heroes

One way to interpret this media trend is that even more of the postfeminist agenda has been championed by the media: Mid-to-late-1990s women are not just convinced they can act out their "choices" through individual (heroic) effort, they want to recuperate the "choice" of wearing high heels (the de-emphasis of this fashion imperative is one of the only things I personally loved about the late 1980s) and makeup to achieve their success. They take for granted that they will marry and have families (and assume they will have the money to take a year or two or forever off work while Dad continues in order to exercise their "natural" mothering skills); however, until that time, they are mostly concerned about "choosing" the manner in which they will

articulate their sexuality. These postfeminists find their individual "activism" primarily in battling what they must first establish to be a legacy of feminist antisexuality based largely upon isolation and demonization of antipornography activists. An example: Andrea Dworkin, who attempts to take all the fun out of sex, another individual behavioral "choice."

A particularly harsh stereotype of the 1970s feminist is of a bitter, angry woman who never has sex because she is too ugly to get a man. Never mind that the stereotype of the angry young man is often perceived as heroic and sexy (France 36). Young women in the 1990s do not want to be associated with the humorless, unhappy, lonely prude. For these women, says Andrea Juno (editor of the anthology *Angry Women in Rock*), association with feminism means "they [are] gonna be delibidinized: You're unsexy, you won't be loved, and you won't get screwed" (quoted in France 36). Difficult questions follow: "[Can] a healthy sexual libido be reconciled with good movement politics? [Are] we tools of the patriarchy just because we [enjoy] renting the occasional porno movie with our boyfriends? Or if we read *Vogue* and profoundly [believe] in the magic of Maybelline?" (France 38). Some women have simply rejected feminism outright based upon its links to an antipornography (and presumed antisexuality) perspective. Others, however, realize that a prosexuality attitude does not conflict with the goals of feminism. "[A]s I always understood it—and I was somebody who read a lot of Germaine Greer and stuff like that—part of the [feminist] manifesto was to find a way for women to reclaim their own sexuality, to not only be the object of male desire but discover what their own desire was about, and claim that for themselves," argues singer Joan Osborne, for example (quoted in France 40).

I submit that the most popular 1990s perspective on this issue is the form of postfeminism Kim France dubbed "rock-me feminism." As I read it, rock-me feminism—also identifiable as "do-me" (France 36) or Madonna feminism—displaces (or at least reinterprets) the pro-family element of postfeminism for the young, thin, and beautiful woman who completely expects a solid career and perfect marriage and kids *later*, but wants a lot of attention through sexual magnetism now. The rock world of the 1990s, with its many female stars, is a powerful site for postfeminist pro-sex modeling, especially thanks to Madonna who "made it okay to be entirely about sex and still be in control" (France 38). Young women seek to "project" their sexuality as a form of individualist empowerment; however, this "projection" tends to be aimed directly at men, to attract their attention and, ultimately, approval. Rock-me feminism thus emerges as a new arrangement of an old song. Women's sexuality has long been mobilized in service of a patriarchal agenda linking women with sex and the body and not with other kinds of power (economic, political).

Exene Cervenka (a member of the 1980s Los Angeles band X) labels this active sexual projection "Rod Stewart Feminism," demonstrating an "if it's ok for guys to do it, it's okay for girls to do it" mentality (quoted in France 39). And this mentality leaves her questioning its effectiveness as a feminist strategy. She ponders the image of 1990s cult star Tori Amos "straddling a piano bench"; she asks, "is that empowering women or is that *Penthouse*-ing women?" Her conclusion: "I don't know" (quoted in France 39). Amos herself, responding to a writer's argument that "[y]ou can't fight the patriarchy in a tube top," well exemplifies the postfeminist/rock-me feminist individualist response: "Okay, so why don't I wait for that writer to fax me on what I should wear to fight the patriarchy?" (quoted in France 39). Limiting a woman's clothing (to avoid accusations of being a "slut" or to "protect" against rape) has generally been a victim-blaming strategy unacceptable to feminist; however, it *has* been essential to feminism that women recognize the oppressive nature of the objectification and control of women's bodies through clothing/fashion. There is no easy answer to this dilemma, and the comment tossed at Amos about her "tube-top" feminism is unhelpful. Nonetheless, it is worth noting that both question and response clearly identify individual "choice" as central to defining feminism (exemplifying faith in "choiceoisie") and dismiss feminist ideology and its fundamental insight that "women operate within a sex/gender system that limits choices" (Dow 96).

Interestingly, both strong feminists protesting pornography and women who actively project their sexuality can threaten men. Andrea Dworkin's infamous linking of heterosexual sex acts with rape scares many men less than Roseanne's joke that her response to people who tell her she's not very feminine is "suck my dick!" Similarly, sexually aggressive rock star personas, like that of Tina Turner (especially as she ages and maintains this persona), or dangerous/animalistic sexualities, like that of Grace Jones, can threaten male audiences while revealing the degree to which race plays a role in how appealing or threatening projected sexuality may be.

Stereotypes and myths of African American women's sexuality, for example, have been mobilized, beginning with the slave trade, to legitimize (sexual) violence against them. Black women have traditionally been represented as sexually exotic, naturally provocative, and oversexed (see Onwurah). Nevertheless, projected rock-me sexuality may function as resistance to assimilation into the still-Victorian, anti-body norms of mainstream white culture. Tina Turner's stage persona is arguably about claiming a sexual power against the controls over black women's bodies in a white- and male-supremacist culture. The danger, however, of other (mis)readings remains present: Are we seeing evidence

of an alternative to white uptightness or validation of the stereotype of the hypersexual black female? (Onwurah) White women, in contrast, can display themselves with a presumption of sexual purity, often regardless of their behavior. Madonna, for example, reflects and exploits the hypersexualized black woman stereotype in her videos. She displays white privilege as she plays the sexual bad girl (perhaps most obviously as black woman in "Human Nature"), then easily sheds this image for a less sexualized one (her most recent New Age persona in "Frozen," for instance) in a way black women necessarily cannot (see hooks 160).

Parody is one effective strategy for articulating the dangers of using projected sexuality for empowerment. Comedian Sandra Bernhardt provides a wonderful performative demonstration of how aggressive sexuality in women is not always a turn-on. In her stand-up routines, she often combines sexualized body display (low-cut, "glamorous" dresses, thick makeup, overly coiffed hair, and high heels) with outspoken dialogue that criticizes men and favors lesbianism. More often, however, female media stars who project images of sexual "power"—like rock-me feminists Madonna or Salt-N-Pepa—do not threaten but arouse men, and encourage women to model their appearance and behavior after these allegedly "new images of strength and sexuality" (France 38). Ultimately, the portrait of the young 1990s postfeminist we are left with is a woman who tips her hat to past feminist gains but now considers them unnecessary and excessive. She rejects the concept of group oppression in favor of a valorization of individual effort and "choice" and repudiates concerns over sexual objectification through sexual projection. This brings us to *Tank Girl*.

POSITIONING *TANK GIRL*

I read Rachel Talalay's *Tank Girl* (1995) as an instructive representation of the compromises and contradictions of the 1990s brand of postfeminism. The film is a speculative action-adventure/comedy set in the year 2033 in the Australian Outback, where years of drought have resulted in an evil corporate executive taking over the culture through his Department of Water and Power (DWP). The action centers around Rebecca Buck, a young white woman who lives in a commune with her young white boyfriend, Richard, and a ten-year-old girl named Sam, among others. When the commune is raided by the DWP, her boyfriend is killed and Sam is kidnapped, and Rebecca is recruited for espionage. She refuses to cooperate and is sent to work in the mines, where she meets a shy but talented female mechanic named Jet. Eventually, Jet and Rebecca escape in a tank (the impressive sexualized power that yields the "Tank Girl" nickname) and rescue Sam from a men's club/brothel, only to lose her again to the DWP. To save her, Tank Girl and Jet seek the help of the Rippers, genetically engineered killing machines (who, in their armor, look a lot like the aliens in *Aliens*). These male half-human/half-kangaroos turn out to be less threatening than they first appear. After proving their loyalty, Tank Girl and Jet work together with the Rippers to invade the DWP headquarters and save Sam. The film ends with Tank Girl happily paired with the "big loveable [sic] Ewokish" (Pinsky and Sullivan 17) Ripper Booga, and water flows freely to all.

Tank Girl is based upon the British comic book of the same name, created by the male artist and writer team Jamie Hewlett and Alan Martin. Their heroine can be read as a "blueprint, positive or negative, for a new academy of funky Bad Girls. She shoots, she farts, she bares her tits, she shags kangaroos" (Romney 35). In the comic books, she is always covered with Band-Aids, hair patchily shaved, scrawny and combat-booted, sexualized but not model pretty. Writing in the *New Statesman and Society*, Johnathan Romney says she is "different from frame to frame, story to story—one minute a fierce avenging slaphead, the next a parodically fleshy cheesecake fantasy" (35). The comic books are nonlinear, often downright difficult to follow, "an art-school slacker's incoherent babble masquerading as a cartoon; spiked with digressions, gratuitous stylisation, graffiti as meaningless as the English inscriptions on Japanese-made leisurewear" (35). Importantly, Tank Girl is also subversively polysexual;[5] she screws men, women, and kangaroo creatures with equal abandon. Thus, although no feminist icon, Hewlett and Martin's Tank Girl challenges a lot of traditional gender norms through her behavior, appearance, and placement within a nonrealist, nonlinear narrative that "plays with the frame and generally subverts conventions" (Felperin 55).[4]

Tank Girl is, in many ways, an excellent choice for a new female action-adventure hero for the 1990s. She displays the aggressive individualism and "projected" sexuality of rock-me/postfeminism while kicking in some actual feminist rage at gender inequities and oppression through words and actions. *Off our backs* film critics Rachel Pinsky and Suzanne Sullivan, for example, praise the feminist issues the film raises, including "sexual harassment, female rebellion and female friendship" (17). When Tank Girl rescues Jet from enslavement and sexual exploitation and rebels against the oppressive evil of the DWP, we see effective challenges to the antifeminist Hollywood film female status quo.

In addition to these strengths, we can add another. Tank Girl bonds with the isolationist Rippers, illustrating a form of coalition building across difference. Though the Rippers include dominant individuals, they seem to operate in a relatively egalitarian fashion, voting democratically on all significant issues. Pinsky and Sullivan call them a "committee" (17), offering a compelling alternative to DWP's white patriarchal structure, similar to the little we see of Tank Girl's anti-establishment commune. Like Tank Girl's former communal family, the Rippers are another disenfranchised group. They lead Pinsky and Sullivan to conclude that the film sets "women and minorities against the all white male power force that sought to control the world" (17). This truly would be a powerful representation if Tank Girl was not the necessary catalyst and leader for the activism of the Rippers, who, before her arrival, made attacks and raids, but never brought down the DWP.

Pinsky and Sullivan also link the Rippers to African Americans (based only on the evidence that Ice T is cast as one of them) (17). This is provocative, if unpersuasive. The Rippers are played by actors of various races, though Ice T's character is clearly coded as stereotypically black through his dreadlocks and "gangsta" speech. The fact that all the Rippers are men is perhaps most interesting in this context, for it supports the media-constructed myth of black activism as a predominantly or solely male interest and pursuit. The common notion that activism among African Americans is exclusively male terrain would thus be supported by *Tank Girl* if we read the Rippers as black. I do not, however; to me, the Rippers' all-male status is most significant as a retreat—even within a film centered on a strong female protagonist and her female sidekick—from the possibilities of women warriors. When these perfect soldiers were genetically engineered, why were none female? In a film less centered on action-adventure, one could find this choice feminist (if essentialist), emphasizing pacifist leanings among feminists. However, in the violent world of *Tank Girl*, the fully male Rippers (however ethnicized) represent a sexist retreat from even postfeminist representations of heroic women.

The dominant feel of the film, nevertheless, is wholly postfeminist. One of the film's most striking aspects is the insistence upon a sexualization of power. "According to this ideology women can only be powerful if they get some man hard" (Pinsky and Sullivan 17). We see this exemplified clearly during an early scene in which Rebecca (Tank Girl) has been caught by DWP soldiers. In the truck, where she is heavily guarded by these violent misogynists, she must find a way to show that though her body is bound, she still has power. Her strategy is to offer to give one of the soldiers a blow job (her plucked eyebrows, heavily made up eyes, shiny painted lips, and model-thin body guarantee the men will desire her). When he stands before her and unzips, she makes the clichéd adolescent joke that his penis is so small she needs tweezers and a magnifying glass to see it; then she swiftly breaks his neck between her legs when he goes to punish her for this humiliation. There is no doubt that Tank Girl's "delight becomes the angry female viewer's delight" here; however, it is equally true that "[a]lthough it is fun to fuck with men because they want in your pants[,] this is not real power" (17).

We see the sexualization of power in many other scenes as well, from an early moment in which Tank Girl is forced at gunpoint to strip for a soldier and uses her talents to take his mind off her dangerousness long enough to blow him up with a grenade to a conversation in which Jet's concern that Tank Girl will be killed by the soldiers is rebuffed with this exclamation: "Jet, they're men!" However, there are times when her sexualization is more clearly disempowering. Like the shot of Sarah Connor's chin-ups in the prison cell in *Terminator 2* or Ripley's tank-top and undies moment in *Aliens,* the sand shower scene in *Tank Girl* provides a powerful opportunity to establish the male gaze in the film. Because the future world in which *Tank Girl* takes place is characterized by a scarcity of water, when Tank Girl is imprisoned and working as a mine slave for the DWP, she can only clean the day's grime with a sand shower. The shower, a minor thematic reminder, is clearly intended to serve the traditional function of every film shower scene that features a young, thin, beautiful woman: objectifying the female body. The camera moves slowly over Lori Petty's body, while an overlay of uncharacteristically slow music with a heavy beat and a moaning woman's voice guide our viewing. (It is perhaps no coincidence that rock-me diva Courtney Love is the executive music coordinator for the film and that Bonnie Greenberg, the film's music supervisor, reads the character of Tank Girl as "a punkish super-hero that is sexy, but has a tough edge" [quoted in Rosen 10].)

In addition, though the shower scene is the only one of its kind in the film, Tank Girl is generally "barely dressed and the camera is often focused on her spread legs" (Pinsky and Sullivan 17). This dismays critic Leslie Felperin. She condemns the script, "written by a man, wouldn't you know," and concludes: "Our heroine was once [in the comic books] a vicious, nut-crunching, kangaroo-bonking baldy bitch. Hollywood has castrated our phallic mother of destruction, given her more hair, a child to protect and—the cruellest [sic] cut of all—plucked her eyebrows severely enough to make her look like Marlene Dietrich slumming it at Glastonbury festival" (55).

Even if we reject this harsh critique and argue that the sexualization of Tank Girl is truly empowering, it is most so when it challenges heteronormativity. Sadly, Talalay's Tank Girl, unlike her comic book predecessor, fails this challenge. Romney, for example, argues, "she dresses like a lesbian situationist performance artist but has a nice boyfriend who gets killed in the first five minutes (he was added just so that, heaven forbid, people wouldn't think she was a lesbian situationist performance artist)" (35). And Felperin notes, "Once [in the comic books] she had an aggressive polymor-

phously perverse sexuality and was an icon for lesbians worldwide; here [in the film] she only kisses Jet to get her [Jet] out of a spot of trouble" (55). The only arguable challenge to gender roles we see is between Rebecca and her boyfriend, Richard, at the beginning of the film, in which, before we know they are a couple, she demands at gunpoint that he strip for her. This may be momentary gender role reversal (if a common pornographic one). It is also just a game. The couple is interrupted by Sam, a girl who lives in their commune and is Richard's daughter, according to Felperin (55). Even this minor sexual role reversal instantly becomes an embarrassing nuclear family (sitcom) moment (with Rebecca blushing and giggling). The scene is then demolished minutes later by the DWP raid. Once Richard is killed, rescuing Sam drives the rest of the narrative. This rescue is a traditional individualist action-adventure hero motive. It is particularly gender role significant for Tank Girl as step-mom figure (or at least mother surrogate because the dialogue never officially declares Sam to be Richard's daughter).

Removing the boyfriend is important in other ways, too. Richard (and Rebecca's serious if brief signs of emotional distress as she sees him shot and killed) establishes from the beginning of the film Rebecca's ability to have a traditional, heterosexual relationship (backlash/antifeminist). Yet, he is killed precisely to ensure that she can display her sexuality to others (rock-me/postfeminist).[5] Tank Girl's "other" lovers are, however, all male. As Felperin mentions (and I cite her above), the lesbianism of the comic book Tank Girl character is limited in the film to one scene in which, in order to save Jet from the menacing clutches of the sexist Sergeant Small, Tank Girl kisses Jet and tells Small to leave her "girlfriend" alone. When Small is gone, Jet expresses her thanks to Tank Girl, though she is obviously disgusted by the kiss and wipes her mouth as soon as she can. Tank Girl derives subversive sexual pleasure from Jet's discomfort and smilingly pretends the kiss is an expression of desire, not a rescue. This scene, however, is where the exploration of Tank Girl's sexual interest in women ends. She never again flirts with Jet or any other woman. Jet remains shy and uncomfortable with sexual advances of any kind (from either gender) throughout the film.

It is possible to read this scene through what seems a rock-me/do-me feminist "lesbian chic." It is equally tempting to read the lesbianism of Hewlett and Martin's comic book version of Tank Girl through this same superficial perspective. In other words, though Hewlett and Martin's Tank Girl plays sexually with women more often than Talalay's, this is no guarantee that the representation is meant to be anything more than titillation for a porn fed male audience. After all, "[l]esbians have been a source of intrigue for straight people much longer than since 1993, when k. d. lang appeared on the cover of *New York* magazine's 'lesbian chic' issue. The porn industry has exploited sex between women for decades" (Daly 63). Certainly, the complexity of lesbian desire, sexuality, and life outside the bedroom is not explored in either the comics or the film. Meg Daly writes, "While we may be political and/or stylish, lesbians do not choose the double oppression of being gay and female. Earning less money than men and being subject to discrimination and violence due to our gender and sexual orientation is not glamorous. Being a lesbian is more than getting down with your good friend on the dance floor, or that sexy *Guess* ad in a magazine" (63). Sadly, the moment of shock or titillation for viewers during *Tank Girl*'s brief woman/woman kiss scene seems exploitative rather than explorative—or at least an example of commercial co-optation. As Daly concludes, "One paradox of our society is that each new step toward understanding and equality, while truly felt and explored by some, is squandered on billboards somewhere else. Just as some women are deepening their understanding of erotic bonds, so too are those bonds plasticized through advertisements, movies, and fashion" (63).

The obvious political limits of Tank Girl's kiss scene with Jet might be stretched by her choice of a nonhuman lover at the end of the film, the gentle and naive kangaroo-being Booga; however, he is clearly a male character played by a male actor. He, like Richard (at least in the short scene we see him in), is kind, affectionate, and obedient. But, the fact that Tank Girl likes such "sensitive" men does not satisfy a desire to see feminist or lesbian sexual politics enacted in the film. As Felperin concludes, "her relationship with Booga, part kangaroo or not, is all fluffy love without the bestiality" (55). Writer/artist Diane DiMassa (creator of the radical feminist comic *Hothead Paisan, Homocidal Lesbian Terrorist*) goes further, identifying the relationship between Tank Girl and Booga as simply a part of the film's reliance on pornographic exploitation of the female. In one panel of a *Hothead Paisan* comic, we see DiMassa's parody of a *Tank Girl* film poster, announcing: "Toilet Tank Gurl: I suck kangaroo dick to appease my male audience" (23).

Perhaps the most compelling strategy worthy of note for the feminist viewer looking for critique of rock-me/do-me images are the film's moments of sexual parody and mockery. Historically, "women have been the object of jokes in traditional humour at the same time that they have been considered to be humourless and learned that they are not supposed to be funny" (Lee 90). Some feminists may stand by the humorless stereotype, considering the subject of feminist politics too serious to risk ridicule when it is already denounced so easily and so often within contemporary media culture (Franzini 811). Most feminists, however, embrace humor, especially feminist humor that "reveals and ridicules the ab-surdity of gender stereotypes and gender based inequality" (Gallivan quoted in Franzini 812). Feminist humor is thus, according to Emily Toth, about "creating new norms, a new culture" (quoted in Lee 90).

Exposure and ridicule of gender stereotypes dominate the humor of *Tank Girl,* primarily through the protagonist's challenge to the power and supremacy of the phallus. As already discussed, she uses juvenile jokes about insecurity over penis size to kill a soldier who threatens her. Similarly, her relationship with her tank clearly exemplifies her tendency to ridicule male power via attacks on male sexuality. In several scenes, Tank Girl caresses and sits (in parodic seductiveness) on the barrel of the tank and once, when she aims it at a group of male aggressors, asks, "Feeling a little inadequate?" This mockery is particularly noteworthy because it functions as a critique of masculine power, which is even stronger than her (sexualized) use of physical violence. She ridicules patriarchal sexual politics in every scene in which she is endangered.

A more developed example of Tank Girl's feminist critique through humor occurs when she rescues Sam from "Liquid Silver," a sexual club/brothel. Tank Girl first finds a disguise for herself, choosing a parody of the sexy silver costumes worn by the (enslaved) prostitutes. She locates Sam, fleeing from the clutches of a child molester, and tries to complete the rescue and escape with Jet. When Tank Girl is trapped, she holds the club's Madam hostage. The scene is played with some seriousness, for the threat to Sam, Tank Girl, and Jet is real. We see post-feminism in Tank Girl's role as action-adventure hero here. We also see some suggestion of feminism in her subversion of the Liquid Silver costuming (a critique of feminine norms of appearance and behavior) and her scorn for child prostitution. However, the politics quickly turn to slapstick as Tank Girl threatens to snip off the Madam's ridiculously coiffed locks if she does not sing Cole Porter's "Let's Do It." The song and dance number that follows is Busby Berkeley meets Mel Brooks; it is completely juvenile, and "joyfully superfluous" (Felperin 55). The innocence and ridiculousness of Cole Porter's horribly outdated "love" song, coupled with the chorus line of prostitutes (with Tank Girl failing to raise her combat boot-clad legs high or straight enough) is obviously parodic. And, though the dancers are women and not men in drag, the scene seems to be far more about female impersonation than about females.

In addition, the rescue of Sam is completed without the violence we see in the rest of the film, making it akin to the isolated sand shower scene. But this time the exceptional scene challenges (through humor) traditional filmic depictions of the female body and feminine sexuality rather than replicating them. If there is a "female gaze" in film, it must be a self-reflexive, mocking gaze;

a group of idealized femme Liquid Silver beauties stopping their forced sexual duties to sing and dance to a 1930s tune along with clutzy Tank Girl and friends surely helps viewers—if only for a moment as we shake our heads and laugh—to rethink the objectification apparent in the "beauty" of the kickline and the artificial, heterosexist romance of the Hollywood musical.

We can also go further and label this scene a self-conscious feminist representation of feminine excess, not the postfeminist challenge of combat boots via false eyelashes, but the foregrounding and flaunting of femininity as masquerade. Mary Ann Doane, building from the theoretical work of Joan Riviere, argues that "masquerade, in flaunting femininity, holds it at a distance" (235). In Michèle Montreley's words, "the woman uses her own body as a disguise" (quoted in Doane 235), effecting what Doane calls a "defamiliarization of female iconography" (235). In other words, there is an active "using" of the overly and actively feminized body to challenge the male gaze and traditional (voyeuristic, fetishistic) systems of viewing. This emphasis, according to Doane, "carries a threat" of import to feminists attempting to articulate a female gaze (235).

However feminist the musical number may be, though, it is dwarfed in importance by the dominance of postfeminist images in the film. Yet to feminism and even postfeminism is added antifeminism in Tank Girl's unpredictability. Pinsky and Sullivan label her a cross between Pippi Longstocking, Pee Wee Herman, and Sigourney Weaver (in *Aliens*) who "runs around making little explosion noises, like a child" (17). Some moments in the film may invite harsher critique, rendering Tank Girl no endearing preadolescent but "a valley girl rebelling against middle-class parents by shopping in thrift stores" (Felperin 55). Or, worse yet, an "abrasive, hyperactive and mean-spirited Bronx brat" (Romney 35). This less adult but equally traditionally feminized image (the spoiled girl) is important for understanding the tendency of Tank Girl to veer from rock-me dynamo to anarchic brat, to move from postfeminist hero to antifeminist rebel without a cause.

On the one hand, when she kisses Jet, Tank Girl enjoys Jet's discomfort; however, there is purpose in her action. On the other hand, there is no purpose (other than self-absorption) when Tank Girl gets so excited with her new tank that she swings the barrel around wildly and knocks Jet out cold. The scene is played for laughs; yet the slapstick, when read politically, is obviously not about subversive feminist humor. Rather, it is about chaos for chaos's sake, and it challenges any power or integrity the character possesses. Similarly, Tank Girl's decision to enact a parodic dance number during the middle of Sam's rescue could feasibly have resulted in the deaths of Sam, Jet, and Tank Girl herself. Over the course of the film we learn that "[w]hen Tank Girl arrives, chaos erupts" (Pinsky and Sullivan 17). Often the anarchy is channeled into productive if wild acts that support feminist or at least postfeminist goals. However, if her love of chaos sometimes means lives are risked or political goals are put on a backburner to immature or selfish play, so be it.

It is hard not to read Tank Girl's rebelliousness in such problematic moments as a combination of entertainment over politics and antifeminist critique of the feminist-as-humorless stereotype. If we return a final time to the Liquid Silver scene, we see overall that Tank Girl enacts feminist critique of proper feminine (prostitute) behavior and clothing, challenges the artificiality/predictability of the traditional action-adventure hero in a feminist manner by refusing to do violence to the Madam, tosses in a critique of traditional Hollywood romance narrative, and enacts a nearly single-handed postfeminist rescue of Sam. Nevertheless, she also risks everyone's life by insisting upon comedy over rescue, forcing even a hesitant Jet and traumatized Sam to join in the "fun" of the song-and-dance number. To ensure the attention of an audience uninvested in or perhaps openly resistant to feminism (of any variety), the repudiation of traditional femininity throughout this scene is not only tempered by irreverent humor but contradicted by an act of childishness that makes of our action-adventure hero an irresponsible brat. Just as she must be sexualized (in however projected a fashion), so too must she be made occasionally obnoxious—a spoiled, overconfident child who, due to luck, achieves success despite doing stupid things like risking others' lives to make jokes or clobbering her sidekick when she gets overexcited about her armaments.

It is this typical and historic media compromise between feminine and feminist, even between feminine and already highly compromised postfeminist, that causes such pain for me as a feminist viewer. I want to argue that the shower and "Let's Do It" scenes are ruptures in the linear narrative and, hence, subversive. I want to argue that Tank Girl's combination of tight, revealing clothes and heavy makeup with chopped hair and combat boots offers critique of fashion and beauty norms for women. I want to argue that the film does raise a few serious feminist issues and at least offers a strong female lead character. I do know that, watching the film for the first time, I agreed with Pinsky and Sullivan, who claim that it "felt so good that I would definitely recommend it to women who need an outlet for their anger and frustration" (17). However, I must also concur with Pinsky and Sullivan: this is no feminist film. The film's strongest message does truly seem to be "Sexy Women Can Kick Ass, O Indeed!" (17). However, even scarier is that the limited popularity of the film (though it enjoys a modest cult status) may reveal that this weak message still "was too strong for some folks" (17). Independent company Dark Horse Comics, who entered the film industry through participating in the production of *Tank Girl,* was deeply disappointed in the film's lack of commercial success. What is their next filmic excursion? *Barb Wire,* a rock-me/antifeminist action-adventure flick without even the subversive moments of *Tank Girl,* starring *Baywatch*'s T & A queen Pamela Anderson.

I did ultimately enjoy *Tank Girl,* despite its contradictory and problematic politics. Unlike Leslie Felperin, I am not so unhappy with the final product that I feel it necessary simply to "give director Rachel Talalay the benefit of the doubt and assume that the studio forced her to mangle this film" (55). Unlike Hewlett and Martin devotee Jonathan Romney, I do not lament the film as "a textbook example of Hollywood snapping up an interesting property and getting it wrong" (35). However, I do find myself thinking about what active concessions to the compromises of postfeminism and an imagined sexist male audience necessitate in even "strong" media images of women. More purposefulness to Tank Girl's chaos, less rock-me and more feminism, and the film would still not have been what "young women want." But it might have been a little less of what they don't need.

Notes

I am grateful to Chad Crouse for his insightful feedback in regard to this chapter, including his arguments that Tank Girl should be read through the discourse of "lesbian chic" and as an irresponsible child. Thanks also to this anthology's editor, Marleen S. Barr, who has been a source of support and inspiration to me from my graduate school days to the present. And much appreciation goes to Kelli Allen, a graduate assistant at Middle Tennessee State University, who helped me collect material during the early stages of my research into postfeminism and Tank Girl.

1. Interestingly, the marines are all male but for the exception of another chin-up pro, the Latina character Vasquez, whose gender and sexuality are questioned by a white male foil. She is "retrieved" for the heterosexual male gaze through brief acknowledgment within the narrative of her love relationship with a white male marine. Interestingly, he is the marine squad's seemingly least intelligent and least physically attractive member, thus coding Vasquez as accessible and desirable to the "average" male viewer.

2. It must be acknowledged here that the sexualization of the pumped-up body in the 1980s and early 1990s was by no means limited to women's bodies. Arnold Schwarzenegger was the Reagan/Bush era symbol of the sexiness of massive muscles and inspiration for and reflection of the era's steroid craze. The scene from the original *Terminator*

film when Schwarzenegger travels back in time and arrives, completely naked, in the city at night is clearly intentionally sexualized; the camera pauses over his crouched form as he stands to provide a full back shot of his enormously muscled back, huge legs, and tight buttocks.

3. I am grateful to Andy "Sunfrog" Smith for introducing me to this term, intended to challenge the "gay/straight" binary and reach beyond "bisexual." Just as there are many genders, there are many sexualities—particularly in a world with kangaroo people (and even without them).

4. John Fiske makes plain the potential subversiveness of nonrealist narrative through his condemnation of the politics of realism. He explains that realism "is not a matter of any fidelity to an empirical reality, but of the discursive conventions by which and for which a sense of reality is constructed" (21). He concludes that realism is "inevitably reactionary" because "it finally represents the world to us in a way that naturalizes the status quo" (33). Nonrealist narratives, such as that of the disjointed, nonlinear comic book *Tank Girl,* thus provide a potentially subversive textual site. This is far less true of the film, which, although nontraditional in its use of animated interruptions and fantasy elements, does follow a linear plot line.

5. Pinsky and Sullivan argue that Richard's death has even greater significance. They state that killing the only "good male" in the film is part of the text's retaliatory "male degradation scenes" (including Richard's gunpoint strip, the oral sex/neck-breaking scene with the soldiers, Tank Girl and Jet's attempt to get information about a DWP weapons shipment by pretending to photograph unattractive male workers in sexy poses for a "Men of Water and Power" calendar, and the violent wounding of a pedophile) that can be read as challenges to the tradition of female degradation in films. Sullivan concludes that "there was only one redeemable male (human) in the flick, and he got wasted almost instantly. That would piss me off if the reverse had been true (as it usually is!) but here, I was delighted!" In contrast, Pinsky is less optimistic about the implications: "I think the male degradation scenes worked; however, this is only one film and not many people even went to see it so I don't think it outweighs the degradation of women we see on a daily basis" (17).

References

Cloud, Dana L. "Hegemony or Concordance? The Rhetoric of Tokenism in 'Oprah' Winfrey's Rags-to-Riches Biography." *Critical Studies in Mass Communication* 13 (1996), 115-137.

Daly, Meg. "A Positive Image." *Tikkun* (March/April 1996), 63+.

DiMassa, Diane. 1995. *The Revenge of Hothead Paisan, Homocidal Lesbian Terrorist.* San Francisco: Cleis Press.

Doane, Mary Ann. 1992. "Film and the Masquerade: Theorizing the Female Spectator." *Screen* 23.3-4 (1982), 74-87. Rpt. in *The Sexual Subject: A Screen Reader in Sexuality,* eds. John Caughie, Annette Kuhn, Mandy Merck, and Barbara Creed. London: Routledge, 227-243.

Douglas, Susan. 1995. *Where the Girls Are: Growing Up Female with the Mass Media.* New York: Random House.

Dow, Bonnie. 1996. *Prime-Time Feminism: Television, Media Culture, and the Women's Movement Since 1970.* Philadelphia: University of Pennsylvania Press.

Felperin, Leslie. Review of *Tank Girl. Sight and Sound.* July 1995, 54-55.

Fiske, John. 1987. *Television Culture.* New York: Routledge.

France, Kim. "Rock-Me Feminism." *New York.* 3 June 1996, 36-41.

Franzini, L. fR. "Feminism and Women's Sense of Humor." *Sex Roles: A Journal of Research* 35.11-12 (1996), 811-819.

hooks, bell. 1992. "Madonna: Plantation Mistress or Soul Sister?" *Black Looks.* Boston: South End.

Kaminer, Wendy. "Feminism's Third Wave: What Do Young Women Want?" *The New York Times Book Review.* 4 June 1995, 3, 22-23.

Lee, Janet. "Subversive Sitcoms: *Roseanne* as Inspiration for Feminist Resistance." *Women's Studies* 21 (1992), 87-101.

Mulvey, Laura. "Visual Pleasure and Narrative Cinema." *Screen* 16.3 (1975), 6-18. Rpt. in *The Sexual Subject: A Screen Reader in Sexuality,* eds. John Caughie, Annette Kuhn, Mandy Merck, and Barbara Creed. London: Routledge, 1992, 22-34.

Onwurah, Nozi, dir. *And Still I Rise.* Women Make Movies, 1993.

Pinsky, Rachel, and Suzanne Sullivan. Review of *Tank Girl. off our backs* May 1996, 17.

Romney, Jonathan. Review of *Tank Girl. New Statesman and Society.* 23 June 1995, 35.

Rosen, Craig. "'Tank Girl' Set Shoots from Hip." Review of Motion Picture Soundtrack. *Billboard.* 25 March 1995, 10.

Stacey, Judith. "The New Conservative Feminism." *Feminist Studies* 9.3 (Fall 1983), 559-583.

Tank Girl. Trilogy Entertainment Group. United Artists Pictures/MGM. 1995.

Stacey Abbott (essay date March 2006)

SOURCE: Abbott, Stacey. "Final Frontiers: Computer-Generated Imagery and the Science Fiction Film." *Science Fiction Studies* 33, no. 98 (March 2006): 89-108.

[*In the following essay, Abbott investigates the relationship between computer-generated special effects technology and science fiction film, asserting that science fiction films have led to spectacular advances in computer-generated effects.*]

> "There were a lot of concerns about just what these invisibility effects would look like. . . . I knew they were doable, it was just a question of how we would do them—and at the time we had no clue."
>
> Scott E. Anderson. Visual Effects Supervisor on *Hollow Man*

The February 2005 edition of *SFX* magazine produced a list of the "50 Greatest Special Effects" voted upon by their readers. At least thirty of the effects listed came from films that can be categorized as science fiction, demonstrating that ever since George Méliès's *Le Voyage dans la Lune* (1902; *Trip to the Moon*), the sf genre on film has been indelibly linked to special effects. As Geoff King has argued with respect to the contemporary blockbuster, this association with spectacle has often led to accusations of the impoverishment of narrative and depth (2). Robin Wood has described the use of special effects in such sf films as *Star Wars* (1977), *Close Encounters of the Third Kind* (1977), and *E.T.* (1982) as representing "the essence of Wonderland Today," becoming ever more "dazzling, more extravagant, more luxuriously unnecessary" (166).

Recent genre theorists have attempted to rethink this dismissal of the sf film by reconsidering how the genre makes film technology its subject. As Annette Kuhn has argued, the genre is ideally suited to display technological advances and developments through its futuristic narratives. In the sf film, the narrative will often stop for the contemplation of the spectacular special effects being used to represent the depicted world. As Kuhn suggests, "since the films themselves are often about new or imagined future technologies, this must be a perfect example of the medium fitting, if not exactly being, the message" (7). Brooks London, in his discussion of contemporary digital effects, takes the argument further by suggesting that the medium *is* in fact the message and that the emphasis on the spectacle of film technology is enough to make a film science fiction regardless of its narrative content. He calls for a "revisionist discussion that would start by attempting to re-think science-fiction film in film-specific terms, opting variously for epistemologically based or image-based criteria instead of source-based or narrative based assumptions that have so far shaped most discussions of science-fiction film" ("Diegetic" 35).

Furthermore, the relationship between science fiction and special effects (FX) is often mutually dependent since the genre needs special effects to showcase its future worlds and technologies while the imaginative demands of the stories themselves have spearheaded new developments of FX technologies.[1] Films from *Metropolis* (1927) to *Star Wars* (1977), from *The Incredible Shrinking Man* (1957) to *Starship Troopers* (1997) have all forced FX artists to answer the question raised by Scott E. Anderson when making *Hollow Man* (2000): "I knew they [the effects] were doable, it was just a question of how we would do them" (qtd in Shay 108). As Michele Pierson explains, however, that period of synergy between the futuristic visions of science fiction and the futuristic quality of the new special effects is short-lived since the "phantasmagorical projections of the future often only achieve the glamour and allure of the truly novel in that brief moment before the techniques used to bring them to the cinema screen have grown too familiar" (102).

Nowhere has this been more evident than in developments of computer-generated special effects over the last twenty-five years. Science-fiction films from *Alien* (1979) to *The Matrix* (1999) have led the way in developing computer-generated imagery (CGI) and revolutionized digital filmmaking within the American film industry, with each film presenting new challenges for the FX artists to overcome. Furthermore, while effects designers throughout the history of cinema have walked a fine line between technician and artist, magician and inventor, the increasing use of computer technology for special effects has made them seem more like modern scientists than their predecessors. Not only does the hardware and software require the highest level of computer expertise to operate, but the technicians must research, develop, and experiment with the technology in order to achieve the desired effects. In recent years, however, CGI has become increasingly familiar to audiences and domesticated by its use to produce invisible effects such as crowd scenes, color alteration, and weather effects, as well as by its use in television. In addition, new developments have been achieved in recent years for genres such as the epic (*Gladiator* [2000]), disaster (*Titanic* [1997]), and fantasy (*The Lord of the Rings* [2001-03]) genres. Despite this, it is the computer-effects artists who continue to bring the science to these fictions.

There is a long-standing debate within genre studies over what films count as legitimate examples of film sf, as opposed to horror or fantasy, with some critics arguing that there is no legitimate science fiction in the cinema at all. As the films I will be discussing are examples of post-classical cinema and blockbuster productions, with budgets to sustain the expense of computer-generated special effects, they are by their very nature hybrid films. They are produced with the intention of crossing genre boundaries with the hope that this will broaden their appeal to a wide range of audiences and thus secure the level of box office intake that is necessary to make a film a blockbuster.

In this article, I will demonstrate that the use of computer imagery specifically transforms genres such as horror, fantasy, and the martial arts film into a form of hybridized science fiction. I will trace how sf films have contributed to the development of computer-generated effects and then consider how the genre has responded to the domestication of the technology by turning away from brave new worlds to explore the new frontier for CGI, the representation of the body. I will therefore not focus on the spectacular nature of these effects but rather on how the infinite malleability of digital technology has extended our understanding of the "indexicality" of the image (as discussed by Laura Mulvey and Philip Rosen) by challenging and reshaping our conception of the body and its boundaries. While Brooks Landon once predicted a future for science fiction in which the media offers the "realization rather than just the representation of SF narrative" (*The Aesthetics of Ambivalence* xxv), the real developments and applications of computer technologies within film production at the turn of the twenty-first century have increasingly led to a convergence between "realization" and "representation." This convergence is located within this reconception of the body both on-screen and off, as the traditional sf cyborg has escaped the confines of the representational space and entered the real world of film production, where actor and computer technology are increasingly being merged into a new form of digital/human hybrid.[2]

THE DEVELOPMENT OF CGI THROUGH SCIENCE FICTION

A computer-generated image can either be a pre-existing image that has been scanned into a computer or a wholly animated image drawn directly within the computer with specially designed software (Netzley 47). Once in the computer the image can be altered or manipulated to suit the needs of the desired effect, and then later combined with the live-action footage and rescanned back onto film. It has taken twenty-five years of experimentation and development for the CG image to achieve the degree of realism and malleability that we expect from contemporary cinema.

Lev Manovich, in his discussion of the language of new media and computer technology, has, however, demonstrated that realism in the cinema is a complex concept that has had numerous practical applications in the development and application of computer-generated imagery. As he explains, the history of cinema has consistently perpetuated the myth of "capturing" reality through the technology's photographic properties and as a result the history of realism in the cinema is "one of addition," in which each new technology—such as sound, panchromatic stock, and color—is presented as offering enhanced realism to the photographic image and emphasizing just how "unrealistic" previous images were (186).[3] This movement towards increased realism was, he argues, not a linear progression but a process of substitution as certain techniques took priority over others. With developments in CGI, however, the concept of realism takes on new meanings. According to Manovich, "achieving synthetic realism means attaining two goals—the simulation of the codes of traditional cinematography and the simulation of the perceptual properties of real life objects and environments" (191-92). In other words, the computer-generated images must look "real"—i.e., must reproduce the necessary proportions and textures of the original object—but they must also look as if they were filmed with a "real" camera, therefore maintaining certain photographic properties such as motion blurring, depth of focus, and the grain of the film stock. As Manovich argues, "although we normally think that synthetic photographs produced with computer graphics are inferior to real photographs, in fact, they are too perfect. But beyond that we can also say that, paradoxically, they are also too "real" (202). With the increasing implementation of CGI in cinema, the development of the technology required an engagement with a language of "realisms" that acknowledged the individual characteristics of vision and perception. The sf genre, a genre of *imagined* realities, became the locus through which the technology could develop and increasingly attain these realisms.

Initially in the 1970s, computers were used primarily as tools, offering alternatives to traditional methods of effects because they were less expensive. In 1979, Ridley Scott used a computer to create all the images on the bridge's computer terminals on the spaceship *Nostromo* in *Alien*. This was a single effect that could have been achieved by alternative means but the filmmakers realized that it was easier to use a computer. *Star Trek: The Wrath of Khan* (1982) featured one of the earliest entirely computer-generated sequences in a feature film. The Genesis sequence is a simulation of the implementation and effect of a device designed to create new worlds from dead ones, "life from lifelessness." Since the sequence is presented as a computer simulation, the film was able to showcase the spectacle of this new FX technology without concerning itself with issues of realism: the technology, while three-dimensional, still gave the impression of animation. In the same year, Walt Disney Studios released their computer-generated extravaganza *Tron* (1982). Set within a computer game, the film features sixteen minutes of completely computer-generated imagery. It was supposed to contain much more, but due to the prohibitive costs and the limitations of the technology at this time, traditional animation methods were used throughout much of the film to create the look of a computer game. In each of these cases computers were used to reproduce the effects and images supposedly generated within the narrative by computers.

It was the film *The Abyss* (1989) that first managed to use CGI to create an artificial entity that seemed seamlessly to exist within the "real" (represented) world. In this sequence, a tentacle made exclusively from water emerges from the diving pool of an underwater mining installation and explores the rig until finally finding its human residents. The tentacle moves effortlessly through the space and stops to interact with the crew, making gestures and faces, and reflecting back the images that surround it. Robin Baker explains that

> it took ILM [Industrial Light and Magic] six months of intensive work and constant checking with the director on the form and realism required for *The Abyss* before its magnificent pod became a convincing animated object, reflecting the interior of the rig through which it passed. Cameron wanted the surface of the pod to be constantly undulating like the surface of a swimming pool.
>
> (39-40)

ILM's team of special effects technicians took what they had accomplished in *The Abyss* and put it to the more challenging task of developing the new, more sophisticated terminator, the T-1000, in *Terminator 2: Judgement Day* (1991). No longer simply the fusion of flesh and a metal endo-skeleton, the new terminator was supposedly made of liquid metal able to transform from one shape to another. The differences between the two cyborgs capture the shift in FX technology from the industrial special make-up and mechanical effects of the T-800, achieved through prosthetics and animatronics, to the post-industrial digital imaging and computer graphics of the T-1000. As with *The Abyss,* the challenge in using digital effects in *Terminator 2* (*T2*) was to enable the T-1000 effortlessly to blend with the real world and believably to transform from one form to another. While the first terminator was able to mimic voices when necessary, this terminator, played by the actor Robert Patrick, was able to copy any living tissue with which he came into contact as well as transforming parts of his body into simple but deadly weapons. The transformations of Patrick's body were achieved through a combination of digital alterations to previously filmed images (such as when the T-1000 walks through the metal bars of an asylum ward by seeming to dissolve through the metal) and also through computer-generated graphics (such as when the T-1000 emerges from a fiery explosion in a glistening metallic state before returning to his borrowed human appearance). To achieve most of these transformations

> a new software technique called "morph" was used which allows a very smooth transition between one form and another so that it looks continuous, making it impossible to detect where the boundary of one character finishes and the other begins. It was necessary to keep the transition realistic so that when the human actor took over, and T-1000 became the police officer, it appeared convincing. To do this the morph software provides a cross dissolve allowing the key features—nose, eyes, and ears—to stay in the same locations as the transformation takes place.
>
> (Baker 40)

The computer technology proved incredibly malleable at smoothly "morphing" from one live-action image to another, suggesting a seamless and painless transformation. While reminiscent of the optical transformations of the Universal Wolfman films of the 1940s, morphing lends the image an unprecedented degree of realism, as the two images are seamlessly merged at the point of transition. In this case the "more real than real" quality of the CGI significantly enhanced the representation of the T-1000 in his natural, liquid-metal state. Here the shiny and fluid quality of the animation was used to emphasize the futuristic and strange quality of this new form of cyborg. The technology is designed to make the CGI character blend within the live-action footage, while also making him stand out within the fictional world of the narrative.

In addition to making the impossible possible through the photo-realistic quality of these transformations (or, in the case of *The Abyss*, the alien effects), these sequences introduced to the sf film an increased self-awareness of the wonders of this new technology, which has increasingly been built into the texts themselves. As Michele Pierson explains, the films provide a narrative space within which to gaze in awe at the magic of the effect:

> sequences featuring CGI commonly exhibit a mode of spectatorial address that—with its tableau-style framing, longer takes, and strategic intercutting between shots of the computer-generated object and reaction shots of characters—solicits an attentive and even contemplative viewing of the computer-generated image.
>
> (124)

In *The Abyss* the crew of the oil rig stare in wonder at the beauty of the water tentacle, while Sarah Connor freezes in horror as she sees the new terminator walk through the bars that separate it from her and her son in *T2*. The best example of this moment of spectatorial address, however, takes place in Steven Spielberg's *Juras-*

sic Park (1993), the first film to use CG effects to create live creatures rather than aliens or machines. In this film the link between the science-content of the film and the technological effect is clearly established in the first scene to display the CGI dinosaurs. The film tells the story of scientists who have used developments in genetic cloning to clone dinosaurs from dino-dna found in fossilized mosquitoes. The film uses developments in CGI technology to bring the dinosaurs to life on the screen in full view, realistically portrayed in three-dimensional space. The moment when palaeontologists Alan Grant and Elly Saddler arrive on the island and see their first "real" dinosaur is designed to instruct the audience in how to respond to this wondrous sight. The dinosaurs are withheld for the first forty seconds of the scene and instead we see repeated shots of Alan and Elly turning, looking up, and staring in wonder at what is out frame. The emphasis in these shots is on the amazement on their faces, enhanced by the camera moving into close-ups of each of them as they look beyond the camera.

That we don't simply cut to the scientists' points of view, but rather to a long shot of the dinosaurs with the human characters in the frame, demonstrates that the wonder of the moment is not simply the narrative revelation of living dinosaurs but the amazing special effects that have produced a realistic, three-dimensional, computer-generated image of a dinosaur smoothly integrated into the live-action shot of the actors. This is summed up by Alan's remark as he looks up and says in astonishment, "that's a dinosaur." While he is shocked to find himself standing next to a living fossil, the audience is equally shocked to see *him* standing next to such a creature. This is a classic moment of the effect and the narrative merging into one spectacular gestalt. While the story goes on to criticize the recklessness of modern science's creation of dinosaurs, the film allows the audience to enjoy the wonder and thrills associated with this recklessness. This film, however, demonstrates another key element of modern special effects, which is the short-lived nature of that wonder at the novel and the spectacular. While FX artists continued to outdo the realism of the dinosaur effects in the film's two sequels, *The Lost World: Jurassic Park* (1997) and *Jurassic Park 3* (2001), that first moment of seeing a dinosaur achieved with such realism and romanticism can never be repeated.

While *Jurassic Park* challenged FX artists to create realistic living creatures, *The Matrix* (1999) gave them the opportunity to experiment with computerized methods to manipulate and control the representation of space and time. The film tells a dystopian narrative in which the world as we know it is revealed to be a virtual reality (the Matrix) maintained by a computer program, while the real world is an apocalyptic landscape in which the last free humans are at war with the machines they have created. To construct these two distinct realities, FX technicians created numerous physical and digital effects, but where the film broke new ground was in its representation of the virtual world in which motion can be controlled by the mind.

When in the Matrix, the hero Neo and his fellow freedom fighters have to be able to defy the laws of nature. To achieve this, visual effects supervisor John Gaeta invented bullet-time, a form of virtual camera technology. Bullet time is created through filming an actor at normal speed and scanning the footage into a computer so the director and FX supervisors can work out the digital camera movement for the scene. Then a series of laser-calibrated still cameras are placed in the studio along the line of the planned camera movement and the action is photographed by each of the still cameras, scanned into the computer, and animated at the required speed (Netzley 142-43). In this manner the image can be slowed down or sped up in the computer to suggest that the characters are able to defy the laws of physics, while the camera "appears to move in ways that a physical camera could not" (John Gaeta, qtd. in Fordham, "Neo-Realism" 85). The result of their experiments with this new virtual technology were the impressive martial arts sequences in which Neo bends the laws of nature to his will as he slows down time, flies through the air and dodges bullets.

While many critics praised the film for its cunning combination of spectacular action with a metaphysical narrative exploring the dehumanizing threat of technology, it was ultimately upon the quality and innovation of the special effects that the reviews focused. Nicola Godwin points out that "what makes it [*The Matrix*] extraordinary are the sheer volume of those effects, and the efforts of its creators to generate entirely new ones" (10), while Jonathan Romney argues that what distinguishes the effects is not simply the spectacle but how they both suggest and subvert notions of illusion and reality ("Cause" 38-39). Even Alexander Walker, who bemoans what he sees as the film's lack of meaning, gives credit to the film's "visual and visceral exhibitionism"—so much so that while he admits to being impressed, he suggests that the film's success will lead to commercial imitation (29). Walker was quite right: these effects were immediately parodied and copied by other genre films without the sf narrative, including *Scary Movie* (2000), *Charlie's Angels* (2000), and even the television series *Angel* (1999-2004). *Shrek* (2001) further parodies *The Matrix* by mimicking its effects through computer animation when Princess Fiona fights off her attackers, freezing in mid-air as the virtual camera swivels around the action before she delivers her final kicks. The effect thus changed from being cutting-edge technology to being overly familiar and the subject of humorous pastiche.

The success of *The Matrix* did, however, raise the standard for what was expected of the film's sequels, *The Matrix Reloaded* (2003) and *The Matrix Revolutions* (2003). The filmmakers and their effects teams faced the challenge of exceeding their previous achievements. Over 2000 visual effects were planned across the two films, drastically exceeding the 400 effects shots in the original (Fordham, "Neo-Realism" 85). Yet despite the technical virtuosity of both sequels, they did not generate the same level of excitement. While critics who both liked and disliked *The Matrix* acknowledged the significance of the film's technical achievements, the reviewers' response to the sequels suggests that this time the effects were not enough. James Veriere points out that since "so many films have already copied the original . . . the sequel [*The Matrix Reloaded*] seems dated" (qtd in Gibbons 11), while Ty Burr argues that "the thrill isn't gone from the sequel, but the surprise is" (qtd in Gibbons 11). More than simply suffering from over-familiarity to the technology, some reviews expressed weariness at the efforts to exceed the effects of the previous film. Philip Strick suggests that while the action scenes in *The Matrix Reloaded* are "enthralling to watch for their technical ingenuity[, they] cannot quite prevent a certain fatigue by the time the Architect reveals it has all happened five times already" (53). Kate Stables describes the martial arts scenes in *The Matrix Revolutions* as being "disconcertingly bloated with CGI" (55). In this case the special effects could not achieve the excitement and tension that were such an indelible part of *The Matrix*.

Between the release of *The Matrix* in 1999 and its sequels in 2003, the public excitement surrounding computer FX had moved to fantasy with the release of Peter Jackson's *The Lord of the Rings* trilogy (2001-2003). And it wasn't the spectacle of the Mines of Moria or the vast Orc armies fighting in the Battle at Helm's Deep that captured the most public and critical attention, but rather the sadly emaciated and shrivelled body of Gollum, the former ring-bearer. The superhuman antics of Neo flying around the world and fighting a hundred Agent Smiths were no match for the pathos of a digitally-created Gollum diving for fish while singing a song in the pond of Osgiliath.

SCIENCE FICTION AND THE CG-BODY

With computer-generated effects increasingly being used by other genres to convey different forms of spectacle, the sf film has turned toward its own limitations to form the subject of its fictions, especially in terms of the representation and manipulation of the body. Barry Keith Grant argues that the body is not conventionally the source of inspiration for science fiction, which is generally pre-occupied with the mind and its cognitive wonders, but is instead the terrain of the horror genre (20). Furthermore, Alex Proyas, director of *I, Robot*

(2004), claims that "CG is often unconvincing when it comes to creating flesh and blood creatures," suggesting that the representation of the body has been one of the most difficult challenges facing computer FX artists (qtd in Duncan 96). While the smooth and sleek surfaces of the water tentacle or the T-1000 are easily created through computer imaging, natural mannerisms and the textured features of human skin have been most difficult to recreate realistically.

The challenge to overcome these limitations has fueled recent advances in computer-generated images, once again demonstrating an interdependent relationship between FX technology and science fiction. Sf films such as *AI* (2001), *Minority Report* (2002), and *I, Robot* have turned their futuristic narratives away from outer space and toward the imbrication of humanity and technology. This is not a new priority within science fiction, of course. Films such as *Metropolis, Star Trek: The Motion Picture* (1979), *Alien* (1979), *The Terminator* (1984), and *Total Recall* (1990) have previously engaged with these themes; *Minority Report* and *I, Robot*, both loosely based on classic sf stories by Philip K. Dick and Isaac Asimov respectively, demonstrate that these are long-standing concerns of the sf literary genre. The use of computer-generated technologies within these films, however, has relocated the emphasis from society to the body itself.

Digital effects are able to manipulate the representation of the body in such a way that they visually embody the fusion of human tissue with technological hardware, enabling the human body to be distorted beyond its physical capabilities. Mary Ann Doane has suggested that traditionally the body has been represented as finite and absolute, a simple empirical fact (182). This reading of the body is supported by contemporary obsessions in popular culture with forensic pathology, as demonstrated by the television series *CSI* (2000-present), the serial killer films *Silence of the Lambs* (1991) and *Seven* (1995), and the novels of Patricia Cornwell, all of which present the corpse as a source of physical evidence. As Maria Angel argues, the modern view of anatomy is to see the "opened body replac[ing] the opened book as the source of anatomical knowledge" (29). She explains that "this modern fascination with the contortions and folds of things, their hidden depths and structures, corresponds to an epistemological obsession with hidden interiors in which knowledge is sought and from which knowledge can be withdrawn" (35).

In the 1980s the horror genre exploited contemporary anxieties about maintaining the sanctity of the body by using special make-up effects to rupture its boundaries in such films as *Alien, An American Werewolf in London* (1981), *The Thing* (1982), and *The Fly* (1986), and to represent the body as an enigma full of unanswered questions about its constitution and health rather than as an empirical resource. Today science fiction film uses digital technology not to rupture the boundaries of the body but rather to stretch and extend the body beyond its usual limits. It also serves to make the invisible visible. The television series *CSI*, which treats the body as a source of evidence, uses digital technology to create a virtual penetration of the skin's surface to envision the results of trauma on the internal organs. Known as the "CSI Shot," these effects are part of the series' strategy for visual exposition. According to associate producer Brad Tenenbaum, "[we need to] explain what the bullet does when it strikes someone's body. We show and tell at the same time" (qtd in Hamit 101). This effect, originated for *Three Kings* (1999) but made familiar by *CSI*, has since been borrowed and parodied in the action film *Charlie's Angels: Full Throttle* (2003). Even the vampire-vs.-werewolf movie *Underworld* (2003) uses the same effect to show the transformation of man into werewolf from the inside as bones and tissue shift and reshape themselves. *Blade Trinity* (2004) uses the effect to show the entry of a virus into Dracula's blood system: the virtual camera follows the virus as it races toward his heart and then, once mixed with his blood, as it exits his body and circulates through the air, infecting all of the other vampires.

Hollow Man, Paul Verhoeven's contemporary version of *The Invisible Man* (1933), does more than simply offer an internal glimpse of the body, but uses the process of making a man invisible to reveal its inner workings and mechanics, layer by layer, as the character Sebastian Caine is made to disappear. When approaching the film, the director and his team of visual-effects artists wanted to present this process as it had never been seen before and without giving in to the gimmicks of earlier films. This meant that they were required to push the boundaries of computer effects, mirroring the efforts of the on-screen team of scientists—each trying to find a way to make a man invisible. The analogy between the film scientists and their effects technicians is strengthened by the fact that the technicians were required to study anatomy, analyze artistic and medical illustrations, and even witness human dissections in order to understand every layer of the body and its function (Shay 108). Furthermore, in order to create their computer-generated version of Sebastian, they had to study, measure, scan, photograph, and motion-test the actor Kevin Bacon, in order to use his body as "reference data" upon which to base their CGI Sebastian during the various stages of his dissolution (Shay 112). The result was a spectacular transformation: as the serum begins to take effect, Sebastian's body goes into convulsions as portions of his skin seemingly burn away, revealing the muscles and veins beneath; then, as he continues to contort and strain, his muscles and ligaments fade, revealing the body's organs and then eventually its skeleton before it finally fades into nothingness. The convulsions not only convey the intense physicality of the process but also provide an opportunity for the camera to explore his body in motion from every angle. Through digital technology the threshold of the body can now be crossed to gain access to the anatomical mysteries hidden within.

Digital technology is, however, not only used to traverse bodily boundaries but to extend and distort them. What is unsettling about the new technology is the manner in which it can take an indexical image and effortlessly transform and reshape it in ways far beyond the capabilities of photographic manipulation. Indexicality, a subject addressed in the works of André Bazin, Roland Barthes, and more recently Laura Mulvey, is a sign produced by "the 'thing' it represents" such as a fingerprint, a shadow or a photograph (Mulvey, "Index" 141). While recognizing to varying degrees that the photographic image can be manipulated, each of these theorists sees in the photograph both a record of the subject being photographed (what Mulvey calls its "here and now-ness") and the moment the photo was taken suspended in time, its "there and then-ness" ("Death"). As Mulvey explains, "when rays of light inscribe an object's image onto photosensitive paper at a particular moment, they record the object's present but they also inscribe that moment of time, henceforth suspended" ("Index" 142).

Digital technology, however, does not necessarily require a pro-filmic referent; it can be a sign that bears no physical relationship to the "thing" it represents and, as a result, is often interpreted as being opposed to indexicality. As Philip Rosen points out, however, "digital information and images can [and often do] have indexical origins, the digital often appropriates or conveys indexical images, and it is common for the digital image to retain compositional forms associated with indexicality"—either an indexical image scanned into the computer or the recorded data that is subsequently interpreted by the computer and presented as an image (314). What this does is introduce to the indexical image the "infinite manipulability" that is available within the digital domain, as Jonathan Romney explains:

> Rather than being a simple "preservation" of life, digital imagery aspires to be something more—its crystallisation, its liquefaction. It has the mystique of an alchemical process in which all matter, transmogrified through the medium of light, can become other matter in which flesh becomes unstable, or passes through various liquid, metallic or crystalline avatars. Digital imagery may as a rule incline to hyper-realism, but to hyper-realism at its most unstable. Any form, however complete, can morph into another; there's no reason why the most convincingly solid object, or indeed the whole screen, shouldn't suddenly dissolve into a shower of its constituent pixels.
>
> ("Million" 210)

According to Mulvey, "the cinema literally transforms the living human body into its inorganic replica. Once projected, these static images then became animated, reproducing the living actions once recorded by the camera" ("Death"). Digital technology, however, creates something like-but-more-than its indexical referent, released from this suspension in time. When applied to the human frame, this technology offers the potential for a completely new representation that challenges the conventional perception of the body as absolute and finite and the photographic image of the body as fixed. Where photography and cinematography can be seen as creating ghosts, images of the dead trapped in time, digital technology creates cyborgs, images that are a combination of their living referent and the technology that has reinterpreted them, no longer forced to repeat their motions as recorded but instead programmed to perform entirely new functions. The cinema has therefore been able to use the technology to redefine our perception of the body for the cyber-age and to create a new form of science fiction. Numerous sf films in recent years have offered fresh visions of the body, altered both internally and externally by its relationship to technology and conveyed through the processes of digital FX, creating cinematic cyborgs.

Donna Haraway has famously defined the cyborg as "a hybrid of machine and organism, a creature of social reality as well as a creature of fiction"; the cyborg in fiction, she argues, serves to map "our social and bodily reality" (158). Hassan Melehy further argues that the cyborg provides, "in the destabilization of the organic structure of the human being, a site for different sorts of production, reproduction, and transformation that strongly challenge the age-old notion of the human as both creator and procreator" (315). By these definitions cyborgs represent more than simply the fusion of flesh and metal; they offer a space in which the interdependence of humanity and technology can be explored and, more significantly, deconstructed. The cyborg body acts as a microcosm for the ways in which humanity is, as Jennifer González suggests, "caught in the process of transformation" as it is constantly being reinvented through technology (540). Furthermore, her argument that "photomontage has served as a particularly appropriate medium for the visual exploration of cyborgs" since "[i]t allows apparently 'real' or at least indexically grounded representations of body parts, objects and spaces to be rearranged and to function as fantastic environments or corporal mutations" (544), equally applies to CG imagery, which can also take an indexical image and reshape it.

In *Minority Report,* for instance, digital technology is used to represent a technological connection between humanity and its environment through the integration of a range of complex digital imagery with live-action footage. Set in the near future, the film tells the story of cybernetic psychics whose predictions of murder are recorded and analyzed by police officers attempting to prevent the crime. The process of analyzing their visions—known as "scrubbing" and based on MIT predictions for a future of "global graphic language and gestural recognition" (Fordham, "Future" 41)—involves the police officer breaking down the images into elements and analyzing and manipulating them individually on transparent screens through precise hand movements. This effect was achieved through the production of seventy layers of computer-generated images, each being made to move independently and seemingly in response to Tom Cruise's well choreographed gestures. Here the process of police investigation has been reduced to a form of computerized image analysis that relies on the investigator's physical attunement to the technology. Furthermore, society's dependence on computer technology, from grocery store scanners to the Internet, is taken to its logical extreme by having each member of society hooked into a computerized system that reads identity through retina scans that serve as identity cards and security passes, as well as facilitating direct advertising. Everywhere they go, the inhabitants of this world are bombarded by holographic commercials, similar to online pop-up ads, which respond to retina scans with personalized promotions. These promotions are computer-generated images inserted to create a panoramic mise-en-scène, demonstrating how the over-stimulation of the information age has spilled over from the electronic screen into everyday life, creating a thoroughly cybernetic society.

While *Minority Report* uses CGI to present a futuristic world based on human and machine hybridity, other films use the digital manipulation of photographic images of the human body to explore the physicality of cyborgs. Steven Spielberg's *AI,* a film about a world split between Organics and Mechas (human and machines), features numerous sequences in which images of humanity are undermined by their technological manipulation. Originally developed by Stanley Kubrick (who debated for years over whether CGI or puppetry would be better suited to create the film's main character, a robot boy named David), the film was taken over by Steven Spielberg, who decided to use a real child actor combined with technological enhancements to make him seem more robotic (Fordham, "Mecha" 70). This mixture of human actor with computerized FX enabled the technicians to showcase the mechanization of the body and to deconstruct digitally what it means to be human.

For instance, David quite humanly responds to childish taunting that he is only a robot and so cannot eat by stuffing his mouth full of spinach, resulting in a malfunction. The flesh on the left side of his face begins to droop, revealing the mechanism beneath. This effect was achieved by scanning the image of the actor's face into a computer so that the skin around his eye and mouth could be digitally warped, while creating a synthetic facial structure within the computer that was applied to the image of the actor's face. There are numerous such instances within the film that deliberately highlight the breakdown of the real human form to reveal the mechanisms within. The film begins with a demonstration of state-of-the-art robotics, showing the face of a woman being opened up to reveal internal machinery. Here the indexical image of the actor is digitally altered to make it appear to crank up like a "garage door" (Scott Farrar, qtd in Fordham, "Mecha" 69). Later, David comes across a group of robots scrounging through a junkyard looking for replacements parts. These robots are a motley crew of decimated androids created through a combination of make-up, animatronics, and digital effects. The most notable digital effects show robots that are missing substantial chunks of their flesh, revealing only the mechanics beneath; one robot has had the entire left side of his face stripped down to its most basic mechanical elements, while another has been left with only her faceplate. From the front she looks normal, but when she turns to the side we see only the remnants of an internal mechanism and what remains of her ponytail—the substance of the human head has been digitally erased. The incompleteness of the bodies in this sequence undermines the conception of the human as physically whole and presents a new form of existence that is not only a collage of flesh and metal but also a curious mix of hybrid mechanical parts.

In Robert Zemeckis's *Contact* (1997), the cyborg does not exist within the narrative but rather is a product of the film's production. The CGI here is used to question human perception by digitally altering or enhancing virtually every shot, including the image of the actress Jodie Foster, in order to evoke her character's perceptual experience of traveling through space (Craig 162). Initially, as Ellie Arroway (Foster) begins her journey to the Vega star system, the lights and colors of space are digitally reflected onto the contours of her face. As the journey accelerates, the dislocation of time and space caused by such speeds is shown through the appearance of a ghostly echo of her face that emerges and stretches beyond the boundaries of her body. Later, as she looks out at a celestial event, her image is digitally altered to create a surreal ripple effect, as if her countenance were being sculpted and reformed before the camera. The audience is looking at an image of the actress reinterpreted through computer technology. The creation of such an effect suggests a genuine fusion between the human actor and digital technology to produce an on-screen cyborg.

The increasing presence of such cyborgs within popular cinema has gradually transformed other genres into a curious hybrid of the sf film. The bodies of actors can now be altered, extended, or made to perform in ways that defy the laws of nature, fusing the body with film-making technologies. One genre that has been transformed is the martial arts film, particularly the kung-fu movie. According to Leon Hunt, the genre has traditionally been obsessed with issues of authenticity and the performing body, emphasizing the actual skills of such artists as Bruce Lee and Jackie Chan (22). With the advent of new technologies, however, not only are actors such as Keanu Reeves, Carrie-Anne Moss, Drew Barrymore, and Cameron Diaz able to perform kung fu on-screen, they are able to transcend the limitations of the performing body and do the impossible. In *The Matrix*, Trinity is able to defy gravity and hover in the air before delivering her fatal kicks, because actress Carrie-Anne Moss was filmed performing the real-time kicks through the process of bullet time, which slowed her movements down. This technological intervention, an extension of existing practices of wirework and cinematic editing, transforms the discourse of the genre away from the "real performing body" to the "hyper-real" performing body. As Leon Hunt argues, "martial arts films have had to respond to this logic, where the 'real' has been refashioned by hypermedia" (187).

It is not that the fight scenes are not real (in fact, most of these films emphasize that the actors have been specially trained in martial arts and perform all their own stunts), but rather that they are technologically enhanced. This is best demonstrated in the American films of "real" martial artist Jet Li (*Romeo Must Die* [2000], *Kiss of the Dragon* [2001], *The One* [2001]), who has fully embraced the technologies through which his real skill is presented hyperbolically on screen. For instance, in the sf film *The One*—a futuristic narrative about parallel universes and a character's desire to destroy his alternate selves in order to absorb their energy—Li's strength, speed, and agility are enhanced exponentially with each life his character absorbs. This is represented through computer-generated manipulation to extend his real body movements beyond his natural abilities. In a confrontation with the police, his leaps defy gravity, his kicks stretch beyond his body span, and his agility enables him to twist and bend beyond his limits. Through this technological mediation, the martial arts film has been transformed into a hybrid sf film both narratively and aesthetically.

In the *Blade* trilogy (*Blade* [1998], *Blade II* [2002], *Blade Trinity* [2004]), computer-generated effects are used to transform the vampire genre by portraying the extension of the vampire body beyond its most basic element, the reanimated corpse, into a new form of being that seems less mystical than quasi-scientific. While not conventionally science fiction, the *Blade* films relocate the vampire into a contemporary world where vampirism is no longer a product of folklore and superstition. John Jordan argues that Blade, a half-vampire/half-human who uses modern technology to hunt vampires

and a scientifically-developed serum to suppress his own bloodlust, embodies the modern cyborg. He "represent[s] a mystical figure surrounded internally and externally by science. Even Blade's name refers both to him as a person and to his signature weapon—a specially crafted sword he carries on his back—blurring the boundary where the body ends and the weapon begins" (10). Throughout the films, however, the vampires are themselves presented as products and/or users of science and technology. They are variously described as a virus, disease, genetic mutation, experiment, or genetically engineered super-race. The weapons that destroy them are no longer religious artifacts like the crucifix, holy water, or holy communion, but silver-nitrate bullets, ultra-violet lamps, grenades, bombs, an anticoagulant super-agent, and a biological weapon called "Daystar." The vampires themselves use science and technology: in *Blade*, Deacon Frost uses a computer program to decrypt an ancient vampire prophecy, while in *Blade 2*, a superior "Reaper" strain of vampires, genetically engineered to transcend traditional undead weaknesses, turns on its creators. Finally, in *Blade Trinity* old and new vampire mythologies merge when a group of contemporary vampires locate the whereabouts of the super vampire, Drake (Dracula), whose DNA they want to study in order to improve their own genetic constitution.

This reconception of the vampires through the language of biological science is enhanced by their visual reinvention through computer-generated effects. In each film, CG effects are used to embody the vampires' attempts to extend the limits of their bodies. In *Blade*, Deacon Frost uses an elaborate ritual to invoke a vampire deity, La Magra the Blood God. While the ritual is mystical in origin, its effect is achieved through computer-generated imagery: Frost is transformed into La Magra, but not on the surface; he still looks like Frost, but internally he has changed, as becomes apparent when Blade bisects him with his sword. Instead of bursting into dust like every vampire before him, Frost's blood corpuscles and tissue reshape themselves in one fluid motion. Frost is no longer confined by the limitations and boundaries of his body but rather has been redefined by the endless computational possibilities of CGI. In *Blade 2*, Nomak, patient-zero of the Reaper strain, is stronger, faster, and more agile than traditional vampires, while also possessing a more powerful bite and an augmented bone structure that protects his heart from being staked. Like Blade, Nomak has been redefined both internally and externally by technoscience. Nomak's cyborg nature is conveyed through digital technology that creates exaggerated and "hyper-real" forms of movement, such as crawling up walls, leaping across rooms, and moving at accelerated speeds, all of which would be impossible without the use of CGI to digitally manipulate the movements of the actor.

In *Blade Trinity,* CGI is used to depict Drake, a genetically purified vampire who, much like the T-1000 in *Terminator 2,* is able to transform himself into anyone with whom he comes into contact, an effect achieved through morphing one image into the next. His vampiric form itself appears to be cybernetic in that his red, scale-like flesh is stretched around a kind of organic body armor; morphing technology depicts his vampire face concealed beneath his human visage, pushing out from within. Like the shot of Jodie Foster in *Contact,* Drake's face is physically reinterpreted by the technology, but in this case to portray the character as a cybernetic fusion of human and monster, flesh and technology.

While these films begin with the indexical image of an actor manipulated through technology, more recent films have taken that fusion one step further by digitally recording and translating the human performance into digital code and recreating the performance within the computer. Donna Haraway argues that communications systems and biotechnologies have made all of humanity into cyborgs, translating "our own bodies" into code (mathematical, genetic, etc.) (107). This translation of humanity into code is precisely what is achieved when the specifics of the human form are digitally recorded through motion capture to create an "artificial" animated human in the computer. The most complex version of this cinematic cyborg was used to create Gollum for the *Lord of the Rings* trilogy. The way this character is described in the novel—physically twisted, emaciated, wretched, walking on all fours, and crawling up and down cliff faces—made it impossible to achieve with a human actor, and yet the importance of the character meant that it needed to be more than a photorealistic CG creation. It needed to give a genuine dramatic performance. As a result, the team developed the most sophisticated combination of CG animation, motion capture, rotoscoping, and actor performance yet to be achieved in cinema.

Originally conceived as CG animation (i.e., designed purely within the computer), with actor Andy Serkis providing the voice, it was Serkis's intensely physical performance while recording the dialogue—complete with facial expressions, hand gestures, and body motions—that made Jackson realize that the actor could provide so much more than a voice. It was decided that Serkis would be the physical model for Gollum in three key ways. He would be present on set to perform as Gollum with the other actors, to provide an animation reference for the animators as they modelled their own 3-D creature. In cases where Serkis's performance achieved the precise intention for the scene, animators also superimposed the CG Gollum over the actor and matched his movements precisely, then painted Serkis out of the scene. Finally, motion capture was used to translate Serkis's body into digital code to recreate his movements in the computer. This was achieved by photographing the actor wearing a specially designed suit with dots that matched up with the joints of his body; special cameras "gather[ed] the electronic data that is reflecting off of these little points" (Jackson, qtd in "Taming"). According to Remington Scott (Motion Capture Supervisor), this arrangement enabled the FX crew to create a three-dimensional representation of Serkis's movements in the digital world, "capturing the essence of Andy" (Scott, qtd in *Taming*).

The significance of these layers of techniques used to create Gollum is the degree to which the actor/character truly reflects a cyborg existence. The character is not only a fusion of flesh and machine (Serkis and the computer-animated Gollum), but the expression of a range of representational technologies. Furthermore, Gollum's cyborg nature has been absolutely key to how the character, and its technological creation, has been received by critics and the public, who have praised both the technology and the performance. Anthony Quinn claims that Gollum lends the film "a psychological edge" (5), while Oliver Pool asks "Can Gollum Get the Precious Oscar Nod?" Elijah Wood, star of *The Lord of the Rings* trilogy, sums up the overall response to this technical accomplishment:

> a lot of people would see it [Gollum] as this amazing digital achievement, but I know that there was so much more behind that. I mean obviously it is an incredible digital achievement and Weta's work is some of the best I've ever seen, but it is also Andy because emotionally you invest because of the performance.
>
> (Wood, qtd in "Taming")

Serkis, who has enjoyed star treatment around the world thanks to a role in which he does not appear on-screen, recognizes the fusion of actor and technology in the realistic creation of his character. "I am so in awe of what the animators have done really," he says; "they have been able to interpret my performance and give it that level of photorealism and reality" (Serkis, qtd in "Taming"). So while *The Lord of the Rings* trilogy is an epic of the fantasy genre, it is also a hybridized form of science fiction due to the central role played by this hyper-real cinematic cyborg.

Conclusion

In the late 1980s and early 1990s, as computer technology was developing in leaps and bounds, there was an increasing concern (or aspiration) that the technology would eventually be so sophisticated as to make actors obsolete, replacing them with computer-generated performers (see Landon, *Aesthetics* 154). The technological developments as outlined above have, however, demonstrated that the situation is becoming more complex than this simple replacement. Actors are not obsolete but are increasingly called upon to interact with FX technology, either by performing in soundstage environments destined to be supplanted by computer-generated virtual worlds—as in *Sky Captain and the World of Tomorrow* (2004), *Sin City* (2005), and the recent *Star Wars* films (*The Phantom Menace* [1999], *Attack of the Clones* [2002], and *Revenge of the Sith* [2005])—or, more significantly, by having their performances technologically mediated through an enhancement of their physical bodies or through the creation of actor/computer cyborgs (e.g., Gollum or, more recently, the robots in *I, Robot* and the vampire brides and Mr. Hyde in *Van Helsing* [2004]). As Lev Manovich argues:

> Live-action footage is now only raw material to be manipulated by hand—animated, combined with 3-D computer generated scenes, and painted over. The final images are constructed manually from different elements, and all the elements are either created entirely from scratch or modified by hand.

(302)

As a result of this mediation, film genres have become increasingly hybridized as the new technology facilitates a rethinking of the body and transforms genres such as horror, martial arts, and fantasy into a form of science fiction.[4] The interdependence of humanity and technology is seen not only in the stories projected on the screen but in the production process itself, with its creation of ever more elaborate CGI cyborgs. The very techniques of filmmaking are increasingly the science fiction of today.

Notes

1. Lev Manovich notes that the special-effects wing of Lucasfilm, Ltd, Industrial Light and Magic, "hired the best computer scientists in the field to produce animations for special effects." As a result, "research for the effects in such films as *Start Trek II: The Wrath of Khan* and *Return of the Jedi* led to the development of important algorithms that became widely used" (194).

2. A second form of synergy between "representation" and "realization" is of course between film and video/computer games and theme park rides. In games, one is offered "the opportunity to enter into the world of a favourite movie, to repeat the actions of its heroes or to linger and explore areas passed over too rapidly on screen" (King and Krzywinska 91), while in theme park rides, one is given the "illusion of participation" (92). The distinctions between these media have been blurred by the computer-generated effects used to create the seamless fantasy world of the film, the game, and the ride.

3. That the notion of "capturing" reality, which has underscored much of the discussion of realism in the cinema, is a "myth" should be mentioned as

the cinema has a long history, pre-CGI, of constructing an image of realism through cinematic and optical techniques, including dissolves, optical printing, rear projection, model work, blue screen, editing, animation, and sound effects. Any discussion of CGI needs to be placed within this historical context, for as Manovich explains, CGI has in many ways simply relocated these techniques from the margins of filmmaking to the center of the industrial practice (300). The sf genre did contribute to this re-centering of the technology.

4. In fact, with the technology available, no genre remains untouched. See the use of computer-generated technology in the small-town family melodrama *Pleasantville* (1998); the Shakespeare adaptation *Titus* (1999); the musicals *O Brother, Where Art Thou?* (2000), *Moulin Rouge* (2001), and *Phantom of the Opera* (2004); and the comic superhero films *X-Men* (2000), *Spider-Man* (2002), and *The Fantastic Four* (2005).

Works Cited

Angel, Maria. "Physiology and Fabrication: The Art of Making Visible." *Images of the Corpse: From the Renaissance to Cyberspace.* Ed. Elizabeth Klaver. Madison: U Wisconsin P, 2004. 16-38.

Baker, Robin. "Computer Technology and Special Effects in Contemporary Cinema." *Future Visions: New Technologies of the Screen.* Ed. Philip Hayward and Tana Wollen. London: British Film Institute, 1993. 31-45.

Craig, J. Robert. "Establishing New Boundaries for Special Effects: Robert Zemeckis's *Contact* and Computer-Generated Imagery." *Journal of Popular Film and Television* 28.4 (Winter 2001): 158-65.

Doane, Mary Ann. "Technophilia: Technology, Representation and the Feminine." *Liquid Metal: The Science Fiction Film Reader.* Ed. Sean Redmond. London: Wallflower, 2004. 182-90.

Duncan, Jody. "Ghosts in the Machine." *Cinefex* 99 (October 2004): 95-118, 126.

"The 50 Greatest Special Effects Ever!" *SFX* February 2005: 42-55.

Fordham, Joe. "Mecha Odyssey." *Cinefex* 87 (October 2001): 62-93.

———. "Future Reality." *Cinefex* 91 (October 2002): 36-77.

———. "Neo-Realism," *Cinefex* 95 (October 2003): 82-127.

Gibbons, Fiachra. "Matrix Makers Declare." *The Guardian* (May 16, 2003): 11.

Godwin, Nicola. "In Effect, Anything but a Conventional Blockbuster." *Daily Telegraph* (June 3, 1999): 10-11.

González, Jennifer. "Envisioning Cyborg Bodies: Notes from Current Research." *The Cyberculture Reader.* Ed. David Bell and Barbara M. Kennedy. New York: Routledge, 2000. 540-51.

Grant, Barry Keith. "'Sensuous Elaboration': Reason and the Visible in the Science-Fiction Film." *Alien Zone II: The Spaces of Science Fiction Cinema.* Ed. Annette Kuhn. New York: Verso, 1999. 16-30.

Hamit, Francis. "The *CSI* Shot." *Emmy* 24.3 (June 2002): 101.

Haraway, Donna J. "A Manifesto for Cyborgs: Science, Technology and Socialist Feminism in the 1980s." 1985. *Liquid Metal: The Science Fiction Film Reader.* Ed. Sean Redmond. London: Wallflower, 2004. 158-81.

Hunt, Leon. *Kung Fu Cult Masters: From Bruce Lee to Crouching Tiger.* London: Wallflower, 2003.

Jordan, John J. "Vampire Cyborgs and Scientific Imperialism." *Journal of Popular Film and Television* 27.2 (Summer 1999): 4-15.

King, Geoff. *Spectacular Narratives: Hollywood in the Age of the Blockbuster.* New York: I.B. Tauris, 2000.

———, and Tanya Krzywinska. *Science Fiction Cinema: From Outerspace to Cyberspace.* London: Wallflower, 2000.

Kuhn, Annette. "Cultural Theory and Science Fiction Cinema." *Alien Zone.* Ed. Annette Kuhn. London: Verso, 1990. 1-12.

Landon, Brooks. *The Aesthetics of Ambivalence: Rethinking Science Fiction Film in the Age of Electronic (Re)Production.* London: Greenwood, 1992.

———. "Diegetic or Digital? The Convergence of Science-Fiction Literature and Science-Fiction Film in Hypermedia." *Alien Zone II: The Spaces of Science-Fiction Cinema.* Ed. Annette Kuhn. New York: Verso, 1999. 31-49.

Melchy, Hassan. "Bodies Without Organs: Cyborg Cinema of the 1980s." *The Science Fiction Film Reader.* Ed. Gregg Rickman. New York: Limelight, 2004. 315-33.

Manovich, Lev. *The Language of New Media.* Cambridge, MA: MIT, 2001.

Mulvey, Laura. "Death 24 Times a Second: The Tension Between Movement and Stillness in the Cinema." Unpublished manuscript, forthcoming in *Death Twenty-four Times a Second: Reflections on Stillness in the Moving Image.* London: Reaktion, 2005.

———. "The Index and the Uncanny." *Time and the Image.* Ed. Carolyn Bailey Gill. Manchester: Manchester UP, 2000. 139-48.

Netzley, Patricia D. *Encyclopedia of Movie Special Effects.* Phoenix: Oryx, 2000.

Pierson, Michele. *Special Effects: Still in Search of Wonder.* New York: Columbia UP, 2002.

Pool, Oliver. "Can Gollum Get the Previous Oscar Nod?" *Daily Telegraph* (February 12, 2003): 19.

Quinn, Anthony. "Towering Epic Proves that a Blockbuster Can Still have the Human Touch." *Independent* (December 2, 2002): 5.

Romney, Jonathan. "Million-Dollar Graffiti: Notes From the Digital Domain." *Short Orders: Film Writing.* London: Serpent's Tail, 1997. 205-26.

———. "Cause and Effects." *New Statesman* (July 12, 1999): 38-39.

Rosen, Philip. *Change Mummified: Cinema, History, Theory.* Minneapolis: U Minnesota P, 2001.

Shay, Estelle. "Disappearing Act." *Cinefex* 83 (October 2000): 104-31.

Stables, Kate. Review of *The Matrix Revolutions. Sight and Sound* 14.1 (January 2004): 54-55.

Strick, Philip. Review of *The Matrix Reloaded. Sight and Sound* 13.7 (July 2003): 50, 52-53.

"Taming of Sméagol." Documentary included on the Special Extended DVD Edition of *The Lord of the Rings: The Two Towers.* New Line Cinema, 2003.

Walker, Alexander. "For Your Eyes Only." *Evening Standard* (June 10, 1999): 29.

Wood, Robin. *Hollywood from Vietnam to Reagan.* New York: Columbia UP, 1986.

Filmography

Abyss, The (James Cameron, US, 1989)

Angel (TV Series, 1999-2004)

Artificial Intelligence: A.I. (Steven Spielberg, US, 2001)

Alien (Ridley Scott, UK, 1979)

American Werewolf in London, An (John Landis, US/UK, 1981)

Blade (Stephen Norrington, US, 1998)

Blade 2 (Guillermo Del Toro, US, 2002)

Blade Trinity (David S. Goyer, US, 2004)

Charlie's Angels (McG, US, 2000)

Charlie's Angels: Full Throttle (McG, US, 2003)

Close Encounters of the Third Kind (Steven Spielberg, US, 1977)

Contact (Robert Zemeckis, US, 1997)

CSI (TV series, 2000-Present)

E.T.: The Extra-Terrestrial (Stcvcn Spiclbcrg, US, 1982)

Fly, The (David Cronenberg, US, 1986)

Gladiator (Ridley Scott, US/UK, 2000)

Hollow Man (Paul Verhoeven, US, 2000)

I, Robot (Alex Proyas, US, 2004)

Incredible Shrinking Man, The (Jack Arnold, US, 1957)

Invisible Man, The (James Whale, US, 1933)

Jurassic Park (Steven Spielberg, US, 1993)

Jurassic Park 3 (Joe Johnston, US, 2001)

Kiss of the Dragon (Chris Nahon, US/Fr, 2001)

Lord of the Rings: The Fellowship of the Ring (Peter Jackson, US/NZ, 2001

Lord of the Rings: The Two Towers (Peter Jackson, US/NZ, 2002)

Lord of the Rings: The Return of the King (Peter Jackson, US/NZ, 2003)

Lost World: Jurassic Park, The (Steven Spielberg, US, 1997)

Matrix, The (Andy and Larry Wachowski, US, 1999)

Matrix Reloaded, The (Andy and Larry Wachowski, US, 2003)

Matrix Revolutions, The (Andy and Larry Wachowski, US, 2003)

Metropolis (Fritz Lang, Ger, 1927)

Minority Report (Steven Spielberg, US, 2002)

One, The (James Wong, US, 2001)

The Phantom Menace (George Lucas, US, 1999)

Revenge of the Sith (George Lucas, US, 2005)

Romeo Must Die (Andrzej Bartkowiak, US, 2000)

Scary Movie (Keenen Ivory Wayans, US, 2000)

Se7en (David Fincher, US, 1995)

Shrek (Andrew Adamson and Vicky Jenson, US, 2001)

Silence of the Lambs (Jonathan Demme, US, 1991)

Sin City (Robert Rodriguez and Frank Miller, US, 2005)

Sky Captain and the World of Tomorrow (Kerry Conran, US/UK/Italy, 2004)

Star Trek: The Motion Picture (Robert Wise, US, 1979)

Star Trek: The Wrath of Khan (Nicholas Meyer, US, 1982)

Star Wars (George, Lucas, US, 1977)

Star Wars: Episode II - Attack of the Clones (George Lucas, US, 2002)

Starship Troopers (Paul Verhoeven, US, 1997)

Terminator, The (James Cameron, US, 1984)

Terminator 2: Judgement Day (James Cameron, US, 1991)

Thing, The (John Carpenter, US, 1982)

Three Kings (David O. Russell, US, 1999)

Titanic (James Cameron, US, 1997)

Total Recall (Paul Verhoeven, US, 1990)

Tron (Steven Lisberger, US, 1982)

Underworld (Len Wiseman, US/UK/Hungary, 2003)

Van Helsing (Stephen Summers, US/Czech Republic, 2004)

Voyage dans la Lune, Le (Trip to the Moon) (George Méliès, Fr, 1902)

M. Keith Booker (essay date 2006)

SOURCE: Booker, M. Keith. Introduction to *Alternate Americas: Science Fiction Film and American Culture*, pp. 1-25. Westport, Conn.: Praeger, 2006.

[*In the following essay, Booker traces the development of science fiction films from the early twentieth century to the early twenty-first century, elucidating the genre's central thematic concerns and key developments.*]

Science fiction film is essentially as old as film itself. It was, for example, central to the work of the pioneering French filmmaker Georges Méliès, who found in the genre a perfect opportunity for the exploration of his belief that the true potential of film lay not in the simple photographic representation of reality but in illusion and visual trickery. A magician by trade, Méliès made dozens of films that relied centrally on what would now be referred to as special effects to create worlds of visual fantasy for his audiences. By 1902, he had made what is still his best-known film, the fourteen-minute *Voyage dans la Lune* (*A Trip to the Moon*). This work of whimsical imagination, based on a novel by Jules Verne, was a major milestone in cinema history and still has the ability to entertain and fascinate audiences even today.

Following the work of Méliès, films that might be described as science fiction quickly became a staple of the new industry, though many of these early works might equally well be described as horror films, establishing a generic uncertainty that continues to the present day. Thus, the Edison studio had, by 1910, produced the first film adaptation of *Frankenstein,* and, in 1920, German expressionism came to the screen with the production of *Das Kabinett des Doktor Caligari (The Cabinet of Dr. Caligari)*, which deals with a sort of mad scientist but which, more importantly, features extreme lighting and distorted sets that effectively combine to create a mood of strangeness and horror.

Similar techniques were put to good use in Fritz Lang's *Metropolis* (1927), in many ways the culmination of German expressionist cinema and a film that is widely regarded as the first truly great work of science fiction cinema. *Metropolis* involves a towering futuristic city in which the rich live in utopian luxury while legions of poor workers slave away like automatons beneath the surface, tending the gigantic machines that power the golden world above. The film includes numerous visions of advanced technology, the most important of which is the humanoid robot developed by the inventor Rotwang (Rudolf Klein-Rogge), which is used to impersonate the woman Maria (Brigitte Helm), spiritual leader of the workers. The ersatz Maria leads the workers in a doomed rebellion, presumably to preclude the possibility of a more genuine (and successful) revolution, though she is ultimately destroyed by the rioting workers. The real Maria is saved from the clutches of the deranged Rotwang by Freder Fredersen (Gustav Fröhlich), son of the city's ruler, who then serves as a mediator between his father and the workers, heralding a new era of cooperation between the classes.

Many critics have complained about the facile ending of *Metropolis,* which certainly makes it weak as a film about a class-based revolution, but this is a film in which image and atmosphere are far more important than plot or characterization. The special effects (especially those involved in the scene in which the metallic robot is transformed into a Maria lookalike) are quite impressive and have been widely imitated. However, the real secret to the success of *Metropolis* is the ability of the expressionist lighting and sets to convey effectively the feeling of a machine-dominated urban future, even if the actual details are not particularly convincing or realistic.

Envisioning the future is very much the project of the British-produced *Things to Come* (1936), which is probably the first truly important science fiction film of the sound era. Scripted by science fiction pioneer H. G. Wells and based on his book *The Shape of Things to Come* (1933), this film well illustrates Wells's belief late in his life that a utopian future was attainable, but only after the current order of civilization had been destroyed. The film is a speculative "history" of the future that projects the development of human civilization over the next hundred years, beginning with a thirty-year-long world war that begins in 1940 and eventually leaves civilization in ruins, largely as the result of bio-weapons that trigger a deadly plague that sweeps the globe. It focuses on the city of Everytown, which begins as a London-like metropolis, but which, by the end of the war, is in decay, ruled by a warlord engaged in primitive warfare with the surrounding "Hill People." The city, like the rest of civilization, is then rebuilt under the leadership of a visionary group of aviators and engineers who use technology (and superior air power) to enforce their vision of an enlightened world government.

By the year 2036, Everytown is a high-tech paradise, a futuristic city of light and open spaces, almost entirely lacking in the ominous undertones that inform the city of *Metropolis*. The city's leaders, however, are not content to rest on their accomplishments but now set their sights on outer space in the belief that humanity as a species must face continual challenges in order to flourish and prosper. Some in the population bitterly oppose this new project, believing that the insatiable drive for progress only threatens to undermine what is already an idyllic life for the citizens of Everytown. However, these protestors are unable to stop the initial launch in the new space program. As the film ends, they angrily look on as a rocket is fired toward the moon from a giant "space gun," ushering in a new era of exploration. "All the universe or nothing!" cries the leader of the city's ruling council. "Which shall it be?"

Directed by William Cameron Menzies and produced by Alexander Korda, *Things to Come* was a big-budget film whose impressive scenes of a futuristic city made it in many ways the direct forerunner of later science fiction blockbusters from *Star Wars* to *The Matrix.* Its images of the urban future (and the costumes of its future citizenry) would set the style for any number of future films, just as its basic faith in technology and its vision of a humanity that could never rest until it had explored the stars would remain crucial components of science fiction in both the cinema and television for the rest of the century.

Other than monster movies such as James Whale's *Frankenstein* (1931), American science fiction film of the 1930s was largely confined to low-budget serials, such as those featuring Flash Gordon and Buck Rogers as the protagonists, all of which starred Buster Crabbe in the central roles. These serials were based on popular syndicated comic strips, and they definitely had a comic-strip quality to them. Produced in episodes of 15-20 minutes in length, each serial ran for 12-15 episodes that were shown weekly in theaters in an attempt to attract young audiences. By today's standards (or even in comparison to a contemporary film such as *Things to Come*), the special effects of these serials were extremely crude. However, to a generation of young Americans, they offered thrilling images of other planets and other times that presented an exciting alternative to a dreary Depression-era world that was drifting toward global war.

American science fiction came of age as a film genre in 1950 with the release of *Destination Moon,* directed by Irving Pichel and produced by George Pal, who would go on to become one of the leading figures in SF (science fiction) film in the next decade, when his productions included such films as *When Worlds Collide* (1951), *War of the Worlds* (1953), *Conquest of Space* (1955), and *The Time Machine* (1960), the last of which he also directed. The Hungarian-born Pal, who had worked as a production designer for Germany's UFA Studios (makers of *Metropolis*) before fleeing Germany when the Nazis came to power in 1933, served as a sort of transition between the early achievement of European SF films and the later dominance of American SF films. Pal's films typically feature higher budgets, better special effects, and better acting than most other SF films of the 1950s. In addition, several of Pal's films gained respectability by drawing on the works of major science fiction writers, as in the case of *War of the Worlds* and *The Time Machine,* both based on novels by Wells, still at that time the best known international writer of science fiction.

Destination Moon was based on *Rocket Ship Galileo,* a 1947 juvenile novel by Robert A. Heinlein, who also co-wrote the script. Heinlein himself would go on to become one of the best-known novelists in SF history, though he had not yet written any of the classic novels (*The Puppet Masters, Double Star, The Door into Summer, Starship Troopers, Stranger in a Strange Land, The Moon Is a Harsh Mistress*) on which his later fame would be based. Filmed in brilliant Technicolor, *Destination Moon* projects the first American trip to the moon. It includes a number of realistic details that combine to convey a very believable picture of future space travel. Meanwhile, the film clearly shows its Cold War context, while strikingly anticipating the coming space race. In particular, the American mission is propelled by the perceived urgency to reach the moon before some less scrupulous nation (obviously meant to be the Soviet Union) can establish a base there. The success of the American effort is a distinct victory for free-market capitalism, not only over communism, but over government in general. The mission is a purely private affair, funded and carried out by enlightened capitalists, who in fact are forced to overcome opposition from the United States government in order to complete the mission.

Destination Moon ends with the vaguely utopian message "THIS IS THE END OF THE BEGINNING" displayed on the screen, suggesting that this mission has initiated a new era in human endeavor. In retrospect, the message also announces the way in which the success of the movie would usher in the 1950s craze for science fiction films, many of which seemed to go out of their way to reproduce various elements of *Destination Moon.* The Pal-produced *Conquest of Space* (directed by Byron Haskin) may be the best example of a film that attempted a realistic portrayal of space travel in the manner of *Destination Moon,* but there were many others. Indeed, Kurt Neumann's *Rocketship X-M* was rushed through production and released slightly before *Destination Moon,* attempting to ride on the coattails of the advance publicity of the latter film. This attempt was so blatant that *Rocketship X-M,* originally conceived as a story about a trip to the moon, was reformulated as the story of a trip to Mars after a threatened lawsuit from Pal.

Fred Wilcox's *Forbidden Planet* (1956), one of the most stylish SF films of the decade, also drew upon interest in the future possibilities of space travel. Memorable for the technological marvel of Robby the Robot, this film nevertheless warns against the dangers of science and technology, which in this case threaten to unleash sinister and devastating forces. Indeed, the SF films of the 1950s were remarkable for the way in which they reflected the various anxieties and tensions of the era. A large number of alien-invasion films addressed the widespread sense among Americans of the time of being surrounded by powerful and sometimes mysterious enemies. Meanwhile, a side genre of monster movies reflected a similar fear, while often directly dealing with the threats posed by the nuclear arms race. Finally, a plethora of postapocalypse films also spoke to the decade's fears of potential nuclear holocaust. At the same time, looked at more carefully, most films in all three categories reflected not only anxieties over international threats to the American way of life but concerns that the American way itself might have a decidedly dark and dehumanizing side.

Some SF films of the 1950s, including *Invasion U.S.A.* (1952), *Red Planet Mars* (1952), and *The 27th Day* (1957) overtly promoted a paranoid fear (and hatred) of communism as a dehumanizing force, often with aliens standing in for communists. On the other hand, Jack Arnold's *It Came from Outer Space* (1954) features benevolent aliens who stop off on Earth simply to make repairs and find themselves confronted by hysterical violence at the hands of humans. Meanwhile, Robert Wise's *The Day the Earth Stood Still* (1951) is essentially a plea for global peace and understanding. Here, in one of the first alien-invasion films of the decade, the Christ-like alien Klaatu (Michael Rennie) is essentially benevolent, though he also issues a stern warning: Earth will be destroyed if it seeks to extend its violent ways beyond Earth. This rejection of the Cold War arms race was a courageous gesture in a film that was produced at the height of American Cold War hysteria and at a time when Hollywood itself was under siege by anti-communist zealots in Washington. The success of the film thus demonstrated the way in which science fiction, because it is perceived by many as divorced from contemporary reality, can serve as a venue for trenchant social and political commentary that might have been judged too controversial in a more "mainstream" form.

Christian Nyby's *The Thing from Another World* (also 1951) was more prototypical of the alien-invasion films to come in the next decade. It was also more representative of American paranoia in the early 1950s, when Americans felt threatened not only by the Soviet Union but also the impoverished masses of the Third World, with which America was increasingly coming into contact as a result of the global politics of the Cold War. In this case, the eponymous Thing, a sort of vegetable creature (it is described at one point in the film as "some form of super carrot"), has come to Earth to colonize the planet for itself and its kind, planning to use the human race as a source of their favorite plant food, blood. The Thing is powerful, highly intelligent, and able to multiply rapidly, thus posing a very serious threat to Earth, though it is, in fact, defeated relatively easily. Then again, the most important and interesting battle in the film is not between the Thing and the humans, but among the humans themselves. In this sense, the primary opposition is between the military men and the scientists, with the film ultimately siding with the former, though only after Captain Patrick Hendry (Kenneth Tobey) defies the military bureaucracy and obeys his own judgment in destroying the Thing.

Even more paranoid about alien threats is Menzies's much-admired *Invaders from Mars* (1953, remade with tongue-in-cheek in 1986 by Tobe Hooper), though there is a vague suggestion that the invasion of that film is really a defensive measure designed as a preemptive strike against the U.S. space program to prevent the earthlings from reaching Mars. In the film, young David Maclean (Jimmy Hunt) can initially get no one to believe that he has seen a Martian saucer land, especially as the saucer has taken refuge underground, doing its work there by sucking anyone who approaches down through the sand that covers it. David watches in horror as his parents and various other adult authority figures turn into robot-like zombies, controlled by the Martians. Luckily, he is eventually able to get the authorities to believe his story, and the U.S. military quickly dispatches the invaders, thus providing audiences with at least some assurance that the military would be able to repel whatever threats that might arise. Perhaps the most memorable thing about *Invaders from Mars,* however, was the design of its aliens. In particular, the head Martian is a metallic-looking creature that is essentially all brain, living in a glass globe, waving its weird tentacles, and controlling, through telepathy, a troop of drone-like mutant slaves, who do all of its physical work.

Haskin's *The War of the Worlds,* again based on a Wells novel, was probably the slickest and most technically impressive of all of the science fiction films produced by Pal during the 1950s. In the film, the Martian invaders are quickly opposed by conventional military forces after scientist Clayton Forrester (Gene Barry), a famous "astro- and nuclear physicist," learns of their existence and alerts the authorities, who quickly mobilize. Unfortunately, the Martians prove invulnerable to conventional attack, surrounding their hovercraft with force fields that are impermeable to the bombs and bullets that are launched against them. Desperate, the top American brass order an atomic attack, but the Martians prove impervious even to a bomb that is "ten times more powerful than anything used before." All seems lost, when the Martians suddenly die off due to their lack of resistance to the germs that inhabit Earth's atmosphere. This is literally a *deus ex machina* ending, the Martians having been destroyed by what is essentially presented as divine intervention. As the film closes, church bells ring and a chorus sings "amen," while the narrator informs us that the Martians have been killed by "the littlest of things, which God in His wisdom had put upon this Earth."

If *War of the Worlds* privileges religion over science, *This Island Earth* (1955) is far more positive in its figuration of science, though its alien invaders are themselves scientists. These aliens, from the besieged planet of Metaluna, have come to Earth, not to colonize the planet or to prevent the evolution of Earth's technology, but to recruit Earth scientists to help them develop better sources of nuclear power so they can fight off their enemies on the neighboring planet of Zahgon. We are told that this recruitment is necessary because most of the Metalunan scientists have already been killed in the war, but it is fairly clear that the depiction of the Metalunans picking the brains of American scientists in this film heavily partakes of the same mindset that convinced Americans in the 1950s that the primitive Soviets could not possibly have developed nuclear weapons without somehow stealing the technology from their more advanced American rivals (who had boosted their own scientific advancement by importing former Nazi scientists after World War II). In the film, he-man scientist Cal Meacham (Rex Reason) and beautiful female scientist Ruth Adams (Faith Domergue) are able to escape from the Metalunans and return to Earth, where they will no doubt get married and breed several beautiful and intelligent American children.

Scientist Russell Marvin (Hugh Marlowe) and new wife Carol (Joan Taylor) have a similarly bright future at the end of *Earth vs. the Flying Saucers* (1956), but only after helping to mobilize the American military-industrial complex to defeat an invasion of aliens, who again do not seem all that evil, other than the fact that they hope to come to Earth to live, their own planet having been rendered uninhabitable. But this in itself is a frightening prospect, just as Americans of the 1950s were widely hostile to the idea of all those Third World masses moving here to take our jobs and use up our resources. So the relatively peaceful aliens are greeted with military force, resulting in an all-out war. The Earthlings win, again providing a reassuring ending.

If the aliens of *Earth vs. the Flying Saucers* are forced to turn to violence largely because of the belligerence of the Earthlings who greet them, there is no such ambivalence in the depiction of the aliens of *Invasion of the Body Snatchers* (1956), perhaps *the* signature alien-invasion film of the 1950s. Here, alien replicants begin replacing the inhabitants of a small California town, with the clear implication that they plan eventually to take over the entire country and perhaps the entire world. While this film is particularly easy to read as an allegory about the threat of communist infiltration in the United States, it is also a complex film that can be read as a commentary on a variety of domestic threats, including conformism and McCarthyism.

Gene Fowler's *I Married a Monster from Outer Space* (1958) resembles *Invasion of the Body Snatchers* in its paranoia about aliens who look just like us, but also indicates the extent to which anxieties over gender roles were central to the decade. In fact, in its focus on male aliens who have come to Earth to mate with human women in order to save their species from dying out, this film addresses a number of concerns surrounding the centrality of marriage and family to American life in the 1950s. It was unusual for the time in that the lone individual who warns of the alien invasion is a woman, who thereby finds herself aligned against Norrisville's masculine authorities, most of whom are already aliens. Nevertheless, the film, despite its apparent suggestion that you never know when your spouse might be an alien, or a communist, or something similarly sinister, ultimately makes a statement in favor of the conventional nuclear family. Indeed, the aliens are finally routed by a group of responsible males who have recently performed their familial duties by producing offspring.

In some cases, such as *The Blob* (1958), the alien invaders in 1950s SF films do not resemble humans but are quite clearly monstrous. Here, the line between alien invasion and monster films often becomes quite thin. Also notable are films in which the monsters were created by radiation, addressing the decade's fear of nuclear catastrophe. One of the earliest of these films was Sam Newfield's *Lost Continent* (1951), in which a team of scientists and soldiers goes to a remote Pacific island to try to retrieve some crucial data from an experimental rocket that has crashed there. Not only are the prehistoric monsters that inhabit the island apparently the result of the high levels of radiation on the island, but the team is also racing to retrieve the top-secret rocket before the Russians can get to it. The monsters of *The Beast from 20,000 Fathoms* (1953), *Them!* (1954), *It Came from Beneath the Sea* (1955), *Tarantula* (1955), *Attack of the Crab Monsters* (1957), and *Attack of the Giant Leeches* (1960) are all either produced or stirred to aggressive action as a result of nuclear testing or radiation experiments.

One of the most interesting sequences of monster films from the 1950s was the trilogy *The Creature from the Black Lagoon* (1954), *Revenge of the Creature* (1955), and *The Creature Walks among Us* (1956), the first two directed by Arnold, one of the most prolific directors of the decade. Clearly reptilian and thus seemingly just as foreign to the human species as the insects and spiders of *Them!* and *Tarantula,* the creature is nevertheless a biped, essentially humanoid in its overall shape, as is indicated by the tendency of the humans in the films to refer to it as the "Gill Man." It is, in fact, an evolutionary missing link between reptiles and mammals, discovered in the remote Third World setting of the Amazon. The basic primitive-critter-from-the-Third-World premise of the creature sequence also places those films in the tradition of *King Kong.* Moreover, the creature itself follows very much in the huge footsteps of Kong in that it is ultimately more sinned against than sinning, so sensitive to the cruel treatment meted out to it by its human captors that audiences could not avoid feeling a certain sympathy with it.

If the Gill Man is almost human, it is also the case that many films of the 1950s blurred the boundary between humans and monsters in general. In particular, unrestrained scientific research always threatens, in the science fiction films of the 1950s, to deprive humans of their humanity in one way or another. In Kurt Neumann's *The Fly* (1958), for example, well-meaning scientist André Delambre (David Hedison) develops a teleportation apparatus, then teleports himself as an experiment. Unfortunately, a common housefly accidentally gets into the machine with him and when they come out on the other end their atoms have become intermixed. Though a somewhat silly film, *The Fly* supplied one of the iconic moments of 1950s science fiction film in a scene near the end in which the fly with a human head, trapped in a spider web, cries out "Help me!" in a tiny voice—only to be smashed with a rock by Police Inspector Charas (Herbert Marshall). The film became a cult classic and was eventually remade into a much more interesting film by David Cronenberg in 1986. In Arnold's *The Incredible Shrinking Man* (1957), radioactive pollution causes protagonist Robert Scott Carey (Grant Williams) to shrink continually, until he literally fades out of existence. This film, however, stands out among the SF films of the decade in its focus on the psychic impact on Carey of his gradually decreasing size. At the other end of the size spectrum was Glenn Manning (Glenn Langan), the protagonist of Bert I. Gordon's *The Amazing Colossal Man* (1957), who grew to colossal size (but also experienced 1950s-style existential trauma), as did Nancy Fowler Archer (Allison Hayes) in Nathan Juran's cult classic *Attack of the 50 Foot Woman* (1958).

Roger Corman, whose trademark campy, low-budget films would make him an important force in American cinema, began his SF film career with the post-apocalypse film *The Day the World Ended* (1955), which also featured a humans-into-monsters motif. Like most of the films directed (or produced) by Corman, *The Day the World Ended,* however silly, has its interesting moments. In a graphic reminder of the horrors of radiation, the film suggests that radiation poisoning can transform humans into monstrous mutant cannibals. In the end, one man and one woman survive, preparing to restart the human race, Adam-and-Eve style. Hackneyed plot, stock characters, and cheesy-looking monster aside, *The Day the World Ended* is still notable as one of the few films of the 1950s that actually showed the effects of radiation on humans, however unrealistic its depiction of those effects might have been. It thus differs from the most popular post-holocaust film of the 1950s, Stanley Kramer's *On the Beach* (1959), which shows no such effects. Here, a global nuclear war has apparently destroyed all human life everywhere on earth, except Australia, which has been spared because of its remote location. Unfortunately, the clouds of deadly radiation that cover the rest of the globe are headed for Australia as well, so the Australians themselves have only a few months before what seems to be inevitable death. The film concentrates on the attempts of the various characters to cope with their impending doom. Indeed, while the how-could-we-be-so-stupid senselessness of the nuclear war looms in the margin as a message throughout, Kramer also seems to have wanted to make the film a sort of universal commentary on how human beings come to grips with the realization of their own certain mortality.

Other post-holocaust films of the long 1950s were even more indirect in their representation of nuclear war and its aftermath. For example, in Edward Bernds's *World without End* (1956), the nuclear holocaust is projected hundreds of years into the future, and the film itself is set hundreds of years after that, when radiation levels have essentially returned to normal. Pal's 1960 film adaptation of Wells's classic 1895 novel *The Time Machine* also focuses on a far-future post-apocalyptic world. At one point, Pal has his time traveler (who begins his journey on New Year's Eve, 1899) stop off in 1966, where he is nearly killed in a nuclear assault on

London, placing the nuclear holocaust itself in the near future of the film. Then, he travels into the far future (he ends up in the year 802,701, just as in Wells's book), where the human race has evolved (actually, devolved) into two separate species. The passive Eloi live on the garden-like surface of the planet, enjoying lives of mindless leisure. They are completely indolent, illiterate, and incapable of creative thought or action. Meanwhile, the aggressive and animalistic Morlocks live beneath the surface, where they still have at least some operating technology. It turns out that they are raising the Eloi essentially as cattle, taking them, at full maturity, beneath the surface to be slaughtered for food. The time-traveling protagonist (Wells himself, played by Rod Taylor) stirs the Eloi to revolt, destroying the Morlocks. As the film ends, he returns to 802,701 to help lead the Eloi in their attempt to build a new world and regenerate their ability for creative action.

By 1962, science fiction films began to deal a bit more directly (and less optimistically) with nuclear holocaust, though a film such as Ray Milland's *Panic in Year Zero* still resembles *On the Beach* in its focus on the human drama of the survivors of the disaster, not the human tragedy of the victims. There are again no actual signs of nuclear destruction, though the film does depict certain negative consequences, such as the looting, rape, and murder that occur in the wake of a nuclear attack. By and large, however, *Panic in Year Zero* is essentially a survivalist adventure, in which the resourceful Baldwin family meet all challenges and ultimately survive the nuclear war unscathed.

The cycle of post-apocalyptic films that marked the 1950s came to a close in 1964 with Stanley Kubrick's *Dr. Strangelove, or How I Learned to Stop Worrying and Love the Bomb.* This highly effective absurdist farce brilliantly captures the insanity of the mutually-assured-destruction mentality of the arms race and may very well have made a significant contribution to the easing of the anti-Soviet hysteria that had marked the 1950s. On the other hand, by providing a sort of final word on this hysteria, the film also brought to a halt the Golden Age of SF film production that had marked the earlier decade, though it was certainly the case that numerous other aspects of American life in the 1960s created an environment in which SF film did not thrive. The decade's emphasis on "relevance," and the clear importance of such phenomena as the anti-war movement, the Civil Rights movement, and the women's movement, made SF film seem frivolous to many.

Some SF films of the 1960s, such as Roger Vadim's sex farce *Barbarella* (1968), attempted to appeal to the ethos of the decade in intentionally frivolous ways. On the other hand, films such as François Truffaut's *Fahrenheit 451* (1966) and Franklin Schaffner's *Planet of the Apes* (1968), the latter of which would become one of the signature films of American popular culture, attempted seriously to engage the issues of the day. Meanwhile, Kubrick's *2001: A Space Odyssey* (1968) strove more for artistic seriousness, bringing unprecedented critical attention and respect to the genre of science fiction film.

In the wake of the success of such films, SF cinema made something of a comeback in the early 1970s. A cycle of SF films in the first half of that decade continued to strive for relevance and artistic seriousness, usually with a dark tone that reflected the era's growing skepticism and increasing sense (driven by such events as the Watergate scandal) that the new and better world envisioned by the political movements of the 1960s didn't seem that different from the old and darker world that had preceded it. In 1971 alone, several films projected a dystopian future, including Kubrick's *A Clockwork Orange* (1971), Wise's *The Andromeda Strain* (1971), and Boris Sagal's *The Omega Man* (1971). Other dark visions of the future followed, including Douglas Trumbull's *Silent Running* (1972), Richard Fleischer's *Soylent Green* (1973), Norman Jewison's *Rollerball* (1975), and Michael Anderson's *Logan's Run* (1976). These dystopian visions of the future set a precedent for important films such as Michael Radford's 1984 adaptation of George Orwell's *Nineteen Eighty-Four* (1949), perhaps the most important of all dystopian novels. By contrast, Woody Allen's *Sleeper* (1973) was a farcical parody of the dystopian genre, while former Monty Python member Terry Gilliam followed in 1985 with *Brazil,* which also presented what was essentially a parodic dystopia, though one that continued to make many of the same serious satirical points for which the sub-genre is well known. Films such as John Carpenter's *They Live* (1988), Andrew Niccol's *Gattaca* (1997), Alex Proyas's *Dark City* (1998), and Kurt Wimmer's *Equilibrium* (2002) continued this tradition into the twenty-first century.

One of the most visually effective dystopian films of the early 1970s was *THX 1138* (1971), the first film by *Star Wars* creator George Lucas. Then, in 1977, *Star Wars* itself took science fiction film in whole new directions. *Star Wars* appealed greatly to the sensibilities of a late-1970s America that, after the disappointments of Vietnam and Watergate, was hungry for a rousing, old-fashioned adventure in which good triumphed over evil. Moreover, *Star Wars* defined "good" in traditional American terms in which individual conscience trumped obedience to official authority. In addition to its charming optimism (and its targeting of juvenile audiences, which was also a key to its commercial success), *Star Wars* was a technical triumph that wowed audiences with its unprecedented special effects. In many ways the most successful SF film of all time, *Star Wars* began one of the most important phenomena in the history of science fiction cinema. For one thing, *Star Wars*

inspired no fewer than five sequels (so far), including *The Empire Strikes Back* (1980), *The Return of the Jedi* (1983), *The Phantom Menace* (1999), *Attack of the Clones* (2002), and *Revenge of the Sith* (2005). *Star Wars* also took the phenomenon of merchandising to unprecedented levels, as a seemingly limitless array of related books, toys, and various kinds of collectibles produced even more income than the blockbuster films themselves.

Star Wars appeared at the beginning of a several-year period that was the richest in the history of SF film, while its old-fashioned, nostalgic appeal also marked the beginning of a rightward turn in American politics that would lead to the election of Ronald Reagan to the presidency in 1980. Indeed, looking at the Cold War years of the 1950s, then at the late 1970s and early 1980s, some critics have concluded that science fiction film seems particularly to flourish in conservative times, perhaps because of their escapist appeal to audiences appalled by contemporary reality. Even seemingly "liberal" SF films of this period—such as Steven Spielberg's *Close Encounters of the Third Kind,* released the same year as *Star Wars*—contained a strong escapist component. Here, however, the escape is not from what many saw as the leftist drift of global politics but from the soul-destroying nature of life in modern capitalist America. The box-office success of the more adult-oriented *Close Encounters* verified the commercial potential of SF film that had been suggested by *Star Wars,* while demonstrating that such film could appeal to a variety of ages and ideologies. On the other hand, Spielberg's *E. T. the Extra-Terrestrial* (1982) turned back to a more youthful audience, aiming more at the sentiments than the intellects of its viewers—and with hugely successful commercial results.

Partly inspired by the recent commercial and technical success of *Star Wars,* Wise's *Star Trek: The Motion Picture* (1979) was an attempt to update the *Star Trek* franchise for a new generation of fans, building upon recent dramatic advances in special effects technology. With nearly three times the budget of *Star Wars* and with special effects wizards such as Douglas Trumbull and John Dykstra on board, *Star Trek* is indeed an impressive-looking film, even if it is not really groundbreaking in the way *Star Wars* had been. It is grander than *Star Wars* (and intended for a more adult audience), but the plot is a bit weak, and the interpersonal relationships (especially among Kirk, Spock, and McCoy) that had provided so much of the energy of the original television series never really quite come off in the film. Still, the built-in audience from fans of the series made the first *Star Trek* film a substantial commercial success, leading to the longest series of sequels in SF film history. For most fans (and critics), *Star Trek: The Wrath of Khan* (1982) was a great improvement over the first film, returning more to the spirit of the original series.

Star Trek III: The Search for Spock (1984), *Star Trek IV: The Voyage Home* (1986), *Star Trek V: The Final Frontier* (1989), and *Star Trek VI: The Undiscovered Country* (1991) found fans as well, though the aging original cast was beginning to creak a bit by the last film. *Star Trek: Generations* (1994) handed the mantle over to the younger cast of television's *Star Trek: The Next Generation,* who continued the film series in *Star Trek: First Contact* (1996), *Star Trek: Insurrection* (1998), and *Star Trek: Nemesis* (2002). Together, these films represented a rare example of SF crossover from television to film (the reverse is more common), though one might also mention Rob Bowman's *The X-Files: Fight the Future* (1998) as a fine SF thriller based on the popular *X-Files* television series. That series, incidentally, drew much of its inspiration from the same 1960s-style oppositional politics that had fueled the original *Star Trek,* except that *The X-Files* series and film were both heavily influenced by the greater cynicism and skepticism of the 1990s.

1979 also saw the beginning of another major SF film franchise with the release of Ridley Scott's *Alien* (1979). Mixing the genres of horror and science fiction with an unprecedented sophistication—and presenting film audiences with a dark, but detailed vision of future technology that they had never before seen—*Alien* was a genuine breakthrough in SF film, not the least because of the effectiveness of its presentation of a tough female heroine, the formidable Ellen Ripley (Sigourney Weaver). Meanwhile, the titular alien was one of the most effective-looking SF film monsters of all time, impacting the look of any number of future alien creatures in SF film. James Cameron's *Aliens* (1986) was in many ways an even greater success, while David Fincher's *Alien³* (1992) and Jean-Pierre Jeunet's visually striking *Alien: Resurrection* (1997) were solid efforts as well, with the latter adding new touches of irony and humor to the sequence.

Blade Runner (1982), Scott's own follow-up to *Alien,* was perhaps the most visually influential SF film of all time, rivaled only by *2001: A Space Odyssey.* Together with *Alien* it ushered in the postmodern era in SF film, a phenomenon that has drawn substantial attention from academic critics, who have found science fiction film (and science fiction in general) to be among the paradigmatic cultural expressions of postmodernism. *Blade Runner* was distinctive for its blurring of the boundary between detective fiction and science fiction, both in its plot and its visual style, while its interrogation of the distinction between humans and the products of their technology addressed numerous contemporary concerns about human identity. Meanwhile, the dark, oddly indeterminate, multicultural city of the film provided some of the most striking visuals in the history of cinema.

Based on a novel by Philip K. Dick, *Blade Runner* also announced a new level of maturity for SF film in which the genre felt able to tackle some of the same kinds of serious issues that had long been the stuff of science fiction novels and stories. Dick's stories, for example, provided the basis for such successful later films as Paul Verhoeven's *Total Recall* (1990) and Steven Spielberg's *Minority Report* (2002). On the other hand, the adaptation of serious SF literature to film is a difficult project that has generally met with relatively little success. Even David Lynch's *Dune* (1984), which provides some striking examples of the director's unique visual style, was largely reviled by fans of the classic Frank Herbert novel—and ultimately rejected as a failure by Lynch himself.

The year 1984 also saw the release of James Cameron's *The Terminator,* another key example of postmodern SF cinema. This film made Arnold Schwarzenegger a star, made the SF action film a major genre, and triggered any number of imitations, including its own two sequels, *Terminator 2: Judgment Day* (1991) and *Terminator 3: Rise of the Machines* (2003). One of the films influenced by *The Terminator* was Paul Verhoeven's *Robocop* (1987), a work that included a substantial amount of social satire but also provided ironic commentary on the science fiction genre itself. Both *The Terminator* and *Robocop* showed a fear of the dehumanizing potential of technology that was typical of the Reagan years, in which nostalgic visions of a return to a simpler past were prominent in the popular American imagination. Indeed, by the end of the 1980s, SF film itself had begun to take a new kind of nostalgic turn enabled by the fact that the genre had become so well established that all subsequent works inevitably entered into dialogues with their predecessors. Even a film as innovative as Cameron's *The Abyss* (1989) had underwater adventure predecessors such as Disney's *20,000 Leagues under the Sea* (1954) and Irwin Allen's *Voyage to the Bottom of the Sea* (1961), while reaching back to *The Day the Earth Stood Still* in the way its alien visitors use their advanced technology to try to put a stop to the Cold War arms race.

The Abyss, however, went well beyond its undersea predecessors in the quality of its special effects, which among other things pioneered computer generated imaging (CGI), leading into a new era of special effects-driven films that relied heavily on such techniques. Though itself a thoughtful film, *The Abyss* in this sense continued the movement toward increased emphasis on special effects that had been a key factor in the evolution of SF film from *Star Wars* onward. This tendency reached new levels in the 1990s with the production of a number of big-budget, high-profit special-effects spectaculars, including Spielberg's *Jurassic Park* (1993), Roland Emmerich's *Stargate* (1994) and *Independence Day* (1996), and Verhoeven's *Starship Troopers* (1997).

The latter two films were indicative of other new trends in SF film in the 1990s as well. Featuring advanced aliens who warn Earth of the follies of the Cold War arms race, *The Abyss* joins *The Day the Earth Stood Still* as anti-war SF films that bracket the Cold War years. Meanwhile, the Cold War had provided background for any number of science fiction films during those years, suggesting that the genre might move in new directions after the end of the Cold War at the beginning of the 1990s. For example, cultural historians such as Richard Slotkin and Tom Engelhardt have argued that the national identity of the United States has from the beginning been defined in opposition to enemies who could be construed as savage and evil.[1] With the loss of the Soviet bloc as such an enemy, American culture seemed to be seeking new enemies to be defeated, as reflected in such films as *Independence Day* and *Starship Troopers.*

The computer simulation of reality was the other major new trend in SF film in the 1990s. While the video-game inspired *Tron* had explored virtual reality as early as 1982, the growing importance of computers and the Internet as part of the texture of everyday life in America in the 1990s led to the production of a number of virtual-reality films, taking SF film in genuinely new directions. Such films included *Johnny Mnemonic* (Robert Longo, 1995), *Strange Days* (Kathryn Bigelow, 1995), and *Virtuosity* (Brett Leonard, 1995). Films such as Alex Proyas's *Dark City* (1998), David Cronenberg's *eXistenZ* (1999), and Josef Rusnak's *The Thirteenth Floor* (1999) took such films to a new level of sophistication in the late 1990s, though by far the most important of such films was Andy and Larry Wachowski's *The Matrix* (1999), which was followed by two sequels in 2003, *The Matrix Reloaded* and *The Matrix Revolutions.* Appropriately enough, virtual-reality films (especially the *Matrix* trilogy) were among those that made the best and most innovative use of computer generated imagery in the production of special effects.

If such films were made possible by advances in computer technology in Hollywood, they were made popular by computer advances in the world at large, in which the growth of the Internet and video gaming spurred a popular fascination with the possibilities of virtual reality. This fascination also grew out of a growing sense of the unreality of reality itself. As described by cultural theorists such as Jean Baudrillard, life in the postmodern era (especially in the United States) has been characterized by a growing sense of unreality and by a collapse of the once seemingly-solid boundary between fiction and reality, between authenticity and simulation.

This phenomenon would only become more prominent in the early years of the twenty-first century, just as CGI became increasingly important in SF film. Computer simulation is especially important in a series of films in which the technology allowed comic books to come to life. Many of the latter were semi-SF super-hero films such as Sam Raimi's hugely successful *Spider-Man* (2002) and *Spider-Man 2* (2004), though films such as Bryan Singer's *X-Men* (2000) and *X2* (2003) fit more comfortably into the category of science fiction. CGI was also ideal for the conversion of popular video games into film, among which Paul W. S. Anderson's *Resident Evil* (2002) and Alexander Witt's *Resident Evil: Apocalypse* (2004) were particularly interesting. Films such as Alex Proyas's *I, Robot* (2004) drew upon the classic science fiction of the past (in this case the robot stories of Isaac Asimov from the 1950s) as material for special-effects extravaganzas. Kerry Conran's *Sky Captain and the World of Tomorrow* (2004), like *Star Wars,* looked back to the 1930s, while introducing new CGI techniques in which virtually everything except the human actors themselves (and even one of the actors) was computer-generated.

The campy nostalgia of *Sky Captain* also placed it in the tradition of films that have played with science fiction convention, sometimes in highly ironic ways. Of course, the addition of an element of camp to SF films goes back at least to the 1950s, when campiness in the films of directors such as Corman sometimes compensated for budget shortages. Campiness in SF film reached its zenith in Jim Sharman's ultra-campy cult classic *The Rocky Horror Picture Show* (1975), a comic rock sendup of the horror genre that includes numerous science fictional elements as well. Indeed, the film's opening number is a 1950s-style rock homage to 1950s-style science fiction, including references to such classics as *The Day the Earth Stood Still* and *Forbidden Planet,* but treating the genre as the stuff of late night double features. The film's central figure, transvestite Frankensteinian mad scientist Frank-N-Furter (Tim Curry, in an inimitable performance) turns out to be an alien emissary from the planet Transsexual in the galaxy Transylvania.

In the 1980s, films such as Lamont Johnson's *Spacehunter: Adventures in the Forbidden Zone* (1983) and John Carpenter's *They Live* (1988) employed campiness to beef up weak plots and low-budget looks, though the latter also uses its cheesy feel to cloak an extremely serious—and unusually radical—critique of consumer capitalist society. It was, however, in the 1990s that the addition of campy elements to basic science fiction plots became a major strategy of SF film. For example, the Sylvester Stallone vehicle *Demolition Man* (1993) is essentially an action film (with a futuristic setting) in which unconventional cop John Spartan (Stallone) battles against arch-criminal Simon Phoenix (Wesley Snipes). It is also a dystopian critique of conformism in its future society, though not a very inventive one. Most of its ideas are mere clichés, though it is an entertaining film, not only for its spectacular action scenes but also for its humor and for its clear understanding that it belongs to a genre that is always in danger of plunging into silliness. Snipes's campy performance as Phoenix is particularly effective, though Stallone has some good comic moments as well, especially in the (potentially prophetic) scene where Spartan, having been transported into the future from 1996, is stunned to learn that Arnold Schwarzenegger (in whose shadow Stallone remained as a SF action star in the 1990s) has served a term as President of the United States.

In a similar way, Stuart Gordon's *Space Truckers* (1996) seems awful on the surface, but is actually a perfectly effective medium-budget space opera that scores a number of satirical points about the excesses and abuses of capitalism. It also substitutes campiness for big-time special effects and draws considerable energy from the over-the-top performances of Dennis Hopper (as a working-class space pilot battling against his exploitative corporate bosses) and Charles Dance (as a former corporate scientist turned rapacious—but hilariously dysfunctional—cyborg). Rachel Talalay's *Tank Girl* (1995) lacks the satirical punch of *Space Truckers,* though its vision of an evil corporate entity that controls the water and power supply of a post-apocalyptic future world has some possibilities. The film proudly displays its origins in a British cult comic-strip, and what could have been a truly awful film has a number of highly entertaining moments thanks to the sheer excess of Lori Petty's performance as the ass-kicking title character and the very zaniness of concepts such as an underground guerrilla band of half-man, half-kangaroo freedom fighters.

In other cases, relatively high-quality, high-budget films used campy, comic elements to good effect, mixing farce with genuine drama in a highly postmodern fashion. Terry Gilliam's *Twelve Monkeys* (1995), for example, is a superb time-travel thriller in which scientists from a dystopian, post-apocalyptic future send agents back to the past to help them learn more about a deadly plague that wiped out most of the Earth's population in 1996 and 1997. In a twist on the usual time-travel plot, the film stipulates that the past cannot be changed, so that there is no question of averting the plague. Instead, the future scientists hope simply to gain information to help the human race to fight the plague in the future. The film features some of the same weirdly old-fashioned "steampunk" future technology that had marked the distinctive visual style of Gilliam's *Brazil,* supplemented by excellent lead performances from A-list actors such as Bruce Willis and Madeleine Stowe. However, some of its most memorable moments come from Brad Pitt's (Oscar-nominated) over-the-top performance as a mental patient and would-be terrorist—not to mention the whacked-out future scientists, who in many ways recall the strange hospital doctors of Dennis Potter's classic BBC ministeries *The Singing Detective* (1986).

In *Twelve Monkeys,* Willis plays a genuinely vulnerable man on the verge of complete mental collapse. In Luc Besson's *The Fifth Element* (1997), he returns to his more usual role of action hero (much in the vein of his portrayal of troubled cop John McClane in the *Die Hard* films). This time, Willis plays a retired military operative who returns to duty from his job as a cab driver (in a futuristic hovercraft cab) in order to save Earth from total destruction. Little else about this film is predictable, however, as it plays with a number of SF clichés. To save Earth, Willis's Korben Dallas must locate and retrieve the five "elements" of an ancient high-tech weapon, the fifth of which is one Leeloo (Milla Jovovich), a sort of goddess whose physical perfection becomes a running joke throughout the film. In fact, though the action plot is perfectly functional and though Willis and Jovovich perform well in the lead roles, the slightly excessive visuals and the outrageous performances of Gary Oldman as a key villain and Chris Tucker as a glitzy media personality lend the entire film a campy air. *The Fifth Element* is a virtual compendium of SF film elements, all of which seem just a bit out of kilter, making the film both a successful space opera and a running commentary on the entire genre of SF film.

Other SF film parodies have addressed specific individual predecessors in the genre. *Death Machine* (1995) is largely an extended riff on *Alien,* with clear echoes of *Robocop* and *The Terminator* tossed in for good measure. Actually, *Death Machine,* directed by Stephen Norrington (who would go on to direct the 1998 vampire action flick *Blade* and who had worked on the creature effects crew for *Aliens*), is a fairly effective (and rather dark) SF thriller. However, the performance by Brad Dourif as a crazed sex-maniac mad scientist adds a strong dose of campiness to the mix, as do the often light-hearted allusions to other films—including the use of character names such as "John Carpenter" and "Sam Raimi," nodding toward the well-known horror-film directors, as well as "Scott Ridley," "Weyland" and "Yutani," which wink at the director of *Alien,* as well as the evil Weyland-Yutani Corporation that figures so prominently in the *Alien* films. In a lighter vein, Mel Brooks's *Spaceballs* (1987) is a hilarious spoof of the *Star Wars* franchise (with side nods to a variety of other SF films), employing an unending stream of sight gags and puns that work only because Brooks can assume that his audience has extensive familiarity with the works being parodied. Dean Parisot's *Galaxy Quest* (1999) similarly relies largely on references to *Star Trek* (and the phenomenon of *Star Trek* fandom), though it also gains energy from the presence of SF superstar Sigourney Weaver as the actress who plays busty blonde space babe Lt. Tawny Madison (the antithesis of Weaver's Ripley in the *Alien* films) in a television series that bears a remarkable resemblance to the original *Star Trek.*

The frequent excesses of the alien-invasion genre have made it a prime target of SF films spoofs. For example, in Ivan Reitman's *Evolution* (2001), David Duchovny virtually resurrects his wise-cracking Fox Mulder character from television's alien-invasion drama *The X-Files,* complete with an evolving romantic tension between himself and a red-haired government scientist (played by Julianne Moore) who looks a bit like Gillian Anderson's Dana Sculley. Orlando Jones adds comic energy as well, and this tale of alien microbes that arrive on Earth inside a meteorite then evolve at breakneck pace into more complex (and more dangerous) alien invaders definitely has its moments. However, Duchovny and Moore's characters lack the on-screen chemistry of Mulder and Sculley, while Reitman's obvious attempts to draw upon his own *Ghost Busters* (1984) formula are unable to keep the film from going flat about halfway through.

Sometimes, as in the notorious case of Ed Wood's *Plan 9 from Outer Space* (1959), alien-invasion films had been so awful as to be unintentionally self-parodic. Tim Burton's *Ed Wood* (1994) drew upon Wood's campy reputation in a fine non-SF film, then Burton himself, in *Mars Attacks!* (1996) made what may be the finest—or at least funniest—comic science fiction film ever made. Like *Ed Wood, Mars Attacks!* plays on nostalgia for the notorious science fiction films of the 1950s and even earlier. The title, for example, looks back to the 1938 Flash Gordon serial *Mars Attacks the World.* Burton's film draws much of its plot and imagery from classic alien-invasion films such as *The Day the Earth Stood Still, War of the Worlds, Invaders from Mars,* and *Earth vs. the Flying Saucers,* though it functions particularly directly (and effectively) as a parody of *Independence Day,* a huge blockbuster that had been released only five months earlier. *Mars Attacks!* is one of Burton's campiest films and, as such, it tends to make the films on which it is based seem a bit ridiculous. At the same time, it remembers those films almost tenderly, seeming wistfully to wish for a time when it was possible to make such simple films in a (mostly) serious way. *Mars Attacks!* itself is anything but simple. A relatively big-budget production, it features an impressive all-star cast (headed by Jack Nicholson) and an array of expensive high-tech special effects, thus differing dramatically from the 1950s films to which it centrally refers. At the same time, the film also includes a number of cheap, old-fashioned effects, as when the Martians zap Earthlings with hokey ray guns that look like children's toys or when they approach Earth in an armada of 1950s-style flying saucers that one character describes as looking suspiciously like hub caps. In the end, the Earthlings triumph in a way that comments on the unlikely nature of such triumphs in many earlier films: it turns out that the Martians have no resistance to the music of Slim Whitman, the sound of which tends to make their brains explode.

Mars Attacks! may have a great deal of fun at the expense of science fiction, but it also draws much of its energy from the same phenomenon. The same might be said for another alien-invasion comedy, Barry Sonnenfeld's *Men in Black* (1997) and its sequel, *Men in Black II* (2002). The films have a great deal of fun with the whole tradition of UFO lore, positing the presence on Earth of a wide array of bizarre alien invaders and the existence of an extensive secret organization that battles against the invaders. Both films star Will Smith and Tommy Lee Jones as the titular men in black, agents of this secret organization. Partly building on Smith's momentum as a central figure in *Independence Day,* the *Men in Black* films together grossed more than a billion dollars worldwide, making them easily the most commercially successful comic SF films ever.

If comedies such as *Men in Black* and *Mars Attacks!* gained ironic energy from a certain nostalgia for earlier SF films, it is also the case that turn-of-the-century SF film seemed in general to look backward more than forward. For example, not only was the the the second *Star Wars* trilogy (released in the years 1999-2005) a prequel to the first trilogy, but it clearly built on nostalgic memories of that first trilogy, which had appeared almost a generation earlier. The years 2000 and 2001, meanwhile, were marked by a series of Mars-exploration films, which clearly looked back to such predecessors as *Rocketship X-M, Conquest of Space* (1955), and *Robinson Crusoe on Mars* (1964), while renewing a fascination with the planet Mars that had marked science fiction since the time of Wells. Some of these films were quite ambitious. In *Mission to Mars* (2000) renowned director Brian de Palma produces a film that contains some genuine moments of wonder, while working hard to place itself within the tradition of SF film. Visually and thematically reminiscent of *2001: A Space Odyssey,* the film focuses on the first manned mission to Mars, and particularly on a rescue mission mounted when a strange phenomenon kills off most of the members of the first expedition. This second mission leads to the discovery of a repository left behind by an ancient, highly-advanced race that once lived on Mars. The virtual-reality archive left in this repository reveals that Mars had been rendered unlivable by a sudden catastrophe, apparently a strike by a large asteroid. The inhabitants of the planet were thus forced to evacuate to the stars, though they also sent a ship to Earth, seeding it with DNA and leading to the evolution of life on Earth. Humans are thus in a very real sense the cousins of the ancient inhabitants of Mars. In fact, one of the human astronauts, Jim McConnell (Gary Sinise), rather than return to Earth, decides to stay on the alien ship that is in the repository and that is about to take off, presumably to follow its makers to their new home in the stars.

In the somewhat confused *Red Planet* (Antony Hoffman, 2000), overpopulation and environmental degradation on Earth have forced humanity to look to Mars for a new home. However, a project to terraform the planet by sending algae there to grow and produce oxygen has gone awry and oxygen levels have started inexplicably to drop. The film begins as an American crew travels to Mars to investigate the situation. A solar flare damages their ship severely just as they reach Martian orbit, triggering a series of misfortunes (including the by-now-obligatory damaged robot that turns on the crew) in which three of the original five crew members are killed. However, they also find that oxygen levels on Mars have now risen dramatically, so much so that humans can breathe on the surface. Mission Commander Kate Bowman (Carrie-Anne Moss) and mechanical systems analyst Robby Gallagher (Val Kilmer) survive to return to Earth and report that the surface of Mars is now swarming with "nematodes" (of unknown origin and looking more like insects than nematodes) and that these creatures have eaten the original algae but are now themselves producing oxygen in large quantities. The implication is that the human project to colonize Mars has been saved, though it is not at all clear that the nematodes (who had already almost completely depleted their algae-food supply) can survive long-term (and co-exist with humans, whom they also find appetizing) on Mars. Meanwhile, there are vague attempts at quasi-religious hints that the nematodes may have a supernatural, even divine origin.

John Carpenter's *Ghosts of Mars* (2001) is more of a pure action flick. Here, a mining operation on a colonized and partly terraformed Mars uncovers the ghosts of an ancient Martian civilization. In an attempt to defend their planet from human occupation, the ghosts then possess the miners, turning them into crazed killers who then attack every human in sight. After a terrific, high-action battle, the ghosts seem to have been defeated by a contingent of Martian police, led by Melanie Ballard (Natasha Henstridge) and joined by notorious criminal James "Desolation" Williams (Ice Cube). Unfortunately, the ghosts reappear, attacking the major human settlement at Chryse. Ballard and Williams prepare to rush back into battle as the film ends.

One of the most obvious signs of a turn to nostalgia was the number of remakes of earlier SF films that appeared at the beginning of the new century, starting with John Harrison's Sci Fi Channel miniseries remake of *Dune* (2000), which sticks more closely to the original novel in plot but falls far short of the original Lynch film as a work of cinematic art. Tim Burton's 2001 remake of *Planet of the Apes,* on the other hand, is vastly superior to the original as a work of visual art, but falls far short of the original's intelligent social and political commentary. Simon Wells's *The Time Machine* (2002) lacks Burton's special visual flair but still makes good

use in advances in special effects technology to spice up its look, though somehow lacking the energy and impact of the original. Big-time action director John McTiernan remade *Rollerball* in 2002 with even worse results, turning a film that at least attempted to critique our culture's fascination with violence into one that simply celebrated violence as spectacle. Finally, in 2005, Spielberg directed a remake of *War of the Worlds* (2005), updating that classic with state-of-the-art big-budget special effects, while in many ways remaining more faithful to the original Wells novel than had the 1953 film adaptation.

With the notable exception of Spielberg's *War of the Worlds,* almost all of these remakes fall far short of the originals, suggesting that it takes more than impressive special effects to make an effective SF film. It also suggests that SF film may be at its best not when it looks back to the past (including its own past) but when it looks toward the future. Thus, while the new century does not appear to be off to a good start in the production of interesting science fiction cinema, recent examples such as the *Matrix* trilogy and Spielberg's excellent *Minority Report* suggest that SF film has far from exhausted itself and that we can probably anticipate a number of new breakthroughs in the coming years.

Note

1. See Tom Engelhardt, *The End of Victory Culture* (Basic Books, 1995) and Richard Slotkin, *Gunfighter Nation: The Myth of the Frontier in Twentieth-Century American Culture* (University of Oklahoma Press, 1988).

MAJOR SCIENCE FICTION FILMS

James Chapman (essay date 1999)

SOURCE: Chapman, James. "'A bit of the old ultra-violence': *A Clockwork Orange.*" In *British Science Fiction Cinema,* edited by I. Q. Hunter, pp. 128-37. London: Routledge, 1999.

[*In the following essay, Chapman discusses* A Clockwork Orange *as a dystopian film that can be categorized as a more realist form of futuristic science fiction.*]

'Nothing dates quite so rapidly as our ideas of what the future might be like,' remarks film critic Philip French (French 1990: 87). The main problem for science fiction in the cinema has always been that visions of the future which might seem prescient for their time can quickly become dated, anachronistic and absurd. Given the perishability of the genre, therefore, perhaps the most remarkable thing about Stanley Kubrick's film *A Clockwork Orange* (1971) is that it still seems so fresh some thirty years later. The film's early-1970s apocalyptic vision of a near-future Britain where law and order have collapsed and an authoritarian right-wing government resorts to brainwashing as a method of social control remains a powerful and often disturbing picture of a society in a state of moral and political decay. Indeed, there are some voices on the left which might argue that the film's prophecy was fulfilled by the events between 1979 and 1997: a Tory government in power for a whole generation, presiding over an increasingly divided society in which violent crime has become more and more commonplace. This is not to say that *A Clockwork Orange* should be interpreted as a prophetic allegory of Thatcherism, though clearly some of its themes and ideas did continue to have relevance during the Thatcher years. What can be said, however, is that *A Clockwork Orange* belongs to that particular brand of futurist science fiction which remains close enough to the present that it can legitimately be described as a realist text rather than a fantasy. There are no ray-guns or space-flights in *A Clockwork Orange,* nor even any elaborate special effects. The differences between this and its director's previous film, *2001: A Space Odyssey* (1968), with its technological fantasy and elaborate sci-fi hardware, could not be more pronounced.

A Clockwork Orange was based on the novel by the English author, Anthony Burgess, first published in 1962. The film, which for the most part follows the novel quite closely, tells the story of Alex DeLarge (Malcolm McDowell). It is set in the near future ('Just as soon as you could imagine it, but not too far ahead—it's just not today, that's all,' explains Alex in the opening voice-over). At the beginning of the film the teenage Alex is the leader of a gang of 'droogs', Dim, Pete and Georgie, who spend their evenings hanging around the Korova Milkbar. Stimulated by their intake of 'milkplus' (drugs), they get their fun by indulging their appetite for 'a bit of the old ultra-violence'. Alex's gang kicks to death a tramp and then takes on and beats the rival gang of Billyboy in a gang-fight in a derelict opera house. Stealing a car, Alex and his gang drive around causing mayhem until they arrive at a remote house in the country. Alex tricks his way inside by pretending to have been involved in an accident. Once inside the house, Alex and his companions embark on an orgy of violence, severely beating the owner Mr Alexander (Patrick Magee) and forcing him to watch as they gang-rape his wife (Adrienne Corri). The next day, while his parents are out, Alex is visited by a social worker; later he enjoys sex with two girls he has picked up. Meeting up with his droogs again, Alex slashes

Dim (Warren Clarke) across the hand to assert his authority after Dim has made fun of Alex's fondness for Beethoven (whom he refers to as 'Ludwig Van'). The gang embark on another night of senseless violence, this time raiding a luxury health farm where Alex kills the owner, the Cat Lady (Miriam Karlin) by bludgeoning her to death with her collection of erotic *objects d'art*. However, the police arrive, and, although his droogs escape, Alex is captured and sentenced to prison for fourteen years for murder.

Two years into his prison term, Alex is approached by the Minister of the Interior (Anthony Sharp), who persuades him to volunteer for the government's new experimental programme of aversion therapy, known as the 'Ludovico Technique', to cure him of his violent tendencies. The treatment is no less than a form of brainwashing in which Alex is pumped full of drugs and forced to watch a succession of pornographic and violent images, to the accompaniment of Beethoven's Ninth Symphony, which he can no longer listen to without suffering nausea. After two weeks Alex is released back into society, but upon returning home he finds that his parents have taken in a lodger who has replaced him in their affections. Homeless, he encounters two of his former droogs, Dim and Georgie, who are now policemen and who beat him savagely and leave him for dead in the middle of nowhere. Alex struggles to the nearest house, which happens to be the home of Mr Alexander, now a cripple and a widower, his wife having died after her traumatic ordeal at the hands of Alex's gang. Alex does not recognise his former victim, but Alexander remembers him and takes him in. Alex tells his apparent benefactor all that had happened, including the details of his treatment by the government. It transpires that Alexander, a writer and intellectual, is planning a coup against the government, and he sees in Alex the opportunity to discredit the government while exacting his own personal revenge. He imprisons Alex in the attic and tortures him by playing Beethoven's Ninth Symphony, which Alex can only escape by throwing himself out of the window in a suicide bid. Alex survives the fall, however, and awakening in hospital he is visited by the Minister who tells him that Alexander's conspiracy has been discovered and suppressed. The Minister believes that Alex is cured and wants to show the press and public that the policy of aversion-therapy has been a success. 'I was cured all right,' Alex remarks in voice-over, and the film ends with him lying on his hospital bed, listening contentedly to Beethoven (which no longer induces nausea) whilst fantasising about a life of more sex and violence.

Most commentators agree that, while the film follows the novel quite closely, nevertheless the dominant authorial voice is that of Stanley Kubrick rather than Anthony Burgess. It is placed in the context of Kubrick's *oeuvre,* comparable in both thematic and stylistic terms to his other films. To quote, for example, Philip Strick: 'That it *is* his [Kubrick's] tale . . . is obvious from the parallels in structure, emphasis and technique with all Kubrick's other dramas, from *Day of the Fight* in which arenas and split personalities find an uncanny preface, to *Full Metal Jacket* in which, once again, conditioned killers pursue the excesses of a fiercely private war' (Strick 1997: 218). The precision of Kubrick's *mise-en-scène,* the almost clinical formalism that is a characteristic of his work, is evident here, for example in the long tracking shots which open so many scenes and in the set dressings which add so much background detail (paintings, sculptures) that is not always present in the novel. Kubrick's obsession with aspects of film form is exemplified in the early sequence where Alex and his gang set upon a drunken tramp. The location is an urban underpass and the formal composition of the scene is a textbook example of expressionism: the set is lit by one strong light from the back (the entrance to the tunnel) while the foreground and edges of the frame are in almost total darkness. The gang members are silhouetted against the backlight, casting long shadows, their faces in blackness. The hoodlums therefore merge into the darkness of the tunnel, becoming, as in the classic cinema of German Expressionism, part of the environment which they inhabit. The fight between Alex and Billyboy's rival gangs is another sequence where action is staged for aesthetic effect. The location is a derelict opera house and the fight takes place on the stage, filmed in frontal tableau. The stage is lit by shafts of light across its rubbish-strewn floor, where even the debris is arranged in carefully abstract patterns. Many critics have remarked upon the balletic qualities of the gang-fight, and the movement is choreographed with all the precision of a dance routine in a musical. The most kinetic and violent sequences, moreover, are set to music, ranging from Rossini's 'Thieving Magpie' during the joy-ride in the stolen car, to 'Singin' in the Rain', which Alex sings mockingly during the assault on Mr and Mrs Alexander . . . .

Thematically, as well as stylistically, *A Clockwork Orange* bears relation to Kubrick's other work. In particular, it has been seen as the third in a loose trilogy of futurist films which each, albeit in their very different ways, expose the dark underside of technology and progress and reveal a deep disquiet about the future of humanity. Philip French considers that *A Clockwork Orange* joins *Dr Strangelove* (1964) and *2001* 'to complete a trilogy of admonitory fables set in a bleak, dehumanised future' (French 1990: 86). In certain respects, *A Clockwork Orange* is a counterpoint to *2001*. If *2001* can be interpreted as a text of the late 1960s embodying the spirit of the flourishing counter-cultures in breaking away from oppressive social and political forces—most famously and spectacularly illustrated in the climactic 'stargate' sequence which is often interpreted as a hallucinogenic 'trip'—then *A Clockwork Orange* is a text of the early 1970s in which social control and authority is re-imposed by the ruling elite. Although the films are very different in that *2001* is a technological fantasy whereas *A Clockwork Orange* is much more a down-to-earth Orwellian nightmare of political repression and social control, there are nevertheless some thematic similarities in so far as both films posit a problematic relationship between humanity and science in the future. And both films also, of course, make extensive use of classical music.

In placing the film in the context of the Kubrick *oeuvre,* however, it is important not to lose sight of the contribution made by Anthony Burgess. Although Burgess was not involved in the production of the film—the screenplay was written by Kubrick himself—the finished film does show his influence as well as its director's. *A Clockwork Orange* was one of five novels which Burgess wrote in the course of 1961-2, his prolific output at this time due to the fact that he had been diagnosed (incorrectly as it turned out) as suffering from an inoperable brain tumour and given only a short time to live. It is perhaps his most personal novel in that it was shaped by events which Burgess had experienced at first hand. He wrote it shortly after returning from six years working abroad as an officer in the Colonial Service in Malaya. Upon his return to Britain, Burgess was struck by the development of teenage gangs such as the Mods and Rockers, and the sub-cultures of coffee-bars, dress codes and slang vocabularies which they created for themselves. Living in Hove on the south coast, Burgess was able to observe the Bank Holiday gang-fights in seaside resorts such as Brighton. The novel, set roughly ten years in the future, describes a society where gang violence has escalated out of control and the government has resorted to Pavlovian techniques of brain-washing and conditioned response to control the offenders. One of the specific incidents in the novel had an even more personal basis. During the Second World War, when Burgess was stationed in Gibraltar, his first wife was savagely attacked and raped by a gang of four American GI deserters in London. She suffered a miscarriage, and Burgess always attributed her early death to the trauma. It is hard not to read the novel without seeing the character of Mr Alexander (a writer) as Burgess himself and Mrs Alexander as Burgess's wife, Lynne.

For all his personal and tragic experience of violence, however, the target of Burgess's book was not so much the gang culture itself as the notion that violent behaviour could be controlled by brainwashing. Burgess had been disturbed by accounts of new behaviourist methods of reforming criminals, particularly the work of American psychologist B. F. Skinner, who believed that the experiments conducted by Pavlov in the behaviour modification of animals could be applied to human beings. Burgess believed that this would erode the freedom of people to make moral choices. The freedom of choice, even if it was the choice to commit rape and murder, was, in Burgess's view, essential for humanity. As the literary critic Blake Morrison writes: 'His book, even before Kubrick's film, caught the anti-mechanistic spirit of the culture, or counter-culture, of the sixties, and took its place, somewhat awkwardly, alongside Ken Kesey's *One Flew Over the Cuckoo's Nest,* the works of R. D. Laing, and other books attacking the erosion of individual rights by penal and medical institutions' (Morrison 1996: xxiii).

The novel of *A Clockwork Orange* was published in Britain in May 1962 to generally negative reviews. Many critics complained that it was difficult to read. This was due to the style which Burgess had adopted whereby he used a first-person narration (by Alex) in an invented language which was meant to approximate the language of teenage gangs. 'Nadsat' was a mixture of American-English, colloquial Russian, Slavic gypsy dialect and Cockney rhyming slang. It is the language which Alex and his droogs speak, and the language in which Alex narrates the story. As a result the novel is quite difficult to read, and, indeed, when it was published in an American edition a glossary of 'Nadsat' words was added by the publishers, much to Burgess's disapproval. Furthermore, the American edition omitted the last chapter of the book, which had a profound effect on the story in terms of both structure and content. The British edition had twenty-one chapters structured in three sections of seven chapters each (each of the seven sections beginning with the rhetorical question 'What's it going to be then, eh?'). In the final chapter Alex has been released from hospital and is hanging around the Korova Milkbar again with a new gang of droogs. However, he now renounces violence, and instead has visions of settling down in domestic bliss with a wife and baby. It is symbolic that this occurs in the twenty-first chapter in so far as twenty-one is the age at which children traditionally reach adulthood. And, as the last chapter also begins with the question 'What's it going to be then, eh?', it is clear that Alex has made the conscious choice between right and wrong. But by dropping the last chapter, the American edition not only lacked the structural and numerical unity of the British edition, but it also ended on a much more downbeat and pessimistic note with Alex still in hospital and his future uncertain. 'My book was Kennedyan and accepted the notion of moral progress,' Burgess later remarked. 'What was really wanted was a Nixonian book with no shred of moral optimism in it' (quoted in Morrison 1996: xvii).

The novel aroused interest from Paramount Pictures in the late 1960s, and a script was prepared by Michael Cooper and Terry Southern, but in the event it was Kubrick who was to make the film, in Britain, backed by Warner Bros. However, it was the American edition of the book which Kubrick adapted for the film. Whether this was deliberate on Kubrick's part, or whether he was unaware of the difference between the two editions, is unclear. The result however, was that the film omitted the more affirmative ending which Burgess himself preferred. While the original novel suggested that Alex had mended his ways, the film ends with the implicit suggestion that he is still looking forward to a life of sex and violence. In most other respects, however, the film is a faithful adaptation of Burgess's novel, and shows his original intent. The narrative of the film follows that of the novel in all but the smallest details, and the key sequences are transcribed from page to screen with much fidelity. Crucially, the film maintains Alex's first-person narration through the technique of a voice-over by McDowell and the extensive use of subjective camerawork, brilliantly exemplified in the point-of-view shot of Alex's attempted suicide where the camera was dropped down the side of a building to simulate his view as he falls.

The association of the spectator with Alex's point-of-view in the film is nevertheless uncomfortable and at times disturbing. This is particularly so in the scenes of violence, the most unsettling of which is the rape of Mrs. Alexander. While the novel also describes the rape from Alex's perspective, a certain barrier is created by the use of the 'Nadsat' language which distances the reader from the full horror of the actions which are being described ('So he did the strong-man on the de-votchka, who was still creech creech creeching away in very horrorshow four-in-a-bar, locking her rookers from the back, while I ripped away at this and that and the other, the others going haw haw haw still, and real good horrorshow groodies they were that then exhibited their pink glazzies, O my brothers, while I untrussed and got ready for the plunge' (Burgess 1996: 22).) However, what in a novel is left to the mind's-eye of the reader can be shown graphically through the medium of film. The rape is presented on screen with a degree of explicit and graphic detail that was unprecedented in mainstream cinema. Not only is the terrorised victim shown in full-frontal nudity, but a hand-held camera is used to film the action in close-up. The resulting scene is extremely uncomfortable, implicating the spectator in the rape as a voyeur. Burgess, who had admired *2001* and had hoped that the film of *A Clockwork Orange* would aspire to a similar level of 'visual futurism', felt that the representation of sexual violence was too stark. A Catholic, he privately felt that the film was pornographic, although in public he praised Kubrick for his 'technically brilliant, thoughtful, relevant, poetic, mind-opening' film (quoted in Morrison 1996: xviii). Perhaps surprisingly, given its content, the film was passed uncut by the British censors, a decision which provoked much controversy (Robertson 1993: 143-50).

Kubrick himself argued that the violence perpetrated by Alex in the first part of the film was necessary in dramatic terms as a counterweight to the brainwashing which he then received. In a rare interview he told *Sight and Sound*:

> It was absolutely necessary to give weight to Alex's brutality, otherwise I think there would be a moral confusion with respect to what the government does to him. If he were a lesser villain, then one could say: 'Oh, yes, of course, he should not be given this psychological conditioning; it's all too horrible and he really wasn't all that bad after all.' On the other hand, when you have shown him committing such atrocious acts, and you still realise the immense evil on the part of the government in turning him into something less than human in order to make him good, then I think the essential moral idea of the book is clear. It is necessary for man to have choice to be good or evil, even if he chooses evil. To deprive him of this choice is to make him something less than human—a clockwork orange.
>
> (Strick and Houston 1972: 63)

For Kubrick, then, as for Burgess, the essential theme of the story was the right to free choice. However, this makes it all the more curious that Kubrick should have based the film on the American edition of the novel rather than on the British edition where Alex is shown in the end to have made the choice between good and evil. Furthermore, Kubrick's explanation of the title in this context is also quite interesting in that the film omits to explain it. In the novel, 'A Clockwork Orange' is the title of a manuscript which Mr Alexander is working on and which Alex destroys as he ransacks Alexander's home. The incongruous juxtaposition is noticed by Alex ('That's a fair gloopy title. Who ever heard of a clockwork orange?'). This reference, however, is not included in the film.

Kubrick's justification of the film's violent content notwithstanding, it is that aspect of the film which has dominated critical debate around it. The critical reception at the time was mixed, though, as Charles Barr has shown, most of the serious film critics tended to be favourably inclined towards the film (Barr 1972). However, there was an orchestrated chorus of disapproval from the popular press and from the anti-permissive lobby exemplified by the Festival of Light and the National Viewers and Listeners' Association, with the latter body calling on Robert Carr, the Home Secretary in the Heath government, to ban it. A press campaign was orchestrated against the film, and there were several hysterical though unsubstantiated reports that it had led young people to commit copy-cat acts of violence (Robertson 1993: 146-9). Although *A Clockwork Orange* won acclaim abroad, being nominated for three Oscars (Best Film, Best Director and Best Screenplay) and winning the prize for Best Foreign Film at the 1972 Venice Film Festival, the controversy around the film

caused Kubrick, who owns the domestic distribution rights, to withdraw it from distribution in Britain after its initial run. Thus the film has not been shown publicly in Britain since the early 1970s: the National Film Archive has no viewing copy and there has been no video release (though pirated copies do exist). When the Scala Cinema in London showed the film in 1993, the legal action which followed resulted in the cinema being closed down. Kubrick's decision to withdraw the film, which he has never fully explained, is probably the most effective censorship of a completed film ever implemented in Britain.

The current unavailability of *A Clockwork Orange* in Britain (it continues to be shown freely abroad, and has enjoyed extensive runs in Paris) means that for all the controversy around the film relatively few people in Britain have actually seen it. The film's critical reputation is therefore based mostly on judgements passed down by others. Its notoriety is exemplified by the harsh, opinionated verdict of the most widely read of all popular film critics. 'A repulsive film in which intellectuals have found acres of social and political meaning,' opined Leslie Halliwell; 'the average judgement is likely to remain that it is pretentious and nasty rubbish for sick minds who do not mind jazzed-up images and incoherent sound' (Halliwell 1987: 201). The sort of intellectual analysis which the great populist Halliwell held in such disdain would presumably be exemplified by the entry on Kubrick in the *Oxford History of World Cinema*, a rather more academic work than Halliwell's *Film Guide*, which suggests that in *A Clockwork Orange* 'the choreography of violence acts as a grotesque mask for a deep pessimism towards utopian beliefs in the rational management of social tension and conflict' (Usai 1996: 458-9). A similar point was made, though at rather greater length, by the *Monthly Film Bulletin* upon the film's initial release:

> From *Paths of Glory* to *Lolita*, *Dr Strangelove* to *2001*, Stanley Kubrick has shown himself an intrepid explorer of closed universes. The no-exit situations through which he rotates his characters result from so finely dovetailed a relationship between psychological obsession and social mechanism, that it is impossible to determine whether his characters' minds are intended as metaphors for society's prison or their external universe as a magnifying glass held up to the barren confines of the human soul. Macro- and microcosm become interchangeable in Kubrick's coherent cosmos. A sardonic moralist, he charts the closing—in the name of progress—of the fields of moral choice; and his hermetic worlds breed the heroes they deserve. If *A Clockwork Orange* emerges as his most cynical and disturbing film to date, this is less because—as was already the case in *Dr Strangelove*—the nightmare future which it predicates is a recognisable extension of the present day, than because it so devastatingly and totally re-

duces its audience to the level of its characters, all of them perfectly adapted to the cynical system which contains them.

(Monthly Film Bulletin February 1972: 29)

Thus speaks the voice of the intellectual critic reading acres of social and political meaning into the film. The critic here is a woman (Jan Dawson), and it is significant not only that she attributes all meaning in the film to Kubrick, not Burgess, but also that she seems to side with Alex and finds his violence, even against women, less disturbing than the therapy to which he is then subjected:

> If we are shocked by Alex's violation of bourgeois property (women included), it is only on an intellectual level, since Kubrick carefully distances his effects, postponing our physical discomfort for the moment when the 'therapists' screw their clamps on to Alex's eyes; by the time Alex regains consciousness in his hospital bed, Kubrick has us rooting for him to resume his thuggery—the only way left to us or him of saying 'no' to this dehumanised society.

The inverted commas around 'therapists' (the rapists?) implies what their treatment of Alex amounts to.

The debate around the violence of *A Clockwork Orange* has overshadowed all other aspects of the film to such an extent that its place and status in the history of British cinema, and of British science fiction, has been largely overlooked. It is difficult to place *A Clockwork Orange* in a particular cycle or sub-genre, although comparisons to individual films do suggest themselves. *Things to Come* (1936), for example, had posited a future (albeit after a destructive world war) where civilisation had broken down and authority was exercised by gangster warlords. A benevolent form of social control became necessary, implemented through the 'peace gas' of John Cabal (Raymond Massey) and other scientists in the name of humanity. The difference between the 1930s and the 1970s, however, is that whereas the earlier film had affirmed faith in progress and a utopian future, the later film was pessimistic about that future. On the one hand *A Clockwork Orange* shows a society threatened by the violent anarchy of the young, while on the other hand it asserts that in order to control that anarchy (which is itself a form of free expression) through behavioural conditioning will result in repression and the destruction of humanity. The implication of *A Clockwork Orange* seems to be that, either way, the outlook for the future is bleak. Unlike *Things to Come,* where science and mankind are ultimately shown to be in harmony, *A Clockwork Orange* implies that science and humanity are incompatible. It is a dystopian film rather than a utopian one, and in this context the closest comparison is to George Orwell's *Nineteen Eighty-Four* (1949), which also presents a totalitarian, authoritarian Britain of the near future. The similarities

between Orwell's 'Thought Police' and the 'Ludovico Technique' are obvious. A comparison could also be made with *Fahrenheit 451* (1966), another film made in Britain by an overseas director (François Truffaut), in which a futurist fascist state asserts its social and political control through burning books. And Nicolas Roeg's *The Man Who Fell To Earth* (1976) shares some thematic similarities in its story of an alien visitor who comes to Earth on a mission to save his own planet but is corrupted by the influence of mankind. Like Alex, Newton (David Bowie) comes to revel in sex and drugs as the ultimate expression of freedom. What these films have in common is that they were all imaginative (if not necessarily entirely successful) works by directors of note who also worked in other genres besides science fiction. In the last analysis, then, *A Clockwork Orange* is not a film which can be located easily in the normal generic profile of British cinema, suggesting that it should instead be placed in an authorial context—a context which allows as much for the voice of Anthony Burgess as of Stanley Kubrick.

Bibliography

Barr, Charles (1972) 'Straw Dogs, A Clockwork Orange and the critics', *Screen* 13, 2: 17-31.

Burgess, Anthony (1996) *A Clockwork Orange,* London: Penguin.

French, Philip (1990) 'A Clockwork Orange', *Sight and Sound* Spring: 84-7.

Halliwell, Leslie (1987) *Halliwell's Film Guide,* sixth edn, London: Grafton.

Morrison, Blake (1996) 'Introduction' to Burgess, *A Clockwork Orange.*

Robertson, James C. (1993) *The Hidden Cinema: British Film Censorship in Action 1913-1975,* London: Routledge.

Strick, Philip (1997) 'A Clockwork Orange', in Laurie Collier Hillstrom (ed.), *International Dictionary of Films and Filmmakers,* third edn, vol. I: Films, London: St James Press.

Strick, Philip and Penelope Houston (1972), 'Interview with Stanley Kubrick', *Sight and Sound* Spring: 62-6.

Usai, Paolo Cerchi (1996) 'Stanley Kubrick', in Geoffrey Nowell-Smith (ed.) *The Oxford History of World Cinema,* Oxford: Oxford University Press.

Thomas Morrissey (essay date fall 2004)

SOURCE: Morrissey, Thomas. "Growing Nowhere: Pinocchio Subverted in Spielberg's *A.I. Artificial Intelligence."* *Extrapolation* 45, no. 3 (fall 2004): 249-62.

[*In the following essay, Morrissey determines the influence of Carlo Collodi's iconic children's story* Pinocchio *on Steven Spielberg's* A.I.: Artificial Intelligence, *calling the film "a beautifully crafted but flawed cinematic hybrid that unsuccessfully blends Collodi's and [Stanley] Kubrick's hard-boiled realism with Spielberg's sentimentality."*]

"I am programmed to evolve, to better myself."

—Lt. Commander Data, ST:TNG [*Star Trek: The Next Generation*] *First Contact*

It's hard to compete with Stephen Spielberg, especially from the grave. That's a big disadvantage for Carlo Collodi and, perhaps, even for Stanley Kubrick as well, despite Spielberg's good intentions. With millions of dollars and Hollywood's best at his service, Spielberg has been given audience-reaching power that Collodi could never have imagined. Collodi's tale of a puppet who becomes a boy clearly on the road to manhood first came to life in a serialized children's newspaper in Italy from 1881-83. Even though it became in subsequent decades an international bestseller, it has since been largely eclipsed in the United States by the powerful images and appealing sounds of the 1940 Walt Disney film. Disney's *Pinocchio* is a great entertainment achievement, but it trivializes Collodi's tale of becoming, by transforming it into a paean to impossibly idealized childhood. In *A.I. Artificial Intelligence,* Spielberg, following Kubrick's lead, reaches past Disney and directly back to Collodi by having Monica Swinton, robot David's mommy, read aloud from a good English version of *The Adventures of Pinocchio.* Furthermore, the fictive world of *A.I.* resembles the kind of place one might expect to find if Collodi's worst villains had gained access to advanced technology. It is that technological leap that allows for the Kubrick-style dystopian world of *A.I.,* one that is consistent with the world as portrayed in Kubrick's inspiration, Brian Aldiss's poignant short story, "Supertoys Last All Summer Long." Building on Aldiss's sad commentary on humanity, *A.I.* projects a future in which humans build and torture robots, create at least one sentient robot who is condemned to perpetual childhood, and end biological life on earth through environmental mismanagement—not a proud legacy. Unfortunately, *A.I.'s* Spielbergian coda attempts to put a happy face on this dismal human self-portrait. The result is a beautifully crafted but flawed cinematic hybrid that unsuccessfully blends Collodi's and Kubrick's hard-boiled realism with Spielberg's sentimentality. Thus is a classic dystopian theme—the horror of enforced, perpetual childhood—set adrift.

To begin with, it is important to establish Collodi's story as one worth retelling in our technologically advanced but seriously threatened era. Collodi's villains do not spew greenhouse gasses into the atmosphere or engage in genocide, but they do exhibit behaviors that could very well lead to these crimes. The Fox and the Cat are not simply con-animals but would-be murderers. They not only steal from Pinocchio, but they stab

and hang him as well. The wicked Coachman who bites off a donkey's ear and gleefully sells young human beings into animal bondage willingly sacrifices the next generation for his own profit. The circus in which Pinocchio in donkey form finds himself for a brief time a prime attraction is a cruel public spectacle of subjugation and pain, not unlike *A.I.'s* infamous Flesh Fairs. The civil authority in Collodi's novel is universally corrupt. Pinocchio has good reason to fear the police, who are the agents of such fools and tyrants as the Gorilla Judge and his boss, the Emperor of Trap for Blockheads, the town where the victims of crime, not the perpetrators, are punished. The single-minded quest of self-satisfaction at the expense of others—especially children—is the nature of evil in both Collodi's story and *A.I.*

What Collodi's novel celebrates is self-actualization in the context of community, a process that involves finding one's way imperfectly in a most decidedly imperfect world. Pinocchio's beginning is inauspicious: he is carved kicking and screaming from "a common piece of wood"(7)[1] by a man whose initial motive for bringing him to life is to earn "my bit of bread and my glass of wine"(13) by exhibiting him—so much for kindly old Geppetto on his knees before the wishing star. After smashing with a hammer the hundred-year old Cricket who tactlessly criticizes his irresponsible attitude, Pinocchio ditches school for a puppet show, thereby beginning a picaresque journey during which foolishness and naiveté will cause him to be robbed, hanged, jailed, nearly fried in a pan, chained up as a watch dog, transformed into a donkey, beaten, drowned, and eaten by a school of hungry fish.

Despite these setbacks, the puppet eventually triumphs. The Girl with Blue Hair who becomes the Fairy watches over him and helps him to accentuate his finer character traits by means of some pretty nasty tough love, including scaring him with rabbit pall bearers, letting him spend a miserable night standing on one foot while the other is stuck in her front door, and feeding him a feast of phony food. In the midst of this, Pinocchio learns some valuable lessons about interdependence when he exchanges favors with a variety of animal helpers like the Pigeon, Alidoro the dog, and the philosophical Tuna. The ghost of the squashed Cricket generously and persistently continues to haunt Pinocchio with advice. Thus does the puppet activate his inherently good heart and join a morally upright subset of the corrupt world, a just microcosmic society that offers him and Collodi's readers an alternative to the depravity of the Fox and the Cat, the diabolical Coachman, and the malevolent government.

Collodi's novel is a fairy tale in the sense that a beneficent but not always agreeable supernatural being saves Pinocchio's life so that he can grow into the real boy he is capable of being. But he contributes mightily to his own salvation by reenacting in a tongue-in-cheek way the epic feats of great heroes such as Aeneas, Odysseus and even Jesus. His descent into the belly of *il pesce cane* to save Geppetto is both an act of heroism and a symbolic descent into the depths from whence so often come wisdom and metamorphosis. Collodi's allusions to classical literature may be light-hearted, but they are not trivial; his child-hero has worth, dignity and stature when he willingly risks his life to save Geppetto and when he makes baskets to support his ailing father.

Disney's story, adapted from the work of 1930's Pinocchio revisionists such as Yasha Frank and Roselle Ross, alters Collodi's in several important ways. Collodi's world is dangerous and inequitable, but there can be found within it genuine just communities; Disney's is universally sinister, and anyone outside the immediate family is suspect. Collodi's Geppetto is a very poor man with no identifiable trade for whom hunger is a constant companion; a wall of his humble cottage is decorated with a painting of the blazing fireplace and bubbling cooking pot, even though in actuality he cannot afford either of these luxuries. Disney's Geppetto is a craftsman, a clockmaker, his little cottage looks comfortable and well-appointed, and he can even afford to keep pets. He is not dirt poor, nor is he recognizably Italian. His Tyrolean outfit would surely offend Collodi, who as a young man took up arms against Tuscany's Austrian oppressors. Collodi's puppet learns some very hard lessons, the most important of which is that life is full of chances and that the only way to survive is to ally oneself with those whose values include concern for others and a willingness to cooperate. Disney's puppet becomes an obedient and passive fantasy child whose first loyalty is to the father and the family, not to a larger social grouping, as is the case in Collodi's novel. He is not one of Collodi's *raggazzi* or street kids, children who do the best they can in a world where all the cards are stacked against them, but a quintessentially American boy, who, if he obeys his parents—in the case of the Disney movie Geppetto and the Blue Fairy—will escape from the clutches of ubiquitous crooks and evildoers.

The biggest conscious difference is the alteration in the imagery of the child. Collodi's puppet learns and grows until he becomes a real boy. Not so in Disney's film. In our *Pinocchio Goes Postmodern: Perils of a Puppet in the United States,* my co-author Richard Wunderlich argues that Disney and his sources created a new image of Pinocchio-as-child: "In this new imagery no longer is the child's goal to grow up, mature, and transform. Rather, its goal is to be a good child, a loved and commended child, a child who enhances Family Harmony and promotes Family Solidarity. Its goal is *to continue as a child!*" (86). Disney's puppet's purposeful nongrowth means that he never develops individual initia-

tive or judgment. The ideology of the film requires that the child not question received ideology. As Jack Zipes writes in *Happily Ever After: Fairy Tales, Children and the Culture Industry,* "Pinocchio will aim to please and will repress his desires and wishes first and foremost that his father is happy. Such a boy is easily manipulated for the good of the country, the good of the corporation, and the good of the Disney studio" (87).

Collodi's novel and Disney's film have very different geneses also, and this, too, is important where *A.I.* is concerned. Collodi's serialized story originally ended with Pinocchio's hanging in Chapter 15. Had it not been resumed later, it is unlikely that anyone would remember it, and then only as yet another example of nineteenth century writers' penchant for moralistic tales with hideous punishments for deviant children. Collodi's child audience demanded that his story be continued and that the puppet be saved, and the author complied. Zipes observes in *When Dreams Come True: Classical Fairy Tales and Their Tradition* that, "Collodi was forced to 'develop' or 'educate' his wooden protagonist despite his initial pessimistic perspective" (146). Indeed, in Chapter 16 the Girl with Blue Hair is suddenly endowed with the magical attributes of a fairy tale fairy; from then on, what began as a thoroughly painful didactic story becomes a somewhat less painful fairy tale and Bildungsroman for which a more or less happy ending is ensured.

If Collodi's *Pinocchio* grew *ad hoc,* Disney's was the result of a premeditated vision and a well-conceived marketing plan. That any differences between his film and Collodi's book are intentional is easily proven. Richard Wunderlich observes that, "It is clear that Disney was conscientious in his endeavor to know Collodi's *Pinocchio*: the Studio purchased several copies of the novel in both Italian and various English translations, as well as the plays by Remo Bufano and Adams T. Rice. Furthermore, Disney contracted to have his own translation written by Bianca Majolie (a staff member)" (95). Unlike the journeyman freelancer Collodi, who accepted the invitation to write *Pinocchio* as just another writer's gig, Disney was aiming for a blockbuster. As Wunderlich tells it, "Drawing on the great popularity of his existing cartoon characters, audience familiarity with his studio name, and the tactics already learned and used to merchandise his creations in myriad ways, Disney launched a market saturation campaign to attract audiences for the upcoming film" (94). In this respect, he is a precursor of Spielberg rather than an heir to Collodi.

A.I. is clearly a purposeful addition to the Pinocchio tradition, but whether Collodi's novel or Disney's film is the principal intertext is an important and complicated issue. Certainly *A.I.* alludes directly to the original *Pinocchio,* although in a curious way. In Scene 10,

"A Classic Story," Mommy (Monica Swinton, played by Australian actress Frances O'Connor) reads two separate passages verbatim from the 1944 translation done by another Australian, E. Harden. However, the volume that her son brings to her and which is clearly visible as she and her boys row, row, row their boat gently down the stream is the lavish Macmillan edition of Carol della Chiesa's 1925 translation. The Macmillan edition is strikingly beautiful with lavish illustrations by Attilio Missing; its cover looks good on camera, and I suspect it is the edition that Kubrick gave to Brian Aldiss while they were collaborating on what would become *A.I.* (Aldiss, xi). Whether Kubrick or Spielberg consciously chose the Harden translation from which to quote over the della Chiesa or others, I cannot say, though, as I will explain later, I have reason to think that this was a deliberate choice. What is of immediate importance is that the film uses a faithful translation of Collodi, not a revisionist adaptation, whether from Disney or not. So, the *textual* manifestation of the Pinocchio myth comes from Collodi's novel.

The Swinton household, though dysfunctional emotionally, is equipped with the right *Pinocchio* text for the job. Why? Because Collodi's *Pinocchio* is not only a tale of transformation but one of maturation as well. Mommy first reads fragments from two key scenes in the novel. The first is Pinocchio's encounter with the Fire-Eater. In this episode from chapter 11 of the book, Pinocchio, his life journey having barely begun, willingly offers himself up as firewood in order to save Harlequin, a fellow puppet. What makes Pinocchio's sacrifice all the more amazing is that in chapter 10 Harlequin, fearing his master's wrath, had helped carry Pinocchio screaming for his father to the fire. Pinocchio's inherent goodness and tendency to empathize with others leads him to this noble gesture even though the puppet for whom he would die had done nothing to save him. Though Pinocchio has clearly imprinted on Geppetto, he is quite capable of loving another being with whom he feels kinship to the point where he would lay down his life for that friend. Robot David's imprinting is monomaniacal; his one love is Monica, his one need her undivided attention. Chapter 11 is a key episode in that it underscores what will turn out to be the very reason that Pinocchio finally triumphs: he has a capacity to extend himself on behalf of others because he feels kinship with them, a kinship that does not depend on blood ties or artificial programming.

Likewise, the second scene from which Mommy reads (from Chapter 36) emphasizes the extent of Pinocchio's growth; it is the grand finale. Pinocchio has become an industrious and caring puppet; he makes baskets to sell to support Geppetto, and he willingly offers what little money he has kept aside for new clothes to help the Fairy, who he thinks is in the hospital. Pinocchio's good heart is now housed in a more mature puppet, one who has learned that laziness and selfishness are not consistent with genuine caring for others. He has already grown and changed; his transformation into a real boy will merely confirm it. In *A.I.*, it is painfully obvious that the flesh and blood son Martin (Jake Thomas) requests this family favorite precisely because he knows that his artificial brother cannot possibly undergo the miraculous transformation to boyhood that Pinocchio experiences; his goal is to cause David pain and regain his primacy in the family. By choosing *The Adventures of Pinocchio*, the malicious Martin has really struck pay dirt, a vein richer than he knows. Not only can David not turn into a real boy, but he is also unable to develop psychologically beyond whatever his creator determined to be his permanent, programmed developmental stage. Martin, therefore, spitefully introduces the film's ultimate tragic core: David is Pinocchio-like, but he is not Pinocchio, for if he were, his suffering would have character-building implications. He would have a future. David's no-growth programming is underscored by the spinach-eating contest that Martin instigates which lands David in the repair shop where Mommy cringes in horror at the sight of his inner workings. Only real boys can eat spinach and become Popeye the Sailor Man; robot boys simply get their circuits clogged. Humans, or quasi-humans capable of growth, can aspire to be or resemble mythic or culture heroes; those with no growth potential cannot.

David's inherent inability to mature marks the essential difference between *A.I.* and Collodi's novel; in fact, that this feature has been consciously built into him inverts completely Collodi's themes of sound child mentoring and mutual sacrifice. The scope, if not the character, of villainy is greater in *A.I.* than in *The Adventures of Pinocchio*, but David's range of options is nothing like Pinocchio's because he has been built to be a toy, an intelligent toy, but a toy nonetheless. There are two types of Mecha or robot in *A.I.*: those that do work and those that give pleasure; both are selfless servants. David is the latter, though, unfortunately for him, he has a self. As a number of commentators have pointed out, there are no decent human characters whatsoever in *A.I.* That harsh judgment seems reasonable given that the humans not only wreck the earth, but they also create a mechanical race that they exploit, torture and kill. Collodi's Professor Hobby (William Hurt) sets out to build a robot-boy who "*will* genuinely love the parent or parents it imprints on with a love that will never end" and who will be "the perfect child, caught in freeze-frame, always loving, never ill, never changing" (1: Artificial Intelligence). He does this in order to assuage his own loss and his company's financial interest. And why not? Robots have been developed to replace the labor of those humans who are dead or unborn because of runaway global warming, the climatic disaster that leads to human extinction. Evidently, the leading product of Cybertronics of New Jersey, Hobby's company, are sex robots, beings created for human gratification who are themselves incapable of gratification. We learn later from Gigolo Joe that the humans have created child sex robots so that pedophiles can satisfy their desires without committing a crime. Joe tells David, "We are the guiltless pleasures of the lonely human being" (19: Rouge City).

Guiltless pleasures? *A.I.* reinforces a theme often expressed in SF stories about artificial people: all too often, humans, freed from the moral restraints prescribed (though not necessarily followed) in human relationships, will exploit androids unethically. In one of the classics of the genre, Philip K. Dick's *Do Androids Dream of Electric Sheep?*, a novel which shares theme and to a large extent setting with *A.I.* (that is, a world ruined by people), a snippet from a television ad appeals to the perverse needs of the audience: "—duplicates the halcyon days of the pre-Civil War Southern States! Either as body servants or tireless field hands, the custom-tailored humanoid robot—designed specially for YOUR UNIQUE NEEDS, FOR YOU AND YOU ALONE" (17). Dick's humans have the same lust-hate relationship with robots as do the pathetic humans of *A.I.* In *Androids,* humans make humanoid robots to serve their needs and animal robots to replace the real creatures they killed off with nuclear war. In both the novel and the film, people want robots to mimic human behavior but hate them for doing so. Dick's novel also posits sexual encounters with androids. Bounty hunter Phil Resch callously recommends to central character Rick Deckard that he have sex with a female android before killing her. Deckard, a man deeply troubled by ethical issues, does have sex with android Rachel Rosen (though he does not kill her) without ever considering whether he is cheating on his wife.

By likening androids to American slaves, Dick is suggesting that the tendency to use others predates the invention of robots and is, in fact, as old as coercive behavior itself, which must be very old indeed since slavery is such an ancient human institution. The classically bad SF film *Creation of the Humanoids* (1962) accomplishes much the same by showing the barbaric responses of the Order of Flesh and Blood to the "clickers" they regard as threats to human hegemony. In *A.I.,* Professor Hobby thinks that there is a market for robot children to replace the flesh and blood children that people cannot have or have lost, but they do not want them to grow up—or even reach puberty—for they would then have their own needs, and continued exploitation would be neither possible nor ethical. The Flesh Fair attendees that spare David respond to his human appearance, but their action does not mark a turning point in human attitudes or behavior towards robots in general.

Though *A.I.*'s humans are detestable, some of its pseudo humans are not. Gigolo Joe protects David and even pi-lots him to Manhattan, a very dangerous act considering that it is a Mecha-free zone and he is a fugitive. Teddy the Supertoy truly loves David and has the sentimentality (and, it turns out, the foresight) to save the lock of hair that David clips from Mommy. The tradition of robots exhibiting behavior that is more humane than that of the humans who made them is common in SF, the most popularly known examples occurring in Isaac Asimov's robot stories and in the "person" of Lt. Commander Data of *Star Trek: the Next Generation.* Because they are imprinted via programming, Asimov's humanitarian Three Laws of Robotics have tended to be more powerful than the Ten Commandments that free-willed humans violate with impunity, but programmed or not, they have contributed to SF's many positive robot role models, up to and including the evolved Mechas that appear at the end of *A.I.* In fact, one of the most important elements in the more human than humans robots is that they appear to transcend their programming (or actually do transcend it), so that their actions are clearly laudable choices rather than programmed reflexes. Lester del Rey's "Helen O'Loy" (1938), Tanith Lee's *The Silver Metal Lover* (1985), and Amy Thomson's *Virtual Girl* (1993) are three fictions that present robots worthy of Mr. Data's company.

Asimov's Three Laws of Robotics require absolutely that robots subordinate any ego that they might have to the needs of humans. Fictional robots in this tradition may be created in the image of humans, but without the human penchant for egotistical behavior—what the Dalai Lama, a man who might be said to preach a human version of Asimov's laws, calls "an exaggerated self-centeredness" (Dalai Lama 4) incompatible with human happiness. If Asimov's robots and their descendents have the advantage of knowing in whose image and for what purpose they were created, humans do not necessarily have the same advantage. *A.I.*'s Professor Hobby identifies a little too closely with his putative creator when he provides a justification for his robot-child project by relying on a patriarchal interpretation of *Genesis.* When asked in the opening scene by a Black colleague (and who would appreciate the moral quandary more than a descendent of slaves?) whether it is ethical to create a robot-boy whose sole purpose is to love a human unconditionally and forever, he answers (with an ominous roll of thunder in the background), "Didn't God create Adam to love *him*?" (1: Artificial Intelligence). This heavy-handed example of hubris shows what in this film damns the human race. Professor Hobby, like Victor Frankenstein before him, believes he can play God; so too do all of the humans who have contributed, consciously or not, to the global warming that in *A.I.* dooms life on the planet. In *A.I.* humans have squandered Eden and made a mockery of the stewardship which they have interpreted as God-given dominion and license. Hobby's surname introduces the chilling suggestion that God created Adam because he needed a hobby. Parenting is certainly not a hobby, so it is perhaps no wonder that, rejected by a punishing father and exiled from paradise, Adam develops an obsession with being like his creator that leads his descendents to condemn their own progeny by ruining creation itself. By creating a humanoid child, Professor Hobby is imperfectly mimicking his maker and expressing humans' insatiable need for love and acceptance, so insatiable that in the case of robot substitutes, the end justifies the means. In Genesis the creator expelled humans from Eden and seems, in this film's awful scenario, to have turned His back on His children, to have left them in the wilderness, just as Monica abandons David in a wood made truly wild by vicious humans. Hence David: he is programmed to be the perfect child forever, and what a perfect child is has been predetermined by Professor Hobby, whose own loss of a child combines with marketing genius to produce the image of a boy who will love his owner unconditionally and who, above all, will never leave. And the recipient of this devotion owes him nothing in return.

David is not just a robot; he is Monica's toy, a plaything that she discards—not without misgivings and pain—when he is no longer wanted and needed. Indeed, the story of David and Gigolo Joe the sex toy are remarkably compatible with the four principal motifs that, according to Lois Kuznets, typify toys-come-to-life narratives. Such toys may "embody human anxiety about what it means to be 'real,'" and, like Joe and his robot peers, "the secrets of the night" in what "can be a marginal, liminal, potentially carnival world." David's obsession with his unreality is the core of the film; the underground world of Rouge City is the place where technology and the Dionysian meet. Martin's cruelty, the Flesh Fair, and the Mecha body parts dumping so reminiscent of Nazi atrocities are evidence that "when manipulated by humans—adults or children—toys embody all the temptations and responsibilities of power." Finally and most importantly for Professor Hobby and *A.I.*, "when toys come alive as beings created by humans (usually male), they replicate 'divine' creation and imply vital possibilities for human creativity while arousing concomitant anxiety about human competition with the divine. These creations also threaten human hegemony" (2). Professor Hobby, despite his Geppetto-like vest, is what Kuznets calls the "bad toy maker." Imagine the scene in which David is provoked to violence when he returns to his maker's lab and is addressed by a perfect duplicate of himself as you read Kuznets' description: "the atmosphere that surrounds the bad toy maker can make the toy shop a fiercely threatening place to be" (184). As soon as they are endowed with sentience and self-consciousness, both robots and toys become us, even when we choose to ignore this fact. To be a plaything is to be objectified; to be a self-conscious plaything is to be abused.

Earlier, I wrote that the *textual* manifestation of the Pinocchio myth comes from Collodi's novel. For the most part, however, the *visual* manifestation is from Disney, and this, I suggest, is part of the reason that, as many critics have commented, it is so very clear where Kubrick's dark vision gives way to Spielberg's attempt at a rosy ending. David's rescue by the Mechas who have succeeded humans as masters of the earth and his schmaltzy perfect day with Mommy sugar coat the bitter core of the film. Spielberg quotes from Collodi, but he shows us Disney. Spielberg's winged Blue Fairy is the prime example. David has presumably heard Collodi's story in its entirety. In that story the Fairy is a crafty shape-changer who can be a little girl, a goat, or a woman as befits the occasion. Nonetheless, it is on the Disneyesque icon that David fixates. Likewise, the whale-shaped amphibicopter also recalls Disney's Monstro rather than Collodi's great shark, *il pesce cane*. As I pointed out earlier, Professor Hobby wears a vest like Geppetto's when David meets him in Manhattan. That David himself has somehow internalized the image of the Disney Fairy is clear when the evolved robots of the future create a Fairy look-alike in order to make communication with David easier.

The foregoing is important because the last segment of *A.I.* suggests that David has become as real as he can become and that somehow his one-day visit from Mommy will suffice until his existence is brought to end, which, considering that he is already 2,000 years old, doesn't look like a near-term probability. The evolved robots know that he will always be a child, and they are, therefore, reluctant to grant his wish that Mommy be revived for a day. Their concern for his well-being contrasts sharply with the deplorable treatment he gets from his creator and his adopted human family. The evolved robots—whether programmed to do so or not—live by Asimov's Three Laws of Robotics and have developed an unexplainable devotion to the memory of the humans who began their evolution by creating David in the first place. The robot spokesman puts it this way: "certainly humans beings must be the key to the meaning of all existence" (29: Coming Home). Since it is very clear in the film that humans are directly responsible for doing themselves in and for taking every other species down with them, the robots' nostalgia for the human past does not make a whole lot of sense, especially since these mechanical beings seem capable of a depth of feeling that no human in the film ever shows. We are told that humans had "spirit," some ineffable quality or faculty that robots lack, yet the evolved Mechas form a post-human just community that compares favorably with Collodi's just community and that contrasts vividly with the out of control selfishness and irresponsibility of their human forebears. Even David's contemporary machine friends Teddy and Gigolo Joe seem to be more direct ancestors of the robots of the future than do the film's humans. In this respect, *A.I.* is consistent with what Brian Aldiss said in a 1997 interview in *Wired* (quoted on "The Kubrick Site") was Kubrick's belief that androids would "'be an improvement over the human race'"(1).

A.I.'s conclusion appears to reinforce the Disney image of the all-important family, but it does so at its own peril. David's family and maker treat him about as badly as they can. Henry Swinton (Sam Robards) takes him home to relieve his wife's depression caused by their son's being in cold storage waiting for a cure that is not likely ever to come. He quickly becomes hostile to David and pushes for his return to the manufacturer, which he knows means death, as soon as David begins to perform actions that suggest to the shoot-from-the-hip head of household that he is potentially dangerous to Monica or the miraculously resuscitated Martin. His Geppetto, Professor Hobby, following his own longings and his hubris, sends David unprepared to a family that no good adoption agency would have selected for placement, then allows him to go through the hell of finding his way to New York, where David is confronted with overwhelming and incontrovertible proof that he is absolutely not unique and that he can be mass produced. But it is Monica, the cherished Mommy, whose betrayal is the deepest. Harvey Karten correctly observes that, "the relationship between David and his 'Mommy' is about co-dependency" (2), but she is literally in the driver's seat when, like a wicked stepmother, she abandons David in the woods, regretting that she hasn't told him more about the world. But what could she have said that would have helped him? Would a preprogrammed Mecha have been able better to adjust to separation from his only love object if she had first told him that humans hate Mechas and that all humans are about as selfish as she is? The world of *A.I.* is certainly as frightening as Disney's, but the family, Disney's bastion, is the greatest horror show on earth. The Dalai Lama observes that "we are all born helpless. Without a parent's kindness we could not survive, much less prosper. When children grow up in constant fear, with no one to rely on, they suffer their whole lives. Because the minds of small children are so delicate, their need for kindness is particularly obvious" (3). In *A.I.*, human moral blindness and ego obscure the obvious: that if David is created to be a child, he must be treated as one, and to have created him without adequate growth potential and to have abandoned him to a hostile adult world is to condemn him to suffer his whole life, and he has a very long life indeed.

At the end of the film Spielberg once again pays homage to Collodi when the narrator tells us that after his day with Mommy David slept for the first time and actually dreamed. This echoes the quotation from the Harden translation that Mommy read in Scene 10. In Collodi's novel Pinocchio sleeps and envisions the Fairy just prior to awakening as real boy. Collodi tells us that

Pinocchio's dream ends, but of the major translators, only Harden emphasizes dreaming by introducing the verb right at the beginning of the event: "As he slept, he dreamed he saw the fairy" (228). At the start of Scene 29, the screen is filled with the image of two blue eyes, which recalls Collodi's description as Pinocchio beholds himself in the mirror: "he saw the expressive, intelligent face of a goodlooking boy, with brown hair and blue eyes, who looked contented and full of joy" (231). Are we now to believe that the advanced robots are wrong and that David will now be capable of growth even though nothing has been changed in his programming? Pinocchio's dream has come true. In Disney's *Pinocchio,* the puppet becomes a little boy who is obviously still in need of parenting; fortunately he has the impossibly kind Geppetto, not to mention Jiminy Cricket, a cat and a goldfish. In *A.I.*, there is no need for a change in appearance; David was made "a good-looking boy," but his happiness and contentment are dependent on an impossibility—Monica's eternal love—and, ultimately, he and his dreams are expendable. Harden's emphasis on dreaming serves Spielberg's purposes, since dreaming is a major element in this DreamWorks film. But David appears to have awakened to a perpetual nightmare. He is now truly unique in the world, and he will always be one of kind, a species of one. True, he has Teddy, but Teddy isn't Mommy. Brian Aldiss recalls that Kubrick very much wanted an actual robot for his film (xv). If a Japanese company had been able to build one for him so that the audience would be constantly reminded of his artificiality, there would have been no need for Haley Joel Osmet—unless, of course, Kubrick had intended to make it possible for his robot-boy to become as real as Collodi's puppet becomes, which is exactly what Aldiss says Kubrick wanted when the two were still working together on a possible screenplay (xi). With a little tweaking, *A.I.* could have been a self-consciously tragic retelling of *Pinocchio*; with a lot more work, it could have been *Pinocchio* reborn, a glorious triumph of humanity in the age of artificial intelligence.

A.I.'s disturbing and somewhat incongruous conclusion marks it as a dystopia of childhood, a world in which perpetual childhood leads to endless frustration. Dystopias are often marked by restrictions on genuine maturation. In Lois Lowry's *The Giver,* for example, drugs, propaganda, and peer pressure prevent citizens from attaining meaningful adulthood—they remain essentially impossibly sexless, unquestioning preadolescents despite physical growth. Like shrinking, which is often a frightening metaphor for powerlessness in children's literature, perpetual childhood is the antithesis of growth and self-determination, and it is the foundation of such adult dystopias as *Pleasantville* and Ira Levin's *This Perfect Day.* The residents of Pleasantville not only don't have sex, they don't even go to the bathroom. Ira Levin's novel, which is a kind of updating of *Brave*

New World, is one where the perfect state controls every aspect of everyone's lives. Even the brief outburst of adolescent sexual needs is carefully controlled through chemotherapy. In the truly horrific world of Garth Nix's young adult novel *Shade's Children,* a ruthless race of invading Overlords make adults disappear so that that they can harvest children on their fourteenth or "sad" birthday, after which the children are sent to a Meat Factory where normal development ends and they are turned into one of several kinds of expendable, grotesque fighting cyborgs. Nix probes primal adolescent fears in his nightmare vision. The often uncomfortable, confusing and potentially embarrassing physical changes that mark puberty are transformed into monstrous and purposeful metamorphoses. The love-hate relationship with adult authority manifests itself as the replacement of that authority with something literally not human—the children of this novel are by definition alienated. Nix's dark vision may seem far more malignant Spielberg's in *A.I.,* but they do share some fundamental similarities: paternalistic totalitarianism treats everyone as if they were children and treats children as chattel. That Spielberg's evolved Mechas who rescue David are nothing like the murderous visitors in *Shade's Children* does not negate the fact that the humans they have replaced succumbed to a fatal failure to nurture their world and their children and to their willingness to abuse technology and its products, including androids and robots.

Collodi's *Pinocchio* is not a utopian novel, but by positing a world in which responsible boyhood and adulthood are possible, it distinguishes itself from works like *A.I.,* in which maturation is purposely and systematically denied. Ironically, the production schedule for *A.I.* would have been more leisurely had it been filmed in a world where growing up *is* impossible. According to Dustin Putman, the film was shot in 20 weeks rather than a year because Haley Joel Osmet was maturing too fast for comfort (2).

A.I.'s David is a Mecha, specifically programmed to be the ideal boy his mother craves but whom she refuses ultimately to love. Like Pinocchio, he travels through a dystopian world, hunted by villains and aided by friends. Unlike Pinocchio, his goal is to become the unreal boy his owners, a.k.a. parents, want: a static, perfect, mobile manikin. David is not only denied real boyhood and thus the potential for manhood, he is also transfixed by the tale of a mythic fairy with whose help he thinks he can become real. Whatever Spielberg's intentions might have been, the attempt to brighten Kubrick's dark vision falls flat as David is left looking forward to looking backward on what must forever be his last day of happiness. Pinocchio's life may have been difficult, but at least he had one, and his dreams were his own.

Note

1. Unless otherwise noted, this and subsequent quotations from *Pinocchio* are from the 1944 Harden translation issued in the United States by Puffin Books in 1974. Quotations from the film were transcribed from the soundtrack on the Dream Works DVD, *A.I. Artificial Intelligence,* released March 5, 2002. Scene numbers and titles, cited in parentheses, conform to the DVD scene index.

Works Cited

Aldiss, Brian. Quotation from The Kubrick Site: *www.visualmemory.co.uk/amk/doc/0068.html, 9 pages,* accessed 3/17/02.

————. *Supertoys Last All Summer Long and Other Stories.* (New York: St. Martin's, 2001) ["Supertoys Last All Summer Long" originally published in *Harper's Bazaar,* 1969].

Collodi, Carlo, *[The Adventures of] Pinocchio.* Trans. E. Harden. A Puffin Book. New York: Penguin, 1974.

Creation of the Humanoids (a.k.a. *Revolt of the Humanoids*). Dir. Wesley Barry. With Don Megowan, Erica Elliott, Don Doolittle, and George Milan. Genie Productions Inc. 1962.

Dalai, Lama (His Holiness). *How to Practice: The Way to a Meaningful Life.* Ed. & Trans. Jeffrey Hopkins. New York: Pocket Books, 2002.

Dick, Philip K. *Do Androids Dream of Electric Sheep?* New York: Ballantine (A Del Rey Book), 1996. Originally published by Random House, 1968.

Karten, Harvey. Review of *A.I. Artificial Intelligence.* All Reviews.com/videos-3/ai-artificial-intelligence-4.htm accessed 3/9/02.

Kuznets, Lois. *When Toys Come Alive: Narratives of Animation, Metamorphosis, and Development.* New Haven: Yale University Press, 1994.

Levin, Ira. *This Perfect Day.* New York: Random House, 1970.

Nix, Garth. *Shade's Children.* New York: Harper, 1998.

Putman, Dustin. Review of *A.I. Artificial Intelligence.* All Reviews.com/videos-3/ai-artificial-intelligence-htm accessed 3/9/02.

Star Trek: First Contact (a.k.a. Star Trek 8). Dir. Jonathan Frakes. With Patrick Stewart, Jonathan Frakes, Brent Spiner, LeVar Burton, Michael Dorn, Gates McFadden, and Marina Sirtis. Paramount Pictures. 1996.

Wunderlich, Richard and Thomas J. Morrissey. *Pinocchio Goes Postmodern: Perils of a Puppet in the United States.* New York: Routledge, 2002.

Zipes, Jack. *Happily Ever After: Fairy Tales, Children and the Culture Industry.* New York: Routledge, 1997.

————. *When Dreams Come True: Classical Fairy Tales and Their Traditions.* New York: Routledge, 1999.

Jonathan Bignell (essay date 2004)

SOURCE: Bignell, Jonathan. "Another Time, Another Space: Modernity, Subjectivity and *The Time Machine.*" In *Liquid Metal: The Science Fiction Film Reader,* edited by Sean Redmond, pp. 136-44. London: Wallflower Press, 2004.

[*In the following essay, Bignell draws parallels between George Pal's 1960 cinematic adaptation of H. G. Wells's renowned science fiction novel* The Time Machine *and the medium of film, asserting that "like the newly invented cinema, time travel frees the subject from the present and the real, to replace these with a virtual present and a virtual reality which is novel, exciting and technological."*]

H. G. Wells' science fiction novels have long been attractive to filmmakers. Film versions include *The Island of Dr Moreau* (Erle C. Kenton, 1932 [titled *The Island of Lost Souls*], Don Taylor, 1977, John Frankenheimer, 1996), *The Invisible Man* (James Whale, 1933, sequels Joe May, 1940, Ford Beebe, 1944), *Things to Come* (William Cameron Menzies, 1936), and *War of the Worlds* (Byron Haskin, 1953). I want to focus here on Wells's short novel *The Time Machine,* first published in 1895, and the film adaptation directed by George Pal (1960).[1] *The Time Machine* does feature strange creatures, but not aliens in the usual science fiction sense. The central character, unnamed in the novel but called George Wells in the film, is a late-nineteenth-century inventor who constructs a sled-like vehicle enabling him to travel into the future. In the year 802,701, the Time Traveller discovers two races of humanoids, the Eloi and the Morlocks. In the novel the frail and childlike Eloi are the passive and effete descendants of the elite of an advanced society, living in a sunlit paradise on the surface. The Morlocks are the ape-like cannibal descendants of the workers who operated the subterranean machines that kept this elite supplied with all its needs. This vision of the future counters the Victorian myth of progress, and explores the interdependence of workers and masters, perverted into the dependence of the Morlocks on the flesh of the Eloi who they formerly served. The Time Traveller realises that evolutionary development toward technical refinement and social order will lead to decadence (in the Eloi) and to savagery (in the Morlocks) at the same time.

In Pal's film version, a global war fought with nuclear weapons has exhausted the resources of this future society, and the remnants of the race have divided into those who continued to dwell on the irradiated surface (who became the Eloi) and those who stayed in underground shelters (and became the Morlocks). Clearly, the Cold War nuclear fears of 1960 have informed the future vision of Pal's film, just as anxieties around Darwinism and class conflict fuel the novel. The changes made to the narrative in the film version essentially involve the updating of the journey into the future so that the fears and fantasies of 1960 can be included.[2] Each version of *The Time Machine* explores future times which are by definition alien to the audience, but this alienness is necessarily consonant with familiar ideas.

My focus here is less on the alienness of the creatures in the future than on the alienness yet familiarity of the time travel experience and the futuristic settings of the story. The Time Traveller becomes a spectator who watches time move like a speeded-up film, and stops several times to explore the future scene. Like the cinema spectator, the Time Traveller sits on a red plush seat and watches a marvellous spectacle, and the journey into the future depends on a machine, a technological apparatus rather than magic or dream. The subjective experience being outlined in the novel is a subjectivity to be developed in cinema and in modern consumer culture in general, where technology transports the consumer to a virtual environment primarily experienced visually. Temporal mobility in *The Time Machine,* as in cinema, allows the subject to encounter what is alien, yet necessarily familiarises this as a consumable media experience. But time travel allows more than a cinematic visual spectacle. Since the hundreds of centuries traversed in the Time Traveller's fictional journey involve changes in buildings, people and even the geology of the landscape, the journey through time is in effect a tourist trip to alien spaces that he can leave his seat to explore. The Time Machine itself, as described in the novel and portrayed in Pal's film, looks like a sled with brass rails and over-decorated Victorian ornaments. It has a large revolving dish mounted vertically behind the inventor, and coloured lights and indicators on its control surface. The Time Machine is envisioned on an analogy with a machine for travelling in space rather than time, signalling the association between tem-poral movement and spatial movement.

Both the novel and the film are predicated on what Anne Friedberg has called a 'mobilised virtual gaze', a characteristic aspect of modernity developing through the nineteenth century into the twentieth, whereby movement in space and time is simulated by visual apparatuses of representation: 'The virtual gaze is not a direct perception but a *received* perception mediated through representation. I introduce this compound term in order to describe a gaze that travels in an imaginary *flânerie* through an imaginary elsewhere and an imaginary elsewhen.'[3] Wells's fictional Time Traveller experiences the future directly, but the reader of the story and the viewer of the film experience a mediated version of this, mediated through language in the novel, and through the visual and aural resources of cinema in the film. The reader or spectator becomes a *flâneur* or stroller, led on an exploratory journey through alien worlds. Friedberg continues: 'The cinema developed as an apparatus that combined the 'mobile' with the 'virtual'. Hence, cinematic spectatorship changed, in unprecedented ways, the concepts of the *present* and the *real*.'[4] In both Wells's novel and Pal's film adaptation, travel in time is experienced predominantly as a visual experience. But one of the main attractions of the novel and the film is the ability to stop the headlong rush into the future, so that the Traveller can stop and stroll around in a realistically presented space. Time travel, like cinema, renders the moment virtual in order to allow a real-seeming experience of an alien space-time. Time travellers and cinema spectators are displaced from the reality of their own present and their own real location in order to be transported to 'an imaginary elsewhere and an imaginary elsewhen'.

The opening of Pal's film makes it clear that it is the cinema spectator who will be moved in virtual space and time and who will become the virtual subject of the time travel experience. It begins with a collection of brightly-lit timepieces, appearing in chronological order of their invention, moving out of the black and dimensionless space of the screen towards the spectator. It is as if the spectator is travelling through space, plunging headlong into black emptiness with the cinema screen functioning as a window onto the journey. The final clock is London's Big Ben, tilted at an angle, as the hour is heard to strike. Lightning flashes and thunder crashes as the shot changes to a rapidly rising sun over which the film's title is superimposed. Then leaves and snow blow across a blue sky, succeeding each other rapidly as the seasons rush past. The first scene establishes the interior of the inventor's house, and the camera pans over a large collection of watches, mantel clocks and grandfather clocks, continuing the time motif and associating the spectator's own plunge through time with the interests of the central character. Already we can see that there is a slippage between the spectating subject in the cinema and the central time-travelling character. Furthermore, travel in time is parallel to travel in space, as the rushing forward movement past a series of clocks makes rather literally evident.

George Pal was drawn to Wells' story in part because it provided opportunities for state-of-the-art visual effects. His film version of *The Time Machine* uses many techniques including accelerated motion, reverse motion, pixellation, model shots and mattes to render the experience of time travel, and the future worlds the Traveller encounters, with as much verisimilitude as was possible in 1960. Pal was a specialist in these technologies of illusion. He began his career as a puppeteer making short advertising films in the late 1930s. In 1940 he went to Hollywood and moved on to adventure films where he specialised in trick effects, receiving an Academy Award in 1943 for his development of innovative methods and techniques. The films he worked on included *Destination Moon* (Irving Pichel, 1950), *When Worlds Collide* (Rudolph Maté, 1951), *War of the Worlds, Tom Thumb* (1958, which he also directed) and *The Time Machine*. All of these films won Oscars for their special effects. Pal's special skill, then, was to realise the incredible, to make the alien and strange comprehensible according to visual conventions we can accept. In this respect he was part of a long tradition in cinema where, since the emergence of the medium, film had been used as a support for wondrous spectacles, where what was absent, novel, distant or unfamiliar became vividly present as part of an entertainment for the paying consumer.

Science fiction, historiography and archaeology, which all blossomed in the later decades of the nineteenth century, share an interest in time: representing a future moment, a documented moment in the past, or an arrested time which we can uncover and see. Time travel in literature in the work of Wells or Jules Verne appears at the same period as stories about lost civilisations in Conan Doyle's *The Lost World*, and novels by Bulwer Lytton and Butler. It is in this period that Roman sites in Britain, the pyramids and Mycenae were excavated, and Arthur Evans recreated parts of the Bronze Age city of Knossos in Crete so that tourists could walk around it. The common feature in these different aspects of culture is the refinement of techniques of representation which can make what is past, absent or fantastic into something which can be recreated, simulated and rendered virtually present for an individual subject. Similarly, the beginning of cinema is associated with nineteenth-century science's quest for knowledge of the physical world, with that period's obsession with memory, death and preservation, with fairground trick effects, magic and the supernatural, and with the possibilities of exploiting mechanical inventions for a mass consumer public. All of these aspects of the culture of modernity are signalled near the beginning of *The Time Machine*. The story is told mainly in flashback in both the novel and in Pal's film, as a dishevelled inventor appears late to meet his houseguests, and tells the story of his time travels. The first flashback returns us to the day when his guests were shown a model Time Machine vanishing, an experiment which all four of them believe may be a parlour trick, like the seances, magic lantern shows and short novelty films of the period. Like the spectators of the first films, the Time Traveller's audiences are thrown into doubt about the evidence of their own eyes. For them, the disappearance of the model Time Machine might be real, but more likely a trick, a simulation, a scientific demonstration or an optical illusion. *The Time Machine*, then, exploits the distinction between the virtual and the real, a distinction fundamental to the culture of modernity and to cinema.

Wells' novel was written amid a long-standing fascination with visually-based representational devices in the late nineteenth century, exemplified by the dioramas, panoramas and other proto-cinematic devices of the period. Dioramas and panoramas were buildings where groups of spectators were presented with large back-lit illuminated images painted on semi-transparent screens, and used highly realistic painted backdrops and carefully arranged effects of perspective and depth of field to seem to place the spectator in a remote landscape, or at the occurrence of a famous past event. They offered the viewer a highly realistic visual environment, representing places to which the great majority of people could never go. These devices were enthralling because they transported the spectator to alien places and alien times by means of visual technologies and supporting special effects. What was there to be seen might be alien, a vision of another place and another time, but the whole spectacle depended on the spectator's familiarity with how to look, and on some familiarity with the cultural significance of what was represented. Effects of perspective, of the play of light and shade, were carefully calculated to be as real-seeming as possible, to allow the spectator to immerse himself or herself in the sense of 'being there' in the scene. Although the spectator would never have visited the great cathedral of Chartres, the eve of the Battle of Waterloo or the Swiss Alps, these places and events had already to be culturally established as significant and recognisable, so that there was a peculiar thrill in seeing them in all their grandeur. Like any consumer technology or media experience, the new, the alien, the surprising, had to be balanced with the expected, the familiar and the conventional.

In the novel and the film, time travel is a curious mixture of scientific experiment and fairground thrills. The experience of time travel gives the inventor in the novel 'a feeling exactly like that one has upon a switch-back—of a helpless headlong motion!'[5] The Doctor in Pal's film version, one of the inventor's guests, suggests that the Time Machine is of no use or commercial value. Instead, he recommends that the inventor should do something to help Britain in the ongoing Boer War. The inventor is presented as a scientist who resists the military or commercial potential of his work, and his trip into the future seems to be an escape from war and commerce. As if escaping into the virtual world of the cinema, to a film in which he is both spectator and central character, the Time Traveller quits the time and space of his quotidian present. As Walter Benjamin wrote:

> Our taverns and our metropolitan streets, our railroad stations and our factories appeared to have locked us up hopelessly. Then came the film and burst this prison-world asunder by the dynamite of the tenth of a second, so that now, in the midst of its far-flung ruins and debris, we calmly and adventurously go travelling.[6]

Like the newly invented cinema, time travel frees the subject from the present and the real, to replace these with a virtual present and a virtual reality which is novel, exciting and technological. Like cinema technology, time travel seems to offer opportunities for science as well as tourism and commercial entertainment, yet the appeal of both Wells's story and of Pal's film is based on the pleasures of fantasy and speculation which they offer, rather than the exploration of the geometric and physical principles which each version refers to in order to ground time travel in scientific fact.

While early pioneers used film to explore the science of animal movement and to record contemporary life, entertainment rapidly became the most commercially successful use for the new technology. In 1894 the first Edison Kinetoscope parlour opened in New York, offering films of less than a minute, viewed by individual spectators who peeked into the Kinetoscope cabinets to see vaudeville performers and famous personalities. The film historian Terry Ramsaye wrote to Wells in 1924 asking whether the idea for *The Time Machine* was born from Wells's experience of the Edison Kinetoscope.[7] Wells replied that he did not remember any connection between early motion pictures and the writing of the story, though the description of the Time Traveller's first jaunt into the future is highly suggestive of cinema. The Time Traveller is in his laboratory, and catches sight of his housekeeper just before he accelerates forward in time:

> Mrs. Watchett came in and walked, apparently without seeing me, towards the garden door. I suppose it took her a minute or so to traverse the place, but to me she seemed to shoot across the room like a rocket. I pressed the lever to its extreme position. The night came like the turning out of a lamp, and in another moment came tomorrow. The laboratory grew faint and hazy, then fainter and ever fainter. Tomorrow night came black, then day again, night again, day again, faster and faster still.[8]

The experience is entirely visual and places the Time Traveller in the role of filmmaker (controlling the machine) and spectator at the same time. As he speeds forward, the flickering motion of a film projector is suggested in the rapid alternation of day and night. The Kinetoscope allowed the novelty of seeing simple action speeded up or reversed, which was one of the most entertaining aspects of early films for their spectators. Films showed the acceleration of mechanical or natural processes (like the growth of plants), and this is mirrored when the Time Traveller sees 'great and splendid architecture rising about me, more massive than any buildings of our own time, and yet, as it seemed, built of glimmer and mist. I saw a richer green flow up the hillside, and remain there without any wintry intermission.'[9] When the Time Traveller returns to his original time, he sees accelerated reverse motion:

> I think I have told you that when I set out, before my velocity became very high, Mrs. Watchett had walked across the room, travelling, as it seemed to me, like a rocket. As I returned, I passed again across that minute when she traversed the laboratory. But now every motion appeared to be the exact inversion of her previous ones. The door at the lower end opened, and she glided quietly up the laboratory, back foremost, and disappeared behind the door by which she had previously entered.[10]

What both time travel and cinema can do is to make the familiar appear unfamiliar by changing the manner of its perception. What is rapid can be slowed down, what moves slowly can be speeded up, and forward motion can be reversed. Time travel and cinema seem to show the spectator the workings of the laws of nature, granting him or her a special perception, which makes the ordinary marvellous and strange.

In Pal's film, the first journey through time uses various cinematic trick effects, and the laboratory has a large glazed wall which enables it to function like a cinema screen, through which the inventor seated at the machine can see a panorama of the changing world outside. Special effects include fast-motion shots of the sun and clouds moving across the sky, a snail speeding across the floor, shadow and light flitting across the inventor and the machine, and people moving rapidly in the street across from the laboratory. While the sequence is anchored through shot/reverse-shots to George's point of view, many of the fast motion sequences are not from his spatial position, and function to make us share George's wonder and disorientation (noted in the voice-over narration) as he makes this short hop into the future. Time travel and cinema place the spectator in a privileged position, able to see movement in a way alien to normal experience. Because the Time Traveller is moving so rapidly through time, the people he sees cannot see him, and events unfold as if he were not present. One of the components of cinematic pleasure explored by Christian Metz[11] and other film theorists is exactly this transcendent vision, where the cinema spectator seems to master and control what is seen on the screen, while being excluded from the action and removed from responsibility for it. The Time Traveller at this point, and the cinema spectator, are both apparent masters of vision, and also voyeurs of a world which they cannot enter.

In 1895 the Lumière brothers showed the first publicly projected films in Paris, exhibited at the Empire Music Hall in London in 1896. Also in 1895, the year *The Time Machine* was published, Robert Paul, a scientific instrument-maker from London who had copied and improved the Kinetoscope, designed a motion picture camera with his collaborator the photographer Birt Acres. By 1896 Robert Paul was showing his own films at Olympia in London and the Alhambra music hall, and had made the first British fiction film, *The Soldier's Courtship*. Ramsaye reports that Robert Paul read *The Time Machine* soon after its publication, and it gave him an idea for a new way to use the film medium.[12] Paul wrote to Wells, who visited him at his London studio. After the meeting with Wells, Paul entered patent application no. 19984, dated 24 October 1895, for 'A Novel Form of Exhibition or Entertainment, Means for Presenting the Same'.[13] It begins:

> My invention consists of a novel form of exhibition whereby the spectators have presented to their view scenes which are supposed to occur in the future or the past, while they are given the sensation of voyaging upon a machine through time.[14]

Paul's invention was never built, due to lack of funds, and belonged among a rash of inventions at the turn of the century which were combinations of film with diorama-like attractions or fairground magic effects. In 1904, for instance, at the St Louis Exhibition, George C. Hale presented Hale's Tours, where travelogue films were shown to spectators seated in a railway carriage, with train sound effects and a wobbling floor to simulate movement. The similarities between the descriptions of time travel in Wells's novel and the experience of cinema seem to have triggered Paul's idea for a virtual time travel attraction exploiting aspects of several recently invented technologies.

The mechanism was to be a 'platform, or platforms' which could contain a group of spectators enclosed on three sides, facing a screen on which 'views' were to be projected. The platform would be moved by cranks to produce 'a gentle rocking motion'.[15] While the platform was moving, fans would blow air over the spectators, simulating the effect of motion, or the fans could be visibly attached to the platform as if they were a means of propulsion.

> After the starting of the mechanism, and a suitable period having elapsed, representing, say, a certain number of centuries, during which the platforms may be in darkness, or in alternations of darkness and dim light, the mechanism may be slowed and a pause made at a given epoch, on which the scene upon the screen will gradually come into view of the spectators, increasing in size and distinctness from a small vista, until the figures, etc., may appear lifelike if desired.[16]

Time travel would be simulated, as in Wells' novel, by a motion not unlike a fairground ride, and would involve passages from darkness to light reminiscent of Wells' description. It was important that the scene should be 'realistic', showing a 'hypothetical landscape, containing also the representations of the inanimate objects in the scene', and would use slides showing moving objects like a balloon which could 'traverse the scene'.[17] There would also be 'slides or films, representing in successive instantaneous photographs, after the manner of the kinetoscope, the living persons or creatures in their natural motions'.[18] To produce dissolves and to enlarge or reduce the picture area, the projectors would be mounted on moveable tracks, which could bring them closer to or further from the screen. Paul's invention reproduces Wells's fictional time travel experience quite closely: putting the spectator into a conveyance like a switchback car, so that travel in time felt not unlike travel in space, and presenting the journey through time as a movement through light and darkness where the spectator stops to see a future epoch in the form of a film. While the alienness of the experience is what is attractive, it resembles familiar experiences like a fairground ride and a film show.

In some ways, Paul's invention looks forward to the experience of watching Pal's 1960 film. Pal's film can offer a modern cinematic experience, where trick effects, synchronous sound and music, and the use of cuts and camera movement have been developed to encourage the spectator's identification with the action, a sense of verisimilitude and dramatic pacing. Despite the futuristic settings of the film, and the alienness of the creatures in the future (especially the blue-skinned, shaggy-haired and sharp-toothed Morlocks), by 1960 cinema was calculated to produce an impression of reality. Paul's invention drew on the familiar technology of nineteenth-century amusement parks, such as the movement of the car and the blowing of air over the spectators, to produce similar effects. Following the practice at dioramas and panoramas, Paul also planned to use built sets which the spectators could physically explore:

> In order to increase the realistic effect I may arrange that after a number of scenes from a hypothetical future have been presented to the spectators, they may be allowed to step from the platforms, and be conducted through grounds or buildings arranged to represent exactly one of the epochs through which the spectator is supposed to be travelling.[19]

Here physical movement and temporal movement appear together, and the spectating subject literally becomes a *flâneur* or stroller, on a tourist trip, complete with guide, through a three-dimensional simulation of the future. In Wells's novel and in Pal's film this experience has to be mediated through the spectator's identification with the Time Traveller himself, who narrates his journeys and describes his wonderment at what he sees, and whose point of view in the film is aligned with the camera as he enters buildings and explores new landscapes. In *The Time Machine* the Time Traveller is not only a voyeur but also a tourist having adventures in future locations, and Paul's invention clearly aimed to replicate this kind of experience.

In Pal's film the inventor stops to look around in 1917, 1940 and 1966. These interludes give the film the chance to create street scenes reminiscent of one of Robert Paul's future environments. The immediate space around the Time Traveller is a dressed set in each case, using glass shots for background, and different cars, costumes and shopfronts to establish location in time. In 1940 Pal departs from the Time Traveller's point of view and uses stock shots of blazing fighter planes, and a diorama model of London in the Blitz, but then from the Time Traveller's point of view the spectator witnesses post-war reconstruction. New concrete buildings rise and cranes and scaffolding grow up at high speed accompanied by jaunty music on the soundtrack. Accelerated motion is intended to be comic here, just as it was when the projector's ability to change the speed of natural movement was realised at the turn of the century. So far, the film has represented the known past in 1960, aiming for visual verisimilitude and focusing thematically on the immediate effects of war. In 1966, the projected future from the perspective of 1960 is like a sunny American suburb. The inventor's house (destroyed by a wartime bomb) has been replaced by a park. The local shop, which had become a department store by 1917, is now a glass and concrete shopping mall, and shiny American cars are in the street. The film's thematic emphasis on the effects of war continues as extras rush past and an air-raid siren sounds. As well as continuing the precise simulation of a realistic location, the film presents the future by extrapolation from a relatively pessimistic vision of humankind's folly. This virtual future environment is alien but familiar, all too obviously determined by a 1960 anxiety (but also shared by Wells in the 1895 novel) that the future will be the same as the present, only more so. The 1966 scene ends as an atomic blast devastates the street, volcanoes erupt, seemingly the earth's vengeance against humankind's misuse of atomic power, and lava streams shunt burned-out cars across the set.

The Time Traveller speeds forward to a landscape seen first in a wide establishing shot featuring a futuristic domed hall and tower falling into decay. Like Robert Paul's walk-through simulations of the future, the settings are 'realistic' in terms of visible detail, dimension, props and set dressing. In 802,701 the buildings and sets in Pal's film draw on an eclectic mix of forms familiar to the audience of 1960. The domed pavilions and towers are reminiscent of the structures built for Disneyland (which opened in 1955), the 1951 Festival of Britain, and other realised versions of the future built for the tourist visitor of the period. Settings are to some extent matched with contemporary preconceptions of the relation between architectural form and function, so that the dome in which decayed books and museum exhibits are found has the wide steps and frontage of a European or American palace of culture. The dark caverns inhabited by the cannibal Morlocks contain the heavy-industrial machines of a dank nineteenth-century factory, while the Morlocks' gruesome deserted dining area, littered with the bones and skulls of their Eloi prey, seems like a reconstruction of an archaeological site. The costumes of the sylvan and vegetarian Eloi are toga-like, and they are most often seen in a wooded and verdant setting like an idealised recreation of the civilisation of ancient Greece. Pal's version of the future is not visualised as a consistent environment. It is neither solely utopian nor dystopian in terms of the signification of elements of *mise-en-scène,* but draws on the cultural currency of signs in the physical environment which were in circulation in the period when the film was made. This virtual future is necessarily unlike the present the spectator knows, but far from alien because of the use of a bricolage of elements with familiar connotations and resonances.

Cinema in general, as the film theorist Jean-Louis Baudry argued, proceeds from a 'wish to construct a simulation machine capable of offering the subject perceptions which are really representations mistaken for perceptions'.[20] As theories of spectatorship have shown, the principle of cinema and other audio-visual technologies is to offer what is recognisable and familiar, balanced against the pleasures of the new, the alien, of what cannot be seen or experienced in quotidian reality. The spectator is moved through represented space and time, offered an imaginary spatial and temporary mobility. The case of *The Time Machine,* novel and film, provides a strikingly literal illustration of the principles of pleasure in representation, which cinema became focused on from a very early period in its development. A brief consideration of Paul's time travel spectacle links Wells's novel with cinema historically, showing that the novel was read, at least by someone who knew of the technical possibilities of the new medium, as a proto-cinematic experience. At the same time, as a science fiction story, *The Time Machine* reminds us that science fiction is especially significant in an examination of the subjectivity of modernity. Works in this genre often focus on spatial and temporal mobility and on the realisation of imaginary alien scenarios. The principle of science fiction is the simulation of another world which is both alien yet representable through the conventions, competencies and technologies we already know. In 1902 in France, only a few years after Wells's novel was published and Paul had entered his patent for a time travel entertainment, the first science fiction film, *A Trip to the Moon,* was first shown. It portrayed a journey through space by means of a gigantic projectile to an alien world where strange creatures are encountered, and used theatrical sets, backdrops and trick effects drawing on the capabilities of the film camera. The film's director, Georges Méliès, had formerly made his career as a stage magician. Just a few years after Paul's idea for a time travel attraction, movement in time and space were simulated on the cinema screen, rather than by elaborate combinations of film, static images, built sets, viewing platforms and tour guides. The modern notions of travel in space and time, which Wells's novel narrated in such visual form, began to become the stock in trade of film as commercial entertainment for the individual consumer, enjoying a mobile gaze but sitting still in the auditorium. The subject in modernity, strolling either literally or by means of a mobile gaze, through a virtual reality associated with commodity consumption and mass entertainment, is both necessary to and furthered by the pleasures of cinema, time travel, science fiction and tourism.

Notes

1. Earlier and shorter versions of *The Time Machine* were 'The Chronic Argonauts', serialised in the *Science Schools Journal,* April to June 1888, and an uncredited and unfinished serial 'The Time Machine', March to June 1894 in the *National Observer.* In January to May 1895 the *New Review* published a serial 'The Time Machine' similar to the first book editions published in 1895 by Heinemann, London, and Henry Holt & Co., New York. The 1960 film *The Time Machine* was directed by George Pal, with a screenplay by David Duncan, produced by MGM/Galaxy, and stars Rod Taylor and Yvette Mimieux. Other versions of Wells's story on film and television include a faithful rendition on BBC television adapted and directed by Robert Barr (screened 25 January 1949, revised and repeated 21 February 1949), a Canadian film version directed by Terence McCarthy in 1973, and an American 1978 TV movie adaptation directed by Henning Schellerup.

2. There is insufficient space here to discuss the many differences between the novel and the film. For example, the endings are very different: in the novel, the Time Traveller journeys to a time when the Earth is about to become lifeless, and, depressed, he returns to collect materials for gathering specimens from the future as evidence of his travels. In the film, he falls in love with Weena, an Eloi woman, and after returning briefly to his own time he sets off again to find her.

3. Anne Friedberg, *Window Shopping: Cinema and the Postmodern* (Berkeley, CA: University of California Press, 1993), pp. 2-3.

4. Ibid.

5. H. G. Wells, *The Time Machine,* in Harry M. Geduld (ed.), *The Definitive Time Machine: A Critical Edition of H. G. Wells's Scientific Romance with Introduction and Notes* (Bloomington and Indianapolis: Indiana University Press, 1987), p. 42. Geduld uses the text of Volume I of the Atlantic edition of Wells's work, H. G. Wells, *The*

Time Machine, The Wonderful Visit and Other Stories (New York: Charles Scribner & Sons, 1924).

6. Walter Benjamin, 'The Work of Art in the Age of Mechanical Reproduction', in *Illuminations,* trans. Harry Zorn (New York: Schocken Books, 1969), p. 316.

7. Terry Ramsaye, 'Robert Paul and *The Time Machine*' from T. Ramsaye, *A Million and One Nights* (New York: Simon & Schuster, 1926), reprinted in Geduld, *The Definitive Time Machine,* p. 196.

8. Wells, *Time Machine,* pp. 41-2.

9. Ibid., p. 43.

10. Ibid., p. 87.

11. Christian Metz, *The Imaginary Signifier: Psychoanalysis and the Cinema* (Bloomington: Indiana University Press, 1982).

12. See Ramsaye 'Robert Paul and *The Time Machine*', p. 196.

13. The patent application is reprinted in full in Geduld, *The Definitive Time Machine,* pp. 198-9.

14. Ibid., p. 198.

15. Ibid.

16. Ibid.

17. Ibid.

18. Ibid.

19. Ibid., p. 199.

20. Jean-Louis Baudry, 'The Apparatus: Metapsychological Approaches to the Impression of Reality in Cinema', in P. Rosen (ed.) *Narrative, Apparatus, Ideology* (New York: Columbia University Press, 1986), p. 315.

Dominic Alessio (essay date 2005)

SOURCE: Alessio, Dominic. "Redemption, 'Race,' Religion, Reality, and the Far-Right: Science Fiction Film Adaptations of Philip K. Dick." In *The Blade Runner Experience: The Legacy of a Science Fiction Classic,* edited by Will Brooker, pp. 59-76. London: Wallflower Press, 2005.

[*In the following essay, Alessio elucidates the central thematic concerns of several films inspired by Philip K. Dick's science fiction stories, including* Blade Runner, The Minority Report, Total Recall, *and* Paycheck.]

INTRODUCTION

According to *The Encyclopedia of Science Fiction* Philip K. Dick (PKD) is 'one of the two or three most important figures in 20th century US Science Fiction' (Clute & Nicholls 1999: 328). Likewise, John Mann in *The Mammoth Encyclopedia of Science Fiction* refers to PKD as 'possibly the most important SF writer of the second half of the twentieth century' (2001: 121). Not surprisingly, a number of academic texts have been devoted to examining his vast output of science fiction short stories, which number in the hundreds, as well as his forty-four published novels.[1] These same critical works have, however—albeit with some notable exceptions such as Judith Kerman's *Retrofitting Blade Runner: Issues in Ridley Scott's Blade Runner and Philip K. Dick's Do Androids Dream of Electric Sheep?* (which was first published in 1991 and republished in a 1997 revised edition), or Paul M. Sammon's *Future Noir: The Making of Blade Runner* (1996)—tended to ignore film adaptations of his writing. Indeed, there even appears to be some implied criticism of secondary material that tends to focus on PKD film adaptations on the basis that it ignores 'the novelistic source material' (Butler 2000: 88).

Since the release of Ridley Scott's *Blade Runner* (1982), however—based on PKD's 1968 novel *Do Androids Dream of Electric Sheep?* and considered to be 'the most influential sf film' (*The Encyclopedia of Science Fiction* 1999: 224)—a number of other movies have also been directly inspired by Dick's creative output. These include: Paul Verhoeven's *Total Recall* (1990), based on the short story 'We Can Remember It For You Wholesale' (1966); Ridley Scott's re-released Director's Cut of *Blade Runner* (1992) which added the famous unicorn scene, dropped the Harrison Ford voice-over, and cut the more optimistic climax; Canadian director Christian Duguay's *Screamers* (1995) which was adapted from the short story 'Second Variety' (1952); Gary Fleder's *Impostor* (2002), which was predicated on the 1953 short story of the same name; Steven Spielberg's *Minority Report* (2002), adapted from 'The Minority Report' (1956); and most recently John Woo's *Paycheck* (2004) which was based on the 1953 short story of the same title. In addition to these science fiction films there are at least two other much more loosely-based PKD-inspired films in existence. These are Jérôme Boivin's *Barjo/Confessions D'Un Barjo* (1992), a French film that draws on PKD's only non-science fiction novel *Confessions of a Crap Artist* (1975), as well as Australian director Peter Weir's *The Truman Show* (1998), whose concept of an artifical town was lifted from the story 'Time Out of Joint' (1959).[2] Aaron Barlow's 'Reel Toads and Imaginary Cities', . . . suggests that elements of PKD and *Blade Runner*'s influence can also be seen in a number of other science fiction productions such as *Brazil* (1985), *Terminator 2* (1991), *Strange Days* (1995), *Twelve Monkeys* (1996), *Cube* (1997), *Gattaca* (1997), *Dark City* (1998), *Soldier* (1998), *eXistenz* (1999) and *The Matrix* (1999). With such an international *opus* of PKD-influenced films, many of which involve some of the most powerful and well-known names in Hollywood, it seems high time that more critical attention was directed specifically at the films themselves, especially as his work, according to John Woo, appears 'written for the movies' since it is so 'cinematic' (Woo quoted on *Sci Fi.com*). In fact, with such a large number of PKD-inspired motion pictures in circulation Dick must surely rank as the most dominant late twentieth-century science fiction author in terms of influence on the film industry.[3]

Film adaptations of published work, in particular science fiction, are sometimes subject to criticism, either on the basis of their inability to effectively elucidate complex ideas or their lack of fidelity to the original material (*The Encyclopedia of Science Fiction*, 1999: 219). Nevertheless, divergence in PKD's case 'does not automatically mean the film is a shallow adaptation of the book' (Sammon 1996: 9). Indeed, as Sammon points out with regard to *Blade Runner* and its relationship with *Do Androids Dream of Electric Sheep?*, 'a careful viewing of *BR* actually reveals a surprising number of similarities between it and the novel' (1996: 20). Brooks Landon echoes Sammon's defence of Scott's film. He argues that the exact reproduction of the original PKD text is not the important benchmark for gauging the success of *Blade Runner*. Instead Landon believes that what is significant about the film is the director's ability 'to tap [the novel's] archetypal appeal' (1992: 97).

The purpose of this chapter, therefore, is not to compare and contrast the similarities and differences between PKD's published material and the science fiction films which were inspired by these works, thereby evaluating a film's apparent success or failure based on its adherence to an Ur-text. Indeed, a significant creative divergence from an original source can in fact provide a fascinating alternative. This can be seen by the successful science fiction films *When Worlds Collide* (1951) and *Forbidden Planet* (1956), both of which are modernised epigones of the Noah's Ark tale and Shakespeare's *The Tempest*. It is possible, if somewhat rarer, to see a successsful remake of a film, exemplified by the 1978 production *Invasion of the Body Snatchers* which updated the classic 1956 original. It can also be argued that Dick himself borrowed some of his ideas from other sources: his body of work dealing with androids indubitably owes a debt of gratitude to Mary Shelley's *Frankenstein* (1818). Likewise, the creative minds behind *Blade Runner*, while adapting the script from PKD's novel, simultaneously borrowed from other sources, in particular detective fiction, film noir and John Milton's *Paradise Lost* (see Landon 1992: 54-8). The same holds true of Woo's *Paycheck*, which in addition to PKD also draws heavily upon Alfred Hitchcock's *North By Northwest* (1959).

Subsequently, when evaluating the relationship between a film and the published work (or film) upon which it is based, it must be recognised that the final result is a product of its time and as such tends to tell its own unique story. These films should, therefore, be treated as creative texts in their own right. Thus the PKD-inspired science fiction films *Blade Runner, Total Recall, Screamers, Impostor, Minority Report* and *Paycheck*, while isomorphic in the sense that they enhance some of the central themes which concerned Dick's work, namely 'paranoia about reality not being what it seems, or people who are not what they seem' (Leeper 1995), also address a variety of equally significant themes, including the transformative nature of love; the blurring of boundaries; issues of class, 'race' and the far right; and the significance of the religious.

Redemption

In *Blade Runner* and *Screamers*, the two films that deal substantially with simulacra developed by human beings, the machines are initially designed by their creators as warriors, assassins, sex slaves, *lumpenproletariat* or killers. If, as in Genesis 1:26, God said, 'Let us make man to our image and likeness', what do the androids and their design functions then tell us about their human creators? Like the Golem of mediaeval Jewish legend that is fashioned in the human image and whose characteristics are 'an expression of ourselves' (*The Encyclopedia of Science Fiction*, 1999: 508), humankind—if measured initially by the design functions of the PKD-inspired androids—appears murderous, depraved and divided. In fact, it is the androids in *Blade Runner, Screamers* and *Impostor*, and their symbolic equivalents in the other films (the mutants in *Total Recall* and the pre-cogs in *Minority Report*), who often emotionally rise above their human counterparts and/or draw attention to humanity's own inhumanity. They are the modern equivalents of the Frankenstein monster, the 'creature without a soul who is the most soulful' (Desser 1991: 62).

As in a number of novels by science fiction authors such as Robert Silberberg, C. J. Cherryh and John Brunner, by the end of *Blade Runner*'s story it looks as though the authors 'take the side of the androids against their human masters' (*The Encyclopedia of Science Fiction*, 1999: 34), since the artifical creations exhibit a greater share of positive human characteristics than their flesh and blood creators. These human features can particularly be seen in *Blade Runner* when the replicants work together in common cause (an early signifier of civilisation), grieve at their mutual losses, are anxious about their own mortality, exhibit a capacity for forgiveness, and demonstrate love for each other, and potentially even for humans (assuming that Deckard is not a replicant). The lead android Batty (Rutger Hauer), for example, appears distraught after Pris's (Daryl Hannah) death. Likewise the death of Zhora (Joanna Cassidy), a female android, only serves to highlight her human capabilities. She is shot dead by Deckard in the back whilst running away. Her subsequent slow-motion and tragic fall amongst a store front of inert shop mannequins, when followed by Deckard's apparent repugnance at what he has done, serves to heighten her distinction from the other 'dummies' around her.

The replicants in the film are in no way perfect or ideal creatures, however, as they also seek revenge, mislead and kill. To gain information Pris deceives the gentle Sebastian (William Sanderson), the genetic scientist who helped to create the replicants, by pretending to be a lost innocent in the corrupt city. And Batty eventually kills both Sebastian and Tyrell (Joe Turkel), his own creator. But how could these replicants be perfect since they are human creations? It is in fact their confused and complicated personalities that make them so human. In an extraordinarily touching grand finale, the chase sequence wherein Batty, the ultimate Nexus-6 warrior, lets Deckard live, the replicant even manages to put aside his anger and to forgive Deckard. Both psychologically and physically, Batty's actions come to evoke an image of Jesus Christ. When Batty realises that his lifespan is at the end of its genetically predetermined four years, he inserts nails into his hands in order to feel pain and extend his existence by a few short minutes. By doing so, and by then letting Deckard live, he forgives the blade runner and comes to celebrate life. The scene ends with Batty releasing a dove, a traditional Christian symbol of the Holy Spirit, which in turn suggests the presence of *Kodesh* (the breath of God) in the replicant, and thus humanity.

In the film the only way to identify a replicant's status as an android is through the complicated Voigt-Kampff test that is administered by trained blade runners and measures emotional responses by way of pupil dilation in a replicant's eye. A lack of empathy in response to personal questions is supposed to distinguish replicants from humans. To conduct the test blade runners must meet the replicants 'eye to eye' across a table. Although the face-to-face meeting might stem from the investigative interview of the film noir technique, the set-up may also insinuate that the two beings are more alike than supposed. It is certainly the case that in this advanced near-future age of androids and spaceships it should have been technically possible to develop a quicker and more straightforward genetic test, much like the medical examination attempted by Spencer Olham (Gary Sinese) in *Impostor* when he tries to prove that he is not a walking alien bomb.

By contrast to the replicants in *Blade Runner* the human beings who are given speaking parts and some character development are nearly all without emotion. The first blade runner, Holden (Morgan Paull), appears colder in his questioning than Leon, the replicant subject of his interrogation. Deckard himself acts like a 'hollow man' without morality (Mann 2001: 340). He apparently has no reluctance in killing replicants, just as nineteenth-century bounty hunters in pre-Civil War America presumably would have had no hesitations in capturing or returning escaped black slaves to their masters. And Tyrell, the replicants' infamous creator, looks and acts like Josef Mengele, the Nazi 'scientist' (see Kerman 1997: 2). Only by the end of the film does Deckard's position change when he seems to have been transformed by his love for the replicant Rachel (Sean Young), the tragic circumstances surrounding Zhora's death and his experiences with the Christ-like Batty. At the film's conclusion Deckard even runs away with Rachel and does not hunt her down, thereby consciously transgressing Earth's immigration laws. Only the sensitive Sebastian, the genetic scientist suffering from his own biological problems, and Gaff (Edward James Olmos), the cop who knowingly seems to let Deckard and Rachel escape together, demonstrate any human sincerity and empathy.

Screamers, the other PKD-inspired film to incorporate human-engineered androids into its subject matter and to introduce themes relating to love, redemption and the nature of humanity, is set in the year 2078 on the distant mining colony of the once beautiful planet of Sirius 6B. The story involves a war being waged over a new energy source by powerful Earth syndicates, the NEB or New Economic Block (a mining cartel whose primary interests lie in obtaining this energy source without consideration of the costs), and the Alliance (a group of miners and scientists who had once worked for the NEB and who then became disillusioned about the environmental and health consequences of its rapaciousness). The Alliance scientists eventually develop 'screamers'—small mechanical devices with blades that home onto the human pulse and kill the victim—as their primary defensive weapon. But slowly the screamers evolve independently into androids in the form of lost little boys, wounded soldiers and beautiful women. Soon both the Alliance and New Economic Block bases are wiped out by these machines, leaving only the human Alliance Commander Joseph Henricksson (Peter Weller) to work out which surviving NEB soldiers are human or machine.[4]

The storyline for *Screamers* was based on PKD's first android story 'Second Variety' which was set in the Cold War period between US and Communist troops. The film was directed by Christian Duguay who also directed the lesser-known science fiction sequels *Scanners II: The New Order* (1991) and *Scanners III: The Takeover* (1993), whilst the screenplay was adapted by Dan O'Brien, the 'creative force behind *Alien*' (Leeper 1995). Not surprisingly, in both *Screamers* and *Alien* (Ridley Scott, 1979) the theme of corporate greed and its disastrous consequences is significant. Although the majority of the human characters in *Screamers* do not have Deckard's *sang froid* (in the sense that early on in the film Deckard does not seem to have hesitations about the termination of the androids), it transpires that the Alliance troops created the screamers originally and were deceived by their commanders back on Earth about the direction of the war. Similarly, the NEB used nuclear and biological weapons against their human enemies. Neither side, consequently, appears to have acted with much humanity. The evolved androids in the film, mass-murderers who wipe out both NEB and Alliance human colonies numbering in the thousands, are thereby simply imitating their human creators. Some of the androids themselves, however, even come to exhibit human emotions, with one type lamenting his loneliness before destruction, 'I am my motherfucking self, alone'. By the film's conclusion Henricksson comments that the screamers are 'coming up in the world' by behaving more like humans every day, especially so as they learn to kill one another.

In both *Blade Runner* and *Screamers* love, sorrow and/or empathy are the emotional correlatives that redeem both humans and replicants. Deckard loves Rachel and learns what it is like to be hunted. Batty loves Pris and comes to be aware of the tragedy of loss. Sebastian identifies with what it is like to age quickly and feels the rejection of his genetically inferior outcast status. Gaff, by watching Deckard closely, discerns truth and does not 'blow the gaff' by revealing the lovers' secret. Likewise in *Screamers* a female replicant falls in love with Henricksson and sacrifices herself in battle with another android so that the human commander can live. It should not be forgotten either that Rachel in *Blade Runner* also kills her fellow android Leon because of her love for Deckard. Marilyn Gwaltney suggests in relation to *Blade Runner* that the evolution of Batty's and Rachel's positive human characteristics is similar to the process of experience that children go through: 'Perhaps personhood is developmental and children and androids are in the process of becoming persons, depending on their degree of experience' (Gwaltney 1991: 36). Such a theme would apply to the replicant's love for Henricksson in *Screamers* and, assuming here that Deckard is a replicant, for the blade runner himself and his developing love for Rachel. Gwaltney's thesis is also one suggested by the Pinocchio tale as well as by Steven Spielberg's updated science fiction version of this classic, *Artificial Intelligence: A.I.* (2001), the story of a lost little robot boy who wants to become real so that his human mother can love him again. Intriguingly, love is also a central theme that Woo deliberately inserted into *Paycheck* as he felt it was so essential to Michael Jennings' (Ben Affleck) development:

> Jennings, he's just a simple guy. He's not a superhero. He wanted to change his own fate. But somehow, he has some problems. He cannot change it by himself . . . Maybe love can help him change . . . So that's why I suggested adding more of a love story, and to make the female role bigger.

> (Woo quoted on Sci-Fi.com)

Paycheck is set in Seattle, Washington in 2007, and follows Jennings, a 'reverse engineer' who is happy to have all memories of his computer research erased after he has finished a large corporate project in order to ensure that his employer's concerns over industrial secrecy are assuaged. After working on a three year programme for Allcom and expecting a $100 million paycheck, instead he discovers only a manilla envelope with a variety of apparently everyday objects such as a bus ticket, paper clip, sunglasses and hair spray. Finding himself on the run from both the FBI and Allcom's thugs, Jennings relies on the support and the love of Rachel (Uma Thurman), a female colleague from Allcom, to help him understand the uses behind the contents of the envelope and the secret of his lost past. Like Rachel in *Blade Runner,* Thurman's character also turns against her own kind, in this case her employer.

In *Impostor,* as in *Blade Runner, Screamers, Artificial Intelligence: A.I.* and *Paycheck,* it is Olham's love for his wife Maya (Madeleine Stowe), and empathy for Earth's outcasts, which makes him so determined to prove his humanity. The setting is 2079, and a totalitarian Earth is at war with the genetically superior Alpha Centauri. Most of Earth's inhabitants live in domes protected by forcefields, with a small population of outcasts living in frontier regions on the borders of these protected artificial environments. Olham has been accused by Earth's security services, led by the 'Grand Inquisitor' Major Hathaway (Vincent D'Onofrio), of being an alien 'replicant' with an explosive implant designed to assassinate Earth's President. The use of *Blade Runner*'s term for artificial humans clearly suggests the shaping influence of Scott's film. During Olham's interrogation by Hathaway the Major insists that Olham and his android kind are not human since they lack souls. Yet Olham's determination to demonstrate his innocence and his genuine fear, when coupled with his love for Maya and his concern for Earth's outcasts who live in a kind of third world poverty (and for whom Olham procures expensive medicines pilfered from a military hospital), earn him the viewing audience's sympathies. By contrast, Hathaway's fundamentalist certainty about Olham's guilt, his admission that innocents have died in his search to weed out Centauri repliants ('we lost ten and saved ten thousand'), the fact that he is willing to shoot his own security forces as well as patients in the local hospital to ensure Olham's demise, and the use of a torturous device that would not look out of place in Counter-Reformation Europe to remove the bomb inside Olham, all make the Major look like the real devil. In reality, however, it turns out that Hathaway was correct, although even Olham himself was not aware he has a duplicate until the last millisecond of his existence.

Hathaway's apparent lack of concern for his own personnel in *Impostor* is reminiscent too of the treatment of civilians in *Total Recall*. The latter is set primarily on Mars in the year 2084 after humans have begun to colonise the red planet. Humans and their mutant relatives have to live in protected environments, like the domes in *Impostor,* due to the lack of breathable oxygen. Douglas Quaid (Arnold Schwarzenegger), the central protagonist, lives on Earth but is haunted by recurring dreams about Mars. Visiting REKALL, a company that gives its customers the artificial memories of an exciting holiday (Quaid chooses the Martian secret agent scenario), he discovers that he actually appears to be a real secret agent and begins working against the corrupt rule of Mars' authoritarian leader. He is followed by Martian counteragents who try to kill and/or capture him at every turn and think nothing of firing upon a crowded escalator or subway, a further example of humanity's own inhumanity towards its kind.

A Blurring of Boundaries

Quaid, whose name was originally Quail in the PKD short story but was changed in the film to avoid resembling the then US Vice-President Dan Quayle, is not above jeopardising the lives of innocent civilians either. This suggests that brutality is not necessarily restricted to the villains or the non-human characters, and that boundaries between so-called protagonists and antagonists, or aliens/replicants and humans, can sometimes be blurred. While trying to pass Mars customs Quaid disguises himself as a woman whose head explodes and causes instant decompression in a public spaceport, thereby potentially threatening the lives of hundreds of innocent passengers. Similarly, Deckard in *Blade Runner* starts out as a futuristic bounty-hunter/assassin, who if a replicant turns out to be killing his own kind and if a human is still murdering sentient beings. This human potential for demonstrating violence against its own kind, even by the protagonists of the science fiction stories, draws to mind historical parallels, in particular Allied bombing atrocities in World War Two over Dresden and Hiroshima/Nagasaki. It is also a theme common to science fiction, such as *Alien* and *Aliens* (James Cameron, 1986), wherein human corporate greed results in the deaths of thousands of innocent colonists. Corporate profit at the expense of human beings is also a theme raised in *Paycheck* (with regard to Allcom's desire to maximise the share value of the company even at the cost of a nuclear war), *Total Recall* (the mutations in the Mars colonists are the result of poor mining conditions) and *Screamers* (NEB short sightedeness over the environment and the safety of its workers is the reason for the creation of the Alliance).

When assessing these so-called moral dilemmas in films such as *Total Recall* it must be remembered that the film is a Schwarzenegger movie directed by Paul Verhoeven, who in addition to the shoot-'em-up *RoboCop* (1987) also directed the violent science fiction box-office success *Starship Troopers* (1997). Consequently, there is the possible danger of overdoing critical analysis of this kind in a genre aimed primarily at entertainment and that as a matter of course includes large swathes of violence. Nonetheless, Verhoeven's work is not so black and white either. His use of Nazi uniforms for Earth's secret intelligence in *Starship Troopers* not only draws attention to fascistic criticisms of Robert Heinlein's original 1959 novel, but implies that militarist Earth is not as innocent in the conflict with the bugs as the audience might assume. Once more it seems that the so-called human protagonists might actually be the real villains of these pieces. By contrast to the humans in *Total Recall,* the humanoid mutants, like the replicants in *Blade Runner,* appear to be the most considerate characters, as evidenced by their strong community and family bonds. Nevertheless, there is an exception amongst the mutants too as the treacherous taxi driver demonstrates once again that the so-called 'good guys' can in fact be bad. This switching can also work the other way around. Quaid in *Total Recall* started out life as a secret service agent in the employ of the corrupt Mars government but changed his attitude because of his love for a woman in the resistance, and his developing empathy for the mutant cause. There appears to be quite a lot of Deckard in him.

As in the other PKD-inspired films, questions are raised about the nature of human behaviour in Steven Spielberg's *Minority Report,* which stars Tom Cruise as police chief John Anderton, the head of Pre-Crime in 2054 Washington, D.C. One focus of this human cruelty towards its own kind rests on the condition of the pre-cogs, three psychics kept in a near-permanent state of drug-induced suspension because they are used by the police and government to detect murders before they are committed. The pre-cogs' imprisonment and isolation is explained away in the film by the simple dismissal 'better if you don't think of them as human', and there are disturbing echoes here of Major Olham's justification for his actions ('we lost ten and saved ten thousand'). Another questionable human action by the protagonists in *Minority Report* includes the behaviour of the police technician Wally, who watches over the psychics in their stasis and who resembles a sexual *voyeur* towards the female pre-cog Agatha when he caresses and speaks to her in endearing expressions. However, once Agatha is taken out of her drug bath by Anderton, who is presumed a killer and like Olham in *Impostor* must go on the run in order to prove his innocence, she begins to demonstrate that she too has a personality and physical abilities like any other 'normal' human being. The evolution of Agatha from object to subject in *Minority Report* serves to underline how cruel her 'imprisonment' was, since it humanises her character and allows the audience to relate to her as an individual.

Other actions that raise concerns in *Minority Report* about human beings' viciousness towards their own kind include the way the pre-cogs evolved (by experimentation on drug addicts), the intrusive use of robot surveillance spiders on run-down communities, and questions about committing so many people to cryogenic sleep on the basis that they might commit a future crime, even when it is recognised that pre-cogs can sometimes get it wrong. There are echoes of *Minority Report*'s disturbing surveillance techniques by police, government and corporate forces in other films too, such as the x-ray/infra red machines used on the interzone peoples in *Impostor*, the CCTV-like cameras used on the mutants in *Total Recall*, and the hidden video camera from Uma Thurman's bathroom in *Paycheck*. Surveillance is also, of course, a crucial element in *The Truman Show*.

'RACE' AND THE FAR RIGHT

In *Minority Report*, *Total Recall*, *Blade Runner* and *Impostor* future habitations are blighted by class distinctions, indicating how divided human communities can be. The poor and the mutants live in high-density, public-housing sprawls, eking out a living along the fringes of so called civilised society. By contrast to the dark and lowly mean streets in *Blade Runner*, the corporate leader Tyrell lives far removed from the masses on the top floor of a colossal *ziggurat*, traditionally the abode of the gods and their priests in Mayan and Sumerian culture, and thus a fitting symbol for a creator of replicants. But an association with long-gone empires or peoples such as the Mayans or Sumerians is also a stark warning that imperial powers can come crashing down. It is, therefore, an appropiate apocalyptic warning portending a Tower of Babel-like collapse. As Sumeria was the world's first civilisation, a *ziggurat* in a futuristic L.A. might also be an appropriate symbol for its last civilisation.

These class distinctions also raise some interesting questions about 'race' and fascism in the PKD-inspired films, which serve to address further questions about morality and humanity. The positions of the replicants in *Blade Runner* and the images of the masses in L.A. 2019 highlight ethnic concerns in 1980s America. It is never explained, for instance, why replicants are not allowed on Earth and only on the Off-World colonies. Francavilla (1991: 7) suggests that what we could be witnessing in the films is a fear of displacement at home by the Other, a factor testified to by Bryant in the film referring to the replicants as 'skin-jobs', which Deckard in the 1982 voice-over explains is akin to calling them 'niggers'.

Official concern about replicants posing as humans, and the need for a police state with scientific tests to determine identity, call to mind comparisons with apartheid South Africa. The purpose of the Voigt-Kampff test is strikingly similar to the so-called 'scientific' tests conducted by South Africa's Race Classifaction Board to determine a person's colour. Likewise, why does the Nazi look-alike Tyrell create only white replicants, especially the genetically super strong and intelligent Batty whom Kerman suggests resembles an 'Aryan superman'? (1997: 22). The Nazi and South African parallels with regard to *Blade Runner* are also intriguing as Earth, or at least L.A., seems to resemble a crowded World War Two Eastern European ghetto or 1980s South African Bantustan, both of which were designed specifically for ethnic division. The choice of Los Angeles as the locale of *Blade Runner* is intriguing too considering that the city, the Watts district especially, has historically been the site of a number of violent twentieth-century racial conflagrations.

If Deckard is a replicant working for a future military industrial power, then taking the fascist parallels even further, he is the equivalent of Primo Levi's *prominenz*, the Jewish volunteers who helped to sort out arrivals at Auschwitz and who assisted in the attempted genocide of their own kind by the Nazis. At the very least, if he is human, then he is a member of a futuristic *Einsatzgruppen*, the German police battalions who brutally hunted down Jews and Communists in Eastern Europe during Operation Barbarossa. Continuing with the racial and fascist premises, the death of Zhora amongst panes of shattering shop glass might even be an oblique reference to *Kristallnacht* when some 91 Jews were killed by Nazi-inspired purges against Jewish-owned businesses, the event taking its name from the millions of glass fragments that resulted from these pogroms. Perhaps it is not so surprising, after considering the far-right German parallels, that Batty and Leon eventually kill both Sebastian as well as the Chinese eye surgeon, since these two scientists were also complicit in the Tyrell Corporation's genetic creations. The replicants' actions are equivalent to those of post-war partisans in countries like France, Greece and Italy who hunted down and executed any who had collaborated with the occupying Nazi and fascist officials. Is it any wonder then that the mutants who fight the authoritarian forces on Mars in *Total Recall* are called the 'resistance'?

Apart from the genetically inferior Sebastian, it seems that the only whites at street level in *Blade Runner* are cops or replicants. The rest of the city looks like a jumbling mass of Chinese, Japanese and Arabs, with the city's culture dominated by Japanese corporations such as Atari, Chinese food vendors and Eastern belly dancers. In part this emphasis upon a non-white population and Oriental dominance could be a reflection of American grumbling during the Reagan Presidency about US trade inbalances with Japan and illegal Latino immigration to California. If the propaganda from the floating dirigibles is to be believed, in early twenty-first-century Earth it appears to be the case that the mass of healthy white people have sought a Nazi-like *lebensraum* (living space) in a pigmentopia (a utopian discourse with a strong or prevailing ethnocentric/racist world view) amongst the stars.[5] The racist agenda of this pigmentopia is further underlined by the fact that it uses replicant slave labour for its wars and its work force, leaving everyone too sick or too ancient back on the Old World Earth. Earth thereby becomes a dumping ground for the infirm, much like the intention of the so-called 'Homelands' of white South Africa's apartheid regime in the mid-1980s.

While 'race' does not appear to be a significant factor in most of the other PKD film adaptations, it may be worth noting that in *Impostor,* Olham's only friend is the black Kyle. Furthermore, Kyle and the other black characters in the film all appear to be relegated to the interzone places and are poor, sick and without medicine. There is also more than a whiff of fascistic iconography in *Impostor* with regard to the media reports surrounding Earth's President (her television appearances shot from ground up and in large halls full of attendants mirror Leni Riefenstahl's infamous film portayals of Hitler), as well as in the authoritarian and militarised nature of Earth's regime (which is encapsulated by Hathaway's ruthlessness and his uniformed marching goons). With so many far-right parallels in *Impostor,* particularly with regard to the authoritarian portrayal of Earth's political and military leaders, it seems that Fleder borrowed as much from *Starship Troopers* as from PKD.

RELIGIOUS SYMBOLISM

PKD was very much interested in theology from the late 1960s onwards, even conducting séances with a bishop in California and later becoming convinced that he had been directly contacted by a superior power (see Butler 2000: 9-10). A number of religious references also infiltrate the film adaptations of his work, in turn compounding questions of identity, morality and meaning. In *Minority Report* the pre-cog chamber is described as a 'temple' and the name Gideon (an Old Testament judge) is used by the overseer of the cryogenic complex. In *Impostor,* Hathaway enters into a inquisitorial diatribe on the nature of souls, and discusses Olham's predicament in a futuristic chapel setting. There is also *Blade Runner*'s apocalyptic vision of a dark and nightmarish Hieronymus Bosch hell, kindled by the opening sequence of a flame-filled L.A. cityscape into which the replicants have crashed. This in turn draws parallels to Lucifer's exile and descent from Heaven (Desser 1991: 54). The Biblical association is supported by the fact that Tyrell refers to Batty's

life as being 'bright', recalling the name Lucifer, derived from the Latin for 'lightbringer'.

According to Kerman, Biblically-inspired apocalyptic themes dominate *Blade Runner,* including the debased future L.A. as akin to Sodom and Gomorrah, the endless rain as a symbol (and warning) of the Flood, as well as issues of Exodus with humans leaving the Earth in search of new Promised Lands (see Kerman in this volume). This theme of the end of the world in PKD's work is not surprising considering the fact that he was a child of the Cold War and thus lived under the threat of atomic annihilation. Among all the signs and symbols of humankind's potential evil and harmful capability towards its own kind, the destruction of life on Earth is perhaps the ultimate example. Not surprisingly, nuclear holocaust is a theme in many of the film adaptations as well. Alamorgodo (the site of America's first nuclear test) is where Commander Hendricksson found his escape rocket in *Screamers.* At the start of *Impostor* Olham likens the possible defeat of the Centauri to the atomic defeat that wiped out Hiroshima and Nagasaki in Japan in 1945. He too includes Alamorgodo in his speech. There may then be a warning in these two films about the *hubris* of humankind, as Olham does eventually blow himself up and it turns out that Hendricksson's escape rocket contains a mechanical screamer that if returned to Earth has the potential to wipe out all life. As the female android remarks to Henricksson: 'You don't know what the hell you have started up.' Nuclear war also threatens to end humanity in *Paycheck* after Jennings discovers that the machine which he built for Allcom foretells the future, in the process inadvertently initiating an atomic conflict.

In addition to the apocalyptic imagery, much of it taken from Revelations and Genesis, the nomenclature in some of the films is also provocative for its religious associations. According to *Genesis,* the Biblical Rachel was surrounded by questions of identity as her husband Jacob was originally deceived by Rachel's father and given her covered elder sister as a bride instead. Both she and Jacob had to flee their homeland after quarreling with her father. Jennings and the other Rachel in *Paycheck* also have to go on the run from the FBI and Allcom hitmen, and there are similar questions of identity surrounding Uma Thurman's character. Allcom, for example, tries to dupe Jennings by using a dummy of Thurman. This ruse, however, is revealed to Jennings by the imposter's kiss. The use of the kiss as a mark of treachery is also a common Biblical occurence, most famously in the New Testament when Judas betrays Christ (Mark 14:45-6), but also in Genesis (27:26-7) when Jacob gives a kiss to Isaac, Rachel's father, as part of his own deception.

Paycheck is not the only science fiction film in which a false declaration of love and an imposter is discovered by way of a kiss. In *Invasion of the Body Snatchers*

Miles finds out that his girlfriend Becky has been replaced by a pod person after she kisses him in an old mining shaft. The treacherous nature of the kiss is also central to *Blade Runner* wherein Batty kisses his creator Tyrell before he kills him, literally echoing Judas' betrayal of Christ and inverting Batty's later Christ-like role. A kiss is also used by Quaid's wife (Sharon Stone) in *Total Recall* to try and delay the hero so that Mars secret agents can catch him, and the theme is picked up in the same film by the mutant leader Kuato, who like Christ is not only killed by his enemies but is also betrayed by one of his own, the taxi driver.

According to *The Encyclopedia of Science Fiction,* 'the landscapes of decay and imposture' in PKD's work mirrored the psychological conditions of his characters (1999: 329). In the films too, landscapes and cityscapes are also thematically significant, both for drawing attention to the results of an over-reliance of technology that could lead to Earth's destruction and as a manifestation of the damaging selfishness of humankind. As Kerman suggests in relation to *Blade Runner,* the cityscapes are reminders of God's vow after humankind's expulsion from Paradise: 'cursed is the earth' (Gen 3:17). The future L.A. of *Blade Runner,* at least in the Director's Cut where the rural forest escape of the 1982 version is removed, appears as a barren polluted wasteland in which it always seems to be dark and raining. In the original novel by PKD nearly all animals were wiped out because of nuclear war, but it is never fully explained why L.A. is portrayed so drearily in the film adaptation and we can only assume that it is due to over-crowding and pollution. Likewise in *Screamers,* the once-beautiful colony of Sirius 6B has been reduced to an atomic wasteland. Posters for the planet had once promoted it as 'paradise', but after the war it is more like Paradise Lost. In *Impostor* Earth is a burnt-out wreck following the war with the Centauri. Even nature trails under protected forcefields look like barren brown field sites, and the park where Olham and Maya went on a hiking holiday is burned down twice during the film.

Intriguingly, at least in the 1982 version of *Blade Runner* wherein Deckard and Rachel escape into the wilderness, or the end of *Minority Report* when the liberated pre-cogs begin to build new lives for themselves in an isolated log-cabin in the woods, it seems that the dream of a rural frontier America is also still alive. Herein lies a vision of a New Jerusalem that was so central to Puritan settler thinking in the early history of the United States (again, see Kerman in this volume). Fittingly, the central protagonists of *Paycheck* end up opening a garden centre as a full-time occupation after all of their experiences with high-tech adventure. In this context of rural versus urban, and the religious allusions between corrupt city and paradise/Eden, it might also be significant to note that the cop in *Blade Runner* who allows Deckard and Rachel to escape might have

also had his name (Gaff) derived from 'Gaffer', which traditionally means an old country fellow. The association of this name with the pastoral underlines once more the redeeming character of a more natural environment.

REALITY

Philip K. Dick has been described as 'the Poet Laureate of false memories and fake experiences' (Butler 2001: 7) while *The Encyclopedia of Science Fiction* states that the quintessential PKD theme is 'the juxtaposition of two "levels of reality"' (1999: 328). The central motif of things not always being what they appear to be was developed by Dick as early as his first novel *Solar Lottery* (1955), which depicted a future Earth organised around a draw that turns out to be fixed. This theme of obfuscation and confusion is further underlined by the questions raised in the section above with regard to human nature and human-replicant characteristics. In part such concerns about compound tiers of existence and shifting boundaries appear to be a consequence of PKD's heavy use of drugs, including LSD, cannabis and speed, which in turn seemed to have caused him to become paranoid and to query reality (Sammon 1996: 10-12). Drugs also appear central to the plot of many PKD-inspired films, and transform the lives of the characters involved. In *Total Recall* they are used to induce Quaid into a state that enables him to accept the implanted memory programme he requested. In *Minority Report* drugs help Anderton to forget the disappearance of his child and are also inadvertently the cause of the precogs' condition as they bring on their psychic abilities and cause their imprisonment. A chemical drug was also used to make Jennings forget three years of work on Allcom's top-secret project designed to foretell the future in *Paycheck.* And drugs are also what Kyle is seeking when he teams up with Olham in *Impostor.* Depending on the circumstances and the film, therefore, drugs can either heal, hide or reveal.

Questions of identity and reality are especially prevalent in *Blade Runner,* and much has been written on the question of Deckard's status as a potential replicant. Like the replicants Rachel and Leon, Deckard also relies on photographs as evidence that his past was real, which in turn only ironically serves to insinuate that Deckard's memories have been fabricated. It is never explained why Deckard retired as a blade runner in the first place, implying perhaps that his history, like Rachel's memories of spiders or a brother/sister visit to the basement, were also made up. The fact that Deckard has never taken the Voigt-Kampff test himself suggests too that he might have failed it. Furthermore, that Deckard is such a good blade runner might be due to the maxim that 'it takes one to know one'. Even the name, Deckard, might be a subtle reference to the French philosopher Descartes and his emphasis on hyperbolic doubt. The use of a Coca-Cola product placement in

Blade Runner, while on the one hand a clever marketing device utilised initially by Spielberg in *E. T. The Extra-Terrestrial* (1982) and possibly added to Scott's film for future authenticity, also ironically emphasises a product that promotes itself as 'the real thing', in turn reminding the viewing audience that all is not what it appears.

Nevertheless, according to some critics, what really seals the case on Deckard's status as a replicant is the unicorn dream sequence added to the Director's Cut. The fact that Gaff at the end of the film leaves an origami unicorn at Deckard's apartment implies that he knows Deckard's dreams just as Deckard knows Rachel's memories. The choice of a unicorn might not be accidental either. According to the thirteenth-century Norman clerk de Guillaume, the unicorn's horn was a mediaeval symbol of truth (Evans 1970: 1115), suggesting perhaps that Deckard's past is as equally mythical as this fabulous beast. Although there are arguments against the possibility that Deckard is a replicant, namely that he is not as strong as Batty and that androids are not allowed on Earth (although Rachel is an obvious exception), there are hints elsewhere in the film that all is not as it appears. The euphemism 'retirement', for example, only serves to hide the true barbarity of the act.

Total Recall also problematises memory and the nature of reality to the point that one is left questioning if the events depicted in the film actually occurred in this fictional future world or if Quaid was just experiencing the secret agent vacation package that he signed up for, complete with the athletic brunette love interest. Characters in the film repeatedly suggest that the entire episode was invented. Schwarzenegger's wife tells him that his 'whole life is just a dream', while Quaid himself questions his very existence, remarking 'Who am I?', and then in an earlier computer conversation with himself states that 'you are not you, you are me'. Similarly the totalitarian leader of Mars warns Quaid that he is merely 'a stupid dream' that will come to an end, while Quaid's Martian love interest Melina (Rachel Ticotin) at the film's conclusion suggests that their victory is 'like a dream' and that Quaid should kiss her quickly before he wakes up. As in *Sleeping Beauty* the kiss is important as it usually does result in the princess being woken from her slumber.

There are a number of other hints that what is seen or heard in *Total Recall* is not to be trusted. The breakfast news programme shows Mars security forces brutally slaughtering opponents while the newsreader comments that 'minimum use of force' was employed. The video images of mountains and lakes in Quaid's kitchen are also fake, while the James Bond-style holograph watch creates yet another duplicate of Quaid. Once again, however, as in *Blade Runner*, contrary positions can be argued. If Quaid is experiencing a dream sequence, then how is the audience or Quaid aware of what goes on when he is not in the room? Similarly, Quaid himself deliberately shoots a possible REKALL employee who tries to convince him that the entire Mars scenario is a dream sequence gone badly wrong. Quaid's justification for this killing is that this so-called employee would not be perspiring so heavily if he did not really think his life was at risk. Yet there also remains the intriguing possibility in this game world of REKALL unreality that the perspiring employee could also be a well thought-out detail of the simulation.

Photographs and video recordings in *Impostor, Blade Runner, Minority Report* and *Paycheck* are used as potential visual testimony by the protagonists to help verify their identities. However, these images too are often subject to distortion and are not ideologically jejune, further emphasising the theme of half-truths and distortion. Olham in *Impostor* stops to focus on an image of his wife Maya as if to remind himself that he had a 'real' past and that he does love his wife. Although this reminder of love might prove to him that he is really human and not a machine, we eventually discover that the Maya in the photo is not the same Maya as his wife: indeed, it turns out at the end of the film that Olham himself is not the real Olham. Similarly in *Blade Runner* Deckard's piano is littered with family portraits, again an apparent signifier of historical evidence, although the images in this scene appear antiquated and thus out-of-place. Following the earlier scenes that emphasised Leon's and Rachel's fabricated photographs and memories, these images in Deckard's apartment cannot be taken at face value. Rachel in *Paycheck* also shows Jennings their personal videos and snapshots to prove to him that he is her partner of three years. Although Jennings responds emotionally to these images they are only used as secondary proof and after the fact; the real evidence of Rachel's authenticity was in her kiss. And visual deception is intriguingly the basis of Tom Cruise's dilemma in *Minority Report*: Anderton keeps replaying 3D footage of his missing son, which when taken with an illegal drug seems to give the police chief some respite from his personal horror by making him believe that he still has a real relationship with the lost little boy. Agatha has her precognition substituted, thereby making Anderton look guilty of a crime that he did not commit; and hundreds of faked photos of murdered children become the basis of an attempt to frame Anderton. In all three cases of *Minority Report* what you see is not what you get.

In both *Screamers* and *Impostor* the directors also play guessing games with the viewers. The former opens with soldiers viewing a desolate landscape from inside of a military fortress, suggesting that people tend to have a kind of blinkered vision or bunker-like mentality about events. Yet as Hendricksson attests in conversation with his second-in-command when he states that 'we were all NEBs once', things are not so black and white and positions can change. To quote Ace, Hendersson's aide: 'It's a bit blurry.' Although Hendricksson also criticises the NEB's use of nuclear weapons on a number of occasions he too is eventually forced to employ them against the 'Davids', androids in the form of lost little boys with teddy-bears, again suggesting the deceptiveness of appearances.

Questions about identity and reality are also raised by Fleder, the director of *Impostor,* who positively encourages the viewer to deliberate over the issue of Olham's innocence and whether he really is the victim of a Centauri plot. After being arrested near the beginning of the film for being an alien explosive device, Olham (who does not believe the charges against him) is forced to pretend to be a bomb in order to frighten his paramilitary escort and escape in the hope that he can then prove his innocence. There is a build-up of suspense with news reports about the Centauri overcoming Earth's forward bases and getting closer and closer all the time, and Olham's neighbour warning him that the enemy can and will get through. Fleder seems to be borrowing here from 1950s anti-Communist hysteria, and the sense of a forthcoming takeover is not too dissimilar from the sense of urgency about alien invasion in the first *Invasion of the Body Snatchers.* Nor do we ever see the Centauri themselves in *Impostor,* which only adds to their mystery. One even begins to wonder if in fact the Centauri actually exist or if the entire war is just a clever scenario to keep the authoritarian leaders of Earth in power, much like the concluding epiphany to the film version of Margaret Atwood's *The Handmaid's Tale* (Volker Schlöndorff, 1990). Is Olham subsequently singled out for termination by Earth's fascist-like government because he has developed a bomb that can end the war, thus also ending the *raison d'être* of the military government too?

Suspense about the nature of what is real is further helped by Olham lamenting that 'I can't trust my mind', much as Quaid in *Total Recall* questions his own grip on reality. The tension is also heightened in *Impostor* by the fact that Olham's wife seems to doubt her husband, eventually betraying him to Hathaway's security forces. Yet in a twist of fate she is shown to be a bomb; and although viewers might begin to think that Olham is innocent, it transpires that Maya is just a red herring, since both husband and wife are supposed Centauri plants.

CONCLUSION

Themes of redemption through love and empathy, the blurring of boundaries, 'race' and the far-right, the religious, and the question of what is real, dominate the Philip K. Dick film adaptations. Although many of these themes were common to PKD's original work, the adaptations are the result of a number of other influences as well, from the literary and cinematic to the personal. With regard to the last point, what is especially intriguing is that most of the directors of these US adaptions are not American-born. Scott is British, Woo is Hong Kong-Chinese, Duguay is French-Canadian, Verhoeven is Dutch and Weir is Australian. Spielberg, although American born, is also Jewish. As foreign or Jewish directors working in Hollywood, questions about identity, boundaries, and 'race' might have proven to be particularly relevant to their own personal histories, even if only at the subconscious level.

Notes

1. For a discussion on secondary reading relating to PKD see Andrew M. Butler, *Philip K. Dick* (Harpenden: Pocket Essentials, 2000), 87-90. The information on Dick's total output of published work comes from http://www.philipkdick.com/works_novels.html (accessed 05/10/05).

2. *The Truman Show* stars Jim Carrey as a young paranoid man who, sensing that something is not quite right with his seemingly utopian existence, discovers that he is the protagonist of a high-tech television soap opera and tries to escape his artificial environment. In contrast to the film the short story deals with a much more science fiction theme, namely an interstellar war between Luna and Earth.

3. Butler (2000: 91) suggested that PKD's *A Scanner Darkly* was also forthcoming, although at the time of writing it had yet to be released.

4. Peter Weller also starred in Paul Verhoeven's science fiction film *RoboCop* (1987) about a part human/part machine cyborg whose personality was blocked by circuitry but who finally managed to regain his past and his humanity.

5. See Dominic Alessio (2004) 'Race, Gender and Proto-Nationalism in Julius Vogel's *Anno Domini 2000*', *Foundation,* 91, 36-54, 45.

Bibliography

Alessio, D. (2004) '"Race', Gender and Proto-Nationalism in Julius Vogel's *Anno Domini 2000*', *Foundation,* 91, 36-54.

Barlow, A. (1997) 'Philip K. Dick's Androids: Victimized Victimizers', in J. B. Kerman, *Retrofitting Blade Runner: Issues in Ridley Scott's Blade Runner and Philip K. Dick's Do Androids Dream of Electric Sheep?* (second edition). Bowling Green: Popular Press, 76-89.

Butler, A. M. (2000) *Philip K. Dick.* Harpenden: Pocket Essentials.

Clute, J. and P. Nicholls (eds) (1999) *The Encyclopedia of Science Fiction.* London: Orbit.

Desser, D. (1997) 'The New Eve: The Influence of *Paradise Lost* and *Frankenstein* on *Blade Runner*', in J. B. Kerman (ed.) *Retrofitting Blade Runner: Issues in Ridley Scott's Blade Runner and Philip K. Dick's Do Androids Dream of Electric Sheep?* (second edition). Bowling Green, OH: Popular Press, 53-65.

Dick, P. K. (1987 [1952]) 'Second Variety' in *Second Variety: The Collected Stories of Philip K. Dick, Vol. 2,* Los Angeles: Underwood/Miller, 15-52.

———. (1987 [1953]) 'Paycheck', in *Beyond Lies the Wub: The Collected Stories of Philip K. Dick, Vol. 1.* Los Angeles: Underwood/Miller, 279-308.

———. (1996 [1968]) *Do Androids Dream of Electric Sheep?.* New York: Del Rey/Ballantine.

———. (2002 [1956]) 'The Minority Report', *Minority Report,* London: Orion/Gollancz, 1-44.

———. (2002 [1966]) 'We Can Remember It For You Wholesale', *Minority Report,* London: Orion/Gollancz, 267-290.

Evans, I. H. (1970) (ed.) *The Wordsworth Dictionary of Phrase and Fable.* London: Wordsworth Editions.

Francavilla, J. (1997) 'The Android as Doppelganger', in J. B. Kerman (ed.) *Retrofitting Blade Runner: Issues in Ridley Scott's Blade Runner and Philip K. Dick's Do Androids Dream of Electric Sheep?* (second edition). Bowling Green, OH: Popular Press, 4-15.

Gwaltney, M. (1997) 'Androids as a Device for Reflection on Personhood' in J. B. Kerman (ed.) *Retrofitting Blade Runner: Issues in Ridley Scott's Blade Runner and Philip K. Dick's Do Androids Dream of Electric Sheep?* (second edition). Bowling Green, OH: Popular Press, 32-39.

Kerman, J. B. (ed.) (1997) *Retrofitting Blade Runner: Issues in Ridley Scott's Blade Runner and Philip K. Dick's Do Androids Dream of Electric Sheep?* (second edition). Bowling Green, OH: Popular Press.

Landon, B. (1992) *The Aesthetics of Ambivalence: Rethinking Science Fiction Film in the Age of Electronic (Re)production.* Westport, CT: Greenwood Press.

Leeper, M. R. (1995) 'Review of *Screamers*'. Available online: http://reviews.imdb.com/Reviews/46/4615 (accessed 5 May 2004).

Mann, J. (ed.) (2001) *The Mammoth Encyclopedia of Science Fiction.* London: Robinson.

Sammon, P. M. (1996) *Future Noir: The Making of Blade Runner.* New York: Harper-Prism.

Ken Weiss (essay date 2006)

SOURCE: Weiss, Ken. "The Brave New World of *Starship Troopers.*" In *Science Fiction America: Essays on SF Cinema,* edited by David J. Hogan, pp. 246-55. Jefferson, N.C.: McFarland & Company, 2006.

[*In the following essay, Weiss contends that* Starship Troopers *(1997) "serves as a predictor of the future, most notably by demonstrating the timelessly effective techniques of propaganda."*]

In *Brave New World,* Aldous Huxley predicted a society in which human beings are genetically engineered for commercial and industrial purposes. They don't protest because they are designed "to love their servitude."

All propaganda, as every advertising and public relations professional knows, requires several ingredients—comprehensibility, consistency of message, and repetition being the three most important ("Keep it simple, keep it straight, and keep it coming"). In public relations, when dealing with large national issues, an added fillip is the demonization, real or created, of the intended enemy. The rules are timeless: In *Mein Kampf* (1925) Adolf Hitler made the same points when he noted that "all propaganda must be popular and its intellectual level must be adjusted to the most limited intelligence among those it is addressed to," and that propaganda "must confine itself to a few points and repeat them over and over."

The subtext for these rules, rarely admitted by those in the business, is the belief that the public in general is ignorant and easily duped. Recognition that "a lie repeated often enough over time will be believed as true" is probably as old as civilization itself and remains the basis of many advertising and public relations campaigns. Julius Caesar warned against leaders who bang "the drums of war to whip the citizenry into a political fervor, for patriotism is indeed a double edged sword. It emboldens the blood, just as it narrows the mind." And when the populace has been properly motivated, "the leader will have no need in seizing the rights of the citizenry. Rather the citizenry, infused with fear and blinded by patriotism, will offer up all their rights unto the leader and gladly so." Two thousand years later, Nazi Hermann Goering told a friend, "Of course the people don't want war. But after all, it's the leaders of the country who determine policy, and it's always a simple matter to drag the people along whether it's a democracy, a fascist dictatorship, or a parliament or a communist dictatorship. Voice or no voice, the people can always be brought to the bidding of their leaders. That is easy. All you have to do is tell them they are being attacked, and denounce the pacifists for lack of patriotism and exposing the country to greater danger. It works the same in any country."

When *Starship Troopers* was released in 1997 it was generally dismissed as just another "sci-fi bug movie." Produced on a healthy $95 million budget, the picture managed a domestic box-office take of just $54.7 million. The director, Paul Verhoeven, had claimed the film's goal was to "evoke old Westerns, World War II movies and adventure tales"—and carefully avoided mention of its political content. Janet Maslin, demonstrating typical perspicacity in *The New York Times,* said it was "about the cute young co-ed army and the big bugs from space"—which it is. It also has a lot of comic-book blood and gore, the cast is ridiculously gorgeous, and there's no dearth of violence, humorous and otherwise. But there is also much more. As would be expected, almost all the mass-media reviewers missed the issues raised by the film: its cynical, satirical, and scary predictions of things to come; its observations about militarism and war; and its "don't trust authority" signals. They also missed what the film was saying about a society totally influenced by media that march in lockstep with government. They missed all these things back in 1997. It's doubtful they'd miss them today. *Starship Troopers* serves as a predictor of the future, most notably by demonstrating the timelessly effective techniques of propaganda. The movie serves as a warning, in the grand tradition of Aldous Huxley's *Brave New World* and George Orwell's *1984,* in which the authors used the device of a future society to comment on the world they saw evolving around them. The film is based on the novel by science-fiction legend Robert A. Heinlein, who probably would have been delighted with Hollywood's adaptation of his book.

The novel, set thousands of years in the future, is a first-person account by Juan "Johnny" Rico, a mobile infantryman in the Terran-based Federation Army, at war with the "Bugs," an insectlike race from another galaxy. Johnny takes us through his last semester in high school, his enlistment in the Federation Mobile Infantry, basic training and, primarily, his various adventures in combat, fighting the Bugs on far-off planets. The novel can be divided into two unequal parts: The larger one is a detailed look at the mobile infantry, its equipment, weapons, rules, traditions and battles. Heinlein, a brilliant storyteller, loves that stuff. He can go on for pages explaining the ins and outs of future legalities and protocols on other planets. A trainee punches an officer in the face—there are ten pages detailing his military trial and his punishment. Mobile infantry troopers wear "powered armor," a suit that "isn't a space suit" but can serve as one, that isn't a tank, although a suited trooper could easily defeat a squadron of tanks, and isn't a ship, although "it can fly a little." Heinlein devotes five pages to a description of the suit's various features.

The novel's other part, equal in significance though not as lengthy, is an exploration of the meaning of personal civic responsibility and a citizen's obligation to the state, a la Heinlein. As always, he offers an enormous menu of viewpoints to choose from, each presented and defended or demolished brilliantly. Everything from "inalienable rights" like life, liberty and the pursuit of happiness (he's against 'em), "communal entities," social workers, and child psychologists (he doesn't like them either), to corporal punishment and self-sacrifice (he's for them). He seems to posit the view that personal sacrifice for the state is the highest form of virtue, the individual sacrificing for the good of the many—the mobile infantryman being a prime example. Late in the book, Johnny's businessman-father, who had been vehemently opposed to his son's signing-up, joins the MI, and explains why: Johnny had exposed the father's cowardice. "You had done something that I knew, buried deep in my heart, I should have done. I had to perform an act of faith. I had to prove to myself that I was a man. Not just a producing-consuming economic animal, but a man." It is difficult not to hear Heinlein speaking.

Readers might remember the Federation (the government that followed the collapse of twentieth century society) from *Stranger in a Strange Land* and many other Heinlein novels. It's the same old mind-numbing Federation, although the satisfied populace would never recognize it as such. In Heinlein's *Starship Troopers,* as in *Stranger,* the Federation is depicted as untrustworthy and deceptive. It's clear that the people of the Federation are being lied to, and that the whole point and direction of the war are questionable. Johnny's first combat drop is a disaster. Most of the men and officers are killed, but the Federation calls it a "strategic victory."

Johnny isn't overly bright. He tells us he hadn't intended to join the MI, but his best friend, Carl, had decided to join up, and cute Carmencita Ibanez, his sort-of girlfriend, was joining up, too, and, well, it seemed the thing to do. And besides, military service was the only way to achieve full citizenship and the right to run for public office. As always, Heinlein is merciless in his disdain for the brainwashed. A one-armed, legless enlistment sergeant does his best to discourage the new recruits, pointing to himself as a product of service. Undeterred, they join up anyway. During the physical Johnny asks the examiner if he'd been a doctor before joining the military. The man is shocked. "Do I look that silly?" he says, and assures Johnny he's a civilian. "No offense," he continues, "but military service is for ants." This makes no particular impression on Johnny.

Although there are few signs of media in the novel, we know from Johnny's narrative that the information he's getting reinforces the belief that while the Federation is winning the war, victory is still a long way off. The obliteration of Buenos Aires is noted offhandedly by Johnny, except for its effect on him (his mother is killed in the attack). The destruction of San Francisco and the

San Joaquin Valley is referred to after the fact, with no details. Johnny mentions that the last thing he suspected was that they were actually *losing* the war. Everyone is led to believe the Bugs operate almost entirely on instinct. Gradually we realize that the Bugs, while organized differently, are probably as intelligent as Terrans. It's made clear that the Worker and Warrior Bugs follow orders and have little imagination. Brain Bugs are the heavy thinkers and leaders, but no Brain Bug has ever been caught. Heinlein doesn't mention the similarity of organization between the two forces. He doesn't have to.

Nor does he address the question of personal responsibility when one's cause happens to be wrong, although his contempt for the Federation is obvious even while he's idealizing the men who fight and die for it, and apparently sees no contradiction in this. The absence of media in the novel is matched by the almost total lack of information about Terran existence outside the military. There are several flashbacks of Johnny in high school, particularly his class in History and Moral Philosophy, whose teacher, Mr. Dubois, pointing his "stump of a left arm," reinforced the notions that violence and force are the ultimate arbiters of what is right, and a soldier is the prime example of civic virtue because he defends the body politic with his life, while the civilian does not. There is little sign of specific commerce or other aspects of civilian society. We know that Johnny's father is a businessman, but that's all. Economic interests do not seem to exist. Heinlein does provide his always-convincing picture of a population totally and willingly dominated by big government, but, as usual, there is no exploration of motives (who is doing this and why?), no reasons given for the war (how did it start?), and never a vision of what he himself might consider a just, equitable and workable society. Despite considerable railing about personal freedom, self-sacrifice, and responsibility (concepts with little objective meaning), in the end Heinlein offers a philosophy of hopelessness. Despite an obviously vibrant imagination and enormous knowledge, perhaps he felt that a just society was not possible, in itself a useful wake-up call to anyone who values democracy.

The movie version of *Starship Troopers* removes some of the novel's ambiguities. It attempts to be true to Heinlein's vision of hegemonic subjugation, with a few additions to satisfy box-office needs, like romantic complications. The movie creates a society in which all information comes from one source, to the complete satisfaction of the populace, who enjoy every luxury except individualism and the ability to think critically. The young people in the movie might have stepped out of a Guess or Calvin Klein commercial—visual symbols of their vacuity. As science-fiction historian Paul Sammon explained, "This is a right wing group of empty-headed beautiful people doing exactly what they're told to do."

The novel and movie differ most in their handling of male and female relationships, and the influence of media. The film's take on gender differences probably would have displeased Heinlein. In the novel the mobile infantry is strictly male and macho. Troopers sometimes go for many months without seeing a woman. For female companionship they head for Sanctuary, an Earth-like planet used for R & R. This is typical Heinlein, whose "wise" characters are, by today's standards, hopelessly chauvinistic. (See the all-knowing Jubal Harshaw, in *Stranger,* and his harem of beautiful women.) Although Heinlein's novels are set in the far future the societies are pretty much the same sexist ones we're familiar with. In the film, the mobile infantry is completely co-ed. Men and women train together, share the same quarters, take showers together and fight side by side. In a happy combination of political commitment and box office savvy the producers present a prolonged nude shower scene involving a lot of very attractive young people that offers considerable T & A to make a political point. For despite the ribald talk and abundance of bare breasts and buttocks, there is no condescension, no leering, nor groping, nor wise-ass comment regarding nudity. Instead, it is handled matter of factly, as something so normal it's unnoticeable to the characters. The training and combat scenes are no different. The women are equals, as tough and resourceful as the men, sometimes more so.

Practically invisible in the novel, media are prominent and set the desired tone for the movie, which opens with a Federation Network television news broadcast that instantly establishes the level of public awareness and the form of government that prevails. In this first broadcast (and all others) the Federation's decor and architecture, its logo—an angular, wings-spread bird of prey, its officers' uniforms, its army training ground scenes, all clearly authoritarian in nature and design, were, in fact, inspired by close study of Leni Riefenstahl's Nazi propaganda masterpiece, *Triumph of the Will,* which provided the tone the producers were trying to establish. *Troopers'* director of cinematography, Jost Vacano, wanted to show "what would have happened if Hitler had won. What would the world look like?" Despite this in-your-face blatancy, most film critics missed the point completely, and a few even thought director Verhoeven was *endorsing* fascism.

The film's opening shot is the Federal Network logo, followed by a long shot of a training field with hundreds of fully uniformed and armed troopers in formation. The visual and sound techniques are those of a slick television commercial. "Join up Now!" a title declares, as the camera zooms in on individual troopers, each young and attractive, and a voiceover tells us, "Young people from all over the globe are joining up to fight for the future." "I'm doing my part," a female trooper says to the camera. "I'm doing my part," a male trooper adds. "I'm doing my part, too," a uniformed, gun-toting preadolescent boy pipes in, to the amused laughter of the troopers. "They're doing their part. Are you?" A caption asks, "Would you like to know more?," and the screen is filled with a Federation Mobile Infantry flag waving in the wind as the voiceover exhorts, "Join the mobile infantry and save the world. Service. Guaranteed citizenship." The inspirational music fades and turns ominous as a headline, "Bug Meteor," appears over a giant meteor hurtling through space. "Klendathu sent another meteor our way. But this time we're ready. Planetary defenses are better than ever." We see a huge Federation starship fire its cannons at the meteor and blast it to space dust. "Would you like to know more?" a caption asks, as another segment titled "Why We Fight" shows a simulation of a deadly asteroid belt of meteors launched from Klendathu to Terra as the narrator warns, "To ensure the safety of our solar system Klendathu must be eliminated."

Bold metallic letters flash on screen: "Invasion!," and we see an armada of huge Federation battleships flying toward the enemy planet. A "Live TV" announcement flashes on and off as "FedNet takes you live to Klendathu where the invasion has begun." The sounds of gunfire, explosions, and yelling troopers are almost deafening. Amidst the din a reporter covering the invasion gives us the lowdown. "It's an ugly planet," he shouts into the camera, "a Bug planet, a planet hostile to life." He doesn't notice that all the troopers are fleeing, nor the giant Bug that appears, until it lifts him into the air and rips him to shreds. The cinéma vérité camera weaves wildly, finally focusing on an MI trooper (we'll later recognize him as Johnny) who shouts, "Get outta here now!" One trooper stands his ground and blasts away at a Bug but can't prevent it from killing him. Johnny, trying to help, is impaled through the thigh by a Bug claw, but manages to pull himself free. The TV screen offers a close up of his face in pain as interference terminates the broadcast. The screen goes black and there is silence. A caption says, "One year earlier."

The style of the broadcast is as fast-paced as tomorrow's commercials (whose purpose, too, is to sell things), disturbingly similar to the TV we're accustomed to. As examples of propaganda the Federation broadcasts (which appear every half hour or so) illustrate what can happen when news becomes entertainment. Successful propaganda is not possible without the complicity of media. (At first, Hitler didn't have to take over the German press. Publishers got the message quickly enough, and the ones that didn't found their offices wrecked by patriotic vigilante groups.)

The Bugs are demonized on every broadcast, but let's face it, it's the Bugs who steal the show. These fantastic creatures, created by Phil Tippett, a two-time Oscar-winning special effects, animation, and computer graphics genius (he's the creator of Jabba the Hutt, among

others) are wonders to behold—part ant, part roach, nine feet tall, fearless, practically indestructible and entirely fascinating, although witnessing them in action is not for the squeamish. Unlike MI troopers, Bug warriors carry no weapons, depending instead on their greater number, their courage, their chit armory, their mandibles and sharp claws. There's plenty of tongue-in-cheek dismemberment, including a moment when an MI officer (Michael Ironside), his finger probing a hole in the top of the head of a dead trooper, says grimly into the camera, "They sucked his brains out."

The second FedNet broadcast starts with "A World that Works" emblazoned across the screen as an MI trooper holds up a large, "fully automatic Baretta" rifle and asks a bunch of preadolescent children, "Who'd like to hold it?" The kids all yell, "Me!" and grab at the rifle as troopers laugh appreciatively and start handing out bullets. The voiceover tells us, "Citizen rule is people, making a better tomorrow." The familiar "Would you like to know more?" caption appears on the lower part of the screen. "Crime and Punishment" introduces an intimidating courtroom whose style and decor are again strongly reminiscent of the Third Reich. The accused appears helpless and somehow innocent as he hears himself sentenced to death: "A murderer was captured this morning and tried today." A gavel slams. "Guilty," a stern-faced judge declares. The screen shows a glass-enclosed room containing a sleek, futuristic, stainless steel reclining electric chair. "The sentence—death. Execution tonight at six, all net, all channels"—an announcement repeated via onscreen flashing captions. "Would you like to know more?" Eerie music follows as a segment encourages viewers to explore their "psychic power" and to be aware that "Federal studies are being conducted in your community. Would you like to know more?"

A cow is pushed into a steel room with a captured Bug and the door slides shut. "Every schoolkid knows that arachnids are dangerous," the voiceover comments. The Bug rips the cow to shreds, as a "Censored" sign discreetly blocks out the goriest parts. "However, Mormon extremists disregarded Federal warnings and established Port Joe Smith deep inside the arachnid quarantine zone." The camera shows an isolated outpost stained by blood and strewn with mutilated chunks of bodies. They realized too late, the voiceover continues, that the area "had been already been chosen by other colonists—arachnids. Would you like to know more?"

Two requirements of a true democracy are an informed, participative citizenry, and a government that provides adequate, accurate information. The "Would you like to know more?" question at the end of each segment serves as ostensible evidence of the Federation's willingness to provide information. There is little doubt but that the information will simply be more propaganda designed to prevent critical thought. So the movie, like the novel, invites the viewer to consider the nature of a democracy whose government can not be trusted. And like the novel, it offers no solutions.

Buenos Aires is destroyed by meteors launched from Klendathu. Johnny's parents are killed in the attack, which he learns from a FedNet report: "8,764,590 Dead." The city has been wiped off the face of the earth. For Johnny, the war against the Bugs takes on greater urgency. Until the attack the war had been an undeclared one. Now the Federation makes it formal. In the next FedNet broadcast flaming metallic letters announce "War," as footage of the devastated city appears on screen. "Out of the ashes of Buenos Aires comes first, sorrow." A family photograph among the debris. "Anger." A dog buried under large slabs of concrete. "The only good Bug is a dead Bug," an enraged Terran yells. "In Geneva, the Federal Council convenes." Sky Marshal Dienes, the symbol of authority, law and order, appears to be a Hollywood World War II caricature of a Nazi. "We must meet the threat with our valor, with our blood, indeed with our very lives, to ensure that human civilization, not insects, dominates this galaxy now and always," he exhorts. Another segment, "Know Your Foe!," describes how "Federation scientists are looking for new ways to kill Bugs." A military specialist tells us a "basic arachnid warrior isn't too smart, but you can blow off a limb—" he fires an automatic weapon at a Bug in a cage, crippling it, "and it's still 86 percent combat effective. Here's a tip: aim for the nerve stem, and put it down for good." Another blast—in the right spot—kills it. "Would you like to know more?"

"Do Your Part!" a title declares, as we see young schoolkids enthusiastically stomping insects (the common garden variety of beetles and grubs). "Everyone's doing their part. Are you?" The gleeful kids keep squashing the insects till the soles of their boots are covered with mush. "The war effort needs your effort. At work. At home. In your community." An adult woman urges the children on, laughing. Fade to a huge armada of spaceships, each one the size of a city. "We break Net and take you live to Fleet Battle Station Ticonderoga, deep inside the arachnid quarantine zone, where the men and women of the Federal Armed Services prepare to attack." A reporter, followed by a camera, is aboard the *Fort Ticonderoga*. He interviews a few of Johnnie's buddies, all of whom can't wait to take on the Bugs. When the reporter mentions that some people had suggested a "live and let live" approach to the Bugs, Johnnie irately grabs the mike and declares, "I'm from Buenos Aires and I say kill 'em all."

The next time we see FedNet is during the invasion of Klendathu, which returns us to the movie's starting point. There's the reporter, saying, "It's an ugly planet. A Bug planet. A planet hostile to life," and being seized by the Bug while the cameraman moves closer for a better shot. And there's Johnny, getting his thigh pierced by a giant hornlike, needle-sharp claw. (It's okay—he'll be submerged in a liquid healing tank that will have him up and around in a few days.) The scene ends with the MI in full retreat. "100,000 Dead in an Hour" is the leadoff story on FedNet. We see acres of barren terrain littered with bloody body parts. "Crisis for humankind," a voice-over intones. "Fleet officials admit they underestimated the arachnid's defensive capability." We move next to the spacious chamber of the Federation Council, where Sky Marshal Dienes resigns and the new sky marshal, Tahat Maru, explains her strategy. "To fight the Bug, we must understand the Bug. We can ill afford another Klendathu," she proclaims to applause. Then the familiar voiceover, "Would you like to know more?"

"Bugs That Think" is the next segment. A man and a woman sit opposite each other, shouting to make a point, parodying contemporary midday talk shows. "Insects with intelligence?" shouts the man. "Have you ever met one? I can't believe I'm hearing this nonsense."

The FedNet broadcasts frame the film and give it context outside the world of the military. Each broadcast is a fast-paced compilation of Federation-selected scenes buttressed by stimulating headlines and simplistic, manipulative voiceovers. No event is covered in depth and words and images flash by, competing with each other for the viewer's attention. In this regard, the movie is predictive. As a phenomenon of everyday American life, news broadcasts in 1997 had not yet accepted competing onscreen imagery and messages. Hardly more than five years later they had become common on CNN, Fox, and Bloomberg. Content shrinks as viewers are conditioned toward shorter attention spans. In 1997, with most media owned by a handful of multinational corporations, writer Ed Neumeier and director Verhoeven could intuit which way the wind was blowing, and their perception is embedded in the film. With *Starship Troopers* Verhoeven set out to show the world a functioning fascist society, full of attractive people the audience feels compelled to identify with. But Gestapo-type uniforms and the overbearing authority of the State present a disturbing contradiction to the beautiful people we're rooting for, forcing us to consider one of Verhoeven's points: Don't be fooled by appearances.

The final FedNet broadcast appears shortly after a successful battle in which the first Brain Bug is captured. "Know Your Foe" is the lead-off segment. We see orange-cloaked and hooded technicians with the captured Bug, an enormous, slug-like, gelatinous creature with a mucousy hole of mouth surrounded by eight large, soulful eyes. "What mystery will the Brain Bug reveal? Federal scientists are working around the clock to probe its secrets. Once we understand the Bug, we will defeat it." A scientist with a two-foot injection probe sticks it into the creature's side, another pushes a multi-pronged probe into its mouth, a "censored" sign blocking the penetration but leaving the sad eyes visible. It is a tribute to Verhoeven and Tippett's skills that we actually feel sympathy for this otherwise repulsive Bug. "Join up Now!" appears onscreen over an enormous armada of Federation battle ships. "We have the ships. We have the weapons. We need soldiers." Soldiers like Lieutenant John Rico, who is seen leading his men to the drop chamber of a starship and screaming, "C'mon you apes, you want to live forever?" "We need you all," the voiceover continues. "Service. Guaranteed citizenship." A headline declares, "They'll Keep Fighting," as the mighty armada sails through space. "And they'll win!" It's the last image on screen so the movie ends where it began, with an exhortation—to a population that has learned to love its servitude—for support in a war apparently without end.

Starship Troopers is distinctive in that it's the only film to present an American-type democratic society in which all citizens accept the enforced hegemony and are unquestioning believers in the propaganda being fed them. In other films, such as *1984* (1956), *Fahrenheit 451* (1966), or *Soylent Green* (1973), there is always someone, a protagonist or band, who challenges the system. But like the novel, the movie is unsparing. *Everyone is brainwashed.* It is the society that Heinlein anticipated and the one Paul Verhoeven could sense emerging in 1997. The accuracy of their predictions is yet to be determined. The signs are not encouraging.

Works Cited

Hitler, Adolf. *Mein Kampf,* Boston: Houghton Mifflin, 1971 [1925].

Gilbert, Gustave M. *Nuremberg Diary.* New York: Farrar, Straus, 1947.

Maslin, Janet. "No Bugs Too Large." *New York Times,* Nov. 7, 1997.

Heinlein, Robert. *Starship Troopers.* New York: Ace Books, 1987 [1959].

Production comments by Verhoeven, Tippett, Vacano and Sammon from *Death from Above* and *Paul Verhoeven and Ed Neumeier Commentary. Starship Troopers* Special Edition DVD. Columbia/Tri-Star.

TEXT AND REPRESENTATION

John Trushell (essay date summer 1999)

SOURCE: Trushell, John. "*The Thing*: Of 'Monsters, Madmen, and Murderers'—A Morality Play on Ice." *Foundation* 28, no. 76 (summer 1999): 76-89.

[In the following essay, Trushell examines the two film adaptations of John W. Campbell, Jr.'s science fiction story "Who Goes There?," The Thing *(from Another* World) *(1951) and* The Thing *(1982), arguing that the movies reflect the political, cultural, and social concerns of their eras.]*

The wreck of a spacecraft and the remains of an alien life form have been discovered, entombed in polar ice, by a scientific expedition. The alien remains have been retrieved, although an attempt to salvage the wrecked craft has led to its destruction. All thirty-seven members of the expedition have gathered to discuss whether thawing the remains for examination "may release a plague unknown to Earth". The expedition members resolve to thaw the remains as the life form does not "have a life-chemistry sufficiently like ours to make cross-infection remotely possible". But the life form has "an unearthly, unkillable vitality" and revives when thawed: this alien "has learned the deepest secrets of biology" and "can control [its] cells *at will*" and—once having absorbed the original—"can imitate anything". Unless contained—and destroyed—the scientists believe that the alien could "Take over the world" not as "lone dictator" but—by absorption and imitation—as "the population of the world".[1]

So begins the story entitled "Who Goes There?" by John W. Campbell, Jr.—published pseudonymously as by Don A. Stuart in *Astounding Science-Fiction,* August 1938—with an editorial blurb that demands "Who—is that your closest friend—or a monstrous imitation, breed of an alien, deadly world?"[2]

Thereafter, the story concerns the means by which the expedition attempts to discern friend from foe: first, a serum test of human-immune husky blood to screen samples of blood drawn from humans and/or aliens which fails; second, a searing of blood drawn from humans/aliens which succeeds as each particle of an alien is separate, self-sufficient and selfish—with a "desire to protect its own life" when threatened—thus betraying "the main mass from which it was split" by attempting to escape. Thus, fifteen members of the expedition are betrayed as aliens and destroyed by the twenty-two humans remaining.[3]

While commentators have alleged that science fiction "eschews the psychological dimension . . . of character portrayal for a more all-encompassing look at . . . [those] various institutions that govern behaviour", this story—set in a polar waste—is concerned indirectly with the sociology of institutions but directly with social psychology.[4]

Critics have described the conduct of the expedition as "paranoia and distrust run wild", but instances of marked paranoia are manifested only by members of the expedition who are imitations—the pseudo-Blair, the "demented" biologist, the pseudo-Kinner, the cook with "praying hysteria", and the pseudo-Clark, the dog-handler who "murders" the "hysterical" pseudo-Kinner—while the humans maintain a certain *sang-froid* in their collective dealings with the imitations who comprise the "monsters, madmen and murderers" of the expedition.[5]

Campbell's "Who Goes There?" evokes contemporary discussions—in elite and popular fiction and speculative non-fiction of the 1930s—concerning the future of biology in general and, in particular, the manipulation and control of living cells. The popular literary convention was for an aspiring experimental biologist to meet an individual fate—customarily meted out by the experimental subject—but "rarely with any effect on the wider society". While the fate of Blair, the biologist, is consistent with this convention, his nemesis is an alien which "has learned the deepest secrets of biology, and turned them to its use" from whom members of the scientific expedition must protect the wider society.[6]

"Who Goes There?"—accounted as "one of the most significant stories of the 1930s"—has correspondences with other contemporary and anterior texts drawn from popular and elite culture: Eco defines this "phenomenon by which a given text echoes previous texts" as intertextual dialogue. These correspondences may be "explicit and recognizable"—the thaw and revival of the alien is likened to the opening of Pandora's Box—or less perceptible. Campbell's descriptions of the alien—three red eyes in "a face ringed with a writhing, loathsome nest of . . . blue mobile worms that crawled where hair should grow" and a scrawny neck from which blue, rubbery tentacles sprouted—evoke both the severed head of the Gorgon, with her deadly gaze and crown of serpents, and the Martian of H. G. Wells's *The War of the Worlds* (1898), with its round body "having in front of it a face" with "a pair of very large, dark-coloured eyes" and "a kind of fleshy beak" around which were "sixteen slender, almost whip-like tentacles".[7]

The scientists' debate as to whether thawing the alien "may release a plague—some germ disease unknown to Earth . . . [against which] man will be utterly defenceless" also recalls *The War of the Worlds* in which invading aliens were:

> slain by the putrefactive and disease bacteria against which their systems were unprepared . . . slain, after all man's devices had failed, by the humblest things that God, in his wisdom, has put upon the Earth."[8]

But, in a neat inversion of Wells, this Thing is not slain by micro-organisms but composed of micro-organisms: "every cell, every drop of blood" is an individual animal. The composition of the alien imbues it with "powers of imitation beyond any conception of man" which recall Proteus, the Greek god, who could metamorphose to bristly boar, to scaly dragon and to tawny lion. Yet

the Thing's composition also causes its downfall: each separate cell or drop of blood "is all for itself" and will betray the imitation from which it was taken.[9]

A social psychological reading of the story would hold that the text is indicative of a contemporary collective consciousness—that is the "mental states shared across a culture at a particular historical moment"—marked by disillusion with that individualism implicated in the Wall Street Crash in 1929 and the Great Depression of the 1930s, and disillusion with a political system which had permitted this "selfish and materialistic betrayal of the American dream".[10]

First, as one commentator contended:

> "individualism, it now appeared to millions, had brought disaster upon the nation by encouraging the wildcatters of speculation and endorsing the socially irresponsible actions of self-centred industrialists who cared for nothing but the dimensions of their profit margins—and the people be damned."[11]

Successful entrepreneurs and financiers—operating "in harmony with the visions of [Frederick W.] Taylor and [Henry] Ford" for "a fully rational and scientific economy and society"—had been the heroes of popular magazine fiction in the 1920s. But the entrepreneur and financier were displaced by "the professional and the little man . . . as the typical hero" of popular fiction during the Depression and, by the end of 1934, the great popular heroes were the "G-Men" of the Federal Bureau of Investigation, collectivist law enforcers in pursuit of such rank individualists as the "public enemies" John Dillinger, "Pretty Boy" Floyd and "Baby Face" Nelson. Disillusioned with an individualism which had "hardened into ruthless self-interest and openly callous toughness", the American people placed a "new emphasis on social security and collective action".[12]

Second, "the mood of the country," as another commentator contended, was marked by "disillusionment with parliamentary politics, so often the prelude to totalitarianism in Europe". People feared revolution in the depth of the Depression and, throughout the 1930s, the "'fascist menace' . . . of an American fascist movement".[13]

Franklin Delano Roosevelt, in his inaugural presidential address in 1933 may have reassured the people that "the only thing we have to fear is fear itself" but he also expressed a willingness to exercise "broad Executive power to wage war against the emergency, as great as the power that would be given to me if we were in fact invaded by a foreign foe." Prior to the presidential inauguration, *Barron's National Business and Financial Weekly* had remarked of Roosevelt that "a genial and lighthearted dictator might be a relief from the pompous futility of such a Congress as we have recently had".[14] But the "fascist menace" of which alarmists warned more often was imagined as being led by Huey Long and Charles Coughlin, disaffected Roosevelt supporters who championed "the little man"—and voiced popular protest on his behalf—against the encroaching impersonality and bureaucracy of Roosevelt's New Deal policies. Father Coughlin, the vociferous "Radio Priest" of the CBS national network, having founded the National Union for Social Justice in 1934, denounced the New Deal as a "Pagan Deal" and a communist conspiracy. "Kingfish" Long, the demagogic Senator from Louisiana, expressed popular resentments toward "wealthy plutocrats" and "bloated fortunes" and advocated the redistribution of wealth, founding the national political organisation Share the Wealth Society—with the slogan "Every Man a King"—in 1934. A Roosevelt aide warned, in 1935: "You can laugh at Father Coughlin, you can snort at Huey Long, but this country was never under a greater threat".[15] Father Coughlin "could not be a rival for the White House because of his Canadian birth and his clerical collar" but could have been "one of those who would determine just who *would* sit there". Coughlin established the Union Party to contest the 1936 presidential election, but the assassination of Huey Long denied the party a credible presidential candidate.[16]

Campaigning for the Democratic nomination for presidential candidate, Roosevelt contended that: "I should like to have it said of my first Administration that in it the forces of selfishness and of lust for power met their match . . . I should like to have it said of my second Administration that in it these forces met their master." Securing the nomination, Roosevelt declared, in his acceptance speech, that:

> "This generation of Americans has a rendezvous with destiny . . . we are waging a great and successful war. It is not alone a war against want and destitution and economic demoralisation. It is more than that; it is a war for the survival of democracy."

Roosevelt won his second term in the White House but, throughout the 1930s, the political rhetoric of "Roosevelt and other politicians helped to foment a 'Brown Scare'" of fascism which—although "directed at different targets and practised on a lesser scale"—resembled the "Red Scare" of communism which followed the Second World War.[17]

But this is to complement a social psychological reading of "Who Goes There?" with a conventional sociological reading which would hold that the text is "indicative of the problems and issues of the societies in which . . . [it was] produced and originally consumed", discerning correspondences between alleged "forces of selfishness and of lust for power" and the selfish alien foe which could "*rule—be—all Earth's inhabitants*".[18]

Campbell was a political conservative whose publications addressed a readership that was "middle class, very well educated, and startlingly above average in terms of income." The protagonists of his early fiction were individualists, "the sons of corporate entrepreneurs, or of distinguished scientists otherwise associated with great wealth": "people to whom battles and tactics, even heroics, are secondary to the importance of efficiency, high rates of productivity, and technological development."[19]

While, in popular fiction generally, entrepreneurs were displaced by professionals and "the little man" as protagonists, in science fiction the individualist scientist's exploits tended to be displaced by group scientific endeavours such as the expedition in "Who Goes There?" However, such scientific collectivism could correspond with social elitism and authoritarianism.[20]

Certainly, Campbell was unsympathetic to "the little man"—most noticeable among the Thing's victims were Kinner, the cook, and the Clark, the dog-handler—and was critical of the susceptibility of ordinary people to manipulation by demagogues such as Long and Coughlin. Nor was Campbell a supporter of the New Deal but, rather, he placed faith in the formation of a social elite of scientists—particularly physicists—and engineers who would impose social security: ironically, the function of such an elite would not have been inconsistent with that of those "droves of professors [who] descended on Washington to take part in the New Deal" and who were dubbed the "Brains Trust" by the *New York Times*.[21]

Collectivist action was endorsed by the first translation of the story "Who Goes There?" into the 1951 film *The Thing (from Another World)*, "considered to be the first real space-monster film". Although the film retained a polar setting and a wrecked spacecraft and a thawed alien menace, the collective comprised a military flight crew and civilians—including a secretary and a reporter—while scientists became "villains . . . who [cared] more for the Thing than for their fellow humans". This recasting is consistent with a post-war consciousness which was marked by mistrust of scientists and professors, and valorisation of the military and, incidentally, entrepreneurs and financiers who—vilified as "Robber Barons in the 1920s and 1930s"—were depicted in "scholarly books of the 1940s and 1950s as constructive captains of industry". Rather than "warriors in the marketplace", "captains of industry" came to be perceived as leaders of a company team and attempts by the state—and by its professorial and social scientific advisors—to manage the economy and administer social welfare could be resented as external impositions. The Republican presidential candidate, war-hero General Dwight Eisenhower, campaigned against the "creeping socialism" of the New Deal, and criticised those "long-haired academic men in Washington" as lacking the masculinity to defend the United States.[22]

The shift in social psychology apparent in the recasting of the collective heroes and the scientific villains in the film was complemented by shifts in the setting and spacecraft which reflected contemporary controversies: while the story was set in the Antarctic, the film was resited to Alaska and the Arctic, reflecting the spate of sightings of unidentified flying objects [UFOs] in the Pacific North-West during 1947; and the spacecraft in the story—"like a submarine without a conning tower or directive vanes"—was replaced in the film by a "flying saucer", the term coined by journalists to describe these UFOs in 1947.[23]

Furthermore, there was a shift in the Thing: a focus of the story on the head of the alien—associated with a fear of possession—became a focus on the alien's "crazy hands" reminiscent of a "B" horror feature film; a man-imitating monster became a monster-suited man; and the alien shifted from interior threat in the story to exterior threat in the film. A contemporary critic observed that the film "is a horror movie where you barely see the monster . . . It occasionally appears in silhouette . . . it's a very exteriorized figure . . ."[24]

This exteriorisation of the alien menace was also an effect of a translation from story to film which did "not produce an identical meaning-content in [the other] medium": whereas the Thing of the story could become a monstrous imitation of Man in text, constraints of 1950s' special effects restricted the Thing of this film to a travesty: "nothing more than [a man] dressed up in a monster suit and rampaging . . . as only a man in a monster suit can do".[25]

This Thing recalls, or perpetuates, those monsters which had become the convention in horror movies of the 1930s and 1940s: Dracula, Frankenstein, the Mummy and the Invisible Man. This recollection, or perpetuation, is often cited to support an argument that *The Thing (from Another World)* is not science fiction but a horror film: however, in such horror films, monsters are seen as complex beings which may engage sympathy whereas, in science fiction films, monsters may have certain attributes and an inferred purpose—say, world domination—but resist anthropomorphisation and remain alien.[26]

Furthermore, these earlier monsters had been human in origin—and amenable to anthropomorphism—whereas this Thing is revealed to be merely an anthropomorphous vegetable—an "intellectual carrot"—when a forearm, severed during its escape, is analysed by the leader of the scientific expedition. The scientist expresses admiration for the Thing's "neat and unconfused reproductive technique of vegetation" and for other attributes:

"Its development was not handicapped by emotional or sexual factors . . . No pain or pleasure as we know it. No emotions. No heart. Our superior, our superior in every way . . . If we can only communicate with it, we can learn secrets that have been hidden from mankind since the beginning . . ."

The critic Jancovich contends that the scientist's inference from this "technique of asexual reproduction" that the Thing is as "a creature without personal or irrational features" corresponds with a preference for "scientific-technical rationality . . . a system directed and managed by experts" within which such a creature would function as "a mere interchangeable component". Although the Thing proves uncommunicative and unmanageable—slaughtering humans for their blood—the scientist persists to the leader of the flight crew that "Knowledge is more important than life, Captain. We owe it to the brain of our species to stand here and die without destroying a source of wisdom . . . Civilization has given us orders . . ."[27]

The leader of the scientific expedition is depicted as an eminent scientist—a Nobel Prize winner—but the military and civilians refer to him and scientists generally as immature: the Captain comments that scientists are "kids, most of 'em, like nine-year-olds drooling over a new fire engine" while the secretary compares the attitude of the leading scientist to the Thing with that of "a kid with a new toy". Although knowledgeable, the leading scientist has not the wisdom to discern the menace of the Thing, remarking that "There are no enemies in science . . . there are only phenomena to study".

The respective conflicts with the leading scientist and the Thing are presented as collective efforts of the flight crew and civilians: the leading scientist is confined to his quarters and laboratory; and while a first attempt by the collective to burn the Thing—which proves hardy, even having grown a new forearm—fails, a second attempt to electrocute the Thing succeeds. The reporter who has witnessed the events concludes that:

"One of the world's greatest battles was fought and won today by the human race. Here at the top of the world, a handful of American soldiers and civilians met the first invasion from another planet . . . Noah once saved the earth with an ark of wood, here . . . a few men performed a similar service with an arc of electricity."

Despite this evocation of a "mythical, biblical past", it is the adept "use of domestic knowledge in conjunction with scientific knowledge . . . [that] wins the day": the female secretary has suggested that the ways to kill a vegetable are to "Boil it, stew it, bake it, fry it". While critics and "purists" may have tended to deplore this inclusion of female characters in the translation from story to film and the introduction of a "love interest" (which became a convention of science fiction films of the 1950s), the asexuality and inferred rationality of the Thing—and the immaturity of the leading scientist—were thereby contrasted with an irrational but mature sexual relationship of 1950s America in which "the boy . . . was the object of peer pressure to advance as far as possible . . . [while] the girl had to give up as little as possible and not surrender her virginity . . . [yet] keep the boy interested in her".[28]

Previously, the Captain's advances to the secretary have been marred by drunken licentiousness—and there are allusions to other episodes involving the Captain in San Francisco and Honolulu—which she has repelled, describing him as "a wolf". But when the Captain has defied the leading scientist and posted an around-the-clock watch on the Thing, he wins her admiration: "I like the way you handled this whole mess . . . you're much nicer when you're . . . when you're not mad."

The finale is marked by two successes: the betrothal of the Captain and the secretary and the repulse of an alien incursion, possibly "to conquer the Earth, start growing some kind of horrible army, turn the human race into food for it". Whereas the monster in the story would have reproduced—by absorption and imitation—to become the population of the world, the Thing in the film could have reproduced—from seed pods contained in its hand—to consume the population of the world. There has been a tendency for critics to consider the film as one of those "thinly veiled allegories" of Cold War invasion: notably, the film contains one explicit reference to Russians, the Captain's remark that "They're all over the Pole, like flies" which is recalled when the collective discuss "rigging an electric fly trap" for the Thing. Rather, the film is concerned with readiness and resistance, anxieties consistent with those expressed by the Democratic liberal historian Arthur Schlesinger Jr.—in such works as *The Vital Center* (1949)—about the "moral decay, impersonality, and immaturity of Americans in a time of peril". The film ends with the reporter's admonition, "Keep watching the skies."[29]

Three decades of Cold War watchfulness were to pass before the story "Who Goes There?" was retranslated into film, *The Thing* of 1982. If the 1950s had been an "age of anxiety"—marked by "militant masculinity, competitiveness and aggressiveness"—and the 1960s had been "an age of commitment"—marked by youthful protest against materialism and oppression, but for equality and pacifism—then the 1970s had been marred by disillusion and introspection. This perception of America in the 1970s was endorsed by the Democrat President Carter who, in July 1979, indicted Americans for their tendency "to worship self-indulgence and consumption" in a vain effort to "fill the emptiness of lives which have no confidence or purpose": this "concern with self over community" was compounded by "a loss

of faith in institutions because of political assassination, Vietnam, and the shame of Watergate". American faith was further shaken when, in November 1979, fifty-three Americans were taken hostage in Iran by the Islamic revolutionary regime and, in December 1979, by the Russian invasion of Afghanistan to support a Marxist regime. Americans were reduced to drawing self-esteem from the defeat of Russia by the United States at ice-hockey in the Winter Olympics at Lake Placid, New York, "a symbolic victory in the Cold War" which was hailed by *Newsweek* as "a morality play on ice".[30]

The retranslation of "Who Goes There?" had been under negotiation from 1975 to 1979, but went into production only after the box-office success of the film *Alien*. One contemporary commentator remarks that "mindlessly destructive BEMs [Bug-Eyed Monsters] of the '50s . . . found popular contemporary counterparts only in the 1979 *Alien*, and two remakes of '50s films: *Invasion of the Body Snatchers* . . . and *The Thing*".[31]

This overlooks that *Alien*, too, was the remake of a 1950s film—*It! The Terror From Beyond Space*—which was a translation of two short stories by A. E. Van Vogt, "Black Destroyer" and "Discord in Scarlet" (published in *Astounding Science-Fiction* in, respectively, July and December 1939). The 1978 *Invasion of the Body Snatchers* was a remake of the 1956 film which was the translation of a serial—*The Body Snatchers*—published in *Collier's* magazine in 1954. Each of these films featured the incursion of a BEM capable of metamorphosis or mimesis—"lingering on the lurid biomechanics with an almost affectionate disgust"—but each film was as concerned with the unreadiness of communities to resist the peril: the San Franciscans in *Invasion of the Body Snatchers* are so stupefied by self-absorption as to have become indistinguishable from their emotionless pod replicas; the crew of the spacecraft in *Alien* are corporate personnel whose "feelings and bonds are so severely truncated" as to have become "essentially indistinguishable from the corporation's literal, and malevolently controlled, robots"; and the members of the polar expedition in *The Thing* are isolated not only from the world but from one another.[32]

Rather than the elitist scientific collective of the 1938 story, or the military-civilian collective of the 1951 film, there is no collectivism or factionalism in the 1982 film merely, as Schelde remarks, "a sense of strained normalcy . . . and alcohol-induced mellowness . . . an equilibrium of sorts" among members of an American Antarctic expedition. The fragility of this mellowness is shown when the protagonist, MacReady, plays a computer programmed for chess: placed in check-mate, Mac tips his glass of whisky into the computer which short-circuits. This chess-playing evokes a scene from the 1951 film when the military flight crew arrive at the Arctic base to find two scientists apparently engrossed in a game of chess underway during the previous visit, and the Captain banters, "Hello, Doctor, Professor . . . the same game?"[33]

This recreation—and social intercourse—is replayed as solitary distraction. Characters other than Mac engage in solitary distractions: for example Nauls, the cook, who roller-skates the corridors and kitchen, and plays his portable stereo too loudly for other members of the expedition, and Palmer, a helicopter pilot, who smokes dope and changes videos without consulting other viewers. Such solitariness imperils the expedition as a monstrous Thing preys upon solitary members: the earliest manifestation of the Thing—as a runaway husky from a Norwegian Antarctic base—pads about the American base until it finds a human alone.

The Thing has been described as a "reconceptualisation" rather than a remake as this film returns to the "premise of John W. Campbell's original story"—and to such details as names of characters and to dialogue—but pays homage to the earlier film. The 1982 film corresponds to the story insofar as the setting is the Antarctic, the alien absorbs and imitates life-forms, the demented biologist Blair sabotages the transport, the test of humans/aliens is a searing of blood drawn from humans/ aliens, and the pseudo-Blair—an apparent madman—is revealed to be an alien imitation at the dénouement. But the 1982 film also includes images from the earlier film: the discovery of the alien remains and the attempt to salvage the alien craft by a Norwegian expedition, shown on a videotape retrieved from the smouldering ruins of the Norwegian base.[34]

Eventually, the pseudo-husky, consigned to the kennels at the American base, attempts to absorb real huskies—as in the 1938 story—revealing the presence of the Thing. Members of the American expedition incinerate the monster and then—from viewing the Norwegian videotapes—locate the site of the crash-landed alien craft. While the submarine-like craft of the 1938 story was replaced in the 1951 film by a contemporary flying saucer, the 1982 film refers to Erich von Däniken's 1968 image of the *Chariots of the Gods*:[35] as Palmer remarks of the remains of the alien spacecraft, "They're falling out of the skies like flies"—an evocation of the 1951 film—"Chariots of the Gods, man. They practically own South America".

Meanwhile, on-screen computer analyses of the alien remains predict:

PROBABILITY THAT ONE OR MORE TEAM MEMBERS MAY BE INFECTED BY INTRUDER ORGANISM: 75% PROJECTION: IF INTRUDER ORGANISM REACHES CIVILISED AREAS . . . ENTIRE WORLD POPULATION INFECTED 27,000 HOURS FROM FIRST CONTACT.

"Paranoia time," as Billson remarks. After the revival of alien remains in a storeroom of the base—a further evocation of the 1951 film—and the absorption of a member of the expedition, the survivors succumb to madness and murderousness: dazed and confused, the radio operator, Windows, menaces the base commander, Garry, with a rifle; a hysterical Nauls maroons Mac in a blizzard to freeze; the panicked dog-handler, Clark, attacks Mac with a scalpel; and, albeit in self-defence, Mac shoots him dead.[36]

"Trust," as Mac has informed Blair/pseudo-Blair, "is a tough thing to come by these days" and, later, as Mac confides to a tape recorder, "Nobody trusts anybody now." Mac cannot even trust himself: "I know I'm human," he asserts but, as one critic contends, "this has become a hollow, and even a useless, knowledge". As Kinner/pseudo-Kinner, the hysterical cook of the 1938 story, demanded, "Mac, would I know if I was a monster? Would I know if the monster had already got me? Oh Lord, I may be a monster already".[37]

Thus, the apprehension of survivors—and Clark's panic—prior to the searing of blood in the 1982 film may be due to not only the identification of alien others but also revelations as to their own identity. The outcome of the blood-test—as pseudo-blood shies away from a heated wire—is that Palmer, "the clown of the group" with his "stoned sense of humour", is a Thing. The pseudo-Palmer is incinerated, but not before infecting Windows who is incinerated in turn.[38]

Further investigation reveals that pseudo-Blair—consistent with the 1938 story—has constructed a craft with which to reach populated areas. McReady, in the story, reduces pseudo-Blair to "a glowing coal" with a blowtorch—as in the 1951 film the "intellectual carrot" is electrocuted—but in the 1982 film, there is no conclusive destruction of the elusive pseudo-Blair. The only recourse for Mac is to raze the Antarctic base: a pyrrhic victory recalling his final gambit with the chess program.[39]

The dénouements of the three texts trace a decline from optimism toward pessimism: the collectivist scientists who keep their world from an alien menace and acquire alien artefacts which reveal the secrets of atomic power and antigravity; the military-civilian collective who keep the world from an alien menace—"destroying a [potential] source of wisdom"—and acquire no alien artefacts; and the loners—and losers—who can merely stalemate the alien menace.[40] But these three texts addressed different readerships quite differently. The earliest text was representative of Campbell's work—both as a writer and as editor of *Astounding Science-Fiction*—intended for a readership appreciative of the "particular care [taken] with the scientific underpinning of his stories". "Who Goes There?" affirmed faith in scientists and the laws of science: for instance, the unearthly Thing was defeated due to scientific deductions which were predicated on "it [obeying] exactly the same laws . . . as any other manifestation of life".[41]

The earlier film eschewed a science-fiction readership while addressing a wider cinema readership of "affluent, conformist America" to whom the individual seemed superfluous and for whom the "'organization man' mentality of a newly powerful corporate capitalism" provided an ideal. Yet this readership was opposed to the reduction of any individual to "a mere interchangeable component" in a scientific-technical rational system. If, as Franklin contended, "science fiction [was moving] inexorably towards the centre of American culture", the science fiction of *The Thing (from Another World)* (1951) was devoid of faith in science and scientists.[42]

The later film—poorly received critically but currently gaining appreciation—addressed an American readership "brooding upon apocalypse" after a succession of disasters, including "Three Mile Island, the plunging dollar, [and] the spectacle of the American imperium held hostage by shabby ideologues". Any faith in a scientific-technical rational system would have been sorely tried by the near meltdown of the nuclear generator at Three Mile Island in 1979, and by the simultaneous increase of economic stagnation and inflation—"stagflation"—between 1975 and 1980. President Carter alleged that Americans no longer "believed in something called progress . . . a faith that the days of our children will be better than our own". *The Thing* (1982) was, for paranoid and isolated Americans, a cautionary tale—a morality play on ice—for which a moral may be found in the past in the lyrics of "The Liberty Song" (1768) which American colonists sang after the Boston Tea Party:

> "Then join in hand brave Americans all,
> By uniting we stand, by dividing we fall."[43]

Notes

1. John W. Campbell [as Don A. Stuart], "Who Goes There?", *Astounding Science-Fiction*, vol. 21 (6) August 1938, pp. 60-97, at pp. 63-76.

2. Ibid., p. 60.

3. Ibid., pp. 92-93.

4. Greg Tate to Mark Dery, "Black to the Future: Interviews with Samuel R. Delany, Greg Tate and Tricia Rose", in Mark Dery, ed., *Flame Wars* (Durham, NC: Duke University Press, 1994), pp. 179-222, at p. 211.

5. Anne Billson, *The Thing* (London: British Film Institute, 1997) p. 16; Campbell, op. cit., p. 94; ibid. p. 90.

6. See Jon Turney, *Frankenstein's Footsteps: Science, Genetics and Popular Culture* (New York: Yale University Press, 1998), pp. 96-120, especially p. 108; Campbell, op. cit., p. 75.

7. See Edward James, *Science Fiction in the Twentieth Century* (Oxford: Oxford University Press, 1994), p. 50; Umberto Eco, "Innovation and repetition: between modern and post-modern aesthetics", *Dædalus,* vol. 14 (4) (Fall 1985), pp. 161-184, at p. 170; Campbell, op. cit., p. 76; notably, this is consistent with Campbell's interest in mythology and folklore, see Albert Berger, *The Magic That Works: John W. Campbell and the American Response to Technology* (San Bernardino: Borgo Press, 1993), p. 16; Campbell, op. cit., p. 68 and pp. 71-72; Virgil (trans. André Bellessort and ed. R. Durand), *Énéide: Books VII-XII,* (Paris: Les Belles Lettres, 1957), Book VIII, l. 438, at p. 63; H. G. Wells, *The War of the Worlds* (London: Everyman, 1993), p. 118.

8. Campbell, op. cit., p. 66; Wells, op. cit., p. 161.

9. Per Schelde, *Androids, Humanoids and Other Science Fiction Monsters* (New York: New York University Press, 1993). p. 95; Campbell, p. 78; Virgil (trans. and ed., Eugène de Saint-Denis), *Les Géorgiques,* (Paris: Les Belles Lettres, 1974), Book IV, ll. 406-408, at p. 71; Campbell, op. cit., p. 83.

10. Annette Kuhn, "Reflections", in Annette Kuhn, ed., *Alien Zone* (London: Verso, 1990), pp. 15-18, at p. 17; Charles R Hearn, *The American Dream in the Depression* (Westport, Connecticut: Greenwood Press, 1977) at p. 96; see also William E. Leuchtenburg, *Franklin D. Roosevelt and the New Deal* (New York: Harper and Row, 1963), pp. 26-28.

11. T. H. Watkins, *The Great Depression* (Boston: Little, Brown & Co, 1993) at p. 16.

12. Peter N. Carroll and David W. Noble, *The Free and the Unfree* (Harmondsworth: Penguin, 1977) at p. 329; Hearn, op. cit., p. 109; see Watkins, op. cit., p. 16, and Leuchtenburg, op. cit., p. 334; see also Robert Warshow, "The gangster as tragic hero", in *The Immediate Experience* (New York: Atheneum, 1975), pp. 127-133—an article reprinted from *Partisan Review* February, 1948—in which the critic contends that "the very conditions of success make it impossible not to be alone, for success is always the establishment of an *individual* pre-eminence that must be imposed on others, in whom it automatically arouses hatred; the successful man is an outlaw" p. 133; Hearn, op. cit., p. 190; Leuchtenburg, op. cit., p. 340.

13. Ibid., pp. 26-28; Frederick W. Allen, *Since Yesterday: The Nineteen-Thirties in America* (New York:

Harper and Row, 1961), p. 129-130; see also Patrick Renshaw, "Organised labour and the Keynsian revolution", in Stephen W. Baskerville and Ralph Willett, eds., *Nothing Else to Fear* (Manchester: Manchester University Press, 1985) pp. 216-235, at p. 217.

14. *Barron's National Business and Financial Weekly,* XIII 13 February 1933, cited in Leuchtenburg, op. cit., p. 30.

15. See Alan Brinkley, *Voices of Protest: Huey Long, Father Coughlin and the Great Depression* (New York: Knopf, 1982); Leuchtenburg, op. cit., p. 102; Michael R. Beschloss, *Kennedy and Roosevelt* (New York: Norton, 1980), p. 113.

16. Leuchtenburg, op. cit., p. 103; Watkins, op. cit., p. 235.

17. Michael S. Sherry, *In the Shadow of War* (New Haven: Yale University Press, 1995), p. 51.

18. Kuhn, op. cit., at p. 16; Campbell, op. cit., p. 76.

19. Berger, op. cit., pp. 12-13; ibid., p. 19; ibid., p. 17.

20. Ibid., pp. 47-48; see also Walter Hirsch, "The Image of the Scientist in Science Fiction", *American Journal of Sociology,* 63 (March 1958), pp. 506-512.

21. Berger, op. cit., p. 165; ibid., p. 59; Leuchtenberg, ibid., p. 25; Elliot A. Rosen, *Hoover, Roosevelt, and the Brains Trust* (New York: Columbia University Press, 1977), p. 239.

22. Christian Nyby, [dir] *The Thing (from Another World)* (US, RKO, 1951): critics have attributed elements of the direction to Howard Hawks—see e.g. Jacques Rivette, "The genius of Howard Hawks" in Jim Hillier, ed., *Cahiers du Cinéma: Vol. I. The 1950s* (Routledge and Kegan Paul: London, 1985), pp. 126-131, reprinted from *Cahiers du Cinéma* 23 (May 1953)—for whom Nyby had been an editor, and elements of the screenplay, ascribed to Charles Lederer, also have been attributed to Ben Hecht, a Hawks-Lederer collaborator; Vicky Allan, Ben Bachley, Leslie Felperin and Nick James, "Film Chronicle" in *Cloning the Future: Science Fiction Film 1895-1996—Sight and Sound Supplement* vol. 6 (11) November 1996, p. 10; Schelde, op. cit., p. 94; Carroll and Noble, op. cit., p. 363; ibid., p. 375; Mark Jancovich, *Horror* (London: Batsford, 1992), at p. 62; Carroll and Noble, op. cit., p. 357.

23. Campbell, op. cit., p. 61; June, 1947 had witnessed a wave of UFO sightings—including at Douglas, Arizona (June 10), Maury Island, near Tacoma, Washington (June 21), Spokane, Wash-

ington (June 21), Mount Rainier, Washington (June 24), Bisbee, Arizona (June 27), and Grand Canyon, Arizona (June 30)—see Jenny Randles and Peter Warrington, *Science and the UFOs* (Oxford: Blackwell, 1985), p. 2 and Jacques Vallée, *Passport to Magonia* (Chicago: Contemporary Books, 1969), p. 191, which the US Air Force had dismissed as "natural phenomena" such as meteors, swamp gas and weather balloons, see John A Keel, *Operation Trojan Horse* (London: Souvenir Press, 1970) p. 36—and the film draws upon this contemporary controversy in image and for dialogue; Campbell op. cit., p. 63; the term "flying saucers" was first used to describe a formation of nine UFOs sighted by a private pilot, Kenneth Arnold, on June 24, 1947, see Jim Schnabel, *Dark White* (Harmondsworth: Penguin, 1995), p. 13.

24. See Charles Tesson, *Photogénie de la Série B* (Paris: Cahiers du Cinéma, 1997), at p. 42, who cites such precedents as Karl Freund [dir.] *The Hands of Orlac* (aka *Mad Love,* US, Metro Goldwyn Mayer, 1934) and Robert Florey R. [dir.] *The Beast with Five Fingers* (US, Warner Brothers, 1946); Judith Williamson, *Deadline at Dawn* (London: Marion Boyars, 1993), at p. 300.

25. Ian Angus, "Inscription and horizon: a postmodern civilizing effect?" in Herbert W Simons and Michael Billig, eds., *After Postmodernism* (London: Sage, 1994), pp. 79-100, at p. 94; Billson, op. cit., p. 16.

26. See Tesson, op. cit., p. 49, who cites Tod Browning [dir.] *Dracula* (US, Universal, 1931), James Whale [dir.] *Frankenstein* (US, Universal, 1931), Karl Freund [dir.] *The Mummy* (US, Universal, 1932) and James Whale [dir.] *The Invisible Man* (US, Universal, 1933) and the respective sequels; Vivian Sobchack, *Screening Space* [2nd ed.] (New Brunswick NJ: Rutgers University Press, 1997) p. 22; Mark Jancovich, *Rational Fears* (Manchester: Manchester Univ. Press, 1996), p. 12.

27. Jancovich, op. cit., pp. 64-65.

28. Bernard Shapiro, "Universal Truths", *Journal of Popular Film and Television,* 18 (3) (1990), pp. 103-111, at p. 107; Jancovich (1996), op. cit., p. 66; Margaret Tarratt, "Monsters from the Id", *Films and Filming,* 17 (3) (December 1970), pp. 38-42, at p. 38; Carroll and Noble, op. cit., p. 376.

29. Sherry, op. cit., p. 158; see Billson, op. cit., p. 18 and p. 164.

30. John Carpenter, J. [dir.] *The Thing* (US, Universal, 1982); W. H. Auden published the dramatic poem *The Age of Anxiety: A Baroque Eclogue* (1947) and Leonard Bernstein entitled his second sym-

phony *The Age of Anxiety* (1949), while Arthur Schlesinger Jr. contended, in *The Vital Center* (1949), that Americans lived in an "age of anxiety", p. 1; see Sherry, op. cit., pp. 157 and 163; Carroll and Noble, op. cit., p. 373; Christopher Lasch, *The Culture of Narcissism* (New York: W.W. Norton & Co., 1991), at p. 237; Kenneth Keniston, *Youth and Dissent* (New York: Harcourt Brace Jovanovich, 1971), at p. 160; Lasch, op. cit.; William H. Chafe, *The Unfinished Journey* (Oxford: Oxford University Press, 1986), p. 453; see also Sherry, op. cit., pp. 363-4 and pp. 374-375.

31. Ridley Scott [dir.] *Alien* (US, Twentieth Century Fox, 1979), see Billson, op. cit., p. 21; Sobchack, op. cit., p. 293, see also Scott Bukatman, *Terminal Identity* (Durham, NC: Duke University Press, 1993), p. 261; Don Siegel, D [dir.], *Invasion of the Body Snatchers* (US, Allied Artists, 1956).

32. Edward Cahn [dir.] *It! The Terror From Beyond Space* (US, Vogue, 1958); A. E. Van Vogt, "Black Destroyer", *Astounding Science-Fiction* 23 (5) (July 1939), pp. 9-31 and A. E. Van Vogt, "Discord in Scarlet", *Astounding Science-Fiction* 24 (4) (December 1939), pp. 2-24; notably Van Vogt "successfully sued the makers of the film *Alien* for plagiarism of his original plot in 'Black Destroyer' and 'Discord in Scarlet'", see George Hay, "Sleep No More", *Foundation* 24 (February 1982), pp. 68-76, at p. 70, Philip Kaufman [dir.], *Invasion of the Body Snatchers* (US, Solofilm/United Artists, 1978); Jack Finney "The Body Snatchers", *Collier's* 134 (11) (26 November 1954), pp. 26 & 90-99; 134 (12) (10 December, 1954), pp. 114 & 116-125; and 134 (13) (24 December 1954), pp. 62, 64-65 & 68-69 & 71-73; Bukatman, op. cit.; H. Bruce Franklin, "Visions of the future in science fiction films from 1970 to 1982", in Annette Kuhn, ed., *Alien Zone* (London: Verso, 1990), pp. 19-31, at p. 21; for further discussion, see John Trushell, "'Body Snatchers': Spectres that haunt an American Century", *Over Here: A European Journal of American Culture*, 16 (2) (Winter 1996), pp. 89-104, at pp. 93-95; Thomas B. Byers "Commodity Futures", in Annette Kuhn, ed., *Alien Zone* (London: Verso, 1990) pp. 39-50, at pp. 39-42; see Jancovich (1992), op. cit., p. 114.

33. Schelde, op. cit., p. 94.

34. Jancovich (1992), op. cit., pp. 113-114; see Billson, op. cit., pp. 32, 52, and 81.

35. Erich von Däniken, *Chariots of the Gods* (New York: Berkeley Books, 1968), described by Thomas Disch as "an unsavoury amalgam of Darwin, the Old Testament, and the eugenic fantasies of the Third Reich [with which] Von Däniken scored a huge publishing success"—Thomas M. Disch, *The Dreams Our Stuff Is Made Of* (New York: Free Press 1998), p. 28.

36. Billson, op. cit., p. 53.

37. Bukatman, op. cit., p. 267; Campbell, op. cit., p. 85; for further discussion, see Billson, op. cit., p. 63.

38. Billson, op. cit., p. 79; notably, when an upsidedown pseudo-human severed head stalks away on spider legs from a flame-thrower, Palmer intones the film's best known line, "You've got to be fucking kidding!"—for further discussion, see Steve Neale, "'You've got to be fucking kidding!' Knowledge, belief and judgment in science fiction", in Annette Kuhn, ed. *Alien Zone* (London: Verso, 1990) pp. 160-168, at pp. 160-161, and Billson, op. cit., pp. 73-74.

39. Campbell, op. cit., p. 96.

40. Ibid., p. 97.

41. Lorris Murail, *Les Maîtres de la Science Fiction* (Paris: Bordas, 1993) p. 99; Campbell, op. cit., p. 75.

42. Jancovich (1996), op. cit., p. 30; Malcolm Bradbury, "From here to modernity", *Prospect* 3, December 1995, pp. 34-39, at p. 36; Scott Bukatman, "X-bodies", in Rodney Sappington and Tyler Stallings, eds., *Uncontrollable Bodies* (Seattle: Washington, Bay Press, 1994), pp. 93-129, at p. 104; Jancovich (1996) op. cit., pp. 64-65; H. Bruce Franklin, *Robert A. Heinlein: America as Science Fiction* (Oxford: Oxford University Press: 1980), p. 3.

43. See, for example, Nicholas Lezard who, reviewing Billson (op. cit.) in "Paperbacks" *The Guardian: Tabloid*, 7 August 1997, p. 15, remarked that *The Thing* (1982) "was rubbished by the critics at the time, a terribly depressing thought. One hopes . . . that the guilty people will be paraded through the streets with placards round their necks saying 'I gave John Carpenter's *The Thing* a bad review' while a gleeful populace points and laughs at them"; Harvey R Greenberg, "Reimagining the gargoyle: psychoanalytic notes on *Alien*", in Constance Penley, Elisabeth Lyon, Lynn Spigel and Janet Bergstrom, eds., *Close Encounters: Film, Feminism and Science Fiction* (Minneapolis: University of Minnesota Press, 1991) pp. 83-104, at p. 83; "A Song for American Freedom (The Liberty Song)"—published in the *Boston Gazette* on 18th July 1768—was written by John Dickinson (1732-1808), who compiled the *Declaration of the Causes and Necessity of Taking Up Arms* (1775) which preceded the *Declaration of Independence* (1776).

J. P. Telotte (essay date 2001)

SOURCE: Telotte, J. P. "Heinlein, Verhoeven, and the Problem of the Real: *Starship Troopers*." *Literature/Film Quarterly* 29, no. 3 (2001): 196-202.

[*In the following essay, Telotte compares Robert Heinlein's science fiction novel* Starship Troopers *with its 1997 film adaptation, maintaining that director Paul Verhoeven emphasizes the theme of alienation in all of his science fiction films by suggesting "how we have come to inhabit a very unnatural and ultimately threatening place, how we have, in great part through our audiovisual media, come to fashion a very* unreal *world for ourselves."*]

> The typical modern human is characterized by a life under the dictatorship of the screen.
>
> —Paul Virilio

> No wonder you're having nightmares: you're always watching the news.
>
> —*Total Recall*

As the above comments suggest, the "typical modern human," as Paul Virilio offers, seems to live a rather precarious, even nightmarish existence, partly as a result of the audiovisual culture we inhabit. And as a character in Paul Verhoeven's *Total Recall* (1991) attests, within that culture even the "news," which we might think of as a means of linking us to the world, of tying us to events just beyond the small circle of personal experience, even of a kind of liberating potential, can produce an unsettling sense of reality. In his various efforts to explain this contemporary situation, Virilio suggests that we have become subject to a process of what he terms "cinematic derealization," thanks to the way media culture has "denatured direct observation" and even "common sense," providing us with a kind of "substitute" reality (*Lost* 111). Within this context, the world around us increasingly comes to seem little more than a kind of detached spectacle, and we find ourselves essentially reconstituted as its spectators. In his various science fiction films especially, Verhoeven has repeatedly explored this same problem, although it shows up most clearly in his, *Starship Troopers* (1997), an adaptation of Robert Heinlein's famous Cold War-era novel. In fact, as we compare the novel source to the film, we find one of the major shifts is its focus on our position within an audiovisual culture, as the film foregrounds its own mechanisms and explores the ways in which that culture conditions our sense of reality.

Of course, the science fiction genre has always made great capital from visualizing alien, futuristic, and apocalyptic environments, from catering to our wonder at what strange realities "could be"—usually elsewhere and in other times. All of Verhoeven's science fiction films clearly follow this pattern, as they evoke various sorts of strained and artificial contexts, environments hostile in diverse ways to the human, both on and off Earth. An obvious example is *Robocop*'s (1987) depiction of a crumbling Old Detroit and its intended replacement by a new, gleaming Delta City, a world that is essentially a corporate dream—and exploitation—of what modern life should be like (even to its "planned" and corporate-controlled crime and corruption) and one that is already being sold to people through the various commercials interspersed in the narrative. While *Total Recall* begins as a dream, that dream quickly turns into a nightmare about being trapped in a depressurized space suit in the airless atmosphere of Mars. And the film ends with more than a hint that its central characters may still just be living in this dream, despite their seemingly happy ending on a transformed Martian world. Although *Starship Troopers* doesn't interrogate its reality in quite this problematic way, it places its key figures constantly on alien worlds, in damaged space ships, in nightmarish, seemingly hopeless situations, far removed from their home planet and out of contact with their fellow human beings. In fact, we might say that alienization is the order of the day here and in Verhoeven's other science fiction films, as they repeatedly suggest how we have come to inhabit a very unnatural and ultimately threatening place, how we have, in great part through our audiovisual media, come to fashion a very *unreal* world for ourselves.

Such a perspective might seem a strange one to be drawn out of the work of Heinlein, an author often praised for his efforts at realistically grounding his science fiction narratives. Yet while Heinlein has been described as "the most mature, forceful, and influential" of the early modern science fiction writers, particularly for his attention to convincingly detailing even his most fantastic environments, some of his work has also been criticized for the larger context of its detailing. In the 1940s and 1950s, like other noted science fiction authors such as Andre Norton, he produced a body of what has been termed "juvenile" science fiction, most of it published in a Scribner's series aimed at an audience typically conceived of as pre- and early-adolescent males.[1] These dozen early novels, as Jack Williamson explains, follow a fairly consistent "story-of-education pattern" (30) and emphasize an "optimistic vision of space conquest" (31). And some of them, as Edward James judges, could well be ranked "among the best novels he wrote, introducing young readers to the excitement of frontier life on the planets and to the challenge of different social structures and difficult moral dilemmas" (84-85). In short, they contain many of the hallmarks of Heinlein's most effective work, including very clear reference to the social context in which he was then writing.

At the same time, all of these early works are clearly marked by exaggeration, often veering into what Heinlein himself termed the "romantic" (*Grumbles* 43), and—more significantly—frequently push in the direction of what he called "my own propaganda purposes" (41). On the one hand, Heinlein seems to have been under no illusions about his efforts for the juvenile market. He obviously saw them as a somewhat different sort of writing from his "adult novels," as constituting an attempt "to write wholesome stories which were able to compete with the lurid excitements of comic books" (72). Yet on the other hand, these juveniles betray a typical Heinlein signature, his own sense of the "wholesome." Like the adult novels, they consistently emphasize the hard details of science—such as the complexities of colonizing the planets and the difficulties of space flight (seen especially in his contributions to the script of the landmark film *Destination Moon* [1950])—portray the problems of everyday living (on Earth and elsewhere), and detail the psychological life of their characters. The result of this dual pull, of a juvenile exaggeration and of Heinlein's trademark fascination with detail, would result in what we might term a rather problematic sense of reality.

We can partly measure out this tension between the requirements of the juvenile genre and an emphasis on what James describes as "not only some hard-headed extrapolation but also . . . a carefully realized social and cultural context, with a 'lived-in' feel" (66), in some of the strained responses to the novels. Well chronicled are Heinlein's frequent censorship battles with his Scribner's editor Alice Dalgliesh and the reactions of reviewers who objected to elements of sex, violence, and the Heinlein world view that inevitably surfaced even in the juveniles, particularly, as Philip E. Smith argues, the pattern of a cold and inescapable "social Darwinism" (137). Many of his stories finally seem to be about a kind of cosmic survival of the fittest and the difficulties his young protagonists face in learning this fundamental truth of life. Their emphasis is frequently on the sort of discipline that would be needed to endure in new and often harsh environments—and by extension, for his juvenile readers to survive in a potentially harsh and constantly challenging future, such as he saw facing the United States in the Cold War era. That emphasis has led many to see in all of his work a rather troubling ideology. Thus, Barton Levenson sums up one focus of recent Heinlein criticism when he argues that, "in the clearest sense of the word, his political and ethical beliefs were fascist" (10).[2]

That charge certainly resonates with the novel *Starship Troopers,* for its militaristic focus, emphasis on the unquestioning obedience to orders, and championing of the elitist group easily suggest such an authoritarian and nationalistic ideology. And partly as a result of that ideology, along with its emphasis on the violent details of war and, as Williamson says, its "glorification of the fighting man," *Starship Troopers* was rejected for the Scribner's juvenile series. While the novel shares many characteristics with the other, more "innocent" works of the juvenile group, it also points toward a more troubling dimension of Heinlein's canon, one that might help us see how it appealed to Verhoeven as a possible vehicle for his own science fiction perspective.

Certainly, all of Verhoeven's work in this genre suggests a similar tension between the real and the exaggerated, even excessive effect. In assessing his own career, he notes that, while working in his home country of the Netherlands, particularly in collaboration with screenwriter Gerard Soeteman, he "went much more to a realistic approach"; at this point his sense of "reality and realism" generally dominated his films (Shea 11).[3] However, upon coming to America to work on *Robocop,* he says, he felt as if he "was going back to my childhood," to the sort of "special-effect movies" he liked as a kid (Shea 11). In fact, he cites a rather obvious ancestor of *Starship Troopers, The War of the Worlds* (1953), as one of the formative films of this juvenile period. While Verhoeven might have initially seen working on *Robocop* as his own kind of juvenile turn, he also found in it something more— an opportunity to deal with elements he "had repressed . . . for twelve or fifteen years" (Shea 11). The end result seems to have been a rather different approach to reality itself. By the time of *Total Recall,* that developing perception produced a narrative that resolutely refuses to situate its audience in a verifiable actuality; rather, it suggests, as Verhoeven says, "that there are different realities possible at the same moment. What I wanted to do in *Total Recall* is . . . a movie where both levels are true" (Shea 19). The very indeterminacy built into this approach not only let him draw on his own juvenile perceptions of his world—perceptions honed during the violent Nazi occupation of his homeland and ones that saw violence as "normal" and peace as "a-normal" (Shea 5)—but also allowed him to reflect on how, as a culture, we have managed to construct such a strange and pervasive sense of reality.

The film *Starship Troopers* certainly seems to many like a comic-book exaggeration of reality, much in the vein of *Robocop*; thus Roger Ebert described it as "the most violent kiddie movie ever made." And in a tone that might recall much later Heinlein criticism, it has been scored for its political posture—or more precisely for lacking one. Richard Schickel, for example, suggests that a key "unexplored premise" of the film is the way that it simply depicts without question "a happily fascist world." And in this same vein, Mike Clark describes the seductive lure of the film's "army of sweet-tempered, fresh-faced fascists." Perhaps these and other reviewers were drawing in part on Heinlein's own political reputation in this regard, yet what they seem to miss is the great extent to which the film diverges from its novelistic source, particularly as it deploys its exaggerations to explore the very reality from which such a politics would arise—in effect, the extent to which it very precisely examines that "premise." For while Heinlein, in *Starship Troopers* and elsewhere, carefully constructs his world and his characters in painstaking detail and with the sort of rigorous attention to scientific possibility that his pulp editor, Joseph W. Campbell, Jr., early on demanded of him, and also emphasizes the sort of dictatorial, authoritarian figures that he saw as necessary for survival in such a world, Verhoeven plays rather loosely with his science, instead focusing his attention on how our culture does the constructing—of both our world and our selves.

Of course, Verhoeven's adaptation of the novel undeniably shows many traces of the juvenile tale's influence. For all of its changes, the film still follows the Heinlein pattern of youthful education, in large part because, the movie implies, we have all become very much like juveniles in the process of being molded by today's media culture and its powerful methods of "derealization." *Starship Troopers* takes Johnny Rico and his friends from high school, Diz, Carmen, and Carl, through various forms of military training; it emphasizes the rigors and even deadly dangers of that training; and then it shows several of these figures in combat against the insect foe from the planet Klendathu. Yet its focus is never the same as Heinlein's, on what these characters learn, on Johnny's maturation in particular; rather, it consistently focuses on *how* people are educated in this future world, indoctrinated on every level, from the classroom, to the sports they play, to the training they undergo in the military, to the pervasive media, to the very structure of society which rewards those who follow the paths it lays out. When early in the film Johnny rebels against one sort of indoctrination, his parents' efforts to send him on an expensive vacation and then to Harvard for college education, arguing that "It's my decision, not yours," it is less the sort of triumphant assertion of individuality that we would expect to find in a Heinlein novel than an ironic note in the face of the many factors we have seen that are already shaping Johnny's future, determining his path to Federal Service more surely than any conscious decisions he makes.[4]

Especially telling in this case of reality construction are a number of things that disappear from the original story, as well as several others that have been grafted on. Foremost among the missing is the variety of dominant, authoritarian figures. Johnny's father, for example, is killed off early in the film, rather than, as in the novel, reappearing as one of Johnny's own troopers who has accepted and adopted his son's world view. That early death provides Johnny with a purely emotional stimulus for his desire to fight the bugs of Klendathu, in place of the novel's gradually developed and thoroughly rationalized devotion to duty and to behaving as a citizen should. The authoritarian, yet beneath a gruff exterior, fundamentally caring Sergeant Zim simply becomes the hard taskmaster, the stereotyped drill sergeant who teaches through violence, breaking one recruit's arm and throwing a knife through another's hand—both vivid teaching tactics and further steps in the mental conditioning of these would-be soldiers. Although he disappears from most of the film, Zim reappears at the narrative's end as the person who has succeeded in capturing a "brain" bug—in effect, one who has managed to bring an unruly and threatening rational impulse under his violent control, under the control of a race that apparently believes, as Mr. Rasczak asserts, that "violence [is] the supreme authority from which all other authority derives." A key scene added to the film is a live-fire training exercise in which Johnny allows a squad member to remove a protective helmet because he cannot see with it on. When the cadet is subsequently shot in the head and killed, Johnny is blamed and receives a public lashing for his negligence—essentially, for allowing one of his charges to remove the sort of blinders that this culture places on those it wishes to use and control.

Just as important is a significant shift in the narrative mechanism itself. For while Heinlein's novel is a first-person narrative, told from Johnny Rico's vantage point, Verhoeven's film unfolds not from the perspective of any individual, but rather from the point of view offered by the audiovisual culture itself. It is a most fitting shift, for with it, the film is able to establish a rather different authoritarian voice, and indeed a subtly tyrannical power, one that is the real heart of its satiric vision. Here, the book's multiple, powerful authoritarian figures are largely transformed into the media, which, through their substitute reality, become precisely the sort of dictatorial voice of which Paul Virilio speaks.

While the repeated use of commercials in both *Robocop* and *Total Recall* pointed out the extent to which our media have influenced the formation of contemporary consciousness, *Starship Troopers* from its very start establishes the media context of all that we see. In fact, the entire narrative is framed in "reports," news coverage of the struggle with the bug adversary of Klendathu. The film opens on a recruiting video for Federal Service, showing a young boy in the ranks with regular soldiers, suggesting just how early this culture begins constructing its violent regime. That introductory video is interrupted by images of what those recruits must realistically face in a newsfeed that is being beamed live to Earth, showing the Mobile Infantry invading Klendathu. The disastrous results of this first action, though, emphasize the problems of such "reality" reporting, as both the on-air reporter and cameraman are killed. Clearly, reality does not want to follow the "script" of heroic warfare and victory that the media has, as we see, already begun shaping for the public back home. The conclusion too is a combination recruiting appeal and newsfeed, detailing a single victory over the bugs, the capture of a "brain bug," and the subsequent testing and experimentation on the creature. A carefully shaped presentation, this last video suggests how the calamitous situation of the war has been carefully reconfigured for public consumption, particularly with its closing affirmation that our forces will "keep on fighting" until they win. And that shaping reminds us how, as Virilio contends, "the concept of reality is always the first victim of war" (*War* 33).

Perhaps the most pointed reminder, though, is the form Verhoeven gives the various other interpolated newsreels/newsfeeds that, from time to time, intrude into and give shape to the narrative. They are a curious combination of the old and the new, of World War II propaganda films and present-day webcasts that together fashion an illusion of the democratic dissemination of information and freedom of choice. On the one hand, the titles of these media messages pointedly evoke Frank Capra's famous World War II *Why We Fight* series and his *Know Your Enemy* films. As Capra explains, while his films were certainly propaganda, they were a necessary part of the "struggle for men's minds" (329) in that era. Couched in the form of rhetorical argument, they examined the causes leading up to the war, examined documents that clarified the ideologies of the combatants, and compared and contrasted the aims of the countries involved; in short, they gave the illusion of a thoughtful, reasoned debate. However, *Starship Troopers'* videos offer no pretense at argument. Instead, they provide us with exaggerations, sloganeering, and cheerleading, as if the audience were much like the fans we see earlier rooting for Johnny Rico's football team. When one of these feeds does offer something akin to hard information, in a piece titled *Know Your Foe*, it is footage of a cow being slaughtered by a captured bug to demonstrate that species' capabilities and its ferocity; interestingly, much of the slaughter occurs behind a "censored" patch across the screen. In turn, another feed shows a bug, perhaps the same one, being blasted to bits by soldiers who are instructed how to hit its central nervous system in order to make a quicker kill—and here nothing is censored. It is a telling illustration of just what this culture sees as obscene, as a censorable reality, and a clear indication of how it has set about sanctioning a most horrific violent response to the bug foe. More importantly, it drives home the extent to which the sense of reality here seems driven by emotion, impulsive reactions, and spectacular effects.

The film couches this display of propagandistic technique, though, in a thoroughly contemporary context by letting us see these video feeds on screens that suggest the streaming news formats that have become familiar on web sites like CNN Interactive and MSNBC. Along with each "news bite" we see a question, "Want to know more?" and a prompt to a hypertext link that is supposed to bring us that "more." However, the narrative's rapid movements from one brief clip to another never follow any of these links, never provide us any in-depth coverage, just the sort of superficial, headline-style information with which both the contemporary evening news and the internet have made us so familiar. More than just logical, futuristic extensions of the "Mediabreak" news show that begins and frequently cuts into *Robocop*'s narrative—a show that promises, "You give us three minutes and we'll give you the world"—these brief video feeds mock the promise of today's electronic communications, the internet, and the democratic diffusion of information supposedly available through the world wide web. For in one chief respect these offerings differ little from those propaganda films produced by Capra for the US government in World War II: the illusion of choice and access to "more" information offered here is no great gain in a world where no one seems to have even those three minutes *Robocop* mentions for thoughtful consideration.

Still, the film emphasizes how the people here are all linked together through the latest in communication devices, essential parts of the artificial technological environment that has been crafted for them. Even from deepest space, Johnny can talk to his parents on a video link—at least until that link completely fails when a bug-sent meteor hits Earth. Carmen seems to be talking to Johnny, until a track back reveals that she is simply watching a disk he has sent her. In nearly similar fashion, we see Johnny view a communication from Carmen, a video "Dear John" letter—appropriately for this context, a communication that terminates a human relationship. Later, Carmen sends out a distress signal prior to crashing into a bug-occupied planet, but the signal breaks up and is lost before Johnny's squad can get a fix on it. What these and numerous other such failed, interrupted, or faulty communications suggest is the difficulty of living in a mediated world. For as those various technological links, the very ones that so condition our sense of reality, repeatedly fail, leaving humans stranded, alone, trapped by the bug enemy, trapped essentially by our own flight from our humanity, they also point out the fragility of that constructing network on which these people have come to rely.

And yet, as Verhoeven's film suggests with its final lines, we probably shall "keep on fighting" in this alien environment; we shall, for all of our efforts, probably remain a most violent and even self-destructive species, far-removed from its home reality. It simply seems, as the title of another of his films suggests, one more "basic instinct" of postmodern humanity. But while for Heinlein this combative nature and predilection for artificial environments are keys to our destiny, a sign of our species' strength, even a mark of our ability to cope with the various challenges with which the conquest of the universe—which he sees as humanity's inescapable destiny—presents us, for Verhoeven it is only a terrible postmodern symptom, part of our retreat from reality itself, a sign of how much we have lost touch with, lost the signal from, or been Dear John-ed by the very real, human world into which we were born. Within this strange, artificial, and ultimately quite fragile environment we have fashioned for ourselves, within the bubble of audiovisual culture, we see—and understand—only what we have culturally decreed that we should see and understand. We almost blindly follow not some fascist leader, but a fascist spirit of control incubated in a derealized environment.

Verhoeven's films, then, much like Virilio's work, suggest that today we face something far more disturbing than anything Heinlein might have conceived, more repressive than any political system, in fact, something that all ideologies seem intent on mobilizing for their benefit. That is the cinematic derealization of our world. In response to this pervasive effect, he has in his films tried to trace the shape and visualize the power of this strange audiovisual environment we inhabit. And it is in this respect that he does share a real kinship with an author like Heinlein. *Starship Troopers,* like Verhoeven's earlier science fiction forays, conveys a sense of purpose akin to that which propelled its novelistic origin. For while Heinlein set about trying to awaken his readers from what he saw as an ideological apathy—an apathy that, he feared, could help pave the way for a communist subversion and takeover—Verhoeven seems intent on exposing another kind of apathy: our passive acceptance of an increasingly cinematic or mediated reality. He does so by painting that world in broad, satiric strokes, by offering us images that foreground and, in the process, challenge the very ways in which we see our world—or are allowed to see it by the supposedly protective blinders we wear. By exposing our own sort of disconnected, ungrounded astronautic identity, as Jean Baudrillard has described this postmodern condition,[5] his films attack the much greater and subtler subversion we face in a post-Cold War, postmodern world, that of derealization itself.

Notes

1. For a discussion of the science fiction "juvenile" and its role in helping to create a dedicated adult readership for the genre, see James's *Science Fiction in the Twentieth Century,* especially pp. 84-85.

2. Levenson bases this conclusion on Heinlein's consistent embrace of what he terms five fundamental tenets of fascism: his fondness for autocratic leaders, his support of militarism, his elitist attitudes, a consistent resorting to consequentialist ethics, and a general contempt for the mechanism of tra-

ditional democracy. These elements, he argues, surface repeatedly across the Heinlein canon and are all forthrightly supported in *Starship Troopers.* See his "The Ideology of Robert A. Heinlein."

3. As Verhoeven explains, all of his European work "was based on reality. I mean *Soldier of Orange* was an autobiographical book, *Keetje Tippel* was autobiographical, *Turkish Delight* was, *Spetters* was based on newspaper articles and all taken from magazines—all real things. Even *The Fourth Man,* even though it looks like a fantasy, was for eighty percent an autobiographical novel" (Shea 11).

4. In the novel Johnny's father rather easily dismisses his son's initial assertion that he will join the Federal Service, noting that "this family has stayed out of politics and cultivated its own garden for over a hundred years—I see no reason for you to break that fine record" (23). And Johnny's actual enlistment suggests no well devised rebellion against this traditional apolitical stance, but rather a sudden surge of youthful enthusiasm; as he notes, "my mouth was leading its own life" (28). To Heinlein's credit, such initial stances and nearly knee-jerk reactions pave the way for his characters to gradually and credibly move toward their true commitments.

5. Baudrillard offers this astronautic metaphor in his *The Ecstasy of Communication* wherein he describes the postmodern human as one who "sees himself promoted to the controls of a hypothetical machine, isolated in a position of perfect sovereignty, at an infinite distance from his original universe; that is to say, in the same position as the astronaut in his bubble, existing in a state of weightlessness which compels the individual to remain in perpetual orbital flight" (15).

Works Cited

Baudrillard, Jean. *The Ecstasy of Communication.* Trans. Bernard and Caroline Schutze. New York: Semiotext(e), 1988.

Clark, Mike. "'Troopers' on Beeline to Blockbuster." *USA Today.* www.usatoday.com/life/enter/movies/lef029.

Ebert, Roger. Review of *Starship Troopers.* www.suntimes.com/ebert/ebert.reviews/1997.

Heinlein, Robert A. *Grumbles from the Grave.* Ed. Virginia Heinlein. New York: Ballantine, 1989.

———. *Starship Troopers.* New York: Ace Books, 1987.

James, Edward. *Science Fiction in the Twentieth Century.* Oxford: Oxford UP, 1994.

Levenson, Barton Paul. "The Ideology of Robert A. Heinlein." *The New York Review of Science Fiction* 116 (1998): 1, 8-11.

Schickel, Richard. "All Bugged Out, Again." *Time.* www.pathfinder.com/time/magazine/1977/dom/971110/the_arts_cine.all_bugged_on.

Shea, Chris, and Wade Jennings. "Paul Verhoeven: An Interview." *Post Script* 12.3 (1993): 3-24.

Smith, Philip E., II. "The Evolution of Politics and the Politics of Evolution: Social Darwinism in Heinlein's Fiction." *Robert A. Heinlein.* Eds. Joseph D. Olander and Martin Harry Greenberg. New York: Taplinger, 1978. 137-71.

Virilio, Paul. *The Lost Dimension.* Trans. Daniel Moshenberg. New York: Semiotext(e), 1991.

———. *War and Cinema: The Logistics of Perception.* Trans. Patrick Camiller. London: Verso, 1989.

Williamson, Jack. "Youth Against Space: Heinlein's Juveniles Revisited." *Robert A. Heinlein.* Eds. Joseph D. Olander and Martin Harry Greenberg. New York: Taplinger, 1978. 15-31.

John Trushell (essay date winter 2002)

SOURCE: Trushell, John. "Mirages in the Desert: *The War of the Worlds* and *Fin du Globe.*" *Extrapolation* 43, no. 4 (winter 2002): 439-55.

[*In the following essay, Trushell explores the major themes of the infamous radio broadcast and films inspired by H. G. Wells's* War of the Worlds, *particularly* The War of the Worlds *(1953) and* Independence Day *(1996).*]

> "And as thirst can create images on the desert, fear can conjure up sensory images that have no objective reality"
>
> (Koch 16)[1]

8:12 P.M., Sunday 30th October 1938. Over 30 million listeners had been tuned to the NBC network to hear America's most successful radio show, "The Chase and Sanborn Hour" featuring ventriloquist Edgar Bergen and his dummy Charlie McCarthy. The first act—the comedy banter of Bergen/McCarthy—had ended and the second act—Nelson Eddy performing "Neapolitan Love Song"[2]—had been announced, evidently prompting listeners to skim the airwaves for a more entertaining item. These listeners happened upon the CBS network on which a reporter was describing, in a special bulletin, a huge cylinder that had fallen from the skies and come to earth on the New Jersey farmlands at Grovers Mill.[3]

> "I wish I could convey the atmosphere . . . the background to this . . . fantastic scene. Hundreds of cars are parked in a field in back of us. Police are trying to rope off the roadway leading into the farm. But it's no use. They're breaking right through. Their headlights throw an enormous spot on the pit where the object's half-buried. Some of the more daring souls are venturing near the edge. Their silhouettes stand out against the metal sheen."[4]

Many listeners continued to skim—or retuned to "The Chase and Sanborn Hour"—but others were intrigued and stayed tuned to CBS. The CBS audience ranged between 4 to 6 million, and Cantril, in *The Invasion from Mars: A Study in the Psychology of Panic,* estimated 1.7 million listeners believed the special bulletin (56-8).

> "Ladies and gentlemen, this is the most terrifying thing I have ever witnessed . . . Wait a minute! Someone's crawling out of the hollow top. Someone or . . . something. I can see peering out of that black hole two luminous disks . . . are they eyes? It might be a face. It might be . . ."[5]

An estimated 1.2 million of CBS listeners were frightened or disturbed (Cantril 58).

> "A humped shape is rising out of the pit. I can make out a small beam of light against a mirror. What's that? There's a jet of flame springing from that mirror. and it leaps right at the advancing men. It strikes them head on! Good Lord, they're turning into flame! Now the whole field's caught fire. The woods . . . the barns . . . the gas tanks of automobiles . . . it's spreading everywhere. It's coming this way. About twenty yards to my right . . ."[6]

And the bulletin ended with a crash of the microphone, then dead silence. But the bulletin was part of a dramatization of H. G. Wells' *The War of the Worlds*[7]—the latest production in "The First Person Singular" series presented by Orson Welles' "The Mercury Theater of the Air"[8]—as would have been revealed in the programme listings of any Sunday newspaper (Brady 169).

Some ill-informed listeners—deemed to be "insecure or inadequate, who suddenly (sometimes with relief) found public embodiment for their fears" (Draper 36)[9]—became convinced that America was being invaded. By 8:32 P.M., John Houseman, the co-producer of the dramatization, recalled: "CBS switchboards had been swamped into uselessness but from outside sources vague rumors were coming in of deaths and suicides and panic injuries" (Koch 85). The ensuing blind and unreasoning panic might have been prevented—John W. Campbell contended in January and June 1939 editorials of *Astounding Science-Fiction*—by listeners' greater familiarity with science fiction (Berger 54). "Smart" listeners (Eco 1985, 174)[10] would have discerned correspondences between this broadcast and antecedent texts: the serializations in the American magazine *Cosmopolitan* (April-Dec 1897, vols. 22-4), unauthorized newspaper adaptations in the New York *Evening Journal* (Dec. 15, 1897—Jan. 11, 1898) and the *Boston Post* (Jan. 9, 1898—Feb. 3, 1898)[11] and the novel published in 1898 (Hughes 639-40).

Moreover, "smart" listeners would have discerned "the strategy of variations" (Eco 1985, 174) between the broadcast and its antecedent texts and, possibly, have appreciated the selection of music interrupted by the special bulletins: the play opened with "*La Cumparsita*,"[12] or "Little Masked Carnival," then—after the initial bulletin reporting "several explosions of incandescent gas, occurring at regular intervals on the Planet Mars" (Koch 37)—"Stardust" and—after an interview with "Professor Richard Pierson, noted astronomer" (Koch 42)—"I'm Always Chasing Rainbows."[13]

However, for "naive" listeners (Eco 1985, 174), "music program" and "news bulletin" constituted model-texts which were more readily identifiable than the conventions, variations and allusions by which these model-texts were produced, as Eco (1994) suggested:

> "The conventions of production through which the author made his fiction explicit were not understood by the audience, which had instead identified the higher unit of broadcasting constituted by the format 'live reporting' and acted on the basis of this unit of expression and content."
>
> (98)

Listeners had become accustomed, during September and October 1938, to the interruption of scheduled broadcasts by news bulletins concerning Adolf Hitler and the Munich crisis: "For the first time in history, the public could tune into their radios every night and hear, boot by boot, accusation by accusation, threat by threat, the rumbling that seemed inevitably leading to a world war" (Brady 164-5).

Statistics for radio listenership "indicated a massive and concerned audience . . . the shadow of war was constantly in and on the air" (Brady 165). Yet—while the "orgy of alarm generated by [the broadcast] occurred within a month of the Munich crisis"—the episode equally may have been: "a mirror to the mood of the decade as a whole, the capstone to a wall of suspicion and paranoia that had been under construction ever since the Wall Street Crash" (Baskerville and Willet 10-11). The Wall Street Crash in 1929, the Great Depression of the 1930s, disillusion with the political system which had permitted "selfish and materialistic betrayal of the American dream" (Hearne 96) and a "Brown Scare" of fascism—fomented by the rhetoric of the president, Franklin Delano Roosevelt, and other political figures (Sherry 51)—during the late 1930s had contributed to a sense of the imminent dissolution of social order which Bergonzi has termed *fin du globe* (4).

Bergonzi considered that *fin du globe* had been "one of the dominant preoccupations of the *fin de siécle* period" (131) in Victorian England and a predominant motif in H. G. Wells' *The War of The Worlds* (15) which enacted "the secret fears and lack of confidence of late Victorian bourgeois society" (144). Orson Welles may have happened upon the *The War of the Worlds* (Brady 162)—reprinted in a pulp magazine, *The Witch's Tales* (1936), from the serialization in the English *Pearson's Magazine* (April-Dec. 1897)—but the radio dramatization retained the *fin du globe* motif of the novel: the Martians' inferred objective was "to disorganize human society"[14] with the outcome "Cities, nations, civilization, progress . . . done."[15] The radio play stressed—as had the novel—the demise of bourgeois culture: "There won't be any more concerts for a million years or so, and no more nice little dinners at restaurants. If it's amusements you're after, I guess the game's up."[16] However, the inference should not be drawn that the dramatization merely traced, repetitiously, the antecedent novel: the translation from print to radio provided an opportunity for innovation to remedy a perceived flaw in Wells' text.

Wells' *The War of the Worlds* had correspondences with contemporary issues and texts—contemporary and anterior—from popular and elite culture. The text has been considered an "ironical inversion of nineteenth century imperialism" (Clarke 84): "Martians [were] to Europeans [as] the Europeans [had been] to the natives of Tasmania, who were wiped out after 'a war of extermination'" (Parrinder 75). Elements from contemporary science fiction texts have been discerned: the setting in the first chapter has affinities with Camille Flammarion's novels *La Fin du Monde* (1892) and *La Planéte Mars* (1895) (Raknem 400-1); and the *dénouement* in which the Martians die from infection by the bacteria on Earth—which "obviously struck [critics] as an unexpected and absolutely convincing proof of [Wells'] genius" (31)—was indebted to Percy Greg's *Across the Zodiac* (1880) (Haynes 265).[17] Critics have observed Biblical allusions—"traces of the religion [Wells] was steeped in as a child" (Kemp 211)—such as the evocation by the Martian's tentacles and eyes of "the snake . . . strongly associated with the Judeo-Christian myth of the Fall" (Lowentrout 354) and "a pillar of fire by night that becomes a pillar of smoke by day" which evokes the Flight from Egypt (Kemp 211). However, as one commentator has noted, Wells' novel corresponds, in plot and fictional technique, to Daniel Defoe's *A Journal of the Plague Year* (1722), remarking that "both novels are offered as eyewitness accounts of a great disaster which befalls mankind and particularly the inhabitants of London" (Hillegas 23).

The perceived flaw in the novel is the awkward "division of the narrative between the philosopher in Woking and his brother, the medical student, in London" which enabled Wells to combine "immediacy of first-person narration" with "the largeness of design that he was obviously seeking" (Bergonzi 126). The principal narrator—the philosopher of Woking—provides an eyewitness account of the Martians' arrival and advance upon London and of the state of the capital under Martian occupation. The complementary narrative of the medical student—interposed between the Martians' arrival and occupation of London—provides an account of the flight of the populace from London concurrent with the advance of the Martians. However, the interposition is disjunctive and the complementary narrative remains unresolved.

The innovation implemented in the translation from print to radio was to provide a multivocal narrative—concerning the Martians' arrival and advance upon New York—by means of news bulletins, interviews—with the astronomer, Professor Pierson—and public announcements by the commander of the state militia, the vice-president of CBS, and the Secretary of the Interior. The multivocal narrative ended with a radio "ham" calling:

"2X2L calling CQ . . . New York.

Isn't there anyone on the air?

Isn't there anyone . . ."

(Koch 67)

Thereafter, following an intermission, the dramatization resumed with the narrative of Professor Pierson which described the state of New York under Martian occupation and the *dénouement*.

The *succès de scandale* of the radio dramatization convinced RKO film executives that—as "the world situation, along with previous publicity, could stimulate much activity at the box office"—Welles should direct *The War of the Worlds* as his first feature. But Welles—while not averse to filming *The War of the Worlds*—"was adamant about not producing it as his *first* picture" (Brady 201). Welles never produced a film of *The War of the Worlds* but the film that was released fifteen years later was indebted to the radio dramatization and to the original novel.

The film translation *The War of the Worlds*—produced by George Pal—was released in 1953. George Pal, an award winning animator, previously had produced the films *Destination Moon* and *When Worlds Collide*.[18] These films—literary adaptations to color film and with "meticulous special effects" (Newman 114) for which both films received Oscars—marked the transition of science fiction serials—from *Flash Gordon* (1936) to *Flying Disc Man from Mars* (1950)[19]—to science fiction features (Tesson 42).[20] Considered as special effects spectacle, featuring Martian invasion machines—resembling manta rays with cobra-like heat weaponry—wreaking destruction, *The War of the Worlds* also received an Oscar. But considered as text, the film *The War of the Worlds* attempted to reconcile Wells' novel, mediated by Welles' radio adaptation, with contemporary issues.

The film opens—before the titles—with documentary footage and a voice-over which explains that, during the twentieth century, weapons of warfare became more powerful, destructive and deadly, conveying "the fear that civilization has run amok and is about to destroy itself" (Ruppersberg 32). The evocation of newsreel as "model-text"—rather than news bulletins—recalls Welles' radio adaptation. The film continues—following the titles—with a sequence of "glorious astronomical paintings" (Sobchack 191) of "Mars and her surrounding planets viewed objectively" (101) which is accompanied by a sonorous narration which tells of the doomed Martian civilization, recalling the opening of Well's novel. Although one critic has contended that the film "presents a perfect Earth as the only desirable spot in the solar system (who *wouldn't* want to invade us?)" (Bukatman 17), this presentation traces the novel's depiction of Earth as "a morning star of hope, [a] warmer planet, green with vegetation and gray with water, with a cloudy atmosphere eloquent of fertility" (Wells 6). Thereafter, the film relates the arrival of the Martians in rural Linda Rosa, California, and their advance upon metropolitan Los Angeles: this progression recalls both the advance of the Martians from Grovers Mill to New York and their earlier advance from Woking to London. However, the inferred purpose of the Martian advances in the novel and the radio dramatization was to disorganize human society while preserving humans as a source of sustenance: the film concentrates—as did the unauthorized newspaper adaptations of the novel—on "Martian marvels and atrocities" (Hughes 642): the Martian machines are rendered impervious by "protective blisters, electromagnetic covering" and the Martians seem bent upon total destruction. The depredations of the Martians are covered by radio reports: "smart" readers may discern allusions to the radio dramatization when—live from Linda Rosa—a KGEB reporter interviews eminent scientists but is cut off when his radio-truck is destroyed by a heat-ray. Later, when radio broadcasts have become impossible, a reporter tape-records his coverage of resistance to the Martians "for the sake of future history, if any."

The principal narrative counterpart to the philosopher of Woking or the astronomer from Princeton is an atomic engineer, Clayton Forrester, from Pacific Tech. While the exploits of the philosopher and astronomer are mostly solitary, Forrester is accompanied by a lecturer in Library Science, Sylvia Van Buren, who provides the "love interest" conventional in science fiction films of the 1950s (Tarratt 38). Van Buren is the niece of the local pastor who "argues that '[the Martians] are more advanced than [humans] are and therefore nearer to the creator'" (Jancovich 56) and who attempts to parley as an emissary, but is incinerated by a heat-ray. The faith and conduct, albeit foolhardy, of the pastor in the film contrasts with that of the curate in the novel who—consistent with "Well's numerous clergymen"—is "stupid, timid, and afraid of asserting [himself]" (Raknem 185). Moreover, Wells may have depicted the destruction of churches as incidental—for instance, "the Oriental College burst into smoky red flame, and the tower of the little church beside it slid down into ruin" (Wells 37-8)—but the desecration of the churches of Los Angeles precedes the *deus ex biologia* of the Martians' death by bacteria.[21]

While Wells' novel—and Welles' radio play—closed with the Martians "slain, after all man's devices had failed, by the humblest things that God, in his wisdom, has put upon this earth,"[22] this was "a profound humiliation for man [as] men had not conquered" (Clarke 85): "hubris followed by nemesis . . . logic so neatly rounded that it speaks of poetic even more than of scientific or cognitive justice" (Parrinder 11).

But, in Pal's film, deliverance by bacteria smacks of divine retribution upon the desecrators and intercession for mankind which "serves only to affirm humanity's triumphal destiny" (Bukatman 17). The religious *dénouement* of the film corresponds with the contemporary mass revival of religion in America throughout the 1950s (Chafe 120), a revival marked "not so much [by] religious belief as [by] belief in the *value* of religion" and not least in the value of religion as a social institution (Whitfield 86-7). Moreover, there was a "conviction that religion was virtually synonymous with American nationalism" (Whitfield 86) as "free exercise of religion [provided] yet another way of differentiating the American way of life from life under communism" (Foner 268).

However, the film may affirm the value of American religion and freedom—as opposed to communism—but it is also indicts American materialism, the "greed, selfishness and indifference to the welfare of others" indicted in the American religious revival of the early nineteenth century (Foner 55-7; Carroll & Noble 147-8). When the Martian's "meteorite" falls to Earth at Linda Rosa, the locals grasp its commercial potential: "It'll be a real good attraction for Sunday drivers," "Better than a lion farm or a snake pit," "We can sell *tamales, enchiladas,* and hot dogs too," "Yeah, ice cream, cold drinks, and souvenirs." As one Linda Rosan concludes, "It's gonna be like having a gold mine in our own backyard." Later, when the Martians approach Los Angeles, rioters and looters—"thieves, robbers, worse"—lay waste to the convoy of scientists from Pacific Tech who represent the world's best hope of salvation.

The critic Newman considers the film to have been "an inflated version of the Cold War hysteria that had been behind smaller invasions like the one in *The Thing from Another World*" (122).[23] However, *The Thing from Another World* and *The War of the Worlds* are more concerned with "readiness and resistance, anxieties consistent with those expressed by the Democratic liberal historian Arthur Schlesinger . . . in such works as *The Vital Center* (1949)" (Trushell 82). *The War of the Worlds* has one reference to contemporary terrestrial enmity: when the "meteorite" bearing the Martians begins opening, a deputy posted on fire-watch exclaims, "It's an enemy sneak attack—let's get out of here!" But early 1950s American cinemagoers would have been posed a problem to decide whether the enemy were North Korea, China and/or Russia.

The North Koreans had invaded South Korea in June 1950. The response of President Harry Truman, a Democrat, was consistent with the doctrine that he laid before a joint session of the houses of Congress on March 12, 1947: "I believe that it must be the policy of the United States to support free peoples who are resisting attempted subjugation by armed minorities or by outside pressures." Truman perceived the invasion of South Korea as a test of American resolution, a test posed by North Korea but instigated by Russia (Chafe 250-1; Sherry 178). When the United Nations Security Council condemned the invasion and sanctioned "police action" against North Korea, Truman dispatched two American divisions, twenty percent of the total strength of the American army. North Korean forces were repulsed but, when the "police action" advanced into North Korea, China deployed forces to repel the United Nations. The opposing armies, by March 1951, were poised at the 38th parallel, the border between North and South Korea: "The war became a contest among entrenched forces on a scarred and cold landscape, with the enemy making futile charges and allied forces unable to gain a decision" (Sherry 181).

General Douglas MacArthur, commander of the United Nations forces, publicly criticized President Truman for denying him nuclear weapons and was relieved of his command (Carroll & Noble 356). The war remained in deadlock—costing nearly 100,000 American casualties—until Spring 1953 when President Dwight Eisenhower—a Republican who had pledged during his election campaign, "If elected, I shall go to Korea"—issued a threat, indirectly by Secretary of State John Foster Dulles, to China that, unless an armistice was achieved, America would deploy nuclear weapons (Brogan 628; Chafe 138 & 389; Sherry 197).

This was consistent with Eisenhower's "New Look" strategy that relied "on enhanced nuclear forces, as well as alliances and covert action, rather than on costly conventional forces to counter enemy initiatives."[24]

Dulles called for "the deterrent of massive retaliatory power" in a world where "the forces of good and evil are massed and armed and opposed as rarely before in history,"[25] but Eisenhower preferred to use the Central Intelligence Agency—under the directorship of Allen Welsh Dulles, the brother of the secretary of state—to sponsor the overthrow of reformist regimes by covert action. When, in 1953, the Iranian premier, Mohammed Mossadegh, nationalized Iranian oil fields, the CIA sponsored a coup d'état which restored the Shah to the throne (Brogan 630; Sherry 200) and when, in 1954, the Guatemalan premier, Jacobo Arbenz, threatened to nationalize landholdings of the American United Fruit Company, the CIA sponsored the replacement of the reformist government by a reactionary clique (Chafe 259; Sherry 200). Moreover, in 1954, Eisenhower prepared America to replace France as a post-imperialist power in Asia, declaring that: "countries in Southeast Asia would be menaced by . . . the loss of South Vietnam [which] would have grave consequences for [America] and for freedom"

Despite Eisenhower's aversion to overt action and the threat of nuclear weapons, the "New Look" policy "accelerated [militarization] at its most technically exquisite, and exquisitely dangerous, nuclear core" (Sherry 203). Thus, the deployment of nuclear weapons against the Martians in *The War of the Worlds* is consistent with contemporary American policy. But the machines are defended by "protective blisters" and the Martians, depicted as "puny and infantile—little more than high-tech third worlders" (Bukatman 17)—prove less susceptible than the North Koreans and the Chinese against whom Eisenhower threatened nuclear response—in 1955 and 1958—if the Taiwanese islands of Quemoy and Matsu were invaded (Sherry 199). These crises—revealing how little it would take to involve America and China in even a limited nuclear war—discredited the strategy of massive retaliatory power and brinksmanship (Gaddis 170-1).

Reminiscent of "New Look" policy, commentators have discerned two very different forms of extraterrestrial invasion in 1950s science fiction film: the overt and unsubtle mass invasion—of which *The War of the Worlds* is the best instance—and the covert and "far more subtle plan . . . of aliens assuming human form" (Simpson 58). Such films as *Invaders from Mars,*[26] in which aliens—large-headed with truncated bodies and small tentacles—transform humans into automata by means of red crystals embedded in the base of the neck (Tesson 140) and *Invasion of the Bodysnatchers,*[27] in which alien seed pods replicate humans who then disintegrate, depict covert invasions which "dramatized the fear of aliens in our midst" and these invasions and fears were translated into television series from the 1960s onwards (Spigel 220).

There is a discernible shift in emphasis from the television series "The Invaders" (1967-68),[28] in which a solitary, disbelieved and persecuted hero defends America against infiltration and sabotage by aliens who replicate humans, to the television mini-series "V" (1983-84)[29] in which occupation by aliens in human guise is met by "romanticized . . . guerilla-like small-group resistance" (Penley 64). The former series reaffirms Cold War fears—a complacent population, a pervasive conspiracy and elusive conspirators who vaporize to leave "Hiroshima shadows"—but the latter series rejects the Cold War legacy—"the ambiguous outcome of the Korean War and the unprecedented divisiveness spawned by Vietnam"—and recalls the Second World War as "the Good War" (Foner 219) drawing "heavily from the resistance-and-collaboration clichés" of that earlier conflict (Newman 124).

The subsequent translation of *War of the Worlds* as a television series (1988-99)[30] re-visions the Cold War: infiltration and sabotage by aliens who possess humans are countered by a covert scientific-military team, the Blackwood Project. The promotional material for the series states:

> In 1953, Earth experienced a War of the Worlds. Common bacteria stopped the aliens, but it didn't kill them. Instead the aliens lapsed into a state of deep hibernation. Now the aliens have been resurrected, more terrifying than before. Today they're after our bodies.

The series bore out the declaration of Republican President Ronald Reagan that America's "Vietnam syndrome" was over (Chafe 476-7): the Cold War had been resumed. Reagan's pronouncements—which described the arms race between America and Russia as "good versus evil, right against wrong"—recalled "the Eisenhower administration's posture of rhetorical bluster and practical caution" (Sherry 395) and were consistent with Reagan's assumption of the role of "the ultimate Cold Warrior" (Chafe 470). Reagan championed the renewal of America's military strength "but geared less to the wider world and more to Americans' sense of their own needs" (Sherry 392): the renewed Cold War—which was waged more within American borders than against external enemies—included a largely rhetorical war against terrorism (Sherry 445-6).

The premise of the television series "War of the Worlds" was that a terrorist attack on a nuclear waste depot in which were stored Martian remains had caused radiation leaks which revived the invaders. Subsequently, the Martians' possession of the terrorists' bodies and their acts of infiltration and sabotage recall the earlier television series "The Invaders"—and the film "Invaders from Mars" in which human automata sabotage "top-secret military plants" (Seed 133)—and covert invasion (Trushell 93). The aliens' attempts to reassemble their manta ray invasion machines and heat weaponry feature images from the 1953 film[31] which recall overt invasion.

The series traces certain themes of the "Golden Age of Science Fiction"—a term "most frequently applied to the period characterized by the first successes of Campbell's regime at *Astounding Science Fiction* (Berger 110)—insofar as the head of the covert scientific-military resistance to the aliens, Harrison Blackwood the astrophysicist, is an unorthodox and intuitive genius—"always . . . important to the science fiction picture of the scientist" (Berger 135)—and his team are "a heroic elite [set] to save the nation" (Seed 29). Notably, the composition of the team is consistent with more contemporary sensibilities: Norton Drake, the computer scientist, is a paraplegic African-American; Lieutenant-Colonel Paul Ironhorse is a Native-American; and Suzanne McCullough, a microbiologist, is a single mother.

Contemporary sensibilities are evident also in the assembly of "good men who put aside their racial and ethnic differences to come together in a common cause" (Taubin 6)—to avert the end of the world—in the film *Independence Day* (1996),[32] a *fin du globe*—even *fin de siécle*—film which almost marks the centenary of Wells' serialization. A Jewish cable television engineer, David Levinson, provides the unorthodox and intuitive genius while an African-American United States Air Force pilot, Captain Steven Hiller, a "white-trash alcoholic" Vietnam veteran (Dargis 54) Russell Casse, and the White Anglo-Saxon Protestant President Whitmore—a Gulf War veteran—constitute the heroic elite. However, *Independence Day*—or *ID4*—has correspondences with the earlier film, the radio broadcast and the original text of Wells.

ID4 opens on a moonscape, the lunar landing site, marked by an American Stars-and-Stripes pennant, a commemorative plaque—"One small step for a man, one giant leap for mankind"—and astronauts' footprints. The lunar surface is shaken—erasing the footprints—and the plaque and pennant are overshadowed by the passage of a giant spacecraft: mankind may be, as Wells noted, "serene in their assurance of their empire over matter" but are about to be shaken from "infinite complacency" (Wells 5). Flying saucers appear over cities, notably New York, Washington and Los Angeles, and—after a countdown during which only Levinson the "cable TV engineer . . . intuits what might happen" (Newman 124)—wreak destruction, each with a beam which resembles a pillar of blue fire: so begins, in the words of Wells, "the rout of civilization, the massacre of mankind" (Wells 97). *ID4* dwells on alien atrocities—the destruction of helicopter-borne emissaries and skyscraper-top "New Age" revelers, and the incineration of fleeing city populations—and depicts the aliens as bent upon the annihilation of humanity. President Whitmore asks a captive alien, "What do you want us to do?" And the alien replies, "Die."

Unlike the Martians of Wells and Welles, these aliens do not preserve humans for consumption, nor possess humans for convenience as in the television series, nor even manifest curiosity for humans as in the film: the aliens of *ID4* are "environmentally despoiling capitalists who strip-mine and abandon entire planets" (Newman 124) utterly indifferent to the inhabitants. These aliens, as did Wells' Martians, "regarded this earth with envious eyes" (Wells 5) yet not, as in the 1953 film, "as the only desirable spot in the solar system" (Bukatman 17) but materialistically. Materialism becomes an alien attribute while humans are depicted as fundamentally good, "and never so much as when they co-operate and play together as a team" (Taubin 8).

The fleeing survivors of alien destruction provide a polyphonic narrative—achieving the immediacy of a first-person chronicle of disaster attempted by Wells—as these representatives of diverse communities pursue mutually-assured survival. But this polyphony—manifesting "a multiplicity of social accents having to do with gender, class and locale" (Stam 129)—is ultimately subordinated to a survivalist masculine ethos. Moreover, the convergence of these narratives—at Roswell, New Mexico, a top-secret installation where scientists have been studying an alien craft which crashed in the 1950s—strains credulity: lovers are reunited and interdenominational prayers are offered while the masculine heroic elite coordinate a counter-offensive.

Against the aliens—"a horde of interplanetary locusts"—the film "pits a gaggle of hyped-up flyboys" (Hoberman 7)—including President Whitmore and the Vietnam veteran—who must breach protective force fields before engaging the flying saucers in combat. Captain Hiller commandeers the alien craft from Roswell to reach the giant spacecraft in orbit, delivering Levinson and the virus which he has devised to infect the computers of the alien fleet. Thus, the viral *deus ex biologia* of Wells' text, Welles' radio play and the 1953 film—and the biological weapon sought by scientists in the 1953 film and the television series—is supplanted by the *deus ex machina* of *ID4*. Salvation is due to a technological fix rather than divine intervention.

The assaults on alien spacecraft occur on American Independence Day, and President Whitmore pronounces that, "If we take the day, July the Fourth will no longer just be an American holiday": hence the acronymic *ID4*. The film dispenses with the ironic inversion of Wells' text—whereby an imperialistic European war of extermination against Tasmanians was recalled in the Martian war against Europeans—and depicts American intercession to avert the annihilation of humanity. *ID4* celebrates *Pax Americana,* showing America—almost incidentally imperialistic—"organizing the world to establish 4 July as a global celebration of independence" (Hoberman 7)

American triumphalism is understandable. *ID4* was released in 4 A.B. (After Bipolarity), dating from the final self-dismemberment of Union of Soviet Socialist Republics on Christmas Day 1991 (Joffe 13). But as Georgiy Arbatov, Russian Academician and one-time Director of the Institute for American and Canadian Studies, remarked, "We are doing something really terrible to you—we are depriving you of an enemy."

The United States of America, as Huntington observed, may need "an other to maintain its unity" and to resist those "domestic forces pushing toward heterogeneity, diversity, multiculturalism, and ethnic and racial division" (Huntington 32). Without this other, the United States might experience "its own sense of chaos and impending dissolution" (Robins 307). As Hughes has contended:

> Two hundred and sixty million people make up the same country, but this does not mean that they are all the same kind of people, with the same beliefs and mores . . . America is a collective work of the imagination . . . and once that sense of collectivity and mutual respect is broken the possibilities of Americanness begin to unravel.
>
> (16)

Contemporaneous with the self-dismemberment of the Soviet bloc, the Iraqi President Sadam Hussein ordered an invasion of Kuwait: Hussein was dubbed the new Hitler (Robins 305; Levidow 318) and the Kuwait crisis was compared with the Korean crisis, "insofar as "both were border crises just waiting for escalation" (Levidow 325). Hussein and this Gulf War were poor substitutes for the pervasive threat of the Soviet bloc and, as Robins observes, only for "a brief moment, this epic spectacle sustained a sense of national integrity and regeneration" (Robins 307).

Fear of fascism and communism justified foreign expansion and domestic repression (Haut 17) for half a century, but the demise of the Soviet bloc poses a different fear: the absence of the other abroad which fosters chaos and dissolution at home. *ID4* provides an epic spectacle—images that have no objective reality—which fosters a collective work of the imagination and assuages American fears of chaos and impending dissolution.

Notes

The author wishes to express his gratitude to Robert Byron of "Time Trek"—science fiction bookshop—in Bromley, and to the staff of the H. G. Wells Collection at Bromley Libraries.

1. Howard Koch was an adapter of *The War of the Worlds* as a radio play. Notably, the adaptation was accomplished in three days by Koch, his assistant Ann Froelich and John Houseman, co-producer of the radio play (Thomson 100).

2. "Neapolitan Love Song (*T'Amo*)" (Blossom, Henry and Herbert, Victor, Witmark and Sons, 1915) had been a "standard" for twenty years during which some listeners' familiarity had bred contempt.

3. See Koch's *The Panic Broadcast* for a memoir; see Cantril's *The Invasion from Mars* (55-6) for a contemporary social scientific account; for narrative/biographical accounts, see Brady's *Citizen Welles* (169-77), Higham's *Orson Welles: The Rise and Fall of an American Genius* (126) and Thomson's, *Rosebud* (102).

4. Note the correspondence between this passage (Koch 47) and the original passage from Wells' *The War of the Worlds* (18):

> "The crowd around the pit had increased, and stood out black against the lemon-yellow of the sky—a couple of hundred people, perhaps. There were raised voices, and some sort of struggle appeared to be going on about the pit."

5. Note the correspondence (Koch 49) with the original passage (Wells 19):

> "But, looking, I presently saw something stirring within the shadow: gray, billowy movements, one above another, and then two luminous disks—like eyes."

6. Note the correspondence (Koch 51-2) with the original passage (Wells 23):

> "Slowly a humped shape rose out of the pit, and the ghost of a beam of light seemed to flicker out from it.
>
> "Forthwith flashes of actual flame, a bright glare leaping from one to another, sprang from the scattered group of men. It was as if some invisible jet impinged upon them and flashed into white flame. It was as if each man were suddenly and momentarily turned to fire."

7. The dramatization drew upon the novel (1898) as the radio play features an episode which did not appear in the earlier magazine serializations, "the episode of the drunken artilleryman who proposes in about five thousand words that men recapture the earth by first disappearing into drains and sewers" (Hughes 644).

8. The Mercury Theater repertory company had been founded by Orson Welles and John Houseman in 1937.

9. See also Kennedy (392-3) who notes that the reaction to the Mercury dramatization provided for Adolf Hitler "ratification of his low estimate of American intelligence" and for his perception that America posed no threat to German expansionism.

10. For a discussion of "smart" and "naive" readers, see Eco (1985).

11. The unauthorized newspaper adaptations substituted American for English locations and sensationalized the novel by the deletion of passages which "deviated from the straight chronicle of death and destruction" and interpolated passages describing further atrocities (Hughes 642).

12. The title *"La Cumparsita"* (Matos Rodriguez, Gerardo, Breyer, 1917) denotes a group of carnival-goers dressed in a similar fashion, and usually masked.

13. "Stardust" (Carmichael, Hoagy and Parish, Mitchell, Mills Music Inc., 1929) and "I'm Always Chasing Rainbows" (Carroll, Harry and McCarthy, Joseph, McCarthy and Fisher, 1918) after Chopin, Frederic, Fantasie Impromptu in C Sharp Minor.

14. Note the full passage from the radio script (Koch 59):

> They seem to be making conscious effort to avoid destruction of cities and countryside. They stop to uproot power lines, bridges and railway tracks. Their apparent objective is to crush resistance, paralyze communication, and disorganize human society.

The radio script recalls a passage from the original text (Wells 98):

> They do not seem to have aimed at extermination so much as at complete demoralization and the destruction of any opposition. They exploded any stores of powder they came upon, cut every telegraph, and wrecked the railways here and there. They were hamstringing mankind.

15. Compare the quotation (Koch 73) with the dialogue from the novel (Wells 148): "Cities, nations, progress—it's all over. That game's up."

16. Note, the correspondence (Koch 73) with the original passage (Wells 148): "There won't be any more blessed concerts for a million years or so; there won't be any Royal Academy of Arts, and no nice little feeds at restaurants. If it's amusement you're after, I reckon the game is up."

17. Arthur C. Clarke in his "Introduction" to *The War of the Worlds* (xxxii-xxxiii) contends that "Talent borrows—Genius steals" and that Wells "brilliantly anticipated a problem which has become of real practical concern . . . planetary quarantine."

18. These films were each adaptations from science fiction novels: director Byron Haskin's *War of the Worlds* (U.S., Paramount, 1953) from Wells; director Irving Pichel's *Destination Moon* (U.S., Eagle Lion, 1950) from Robert Heinlein's *Rocket Ship Galileo*; and director Rudolph Maté's *When Worlds Collide* (U.S., Paramount, 1951) from Edwin Balmer and Philip Wylie's *When Worlds Collide*.

19. Stephani, Frederick and Taylor, Ray [dirs.] *Flash Gordon* (U.S., Universal, 1936); Bannon, Fred [dir.] *Flying Disc Man from Mars* (U.S., Republic, 1950).

20. Notably, Kurt Neumann produced, directed and wrote the monochrome feature *Rocketship X-M* (U.S., Lippert, 1950)—at the behest of distributor Robert Lippert—which was released before *Destination Moon* (Tesson 42).

21. For desecration, see Strick (763), and for *deus ex biologia*, see Bukatman (17).

22. This passage (Wells 161) may be traced in this passage from the radio playscript (Koch 77): "slain after all man's defenses had failed, by the humblest thing that God in His wisdom put upon this earth."

23. Nyby, Christian [dir.] *The Thing (from Another World)* (U.S., RKO, 1951).

24. The "New Look" strategy was stated in National Security Council 162/2 and approved by Eisenhower in October 1953 (Sherry 192).

25. Speech to the Council on Foreign Relations on January 12, 1954, published in amended form in Foreign Affairs (Dulles 357-359).

26. Menzies, William Cameron [dir.], *Invaders from Mars* (U.S., Twentieth Century Fox, 1953).

27. Siegel, Don [dir.], *Invasion of the Body Snatchers* (U.S., Allied Artists, 1956).

28. Cohen, Larry [creator] and Armer, Alan [prod.], "The Invaders" (U.S., ABC/Quinn-Martin Productions, 1967-68).

29. Johnson, Kenneth [creator and prod.] "V" (U.S., NBC, 1983/84).

30. Strangis, Greg [creator] and Strangis, Greg and Strangis Sam [prods.] *War of the Worlds* (U.S., Paramount, 1988/89)

31. Images from the 1953 film are used in the 1988/89 television series for flashbacks and for special effects, thus conflating the past and the present.

32. Emmerich, Roland [dir.] *Independence Day* (U.S., 20th Century Fox, 1996)

Works Cited

Balmer, Edwin and Wylie, Philip. *When Worlds Collide.* Philadelphia: J.B. Lippincott, 1933.

Baskerville, Stephen and Willett, Ralph. "Nothing Else to Fear: an Introduction." In *Nothing Else to Fear.* Ed. Stephen Baskerville and Ralph Willett. Manchester: Manchester University Press, 1985. 1-12.

Berger, Albert. *The Magic That Works: John W. Campbell and the American Response to Technology.* San Bernadino: Borgo Press, 1993.

Bergonzi, Bernard. *The Early H. G. Wells: A Study of the Scientific Romances.* Manchester: Manchester University Press, 1961.

Brady, Frank. *Citizen Welles.* London: Hodder and Stoughton, 1990.

Brogan, Hugh. *Longman History of the United States of America.* London: Longman, 1985.

Bukatman, Scott. *Terminal Identity.* Durham, North Carolina: Duke University Press, 1993.

Cantril, Hadley. *The Invasion from Mars: A Study in the Psychology of Panic.* Princeton: Princeton University Press, 1940.

Carroll, Peter, and Noble, David. *The Free and the Unfree: A New History of the United States.* Harmondsworth: Penguin, 1977.

Chafe, William H. *The Unfinished Journey.* Oxford: Oxford University Press, 1995.

Clarke, Arthur C. "Introduction." In *The War of the Worlds.* London: J. M. Dent, 1993. xxix-xxxiv.

Clarke, I. F. *Voices Prophesying War.* Oxford: Oxford University Press, 1992.

Dargis, Manohla. "*Independence Day.*" *Sight and Sound* 6 (8) (August 1996): 53-54.

Draper, Michael. "The Martians in Ecuador." *Wellsian: The Journal of the H. G. Wells Society* New Series 5 (Summer 1982): 35-36.

Dulles, John Foster. "Policy for Security and Peace." *Foreign Affairs* XXXII (April 1954): 357-359

Eco, Umberto. "Innovation and repetition: between modern and post-modern aesthetics." *Dædelus* 114 (4) (Fall 1985): 161-184.

———. "Does the audience have bad effects on television?" In *Apocalypse Postponed.* Ed. Umberto Eco with Robert Lumley. Bloomington, Indiana: Indiana University Press/London: British Film Institute, 1994. 87-102.

Foner, Eric. *The Story of American Freedom.* London: Picador, 1998.

Gaddis, John Lewis. *Strategies of Containment.* Oxford: Oxford University Press, 1982.

Haut, Woody. *Pulp Culture: Hardboiled Fiction and the Cold War.* London: Serpent's Tail, 1995.

Haynes, Roslynn D. *H. G. Wells: Discoverer of the Future.* London: Macmillan, 1980

Hearne, C. R. *The American Dream in the Depression.* Westport, Connecticut: Greenwood Press, 1977.

Heinlein, Robert. *Rocket Ship Galileo.* New York: Scribner, 1947.

Higham, Charles. *Orson Welles: The Rise and Fall of an American Genius.* London: New English Library, 1986.

Hillegas, Mark R. *The Future as Nightmare: H. G. Wells and the Anti-Utopians.* New York: Oxford University Press, 1967.

Hoberman, J. "Pax Americana." *Sight and Sound* 7 (2) (February 1997): 6-9.

Hughes, David Y. "*The War of the Worlds* in the Yellow Press." *Journalism Quarterly* 43 (4) (Winter 1966): 639-646.

Hughes, Robert. *Culture of Complaint.* London: Harvill Press, 1993.

Huntington, Samuel. "The erosion of American national interests." *Foreign Affairs* 76 (5) (September/October 1997): 28-49.

Joffe, Josef, "How America does it." *Foreign Affairs* 76 (5) (September/October 1997): 13-27.

Kemp, Peter, *H. G. Wells and the Culminating Ape.* London: Macmillan, 1982.

Kennedy, David M. *Freedom from Fear: The American People in Depression and War, 1929-1945.* New York: Oxford University Press, 1999.

Koch, Howard. *The Panic Broadcast: The Portrait of an Event.* Boston, Mass.: Little, Brown and Co., 1970.

Levidow, Les, "The Gulf Massacre as paranoid rationality." In *Culture on the Brink.* Ed. Gretchen Bender and Timothy Druckery. Seattle: Bay Press, 1994. 317-327.

Lowentrout, Peter. "*The War of the Worlds* revisited: science fiction and the angst of secularization." *Extrapolation* 33 (4) (Winter 1992): 351-9

Newman, Kim. *Millennium Movies.* London: Titan Books, 1999.

Parrinder, Patrick. *Shadows of the Future.* Liverpool: Liverpool University Press, 1995.

Penley, Constance, "Time travel, primal scene, and the critical dystopia." In *Close Encounters.* Ed. Constance Penley, Elisabeth Lyon, Lynn Spigel and Janet Bergstrom. Minneapolis: University of Minnesota Press, 1991. 63-80.

Raknem, Ingvald. *H. G. Wells and his Critics* (Trondheim, Norway: Universitetsforlaget/George Allen & Unwin, 1962.

Robins, Kevin. "The haunted screen." In *Culture on the Brink.* Ed. Gretchen Bender and Timothy Druckery. Seattle: Bay Press, 1994. 305-315.

Ruppersberg, Hugh. "The alien messiah." In *Alien Zone.* Ed. Annette Kuhn. London: Verso, 1990. 32-38.

Seed, David. *American Science Fiction and the Cold War.* Edinburgh: Edinburgh University Press, 1999.

Sherry, Michael S. *In the Shadow of War.* New Haven: Yale University Press, 1995.

Simpson, M. J. "I married a 1950s B-movie." *SFX* 50 (April 1999): 56-61.

Sobchack, Vivian. *Screening Space: The American Science Fiction Film.* New Brunswick, N.J.: Rutgers University Press, 1997.

Spigel, Lynn, "From domestic space to outer space: the 1960s fantastic family sit-com." In *Close Encounters.* Ed. Constance Penley, Elisabeth Lyon, Lynn Spigel and Janet Bergstrom. Minneapolis: University of Minnesota Press, 1991. 205-235.

Stam, Robert. "Mikhail Bakhtin and left cultural critique." In *Postmodernism and its Discontents.* Ed. Ann E. Kaplan. London: Verso, 1988. 116-145.

Strick, Philip. "Space invaders." *The Movie* 39 (1980): 761-764

Tarratt, Margaret. "Monsters from the Id." *Films and Filming* 17 (3) (December 1970): 38-42.

Taubin, Amy. "Playing it straight." *Sight and Sound* 6 (8) (August 1996): 6-8.

Tesson, Charles. *Photogénie de la Série B.* Paris: Cahiers du Cinéma, 1997.

Thomson, David. *Rosebud: The Story of Orson Welles.* London: Little, Brown & Co., 1996.

Trushell, John, "Body Snatchers: Spectres that Haunt an American Century." *Over Here: A European Journal of American Culture* 16 (2) (Winter 1996): 89-104.

————. "*The Thing*: Of 'Monsters, Madmen and Murderers'—A Morality Play on Ice." *Foundation* 76 (Summer 1999): 76-89.

Wells, Herbert George. *The War of the Worlds.* London: J.M. Dent, 1993.

Whitfield, Stephen J. *The Culture of the Cold War.* Baltimore: John Hopkins University Press, 1991.

FURTHER READING

Criticism

Badmington, Neil. *Alien Chic: Posthumanism and the Other Within.* London: Routledge, 2004, 203 p.

Examines the central role aliens play in the genre of science fiction cinema.

Bleiler, Everett. "A Book That Fails to Work Miracles." *Science Fiction Films* 31, no. 92 (March 2004): 127-31.

Explores the collaboration between H. G. Wells and Lajos Biro on the film *The Man Who could Work Miracles.*

Dimitrakaki, Angela, and Miltos Tsiantis. "Terminators, Monkeys and Mass Culture: The Carnival of Time in Science Fiction Films." *Time & Society* 11, nos. 2-3 (2002): 209-31.

Analyzes the theme of time in science fiction films.

Hardy, Sylvia. "H. G. Wells and British Cinema: The War of the Worlds." *Foundation* 28, no. 77 (autumn 1999): 46-58.

Traces H. G. Wells's involvement in the developing British film industry in the early twentieth century, noting that "his enthusiasm for cinema was in marked contrast to the response of many influential figures in the literary world who deplored the influence of the new medium."

Jones, Robert A. "Science Fiction, Solid Fact and Social Formations in *Spaceways.*" *Foundation* 35, no. 98 (autumn 2006): 44-58.

Investigates the scientific sources used to create the rocket and space equipment found in the 1952 film *Spaceways.*

Landon, Brooks. *The Aesthetics of Ambivalence: Rethinking Science Fiction Film in the Age of Electronic (Re)Production.* Westport, Conn.: Greenwood Press, 1992, 187 p.

Considers the relationship between science fiction film and literature.

Martin, Sara. "In Mary Shelley's Loving Arms: Brian Aldiss's *Frankenstein Unbound* and Its Film Adaptation by Roger Corman." *Foundation* 32, no. 89 (autumn 2003): 76-92.

Notes that both Brian Aldiss's 1973 novel *Frankenstein Unbound* and Roger Corman's 1990 adaptation of Aldiss's novel both focus exclusively on the masculine identity of Victor Frankenstein and his monster and ignore the scholarship that has emerged in recent years on Mary Shelley's role as woman writer and feminist icon.

Palumbo, Donald E. "The Politics of Entropy: Revolution vs. Evolution in George Pal's 1960 Film Version of H. G. Wells's *The Time Machine.*" In *Modes of the Fantastic: Selected Essays from the Twelfth International Conference on the Fantastic in the Arts,* edited by Robert A. Latham and Robert A. Collins, pp. 204-11. Westport, Conn.: Greenwood Press, 1995.

Shows that George Pal's 1960 film adaptation of *The Time Machine* deliberately subverts many of the key themes in Wells's novella in order to appeal to a mass audience.

Penley, Constance, Elisabeth Lyon, Lynn Spigel, and Janet Bergstrom, eds. *Close Encounters: Film, Feminism, and Science Fiction.* Minneapolis: University of Minnesota Press, 1991, 298 p.
    Collection of essays that explore feminist themes in science fiction film and literature.

Redmond, Sean, ed. *Liquid Metal: The Science Fiction Film Reader.* London: Wallflower Press, 2004, 352 p.
    Compilation of seminal essays on science fiction film.

Russell, Sharon A. "The Problem of Novelization: *Dead and Buried* and *Nomads* by Chelsea Quinn Yarbo." In *Contours of the Fantastic: Selected Essays from the Eighth International Conference on the Fantastic in the Arts,* edited by Michele K. Langford, pp. 121-30. New York: Greenwood Press, 1990.
    Delineates the challenges with Chelsea Quinn Yarbo's novelization of the films *Dead and Buried* and *Nomads,* arguing that the changes made from the film to the novel "suggest a great deal about the differences between reading and seeing when the traditional movement from literature to film is reversed."

Smith, Don G. *H. G. Wells on Film: The Utopian Nightmare.* Jefferson, N.C.: McFarland & Company, Inc., 2002, 197 p.

Full-length study of the cinematic adaptations of H. G. Wells's science fiction stories and novels.

Strugatsky, Boris Natanovich. "Working for Tarkovsky." *Science Fiction Films* 31, no. 94 (November 2004): 418-20.
    Recollects working on the film *Stalker* with renowned director Andrei Tarkovsky.

Swope, Richard. "Science Fiction Cinema and the Crime of Social-Spatial Reality." *Science Fiction Studies* 29, no. 87 (July 2002): 221-46.
    Analyzes the relationship between science fiction cinema and contemporary space through a study of Alex Proyas's *Dark City* and Josef Rusnak's *The Thirteenth Floor.*

Telotte, J. P. *Replications: A Robotic History of the Science Fiction Film.* Urbana: University of Illinois Press, 1995, 222 p.
    Investigates science fiction film's concern with human artifice throughout the years.

————. *Science Fiction Film.* Cambridge: Cambridge University Press, 2001, 254 p.
    Provides an historical overview of science fiction film and delineates various critical approaches to the genre.

Wykes, Alan. "H. G. Wells in the Cinema." In *H. G. Wells in the Cinema,* pp. 13-24. London: Jupiter, 1977.
    Considers H. G. Wells's personal and artistic development in relation to the emerging film industry in the early twentieth century.

How to Use This Index

CDALBS = *Concise Dictionary of American Literary Biography Supplement*
CDBLB = *Concise Dictionary of British Literary Biography*
CMW = *St. James Guide to Crime & Mystery Writers*
CN = *Contemporary Novelists*
CP = *Contemporary Poets*
CPW = *Contemporary Popular Writers*
CSW = *Contemporary Southern Writers*
CWD = *Contemporary Women Dramatists*
CWP = *Contemporary Women Poets*
CWRI = *St. James Guide to Children's Writers*
CWW = *Contemporary World Writers*
DA = *DISCovering Authors*
DA3 = *DISCovering Authors 3.0*
DAB = *DISCovering Authors: British Edition*
DAC = *DISCovering Authors: Canadian Edition*
DAM = *DISCovering Authors: Modules*
   DRAM: *Dramatists Module;* **MST:** *Most-studied Authors Module;*
   MULT: *Multicultural Authors Module;* **NOV:** *Novelists Module;*
   POET: *Poets Module;* **POP:** *Popular Fiction and Genre Authors Module*
DFS = *Drama for Students*
DLB = *Dictionary of Literary Biography*
DLBD = *Dictionary of Literary Biography Documentary Series*
DLBY = *Dictionary of Literary Biography Yearbook*
DNFS = *Literature of Developing Nations for Students*
EFS = *Epics for Students*
EXPN = *Exploring Novels*
EXPP = *Exploring Poetry*
EXPS = *Exploring Short Stories*
EW = *European Writers*
FANT = *St. James Guide to Fantasy Writers*
FW = *Feminist Writers*
GFL = *Guide to French Literature,* Beginnings to 1789, 1798 to the Present
GLL = *Gay and Lesbian Literature*
HGG = *St. James Guide to Horror, Ghost & Gothic Writers*
HW = *Hispanic Writers*
IDFW = *International Dictionary of Films and Filmmakers: Writers and Production Artists*
IDTP = *International Dictionary of Theatre: Playwrights*
LAIT = *Literature and Its Times*
LAW = *Latin American Writers*
JRDA = *Junior DISCovering Authors*
MAICYA = *Major Authors and Illustrators for Children and Young Adults*
MAICYAS = *Major Authors and Illustrators for Children and Young Adults Supplement*
MAWW = *Modern American Women Writers*
MJW = *Modern Japanese Writers*
MTCW = *Major 20th-Century Writers*
NCFS = *Nonfiction Classics for Students*
NFS = *Novels for Students*
PAB = *Poets: American and British*
PFS = *Poetry for Students*
RGAL = *Reference Guide to American Literature*
RGEL = *Reference Guide to English Literature*
RGSF = *Reference Guide to Short Fiction*
RGWL = *Reference Guide to World Literature*
RHW = *Twentieth-Century Romance and Historical Writers*
SAAS = *Something about the Author Autobiography Series*
SATA = *Something about the Author*
SFW = *St. James Guide to Science Fiction Writers*
SSFS = *Short Stories for Students*
TCWW = *Twentieth-Century Western Writers*
WLIT = *World Literature and Its Times*
WP = *World Poets*
YABC = *Yesterday's Authors of Books for Children*
YAW = *St. James Guide to Young Adult Writers*

Literary Criticism Series
Cumulative Author Index

Aeschines c. 390B.C.-c. 320B.C. .... **CMLC 47**
See also DLB 176

Aeschylus 525(?)B.C.-456(?)B.C. .. **CMLC 11, 51, 94; DC 8; WLCS**
See also AW 1; CDWLB 1; DA; DAB; DAC; DAM DRAM, MST; DFS 5, 10; DLB 176; LMFS 1; RGWL 2, 3; TWA; WLIT 8

Aesop 620(?)B.C.-560(?)B.C. .... **CMLC 24**
See also CLR 14; MAICYA 1, 2; SATA 64

Affable Hawk
See MacCarthy, Sir (Charles Otto) Desmond

Africa, Ben
See Bosman, Herman Charles

Afton, Effie
See Harper, Frances Ellen Watkins

Agapida, Fray Antonio
See Irving, Washington

Agee, James (Rufus) 1909-1955 ...... **TCLC 1, 19, 180**
See also AAYA 44; AITN 1; AMW; CA 148; CAAE 108; CANR 131; CDALB 1941-1968; DAM NOV; DLB 2, 26, 152; DLBY 1989; EWL 3; LAIT 3; LATS 1:2; MAL 5; MTCW 2; MTFW 2005; NFS 22; RGAL 4; TUS

A Gentlewoman in New England
See Bradstreet, Anne

A Gentlewoman in Those Parts
See Bradstreet, Anne

Aghill, Gordon
See Silverberg, Robert

Agnon, S(hmuel) Y(osef Halevi) 1888-1970 .... **CLC 4, 8, 14; SSC 30; TCLC 151**
See also CA 17-18; CAAS 25-28R; CANR 60, 102; CAP 2; DLB 329; EWL 3; MTCW 1, 2; RGHL; RGSF 2; RGWL 2, 3; WLIT 6

Agrippa von Nettesheim, Henry Cornelius 1486-1535 .... **LC 27**

Aguilera Malta, Demetrio 1909-1981 .... **HLCS 1**
See also CA 124; CAAE 111; CANR 87; DAM MULT, NOV; DLB 145; EWL 3; HW 1; RGWL 3

Agustini, Delmira 1886-1914 .... **HLCS 1**
See also CA 166; DLB 290; HW 1, 2; LAW

Aherne, Owen
See Cassill, R(onald) V(erlin)

Ai 1947- .... **CLC 4, 14, 69; PC 72**
See also CA 85-88; 13; CANR 70; CP 6, 7; DLB 120; PFS 16

Aickman, Robert (Fordyce) 1914-1981 .... **CLC 57**
See also CA 5-8R; CANR 3, 72, 100; DLB 261; HGG; SUFW 1, 2

Aidoo, (Christina) Ama Ata 1942- .... **BLCS; CLC 177**
See also AFW; BW 1; CA 101; CANR 62, 144; CD 5, 6; CDWLB 3; CN 6, 7; CWD; CWP; DLB 117; DNFS 1, 2; EWL 3; FW; WLIT 2

Aiken, Conrad (Potter) 1889-1973 .... **CLC 1, 3, 5, 10, 52; PC 26; SSC 9**
See also AMW; CA 5-8R; CAAS 45-48; CANR 4, 60; CDALB 1929-1941; CN 1; CP 1; DAM NOV, POET; DLB 9, 45, 102; EWL 3; EXPS; HGG; MAL 5; MTCW 1, 2; MTFW 2005; PFS 24; RGAL 4; RGSF 2; SATA 3, 30; SSFS 8; TUS

Aiken, Joan (Delano) 1924-2004 ...... **CLC 35**
See also AAYA 1, 25; CA 182; 9-12R, 182; CAAS 223; CANR 4, 23, 34, 64, 121; CLR 1, 19, 90; DLB 161; FANT; HGG; JRDA; MAICYA 1, 2; MTCW 1; RHW; SAAS 1; SATA 2, 30, 73; SATA-Essay 109; SATA-Obit 152; SUFW 2; WYA; YAW

Ainsworth, William Harrison 1805-1882 .... **NCLC 13**
See also DLB 21; HGG; RGEL 2; SATA 24; SUFW 1

Aitmatov, Chingiz (Torekulovich) 1928- .... **CLC 71**
See Aytmatov, Chingiz
See also CA 103; CANR 38; CWW 2; DLB 302; MTCW 1; RGSF 2; SATA 56

Akers, Floyd
See Baum, L(yman) Frank

Akhmadulina, Bella Akhatovna 1937- .... **CLC 53; PC 43**
See also CA 65-68; CWP; CWW 2; DAM POET; EWL 3

Akhmatova, Anna 1888-1966 ..... **CLC 11, 25, 64, 126; PC 2, 55**
See also CA 19-20; CAAS 25-28R; CANR 35; CAP 1; DA3; DAM POET; DLB 295; EW 10; EWL 3; FL 1:5; MTCW 1, 2; PFS 18, 27; RGWL 2, 3

Aksakov, Sergei Timofeevich 1791-1859 .... **NCLC 2, 181**
See also DLB 198

Aksenov, Vasilii (Pavlovich)
See Aksyonov, Vassily (Pavlovich)
See also CWW 2

Aksenov, Vassily
See Aksyonov, Vassily (Pavlovich)

Akst, Daniel 1956- .... **CLC 109**
See also CA 161; CANR 110

Aksyonov, Vassily (Pavlovich) 1932- .... **CLC 22, 37, 101**
See Aksenov, Vasilii (Pavlovich)
See also CA 53-56; CANR 12, 48, 77; DLB 302; EWL 3

Akutagawa Ryunosuke 1892-1927 ... **SSC 44; TCLC 16**
See also CA 154; CAAE 117; DLB 180; EWL 3; MJW; RGSF 2; RGWL 2, 3

Alabaster, William 1568-1640 .... **LC 90**
See also DLB 132; RGEL 2

Alain 1868-1951 .... **TCLC 41**
See also CA 163; EWL 3; GFL 1789 to the Present

Alain de Lille c. 1116-c. 1203 .... **CMLC 53**
See also DLB 208

Alain-Fournier .... **TCLC 6**
See Fournier, Henri-Alban
See also DLB 65; EWL 3; GFL 1789 to the Present; RGWL 2, 3

Al-Amin, Jamil Abdullah 1943- ...... **BLC 1:1**
See also BW 1, 3; CA 125; CAAE 112; CANR 82; DAM MULT

Alanus de Insluis
See Alain de Lille

Alarcon, Pedro Antonio de 1833-1891 .... **NCLC 1; SSC 64**

Alas (y Urena), Leopoldo (Enrique Garcia) 1852-1901 .... **TCLC 29**
See also CA 131; CAAE 113; HW 1; RGSF 2

Albee, Edward (III) 1928- ..... **CLC 1, 2, 3, 5, 9, 11, 13, 25, 53, 86, 113; DC 11; WLC 1**
See also AAYA 51; AITN 1; AMW; CA 5-8R; CABS 3; CAD; CANR 8, 54, 74, 124; CD 5, 6; CDALB 1941-1968; DA; DA3; DAB; DAC; DAM DRAM, MST; DFS 2, 3, 8, 10, 13, 14; DLB 7, 266; EWL 3; INT CANR-8; LAIT 4; LMFS 2; MAL 5; MTCW 1, 2; MTFW 2005; RGAL 4; TUS

Alberti (Merello), Rafael
See Alberti, Rafael
See also CWW 2

Alberti, Rafael 1902-1999 .... **CLC 7**
See Alberti (Merello), Rafael
See also CA 85-88; CAAS 185; CANR 81; DLB 108; EWL 3; HW 2; RGWL 2, 3

Albert the Great 1193(?)-1280 ...... **CMLC 16**
See also DLB 115

Alcaeus c. 620B.C.- .... **CMLC 65**
See also DLB 176

Alcala-Galiano, Juan Valera y
See Valera y Alcala-Galiano, Juan

Alcayaga, Lucila Godoy
See Godoy Alcayaga, Lucila

Alciato, Andrea 1492-1550 .... **LC 116**

Alcott, Amos Bronson 1799-1888 ... **NCLC 1, 167**
See also DLB 1, 223

Alcott, Louisa May 1832-1888 . **NCLC 6, 58, 83; SSC 27, 98; WLC 1**
See also AAYA 20; AMWS 1; BPFB 1; BYA 2; CDALB 1865-1917; CLR 1, 38, 109; DA; DA3; DAB; DAC; DAM MST, NOV; DLB 1, 42, 79, 223, 239, 242; DLBD 14; FL 1:2; FW; JRDA; LAIT 2; MAICYA 1, 2; NFS 12; RGAL 4; SATA 100; TUS; WCH; WYA; YABC 1; YAW

Alcuin c. 730-804 .... **CMLC 69**
See also DLB 148

Aldanov, M. A.
See Aldanov, Mark (Alexandrovich)

Aldanov, Mark (Alexandrovich) 1886-1957 .... **TCLC 23**
See also CA 181; CAAE 118; DLB 317

Aldhelm c. 639-709 .... **CMLC 90**

Aldington, Richard 1892-1962 .... **CLC 49**
See also CA 85-88; CANR 45; DLB 20, 36, 100, 149; LMFS 2; RGEL 2

Aldiss, Brian W. 1925- .. **CLC 5, 14, 40; SSC 36**
See also AAYA 42; CA 190; 5-8R, 190; 2; CANR 5, 28, 64, 121, 168; CN 1, 2, 3, 4, 5, 6, 7; DAM NOV; DLB 14, 261, 271; MTCW 1, 2; MTFW 2005; SATA 34; SCFW 1, 2; SFW 4

Aldiss, Brian Wilson
See Aldiss, Brian W.

Aldrich, Bess Streeter 1881-1954 .... **TCLC 125**
See also CLR 70; TCWW 2

Alegria, Claribel
See Alegria, Claribel
See also CWW 2; DLB 145, 283

Alegria, Claribel 1924- .... **CLC 75; HLCS 1; PC 26**
See Alegria, Claribel
See also CA 131; 15; CANR 66, 94, 134; DAM MULT; EWL 3; HW 1; MTCW 2; MTFW 2005; PFS 21

Alegria, Fernando 1918-2005 .... **CLC 57**
See also CA 9-12R; CANR 5, 32, 72; EWL 3; HW 1, 2

Aleixandre, Vicente 1898-1984 .... **HLCS 1; TCLC 113**
See also CANR 81; DLB 108, 329; EWL 3; HW 2; MTCW 1, 2; RGWL 2, 3

Alekseev, Konstantin Sergeivich
See Stanislavsky, Constantin

Alekseyer, Konstantin Sergeyevich
See Stanislavsky, Constantin

Aleman, Mateo 1547-1615(?) .... **LC 81**

Alencar, Jose de 1829-1877 .... **NCLC 157**
See also DLB 307; LAW; WLIT 1

Alencon, Marguerite d'
See de Navarre, Marguerite

Alepoudelis, Odysseus
See Elytis, Odysseus
See also CWW 2

Aleshkovsky, Joseph 1929-
See Aleshkovsky, Yuz
See also CA 128; CAAE 121

Aleshkovsky, Yuz .... **CLC 44**
  See Aleshkovsky, Joseph
  See also DLB 317
Alexander, Barbara
  See Ehrenreich, Barbara
Alexander, Lloyd 1924-2007 .... **CLC 35**
  See also AAYA 1, 27; BPFB 1; BYA 5, 6,
  7, 9, 10, 11; CA 1-4R; CAAS 260; CANR
  1, 24, 38, 55, 113; CLR 1, 5, 48; CWRI
  5; DLB 52; FANT; JRDA; MAICYA 1, 2;
  MAICYAS 1; MTCW 1; SAAS 19; SATA
  3, 49, 81, 129, 135; SATA-Obit 182;
  SUFW; TUS; WYA; YAW
Alexander, Lloyd Chudley
  See Alexander, Lloyd
Alexander, Meena 1951- .... **CLC 121**
  See also CA 115; CANR 38, 70, 146; CP 5,
  6, 7; CWP; DLB 323; FW
Alexander, Samuel 1859-1938 .... **TCLC 77**
Alexeiev, Konstantin
  See Stanislavsky, Constantin
Alexeyev, Constantin Sergeivich
  See Stanislavsky, Constantin
Alexeyev, Konstantin Sergeyevich
  See Stanislavsky, Constantin
Alexie, Sherman 1966- .... **CLC 96, 154;**
  NNAL; PC 53; SSC 107
  See also AAYA 28; BYA 15; CA 138;
  CANR 65, 95, 133; CN 7, DA3; DAM
  MULT; DLB 175, 206, 278; LATS 1:2;
  MTCW 2; MTFW 2005; NFS 17; SSFS
  18
Alexie, Sherman Joseph, Jr.
  See Alexie, Sherman
al-Farabi 870(?) 950 .... **CMLC 58**
  See also DLB 115
Alfau, Felipe 1902-1999 .... **CLC 66**
  See also CA 137
Alfieri, Vittorio 1749-1803 .... **NCLC 101**
  See also EW 4; RGWL 2, 3; WLIT 7
Alfonso X 1221-1284 .... **CMLC 78**
Alfred, Jean Gaston
  See Ponge, Francis
Alger, Horatio, Jr. 1832-1899 .... **NCLC 8, 83**
  See also CLR 87; DLB 42; LAIT 2; RGAL
  4; SATA 16; TUS
Al-Ghazali, Muhammad ibn Muhammad
  1058-1111 .... **CMLC 50**
  See also DLB 115
Algren, Nelson 1909-1981 ..... **CLC 4, 10, 33;**
  SSC 33
  See also AMWS 9; BPFB 1; CA 13-16R;
  CAAS 103; CANR 20, 61; CDALB 1941-
  1968; CN 1, 2; DLB 9; DLBY 1981,
  1982, 2000, EWL 3; MAL 5; MTCW 1,
  2; MTFW 2005; RGAL 4; RGSF 2
al-Hamadhani 967-1007 .... **CMLC 93**
  See also WLIT 6
**al-Hariri, al-Qasim ibn 'Ali Abu
  Muhammad al-Basri**
  1054-1122 .... **CMLC 63**
  See also RGWL 3
Ali, Ahmed 1908-1998 .... **CLC 69**
  See also CA 25-28R; CANR 15, 34; CN 1,
  2, 3, 4, 5; DLB 323; EWL 3
Ali, Tariq 1943- .... **CLC 173**
  See also CA 25-28R; CANR 10, 99, 161
Alighieri, Dante
  See Dante
  See also WLIT 7
al-Kindi, Abu Yusuf Ya'qub ibn Ishaq c.
  801-c. 873 .... **CMLC 80**
Allan, John B.
  See Westlake, Donald E.
Allan, Sidney
  See Hartmann, Sadakichi
Allan, Sydney
  See Hartmann, Sadakichi

Allard, Janet .... **CLC 59**
Allen, Edward 1948- .... **CLC 59**
Allen, Fred 1894-1956 .... **TCLC 87**
Allen, Paula Gunn 1939- .... **CLC 84, 202;**
  NNAL
  See also AMWS 4; CA 143; CAAE 112;
  CANR 63, 130; CWP; DA3; DAM
  MULT; DLB 175; FW; MTCW 2; MTFW
  2005; RGAL 4; TCWW 2
Allen, Roland
  See Ayckbourn, Alan
Allen, Sarah A.
  See Hopkins, Pauline Elizabeth
Allen, Sidney H.
  See Hartmann, Sadakichi
Allen, Woody 1935- .... **CLC 16, 52, 195**
  See also AAYA 10, 51; AMWS 15; CA 33-
  36R; CANR 27, 38, 63, 128, 172; DAM
  POP; DLB 44; MTCW 1; SSFS 21
Allende, Isabel 1942- ... **CLC 39, 57, 97, 170;**
  HLC 1; SSC 65; WLCS
  See also AAYA 18, 70; CA 130; CAAE 125;
  CANR 51, 74, 129, 165; CDWLB 3; CLR
  99; CWW 2; DA3; DAM MULT, NOV;
  DLB 145; DNFS 1; EWL 3; FL 1:5; FW;
  HW 1, 2; INT CA-130; LAIT 5; LAWS
  1; LMFS 2; MTCW 1, 2; MTFW 2005;
  NCFS 1; NFS 6, 18; RGSF 2; RGWL 3;
  SATA 163; SSFS 11, 16; WLIT 1
Alleyn, Ellen
  See Rossetti, Christina
Alleyne, Carla D. .... **CLC 65**
Allingham, Margery (Louise)
  1904-1966 .... **CLC 19**
  See also CA 5-8R; CAAS 25-28R; CANR
  4, 58; CMW 4; DLB 77; MSW; MTCW
  1, 2
Allingham, William 1824-1889 ...... **NCLC 25**
  See also DLB 35; RGEL 2
Allison, Dorothy E. 1949- .... **CLC 78, 153**
  See also AAYA 53; CA 140; CANR 66, 107;
  CN 7; CSW; DA3; FW; MTCW 2; MTFW
  2005; NFS 11; RGAL 4
Alloula, Malek .... **CLC 65**
Allston, Washington 1779-1843 .... **NCLC 2**
  See also DLB 1, 235
Almedingen, E. M. .... **CLC 12**
  See Almedingen, Martha Edith von
  See also SATA 3
Almedingen, Martha Edith von 1898-1971
  See Almedingen, E. M.
  See also CA 1-4R; CANR 1
Almodovar, Pedro 1949(?)- .... **CLC 114, 229;**
  HLCS 1
  See also CA 133; CANR 72, 151; HW 2
Almqvist, Carl Jonas Love
  1793-1866 .... **NCLC 42**
**al-Mutanabbi, Ahmad ibn al-Husayn Abu
  al-Tayyib al-Juli al-Kindi**
  915-965 .... **CMLC 66**
  See Mutanabbi, Al-
  See also RGWL 3
Alonso, Damaso 1898-1990 .... **CLC 14**
  See also CA 131; CAAE 110; CAAS 130;
  CANR 72; DLB 108; EWL 3; HW 1, 2
Alov
  See Gogol, Nikolai (Vasilyevich)
al'Sadaawi, Nawal
  See El Saadawi, Nawal
  See also FW
al-Shaykh, Hanan 1945- .... **CLC 218**
  See Shaykh, al- Hanan
  See also CA 135; CANR 111; WLIT 6
Al Siddik
  See Rolfe, Frederick (William Serafino Aus-
  tin Lewis Mary)
  See also GLL 1; RGEL 2
Alta 1942- .... **CLC 19**
  See also CA 57-60

Alter, Robert B. 1935- .... **CLC 34**
  See also CA 49-52; CANR 1, 47, 100, 160
Alter, Robert Bernard
  See Alter, Robert B.
Alther, Lisa 1944- .... **CLC 7, 41**
  See also BPFB 1; CA 65-68; 30; CANR 12,
  30, 51; CN 4, 5, 6, 7; CSW; GLL 2;
  MTCW 1
Althusser, L.
  See Althusser, Louis
Althusser, Louis 1918-1990 .... **CLC 106**
  See also CA 131; CAAS 132; CANR 102;
  DLB 242
Altman, Robert 1925-2006 .... **CLC 16, 116,**
  242
  See also CA 73-76; CAAS 254; CANR 43
Alurista .... **HLCS 1; PC 34**
  See Urista (Heredia), Alberto (Baltazar)
  See also CA 45-48R; DLB 82; LLW
Alvarez, A. 1929- .... **CLC 5, 13**
  See also CA 1-4R; CANR 3, 33, 63, 101,
  134; CN 3, 4, 5, 6; CP 1, 2, 3, 4, 5, 6, 7;
  DLB 14, 40; MTFW 2005
Alvarez, Alejandro Rodriguez 1903-1965
  See Casona, Alejandro
  See also CA 131; CAAS 93-96; HW 1
Alvarez, Julia 1950- .... **CLC 93; HLCS 1**
  See also AAYA 25; AMWS 7; CA 147;
  CANR 69, 101, 133, 166; DA3; DLB 282;
  LATS 1:2; LLW; MTCW 2; MTFW 2005;
  NFS 5, 9; SATA 129; WLIT 1
Alvaro, Corrado 1896-1956 .... **TCLC 60**
  See also CA 163, DLB 264; EWL 3
Amado, Jorge 1912-2001 ... **CLC 13, 40, 106,**
  232; HLC 1
  See also CA 77-80; CAAS 201; CANR 35,
  74, 135; CWW 2; DAM MULT, NOV;
  DLB 113, 307; EWL 3; HW 2; LAW;
  LAWS 1; MTCW 1, 2; MTFW 2005;
  RGWL 2, 3; TWA; WLIT 1
Ambler, Eric 1909-1998 .... **CLC 4, 6, 9**
  See also BRWS 4; CA 9-12R; CAAS 171;
  CANR 7, 38, 74; CMW 4; CN 1, 2, 3, 4,
  5, 6; DLB 77; MSW; MTCW 1, 2; TEA
Ambrose, Stephen E. 1936-2002 .... **CLC 145**
  See also AAYA 44; CA 1-4R; CAAS 209;
  CANR 3, 43, 57, 83, 105; MTFW 2005;
  NCFS 2; SATA 40, 138
Amichai, Yehuda 1924-2000 .. **CLC 9, 22, 57,**
  116; PC 38
  See also CA 85-88; CAAS 189; CANR 46,
  60, 99, 132; CWW 2; EWL 3; MTCW 1,
  2; MTFW 2005; PFS 24; RGHL; WLIT 6
Amichai, Yehudah
  See Amichai, Yehuda
Amiel, Henri Frederic 1821-1881 .... **NCLC 4**
  See also DLB 217
Amis, Kingsley 1922-1995 . **CLC 1, 2, 3, 5, 8,**
  13, 40, 44, 129
  See also AAYA 77; AITN 2; BPFB 1;
  BRWS 2; CA 9-12R; CAAS 150; CANR
  8, 28, 54; CDBLB 1945-1960; CN 1, 2,
  3, 4, 5, 6; CP 1, 2, 3, 4; DA; DA3; DAB;
  DAC; DAM MST, NOV; DLB 15, 27,
  100, 139, 326; DLBY 1996; EWL 3;
  HGG; INT CANR-8; MTCW 1, 2; MTFW
  2005; RGEL 2; RGSF 2; SFW 4
Amis, Martin 1949- ... **CLC 4, 9, 38, 62, 101,**
  213
  See also BEST 90:3; BRWS 4; CA 65-68;
  CANR 8, 27, 54, 73, 95, 132, 166; CN 5,
  6, 7; DA3; DLB 14, 194; EWL 3; INT
  CANR-27; MTCW 2; MTFW 2005
Amis, Martin Louis
  See Amis, Martin
Ammianus Marcellinus c. 330-c.
  395 .... **CMLC 60**
  See also AW 2; DLB 211

Ammons, A.R. 1926-2001 .. **CLC 2, 3, 5, 8, 9, 25, 57, 108; PC 16**
See also AITN 1; AMWS 7; CA 9-12R; CAAS 193; CANR 6, 36, 51, 73, 107, 156; CP 1, 2, 3, 4, 5, 6, 7; CSW; DAM POET; DLB 5, 165; EWL 3; MAL 5; MTCW 1, 2; PFS 19; RGAL 4; TCLE 1:1

Ammons, Archie Randolph
See Ammons, A.R.

Amo, Tauraatua i
See Adams, Henry (Brooks)

Amory, Thomas 1691(?)-1788 .... **LC 48**
See also DLB 39

Anand, Mulk Raj 1905-2004 ..... **CLC 23, 93, 237**
See also CA 65-68; CAAS 231; CANR 32, 64; CN 1, 2, 3, 4, 5, 6, 7; DAM NOV; DLB 323; EWL 3; MTCW 1, 2; MTFW 2005; RGSF 2

Anatol
See Schnitzler, Arthur

Anaximander c. 611B.C.-c. 546B.C. .... **CMLC 22**

Anaya, Rudolfo A. 1937- .... **CLC 23, 148; HLC 1**
See also AAYA 20; BYA 13; CA 45-48; 4; CANR 1, 32, 51, 124, 169; CLR 129; CN 4, 5, 6, 7; DAM MULT, NOV; DLB 82, 206, 278; HW 1; LAIT 4; LLW; MAL 5; MTCW 1, 2; MTFW 2005; NFS 12; RGAL 4; RGSF 2; TCWW 2; WLIT 1

Anaya, Rudolpho Alfonso
See Anaya, Rudolfo A.

Andersen, Hans Christian 1805-1875 .... **NCLC 7, 79; SSC 6, 56; WLC 1**
See also AAYA 57; CLR 6, 113; DA; DA3; DAB; DAC; DAM MST, POP; EW 6; MAICYA 1, 2; RGSF 2; RGWL 2, 3; SATA 100; TWA; WCH; YABC 1

Anderson, C. Farley
See Mencken, H(enry) L(ouis); Nathan, George Jean

Anderson, Jessica (Margaret) Queale 1916- .... **CLC 37**
See also CA 9-12R; CANR 4, 62; CN 4, 5, 6, 7; DLB 325

Anderson, Jon (Victor) 1940- .... **CLC 9**
See also CA 25-28R; CANR 20; CP 1, 3, 4, 5; DAM POET

Anderson, Lindsay (Gordon) 1923-1994 .... **CLC 20**
See also CA 128; CAAE 125; CAAS 146; CANR 77

Anderson, Maxwell 1888-1959 .... **TCLC 2, 144**
See also CA 152; CAAE 105; DAM DRAM; DFS 16, 20; DLB 7, 228; MAL 5; MTCW 2; MTFW 2005; RGAL 4

Anderson, Poul 1926-2001 .... **CLC 15**
See also AAYA 5, 34; BPFB 1; BYA 6, 8, 9; CA 181; 1-4R, 181; 2; CAAS 199; CANR 2, 15, 34, 64, 110; CLR 58; DLB 8; FANT; INT CANR-15; MTCW 1, 2; MTFW 2005; SATA 90; SATA-Brief 39; SATA-Essay 106; SCFW 1, 2; SFW 4; SUFW 1, 2

Anderson, Robert (Woodruff) 1917- .... **CLC 23**
See also AITN 1; CA 21-24R; CANR 32; CD 6; DAM DRAM; DLB 7; LAIT 5

Anderson, Roberta Joan
See Mitchell, Joni

Anderson, Sherwood 1876-1941 ... **SSC 1, 46, 91; TCLC 1, 10, 24, 123; WLC 1**
See also AAYA 30; AMW; AMWC 2; BPFB 1; CA 121; CAAE 104; CANR 61; CDALB 1917-1929; DA; DA3; DAB; DAC; DAM MST, NOV; DLB 4, 9, 86;

DLBD 1; EWL 3; EXPS; GLL 2; MAL 5; MTCW 1, 2; MTFW 2005; NFS 4; RGAL 4; RGSF 2; SSFS 4, 10, 11; TUS

Anderson, Wes 1969- .... **CLC 227**
See also CA 214

Andier, Pierre
See Desnos, Robert

Andouard
See Giraudoux, Jean(-Hippolyte)

Andrade, Carlos Drummond de ..... **CLC 18**
See Drummond de Andrade, Carlos
See also EWL 3; RGWL 2, 3

Andrade, Mario de .... **TCLC 43**
See de Andrade, Mario
See also DLB 307; EWL 3; LAW; RGWL 2, 3; WLIT 1

Andreae, Johann V(alentin) 1586-1654 .... **LC 32**
See also DLB 164

Andreas Capellanus fl. c. 1185- .... **CMLC 45**
See also DLB 208

Andreas-Salome, Lou 1861-1937 ... **TCLC 56**
See also CA 178; DLB 66

Andreev, Leonid
See Andreyev, Leonid (Nikolaevich)
See also DLB 295; EWL 3

Andress, Lesley
See Sanders, Lawrence

Andrewes, Lancelot 1555-1626 .... **LC 5**
See also DLB 151, 172

Andrews, Cicily Fairfield
See West, Rebecca

Andrews, Elton V.
See Pohl, Frederik

Andrews, Peter
See Soderbergh, Steven

Andrews, Raymond 1934-1991 .... **BLC 2:1**
See also BW 2; CA 81-84; CAAS 136; CANR 15, 42

Andreyev, Leonid (Nikolaevich) 1871-1919 .... **TCLC 3**
See Andreev, Leonid
See also CA 185; CAAE 104

Andric, Ivo 1892-1975 .... **CLC 8; SSC 36; TCLC 135**
See also CA 81-84; CAAS 57-60; CANR 43, 60; CDWLB 4; DLB 147, 329; EW 11; EWL 3; MTCW 1; RGSF 2; RGWL 2, 3

Androvar
See Prado (Calvo), Pedro

Angela of Foligno 1248(?)-1309 .... **CMLC 76**

Angelique, Pierre
See Bataille, Georges

Angell, Roger 1920- .... **CLC 26**
See also CA 57-60; CANR 13, 44, 70, 144; DLB 171, 185

Angelou, Maya 1928- ...... **BLC 1:1; CLC 12, 35, 64, 77, 155; PC 32; WLCS**
See also AAYA 7, 20; AMWS 4; BPFB 1; BW 2, 3; BYA 2; CA 65-68; CANR 19, 42, 65, 111, 133; CDALBS; CLR 53; CP 4, 5, 6, 7; CPW; CSW; CWP; DA; DA3; DAB; DAC; DAM MST, MULT, POET, POP; DLB 38; EWL 3; EXPN; EXPP; FL 1:5; LAIT 4; MAICYA 2; MAICYAS 1; MAL 5; MBL; MTCW 1, 2; MTFW 2005; NCFS 2; NFS 2; PFS 2, 3; RGAL 4; SATA 49, 136; TCLE 1:1; WYA; YAW

Angouleme, Marguerite d'
See de Navarre, Marguerite

Anna Comnena 1083-1153 .... **CMLC 25**

Annensky, Innokentii Fedorovich
See Annensky, Innokenty (Fyodorovich)
See also DLB 295

Annensky, Innokenty (Fyodorovich) 1856-1909 .... **TCLC 14**
See also CA 155; CAAE 110; EWL 3

Annunzio, Gabriele d'
See D'Annunzio, Gabriele

Anodos
See Coleridge, Mary E(lizabeth)

Anon, Charles Robert
See Pessoa, Fernando (Antonio Nogueira)

Anouilh, Jean 1910-1987 ..... **CLC 1, 3, 8, 13, 40, 50; DC 8, 21; TCLC 195**
See also AAYA 67; CA 17-20R; CAAS 123; CANR 32; DAM DRAM; DFS 9, 10, 19; DLB 321; EW 13; EWL 3; GFL 1789 to the Present; MTCW 1, 2; MTFW 2005; RGWL 2, 3; TWA

Ansa, Tina McElroy 1949- .... **BLC 2:1**
See also BW 2; CA 142; CANR 143; CSW

Anselm of Canterbury 1033(?)-1109 .... **CMLC 67**
See also DLB 115

Anthony, Florence
See Ai

Anthony, John
See Ciardi, John (Anthony)

Anthony, Peter
See Shaffer, Anthony; Shaffer, Peter

Anthony, Piers 1934- .... **CLC 35**
See also AAYA 11, 48; BYA 7; CA 200; 200; CANR 28, 56, 73, 102, 133; CLR 118; CPW; DAM POP; DLB 8; FANT; MAICYA 2; MAICYAS 1; MTCW 1, 2; MTFW 2005; SAAS 22; SATA 84, 129; SATA-Essay 129; SFW 4; SUFW 1, 2; YAW

Anthony, Susan B(rownell) 1820-1906 .... **TCLC 84**
See also CA 211; FW

Antiphon c. 480B.C.-c. 411B.C. .... **CMLC 55**

Antoine, Marc
See Proust, (Valentin-Louis-George-Eugene) Marcel

Antoninus, Brother
See Everson, William (Oliver)
See also CP 1

Antonioni, Michelangelo 1912-2007 .... **CLC 20, 144**
See also CA 73-76; CAAS 262; CANR 45, 77

Antschel, Paul 1920-1970
See Celan, Paul
See also CA 85-88; CANR 33, 61; MTCW 1; PFS 21

Anwar, Chairil 1922-1949 .... **TCLC 22**
See Chairil Anwar
See also CA 219; CAAE 121; RGWL 3

Anyidoho, Kofi 1947- .... **BLC 2:1**
See also BW 3; CA 178; CP 5, 6, 7; DLB 157; EWL 3

Anzaldua, Gloria (Evanjelina) 1942-2004 .... **CLC 200; HLCS 1**
See also CA 175; CAAS 227; CSW; CWP; DLB 122; FW; LLW; RGAL 4; SATA-Obit 154

Apess, William 1798-1839(?) .... **NCLC 73; NNAL**
See also DAM MULT; DLB 175, 243

Apollinaire, Guillaume 1880-1918 .... **PC 7; TCLC 3, 8, 51**
See Kostrowitzki, Wilhelm Apollinaris de
See also CA 152; DAM POET; DLB 258, 321; EW 9; EWL 3; GFL 1789 to the Present; MTCW 2; PFS 24; RGWL 2, 3; TWA; WP

Apollonius of Rhodes
See Apollonius Rhodius
See also AW 1; RGWL 2, 3

Apollonius Rhodius c. 300B.C.-c. 220B.C. .... **CMLC 28**
See Apollonius of Rhodes
See also DLB 176

Appelfeld, Aharon 1932- ... **CLC 23, 47; SSC 42**
See also CA 133; CAAE 112; CANR 86, 160; CWW 2; DLB 299; EWL 3; RGHL; RGSF 2; WLIT 6

Appelfeld, Aron
See Appelfeld, Aharon

Apple, Max (Isaac) 1941- .... **CLC 9, 33; SSC 50**
See also AMWS 17; CA 81-84; CANR 19, 54; DLB 130

Appleman, Philip (Dean) 1926- .... **CLC 51**
See also CA 13-16R; 18; CANR 6, 29, 56

Appleton, Lawrence
See Lovecraft, H. P.

Apteryx
See Eliot, T(homas) S(tearns)

Apuleius, (Lucius Madaurensis) c. 125-c. 164 .... **CMLC 1, 84**
See also AW 2; CDWLB 1; DLB 211; RGWL 2, 3; SUFW; WLIT 8

Aquin, Hubert 1929-1977 .... **CLC 15**
See also CA 105; DLB 53; EWL 3

Aquinas, Thomas 1224(?)-1274 ..... **CMLC 33**
See also DLB 115; EW 1; TWA

Aragon, Louis 1897-1982 .... **CLC 3, 22; TCLC 123**
See also CA 69-72; CAAS 108; CANR 28, 71; DAM NOV, POET; DLB 72, 258; EW 11; EWL 3; GFL 1789 to the Present; GLL 2; LMFS 2; MTCW 1, 2; RGWL 2, 3

Arany, Janos 1817-1882 .... **NCLC 34**

Aranyos, Kakay 1847-1910
See Mikszath, Kalman

Aratus of Soli c. 315B.C.-c. 240B.C. .... **CMLC 64**
See also DLB 176

Arbuthnot, John 1667-1735 .... **LC 1**
See also DLB 101

Archer, Herbert Winslow
See Mencken, H(enry) L(ouis)

Archer, Jeffrey 1940- .... **CLC 28**
See also AAYA 16; BEST 89:3; BPFB 1; CA 77-80; CANR 22, 52, 95, 136; CPW; DA3; DAM POP; INT CANR-22; MTFW 2005

Archer, Jeffrey Howard
See Archer, Jeffrey

Archer, Jules 1915- .... **CLC 12**
See also CA 9-12R; CANR 6, 69; SAAS 5; SATA 4, 85

Archer, Lee
See Ellison, Harlan

Archilochus c. 7th cent. B.C.- .... **CMLC 44**
See also DLB 176

Ard, William
See Jakes, John

Arden, John 1930- .... **CLC 6, 13, 15**
See also BRWS 2; CA 13-16R; 4; CANR 31, 65, 67, 124; CBD; CD 5, 6; DAM DRAM; DFS 9; DLB 13, 245; EWL 3; MTCW 1

Arenas, Reinaldo 1943-1990 .. **CLC 41; HLC 1; TCLC 191**
See also CA 128; CAAE 124; CAAS 133; CANR 73, 106; DAM MULT; DLB 145; EWL 3; GLL 2; HW 1; LAW; LAWS 1; MTCW 2; MTFW 2005; RGSF 2; RGWL 3; WLIT 1

Arendt, Hannah 1906-1975 .... **CLC 66, 98; TCLC 193**
See also CA 17-20R; CAAS 61-64; CANR 26, 60, 172; DLB 242; MTCW 1, 2

Aretino, Pietro 1492-1556 .... **LC 12**
See also RGWL 2, 3

Arghezi, Tudor .... **CLC 80**
See Theodorescu, Ion N.
See also CA 167; CDWLB 4; DLB 220; EWL 3

Arguedas, Jose Maria 1911-1969 .... **CLC 10, 18; HLCS 1; TCLC 147**
See also CA 89-92; CANR 73; DLB 113; EWL 3; HW 1; LAW; RGWL 2, 3; WLIT 1

Argueta, Manlio 1936- .... **CLC 31**
See also CA 131; CANR 73; CWW 2; DLB 145; EWL 3; HW 1; RGWL 3

Arias, Ron 1941- .... **HLC 1**
See also CA 131; CANR 81, 136; DAM MULT; DLB 82; HW 1, 2; MTCW 2; MTFW 2005

Ariosto, Lodovico
See Ariosto, Ludovico
See also WLIT 7

Ariosto, Ludovico 1474-1533 ... **LC 6, 87; PC 42**
See Ariosto, Lodovico
See also EW 2; RGWL 2, 3

Aristides
See Epstein, Joseph

Aristophanes 450B.C.-385B.C. .... **CMLC 4, 51; DC 2; WLCS**
See also AW 1; CDWLB 1; DA; DA3; DAB; DAC; DAM DRAM, MST; DFS 10; DLB 176; LMFS 1; RGWL 2, 3; TWA; WLIT 8

Aristotle 384B.C.-322B.C. .... **CMLC 31; WLCS**
See also AW 1; CDWLB 1; DA; DA3; DAB; DAC; DAM MST; DLB 176; RGWL 2, 3; TWA; WLIT 8

Arlt, Roberto (Godofredo Christophersen) 1900-1942 .... **HLC 1; TCLC 29**
See also CA 131; CAAE 123; CANR 67; DAM MULT; DLB 305; EWL 3; HW 1, 2; IDTP; LAW

Armah, Ayi Kwei 1939- . **BLC 1:1, 2:1; CLC 5, 33, 136**
See also AFW; BRWS 10; BW 1; CA 61-64; CANR 21, 64; CDWLB 3; CN 1, 2, 3, 4, 5, 6, 7; DAM MULT, POET; DLB 117; EWL 3; MTCW 1; WLIT 2

Armatrading, Joan 1950- .... **CLC 17**
See also CA 186; CAAE 114

Armin, Robert 1568(?)-1615(?) .... **LC 120**

Armitage, Frank
See Carpenter, John (Howard)

Armstrong, Jeannette (C.) 1948- .... **NNAL**
See also CA 149; CCA 1; CN 6, 7; DAC; DLB 334; SATA 102

Arnette, Robert
See Silverberg, Robert

Arnim, Achim von (Ludwig Joachim von Arnim) 1781-1831 .. **NCLC 5, 159; SSC 29**
See also DLB 90

Arnim, Bettina von 1785-1859 ...... **NCLC 38, 123**
See also DLB 90; RGWL 2, 3

Arnold, Matthew 1822-1888 ..... **NCLC 6, 29, 89, 126; PC 5; WLC 1**
See also BRW 5; CDBLB 1832-1890; DA; DAB; DAC; DAM MST, POET; DLB 32, 57; EXPP; PAB; PFS 2; TEA; WP

Arnold, Thomas 1795-1842 .... **NCLC 18**
See also DLB 55

Arnow, Harriette (Louisa) Simpson 1908-1986 ...... **CLC 2, 7, 18; TCLC 196**
See also BPFB 1; CA 9-12R; CAAS 118; CANR 14; CN 2, 3, 4; DLB 6; FW; MTCW 1, 2; RHW; SATA 42; SATA-Obit 47

Arouet, Francois-Marie
See Voltaire

Arp, Hans
See Arp, Jean

Arp, Jean 1887-1966 .... **CLC 5; TCLC 115**
See also CA 81-84; CAAS 25-28R; CANR 42, 77; EW 10

Arrabal
See Arrabal, Fernando

Arrabal (Teran), Fernando
See Arrabal, Fernando
See also CWW 2

Arrabal, Fernando 1932- ... **CLC 2, 9, 18, 58**
See Arrabal (Teran), Fernando
See also CA 9-12R; CANR 15; DLB 321; EWL 3; LMFS 2

Arreola, Juan Jose 1918-2001 .... **CLC 147; HLC 1; SSC 38**
See also CA 131; CAAE 113; CAAS 200; CANR 81; CWW 2; DAM MULT; DLB 113; DNFS 2; EWL 3; HW 1, 2; LAW; RGSF 2

Arrian c. 89(?)-c. 155(?) .... **CMLC 43**
See also DLB 176

Arrick, Fran .... **CLC 30**
See Gaberman, Judie Angell
See also BYA 6

Arley, Richmond
See Delany, Samuel R., Jr.

Artaud, Antonin (Marie Joseph) 1896-1948 .... **DC 14; TCLC 3, 36**
See also CA 149; CAAE 104; DA3; DAM DRAM; DFS 22; DLB 258, 321; EW 11; EWL 3; GFL 1789 to the Present; MTCW 2; MTFW 2005; RGWL 2, 3

Arthur, Ruth M(abel) 1905-1979 .... **CLC 12**
See also CA 9-12R; CAAS 85-88; CANR 4; CWRI 5; SATA 7, 26

Artsybashev, Mikhail (Petrovich) 1878-1927 .... **TCLC 31**
See also CA 170; DLB 295

Arundel, Honor (Morfydd) 1919-1973 .... **CLC 17**
See also CA 21-22; CAAS 41-44R; CAP 2; CLR 35; CWRI 5; SATA 4; SATA-Obit 24

Arzner, Dorothy 1900-1979 .... **CLC 98**

Asch, Sholem 1880-1957 .... **TCLC 3**
See also CAAE 105; DLB 333; EWL 3; GLL 2; RGHL

Ascham, Roger 1516(?)-1568 .... **LC 101**
See also DLB 236

Ash, Shalom
See Asch, Sholem

Ashbery, John 1927- ... **CLC 2, 3, 4, 6, 9, 13, 15, 25, 41, 77, 125, 221; PC 26**
See also AMWS 3; CA 5-8R; CANR 9, 37, 66, 102, 132, 170; CP 1, 2, 3, 4, 5, 6, 7; DA3; DAM POET; DLB 5, 165; DLBY 1981; EWL 3; GLL 1; INT CANR-9; MAL 5; MTCW 1, 2; MTFW 2005; PAB; PFS 11; RGAL 4; TCLE 1:1; WP

Ashbery, John Lawrence
See Ashbery, John

Ashbridge, Elizabeth 1713-1755 .... **LC 147**
See also DLB 200

Ashdown, Clifford
See Freeman, R(ichard) Austin

Ashe, Gordon
See Creasey, John

Ashton-Warner, Sylvia (Constance) 1908-1984 .... **CLC 19**
See also CA 69-72; CAAS 112; CANR 29; CN 1, 2, 3; MTCW 1, 2

Asimov, Isaac 1920-1992 ..... **CLC 1, 3, 9, 19, 26, 76, 92**
See also AAYA 13; BEST 90:2; BPFB 1; BYA 4, 6, 7, 9; CA 1-4R; CAAS 137; CANR 2, 19, 36, 60, 125; CLR 12, 79; CMW 4; CN 1, 2, 3, 4, 5; CPW; DA3; DAM POP; DLB 8; DLBY 1992; INT

Barker, Clive 1952- .... **CLC 52, 205; SSC 53**
See also AAYA 10, 54; BEST 90:3; BPFB
1; CA 129; CAAE 121; CANR 71, 111,
133; CPW; DA3; DAM POP; DLB 261;
HGG; INT CA-129; MTCW 1, 2; MTFW
2005; SUFW 2

Barker, George Granville
1913-1991 .... **CLC 8, 48; PC 77**
See also CA 9-12R; CAAS 135; CANR 7,
38; CP 1, 2, 3, 4, 5; DAM POET; DLB
20; EWL 3; MTCW 1

Barker, Harley Granville
See Granville-Barker, Harley
See also DLB 10

Barker, Howard 1946- .... **CLC 37**
See also CA 102; CBD; CD 5, 6; DLB 13,
233

Barker, Jane 1652-1732 .... **LC 42, 82**
See also DLB 39, 131

Barker, Pat 1943- .... **CLC 32, 94, 146**
See also BRWS 4; CA 122; CAAE 117;
CANR 50, 101, 148; CN 6, 7; DLB 271,
326; INT CA-122

Barker, Patricia
See Barker, Pat

Barlach, Ernst (Heinrich)
1870-1938 .... **TCLC 84**
See also CA 178; DLB 56, 118; EWL 3

Barlow, Joel 1754-1812 .... **NCLC 23**
See also AMWS 2; DLB 37; RGAL 4

Barnard, Mary (Ethel) 1909- .... **CLC 48**
See also CA 21-22; CAP 2; CP 1

Barnes, Djuna 1892-1982 .... **CLC 3, 4, 8, 11,
29, 127; SSC 3**
See Steptoe, Lydia
See also AMWS 3; CA 9-12R; CAAS 107;
CAD; CANR 16, 55; CN 1, 2, 3; CWD;
DLB 4, 9, 45; EWL 3; GLL 1; MAL 5;
MTCW 1, 2; MTFW 2005; RGAL 4;
TCLE 1:1; TUS

Barnes, Jim 1933- .... **NNAL**
See also CA 175; 108, 175; 28; DLB 175

Barnes, Julian 1946- .... **CLC 42, 141**
See also BRWS 4; CA 102; CANR 19, 54,
115, 137; CN 4, 5, 6, 7; DAB; DLB 194;
DLBY 1993; EWL 3; MTCW 2; MTFW
2005; SSFS 24

Barnes, Julian Patrick
See Barnes, Julian

Barnes, Peter 1931-2004 .... **CLC 5, 56**
See also CA 65-68; 12; CAAS 230; CANR
33, 34, 64, 113; CBD; CD 5, 6; DFS 6;
DLB 13, 233; MTCW 1

Barnes, William 1801-1886 .... **NCLC 75**
See also DLB 32

Baroja, Pio 1872-1956 .... **HLC 1; TCLC 8**
See also CA 247; CAAE 104; EW 9

Baroja y Nessi, Pio
See Baroja, Pio

Baron, David
See Pinter, Harold

Baron Corvo
See Rolfe, Frederick (William Serafino Austin Lewis Mary)

Barondess, Sue K(aufman)
1926-1977 .... **CLC 8**
See Kaufman, Sue
See also CA 1-4R; CAAS 69-72; CANR 1

Baron de Teive
See Pessoa, Fernando (Antonio Nogueira)

Baroness Von S.
See Zangwill, Israel

Barres, (Auguste-)Maurice
1862-1923 .... **TCLC 47**
See also CA 164; DLB 123; GFL 1789 to
the Present

Barreto, Afonso Henrique de Lima
See Lima Barreto, Afonso Henrique de

Barrett, Andrea 1954- .... **CLC 150**
See also CA 156; CANR 92; CN 7; DLB
335; SSFS 24

Barrett, Michele .... **CLC 65**

Barrett, (Roger) Syd 1946-2006 .... **CLC 35**

Barrett, William (Christopher)
1913-1992 .... **CLC 27**
See also CA 13-16R; CAAS 139; CANR
11, 67; INT CANR-11

Barrett Browning, Elizabeth
1806-1861 ...... **NCLC 1, 16, 61, 66, 170;
PC 6, 62; WLC 1**
See also AAYA 63; BRW 4; CDBLB 1832-
1890; DA; DA3; DAB; DAC; DAM MST,
POET; DLB 32, 199; EXPP; FL 1:2; PAB;
PFS 2, 16, 23; TEA; WLIT 4; WP

Barrie, J(ames) M(atthew)
1860-1937 .... **TCLC 2, 164**
See also BRWS 3; BYA 4, 5; CA 136;
CAAE 104; CANR 77; CDBLB 1890-
1914; CLR 16, 124; CWRI 5; DA3; DAB;
DAM DRAM; DFS 7; DLB 10, 141, 156;
EWL 3; FANT; MAICYA 1, 2; MTCW 2;
MTFW 2005; SATA 100; SUFW; WCH;
WLIT 4; YABC 1

Barrington, Michael
See Moorcock, Michael

Barrol, Grady
See Bograd, Larry

Barry, Mike
See Malzberg, Barry N(athaniel)

Barry, Philip 1896-1949 .... **TCLC 11**
See also CA 199; CAAE 109; DFS 9; DLB
7, 228; MAL 5; RGAL 4

Bart, Andre Schwarz
See Schwarz-Bart, Andre

Barth, John (Simmons) 1930- ... **CLC 1, 2, 3,
5, 7, 9, 10, 14, 27, 51, 89, 214; SSC 10,
89**
See also AITN 1, 2; AMW; BPFB 1; CA
1-4R; CABS 1; CANR 5, 23, 49, 64, 113;
CN 1, 2, 3, 4, 5, 6, 7; DAM NOV; DLB
2, 227; EWL 3; FANT; MAL 5; MTCW
1; RGAL 4; RGSF 2; RHW; SSFS 6; TUS

Barthelme, Donald 1931-1989 ... **CLC 1, 2, 3,
5, 6, 8, 13, 23, 46, 59, 115; SSC 2, 55**
See also AMWS 4; BPFB 1; CA 21-24R;
CAAS 129; CANR 20, 58; CN 1, 2, 3, 4;
DA3; DAM NOV; DLB 2, 234; DLBY
1980, 1989; EWL 3; FANT; LMFS 2;
MAL 5; MTCW 1, 2; MTFW 2005;
RGAL 4; RGSF 2; SATA 7; SATA-Obit
62; SSFS 17

Barthelme, Frederick 1943- ...... **CLC 36, 117**
See also AMWS 11; CA 122; CAAE 114;
CANR 77; CN 4, 5, 6, 7; CSW; DLB 244;
DLBY 1985; EWL 3; INT CA-122

Barthes, Roland (Gerard)
1915-1980 .... **CLC 24, 83; TCLC 135**
See also CA 130; CAAS 97-100; CANR
66; DLB 296; EW 13; EWL 3; GFL 1789
to the Present; MTCW 1, 2; TWA

Bartram, William 1739-1823 .... **NCLC 145**
See also ANW; DLB 37

Barzun, Jacques (Martin) 1907- ..... **CLC 51,
145**
See also CA 61-64; CANR 22, 95

Bashevis, Isaac
See Singer, Isaac Bashevis

Bashevis, Yitskhok
See Singer, Isaac Bashevis

Bashkirtseff, Marie 1859-1884 .... **NCLC 27**

Basho, Matsuo
See Matsuo Basho
See also RGWL 2, 3; WP

Basil of Caesaria c. 330-379 .... **CMLC 35**

Basket, Raney
See Edgerton, Clyde (Carlyle)

Bass, Kingsley B., Jr.
See Bullins, Ed

Bass, Rick 1958- .... **CLC 79, 143; SSC 60**
See also AMWS 16; ANW; CA 126; CANR
53, 93, 145; CSW; DLB 212, 275

Bassani, Giorgio 1916-2000 .... **CLC 9**
See also CA 65-68; CAAS 190; CANR 33;
CWW 2; DLB 128, 177, 299; EWL 3;
MTCW 1; RGHL; RGWL 2, 3

Bastian, Ann .... **CLC 70**

Bastos, Augusto Roa
See Roa Bastos, Augusto

Bataille, Georges 1897-1962 .... **CLC 29;
TCLC 155**
See also CA 101; CAAS 89-92; EWL 3

Bates, H(erbert) E(rnest)
1905-1974 .... **CLC 46; SSC 10**
See also CA 93-96; CAAS 45-48; CANR
34; CN 1; DA3; DAB; DAM POP; DLB
162, 191; EWL 3; EXPS; MTCW 1, 2;
RGSF 2; SSFS 7

Bauchart
See Camus, Albert

Baudelaire, Charles 1821-1867 . **NCLC 6, 29,
55, 155; PC 1; SSC 18; WLC 1**
See also DA; DA3; DAB; DAC; DAM
MST, POET; DLB 217; EW 7; GFL 1789
to the Present; LMFS 2; PFS 21; RGWL
2, 3; TWA

Baudouin, Marcel
See Peguy, Charles (Pierre)

Baudouin, Pierre
See Peguy, Charles (Pierre)

Baudrillard, Jean 1929-2007 .... **CLC 60**
See also CA 252; CAAS 258; DLB 296

Baum, L(yman) Frank 1856-1919 .. **TCLC 7,
132**
See also AAYA 46; BYA 16; CA 133;
CAAE 108; CLR 15, 107; CWRI 5; DLB
22; FANT; JRDA; MAICYA 1, 2; MTCW
1, 2; NFS 13; RGAL 4; SATA 18, 100;
WCH

Baum, Louis F.
See Baum, L(yman) Frank

Baumbach, Jonathan 1933- .... **CLC 6, 23**
See also CA 13-16R; 5; CANR 12, 66, 140;
CN 3, 4, 5, 6, 7; DLBY 1980; INT CANR-
12; MTCW 1

Bausch, Richard 1945- .... **CLC 51**
See also AMWS 7; CA 101; 14; CANR 43,
61, 87, 164; CN 7; CSW; DLB 130; MAL
5

Bausch, Richard Carl
See Bausch, Richard

Baxter, Charles 1947- .... **CLC 45, 78**
See also AMWS 17; CA 57-60; CANR 40,
64, 104, 133; CPW; DAM POP; DLB
130; MAL 5; MTCW 2; MTFW 2005;
TCLE 1:1

Baxter, George Owen
See Faust, Frederick (Schiller)

Baxter, James K(eir) 1926-1972 .... **CLC 14**
See also CA 77-80; CP 1; EWL 3

Baxter, John
See Hunt, E. Howard

Bayer, Sylvia
See Glassco, John

Bayle, Pierre 1647-1706 .... **LC 126**
See also DLB 268, 313; GFL Beginnings to
1789

Baynton, Barbara 1857-1929 .... **TCLC 57**
See also DLB 230; RGSF 2

Beagle, Peter S. 1939- .... **CLC 7, 104**
See also AAYA 47; BPFB 1; BYA 9, 10,
16; CA 9-12R; CANR 4, 51, 73, 110;
DA3; DLBY 1980; FANT; INT CANR-4;
MTCW 2; MTFW 2005; SATA 60, 130;
SUFW 1, 2; YAW

Blaise, Clark 1940- .... **CLC 29**
See also AITN 2; CA 231; 53-56, 231; 3;
CANR 5, 66, 106; CN 4, 5, 6, 7; DLB 53;
RGSF 2

Blake, Fairley
See De Voto, Bernard (Augustine)

Blake, Nicholas
See Day Lewis, C(ecil)
See also DLB 77; MSW

Blake, Sterling
See Benford, Gregory

Blake, William 1757-1827 . **NCLC 13, 37, 57,
127, 173, 190; PC 12, 63; WLC 1**
See also AAYA 47; BRW 3; BRWR 1; CD-
BLB 1789-1832; CLR 52; DA; DA3;
DAB; DAC; DAM MST, POET; DLB 93,
163; EXPP; LATS 1:1; LMFS 1; MAI-
CYA 1, 2; PAB; PFS 2, 12, 24; SATA 30;
TEA; WCH; WLIT 3; WP

Blanchot, Maurice 1907-2003 .... **CLC 135**
See also CA 144; CAAE 117; CAAS 213;
CANR 238; DLB 72, 296; EWL 3

Blasco Ibanez, Vicente 1867-1928 . **TCLC 12**
See Ibanez, Vicente Blasco
See also BPFB 1; CA 131; CAAE 110;
CANR 81; DA3; DAM NOV; EW 8;
EWL 3; HW 1, 2; MTCW 1

Blatty, William Peter 1928- .... **CLC 2**
See also CA 5-8R; CANR 9, 124; DAM
POP; HGG

Bleeck, Oliver
See Thomas, Ross (Elmore)

Blessing, Lee (Knowlton) 1949- .... **CLC 54**
See also CA 236; CAD; CD 5, 6; DFS 23

Blight, Rose
See Greer, Germaine

Blish, James (Benjamin) 1921-1975 . **CLC 14**
See also BPFB 1; CA 1-4R; CAAS 57-60;
CANR 3; CN 2; DLB 8; MTCW 1; SATA
66; SCFW 1, 2; SFW 4

Bliss, Frederick
See Card, Orson Scott

Bliss, Gillian
See Paton Walsh, Jill

Bliss, Reginald
See Wells, H(erbert) G(eorge)

Blixen, Karen (Christentze Dinesen)
1885-1962
See Dinesen, Isak
See also CA 25-28; CANR 22, 50; CAP 2;
DA3; DLB 214; LMFS 1; MTCW 1, 2;
SATA 44; SSFS 20

Bloch, Robert (Albert) 1917-1994 .... **CLC 33**
See also AAYA 29; CA 179; 5-8R, 179; 20;
CAAS 146; CANR 5, 78; DA3; DLB 44;
HGG; INT CANR-5; MTCW 2; SATA 12;
SATA-Obit 82; SFW 4; SUFW 1, 2

Blok, Alexander (Alexandrovich)
1880-1921 .... **PC 21; TCLC 5**
See also CA 183; CAAE 104; DLB 295;
EW 9; EWL 3; LMFS 2; RGWL 2, 3

Blom, Jan
See Breytenbach, Breyten

Bloom, Harold 1930- .... **CLC 24, 103, 221**
See also CA 13-16R; CANR 39, 75, 92,
133; DLB 67; EWL 3; MTCW 2; MTFW
2005; RGAL 4

Bloomfield, Aurelius
See Bourne, Randolph S(illiman)

Bloomfield, Robert 1766-1823 ..... **NCLC 145**
See also DLB 93

Blount, Roy (Alton), Jr. 1941- .... **CLC 38**
See also CA 53-56; CANR 10, 28, 61, 125;
CSW; INT CANR-28; MTCW 1, 2;
MTFW 2005

Blowsnake, Sam 1875-(?) .... **NNAL**

Bloy, Leon 1846-1917 .... **TCLC 22**
See also CA 183; CAAE 121; DLB 123;
GFL 1789 to the Present

Blue Cloud, Peter (Aroniawenrate)
1933- .... **NNAL**
See also CA 117; CANR 40; DAM MULT

Bluggage, Oranthy
See Alcott, Louisa May

Blume, Judy (Sussman) 1938- .... **CLC 12, 30**
See also AAYA 3, 26; BYA 1, 8, 12; CA 29-
32R; CANR 13, 37, 66, 124; CLR 2, 15,
69; CPW; DA3; DAM NOV, POP; DLB
52; JRDA; MAICYA 1, 2; MAICYAS 1;
MTCW 1, 2; MTFW 2005; NFS 24;
SATA 2, 31, 79, 142; WYA; YAW

Blunden, Edmund (Charles)
1896-1974 .... **CLC 2, 56; PC 66**
See also BRW 6; BRWS 11; CA 17-18;
CAAS 45-48; CANR 54; CAP 2; CP 1, 2;
DLB 20, 100, 155; MTCW 1; PAB

Bly, Robert (Elwood) 1926- .... **CLC 1, 2, 5,
10, 15, 38, 128; PC 39**
See also AMWS 4; CA 5-8R; CANR 41,
73, 125; CP 1, 2, 3, 4, 5, 6, 7; DA3; DAM
POET; DLB 5; EWL 3; MAL 5; MTCW
1, 2; MTFW 2005; PFS 6, 17; RGAL 4

Boas, Franz 1858-1942 .... **TCLC 56**
See also CA 181; CAAE 115

Bobette
See Simenon, Georges (Jacques Christian)

Boccaccio, Giovanni 1313-1375 ... **CMLC 13,
57; SSC 10, 87**
See also EW 2; RGSF 2; RGWL 2, 3; TWA;
WLIT 7

Bochco, Steven 1943- .... **CLC 35**
See also AAYA 11, 71; CA 138; CAAE 124

Bode, Sigmund
See O'Doherty, Brian

Bodel, Jean 1167(?)-1210 .... **CMLC 28**

Bodenheim, Maxwell 1892-1954 .... **TCLC 44**
See also CA 187; CAAE 110; DLB 9, 45;
MAL 5; RGAL 4

Bodenheimer, Maxwell
See Bodenheim, Maxwell

Bodker, Cecil 1927-
See Bodker, Cecil

Bodker, Cecil 1927- .... **CLC 21**
See also CA 73-76; CANR 13, 44, 111;
CLR 23; MAICYA 1, 2; SATA 14, 133

Boell, Heinrich (Theodor)
1917-1985 ..... **CLC 2, 3, 6, 9, 11, 15, 27,
32, 72; SSC 23; WLC 1**
See Boll, Heinrich (Theodor)
See also CA 21-24R; CAAS 116; CANR
24; DA; DA3; DAB; DAC; DAM MST,
NOV; DLB 69; DLBY 1985; MTCW 1,
2; MTFW 2005; SSFS 20; TWA

Boerne, Alfred
See Doeblin, Alfred

Boethius c. 480-c. 524 .... **CMLC 15**
See also DLB 115; RGWL 2, 3; WLIT 8

Boff, Leonardo (Genezio Darci)
1938- .... **CLC 70; HLC 1**
See also CA 150; DAM MULT; HW 2

Bogan, Louise 1897-1970 .... **CLC 4, 39, 46,
93; PC 12**
See also AMWS 3; CA 73-76; CAAS 25-
28R; CANR 33, 82; CP 1; DAM POET;
DLB 45, 169; EWL 3; MAL 5; MBL;
MTCW 1, 2; PFS 21; RGAL 4

Bogarde, Dirk
See Van Den Bogarde, Derek Jules Gaspard
Ulric Niven
See also DLB 14

Bogosian, Eric 1953- .... **CLC 45, 141**
See also CA 138; CAD; CANR 102, 148;
CD 5, 6

Bograd, Larry 1953- .... **CLC 35**
See also CA 93-96; CANR 57; SAAS 21;
SATA 33, 89; WYA

Boiardo, Matteo Maria 1441-1494 .... **LC 6**

Boileau-Despreaux, Nicolas 1636-1711 . **LC 3**
See also DLB 268; EW 3; GFL Beginnings
to 1789; RGWL 2, 3

Boissard, Maurice
See Leautaud, Paul

Bojer, Johan 1872-1959 .... **TCLC 64**
See also CA 189; EWL 3

Bok, Edward W(illiam)
1863-1930 .... **TCLC 101**
See also CA 217; DLB 91; DLBD 16

Boker, George Henry 1823-1890 . **NCLC 125**
See also RGAL 4

Boland, Eavan 1944- ... **CLC 40, 67, 113; PC
58**
See also BRWS 5; CA 207; 143, 207;
CANR 61; CP 1, 6, 7; CWP; DAM POET;
DLB 40; FW; MTCW 2; MTFW 2005;
PFS 12, 22

Boll, Heinrich (Theodor) .... **TCLC 185**
See Boell, Heinrich (Theodor)
See also BPFB 1; CDWLB 2; DLB 329;
EW 13; EWL 3; RGHL; RGSF 2; RGWL
2, 3

Bolt, Lee
See Faust, Frederick (Schiller)

Bolt, Robert (Oxton) 1924-1995 ...... **CLC 14;
TCLC 175**
See also CA 17-20R; CAAS 147; CANR
35, 67; CBD; DAM DRAM; DFS 2; DLB
13, 233; EWL 3; LAIT 1; MTCW 1

Bombal, Maria Luisa 1910-1980 .... **HLCS 1;
SSC 37**
See also CA 127; CANR 72; EWL 3; HW
1; LAW; RGSF 2

Bombet, Louis-Alexandre-Cesar
See Stendhal

Bomkauf
See Kaufman, Bob (Garnell)

Bonaventura .... **NCLC 35**
See also DLB 90

Bonaventure 1217(?)-1274 .... **CMLC 79**
See also DLB 115; LMFS 1

Bond, Edward 1934- .... **CLC 4, 6, 13, 23**
See also AAYA 50; BRWS 1; CA 25-28R;
CANR 38, 67, 106; CBD; CD 5, 6; DAM
DRAM; DFS 3, 8; DLB 13, 310; EWL 3;
MTCW 1

Bonham, Frank 1914-1989 .... **CLC 12**
See also AAYA 1, 70; BYA 1, 3; CA 9-12R;
CANR 4, 36; JRDA; MAICYA 1, 2;
SAAS 3; SATA 1, 49; SATA-Obit 62;
TCWW 1, 2; YAW

Bonnefoy, Yves 1923- . **CLC 9, 15, 58; PC 58**
See also CA 85-88; CANR 33, 75, 97, 136;
CWW 2; DAM MST, POET; DLB 258;
EWL 3; GFL 1789 to the Present; MTCW
1, 2; MTFW 2005

Bonner, Marita . **HR 1:2; PC 72; TCLC 179**
See Occomy, Marita (Odette) Bonner

Bonnin, Gertrude 1876-1938 .... **NNAL**
See Zitkala-Sa
See also CA 150; DAM MULT

Bontemps, Arna(ud Wendell)
1902-1973 ..... **BLC 1:1; CLC 1, 18; HR
1:2**
See also BW 1; CA 1-4R; CAAS 41-44R;
CANR 4, 35; CLR 6; CP 1; CWRI 5;
DA3; DAM MULT, NOV, POET; DLB
48, 51; JRDA; MAICYA 1, 2; MAL 5;
MTCW 1, 2; SATA 2, 44; SATA-Obit 24;
WCH; WP

Boot, William
See Stoppard, Tom

Booth, Martin 1944-2004 .... **CLC 13**
See also CA 188; 93-96, 188; 2; CAAS 223;
CANR 92; CP 1, 2, 3, 4

Buchner, (Karl) Georg
1813-1837 .... NCLC 26, 146
See also CDWLB 2; DLB 133; EW 6;
RGSF 2; RGWL 2, 3; TWA

Buchwald, Art 1925-2007 .... CLC 33
See also AITN 1; CA 5-8R; CAAS 256;
CANR 21, 67, 107; MTCW 1, 2; SATA
10

Buchwald, Arthur
See Buchwald, Art

Buck, Pearl S(ydenstricker)
1892-1973 .... CLC 7, 11, 18, 127
See also AAYA 42; AITN 1; AMWS 2;
BPFB 1; CA 1-4R; CAAS 41-44R; CANR
1, 34; CDALBS; CN 1; DA; DA3; DAB;
DAC; DAM MST, NOV; DLB 9, 102,
329; EWL 3; LAIT 3; MAL 5; MTCW 1,
2; MTFW 2005; NFS 25; RGAL 4; RHW;
SATA 1, 25; TUS

Buckler, Ernest 1908-1984 .... CLC 13
See also CA 11-12; CAAS 114; CAP 1;
CCA 1; CN 1, 2, 3; DAC; DAM MST;
DLB 68; SATA 47

Buckley, Christopher 1952- .... CLC 165
See also CA 139; CANR 119

Buckley, Christopher Taylor
See Buckley, Christopher

Buckley, Vincent (Thomas)
1925-1988 .... CLC 57
See also CA 101; CP 1, 2, 3, 4; DLB 289

Buckley, William F., Jr. 1925-2008 ... CLC 7,
18, 37
See also AITN 1; BPFB 1; CA 1-4R; CANR
1, 24, 53, 93, 133; CMW 4; CPW; DA3;
DAM POP; DLB 137; DLBY 1980; INT
CANR-24; MTCW 1, 2; MTFW 2005;
TUS

Buechner, Frederick 1926- ..... CLC 2, 4, 6, 9
See also AMWS 12; BPFB 1; CA 13-16R;
CANR 11, 39, 64, 114, 138; CN 1, 2, 3,
4, 5, 6, 7; DAM NOV; DLBY 1980; INT
CANR-11; MAL 5; MTCW 1, 2; MTFW
2005; TCLE 1:1

Buell, John (Edward) 1927- .... CLC 10
See also CA 1-4R; CANR 71; DLB 53

Buero Vallejo, Antonio 1916-2000 ... CLC 15,
46, 139, 226; DC 18
See also CA 106; CAAS 189; CANR 24,
49, 75; CWW 2; DFS 11; EWL 3; HW 1;
MTCW 1, 2

Bufalino, Gesualdo 1920-1996 .... CLC 74
See also CA 209; CWW 2; DLB 196

Bugayev, Boris Nikolayevich
1880-1934 .... PC 11; TCLC 7
See Bely, Andrey; Belyi, Andrei
See also CA 165; CAAE 104; MTCW 2;
MTFW 2005

Bukowski, Charles 1920-1994 ... CLC 2, 5, 9,
41, 82, 108; PC 18; SSC 45
See also CA 17-20R; CAAS 144; CANR
40, 62, 105; CN 4, 5; CP 1, 2, 3, 4, 5;
CPW; DA3; DAM NOV, POET; DLB 5,
130, 169; EWL 3; MAL 5; MTCW 1, 2;
MTFW 2005

Bulgakov, Mikhail 1891-1940 .... SSC 18;
TCLC 2, 16, 159
See also AAYA 74; BPFB 1; CA 152;
CAAE 105; DAM DRAM, NOV; DLB
272; EWL 3; MTCW 2; MTFW 2005;
NFS 8; RGSF 2; RGWL 2, 3; SFW 4;
TWA

Bulgakov, Mikhail Afanasevich
See Bulgakov, Mikhail

Bulgya, Alexander Alexandrovich
1901-1956 .... TCLC 53
See Fadeev, Aleksandr Aleksandrovich;
Fadeev, Alexandr Alexandrovich; Fadeyev,
Alexander
See also CA 181; CAAE 117

Bullins, Ed 1935- ...... BLC 1:1; CLC 1, 5, 7;
DC 6
See also BW 2, 3; CA 49-52; 16; CAD;
CANR 24, 46, 73, 134; CD 5, 6; DAM
DRAM, MULT; DLB 7, 38, 249; EWL 3;
MAL 5; MTCW 1, 2; MTFW 2005;
RGAL 4

Bulosan, Carlos 1911-1956 .... AAL
See also CA 216; DLB 312; RGAL 4

Bulwer-Lytton, Edward (George Earle
Lytton) 1803-1873 .... NCLC 1, 45
See also DLB 21; RGEL 2; SFW 4; SUFW
1; TEA

Bunin, Ivan
See Bunin, Ivan Alexeyevich

Bunin, Ivan Alekseevich
See Bunin, Ivan Alexeyevich

Bunin, Ivan Alexeyevich 1870-1953 ... SSC 5;
TCLC 6
See also CAAE 104; DLB 317, 329; EWL
3; RGSF 2; RGWL 2, 3; TWA

Bunting, Basil 1900-1985 ...... CLC 10, 39, 47
See also BRWS 7; CA 53-56; CAAS 115;
CANR 7; CP 1, 2, 3, 4; DAM POET; DLB
20; EWL 3; RGEL 2

Bunuel, Luis 1900-1983 ... CLC 16, 80; HLC
1
See also CA 101; CAAS 110; CANR 32,
77; DAM MULT; HW 1

Bunyan, John 1628-1688 .. LC 4, 69; WLC 1
See also BRW 2; BYA 5; CDBLB 1660-
1789; CLR 124; DA; DAB; DAC; DAM
MST; DLB 39; RGEL 2; TEA; WCH;
WLIT 3

Buravsky, Alexandr .... CLC 59

Burchill, Julie 1959- .... CLC 238
See also CA 135; CANR 115, 116

Burckhardt, Jacob (Christoph)
1818-1897 .... NCLC 49
See also EW 6

Burford, Eleanor
See Hibbert, Eleanor Alice Burford

Burgess, Anthony . CLC 1, 2, 4, 5, 8, 10, 13,
15, 22, 40, 62, 81, 94
See Wilson, John (Anthony) Burgess
See also AAYA 25; AITN 1; BRWS 1; CD-
BLB 1960 to Present; CN 1, 2, 3, 4, 5;
DAB; DLB 14, 194, 261; DLBY 1998;
EWL 3; RGEL 2; RHW; SFW 4; YAW

Buridan, John c. 1295-c. 1358 ...... CMLC 97

Burke, Edmund 1729(?)-1797 .... LC 7, 36,
146; WLC 1
See also BRW 3; DA; DA3; DAB; DAC;
DAM MST; DLB 104, 252, 336; RGEL
2; TEA

Burke, Kenneth (Duva) 1897-1993 ... CLC 2,
24
See also AMW; CA 5-8R; CAAS 143;
CANR 39, 74, 136; CN 1, 2; CP 1, 2, 3,
4, 5; DLB 45, 63; EWL 3; MAL 5;
MTCW 1, 2; MTFW 2005; RGAL 4

Burke, Leda
See Garnett, David

Burke, Ralph
See Silverberg, Robert

Burke, Thomas 1886-1945 .... TCLC 63
See also CA 155; CAAE 113; CMW 4;
DLB 197

Burney, Fanny 1752-1840 .... NCLC 12, 54,
107
See also BRWS 3; DLB 39; FL 1:2; NFS
16; RGEL 2; TEA

Burney, Frances
See Burney, Fanny

Burns, Robert 1759-1796 ... LC 3, 29, 40; PC
6; WLC 1
See also AAYA 51; BRW 3; CDBLB 1789-
1832; DA; DA3; DAB; DAC; DAM MST,
POET; DLB 109; EXPP; PAB; RGEL 2;
TEA; WP

Burns, Tex
See L'Amour, Louis

Burnshaw, Stanley 1906-2005 ..... CLC 3, 13,
44
See also CA 9-12R; CAAS 243; CP 1, 2, 3,
4, 5, 6, 7; DLB 48; DLBY 1997

Burr, Anne 1937- .... CLC 6
See also CA 25-28R

Burroughs, Edgar Rice 1875-1950 . TCLC 2,
32
See also AAYA 11; BPFB 1; BYA 4, 9; CA
132; CAAE 104; CANR 131; DA3; DAM
NOV; DLB 8; FANT; MTCW 1, 2;
MTFW 2005; RGAL 4; SATA 41; SCFW
1, 2; SFW 4; TCWW 1, 2; TUS; YAW

Burroughs, William S. 1914-1997 . CLC 1, 2,
5, 15, 22, 42, 75, 109; TCLC 121; WLC
1
See Lee, William; Lee, Willy
See also AAYA 60; AITN 2; AMWS 3; BG
1:2; BPFB 1; CA 9-12R; CAAS 160;
CANR 20, 52, 104; CN 1, 2, 3, 4, 5, 6;
CPW; DA; DA3; DAB; DAC; DAM MST,
NOV, POP; DLB 2, 8, 16, 152, 237;
DLBY 1981, 1997; EWL 3; HGG; LMFS
2; MAL 5; MTCW 1, 2; MTFW 2005;
RGAL 4; SFW 4

Burroughs, William Seward
See Burroughs, William S.

Burton, Sir Richard F(rancis)
1821-1890 .... NCLC 42
See also DLB 55, 166, 184; SSFS 21

Burton, Robert 1577-1640 .... LC 74
See also DLB 151; RGEL 2

Buruma, Ian 1951- .... CLC 163
See also CA 128; CANR 65, 141

Busch, Frederick 1941-2006 .. CLC 7, 10, 18,
47, 166
See also CA 33-36R; 1; CAAS 248; CANR
45, 73, 92, 157; CN 1, 2, 3, 4, 5, 6, 7;
DLB 6, 218

Busch, Frederick Matthew
See Busch, Frederick

Bush, Barney (Furman) 1946- .... NNAL
See also CA 145

Bush, Ronald 1946- .... CLC 34
See also CA 136

Busia, Abena, P. A. 1953- .... BLC 2:1

Bustos, F(rancisco)
See Borges, Jorge Luis

Bustos Domecq, H(onorio)
See Bioy Casares, Adolfo; Borges, Jorge
Luis

Butler, Octavia E. 1947-2006 .... BLCS; BLC
2:1; CLC 38, 121, 230, 240
See also AAYA 18, 48; AFAW 2; AMWS
13; BPFB 1; BW 2, 3; CA 73-76; CAAS
248; CANR 12, 24, 38, 73, 145, 240; CLR
65; CN 7; CPW; DA3; DAM MULT,
POP; DLB 33; LATS 1:2; MTCW 1, 2;
MTFW 2005; NFS 8, 21; SATA 84; SCFW
2; SFW 4; SSFS 6; TCLE 1:1; YAW

Butler, Octavia Estelle
See Butler, Octavia E.

Butler, Robert Olen, (Jr.) 1945- ...... CLC 81,
162
See also AMWS 12; BPFB 1; CA 112;
CANR 66, 138; CN 7; CSW; DAM POP;
DLB 173, 335; INT CA-112; MAL 5;
MTCW 2; MTFW 2005; SSFS 11, 22

Butler, Samuel 1612-1680 .... LC 16, 43
See also DLB 101, 126; RGEL 2

Butler, Samuel 1835-1902 .... TCLC 1, 33;
WLC 1
See also BRWS 2; CA 143; CDBLB 1890-
1914; DA; DA3; DAB; DAC; DAM MST,
NOV; DLB 18, 57, 174; RGEL 2; SFW 4;
TEA

Butler, Walter C.
See Faust, Frederick (Schiller)

Butor, Michel (Marie Francois)
1926- .... **CLC 1, 3, 8, 11, 15, 161**
See also CA 9-12R; CANR 33, 66; CWW
2; DLB 83; EW 13; EWL 3; GFL 1789 to
the Present; MTCW 1, 2; MTFW 2005

Butts, Mary 1890(?)-1937 .... **TCLC 77**
See also CA 148; DLB 240

Buxton, Ralph
See Silverstein, Alvin; Silverstein, Virginia
B(arbara Opshelor)

Buzo, Alex
See Buzo, Alexander (John)
See also DLB 289

Buzo, Alexander (John) 1944- .... **CLC 61**
See also CA 97-100; CANR 17, 39, 69; CD
5, 6

Buzzati, Dino 1906-1972 .... **CLC 36**
See also CA 160; CAAS 33-36R; DLB 177;
RGWL 2, 3; SFW 4

Byars, Betsy 1928- .... **CLC 35**
See also AAYA 19; BYA 3; CA 183; 33-
36R, 183; CANR 18, 36, 57, 102, 148;
CLR 1, 16, 72; DLB 52; INT CANR-18;
JRDA; MAICYA 1, 2; MAICYAS 1;
MTCW 1; SAAS 1; SATA 4, 46, 80, 163;
SATA-Essay 108; WYA; YAW

Byars, Betsy Cromer
See Byars, Betsy

Byatt, Antonia Susan Drabble
See Byatt, A.S.

Byatt, A.S. 1936- .... **CLC 19, 65, 136, 223;
SSC 91**
See also BPFB 1; BRWC 2; BRWS 4; CA
13-16R; CANR 13, 33, 50, 75, 96, 133;
CN 1, 2, 3, 4, 5, 6; DA3; DAM NOV;
POP; DLB 14, 194, 319, 326; EWL 3;
MTCW 1, 2; MTFW 2005; RGSF 2;
RHW; TEA

Byrd, William II 1674-1744 .... **LC 112**
See also DLB 24, 140; RGAL 4

Byrne, David 1952- .... **CLC 26**
See also CA 127

Byrne, John Keyes 1926-
See Leonard, Hugh
See also CA 102; CANR 78, 140; INT CA-
102

Byron, George Gordon (Noel)
1788-1824 ..... **DC 24; NCLC 2, 12, 109,
149; PC 16; WLC 1**
See also AAYA 64; BRW 4; BRWC 2; CD-
BLB 1789-1832; DA; DA3; DAB; DAC;
DAM MST, POET; DLB 96, 110; EXPP;
LMFS 1; PAB; PFS 1, 14; RGEL 2; TEA;
WLIT 3; WP

Byron, Robert 1905-1941 .... **TCLC 67**
See also CA 160; DLB 195

C. 3. 3.
See Wilde, Oscar

Caballero, Fernan 1796-1877 .... **NCLC 10**

Cabell, Branch
See Cabell, James Branch

Cabell, James Branch 1879-1958 .... **TCLC 6**
See also CA 152; CAAE 105; DLB 9, 78;
FANT; MAL 5; MTCW 2; RGAL 4;
SUFW 1

Cabeza de Vaca, Alvar Nunez
1490-1557(?) .... **LC 61**

Cable, George Washington
1844-1925 .... **SSC 4; TCLC 4**
See also CA 155; CAAE 104; DLB 12, 74;
DLBD 13; RGAL 4; TUS

Cabral de Melo Neto, Joao
1920-1999 .... **CLC 76**
See Melo Neto, Joao Cabral de
See also CA 151; DAM MULT; DLB 307;
LAW; LAWS 1

Cabrera Infante, G. 1929-2005 ... **CLC 5, 25,
45, 120; HLC 1; SSC 39**
See also CA 85-88; CAAS 236; CANR 29,
65, 110; CDWLB 3; CWW 2; DA3; DAM
MULT; DLB 113; EWL 3; HW 1, 2;
LAW; LAWS 1; MTCW 1, 2; MTFW
2005; RGSF 2; WLIT 1

Cabrera Infante, Guillermo
See Cabrera Infante, G.

Cade, Toni
See Bambara, Toni Cade

Cadmus and Harmonia
See Buchan, John

Caedmon fl. 658-680 .... **CMLC 7**
See also DLB 146

Caeiro, Alberto
See Pessoa, Fernando (Antonio Nogueira)

Caesar, Julius .... **CMLC 47**
See Julius Caesar
See also AW 1; RGWL 2, 3; WLIT 8

Cage, John (Milton), (Jr.)
1912-1992 .... **CLC 41; PC 58**
See also CA 13-16R; CAAS 169; CANR 9,
78; DLB 193; INT CANR-9; TCLE 1:1

Cahan, Abraham 1860-1951 .... **TCLC 71**
See also CA 154; CAAE 108; DLB 9, 25,
28; MAL 5; RGAL 4

Cain, G.
See Cabrera Infante, G.

Cain, Guillermo
See Cabrera Infante, G.

Cain, James M(allahan) 1892-1977 .. **CLC 3,
11, 28**
See also AITN 1; BPFB 1; CA 17-20R;
CAAS 73-76; CANR 8, 34, 61; CMW 4;
CN 1, 2; DLB 226; EWL 3; MAL 5;
MSW; MTCW 1; RGAL 4

Caine, Hall 1853-1931 .... **TCLC 97**
See also RHW

Caine, Mark
See Raphael, Frederic (Michael)

Calasso, Roberto 1941- .... **CLC 81**
See also CA 143; CANR 89

Calderon de la Barca, Pedro
1600-1681 . **DC 3; HLCS 1; LC 23, 136**
See also DFS 23; EW 2; RGWL 2, 3; TWA

Caldwell, Erskine 1903-1987 ... **CLC 1, 8, 14,
50, 60; SSC 19; TCLC 117**
See also AITN 1; AMW; BPFB 1; CA 1-4R;
1, CAAS 121; CANR 2, 33; CN 1, 2, 3,
4; DA3; DAM NOV; DLB 9, 86; EWL 3;
MAL 5; MTCW 1, 2; MTFW 2005;
RGAL 4; RGSF 2; TUS

Caldwell, (Janet Miriam) Taylor (Holland)
1900-1985 .... **CLC 2, 28, 39**
See also BPFB 1; CA 5-8R; CAAS 116;
CANR 5; DA3; DAM NOV, POP; DLBD
17; MTCW 2; RHW

Calhoun, John Caldwell
1782-1850 .... **NCLC 15**
See also DLB 3, 248

Calisher, Hortense 1911- ..... **CLC 2, 4, 8, 38,
134; SSC 15**
See also CA 1-4R; CANR 1, 22, 117; CN
1, 2, 3, 4, 5, 6, 7; DA3; DAM NOV; DLB
2, 218; INT CANR-22; MAL 5; MTCW
1, 2; MTFW 2005; RGAL 4; RGSF 2

Callaghan, Morley Edward
1903-1990 ..... **CLC 3, 14, 41, 65; TCLC
145**
See also CA 9-12R; CAAS 132; CANR 33,
73; CN 1, 2, 3, 4; DAC; DAM MST; DLB
68; EWL 3; MTCW 1, 2; MTFW 2005;
RGEL 2; RGSF 2; SSFS 19

Callimachus c. 305B.C.-c.
240B.C. .... **CMLC 18**
See also AW 1; DLB 176; RGWL 2, 3

Calvin, Jean
See Calvin, John
See also DLB 327; GFL Beginnings to 1789

Calvin, John 1509-1564 .... **LC 37**
See Calvin, Jean

Calvino, Italo 1923-1985 .... **CLC 5, 8, 11, 22,
33, 39, 73; SSC 3, 48; TCLC 183**
See also AAYA 58; CA 85-88; CAAS 116;
CANR 23, 61, 132; DAM NOV; DLB
196; EW 13; EWL 3; MTCW 1, 2; MTFW
2005; RGHL; RGSF 2; RGWL 2, 3; SFW
4; SSFS 12; WLIT 7

Camara Laye
See Laye, Camara
See also EWL 3

Camden, William 1551-1623 .... **LC 77**
See also DLB 172

Cameron, Carey 1952- .... **CLC 59**
See also CA 135

Cameron, Peter 1959- .... **CLC 44**
See also AMWS 12; CA 125; CANR 50,
117; DLB 234; GLL 2

Camoens, Luis Vaz de 1524(?)-1580
See Camoes, Luis de
See also EW 2

Camoes, Luis de 1524(?)-1580 . **HLCS 1; LC
62; PC 31**
See Camoens, Luis Vaz de
See also DLB 287; RGWL 2, 3

Camp, Madeleine L'Engle
See L'Engle, Madeleine

Campana, Dino 1885-1932 .... **TCLC 20**
See also CA 246; CAAE 117; DLB 114;
EWL 3

Campanella, Tommaso 1568-1639 .... **LC 32**
See also RGWL 2, 3

Campbell, Bebe Moore 1950-2006 . **BLC 2:1;
CLC 246**
See also AAYA 26; BW 2, 3; CA 139;
CAAS 254; CANR 81, 134; DLB 227;
MTCW 2; MTFW 2005

Campbell, John Ramsey
See Campbell, Ramsey

Campbell, John W(ood, Jr.)
1910-1971 .... **CLC 32**
See also CA 21-22; CAAS 29-32R; CANR
34; CAP 2; DLB 8; MTCW 1; SCFW 1,
2; SFW 4

Campbell, Joseph 1904-1987 .... **CLC 69;
TCLC 140**
See also AAYA 3, 66; BEST 89:2; CA 1-4R;
CAAS 124; CANR 3, 28, 61, 107; DA3;
MTCW 1, 2

Campbell, Maria 1940- .... **CLC 85; NNAL**
See also CA 102; CANR 54; CCA 1; DAC

Campbell, Ramsey 1946- ... **CLC 42; SSC 19**
See also AAYA 51; CA 228; 57-60, 228;
CANR 7, 102, 171; DLB 261; HGG; INT
CANR-7; SUFW 1, 2

Campbell, (Ignatius) Roy (Dunnachie)
1901-1957 .... **TCLC 5**
See also AFW; CA 155; CAAE 104; DLB
20, 225; EWL 3; MTCW 2; RGEL 2

Campbell, Thomas 1777-1844 .... **NCLC 19**
See also DLB 93, 144; RGEL 2

Campbell, Wilfred .... **TCLC 9**
See Campbell, William

Campbell, William 1858(?)-1918
See Campbell, Wilfred
See also CAAE 106; DLB 92

Campbell, William Edward March
1893-1954
See March, William
See also CAAE 108

Campion, Jane 1954- .... **CLC 95, 229**
See also AAYA 33; CA 138; CANR 87

Campion, Thomas 1567-1620 .... **LC 78**
See also CDBLB Before 1660; DAM POET;
DLB 58, 172; RGEL 2

Defoe, Daniel 1660(?)-1731 .... **LC 1, 42, 108; WLC 2**
  See also AAYA 27; BRW 3; BRWR 1; BYA 4; CDBLB 1660-1789; CLR 61; DA; DA3; DAB; DAC; DAM MST, NOV; DLB 39, 95, 101, 336; JRDA; LAIT 1; LMFS 1; MAICYA 1, 2; NFS 9, 13; RGEL 2; SATA 22; TEA; WCH; WLIT 3
de Gouges, Olympe
  See de Gouges, Olympe
de Gouges, Olympe 1748-1793 .... **LC 127**
  See also DLB 313
de Gourmont, Remy(-Marie-Charles)
  See Gourmont, Remy(-Marie-Charles) de
de Gournay, Marie le Jars
  1566-1645 .... **LC 98**
  See also DLB 327; FW
de Hartog, Jan 1914-2002 .... **CLC 19**
  See also CA 1-4R; CAAS 210; CANR 1; DFS 12
de Hostos, E. M.
  See Hostos (y Bonilla), Eugenio Maria de
de Hostos, Eugenio M.
  See Hostos (y Bonilla), Eugenio Maria de
Deighton, Len .... **CLC 4, 7, 22, 46**
  See Deighton, Leonard Cyril
  See also AAYA 6; BEST 89:2; BPFB 1; CD-BLB 1960 to Present; CMW 4; CN 1, 2, 3, 4, 5, 6, 7; CPW; DLB 87
Deighton, Leonard Cyril 1929-
  See Deighton, Len
  See also AAYA 57; CA 9-12R; CANR 19, 33, 68; DA3; DAM NOV, POP; MTCW 1, 2; MTFW 2005
Dekker, Thomas 1572(?)-1632 ..... **DC 12; LC 22**
  See also CDBLB Before 1660; DAM DRAM; DLB 62, 172; LMFS 1; RGEL 2
de Laclos, Pierre Ambroise Franols
  See Laclos, Pierre-Ambroise Francois
Delacroix, (Ferdinand-Victor-)Eugene
  1798-1863 .... **NCLC 133**
  See also EW 5
Delafield, E. M. .... **TCLC 61**
  See Dashwood, Edmee Elizabeth Monica de la Pasture
  See also DLB 34; RHW
de la Mare, Walter (John)
  1873-1956 ..... **PC 77; SSC 14; TCLC 4, 53; WLC 2**
  See also CA 163; CDBLB 1914-1945; CLR 23; CWRI 5; DA3; DAB; DAC; DAM MST, POET; DLB 19, 153, 162, 255, 284; EWL 3; EXPP; HGG; MAICYA 1, 2; MTCW 2; MTFW 2005; RGEL 2; RGSF 2; SATA 16; SUFW 1; TEA; WCH
de Lamartine, Alphonse (Marie Louis Prat)
  See Lamartine, Alphonse (Marie Louis Prat) de
Delaney, Franey
  See O'Hara, John (Henry)
Delaney, Shelagh 1939- .... **CLC 29**
  See also CA 17-20R; CANR 30, 67; CBD; CD 5, 6; CDBLB 1960 to Present; CWD; DAM DRAM; DFS 7; DLB 13; MTCW 1
Delany, Martin Robison
  1812-1885 .... **NCLC 93**
  See also DLB 50; RGAL 4
Delany, Mary (Granville Pendarves)
  1700-1788 .... **LC 12**
Delany, Samuel R., Jr. 1942- .... **BLC 1:1; CLC 8, 14, 38, 141**
  See also AAYA 24; AFAW 2; BPFB 1; BW 2, 3; CA 81-84; CANR 27, 43, 116, 172; CN 2, 3, 4, 5, 6, 7; DAM MULT; DLB 8, 33; FANT; MAL 5; MTCW 1, 2; RGAL 4; SATA 92; SCFW 1, 2; SFW 4; SUFW 2

Delany, Samuel Ray
  See Delany, Samuel R., Jr.
de la Parra, (Ana) Teresa (Sonojo)
  1890(?)-1936 .... **TCLC 185**
  See Parra Sanojo, Ana Teresa de la
  See also CA 178; HW 2
De La Ramee, Marie Louise 1839-1908
  See Ouida
  See also CA 204; SATA 20
de la Roche, Mazo 1879-1961 .... **CLC 14**
  See also CA 85-88; CANR 30; DLB 68; RGEL 2; RHW; SATA 64
De La Salle, Innocent
  See Hartmann, Sadakichi
de Laureamont, Comte
  See Lautreamont
Delbanco, Nicholas 1942- ..... **CLC 6, 13, 167**
  See also CA 189; 17-20R, 189; 2; CANR 29, 55, 116, 150; CN 7; DLB 6, 234
Delbanco, Nicholas Franklin
  See Delbanco, Nicholas
del Castillo, Michel 1933- .... **CLC 38**
  See also CA 109; CANR 77
Deledda, Grazia (Cosima)
  1875(?)-1936 .... **TCLC 23**
  See also CA 205; CAAE 123; DLB 264, 329; EWL 3; RGWL 2, 3; WLIT 7
Deleuze, Gilles 1925-1995 .... **TCLC 116**
  See also DLB 296
Delgado, Abelardo (Lalo) B(arrientos)
  1930-2004 .... **HLC 1**
  See also CA 131; 15; CAAS 230; CANR 90; DAM MST, MULT; DLB 82; HW 1, 2
Delibes, Miguel .... **CLC 8, 18**
  See Delibes Setien, Miguel
  See also DLB 322; EWL 3
Delibes Setien, Miguel 1920-
  See Delibes, Miguel
  See also CA 45-48, CANR 1, 32; CWW 2; HW 1; MTCW 1
DeLillo, Don 1936- ..... **CLC 8, 10, 13, 27, 39, 54, 76, 143, 210, 213**
  See also AMWC 2; AMWS 6; BEST 89:1; BPFB 1; CA 81-84; CANR 21, 76, 92, 133, 173; CN 3, 4, 5, 6, 7; CPW; DA3; DAM NOV, POP; DLB 6, 173; EWL 3; MAL 5; MTCW 1, 2; MTFW 2005; RGAL 4; TUS
de Lisser, H. G.
  See De Lisser, H(erbert) G(eorge)
  See also DLB 117
De Lisser, H(erbert) G(eorge)
  1878-1944 .... **TCLC 12**
  See de Lisser, H. G.
  See also BW 2; CA 152; CAAE 109
Deloire, Pierre
  See Peguy, Charles (Pierre)
Deloney, Thomas 1543(?)-1600 .... **LC 41; PC 79**
  See also DLB 167; RGEL 2
Deloria, Ella (Cara) 1889-1971(?) ..... **NNAL**
  See also CA 152; DAM MULT; DLB 175
Deloria, Vine, Jr. 1933-2005 .... **CLC 21, 122; NNAL**
  See also CA 53-56; CAAS 245; CANR 5, 20, 48, 98; DAM MULT; DLB 175; MTCW 1; SATA 21; SATA-Obit 171
Deloria, Vine Victor, Jr.
  See Deloria, Vine, Jr.
del Valle-Inclan, Ramon (Maria)
  See Valle-Inclan, Ramon (Maria) del
  See also DLB 322
Del Vecchio, John M(ichael) 1947- .. **CLC 29**
  See also CA 110; DLBD 9
de Man, Paul (Adolph Michel)
  1919-1983 .... **CLC 55**
  See also CA 128; CAAS 111; CANR 61; DLB 67; MTCW 1, 2

DeMarinis, Rick 1934- .... **CLC 54**
  See also CA 184; 57-60, 184; 24; CANR 9, 25, 50, 160; DLB 218; TCWW 2
de Maupassant, (Henri Rene Albert) Guy
  See Maupassant, (Henri Rene Albert) Guy de
Dembry, R. Emmet
  See Murfree, Mary Noailles
Demby, William 1922- ...... **BLC 1:1; CLC 53**
  See also BW 1, 3; CA 81-84; CANR 81; DAM MULT; DLB 33
de Menton, Francisco
  See Chin, Frank (Chew, Jr.)
Demetrius of Phalerum c.
  307B.C.- .... **CMLC 34**
Demijohn, Thom
  See Disch, Thomas M.
De Mille, James 1833-1880 .... **NCLC 123**
  See also DLB 99, 251
Deming, Richard 1915-1983
  See Queen, Ellery
  See also CA 9-12R; CANR 3, 94; SATA 24
Democritus c. 460B.C.-c. 370B.C. . **CMLC 47**
de Montaigne, Michel (Eyquem)
  See Montaigne, Michel (Eyquem) de
de Montherlant, Henry (Milon)
  See Montherlant, Henry (Milon) de
Demosthenes 384B.C.-322B.C. ... **CMLC 13**
  See also AW 1; DLB 176; RGWL 2, 3; WLIT 8
de Musset, (Louis Charles) Alfred
  See Musset, Alfred de
de Natale, Francine
  See Malzberg, Barry N(athaniel)
de Navarre, Marguerite 1492-1549 ... **LC 61; SSC 85**
  See Marguerite d'Angouleme; Marguerite de Navarre
  See also DLB 327
Denby, Edwin (Orr) 1903-1983 .... **CLC 48**
  See also CA 138; CAAS 110; CP 1
de Nerval, Gerard
  See Nerval, Gerard de
Denham, John 1615-1669 .... **LC 73**
  See also DLB 58, 126; RGEL 2
Denis, Julio
  See Cortazar, Julio
Denmark, Harrison
  See Zelazny, Roger
Dennis, John 1658-1734 .... **LC 11**
  See also DLB 101; RGEL 2
Dennis, Nigel (Forbes) 1912-1989 ...... **CLC 8**
  See also CA 25-28R; CANR 3; CN 1, 2, 3, 4; DLB 13, 15, 233; EWL 3; MTCW 1
Dent, Lester 1904-1959 .... **TCLC 72**
  See also CA 161; CAAE 112; CMW 4; DLB 306; SFW 4
De Palma, Brian 1940- .... **CLC 20, 247**
  See also CA 109
De Palma, Brian Russell
  See De Palma, Brian
de Pizan, Christine
  See Christine de Pizan
  See also FL 1:1
De Quincey, Thomas 1785-1859 ..... **NCLC 4, 87**
  See also BRW 4; CDBLB 1789-1832; DLB 110, 144; RGEL 2
Deren, Eleanora 1908(?)-1961
  See Deren, Maya
  See also CA 192; CAAS 111
Deren, Maya .... **CLC 16, 102**
  See Deren, Eleanora

Doblin, Alfred .... **TCLC 13**
　See Doeblin, Alfred
　See also CDWLB 2; EWL 3; RGWL 2, 3

Dobroliubov, Nikolai Aleksandrovich
　See Dobrolyubov, Nikolai Alexandrovich
　See also DLB 277

Dobrolyubov, Nikolai Alexandrovich
　1836-1861 .... **NCLC 5**
　See Dobroliubov, Nikolai Aleksandrovich

Dobson, Austin 1840-1921 .... **TCLC 79**
　See also DLB 35, 144

Dobyns, Stephen 1941- .... **CLC 37, 233**
　See also AMWS 13; CA 45-48; CANR 2,
　18, 99; CMW 4; CP 4, 5, 6, 7; PFS 23

Doctorow, Edgar Laurence
　See Doctorow, E.L.

Doctorow, E.L. 1931- . **CLC 6, 11, 15, 18, 37,
　44, 65, 113, 214**
　See also AAYA 22; AITN 2; AMWS 4;
　BEST 89:3; BPFB 1; CA 45-48; CANR
　2, 33, 51, 76, 97, 133, 170; CDALB 1968-
　1988; CN 3, 4, 5, 6, 7; CPW; DA3; DAM
　NOV, POP; DLB 2, 28, 173; DLBY 1980;
　EWL 3; LAIT 3; MAL 5; MTCW 1, 2;
　MTFW 2005; NFS 6; RGAL 4; RGHL;
　RHW; TCLE 1:1; TCWW 1, 2; TUS

Dodgson, Charles L(utwidge) 1832-1898
　See Carroll, Lewis
　See also CLR 2; DA; DA3; DAB; DAC;
　DAM MST, NOV, POET; MAICYA 1, 2;
　SATA 100; YABC 2

Dodsley, Robert 1703-1764 .... **LC 97**
　See also DLB 95; RGEL 2

Dodson, Owen (Vincent)
　1914-1983 .... **BLC 1:1; CLC 79**
　See also BW 1; CA 65-68; CAAS 110;
　CANR 24; DAM MULT; DLB 76

Doeblin, Alfred 1878-1957 .... **TCLC 13**
　See Doblin, Alfred
　See also CA 141; CAAE 110; DLB 66

Doerr, Harriet 1910-2002 .... **CLC 34**
　See also CA 122; CAAE 117; CAAS 213;
　CANR 47; INT CA-122; LATS 1:2

Domecq, H(onorio Bustos)
　See Bioy Casares, Adolfo

Domecq, H(onorio) Bustos
　See Bioy Casares, Adolfo; Borges, Jorge
　Luis

Domini, Rey
　See Lorde, Audre
　See also GLL 1

Dominique
　See Proust, (Valentin-Louis-George-Eugene)
　Marcel

Don, A
　See Stephen, Sir Leslie

Donaldson, Stephen R. 1947- ... **CLC 46, 138**
　See also AAYA 36; BPFB 1; CA 89-92;
　CANR 13, 55, 99; CPW; DAM POP;
　FANT; INT CANR-13; SATA 121; SFW
　4; SUFW 1, 2

Donleavy, J(ames) P(atrick) 1926- .... **CLC 1,
　4, 6, 10, 45**
　See also AITN 2; BPFB 1; CA 9-12R;
　CANR 24, 49, 62, 80, 124; CBD; CD 5,
　6; CN 1, 2, 3, 4, 5, 6, 7; DLB 6, 173; INT
　CANR-24; MAL 5; MTCW 1, 2; MTFW
　2005; RGAL 4

Donnadieu, Marguerite
　See Duras, Marguerite

Donne, John 1572-1631 ... **LC 10, 24, 91; PC
　1, 43; WLC 2**
　See also AAYA 67; BRW 1; BRWC 1;
　BRWR 2; CDBLB Before 1660; DA;
　DAB; DAC; DAM MST, POET; DLB
　121, 151; EXPP; PAB; PFS 2, 11; RGEL
　3; TEA; WLIT 3; WP

Donnell, David 1939(?)- .... **CLC 34**
　See also CA 197

Donoghue, Denis 1928- .... **CLC 209**
　See also CA 17-20R; CANR 16, 102

Donoghue, Emma 1969- .... **CLC 239**
　See also CA 155; CANR 103, 152; DLB
　267; GLL 2; SATA 101

Donoghue, P.S.
　See Hunt, E. Howard

Donoso (Yanez), Jose 1924-1996 ... **CLC 4, 8,
　11, 32, 99; HLC 1; SSC 34; TCLC 133**
　See also CA 81-84; CAAS 155; CANR 32,
　73; CDWLB 3; CWW 2; DAM MULT;
　DLB 113; EWL 3; HW 1, 2; LAW; LAWS
　1; MTCW 1, 2; MTFW 2005; RGSF 2;
　WLIT 1

Donovan, John 1928-1992 .... **CLC 35**
　See also AAYA 20; CA 97-100; CAAS 137;
　CLR 3; MAICYA 1, 2; SATA 72; SATA-
　Brief 29; YAW

Don Roberto
　See Cunninghame Graham, Robert
　(Gallnigad) Bontine

Doolittle, Hilda 1886-1961 . **CLC 3, 8, 14, 31,
　34, 73; PC 5; WLC 3**
　See H. D.
　See also AAYA 66; AMWS 1; CA 97-100;
　CANR 35, 131; DA; DAC; DAM MST,
　POET; DLB 4, 45; EWL 3; FW; GLL 1;
　LMFS 2; MAL 5; MBL; MTCW 1, 2;
　MTFW 2005; PFS 6; RGAL 4

Doppo, Kunikida .... **TCLC 99**
　See Kunikida Doppo

Dorfman, Ariel 1942- .... **CLC 48, 77, 189;
　HLC 1**
　See also CA 130; CAAE 124; CANR 67,
　70, 135; CWW 2; DAM MULT; DFS 4;
　EWL 3; HW 1, 2; INT CA-130; WLIT 1

Dorn, Edward (Merton)
　1929-1999 .... **CLC 10, 18**
　See also CA 93-96; CAAS 187; CANR 42,
　79; CP 1, 2, 3, 4, 5, 6, 7; DLB 5; INT
　CA-93-96; WP

Dor-Ner, Zvi .... **CLC 70**

Dorris, Michael 1945-1997 .... **CLC 109;
　NNAL**
　See also AAYA 20; BEST 90:1; BYA 12;
　CA 102; CAAS 157; CANR 19, 46, 75;
　CLR 58; DA3; DAM MULT, NOV; DLB
　175; LAIT 5; MTCW 2; MTFW 2005;
　NFS 3; RGAL 4; SATA 75; SATA-Obit
　94; TCWW 2; YAW

Dorris, Michael A.
　See Dorris, Michael

Dorsan, Luc
　See Simenon, Georges (Jacques Christian)

Dorsange, Jean
　See Simenon, Georges (Jacques Christian)

Dorset
　See Sackville, Thomas

Dos Passos, John (Roderigo)
　1896-1970 . **CLC 1, 4, 8, 11, 15, 25, 34,
　82; WLC 2**
　See also AMW; BPFB 1; CA 1-4R; CAAS
　29-32R; CANR 3; CDALB 1929-1941;
　DA; DA3; DAB; DAC; DAM MST, NOV;
　DLB 4, 9, 274, 316; DLBD 1, 15; DLBY
　1996; EWL 3; MAL 5; MTCW 1, 2;
　MTFW 2005; NFS 14; RGAL 4; TUS

Dossage, Jean
　See Simenon, Georges (Jacques Christian)

Dostoevsky, Fedor Mikhailovich
　1821-1881 .. **NCLC 2, 7, 21, 33, 43, 119,
　167; SSC 2, 33, 44; WLC 2**
　See Dostoevsky, Fyodor
　See also AAYA 40; DA; DA3; DAB; DAC;
　DAM MST, NOV; EW 7; EXPN; NFS 3,
　8; RGSF 2; RGWL 2, 3; SSFS 8; TWA

Dostoevsky, Fyodor
　See Dostoevsky, Fedor Mikhailovich
　See also DLB 238; LATS 1:1; LMFS 1, 2

Doty, Mark 1953(?)- .... **CLC 176; PC 53**
　See also AMWS 11; CA 183; 161, 183;
　CANR 110, 173; CP 7

Doty, Mark A.
　See Doty, Mark

Doty, Mark Alan
　See Doty, Mark

Doty, M.R.
　See Doty, Mark

Doughty, Charles M(ontagu)
　1843-1926 .... **TCLC 27**
　See also CA 178; CAAE 115; DLB 19, 57,
　174

Douglas, Ellen .... **CLC 73**
　See Haxton, Josephine Ayres; Williamson,
　Ellen Douglas
　See also CN 5, 6, 7; CSW; DLB 292

Douglas, Gavin 1475(?)-1522 .... **LC 20**
　See also DLB 132; RGEL 2

Douglas, George
　See Brown, George Douglas
　See also RGEL 2

Douglas, Keith (Castellain)
　1920-1944 .... **TCLC 40**
　See also BRW 7; CA 160; DLB 27; EWL
　3; PAB; RGEL 2

Douglas, Leonard
　See Bradbury, Ray

Douglas, Michael
　See Crichton, Michael

Douglas, (George) Norman
　1868-1952 .... **TCLC 68**
　See also BRW 6; CA 157; CAAE 119; DLB
　34, 195; RGEL 2

Douglas, William
　See Brown, George Douglas

Douglass, Frederick 1817(?)-1895 .. **BLC 1:1;
　NCLC 7, 55, 141; WLC 2**
　See also AAYA 48; AFAW 1, 2; AMWC 1;
　AMWS 3; CDALB 1640-1865; DA; DA3;
　DAC; DAM MST, MULT; DLB 1, 43, 50,
　79, 243; FW; LAIT 2; NCFS 2; RGAL 4;
　SATA 29

Dourado, (Waldomiro Freitas) Autran
　1926- .... **CLC 23, 60**
　See also CA 25-28R, 179; CANR 34, 81;
　DLB 145, 307; HW 2

Dourado, Waldomiro Freitas Autran
　See Dourado, (Waldomiro Freitas) Autran

Dove, Rita 1952- . **BLCS; BLC 2:1; CLC 50,
　81; PC 6**
　See also AAYA 46; AMWS 4; BW 2; CA
　109; 19; CANR 27, 42, 68, 76, 97, 132;
　CDALBS; CP 5, 6, 7; CSW; CWP; DA3;
　DAM MULT, POET; DLB 120; EWL 3;
　EXPP; MAL 5; MTCW 2; MTFW 2005;
　PFS 1, 15; RGAL 4

Dove, Rita Frances
　See Dove, Rita

Doveglion
　See Villa, Jose Garcia

Dowell, Coleman 1925-1985 .... **CLC 60**
　See also CA 25-28R; CAAS 117; CANR
　10; DLB 130; GLL 2

Downing, Major Jack
　See Smith, Seba

Dowson, Ernest (Christopher)
　1867-1900 .... **TCLC 4**
　See also CA 150; CAAE 105; DLB 19, 135;
　RGEL 2

Doyle, A. Conan
　See Doyle, Sir Arthur Conan

Doyle, Sir Arthur Conan
　1859-1930 ..... **SSC 12, 83, 95; TCLC 7;
　WLC 2**
　See Conan Doyle, Arthur
　See also AAYA 14; BRWS 2; CA 122;
　CAAE 104; CANR 131; CDBLB 1890-
　1914; CLR 106; CMW 4; DA; DA3;

Dunn, Douglas (Eaglesham) 1942- .... **CLC 6, 40**
See also BRWS 10; CA 45-48; CANR 2, 33, 126; CP 1, 2, 3, 4, 5, 6, 7; DLB 40; MTCW 1

Dunn, Katherine 1945- .... **CLC 71**
See also CA 33-36R; CANR 72; HGG; MTCW 2; MTFW 2005

Dunn, Stephen 1939- .... **CLC 36, 206**
See also AMWS 11; CA 33-36R; CANR 12, 48, 53, 105; CP 3, 4, 5, 6, 7; DLB 105; PFS 21

Dunn, Stephen Elliott
See Dunn, Stephen

Dunne, Finley Peter 1867-1936 ...... **TCLC 28**
See also CA 178; CAAE 108; DLB 11, 23; RGAL 4

Dunne, John Gregory 1932-2003 ..... **CLC 28**
See also CA 25-28R; CAAS 222; CANR 14, 50; CN 5, 6, 7; DLBY 1980

Dunsany, Lord .... **TCLC 2, 59**
See Dunsany, Edward John Moreton Drax Plunkett
See also DLB 77, 153, 156, 255; FANT; IDTP; RGEL 2; SFW 4; SUFW 1

Dunsany, Edward John Moreton Drax Plunkett 1878-1957
See Dunsany, Lord
See also CA 148; CAAE 104; DLB 10; MTCW 2

Duns Scotus, John 1266(?)-1308 ... **CMLC 59**
See also DLB 115

du Perry, Jean
See Simenon, Georges (Jacques Christian)

Durang, Christopher 1949- .... **CLC 27, 38**
See also CA 105; CAD; CANR 50, 76, 130; CD 5, 6; MTCW 2; MTFW 2005

Durang, Christopher Ferdinand
See Durang, Christopher

Duras, Claire de 1777-1832 .... **NCLC 154**

Duras, Marguerite 1914-1996 .. **CLC 3, 6, 11, 20, 34, 40, 68, 100; SSC 40**
See also BPFB 1; CA 25-28R; CAAS 151; CANR 50; CWW 2; DFS 21; DLB 83, 321; EWL 3; FL 1:5; GFL 1789 to the Present; IDFW 4; MTCW 1, 2; RGWL 2, 3; TWA

Durban, (Rosa) Pam 1947- .... **CLC 39**
See also CA 123; CANR 98; CSW

Durcan, Paul 1944- .... **CLC 43, 70**
See also CA 134; CANR 123; CP 1, 5, 6, 7; DAM POET; EWL 3

d'Urfe, Honore
See Urfe, Honore d'

Durfey, Thomas 1653-1723 .... **LC 94**
See also DLB 80; RGEL 2

Durkheim, Emile 1858-1917 .... **TCLC 55**
See also CA 249

Durrell, Lawrence (George) 1912-1990 ..... **CLC 1, 4, 6, 8, 13, 27, 41**
See also BPFB 1; BRWS 1; CA 9-12R; CAAS 132; CANR 40, 77; CDBLB 1945-1960; CN 1, 2, 3, 4; CP 1, 2, 3, 4, 5; DAM NOV; DLB 15, 27, 204; DLBY 1990; EWL 3; MTCW 1, 2; RGEL 2; SFW 4; TEA

Durrenmatt, Friedrich
See Duerrenmatt, Friedrich
See also CDWLB 2; EW 13; EWL 3; RGHL; RGWL 2, 3

Dutt, Michael Madhusudan 1824-1873 .... **NCLC 118**

Dutt, Toru 1856-1877 .... **NCLC 29**
See also DLB 240

Dwight, Timothy 1752-1817 .... **NCLC 13**
See also DLB 37; RGAL 4

Dworkin, Andrea 1946-2005 ..... **CLC 43, 123**
See also CA 77-80; 21; CAAS 238; CANR 16, 39, 76, 96; FL 1:5; FW; GLL 1; INT CANR-16; MTCW 1, 2; MTFW 2005

Dwyer, Deanna
See Koontz, Dean R.

Dwyer, K. R.
See Koontz, Dean R.

Dybek, Stuart 1942- .... **CLC 114; SSC 55**
See also CA 97-100; CANR 39; DLB 130; SSFS 23

Dye, Richard
See De Voto, Bernard (Augustine)

Dyer, Geoff 1958- .... **CLC 149**
See also CA 125; CANR 88

Dyer, George 1755-1841 .... **NCLC 129**
See also DLB 93

Dylan, Bob 1941- .... **CLC 3, 4, 6, 12, 77; PC 37**
See also CA 41-44R; CANR 108; CP 1, 2, 3, 4, 5, 6, 7; DLB 16

Dyson, John 1943- .... **CLC 70**
See also CA 144

Dzyubin, Eduard Georgievich 1895-1934
See Bagritsky, Eduard
See also CA 170

E. V. L.
See Lucas, E(dward) V(errall)

Eagleton, Terence (Francis) 1943- .. **CLC 63, 132**
See also CA 57-60; CANR 7, 23, 68, 115; DLB 242; LMFS 2; MTCW 1, 2; MTFW 2005

Eagleton, Terry
See Eagleton, Terence (Francis)

Early, Jack
See Scoppettone, Sandra
See also GLL 1

East, Michael
See West, Morris L(anglo)

Eastaway, Edward
See Thomas, (Philip) Edward

Eastlake, William (Derry) 1917-1997 .... **CLC 8**
See also CA 5-8R; 1; CAAS 158; CANR 5, 63; CN 1, 2, 3, 4, 5, 6; DLB 6, 206; INT CANR-5; MAL 5; TCWW 1, 2

Eastman, Charles A(lexander) 1858-1939 .... **NNAL; TCLC 55**
See also CA 179; CANR 91; DAM MULT; DLB 175; YABC 1

Eaton, Edith Maude 1865-1914 .... **AAL**
See Far, Sui Sin
See also CA 154; DLB 221, 312; FW

Eaton, (Lillie) Winnifred 1875-1954 .... **AAL**
See also CA 217; DLB 221, 312; RGAL 4

Eberhart, Richard 1904-2005 ...... **CLC 3, 11, 19, 56; PC 76**
See also AMW; CA 1-4R; CAAS 240; CANR 2, 125; CDALB 1941-1968; CP 1, 2, 3, 4, 5, 6, 7; DAM POET; DLB 48; MAL 5; MTCW 1; RGAL 4

Eberhart, Richard Ghormley
See Eberhart, Richard

Eberstadt, Fernanda 1960- .... **CLC 39**
See also CA 136; CANR 69, 128

Ebner, Margaret c. 1291-1351 ...... **CMLC 98**

Echegaray (y Eizaguirre), Jose (Maria Waldo) 1832-1916 .... **HLCS 1; TCLC 4**
See also CAAE 104; CANR 32; DLB 329; EWL 3; HW 1; MTCW 1

Echeverria, (Jose) Esteban (Antonino) 1805-1851 .... **NCLC 18**
See also LAW

Echo
See Proust, (Valentin-Louis-George-Eugene) Marcel

Eckert, Allan W. 1931- .... **CLC 17**
See also AAYA 18; BYA 2; CA 13-16R; CANR 14, 45; INT CANR-14; MAICYA 2; MAICYAS 1; SAAS 21; SATA 29, 91; SATA-Brief 27

Eckhart, Meister 1260(?)-1327(?) .. **CMLC 9, 80**
See also DLB 115; LMFS 1

Eckmar, F. R.
See de Hartog, Jan

Eco, Umberto 1932- .... **CLC 28, 60, 142, 248**
See also BEST 90:1; BPFB 1; CA 77-80; CANR 12, 33, 55, 110, 131; CPW; CWW 2; DA3; DAM NOV, POP; DLB 196, 242; EWL 3; MSW; MTCW 1, 2; MTFW 2005; NFS 22; RGWL 3; WLIT 7

Eddison, E(ric) R(ucker) 1882-1945 .... **TCLC 15**
See also CA 156; CAAE 109; DLB 255; FANT; SFW 4; SUFW 1

Eddy, Mary (Ann Morse) Baker 1821-1910 .... **TCLC 71**
See also CA 174; CAAE 113

Edel, (Joseph) Leon 1907-1997 .. **CLC 29, 34**
See also CA 1-4R; CAAS 161; CANR 1, 22, 112; DLB 103; INT CANR-22

Eden, Emily 1797-1869 .... **NCLC 10**

Edgar, David 1948- .... **CLC 42**
See also CA 57-60; CANR 12, 61, 112; CBD; CD 5, 6; DAM DRAM; DFS 15; DLB 13, 233; MTCW 1

Edgerton, Clyde (Carlyle) 1944- ...... **CLC 39**
See also AAYA 17; CA 134; CAAE 118; CANR 64, 125; CN 7; CSW; DLB 278; INT CA-134; TCLE 1:1; YAW

Edgeworth, Maria 1768-1849 ... **NCLC 1, 51, 158; SSC 86**
See also BRWS 3; DLB 116, 159, 163; FL 1:3; FW; RGEL 2; SATA 21; TEA; WLIT 3

Edmonds, Paul
See Kuttner, Henry

Edmonds, Walter D(umaux) 1903-1998 .... **CLC 35**
See also BYA 2; CA 5-8R; CANR 2; CWRI 5; DLB 9; LAIT 1; MAICYA 1, 2; MAL 5; RHW; SAAS 4; SATA 1, 27; SATA-Obit 99

Edmondson, Wallace
See Ellison, Harlan

Edson, Margaret 1961- ...... **CLC 199; DC 24**
See also CA 190; DFS 13; DLB 266

Edson, Russell 1935- .... **CLC 13**
See also CA 33-36R; CANR 115; CP 2, 3, 4, 5, 6, 7; DLB 244; WP

Edwards, Bronwen Elizabeth
See Rose, Wendy

Edwards, G(erald) B(asil) 1899-1976 .... **CLC 25**
See also CA 201; CAAS 110

Edwards, Gus 1939- .... **CLC 43**
See also CA 108; INT CA-108

Edwards, Jonathan 1703-1758 .... **LC 7, 54**
See also AMW; DA; DAC; DAM MST; DLB 24, 270; RGAL 4; TUS

Edwards, Sarah Pierpont 1710-1758 .. **LC 87**
See also DLB 200

Efron, Marina Ivanovna Tsvetaeva
See Tsvetaeva (Efron), Marina (Ivanovna)

Egeria fl. 4th cent. - .... **CMLC 70**

Eggers, Dave 1970- .... **CLC 241**
See also AAYA 56; CA 198; CANR 138; MTFW 2005

Egoyan, Atom 1960- .... **CLC 151**
See also AAYA 63; CA 157; CANR 151

Ehle, John (Marsden, Jr.) 1925- ...... **CLC 27**
See also CA 9-12R; CSW

Ehrenbourg, Ilya (Grigoryevich)
See Ehrenburg, Ilya (Grigoryevich)

Emerson, Mary Moody
1774-1863 .... **NCLC 66**

Emerson, Ralph Waldo 1803-1882 . **NCLC 1, 38, 98; PC 18; WLC 2**
See also AAYA 60; AMW; ANW; CDALB 1640-1865; DA; DA3; DAB; DAC; DAM MST, POET; DLB 1, 59, 73, 183, 223, 270; EXPP; LAIT 2; LMFS 1; NCFS 3; PFS 4, 17; RGAL 4; TUS; WP

Eminem 1972- .... **CLC 226**
See also CA 245

Eminescu, Mihail 1850-1889 .. **NCLC 33, 131**

Empedocles 5th cent. B.C.- .... **CMLC 50**
See also DLB 176

Empson, William 1906-1984 ... **CLC 3, 8, 19, 33, 34**
See also BRWS 2; CA 17-20R; CAAS 112; CANR 31, 61; CP 1, 2, 3; DLB 20; EWL 3; MTCW 1, 2; RGEL 2

Enchi, Fumiko (Ueda) 1905-1986 ..... **CLC 31**
See Enchi Fumiko
See also CA 129; CAAS 121; FW; MJW

Enchi Fumiko
See Enchi, Fumiko (Ueda)
See also DLB 182; EWL 3

Ende, Michael (Andreas Helmuth)
1929-1995 .... **CLC 31**
See also BYA 5; CA 124; CAAE 118; CAAS 149; CANR 36, 110; CLR 14; DLB 75; MAICYA 1, 2; MAICYAS 1; SATA 61, 130; SATA-Brief 42; SATA-Obit 86

Endo, Shusaku 1923-1996 ..... **CLC 7, 14, 19, 54, 99; SSC 48; TCLC 152**
See Endo Shusaku
See also CA 29-32R; CAAS 153; CANR 21, 54, 131; DA3; DAM NOV; MTCW 1, 2; MTFW 2005; RGSF 2; RGWL 2, 3

Endo Shusaku
See Endo, Shusaku
See also CWW 2; DLB 182; EWL 3

Engel, Marian 1933-1985 .... **CLC 36; TCLC 137**
See also CA 25-28R; CANR 12; CN 2, 3; DLB 53; FW; INT CANR-12

Engelhardt, Frederick
See Hubbard, L. Ron

Engels, Friedrich 1820-1895 .. **NCLC 85, 114**
See also DLB 129; LATS 1.1

Enright, D(ennis) J(oseph)
1920-2002 .... **CLC 4, 8, 31**
See also CA 1-4R; CAAS 211; CANR 1, 42, 83; CN 1, 2; CP 1, 2, 3, 4, 5, 6, 7; DLB 27; EWL 3; SATA 25; SATA-Obit 140

Ensler, Eve 1953- .... **CLC 212**
See also CA 172; CANR 126, 163; DFS 23

Enzensberger, Hans Magnus
1929- .... **CLC 43; PC 28**
See also CA 119; CAAE 116; CANR 103; CWW 2; EWL 3

Ephron, Nora 1941- .... **CLC 17, 31**
See also AAYA 35; AITN 2; CA 65-68; CANR 12, 39, 83, 161; DFS 22

Epicurus 341B.C.-270B.C. .... **CMLC 21**
See also DLB 176

Epinay, Louise d' 1726-1783 .... **LC 138**
See also DLB 313

Epsilon
See Betjeman, John

Epstein, Daniel Mark 1948- .... **CLC 7**
See also CA 49-52; CANR 2, 53, 90

Epstein, Jacob 1956- .... **CLC 19**
See also CA 114

Epstein, Jean 1897-1953 .... **TCLC 92**

Epstein, Joseph 1937- .... **CLC 39, 204**
See also AMWS 14; CA 119; CAAE 112; CANR 50, 65, 117, 164

Epstein, Leslie 1938- .... **CLC 27**
See also AMWS 12; CA 215; 73-76, 215; 12; CANR 23, 69, 162; DLB 299; RGHL

Equiano, Olaudah 1745(?)-1797 ..... **BLC 1:2; LC 16, 143**
See also AFAW 1, 2; CDWLB 3; DAM MULT; DLB 37, 50; WLIT 2

Erasmus, Desiderius 1469(?)-1536 ..... **LC 16, 93**
See also DLB 136; EW 2; LMFS 1; RGWL 2, 3; TWA

Erdman, Paul E. 1932-2007 .... **CLC 25**
See also AITN 1; CA 61-64; CAAS 259; CANR 13, 43, 84

Erdman, Paul Emil
See Erdman, Paul E.

Erdrich, Karen Louise
See Erdrich, Louise

Erdrich, Louise 1954- .... **CLC 39, 54, 120, 176; NNAL; PC 52**
See also AAYA 10, 47; AMWS 4; BEST 89:1; BPFB 1; CA 114; CANR 41, 62, 118, 138; CDALBS; CN 5, 6, 7; CP 6, 7; CPW; CWP; DA3; DAM MULT, NOV, POP; DLB 152, 175, 206; EWL 3; EXPP; FL 1:5; LAIT 5; LATS 1:2; MAL 5; MTCW 1, 2; MTFW 2005; NFS 5; PFS 14; RGAL 4; SATA 94, 141; SSFS 14, 22; TCWW 2

Erenburg, Ilya (Grigoryevich)
See Ehrenburg, Ilya (Grigoryevich)

Erickson, Stephen Michael
See Erickson, Steve

Erickson, Steve 1950- .... **CLC 64**
See also CA 129; CANR 60, 68, 136; MTFW 2005; SFW 4; SUFW 2

Erickson, Walter
See Fast, Howard

Ericson, Walter
See Fast, Howard

Eriksson, Buntel
See Bergman, Ingmar

Eriugena, John Scottus c. 810-877 .... **CMLC 65**
See also DLB 115

Ernaux, Annie 1940- .... **CLC 88, 184**
See also CA 147; CANR 93; MTFW 2005; NCFS 3, 5

Erskine, John 1879-1951 .... **TCLC 84**
See also CA 159; CAAE 112; DLB 9, 102; FANT

Erwin, Will
See Eisner, Will

Eschenbach, Wolfram von
See von Eschenbach, Wolfram
See also RGWL 3

Eseki, Bruno
See Mphahlele, Ezekiel

Esenin, S.A.
See Esenin, Sergei
See also EWL 3

Esenin, Sergei 1895-1925 .... **TCLC 4**
See Esenin, S.A.
See also CAAE 104; RGWL 2, 3

Esenin, Sergei Aleksandrovich
See Esenin, Sergei

Eshleman, Clayton 1935- .... **CLC 7**
See also CA 212; 33-36R, 212; 6; CANR 93; CP 1, 2, 3, 4, 5, 6, 7; DLB 5

Espada, Martin 1957- .... **PC 74**
See also CA 159; CANR 80; CP 7; EXPP; LLW; MAL 5; PFS 13, 16

Espriella, Don Manuel Alvarez
See Southey, Robert

Espriu, Salvador 1913-1985 .... **CLC 9**
See also CA 154; CAAS 115; DLB 134; EWL 3

Espronceda, Jose de 1808-1842 ..... **NCLC 39**

Esquivel, Laura 1950(?)- ... **CLC 141; HLCS 1**
See also AAYA 29; CA 143; CANR 68, 113, 161; DA3; DNFS 2; LAIT 3; LMFS 2; MTCW 2; MTFW 2005; NFS 5; WLIT 1

Esse, James
See Stephens, James

Esterbrook, Tom
See Hubbard, L. Ron

Esterhazy, Peter 1950- .... **CLC 251**
See also CA 140; CANR 137; CDWLB 4; CWW 2; DLB 232; EWL 3; RGWL 3

Estleman, Loren D. 1952- .... **CLC 48**
See also AAYA 27; CA 85-88; CANR 27, 74, 139; CMW 4; CPW; DA3; DAM NOV, POP; DLB 226; INT CANR-27; MTCW 1, 2; MTFW 2005; TCWW 1, 2

Etherege, Sir George 1636-1692 . **DC 23; LC 78**
See also BRW 2; DAM DRAM; DLB 80; PAB; RGEL 2

Euclid 306B.C.-283B.C. .... **CMLC 25**

Eugenides, Jeffrey 1960(?)- .... **CLC 81, 212**
See also AAYA 51; CA 144; CANR 120; MTFW 2005; NFS 24

Euripides c. 484B.C.-406B.C. .... **CMLC 23, 51; DC 4; WLCS**
See also AW 1; CDWLB 1; DA; DA3; DAB; DAC; DAM DRAM, MST; DFS 1, 4, 6; DLB 176; LAIT 1; LMFS 1; RGWL 2, 3; WLIT 8

Evan, Evin
See Faust, Frederick (Schiller)

Evans, Caradoc 1878-1945 ... **SSC 43; TCLC 85**
See also DLB 162

Evans, Evan
See Faust, Frederick (Schiller)

Evans, Marian
See Eliot, George

Evans, Mary Ann
See Eliot, George
See also NFS 20

Evarts, Esther
See Benson, Sally

Evelyn, John 1620-1706 .... **LC 144**
See also BRW 2; RGEL 2

Everett, Percival
See Everett, Percival L.
See also CSW

Everett, Percival L. 1956- .... **CLC 57**
See Everett, Percival
See also BW 2; CA 129; CANR 94, 134; CN 7; MTFW 2005

Everson, R(onald) G(ilmour)
1903-1992 .... **CLC 27**
See also CA 17-20R; CP 1, 2, 3, 4; DLB 88

Everson, William (Oliver)
1912-1994 .... **CLC 1, 5, 14**
See Antoninus, Brother
See also BG 1:2; CA 9-12R; CAAS 145; CANR 20; CP 2, 3, 4, 5; DLB 5, 16, 212; MTCW 1

Evtushenko, Evgenii Aleksandrovich
See Yevtushenko, Yevgeny (Alexandrovich)
See also CWW 2; RGWL 2, 3

Ewart, Gavin (Buchanan)
1916-1995 .... **CLC 13, 46**
See also BRWS 7; CA 89-92; CAAS 150; CANR 17, 46; CP 1, 2, 3, 4, 5, 6; DLB 40; MTCW 1

Ewers, Hanns Heinz 1871-1943 ..... **TCLC 12**
See also CA 149; CAAE 109

Ewing, Frederick R.
See Sturgeon, Theodore (Hamilton)

Ferling, Lawrence
See Ferlinghetti, Lawrence

Ferlinghetti, Lawrence 1919(?)- .... **CLC 2, 6, 10, 27, 111; PC 1**
See also AAYA 74; BG 1:2; CA 5-8R; CAD; CANR 3, 41, 73, 125, 172; CDALB 1941-1968; CP 1, 2, 3, 4, 5, 6, 7; DA3; DAM POET; DLB 5, 16; MAL 5; MTCW 1, 2; MTFW 2005; RGAL 4; WP

Ferlinghetti, Lawrence Monsanto
See Ferlinghetti, Lawrence

Fern, Fanny
See Parton, Sara Payson Willis

Fernandez, Vicente Garcia Huidobro
See Huidobro Fernandez, Vicente Garcia

Fernandez-Armesto, Felipe .... **CLC 70**
See Fernandez-Armesto, Felipe Fermin Ricardo
See also CANR 153

Fernandez-Armesto, Felipe Fermin Ricardo 1950-
See Fernandez-Armesto, Felipe
See also CA 142; CANR 93

Fernandez de Lizardi, Jose Joaquin
See Lizardi, Jose Joaquin Fernandez de

Ferre, Rosario 1938- ...... **CLC 139; HLCS 1; SSC 36, 106**
See also CA 131; CANR 55, 81, 134; CWW 2; DLB 145; EWL 3; HW 1, 2; LAWS 1; MTCW 2; MTFW 2005; WLIT 1

Ferrer, Gabriel (Francisco Victor) Miro
See Miro (Ferrer), Gabriel (Francisco Victor)

Ferrier, Susan (Edmonstone) 1782-1854 .... **NCLC 8**
See also DLB 116; RGEL 2

Ferrigno, Robert 1948(?)- .... **CLC 65**
See also CA 140; CANR 125, 161

Ferron, Jacques 1921-1985 .... **CLC 94**
See also CA 129; CAAE 117; CCA 1; DAC; DLB 60; EWL 3

Feuchtwanger, Lion 1884-1958 .... **TCLC 3**
See also CA 187; CAAE 104; DLB 66; EWL 3; RGHL

Feuerbach, Ludwig 1804-1872 ..... **NCLC 139**
See also DLB 133

Feuillet, Octave 1821-1890 .... **NCLC 45**
See also DLB 192

Feydeau, Georges (Leon Jules Marie) 1862-1921 .... **TCLC 22**
See also CA 152; CAAE 113; CANR 84; DAM DRAM; DLB 192; EWL 3; GFL 1789 to the Present; RGWL 2, 3

Fichte, Johann Gottlieb 1762-1814 .... **NCLC 62**
See also DLB 90

Ficino, Marsilio 1433-1499 .... **LC 12**
See also LMFS 1

Ficdeler, Hans
See Doeblin, Alfred

Fiedler, Leslie A(aron) 1917-2003 ..... **CLC 4, 13, 24**
See also AMWS 13; CA 9-12R; CAAS 212; CANR 7, 63; CN 1, 2, 3, 4, 5, 6; DLB 28, 67; EWL 3; MAL 5; MTCW 1, 2; RGAL 4; TUS

Field, Andrew 1938- .... **CLC 44**
See also CA 97-100; CANR 25

Field, Eugene 1850-1895 .... **NCLC 3**
See also DLB 23, 42, 140; DLBD 13; MAICYA 1, 2; RGAL 4; SATA 16

Field, Gans T.
See Wellman, Manly Wade

Field, Michael 1915-1971 .... **TCLC 43**
See also CAAS 29-32R

Fielding, Helen 1958- .... **CLC 146, 217**
See also AAYA 65; CA 172; CANR 127; DLB 231; MTFW 2005

Fielding, Henry 1707-1754 .... **LC 1, 46, 85; WLC 2**
See also BRW 3; BRWR 1; CDBLB 1660-1789; DA; DA3; DAB; DAC; DAM DRAM, MST, NOV; DLB 39, 84, 101; NFS 18; RGEL 2; TEA; WLIT 3

Fielding, Sarah 1710-1768 .... **LC 1, 44**
See also DLB 39; RGEL 2; TEA

Fields, W. C. 1880-1946 .... **TCLC 80**
See also DLB 44

Fierstein, Harvey (Forbes) 1954- ..... **CLC 33**
See also CA 129; CAAE 123; CAD; CD 5, 6; CPW; DA3; DAM DRAM, POP; DFS 6; DLB 266; GLL; MAL 5

Figes, Eva 1932- .... **CLC 31**
See also CA 53-56; CANR 4, 44, 83; CN 2, 3, 4, 5, 6, 7; DLB 14, 271; FW; RGHL

Filippo, Eduardo de
See de Filippo, Eduardo

Finch, Anne 1661-1720 ..... **LC 3, 137; PC 21**
See also BRWS 9; DLB 95

Finch, Robert (Duer Claydon) 1900-1995 .... **CLC 18**
See also CA 57-60; CANR 9, 24, 49; CP 1, 2, 3, 4, 5, 6; DLB 88

Findley, Timothy (Irving Frederick) 1930-2002 .... **CLC 27, 102**
See also CA 25-28R; CAAS 206; CANR 12, 42, 69, 109; CCA 1; CN 4, 5, 6, 7; DAC; DAM MST; DLB 53; FANT; RHW

Fink, William
See Mencken, H(enry) L(ouis)

Firbank, Louis 1942-
See Reed, Lou
See also CAAE 117

Firbank, (Arthur Annesley) Ronald 1886-1926 .... **TCLC 1**
See also BRWS 2; CA 177; CAAE 104; DLB 36; EWL 3; RGEL 2

Firdawsi, Abu al-Qasim
See Ferdowsi, Abu'l Qasem
See also WLIT 6

Fish, Stanley
See Fish, Stanley Eugene

Fish, Stanley E.
See Fish, Stanley Eugene

Fish, Stanley Eugene 1938- .... **CLC 142**
See also CA 132; CAAE 112; CANR 90; DLB 67

Fisher, Dorothy (Frances) Canfield 1879-1958 .... **TCLC 87**
See also CA 136; CAAE 114; CANR 80; CLR 71; CWRI 5; DLB 9, 102, 284; MAICYA 1, 2; MAL 5; YABC 1

Fisher, M(ary) F(rances) K(ennedy) 1908-1992 .... **CLC 76, 87**
See also AMWS 17; CA 77-80; CAAS 138; CANR 44; MTCW 2

Fisher, Roy 1930- .... **CLC 25**
See also CA 81-84; 10; CANR 16; CP 1, 2, 3, 4, 5, 6, 7; DLB 40

Fisher, Rudolph 1897-1934 ...... **BLC 1:2; HR 1:2; SSC 25; TCLC 11**
See also BW 1, 3; CA 124; CAAE 107; CANR 80; DAM MULT; DLB 51, 102

Fisher, Vardis (Alvero) 1895-1968 .... **CLC 7; TCLC 140**
See also CA 5-8R; CAAS 25-28R; CANR 68; DLB 9, 206; MAL 5; RGAL 4; TCWW 1, 2

Fiske, Tarleton
See Bloch, Robert (Albert)

Fitch, Clarke
See Sinclair, Upton

Fitch, John IV
See Cormier, Robert

Fitzgerald, Captain Hugh
See Baum, L(yman) Frank

FitzGerald, Edward 1809-1883 ...... **NCLC 9, 153; PC 79**
See also BRW 4; DLB 32; RGEL 2

Fitzgerald, F(rancis) Scott (Key) 1896-1940 ... **SSC 6, 31, 75; TCLC 1, 6, 14, 28, 55, 157; WLC 2**
See also AAYA 24; AITN 1; AMW; AMWC 2; AMWR 1; BPFB 1; CA 123; CAAE 110; CDALB 1917-1929; DA; DA3; DAB; DAC; DAM MST, NOV; DLB 4, 9, 86, 219, 273; DLBD 1, 15, 16; DLBY 1981, 1996; EWL 3; EXPN; EXPS; LAIT 3; MAL 5; MTCW 1, 2; MTFW 2005; NFS 2, 19, 20; RGAL 4; RGSF 2; SSFS 4, 15, 21, 25; TUS

Fitzgerald, Penelope 1916-2000 . **CLC 19, 51, 61, 143**
See also BRWS 5; CA 85-88; 10; CAAS 190; CANR 56, 86, 131; CN 3, 4, 5, 6, 7; DLB 14, 194, 326; EWL 3; MTCW 2; MTFW 2005

Fitzgerald, Robert (Stuart) 1910-1985 .... **CLC 39**
See also CA 1-4R; CAAS 114; CANR 1; CP 1, 2, 3, 4; DLBY 1980; MAL 5

FitzGerald, Robert D(avid) 1902-1987 .... **CLC 19**
See also CA 17-20R; CP 1, 2, 3, 4; DLB 260; RGEL 2

Fitzgerald, Zelda (Sayre) 1900-1948 .... **TCLC 52**
See also AMWS 9; CA 126; CAAE 117; DLBY 1984

Flanagan, Thomas (James Bonner) 1923-2002 .... **CLC 25, 52**
See also CA 108; CAAS 206; CANR 55; CN 3, 4, 5, 6, 7; DLBY 1980; INT CA-108; MTCW 1; RHW; TCLE 1:1

Flaubert, Gustave 1821-1880 .... **NCLC 2, 10, 19, 62, 66, 135, 179, 185; SSC 11, 60; WLC 2**
See also DA; DA3; DAB; DAC; DAM MST, NOV; DLB 119, 301; EW 7; EXPS; GFL 1789 to the Present; LAIT 2; LMFS 1; NFS 14; RGSF 2; RGWL 2, 3; SSFS 6; TWA

Flavius Josephus
See Josephus, Flavius

Flecker, Herman Elroy
See Flecker, (Herman) James Elroy

Flecker, (Herman) James Elroy 1884-1915 .... **TCLC 43**
See also CA 150; CAAE 109; DLB 10, 19; RGEL 2

Fleming, Ian 1908-1964 ... **CLC 3, 30; TCLC 193**
See also AAYA 26; BPFB 1; CA 5-8R, CANR 59; CDBLB 1945-1960; CMW 4; CPW; DA3; DAM POP; DLB 87, 201; MSW; MTCW 1, 2; MTFW 2005; RGEL 2; SATA 9; TEA; YAW

Fleming, Ian Lancaster
See Fleming, Ian

Fleming, Thomas 1927- .... **CLC 37**
See also CA 5-8R; CANR 10, 102, 155; INT CANR-10; SATA 8

Fleming, Thomas James
See Fleming, Thomas

Fletcher, John 1579-1625 .... **DC 6; LC 33**
See also BRW 2; CDBLB Before 1660; DLB 58; RGEL 2; TEA

Fletcher, John Gould 1886-1950 .... **TCLC 35**
See also CA 167; CAAE 107; DLB 4, 45; LMFS 2; MAL 5; RGAL 4

Fleur, Paul
See Pohl, Frederik

Flieg, Helmut
See Heym, Stefan

Flooglebuckle, Al
See Spiegelman, Art

Goines, Donald 1937(?)-1974 .... **BLC 1:2; CLC 80**
See also AITN 1; BW 1, 3; CA 124; CAAS 114; CANR 82; CMW 4; DA3; DAM MULT, POP; DLB 33

Gold, Herbert 1924- ... **CLC 4, 7, 14, 42, 152**
See also CA 9-12R; CANR 17, 45, 125; CN 1, 2, 3, 4, 5, 6, 7; DLB 2; DLBY 1981; MAL 5

Goldbarth, Albert 1948- .... **CLC 5, 38**
See also AMWS 12; CA 53-56; CANR 6, 40; CP 3, 4, 5, 6, 7; DLB 120

Goldberg, Anatol 1910-1982 .... **CLC 34**
See also CA 131; CAAS 117

Goldemberg, Isaac 1945- .... **CLC 52**
See also CA 69-72; 12; CANR 11, 32; EWL 3; HW 1; WLIT 1

Golding, Arthur 1536-1606 .... **LC 101**
See also DLB 136

Golding, William 1911-1993 . **CLC 1, 2, 3, 8, 10, 17, 27, 58, 81; WLC 3**
See also AAYA 5, 44; BPFB 2; BRWR 1; BRWS 1; BYA 2; CA 5-8R; CAAS 141; CANR 13, 33, 54; CD 5; CDBLB 1945-1960; CLR 94, 130; CN 1, 2, 3, 4; DA; DA3; DAB; DAC; DAM MST, NOV; DLB 15, 100, 255, 326, 330; EWL 3; EXPN; HGG; LAIT 4; MTCW 1, 2; MTFW 2005; NFS 2; RGEL 2; RHW; SFW 4; TEA; WLIT 4; YAW

Golding, William Gerald
See Golding, William

Goldman, Emma 1869-1940 .... **TCLC 13**
See also CA 150; CAAE 110; DLB 221; FW; RGAL 4; TUS

Goldman, Francisco 1954- .... **CLC 76**
See also CA 162

Goldman, William 1931- .... **CLC 1, 48**
See also BPFB 2; CA 9-12R; CANR 29, 69, 106; CN 1, 2, 3, 4, 5, 6, 7; DLB 44; FANT; IDFW 3, 4

Goldman, William W.
See Goldman, William

Goldmann, Lucien 1913-1970 .... **CLC 24**
See also CA 25-28; CAP 2

Goldoni, Carlo 1707-1793 .... **LC 4**
See also DAM DRAM; EW 4; RGWL 2, 3; WLIT 7

Goldsberry, Steven 1949- .... **CLC 34**
See also CA 131

Goldsmith, Oliver 1730(?)-1774 .... **DC 8; LC 2, 48, 122; PC 77; WLC 3**
See also BRW 3; CDBLB 1660-1789; DA; DAB; DAC; DAM DRAM, MST, NOV; POET; DFS 1; DLB 39, 89, 104, 109, 142, 336; IDTP; RGEL 2; SATA 26; TEA; WLIT 3

Goldsmith, Peter
See Priestley, J(ohn) B(oynton)

Goldstein, Rebecca 1950- .... **CLC 239**
See also CA 144; CANR 99, 165; TCLE 1:1

Goldstein, Rebecca Newberger
See Goldstein, Rebecca

Gombrowicz, Witold 1904-1969 .... **CLC 4, 7, 11, 49**
See also CA 19-20; CAAS 25-28R; CANR 105; CAP 2; CDWLB 4; DAM DRAM; DLB 215; EW 12; EWL 3; RGWL 2, 3; TWA

Gomez de Avellaneda, Gertrudis 1814-1873 .... **NCLC 111**
See also LAW

Gomez de la Serna, Ramon 1888-1963 .... **CLC 9**
See also CA 153; CAAS 116; CANR 79; EWL 3; HW 1, 2

Goncharov, Ivan Alexandrovich 1812-1891 .... **NCLC 1, 63**
See also DLB 238; EW 6; RGWL 2, 3

Goncourt, Edmond (Louis Antoine Huot) de 1822-1896 .... **NCLC 7**
See also DLB 123; EW 7; GFL 1789 to the Present; RGWL 2, 3

Goncourt, Jules (Alfred Huot) de 1830-1870 .... **NCLC 7**
See also DLB 123; EW 7; GFL 1789 to the Present; RGWL 2, 3

Gongora (y Argote), Luis de 1561-1627 .... **LC 72**
See also RGWL 2, 3

Gontier, Fernande 19(?)- .... **CLC 50**

Gonzalez Martinez, Enrique
See Gonzalez Martinez, Enrique
See also DLB 290

Gonzalez Martinez, Enrique 1871-1952 .... **TCLC 72**
See Gonzalez Martinez, Enrique
See also CA 166; CANR 81; EWL 3; HW 1, 2

Goodison, Lorna 1947- .... **BLC 2:2; PC 36**
See also CA 142; CANR 88; CP 5, 6, 7; CWP; DLB 157; EWL 3; PFS 25

Goodman, Allegra 1967- .... **CLC 241**
See also CA 204; CANR 162; DLB 244

Goodman, Paul 1911-1972 ..... **CLC 1, 2, 4, 7**
See also CA 19-20; CAAS 37-40R; CAD; CANR 34; CAP 2; CN 1; DLB 130, 246; MAL 5; MTCW 1; RGAL 4

GoodWeather, Hartley
See King, Thomas

Googe, Barnabe 1540-1594 .... **LC 94**
See also DLB 132; RGEL 2

Gordimer, Nadine 1923- ...... **CLC 3, 5, 7, 10, 18, 33, 51, 70, 123, 160, 161; SSC 17, 80; WLCS**
See also AAYA 39; AFW; BRWS 2; CA 5-8R; CANR 3, 28, 56, 88, 131; CN 1, 2, 3, 4, 5, 6, 7; DA; DA3; DAB; DAC; DAM MST, NOV; DLB 225, 326, 330; EWL 3; EXPS; INT CANR-28; LATS 1:2; MTCW 1, 2; MTFW 2005; NFS 4; RGEL 2; RGSF 2; SSFS 2, 14, 19; TWA; WLIT 2; YAW

Gordon, Adam Lindsay 1833-1870 .... **NCLC 21**
See also DLB 230

Gordon, Caroline 1895-1981 . **CLC 6, 13, 29, 83; SSC 15**
See also AMW; CA 11-12; CAAS 103; CANR 36; CAP 1; CN 1, 2; DLB 4, 9, 102; DLBD 17; DLBY 1981; EWL 3; MAL 5; MTCW 1, 2; MTFW 2005; RGAL 4; RGSF 2

Gordon, Charles William 1860-1937
See Connor, Ralph
See also CAAE 109

Gordon, Mary 1949- .. **CLC 13, 22, 128, 216; SSC 59**
See also AMWS 4; BPFB 2; CA 102; CANR 44, 92, 154; CN 4, 5, 6, 7; DLB 6; DLBY 1981; FW; INT CA-102; MAL 5; MTCW 1

Gordon, Mary Catherine
See Gordon, Mary

Gordon, N. J.
See Bosman, Herman Charles

Gordon, Sol 1923- .... **CLC 26**
See also CA 53-56; CANR 4; SATA 11

Gordone, Charles 1925-1995 .... **BLC 2:2; CLC 1, 4; DC 8**
See also BW 1, 3; CA 180; 93-96, 180; CAAS 150; CAD; CANR 55; DAM DRAM; DLB 7; INT CA-93-96; MTCW 1

Gore, Catherine 1800-1861 .... **NCLC 65**
See also DLB 116; RGEL 2

Gorenko, Anna Andreevna
See Akhmatova, Anna

Gorky, Maxim .... **SSC 28; TCLC 8; WLC 3**
See Peshkov, Alexei Maximovich
See also DAB; DFS 9; DLB 295; EW 8; EWL 3; TWA

Goryan, Sirak
See Saroyan, William

Gosse, Edmund (William) 1849-1928 .... **TCLC 28**
See also CAAE 117; DLB 57, 144, 184; RGEL 2

Gotlieb, Phyllis (Fay Bloom) 1926- .. **CLC 18**
See also CA 13-16R; CANR 7, 135; CN 7; CP 1, 2, 3, 4; DLB 88, 251; SFW 4

Gottesman, S. D.
See Kornbluth, C(yril) M.; Pohl, Frederik

Gottfried von Strassburg fl. c. 1170-1215 .... **CMLC 10, 96**
See also CDWLB 2; DLB 138; EW 1; RGWL 2, 3

Gotthelf, Jeremias 1797-1854 .... **NCLC 117**
See also DLB 133; RGWL 2, 3

Gottschalk, Laura Riding
See Jackson, Laura (Riding)

Gould, Lois 1932(?)-2002 .... **CLC 4, 10**
See also CA 77-80; CAAS 208; CANR 29; MTCW 1

Gould, Stephen Jay 1941-2002 .... **CLC 163**
See also AAYA 26; BEST 90:2; CA 77-80; CAAS 205; CANR 10, 27, 56, 75, 125; CPW; INT CANR-27; MTCW 1, 2; MTFW 2005

Gourmont, Remy(-Marie-Charles) de 1858-1915 .... **TCLC 17**
See also CA 150; CAAE 109; GFL 1789 to the Present; MTCW 2

Gournay, Marie le Jars de
See de Gournay, Marie le Jars

Govier, Katherine 1948- .... **CLC 51**
See also CA 101; CANR 18, 40, 128; CCA 1

Gower, John c. 1330-1408 .... **LC 76; PC 59**
See also BRW 1; DLB 146; RGEL 2

Goyen, (Charles) William 1915-1983 .... **CLC 5, 8, 14, 40**
See also AITN 2; CA 5-8R; CAAS 110; CANR 6, 71; CN 1, 2, 3; DLB 2, 218; DLBY 1983; EWL 3; INT CANR-6; MAL 5

Goytisolo, Juan 1931- .... **CLC 5, 10, 23, 133; HLC 1**
See also CA 85-88; CANR 32, 61, 131; CWW 2; DAM MULT; DLB 322; EWL 3; GLL 2; HW 1, 2; MTCW 1, 2; MTFW 2005

Gozzano, Guido 1883-1916 .... **PC 10**
See also CA 154; DLB 114; EWL 3

Gozzi, (Conte) Carlo 1720-1806 .... **NCLC 23**

Grabbe, Christian Dietrich 1801-1836 .... **NCLC 2**
See also DLB 133; RGWL 2, 3

Grace, Patricia Frances 1937- .... **CLC 56**
See also CA 176; CANR 118; CN 4, 5, 6, 7; EWL 3; RGSF 2

Gracian y Morales, Baltasar 1601-1658 .... **LC 15**

Gracq, Julien 1910-2007 .... **CLC 11, 48**
See also CA 126; CAAE 122; CANR 141; CWW 2; DLB 83; GFL 1789 to the present

Grade, Chaim 1910-1982 .... **CLC 10**
See also CA 93-96; CAAS 107; DLB 333; EWL 3; RGHL

Grade, Khayim
See Grade, Chaim

Greve, Felix Paul (Berthold Friedrich)
1879-1948
See Grove, Frederick Philip
See also CA 141, 175; CAAE 104; CANR 79; DAC; DAM MST

Greville, Fulke 1554-1628 .... **LC 79**
See also BRWS 11; DLB 62, 172; RGEL 2

Grey, Lady Jane 1537-1554 .... **LC 93**
See also DLB 132

Grey, Zane 1872-1939 .... **TCLC 6**
See also BPFB 2; CA 132; CAAE 104; DA3; DAM POP; DLB 9, 212; MTCW 1, 2; MTFW 2005; RGAL 4; TCWW 1, 2; TUS

Griboedov, Aleksandr Sergeevich
1795(?)-1829 .... **NCLC 129**
See also DLB 205; RGWL 2, 3

Grieg, (Johan) Nordahl (Brun)
1902-1943 .... **TCLC 10**
See also CA 189; CAAE 107; EWL 3

Grieve, C(hristopher) M(urray)
1892-1978 .... **CLC 11, 19**
See MacDiarmid, Hugh; Pteleon
See also CA 5-8R; CAAS 85-88; CANR 33, 107; DAM POET; MTCW 1; RGEL 2

Griffin, Gerald 1803-1840 .... **NCLC 7**
See also DLB 159; RGEL 2

Griffin, John Howard 1920-1980 ..... **CLC 68**
See also AITN 1; CA 1-4R; CAAS 101; CANR 2

Griffin, Peter 1942- .... **CLC 39**
See also CA 136

Griffith, D(avid Lewelyn) W(ark)
1875(?)-1948 .... **TCLC 68**
See also CA 150; CAAE 119; CANR 80

Griffith, Lawrence
See Griffith, D(avid Lewelyn) W(ark)

Griffiths, Trevor 1935- .... **CLC 13, 52**
See also CA 97-100; CANR 45; CBD; CD 5, 6; DLB 13, 245

Griggs, Sutton (Elbert)
1872-1930 .... **TCLC 77**
See also CA 186; CAAE 123; DLB 50

Grigson, Geoffrey (Edward Harvey)
1905-1985 .... **CLC 7, 39**
See also CA 25-28R; CAAS 118; CANR 20, 33; CP 1, 2, 3, 4; DLB 27; MTCW 1, 2

Grile, Dod
See Bierce, Ambrose (Gwinett)

Grillparzer, Franz 1791-1872 .... **DC 14; NCLC 1, 102; SSC 37**
See also CDWLB 2; DLB 133; EW 5; RGWL 2, 3; TWA

Grimble, Reverend Charles James
See Eliot, T(homas) S(tearns)

Grimke, Angelina (Emily) Weld
1880-1958 .... **HR 1:2**
See Weld, Angelina (Emily) Grimke
See also BW 1; CA 124; DAM POET; DLB 50, 54

Grimke, Charlotte L(ottie) Forten
1837(?)-1914
See Forten, Charlotte L.
See also BW 1; CA 124; CAAE 117; DAM MULT, POET

Grimm, Jacob Ludwig Karl
1785-1863 .... **NCLC 3, 77; SSC 36**
See Grimm Brothers
See also CLR 112; DLB 90; MAICYA 1, 2; RGSF 2; RGWL 2, 3; SATA 22; WCH

Grimm, Wilhelm Karl 1786-1859 .. **NCLC 3, 77; SSC 36**
See Grimm Brothers
See also CDWLB 2; CLR 112; DLB 90; MAICYA 1, 2; RGSF 2; RGWL 2, 3; SATA 22; WCH

Grimm and Grim
See Grimm, Jacob Ludwig Karl; Grimm, Wilhelm Karl

Grimm Brothers .... **SSC 88**
See Grimm, Jacob Ludwig Karl; Grimm, Wilhelm Karl
See also CLR 112

Grimmelshausen, Hans Jakob Christoffel von
See Grimmelshausen, Johann Jakob Christoffel von
See also RGWL 2, 3

Grimmelshausen, Johann Jakob Christoffel von 1621-1676 .... **LC 6**
See Grimmelshausen, Hans Jakob Christoffel von
See also CDWLB 2; DLB 168

Grindel, Eugene 1895-1952
See Eluard, Paul
See also CA 193; CAAE 104; LMFS 2

Grisham, John 1955- .... **CLC 84**
See also AAYA 14, 47; BPFB 2; CA 138; CANR 47, 69, 114, 133; CMW 4; CN 6, 7; CPW; CSW; DA3; DAM POP; MSW; MTCW 2; MTFW 2005

Grosseteste, Robert 1175(?)-1253 . **CMLC 62**
See also DLB 115

Grossman, David 1954- .... **CLC 67, 231**
See also CA 138; CANR 114; CWW 2; DLB 299; EWL 3; RGHL; WLIT 6

Grossman, Vasilii Semenovich
See Grossman, Vasily (Semenovich)
See also DLB 272

Grossman, Vasily (Semenovich)
1905-1964 .... **CLC 41**
See Grossman, Vasilii Semenovich
See also CA 130; CAAE 124; MTCW 1; RGHL

Grove, Frederick Philip .... **TCLC 4**
See Greve, Felix Paul (Berthold Friedrich)
See also DLB 92; RGEL 2; TCWW 1, 2

Grubb
See Crumb, R.

Grumbach, Doris 1918- .... **CLC 13, 22, 64**
See also CA 5-8R; 2; CANR 9, 42, 70, 127; CN 6, 7; INT CANR-9; MTCW 2; MTFW 2005

Grundtvig, Nikolai Frederik Severin
1783-1872 .... **NCLC 1, 158**
See also DLB 300

Grunge
See Crumb, R.

Grunwald, Lisa 1959- .... **CLC 44**
See also CA 120; CANR 148

Gryphius, Andreas 1616-1664 .... **LC 89**
See also CDWLB 2; DLB 164; RGWL 2, 3

Guare, John 1938- .... **CLC 8, 14, 29, 67; DC 20**
See also CA 73-76; CAD; CANR 21, 69, 118; CD 5, 6; DAM DRAM; DFS 8, 13; DLB 7, 249; EWL 3; MAL 5; MTCW 1, 2; RGAL 4

Guarini, Battista 1538-1612 .... **LC 102**
See also DLB 339

Gubar, Susan 1944- .... **CLC 145**
See also CA 108; CANR 45, 70, 139; FW; MTCW 1; RGAL 4

Gubar, Susan David
See Gubar, Susan

Gudjonsson, Halldor Kiljan 1902-1998
See Halldor Laxness
See also CA 103; CAAS 164

Guenter, Erich
See Eich, Gunter

Guest, Barbara 1920-2006 ... **CLC 34; PC 55**
See also BG 1:2; CA 25-28R; CAAS 248; CANR 11, 44, 84; CP 1, 2, 3, 4, 5, 6, 7; CWP; DLB 5, 193

Guest, Edgar A(lbert) 1881-1959 ... **TCLC 95**
See also CA 168; CAAE 112

Guest, Judith 1936- .... **CLC 8, 30**
See also AAYA 7, 66; CA 77-80; CANR 15, 75, 138; DA3; DAM NOV, POP; EXPN; INT CANR-15; LAIT 5; MTCW 1, 2; MTFW 2005; NFS 1

Guevara, Che .... **CLC 87; HLC 1**
See Guevara (Serna), Ernesto

Guevara (Serna), Ernesto
1928-1967 .... **CLC 87; HLC 1**
See Guevara, Che
See also CA 127; CAAS 111; CANR 56; DAM MULT; HW 1

Guicciardini, Francesco 1483-1540 ..... **LC 49**

Guido delle Colonne c. 1215-c.
1290 .... **CMLC 90**

Guild, Nicholas M. 1944- .... **CLC 33**
See also CA 93-96

Guillemin, Jacques
See Sartre, Jean-Paul

Guillen, Jorge 1893-1984 . **CLC 11; HLCS 1; PC 35**
See also CA 89-92; CAAS 112; DAM MULT, POET; DLB 108; EWL 3; HW 1; RGWL 2, 3

Guillen, Nicolas (Cristobal)
1902-1989 .... **BLC 1:2; CLC 48, 79; HLC 1; PC 23**
See also BW 2; CA 125; CAAE 116; CAAS 129; CANR 84; DAM MST, MULT, POET; DLB 283; EWL 3; HW 1; LAW; RGWL 2, 3; WP

Guillen y Alvarez, Jorge
See Guillen, Jorge

Guillevic, (Eugene) 1907-1997 .... **CLC 33**
See also CA 93-96; CWW 2

Guillois
See Desnos, Robert

Guillois, Valentin
See Desnos, Robert

Guimaraes Rosa, Joao 1908-1967 .... **HLCS 2**
See Rosa, Joao Guimaraes
See also CA 175; LAW; RGSF 2; RGWL 2, 3

Guiney, Louise Imogen
1861-1920 .... **TCLC 41**
See also CA 160; DLB 54; RGAL 4

Guinizelli, Guido c. 1230-1276 .... **CMLC 49**
See Guinizzelli, Guido

Guinizzelli, Guido
See Guinizelli, Guido
See also WLIT 7

Guiraldes, Ricardo (Guillermo)
1886-1927 .... **TCLC 39**
See also CA 131; EWL 3; HW 1; LAW; MTCW 1

Gumilev, Nikolai (Stepanovich)
1886-1921 .... **TCLC 60**
See Gumilyov, Nikolay Stepanovich
See also CA 165; DLB 295

Gumilyov, Nikolay Stepanovich
See Gumilev, Nikolai (Stepanovich)
See also EWL 3

Gump, P. Q.
See Card, Orson Scott

Gunesekera, Romesh 1954- .... **CLC 91**
See also BRWS 10; CA 159; CANR 140, 172; CN 6, 7; DLB 267, 323

Gunn, Bill .... **CLC 5**
See Gunn, William Harrison
See also DLB 38

Gunn, Thom(son William)
1929-2004 . **CLC 3, 6, 18, 32, 81; PC 26**
See also BRWS 4; CA 17-20R; CAAS 227; CANR 9, 33, 116; CDBLB 1960 to Present; CP 1, 2, 3, 4, 5, 6, 7; DAM POET; DLB 27; INT CANR-33; MTCW 1; PFS 9; RGEL 2

Hoffman, Alice 1952- .... **CLC 51**
  See also AAYA 37; AMWS 10; CA 77-80;
  CANR 34, 66, 100, 138, 170; CN 4, 5, 6,
  7; CPW; DAM NOV; DLB 292; MAL 5;
  MTCW 1, 2; MTFW 2005; TCLE 1:1

Hoffman, Daniel (Gerard) 1923- . **CLC 6, 13, 23**
  See also CA 1-4R; CANR 4, 142; CP 1, 2,
  3, 4, 5, 6, 7; DLB 5; TCLE 1:1

Hoffman, Eva 1945- .... **CLC 182**
  See also AMWS 16; CA 132; CANR 146

Hoffman, Stanley 1944- .... **CLC 5**
  See also CA 77-80

Hoffman, William 1925- .... **CLC 141**
  See also CA 21-24R; CANR 9, 103; CSW;
  DLB 234; TCLE 1:1

Hoffman, William M.
  See Hoffman, William M(oses)
  See also CAD; CD 5, 6

Hoffman, William M(oses) 1939- ..... **CLC 40**
  See Hoffman, William M.
  See also CA 57-60; CANR 11, 71

Hoffmann, E(rnst) T(heodor) A(madeus)
  1776-1822 ..... **NCLC 2, 183; SSC 13, 92**
  See also CDWLB 2; DLB 90; EW 5; GL 2;
  RGSF 2; RGWL 2, 3; SATA 27; SUFW
  1; WCH

Hofmann, Gert 1931-1993 .... **CLC 54**
  See also CA 128; CANR 145; EWL 3;
  RGHL

Hofmannsthal, Hugo von 1874-1929 ... **DC 4; TCLC 11**
  See also CA 153; CAAE 106; CDWLB 2;
  DAM DRAM; DFS 17; DLB 81, 118; EW
  9; EWL 3; RGWL 2, 3

Hogan, Linda 1947- ..... **CLC 73; NNAL; PC 35**
  See also AMWS 4; ANW; BYA 12; CA 226;
  120, 226; CANR 45, 73, 129; CWP; DAM
  MULT; DLB 175; SATA 132; TCWW 2

Hogarth, Charles
  See Creasey, John

Hogarth, Emmett
  See Polonsky, Abraham (Lincoln)

Hogarth, William 1697-1764 .... **LC 112**
  See also AAYA 56

Hogg, James 1770-1835 .... **NCLC 4, 109**
  See also BRWS 10; DLB 93, 116, 159; GL
  2; HGG; RGEL 2; SUFW 1

Holbach, Paul-Henri Thiry
  1723-1789 .... **LC 14**
  See also DLB 313

Holberg, Ludvig 1684-1754 .... **LC 6**
  See also DLB 300; RGWL 2, 3

Holcroft, Thomas 1745-1809 .... **NCLC 85**
  See also DLB 39, 89, 158; RGEL 2

Holden, Ursula 1921- .... **CLC 18**
  See also CA 101; 8; CANR 22

Holderlin, (Johann Christian) Friedrich
  1770-1843 .... **NCLC 16, 187; PC 4**
  See also CDWLB 2; DLB 90; EW 5; RGWL
  2, 3

Holdstock, Robert 1948- .... **CLC 39**
  See also CA 131; CANR 81; DLB 261;
  FANT; HGG; SFW 4; SUFW 2

Holdstock, Robert P.
  See Holdstock, Robert

Holinshed, Raphael fl. 1580- .... **LC 69**
  See also DLB 167; RGEL 2

Holland, Isabelle (Christian)
  1920-2002 .... **CLC 21**
  See also AAYA 11, 64; CA 181; 21-24R;
  CAAS 205; CANR 10, 25, 47; CLR 57;
  CWRI 5; JRDA; LAIT 4; MAICYA 1, 2;
  SATA 8, 70; SATA-Essay 103; SATA-Obit
  132; WYA

Holland, Marcus
  See Caldwell, (Janet Miriam) Taylor
  (Holland)

Hollander, John 1929- .... **CLC 2, 5, 8, 14**
  See also CA 1-4R; CANR 1, 52, 136; CP 1,
  2, 3, 4, 5, 6, 7; DLB 5; MAL 5; SATA 13

Hollander, Paul
  See Silverberg, Robert

Holleran, Andrew .... **CLC 38**
  See Garber, Eric
  See also CA 144; GLL 1

Holley, Marietta 1836(?)-1926 .... **TCLC 99**
  See also CAAE 118; DLB 11; FL 1:3

Hollinghurst, Alan 1954- .... **CLC 55, 91**
  See also BRWS 10; CA 114; CN 5, 6, 7;
  DLB 207, 326; GLL 1

Hollis, Jim
  See Summers, Hollis (Spurgeon, Jr.)

Holly, Buddy 1936-1959 .... **TCLC 65**
  See also CA 213

Holmes, Gordon
  See Shiel, M(atthew) P(hipps)

Holmes, John
  See Souster, (Holmes) Raymond

Holmes, John Clellon 1926-1988 ...... **CLC 56**
  See also BG 1:2; CA 9-12R; CAAS 125;
  CANR 4; CN 1, 2, 3, 4; DLB 16, 237

Holmes, Oliver Wendell, Jr.
  1841-1935 .... **TCLC 77**
  See also CA 186; CAAE 114

Holmes, Oliver Wendell
  1809-1894 .... **NCLC 14, 81; PC 71**
  See also AMWS 1; CDALB 1640-1865;
  DLB 1, 189, 235; EXPP; PFS 24; RGAL
  4; SATA 34

Holmes, Raymond
  See Souster, (Holmes) Raymond

Holt, Victoria
  See Hibbert, Eleanor Alice Burford
  See also BPFB 2

Holub, Miroslav 1923-1998 .... **CLC 4**
  See also CA 21-24R; CAAS 169; CANR
  10; CDWLB 4; CWW 2; DLB 232; EWL
  3; RGWL 3

Holz, Detlev
  See Benjamin, Walter

Homer c. 8th cent. B.C.- .... **CMLC 1, 16, 61; PC 23; WLCS**
  See also AW 1; CDWLB 1; DA; DA3;
  DAB; DAC; DAM MST, POET; DLB
  176; EFS 1; LAIT 1; LMFS 1; RGWL 2,
  3; TWA; WLIT 8; WP

Hongo, Garrett Kaoru 1951- .... **PC 23**
  See also CA 133; 22; CP 5, 6, 7; DLB 120,
  312; EWL 3; EXPP; PFS 25; RGAL 4

Honig, Edwin 1919- .... **CLC 33**
  See also CA 5-8R; 8; CANR 4, 45, 144; CP
  1, 2, 3, 4, 5, 6, 7; DLB 5

Hood, Hugh (John Blagdon) 1928- . **CLC 15, 28; SSC 42**
  See also CA 49-52; 17; CANR 1, 33, 87;
  CN 1, 2, 3, 4, 5, 6, 7; DLB 53; RGSF 2

Hood, Thomas 1799-1845 .... **NCLC 16**
  See also BRW 4; DLB 96; RGEL 2

Hooker, (Peter) Jeremy 1941- .... **CLC 43**
  See also CA 77-80; CANR 22; CP 2, 3, 4,
  5, 6, 7; DLB 40

Hooker, Richard 1554-1600 .... **LC 95**
  See also BRW 1; DLB 132; RGEL 2

Hooker, Thomas 1586-1647 .... **LC 137**
  See also DLB 24

hooks, bell 1952(?)- .... **BLCS; CLC 94**
  See also BW 2; CA 143; CANR 87, 126;
  DLB 246; MTCW 2; MTFW 2005; SATA
  115, 170

Hooper, Johnson Jones
  1815-1862 .... **NCLC 177**
  See also DLB 3, 11, 248; RGAL 4

Hope, A(lec) D(erwent) 1907-2000 .... **CLC 3, 51; PC 56**
  See also BRWS 7; CA 21-24R; CAAS 188;
  CANR 33, 74; CP 1, 2, 3, 4, 5; DLB 289;
  EWL 3; MTCW 1, 2; MTFW 2005; PFS
  8; RGEL 2

Hope, Anthony 1863-1933 .... **TCLC 83**
  See also CA 157; DLB 153, 156; RGEL 2;
  RHW

Hope, Brian
  See Creasey, John

Hope, Christopher (David Tully)
  1944- .... **CLC 52**
  See also AFW; CA 106; CANR 47, 101;
  CN 4, 5, 6, 7; DLB 225; SATA 62

Hopkins, Gerard Manley
  1844-1889 .... **NCLC 17, 189; PC 15; WLC 3**
  See also BRW 5; BRWR 2; CDBLB 1890-
  1914; DA; DA3; DAB; DAC; DAM MST,
  POET; DLB 35, 57; EXPP; PAB; PFS 26;
  RGEL 2; TEA; WP

Hopkins, John (Richard) 1931-1998 .. **CLC 4**
  See also CA 85-88; CAAS 169; CBD; CD
  5, 6

Hopkins, Pauline Elizabeth
  1859-1930 .... **BLC 1:2; TCLC 28**
  See also AFAW 2; BW 2, 3; CA 141; CANR
  82; DAM MULT; DLB 50

Hopkinson, Francis 1737-1791 .... **LC 25**
  See also DLB 31; RGAL 4

Hopley-Woolrich, Cornell George 1903-1968
  See Woolrich, Cornell
  See also CA 13-14; CANR 58, 156; CAP 1;
  CMW 4; DLB 226; MTCW 2

Horace 65B.C.-8B.C. .... **CMLC 39; PC 46**
  See also AW 2; CDWLB 1; DLB 211;
  RGWL 2, 3; WLIT 8

Horatio
  See Proust, (Valentin-Louis-George-Eugene)
  Marcel

Horgan, Paul (George Vincent
  O'Shaughnessy) 1903-1995 .. **CLC 9, 53**
  See also BPFB 2; CA 13-16R; CAAS 147;
  CANR 9, 35; CN 1, 2, 3, 4, 5; DAM
  NOV; DLB 102, 212; DLBY 1985; INT
  CANR-9; MTCW 1, 2; MTFW 2005;
  SATA 13; SATA-Obit 84; TCWW 1, 2

Horkheimer, Max 1895-1973 .... **TCLC 132**
  See also CA 216; CAAS 41-44R; DLB 296

Horn, Peter
  See Kuttner, Henry

Hornby, Nick 1957(?)- .... **CLC 243**
  See also AAYA 74; CA 151; CANR 104,
  151; CN 7; DLB 207

Horne, Frank (Smith) 1899-1974 ...... **HR 1:2**
  See also BW 1; CA 125; CAAS 53-56; DLB
  51, WP

Horne, Richard Henry Hengist
  1802(?)-1884 .... **NCLC 127**
  See also DLB 32; SATA 29

Hornem, Horace Esq.
  See Byron, George Gordon (Noel)

Horney, Karen (Clementine Theodore
  Danielsen) 1885-1952 .... **TCLC 71**
  See also CA 165; CAAE 114; DLB 246;
  FW

Hornung, E(rnest) W(illiam)
  1866-1921 .... **TCLC 59**
  See also CA 160; CAAE 108; CMW 4;
  DLB 70

Horovitz, Israel (Arthur) 1939- .... **CLC 56**
  See also CA 33-36R; CAD; CANR 46, 59;
  CD 5, 6; DAM DRAM; DLB 7; MAL 5

Horton, George Moses
  1797(?)-1883(?) .... **NCLC 87**
  See also DLB 50

Jean Paul 1763-1825 .... NCLC 7

Jefferies, (John) Richard
   1848-1887 .... NCLC 47
   See also DLB 98, 141; RGEL 2; SATA 16;
   SFW 4

Jeffers, John Robinson
   See Jeffers, Robinson

Jeffers, Robinson 1887-1962 .... CLC 2, 3, 11,
   15, 54; PC 17; WLC 3
   See also AMWS 2; CA 85-88; CANR 35;
   CDALB 1917-1929; DA; DAC; DAM
   MST, POET; DLB 45, 212; EWL 3; MAL
   5; MTCW 1, 2; MTFW 2005; PAB; PFS
   3, 4; RGAL 4

Jefferson, Janet
   See Mencken, H(enry) L(ouis)

Jefferson, Thomas 1743-1826 . NCLC 11, 103
   See also AAYA 54; ANW; CDALB 1640-
   1865; DA3; DLB 31, 183; LAIT 1; RGAL
   4

Jeffrey, Francis 1773-1850 .... NCLC 33
   See Francis, Lord Jeffrey

Jelakowitch, Ivan
   See Heijermans, Herman

Jelinek, Elfriede 1946- .... CLC 169
   See also AAYA 68; CA 154; CANR 169;
   DLB 85, 330; FW

Jellicoe, (Patricia) Ann 1927- .... CLC 27
   See also CA 85-88; CBD; CD 5, 6; CWD;
   CWRI 5; DLB 13, 233; FW

Jelloun, Tahar ben
   See Ben Jelloun, Tahar

Jemyma
   See Holley, Marietta

Jen, Gish .... AAL; CLC 70, 198
   See Jen, Lillian
   See also AMWC 2; CN 7; DLB 312

Jen, Lillian 1955-
   See Jen, Gish
   See also CA 135; CANR 89, 130

Jenkins, (John) Robin 1912- .... CLC 52
   See also CA 1-4R; CANR 1, 135; CN 1, 2,
   3, 4, 5, 6, 7; DLB 14, 271

Jennings, Elizabeth (Joan)
   1926-2001 .... CLC 5, 14, 131
   See also BRWS 5; CA 61-64; 5; CAAS 200;
   CANR 8, 39, 66, 127; CP 1, 2, 3, 4, 5, 6,
   7; CWP; DLB 27; EWL 3; MTCW 1;
   SATA 66

Jennings, Waylon 1937-2002 .... CLC 21

Jensen, Johannes V(ilhelm)
   1873-1950 .... TCLC 41
   See also CA 170; DLB 214, 330; EWL 3;
   RGWL 3

Jensen, Laura (Linnea) 1948- .... CLC 37
   See also CA 103

Jerome, Saint 345-420 .... CMLC 30
   See also RGWL 3

Jerome, Jerome K(lapka)
   1859-1927 .... TCLC 23
   See also CA 177; CAAE 119; DLB 10, 34,
   135; RGEL 2

Jerrold, Douglas William
   1803-1857 .... NCLC 2
   See also DLB 158, 159; RGEL 2

Jewett, (Theodora) Sarah Orne
   1849-1909 .... SSC 6, 44; TCLC 1, 22
   See also AAYA 76; AMW; AMWC 2;
   AMWR 2; CA 127; CAAE 108; CANR
   71; DLB 12, 74, 221; EXPS; FL 1:3; FW;
   MAL 5; MBL; NFS 15; RGAL 4; RGSF
   2; SATA 15; SSFS 4

Jewsbury, Geraldine (Endsor)
   1812-1880 .... NCLC 22
   See also DLB 21

Jhabvala, Ruth Prawer 1927- . CLC 4, 8, 29,
   94, 138; SSC 91
   See also BRWS 5; CA 1-4R; CANR 2, 29,
   51, 74, 91, 128; CN 1, 2, 3, 4, 5, 6, 7;
   DAB; DAM NOV; DLB 139, 194, 323,
   326; EWL 3; IDFW 3, 4; INT CANR-29;
   MTCW 1, 2; MTFW 2005; RGSF 2;
   RGWL 2; RHW; TEA

Jibran, Kahlil
   See Gibran, Kahlil

Jibran, Khalil
   See Gibran, Kahlil

Jiles, Paulette 1943- .... CLC 13, 58
   See also CA 101; CANR 70, 124, 170; CP
   5; CWP

Jimenez (Mantecon), Juan Ramon
   1881-1958 .... HLC 1; PC 7; TCLC 4,
   183
   See also CA 131; CAAE 104; CANR 74;
   DAM MULT, POET; DLB 134, 330; EW
   9; EWL 3; HW 1; MTCW 1, 2; MTFW
   2005; RGWL 2, 3

Jimenez, Ramon
   See Jimenez (Mantecon), Juan Ramon

Jimenez Mantecon, Juan
   See Jimenez (Mantecon), Juan Ramon

Jin, Ba 1904-2005
   See Pa Chin
   See also CAAS 244; CWW 2; DLB 328

Jin, Xuefei
   See Ha Jin

Jodelle, Etienne 1532-1573 .... LC 119
   See also DLB 327; GFL Beginnings to 1789

Joel, Billy .... CLC 26
   See Joel, William Martin

Joel, William Martin 1949-
   See Joel, Billy
   See also CA 108

John, St.
   See John of Damascus, St.

John of Damascus, St. c.
   675-749 .... CMLC 27, 95

John of Salisbury c. 1115-1180 ..... CMLC 63

John of the Cross, St. 1542-1591 .... LC 18,
   146
   See also RGWL 2, 3

John Paul II, Pope 1920-2005 .... CLC 128
   See also CA 133; CAAE 106; CAAS 238

Johnson, B(ryan) S(tanley William)
   1933-1973 .... CLC 6, 9
   See also CA 9-12R; CAAS 53-56; CANR
   9; CN 1; CP 1, 2; DLB 14, 40; EWL 3;
   RGEL 2

Johnson, Benjamin F., of Boone
   See Riley, James Whitcomb

Johnson, Charles (Richard) 1948- . BLC 1:2;
   CLC 7, 51, 65, 163
   See also AFAW 2; AMWS 6; BW 2, 3; CA
   116; 18; CANR 42, 66, 82, 129; CN 5, 6,
   7; DAM MULT; DLB 33, 278; MAL 5;
   MTCW 2; MTFW 2005; RGAL 4; SSFS
   16

Johnson, Charles S(purgeon)
   1893-1956 .... HR 1:3
   See also BW 1, 3; CA 125; CANR 82; DLB
   51, 91

Johnson, Denis 1949- . CLC 52, 160; SSC 56
   See also CA 121; CAAE 117; CANR 71,
   99; CN 4, 5, 6, 7; DLB 120

Johnson, Diane 1934- ...... CLC 5, 13, 48, 244
   See also BPFB 2; CA 41-44R; CANR 17,
   40, 62, 95, 155; CN 4, 5, 6, 7; DLBY
   1980; INT CANR-17; MTCW 1

Johnson, E(mily) Pauline 1861-1913 . NNAL
   See also CA 150; CCA 1; DAC; DAM
   MULT; DLB 92, 175; TCWW 2

Johnson, Eyvind (Olof Verner)
   1900-1976 .... CLC 14
   See also CA 73-76; CAAS 69-72; CANR
   34, 101; DLB 259, 330; EW 12; EWL 3

Johnson, Fenton 1888-1958 .... BLC 2
   See also BW 1; CA 124; CAAE 118; DAM
   MULT; DLB 45, 50

Johnson, Georgia Douglas (Camp)
   1880-1966 .... HR 1:3
   See also BW 1; CA 125; DLB 51, 249; WP

Johnson, Helene 1907-1995 .... HR 1:3
   See also CA 181; DLB 51; WP

Johnson, J. R.
   See James, C(yril) L(ionel) R(obert)

Johnson, James Weldon
   1871-1938 .... BLC 1:2; HR 1:3; PC 24;
   TCLC 3, 19, 175
   See also AAYA 73; AFAW 1, 2; BW 1, 3;
   CA 125; CAAE 104; CANR 82; CDALB
   1917-1929; CLR 32; DA3; DAM MULT,
   POET; DLB 51; EWL 3; EXPP; LMFS 2;
   MAL 5; MTCW 1, 2; MTFW 2005; NFS
   22; PFS 1; RGAL 4; SATA 31; TUS

Johnson, Joyce 1935- .... CLC 58
   See also BG 1:3; CA 129; CAAE 125;
   CANR 102

Johnson, Judith (Emlyn) 1936- .... CLC 7, 15
   See Sherwin, Judith Johnson
   See also CA 25-28R; 153; CANR 34; CP 6,
   7

Johnson, Lionel (Pigot)
   1867-1902 .... TCLC 19
   See also CA 209; CAAE 117; DLB 19;
   RGEL 2

Johnson, Marguerite Annie
   See Angelou, Maya

Johnson, Mel
   See Malzberg, Barry N(athaniel)

Johnson, Pamela Hansford
   1912-1981 .... CLC 1, 7, 27
   See also CA 1-4R; CAAS 104; CANR 2,
   28; CN 1, 2, 3; DLB 15; MTCW 1, 2;
   MTFW 2005; RGEL 2

Johnson, Paul 1928- .... CLC 147
   See also BEST 89:4; CA 17-20R; CANR
   34, 62, 100, 155

Johnson, Paul Bede
   See Johnson, Paul

Johnson, Robert .... CLC 70

Johnson, Robert 1911(?)-1938 .... TCLC 69
   See also BW 3; CA 174

Johnson, Samuel 1709-1784 . LC 15, 52, 128;
   PC 81; WLC 3
   See also BRW 3; BRWR 1; CDBLB 1660-
   1789; DA; DAB; DAC; DAM MST; DLB
   39, 95, 104, 142, 213; LMFS 1; RGEL 2;
   TEA

Johnson, Uwe 1934-1984 .. CLC 5, 10, 15, 40
   See also CA 1-4R; CAAS 112; CANR 1,
   39; CDWLB 2; DLB 75; EWL 3; MTCW
   1; RGWL 2, 3

Johnston, Basil H. 1929- .... NNAL
   See also CA 69-72; CANR 11, 28, 66;
   DAC; DAM MULT; DLB 60

Johnston, George (Benson) 1913- .... CLC 51
   See also CA 1-4R; CANR 5, 20; CP 1, 2, 3,
   4, 5, 6, 7; DLB 88

Johnston, Jennifer (Prudence)
   1930- .... CLC 7, 150, 228
   See also CA 85-88; CANR 92; CN 4, 5, 6,
   7; DLB 14

Joinville, Jean de 1224(?)-1317 ..... CMLC 38

Jolley, Elizabeth 1923-2007 ..... CLC 46; SSC
   19
   See also CA 127; 13; CAAS 257; CANR
   59; CN 4, 5, 6, 7; DLB 325; EWL 3;
   RGSF 2

Jolley, Monica Elizabeth
   See Jolley, Elizabeth

Kaiser, Georg 1878-1945 .... **TCLC 9**
  See also CA 190; CAAE 106; CDWLB 2;
  DLB 124; EWL 3; LMFS 2; RGWL 2, 3

Kaledin, Sergei .... **CLC 59**

Kaletski, Alexander 1946- .... **CLC 39**
  See also CA 143; CAAE 118

Kalidasa fl. c. 400-455 .... **CMLC 9; PC 22**
  See also RGWL 2, 3

Kallman, Chester (Simon)
  1921-1975 .... **CLC 2**
  See also CA 45-48; CAAS 53-56; CANR 3;
  CP 1, 2

Kaminsky, Melvin .... **CLC 12, 217**
  See Brooks, Mel
  See also AAYA 13, 48; DLB 26

Kaminsky, Stuart M. 1934- .... **CLC 59**
  See also CA 73-76; CANR 29, 53, 89, 161;
  CMW 4

Kaminsky, Stuart Melvin
  See Kaminsky, Stuart M.

Kamo no Chomei 1153(?)-1216 .... **CMLC 66**
  See also DLB 203

Kamo no Nagaakira
  See Kamo no Chomei

Kandinsky, Wassily 1866-1944 .... **TCLC 92**
  See also AAYA 64; CA 155; CAAE 118

Kane, Francis
  See Robbins, Harold

Kane, Henry 1918-
  See Queen, Ellery
  See also CA 156; CMW 4

Kane, Paul
  See Simon, Paul

Kane, Sarah 1971-1999 .... **DC 31**
  See also BWS 8; CA 190; CD 5, 6; DLB
  310

Kanin, Garson 1912-1999 .... **CLC 22**
  See also AITN 1; CA 5-8R; CAAS 177;
  CAD; CANR 7, 78; DLB 7; IDFW 3, 4

Kaniuk, Yoram 1930- .... **CLC 19**
  See also CA 134; DLB 299; RGHL

Kant, Immanuel 1724-1804 .... **NCLC 27, 67**
  See also DLB 94

Kantor, MacKinlay 1904-1977 .... **CLC 7**
  See also CA 61-64; CAAS 73-76; CANR
  60, 63; CN 1, 2; DLB 9, 102; MAL 5;
  MTCW 2; RHW; TCWW 1, 2

Kanze Motokiyo
  See Zeami

Kaplan, David Michael 1946- .... **CLC 50**
  See also CA 187

Kaplan, James 1951- .... **CLC 59**
  See also CA 135; CANR 121

Karadzic, Vuk Stefanovic
  1787-1864 .... **NCLC 115**
  See also CDWLB 4; DLB 147

Karageorge, Michael
  See Anderson, Poul

Karamzin, Nikolai Mikhailovich
  1766-1826 .... **NCLC 3, 173**
  See also DLB 150; RGSF 2

Karapanou, Margarita 1946- .... **CLC 13**
  See also CA 101

Karinthy, Frigyes 1887-1938 .... **TCLC 47**
  See also CA 170; DLB 215; EWL 3

Karl, Frederick R(obert)
  1927-2004 .... **CLC 34**
  See also CA 5-8R; CAAS 226; CANR 3,
  44, 143

Karr, Mary 1955- .... **CLC 188**
  See also AMWS 11; CA 151; CANR 100;
  MTFW 2005; NCFS 5

Kastel, Warren
  See Silverberg, Robert

Kataev, Evgeny Petrovich 1903-1942
  See Petrov, Evgeny
  See also CAAE 120

Kataphusin
  See Ruskin, John

Katz, Steve 1935- .... **CLC 47**
  See also CA 25-28R; 14, 64; CANR 12;
  CN 4, 5, 6, 7; DLBY 1983

Kauffman, Janet 1945- .... **CLC 42**
  See also CA 117; CANR 43, 84; DLB 218;
  DLBY 1986

Kaufman, Bob (Garnell)
  1925-1986 .... **CLC 49; PC 74**
  See also BG 1:3; BW 1; CA 41-44R; CAAS
  118; CANR 22; CP 1; DLB 16, 41

Kaufman, George S. 1889-1961 ...... **CLC 38;**
  DC 17
  See also CA 108; CAAS 93-96; DAM
  DRAM; DFS 1, 10; DLB 7; INT CA-108;
  MTCW 2; MTFW 2005; RGAL 4; TUS

Kaufman, Moises 1964- .... **DC 26**
  See also CA 211; DFS 22; MTFW 2005

Kaufman, Sue .... **CLC 3, 8**
  See Barondess, Sue K(aufman)

Kavafis, Konstantinos Petrou 1863-1933
  See Cavafy, C(onstantine) P(eter)
  See also CAAE 104

Kavan, Anna 1901-1968 .... **CLC 5, 13, 82**
  See also BRWS 7; CA 5-8R; CANR 6, 57;
  DLB 255; MTCW 1; RGEL 2; SFW 4

Kavanagh, Dan
  See Barnes, Julian

Kavanagh, Julie 1952- .... **CLC 119**
  See also CA 163

Kavanagh, Patrick (Joseph)
  1904-1967 .... **CLC 22; PC 33**
  See also BRWS 7; CA 123; CAAS 25-28R;
  DLB 15, 20; EWL 3; MTCW 1; RGEL 2

Kawabata, Yasunari 1899-1972 ..... **CLC 2, 5,**
  9, 18, 107; SSC 17
  See Kawabata Yasunari
  See also CA 93-96; CAAS 33-36R; CANR
  88; DAM MULT; DLB 330; MJW;
  MTCW 2; MTFW 2005; RGSF 2; RGWL
  2, 3

Kawabata Yasunari
  See Kawabata, Yasunari
  See also DLB 180; EWL 3

Kaye, Mary Margaret
  See Kaye, M.M.

Kaye, M.M. 1908-2004 .... **CLC 28**
  See also CA 89-92; CAAS 223; CANR 24,
  60, 102, 142; MTCW 1, 2; MTFW 2005;
  RHW; SATA 62; SATA-Obit 152

Kaye, Mollie
  See Kaye, M.M.

Kaye-Smith, Sheila 1887-1956 .... **TCLC 20**
  See also CA 203; CAAE 118; DLB 36

Kaymor, Patrice Maguilene
  See Senghor, Leopold Sedar

Kazakov, Iurii Pavlovich
  See Kazakov, Yuri Pavlovich
  See also DLB 302

Kazakov, Yuri Pavlovich 1927-1982 . **SSC 43**
  See Kazakov, Iurii Pavlovich; Kazakov,
  Yury
  See also CA 5-8R; CANR 36; MTCW 1;
  RGSF 2

Kazakov, Yury
  See Kazakov, Yuri Pavlovich
  See also EWL 3

Kazan, Elia 1909-2003 .... **CLC 6, 16, 63**
  See also CA 21-24R; CAAS 220; CANR
  32, 78

Kazantzakis, Nikos 1883(?)-1957 .... **TCLC 2,**
  5, 33, 181
  See also BPFB 2; CA 132; CAAE 105;
  DA3; EW 9; EWL 3; MTCW 1, 2; MTFW
  2005; RGWL 2, 3

Kazin, Alfred 1915-1998 ..... **CLC 34, 38, 119**
  See also AMWS 8; CA 1-4R; 7; CANR 1,
  45, 79; DLB 67; EWL 3

Keane, Mary Nesta (Skrine) 1904-1996
  See Keane, Molly
  See also CA 114; CAAE 108; CAAS 151;
  RHW

Keane, Molly .... **CLC 31**
  See Keane, Mary Nesta (Skrine)
  See also CN 5, 6; INT CA-114; TCLE 1:1

Keates, Jonathan 1946(?)- .... **CLC 34**
  See also CA 163; CANR 126

Keaton, Buster 1895-1966 .... **CLC 20**
  See also CA 194

Keats, John 1795-1821 ...... **NCLC 8, 73, 121;**
  PC 1; WLC 3
  See also AAYA 58; BRW 4; BRWR 1; CD-
  BLB 1789-1832; DA; DA3; DAB; DAC;
  DAM MST, POET; DLB 96, 110; EXPP;
  LMFS 1; PAB; PFS 1, 2, 3, 9, 17; RGEL
  2; TEA; WLIT 3; WP

Keble, John 1792-1866 .... **NCLC 87**
  See also DLB 32, 55; RGEL 2

Keene, Donald 1922- .... **CLC 34**
  See also CA 1-4R; CANR 5, 119

Keillor, Garrison 1942- ..... **CLC 40, 115, 222**
  See also AAYA 2, 62; AMWS 16; BEST
  89:3; BPFB 2; CA 117; CAAE 111;
  CANR 36, 59, 124; CPW; DA3; DAM
  POP; DLBY 1987; EWL 3; MTCW 1, 2;
  MTFW 2005; SATA 58; TUS

Keith, Carlos
  See Lewton, Val

Keith, Michael
  See Hubbard, L. Ron

Keller, Gottfried 1819-1890 .... **NCLC 2; SSC**
  26, 107
  See also CDWLB 2; DLB 129; EW; RGSF
  2; RGWL 2, 3

Keller, Nora Okja 1965- .... **CLC 109**
  See also CA 187

Kellerman, Jonathan 1949- .... **CLC 44**
  See also AAYA 35; BEST 90:1; CA 106;
  CANR 29, 51, 150; CMW 4; CPW; DA3;
  DAM POP; INT CANR-29

Kelley, William Melvin 1937- .... **BLC 2:2;**
  CLC 22
  See also BW 1; CA 77-80; CANR 27, 83;
  CN 1, 2, 3, 4, 5, 6, 7; DLB 33; EWL 3

Kellogg, Marjorie 1922-2005 .... **CLC 2**
  See also CA 81-84; CAAS 246

Kellow, Kathleen
  See Hibbert, Eleanor Alice Burford

Kelly, Lauren
  See Oates, Joyce Carol

Kelly, M(ilton) T(errence) 1947- ...... **CLC 55**
  See also CA 97-100; 22; CANR 19, 43, 84;
  CN 6

Kelly, Robert 1935- .... **SSC 50**
  See also CA 17-20R; 19; CANR 47; CP 1,
  2, 3, 4, 5, 6, 7; DLB 5, 130, 165

Kelman, James 1946- .... **CLC 58, 86**
  See also BRWS 5; CA 148; CANR 85, 130;
  CN 5, 6, 7; DLB 194, 319, 326; RGSF 2;
  WLIT 4

Kemal, Yasar
  See Kemal, Yashar
  See also CWW 2; EWL 3; WLIT 3

Kemal, Yashar 1923(?)- .... **CLC 14, 29**
  See also CA 89-92; CANR 44

Kemble, Fanny 1809-1893 .... **NCLC 18**
  See also DLB 32

Kemelman, Harry 1908-1996 .... **CLC 2**
  See also AITN 1; BPFB 2; CA 9-12R;
  CAAS 155; CANR 6, 71; CMW 4; DLB
  28

Kempe, Margery 1373(?)-1440(?) ... **LC 6, 56**
  See also BRWS 12; DLB 146; FL 1:1;
  RGEL 2

Author Index

Lindsay, (Nicholas) Vachel
1879-1931 .... **PC 23; TCLC 17; WLC 4**
See also AMWS 1; CA 135; CAAE 114;
CANR 79; CDALB 1865-1917; DA;
DA3; DAC; DAM MST, POET; DLB 54;
EWL 3; EXPP; MAL 5; RGAL 4; SATA
40; WP

Linke-Poot
See Doeblin, Alfred

Linney, Romulus 1930- .... **CLC 51**
See also CA 1-4R; CAD; CANR 40, 44,
79; CD 5, 6; CSW; RGAL 4

Linton, Eliza Lynn 1822-1898 .... **NCLC 41**
See also DLB 18

Li Po 701-763 .... **CMLC 2, 86; PC 29**
See also PFS 20; WP

Lipsius, Justus 1547-1606 .... **LC 16**

Lipsyte, Robert 1938- .... **CLC 21**
See also AAYA 7, 45; CA 17-20R; CANR
8, 57, 146; CLR 23, 76; DA; DAC; DAM
MST, NOV; JRDA; LAIT 5; MAICYA 1,
2; SATA 5, 68, 113, 161; WYA; YAW

Lipsyte, Robert Michael
See Lipsyte, Robert

Lish, Gordon 1934- .... **CLC 45; SSC 18**
See also CA 117; CAAE 113; CANR 79,
151; DLB 130; INT CA-117

Lish, Gordon Jay
See Lish, Gordon

Lispector, Clarice 1925(?)-1977 .... **CLC 43;**
HLCS 2; SSC 34, 96
See also CA 139; CAAS 116; CANR 71;
CDWLB 3; DLB 113, 307; DNFS 1; EWL
3; FW; HW 2; LAW; RGSF 2; RGWL 2,
3; WLIT 1

Littell, Robert 1935(?)- .... **CLC 42**
See also CA 112; CAAE 109; CANR 64,
115, 162; CMW 4

Little, Malcolm 1925-1965
See Malcolm X
See also BW 1, 3; CA 125; CAAS 111;
CANR 82; DA; DA3; DAB; DAC; DAM
MST, MULT; MTCW 1, 2; MTFW 2005

Littlewit, Humphrey Gent.
See Lovecraft, H. P.

Litwos
See Sienkiewicz, Henryk (Adam Alexander
Pius)

Liu, E. 1857-1909 .... **TCLC 15**
See also CA 190; CAAE 115; DLB 328

Lively, Penelope 1933- .... **CLC 32, 50**
See also BPFB 2; CA 41-44R; CANR 29,
67, 79, 131, 172; CLR 7; CN 5, 6, 7;
CWRI 5; DAM NOV; DLB 14, 161, 207,
326; FANT; JRDA; MAICYA 1, 2;
MTCW 1, 2; MTFW 2005; SATA 7, 60,
101, 164; TEA

Lively, Penelope Margaret
See Lively, Penelope

Livesay, Dorothy (Kathleen)
1909-1996 .... **CLC 4, 15, 79**
See also AITN 2; CA 25-28R; 8; CANR 36,
67; CP 1, 2, 3, 4, 5; DAC; DAM MST,
POET; DLB 68; FW; MTCW 1; RGEL 2;
TWA

Livy c. 59B.C.-c. 12 .... **CMLC 11**
See also AW 2; CDWLB 1; DLB 211;
RGWL 2, 3; WLIT 8

Lizardi, Jose Joaquin Fernandez de
1776-1827 .... **NCLC 30**
See also LAW

Llewellyn, Richard
See Llewellyn Lloyd, Richard Dafydd Vivian
See also DLB 15

Llewellyn Lloyd, Richard Dafydd Vivian
1906-1983 .... **CLC 7, 80**
See Llewellyn, Richard
See also CA 53-56; CAAS 111; CANR 7,
71; SATA 11; SATA-Obit 37

Llosa, Jorge Mario Pedro Vargas
See Vargas Llosa, Mario
See also RGWL 3

Llosa, Mario Vargas
See Vargas Llosa, Mario

Lloyd, Manda
See Mander, (Mary) Jane

Lloyd Webber, Andrew 1948-
See Webber, Andrew Lloyd
See also AAYA 1, 38; CA 149; CAAE 116;
DAM DRAM; SATA 56

Llull, Ramon c. 1235-c. 1316 .... **CMLC 12**

Lobb, Ebenezer
See Upward, Allen

Locke, Alain (Le Roy)
1886-1954 .... **BLCS; HR 1:3; TCLC 43**
See also AMWS 14; BW 1, 3; CA 124;
CAAE 106; CANR 79; DLB 51; LMFS
2; MAL 5; RGAL 4

Locke, John 1632-1704 .... **LC 7, 35, 135**
See also DLB 31, 101, 213, 252; RGEL 2;
WLIT 3

Locke-Elliott, Sumner
See Elliott, Sumner Locke

Lockhart, John Gibson 1794-1854 .. **NCLC 6**
See also DLB 110, 116, 144

Lockridge, Ross (Franklin), Jr.
1914-1948 .... **TCLC 111**
See also CA 145; CAAE 108; CANR 79;
DLB 143; DLBY 1980; MAL 5; RGAL
4; RHW

Lockwood, Robert
See Johnson, Robert

Lodge, David 1935- .... **CLC 36, 141**
See also BEST 90:1; BRWS 4; CA 17-20R;
CANR 19, 53, 92, 139; CN 1, 2, 3, 4, 5,
6, 7; CPW; DAM POP; DLB 14, 194;
EWL 3; INT CANR-19; MTCW 1, 2;
MTFW 2005

Lodge, Thomas 1558-1625 .... **LC 41**
See also DLB 172; RGEL 2

Loewinsohn, Ron(ald William)
1937- .... **CLC 52**
See also CA 25-28R; CANR 71; CP 1, 2, 3,
4

Logan, Jake
See Smith, Martin Cruz

Logan, John (Burton) 1923-1987 .... **CLC 5**
See also CA 77-80; CAAS 124; CANR 45;
CP 1, 2, 3, 4; DLB 5

Lo Kuan-chung 1330(?)-1400(?) .... **LC 12**

Lombard, Nap
See Johnson, Pamela Hansford

Lombard, Peter 1100(?)-1160(?) ... **CMLC 72**

Lombino, Salvatore
See Hunter, Evan

London, Jack 1876-1916 .. **SSC 4, 49; TCLC**
9, 15, 39; WLC 4
See London, John Griffith
See also AAYA 13; AITN 2; AMW; BPFB
2; BYA 4, 13; CDALB 1865-1917; CLR
108; DLB 8, 12, 78, 212; EWL 3; EXPS;
LAIT 3; MAL 5; NFS 8; RGAL 4; RGSF
2; SATA 18; SFW 4; SSFS 7; TCWW 1,
2; TUS; WYA; YAW

London, John Griffith 1876-1916
See London, Jack
See also AAYA 75; CA 119; CAAE 110;
CANR 73; DA; DA3; DAB; DAC; DAM
MST, NOV; JRDA; MAICYA 1, 2;
MTCW 1, 2; MTFW 2005; NFS 19

Long, Emmett
See Leonard, Elmore

Longbaugh, Harry
See Goldman, William

Longfellow, Henry Wadsworth
1807-1882 .... **NCLC 2, 45, 101, 103; PC**
30; WLCS
See also AMW; AMWR 2; CDALB 1640-
1865; CLR 99; DA; DA3; DAB; DAC;
DAM MST, POET; DLB 1, 59, 235;
EXPP; PAB; PFS 2, 7, 17; RGAL 4;
SATA 19; TUS; WP

Longinus c. 1st cent. - .... **CMLC 27**
See also AW 2; DLB 176

Longley, Michael 1939- .... **CLC 29**
See also BRWS 8; CA 102; CP 1, 2, 3, 4, 5,
6, 7; DLB 40

Longstreet, Augustus Baldwin
1790-1870 .... **NCLC 159**
See also DLB 3, 11, 74, 248; RGAL 4

Longus fl. c. 2nd cent. - .... **CMLC 7**

Longway, A. Hugh
See Lang, Andrew

Lonnbohm, Armas Eino Leopold 1878-1926
See Leino, Eino
See also CAAE 123

Lonnrot, Elias 1802-1884 .... **NCLC 53**
See also EFS 1

Lonsdale, Roger .... **CLC 65**

Lopate, Phillip 1943- .... **CLC 29**
See also CA 97-100; CANR 88, 157; DLBY
1980; INT CA-97-100

Lopez, Barry (Holstun) 1945- .... **CLC 70**
See also AAYA 9, 63; ANW; CA 65-68;
CANR 7, 23, 47, 68, 92; DLB 256, 275,
335; INT CANR-7, CANR-23; MTCW 1;
RGAL 4; SATA 67

Lopez de Mendoza, Inigo
See Santillana, Inigo Lopez de Mendoza,
Marques de

Lopez Portillo (y Pacheco), Jose
1920-2004 .... **CLC 46**
See also CA 129; CAAS 224; HW 1

Lopez y Fuentes, Gregorio
1897(?)-1966 .... **CLC 32**
See also CA 131; EWL 3; HW 1

Lorca, Federico Garcia .... **TCLC 197**
See Garcia Lorca, Federico
See also DFS 4; EW 11; PFS 20; RGWL 2,
3; WP

Lord, Audre
See Lorde, Audre
See also EWL 3

Lord, Bette Bao 1938- .... **AAL; CLC 23**
See also BEST 90:3; BPFB 2; CA 107;
CANR 41, 79; INT CA-107; SATA 58

Lord Auch
See Bataille, Georges

Lord Brooke
See Greville, Fulke

Lord Byron
See Byron, George Gordon (Noel)

Lorde, Audre 1934-1992 . **BLC 1:2; CLC 18,**
71; PC 12; TCLC 173
See Domini, Rey; Lord, Audre
See also AFAW 1, 2; BW 1, 3; CA 25-28R;
CAAS 142; CANR 16, 26, 46, 82; CP 2,
3, 4, 5; DA3; DAM MULT, POET; DLB
41; FW; MAL 5; MTCW 1, 2; MTFW
2005; PFS 16; RGAL 4

Lorde, Audre Geraldine
See Lorde, Audre

Lord Houghton
See Milnes, Richard Monckton

Lord Jeffrey
See Jeffrey, Francis

Loreaux, Nichol .... **CLC 65**

Lorenzini, Carlo 1826-1890
See Collodi, Carlo
See also MAICYA 1, 2; SATA 29, 100

Margulies, Donald 1954- .... **CLC 76**
　See also AAYA 57; CA 200; CD 6; DFS 13;
　DLB 228

Marias, Javier 1951- .... **CLC 239**
　See also CA 167; CANR 109, 139; DLB
　322; HW 2; MTFW 2005

Marie de France c. 12th cent. - ..... **CMLC 8;
　PC 22**
　See also DLB 208; FW; RGWL 2, 3

Marie de l'Incarnation 1599-1672 ...... **LC 10**

Marier, Captain Victor
　See Griffith, D(avid Lewelyn) W(ark)

Mariner, Scott
　See Pohl, Frederik

Marinetti, Filippo Tommaso
　1876-1944 .... **TCLC 10**
　See also CAAE 107; DLB 114, 264; EW 9;
　EWL 3; WLIT 7

Marivaux, Pierre Carlet de Chamblain de
　1688-1763 .... **DC 7; LC 4, 123**
　See also DLB 314; GFL Beginnings to
　1789; RGWL 2, 3; TWA

Markandaya, Kamala .... **CLC 8, 38**
　See Taylor, Kamala
　See also BYA 13; CN 1, 2, 3, 4, 5, 6, 7;
　DLB 323; EWL 3

Markfield, Wallace (Arthur)
　1926-2002 .... **CLC 8**
　See also CA 69-72; 3; CAAS 208; CN 1, 2,
　3, 4, 5, 6, 7; DLB 2, 28; DLBY 2002

Markham, Edwin 1852-1940 .... **TCLC 47**
　See also CA 160; DLB 54, 186; MAL 5;
　RGAL 4

Markham, Robert
　See Amis, Kingsley

Marks, J.
　See Highwater, Jamake (Mamake)

Marks-Highwater, J.
　See Highwater, Jamake (Mamake)

Markson, David M. 1927- .... **CLC 67**
　See also AMWS 17; CA 49-52; CANR 1,
　91, 158; CN 5, 6

Markson, David Merrill
　See Markson, David M.

Marlatt, Daphne (Buckle) 1942- .... **CLC 168**
　See also CA 25-28R; CANR 17, 39; CN 6,
　7; CP 4, 5, 6, 7; CWP; DLB 60; FW

Marley, Bob .... **CLC 17**
　See Marley, Robert Nesta

Marley, Robert Nesta 1945-1981
　See Marley, Bob
　See also CA 107; CAAS 103

Marlowe, Christopher 1564-1593 . **DC 1; LC
　22, 47, 117; PC 57; WLC 4**
　See also BRW 1; BRWR 1; CDBLB Before
　1660; DA; DA3; DAB; DAC; DAM
　DRAM, MST, DFS 1, 5, 13, 21; DLB 62;
　EXPP; LMFS 1; PFS 22; RGEL 2; TEA;
　WLIT 3

Marlowe, Stephen 1928-2008 .... **CLC 70**
　See Queen, Ellery
　See also CA 13-16R; CANR 6, 55; CMW
　4; SFW 4

Marmion, Shakerley 1603-1639 .... **LC 89**
　See also DLB 58; RGEL 2

Marmontel, Jean-Francois 1723-1799 .. **LC 2**
　See also DLB 314

Maron, Monika 1941- .... **CLC 165**
　See also CA 201

Marot, Clement c. 1496-1544 .... **LC 133**
　See also DLB 327; GFL Beginnings to 1789

Marquand, John P(hillips)
　1893-1960 .... **CLC 2, 10**
　See also AMW; BPFB 2; CA 85-88; CANR
　73; CMW 4; DLB 9, 102; EWL 3; MAL
　5; MTCW 2; RGAL 4

Marques, Rene 1919-1979 .. **CLC 96; HLC 2**
　See also CA 97-100; CAAS 85-88; CANR
　78; DAM MULT; DLB 305; EWL 3; HW
　1, 2; LAW; RGSF 2

Marquez, Gabriel Garcia
　See Garcia Marquez, Gabriel

Marquis, Don(ald Robert Perry)
　1878-1937 .... **TCLC 7**
　See also CA 166; CAAE 104; DLB 11, 25;
　MAL 5; RGAL 4

Marquis de Sade
　See Sade, Donatien Alphonse Francois

Marric, J. J.
　See Creasey, John
　See also MSW

Marryat, Frederick 1792-1848 .... **NCLC 3**
　See also DLB 21, 163; RGEL 2; WCH

Marsden, James
　See Creasey, John

Marsh, Edward 1872-1953 .... **TCLC 99**

Marsh, (Edith) Ngaio 1895-1982 .. **CLC 7, 53**
　See also CA 9-12R; CANR 6, 58; CMW 4;
　CN 1, 2, 3; CPW; DAM POP; DLB 77;
　MSW; MTCW 1, 2; RGEL 2; TEA

Marshall, Allen
　See Westlake, Donald E.

Marshall, Garry 1934- .... **CLC 17**
　See also AAYA 3; CA 111; SATA 60

Marshall, Paule 1929- ..... **BLC 1:3; CLC 27,
　72; SSC 3**
　See also AFAW 1, 2; AMWS 11; BPFB 2;
　BW 2, 3; CA 77-80; CANR 25, 73, 129;
　CN 1, 2, 3, 4, 5, 6, 7; DA3; DAM MULT;
　DLB 33, 157, 227; EWL 3; LATS 1:2;
　MAL 5; MTCW 1, 2; MTFW 2005;
　RGAL 4; SSFS 15

Marshallik
　See Zangwill, Israel

Marsten, Richard
　See Hunter, Evan

Marston, John 1576-1634 .... **LC 33**
　See also BRW 2; DAM DRAM; DLB 58,
　172; RGEL 2

Martel, Yann 1963- .... **CLC 192**
　See also AAYA 67; CA 146; CANR 114;
　DLB 326, 334; MTFW 2005

Martens, Adolphe-Adhemar
　See Ghelderode, Michel de

Martha, Henry
　See Harris, Mark

Marti, Jose .... **PC 76**
　See Marti (y Perez), Jose (Julian)
　See also DLB 290

Marti (y Perez), Jose (Julian)
　1853-1895 .... **HLC 2; NCLC 63**
　See Marti, Jose
　See also DAM MULT; HW 2; LAW; RGWL
　2, 3; WLIT 1

Martial c. 40-c. 104 .... **CMLC 35; PC 10**
　See also AW 2; CDWLB 1; DLB 211;
　RGWL 2, 3

Martin, Ken
　See Hubbard, L. Ron

Martin, Richard
　See Creasey, John

Martin, Steve 1945- .... **CLC 30, 217**
　See also AAYA 53; CA 97-100; CANR 30,
　100, 140; DFS 19; MTCW 1; MTFW
　2005

Martin, Valerie 1948- .... **CLC 89**
　See also BEST 90:2; CA 85-88; CANR 49,
　89, 165

Martin, Violet Florence 1862-1915 .. **SSC 56;
　TCLC 51**

Martin, Webber
　See Silverberg, Robert

Martindale, Patrick Victor
　See White, Patrick (Victor Martindale)

Martin du Gard, Roger
　1881-1958 .... **TCLC 24**
　See also CAAE 118; CANR 94; DLB 65,
　331; EWL 3; GFL 1789 to the Present;
　RGWL 2, 3

Martineau, Harriet 1802-1876 ...... **NCLC 26,
　137**
　See also DLB 21, 55, 159, 163, 166, 190;
　FW; RGEL 2; YABC 2

Martines, Julia
　See O'Faolain, Julia

Martinez, Enrique Gonzalez
　See Gonzalez Martinez, Enrique

Martinez, Jacinto Benavente y
　See Benavente (y Martinez), Jacinto

Martinez de la Rosa, Francisco de Paula
　1787-1862 .... **NCLC 102**
　See also TWA

Martinez Ruiz, Jose 1873-1967
　See Azorin; Ruiz, Jose Martinez
　See also CA 93-96; HW 1

Martinez Sierra, Gregorio
　See Martinez Sierra, Maria

Martinez Sierra, Gregorio
　1881-1947 .... **TCLC 6**
　See also CAAE 115; EWL 3

Martinez Sierra, Maria 1874-1974 .. **TCLC 6**
　See also CA 250; CAAS 115; EWL 3

Martinsen, Martin
　See Follett, Ken

Martinson, Harry (Edmund)
　1904-1978 .... **CLC 14**
　See also CA 77-80; CANR 34, 130; DLB
　259, 331; EWL 3

Martyn, Edward 1859-1923 .... **TCLC 131**
　See also CA 179; DLB 10; RGEL 2

Marut, Ret
　See Traven, B.

Marut, Robert
　See Traven, B.

Marvell, Andrew 1621-1678 .... **LC 4, 43; PC
　10, 86; WLC 4**
　See also BRW 2; BRWR 2; CDBLB 1660-
　1789; DA; DAB; DAC; DAM MST,
　POET; DLB 131; EXPP; PFS 5; RGEL 2;
　TEA; WP

Marx, Karl (Heinrich)
　1818-1883 .... **NCLC 17, 114**
　See also DLB 129; LATS 1:1; TWA

Masaoka, Shiki -1902 .... **TCLC 18**
　See Masaoka, Tsunenori
　See also RGWL 3

Masaoka, Tsunenori 1867-1902
　See Masaoka, Shiki
　See also CA 191; CAAE 117; TWA

Masefield, John (Edward)
　1878-1967 .... **CLC 11, 47; PC 78**
　See also CA 19-20; CAAS 25-28R; CANR
　33; CAP 2; CDBLB 1890-1914, DAM
　POET; DLB 10, 19, 153, 160; EWL 3;
　EXPP; FANT; MTCW 1, 2; PFS 5; RGEL
　2; SATA 19

Maso, Carole 1955(?)- .... **CLC 44**
　See also CA 170; CANR 148; CN 7; GLL
　2; RGAL 4

Mason, Bobbie Ann 1940- ... **CLC 28, 43, 82,
　154; SSC 4, 101**
　See also AAYA 5, 42; AMWS 8; BPFB 2;
　CA 53-56; CANR 11, 31, 58, 83, 125,
　169; CDALBS; CN 5, 6, 7; CSW; DA3;
　DLB 173; DLBY 1987; EWL 3; EXPS;
　INT CANR-31; MAL 5; MTCW 1, 2;
　MTFW 2005; NFS 4; RGAL 4; RGSF 2;
　SSFS 3, 8, 20; TCLE 1:2; YAW

Mason, Ernst
　See Pohl, Frederik

Mason, Hunni B.
　See Sternheim, (William Adolf) Carl

DA3; DLB 2; DLBY 1981; EWL 3; FW; INT CANR-16; MAL 5; MBL; MTCW 1, 2; MTFW 2005; RGAL 4; TUS

McCartney, James Paul
See McCartney, Paul

McCartney, Paul 1942- .... **CLC 12, 35**
See also CA 146; CANR 111

McCauley, Stephen (D.) 1955- .... **CLC 50**
See also CA 141

McClaren, Peter .... **CLC 70**

McClure, Michael (Thomas) 1932- ... **CLC 6, 10**
See also BG 1:3; CA 21-24R; CAD; CANR 17, 46, 77, 131; CD 5, 6; CP 1, 2, 3, 4, 5, 6, 7; DLB 16; WP

McCorkle, Jill (Collins) 1958- .... **CLC 51**
See also CA 121; CANR 113; CSW; DLB 234; DLBY 1987; SSFS 24

McCourt, Frank 1930- .... **CLC 109**
See also AAYA 61; AMWS 12; CA 157; CANR 97, 138; MTFW 2005; NCFS 1

McCourt, James 1941- .... **CLC 5**
See also CA 57-60; CANR 98, 152

McCourt, Malachy 1931- .... **CLC 119**
See also SATA 126

McCoy, Horace (Stanley)
1897-1955 .... **TCLC 28**
See also AMWS 13; CA 155; CAAE 108; CMW 4; DLB 9

McCrae, John 1872-1918 .... **TCLC 12**
See also CAAE 109; DLB 92; PFS 5

McCreigh, James
See Pohl, Frederik

McCullers, (Lula) Carson (Smith)
1917-1967 .... **CLC 1, 4, 10, 12, 48, 100; SSC 9, 24, 99; TCLC 155; WLC 4**
See also AAYA 21; AMW; AMWC 2; BPFB 2; CA 5-8R; CAAS 25-28R; CABS 1, 3; CANR 18, 132; CDALB 1941-1968; DA; DA3; DAB; DAC; DAM MST, NOV; DFS 5, 18; DLB 2, 7, 173, 228, EWL 3; EXPS; FW; GLL 1; LAIT 3, 4; MAL 5; MBL; MTCW 1, 2; MTFW 2005; NFS 6, 13; RGAL 4; RGSF 2; SATA 27; SSFS 5; TUS; YAW

McCulloch, John Tyler
See Burroughs, Edgar Rice

McCullough, Colleen 1937- ...... **CLC 27, 107**
See also AAYA 36; BPFB 2; CA 81-84; CANR 17, 46, 67, 98, 139; CPW; DA3; DAM NOV, POP; MTCW 1, 2; MTFW 2005; RHW

McCunn, Ruthanne Lum 1946- .... **AAL**
See also CA 119; CANR 43, 96; DLB 312; LAIT 2; SATA 63

McDermott, Alice 1953- .... **CLC 90**
See also CA 109; CANR 40, 90, 126; CN 7; DLB 292; MTFW 2005; NFS 23

McElroy, Joseph 1930- .... **CLC 5, 47**
See also CA 17-20R; CANR 149; CN 3, 4, 5, 6, 7

McElroy, Joseph Prince
See McElroy, Joseph

McEwan, Ian 1948- ... **CLC 13, 66, 169; SSC 106**
See also BEST 90:4; BRWS 4; CA 61-64; CANR 14, 41, 69, 87, 132; CN 3, 4, 5, 6, 7; DAM NOV; DLB 14, 194, 319, 326; HGG; MTCW 1, 2; MTFW 2005; RGSF 2; SUFW 2; TEA

McFadden, David 1940- .... **CLC 48**
See also CA 104; CP 1, 2, 3, 4, 5, 6, 7; DLB 60; INT CA-104

McFarland, Dennis 1950- .... **CLC 65**
See also CA 165; CANR 110

McGahern, John 1934-2006 .... **CLC 5, 9, 48, 156; SSC 17**
See also CA 17-20R; CAAS 249; CANR 29, 68, 113; CN 1, 2, 3, 4, 5, 6, 7; DLB 14, 231, 319; MTCW 1

McGinley, Patrick (Anthony) 1937- . **CLC 41**
See also CA 127; CAAE 120; CANR 56; INT CA-127

McGinley, Phyllis 1905-1978 .... **CLC 14**
See also CA 9-12R; CAAS 77-80; CANR 19; CP 1, 2; CWRI 5; DLB 11, 48; MAL 5; PFS 9, 13; SATA 2, 44; SATA-Obit 24

McGinniss, Joe 1942- .... **CLC 32**
See also AITN 2; BEST 89:2; CA 25-28R; CANR 26, 70, 152; CPW; DLB 185; INT CANR-26

McGivern, Maureen Daly
See Daly, Maureen

McGivern, Maureen Patricia Daly
See Daly, Maureen

McGrath, Patrick 1950- .... **CLC 55**
See also CA 136; CANR 65, 148; CN 5, 6, 7; DLB 231; HGG; SUFW 2

McGrath, Thomas (Matthew)
1916-1990 .... **CLC 28, 59**
See also AMWS 10; CA 9-12R; CAAS 132; CANR 6, 33, 95; CP 1, 2, 3, 4, 5; DAM POET; MAL 5; MTCW 1; SATA 41; SATA-Obit 66

McGuane, Thomas 1939- .. **CLC 3, 7, 18, 45, 127**
See also AITN 2; BPFB 2; CA 49-52; CANR 5, 24, 49, 94, 164; CN 2, 3, 4, 5, 6, 7; DLB 2, 212; DLBY 1980; EWL 3; INT CANR-24; MAL 5; MTCW 1; MTFW 2005; TCWW 1, 2

McGuane, Thomas Francis III
See McGuane, Thomas

McGuckian, Medbh 1950- .... **CLC 48, 174; PC 27**
See also BRWS 5; CA 143; CP 4, 5, 6, 7; CWP; DAM POET; DLB 40

McHale, Tom 1942(?)-1982 .... **CLC 3, 5**
See also AITN 1; CA 77-80; CAAS 106; CN 1, 2, 3

McHugh, Heather 1948- .... **PC 61**
See also CA 69-72; CANR 11, 28, 55, 92; CP 4, 5, 6, 7; CWP; PFS 24

McIlvanney, William 1936- .... **CLC 42**
See also CA 25-28R; CANR 61; CMW 4; DLB 14, 207

McIlwraith, Maureen Mollie Hunter
See Hunter, Mollie
See also SATA 2

McInerney, Jay 1955- .... **CLC 34, 112**
See also AAYA 18; BPFB 2; CA 123; CAAE 116; CANR 45, 68, 116; CN 5, 6, 7; CPW; DA3; DAM POP; DLB 292; INT CA-123; MAL 5; MTCW 2; MTFW 2005

McIntyre, Vonda N. 1948- .... **CLC 18**
See also CA 81-84; CANR 17, 34, 69; MTCW 1; SFW 4; YAW

McIntyre, Vonda Neel
See McIntyre, Vonda N.

McKay, Claude .... **BLC 1:3; HR 1:3; PC 2; TCLC 7, 41; WLC 4**
See McKay, Festus Claudius
See also AFAW 1, 2; AMWS 10; DAB; DLB 4, 45, 51, 117; EWL 3; EXPP; GLL 2; LAIT 2; LMFS 2; MAL 5; PAB; PFS 4; RGAL 4; WP

McKay, Festus Claudius 1889-1948
See McKay, Claude
See also BW 1, 3; CA 124; CAAE 104; CANR 73; DA; DAC; DAM MST, MULT, NOV, POET; MTCW 1, 2; MTFW 2005; TUS

McKuen, Rod 1933- .... **CLC 1, 3**
See also AITN 1; CA 41-44R; CANR 40; CP 1

McLoughlin, R. B.
See Mencken, H(enry) L(ouis)

McLuhan, (Herbert) Marshall
1911-1980 .... **CLC 37, 83**
See also CA 9-12R; CAAS 102; CANR 12, 34, 61; DLB 88; INT CANR-12; MTCW 1, 2; MTFW 2005

McManus, Declan Patrick Aloysius
See Costello, Elvis

McMillan, Terry 1951- .. **BLCS; CLC 50, 61, 112**
See also AAYA 21; AMWS 13; BPFB 2; BW 2, 3; CA 140; CANR 60, 104, 131; CN 7; CPW; DA3; DAM MULT, NOV, POP; MAL 5; MTCW 2; MTFW 2005; RGAL 4; YAW

McMurtry, Larry 1936- .... **CLC 2, 3, 7, 11, 27, 44, 127, 250**
See also AAYA 15; AITN 2; AMWS 5; BEST 89:2; BPFB 2; CA 5-8R; CANR 19, 43, 64, 103, 170; CDALB 1968-1988; CN 2, 3, 4, 5, 6, 7; CPW; CSW; DA3; DAM NOV, POP; DLB 2, 143, 256; DLBY 1980, 1987; EWL 3; MAL 5; MTCW 1, 2; MTFW 2005; RGAL 4; TCWW 1, 2

McMurtry, Larry Jeff
See McMurtry, Larry

McNally, Terrence 1939- ... **CLC 4, 7, 41, 91, 252; DC 27**
See also AAYA 62; AMWS 13; CA 45-48; CAD; CANR 2, 56, 116; CD 5, 6; DA3; DAM DRAM; DFS 16, 19; DLB 7, 249; EWL 3; GLL 1; MTCW 2; MTFW 2005

McNally, Thomas Michael
See McNally, T.M.

McNally, T.M. 1961- .... **CLC 82**
See also CA 246

McNamer, Deirdre 1950- .... **CLC 70**
See also CA 188; CANR 163

McNeal, Tom .... **CLC 119**
See also CA 252

McNeile, Herman Cyril 1888-1937
See Sapper
See also CA 184; CMW 4; DLB 77

McNickle, (William) D'Arcy
1904-1977 .... **CLC 89; NNAL**
See also CA 9-12R; CAAS 85-88; CANR 5, 45; DAM MULT; DLB 175, 212; RGAL 4; SATA-Obit 22; TCWW 1, 2

McPhee, John 1931- .... **CLC 36**
See also AAYA 61; AMWS 3; ANW; BEST 90:1; CA 65-68; CANR 20, 46, 64, 69, 121, 165; CPW; DLB 185, 275; MTCW 1, 2; MTFW 2005; TUS

McPhee, John Angus
See McPhee, John

McPherson, James Alan 1943- . **BLCS; CLC 19, 77; SSC 95**
See also BW 1, 3; CA 25-28R; 17; CANR 24, 74, 140; CN 3, 4, 5, 6; CSW; DLB 38, 244; EWL 3; MTCW 1, 2; MTFW 2005; RGAL 4; RGSF 2; SSFS 23

McPherson, William (Alexander)
1933- .... **CLC 34**
See also CA 69-72; CANR 28; INT CANR-28

McTaggart, J. McT. Ellis
See McTaggart, John McTaggart Ellis

McTaggart, John McTaggart Ellis
1866-1925 .... **TCLC 105**
See also CAAE 120; DLB 262

Mda, Zakes 1948- .... **BLC 2:3**
See also CA 205; CANR 151; CD 5, 6; DLB 225

Mead, George Herbert 1863-1931 . **TCLC 89**
See also CA 212; DLB 270

Mo, Timothy (Peter) 1950- .... **CLC 46, 134**
See also CA 117; CANR 128; CN 5, 6, 7;
DLB 194; MTCW 1; WLIT 4; WWE 1

Modarressi, Taghi (M.) 1931-1997 ... **CLC 44**
See also CA 134; CAAE 121; INT CA-134

Modiano, Patrick (Jean) 1945- .... **CLC 18, 218**
See also CA 85-88; CANR 17, 40, 115;
CWW 2; DLB 83, 299; EWL 3; RGHL

Mofolo, Thomas (Mokopu)
1875(?)-1948 .... **BLC 1:3; TCLC 22**
See also AFW; CA 153; CAAE 121; CANR
83; DAM MULT; DLB 225; EWL 3;
MTCW 2; MTFW 2005; WLIT 2

Mohr, Nicholasa 1938- .... **CLC 12; HLC 2**
See also AAYA 8, 46; CA 49-52; CANR 1,
32, 64; CLR 22; DAM MULT; DLB 145;
HW 1, 2; JRDA; LAIT 5; LLW; MAICYA
2; MAICYAS 1; RGAL 4; SAAS 8; SATA
8, 97; SATA-Essay 113; WYA; YAW

Moi, Toril 1953- .... **CLC 172**
See also CA 154; CANR 102; FW

Mojtabai, A(nn) G(race) 1938- ..... **CLC 5, 9, 15, 29**
See also CA 85-88; CANR 88

Moliere 1622-1673 ..... **DC 13; LC 10, 28, 64, 125, 127; WLC 4**
See also DA; DA3; DAB; DAC; DAM
DRAM, MST; DFS 13, 18, 20; DLB 268;
EW 3; GFL Beginnings to 1789; LATS
1:1; RGWL 2, 3; TWA

Molin, Charles
See Mayne, William (James Carter)

Molnar, Ferenc 1878-1952 .... **TCLC 20**
See also CA 153; CAAE 109; CANR 83;
CDWLB 4; DAM DRAM; DLB 215;
EWL 3; RGWL 2, 3

Momaday, N. Scott 1934- ...... **CLC 2, 19, 85, 95, 160; NNAL; PC 25; WLCS**
See also AAYA 11, 64; AMWS 4; ANW;
BPFB 2; BYA 12; CA 25-28R; CANR 14,
34, 68, 134; CDALBS; CN 2, 3, 4, 5, 6,
7; CPW; DA; DA3; DAB; DAC; DAM
MST, MULT, NOV, POP; DLB 143, 175,
256; EWL 3; EXPP; INT CANR-14;
LAIT 4; LATS 1:2; MAL 5; MTCW 1, 2;
MTFW 2005; NFS 10; PFS 2, 11; RGAL
4; SATA 48; SATA-Brief 30; TCWW 1,
2; WP; YAW

Monette, Paul 1945-1995 .... **CLC 82**
See also AMWS 10; CA 139; CAAS 147;
CN 6; GLL 1

Monroe, Harriet 1860-1936 .... **TCLC 12**
See also CA 204; CAAE 109; DLB 54, 91

Monroe, Lyle
See Heinlein, Robert A.

Montagu, Elizabeth 1720-1800 .... **NCLC 7, 117**
See also FW

Montagu, Mary (Pierrepont) Wortley
1689-1762 .... **LC 9, 57; PC 16**
See also DLB 95, 101; FL 1:1; RGEL 2

Montagu, W. H.
See Coleridge, Samuel Taylor

Montague, John (Patrick) 1929- ..... **CLC 13, 46**
See also CA 9-12R; CANR 9, 69, 121; CP
1, 2, 3, 4, 5, 6, 7; DLB 40; EWL 3;
MTCW 1; PFS 12; RGEL 2; TCLE 1:2

Montaigne, Michel (Eyquem) de
1533-1592 .... **LC 8, 105; WLC 4**
See also DA; DAB; DAC; DAM MST;
DLB 327; EW 2; GFL Beginnings to
1789; LMFS 1; RGWL 2, 3; TWA

Montale, Eugenio 1896-1981 ... **CLC 7, 9, 18; PC 13**
See also CA 17-20R; CAAS 104; CANR
30; DLB 114, 331; EW 11; EWL 3;
MTCW 1; PFS 22; RGWL 2, 3; TWA;
WLIT 7

Montesquieu, Charles-Louis de Secondat
1689-1755 .... **LC 7, 69**
See also DLB 314; EW 3; GFL Beginnings
to 1789; TWA

Montessori, Maria 1870-1952 ...... **TCLC 103**
See also CA 147; CAAE 115

Montgomery, (Robert) Bruce 1921(?)-1978
See Crispin, Edmund
See also CA 179; CAAS 104; CMW 4

Montgomery, L(ucy) M(aud)
1874-1942 .... **TCLC 51, 140**
See also AAYA 12; BYA 1; CA 137; CAAE
108; CLR 8, 91; DA3; DAC; DAM MST;
DLB 92; DLBD 14; JRDA; MAICYA 1,
2; MTCW 2; MTFW 2005; RGEL 2;
SATA 100; TWA; WCH; WYA; YABC 1

Montgomery, Marion, Jr. 1925- .... **CLC 7**
See also AITN 1; CA 1-4R; CANR 3, 48,
162; CSW; DLB 6

Montgomery, Marion H. 1925-
See Montgomery, Marion, Jr.

Montgomery, Max
See Davenport, Guy (Mattison, Jr.)

Montherlant, Henry (Milon) de
1896-1972 .... **CLC 8, 19**
See also CA 85-88; CAAS 37-40R; DAM
DRAM; DLB 72, 321; EW 11; EWL 3;
GFL 1789 to the Present; MTCW 1

Monty Python
See Chapman, Graham; Cleese, John
(Marwood); Gilliam, Terry; Idle, Eric;
Jones, Terence Graham Parry; Palin,
Michael (Edward)
See also AAYA 7

Moodie, Susanna (Strickland)
1803-1885 .... **NCLC 14, 113**
See also DLB 99

Moody, Hiram 1961-
See Moody, Rick
See also CA 138; CANR 64, 112; MTFW
2005

Moody, Minerva
See Alcott, Louisa May

Moody, Rick .... **CLC 147**
See Moody, Hiram

Moody, William Vaughan
1869-1910 .... **TCLC 105**
See also CA 178; CAAE 110; DLB 7, 54;
MAL 5; RGAL 4

Mooney, Edward 1951-
See Mooney, Ted
See also CA 130

Mooney, Ted .... **CLC 25**
See Mooney, Edward

Moorcock, Michael 1939- ...... **CLC 5, 27, 58, 236**
See Bradbury, Edward P.
See also AAYA 26; CA 45-48; 5; CANR 2,
17, 38, 64, 122; CN 5, 6, 7; DLB 14, 231,
261, 319; FANT; MTCW 1, 2; MTFW
2005; SATA 93, 166; SCFW 1, 2; SFW 4;
SUFW 1, 2

Moorcock, Michael John
See Moorcock, Michael

Moorcock, Michael John
See Moorcock, Michael

Moore, Alan 1953- .... **CLC 230**
See also AAYA 51; CA 204; CANR 138;
DLB 261; MTFW 2005; SFW 4

Moore, Brian 1921-1999 ... **CLC 1, 3, 5, 7, 8, 19, 32, 90**
See Bryan, Michael
See also BRWS 9; CA 1-4R; CAAS 174;
CANR 1, 25, 42, 63; CCA 1; CN 1, 2, 3,
4, 5, 6; DAB; DAC; DAM MST; DLB
251; EWL 3; FANT; MTCW 1, 2; MTFW
2005; RGEL 2

Moore, Edward
See Muir, Edwin
See also RGEL 2

Moore, G. E. 1873-1958 .... **TCLC 89**
See also DLB 262

Moore, George Augustus
1852-1933 .... **SSC 19; TCLC 7**
See also BRW 6; CA 177; CAAE 104; DLB
10, 18, 57, 135; EWL 3; RGEL 2; RGSF
2

Moore, Lorrie .... **CLC 39, 45, 68**
See Moore, Marie Lorena
See also AMWS 10; CN 5, 6, 7; DLB 234;
SSFS 19

Moore, Marianne (Craig)
1887-1972 .... **CLC 1, 2, 4, 8, 10, 13, 19, 47; PC 4, 49; WLCS**
See also AMW; CA 1-4R; CAAS 33-36R;
CANR 3, 61; CDALB 1929-1941; CP 1;
DA; DA3; DAB; DAC; DAM MST,
POET; DLB 45; DLBD 7; EWL 3; EXPP;
FL 1:6; MAL 5; MBL; MTCW 1, 2;
MTFW 2005; PAB; PFS 14, 17; RGAL 4;
SATA 20; TUS; WP

Moore, Marie Lorena 1957- .... **CLC 165**
See Moore, Lorrie
See also CA 116; CANR 39, 83, 139; DLB
234; MTFW 2005

Moore, Michael 1954- .... **CLC 218**
See also AAYA 53; CA 166; CANR 150

Moore, Thomas 1779-1852 .... **NCLC 6, 110**
See also DLB 96, 144; RGEL 2

Moorhouse, Frank 1938- .... **SSC 40**
See also CA 118; CANR 92; CN 3, 4, 5, 6,
7; DLB 289; RGSF 2

Mora, Pat 1942- .... **HLC 2**
See also AMWS 13; CA 129; CANR 57,
81, 112, 171; CLR 58; DAM MULT; DLB
209; HW 1, 2; LLW; MAICYA 2; MTFW
2005; SATA 92, 134, 186

Moraga, Cherrie 1952- ... **CLC 126, 250; DC 22**
See also CA 131; CANR 66, 154; DAM
MULT; DLB 82, 249; FW; GLL 1; HW 1,
2; LLW

Morand, Paul 1888-1976 .... **CLC 41; SSC 22**
See also CA 184; CAAS 69-72; DLB 65;
EWL 3

Morante, Elsa 1918-1985 .... **CLC 8, 47**
See also CA 85-88; CAAS 117; CANR 35;
DLB 177; EWL 3; MTCW 1, 2; MTFW
2005; RGHL; RGWL 2, 3; WLIT 7

Moravia, Alberto .... **CLC 2, 7, 11, 27, 46; SSC 26**
See Pincherle, Alberto
See also DLB 177; EW 12; EWL 3; MTCW
2; RGSF 2; RGWL 2, 3; WLIT 7

More, Hannah 1745-1833 ...... **NCLC 27, 141**
See also DLB 107, 109, 116, 158; RGEL 2

More, Henry 1614-1687 .... **LC 9**
See also DLB 126, 252

More, Sir Thomas 1478(?)-1535 ... **LC 10, 32, 140**
See also BRWC 1; BRWS 7; DLB 136, 281;
LMFS 1; RGEL 2; TEA

Moreas, Jean .... **TCLC 18**
See Papadiamantopoulos, Johannes
See also GFL 1789 to the Present

Moreton, Andrew Esq.
See Defoe, Daniel

Morgan, Berry 1919-2002 .... **CLC 6**
See also CA 49-52; CAAS 208; DLB 6

Morgan, Claire
See Highsmith, Patricia
See also GLL 1

Morgan, Edwin 1920- .... **CLC 31**
See also BRWS 9; CA 5-8R; CANR 3, 43,
90, CP 1, 2, 3, 4, 5, 6, 7; DLB 27

Nekrasov, Nikolai Alekseevich
1821-1878 .... **NCLC 11**
See also DLB 277

Nelligan, Emile 1879-1941 .... **TCLC 14**
See also CA 204; CAAE 114; DLB 92;
EWL 3

Nelson, Willie 1933- .... **CLC 17**
See also CA 107; CANR 114

Nemerov, Howard 1920-1991 .... **CLC 2, 6, 9, 36; PC 24; TCLC 124**
See also AMW; CA 1-4R; CAAS 134;
CABS 2; CANR 1, 27, 53; CN 1, 2, 3;
CP 1, 2, 3, 4, 5; DAM POET; DLB 5, 6;
DLBY 1983; EWL 3; INT CANR-27;
MAL 5; MTCW 1, 2; MTFW 2005; PFS
10, 14; RGAL 4

Nepos, Cornelius c. 99B.C.-c.
24B.C. .... **CMLC 89**
See also DLB 211

Neruda, Pablo 1904-1973 .. **CLC 1, 2, 5, 7, 9, 28, 62; HLC 2; PC 4, 64; WLC 4**
See also CA 19-20; CAAS 45-48; CANR
131; CAP 2; DA; DA3; DAB; DAC;
DAM MST, MULT, POET; DLB 283,
331; DNFS 2; EWL 3; HW 1; LAW;
MTCW 1, 2; MTFW 2005; PFS 11;
RGWL 2, 3; TWA; WLIT 1; WP

Nerval, Gerard de 1808-1855 ... **NCLC 1, 67; PC 13; SSC 18**
See also DLB 217; EW 6; GFL 1789 to the
Present; RGSF 2; RGWL 2, 3

Nervo, (Jose) Amado (Ruiz de)
1870 1919 .... **HLCS 2; TCLC 11**
See also CA 131; CAAE 109; DLB 290;
EWL 3; HW 1; LAW

Nesbit, Malcolm
See Chester, Alfred

Nessi, Pio Baroja y
See Baroja, Pio

Nestroy, Johann 1801-1862 .... **NCLC 42**
See also DLB 133; RGWL 2, 3

Netterville, Luke
See O'Grady, Standish (James)

Neufeld, John (Arthur) 1938- .... **CLC 17**
See also AAYA 11; CA 25-28R; CANR 11,
37, 56; CLR 52; MAICYA 1, 2; SAAS 3;
SATA 6, 81, 131; SATA-Essay 131; YAW

Neumann, Alfred 1895-1952 .... **TCLC 100**
See also CA 183; DLB 56

Neumann, Ferenc
See Molnar, Ferenc

Neville, Emily Cheney 1919- .... **CLC 12**
See also BYA 2; CA 5-8R; CANR 3, 37,
85; JRDA; MAICYA 1, 2; SAAS 2; SATA
1; YAW

Newbound, Bernard Slade 1930-
See Slade, Bernard
See also CA 81-84; CANR 49; CD 5; DAM
DRAM

Newby, P(ercy) H(oward)
1918-1997 .... **CLC 2, 13**
See also CA 5-8R; CAAS 161; CANR 32,
67; CN 1, 2, 3, 4, 5, 6; DAM NOV; DLB
15, 326; MTCW 1; RGEL 2

Newcastle
See Cavendish, Margaret Lucas

Newlove, Donald 1928- .... **CLC 6**
See also CA 29-32R; CANR 25

Newlove, John (Herbert) 1938- .... **CLC 14**
See also CA 21-24R; CANR 9, 25; CP 1, 2,
3, 4, 5, 6, 7

Newman, Charles 1938-2006 .... **CLC 2, 8**
See also CA 21-24R; CAAS 249; CANR
84; CN 3, 4, 5, 6

Newman, Charles Hamilton
See Newman, Charles

Newman, Edwin (Harold) 1919- ...... **CLC 14**
See also AITN 1; CA 69-72; CANR 5

Newman, John Henry 1801-1890 . **NCLC 38, 99**
See also BRWS 7; DLB 18, 32, 55; RGEL
2

Newton, (Sir) Isaac 1642-1727 ...... **LC 35, 53**
See also DLB 252

Newton, Suzanne 1936- .... **CLC 35**
See also BYA 7; CA 41-44R; CANR 14;
JRDA; SATA 5, 77

New York Dept. of Ed. .... **CLC 70**

Nexo, Martin Andersen
1869-1954 .... **TCLC 43**
See also CA 202; DLB 214; EWL 3

Nezval, Vitezslav 1900-1958 .... **TCLC 44**
See also CAAE 123; CDWLB 4; DLB 215;
EWL 3

Ng, Fae Myenne 1957(?)- .... **CLC 81**
See also BYA 11; CA 146

Ngcobo, Lauretta 1931- .... **BLC 2:3**
See also CA 165

Ngema, Mbongeni 1955- .... **CLC 57**
See also BW 2; CA 143; CANR 84; CD 5,
6

Ngugi, James T. .... **CLC 3, 7, 13, 182**
See Ngugi wa Thiong'o
See also CN 1, 2

Ngugi, James Thiong'o
See Ngugi wa Thiong'o

Ngugi wa Thiong'o 1938- ...... **BLC 1:3; CLC 36, 182**
See Ngugi, James T.
See also AFW; BRWS 8; BW 2; CA 81-84;
CANR 27, 58, 164; CD 3; CD 5, 6; CD-
WLB 3; DAM MULT, NOV; DLB 125;
DNFS 2; EWL 3; MTCW 1, 2; MTFW
2005; RGEL 2; WWE 1

Niatum, Duane 1938- .... **NNAL**
See also CA 41-44R; CANR 21, 45, 83;
DLB 175

Nichol, B(arrie) P(hillip) 1944-1988 . **CLC 18**
See also CA 53-56; CP 1, 2, 3, 4; DLB 53;
SATA 66

Nicholas of Cusa 1401-1464 .... **LC 80**
See also DLB 115

Nichols, John 1940- .... **CLC 38**
See also AMWS 13; CA 190; 9-12R, 190;
2; CANR 6, 70, 121; DLBY 1982; LATS
1:2; MTFW 2005; TCWW 1, 2

Nichols, Leigh
See Koontz, Dean R.

Nichols, Peter (Richard) 1927- .... **CLC 5, 36, 65**
See also CA 104; CANR 33, 86; CBD; CD
5, 6; DLB 13, 245; MTCW 1

Nicholson, Linda .... **CLC 65**

Ni Chuilleanain, Eilean 1942- .... **PC 34**
See also CA 126; CANR 53, 83; CP 5, 6, 7;
CWP; DLB 40

Nicolas, F. R. E.
See Freeling, Nicolas

Niedecker, Lorine 1903-1970 ..... **CLC 10, 42; PC 42**
See also CA 25-28; CAP 2; DAM POET;
DLB 48

Nietzsche, Friedrich (Wilhelm)
1844-1900 .... **TCLC 10, 18, 55**
See also CA 121; CAAE 107; CDWLB 2;
DLB 129; EW 7; RGWL 2, 3; TWA

Nievo, Ippolito 1831-1861 .... **NCLC 22**

Nightingale, Anne Redmon 1943-
See Redmon, Anne
See also CA 103

Nightingale, Florence 1820-1910 ... **TCLC 85**
See also CA 188; DLB 166

Nijo Yoshimoto 1320-1388 .... **CMLC 49**
See also DLB 203

Nik. T. O.
See Annensky, Innokenty (Fyodorovich)

Nin, Anais 1903-1977 ..... **CLC 1, 4, 8, 11, 14, 60, 127; SSC 10**
See also AITN 2; AMWS 10; BPFB 2; CA
13-16R; CAAS 69-72; CANR 22, 53; CN
1, 2; DAM NOV, POP; DLB 2, 4, 152;
EWL 3; GLL 2; MAL 5; MBL; MTCW 1,
2; MTFW 2005; RGAL 4; RGSF 2

Nisbet, Robert A(lexander)
1913-1996 .... **TCLC 117**
See also CA 25-28R; CAAS 153; CANR
17; INT CANR-17

Nishida, Kitaro 1870-1945 .... **TCLC 83**

Nishiwaki, Junzaburo 1894-1982 .... **PC 15**
See Junzaburo, Nishiwaki
See also CA 194; CAAS 107; MJW; RGWL
3

Nissenson, Hugh 1933- .... **CLC 4, 9**
See also CA 17-20R; CANR 27, 108, 151;
CN 5, 6; DLB 28, 335

Nister, Der
See Der Nister
See also DLB 333; EWL 3

Niven, Larry 1938-
See Niven, Laurence VanCott
See also CA 207; 21-24R, 207; 12; CANR
14, 44, 66, 113, 155; CPW; DAM POP;
MTCW 1, 2; SATA 95, 171; SFW 4

Niven, Laurence VanCott .... **CLC 8**
See Niven, Larry
See also AAYA 27; BPFB 2; BYA 10; DLB
8; SCFW 1, 2

Nixon, Agnes Eckhardt 1927- .... **CLC 21**
See also CA 110

Nizan, Paul 1905-1940 .... **TCLC 40**
See also CA 161; DLB 72; EWL 3; GFL
1789 to the Present

Nkosi, Lewis 1936- .... **BLC 1:3; CLC 45**
See also BW 1, 3; CA 65-68; CANR 27,
81; CBD; CD 5, 6; DAM MULT; DLB
157, 225; WWE 1

Nodier, (Jean) Charles (Emmanuel)
1780-1844 .... **NCLC 19**
See also DLB 119; GFL 1789 to the Present

Noguchi, Yone 1875-1947 .... **TCLC 80**

Nolan, Christopher 1965- .... **CLC 58**
See also CA 111; CANR 88

Noon, Jeff 1957- .... **CLC 91**
See also CA 148; CANR 83; DLB 267;
SFW 4

Norden, Charles
See Durrell, Lawrence (George)

Nordhoff, Charles Bernard
1887-1947 .... **TCLC 23**
See also CA 211; CAAE 108; DLB 9; LAIT
1; RHW 1; SATA 23

Norfolk, Lawrence 1963- .... **CLC 76**
See also CA 144; CANR 85; CN 6, 7; DLB
267

Norman, Marsha (Williams) 1947- . **CLC 28, 186; DC 8**
See also CA 105; CABS 3; CAD; CANR
41, 131; CD 5, 6; CSW; CWD; DAM
DRAM; DFS 2; DLB 266; DLBY 1984;
FW; MAL 5

Normyx
See Douglas, (George) Norman

Norris, (Benjamin) Frank(lin, Jr.)
1870-1902 .... **SSC 28; TCLC 24, 155**
See also AAYA 57; AMW; AMWC 2; BPFB
2; CA 160; CAAE 110; CDALB 1865-
1917; DLB 12, 71, 186; LMFS 2; MAL
5; NFS 12; RGAL 4; TCWW 1, 2; TUS

Norris, Kathleen 1947- .... **CLC 248**
See also CA 160; CANR 113

Norris, Leslie 1921-2006 .... **CLC 14**
See also CA 11-12; CAAS 251; CANR 14,
117; CAP 1; CP 1, 2, 3, 4, 5, 6, 7; DLB
27, 256

Parkman, Francis, Jr. 1823-1893 .. **NCLC 12**
See also AMWS 2; DLB 1, 30, 183, 186, 235; RGAL 4

Parks, Gordon 1912-2006 . **BLC 1:3; CLC 1, 16**
See also AAYA 36; AITN 2; BW 2, 3; CA 41-44R; CAAS 249; CANR 26, 66, 145; DA3; DAM MULT; DLB 33; MTCW 2; MTFW 2005; SATA 8, 108; SATA-Obit 175

Parks, Suzan-Lori 1964(?)- ..... **BLC 2:3; DC 23**
See also AAYA 55; CA 201; CAD; CD 5, 6; CWD; DFS 22; RGAL 4

Parks, Tim(othy Harold) 1954- ...... **CLC 147**
See also CA 131; CAAE 126; CANR 77, 144; CN 7; DLB 231; INT CA-131

Parmenides c. 515B.C.-c. 450B.C. .... **CMLC 22**
See also DLB 176

Parnell, Thomas 1679-1718 .... **LC 3**
See also DLB 95; RGEL 2

Parr, Catherine c. 1513(?)-1548 .... **LC 86**
See also DLB 136

Parra, Nicanor 1914- ... **CLC 2, 102; HLC 2; PC 39**
See also CA 85-88; CANR 32; CWW 2; DAM MULT; DLB 283; EWL 3; HW 1; LAW; MTCW 1

Parra Sanojo, Ana Teresa de la 1890-1936 .... **HLCS 2**
See de la Parra, (Ana) Teresa (Sonojo)
See also LAW

Parrish, Mary Frances
See Fisher, M(ary) F(rances) K(ennedy)

Parshchikov, Aleksei 1954- .... **CLC 59**
See Parshchikov, Aleksei Maksimovich

Parshchikov, Aleksei Maksimovich
See Parshchikov, Aleksei
See also DLB 285

Parson, Professor
See Coleridge, Samuel Taylor

Parson Lot
See Kingsley, Charles

Parton, Sara Payson Willis 1811-1872 .... **NCLC 86**
See also DLB 43, 74, 239

Partridge, Anthony
See Oppenheim, E(dward) Phillips

Pascal, Blaise 1623-1662 .... **LC 35**
See also DLB 268; EW 3; GFL Beginnings to 1789; RGWL 2, 3; TWA

Pascoli, Giovanni 1855-1912 .... **TCLC 45**
See also CA 170; EW 7; EWL 3

Pasolini, Pier Paolo 1922-1975 .. **CLC 20, 37, 106; PC 17**
See also CA 93-96; CAAS 61-64; CANR 63; DLB 128, 177; EWL 3; MTCW 1; RGWL 2, 3

Pasquini
See Silone, Ignazio

Pastan, Linda (Olenik) 1932- .... **CLC 27**
See also CA 61-64; CANR 18, 40, 61, 113; CP 3, 4, 5, 6, 7; CSW; CWP; DAM POET; DLB 5; PFS 8, 25

Pasternak, Boris 1890-1960 ... **CLC 7, 10, 18, 63; PC 6; SSC 31; TCLC 188; WLC 4**
See also BPFB 3; CA 127; CAAS 116; DA; DA3; DAB; DAC; DAM MST, NOV; POET; DLB 302, 331; EW 10; MTCW 1, 2; MTFW 2005; NFS 26; RGSF 2; RGWL 2, 3; TWA; WP

Patchen, Kenneth 1911-1972 .... **CLC 1, 2, 18**
See also BG 1:3; CA 1-4R; CAAS 33-36R; CANR 3, 35; CN 1; CP 1; DAM POET; DLB 16, 48; EWL 3; MAL 5; MTCW 1; RGAL 4

Patchett, Ann 1963- .... **CLC 244**
See also AAYA 69; AMWS 12; CA 139; CANR 64, 110, 167; MTFW 2005

Pater, Walter (Horatio) 1839-1894 . **NCLC 7, 90, 159**
See also BRW 5; CDBLB 1832-1890; DLB 57, 156; RGEL 2; TEA

Paterson, A(ndrew) B(arton) 1864-1941 .... **TCLC 32**
See also CA 155; DLB 230; RGEL 2; SATA 97

Paterson, Banjo
See Paterson, A(ndrew) B(arton)

Paterson, Katherine 1932- .... **CLC 12, 30**
See also AAYA 1, 31; BYA 1, 2, 7; CA 21-24R; CANR 28, 59, 111, 173; CLR 7, 50, 127; CWRI 5; DLB 52; JRDA; LAIT 4; MAICYA 1, 2; MAICYAS 1; MTCW 1; SATA 13, 53, 92, 133; WYA; YAW

Paterson, Katherine Womeldorf
See Paterson, Katherine

Patmore, Coventry Kersey Dighton 1823-1896 .... **NCLC 9; PC 59**
See also DLB 35, 98; RGEL 2; TEA

Paton, Alan 1903-1988 ..... **CLC 4, 10, 25, 55, 106; TCLC 165; WLC 4**
See also AAYA 26; AFW; BPFB 3; BRWS 2; BYA 1; CA 13-16; CAAS 125; CANR 22; CAP 1; CN 1, 2, 3, 4; DA; DA3; DAB; DAC; DAM MST, NOV; DLB 225; DLBD 17; EWL 3; EXPN; LAIT 4; MTCW 1, 2; MTFW 2005; NFS 3, 12; RGEL 2; SATA 11; SATA-Obit 56; TWA; WLIT 2; WWE 1

Paton Walsh, Gillian
See Paton Walsh, Jill
See also AAYA 47; BYA 1, 8

Paton Walsh, Jill 1937- .... **CLC 35**
See Paton Walsh, Gillian; Walsh, Jill Paton
See also AAYA 11; CA 262; 262; CANR 38, 83, 158; CLR 2, 65; DLB 161; JRDA; MAICYA 1, 2; SAAS 3; SATA 4, 72, 109; YAW

Patsauq, Markoosie 1942- .... **NNAL**
See also CA 101; CLR 23; CWRI 5; DAM MULT

Patterson, (Horace) Orlando (Lloyd) 1940- .... **BLCS**
See also BW 1; CA 65-68; CANR 27, 84; CN 1, 2, 3, 4, 5, 6

Patton, George S(mith), Jr. 1885-1945 .... **TCLC 79**
See also CA 189

Paulding, James Kirke 1778-1860 ... **NCLC 2**
See also DLB 3, 59, 74, 250; RGAL 4

Paulin, Thomas Neilson
See Paulin, Tom

Paulin, Tom 1949- .... **CLC 37, 177**
See also CA 128; CAAE 123; CANR 98; CP 3, 4, 5, 6, 7; DLB 40

Pausanias c. 1st cent. - .... **CMLC 36**

Paustovsky, Konstantin (Georgievich) 1892-1968 .... **CLC 40**
See also CA 93-96; CAAS 25-28R; DLB 272; EWL 3

Pavese, Cesare 1908-1950 .... **PC 13; SSC 19; TCLC 3**
See also CA 169; CAAE 104; DLB 128, 177; EW 12; EWL 3; PFS 20; RGSF 2; RGWL 2, 3; TWA; WLIT 7

Pavic, Milorad 1929- .... **CLC 60**
See also CA 136; CDWLB 4; CWW 2; DLB 181; EWL 3; RGWL 3

Pavlov, Ivan Petrovich 1849-1936 . **TCLC 91**
See also CA 180; CAAE 118

Pavlova, Karolina Karlovna 1807-1893 .... **NCLC 138**
See also DLB 205

Payne, Alan
See Jakes, John

Payne, Rachel Ann
See Jakes, John

Paz, Gil
See Lugones, Leopoldo

Paz, Octavio 1914-1998 . **CLC 3, 4, 6, 10, 19, 51, 65, 119; HLC 2; PC 1, 48; WLC 4**
See also AAYA 50; CA 73-76; CAAS 165; CANR 32, 65, 104; CWW 2; DA; DA3; DAB; DAC; DAM MST, MULT, POET; DLB 290, 331; DLBY 1990, 1998; DNFS 1; EWL 3; HW 1, 2; LAW; LAWS 1; MTCW 1, 2; MTFW 2005; PFS 18; RGWL 2, 3; SSFS 13; TWA; WLIT 1

p'Bitek, Okot 1931-1982 . **BLC 1:3; CLC 96; TCLC 149**
See also AFW; BW 2, 3; CA 124; CAAS 107; CANR 82; CP 1, 2, 3; DAM MULT; DLB 125; EWL 3; MTCW 1, 2; MTFW 2005; RGEL 2; WLIT 2

Peabody, Elizabeth Palmer 1804-1894 .... **NCLC 169**
See also DLB 1, 223

Peacham, Henry 1578-1644(?) .... **LC 119**
See also DLB 151

Peacock, Molly 1947- .... **CLC 60**
See also CA 262; 103, 262; 21; CANR 52, 84; CP 5, 6, 7; CWP; DLB 120, 282

Peacock, Thomas Love 1785-1866 .... **NCLC 22**
See also BRW 4; DLB 96, 116; RGEL 2; RGSF 2

Peake, Mervyn 1911-1968 .... **CLC 7, 54**
See also CA 5-8R; CAAS 25-28R; CANR 3; DLB 15, 160, 255; FANT, MTCW 1; RGEL 2; SATA 23; SFW 4

Pearce, Philippa 1920-2006
See Christie, Philippa
See also CA 5-8R; CAAS 255; CANR 4, 109; CWRI 5; FANT; MAICYA 2; SATA-Obit 179

Pearl, Eric
See Elman, Richard (Martin)

Pearson, Jean Mary
See Gardam, Jane

Pearson, T. R. 1956- .... **CLC 39**
See also CA 130; CAAE 120; CANR 97, 147; CSW; INT CA-130

Pearson, Thomas Reid
See Pearson, T. R.

Peck, Dale 1967- .... **CLC 81**
See also CA 146; CANR 72, 127; GLL 2

Peck, John (Frederick) 1941- .... **CLC 3**
See also CA 49-52; CANR 3, 100; CP 4, 5, 6, 7

Peck, Richard 1934- .... **CLC 21**
See also AAYA 1, 24; BYA 1, 6, 8, 11; CA 85-88; CANR 19, 38, 129; CLR 15; INT CANR-19; JRDA; MAICYA 1, 2; SAAS 2; SATA 18, 55, 97, 110, 158; SATA-Essay 110; WYA; YAW

Peck, Richard Wayne
See Peck, Richard

Peck, Robert Newton 1928- .... **CLC 17**
See also AAYA 3, 43; BYA 1, 6; CA 182; 81-84, 182; CANR 31, 63, 127; CLR 45; DA; DAC; DAM MST; JRDA; LAIT 3; MAICYA 1, 2; SAAS 1; SATA 21, 62, 111, 156; SATA-Essay 108; WYA; YAW

Peckinpah, David Samuel
See Peckinpah, Sam

Peckinpah, Sam 1925-1984 .... **CLC 20**
See also CA 109; CAAS 114; CANR 82

Pedersen, Knut 1859-1952
See Hamsun, Knut
See also CA 119; CAAE 104; CANR 63; MTCW 1, 2

Pincherle, Alberto 1907-1990 ...... **CLC 11, 18**
    See Moravia, Alberto
    See also CA 25-28R; CAAS 132; CANR
        33, 63, 142; DAM NOV; MTCW 1;
        MTFW 2005
Pinckney, Darryl 1953- .... **CLC 76**
    See also BW 2, 3; CA 143; CANR 79
Pindar 518(?)B.C.-438(?)B.C. .... **CMLC 12;**
    PC 19
    See also AW 1; CDWLB 1; DLB 176;
        RGWL 2
Pineda, Cecile 1942- .... **CLC 39**
    See also CA 118; DLB 209
Pinero, Arthur Wing 1855-1934 .... **TCLC 32**
    See also CA 153; CAAE 110; DAM DRAM;
        DLB 10; RGEL 2
Pinero, Miguel (Antonio Gomez)
    1946-1988 .... **CLC 4, 55**
    See also CA 61-64; CAAS 125; CAD;
        CANR 29, 90; DLB 266; HW 1; LLW
Pinget, Robert 1919-1997 .... **CLC 7, 13, 37**
    See also CA 85-88; CAAS 160; CWW 2;
        DLB 83; EWL 3; GFL 1789 to the Present
Pink Floyd
    See Barrett, (Roger) Syd; Gilmour, David;
        Mason, Nick; Waters, Roger; Wright, Rick
Pinkney, Edward 1802-1828 .... **NCLC 31**
    See also DLB 248
Pinkwater, D. Manus
    See Pinkwater, Daniel Manus
Pinkwater, Daniel
    See Pinkwater, Daniel Manus
Pinkwater, Daniel M.
    See Pinkwater, Daniel Manus
Pinkwater, Daniel Manus 1941- .... **CLC 35**
    See also AAYA 1, 46; BYA 9; CA 29-32R;
        CANR 12, 38, 89, 143; CLR 4; CSW;
        FANT; JRDA; MAICYA 1, 2; SAAS 3;
        SATA 8, 46, 76, 114, 158; SFW 4; YAW
Pinkwater, Manus
    See Pinkwater, Daniel Manus
Pinsky, Robert 1940- .... **CLC 9, 19, 38, 94,**
    121, 216; PC 27
    See also AMWS 6; CA 29-32R; 4; CANR
        58, 97, 138; CP 3, 4, 5, 6, 7; DA3; DAM
        POET; DLBY 1982, 1998; MAL 5;
        MTCW 2; MTFW 2005; PFS 18; RGAL
        4; TCLE 1:2
Pinta, Harold
    See Pinter, Harold
Pinter, Harold 1930- .. **CLC 1, 3, 6, 9, 11, 15,**
    27, 58, 73, 199; DC 15; WLC 4
    See also BRWR 1; BRWS 1; CA 5-8R;
        CANR 33, 65, 112, 145; CBD; CD 5, 6;
        CDBLB 1960 to Present; CP 1; DA; DA3;
        DAB; DAC; DAM DRAM, MST; DFS 3,
        5, 7, 14; DLB 13, 310, 331; EWL 3;
        IDFW 3, 4; LMFS 2; MTCW 1, 2; MTFW
        2005; RGEL 2; RGHL; TEA
Piozzi, Hester Lynch (Thrale)
    1741-1821 .... **NCLC 57**
    See also DLB 104, 142
Pirandello, Luigi 1867-1936 .. **DC 5; SSC 22;**
    TCLC 4, 29, 172; WLC 4
    See also CA 153; CAAE 104; CANR 103;
        DA; DA3; DAB; DAC; DAM DRAM,
        MST; DFS 4, 9; DLB 264, 331; EW 8;
        EWL 3; MTCW 2; MTFW 2005; RGSF
        2; RGWL 2, 3; WLIT 7
Pirsig, Robert M(aynard) 1928- ... **CLC 4, 6,**
    73
    See also CA 53-56; CANR 42, 74; CPW 1;
        DA3; DAM POP; MTCW 1, 2; MTFW
        2005; SATA 39
Pisan, Christine de
    See Christine de Pizan
Pisarev, Dmitrii Ivanovich
    See Pisarev, Dmitry Ivanovich
    See also DLB 277

Pisarev, Dmitry Ivanovich
    1840-1868 .... **NCLC 25**
    See Pisarev, Dmitrii Ivanovich
Pix, Mary (Griffith) 1666-1709 ..... **LC 8, 149**
    See also DLB 80
Pixerecourt, (Rene Charles) Guilbert de
    1773-1844 .... **NCLC 39**
    See also DLB 192; GFL 1789 to the Present
Plaatje, Sol(omon) T(shekisho)
    1878-1932 .... **BLCS; TCLC 73**
    See also BW 2, 3; CA 141; CANR 79; DLB
        125, 225
Plaidy, Jean
    See Hibbert, Eleanor Alice Burford
Planche, James Robinson
    1796-1880 .... **NCLC 42**
    See also RGEL 2
Plant, Robert 1948- .... **CLC 12**
Plante, David 1940- .... **CLC 7, 23, 38**
    See also CA 37-40R; CANR 12, 36, 58, 82,
        152; CN 2, 3, 4, 5, 6, 7; DAM NOV;
        DLBY 1983; INT CANR-12; MTCW 1
Plante, David Robert
    See Plante, David
Plath, Sylvia 1932-1963 ..... **CLC 1, 2, 3, 5, 9,**
    11, 14, 17, 50, 51, 62, 111; PC 1, 37;
    WLC 4
    See also AAYA 13; AMWR 2; AMWS 1;
        BPFB 3; CA 19-20; CANR 34, 101; CAP
        2; CDALB 1941-1968; DA; DA3; DAB;
        DAC; DAM MST, POET; DLB 5, 6, 152;
        EWL 3; EXPN; EXPP; FL 1:6; FW; LAIT
        4; MAL 5; MBL; MTCW 1, 2; MTFW
        2005; NFS 1; PAB; PFS 1, 15; RGAL 4;
        SATA 96; TUS; WP; YAW
Plato c. 428B.C.-347B.C. .... **CMLC 8, 75, 98;**
    WLCS
    See also AW 1; CDWLB 1; DA; DA3;
        DAB; DAC; DAM MST; DLB 176; LAIT
        1; LATS 1:1; RGWL 2, 3, WLIT 8
Platonov, Andrei
    See Klimentov, Andrei Platonovich
Platonov, Andrei Platonovich
    See Klimentov, Andrei Platonovich
    See also DLB 272
Platonov, Andrey Platonovich
    See Klimentov, Andrei Platonovich
    See also EWL 3
Platt, Kin 1911- .... **CLC 26**
    See also AAYA 11; CA 17-20R; CANR 11;
        JRDA; SAAS 17; SATA 21, 86; WYA
Plautus c. 254B.C.-c. 184B.C. .... **CMLC 24,**
    92; DC 6
    See also AW 1; CDWLB 1; DLB 211;
        RGWL 2, 3; WLIT 8
Plick et Plock
    See Simenon, Georges (Jacques Christian)
Plieksans, Janis
    See Rainis, Janis
Plimpton, George 1927-2003 .... **CLC 36**
    See also AITN 1; AMWS 16; CA 21-24R;
        CAAS 224; CANR 32, 70, 103, 133; DLB
        185, 241; MTCW 1, 2; MTFW 2005;
        SATA 10; SATA-Obit 150
Pliny the Elder c. 23-79 .... **CMLC 23**
    See also DLB 211
Pliny the Younger c. 61-c. 112 ...... **CMLC 62**
    See also AW 2; DLB 211
Plomer, William Charles Franklin
    1903-1973 .... **CLC 4, 8**
    See also AFW; BRWS 11; CA 21-22; CANR
        34; CAP 2; CN 1; CP 1, 2; DLB 20, 162,
        191, 225; EWL 3; MTCW 1; RGEL 2;
        RGSF 2; SATA 24
Plotinus 204-270 .... **CMLC 46**
    See also CDWLB 1; DLB 176
Plowman, Piers
    See Kavanagh, Patrick (Joseph)

Plum, J.
    See Wodehouse, P(elham) G(renville)
Plumly, Stanley (Ross) 1939- .... **CLC 33**
    See also CA 110; CAAE 108; CANR 97;
        CP 3, 4, 5, 6, 7; DLB 5, 193; INT CA-
        110
Plumpe, Friedrich Wilhelm
    See Murnau, F.W.
Plutarch c. 46-c. 120 .... **CMLC 60**
    See also AW 2; CDWLB 1; DLB 176;
        RGWL 2, 3; TWA; WLIT 8
Po Chu-i 772-846 .... **CMLC 24**
Podhoretz, Norman 1930- .... **CLC 189**
    See also AMWS 8; CA 9-12R; CANR 7,
        78, 135
Poe, Edgar Allan 1809-1849 ..... **NCLC 1, 16,**
    55, 78, 94, 97, 117; PC 1, 54; SSC 1,
    22, 34, 35, 54, 88; WLC 4
    See also AAYA 14; AMW; AMWC 1;
        AMWR 2; BPFB 3; BYA 5, 11; CDALB
        1640-1865; CMW 4; DA; DA3; DAB;
        DAC; DAM MST, POET; DLB 3, 59, 73,
        74, 248, 254; EXPP; EXPS; GL 3; HGG;
        LAIT 2; LATS 1:1; LMFS 1; MSW; PAB;
        PFS 1, 3, 9; RGAL 4; RGSF 2; SATA 23;
        SCFW 1, 2; SFW 4; SSFS 2, 4, 7, 8, 16;
        SUFW; TUS; WP; WYA
Poet of Titchfield Street, The
    See Pound, Ezra (Weston Loomis)
Poggio Bracciolini, Gian Francesco
    1380-1459 .... **LC 125**
Pohl, Frederik 1919- .... **CLC 18; SSC 25**
    See also AAYA 24; CA 188; 61-64, 188; 1;
        CANR 11, 37, 81, 140; CN 1, 2, 3, 4, 5,
        6; DLB 8; INT CANR-11; MTCW 1, 2;
        MTFW 2005; SATA 24; SCFW 1, 2; SFW
        4
Poirier, Louis
    See Gracq, Julien
Poitier, Sidney 1927- .... **CLC 26**
    See also AAYA 60; BW 1; CA 117; CANR
        94
Pokagon, Simon 1830-1899 .... **NNAL**
    See also DAM MULT
Polanski, Roman 1933- .... **CLC 16, 178**
    See also CA 77-80
Poliakoff, Stephen 1952- .... **CLC 38**
    See also CA 106; CANR 116; CBD; CD 5,
        6; DLB 13
Police, The
    See Copeland, Stewart (Armstrong); Sum-
        mers, Andy
Polidori, John William
    1795-1821 .... **NCLC 51; SSC 97**
    See also DLB 116; HGG
Poliziano, Angelo 1454-1494 .... **LC 120**
    See also WLIT 7
Pollitt, Katha 1949- .... **CLC 28, 122**
    See also CA 122; CAAE 120; CANR 66,
        108, 164; MTCW 1, 2; MTFW 2005
Pollock, (Mary) Sharon 1936- .... **CLC 50**
    See also CA 141; CANR 132; CD 5; CWD;
        DAC; DAM DRAM, MST; DFS 3; DLB
        60; FW
Pollock, Sharon 1936- .... **DC 20**
    See also CD 6
Polo, Marco 1254-1324 .... **CMLC 15**
    See also WLIT 7
Polonsky, Abraham (Lincoln)
    1910-1999 .... **CLC 92**
    See also CA 104; CAAS 187; DLB 26; INT
        CA-104
Polybius c. 200B.C.-c. 118B.C. ...... **CMLC 17**
    See also AW 1; DLB 176; RGWL 2, 3
Pomerance, Bernard 1940- .... **CLC 13**
    See also CA 101; CAD; CANR 49, 134;
        CD 5, 6; DAM DRAM; DFS 9; LAIT 2

Ponge, Francis 1899-1988 .... **CLC 6, 18**
  See also CA 85-88; CAAS 126; CANR 40,
  86; DAM POET; DLBY 2002; EWL 3;
  GFL 1789 to the Present; RGWL 2, 3
Poniatowska, Elena 1932- . **CLC 140; HLC 2**
  See also CA 101; CANR 32, 66, 107, 156;
  CDWLB 3; CWW 2; DAM MULT; DLB
  113; EWL 3; HW 1, 2; LAWS 1; WLIT 1
Pontoppidan, Henrik 1857-1943 .... **TCLC 29**
  See also CA 170; DLB 300, 331
Ponty, Maurice Merleau
  See Merleau-Ponty, Maurice
Poole, Josephine .... **CLC 17**
  See Helyar, Jane Penelope Josephine
  See also SAAS 2; SATA 5
Popa, Vasko 1922-1991 . **CLC 19; TCLC 167**
  See also CA 148; CAAE 112; CDWLB 4;
  DLB 181; EWL 3; RGWL 2, 3
Pope, Alexander 1688-1744 ...... **LC 3, 58, 60,
  64; PC 26; WLC 5**
  See also BRW 3; BRWC 1; BRWR 1; CD-
  BLB 1660-1789; DA; DA3; DAB; DAC;
  DAM MST, POET; DLB 95, 101, 213;
  EXPP; PAB; PFS 12; RGEL 2; WLIT 3;
  WP
Popov, Evgenii Anatol'evich
  See Popov, Yevgeny
  See also DLB 285
Popov, Yevgeny .... **CLC 59**
  See Popov, Evgenii Anatol'evich
Poquelin, Jean-Baptiste
  See Moliere
Porete, Marguerite (?)-1310 .... **CMLC 73**
  See also DLB 208
Porphyry c. 233-c. 305 .... **CMLC 71**
Porter, Connie (Rose) 1959(?)- .... **CLC 70**
  See also AAYA 65; BW 2, 3; CA 142;
  CANR 90, 109; SATA 81, 129
Porter, Gene(va Grace) Stratton .. **TCLC 21**
  See Stratton-Porter, Gene(va Grace)
  See also BPFB 3; CAAE 112; CWRI 5;
  RHW
Porter, Katherine Anne 1890-1980 ... **CLC 1,
  3, 7, 10, 13, 15, 27, 101; SSC 4, 31, 43,
  108**
  See also AAYA 42; AITN 2; AMW; BPFB
  3; CA 1-4R; CAAS 101; CANR 1, 65;
  CDALBS; CN 1, 2; DA; DA3; DAB;
  DAC; DAM MST, NOV; DLB 4, 9, 102;
  DLBD 12; DLBY 1980; EWL 3; EXPS;
  LAIT 3; MAL 5; MBL; MTCW 1, 2;
  MTFW 2005; NFS 14; RGAL 4; RGSF 2;
  SATA 39; SATA-Obit 23; SSFS 1, 8, 11,
  16, 23; TCWW 2; TUS
Porter, Peter (Neville Frederick)
  1929- .... **CLC 5, 13, 33**
  See also CA 85-88; CP 1, 2, 3, 4, 5, 6, 7;
  DLB 40, 289; WWE 1
Porter, William Sydney 1862-1910
  See Henry, O.
  See also CA 131; CAAE 104; CDALB
  1865-1917; DA; DA3; DAB; DAC; DAM
  MST; DLB 12, 78, 79; MTCW 1, 2;
  MTFW 2005; TUS; YABC 2
Portillo (y Pacheco), Jose Lopez
  See Lopez Portillo (y Pacheco), Jose
Portillo Trambley, Estela 1927-1998 .. **HLC 2**
  See Trambley, Estela Portillo
  See also CANR 32; DAM MULT; DLB
  209; HW 1
Posey, Alexander (Lawrence)
  1873-1908 .... **NNAL**
  See also CA 144; CANR 80; DAM MULT;
  DLB 175
Posse, Abel .... **CLC 70**
  See also CA 252
Post, Melville Davisson
  1869-1930 .... **TCLC 39**
  See also CA 202; CAAE 110; CMW 4

Postman, Neil 1931(?)-2003 .... **CLC 244**
  See also CA 102; CAAS 221
Potok, Chaim 1929-2002 ... **CLC 2, 7, 14, 26,
  112**
  See also AAYA 15, 50; AITN 1, 2; BPFB 3;
  BYA 1; CA 17-20R; CAAS 208; CANR
  19, 35, 64, 98; CLR 92; CN 4, 5, 6; DA3;
  DAM NOV; DLB 28, 152; EXPN; INT
  CANR-19; LAIT 4; MTCW 1, 2; MTFW
  2005; NFS 4; RGHL; SATA 33, 106;
  SATA-Obit 134; TUS; YAW
Potok, Herbert Harold -2002
  See Potok, Chaim
Potok, Herman Harold
  See Potok, Chaim
Potter, Dennis (Christopher George)
  1935-1994 .... **CLC 58, 86, 123**
  See also BRWS 10; CA 107; CAAS 145;
  CANR 33, 61; CBD; DLB 233; MTCW 1
Pound, Ezra (Weston Loomis)
  1885-1972 .. **CLC 1, 2, 3, 4, 5, 7, 10, 13,
  18, 34, 48, 50, 112; PC 4; WLC 5**
  See also AAYA 47; AMW; AMWR 1; CA
  5-8R; CAAS 37-40R; CANR 40; CDALB
  1917-1929; CP 1; DA; DA3; DAB; DAC;
  DAM MST, POET; DLB 4, 45, 63; DLBD
  15; EFS 2; EWL 3; EXPP; LMFS 2; MAL
  5; MTCW 1, 2; MTFW 2005; PAB; PFS
  2, 8, 16; RGAL 4; TUS; WP
Povod, Reinaldo 1959-1994 .... **CLC 44**
  See also CA 136; CAAS 146; CANR 83
Powell, Adam Clayton, Jr.
  1908-1972 .... **BLC 1:3; CLC 89**
  See also BW 1, 3; CA 102; CAAS 33-36R;
  CANR 86; DAM MULT
Powell, Anthony 1905-2000 ... **CLC 1, 3, 7, 9,
  10, 31**
  See also BRW 7; CA 1-4R; CAAS 189;
  CANR 1, 32, 62, 107; CDBLB 1945-
  1960; CN 1, 2, 3, 4, 5, 6; DLB 15; EWL
  3; MTCW 1, 2; MTFW 2005; RGEL 2;
  TEA
Powell, Dawn 1896(?)-1965 .... **CLC 66**
  See also CA 5-8R; CANR 121; DLBY 1997
Powell, Padgett 1952- .... **CLC 34**
  See also CA 126; CANR 63, 101; CSW;
  DLB 234; DLBY 01; SSFS 25
Powell, (Oval) Talmage 1920-2000
  See Queen, Ellery
  See also CA 5-8R; CANR 2, 80
Power, Susan 1961- .... **CLC 91**
  See also BYA 14; CA 160; CANR 135; NFS
  11
Powers, J(ames) F(arl) 1917-1999 ..... **CLC 1,
  4, 8, 57; SSC 4**
  See also CA 1-4R; CAAS 181; CANR 2,
  61; CN 1, 2, 3, 4, 5, 6; DLB 130; MTCW
  1; RGAL 4; RGSF 2
Powers, John J(ames) 1945-
  See Powers, John R.
  See also CA 69-72
Powers, John R. .... **CLC 66**
  See Powers, John J(ames)
Powers, Richard 1957- .... **CLC 93**
  See also AMWS 9; BPFB 3; CA 148;
  CANR 80; CN 6, 7; MTFW 2005; TCLE
  1:2
Powers, Richard S.
  See Powers, Richard
Pownall, David 1938- .... **CLC 10**
  See also CA 89-92, 180; 18; CANR 49, 101;
  CBD; CD 5, 6; CN 4, 5, 6, 7; DLB 14
Powys, John Cowper 1872-1963 ... **CLC 7, 9,
  15, 46, 125**
  See also CA 85-88; CANR 106; DLB 15,
  255; EWL 3; FANT; MTCW 1, 2; MTFW
  2005; RGEL 2; SUFW

Powys, T(heodore) F(rancis)
  1875-1953 .... **TCLC 9**
  See also BRWS 8; CA 189; CAAE 106;
  DLB 36, 162; EWL 3; FANT; RGEL 2;
  SUFW
Pozzo, Modesta
  See Fonte, Moderata
Prado (Calvo), Pedro 1886-1952 ... **TCLC 75**
  See also CA 131; DLB 283; HW 1; LAW
Prager, Emily 1952- .... **CLC 56**
  See also CA 204
Pratchett, Terence David John
  See Pratchett, Terry
Pratchett, Terry 1948- .... **CLC 197**
  See also AAYA 19, 54; BPFB 3; CA 143;
  CANR 87, 126, 170; CLR 64; CN 6, 7;
  CPW; CWRI 5; FANT; MTFW 2005;
  SATA 82, 139, 185; SFW 4; SUFW 2
Pratolini, Vasco 1913-1991 .... **TCLC 124**
  See also CA 211; DLB 177; EWL 3; RGWL
  2, 3
Pratt, E(dwin) J(ohn) 1883(?)-1964 . **CLC 19**
  See also CA 141; CAAS 93-96; CANR 77;
  DAC; DAM POET; DLB 92; EWL 3;
  RGEL 2; TWA
Premchand .... **TCLC 21**
  See Srivastava, Dhanpat Rai
  See also EWL 3
Prescott, William Hickling
  1796-1859 .... **NCLC 163**
  See also DLB 1, 30, 59, 235
Preseren, France 1800-1849 .... **NCLC 127**
  See also CDWLB 4; DLB 147
Preussler, Otfried 1923- .... **CLC 17**
  See also CA 77-80; SATA 24
Prevert, Jacques (Henri Marie)
  1900-1977 .... **CLC 15**
  See also CA 77-80; CAAS 69-72; CANR
  29, 61; DLB 258; EWL 3; GFL 1789 to
  the Present; IDFW 3, 4; MTCW 1; RGWL
  2, 3; SATA-Obit 30
Prevost, (Antoine Francois)
  1697-1763 .... **LC 1**
  See also DLB 314; EW 4; GFL Beginnings
  to 1789; RGWL 2, 3
Price, Reynolds 1933- .. **CLC 3, 6, 13, 43, 50,
  63, 212; SSC 22**
  See also AMWS 6; CA 1-4R; CANR 1, 37,
  57, 87, 128; CN 1, 2, 3, 4, 5, 6, 7; CSW;
  DAM NOV; DLB 2, 218, 278; EWL 3;
  INT CANR-37; MAL 5; MTFW 2005;
  NFS 18
Price, Richard 1949- .... **CLC 6, 12**
  See also CA 49-52; CANR 3, 147; CN 7;
  DLBY 1981
Prichard, Katharine Susannah
  1883-1969 .... **CLC 46**
  See also CA 11-12; CANR 33; CAP 1; DLB
  260; MTCW 1; RGEL 2; RGSF 2; SATA
  66
Priestley, J(ohn) B(oynton)
  1894-1984 .... **CLC 2, 5, 9, 34**
  See also BRW 7; CA 9-12R; CAAS 113;
  CANR 33; CDBLB 1914-1945; CN 1, 2,
  3; DA3; DAM DRAM, NOV; DLB 10,
  34, 77, 100, 139; DLBY 1984; EWL 3;
  MTCW 1, 2; MTFW 2005; RGEL 2; SFW
  4
Prince 1958- .... **CLC 35**
  See also CA 213
Prince, F(rank) T(empleton)
  1912-2003 .... **CLC 22**
  See also CA 101; CAAS 219; CANR 43,
  79; CP 1, 2, 3, 4, 5, 6, 7; DLB 20
Prince Kropotkin
  See Kropotkin, Peter (Aleksieevich)
Prior, Matthew 1664-1721 .... **LC 4**
  See also DLB 95; RGEL 2

Sade, Marquis de
See Sade, Donatien Alphonse Francois

Sadoff, Ira 1945- .... **CLC 9**
See also CA 53-56; CANR 5, 21, 109; DLB 120

Saetone
See Camus, Albert

Safire, William 1929- .... **CLC 10**
See also CA 17-20R; CANR 31, 54, 91, 148

Sagan, Carl 1934-1996 .... **CLC 30, 112**
See also AAYA 2, 62; CA 25-28R; CAAS 155; CANR 11, 36, 74; CPW; DA3; MTCW 1, 2; MTFW 2005; SATA 58; SATA-Obit 94

Sagan, Francoise .... **CLC 3, 6, 9, 17, 36**
See Quoirez, Francoise
See also CWW 2; DLB 83; EWL 3; GFL 1789 to the Present; MTCW 2

Sahgal, Nayantara (Pandit) 1927- .... **CLC 41**
See also CA 9-12R; CANR 11, 88; CN 1, 2, 3, 4, 5, 6, 7; DLB 323

Said, Edward W. 1935-2003 .... **CLC 123**
See also CA 21-24R; CAAS 220; CANR 45, 74, 107, 131; DLB 67; MTCW 2; MTFW 2005

Saikaku, Ihara 1642-1693 .... **LC 141**
See also RGWL 3

Saikaku Ihara
See Saikaku, Ihara

Saint, H(arry) F. 1941- .... **CLC 50**
See also CA 127

St. Aubin de Teran, Lisa 1953-
See Teran, Lisa St. Aubin de
See also CA 126; CAAE 118; CN 6, 7; INT CA-126

Saint Birgitta of Sweden c.
1303-1373 .... **CMLC 24**

Sainte-Beuve, Charles Augustin
1804-1869 .... **NCLC 5**
See also DLB 217; EW 6; GFL 1789 to the Present

Saint-Exupery, Antoine de
1900-1944 .... **TCLC 2, 56, 169; WLC**
See also AAYA 63; BPFB 3; BYA 3; CA 132; CAAE 108; CLR 10; DA3; DAM NOV; DLB 72; EW 12; EWL 3; GFL 1789 to the Present; LAIT 3; MAICYA 1, 2; MTCW 1, 2; MTFW 2005; RGWL 2, 3; SATA 20; TWA

Saint-Exupery, Antoine Jean Baptiste Marie Roger de
See Saint-Exupery, Antoine de

St. John, David
See Hunt, E. Howard

St. John, J. Hector
See Crevecoeur, Michel Guillaume Jean de

Saint-John Perse
See Leger, (Marie-Rene Auguste) Alexis Saint-Leger
See also EW 10; EWL 3; GFL 1789 to the Present; RGWL 2

Saintsbury, George (Edward Bateman)
1845-1933 .... **TCLC 31**
See also CA 160; DLB 57, 149

Sait Faik .... **TCLC 23**
See Abasiyanik, Sait Faik

Saki .... **SSC 12; TCLC 3; WLC 5**
See Munro, H(ector) H(ugh)
See also BRWS 6; BYA 11; LAIT 2; RGEL 2; SSFS 1; SUFW

Sala, George Augustus 1828-1895 . **NCLC 46**

Saladin 1138-1193 .... **CMLC 38**

Salama, Hannu 1936- .... **CLC 18**
See also CA 244; EWL 3

Salamanca, J(ack) R(ichard) 1922- .. **CLC 4, 15**
See also CA 193; 25-28R, 193

Salas, Floyd Francis 1931- .... **HLC 2**
See also CA 119; 27; CANR 44, 75, 93; DAM MULT; DLB 82; HW 1, 2; MTCW 2; MTFW 2005

Sale, J. Kirkpatrick
See Sale, Kirkpatrick

Sale, John Kirkpatrick
See Sale, Kirkpatrick

Sale, Kirkpatrick 1937- .... **CLC 68**
See also CA 13-16R; CANR 10, 147

Salinas, Luis Omar 1937- ... **CLC 90; HLC 2**
See also AMWS 13; CA 131; CANR 81, 153; DAM MULT; DLB 82; HW 1, 2

Salinas (y Serrano), Pedro
1891(?)-1951 .... **TCLC 17**
See also CAAE 117; DLB 134; EWL 3

Salinger, J.D. 1919- . **CLC 1, 3, 8, 12, 55, 56, 138, 243; SSC 2, 28, 65; WLC 5**
See also AAYA 2, 36; AMW; AMWC 1; BPFB 3; CA 5-8R; CANR 39, 129; CDALB 1941-1968; CLR 18; CN 1, 2, 3, 4, 5, 6, 7; CPW 1; DA; DA3; DAB; DAC; DAM MST, NOV, POP; DLB 2, 102, 173; EWL 3; EXPN; LAIT 4; MAICYA 1, 2; MAL 5; MTCW 1, 2; MTFW 2005; NFS 1; RGAL 4; RGSF 2; SATA 67; SSFS 17; TUS; WYA; YAW

Salisbury, John
See Caute, (John) David

Sallust c. 86B.C.-35B.C. .... **CMLC 68**
See also AW 2; CDWLB 1; DLB 211; RGWL 2, 3

Salter, James 1925- .. **CLC 7, 52, 59; SSC 58**
See also AMWS 9; CA 73-76; CANR 107, 160; DLB 130; SSFS 25

Saltus, Edgar (Everton) 1855-1921 . **TCLC 8**
See also CAAE 105; DLB 202; RGAL 4

Saltykov, Mikhail Evgrafovich
1826-1889 .... **NCLC 16**
See also DLB 238;

Saltykov-Shchedrin, N.
See Saltykov, Mikhail Evgrafovich

Samarakis, Andonis
See Samarakis, Antonis
See also EWL 3

Samarakis, Antonis 1919-2003 .... **CLC 5**
See Samarakis, Andonis
See also CA 25-28R; 16; CAAS 224; CANR 36

Sanchez, Florencio 1875-1910 .... **TCLC 37**
See also CA 153; DLB 305; EWL 3; HW 1; LAW

Sanchez, Luis Rafael 1936- .... **CLC 23**
See also CA 128; DLB 305; EWL 3; HW 1; WLIT 1

Sanchez, Sonia 1934- . **BLC 1:3; CLC 5, 116, 215; PC 9**
See also BW 2, 3; CA 33-36R; CANR 24, 49, 74, 115; CLR 18; CP 2, 3, 4, 5, 6, 7; CSW; CWP; DA3; DAM MULT; DLB 41; DLBD 8; EWL 3; MAICYA 1, 2; MAL 5; MTCW 1, 2; MTFW 2005; PFS 26; SATA 22, 136; WP

Sancho, Ignatius 1729-1780 .... **LC 84**

Sand, George 1804-1876 .... **DC 29; NCLC 2, 42, 57, 174; WLC 5**
See also DA; DA3; DAB; DAC; DAM MST, NOV; DLB 119, 192; EW 6; FL 1:3; FW; GFL 1789 to the Present; RGWL 2, 3; TWA

Sandburg, Carl (August) 1878-1967 . **CLC 1, 4, 10, 15, 35; PC 2, 41; WLC 5**
See also AAYA 24; AMW; BYA 1, 3; CA 5-8R; CAAS 25-28R; CANR 35; CDALB 1865-1917; CLR 67; DA; DA3; DAB; DAC; DAM MST, POET; DLB 17, 54, 284; EWL 3; EXPP; LAIT 2; MAICYA 1, 2; MAL 5; MTCW 1, 2; MTFW 2005; PAB; PFS 3, 6, 12; RGAL 4; SATA 8; TUS; WCH; WP; WYA

Sandburg, Charles
See Sandburg, Carl (August)

Sandburg, Charles A.
See Sandburg, Carl (August)

Sanders, (James) Ed(ward) 1939- .... **CLC 53**
See Sanders, Edward
See also BG 1:3; CA 13-16R; 21; CANR 13, 44, 78; CP 1, 2, 3, 4, 5, 6, 7; DAM POET; DLB 16, 244

Sanders, Edward
See Sanders, (James) Ed(ward)
See also DLB 244

Sanders, Lawrence 1920-1998 .... **CLC 41**
See also BEST 89:4; BPFB 3; CA 81-84; CAAS 165; CANR 33, 62; CMW 4; CPW; DA3; DAM POP; MTCW 1

Sanders, Noah
See Blount, Roy (Alton), Jr.

Sanders, Winston P.
See Anderson, Poul

Sandoz, Mari(e Susette) 1900-1966 .. **CLC 28**
See also CA 1-4R; CAAS 25-28R; CANR 17, 64; DLB 9, 212; LAIT 2; MTCW 1, 2; SATA 5; TCWW 1, 2

Sandys, George 1578-1644 .... **LC 80**
See also DLB 24, 121

Saner, Reg(inald Anthony) 1931- .... **CLC 9**
See also CA 65-68; CP 3, 4, 5, 6, 7

Sankara 788-820 .... **CMLC 32**

Sannazaro, Jacopo 1456(?)-1530 .... **LC 8**
See also RGWL 2, 3; WLIT 7

Sansom, William 1912-1976 . **CLC 2, 6; SSC 21**
See also CA 5-8R; CAAS 65-68; CANR 42; CN 1, 2; DAM NOV; DLB 139; EWL 3; MTCW 1; RGEL 2; RGSF 2

Santayana, George 1863-1952 .... **TCLC 40**
See also AMW; CA 194; CAAE 115; DLB 54, 71, 246, 270; DLBD 13; EWL 3; MAL 5; RGAL 4; TUS

Santiago, Danny .... **CLC 33**
See James, Daniel (Lewis)
See also DLB 122

Santillana, Inigo Lopez de Mendoza, Marques de 1398-1458 .... **LC 111**
See also DLB 286

Santmyer, Helen Hooven
1895-1986 .... **CLC 33; TCLC 133**
See also CA 1-4R; CAAS 118; CANR 15, 33; DLBY 1984; MTCW 1; RHW

Santoka, Taneda 1882-1940 .... **TCLC 72**

Santos, Bienvenido N(uqui)
1911-1996 ... **AAL; CLC 22; TCLC 156**
See also CA 101; CAAS 151; CANR 19, 46; CP 1; DAM MULT; DLB 312; EWL; RGAL 4; SSFS 19

Sapir, Edward 1884-1939 .... **TCLC 108**
See also CA 211; DLB 92

Sapper .... **TCLC 44**
See McNeile, Herman Cyril

Sapphire 1950- .... **CLC 99**
See also CA 262

Sapphire, Brenda
See Sapphire

Sappho fl. 6th cent. B.C.- ... **CMLC 3, 67; PC 5**
See also CDWLB 1; DA3; DAM POET; DLB 176; FL 1:1; PFS 20; RGWL 2, 3; WLIT 8; WP

Saramago, Jose 1922- ..... **CLC 119; HLCS 1**
See also CA 153; CANR 96, 164; CWW 2; DLB 287, 332; EWL 3; LATS 1:2; SSFS 23

Sarduy, Severo 1937-1993 .... **CLC 6, 97; HLCS 2; TCLC 167**
See also CA 89-92; CAAS 142; CANR 58, 81; CWW 2; DLB 113; EWL 3; HW 1, 2; LAW

Seton, Cynthia Propper 1926-1982 .. CLC 27
See also CA 5-8R; CAAS 108; CANR 7
Seton, Ernest (Evan) Thompson
1860-1946 .... TCLC 31
See also ANW; BYA 3; CA 204; CAAE
109; CLR 59; DLB 92; DLBD 13; JRDA;
SATA 18
Seton-Thompson, Ernest
See Seton, Ernest (Evan) Thompson
Settle, Mary Lee 1918-2005 .... CLC 19, 61
See also BPFB 3; CA 89-92; 1; CAAS 243;
CANR 44, 87, 126; CN 6, 7; CSW; DLB
6; INT CA-89-92
Seuphor, Michel
See Arp, Jean
Sevigne, Marie (de Rabutin-Chantal)
1626-1696 .... LC 11, 144
See Sevigne, Marie de Rabutin Chantal
See also GFL Beginnings to 1789; TWA
Sevigne, Marie de Rabutin Chantal
See Sevigne, Marie (de Rabutin-Chantal)
See also DLB 268
Sewall, Samuel 1652-1730 .... LC 38
See also DLB 24; RGAL 4
Sexton, Anne (Harvey) 1928-1974 ..... CLC 2,
4, 6, 8, 10, 15, 53, 123; PC 2, 79; WLC
5
See also AMWS 2; CA 1-4R; CAAS 53-56;
CABS 2; CANR 3, 36; CDALB 1941-
1968; CP 1, 2; DA; DA3; DAB; DAC;
DAM MST, POET; DLB 5, 169; EWL 3;
EXPP; FL 1:6; FW; MAL 5; MBL;
MTCW 1, 2; MTFW 2005; PAB; PFS 4,
14; RGAL 4; RGHL; SATA 10; TUS
Shaara, Jeff 1952- .... CLC 119
See also AAYA 70; CA 163; CANR 109,
172; CN 7; MTFW 2005
Shaara, Michael 1929-1988 .... CLC 15
See also AAYA 71; AITN 1; BPFB 3; CA
102; CAAS 125; CANR 52, 85; DAM
POP; DLBY 1983; MTFW 2005; NFS 26
Shackleton, C.C.
See Aldiss, Brian W.
Shacochis, Bob .... CLC 39
See Shacochis, Robert G.
Shacochis, Robert G. 1951-
See Shacochis, Bob
See also CA 124; CAAE 119; CANR 100;
INT CA-124
Shadwell, Thomas 1641(?)-1692 .... LC 114
See also DLB 80; IDTP; RGEL 2
Shaffer, Anthony 1926-2001 .... CLC 19
See also CA 116; CAAE 110; CAAS 200;
CBD; CD 5, 6; DAM DRAM; DFS 13;
DLB 13
Shaffer, Anthony Joshua
See Shaffer, Anthony
Shaffer, Peter 1926- ... CLC 5, 14, 18, 37, 60;
DC 7
See also BRWS 1; CA 25-28R; CANR 25,
47, 74, 118; CBD; CD 5, 6; CDBLB 1960
to Present; DA3; DAB; DAM DRAM,
MST; DFS 5, 13; DLB 13, 233; EWL 3;
MTCW 1, 2; MTFW 2005; RGEL 2; TEA
Shakespeare, William 1564-1616 .... PC 84;
WLC 5
See also AAYA 35; BRW 1; CDBLB Be-
fore 1660; DA; DA3; DAB; DAC; DAM
DRAM, MST, POET; DFS 20, 21; DLB
62, 172, 263; EXPP; LAIT 1; LATS 1:1;
LMFS 1; PAB; PFS 1, 2, 3, 4, 5, 8, 9;
RGEL 2; TEA; WLIT 3; WP; WS; WYA
Shakey, Bernard
See Young, Neil
Shalamov, Varlam (Tikhonovich)
1907-1982 .... CLC 18
See also CA 129; CAAS 105; DLB 302;
RGSF 2

Shamloo, Ahmad
See Shamlu, Ahmad
Shamlou, Ahmad
See Shamlu, Ahmad
Shamlu, Ahmad 1925-2000 .... CLC 10
See also CA 216; CWW 2
Shammas, Anton 1951- .... CLC 55
See also CA 199
Shandling, Arline
See Berriault, Gina
Shange, Ntozake 1948- ...... BLC 1:3; CLC 8,
25, 38, 74, 126; DC 3
See also AAYA 9, 66; AFAW 1, 2; BW 2;
CA 85-88; CABS 3; CAD; CANR 27, 48,
74, 131; CD 5, 6; CP 5, 6, 7; CWD; CWP;
DA3; DAM DRAM, MULT; DFS 2, 11;
DLB 38, 249; FW; LAIT 4, 5; MAL 5;
MTCW 1, 2; MTFW 2005; NFS 11;
RGAL 4; SATA 157; YAW
Shanley, John Patrick 1950- .... CLC 75
See also AAYA 74; AMWS 14; CA 133;
CAAE 128; CAD; CANR 83, 154; CD 5,
6; DFS 23
Shapcott, Thomas W(illiam) 1935- .. CLC 38
See also CA 69-72; CANR 49, 83, 103; CP
1, 2, 3, 4, 5, 6, 7; DLB 289
Shapiro, Jane 1942- .... CLC 76
See also CA 196
Shapiro, Karl 1913-2000 ... CLC 4, 8, 15, 53;
PC 25
See also AMWS 2; CA 1-4R; 6; CAAS 188;
CANR 1, 36, 66; CP 1, 2, 3, 4, 5, 6; DLB
48; EWL 3; EXPP; MAL 5; MTCW 1, 2;
MTFW 2005; PFS 3; RGAL 4
Sharp, William 1855-1905 .... TCLC 39
See Macleod, Fiona
See also CA 160; DLB 156; RGEL 2
Sharpe, Thomas Ridley 1928-
See Sharpe, Tom
See also CA 122; CAAE 114; CANR 85;
INT CA-122
Sharpe, Tom .... CLC 36
See Sharpe, Thomas Ridley
See also CN 4, 5, 6, 7; DLB 14, 231
Shatrov, Mikhail .... CLC 59
Shaw, Bernard
See Shaw, George Bernard
See also DLB 10, 57, 190
Shaw, G. Bernard
See Shaw, George Bernard
Shaw, George Bernard 1856-1950 ..... DC 23;
TCLC 3, 9, 21, 45; WLC 5
See Shaw, Bernard
See also AAYA 61; BRW 6; BRWC 1;
BRWR 2; CA 128; CAAE 104; CDBLB
1914-1945; DA; DA3; DAB; DAC; DAM
DRAM, MST; DFS 1, 3, 6, 11, 19, 22;
DLB 332; EWL 3; LAIT 3; LATS 1:1;
MTCW 1, 2; MTFW 2005; RGEL 2;
TEA; WLIT 4
Shaw, Henry Wheeler 1818-1885 .. NCLC 15
See also DLB 11; RGAL 4
Shaw, Irwin 1913-1984 .... CLC 7, 23, 34
See also AITN 1; BPFB 3; CA 13-16R;
CAAS 112; CANR 21; CDALB 1941-
1968; CN 1, 2, 3; CPW; DAM DRAM,
POP; DLB 6, 102; DLBY 1984; MAL 5;
MTCW 1, 21; MTFW 2005
Shaw, Robert (Archibald)
1927-1978 .... CLC 5
See also AITN 1; CA 1-4R; CAAS 81-84;
CANR 4; CN 1, 2; DLB 13, 14
Shaw, T. E.
See Lawrence, T(homas) E(dward)
Shawn, Wallace 1943- .... CLC 41
See also CA 112; CAD; CD 5, 6; DLB 266
Shaykh, al- Hanan
See al-Shaykh, Hanan
See also CWW 2; EWL 3

Shchedrin, N.
See Saltykov, Mikhail Evgrafovich
Shea, Lisa 1953- .... CLC 86
See also CA 147
Sheed, Wilfrid (John Joseph) 1930- . CLC 2,
4, 10, 53
See also CA 65-68; CANR 30, 66; CN 1, 2,
3, 4, 5, 6, 7; DLB 6; MAL 5; MTCW 1,
2; MTFW 2005
Sheehy, Gail 1937- .... CLC 171
See also CA 49-52; CANR 1, 33, 55, 92;
CPW; MTCW 1
Sheldon, Alice Hastings Bradley
1915(?)-1987
See Tiptree, James, Jr.
See also CA 108; CAAS 122; CANR 34;
INT CA-108; MTCW 1
Sheldon, John
See Bloch, Robert (Albert)
Sheldon, Walter J(ames) 1917-1996
See Queen, Ellery
See also AITN 1; CA 25-28R; CANR 10
Shelley, Mary Wollstonecraft (Godwin)
1797-1851 .... NCLC 14, 59, 103, 170;
SSC 92; WLC 5
See also AAYA 20; BPFB 3; BRW 3;
BRWC 2; BRWS 3; BYA 5; CDBLB
1789-1832; DA; DA3; DAB; DAC; DAM
MST, NOV; DLB 110, 116, 159, 178;
EXPN; FL 1:3; GL 3; HGG; LAIT 1;
LMFS 1, 2; NFS 1; RGEL 2; SATA 29;
SCFW 1, 2; SFW 4; TEA; WLIT 3
Shelley, Percy Bysshe 1792-1822 .. NCLC 18,
93, 143, 175; PC 14, 67; WLC 5
See also AAYA 61; BRW 4; BRWR 1; CD-
BLB 1789-1832; DA; DA3; DAB; DAC;
DAM MST, POET; DLB 96, 110, 158;
EXPP; LMFS 1; PAB; PFS 2, 27; RGEL
2; TEA; WLIT 3; WP
Shepard, James R.
See Shepard, Jim
Shepard, Jim 1956- .... CLC 36
See also AAYA 73; CA 137; CANR 59, 104,
160; SATA 90, 164
Shepard, Lucius 1947- .... CLC 34
See also CA 141; CAAE 128; CANR 81,
124; HGG; SCFW 2; SFW 4; SUFW 2
Shepard, Sam 1943- .... CLC 4, 6, 17, 34, 41,
44, 169; DC 5
See also AAYA 1, 58; AMWS 3; CA 69-72;
CABS 3; CAD; CANR 22, 120, 140; CD
5, 6; DA3; DAM DRAM; DFS 3, 6, 7,
14; DLB 7, 212; EWL 3; IDFW 3, 4;
MAL 5; MTCW 1, 2; MTFW 2005;
RGAL 4
Shepherd, Jean (Parker)
1921-1999 .... TCLC 177
See also AAYA 69; AITN 2; CA 77-80;
CAAS 187
Shepherd, Michael
See Ludlum, Robert
Sherburne, Zoa (Lillian Morin)
1912-1995 .... CLC 30
See also AAYA 13; CA 1-4R; CAAS 176;
CANR 3, 37; MAICYA 1, 2; SAAS 18;
SATA 3; YAW
Sheridan, Frances 1724-1766 .... LC 7
See also DLB 39, 84
Sheridan, Richard Brinsley
1751-1816 . DC 1; NCLC 5, 91; WLC 5
See also BRW 3; CDBLB 1660-1789; DA;
DAB; DAC; DAM DRAM, MST; DFS
15; DLB 89; WLIT 3
Sherman, Jonathan Marc 1968- .... CLC 55
See also CA 230
Sherman, Martin 1941(?)- .... CLC 19
See also CA 123; CAAE 116; CAD; CANR
86; CD 5, 6; DFS 20; DLB 228; GLL 1;
IDTP; RGIIL

Sherwin, Judith Johnson
See Johnson, Judith (Emlyn)
See also CANR 85; CP 2, 3, 4, 5; CWP

Sherwood, Frances 1940- .... **CLC 81**
See also CA 220; 146, 220; CANR 158

Sherwood, Robert E(mmet)
1896-1955 .... **TCLC 3**
See also CA 153; CAAE 104; CANR 86;
DAM DRAM; DFS 11, 15, 17; DLB 7,
26, 249; IDFW 3, 4; MAL 5; RGAL 4

Shestov, Lev 1866-1938 .... **TCLC 56**

Shevchenko, Taras 1814-1861 .... **NCLC 54**

Shiel, M(atthew) P(hipps)
1865-1947 .... **TCLC 8**
See Holmes, Gordon
See also CA 160; CAAE 106; DLB 153;
HGG; MTCW 2; MTFW 2005; SCFW 1,
2; SFW 4; SUFW

Shields, Carol 1935-2003 .. **CLC 91, 113, 193**
See also AMWS 7; CA 81-84; CAAS 218;
CANR 51, 74, 98, 133; CCA 1; CN 6, 7;
CPW; DA3; DAC; DLB 334; MTCW 2;
MTFW 2005; NFS 23

Shields, David 1956- .... **CLC 97**
See also CA 124; CANR 48, 99, 112, 157

Shields, David Jonathan
See Shields, David

Shiga, Naoya 1883-1971 .... **CLC 33; SSC 23;
TCLC 172**
See Shiga Naoya
See also CA 101; CAAS 33-36R; MJW;
RGWL 3

Shiga Naoya
See Shiga, Naoya
See also DLB 180; EWL 3; RGWL 3

Shilts, Randy 1951-1994 .... **CLC 85**
See also AAYA 19; CA 127; CAAE 118;
CAAS 144; CANR 45; DA3; GLL 1; INT
CA-127; MTCW 2; MTFW 2005

Shimazaki, Haruki 1872-1943
See Shimazaki Toson
See also CA 134; CAAE 105; CANR 84;
RGWL 3

Shimazaki Toson .... **TCLC 5**
See Shimazaki, Haruki
See also DLB 180; EWL 3

Shirley, James 1596-1666 .... **DC 25; LC 96**
See also DLB 58; RGEL 2

Shirley Hastings, Selina
See Hastings, Selina

Sholokhov, Mikhail (Aleksandrovich)
1905-1984 .... **CLC 7, 15**
See also CA 101; CAAS 112; DLB 272,
332; EWL 3, MTCW 1, 2; MTFW 2005;
RGWL 2, 3; SATA-Obit 36

Sholom Aleichem 1859-1916 .... **SSC 33;
TCLC 1, 35**
See Rabinovitch, Sholem
See also DLB 333; TWA

Shone, Patric
See Hanley, James

Showalter, Elaine 1941- .... **CLC 169**
See also CA 57-60; CANR 58, 106; DLB
67; FW; GLL 2

Shreve, Susan
See Shreve, Susan Richards

Shreve, Susan Richards 1939- .... **CLC 23**
See also CA 49-52; 5; CANR 5, 38, 69, 100,
159; MAICYA 1, 2; SATA 46, 95, 152;
SATA-Brief 41

Shue, Larry 1946-1985 .... **CLC 52**
See also CA 145; CAAS 117; DAM DRAM;
DFS 7

Shu-Jen, Chou 1881-1936
See Lu Hsun
See also CAAE 104

Shulman, Alix Kates 1932- .... **CLC 2, 10**
See also CA 29-32R; CANR 43; FW; SATA
7

Shuster, Joe 1914-1992 .... **CLC 21**
See also AAYA 50

Shute, Nevil .... **CLC 30**
See Norway, Nevil Shute
See also BPFB 3; DLB 255; NFS 9; RHW;
SFW 4

Shuttle, Penelope (Diane) 1947- .... **CLC 7**
See also CA 93-96; CANR 39, 84, 92, 108;
CP 3, 4, 5, 6, 7; CWP; DLB 14, 40

Shvarts, Elena 1948- .... **PC 50**
See also CA 147

Sidhwa, Bapsi 1939-
See Sidhwa, Bapsy (N.)
See also CN 6, 7; DLB 323

Sidhwa, Bapsy (N.) 1938- .... **CLC 168**
See Sidhwa, Bapsi
See also CA 108; CANR 25, 57; FW

Sidney, Mary 1561-1621 .... **LC 19, 39**
See Sidney Herbert, Mary

Sidney, Sir Philip 1554-1586 .... **LC 19, 39,
131; PC 32**
See also BRW 1; BRWR 2; CDBLB Before
1660; DA; DA3; DAB; DAC; DAM MST,
POET; DLB 167; EXPP; PAB; RGEL 2;
TEA; WP

Sidney Herbert, Mary
See Sidney, Mary
See also DLB 167

Siegel, Jerome 1914-1996 .... **CLC 21**
See Siegel, Jerry
See also CA 169; CAAE 116; CAAS 151

Siegel, Jerry
See Siegel, Jerome
See also AAYA 50

Sienkiewicz, Henryk (Adam Alexander Pius)
1846-1916 .... **TCLC 3**
See also CA 134; CAAE 104; CANR 84;
DLB 332; EWL 3; RGSF 2; RGWL 2, 3

Sierra, Gregorio Martinez
See Martinez Sierra, Gregorio

Sierra, Maria de la O'LeJarraga Martinez
See Martinez Sierra, Maria

Sigal, Clancy 1926- .... **CLC 7**
See also CA 1-4R; CANR 85; CN 1, 2, 3,
4, 5, 6, 7

Siger of Brabant 1240(?)-1284(?) . **CMLC 69**
See also DLB 115

Sigourney, Lydia H.
See Sigourney, Lydia Howard (Huntley)
See also DLB 73, 183

Sigourney, Lydia Howard (Huntley)
1791-1865 .... **NCLC 21, 87**
See Sigourney, Lydia H.; Sigourney, Lydia
Huntley
See also DLB 1

Sigourney, Lydia Huntley
See Sigourney, Lydia Howard (Huntley)
See also DLB 42, 239, 243

Siguenza y Gongora, Carlos de
1645-1700 .... **HLCS 2; LC 8**
See also LAW

Sigurjonsson, Johann
See Sigurjonsson, Johann

Sigurjonsson, Johann 1880-1919 ... **TCLC 27**
See also CA 170; DLB 293; EWL 3

Sikelianos, Angelos 1884-1951 .... **PC 29;
TCLC 39**
See also EWL 3; RGWL 2, 3

Silkin, Jon 1930-1997 .... **CLC 2, 6, 43**
See also CA 5-8R; 5; CANR 89; CP 1, 2, 3,
4, 5, 6; DLB 27

Silko, Leslie 1948- ...... **CLC 23, 74, 114, 211;
NNAL; SSC 37, 66; WLCS**
See also AAYA 14; AMWS 4; ANW; BYA
12; CA 122; CAAE 115; CANR 45, 65,
118; CN 4, 5, 6, 7; CP 4, 5, 6, 7; CPW 1;
CWP; DA; DA3; DAC; DAM MST,
MULT, POP; DLB 143, 175, 256, 275;

EWL 3; EXPP; EXPS; LAIT 4; MAL 5;
MTCW 2; MTFW 2005; NFS 4; PFS 9,
16; RGAL 4; RGSF 2; SSFS 4, 8, 10, 11;
TCWW 1, 2

Sillanpaa, Frans Eemil 1888-1964 ... **CLC 19**
See also CA 129; CAAS 93-96; DLB 332;
EWL 3; MTCW 1

Sillitoe, Alan 1928- .. **CLC 1, 3, 6, 10, 19, 57,
148**
See also AITN 1; BRWS 5; CA 191; 9-12R,
191; 2; CANR 8, 26, 55, 139; CDBLB
1960 to Present; CN 1, 2, 3, 4, 5, 6; CP 1,
2, 3, 4, 5; DLB 14, 139; EWL 3; MTCW
1, 2; MTFW 2005; RGEL 2; RGSF 2;
SATA 61

Silone, Ignazio 1900-1978 .... **CLC 4**
See also CA 25-28; CAAS 81-84; CANR
34; CAP 2; DLB 264; EW 12; EWL 3;
MTCW 1; RGSF 2; RGWL 2, 3

Silone, Ignazione
See Silone, Ignazio

Silver, Joan Micklin 1935- .... **CLC 20**
See also CA 121; CAAE 114; INT CA-121

Silver, Nicholas
See Faust, Frederick (Schiller)

Silverberg, Robert 1935- .... **CLC 7, 140**
See also AAYA 24; BPFB 3; BYA 7, 9; CA
186; 1-4R, 186; 3; CANR 1, 20, 36, 85,
140; CLR 59; CN 6, 7; CPW; DAM POP;
DLB 8; INT CANR-20, MAICYA 1, 2;
MTCW 1, 2; MTFW 2005; SATA 13, 91;
SATA-Essay 104; SCFW 1, 2; SFW 4;
SUFW 2

Silverstein, Alvin 1933- .... **CLC 17**
See also CA 49-52; CANR 2; CLR 25;
JRDA; MAICYA 1, 2; SATA 8, 69, 124

Silverstein, Shel 1932-1999 .... **PC 49**
See also AAYA 40; BW 3; CA 107; CAAS
179; CANR 47, 74, 81; CLR 5, 96; CWRI
5; JRDA; MAICYA 1, 2; MTCW 2;
MTFW 2005; SATA 33, 92; SATA-Brief
27; SATA-Obit 116

Silverstein, Virginia B(arbara Opshelor)
1937- .... **CLC 17**
See also CA 49-52; CANR 2; CLR 25;
JRDA; MAICYA 1, 2; SATA 8, 69, 124

Sim, Georges
See Simenon, Georges (Jacques Christian)

Simak, Clifford D(onald) 1904-1988 . **CLC 1,
55**
See also CA 1-4R; CAAS 125; CANR 1,
35; DLB 8; MTCW 1; SATA-Obit 56;
SCFW 1, 2, SFW 4

Simenon, Georges (Jacques Christian)
1903-1989 .... **CLC 1, 2, 3, 8, 18, 47**
See also BPFB 3; CA 85-88; CAAS 129;
CANR 35; CMW 4; DA3; DAM POP;
DLB 72; DLBY 1989; EW 12; EWL 3;
GFL 1789 to the Present; MSW; MTCW
1, 2; MTFW 2005; RGWL 2, 3

Simic, Charles 1938- .... **CLC 6, 9, 22, 49, 68,
130; PC 69**
See also AMWS 8; CA 29-32R; 4; CANR
12, 33, 52, 61, 96, 140; CP 2, 3, 4, 5, 6,
7; DA3; DAM POET; DLB 105; MAL 5;
MTCW 2; MTFW 2005; PFS 7; RGAL 4;
WP

Simmel, Georg 1858-1918 .... **TCLC 64**
See also CA 157; DLB 296

Simmons, Charles (Paul) 1924- .... **CLC 57**
See also CA 89-92; INT CA-89-92

Simmons, Dan 1948- .... **CLC 44**
See also AAYA 16, 54; CA 138; CANR 53,
81, 126; CPW; DAM POP; HGG; SUFW
2

Simmons, James (Stewart Alexander)
1933- .... **CLC 43**
See also CA 105; 21; CP 1, 2, 3, 4, 5, 6, 7;
DLB 40

Swados, Harvey 1920-1972 .... **CLC 5**
See also CA 5-8R; CAAS 37-40R; CANR
6; CN 1; DLB 2, 335; MAL 5
Swados, Liz
See Swados, Elizabeth
Swan, Gladys 1934- .... **CLC 69**
See also CA 101; CANR 17, 39; TCLE 1:2
Swanson, Logan
See Matheson, Richard
Swarthout, Glendon (Fred)
1918-1992 .... **CLC 35**
See also AAYA 55; CA 1-4R; CAAS 139;
CANR 1, 47; CN 1, 2, 3, 4, 5; LAIT 5;
SATA 26; TCWW 1, 2; YAW
Swedenborg, Emanuel 1688-1772 ..... **LC 105**
Sweet, Sarah C.
See Jewett, (Theodora) Sarah Orne
Swenson, May 1919-1989 ...... **CLC 4, 14, 61,
106; PC 14**
See also AMWS 4; CA 5-8R; CAAS 130;
CANR 36, 61, 131; CP 1, 2, 3, 4; DA;
DAB; DAC; DAM MST, POET; DLB 5;
EXPP; GLL 2; MAL 5; MTCW 1, 2;
MTFW 2005; PFS 16; SATA 15; WP
Swift, Augustus
See Lovecraft, H. P.
Swift, Graham 1949- .... **CLC 41, 88, 233**
See also BRWC 2; BRWS 5; CA 122;
CAAE 117; CANR 46, 71, 128; CN 4, 5,
6, 7; DLB 194, 326; MTCW 2; MTFW
2005; NFS 18; RGSF 2
Swift, Jonathan 1667-1745 ..... **LC 1, 42, 101;
PC 9; WLC 6**
See also AAYA 41; BRW 3; BRWC 1;
BRWR 1; BYA 5, 14; CDBLB 1660-1789;
CLR 53; DA; DA3; DAB; DAC; DAM
MST, NOV, POET; DLB 39, 95, 101;
EXPN; LAIT 1; NFS 6; PFS 27; RGEL 2;
SATA 19; TEA; WCH; WLIT 3
Swinburne, Algernon Charles
1837-1909 ... **PC 24; TCLC 8, 36; WLC
6**
See also DRW 5; CA 140, CAAE 105, CD-
BLB 1832-1890; DA; DA3; DAB; DAC;
DAM MST, POET; DLB 35, 57; PAB;
RGEL 2; TEA
Swinfen, Ann .... **CLC 34**
See also CA 202
Swinnerton, Frank (Arthur)
1884-1982 .... **CLC 31**
See also CA 202; CAAS 108; CN 1, 2, 3;
DLB 34
Swinnerton, Frank Arthur
1884-1982 .... **CLC 31**
See also CAAS 108; DLB 34
Swithen, John
See King, Stephen
Sylvia
See Ashton-Warner, Sylvia (Constance)
Symmes, Robert Edward
See Duncan, Robert
Symonds, John Addington
1840-1893 .... **NCLC 34**
See also DLB 57, 144
Symons, Arthur 1865-1945 .... **TCLC 11**
See also CA 189; CAAE 107; DLB 19, 57,
149; RGEL 2
Symons, Julian (Gustave)
1912-1994 .... **CLC 2, 14, 32**
See also CA 49-52; 3; CAAS 147; CANR
3, 33, 59; CMW 4; CN 1, 2, 3, 4, 5; CP 1,
3, 4; DLB 87, 155; DLBY 1992; MSW;
MTCW 1
Synge, (Edmund) J(ohn) M(illington)
1871-1909 .... **DC 2; TCLC 6, 37**
See also BRW 6; BRWR 1; CA 141; CAAE
104; CDBLB 1890-1914; DAM DRAM;
DFS 18; DLB 10, 19; EWL 3; RGEL 2;
TEA; WLIT 4

Syruc, J.
See Milosz, Czeslaw
Szirtes, George 1948- .... **CLC 46; PC 51**
See also CA 109; CANR 27, 61, 117; CP 4,
5, 6, 7
Szymborska, Wislawa 1923- ... **CLC 99, 190;
PC 44**
See also AAYA 76; CA 154; CANR 91, 133;
CDWLB 4; CWP; CWW 2; DA3; DLB
232, 332; DLBY 1996; EWL 3; MTCW
2; MTFW 2005; PFS 15, 27; RGHL;
RGWL 3
T. O., Nik
See Annensky, Innokenty (Fyodorovich)
Tabori, George 1914-2007 .... **CLC 19**
See also CA 49-52; CAAS 262; CANR 4,
69; CBD; CD 5, 6; DLB 245; RGHL
Tacitus c. 55-c. 117 .... **CMLC 56**
See also AW 2; CDWLB 1; DLB 211;
RGWL 2, 3; WLIT 8
Tadjo, Veronique 1955- .... **BLC 2:3**
See also EWL 3
Tagore, Rabindranath 1861-1941 .... **PC 8;
SSC 48; TCLC 3, 53**
See also CA 120; CAAE 104; DA3; DAM
DRAM, POET; DLB 323, 332; EWL 3;
MTCW 1, 2; MTFW 2005; PFS 18; RGEL
2; RGSF 2; RGWL 2, 3; TWA
Taine, Hippolyte Adolphe
1828-1893 .... **NCLC 15**
See also EW 7; GFL 1789 to the Present
Talayesva, Don C. 1890-(?) .... **NNAL**
Talese, Gay 1932- .... **CLC 37, 232**
See also AITN 1; AMWS 1; CA 1-4R;
CANR 9, 58, 137; DLB 185; INT
CANR-9; MTCW 1, 2; MTFW 2005
Tallent, Elizabeth 1954- .... **CLC 45**
See also CA 117; CANR 72; DLB 130
Tallmountain, Mary 1918-1997 .... **NNAL**
See also CA 146; CAAS 161; DLB 193
Tally, Ted 1952- .... **CLC 42**
See also CA 124; CAAE 120; CAD; CANR
125; CD 5, 6; INT CA-124
Talvik, Heiti 1904-1947 .... **TCLC 87**
See also EWL 3
Tamayo y Baus, Manuel
1829-1898 .... **NCLC 1**
Tammsaare, A(nton) H(ansen)
1878-1940 .... **TCLC 27**
See also CA 164; CDWLB 4; DLB 220;
EWL 3
Tam'si, Tchicaya U
See Tchicaya, Gerald Felix
Tan, Amy 1952- ...... **AAL; CLC 59, 120, 151**
See also AAYA 9, 48; AMWS 10; BEST
89:3; BPFB 3; CA 136; CANR 54, 105,
132; CDALBS; CN 6, 7; CPW 1; DA3;
DAM MULT, NOV, POP; DLB 173, 312;
EXPN; FL 1:6; FW; LAIT 3, 5; MAL 5;
MTCW 2; MTFW 2005; NFS 1, 13, 16;
RGAL 4; SATA 75; SSFS 9; YAW
Tandem, Carl Felix
See Spitteler, Carl
Tandem, Felix
See Spitteler, Carl
Tanizaki, Jun'ichiro 1886-1965 ... **CLC 8, 14,
28; SSC 21**
See Tanizaki Jun'ichiro
See also CA 93-96; CAAS 25-28R; MJW;
MTCW 2; MTFW 2005; RGSF 2; RGWL
2
Tanizaki Jun'ichiro
See Tanizaki, Jun'ichiro
See also DLB 180; EWL 3
Tannen, Deborah 1945- .... **CLC 206**
See also CA 118; CANR 95
Tannen, Deborah Frances
See Tannen, Deborah

Tanner, William
See Amis, Kingsley
Tante, Dilly
See Kunitz, Stanley
Tao Lao
See Storni, Alfonsina
Tapahonso, Luci 1953- .... **NNAL; PC 65**
See also CA 145; CANR 72, 127; DLB 175
Tarantino, Quentin (Jerome)
1963- .... **CLC 125, 230**
See also AAYA 58; CA 171; CANR 125
Tarassoff, Lev
See Troyat, Henri
Tarbell, Ida M(inerva) 1857-1944 . **TCLC 40**
See also CA 181; CAAE 122; DLB 47
**Tardieu d'Esclavelles,
Louise-Florence-Petronille**
See Epinay, Louise d'
Tarkington, (Newton) Booth
1869-1946 .... **TCLC 9**
See also BPFB 3; BYA 3; CA 143; CAAE
110; CWRI 5; DLB 9, 102; MAL 5;
MTCW 2; RGAL 4; SATA 17
Tarkovskii, Andrei Arsen'evich
See Tarkovsky, Andrei (Arsenyevich)
Tarkovsky, Andrei (Arsenyevich)
1932-1986 .... **CLC 75**
See also CA 127
Tartt, Donna 1964(?)- .... **CLC 76**
See also AAYA 56; CA 142; CANR 135;
MTFW 2005
Tasso, Torquato 1544-1595 .... **LC 5, 94**
See also EFS 2; EW 2; RGWL 2, 3; WLIT
7
Tate, (John Orley) Allen 1899-1979 .. **CLC 2,
4, 6, 9, 11, 14, 24; PC 50**
See also AMW; CA 5-8R; CAAS 85-88;
CANR 32, 108; CN 1, 2; CP 1, 2; DLB 4,
45, 63; DLBD 17; EWL 3; MAL 5;
MTCW 1, 2; MTFW 2005; RGAL 4;
RHW
Tate, Ellalice
See Hibbert, Eleanor Alice Burford
Tate, James (Vincent) 1943- .... **CLC 2, 6, 25**
See also CA 21-24R; CANR 29, 57, 114;
CP 1, 2, 3, 4, 5, 6, 7; DLB 5, 169; EWL
3; PFS 10, 15; RGAL 4; WP
Tate, Nahum 1652(?)-1715 .... **LC 109**
See also DLB 80; RGEL 2
Tauler, Johannes c. 1300-1361 ...... **CMLC 37**
See also DLB 179; LMFS 1
Tavel, Ronald 1940- .... **CLC 6**
See also CA 21-24R; CAD; CANR 33; CD
5, 6
Taviani, Paolo 1931- .... **CLC 70**
See also CA 153
Taylor, Bayard 1825-1878 .... **NCLC 89**
See also DLB 3, 189, 250, 254; RGAL 4
Taylor, C(ecil) P(hilip) 1929-1981 .... **CLC 27**
See also CA 25-28R; CAAS 105; CANR
47; CBD
Taylor, Edward 1642(?)-1729 . **LC 11; PC 63**
See also AMW; DA; DAB; DAC; DAM
MST, POET; DLB 24; EXPP; RGAL 4;
TUS
Taylor, Eleanor Ross 1920- .... **CLC 5**
See also CA 81-84; CANR 70
Taylor, Elizabeth 1912-1975 .... **CLC 2, 4, 29;
SSC 100**
See also CA 13-16R; CANR 9, 70; CN 1,
2; DLB 139; MTCW 1; RGEL 2; SATA
13
Taylor, Frederick Winslow
1856-1915 .... **TCLC 76**
See also CA 188
Taylor, Henry (Splawn) 1942- .... **CLC 44**
See also CA 33-36R; 7; CANR 31; CP 6, 7;
DLB 5; PFS 10

Taylor, Kamala 1924-2004
See Markandaya, Kamala
See also CA 77-80; CAAS 227; MTFW 2005; NFS 13

Taylor, Mildred D. 1943- .... **CLC 21**
See also AAYA 10, 47; BW 1; BYA 3, 8; CA 85-88; CANR 25, 115, 136; CLR 9, 59, 90; CSW; DLB 52; JRDA; LAIT 3; MAICYA 1, 2; MTFW 2005; SAAS 5; SATA 135; WYA; YAW

Taylor, Peter (Hillsman) 1917-1994 .. **CLC 1, 4, 18, 37, 44, 50, 71; SSC 10, 84**
See also AMWS 5; BPFB 3; CA 13-16R; CAAS 147; CANR 9, 50; CN 1, 2, 3, 4, 5; CSW; DLB 218, 278; DLBY 1981, 1994; EWL 3; EXPS; INT CANR-9; MAL 5; MTCW 1, 2; MTFW 2005; RGSF 2; SSFS 9; TUS

Taylor, Robert Lewis 1912-1998 .... **CLC 14**
See also CA 1-4R; CAAS 170; CANR 3, 64; CN 1, 2; SATA 10; TCWW 1, 2

Tchekhov, Anton
See Chekhov, Anton (Pavlovich)

Tchicaya, Gerald Felix 1931-1988 .. **CLC 101**
See Tchicaya U Tam'si
See also CA 129; CAAS 125; CANR 81

Tchicaya U Tam'si
See Tchicaya, Gerald Felix
See also EWL 3

Teasdale, Sara 1884-1933 .... **PC 31; TCLC 4**
See also CA 163; CAAE 104; DLB 45; GLL 1; PFS 14; RGAL 4; SATA 32; TUS

Tecumseh 1768-1813 .... **NNAL**
See also DAM MULT

Tegner, Esaias 1782-1846 .... **NCLC 2**

Teilhard de Chardin, (Marie Joseph) Pierre 1881-1955 .... **TCLC 9**
See also CA 210; CAAE 105; GFL 1789 to the Present

Temple, Ann
See Mortimer, Penelope (Ruth)

Tennant, Emma 1937- .... **CLC 13, 52**
See also BRWS 9; CA 65-68; 9; CANR 10, 38, 59, 88; CN 3, 4, 5, 6, 7; DLB 14; EWL 3; SFW 4

Tenneshaw, S. M.
See Silverberg, Robert

Tenney, Tabitha Gilman 1762-1837 .... **NCLC 122**
See also DLB 37, 200

Tennyson, Alfred 1809-1892 ... **NCLC 30, 65, 115; PC 6; WLC 6**
See also AAYA 50; BRW 4; CDBLB 1832-1890; DA; DA3; DAB; DAC; DAM MST, POET; DLB 32; EXPP; PAB; PFS 1, 2, 4, 11, 15, 19; RGEL 2; TEA; WLIT 4; WP

Teran, Lisa St. Aubin de .... **CLC 36**
See St. Aubin de Teran, Lisa

Terence c. 184B.C.-c. 159B.C. ...... **CMLC 14; DC 7**
See also AW 1; CDWLB 1; DLB 211; RGWL 2, 3; TWA; WLIT 8

Teresa de Jesus, St. 1515-1582 .... **LC 18, 149**

Teresa of Avila, St.
See Teresa de Jesus, St.

Terkel, Louis .... **CLC 38**
See Terkel, Studs
See also AAYA 32; AITN 1; MTCW 2; TUS

Terkel, Studs 1912-
See Terkel, Louis
See also CA 57-60; CANR 18, 45, 67, 132; DA3; MTCW 1, 2; MTFW 2005

Terry, C. V.
See Slaughter, Frank G(ill)

Terry, Megan 1932- .... **CLC 19; DC 13**
See also CA 77-80; CABS 3; CAD; CANR 43; CD 5, 6; CWD; DFS 18; DLB 7, 249; GLL 2

Tertullian c. 155-c. 245 .... **CMLC 29**

Tertz, Abram
See Sinyavsky, Andrei (Donatevich)
See also RGSF 2

Tesich, Steve 1943(?)-1996 .... **CLC 40, 69**
See also CA 105; CAAS 152; CAD; DLBY 1983

Tesla, Nikola 1856-1943 .... **TCLC 88**

Teternikov, Fyodor Kuzmich 1863-1927
See Sologub, Fyodor
See also CAAE 104

Tevis, Walter 1928-1984 .... **CLC 42**
See also CA 113; SFW 4

Tey, Josephine .... **TCLC 14**
See Mackintosh, Elizabeth
See also DLB 77; MSW

Thackeray, William Makepeace 1811-1863 ...... **NCLC 5, 14, 22, 43, 169; WLC 6**
See also BRW 5; BRWC 2; CDBLB 1832-1890; DA; DA3; DAB; DAC; DAM MST, NOV; DLB 21, 55, 159, 163; NFS 13; RGEL 2; SATA 23; TEA; WLIT 3

Thakura, Ravindranatha
See Tagore, Rabindranath

Thames, C. H.
See Marlowe, Stephen

Tharoor, Shashi 1956- .... **CLC 70**
See also CA 141; CANR 91; CN 6, 7

Thelwall, John 1764-1834 .... **NCLC 162**
See also DLB 93, 158

Thelwell, Michael Miles 1939- .... **CLC 22**
See also BW 2; CA 101

Theobald, Lewis, Jr.
See Lovecraft, H. P.

Theocritus c. 310B.C.- .... **CMLC 45**
See also AW 1; DLB 176; RGWL 2, 3

Theodorescu, Ion N. 1880-1967
See Arghezi, Tudor
See also CAAS 116

Theriault, Yves 1915-1983 .... **CLC 79**
See also CA 102; CANR 150; CCA 1; DAC; DAM MST; DLB 88; EWL 3

Theroux, Alexander 1939- .... **CLC 2, 25**
See also CA 85-88; CANR 20, 63; CN 4, 5, 6, 7

Theroux, Alexander Louis
See Theroux, Alexander

Theroux, Paul 1941- .... **CLC 5, 8, 11, 15, 28, 46, 159**
See also AAYA 28; AMWS 8; BEST 89:4; BPFB 3; CA 33-36R; CANR 20, 45, 74, 133; CDALBS; CN 1, 2, 3, 4, 5, 6, 7; CP 1; CPW 1; DA3; DAM POP; DLB 2, 218; EWL 3; HGG; MAL 5; MTCW 1, 2; MTFW 2005; RGAL 4; SATA 44, 109; TUS

Thesen, Sharon 1946- .... **CLC 56**
See also CA 163; CANR 125; CP 5, 6, 7; CWP

Thespis fl. 6th cent. B.C.- .... **CMLC 51**
See also LMFS 1

Thevenin, Denis
See Duhamel, Georges

Thibault, Jacques Anatole Francois 1844-1924
See France, Anatole
See also CA 127; CAAE 106; DA3; DAM NOV; MTCW 1, 2; TWA

Thiele, Colin 1920-2006 .... **CLC 17**
See also CA 29-32R; CANR 12, 28, 53, 105; CLR 27; CP 1, 2; DLB 289; MAICYA 1, 2; SAAS 2; SATA 14, 72, 125; YAW

Thiong'o, Ngugi Wa
See Ngugi wa Thiong'o

Thistlethwaite, Bel
See Wetherald, Agnes Ethelwyn

Thomas, Audrey (Callahan) 1935- .... **CLC 7, 13, 37, 107; SSC 20**
See also AITN 2; CA 237; 21-24R, 237; 19; CANR 36, 58; CN 2, 3, 4, 5, 6, 7; DLB 60; MTCW 1; RGSF 2

Thomas, Augustus 1857-1934 .... **TCLC 97**
See also MAL 5

Thomas, D.M. 1935- ..... **CLC 13, 22, 31, 132**
See also BPFB 3; BRWS 4; CA 61-64; 11; CANR 17, 45, 75; CDBLB 1960 to Present; CN 4, 5, 6, 7; CP 1, 2, 3, 4, 5, 6, 7; DA3; DLB 40, 207, 299; HGG; INT CANR-17; MTCW 1, 2; MTFW 2005; RGHL; SFW 4

Thomas, Dylan (Marlais) 1914-1953 .... **PC 2, 52; SSC 3, 44; TCLC 1, 8, 45, 105; WLC 6**
See also AAYA 45; BRWS 1; CA 120; CAAE 104; CANR 65; CDBLB 1945-1960; DA; DA3; DAB; DAC; DAM DRAM, MST, POET; DLB 13, 20, 139; EWL 3; EXPP; LAIT 3; MTCW 1, 2; MTFW 2005; PAB; PFS 1, 3, 8; RGEL 2; RGSF 2; SATA 60; TEA; WLIT 4; WP

Thomas, (Philip) Edward 1878-1917 . **PC 53; TCLC 10**
See also BRW 6; BRWS 3; CA 153; CAAE 106; DAM POET; DLB 19, 98, 156, 216; EWL 3; PAB; RGEL 2

Thomas, Joyce Carol 1938- .... **CLC 35**
See also AAYA 12, 54; BW 2, 3; CA 116; CAAE 113; CANR 48, 114, 135; CLR 19; DLB 33; INT CA-116; JRDA; MAICYA 1, 2; MTCW 1, 2; MTFW 2005; SAAS 7; SATA 40, 78, 123, 137; SATA-Essay 137; WYA; YAW

Thomas, Lewis 1913-1993 .... **CLC 35**
See also ANW; CA 85-88; CAAS 143; CANR 38, 60; DLB 275; MTCW 1, 2

Thomas, M. Carey 1857-1935 .... **TCLC 89**
See also FW

Thomas, Paul
See Mann, (Paul) Thomas

Thomas, Piri 1928- .... **CLC 17; HLCS 2**
See also CA 73-76; HW 1; LLW

Thomas, R(onald) S(tuart) 1913-2000 .... **CLC 6, 13, 48**
See also CA 89-92; 4; CAAS 189; CANR 30; CDBLB 1960 to Present; CP 1, 2, 3, 4, 5, 6, 7; DAB; DAM POET; DLB 27; EWL 3; MTCW 1; RGEL 2

Thomas, Ross (Elmore) 1926-1995 .. **CLC 39**
See also CA 33-36R; CAAS 150; CANR 22, 63; CMW 4

Thompson, Francis (Joseph) 1859-1907 .... **TCLC 4**
See also BRW 5; CA 189; CAAE 104; CD-BLB 1890-1914; DLB 19; RGEL 2; TEA

Thompson, Francis Clegg
See Mencken, H(enry) L(ouis)

Thompson, Hunter S. 1937(?)-2005 .. **CLC 9, 17, 40, 104, 229**
See also AAYA 45; BEST 89:1; BPFB 3; CA 17-20R; CAAS 236; CANR 23, 46, 74, 77, 111, 133; CPW; CSW; DA3; DAM POP; DLB 185; MTCW 1, 2; MTFW 2005; TUS

Thompson, James Myers
See Thompson, Jim (Myers)

Thompson, Jim (Myers) 1906-1977(?) .... **CLC 69**
See also BPFB 3; CA 140; CMW 4; CPW; DLB 226; MSW

Thompson, Judith (Clare Francesca) 1954- .... **CLC 39**
See also CA 143; CD 5, 6; CWD; DFS 22; DLB 334

Thomson, James 1700-1748 .... **LC 16, 29, 40**
See also BRWS 3; DAM POET; DLB 95; RGEL 2

Walker, Ted .... CLC 13
See Walker, Edward Joseph
See also CP 1, 2, 3, 4, 5, 6, 7; DLB 40

Wallace, David Foster 1962- ... CLC 50, 114;
SSC 68
See also AAYA 50; AMWS 10; CA 132;
CANR 59, 133; CN 7; DA3; MTCW 2;
MTFW 2005

Wallace, Dexter
See Masters, Edgar Lee

Wallace, (Richard Horatio) Edgar
1875-1932 .... TCLC 57
See also CA 218; CAAE 115; CMW 4;
DLB 70; MSW; RGEL 2

Wallace, Irving 1916-1990 .... CLC 7, 13
See also AITN 1; BPFB 3; CA 1-4R; 1;
CAAS 132; CANR 1, 27; CPW; DAM
NOV, POP; INT CANR-27; MTCW 1, 2

Wallant, Edward Lewis 1926-1962 ... CLC 5,
10
See also CA 1-4R; CANR 22; DLB 2, 28,
143, 299; EWL 3; MAL 5; MTCW 1, 2;
RGAL 4; RGHL

Wallas, Graham 1858-1932 .... TCLC 91

Waller, Edmund 1606-1687 .... LC 86; PC 72
See also BRW 2; DAM POET; DLB 126;
PAB; RGEL 2

Walley, Byron
See Card, Orson Scott

Walpole, Horace 1717-1797 .... LC 2, 49
See also BRW 3; DLB 39, 104, 213; GL 3;
HGG; LMFS 1; RGEL 2; SUFW 1; TEA

Walpole, Hugh (Seymour)
1884-1941 .... TCLC 5
See also CA 165; CAAE 104; DLB 34;
HGG; MTCW 2; RGEL 2; RHW

Walrond, Eric (Derwent) 1898-1966 . HR 1:3
See also BW 1; CA 125; DLB 51

Walser, Martin 1927- .... CLC 27, 183
See also CA 57-60; CANR 8, 46, 145;
CWW 2; DLB 75, 124; EWL 3

Walser, Robert 1878-1956 ..... SSC 20; TCLC
18
See also CA 165; CAAE 118; CANR 100;
DLB 66; EWL 3

Walsh, Gillian Paton
See Paton Walsh, Jill

Walsh, Jill Paton .... CLC 35
See Paton Walsh, Jill
See also CLR 2, 65, 128; WYA

Walter, Villiam Christian
See Andersen, Hans Christian

Walters, Anna L(ee) 1946- .... NNAL
See also CA 73-76

Walther von der Vogelweide c.
1170-1228 .... CMLC 56

Walton, Izaak 1593-1683 .... LC 72
See also BRW 2; CDBLB Before 1660;
DLB 151, 213; RGEL 2

Walzer, Michael (Laban) 1935- ...... CLC 238
See also CA 37-40R; CANR 15, 48, 127

Wambaugh, Joseph, Jr. 1937- ...... CLC 3, 18
See also AITN 1; BEST 89:3; BPFB 3; CA
33-36R; CANR 42, 65, 115, 167; CMW
4; CPW 1; DA3; DAM NOV, POP; DLB
6; DLBY 1983; MSW; MTCW 1, 2

Wambaugh, Joseph Aloysius
See Wambaugh, Joseph, Jr.

Wang Wei 699(?)-761(?) .... PC 18
See also TWA

Warburton, William 1698-1779 .... LC 97
See also DLB 104

Ward, Arthur Henry Sarsfield 1883-1959
See Rohmer, Sax
See also CA 173; CAAE 108; CMW 4;
HGG

Ward, Douglas Turner 1930- .... CLC 19
See also BW 1; CA 81-84; CAD; CANR
27; CD 5, 6; DLB 7, 38

Ward, E. D.
See Lucas, E(dward) V(errall)

Ward, Mrs. Humphry 1851-1920
See Ward, Mary Augusta
See also RGEL 2

Ward, Mary Augusta 1851-1920 ... TCLC 55
See Ward, Mrs. Humphry
See also DLB 18

Ward, Nathaniel 1578(?)-1652 .... LC 114
See also DLB 24

Ward, Peter
See Faust, Frederick (Schiller)

Warhol, Andy 1928(?)-1987 .... CLC 20
See also AAYA 12; BEST 89:4; CA 89-92;
CAAS 121; CANR 34

Warner, Francis (Robert Le Plastrier)
1937- .... CLC 14
See also CA 53-56; CANR 11; CP 1, 2, 3, 4

Warner, Marina 1946- .... CLC 59, 231
See also CA 65-68; CANR 21, 55, 118; CN
5, 6, 7; DLB 194; MTFW 2005

Warner, Rex (Ernest) 1905-1986 ...... CLC 45
See also CA 89-92; CAAS 119; CN 1, 2, 3,
4; CP 1, 2, 3, 4; DLB 15; RGEL 2; RHW

Warner, Susan (Bogert)
1819-1885 .... NCLC 31, 146
See also DLB 3, 42, 239, 250, 254

Warner, Sylvia (Constance) Ashton
See Ashton-Warner, Sylvia (Constance)

Warner, Sylvia Townsend
1893-1978 .. CLC 7, 19; SSC 23; TCLC
131
See also BRWS 7; CA 61-64; CAAS 77-80;
CANR 16, 60, 104; CN 1, 2; DLB 34,
139; EWL 3; FANT; FW; MTCW 1, 2;
RGEL 2; RGSF 2; RHW

Warren, Mercy Otis 1728-1814 ..... NCLC 13
See also DLB 31, 200; RGAL 4; TUS

Warren, Robert Penn 1905-1989 .. CLC 1, 4,
6, 8, 10, 13, 18, 39, 53, 59; PC 37; SSC
4, 58; WLC 6
See also AITN 1; AMW; AMWC 2; BPFB
3; BYA 1; CA 13-16R; CAAS 129; CANR
10, 47; CDALB 1968-1988; CN 1, 2, 3,
4; CP 1, 2, 3, 4; DA; DA3; DAB; DAC;
DAM MST, NOV, POET; DLB 2, 48, 152,
320; DLBY 1980, 1989; EWL 3; INT
CANR-10; MAL 5; MTCW 1, 2; MTFW
2005; NFS 13; RGAL 4; RGSF 2; RHW;
SATA 46; SATA-Obit 63; SSFS 8; TUS

Warrigal, Jack
See Furphy, Joseph

Warshofsky, Isaac
See Singer, Isaac Bashevis

Warton, Joseph 1722-1800 ... LC 128; NCLC
118
See also DLB 104, 109; RGEL 2

Warton, Thomas 1728-1790 .... LC 15, 82
See also DAM POET; DLB 104, 109, 336;
RGEL 2

Waruk, Kona
See Harris, (Theodore) Wilson

Warung, Price .... TCLC 45
See Astley, William
See also DLB 230; RGEL 2

Warwick, Jarvis
See Garner, Hugh
See also CCA 1

Washington, Alex
See Harris, Mark

Washington, Booker T(aliaferro)
1856-1915 .... BLC 1:3; TCLC 10
See also BW 1; CA 125; CAAE 114; DA3;
DAM MULT; LAIT 2; RGAL 4; SATA
28

Washington, George 1732-1799 .... LC 25
See also DLB 31

Wassermann, (Karl) Jakob
1873-1934 .... TCLC 6
See also CA 163; CAAE 104; DLB 66;
EWL 3

Wasserstein, Wendy 1950-2006 . CLC 32, 59,
90, 183; DC 4
See also AAYA 73; AMWS 15; CA 129;
CAAE 121; CAAS 247; CABS 3; CAD;
CANR 53, 75, 128; CD 5, 6; CWD; DA3;
DAM DRAM; DFS 5, 17; DLB 228;
EWL 3; FW; INT CA-129; MAL 5;
MTCW 2; MTFW 2005; SATA 94; SATA-
Obit 174

Waterhouse, Keith (Spencer) 1929- . CLC 47
See also BRWS 13; CA 5-8R; CANR 38,
67, 109; CBD; CD 6; CN 1, 2, 3, 4, 5, 6,
7; DLB 13, 15; MTCW 1, 2; MTFW 2005

Waters, Frank (Joseph) 1902-1995 .. CLC 88
See also CA 5-8R; 13; CAAS 149; CANR
3, 18, 63, 121; DLB 212; DLBY 1986;
RGAL 4; TCWW 1, 2

Waters, Mary C. .... CLC 70

Waters, Roger 1944- .... CLC 35

Watkins, Frances Ellen
See Harper, Frances Ellen Watkins

Watkins, Gerrold
See Malzberg, Barry N(athaniel)

Watkins, Gloria Jean
See hooks, bell

Watkins, Paul 1964- .... CLC 55
See also CA 132; CANR 62, 98

Watkins, Vernon Phillips
1906-1967 .... CLC 43
See also CA 9-10; CAAS 25-28R; CAP 1;
DLB 20; EWL 3; RGEL 2

Watson, Irving S.
See Mencken, H(enry) L(ouis)

Watson, John H.
See Farmer, Philip Jose

Watson, Richard F.
See Silverberg, Robert

Watts, Ephraim
See Horne, Richard Henry Hengist

Watts, Isaac 1674-1748 .... LC 98
See also DLB 95; RGEL 2; SATA 52

Waugh, Auberon (Alexander)
1939-2001 .... CLC 7
See also CA 45-48; CAAS 192; CANR 6,
22, 92; CN 1, 2, 3; DLB 14, 194

Waugh, Evelyn (Arthur St. John)
1903-1966 .. CLC 1, 3, 8, 13, 19, 27, 44,
107; SSC 41; WLC 6
See also BPFB 3; BRW 7; CA 85-88; CAAS
25-28R; CANR 22; CDBLB 1914-1945;
DA; DA3; DAB; DAC; DAM MST, NOV,
POP; DLB 15, 162, 195; EWL 3; MTCW
1, 2; MTFW 2005; NFS 13, 17; RGEL 2;
RGSF 2; TEA; WLIT 4

Waugh, Harriet 1944- .... CLC 6
See also CA 85-88; CANR 22

Ways, C. R.
See Blount, Roy (Alton), Jr.

Waystaff, Simon
See Swift, Jonathan

Webb, Beatrice (Martha Potter)
1858-1943 .... TCLC 22
See also CA 162; CAAE 117; DLB 190;
FW

Webb, Charles (Richard) 1939- .... CLC 7
See also CA 25-28R; CANR 114

Webb, Frank J. .... NCLC 143
See also DLB 50

Webb, James, Jr.
See Webb, James

Webb, James 1946- .... CLC 22
See also CA 81-84; CANR 156

Webb, James H.
See Webb, James

Wilson, Katharina .... **CLC 65**

Wilson, Lanford 1937- .. **CLC 7, 14, 36, 197; DC 19**
See also CA 17-20R; CABS 3; CAD; CANR 45, 96; CD 5, 6; DAM DRAM; DFS 4, 9, 12, 16, 20; DLB 7; EWL 3; MAL 5; TUS

Wilson, Robert M. 1941- .... **CLC 7, 9**
See also CA 49-52; CAD; CANR 2, 41; CD 5, 6; MTCW 1

Wilson, Robert McLiam 1964- .... **CLC 59**
See also CA 132; DLB 267

Wilson, Sloan 1920-2003 .... **CLC 32**
See also CA 1-4R; CAAS 216; CANR 1, 44; CN 1, 2, 3, 4, 5, 6

Wilson, Snoo 1948- .... **CLC 33**
See also CA 69-72; CBD; CD 5, 6

Wilson, William S(mith) 1932- .... **CLC 49**
See also CA 81-84

Wilson, (Thomas) Woodrow
1856-1924 .... **TCLC 79**
See also CA 166; DLB 47

Winchilsea, Anne (Kingsmill) Finch
1661-1720
See Finch, Anne
See also RGEL 2

Winckelmann, Johann Joachim
1717-1768 .... **LC 129**
See also DLB 97

Windham, Basil
See Wodehouse, P(elham) G(renville)

Wingrove, David 1954- .... **CLC 68**
See also CA 133; SFW 4

Winnemucca, Sarah 1844-1891 .... **NCLC 79; NNAL**
See also DAM MULT; DLB 175; RGAL 4

Winstanley, Gerrard 1609-1676 .... **LC 52**

Wintergreen, Jane
See Duncan, Sara Jeannette

Winters, Arthur Yvor
See Winters, Yvor

Winters, Janet Lewis .... **CLC 41**
See Lewis, Janet
See also DLBY 1987

Winters, Yvor 1900-1968 .. **CLC 4, 8, 32; PC 82**
See also AMWS 2; CA 11-12; CAAS 25-28R; CAP 1; DLB 48; EWL 3; MAL 5; MTCW 1; RGAL 4

Winterson, Jeanette 1959- .... **CLC 64, 158**
See also BRWS 4; CA 136; CANR 58, 116; CN 5, 6, 7; CPW; DA3; DAM POP; DLB 207, 261; FANT; FW; GLL 1; MTCW 2; MTFW 2005; RHW

Winthrop, John 1588-1649 .... **LC 31, 107**
See also DLB 24, 30

Winton, Tim 1960- .... **CLC 251**
See also AAYA 34; CA 152; CANR 118; CN 6, 7; DLB 325; SATA 98

Wirth, Louis 1897-1952 .... **TCLC 92**
See also CA 210

Wiseman, Frederick 1930- .... **CLC 20**
See also CA 159

Wister, Owen 1860-1938 ..... **SSC 100; TCLC 21**
See also BPFB 3; CA 162; CAAE 108; DLB 9, 78, 186; RGAL 4; SATA 62; TCWW 1, 2

Wither, George 1588-1667 .... **LC 96**
See also DLB 121; RGEL 2

Witkacy
See Witkiewicz, Stanislaw Ignacy

Witkiewicz, Stanislaw Ignacy
1885-1939 .... **TCLC 8**
See also CA 162; CAAE 105; CDWLB 4; DLB 215; EW 10; EWL 3; RGWL 2, 3; SFW 4

Wittgenstein, Ludwig (Josef Johann)
1889-1951 .... **TCLC 59**
See also CA 164; CAAE 113; DLB 262; MTCW 2

Wittig, Monique 1935-2003 .... **CLC 22**
See also CA 135; CAAE 116; CAAS 212; CANR 143; CWW 2; DLB 83; EWL 3; FW; GLL 1

Wittlin, Jozef 1896-1976 .... **CLC 25**
See also CA 49-52; CAAS 65-68; CANR 3; EWL 3

Wodehouse, P(elham) G(renville)
1881-1975 . **CLC 1, 2, 5, 10, 22; SSC 2; TCLC 108**
See also AAYA 65; AITN 2; BRWS 3; CA 45-48; CAAS 57-60; CANR 3, 33; CD-BLB 1914-1945; CN 1, 2; CPW 1; DA3; DAB; DAC; DAM NOV; DLB 34, 162; EWL 3; MTCW 1, 2; MTFW 2005; RGEL 2; RGSF 2; SATA 22; SSFS 10

Woiwode, L.
See Woiwode, Larry (Alfred)

Woiwode, Larry (Alfred) 1941- ... **CLC 6, 10**
See also CA 73-76; CANR 16, 94; CN 3, 4, 5, 6, 7; DLB 6; INT CANR-16

Wojciechowska, Maia (Teresa)
1927-2002 .... **CLC 26**
See also AAYA 8, 46; BYA 3; CA 183; 9-12R, 183; CAAS 209; CANR 4, 41; CLR 1; JRDA; MAICYA 1, 2; SAAS 1; SATA 1, 28, 83; SATA-Essay 104; SATA-Obit 134; YAW

Wojtyla, Karol (Josef)
See John Paul II, Pope

Wojtyla, Karol (Jozef)
See John Paul II, Pope

Wolf, Christa 1929- .... **CLC 14, 29, 58, 150**
See also CA 85-88; CANR 45, 123; CD-WLB 2; CWW 2; DLB 75; EWL 3; FW; MTCW 1; RGWL 2, 3; SSFS 14

Wolf, Naomi 1962- .... **CLC 157**
See also CA 141; CANR 110; FW; MTFW 2005

Wolfe, Gene 1931- .... **CLC 25**
See also AAYA 35; CA 57-60; 9; CANR 6, 32, 60, 152; CPW; DAM POP; DLB 8; FANT; MTCW 2; MTFW 2005; SATA 118, 165; SCFW 2; SFW 4; SUFW 2

Wolfe, Gene Rodman
See Wolfe, Gene

Wolfe, George C. 1954- .... **BLCS; CLC 49**
See also CA 149; CAD; CD 5, 6

Wolfe, Thomas (Clayton)
1900-1938 ...... **SSC 33; TCLC 4, 13, 29, 61; WLC 6**
See also AMW; BPFB 3; CA 132; CAAE 104; CANR 102; CDALB 1929-1941; DA; DA3; DAB; DAC; DAM MST, NOV; DLB 9, 102, 229; DLBD 2, 16; DLBY 1985, 1997; EWL 3; MAL 5; MTCW 1, 2; NFS 18; RGAL 4; SSFS 18; TUS

Wolfe, Thomas Kennerly, Jr.
1931- .... **CLC 147**
See Wolfe, Tom
See also CA 13-16R; CANR 9, 33, 70, 104; DA3; DAM POP; DLB 185; EWL 3; INT CANR-9; MTCW 1, 2; MTFW 2005; TUS

Wolfe, Tom .... **CLC 1, 2, 9, 15, 35, 51**
See Wolfe, Thomas Kennerly, Jr.
See also AAYA 8, 67; AITN 2; AMWS 3; BEST 89:1; BPFB 3; CN 5, 6, 7; CPW; CSW; DLB 152; LAIT 5; RGAL 4

Wolff, Geoffrey 1937- .... **CLC 41**
See also CA 29-32R; CANR 29, 43, 78, 154

Wolff, Geoffrey Ansell
See Wolff, Geoffrey

Wolff, Sonia
See Levitin, Sonia (Wolff)

Literary Criticism Series
Cumulative Topic Index

This index lists all topic entries in Gale's *Children's Literature Review* (CLR), *Classical and Medieval Literature Criticism* (CMLC), *Contemporary Literary Criticism* (CLC), *Drama Criticism* (DC), *Literature Criticism from 1400 to 1800* (LC), *Nineteenth-Century Literature Criticism* (NCLC), *Short Story Criticism* (SSC), and *Twentieth-Century Literary Criticism* (TCLC). The index also lists topic entries in the Gale Critical Companion Collection, which includes the following publications: *The Beat Generation* (BG), *Feminism in Literature* (FL), *Gothic Literature* (GL), and *Harlem Renaissance* (HR).

Topic Index

Topic Index

TCLC Cumulative Nationality Index

AMERICAN

Abbey, Edward **160**
Acker, Kathy **191**
Adams, Andy **56**
Adams, Brooks **80**
Adams, Henry (Brooks) **4, 52**
Addams, Jane **76**
Agee, James (Rufus) **1, 19, 180**
Aldrich, Bess (Genevra) Streeter **125**
Allen, Fred **87**
Anderson, Maxwell **2, 144**
Anderson, Sherwood **1, 10, 24, 123**
Anthony, Susan B(rownell) **84**
Arendt, Hannah **193**
Arnow, Harriette **196**
Atherton, Gertrude (Franklin Horn) **2**
Austin, Mary (Hunter) **25**
Baker, Ray Stannard **47**
Baker, Carlos (Heard) **119**
Bambara, Toni Cade **116**
Barry, Philip **11**
Baum, L(yman) Frank **7, 132**
Beard, Charles A(ustin) **15**
Becker, Carl (Lotus) **63**
Belasco, David **3**
Bell, James Madison **43**
Benchley, Robert (Charles) **1, 55**
Benedict, Ruth (Fulton) **60**
Benét, Stephen Vincent **7**
Benét, William Rose **28**
Bettelheim, Bruno **143**
Bierce, Ambrose (Gwinett) **1, 7, 44**
Biggers, Earl Derr **65**
Bishop, Elizabeth **121**
Bishop, John Peale **103**
Black Elk **33**
Boas, Franz **56**
Bodenheim, Maxwell **44**
Bok, Edward W. **101**
Bonner, Marita **179**
Bourne, Randolph S(illiman) **16**
Boyd, James **115**
Boyd, Thomas (Alexander) **111**
Bradford, Gamaliel **36**
Brautigan, Richard **133**
Brennan, Christopher John **17**
Brennan, Maeve **124**
Brodkey, Harold (Roy) **123**
Bromfield, Louis (Brucker) **11**
Broun, Heywood **104**
Bryan, William Jennings **99**
Burroughs, Edgar Rice **2, 32**
Burroughs, William S(eward) **121**
Cabell, James Branch **6**
Cable, George Washington **4**
Cahan, Abraham **71**
Caldwell, Erskine (Preston) **117**
Campbell, Joseph **140**
Capote, Truman **164**
Cardozo, Benjamin N(athan) **65**
Carnegie, Dale **53**
Cather, Willa (Sibert) **1, 11, 31, 99, 132, 152**

Chambers, Robert W(illiam) **41**
Chambers, (David) Whittaker **129**
Chandler, Raymond (Thornton) **1, 7, 179**
Chapman, John Jay **7**
Chase, Mary Ellen **124**
Chesnutt, Charles W(addell) **5, 39**
Childress, Alice **116**
Chopin, Katherine **5, 14, 127, 199**
Cobb, Irvin S(hrewsbury) **77**
Coffin, Robert P(eter) Tristram **95**
Cohan, George M(ichael) **60**
Comstock, Anthony **13**
Cotter, Joseph Seamon Sr. **28**
Cram, Ralph Adams **45**
Crane, (Harold) Hart **2, 5, 80**
Crane, Stephen (Townley) **11, 17, 32**
Crawford, F(rancis) Marion **10**
Crothers, Rachel **19**
Cullen, Countée **4, 37**
Cummings, E. E. **137**
Darrow, Clarence (Seward) **81**
Davis, Rebecca (Blaine) Harding **6**
Davis, Richard Harding **24**
Day, Clarence (Shepard Jr.) **25**
Dent, Lester **72**
De Voto, Bernard (Augustine) **29**
Dewey, John **95**
Dickey, James **151**
Dixon, Thomas, Jr. **163**
di Donato, Pietro **159**
Dreiser, Theodore (Herman Albert) **10, 18, 35, 83**
Du Bois, W. E. B. **169**
Dulles, John Foster **72**
Dunbar, Paul Laurence **2, 12**
Duncan, Isadora **68**
Dunne, Finley Peter **28**
Eastman, Charles A(lexander) **55**
Eddy, Mary (Ann Morse) Baker **71**
Einstein, Albert **65**
Erskine, John **84**
Faulkner, William **141**
Faust, Frederick (Schiller) **49**
Fenollosa, Ernest (Francisco) **91**
Fields, W. C. **80**
Fisher, Dorothy (Frances) Canfield **87**
Fisher, Rudolph **11**
Fisher, Vardis **140**
Fitzgerald, F(rancis) Scott (Key) **1, 6, 14, 28, 55, 157**
Fitzgerald, Zelda (Sayre) **52**
Fletcher, John Gould **35**
Foote, Mary Hallock **108**
Ford, Henry **73**
Forten, Charlotte L. **16**
Freeman, Douglas Southall **11**
Freeman, Mary E(leanor) Wilkins **9**
Fuller, Henry Blake **103**
Futrelle, Jacques **19**
Gale, Zona **7**
Gardner, John **195**
Garland, (Hannibal) Hamlin **3**

Gilman, Charlotte (Anna) Perkins (Stetson) **9, 37, 117, 201**
Ginsberg, Allen **120**
Glasgow, Ellen (Anderson Gholson) **2, 7**
Glaspell, Susan **55, 175**
Goldman, Emma **13**
Green, Anna Katharine **63**
Grey, Zane **6**
Griffith, D(avid Lewelyn) W(ark) **68**
Griggs, Sutton (Elbert) **77**
Guest, Edgar A(lbert) **95**
Guiney, Louise Imogen **41**
Haley, Alex **147**
Hall, James Norman **23**
Hammett, Dashiell **187**
Handy, W(illiam) C(hristopher) **97**
Hansberry, Lorraine **192**
Harper, Frances Ellen Watkins **14**
Harris, Joel Chandler **2**
Harte, (Francis) Bret(t) **1, 25**
Hartmann, Sadakichi **73**
Hatteras, Owen **18**
Hawthorne, Julian **25**
Hearn, (Patricio) Lafcadio (Tessima Carlos) **9**
Hecht, Ben **101**
Heller, Joseph **131, 151**
Hellman, Lillian (Florence) **119**
Hemingway, Ernest (Miller) **115, 203**
Henry, O. **1, 19**
Hergesheimer, Joseph **11**
Heyward, (Edwin) DuBose **59**
Higginson, Thomas Wentworth **36**
Himes, Chester **139**
Holley, Marietta **99**
Holly, Buddy **65**
Holmes, Oliver Wendell Jr. **77**
Hopkins, Pauline Elizabeth **28**
Horney, Karen (Clementine Theodore Danielsen) **71**
Howard, Robert E(rvin) **8**
Howe, Julia Ward **21**
Howells, William Dean **7, 17, 41**
Huneker, James Gibbons **65**
Hurston, Zora Neale **121, 131**
Ince, Thomas H. **89**
Jackson, Shirley **187**
James, Henry **2, 11, 24, 40, 47, 64, 171**
James, William **15, 32**
Jarrell, Randall **177**
Jewett, (Theodora) Sarah Orne **1, 22**
Johnson, James Weldon **3, 19, 175**
Johnson, Robert **69**
Kerouac, Jack **117**
Kinsey, Alfred C(harles) **91**
Kirk, Russell (Amos) **119**
Kornbluth, C(yril) M. **8**
Korzybski, Alfred (Habdank Skarbek) **61**
Kubrick, Stanley **112**
Kuttner, Henry **10**
Lane, Rose Wilder **177**
Lardner, Ring(gold) W(ilmer) **2, 14**
Larsen, Nella **200**
Lewis, (Harry) Sinclair **4, 13, 23, 39**

Nationality Index

ISBN-13: 978-0-7876-9977-2
ISBN-10: 0-7876-9977-2

90000

9 780787 699772